# CRIMINAL LAW

SECOND EDITION

*by*

RICHARD J. BONNIE
John S. Battle Professor of Law
Director, Institute of Law, Psychiatry & Public Policy
University of Virginia

ANNE M. COUGHLIN
Professor of Law
University of Virginia

JOHN C. JEFFRIES, JR.
Emerson Spies Professor of Law
Arnold H. Leon Professor and Dean of the Law School
University of Virginia

PETER W. LOW
Hardy Cross Dillard Professor of Law
University of Virginia

FOUNDATION PRESS

NEW YORK, NEW YORK

2004

© 1997 FOUNDATION PRESS
© 2004 By FOUNDATION PRESS
      395 Hudson Street
      New York, NY 10014
      Phone Toll Free 1–877–888–1330
      Fax (212) 367–6799
      fdpress.com
Printed in the United States of America

**SBN** 1–58778–720–2

 TEXT IS PRINTED ON 10% POST CONSUMER RECYCLED PAPER

# PREFACE

The first edition of this book was published in 1997. That book was in turn a successor to Low, Jeffries, and Bonnie, Criminal Law (Second Edition, 1986), the first edition of which was published in 1982. Over these 22 years, much has changed, as we have sought to develop innovative approaches to the teaching of fundamental ideas, to present traditional topics in contemporary contexts, and to introduce intriguing new subjects. At the same time, we have sought to retain what we regard as the strengths of the preceding volumes, both in particular packages of materials that seem to have taught well and in overall analytic sophistication. If we could claim one virtue for the prior volumes, it would be intellectual challenge. That tradition is continued here in the selection of main cases designed to raise difficult issues on interesting facts, and in the extensive use of notes to provide background, summarize doctrine, and identify analogous problems.

The first change to be noted is the expanded and revitalized Introduction, which now covers not only the purposes of punishment, but also the topic of criminalization that formerly appeared at the end of the book. Both of these foundational inquiries are presented in new factual contexts—the purposes of punishment are explored in the setting of case vignettes involving parents and other caregivers prosecuted for the deaths of children, and criminalization is explored in the context of the U.S. Supreme Court's 2003 decision invalidating the Texas sodomy statute. Teachers who would prefer to defer or omit either topic are able to do so.

In our continuing effort to enable teachers to cover the fundamentals of the criminal act and mens rea efficiently but thoroughly, we have also streamlined, reorganized and enriched Chapters 1 and 2. Our main aims have been to vivify the act requirement, to consolidate the material on common-law mens rea, and to provide even greater flexibility for teachers who want to spend more or less time on the basic principles of culpability.

All of this should enable teachers to dip into the rich body of materials we have assembled on justification and excuse, criminal responsibility, sexual assault, and homicide. The homicide chapter has been reorganized along more traditional lines, and the substantial section on capital homicide now appears at the end of the chapter. Although the structure of the materials on proof and proportionality in Chapter 9 remains unchanged, the content has been significantly expanded to take account of the U.S. Supreme Court's recent activity in these areas.

All in all, we are very excited about the balance we have struck between the old and the new in this edition. We hope you agree.

RJB
AMC
JCJjr
PWL

April 2004
Charlottesville, Virginia

# SUMMARY OF CONTENTS

\*

# TABLE OF CONTENTS

*

# TABLE OF CASES

Principal cases are in bold type. Non-principal cases are in roman type. References are to Pages.

\*

# CRIMINAL LAW

\*

# INTRODUCTION

# WHY AND WHAT WE PUNISH

―――――

## INTRODUCTORY NOTE

This book is about the substantive criminal law. Its focus is on crime definition and the components of criminal liability. Broadly speaking, there are three main elements of criminal liability: the criminal act (the actus reus), the criminal state of mind (the mens rea), and the absence of a defense of justification or excuse. The cases and statutory materials that follow examine each of these concepts in detail.

The subject matter of the book implicates two long-standing and related philosophical debates. The first concerns the functions served by criminal punishment. Conduct prohibited by the criminal law may be and, indeed, often is the subject of civil lawsuits.[a] Persons who commit crimes may be ordered to pay an award of damages in tort to their victims. Why isn't this enough? Why do we need criminal sanctions in addition to the remedial structure available under other sources of law? As H.L.A. Hart observed, "we may well ask what justification there is for [the] criminal law with all the misery which criminal punishment entails."[b] The first section of this introduction is designed to provoke preliminary thought about these questions by outlining in general terms an inquiry into the purposes of punishment.[c]

The second debate focuses on what is often called the "criminalization" decision. What factors are relevant to identifying the specific kinds of behavior that should be punishable by criminal sanctions? Particular criminalization decisions require lawmakers to take account of a broad range of political, social, economic, psychological, and practical variables. The primary purpose of this book is to explore the substantive structure into which conduct will fall once the criminalization decision is made. Yet it is useful at the outset for students of the criminal law to have in mind the general framework of the criminalization debate. Hence, the second section

---

[a] Many lawyers have struggled to identify the distinction between civil and criminal regulation. In an essay prepared for first-year students on the threshold of studying criminal law, Henry Hart explained that "[w]hat distinguishes a criminal from a civil sanction and all that distinguishes it, it is ventured, is the judgment of community condemnation which accompanies and justifies its imposition." Henry Hart, The Aims of the Criminal Law, 23 Law & Contemp. Probs. 401, 404 (1958).

[b] H.L.A. Hart, Immorality and Treason, in Morality and the Law 51 (Richard A. Wasserstrom ed. 1971).

[c] For a helpful collection of essays on this subject, see Andrew von Hirsch & Andrew Ashworth (eds.), Principled Sentencing (1992).

1

of this introduction identifies some of the fundamental, recurring questions for lawmakers faced with determining when behavior should be criminalized and when it should be left to control by other means.

## SECTION 1:   THE PURPOSES OF PUNISHMENT

INTRODUCTORY NOTE ON THE PURPOSES OF PUNISHMENT

For many years, criminal law scholars have identified four main goals of punishment: retribution, deterrence, incapacitation, and rehabilitation. However, there are at bottom only two competing philosophical theories regarding the purpose of punishment. Each theory represents a complex series of moral assertions and aspirations for the criminal justice system. Each rests on a distinct understanding of human nature and of the causes of criminal activity.

The first theory, which is associated with the retributive function of punishment, is deontological in nature. According to this view, "the institution[] of punishment [is] justified by the rightness or fairness of the institution ... not by the good consequences such institution may generate."[a] For the deontologist, the justification for punishment is the moral culpability (or desert) of persons who violate the criminal law. The second theory of punishment is utilitarian in nature, and is associated with the goals of deterrence, incapacitation, and rehabilitation. According to this view, punishment is threatened and imposed in order to achieve beneficial social consequences, namely, to prevent or minimize criminal behavior.

For purposes of clarity, this essay will focus separately on each of these theories and their practical implications for the criminal process. But it bears emphasizing that the criminal justice system rests on a mixture of these philosophies. That is, while it is possible to envision a system wholly governed by deontological premises or one that relies solely on utilitarian policies, neither of these positions dominates the existing system to the exclusion of the other. Rather, the system makes a series of significant, if uneasy, compromises between them. As you would expect, moreover, the purposes of punishment are historically contingent in the sense that different justifications are emphasized at different times.[b] While retributive impulses may wane and instrumental goals wax, or vice-versa, the system nonetheless remains committed to a mixture of justificatory principles.

Of course, the criminal process itself does not negotiate these compromises by means of an abstract philosophical dispute. To the contrary, the process does its work by punishing real people in specific cases. Some

[a] Michael S. Moore, The Moral Worth of Retribution, in Ferdinand Schoeman, Responsibility, Character, and the Emotions 182 (1987).

[b] See Albert W. Alschuler, The Changing Purposes of Criminal Punishment: A Retrospective on the Past Century and Some Thoughts about the Next, 70 U. Chi. L. Rev. 1 (2003).

people go to jail, others are forced to pay fines, while still others are put to death. For that reason, it is useful to have factual contexts in mind when exploring why our culture commits its resources to punishing criminals. The following cases are variations on a theme. In each case, a child dies. The questions for the criminal justice system are whether someone should be punished for the death and, if so, how harsh the penalty should be.

———

## Testing Cases

**1. Donte Phillips.** Sarah Davis picked up 2–year-old Donte Phillips and drove him to his day-care center. Davis was the director of the center, which was run by a local church and provided services to low-income families. Donte was the only passenger in the center's van that day. Davis and Donte arrived at the center at 8:30 a.m. Donte remained in the van until 4:00 p.m., when his aunt came to take him home. After a frantic and fruitless search for the boy on the center's grounds, Davis realized that she must have left him in the van. She screamed and rushed to the van, where she discovered Donte's lifeless body. The doctor who performed the autopsy attributed the death to heat stroke. In a statement made to investigators, Davis said that when she arrived at the center, she observed other children running around the grounds. Concerned for their safety, she parked the van and went to check on them, forgetting about Donte for the rest of the day. Davis's colleagues characterized her as sensitive, conscientious, and extremely upset about Donte's death. They attributed her mistake to the fact that both the church and day-care center were struggling financially, and Davis was performing a variety of different jobs in an effort to keep the facility from closing.[a]

**2. Gregory Gaito.** Robert Gaito parked his car outside his workplace in Colonie, New York, and went inside, leaving his five-month-old son, Gregory, in the car. At about 5:15 p.m., Gaito's wife telephoned to ask him why the child was not at his babysitter's house. Gaito rushed to his car and discovered the baby's corpse. The autopsy report showed that the child had died of heat exhaustion and struggled furiously before his death. In a statement given to the police, Gaito explained that he had intended to drop the child off at the babysitter's house, but forgot to do so.[b]

**3. Michael and Alex Smith.** Susan Smith drove her car to a boat ramp on a lake near her home in Union, South Carolina, and sent the car into the lake. Smith's two young sons were inside the car, strapped into their car seats. Then, Smith ran to a nearby home and reported that her sons had been kidnaped. For nine days, Smith stuck to that story in interviews with the police, and she appeared on national television to plead for the boys' safe return. Ultimately, Smith confessed that she had

[a] See Brad Schmitt & Dorren Klausnitzer, *Toddler Likely Didn't Suffer, Examiner Says*, The Tennesean, June 18, 1994.

[b] See *Charges Dropped Against Man Who Left 5–Month–Old Son in Car*, Buffalo News, July 8, 1994.

drowned her sons, and police divers found her car with their corpses inside it. In her confession, Smith mentioned that she had been distraught because her boyfriend had broken up with her, saying that he was not ready to be a parent. Smith also told the police that she had gone to the lake intending to take her own life, but when the car started rolling into the water, she found that she could not go through with her suicide plan. When Smith was six years old, her father committed suicide. Smith attempted suicide when she was 13. After this incident, a psychologist recommended that Smith be hospitalized for depression, but her mother and stepfather refused. When she was 16, her stepfather began sexually molesting her. Smith's stepfather admitted to police that he had fondled her, but no criminal charges were brought because Smith and her mother did not want him to be prosecuted.[c]

**4. Imani and Jasmine Lawrey.** Khalimba Berry found her daughters, three-year-old twins, dead inside her car, which was parked outside her apartment building in Atlanta, Georgia. The cause of death was hyperthermia. That morning, Berry had returned home from her nightshift job, fed her children breakfast, and watched television with them. At noon, Berry went to sleep, leaving the twins in the care of their 11–year-old brother. When she woke up two hours later, Berry could not find the girls. Berry and her neighbors searched the apartment complex for two hours, with no success. Berry then telephoned 911, and the dispatcher suggested that she check her car. She went to the car, and found her children's bodies. She screamed and held them in her arms. Investigators believe that the girls were playing in the car and that they accidentally locked themselves in.[d]

**5. Devon and Dustin Ducker.** One summer morning, at around 3:30 a.m., Jenny Bain Ducker drove to a Holiday Inn in McMinnville, Tennessee, to visit several co-workers who were staying there. Ducker's two young sons accompanied her to the motel, and she left the boys, who were sleeping in their car seats, alone in the car for about ten hours. In the motel, Ducker drank beer and played video games with her friends. According to Ducker's companions, she left the motel room periodically, presumably to check on the boys. However, at some point she fell asleep, due to the combined effects of the beer and prescription medicine she was taking for bronchitis. When she woke up, it was 1:00 p.m. She immediately went to her car and found that one of her sons appeared to be dead. She rushed the boys to the hospital, where both were pronounced dead from heat exhaustion. Ducker and the boys' father were married briefly; both were high school dropouts. According to her ex-husband, Ducker was a neglectful mother. He thought that she drank too much, and he said that he had been planning to seek custody of the boys because he suspected that she was abusing them physically. Ducker's parents pointed out that until recently she had worked the night shift at a local factory; night-shift

[c] See, e.g., Twila Decker, The Many Faces of Susan Smith, The Dallas Morning News, May 10, 1995.

[d] See Bill Montgomery, Autopsy: Twins Died of Heat Exhaustion, Atlanta Constitution, June 10, 1995, at B6.

workers frequently make early morning social visits. Moreover, the children of other factory workers regularly stayed up late and slept during the day, when their parents did.[e]

**6.   Frances Kelly.** One morning after breakfast, Kevin Kelly took six of his thirteen children out in the family van to do errands. Kelly's wife was visiting family in Ireland, and he was staying at home from his job as an engineer to take care of the children. Kelly and the children returned to their home on Zimbro Avenue in Manassas, Virginia, at about noon, and Kelly asked three of the older children, including his 17–year-old son, Anthony, to take care of the little ones. Kelly spent the rest of the day doing chores and errands around the house, including fixing the backyard fence, ferrying children to and from school, washing clothes, and preparing meals. At about 7:30 p.m., neighbors discovered the body of Kelly's youngest child, 21–month-old Frances, strapped into her car seat in the van. During the day, the temperature inside the van probably reached 140 degrees. Friends and neighbors said that Kelly was a devoted father and a deeply religious man. As one neighbor put it, Kelly's children were his whole life. But other neighbors remarked that this was not the first time that Kelly had lost track of one of his children. Several months earlier, Kelly had left his four-year-old son behind in a video store. The child was restored to the family only after the police used rental records to locate all customers who had come to the store that day; when the police called Kelly, he rushed over to pick up his son. On another occasion, Frances was found wandering by herself down Zimbro Avenue. A police officer brought her home and warned the Kellys to be more careful.[f]

**7.   Jonathan Perry Courtney.** Donna Mutyambizi parked her car outside a home in North Laurel, Maryland, for her first day on the job as house cleaner. Although she had been warned not to do so, Mutyambizi left her 17–month-old son, Jonathan Courtney, alone in the car. She cracked the car windows to provide ventilation, and she placed a bottle of water and cereal near the child's car seat. She checked on him twice and each time found him sleeping. When she returned to the car about three hours later, the boy was lifeless. She asked a neighbor to help resuscitate the child, but he already had died from hyperthermia. Initially, Mutyambizi told the police that she had brought her son into the house with her. Later, she admitted that she had left him alone in the car, and she explained that she did so because she had no money for a babysitter. She had asked her estranged husband for money, but he refused to give her any. Mutyambizi's husband claimed that she could afford to pay a babysitter, but he said that she had lost confidence in the person who had been caring for the child. When Mutyambizi was 6 years old, her father shot and killed her mother; thereafter, she was raised by several different foster parents. Mutyambizi's own marriage was unhappy. She and her husband argued frequently, and they separated about six months before their child's death. Friends charac-

---

[e] See State v. Ducker, 27 S.W.3d 889 (Tenn.2000).

[f] See, e.g., Josh White, Jury Says Father Should Get Jail, The Washington Post, Dec. 5, 2002, at B1.

terized Mutyambizi as a doting parent, and they said she was very worried about making ends meet following her separation from her husband. At the time of Jonathan's death, Mutyambizi was pregnant with her second child.[g]

————

Which, if any, of the following goals would be served by punishing the actors in the foregoing cases?

————

## NOTES ON RETRIBUTION

**1. Introduction.** The retributive function of punishment presupposes that human actors are responsible moral agents who are capable of making choices for good or evil. People who make evil choices deserve to be punished. This premise is a normative assertion; it does not require empirical verification, nor does it depend on pragmatic justification. According to retributivism, it is right to punish one who offends against societal norms because it is wrong to violate these norms. The same point is sometimes put in terms of expiation. It is essential for the offender to right the wrong or, in the vernacular, to "pay" for the crime. The offender "owes a debt to society" for retributive reasons; having violated societal norms, the offender must now atone by suffering punishment for the transgression.[a]

A famous proponent of retributivism is Sir James Fitzjames Stephen, a 19th-century English judge and historian of the criminal law. His view was:

> [N]o one in this country regards murder, rape, arson, robbery, theft, or the like, with any feeling but detestation. I do not think it admits of any doubt that law and morals powerfully support and greatly intensify each other in this matter. Everything which is regarded as enhancing the moral guilt of a particular offence is recognized as a reason for increasing the severity of the punishment awarded to it. On the other hand, the sentence of the law is to the moral sentiment of the public in relation to any offence what a seal is to hot wax. It converts into a permanent final judgment what might otherwise be a transient sentiment. The mere general suspicion or knowledge that a man has done something dishonest may never be brought to a point, and the disappro-

[g] See Michael Rezendes, Maryland Woman Caught in a Cycle of Sorrow, The Washington Post, July 13, 1989.

[a] Cf. H.L.A. Hart, Punishment and Responsibility 158–59 (1968):

> This . . . conception of punishment . . . makes primary the meting out to a responsible wrongdoer of his just deserts. Dostoevsky passionately believed that so-

ciety was morally justified in punishing people simply because they had done wrong; he also believed that psychologically the criminal needed his punishment to heal the laceration of the bonds that joined him to his society. So, in the end, Raskolnikov the murderer thirsts for his punishment.

bation excited by it may in time pass away, but the fact that he has been convicted and punished as a thief stamps a mark upon him for life. In short, the infliction of punishment by law gives definite expression and a solemn ratification and justification to the hatred which is excited by the commission of the offense.... The criminal law thus proceeds upon the principle that it is morally right to hate criminals, and it confirms and justifies that sentiment by inflicting upon criminals punishments which express it....

These views are regarded by many people as being wicked, because it is supposed that we never ought to hate, or wish to be revenged upon, any one. The doctrine that hatred and vengeance are wicked in themselves appears to me to contradict plain facts, and to be unsupported by any argument deserving of attention. Love and hatred, gratitude for benefits, and the desire of vengeance for injuries, imply each other as much as convex and concave. ... The unqualified manner in which [these views] have been denounced is in itself a proof that they are deeply rooted in human nature. No doubt they are peculiarly liable to abuse, and in some states of society are commonly in excess of what is desirable, and so require restraint rather than excitement, but unqualified denunciations of them are as ill-judged as unqualified denunciations of sexual passion. The forms in which deliberate anger and righteous disapprobation are expressed, and the execution of criminal justice is the most emphatic of such forms, stand to the one set of passions in the same relation in which marriage stands to the other....[b]

The perspective expressed by Stephen is deeply embedded in the vocabulary of the criminal law. We speak in terms of "guilt" or "innocence." We talk about "punishment," "blame," and "responsibility." Words like "murderer," "rapist," "pedophile," "burglar," "thief," "convicted felon," carry deeply stigmatic overtones, attesting perhaps to the most significant moral disapprobation that society can express. Stigmatic labels of this intensity and with these consequences are not applied to one who commits a tort, who breaks a lease, or who breaches a contract. "Civil" remedies and sanctions do not carry the same meaning as a "criminal" conviction.

Critics of retributivism insist that the angry and vengeful emotions identified by Stephen do not provide a moral justification for punishment. For example, David Dolinko argues that by valorizing "anger and hatred as ... proper bases for punishment," retributive theory "invites the public and the legal system to indulge the passion for revenge untroubled by moral qualms."[c] Some modern proponents of retributive theory have responded by distinguishing retribution from a simple thirst for revenge.

[b] James Fitzjames Stephen, 2 A History of the Criminal Law of England 81–82 (1883).

[c] David Dolinko, Three Mistakes of Retributivism, 39 U.C.L.A. L. Rev. 1623, 1652 (1992).

Michael Moore insists that the retributive urge springs from a virtuous (rather than "wicked") emotion, and thus provides a moral foundation for the attribution of criminal blame.[d] Moore explains:

> When we make a retributive judgment ... we need not be motivated by [revenge]. Our concern for retributive justice might be motivated by very deep emotions that are nonetheless of a wholly virtuous nature. These are the feelings of guilt we would have if we did the kinds of acts that fill the criminal appellate reports of any state.

Moore invites readers to imagine how they would feel if they committed a vicious crime, say, a brutal homicide, and he suggests that, in such a case, the only virtuous response would be to "feel guilty unto death.... One ought to feel so guilty one wants to die." Moore also argues that it is appropriate, indeed, respectful, to hold actual wrongdoers, no matter what their socio-economic hardships or psychological shortcomings, to the same high standards to which we hold ourselves. "If we experience any reluctance to transfer the guilt and desert *we* would possess," had we committed a brutal crime, to the criminal offender, "we should examine that reluctance carefully." By blaming the offender as harshly as we would blame ourselves, Moore insists, we are giving the offender "the benefit each of us gives himself or herself: the benefit of being the subjective seat of a will that, although caused, is nonetheless capable of both choice and responsibility."

Does Moore's retributive approach help to resolve the questions of whether and how harshly to punish the actors in the testing cases summarized above? From whose perspective should lawmakers make the determination deemed crucial by Moore? Put bluntly, who gets to decide how guilty "*we*" ought to feel in those or other cases?

**2. Retribution and the Blameworthy Actor.** The central ethical predicate of retributivism raises difficult questions. Does it follow that people who are not responsible moral agents should not be punished? How is one to determine whether a person is a responsible moral agent? Does it also follow that punishment is unjust if the underlying misconduct was not the product of free and voluntary choice? How is that determination to be made? How should the law deal with situational circumstances that in a given instance undermine or strongly influence an individual's capacity to make a free and voluntary choice?

Traditionally, the criminal law has answered these questions through several narrowly framed inquiries about the actor and the circumstances surrounding the misconduct. As for the important threshold question of who "qualif[ies] as a blameworthy moral agent," the law's general response is: "Everyone except for the very young, the very crazy, and the severely mentally retarded."[e] As for whether situational circumstances may negate

---

[d] See Michael S. Moore, The Moral Worth of Retribution, in Responsibility, Character, and the Emotions, 179, 212–15 (Ferdinand Schoeman ed., 1987).

[e] Peter Arenella, Convicting the Morally Blameless: Reassessing the Relationship Between Legal and Moral Accountability, 39 U.C.L.A. L. Rev. 1511, 1521 (1992).

free choice, the law is willing to withhold blame only if the actor's capacity to choose a legal option was constrained by overwhelming external pressures. Here, the classic example is the actor who offends because another person threatens to kill her if she refuses to commit the crime. As these references are designed to illustrate, the criminal law treats the vast majority of accused persons as fit candidates for punishment, notwithstanding their internal failings or situational difficulties. As Michael Moore's essay suggests, retributivists insist that such treatment is morally justified, indeed required.

Some lawyers have argued that retribution endorses a theory of responsibility that is empirically false and morally deficient. According to this view, crime is produced not by offenders' vicious choices, but by vicious circumstances in which offenders are born and forced to reside by an uncaring society. By attributing misconduct to offenders' choices—rather than to their impoverished circumstances—retributive theory allows the community to avoid its responsibility for poverty and related cultural ills. For example, in a provocative lecture delivered in 1975, David Bazelon warned that the criminal process would lose its moral credibility unless it became sensitive to the productive relationship between social injustice and crime.[f] To force the system to confront "society's own conduct in relation to the actor," Bazelon suggested that jurors be allowed to acquit in cases where the crime was caused by "physiological, psychological, environmental, cultural, educational, economic, and hereditary factors," rather than by the accused's free choice. Although Bazelon's primary claim was that the victims of poverty and racial discrimination often may not justly be blamed for committing crimes, he conceded that his determinist view of human conduct would be implicated in a wide variety of cases. Thus, he wondered:

> whether a free choice to do wrong can be found in the acts of a poverty-stricken and otherwise deprived black youth from the central city who kills a marine who taunted him with a racial epithet, in the act of a "modern Jean Valjean" who steals to feed his family, in the act of a narcotics addict who buys drugs for his own use, or in the act of a superpatriot steeped in cold war ideology who burglarizes in the name of "national security."

Bazelon's proposal has attracted some favorable commentary,[g] but it is fair to say that most criminal law scholars disagree. In Stephen Morse's view, the empirical and normative assumptions underlying Bazelon's determinist model are flawed. First, Morse argues that Bazelon's assertions concerning the causes of crime "are wrong.... [W]e do not understand *any* of the causes of crime. There are various factors which have a strong positive correlation with violent crime, such as youth and poverty. But

---

[f] David L. Bazelon, The Morality of the Criminal Law, 49 S. Cal. L. Rev. 385 (1976).

[g] See Richard Delgado, "Rotten Social Background": Should the Criminal Law Rec-

ognize a Defense of Severe Environmental Deprivation?, 3 Law & Ineq. J. 9 (1985).

social science is not yet ready to make firm causal statements.''[h] Second, and more important, the definition of responsibility applied by retributive theory rests on an ethical, rather than factual, basis:

> ... There is no bright line between free and unfree choices. Harder and easier choices are arranged along a continuum of choice: there is no scientifically dictated cutting point where legal and moral responsibility begins or ends. Nor is there a higher moral authority which can tell society where to draw the line. All society can do is to determine the cutting point that comports with our collective sense of morality. The real issue is where society ought to draw the line of responsibility—and by whom it should be drawn.

For Morse and others, Bazelon's determinist judgments are unethical because they erode the state's respect for individual autonomy. Even where an offender was faced with a very hard choice to obey the law, it is "respectful to the actor to hold the actor responsible.... [S]uch a view treats all persons as autonomous and capable of that most human capacity, the power to choose. To treat persons otherwise is to treat them as less than human.''

To illustrate the ethical dilemma created by Bazelon's proposal, these commentators ask a practical question, namely, what would the community do with the large numbers of dangerous persons acquitted on grounds of nonresponsibility? Since the community could not tolerate the release of such persons, the system inevitably would replace criminal punishment with other more "repressive measures,'' including coercive therapy and preventive detention of potentially dangerous actors.

Critical race and feminist scholars and practitioners have refocused Morse's question about the political constituents who should inform the criminal law's definition of responsibility. When Morse asked this question—that is, "by whom'' should the line of responsibility be drawn—he was referring to the appropriate allocation of authority between legislatures and courts; his claim is that legislators, not jurors, should identify the moral standards that govern the allocation of criminal blame. By contrast, when critical race and feminist commentators ask this question, they are concerned to demonstrate that legislatures, as well as courts, traditionally have been dominated by affluent white men. Since that is the case, these critics claim that the definition of responsibility serves the political interests of such men, not of African–Americans, women, or the members of other marginalized groups. In particular, they argue, the proposition that criminal blame is respectful of individual autonomy protects only those who already possess the social and economic resources to exercise meaningful choices. While it is too early to identify the ultimate impact of such arguments, they have inspired a number of law reform movements, includ-

[h] Stephen J. Morse, The Twilight of Welfare Criminology: A Reply to Judge Bazelon,     49 S. Cal. L. Rev. 1247, 1261 (1976).

ing efforts to make self-defense doctrine more sensitive to the experiences of women and minorities, and to revise charging and sentencing policies that have a disproportionate impact on African–American offenders.

**3.  Retribution and Grading: Proportionality.** Retribution places an important limitation on the application of criminal blame, namely, the principle of proportionality. Blame is a question of degree. To say that it was bad for someone to do something suggests the further question: How bad? A simple illustration makes the point. Most would agree that a petty thief should not be punished as severely as the person who kills for money. But why not? Our impulse that life imprisonment for the petty thief is grossly disproportionate to the offense is derived from a retributive evaluation of the behavior. The degree of wrong-doing involved in such a case does not justify such extreme punishment. In the language of retribution, this offender did not "deserve" to be punished so severely.

The substantive criminal law implements the principle of proportionality in at least two ways. First, the system grades offenses, *i.e.*, legislatures establish the relative severity of different crimes in the abstract. For centuries, the law has incorporated proportionality by using the category of "felony" for more serious offenses and "misdemeanor" for less serious crimes. Today, legislatures grade offenses by establishing the maximum penalty that can be imposed upon conviction, and the relative seriousness of a given offense is determined by comparing that sanction with those authorized for other offenses. Current legislative grading schemes are considerably more complicated than the traditional distinction between felonies and misdemeanors. For example, the Federal Sentencing Guidelines distribute crimes, according to their relative seriousness, among 43 different offense levels.

Second, the principle of proportionality requires some assessment of whether a sentence actually imposed fairly reflects the blameworthiness of the individual wrongdoer and the gravity of his or her crime. The question here is whether a particular penalty is or is not disproportionate for a particular crime, in the light of all of the surrounding circumstances. Most sentencing schemes give judges some discretion, to a greater or lesser degree, to consider case-specific factors when determining an offender's penalty.

Consider these two aspects of proportionality in connection with the testing cases summarized above. Presumably, some of the actors whose conduct caused a child's death deserve criminal punishment. Should each be charged with homicide? The same degree of homicide (e.g., murder as opposed to manslaughter)? With some other crime? Do some of the cases present mitigating or aggravating factors that should be counted when calculating the sentence?

Critics of retributive theory argue that the principle of proportionality provides no method for calibrating sentences with the type of precision that the criminal justice system requires:

[I]t has long been a stock objection to retributivism that there is simply no workable way to determine just *what* punishment a criminal deserves. Retributivists very commonly direct us to make punishments "proportional" to crimes by punishing a more serious crime more severely than a less serious one. Unfortunately, this prescription by itself cannot tell us what punishment any particular crime actually deserves, even if we could rank every crime in a single scale from least to most serious. For the prescription requires only that we assign greater penalties as we ascend the scale of crimes, without either supplying a starting point (the penalty for the least serious offense) or telling us *by how much* to increase the penalty as we move from one crime to the next in the scale.[i]

Likewise, sentencing officials have commented on the practical difficulties they confront when trying to rationalize their sentencing decisions according to the principle of proportionality. As the United States Sentencing Commissioners put it in the United States Sentencing Guidelines Manual (2003):

[A] sentencing system tailored to fit every conceivable wrinkle of each case can become unworkable.... A bank robber with (or without) a gun, which the robber kept hidden (or brandished), might have frightened (or merely warned), injured seriously (or less seriously), tied up (or simply pushed) a guard, a teller or a customer, at night (or at noon), for a bad (or arguably less bad) motive, in an effort to obtain money for other crimes (or for other purposes), in the company of a few (or many) other robbers, for the first (or fourth) time that day, while sober (or under the influence of drugs and alcohol), and so forth.

Of course, as proponents of retributivism remark, the principle of proportionality does not claim to provide "an invariant, objective deserved punishment for each offensive act." In the view of these commentators, one of the strengths of retributive theory is its sensitivity to contemporary community morality. "It is possible in any society to rank the seriousness of criminal offenses and to assign to each a punishment that the society at that time considers proportional to the seriousness of the offense. This is then the deserved punishment at that time and place."[j]

**4.   Retribution as a Limiting Principle.** As the foregoing sections explain, retributivism treats punishment of blameworthy wrongdoers as an ethical imperative. According to retributive philosophy, retribution *requires* punishment whether or not the punishment produces beneficial social consequences. The subsequent sections of this essay explore the opposing view, under which punishment is justified only where it secures social benefits. Before turning to consequentialist views of punishment, it is

---

[i] David Dolinko, Three Mistakes of Retributivism, 39 U.C.L.A. L. Rev. 1623, 1626 (1992).

[j] Stephen J. Morse, Justice, Mercy, and Craziness, 36 Stan. L. Rev. 1485, 1492–93 (1984).

useful to remark that many consequentialist philosophers accept the ethical postulates of retribution as principles that limit the occasions for, and severity of, punishment that otherwise would be justifiable on purely utilitarian grounds.

For these philosophers, retribution alone is not a sufficient justification for punishment, but they believe that the criminal process achieves good consequences by incorporating retributive premises. For example, H.L.A. Hart explains that the retributivists' definition of human beings as responsible moral agents serves "values quite distinct from those of retributive punishment." Thus, if the criminal law were to be designed solely along utilitarian lines, Hart believes that it would continue to endorse that definition and associated ideas. He offers two examples of the social benefits secured by retributive thinking. First, by insisting that people have the power to choose how they behave, the criminal law enhances their ability to control their lives:

> [It allows us] to predict and plan the future course of our lives within the coercive framework of the law. For the system which makes liability to the law's sanctions dependent upon a voluntary act not only maximizes the power of the individual to determine by his choice his future fate; it also maximizes his power to identify in advance the space which will be left open to him free from the law's interference. Whereas a system from which responsibility was eliminated so that he was liable for that which he did by mistake or accident would leave each individual not only less able to exclude the future interference by the law with his life, but also less able to foresee the times of the law's interference.[k]

Second, by adhering to retributive premises about individual responsibility for misconduct, the criminal law commands widespread public acceptance because those premises describe the way people treat each other in our culture. "[P]ersons interpret each other's movements as manifestations of intention and choices, and these subjective factors are often more important to their social relations than the movements by which they are manifested or their effects." When one person strikes another, Hart argues, "[i]f the blow was light but deliberate, it has a significance for the person struck quite different from an accidental but much heavier blow." He concludes that:

> This is how human nature in society actually is and as yet we have no power to alter it. The bearing of this fundamental fact on law is this. If as our legal moralists maintain it is important for the law to reflect common judgments of morality, it is surely even more important that it should in general reflect in its judgments on human conduct distinctions which not only underlly morality, but pervade the whole of our social life. This it would fail to do if it

[k] H.L.A. Hart, Punishment and Responsibility 180–83 (1968). Copyright © Oxford University Press 1968. The excerpts below are reprinted by permission of the author and Oxford University Press.

treated men as merely alterable, predictable, curable or manipulable things.

--------

## NOTES ON GENERAL DETERRENCE

**1. Introduction.** Deterrence encompasses two distinct concepts, namely, *special* deterrence and *general* deterrence. *Special* deterrence, sometimes called deterrence by intimidation, refers to steps taken to dissuade particular offenders from repeating their crimes. By bringing the costs of lawless behavior to the offenders' attention, the criminal sanction presumably will induce them to refrain from such conduct in the future. *General* deterrence, often called general prevention or deterrence by example, refers to the impact of criminal punishment on other persons. The idea is that members of the public will be deterred from criminal behavior once they see the consequences suffered by those who commit crimes.

Both special and general deterrence rest on the notion that human actors perform a hedonistic calculus of pain and pleasure when choosing among alternative courses of conduct. If the costs of crime are set high enough to assure that the gains to be derived from it are not profitable, the rational person will not commit crimes. Thus, deterrence theory explicitly concedes that human conduct is caused by a variety of factors and requires only that the threat of criminal punishment constitute one such factor. In order to facilitate consideration of deterrence theory, the following paragraphs explore the concept of general deterrence, while special deterrence is included below in the section discussing individual prevention.

**2. The Concept.** In The Rationale of Punishment 19–41 (1830), Jeremy Bentham outlined the classical concept of deterrence:

> Pain and pleasure are the great springs of human action. When a man perceives or supposes pain to be the consequence of an act, he is acted upon in such a manner as tends, with a certain force, to withdraw him, as it were, from the commission of that act. If the apparent magnitude, or rather value* of that pain be greater than the apparent magnitude or value of the pleasure or good he expects to be the consequence of the act, he will be absolutely prevented from performing it. The mischief which would have ensued from the act, if performed, will also by that means be prevented....[a]

\* I say *value*, in order to include the circumstances of *intensity, proximity, certainty*, and *duration*; which magnitude, properly speaking, does not....

[a] As Bentham says later, "[t]he profit of the crime is the force which urges a man to delinquency—the pain of the punishment is the force employed to restrain him from it. If the first of these forces be the greater, the crime will be committed ['that is to say, committed by those who are only restrained by the laws, and not by any other tutelary motives, such as benevolence, religion, or honour']; if the second, the crime will not be committed."—[Footnote by eds.]

General prevention is effected by the denunciation of punishment, and by its application, which, according to the common expression, *serves for an example*. The punishment suffered by the offender presents to every one an example of what he himself will have to suffer if he is guilty of the same offence.

General prevention ought to be the chief end of punishment, as it is its real justification. If we could consider an offence which has been committed as an isolated fact, the like of which would never recur, punishment would be useless. It would only be adding one evil to another. But when we consider that an unpunished crime leaves the path of crime open, not only to the same delinquent, but also to all those who may have the same motives and opportunities for entering upon it, we perceive that the punishment inflicted on the individual becomes a source of security to all. That punishment, which, considered in itself, appeared base and repugnant to all generous sentiments, is elevated to the first rank of benefits, when it is regarded not as an act of wrath or of vengeance against a guilty or unfortunate individual who has given way to mischievous inclinations, but as an indispensable sacrifice to the common safety....

All punishment being in itself evil, upon the principle of utility, if it ought at all to be admitted, it ought only to be admitted in as far as it promises to exclude some greater evil.

Bentham's famous argument captures the utilitarian focus of general deterrence. Unlike retribution, deterrence is not backward-looking in the sense of exacting vengeance for a crime. Rather, it is forward-looking in the sense of preventing or reducing the incidence of future offensive behavior.[b] The central utilitarian premise is that society has the right (and the obligation) to take measures that protect its members from harmful behavior. This premise remains widely influential today.

**3. The Criminal as Rational Calculator.** Bentham himself remarked that critics of his theory doubt that criminal offenders perform the rational calculations that the theory presupposes. The critics concede that the rational calculator model may have some explanatory power for crimes committed for financial gain, but they believe it is wholly unrealistic when applied to crimes motivated by some passion other than greed. By contrast, modern economists support Bentham's assumption that criminals, including those motivated by passions other than cupidity, respond to incentives. As Isaac Ehrlich puts it, "willful engagement in even the most reprehensible violations of legal and moral codes does not preclude an ability to make self-serving choices."[c] Ehrlich offers the following formula to measure the likelihood that a particular actor will decide to participate in criminal activity:

[b] See Kyron Huigens, The Dead End of Deterrence, and Beyond, 41 Wm. & Mary L. Rev. 943, 945 (2000).

[c] Isaac Ehrlich, Crime, Punishment, and the Market for Offenses, 10 J. Econ. Persp. 43 (1996).

[The decision] can be viewed as motivated by the costs and gains from such activity. These include the expected illegitimate payoff (loot) per offense ...; the direct costs incurred by offenders in acquiring the loot (including the costs of self-protection to escape punishment) ...; the wage rate in an alternative legitimate activity ...; the probability of apprehension and conviction ...; the prospective penalty if convicted ...; and finally one's taste (or distaste) for crime—a combination of moral values, proclivity for violence, and preference for risk....

A straightforward combination of these components into an overall expected net return per offense ... might read that this is equal to expected gross payoff [minus] direct costs incurred in acquiring the loot [minus] foregone wages from legitimate activity [minus] (probability of conviction) [times] (prospective penalty if convicted). For crimes that do not involve any material gain, the net return is negative; it can be viewed as the price of crime to the offender.

This formulation includes two additional simplifying assumptions. One is that potential offenders are risk neutral; the other is that "distaste for crime" can be measured as a constant, compensating expected net return that an individual requires to enter a criminal activity. In other words, the net payoff must exceed some threshold level before an individual decides to engage in crime. Given these conditions, the individual supply of offenses will be a function of the personal (expected) net return from crime.[d]

As the foregoing excerpt illustrates, contemporary economic theory is far more sensitive to the diverse determinants of criminal activity than Bentham's blunt assertion that "every one calculates." However, some critics insist that economists will not provide useful suggestions about how to deter crime until they develop a model that is faithful to the psychological characteristics of the persons whom the law most wants to deter. According to John DiIulio, for example, what is needed is a model that takes account of the fact that many young criminals

... are almost completely incapable of deferring gratifications for the sake of future rewards. In their lives, there has never been a stable relationship between doing "what's right" and being rewarded and doing "what's wrong" and being punished.... Such discipline as they may have received ... has been almost purely arbitrary: the first three times they commit a given prohibited act, nothing happens; the fourth time they get screamed at; the fifth and sixth times nothing happens; the seventh time they get punched in the head; the eight time nothing happens; and so on.... Their lived experience, the most powerful teacher of all, counsels that kids who look ahead, stay in school and "do the right

---

[d] Id. Reprinted by permission of the author and American Economic Association.

thing" often end up just as jobless, hopeless and miserable as kids who do crime.

[T]he extraordinary degree to which today's young street criminals are present oriented, and the extent to which they do crime for fun as well as for profit, has yet to be taken fully into account by economists. "You never think about doing thirty," one young prisoner told me, "when you don't expect to live to thirty."

[I]magine a radically present-oriented young man who is also unable to feel joy or pain at the joy or pain of others. He is capable of committing the most heinous acts of physical violence for the most trivial reasons ... without feeling remorse or losing any sleep. He fears neither the stigma of arrest nor the pains of imprisonment.... If he is part of a gang, then going to prison is very nearly a good "career move." And the things he gets for behaving criminally ... —money, drugs, status, sex—are their own immediate rewards. So for as long as his youthful energies hold out, he does what comes naturally: murders, assaults, rapes, robs, burglarizes and deals deadly drugs....

If there is a model of criminal deterrence in the literature that mirrors such behavioral propensities, I have yet to come across it.... Models that assume that young urban street predators are but a highly impulsive breed of middle-aged economics professors are not only intellectually idle, but (should anyone actually be foolish enough to act on them) downright dangerous. The reality simply does not fit the theory; economists need a new theory, one way beyond the confines of the [current rational calculator] model.[e]

How helpful is the rational calculator model when contemplating the appropriate response to misbehavior committed by actors in the testing cases?

**4. How Much Punishment Will Deter?** Critics of deterrence often complain that the theory does not offer a precise standard by which to measure the kind or amount of punishment that the law should inflict. What types of assessments should legislators and judges make when designating sentence levels or selecting the punishment for a particular crime? If deterrence is the goal, why not simply impose uniform, severe penalties for all crimes? Is proportionality a relic of retributive thinking that deterrence theorists rebuff? Richard Posner has considered these and other difficult questions.

[T]here is a place in the criminal justice system, and a big one, for imprisonment; and perhaps for other nonmonetary criminal sanctions as well. Since the cost of murder to the victim approaches infinity, ... even life imprisonment may not impose costs

[e] John J. DiIulio, Jr., Help Wanted: Economists, Crime and Public Policy, 10 J. Econ. Persp. 3, 16–17 (1996). Reprinted by permission of the author and American Economic Association.

on the murderer equal to those of the victim. It might seem, however, that the important thing is not that the punishment for murder equal the cost to the victim but that it be high enough to make the murder not pay—and surely imprisoning the murderer for the rest of his life or, if he is wealthy, confiscating his wealth would cost him more than the murder could possibly have gained him. But this analysis implicitly treats the probability of apprehension and conviction as one. If it is less than one, as of course it is, then the murderer will not be comparing the gain from the crime with the loss if he is caught and sentenced; he will be comparing it with the disutility of the sentence discounted by the probability that it will actually be imposed. . . .

Capital punishment is . . . supported by considerations of marginal deterrence, which require as big a spread as possible between the punishments for the least and most serious crimes. If the maximum punishment for murder is life imprisonment, we may not want to make armed robbery also punishable by life imprisonment, for then armed robbers would have no additional incentive not to murder their victims.[f] But . . . the argument does not lead inexorably to the conclusion that capital punishment should be the punishment for simple murder. For if it is, then we have the problem of marginally deterring the multiple murderer. Maybe capital punishment should be reserved for him, so that murderers have a disincentive to kill witnesses to the murder, though again the number of such complementary murders may be less if the initial murder is punished severely. . . .

Death is not the only modern form of "afflictive" punishment. Flogging is still used by many parents and, in attenuated form, in some schools. The economic objection to punishing by inflicting physical pain is not that it is disgusting or that people have different thresholds of pain that make it difficult to calibrate the severity of the punishment—imprisonment and death are subject to the same problem. The objection is that it may be a poor method of inflicting severe but not lethal punishment. Just to inflict a momentary excruciating pain with no after-effects might

---

[f] Bentham also defended a rule of proportionality in grading:

> *When two offences come in competition, the punishment for the greater offence must be sufficient to induce a man to prefer the less.*

Two offences may be said to be in competition, when it is in the power of an individual to commit both. When thieves break into a house, they may execute their purpose in different manners; by simply stealing, by theft accompanied with bodily injury, or murder, or incendiarism. If the punishment is the same for simple theft, as for theft and murder, you give the thieves a motive for committing murder, because this crime adds to the facility of committing the former, and the chance of impunity when it is committed.

The great inconvenience resulting from the infliction of great punishments for small offenses, is, that the power of increasing them in proportion to the magnitude of the offense is thereby lost.—[Footnote by eds.]

be a trivial deterrent, especially for people who had never experienced such pain; while to inflict a level of pain that would be the equivalent of five years in prison would require measures so drastic that they might endanger the life, or destroy the physical or mental health, of the offender.... Incidentally, I do not mean, by omission, to disparage noneconomic objections to "afflictive punishment." But this is an Article about economics....

[T]here is an argument ... for combining heavy prison terms for convicted criminals with low probabilities of apprehension and conviction. Consider the choice between combining a .1 probability of apprehension and conviction with a ten-year prison term and a .2 probability of apprehension and conviction with a five-year term. Under the second approach twice as many individuals are imprisoned but for only half as long, so the total costs of imprisonment to the government will be the same under the two approaches. But the costs of police, court officials, and the like will probably be lower under the first approach. The probability of apprehension and conviction, and hence the number of prosecutions, is only half as great. Although more resources will be devoted to a trial where the possible punishment is greater, these resources will be incurred in fewer trials because fewer people will be punished, and even if the total litigation resources are no lower, police and prosecution costs will clearly be much lower....

But isn't a system under which probabilities of punishment are low "unfair," because it creates ex post inequality among offenders? Many go scot-free; others serve longer prison sentences than they would if more offenders were caught. However, to object to this result is like saying that all lotteries are unfair because, ex post, they create wealth differences among the players. In an equally significant sense both the criminal justice system that creates low probabilities of apprehension and conviction and the lottery are fair so long as the ex ante costs and benefits are equalized among the participants. Nor is it correct that while real lotteries are voluntary the criminal justice "lottery" is not. The criminal justice lottery is voluntary: you keep out of it by not committing crimes.[g]

As Posner remarks, the magnitude of the criminal sanction is not the only factor that determines the deterrent effect of punishment. The proximity and certainty of punishment—the probability of conviction and imposition of a criminal sanction—must also be taken into account. Johannes Andenaes has spoken to the relationship between these factors:

... Even the simplest kind of common sense indicates that the degree of risk of detection and conviction is of paramount impor-

[g] Richard Posner, An Economic Theory of the Criminal Law, 85 Colum. L. Rev. 1193, 1209–13 (1985). Reprinted by permission of the author and Columbia Law Review Association, Inc.

tance to the preventive effects of the penal law. Very few people would violate law if there were a policeman on every doorstep. It has even been suggested that the insanity of an offender be determined by asking whether he would have performed the prohibited act "with a policeman at his elbow."

Exceptions would occur, however. Some crimes are committed in such a state of excitement that the criminal acts without regard to the consequences. In other cases the actor accepts the penalty as a reasonable price for carrying out the action—we may think of the attitude a busy salesman has toward parking regulations. Further a political assassin may deliberately sacrifice his life to his cause. But there is good reason to believe that certainty of rapid apprehension and punishment would prevent *most* violations.

On the other hand, there is evidence that the lack of enforcement of penal laws designed to regulate behavior in morally neutral fields may rapidly lead to mass infringements. Parking regulations, currency regulations, and price regulations are examples of such laws. The individual's moral reluctance to break the law is not strong enough to secure obedience when the law comes into conflict with his personal interests.[h]

**5. Measuring Deterrence.** As explained above, retribution is a theory of punishment whose validity does not depend on empirical verification. By contrast, the central premise of deterrence theory—that punishment discourages crime—invites empirical validation. However, to date, much of the empirical support for the deterrent effect of punishment remains anecdotal.

In 1978, Daniel Nagin reviewed the empirical literature on deterrence in a report prepared for the National Research Council. His conclusions remain a fair assessment of the current state of scientific research in this area:

> [D]espite the intensity of the research effort, the empirical evidence is still not sufficient for providing a rigorous confirmation of the existence of a deterrent effect. Perhaps more important, the evidence is woefully inadequate for providing a good estimate of the magnitude of whatever effect may exist. . . .
>
> This is in stark contrast to some of the presentations in public discussion that have unequivocally concluded that sanctions deter and that have made sweeping suggestions that sanctioning practices be changed to take advantage of the presumed deterrent effect. Certainly, most people will agree that increasing sanctions will deter crime somewhat, but the critical question is, By how much? There is still considerable uncertainty over whether that

[h] Johannes Andenaes, The General–Preventive Effects of Punishment, 114 U.Pa. L.Rev. 949, 960–70 (1966). Reprinted by permission of the University of Pennsylvania Law Review and Fred B. Rothman & Company from the University of Pennsylvania Law Review, vol. 114, pp. 960–61.

effect is trivial (even if statistically detectable) or profound. Any unequivocal policy conclusion is simply not supported by valid evidence.

Although more punitive sanctioning practices might legitimately be argued as a responsible ethical response to a truly significant crime problem, arguing such a policy on the basis of the empirical evidence is not yet justified because it offers a misleading impression of scientific validity. Policy makers in the criminal justice system are done a disservice if they are left with the impression that the empirical evidence, which they themselves are frequently unable to evaluate, strongly supports the deterrence hypothesis. Furthermore, such distortions ultimately undermine the credibility of scientific evidence as inputs to public-policy choices. A more critical assessment of the evidence is needed if we are to see progress in the development of knowledge about deterrent effectiveness and its application to effective public policy.[i]

Yet, as John DiIulio observes, "On drives to academic conferences I have noted that even criminologists who have critiqued deterrence theories pump their brakes when a highway patrol car appears."[j]

**6. Deterrence and Blameworthiness.** Bentham argued that punishment ought not to be inflicted in cases where it would be "inefficacious." For example, he remarked that punishment "cannot act so as to prevent the mischief" in cases "of extreme infancy, insanity, and intoxication." Presumably, the threat of criminal sanctions does not affect the behavior of young children or actors who are insane or very drunk. For the retributivist, these examples involve persons who would not be blameworthy for having engaged in otherwise criminal behavior. H.L.A. Hart has argued that deterrence theory alone does not support Bentham's position:

> Utilitarians have made strenuous, detailed efforts to show that restriction of the use of punishment to those who have voluntarily broken the law is explicable on purely utilitarian lines. Bentham's efforts are the most complete and their failure is an instructive warning to contemporaries....
>
> Bentham's argument is in fact a spectacular non sequitur. He sets out to prove that to *punish* the mad, the infant child or those who break the law unintentionally or under duress or even under "necessity" must be inefficacious; but all that he proves (at the most) is the quite different proposition that the *threat* of punishment will be ineffective so far as the class of persons who suffer from these conditions is concerned. Plainly it is possible that though (as Bentham says) the *threat* of punishment could not have

[i] Daniel Nagin, General Deterrence: A Review of the Empirical Literature, in Deterrence and Incapacitation: Estimating the Effects of Criminal Sanctions on Crime Rates 135–36 (Alfred Blumstein et al. eds. 1978).

[j] John J. DiIulio, Jr., Help Wanted: Economists, Crime and Public Policy, 10 J. Econ. Persp. 3, 16 (1996).

operated on them, the actual *infliction* of punishment on those persons, may secure a higher measure of conformity to law on the part of normal persons than is secured by the admission of excusing conditions. If this is so and if utilitarian principles only were at stake, we should, without any sense that we were sacrificing any principle of value or were choosing the lesser of two evils, drop from the law the restriction on punishment entailed by the admission of excuses: Unless, of course, we believed that the terror or insecurity or misery produced by the operation of laws so draconic was worse than the lower measure of obedience to law secured by the law which admits excuses.

This objection to Bentham's rationale of excuses is not merely a fanciful one. Any increase in the number of conditions required to establish criminal liability increases the opportunity for deceiving courts or juries by the pretence that some condition is not satisfied. When the condition is a psychological factor the chances of such pretence succeeding are considerable. Quite apart from the provision made for mental disease, the cases where an accused person pleads that he killed in his sleep or accidentally or in some temporary abnormal state of unconsciousness show that deception is certainly feasible. From the utilitarian point of view this may lead to two sorts of "losses." The belief that such deception is feasible may embolden persons who would not otherwise risk punishment to take their chance of deceiving a jury in this way. Secondly, a criminal who actually succeeds in this deception will be left at large, though belonging to the class which the law is concerned to incapacitate.[k]

Although Hart's argument might suggest that utilitarians should abandon blameworthiness as a necessary condition for punishment, Louis Michael Seidman has claimed that the criminal sanction can function as a deterrent only when it reflects community intuitions about culpability. He observed:

Quite by accident, the law and economics literature provides some chilling insights into the law enforcement consequences of divorcing punishment from blame. It is interesting to note that proponents of an economic view of crime repeatedly rely on the model of the traffic violator to make their argument. This choice of example is hardly coincidental. It serves the economists heuristic purposes to choose for study a "crime" where we can imagine both the criminal and society rationally calculating costs and benefits without the encumbrance of moral feelings and inhibitions. Of course, for that very reason the example is highly misleading. [A] person reading this literature might suppose that when Americans complain about crime in the street, they are upset about overtime

[k] H.L.A. Hart, Punishment and Responsibility 18–20 (1968). Copyright © Oxford University Press 1968. The excerpts below are reprinted by permission of the author and Oxford University Press.

parking. Yet the example is also unintentionally revealing. It suggests that if we do succeed in remaking our criminal justice system into a means of imposing pain without blame, we will end up with exactly the sort of compliance we now achieve at a typical parking meter.

Similarly, ... Richard Posner [draws an analogy between the criminal process and a lottery.] Posner may or may not be correct about optimal enforcement levels, but he surely misunderstands the point of his own analogy. Many people have no moral qualms about playing the lotteries, and those who have a taste for risk will play them even when the odds are substantially unfavorable. Thus, if we make our criminal justice system look like a lottery, we can hardly claim surprise when potential criminals choose to play the game.

The evidence is all around us that large numbers of people are willing to play the crime game when the threatened punishment no longer communicates moral disapproval. From the disastrous effort sixty years ago to enforce Prohibition to the current and growing difficulty in deterring tax evasion, it is clear that people do not respond solely to the risk of loss unassociated with moral blame....[1]

———

## NOTES ON INDIVIDUAL PREVENTION

**1.  Introduction.** It is convenient to collect the remaining purposes of punishment under the rubric of individual prevention because each is based on the proposition that the system should devote its resources to preventing those who commit a crime from violating again. The focus here shifts from the effect of punishment on the general population to the effect of punishment on particular offenders. However, the ultimate objective—prevention of future criminality—remains the same. Usually, considerations of individual prevention play a more prominent role in making sentencing decisions than in determining the substantive content of criminal prohibitions.

**2.  Special Deterrence.** Special deterrence refers to steps taken to discourage individual offenders from repeating their misconduct. It is conceptually distinct from rehabilitation, although the two objectives sometimes are confused and the criminal sanction may be intended to serve both objectives simultaneously. The justification for a sentence to probation, for example, might be both to intimidate the offender through exposure to the criminal process and to rehabilitate him through official supervision during the period of probation. Special deterrence presupposes that the actor who

[1] Louis Michael Seidman, Soldiers, Martyrs, and Criminals: Utilitarian Theory and the Problem of Crime Control, 94 Yale L. J. 315, 332–33 (1984). Reprinted by permission of the author and Yale Law Journal.

offends once may desire to commit future violations, but assumes that the costs imposed by the past punishment will discourage him from continuing his criminal career. By contrast, rehabilitation is a therapeutic intervention that proposes to transform the offender's character so that he no longer considers criminal misconduct to be a potentially desirable course of action.

The literature on special deterrence is scant. Most studies of prison effectiveness focus on rehabilitative programs or incapacitative goals rather than on the isolated effect of special deterrence. To the extent that special deterrence is considered on its own terms, some commentators argue that high recidivism rates demonstrate that punishment is not an effective special deterrent. To be sure, there may be types of offenders who do not find punishment intimidating, and these offenders may comprise the bulk of the prison population. However, other types of offenders may learn from the fact of conviction or from realistic exposure to the possibility of severe sanctions that they want to avoid future entanglement in the criminal process. Indeed, the so-called "split sentence" has become more widely used in recent years on just this theory. A "split sentence" is a sentence that uses a short jail term (which gives the offender a taste of confinement, for the purpose of inducing a distaste for it) followed by a period of probation.[a]

Finally, special deterrence is subject to some of the same shortcomings that are said to afflict general deterrence theory. For one thing, the empirical foundation for assertions about special deterrence has not been scientifically established. Moreover, no less than general deterrence, the inexorable pursuit of special deterrence would produce results that the community finds unethical, and, therefore, special deterrence appears to give way in such cases to constraints imposed by retributive theory.[b]

**3. Incapacitation.** "When criminals are deprived of their liberty, as by imprisonment . . ., their ability to commit offenses against citizens is ended. We say these persons have been 'incapacitated'. . . ."[c] At first glance, incapacitation appears to be a foolproof method of crime prevention in that it avoids some of the more vexing empirical questions posed by

---

[a] Its use is described and defended in ABA Standards for Criminal Justice ch. 18, pp. 100–07 (2d ed. 1980); see also Federal Sentencing Guidelines Manual 7 (West 1995) (The United States Sentencing Commission approved the split sentence on the ground that in some cases "the definite prospect of prison, even though the term may be short, will serve as a significant deterrent, particularly when compared with pre-guidelines practice where probation, not prison, was the norm.").

[b] Daniel Farrell offers the following example of the limits that retributivism places on special deterrence:

[I]t is not at all clear that we would feel justified in killing an aggressor's children, even if that were the only way of keeping her from killing us. And we would certainly say that we are much more clearly justified in killing the murderous aggressor, in order to protect ourselves from her, than in killing her children, even if the latter would do the job just as well as the former.

Daniel M. Farrell, The Justification of General Deterrence, in Punishment and Rehabilitation 41 (Jeffrie G. Murphy ed., 1995).

[c] James Q. Wilson, Selective Incapacitation, in Principled Sentencing 148 (Andrew von Hirsch & Andrew Ashworth eds. 1992).

deterrence theory. In a word, incapacitation "works:" as long as the offender is incarcerated, we are confident that he or she is not committing further offenses within the community.

As it turns out, incapacitation presents an empirical problem of imposing dimensions. Consistent with its utilitarian objectives, incapacitation should be used only in cases where it is needed to restrain the offender from committing a future offense. Incapacitation provides no justification for punishing offenders who would not commit another crime anyway. Thus, for one thing, incapacitation theory requires the system to develop a mechanism that distinguishes those offenders who are potentially recidivist from those who are not. Accordingly, law enforcement officials have begun to explore the feasibility of "selective incapacitation" programs. A panel of the National Research Council explains the concept and identifies the different forms selective incapacitation may take:

Under 1970 incarceration policies, incapacitation was estimated to have reduced the number of FBI index crimes [murder, rape, robbery, aggravated assault, burglary, larceny, and auto theft] by 10 to 20 percent. For robberies and burglaries, incapacitation is estimated to have reduced their number by 25–35 percent in 1973; in 1982, after the national inmate population had almost doubled, the incapacitative effect for these offenses is estimated to have increased to about 35–45 percent. For general increases in incarceration to reduce index crimes by an additional 10 to 20 percent from 1982 levels, inmate populations again would have to have more than doubled.

Since the increments to crime control from incapacitation are modest, even with very large general increases in inmate populations, and since considerable pressure on prison and jail resources exists, interest has been stimulated in developing policies that selectively target incapacitation on the most active offenders. Such policies have the potential of achieving the same, or even improved, crime reduction, with much smaller increases in inmate populations. Two forms of selective incapacitation policies have been considered: offender-based policies, which extend the time served for those predicted to be high-rate offenders among all those convicted of the same charge; and charge-based policies, which impose mandatory minimum terms on all offenders convicted of selected offense types in which high-rate offenders tend to engage.

Of the selective incapacitation policies that have been proposed, the estimated crime reduction effects ... are modest, ranging at most up to 10 percent. Compared with the 100 percent increase in inmate populations required to achieve this reduction through general increases in incarceration, however, selective incapacitation policies involve only 10 to 20 percent increases in total inmate populations. The achievable incapacitative effect will be lower, however, if the offenses of incarcerated offenders are continued by others or replaced by new recruits. The degree to which replacement occurs can be expected to vary by crime type (e.g., presumably higher for drug sales than for acts of personal violence), but there are no estimates of rates of replacement.[d]

Apparently impressed by the notion of incapacitation, legislators have begun passing a number of tough sentencing initiatives, including the so-called "three strikes and you're out" laws.[e] Some commentators have criticized these initiatives on the ground that the system is not equipped to make the predictions of future dangerousness that incapacitation theory requires. However, there is a "widespread and growing consensus" among behavioral scientists on the proposition that "clinical predictions of violence have more than chance validity."[f] Moreover, parole boards in some jurisdictions determine the length of offenders' prison terms in part by assessing their likelihood of recidivism. Recidivism assessments rely on a range of offender characteristics identified by social scientists as predictive of future dangerousness. Such factors include "age of initiation of criminal careers, drug use, [length of time spent unemployed], and prior criminal record."[g] Consultants for the National Research Council evaluated several of these assessment instruments and found that they produced a "rate of false positives"[h] that ranged from less than 30 percent to 60 percent.

Since the system is incapable of identifying recidivist offenders with perfect accuracy, incapacitation raises difficult ethical questions for policy makers. What margin of error is acceptable in making predictions of future criminality? If there is only a 30 percent chance that a violent offender with certain characteristics will commit another violent offense, is incapacitation appropriate? For how long? Until the chances are reduced to 10 per cent?

[d] 1 Panel on Research on Criminal Careers, National Research Council, Criminal Careers and "Career Criminals" 6–7 (Alfred Blumstein et al. eds., 1986).

[e] Under the "three strikes" approach to sentencing, offenders who commit the requisite number of crimes ("strikes") of a specified kind (usually felonies) are sentenced to life terms. John DiIulio describes and responds to one criticism of this approach, namely, that the approach is both inefficient and unfair because persons convicted of several trivial violations may be incarcerated for life:

> [F]indings on the amount of serious crime committed by probationers and parolees and the failure of intensive supervision programs have led some to conclude that three-strikes laws are the "only answer." ... Opponents [of three strikes measures argue that such laws will] lead to the lifetime incarceration of mere "nonviolent" offenders.... The much-publicized 1994 case of the California felon whose "third strike" was stealing a slice of pizza in a mall sounds positively damning until you get all the facts. The facts are that this man had four prior felony convictions in nine years, five suspended sentences, and numerous bouts on probation.

John J. DiIulio, Jr., Help Wanted: Economists, Crime and Public Policy, 10 J. Econ. Persp. 3, 14 (1996).

[f] John Monahan, Clinical and Actuarial Predictions of Violence, in West's Companion to Scientific Evidence (D. Faigman et al. eds., 1996).

[g] Panel on Research on Criminal Careers, National Research Council, Criminal Careers and "Career Criminals" 5 (Alfred Blumstein et al. eds., 1986).

[h] As the National Research Council report explains, "false positives" are "offenders classified as high risks [for recidivist conduct] who were not arrested during the follow-up period."

Until there is *no* chance? These problems are exacerbated where the predicted future offense does not involve violence. For how long should a petty thief be incapacitated if there is a 90 percent chance of future petty thefts? By itself, incapacitation theory may justify sentencing this thief to a term of life imprisonment. On the other hand, empirical studies suggest that certain kinds of killers are virtually certain not to repeat their crimes. For example, some of the testing cases may involve one-time homicides. If so, punishment of those and similar killers would not be justified at all according to an incapacitation rationale.

The system resolves some of these problems by making one of the philosophical compromises alluded to at the beginning of this essay. In other words, the system may decide what punishment to impose on the killer by invoking some goal of punishment other than incapacitation and thereby restraining the result that incapacitation theory would achieve on its own. Both retribution and deterrence usually demand a substantial punishment for the killer, notwithstanding a prediction that the particular offender is not likely to perpetrate crimes in the future.

Norval Morris offered a theory of criminal punishment that explicitly combines retributive and incapacitative goals. Under this theory, punishment should rest primarily on retributive grounds, with incapacitation serving as a useful subsidiary objective. In Morris's view, where crimes of serious violence are involved, the criminal process should take account of predictions of future dangerousness even if "the best we can do at present is to predict one in three, in the sense that to be sure of preventing one crime we would have to lock up three people."[i] Thus, once an offender has been convicted and a range of *deserved* punishments identified, it is proper for judges to rely on predictions concerning the offender's dangerousness when selecting a sentence from within the specified range. The idea is that the judge will sentence offenders predicted to be recidivists to the maximum deserved term, while imposing the minimum deserved term on offenders who are unlikely to repeat their crimes. Morris discussed some of the ethical questions raised by his approach:[*]

> Criminals *X* and *Y* had identical criminal records and had committed identical crimes, but *Y* was not a school dropout, *Y* had a job to which he could return if not sent to prison, and *Y* had a supportive family who would take him back if allowed to do so, while the unfortunate *X* was a school dropout, was unemployed, and lacked a supportive family. And let us suppose that past studies reveal that criminals with *X*'s criminal record and with his environmental circumstances have a ... 1 in 10 [chance] of being involved in a crime of personal violence. While no such calculations have been made for criminals like *Y*, it is quite clear that they have a much lower base expectancy rate of future violent criminal-

---

[i] Norval Morris, Incapacitation Within Limits, in Principled Sentencing 140 (Andrew von Hirsch & Andrew Ashworth eds., 1992).

[*] Reprinted with permission from The Record of The Association of the Bar of the City of New York, © 1984. 39 The Record 102.

ity. I suggest that $X$ should be held longer than $Y$ based on these predictions.

[T]he reality in this country at this time will be that my apparently aseptic principles will grossly favor the wealthy to the detriment of the poor, and will be used to justify even more imprisonment of blacks and other underclass minorities than at present obtains—as will the whole "selective incapacitation" process. Put curtly, without knowing more about our hypothetical criminals, we already confidently guess the pigmentation of $X$ and $Y$. As a matter of statistical likelihood, $Y$ is white and $X$ is black.

[L]et me offer one or two comments by way of explanation—not really apology—for my thesis. The sad fact is that in our society predictors of violence are not racially neutral. How could they be racially neutral, when at this moment one of every 20 black males in their twenties is either in prison or in jail.[j] And that really underestimates the difference between blacks and whites in prisons and jails, since when black youths move into the middle class their crime rates are just the same as those of white youths. It is the black underclass, left behind, which has these enormously high rates of imprisonment and jailing and very much higher rates of violence.... And what else is characteristic of the inner-city ghetto? Much else that distinguishes our criminal $X$ from our criminal $Y$—school absenteeism, unemployment, functional illiteracy, generations on welfare, no supportive families. Blackness and a higher base expectancy rate of violence overlap....

What, then, is the conclusion properly to be drawn from these sad realities? Some would say: "Don't base decisions in the criminal justice system at all on predictions of dangerousness; they are racially skewed, and we already lock up too many ... minorities." I sympathize with the reason, but reject the conclusion. The criminal justice system cannot rectify racial inequalities and social injustices; it will do well if it does not exacerbate them.... We cannot properly close our eyes to the different threats that criminal $X$ and criminal $Y$ pose to the community. But it is of first importance that we base our [predictions about violence] on validated knowledge and not on prejudice, particularly racial prejudice, and hence that we insist on the most careful validation of such stereotypes of dangerousness....

Theories of punishment that combine retributive and incapacitative premises create yet another puzzle, when we remark that incapacitation rests on assumptions about human conduct very different from those underlying retribution. Retributive theory dictates that criminal $X$ and criminal $Y$ "deserve" to be punished because each voluntarily chose to

---

[j] A recent study reports that "[a]lmost one in three (32.2%) young black men in the age group 20–29 [was] under criminal justice supervision on any given day [in 1995]—in prison or jail, on probation or parole." The Sentencing Project, Young Black Americans and the Criminal Justice System: Five Years Later 1 (Oct. 1995).—[Footnote by eds.]

commit a crime. None of the facts about criminal $X$'s impoverished background diminishes his responsibility for his offense even though they probably made it very hard for him to obey the law. According to incapacitation theory, by contrast, criminal $X$ is an appropriate candidate for (enhanced) punishment because his impoverished circumstances suggest that he may be unable to avoid offending in the future. Herbert Packer concisely summarized the dilemma:

> The case for incapacitation is strongest in precisely those areas where the offender is least capable of controlling himself, where his conduct bears the least resemblance to the kind of purposeful, voluntary conduct to which we are likely to attach moral condemnation. Baldly put, the incapacitative theory is at its strongest for those who, in retributive terms, are the least deserving of punishment.[k]

**4. Rehabilitation.** The literature concerning rehabilitation as a goal of punishment[l] has tended to fluctuate between extremes of optimism and pessimism. According to the rehabilitative model, criminal conduct is caused by the pathology of individual offenders. Karl Menninger has offered an eloquent argument in favor of the optimistic view of rehabilitation in which he praises rehabilitation as a humanitarian intervention that promises to cure offenders and return them to law-abiding ways. As Menninger points out, the psychiatric community has developed numerous therapeutic "forms and techniques," which are designed to enhance the individual's "impulse control and life satisfaction" and which are successful in achieving those goals. Among the treatments that Menninger mentions are "[p]sychoanalysis; electroshock therapy; psychotherapy; occupational and industrial therapy; family group therapy; milieu therapy; the use of music, art, and horticultural activities; and various drug therapies." Menninger also claims that therapists can and should provide other kinds of assistance that enhance the treatment effect, including advice concerning leisure activities, physical exercise, social companions, and job opportunities. Menninger remarks that these interventions will succeed in effecting a cure, however, only if "[a]ll of the participants . . . are imbued with what we may call a *therapeutic attitude*." According to Menninger, the "therapeutic attitude" rejects "attitudes of avoidance, ridicule, scorn, or punitiveness" towards the patient. While therapists disapprove of their patients'

---

[k] Herbert Packer, The Limits of the Criminal Sanction 50–51 (1968).

[l] A panel of the National Research Council offers the following definition of rehabilitation:

> The definition . . . involves three aspects[:] the desired outcome, the intervening variable(s) to be the assumed target of the rehabilitative treatment, and the intervention itself. [R]ehabilitation [is] the result of any planned intervention that reduces an offender's further criminal activity, whether that reduction is mediated by personality, behavior, abilities, attitudes, values or other factors. The effects of maturation and the effects associated with "fear" or "intimidation" are excluded, the result of the latter having traditionally been labeled as "specific deterrence."

Panel on Research on Rehabilitative Techniques, National Research Council, New Directions in the Rehabilitation of Criminal Offenders 8 (Susan E. Martin et al. eds., 1981).

"offensive" or "obnoxious" conduct, they recognize such conduct "as symptomatic of [the patients'] continued imbalance and disorganization, which is what they are seeking to change." Menninger believes that these various treatment techniques may form part of an effective prison rehabilitation program, but he emphasizes that such programs will not succeed unless program administrators deliberately replace "the punitive attitude with a therapeutic attitude." Finally, Menninger anticipates and responds to critics of his approach:

> "But you were talking about the mentally ill," readers may interject, "those poor, confused, bereft, frightened individuals who yearn for help from you doctors and nurses. Do you mean to imply that willfully perverse individuals, our criminals, can be similarly reached and rehabilitated?" . . .
>
> Do I believe there is effective treatment for offenders, and they *can* be changed? *Most certainly and definitely I do.* Not all cases, to be sure; there are also some physical afflictions which we cannot cure at the moment. Some provision has to be made for incurables—pending new knowledge—and these will include some offenders. But I believe the majority of them would prove to be curable. The willfulness and the viciousness of offenders are part of the thing for which they have to be treated. These must not thwart the therapeutic attitude. . . .[m]

Such assertions have prompted sharp criticisms. A number of authors have attacked the empirical basis for the claim that offenders can be cured of their vicious propensities. In an influential survey, sociologist Robert Martinson reviewed the scientific research on rehabilitation that was published between 1945 and 1967. To say the least, his assessment of the efficacy of rehabilitative programs was negative. Martinson stopped short of concluding that "nothing works" to rehabilitate offenders, but just barely: *"With few exceptions, the rehabilitative efforts that have been reported so far have had no appreciable effect on recidivism."*[n] Martinson did concede that some programs might be working and that researchers had failed to identify rehabilitative effects because of flaws in their experimental methodology. He also agreed that some of the underlying therapies might be imperfectly designed and poorly administered. Nonetheless, he doubted that rehabilitation was a legitimate goal of punishment:

> It may be . . . that there is a more radical flaw in our present strategies—that education at its best, or that psychotherapy at its best, cannot overcome, or even appreciably reduce the powerful tendency for offenders to continue in criminal behavior. Our present treatment programs are based on a theory of crime as a 'disease'—that is to say, as something foreign and abnormal in the individual which can presumably be cured. This theory may well

[m] Karl Menninger, The Crime of Punishment 259–62 (1968).

[n] Robert Martinson, What Works?—Questions and Answers About Prison Reform, 35 Pub. Int. 22, 25 (1974).

be flawed, in that it overlooks—indeed, denies—both the normality of crime in society and the personal normality of a very large proportion of offenders, criminals who are merely responding to the facts and conditions of our society.

In recent years, the empirical literature on rehabilitation has adopted a more moderate outlook. Indeed, Martinson performed a subsequent study, which led him to "withdraw [his] conclusion" that rehabilitation has " 'no appreciable effect on recidivism.' "[o] This time, Martinson found, some kinds of interventions, including especially supervised parole, are effective in reducing rearrest rates. Other commentators continue to urge that there are "good reason[s] for not completely abandoning a faith in rehabilitation." First, "a number of studies have shown that improvements *can* be effected in failure rates." Second, the primary "reason why treatment has so often been shown to have no effect . . . is simply that none has been given."[p] "Why would one expect that one hour per week of group therapy with a poorly trained leader and unwilling participants would produce a major behavior change in incarcerated felons, especially considering the powerful effect of the prison background."[q] According to this view, rehabilitation may well prove to be effective, at least for some categories of offenders, but only if the community is willing to devote substantial resources to the development and implementation of new treatment programs.

For some philosophers, however, evidence that rehabilitation "works" makes it all the more objectionable on ethical grounds. For example, Herbert Morris has argued that the notion that crime is an event caused by the offender's sickness is "basically at odds" with norms that structure not only the criminal process, but also our entire way of life.[r] Morris offers the following criticism of rehabilitation as a legitimate function of punishment:[*]

> First, human beings pride themselves in having capacities that animals do not. . . . In a system where all actions are assimilated to happenings we are assimilated to creatures . . . whom we have always thought possessed of less than we. Fundamental to our practice of praise and order of attainment is that one who can do more . . . is more worthy of respect and admiration. And we have thought of ourselves as capable, where animals are not, of making, of creating, among other things, ourselves. . . .

[o] Robert Martinson, New Findings, New Views: A Note of Caution Regarding Sentencing Reform, 7 Hofstra L. Rev. 243, 252–54 (1979).

[p] Stephen Brody, How Effective Are Penal Treatments?, in Principled Sentencing 12 (Andrew von Hirsch & Andrew Ashworth eds., 1992).

[q] Panel on Research on Rehabilitative Techniques, National Research Council, New Directions in the Rehabilitation of Criminal Offenders 9 (Susan E. Martin et al. eds., 1981).

[r] Herbert Morris, Rehabilitation and Dignity, in Principled Sentencing 17 (Andrew von Hirsch & Andrew Ashworth eds., 1992).

[*] Copyright © 1968, THE MONIST, La-Salle, Illinois 61301. Reprinted by permission.

Second, if all human conduct is viewed as something men undergo, thrown into question would be the appropriateness of that extensive range of peculiarly human satisfactions that derive from a sense of achievement. For these satisfactions we shall have to substitute those mild satisfactions attendant upon a healthy well-functioning body. . . .

Third, in the therapy world nothing is earned and what we receive comes to us through compassion, or through a desire to control us. Resentment is out of place. We can take credit for nothing but must always regard ourselves . . . as fortunate recipients of benefits or unfortunate carriers of disease who must be controlled. We know that within our own world human beings who have been so regarded and who come to accept this view of themselves come to look upon themselves as worthless. When what we do is met with resentment, we are indirectly paid something of a compliment.

Fourth, [t]he logic of cure will push us towards forms of therapy that inevitably involve changes in the person made against his will. The evil in this would be most apparent in those cases where the agent, whose action is determined to be a manifestation of some disease, does not regard his action in this way. He believes that what he has done is, in fact, "right," but his conception of "normality" is not the therapeutically accepted one. [Thus,] we have to change him and his judgments of value. In doing this we display a lack of respect for the moral status of individuals, that is, a lack of respect for the reasoning and choices of individuals. They are but animals who must be conditioned. I think we can understand and, indeed, sympathize with a man's preferring death to being forcibly turned into what he is not.

Finally, perhaps most frightening of all would be the derogation in status of all protests to treatment. [T]he protest will itself be regarded as a sign of some pathological condition, for who would not wish to be cured of an affliction? What this leads to are questions of an important kind about the effect of this conception of man upon what we now understand by reasoning. Here what a person takes to be a reasoned defense of an act is treated, as the action was, on the model of a happening of a pathological kind. Not just a person's acts are taken from him but also his attempt at a reasoned justification for the acts. In a system of punishment a person who has committed a crime may argue that what he did was right. We make him pay the price and we respect his right to retain the judgment he has made. A conception of pathology precludes this form of respect.

According to Edward Rubin, Morris's ethical case proves too much, for, without rehabilitation, we have no coherent explanation for the contemporary preference for incarceration as a mode of punishment. After surveying the origins of the modern prison system, Rubin concludes that, "[f]rom its outset, the penitentiary was conceived as a means of rehabilitation. This was the rationale for relying on confinement, instead of the more familiar sanctions of execution, torture, or exile." Rubin considers and rejects the possibility that incarceration now rests on incapacitative goals rather than rehabilitative impulses:

> The defect in this account ... is that prison necessarily incapacitates, no matter what regime prevails inside the prison walls. Just as a deterrence rationale fails to tell us anything about the mode of punishment, incapacitation, while it does identify prison as the preferred mode of punishment, is equally uninformative about the mode of imprisonment.... To put the matter in practical terms, consider the position of a prison warden who is charged with developing a strategy to deal with the prisoner who comes into his institution. The law tells him that the purpose of imprisonment is incapacitation. To this end, it tells him how long he is to keep the prisoner.... Beyond that, it tells him nothing. It provides no guidance whatsoever about the way the prisoner should be treated in the institution.[s]

In the absence of a rehabilitative ideal, Rubin speculates that the criminal justice system likely would fall back on cheaper modes of punishment, such as corporal and capital punishment. Instead, corrections officials remain committed at least to providing the opportunity for rehabilitation. "Convicted felons are separated from their former life, confined in a secure facility, and subjected to some regimen that will change their attitudes and enable them to be productive, law-abiding citizens once they are released."

As for Morris's claim that rehabilitation is disrespectful of the individual offender's personality and autonomy, Rubin remarks that rehabilitation is far more compatible with our democratic ethos than is incapacitation. According to the familiar metaphor, it is the incapacitative prison that "functions as a warehouse for the prisoner" and thereby treats the human offender as a thing. By contrast, the "central premise [of rehabilitation] is that every human life is valuable, and that government has an affirmative obligation to help offenders return to society and live a normal and productive life."

---

## SECTION 2: CRIMINALIZATION

### INTRODUCTORY NOTE

In contemporary American jurisprudence, criminalization decisions are entrusted to legislatures. As the democratically elected representatives of their communities, legislators are thought to be in the best position to decide when the state's interest in social control should be vindicated by the drastic forms of intervention on individual liberty and privacy that

---

[s] Edward L. Rubin, The Inevitability of Rehabilitation, 19 Law & Ineq. J. 343 (2001).

criminal punishment entails. Of course, many criminalization decisions are not controversial at all. For example, legislators need not think twice about the basic judgments underlying the murder provisions of their states' penal codes. Everyone (in every culture?) agrees that murder is the paradigmatic case for criminal sanctions.

But other criminalization judgments are not so easy, requiring lawmakers to balance carefully the pros and cons of relying on criminal enforcement mechanisms. What precise considerations should be taken into account in deciding whether disapproved behavior should be prohibited by the criminal law? Should it be enough that a majority of lawmakers find the behavior morally objectionable? Or must the lawmakers point to some form of "objective" social harm above and beyond their moral reservations? Do the considerations change when the issue is decriminalization of behavior that arguably should no longer be punished by criminal sanctions?

From another perspective, is it appropriate to criminalize socially undesirable behavior that has no moral significance? How should a lawmaker assess the utility of the criminal sanction in comparison with other legal or social mechanisms of control? How does one know when the costs of criminalization outweigh its benefits? Of what significance is the difficulty of enforcement? Or the pervasiveness of the prohibited behavior? Is it appropriate to make conduct criminal with the expectation that the law will not be enforced or will be significantly under-enforced?

Over the years, these and related issues have received considerable attention in academic commentary and official reports. Much of the criminalization literature has been preoccupied with the controversial questions created by punishment of what are quaintly known as "vice crimes," such as adultery, gay sex, prostitution, gambling, and drug use. Because these offenses test the outer boundaries of a state's criminalization authority, courts in our constitutional system sometimes must get involved in the criminalization debate too.

———

## Lawrence v. Texas

Supreme Court of the United States, 2003.
539 U.S. 558.

■ JUSTICE KENNEDY delivered the opinion of the Court.

Liberty protects the person from unwarranted government intrusions into a dwelling or other private places. In our tradition the State is not omnipresent in the home. And there are other spheres of our lives and existence, outside the home, where the State should not be a dominant presence. Freedom extends beyond spatial bounds. Liberty presumes an autonomy of self that includes freedom of thought, belief, expression, and certain intimate conduct. The instant case involves liberty of the person both in its spatial and more transcendent dimensions.

I.

The question before the Court is the validity of a Texas statute making it a crime for two persons of the same sex to engage in certain intimate sexual conduct.

In Houston, Texas, officers of the Harris County Police Department were dispatched to a private residence in response to a reported weapons disturbance. They entered an apartment where one of the petitioners, John Geddes Lawrence, resided. The right of the police to enter does not seem to have been questioned. The officers observed Lawrence and another man, Tyron Garner, engaging in a sexual act. The two petitioners were arrested, held in custody over night, and charged and convicted before a Justice of the Peace.

The complaints described their crime as "deviate sexual intercourse, namely anal sex, with a member of the same sex (man)." The applicable [Texas penal statute] provides: "A person commits an offense if he engages in deviate sexual intercourse with another individual of the same sex." The statute defines "deviate sexual intercourse" as follows:

(A) any contact between any part of the genitals of one person and the mouth or anus of another person; or

(B) the penetration of the genitals or the anus of another person with an object.

The petitioners exercised their right to a trial de novo in Harris County Criminal Court. They challenged the statute as a violation of the Equal Protection Clause of the 14th Amendment and of a like provision of the Texas Constitution. Those contentions were rejected. The petitioners, having entered a plea of nolo contendere, were each fined $200 and assessed court costs of $141.25.

The Court of Appeals for the Texas Fourteenth District considered the petitioners' federal constitutional arguments under both the Equal Protection and Due Process Clauses of the 14th Amendment.[a] After hearing the case en banc the court, in a divided opinion, rejected the constitutional arguments and affirmed the convictions. The majority opinion ... considered ... Bowers v. Hardwick, 478 U.S. 186 (1986), to be controlling on the federal due process aspect of the case. *Bowers* then being authoritative, this was proper.

We granted certiorari. . . .

II.

We conclude the case should be resolved by determining whether the petitioners were free as adults to engage in the private conduct in the exercise of their liberty under the Due Process Clause of the 14th Amend-

---

[a] The 14th Amendment of the United States Constitution provides in relevant part: "No state shall ... deprive any person of life, liberty, or property, without due process of law; nor deny to any person within its jurisdiction the equal protection of the laws."— [Footnote by eds.]

ment to the Constitution. For this inquiry we deem it necessary to reconsider ... *Bowers*.

There are broad statements of the substantive reach of liberty under the Due Process Clause in earlier cases, ... but the most pertinent beginning point is our decision in Griswold v. Connecticut, 381 U.S. 479 (1965).

In *Griswold* the Court invalidated a state law prohibiting the use of drugs or devices of contraception and counseling or aiding and abetting the use of contraceptives. The Court described the protected interest as a right to privacy and placed emphasis on the marriage relation and the protected space of the marital bedroom.

After *Griswold* it was established that the right to make certain decisions regarding sexual conduct extends beyond the marital relationship. In Eisenstadt v. Baird, 405 U.S. 438 (1972), the Court invalidated a law prohibiting the distribution of contraceptives to unmarried persons. [T]he Court [stated] that the law impaired the exercise of their personal rights ...:

> It is true that in *Griswold* the right of privacy in question inhered in the marital relationship.... If the right of privacy means anything, it is the right of the individual, married or single, to be free from unwarranted governmental intrusion into matters so fundamentally affecting a person as the decision whether to bear or beget a child.

The opinions in *Griswold* and *Eisenstadt* were part of the background for the decision in Roe v. Wade, 410 U.S. 113 (1973). As is well known, the case involved a challenge to the Texas law prohibiting abortions, but the laws of other states were affected as well. Although the Court held the woman's rights were not absolute, her right to elect an abortion did have real and substantial protection as an exercise of her liberty under the Due Process Clause.... *Roe* recognized the right of a woman to make certain fundamental decisions affecting her destiny and confirmed once more that the protection of liberty under the Due Process Clause has a substantive dimension of fundamental significance in defining the rights of the person....

The facts in *Bowers* had some similarities to the instant case. A police officer, whose right to enter seems not to have been in question, observed Hardwick, in his own bedroom, engaging in intimate sexual conduct with another adult male. The conduct was in violation of a Georgia statute making it a criminal offense to engage in sodomy. One difference between the two cases is that the Georgia statute prohibited the conduct whether or not the participants were of the same sex, while the Texas statute, as we have seen, applies only to participants of the same sex.... The Court ... sustained the Georgia law....

The Court began its substantive discussion in *Bowers* as follows: "The issue presented is whether the Federal Constitution confers a fundamental right upon homosexuals to engage in sodomy and hence invalidates the laws of the many States that still make such conduct illegal and have done so for a very long time." That statement ... discloses the Court's own failure to appreciate the extent of the liberty at stake. To say that the issue in *Bowers* was simply the right to engage in certain sexual conduct demeans the claim the individual put forward, just as it would demean a married couple were it to be said marriage is simply about the right to have sexual intercourse. The laws involved in *Bowers* and here are, to be sure, statutes that purport to do no more than prohibit a particular sexual act. Their penalties and purposes, though, have more far-reaching consequences, touching upon the most private human conduct, sexual behavior, and in the most private of places, the home. The statutes do seek to control a personal relationship that, whether or not entitled to formal recognition in the law, is within the liberty of persons to choose without being punished as criminals.

This, as a general rule, should counsel against attempts by the State, or a court, to define the meaning of the relationship or to set its boundaries absent injury to a person or abuse of an institution the law protects. It suffices for us to acknowledge that adults may choose to enter upon this relationship in the confines of their homes and their own private lives and still retain their dignity as free persons. When sexuality finds overt expression in intimate conduct with another person, the conduct can be but one element in a personal bond that is more enduring. The liberty protected by the Constitution allows homosexual persons the right to make this choice.

Having misapprehended the claim of liberty there presented to it, and thus stating the claim to be whether there is a fundamental right to engage in consensual sodomy, the *Bowers* Court said: "Proscriptions against that conduct have ancient roots." In academic writings, and in many of the scholarly amicus briefs filed to assist the Court in this case, there are fundamental criticisms of the historical premises relied upon by ... *Bowers*. [T]he following considerations counsel against adopting the definitive conclusions upon which *Bowers* placed such reliance.

At the outset it should be noted that there is no longstanding history in this country of laws directed at homosexual conduct as a distinct matter. [E]arly American sodomy laws were not directed at homosexuals as such but instead sought to prohibit nonprocreative sexual activity more generally. This does not suggest approval of homosexual conduct. It does tend to show that this particular form of conduct was not thought of as a separate category from like conduct between heterosexual persons.

Laws prohibiting sodomy do not seem to have been enforced against consenting adults acting in private. A substantial number of sodomy prosecutions ... were for predatory acts against those who could not or did not consent, as in the case of a minor or the victim of an assault. As to these, one purpose for the prohibitions was to ensure there would be no lack of coverage if a predator committed a sexual assault that did not constitute rape as defined by the criminal law....

It was not until the 1970's that any State singled out same-sex relations for criminal prosecution, and only nine States have done so. Post-

*Bowers* even some of these States did not adhere to the policy of suppressing homosexual conduct. Over the course of the last decades, States with same-sex prohibitions have moved toward abolishing them....

[O]f course, ... *Bowers* was making the broader point that for centuries there have been powerful voices to condemn homosexual conduct as immoral. The condemnation has been shaped by religious beliefs, conceptions of right and acceptable behavior, and respect for the traditional family. For many persons these are not trivial concerns but profound and deep convictions accepted as ethical and moral principles to which they aspire and which thus determine the course of their lives. These considerations do not answer the question before us, however. The issue is whether the majority may use the power of the State to enforce these views on the whole society through operation of the criminal law. "Our obligation is to define the liberty of all, not to mandate our own moral code."

... In all events we think that our laws and traditions in the past half century are of most relevance here. These references show an emerging awareness that liberty gives substantial protection to adult persons in deciding how to conduct their private lives in matters pertaining to sex. "History and tradition are the starting point but not in all cases the ending point of the substantive due process inquiry."

This emerging recognition should have been apparent when *Bowers* was decided. In 1955 the American Law Institute promulgated the Model Penal Code and made clear that it did not recommend or provide for "criminal penalties for consensual sexual relations conducted in private." It justified its decision on three grounds: (1) The prohibitions undermined respect for the law by penalizing conduct many people engaged in; (2) the statutes regulated private conduct not harmful to others; and (3) the laws were arbitrarily enforced and thus invited the danger of blackmail. In 1961 Illinois changed its laws to conform to the Model Penal Code. Other States soon followed.

In *Bowers* the Court referred to the fact that before 1961 all 50 States had outlawed sodomy, and that at the time of the Court's decision 24 States and the District of Columbia had sodomy laws. [T]hese prohibitions often were being ignored, however. Georgia, for instance, had not sought to enforce its law for decades.

[Nor did *Bowers*] take account of other authorities pointing in an opposite direction. A committee advising the British Parliament recommended in 1957 repeal of laws punishing homosexual conduct. The Wolfenden Report: Report of the Committee on Homosexual Offenses and Prostitution (1963). Parliament enacted the substance of those recommendations 10 years later.

Of even more importance, almost five years before *Bowers* was decided the European Court of Human Rights considered a [parallel] case.... An adult male resident in Northern Ireland alleged he was a practicing homosexual who desired to engage in consensual homosexual conduct. The laws of Northern Ireland forbade him that right. He alleged that he had been questioned, his home had been searched, and he feared criminal prosecution. The court held that the laws proscribing the conduct were invalid under the European Convention on Human Rights. Dudgeon v. United Kingdom, 45 Eur. Ct. H.R. (1981) P52. Authoritative in all countries that are members of the Council of Europe (21 nations then, 45 nations now), the decision is at odds with the premise in *Bowers* that the claim put forward was insubstantial in our Western civilization.

In our own constitutional system the deficiencies in *Bowers* became even more apparent in the years following its announcement. The 25 states with laws prohibiting the relevant conduct ... are reduced now to 13, of which 4 enforce their laws only against homosexual conduct. In those states where sodomy is still proscribed, whether for same-sex or heterosexual conduct, there is a pattern of nonenforcement with respect to consenting adults acting in private. The State of Texas admitted in 1994 that as of that date it had not prosecuted anyone under those circumstances.

[C]ases decided after *Bowers* cast its holding into even more doubt. In Planned Parenthood of Southeastern Pa. v. Casey, 505 U.S. 833 (1992), the Court reaffirmed the substantive force of the liberty protected by the Due Process Clause. The *Casey* decision again confirmed that our laws and tradition afford constitutional protection to personal decisions relating to marriage, procreation, contraception, family relationships, child rearing, and education. In explaining the respect the Constitution demands for the autonomy of the person in making these choices, we stated as follows:

> These matters, involving the most intimate and personal choices a person may make in a lifetime, choices central to personal dignity and autonomy, are central to the liberty protected by the 14th Amendment. At the heart of liberty is the right to define one's own concept of existence, of meaning, of the universe, and of the mystery of human life. Beliefs about these matters could not define the attributes of personhood were they formed under compulsion of the State.

Persons in a homosexual relationship may seek autonomy for these purposes, just as heterosexual persons do. The decision in *Bowers* would deny them this right. . . .

As an alternative argument in this case, counsel for the petitioners and some amici contend that ... the Texas statute [is] invalid under the Equal Protection Clause. That is a tenable argument, but we conclude the instant case requires us to address whether *Bowers* itself has continuing validity. Were we to hold the statute invalid under the Equal Protection Clause some might question whether a prohibition would be valid if drawn differently, say, to prohibit the conduct both between same-sex and different-sex participants.

Equality of treatment and the due process right to demand respect for conduct protected by the substantive guarantee of liberty are linked in important respects. . . . If protected conduct is made criminal and the law which does so remains unexamined for its substantive validity, its stigma might remain even if it were not enforceable as drawn for equal protection reasons. When homosexual conduct is made criminal by the law of the State, that declaration in and of itself is an invitation to subject homosexual persons to discrimination both in the public and in the private spheres. The central holding of *Bowers* has been brought in question by this case, and it should be addressed. Its continuance as precedent demeans the lives of homosexual persons.

The stigma this criminal statute imposes, moreover, is not trivial. The offense, to be sure, is but a class C misdemeanor, a minor offense in the Texas legal system. Still, it remains a criminal offense with all that imports for the dignity of the persons charged. The petitioners will bear on their record the history of their criminal convictions. Just this Term we rejected various challenges to state laws requiring the registration of sex offenders. [A person convicted for violating this statute] would come within the registration laws of at least four States were he or she to be subject to their jurisdiction.... Furthermore, the Texas criminal conviction carries with it the other collateral consequences always following a conviction, such as notations on job application forms, to mention but one example....

The doctrine of stare decisis is essential to the respect accorded to the judgments of the Court and to the stability of the law. It is not, however, an inexorable command. [W]hen a Court is asked to overrule a precedent recognizing a constitutional liberty interest, individual or societal reliance on the existence of that liberty cautions with particular strength against reversing course. The holding in *Bowers*, however, has not induced detrimental reliance comparable to some instances where recognized individual rights are involved....

... In his dissenting opinion in *Bowers*, Justice Stevens came to these conclusions:

> Our prior cases make two propositions abundantly clear. First, the fact that the governing majority in a State has traditionally viewed a particular practice as immoral is not a sufficient reason for upholding a law prohibiting the practice; neither history nor tradition could save a law prohibiting miscegenation from constitutional attack. Second, individual decisions by married persons, concerning the intimacies of their physical relationship, even when not intended to produce offspring, are a form of ''liberty'' protected by the Due Process Clause of the 14th Amendment. Moreover, this protection extends to intimate choices by unmarried as well as married persons.

Justice Stevens' analysis, in our view, should have been controlling in *Bowers* and should control here.

*Bowers* was not correct when it was decided, and it is not correct today. It ought not to remain binding precedent. *Bowers v. Hardwick* should be and now is overruled.

The present case does not involve minors. It does not involve persons who might be injured or coerced or who are situated in relationships where consent might not easily be refused. It does not involve public conduct or prostitution. It does not involve whether the government must give formal recognition to any relationship that homosexual persons seek to enter. The case does involve two adults who, with full and mutual consent from each other, engaged in sexual practices common to a homosexual lifestyle. The petitioners are entitled to respect for their private lives. The State cannot demean their existence or control their destiny by making their private sexual conduct a crime. Their right to liberty under the Due Process Clause gives them the full right to engage in their conduct without intervention of the government.... The Texas statute furthers no legitimate state interest which can justify its intrusion into the personal and private life of the individual.

Had those who drew and ratified the Due Process Clauses of the Fifth Amendment or the 14th Amendment known the components of liberty in its manifold possibilities, they might have been more specific. They did not presume to have this insight. They knew times can blind us to certain truths and later generations can see that laws once thought necessary and proper in fact serve only to oppress. As the Constitution endures, persons in every generation can invoke its principles in their own search for greater freedom.

The judgment of the Court of Appeals for the Texas Fourteenth District is reversed, and the case is remanded for further proceedings not inconsistent with this opinion.

■ JUSTICE O'CONNOR, concurring in the judgment.

The Court today overrules *Bowers v. Hardwick*. I joined *Bowers*, and do not join the Court in overruling it. Nevertheless, I agree with the Court that Texas' statute banning same-sex sodomy is unconstitutional.... I base my conclusion on the 14th Amendment's Equal Protection Clause....

The Texas statute makes homosexuals unequal in the eyes of the law by making particular conduct—and only that conduct—subject to criminal sanction. It appears that prosecutions under Texas' sodomy law are rare. This case shows, however, that prosecutions do occur. And while the penalty imposed on petitioners in this case was relatively minor, the consequences of conviction are not. [P]etitioners' convictions, if upheld, would disqualify them from or restrict their ability to engage in a variety of professions, including medicine, athletic training, and interior design. Indeed, were petitioners to move to one of four States, their convictions would require them to register as sex offenders to local law enforcement.

And the effect of Texas' sodomy law is not just limited to the threat of prosecution or consequence of conviction. Texas' sodomy law brands all homosexuals as criminals, thereby making it more difficult for homosexuals to be treated in the same manner as everyone else. Indeed, Texas itself has previously acknowledged the collateral effects of the law, stipulating in a prior challenge to this action that the law "legally sanctions discrimination against [homosexuals] in a variety of ways unrelated to the criminal law," including in the areas of "employment, family issues, and housing." ...

This case raises a different issue than *Bowers*: whether, under the Equal Protection Clause, moral disapproval is a legitimate state interest to justify by itself a statute that bans homosexual sodomy, but not heterosexual sodomy. It is not. . . .

Moral disapproval of a group cannot be a legitimate governmental interest under the Equal Protection Clause because legal classifications must not be "drawn for the purpose of disadvantaging the group burdened by the law." Texas' invocation of moral disapproval as a legitimate state interest proves nothing more than Texas' desire to criminalize homosexual sodomy. But the Equal Protection Clause prevents a State from creating "a classification of persons undertaken for its own sake." And because Texas so rarely enforces its sodomy law as applied to private, consensual acts, the law serves more as a statement of dislike and disapproval against homosexuals than as a tool to stop criminal behavior. The Texas sodomy law "raises the inevitable inference that the disadvantage imposed is born of animosity toward the class of persons affected."

Texas argues, however, that the sodomy law does not discriminate against homosexual persons. Instead, the State maintains that the law discriminates only against homosexual conduct. While it is true that the law applies only to conduct, the conduct targeted by this law is conduct that is closely correlated with being homosexual. Under such circumstances, Texas' sodomy law is targeted at more than conduct. It is instead directed toward gay persons as a class. "After all, there can hardly be more palpable discrimination against a class than making the conduct that defines the class criminal." When a State makes homosexual conduct criminal, and not "deviate sexual intercourse" committed by persons of different sexes, "that declaration in and of itself is an invitation to subject homosexual persons to discrimination both in the public and in the private spheres." . . .

Whether a sodomy law that is neutral both in effect and application would violate the substantive component of the Due Process Clause is an issue that need not be decided today. I am confident, however, that so long as the Equal Protection Clause requires a sodomy law to apply equally to the private consensual conduct of homosexuals and heterosexuals alike, such a law would not long stand in our democratic society. . . .

That this law as applied to private, consensual conduct is unconstitutional under the Equal Protection Clause does not mean that other laws distinguishing between heterosexuals and homosexuals would similarly fail under rational basis review. Texas cannot assert any legitimate state interest here, such as national security or preserving the traditional institution of marriage. Unlike the moral disapproval of same-sex relations—the asserted state interest in this case—other reasons exist to promote the institution of marriage beyond mere moral disapproval of an excluded group. . . .

■ JUSTICE SCALIA, with whom THE CHIEF JUSTICE and JUSTICE THOMAS join, dissenting.

I.

... The Court's claim that *Planned Parenthood v. Casey* "casts some doubt" upon the holding in *Bowers* (or any other case, for that matter) does not withstand analysis. As far as its holding is concerned, *Casey* provided a less expansive right to abortion than did *Roe*.... And if the Court is referring not to the holding of *Casey*, but to the dictum of its famed sweet-mystery-of-life passage, [that dictum] "casts some doubt" upon either the totality of our jurisprudence or else (presumably the right answer) nothing at all. I have never heard of a law that attempted to restrict one's "right to define" certain concepts; and if the passage calls into question the government's power to regulate actions based on one's self-defined "concept of existence, etc.," it is the passage that ate the rule of law....

[T]he "societal reliance" on the principles confirmed in *Bowers* and discarded today has been overwhelming. Countless judicial decisions and legislative enactments have relied on the ancient proposition that a governing majority's belief that certain sexual behavior is "immoral and unacceptable" constitutes a rational basis for regulation. See, e.g., Williams v. Pryor, 240 F.3d 944, 949 (CA11 2001) (citing *Bowers* in upholding Alabama's prohibition on the sale of sex toys ...). State laws against bigamy, same-sex marriage, adult incest, prostitution, masturbation, adultery, fornication, bestiality, and obscenity are likewise sustainable only in light of *Bowers'* validation of laws based on moral choices. Every single one of these laws is called into question by today's decision; the Court makes no effort to cabin the scope of its decision to exclude them from its holding. The impossibility of distinguishing homosexuality from other traditional "morals" offenses is precisely why *Bowers* rejected the rational-basis challenge. "The law," it said, "is constantly based on notions of morality, and if all laws representing essentially moral choices are to be invalidated under the Due Process Clause, the courts will be very busy indeed."

What a massive disruption of the current social order, therefore, the overruling of *Bowers* entails....

[The Texas statute] undoubtedly imposes constraints on liberty. So do laws prohibiting prostitution, recreational use of heroin, and, for that matter, working more than 60 hours per week in a bakery. But there is no right to "liberty" under the Due Process Clause, though today's opinion repeatedly makes that claim. The 14th Amendment expressly allows States to deprive their citizens of "liberty," so long as "due process of law" is provided....

Our opinions applying the doctrine known as "substantive due process" hold that the Due Process Clause prohibits States from infringing fundamental liberty interests, unless the infringement is narrowly tailored to serve a compelling state interest.... All other liberty interests may be abridged or abrogated pursuant to a validly enacted state law if that law is rationally related to a legitimate state interest....

The Court today does not ... describe homosexual sodomy as a "fundamental right" or a "fundamental liberty interest," nor does it subject the Texas statute to strict scrutiny. Instead, ... the Court concludes that the application of Texas's statute to petitioners' conduct fails the rational-basis test, and overrules *Bowers'* holding to the contrary. "The Texas statute furthers no legitimate state interest which can justify its intrusion into the personal and private life of the individual." ...

III.

... It is ... entirely irrelevant whether the laws in our long national tradition criminalizing homosexual sodomy were "directed at homosexual conduct as a distinct matter." [T]he only relevant point is that it was criminalized—which suffices to establish that homosexual sodomy is not a right "deeply rooted in our Nation's history and tradition." The Court today agrees that homosexual sodomy was criminalized and thus does not dispute the facts on which *Bowers* actually relied.

[T]he Court instead says: "We think that our laws and traditions in the past half century are of most relevance here. These references show an emerging awareness that liberty gives substantial protection to adult persons in deciding how to conduct their private lives in matters pertaining to sex." Apart from the fact that such an "emerging awareness" does not establish a "fundamental right," the statement is factually false. States continue to prosecute all sorts of crimes by adults "in matters pertaining to sex": prostitution, adult incest, adultery, obscenity, and child pornography. Sodomy laws, too, have been enforced "in the past half century," in which there have been 134 reported cases involving prosecutions for consensual, adult, homosexual sodomy. In relying, for evidence of an "emerging recognition," upon the American Law Institute's 1955 recommendation not to criminalize " 'consensual sexual relations conducted in private,' " the Court ignores the fact that this recommendation was "a point of resistance in most of the states that considered adopting the Model Penal Code."

In any event, an "emerging awareness" is by definition not "deeply rooted in this Nation's history and traditions," as we have said "fundamental right" status requires. Constitutional entitlements do not spring into existence because some States choose to lessen or eliminate criminal sanctions on certain behavior. Much less do they spring into existence, as the Court seems to believe, because foreign nations decriminalize conduct.... The Court's discussion of these foreign views (ignoring, of course, the many countries that have retained criminal prohibitions on sodomy) is therefore meaningless dicta. Dangerous dicta, however, since "this Court ... should not impose foreign moods, fads, or fashions on Americans."

IV.

I turn now to the ground on which the Court squarely rests its holding: the contention that there is no rational basis for the law here under attack. This proposition is so out of accord with our jurisprudence—indeed, with the jurisprudence of any society we know—that it requires little discussion.

The Texas statute undeniably seeks to further the belief of its citizens that certain forms of sexual behavior are "immoral and unacceptable,"—

the same interest furthered by criminal laws against fornication, bigamy, adultery, adult incest, bestiality, and obscenity. *Bowers* held that this was a legitimate state interest. The Court today reaches the opposite conclusion [and] effectively decrees the end of all morals legislation. If, as the Court asserts, the promotion of majoritarian sexual morality is not even a legitimate state interest, none of the above-mentioned laws can survive rational-basis review.

V.

Finally, I turn to petitioners' equal-protection challenge, which no Member of the Court save Justice O'Connor embraces: On its face [the Texas statute] applies equally to all persons. Men and women, heterosexuals and homosexuals, are all subject to its prohibition of deviate sexual intercourse with someone of the same sex. To be sure, [the statute] does distinguish between the sexes insofar as concerns the partner with whom the sexual acts are performed: men can violate the law only with other men, and women only with other women. But this cannot itself be a denial of equal protection, since it is precisely the same distinction regarding partner that is drawn in state laws prohibiting marriage with someone of the same sex while permitting marriage with someone of the opposite sex....

Justice O'Connor argues that ... "the conduct targeted by this law is conduct that is closely correlated with being homosexual. Under such circumstances, Texas' sodomy law is ... directed toward gay persons as a class." ... Of course the same could be said of any law. A law against public nudity targets "the conduct that is closely correlated with being a nudist," and hence "is targeted at more than conduct"; it is "directed toward nudists as a class." But be that as it may. Even if the Texas law does deny equal protection to "homosexuals as a class," that denial still does not need to be justified by anything more than a rational basis, which our cases show is satisfied by the enforcement of traditional notions of sexual morality....

... Today's opinion is the product of a Court, which is the product of a law-profession culture, that has largely signed on to the so-called homosexual agenda, by which I mean the agenda promoted by some homosexual activists directed at eliminating the moral opprobrium that has traditionally attached to homosexual conduct. [T]he American Association of Law Schools (to which any reputable law school must seek to belong) excludes from membership any school that refuses to ban from its job-interview facilities a law firm (no matter how small) that does not wish to hire as a prospective partner a person who openly engages in homosexual conduct.

One of the most revealing statements in today's opinion is the Court's grim warning that the criminalization of homosexual conduct is "an invitation to subject homosexual persons to discrimination both in the public and in the private spheres." [T]he Court has taken sides in the culture war, departing from its role of assuring, as neutral observer, that the democratic rules of engagement are observed. Many Americans do not want persons who openly engage in homosexual conduct as partners in their business, as scoutmasters for their children, as teachers in their children's schools, or as boarders in their home. They view this as protecting themselves and their families from a lifestyle that they believe to be immoral and destructive. The Court views it as "discrimination" which it is the function of our judgments to deter. So imbued is the Court with the law profession's anti-anti-homosexual culture, that it is seemingly unaware that the attitudes of that culture are not obviously "mainstream"....

Let me be clear that I have nothing against homosexuals, or any other group, promoting their agenda through normal democratic means.... That homosexuals have achieved some success in that enterprise is attested to by the fact that Texas is one of the few remaining States that criminalize private, consensual homosexual acts. But persuading one's fellow citizens is one thing, and imposing one's views in absence of democratic majority will is something else.... It is indeed true that "later generations can see that laws once thought necessary and proper in fact serve only to oppress;" and when that happens, later generations can repeal those laws. But it is the premise of our system that those judgments are to be made by the people, and not imposed by a governing caste that knows best.

One of the benefits of leaving regulation of this matter to the people rather than to the courts is that the people, unlike judges, need not carry things to their logical conclusion. The people may feel that their disapprobation of homosexual conduct is strong enough to disallow homosexual marriage, but not strong enough to criminalize private homosexual acts—and may legislate accordingly. The Court today pretends that it possesses a similar freedom of action, so that that we need not fear judicial imposition of homosexual marriage, as has recently occurred in Canada (in a decision that the Canadian Government has chosen not to appeal). See Halpern v. Toronto, 2003 WL 34950 (Ontario Ct. App.). At the end of its opinion—after having laid waste the foundations of our rational-basis jurisprudence—the Court says that the present case "does not involve whether the government must give formal recognition to any relationship that homosexual persons seek to enter." Do not believe it....

■ [Justice Thomas's dissenting opinion is omitted.]

---

NOTES ON CRIMINALIZATION

**1. Questions and Comments on *Lawrence v. Texas*.** In *Lawrence v. Texas*, the Supreme Court holds that the Due Process Clause has a "substantive" component that protects citizens' "liberty" against the state's otherwise broad criminalization power. That is, the Due Process Clause does not merely guarantee that the state will follow certain procedures, such as providing notice and a fair trial, before depriving citizens who have committed crimes of their "liberty." Rather, the "liberty" protected by the Due Process Clause completely insulates certain behavior from criminalization. As Justice Kennedy puts it for the *Lawrence* majority, states may not punish adults for intimate sexual activity merely because a governing majority finds the activity morally offensive. Of course, the Court allows that the majority is entitled to criminalize sexual and other activity that causes "injury to a person or abuse of an institution that the law protects," but it invalidates the Texas sodomy statute because the state identified no such injury or abuse in this case. Precisely what conduct is protected by *Lawrence* and the precedents on which it relies? Is Justice Scalia correct when he remarks that *Lawrence* invalidates laws punishing adultery, adult incest, bigamy, prostitution, and obscenity? Is it, as Justice Scalia claims, impossible to distinguish gay sex from other "morals offenses," including the "recreational use of heroin"?

**2. John Stuart Mill.** In connection with *Lawrence*'s statement of constitutional principles, as well as its description of the history and traditions supporting those principles, consider the following excerpt from John Stuart Mill, On Liberty. Published in 1859, the essay is the classic argument for the proposition that there are categorical limits on the purposes for which the government properly may interfere with the individual and, in particular, that enforcement of the prevailing moral code is not, in itself a sufficient reason for criminalization:

> The object of this essay is to assert one very simple principle, as entitled to govern absolutely the dealings of society with the individual in the way of compulsion and control, whether the means used be physical force in the form of legal penalties, or the moral coercion of public opinion. That principle is, that the sole end for which mankind are warranted, individually or collectively, in interfering with the liberty of action of any of their number, is self-protection. That the only purpose for which power can be rightfully exercised over any member of a civilized community, against his will, is to prevent harm to others. His own good, either physical or moral, is not a sufficient warrant. He cannot rightfully be compelled to do or forbear because it will be better for him to do so, because it will make him happier, because, in the opinions of others, to do so would be wise, or even right. These are good reasons for remonstrating with him, or reasoning with him, or persuading him, or entreating him, but not for compelling him, or visiting him with any evil in case he do otherwise. To justify that, the conduct from which it is desired to deter him must be calculated to produce evil to some one else. The only part of the conduct of any one, for which he is amenable to society, is that which concerns others. In the part which merely concerns himself, his independence is, of right, absolute. Over himself, over his own body and mind, the individual is sovereign.

> It is, perhaps, hardly necessary to say that this doctrine is meant to apply only to human beings in the maturity of their faculties. We are not speaking of children, or of young persons below the age which the law may fix as that of manhood or womanhood. Those who are still in a state to require being taken

care of by others, must be protected against their own actions as well as against external injury.

. . . This, then, is the appropriate region of human liberty. It comprises, first, the inward domain of consciousness; demanding liberty of conscience, in the most comprehensive sense; liberty of thought and feeling; absolute freedom of opinion and sentiment on all subjects, practical or speculative, scientific, moral, or theological. The liberty of expressing and publishing opinions may seem to fall under a different principle, since it belongs to that part of the conduct of an individual which concerns other people; but, being almost of as much importance as the liberty of thought itself, and resting in great part on the same reasons, is practically inseparable from it. Secondly, the principle requires liberty of tastes and pursuits; of framing the plan of our life to suit our own character; of doing as we like, subject to such consequences as may follow: without impediment from our fellow creatures, so long as what we do does not harm them, even though they should think our conduct foolish, perverse, or wrong. Thirdly, from this liberty of each individual, follows the liberty, within the same limits, of combination among individuals; freedom to unite, for any purpose not involving harm to others: the persons combining being supposed to be of full age, and not forced or deceived.

No society in which these liberties are not, on the whole, respected, is free, whatever may be its form of government; and none is completely free in which they do not exist absolute and unqualified. The only freedom which deserves the name, is that of pursuing our own good in our own way, so long as we do not attempt to deprive others of theirs, or impede their efforts to obtain it. Each is the proper guardian of his own health, whether bodily, or mental and spiritual. Mankind are greater gainers by suffering each other to live as seems good to themselves, than by compelling each to live as seems good to the rest. . . .

I fully admit that the mischief which a person does to himself may seriously affect, both through their sympathies and their interests, those nearly connected with him, and in a minor degree, society at large. When, by conduct of this sort, a person is led to violate a distinct and assignable obligation to any other person or persons, the case is taken out of the self-regarding class, and becomes amenable to moral disapprobation in the proper sense of the term. If, for example, a man, through intemperance or extravagance, becomes unable to pay his debts, or, having undertaken the moral responsibility of a family, becomes from the same cause incapable of supporting or educating them, he is deservedly reprobated, and might be justly punished; but it is for the breach of duty to his family or creditors, not for the extravagance. . . . Whoever fails in the consideration generally due to the interests and feelings of others, not being compelled by some more imperative duty, or justified by allowable self-preference, is a subject of moral disapprobation for that failure, but not for the cause of it, nor for the errors, merely personal to himself, which may have remotely led to it. In like manner, when a person disables himself, by conduct purely self-regarding, from the performance of some definite duty incumbent on him to the public, he is guilty of a social offence. No person ought to be punished simply for being drunk; but a soldier or a policeman should be punished for being drunk on duty. Whenever, in short, there is a definite damage, or a definite risk of damage, either to an individual or to the public, the case is taken out of the province of liberty, and placed in that of morality or law. . . .

[T]he strongest of all the arguments against the interference of the public with purely personal conduct, is that when it does interfere, the odds are that it interferes wrongly, and in the wrong place. On questions of social morality, of duty to others, the opinion of the public, that is, of an overruling majority, though often wrong, is likely to be still oftener right; because on such questions they are only required to judge of their own interests, of the manner in which some mode of conduct, if allowed to be practised, would affect themselves. But the opinion of a similar majority, imposed as a law on the minority, on questions of self-regarding conduct, is quite as likely to be wrong as right; for in these cases public opinion means, at the best, some people's opinion of what is good or bad for other people; while very often it does not even mean that; the public, with the most perfect indifference, passing over the pleasure or convenience of those whose conduct they censure, and considering only their own preference. There are many who consider as an injury to themselves any conduct which they have a distaste for, and resent it as an outrage to their feelings; as a religious bigot, when charged with disregarding the religious feelings of others, has been known to retort that they disregard his feelings, by persisting in their abominable worship or creed. But there is no parity between the feeling of a person for his own opinion, and the feeling of another who is offended at his holding it; no more than between the desire of a thief to take a purse, and the desire of the right owner to keep it. And a person's taste is as much his own peculiar concern as his opinion or his purse. . . .

The right inherent in society, to ward off crimes against itself by antecedent precautions, suggests the obvious limitations to the maxim, that purely self-regarding misconduct cannot properly be meddled with in the way of prevention or punishment. Drunkenness, for example, in ordinary cases, is not a fit subject for legislative interference; but I should deem it perfectly legitimate that a person, who had once been convicted of any act of violence to others under the influence of drink, should be placed under a special legal restriction, personal to himself; that if he were afterwards found drunk, he should be liable to a penalty, and that if when in that state he committed another offence, the punishment to which he would be liable for that other offence should be increased in severity. The making himself drunk, in a person whom drunkenness excites to do harm to others, is a crime against others. So, again, idleness, except in a person receiving support from the public, or except when it constitutes a breach of contract, cannot without tyranny be made a subject of legal punishment; but if, either from idleness or from any other avoidable cause, a man fails to perform his legal duties to others, as for instance to support his children, it is no tyranny to force him to fulfill that obligation, by compulsory labour, if no other means are available.

Again, there are many acts which, being directly injurious only to the agents themselves, ought not to be legally interdicted, but which, if done publicly, are a violation of good manners, and coming thus within the category of offenses against others, may rightfully be prohibited. Of this kind are offences against decency; ... they are only connected indirectly with our subject, the objection to publicity being equally strong in the case of many actions not in themselves condemnable, nor supposed to be so.

There is another question to which an answer must be found, consistent with the principles which have been laid down. [W]hat the agent is free to do, ought other persons to be equally free to counsel or instigate? This question is not free from difficulty. The case of a person who solicits another to do an act, is not strictly a case of self-regarding conduct. To give advice or offer inducements to any one, is a social act, and may, therefore, like actions in general which affect others, be supposed amenable to social control. But a little reflection corrects the first impression, by showing that if the case is not strictly within the definition of individual liberty, yet the reasons on which the principle of individual liberty is grounded, are applicable to it. If people must be allowed, in whatever concerns only themselves, to act as seems best to themselves at their own peril, they must equally be free to consult with one another about what is fit to be so done; to exchange opinions, and give and receive suggestions. Whatever it is permitted to do, it must be permitted to advise to do. The question is doubtful, only when the instigator derives a personal benefit from his advice; when he makes it his occupation, for subsistence or pecuniary gain, to promote what society and the state consider to be an evil. Then, indeed, a new element of complication is introduced; namely, the existence of classes of persons with an interest opposed to what is considered as the public weal, and whose mode of living is grounded on the counteraction of it. Ought this to be interfered with, or not? Fornication, for example, must be tolerated, and so must gambling; but should a person be free to be a pimp, or to keep a gambling-house? The case is one of those which lie on the exact boundary line between two principles, and it is not at once apparent to which of the two it properly belongs. There are arguments on both sides. On the side of toleration it may be said, that the fact of following anything as an occupation, and living or profiting by the practice of it, cannot make that criminal which would otherwise be admissible; that the act should either be consistently permitted or consistently prohibited; that if the principles which we have hitherto defended are true, society has no business, *as* society, to decide any-thing to be wrong which concerns only the individual; that it cannot go beyond dissuasion, and that one person should be as free to persuade, as another to dissuade. In opposition to this it may be contended, that although the public, or the state, are not warranted in authoritatively deciding, for purposes of repression or punishment, that such or such conduct affecting only the interests of the individual is good or bad, they are fully justified in assuming, if they regard it as bad, that its being so or not is at least a disputable question: That, this being supposed, they cannot be acting wrongly in endeavouring to exclude the influence of solicitations which are not disinterested, of instigators who cannot possibly be impartial—who have a direct personal interest on one side, and that side the one which the state believes to be wrong, and who confessedly promote it for personal objects only. There can surely, it may be urged, be nothing lost, no sacrifice of good, by so ordering matters that persons shall make their election, either wisely or foolishly, on their own prompting, as free as possible from the arts of persons who stimulate their inclinations for interested purposes of their own. . . .

**3. Stephen's Response.** Mill's famous essay was just as famously criticized by Sir James Fitzjames Stephen in Liberty, Equality, Fraternity (1874). "Complete moral tolerance," Stephen said, "is possible only when men have become completely indifferent to each other—that is to say, when society is at an end." The moral coercion of public opinion, he argued, "is the great engine by which the whole mass of beliefs, habits, and customs, which collectively constitute positive morality, are protected and sanctioned." Although Stephen acknowledged that the proper use of the criminal law to enforce positive morality is subject to restraints "independent of general considerations about liberty," he insisted that the penal law ought to prohibit "grossly immoral" or "unquestionably wicked" acts on that ground alone. He summarized his argument as follows:

> [T]here is a sphere, none the less real because it is impossible to define its limits, within which law and public opinion are intruders likely to do more harm than good. To try to regulate the internal affairs of a family, the relations of love or friendship, or many other things of the same sort, by law or by the coercion of public opinion, is like trying to pull an eyelash out of a man's eye with a pair of tongs. They may put out the eye, but they will never get hold of the eyelash.

[T]he principal importance of what is done [in promoting virtue and restraining vice] by criminal law is that in extreme cases it brands gross acts of vice with the deepest mark of infamy which can be impressed upon them, and that in this manner it protects the public and accepted standard of morals from being grossly and openly violated. In short, it affirms in a singularly emphatic manner a principle which is absolutely inconsistent with and contradictory to Mr. Mill's—the principle, namely, that there are acts of wickedness so gross and outrageous that, self-protection apart, they must be prevented as far as possible at any cost to the offender, and punished, if they occur, with exemplary severity.

**4. From the Wolfenden Report to the Model Penal Code to Lawrence.** In *Lawrence v. Texas*, the Supreme Court cites an "emerging awareness" that states should not impose criminal sanctions on adults for their private, consensual, non-commercial sex acts. Among other authorities for this proposition, the Court relies on what is known as the Wolfenden Report, which was published in the middle of the last century by an English Committee on Homosexual Offenses and Prostitution. In the words of the Wolfenden Report:

[T]he function of the criminal law ... is to preserve public order and decency, to protect the citizen from what is offensive or injurious, and to provide sufficient safeguards against exploitation and corruption of others, particularly those who are specially vulnerable because they are young, weak in body or mind, inexperienced, or in a state of special physical, official or economic dependence.

It is not, in our view, the function of the law to intervene in the private lives of citizens, or to seek to enforce any particular pattern of behavior, further than is necessary to carry out the purposes we have outlined.

... Unless a deliberate attempt is to be made by society, acting through the agency of the law, to equate the sphere of crime with that of sin, there must remain a realm of private morality and immorality which is, in brief and crude terms, not the law's business. To say this is not to condone or encourage private immorality.

The Wolfenden Committee's major recommendation was that private homosexual behavior between consenting adults should be decriminalized.[a]

As *Lawrence* remarks, the drafters of the Model Penal Code also argued that "private immorality should be beyond the reach of the penal law" in the absence of a demonstrable secular justification. In particular, the Code's drafters recommended that private sexual activity between consenting adults should be decriminalized. Accordingly, the Model Code

[a] This recommendation was implemented in England in The Sexual Offenses Act, 1967, § 1(1).

does not prohibit adultery, fornication, or other forms of sexual relations between consenting adults.[b]

The Wolfenden Report and the Model Penal Code renewed the controversy initiated by Mill and Stephen a century earlier. Among the leading figures in the ensuing debate were Lord Patrick Devlin, who criticized the libertarian position advanced by Mill and the Wolfenden Committee, and Professor H.L.A. Hart, who defended a modified version of the libertarian position.[c]

**5. Paternalism in Health and Safety.** Recall that Mill found paternalism in matters of health and morals equally objectionable; he insisted that coercion is permissible only to prevent direct harm to others and that the individual's "own good, either physical or moral, is not sufficient warrant" for state regulation. Are these grounds for intervention theoretically distinguishable? Is the ethical basis for criminalization stronger in connection with consumption-related drug offenses, for example, than it is for consensual sex offenses?

In the debate cited above, Lord Devlin and Professor Hart argued over whether it is possible to draw a theoretical distinction between enforcement of morals and paternalism in matters of health or physical safety. Lord Devlin claimed that the function of several criminal offenses "is simply to enforce a moral principle and nothing else," and includes among his examples the bans on euthanasia and duelling. Professor Hart offered this response:

> ... The rules excluding the victim's consent as a defence to charges of murder or assault may perfectly well be explained as a piece of paternalism, designed to protect individuals against themselves. Mill no doubt might have protested against a paternalistic policy of using the law to protect even a consenting victim from bodily harm nearly as much as he protested against laws used merely to enforce positive morality; but this does not mean that these two policies are identical....
>
> Lord Devlin says of the attitude of the criminal law to the victim's consent that if the law existed for the protection of the individual there would be no reason why he should avail himself of it if he did not want it. But paternalism—the protection of people against themselves—is a perfectly coherent policy.... The supply of drugs or narcotics, even to adults, except under medical prescription is punishable by the criminal law, and it would seem very dogmatic to say of the law creating this offence ... that the law was concerned not with the protection of the would-be purchasers

[b] See ALl Model Penal Code and Commentaries, Part II, pp. 357–74 (Comment on Section 213.2 (Deviate Sexual Intercourse by Force or Imposition)) and 430–39 (Note on Adultery and Fornication) (1980).

[c] The famous debate between Lord Devlin and Professor Hart is fully developed in H.L.A. Hart, Law, Liberty and Morality (1963), Patrick Devlin, The Enforcement of Morals (1965), and H.L.A. Hart, Social Solidarity and the Enforcement of Morality, 35 U.Chi.L.Rev. 1 (1967).

against themselves, but only with the punishment of the seller for his immorality. If, as seems obvious, paternalism is a possible explanation of such laws, it is also possible in the case of the rule excluding the consent of the victim as a defence to a charge of assault. In neither case are we forced to conclude with Lord Devlin that the law's "function" is to "enforce a moral principle and nothing else."

   ... Mill carried his protests against paternalism to lengths that may now appear to us fantastic. He cites the example of restrictions of the sale of drugs, and criticises them as interferences with the liberty of the would-be purchaser rather than with that of the seller. No doubt if we no longer sympathise with this criticism this is due, in part, to a general decline in the belief that individuals know their own interests best, and to an increased awareness of a great range of factors which diminish the significance to be attached to an apparently free choice or to consent. Choices may be made or consent given without adequate reflection or appreciation of the consequences; or in pursuit of merely transitory desires; or in various predicaments when the judgment is likely to be clouded; or under inner psychological compulsion; or under pressure by others of a kind too subtle to be susceptible of proof in a law court....

   Certainly a modification in Mill's principles is required, if they are to accommodate the rule of criminal law under discussion or other instances of paternalism. But the modified principles would not abandon the objection to the use of the criminal law merely to enforce positive morality. They would only have to provide that harming others is something we may still seek to prevent by use of the criminal law, even when the victims consent to or assist in the acts which are harmful to them.[d]

Lord Devlin responded that Hart was trying to stake out a position as a "physical paternalist and a moral individualist" and that such a distinction was illogical:

   [If] there is an element of physical paternalism in the law that forbids masochism and euthanasia these crimes seem to me as good examples as any that could be selected to illustrate the difficulty in practice of distinguishing between physical and moral paternalism. Neither in principle nor in practice can a line be drawn between legislation controlling the individual's physical welfare and legislation controlling his moral welfare. If paternalism be the principle, no father of a family would content himself with looking after his children's welfare and leaving their morals to themselves. If society has an interest which permits it to

---

[d] H.L.A. Hart, Law, Liberty and Morality 31–33 (1963). Reprinted with the permission of the publishers, Stanford University Press. © 1963 by the Board of Trustees of the Leland Stanford Junior University.

legislate in the one case, why not in the other? If, on the other hand, we are grown up enough to look after our own morals, why not after our own bodies?[e]

The drug laws provide a useful vehicle for testing one's views on the theoretical questions raised by Mill's essay and debated by Hart and Devlin. Are prohibitions against availability and use of psychoactive drugs ethically defensible? Does it provide "sufficient warrant" that the prevailing public opinion regards use of psychoactive drugs for purposes of "getting high" to be morally wrong? Is it "sufficient warrant" that society is protecting individuals from harming themselves? Does the legitimacy of the prohibition depend upon the social impact of drug consumption? If so, does it depend upon a determination that use of the particular drug is likely to cause disordered or violent behavior that could harm someone else? Or is criminalization permissible if use of the drug would impair the person's health or behavior in a way likely to burden health-care and social-service systems? Would the ethical analysis differ according to whether the prohibition was limited to trafficking offenses or also included possession and use offenses?

---

## NOTES ON THE EFFECTS OF CRIMINALIZATION

**1. Introduction.** Virtually all participants in the criminalization debates acknowledge that there are many practical arguments against state punishment of private vice. Sir James Fitzjames Stephen emphasized that "criminal law is at once by far the most powerful and by far the roughest engine which society can use for any purpose." He continued:

> It strikes so hard that it can be enforced only on the gravest occasions, and with every sort of precaution against abuse or mistake. Before an act can be treated as a crime, it ought to be capable of distinct definition and of specific proof, and it ought also to be of such a nature that it is worthwhile to prevent it at the risk of inflicting great damage, direct and indirect, upon those who commit it. These conditions are seldom, if ever, fulfilled by mere vices. It would obviously be impossible to indict a man for ingratitude or perfidy. Such charges are too vague for specific discussion and distinct proof on the one side, and disproof on the other. Moreover, the expense of the investigations necessary for the legal punishment of such conduct would be enormous. It would be necessary to go into an infinite number of delicate and subtle inquiries which would tear off all privacy from the lives of a large number of persons. These considerations are, I think, conclusive reasons against treating vice in general as a crime.
>
> The excessive harshness of criminal law is also a circumstance which very greatly narrows the range of its application.... A law

[e] Patrick Devlin, The Enforcement of Morals 135–36 (1965).

which enters into a direct contest with fierce imperious passion, which the person who feels it does not admit to be bad, and which is not directly injurious to others, will generally do more harm than good; and this is perhaps the principal reason why it is impossible to legislate directly against unchastity, unless it takes forms which everyone regards as monstrous and horrible....[a]

Surely, Stephen is right when he observes that socially disapproved behavior should not be punished by criminal sanctions if this will "do more harm than good." The question arises, however, whether it is possible to identify more specific criteria for assessing the effects of criminalization and for determining, in a given case, whether its costs outweigh its benefits. The ongoing efforts to identify such criteria are summarized in the following notes.

**2.   Assessing Benefits.** Empirical assessments of the benefits of any particular criminal prohibition are not easily made. Perhaps the main difficulty is the need to isolate the incremental preventive effects of any given scheme of criminalization beyond those that would be achieved in any event by non-criminal methods of legal regulation and other means of social control. Consider, for example, the utility of criminal sanctions to punish parents who physically abuse their children. What would the prevalence of child abuse be if this conduct were not criminally punishable? To what extent does the threatened imposition of criminal punishment supplement the preventive effect of civil schemes for state intervention and termination of parental rights? To what extent does any type of legal control, civil or criminal, shape parental behavior in this context when one takes into account personal pathology and the impact of community expectations and pressures? On the other hand, to what extent does criminalization reinforce and perpetuate proper parental attitudes regarding the use of violence to discipline and control their children? Obviously these questions are not easily researched.[b]

A second problem is presented by the need to quantify the behavioral impact of criminalization. Take the offense of driving while intoxicated (DWI) as an example. Initially it is necessary to determine the degree to which the precise scheme of criminalization being studied reduces the number of incidents of drunken driving.[c] However, as is the case with many criminal offenses, the DWI prohibition is designed to prevent harm by reducing risk-creating conduct. Thus, a precise calculation of the social benefits of the scheme of criminalization requires a further determination regarding the degree to which it reduces the social costs associated with the harms ultimately feared—in the case of DWI, this would mean the health

[a] James Fitzjames Stephen, Liberty, Equality, Fraternity 159–61 (1874).

[b] For an illuminating discussion of this issue, see Michael P. Rosenthal, Physical Abuse of Children by Parents: The Criminalization Decision, 7 Am.J.Crim.L. 141 (1979).

[c] As previous materials have demonstrated, this preventive effect can be achieved in a variety of ways—by deterring potential offenders, by shaping and reinforcing beliefs and attitudes that are unfavorable to the objectionable conduct, and by affording a basis for preventing recidivism through the punishment of individual violators.

and welfare costs associated with accidents and fatalities that are attributable to drunken driving.

A third difficulty involved in assessing the social benefits of criminalization arises from the fact that "criminalization" is a variable that is itself subject to manipulation. For one thing, the behavioral effects obviously will depend on the precise definition of the prohibited conduct. For example, DWI can be defined as: (i) impaired driving due to intoxication; or (ii) driving while one's faculties are impaired by the effects of intoxicating substances; or (iii) having a designated level of alcohol in one's blood, a level which itself can be varied. In addition, the deterrent effect of any particular prohibition will depend upon the probability of apprehension and conviction and the magnitude of the anticipated penalty. Indeed, it is generally believed that the deterrent effect of a prohibition can be affected by manipulating any of these variables.

It must be emphasized, of course, that the use of criminal sanctions for most of the behavior covered in any criminal code is not open to serious question. In these contexts, attention is focused mainly on the determination of the optimal combination of probability and severity of punishment. However, in some contexts, the conclusion that a criminal sanction is useful at all may depend on a set of assumptions about the level of enforcement and the severity of the effective penalty. Specifically, it might be determined that the optimal scheme of legal control will include some or all of the distinctive features of a criminal sanction *only* at a specified level of enforcement, and that otherwise the costs of criminalization will exceed its benefits.

**3. Assessing Costs.** The costs of any scheme of criminal sanctions will also depend directly on the level of enforcement and the characteristics of the penalties imposed on violators. Indeed, some of the distinctive costs of criminalization frequently mentioned in the literature arise only under certain conditions of enforcement and punishment. Moreover, several of the special problems associated with the criminal process are primarily ethical in nature and therefore defy quantitative measurement. These observations should be kept in mind while reviewing the following summary of the considerations usually regarded as relevant to the task of assessing the costs of criminalization.

**(i) Deterrence of Socially Valuable Behavior.** Criminal prohibitions, like other types of legal regulation, can deter lawful behavior on the margins of the forbidden conduct. The magnitude of this effect will vary in relation to the indeterminacy of the prohibition and the instrumental nature of the prohibited behavior. In most situations, of course, the marginally lawful behavior will be without social value and its deterrence therefore will not constitute a cost of the prohibition. However, if the marginal behavior does have social value, its reduction must be counted as a cost of the prohibition.

**(ii) Enforcement Expenditures.** Although the level of enforcement can be varied, the costs of an existing or proposed criminal prohibition include the resources devoted to the detection and punishment of violators. Police departments, prosecutors, courts, and correctional agencies usually do not have line-item budgets linked to various offenses. Still, it is possible to make general estimates of the costs incurred in enforcing a particular prohibition at any given time. Of course, one cannot automatically conclude that these costs would be saved if the criminal prohibition were repealed or if the level of enforcement were reduced. This is because criminal-justice budgets typically do not vary with the number of offenses enforced, and most of the expenditure is attributable to the costs of maintaining the system itself. In any case, resources identifiably related to enforcement of any particular offense are best seen as "opportunity costs"—resources that would otherwise have been spent in enforcing other penal laws.

**(iii) Effects on the Individual.** Not all of the "pains" of punishment are measurable in economic terms, or even in psychological ones. However, it is possible to describe the effects of arrest, prosecution, conviction, and sentence on individual offenders. These include reduced productivity attributable to stigmatization and confinement, adverse impact on dependents, and the psychic and physical harms that can occur as a result of imprisonment. Such effects must be taken into account in a comprehensive assessment of the social costs of any particular criminal prohibition. Obviously, these effects vary among individuals. They also are linked directly to the level of enforcement and the severity of the deprivations (both before and after conviction) that are experienced by the offender in connection with particular offenses.

**(iv) Effects on Privacy.** Stephen and Devlin acknowledges the dangers of criminalizing behavior that occurs in private without direct injury to another. The problem is that enforcement of these laws requires the police to employ intrusive investigative techniques that offend widely-shared expectations of privacy. Professor Herbert Packer argued that any criminal prohibition that requires systematic use of decoys, undercover agents, residential searches, and electronic surveillance in order to detect violations "should be suspect." These techniques, he argued, "are so at odds with values of privacy and human dignity that we should resort to them only under the most exigent circumstances." Professor Packer found the vice laws especially objectionable because they "thrust the police into the role of snoopers and harassers." The enforcement of laws against bribery, weapons transactions, and virtually all possessory offenses also require systematic use of intrusive investigative techniques.[d] Should these offenses be "suspect" also?

**(v) Criminogenic Effects.** Some prohibitions have criminogenic consequences—that is, they create circumstances that increase the likelihood of criminal activity that would not have occurred in the absence of the prohibition. It has been clearly demonstrated, for example, that drug-dependent persons commit property crimes, or engage in prostitution or retail drug trafficking, to obtain money to buy illicit drugs at high prices—

[d] Herbert Packer, The Limits of the Criminal Sanction 283–86 (1968).

drugs that would cost very little if they were legitimately available. Also, prohibitions of drug use and homosexuality are thought to force persons who engage in such behavior into association with persons who engage in other criminal activities, thereby increasing the likelihood that they too will develop deviant lifestyles.

In this connection, consider too the so-called "labeling" hypothesis. According to labeling theorists, official responses to deviance, especially through the stigmatizing processes of the criminal law, increase the likelihood of further deviance by individuals who did not already view themselves as "outsiders" before they were so labeled. To the extent that this phenomenon does occur, it has special implications for the criminalization of conduct, such as drug use and petty shoplifting, that is relatively prevalent among young and otherwise law-abiding persons. It should be noted, however, that the validity of the labeling theory is difficult to test because it requires proof that recidivist offenders would not have continued or diversified their deviant conduct in the absence of official intervention.

**(vi) Costs of Under–Enforcement.** Economic theory demonstrates that the optimal level of enforcement is something less than 100 per cent. Although relatively full enforcement is usually sought in connection with the most serious predatory offenses, the actual level of enforcement is determined by the allocation of investigative and prosecutorial resources as well as by the prevalence of the prohibited behavior. However, violations of some laws are so pervasive and difficult to detect that they will be significantly under-enforced no matter what the police choose to do. Moreover, to the extent that these laws are enforced at all, the conditions are established for arbitrariness in the administration of the penal law. The threat to the rule of law is aggravated even further if the criminal conduct is not uniformly condemned by the prevailing public morality.

Many commentators have suggested that the penal law should not include offenses that will not be enforced, or will be enforced only sporadically. Is it appropriate to enact or retain a criminal prohibition simply to declare and symbolize the prevailing morality with no expectation that it will be enforced? Are the costs of under-enforcement higher in connection with adultery or marijuana use? Why?

**(vii) The Crime Tariff.** Prohibitions against commercial activity in gambling, sex, pornography, and drugs clearly reduce the supply of the prohibited goods and services, but so long as there continue to be willing buyers, an illicit commercial market will develop. Of course, the threat of criminal punishment will reduce the number of producers and sellers; and reduced competition, together with the suppliers' costs of avoiding detection, will drive up the price. As a result, the degree to which the prohibition actually reduces the undesired activity depends on the elasticity of demand—i.e., on the extent to which potential consumers are responsive to the increase in price. Whatever the size of the illegal market, the main economic effect of prohibition in any case is to establish what the economists call "barriers to entry" and to assure a high return for entrepreneurs who are willing to assume the risks of violating the law. Professor Packer referred to this economic effect as a "crime tariff."

What are the social consequences of the crime tariff? For one thing, the tremendous revenues generated by illegal trafficking in prohibited goods and services are untaxed. For another, black-market entrepreneurs obviously have strong incentives, and substantial capital, to take whatever measures are necessary to protect their investment and reduce the risk of punishment. Pervasive corruption of law enforcement officials is an all-too-frequent result. Moreover, high crime tariffs for commerce in drugs, sex, and gambling establish the economic conditions for large-scale criminal organizations to flourish. Finally, to the extent that the illicit good or service can vary in quality, society forgoes the benefits of regulation: prostitutes are not required to be examined and treated for venereal disease; gambling establishments are not monitored for fraudulent practices; and drugs are not tested for purity.

———

# CHAPTER I

# THE CRIMINAL ACT

---

## SECTION 1: THE CONDUCT REQUIREMENT

## Doe v. City of Lafayette

United States Court of Appeals, Seventh Circuit, 2003.
334 F.3d 606.

Before RIPPLE, DIANE P. WOOD, and WILLIAMS, CIRCUIT JUDGES.

■ WILLIAMS, CIRCUIT JUDGE.

John Doe was banned for life from all park property in the City of Lafayette, Indiana—including a golf course, sports stadium, and city pools.... Doe filed suit against the City, arguing that the ban violates his First Amendment[a] right to freedom of thought.... The District Court granted summary judgment in favor of the City. We reverse, finding the ban violates the First Amendment.

## I. BACKGROUND

John Doe is a convicted sex offender. His criminal history includes convictions for child molestation, voyeurism, exhibitionism, and window peeping. His last conviction was in 1991, ten years before this litigation. Doe's crimes were committed in schools, a convenience store, and outside private residences, and he claims that his urges are triggered by emotional vulnerability, typically in the late evening. As a result of these criminal convictions, Doe has been hospitalized, imprisoned, under house arrest, and on probation. He has been in active psychological treatment since 1986, and voluntarily attends a self-help group for sex offenders. Doe admits he still has fantasies about children, and his psychologist opines that he will likely have these urges for the rest of his life, although he recently began taking medication to control his sexual urges.

In January 2000, Doe was driving home from work and began to have sexual thoughts about children. He drove to a City of Lafayette park[1] and

---

[a] The First Amendment to the United States Constitution provides in relevant part that "Congress shall make no law ... abridging the freedom of speech...." This prohibition speaks only to the authority of Congress. The United States Supreme Court has interpreted the 14th Amendment to extend the prohibition to state and local government en-

tities. How and why it has done so is for present purposes unimportant.—[Footnote by eds.]

[1] The dissent points out that Doe came in contact with two parks, but we think his intention in going to the first park, Columbian Park, is far from clear. Doe explained in

61

watched several youths in their early teens playing on a baseball diamond. Doe admits that, while observing them, he thought about having sexual contact with the children. After watching them for 15–30 minutes, and without having any contact with them, Doe left the park. Because he was upset about the incident, Doe contacted his psychologist to report the incident.[2] He also reported the incident to his self-help group.

An anonymous source reported Doe's January visit to the park, and the thoughts he had while he was there, to his former probation officer. Following this unidentified report, the probation officer contacted the Lafayette Police Department, which prompted a conversation between the Police Chief, the Superintendent of the Lafayette Parks Department, and a City attorney regarding Doe's appearance in the park. Their discussion focused on the nature of Doe's January visit to the park and his criminal history, although all acknowledge that Doe was no longer serving a sentence or on probation.[3] As a result of this conversation, the City Parks Department issued an order permanently banning Doe from entering any City park property at any time and for any purpose under threat of arrest for trespass. The City did not provide any preissuance review of the ban, nor was Doe afforded an opportunity to appeal.

The ban order is both geographically and temporally broad. The City of Lafayette's extensive park system includes several large parks, many smaller neighborhood parks, a zoo, a golf course, a sports complex, a baseball stadium, and several pools. Typically, ban orders are issued by the City against those who have vandalized park property or interfered with park patrons. The resulting bans ordinarily are issued for a week or, at most, a summer. In this case, the ban order against Doe has no termination date.

Doe sued the City seeking to lift the ban, challenging it under the First [Amendment]. On cross motions for summary judgment, the district court granted the City's motion, finding [no] First Amendment . . . problem with the ban. Doe appeals.

## II.   ANALYSIS

Given the bases on which Doe appeals, we are faced with a question not typically before a court: may a city constitutionally ban one of its citizens from public property based on its discovery of that individual's immoral thoughts? This scenario is quite unusual, as it is a rare case where thoughts, as separated from deeds, become known. Technology has not yet

---

his deposition that he lived a short distance from that park, and there is no evidence that he got out of his car or even stopped his car at the first park.

[2] Doe's psychologist testified that his ability to go to the park and manage his impulses is a positive step in his treatment and helps integrate Doe into a more normal lifestyle.

[3] Doe was not on probation in January 2000, and was not even restricted from entering the park during his period of house arrest a decade earlier, so we need not consider whether the restrictions imposed by the City might have been appropriate as a condition of release as part of the earlier criminal sentences.

produced a mind-reader,[6] and thus most thinking, unless purposefully revealed to others, remains one's own. Unlike other cases in which the state becomes aware of an individual's mental state because of his or her actions, here the City acknowledges that Doe's own revelation of his thoughts, not any outward indication of his thinking, is the basis for its actions.

The freedom of individuals to control their own thoughts has been repeatedly acknowledged by the Supreme Court.... Indeed, it [has] recognized that freedom to hold beliefs about politics, religion, and other matters is a cornerstone of liberty.... Given the long-standing recognition by the High Court, we analyze the City of Lafayette's ban order with the principle that freedom of the mind occupies a highly-protected position in our constitutional heritage.

The City defends the ban as a measure to protect its youth from a person with a history of sex offenses whom they fear may harm the City's children. As part of this argument, the City seems to imply that Doe's thoughts about children and close proximity to them may encourage him to strike again. This fear—that thoughts alone may encourage action—is not enough to curb protected thinking.... We need not entertain further the exercise of determining what state interests might outweigh a person's right to think, as the City's only articulated interest in this case does not justify its ban order.

We recognize that although pure thoughts are protected by the First Amendment, non-expressive actions are not. First Amendment jurisprudence is fastened upon the critical distinction between thinking and acting on those thoughts. [The] cases focus on the distinction between mere conduct and expression and do not contradict long-standing principles regarding protection of thought....

Our conclusion is further reinforced by a fundamental understanding of the bounds of punishable action. The maxim that cogitationis poenam nemo patitur (no one is punishable solely for his thoughts) is a cornerstone of the American common law system of criminal justice that has shaped many of the constitutional boundaries of criminal law.[9] Perhaps the Victorian legal scholar James Fitzjames Stephen best explained this basic limit on government power: "If it were not so restricted it would be utterly intolerable; all mankind would be criminals, and most of their lives would

---

[6] The form such mind-reading technology might take was recently the topic of a popular Steven Spielberg movie, *Minority Report*. The movie depicts the year 2054, in which police rely on three psychic "precognitives" that see crimes before they happen. Using these projections, the police arrest and incarcerate individuals for crimes committed only in the minds of the arrestees.

[9] The proscription against penalizing for ideas alone has been recognized for centuries, see 4 William Blackstone, Commentaries on Laws of England, 21 (1765) ("[N]o temporal tribunal can search the heart, or fathom the intentions of the mind, otherwise than as they are demonstrated by outward actions, it therefore cannot punish for what it cannot know."), and is reflected in modern codifications of the common law, see Model Penal Code and Commentaries, Comment to § 2.01 at 214–15 (1985) ("It is fundamental that a civilized society does not punish for thoughts alone.").

be passed trying and punishing each other for offenses which could never be proved." 1 James Fitzjames Stephen, A History of the Criminal Law of England 78 (1883).

This axiomatic principle is illustrated by the discernment between punishment for a person's status—impermissible under the Eighth Amendment[b]—and sanctions levied for a person's conduct. See Robinson v. California, 370 U.S. 660, 666 (1962). In *Robinson*, the Supreme Court struck down a California statute that made addiction to narcotics illegal. Because the statute required no illegal act, but criminalized mere status as a drug addict, it violated the Eighth Amendment's prohibition against cruel and unusual punishment. This distinction was further refined in Powell v. Texas, 392 U.S. 514, 532–34 (1968), where the Court explained that although status may not be criminalized, acts undertaken as a result of that status may be. There the Court upheld Powell's arrest for appearing drunk in public because the Texas law did not sanction Powell merely for his status as an alcoholic, but for his act of overimbibing in public. The Court rested its holding on the fact that Powell voluntarily committed sanctionable conduct: "The entire thrust of *Robinson*'s interpretation of the Cruel and Unusual Punishment Clause is that criminal penalties may be inflicted only if the accused has committed some act, has engaged in some behavior, which society has an interest in preventing, or perhaps in historical common law terms, has committed some actus reus." Id. at 533.... Here Doe has committed no such act.

The dissent argues that Doe's steps of driving to the park and watching children constitute punishable action. Yet the circumstances make clear that the ban order issued by the City resulted from its concern about Doe's fantasies about children. The City did not receive any complaints from the children in the park, and it does not allege that anyone was at all affected by Doe's presence there. Presumably, untold numbers of Lafayette residents wander the City's parks every day, many of them potentially thinking offensive or objectionable thoughts. Despite the prevalence of his behavior, only Doe has been banned from the park for it. The City has not suggested that it monitors sex offenders' presence in the City parks, and it could not cite any other example of an individual banned for mere presence in the park. The City does not dispute that it is Doe's thoughts that distinguish him from all other park users.

What is more, Doe's behavior does not rise to the level of an action of sufficient gravity to justify punishment. The error in punishing actions similar to Doe's is more easily seen by way of analogies removed from the sensitive context of child molestation. By way of comparison, we would not sanction criminal punishment of an individual with a criminal history of

[b] The Eighth Amendment to the United States Constitution provides: "Excessive bail shall not be required, nor excessive fines imposed, nor cruel and unusual punishments inflicted." The prohibition on "cruel and unusual punishments" has also been applied by the United States Supreme Court to state and local government through the provisions of the 14th Amendment. Again, how and why it has done so is for present purposes unimportant.—[Footnote by eds.]

bank robbery (a crime, like child molestation, with a high rate of recidivism) simply because she or he stood in the parking lot of a bank and thought about robbing it. It goes without saying that in this hypothetical the individual would not have taken an action that could support punishment. Or, as a different example, punishment of a drug addict who stands outside a dealer's house craving a hit but successfully resists the urge to enter and purchase drugs would be offensive to our understanding of the bounds of the criminal law. Despite the City's suggestions at oral argument, both of these situations, analogous to the actions taken by Doe here, present clear examples of actions that do not reach a level of criminal culpability necessary to justify punishment.

As these illustrations suggest, Doe's behavior may also be understood as the kind that does not come close to what we recognize as punishable under the theory of attempt. Under Indiana law, a person commits attempt when, acting with culpability necessary to commit the crime, he or she "engages in conduct that constitutes a substantial step toward commission of the crime." Ind.Code § 35–41–5–1. Here, the most that can be said of Doe's action is that he drove to the park and watched children. Even if we assume Doe intended to molest children when he stood in the park, Doe's mere presence in the park is not enough to constitute a "substantial step" towards an attempted sex offense. In the same way that the individual with a history of robbing banks could not be charged with attempted bank robbery for standing across the street from the bank and thinking about robbing it, Doe may not be punished for merely thinking perverted thoughts about children.

Finally, Doe's conduct is not akin to stalking, which, while perhaps motivated by thoughts, requires actual threatening conduct by the stalker. Stalking statutes typically require that a defendant 1) knowingly or intentionally; 2) engage in a course of conduct involving continuous or repeated harassment; 3) that would cause a reasonable person to feel terrorized, frightened, intimidated, or threatened; and 4) actually causes that person to feel terrorized, frightened, intimidated, or threatened. See, e.g., Ind.Code § 35–45–10–1. Doe's actions do not come close to criminal conduct punishable as stalking. He did not "continually" or "repeatedly" go to the public park; his ban order was based on a single visit. See Landis v. State, 704 N.E.2d 113, 113 (Ind.1998) (holding that "the crime of stalking by its nature necessitates proof of repeated or continuing acts"). Nor did Doe's gaze or proximity cause any specific person to feel frightened or threatened; indeed, there is no evidence that anyone even *noticed* Doe's presence. Frazier v. Delco Elecs. Corp., 263 F.3d 663, 668 (7th Cir.2001) ("The stalking victim who doesn't know that she is being stalked is not in fear of being injured."). Most importantly, Doe's conduct—going to a public park with improper thoughts about children previously unknown to him—did not harm any of the youths in the park, unlike the terror caused by actions criminalized as stalking.[10]

---

[10] See, e.g., Garza v. State, 736 N.E.2d 323, 325 (Ind.Ct.App.2000) (despite several requests to be left alone, stalker repeatedly contacted victim, sent her flowers with a

We are acutely aware of the critical problem of sex offenses against children. We find the substance of Doe's sexual fantasies about children repugnant and deplorable. But, of course, the fact that this court or the City of Lafayette finds Doe's thoughts offensive does not limit the amount of First Amendment protection they are afforded. Despite our repudiation of the content of his thoughts, the City of Lafayette may not punish Doe for this thinking alone, for without protection from government intrusion into our thoughts, the freedoms guaranteed by the First Amendment would be meaningless.

## III.   CONCLUSION

Accordingly, we reverse the judgment of the district court and remand for proceedings consistent with this opinion.

■ Ripple, Circuit Judge, dissenting.

The majority invalidates the City of Lafayette's ("the City" or "Lafayette") action because, in its view, the ban order against Mr. Doe violates the First Amendment. In my view, the City has adopted a reasonable proscription designed to protect a vulnerable part of the population, its children, against the danger of a relapse by Mr. Doe. Therefore, I respectfully dissent.

The majority and Mr. Doe base their position on the conclusory proposition that banning Mr. Doe from the park constitutes "punishment" for "pure thought." This view requires that we close our eyes to Mr. Doe's actions in that park in January of 2000. It also requires that we give short shrift to Mr. Doe's condition as an admitted pedophile who, despite some progress in dealing with his condition, continues to have difficulty controlling his urges.[2] . . .

The majority opinion rests on the assumption that the ban punishes Mr. Doe solely for his thoughts. In support of that characterization, Mr. Doe relies on the unexceptional proposition that "it would be nonsensical to extend the protection of the Constitution to speech, but allow the government to invade thoughts." In my view, our concern here ought to be stated in terms that recognize, more comprehensively and pragmatically, the actual situation confronting the City as well as the parents and children who look to that City for protection as they go about their everyday

message that began "hate, anger, bitterness, malice, venom, hellish prisons of our own making," and joined her health club); Johnson v. State, 721 N.E.2d 327, 330 (Ind.Ct. App.2000) (stalker threatened to kill former girlfriend, flattened her car tires, and came to her home on many occasions, including three separate times the night he was arrested); Waldon v. State, 684 N.E.2d 206, 207 (Ind.Ct. App.1997) (despite existence of restraining order, victim encountered stalker on at least six separate occasions near her dance studio within one-year period).

[2] It is important to note that Mr. Doe acknowledges that he will never be cured of his pedophilia and that a successful recovery will mean that he has learned to control his urges, not that those urges have gone away. Mr. Doe, therefore, is more likely to act on such urges than individuals without this affliction. Notably, he has three convictions for sexual offenses against minors.

activities. This case is not about Mr. Doe's thoughts. It is about the danger he presents to the children when, because of these thoughts, he goes to the park to be near children and to achieve sexual gratification. Mr. Doe and the majority take the position that the First Amendment requires that the City admit him to its public parks while knowing that he poses an immediate safety threat to the children there.

My colleagues write that the ban punishes Mr. Doe for his fantasies and therefore punishes him for "pure thought." Such a characterization might be accurate if Lafayette had banned him from public parks because he had admitted to having sexual fantasies about children in his home. But Mr. Doe did not simply indulge such fantasies in his own home. Nor did he go to the park simply to think and contemplate. He entered the park in search of sexual gratification induced by the children playing there. Mr. Doe did not simply entertain thoughts; he had sexual urges directed toward children, and he took several steps toward gratifying those urges. He went to not one, but two parks[3] in search of children at play in order to achieve sexual gratification. At the second park, he spent between 15 and 30 minutes observing children at play, and consequently became sexually aroused.[4] In short, he engaged not only in thought but in activity directed toward an illegal and very harmful end. The City's focus in implementing the ban was Mr. Doe's actions—directed toward this dangerous, illegal and harmful end. The City restricted Mr. Doe's ability to enter public parks where children are often unsupervised because Mr. Doe went to a park for the purpose of sexually gratifying himself by his proximity to children.

The City has not tried to curb Mr. Doe's thoughts. It has not enacted an ordinance banning Mr. Doe, or any other individual, from having sexual fantasies about children. Lafayette is justifiably concerned with Mr. Doe's efforts to act on those thoughts and, therefore, with his proximity to unsupervised children. Mr. Doe's actions in January of 2000 demonstrate that his recovery is incomplete and that there is a very real possibility of a future assault. Thus, upon learning of Mr. Doe's trip to Columbian and Murdock Parks in response to his sexual desires, Lafayette banned Mr. Doe from city parks. The Lafayette School Corporation also banned Mr. Doe from its premises, a ban that Mr. Doe does not challenge. Both of these restrictions are reasonable preventative measures designed to keep Mr. Doe away from locations where unsupervised children may be present.

Mr. Doe contends that he is being singled out for this treatment. He points to the many convicted sex offenders living in the Lafayette/West Lafayette area who are not banned from public parks and claims that the City's action is therefore arbitrary. According to the record in this case,

---

[3] The transcript of Mr. Doe's deposition is clear that Mr. Doe drove first to one park (Columbian) and then a second (Murdock). Mr. Doe characterized his activity as "cruising." When the City's attorney asked for clarification, Mr. Doe admitted that he was "mostly" looking for children.

[4] Mr. Doe stated that seeing the children in the park caused him to have thoughts "about the possibility of, you know, having some kind of sexual contact with the kids."

however, the City does not have knowledge that relapses or near-relapses involving other sex offenders have occurred on city property. There is certainly no indication in the record that Lafayette would respond to any other similar case in a different manner. By his own admission, Mr. Doe had entered the park for the purpose of obtaining sexual gratification by observing children. The City certainly need not act in an ostrichlike fashion with respect to this information. It had an obligation to act prudently.

Mr. Doe contends that "[i]t surely would be safer for the City of Lafayette if it could enter the thoughts of every citizen to try to determine the potential for criminal activity.... Such a broad brush approach would banish many innocent persons because of thoughts that would never blossom into reality." This submission might be apt if Lafayette had adopted an ordinance banning all individuals who had sexual fantasies about children from entering public parks. But the City was entitled to take into consideration the reality that, unlike most individuals who have such fantasies, Mr. Doe poses, by his own admission, a far greater probability of acting on those fantasies and endangering the children. As Justice Holmes wrote, "the character of every act depends upon the circumstances in which it is done." See Schenck v. United States, 249 U.S. 47, 52 (1919). We cannot accurately assess the City's action without taking into account Mr. Doe's pedophilia. This affliction certainly ought not doom him to permanent exile from society. Nor may society, acting through the government, harass or marginalize him. His actions do, however, render reasonable some restrictions that would be inappropriate if applied to someone without such a history.

The law has long recognized that not every individual is equally capable of controlling his desires and preventing them from becoming actions that endanger others. Here, we have an individualized finding, based upon an admission, that Mr. Doe belongs to that group of persons who are more susceptible to having sexual desires with respect to children *and* to acting on those urges. The City of Lafayette has a compelling interest in protecting children from these individuals. Mr. Doe moved beyond a momentary desire to seek sexual gratification from children to a calculated effort to act on those desires. The fact that, on that particular day in January 2000, the sexual gratification took the form of merely observing the children at play is fortunate for those children and for Mr. Doe.[5] It does not change, however, the fact that his urge, at least for an hour or so, was able to overpower his ability to control it. The City of Lafayette did not violate his First Amendment rights by taking the action that it did to protect its children. It need not expose the children to the risk that, on a future date, Mr. Doe's loss of control will be as short-lived....

Banning Mr. Doe from Lafayette's parks will not restrict the flow of information and ideas. Nor will it prevent him from participating in public life or realizing his potential as an individual. I do not believe the First

---

[5] Mr. Doe testified that, while in the park he said to himself, "I've got to get out of    here before I do something...."

Amendment argument submitted by Mr. Doe has any merit. Accordingly, I must respectfully dissent.

## NOTES ON THE REQUIREMENT OF CONDUCT

**1.  The Requirement of Conduct.** The law is clear that conduct is an essential component of any crime. This traditional understanding is succinctly stated in Glanville Williams, Criminal Law: The General Part 1 (2d ed. 1961):

> That crime requires an act is invariably true if the proposition be read as meaning that a private thought is not sufficient to found responsibility.... "So long as an act rests in bare intention," said Mansfield, "it is not punishable by our laws"; and this is so even though the intention be abundantly proved by the confession of the accused.

As the quotation suggests, it has long been established that criminal liability may not be premised on a mere intention or bare desire to do wrong. Increasingly, the requirement of conduct is also taken to bar the infliction of punishment for a mere personal characteristic or status. Instead, criminal liability is reserved for behavior. At least within the confines of the Anglo–American tradition, the starting point for any definition of any crime is a statement of proscribed conduct.

Adherence to a conduct requirement does not limit the penal law to the redress of positive acts. On the contrary, the law may proscribe a failure to act. It also may punish possession—a condition begun by an act of acquisition and continued by a failure to divest. But conduct in some form—an act, omission, or possession—remains everywhere accepted as an essential prerequisite of criminal conviction and punishment.

This requirement of conduct is so fundamental to our understanding of the criminal law that it is rarely put in issue. Obvious though it may seem, however, the requirement of conduct is a matter of great significance to the conceptual structure of the penal law.

**2.  Jeffries and Stephan.** A short rationale for the requirement that criminal punishment be based on conduct appears in John C. Jeffries, Jr. and Paul Stephan, Defenses, Presumptions, and Burden of Proof in the Criminal Law, 88 Yale L. J. 1325, 1371 n.130 (1979):*

> The significance of the act requirement should not be understated. First, it serves a critical evidentiary function in corroborating other proof going to the existence of evil intent. The inevitable risk of error in assessing mental attitude is intolerably great when state of mind is not anchored in evidence of objectively demonstrable conduct. Thus, proof of conduct is necessary to establish culpability.

* Reprinted by permission of The Yale Law Journal Company and Fred B. Rothman & Company from The Yale Law Journal, Vol. 88, p. 1371.

Second, the act requirement serves an equally important function in differentiating daydreams from fixed intentions. Mental attitude is not only difficult to demonstrate; it is also evanescent, fluid, and various. When there is no real prospect that evil thought will be translated into evil deed, there is no legitimate occasion for punishment. The act requirement therefore precludes criminal penalty for fantasy, wish, or conjecture. It insists that anti-social thought be manifest in behavior tending toward the harm ultimately feared. Thus, proof of conduct is necessary to establish dangerousness as well as culpability.

Finally, the act requirement preserves the liberty of the individual citizen by constraining penal liability within a tolerable sphere. It states a limit on the coercive power of the state and marks a boundary of individual accountability to the collective will. As Herbert Packer put the point, the act requirement provides a locus poenitentiae to enable the law-abiding citizen to avoid criminal liability. . . .

**3.  Packer.** The final reference in the preceding excerpt is to Herbert Packer, The Limits of the Criminal Sanction 73–75 (1968). Packer's development of the point is sufficiently subtle to warrant extensive quotation:**

It may hardly seem a startling notion that criminal law, or law in general for that matter, is concerned with conduct—people's actions (including their verbal and other expressive actions) and their failures to act. Yet there is nothing in the nature of things that compels this focus. The criminal law could be concerned with people's thoughts and emotions, with their personality patterns and character structures. It is true that if this rather than conduct was the focus, it would still be expedient in most cases to ascertain these essentially internal characteristics through inquiry into conduct. But if these internal characteristics were the focus, conduct would simply be evidence of what we are interested in rather than the thing itself; and we would not hesitate to use other evidence to the extent that it became available. If, for example, we could determine through projective tests like the Rorschach or through other and more sophisticated forms of psychological testing that a given individual was likely to inflict serious physical injury on someone, someday, somewhere, and if we viewed conduct [as merely evidentiary rather than as a prerequisite of liability], we would presumably not hesitate to inflict punishment on that person for his propensities, or, as the old cliche has it, for thinking evil thoughts. . . .

Why do we not do so? The obvious historical answer is that, aside from a few antiquarian anomalies such as the offense of

---

imagining the King's death, we have not been sufficiently stirred by the danger presented or sufficiently confident of our ability to discern propensities in the absence of conduct to use the instruments of the criminal law in this fashion. For some it may be enough to rejoice that historically this was so and to rest on that historical accident for the present and the future, but I think that a further answer is required. This answer turns, in my view, on the idea of culpability. . . .

Among the notions associated with the concept of "culpability" are those of free will and human autonomy. I do not mean this in any deep philosophical sense but in a contingent and practical social sense. It is important, especially in a society that likes to describe itself as "free" and "open," that a government should be empowered to coerce people only for what they do and not for what they are.

If this is important for law generally, it is a fortiori important for that most coercive of legal instruments, the criminal law. Now, this self-denying ordinance can be and often is attacked as being inconsistent with the facts of human nature. People may in fact have little if any greater capacity to control their conduct . . . than their emotions or their thoughts. It is therefore either unrealistic or hypocritical, so the argument runs, to deal with conduct as willed or to treat it differently from personality and character.

This attack is, however, misconceived. Neither philosophic concepts nor psychological realities are actually at issue in the criminal law. The idea of free will in relation to conduct is not, in the legal system, a statement of fact, but rather a value preference having very little to do with the metaphysics of determinism and free will. . . . Very simply, the law treats man's conduct as autonomous and willed, not because it is, but because it is desirable to proceed as if it were. It is desirable because the capacity of the individual human being to live his life in reasonable freedom from socially imposed external constraints (the only kind with which the law is concerned) would be fatally impaired unless the law provided a locus poenitentiae, a point of no return beyond which external constraints may be imposed but before which the individual is free—not free of whatever compulsions determinists tell us he labors under but free of the very specific social compulsions of the law. . . .

**4.   Questions and Comments on the Conduct Requirement.**
Packer mentions, as a hypothetical, the possibility of using sophisticated psychological testing to determine in advance that a given individual is likely to engage in violent conduct. Recent research suggests that the prospect may not be entirely fanciful. And Steven Spielberg speculated about the possibility in the movie referred to in *Doe*.

Suppose, hypothetically, that predictive techniques were sufficiently refined to allow accurate predictions of violent criminal behavior. Suppose, to be specific, that persons extremely likely to engage in violent rape could be identified in advance of such conduct. If such a procedure were feasible, should it be used as a basis for criminal prosecution? Or would it still be preferable to await punishable conduct before coercive state intervention?

Does *Doe* present a closer case? Assume Louisiana adopted a criminal statute providing that it was a crime for a person "to enter a park with intent to have sexual contact with children." Assume further that the term "sexual contact" was precisely defined to include a particularized list of inappropriate behavior. Would such a statute be constitutional under the reasoning in *Doe*? Would it be good policy?

———

## Martin v. State

Alabama Court of Appeals, 1944.
4 Div. 805, 17 So.2d 427.

■ SIMPSON, JUDGE.

Appellant was convicted of being drunk on a public highway, and appeals. Officers of the law arrested him at his home and took him onto the highway, where he allegedly committed the proscribed acts, viz., manifested a drunken condition by using loud and profane language.

The pertinent provisions of our statute are: "Any person who, while intoxicated or drunk, appears in any public place where one or more persons are present, . . . and manifests a drunken condition by boisterous or indecent conduct, or loud and profane discourse, shall, on conviction, be fined," etc. Code 1940, tit., 14, § 120.

Under the plain terms of this statute, a voluntary appearance is presupposed. The rule has been declared, and we think it sound, that an accusation of drunkenness in a designated public place cannot be established by proof that the accused, while in an intoxicated condition, was involuntarily and forcibly carried to that place by the arresting officer.

Conviction of appellant was contrary to this announced principle and, in our view, erroneous. It appears that no legal conviction can be sustained under the evidence, so, consonant with the prevailing rule, the judgment of the trial court is reversed and one here rendered discharging appellant. . . .

## NOTES ON THE REQUIREMENT OF A VOLUNTARY ACT

**1. The Requirement of a Voluntary Act.** Settled doctrine requires not only that criminal liability be based on conduct, but also that the conduct be voluntary. This is called the requirement of a voluntary "act," but it applies as well to omissions and to possession. Criminal liability for omissions and possession is dealt with later in this Chapter.

The classic definition of a "voluntary act" is that it must result from an exercise of will.[a] Note that the requirement is that there be an "exercise" of will. The requirement is *not* that the exercise of will be free from pressure by circumstance or other people. Thus, if a bank is robbed by the victim of the threat, "rob the bank or I will shoot your children," the threat victim would have engaged in a "voluntary act." The bank robber may well and justifiably believe in such a case that there was "no choice" but to rob the bank. The act of robbing the bank, however, would involve a decision, a choice to do what was regarded as a lesser evil. The threat victim would have engaged in an exercise of will, and hence a "voluntary" act.[b]

This formulation raises philosophical questions of some difficulty, and theoretical debate over the meaning of the concept continues.[c] The law, however, has largely been content to "define" by example, which is why most accounts of the voluntary-act requirement feature illustrations of acts that are not voluntary. Among the generally accepted instances of involuntary conduct are the following:

(i) **Physically Coerced Movement.** If *A*, without *B*'s assent or cooperation, shoves *B* into *C* and thus knocks *C* into the path of a passing car, *B*'s act is involuntary. Indeed, it may be more idiomatic in this case to say that *B* has engaged in no "act" at all, for the "act" is attributed to *A*, not *B*. Under either formulation, *B* is not liable.

(ii) **Reflex Movements.** The usual example is the reaction of a person suddenly attacked by a swarm of bees. According to most authorities, a person so afflicted while, say, driving a car could not be held liable for the resulting loss of control over the vehicle.

(iii) **Muscular Contraction or Paralysis Produced by Disease.** Some disorders of the central nervous system, including epilepsy and chorea, cause muscular contractions beyond the control of the individual. Others, such as a stroke, may suddenly restrict movement or induce partial paralysis. A person who has no control over his or her limbs cannot be said to act voluntarily with respect to their movements.

[a] See J. Austin, Lectures in Jurisprudence 284–91 (4th ed. 1873); J. Salmond, Jurisprudence 367–69 (10th ed. 1947); O. Holmes, The Common Law 53–55 (1881).

[b] This does not mean that the bank robber would have no defense in this situation, only that the defense that there was no voluntary act would be denied. The defense that may well be available on these facts is called "duress," which is considered in Chapter 5.

[c] An early attack on the classical formulation is H.L.A. Hart, Acts of Will and Responsibility, in Punishment and Responsibility at 90 (1968). Hart's views were criticized in Jeffrie G. Murphy, Involuntary Acts and Criminal Responsibility, 81 Ethics 332 (1971), where the author proposes a reformulation of the traditional focus on an exercise of the will. For probing philosophical analysis of this and related questions, see Michael S. Moore, Act and Crime (1993), and the symposium on that book in 142 U. Pa. L. Rev. 1443 (1994).

**(iv) Unconsciousness.** A relatively complete obliteration of consciousness, ranging from coma to normal sleep, ordinarily involves a cessation of most motor functions. In some cases, however, unconscious acts may occur. A sleeping mother may roll over her child and smother it. A person may suffer unconsciousness due to stroke, epilepsy, narcolepsy, or some other neurophysiological disturbance. Physical movements or omissions during these intervals are not, in any meaningful sense, voluntary.

The common theme in these situations is that the actor's bodily movement or omission is not directed by conscious mental processes. As H.L.A. Hart once put the point, what is "missing in such a case is the minimum link between mind and body, indispensable for any form of criminal responsibility."[d]

**2. Forms of Impaired Consciousness.** The above examples describe situations where the individual lacks any mental control over physical acts. Such acts are plainly involuntary. In other recognized instances of involuntariness, however, some link between mind and body remains, but that link is sufficiently attenuated to preclude criminal responsibility. These situations characteristically involve disturbances of consciousness in persons who retain the capacity to engage in goal-directed conduct based on prior learned responses. Because conscious awareness of one's acts is absent during such episodes, such behavior may be said to be "automatic" and the individual so afflicted an "automaton." Hence the law sometimes has dealt with such conditions under the rubric of "automatism" even though use of this term is medically appropriate only in cases of epilepsy. The two most important examples are concussion and somnambulism.

**(i) Concussion.** Temporary brain damage due to physical trauma sometimes produces a "black-out" or "confusional state," during which a person may engage in previously learned behavior without full awareness thereof. An example is the football player who continues to go through the motions of the game even though he is not consciously aware of his actions and does not remember them afterwards. Moreover, concussion can compromise the functioning of those brain centers that mediate and inhibit behavioral manifestation of emotion. A person who injures another while in such a state may do what he or she (unconsciously) wanted to do but would not have done had there been conscious control over the behavior. Some courts have found such conduct to be involuntary.[e]

**(ii) Somnambulism.** There is a well-recognized continuum of sleep disorders, ranging from ordinary nightmares to sleepwalking to a more severe form of disturbance known as "night terrors."[f] During mild sleepwalking episodes, the "sleeping" person

---

[d] H.L.A. Hart, Acts of Will and Responsibility, in Punishment and Responsibility at 92 (1968).

[e] See Regina v. Wakefield, 75 W.N. 66 (New South Wales 1957); Coates v. Regina, 96 C.L.R. 353 (1957); Regina v. Minor, 112 Can. Crim. Cases 29 (1959).

[f] See generally Peter Fenwick, Somnambulism and the Law: A Review, 5 Behav. Sci. & the Law 343 (1987).

may move about, although generally in a poorly coordinated, automatic manner. "Night terrors" are characterized by extreme fear and panic, intense vocalization, and frenzied motor activity. Aberrant behavior, including violence, can occur. Moreover, any interference with a person experiencing a somnambulistic episode may precipitate a violent reaction. The courts have generally regarded acts committed during such episodes as involuntary. In one famous English case, an 1859 grand jury refused to indict a woman who, after dreaming that her house was on fire, arose in a panic, screamed "Save my children!," and threw her baby out the window.[g]

**(iii) Hypoglycemia.** There are other situations involving impaired consciousness for which the sufficiency of the "link between mind and body" appears to be an open question. One such instance concerns the behavioral effects of hypoglycemia, or abnormally low blood sugar. Because blood sugar is the exclusive source of energy for brain metabolism, hypoglycemia can lead to impaired functioning of the central nervous system. This condition usually arises when a diabetic takes too much insulin or fails to get sufficient food or sleep. It can also occur, however, in a non-diabetic but biologically susceptible individual whose blood sugar is reduced by starvation or muscular over-exertion. In many such cases, the condition is precipitated by the ingestion of alcohol. Hypoglycemic symptoms include tremors, poor coordination, confusion, and irritation. Although the condition may be associated with aggressive behavior, current understanding does not permit confident generalization about the effect of hypoglycemia on control over one's conduct.[h] The question, simply put, is whether this condition differs significantly from any of a number of other metabolic conditions that may lower a person's threshold for aggressive behavior without rendering such conduct involuntary.

**3. Illustrative Case of Impaired Consciousness.** A Virginia prosecution illustrates the excruciating questions that cases of impaired consciousness can create for the criminal justice system. A baby was found dead in a microwave oven. The medical evidence established that the baby was in the oven for at least 10 minutes and had died from thermal injuries caused by overheating of the blood. The infant's mother had a long, well-documented history of epilepsy, and she claimed that she had no recollection of the events immediately preceding the baby's death. She stated that she got up in the middle of the night to feed the baby, that she could

[g] This case is described in Nigel Walker, Crime and Insanity in England 168–69 (1968). Other well-known somnambulism cases include Fain v. Commonwealth, 78 Ky. 183 (1879), and H.M. Advocate v. Fraser, 4 Couper 70 (Scotland 1878). For an especially intriguing case, see Norval Morris, Somnam- bulistic Homicide: Ghosts, Spiders and North Koreans, 5 Res. Judicatae 29 (1959).

[h] See generally Anthony Whitlock, Some Medicolegal Consequences of Hypoglycaemia in Robert Bluglass and Paul Bowden (eds.), Principles and Practice of Forensic Psychiatry 287–90 (1990).

remember sitting on the couch burping him, and that she must then have suffered a grand-mal seizure after which she accidentally placed the baby in the oven.

In the immediate aftermath of the death, epilepsy experts divided over the question of whether the mother could have committed the killing unconsciously. Epileptic seizures sometimes are followed by trance-like states, which can last for as long as 30 minutes. Yet, some experts dismissed the mother's claim as implausible, arguing that the most the sufferer can do during the trance is perform "simple repetitive actions." See Craig Timberg, Mother Charged in Baby's Oven Death, The Washington Post, Sept. 28, 1999, at B1. Other experts disagreed, saying that a person in such a trance is "able to carry out complex tasks such as undressing, using a curling iron, even driving a car." See Josh White, Baby's Death Stirs Debate on Illness vs. Intent in Va., The Washington Post, Jan. 28, 2001, at C1. Thus, they speculated that the mother may have dropped the baby during her seizure and then reacted to his cries "as an automaton," placing "him in the oven by accident as if he were a bottle." Id.

Initially, the prosecutor believed that the woman was lying about the seizure in order to cover up her murder of her baby, and he charged her with first-degree murder. A court-appointed neurologist evaluated the mother, and his video-taped findings tended to corroborate her story. In a test designed to simulate the activities that occurred on the night the baby died, the neurologist deprived the mother of her medication and kept her awake for three days. During the test, the woman had a seizure, after which she appeared to be in a "wide-eyed daze," indeed, to be so bewildered that she was unable to recognize her mother. More important, while she was in the trance, the woman was "able to operate a tape recorder without much trouble—but also without much comprehension of what she [was] doing." Id. After viewing the videotape, the prosecutor concluded that there was doubt about the mother's state of mind at the time of the killing. As he put it in comments made to the press, "I was convinced that she maliciously killed the child—until I saw that tape. . . . It created doubt for me, and I had to wonder how the jury would respond. I am not convinced it was an accident, but I will accept the concept it could have been an accident." Id. As the case was on the verge of going to trial, the prosecutor reduced the charge to involuntary manslaughter, to which the mother entered a "no contest plea." Josh White, Va. Mother Gets 5 Years in Microwave Death, The Washington Post, Dec. 14, 2000, at B2.

**4. Codification.** As has been noted, the voluntariness requirement was an established feature of common-law doctrine. Accordingly, courts have tended to regard the voluntary-act requirement as existing independent of statute and have enforced the requirement in the absence of supporting legislation.

Older American statutes did sometimes require a "voluntary act" without further explication, e.g., Smith–Hurd Ill.Ann.Stat. § 4–1, or exempt from liability persons who acted "without being conscious thereof," e.g., Cal. Penal Code § 26. More elaborate formulation was undertaken by the drafters of the Model Penal Code, who attempted in § 2.01 to spell out the scope of the voluntary-act requirement:

(1) A person is not guilty of an offense unless his liability is based on conduct which includes a voluntary act or the omission to perform an act of which he is physically capable.

(2) The following are not voluntary acts within the meaning of this Section:

(a) a reflex or convulsion;

(b) a bodily movement during unconsciousness or sleep;

(c) conduct during hypnosis or resulting from hypnotic suggestion;

(d) a bodily movement that otherwise is not a product of the effort or determination of the actor, either conscious or habitual.

See also N.J. Stat. Ann. § 2C:2–1. Note that this formulation continues the tradition of definition by example and that the list of involuntary acts does not purport to be exhaustive. On the contrary, the Model Code provision plainly contemplates that judges will continue the case-by-case development of the voluntary-act requirement under the rubric of identifying acts that are "not [products] of the effort or determination of the actor, either conscious or habitual."

**5.   Content and Function of the Voluntary Act Requirement.** It is probably not possible to devise any test that precisely differentiates voluntary from involuntary acts. Perhaps as good as any is the Model Penal Code formulation of "a bodily movement that . . . is not a product of the effort or determination of the actor, either conscious or habitual." Ultimately, however, the requirement of a voluntary act poses a question of judgment rather than definition. Interpretation of the voluntary-act requirement rests on a normative view of the appropriate reach of penal sanctions and of the appropriate relationship of voluntariness to other exculpatory doctrines of the criminal law.

At the outset, it is important to understand the consequence of invoking the voluntary-act requirement. Under settled principles, commission of a voluntary act is a necessary, though not sufficient, condition of criminal liability. Holding an act involuntary precludes any criminal liability for that act. The result is a complete exoneration of the actor and a correspondingly total sacrifice of the social-control objectives implicated by the actor's conduct.

Not surprisingly, the complete exculpation that results from a finding of involuntariness has constrained the interpretation of that concept. Many acts that in some meaningful sense are coerced by circumstances are found nevertheless to satisfy the voluntary-act requirement. An example might be the person who steals bread because he or she has no other way to feed a child. It may seem a bit strained to describe such a theft as voluntary, but it is everywhere agreed that the voluntary-act requirement would be met in such a case. The point is that the legal construct of voluntariness is not merely descriptive. The meaning of the concept is informed by its function, and the function of the voluntary-act requirement is to identify cases where an individual's responsibility for his own conduct is so sharply interrupted as to preclude altogether any imposition of penal sanctions.

**6.   Involuntary Act in a Voluntary Course of Conduct:** *People v. Decina.* A recurring problem is the case of an involuntary act embedded in an otherwise voluntary course of conduct. Here the Model Penal Code formulation is instructive. It does not flatly preclude liability based on involuntary conduct; instead, it requires that liability be based on "conduct which includes" a voluntary act. The point of this phrasing is to leave open the possibility of penal sanctions for a course of conduct that includes some involuntary aspects.

The issue is raised by the famous case of People v. Decina, 2 N.Y.2d 133, 138 N.E.2d 799 (1956). The defendant suffered an epileptic seizure while driving and ran over and killed several children. He was convicted under a statute punishing negligent homicide in a motor vehicle.[i] Everyone agreed that the seizure itself was involuntary and could not support penal liability, but the prosecution proceeded on the theory that the defendant was liable for the negligent and voluntary act of driving a car with knowledge that he was subject to epileptic seizures. The indictment was sustained on the ground that the admittedly involuntary character of the seizure did not vitiate the defendant's responsibility for his voluntary acts prior to losing consciousness:

> To hold otherwise would be to say that a man may freely indulge himself in liquor in the same hope that it will not affect his driving, and if it later develops that ensuing intoxication causes dangerous and reckless driving resulting in death, his unconsciousness or involuntariness at that time would relieve him from prosecution under the statute. His awareness of a condition which he knows may produce such consequences as these, and his disregard of the consequences, [render] him liable for culpable negligence. . . . To have a sudden sleeping spell, an unexpected heart or other disabling attack, without any prior knowledge or warning thereof, is an altogether different situation. . . .

This is not to say that it is necessarily negligent to drive with knowledge of a potentially disabling medical condition, but only that the act of doing so may serve in an appropriate case as the basis for criminal liability.[j] For

---

[i] N.Y. Penal Law § 1053–a provided punishment for anyone "who operates or drives any vehicle of any kind in a reckless or culpably negligent manner, whereby a human being is killed. . . ."

[j] While this position seems consistent with the voluntary-act requirement, the point is not entirely free from doubt. In particular, debate may arise over whether the specific voluntary act committed by the defendant was the act proscribed by the offense. Essentially, this is an issue of statutory construction. For discussions evidencing concern with this problem, see the dissent in People v. Decina, 2 N.Y.2d 133 at 140, 138 N.E.2d 799 at 804, and the earlier decision in People v. Freeman, 61 Cal.App.2d 110, 142 P.2d 435 (1943).

another example of such a situation, see Frederick Kunkle, Case Moves Forward in Frederick Fatalities, Wash. Post, Jan. 18, 2004, at C1.

**7. Constitutionalizing Voluntariness?: *Robinson* and *Powell*.** At one time, it seemed that the Supreme Court might adopt an expansive notion of involuntariness as a constitutional constraint on criminal punishment. In Robinson v. California, 370 U.S. 660 (1962), the Court ruled that convicting someone for "be[ing] addicted to" the use of narcotics violated the Eighth Amendment guarantee against cruel and unusual punishment. The problem was not the severity of the penalty but the fact of criminal liability for this conduct.

The precise basis for the decision in *Robinson* was never clear. On one reading, the decision merely disallowed criminal liability for a bare "status or condition," such as "being addicted." This proposition is undoubtedly sound. Criminal liability requires an act, omission, or possession and cannot be based on a mere condition or status. But so read, *Robinson* has little practical importance, as the law almost never purports to punish status as such.

A broader reading of *Robinson* focused on voluntariness. On this view, *Robinson* stood for the proposition that drug addiction was involuntary and for that reason could not constitutionally be punished as criminal. Presumably, such involuntariness would apply not only to the condition or status of being addicted, but also to purchase and use of narcotics. Indeed, the involuntariness might even include antecedent acts (such as theft) intended to gain resources for satisfying an addiction. On this reading *Robinson* seemed to imply a constitutional command to decriminalize addictive behavior and relegate social control of such problems to a "medical" model of diagnosis and treatment.

In Powell v. Texas, 392 U.S. 514 (1968), the Supreme Court drew back from this implication. *Powell* involved a prosecution for intoxication in a public place. The defendant tried to bring his case within the ambit of *Robinson* by showing that he was a "chronic alcoholic" and therefore under a compulsion to drink. By a vote of five-four, the Supreme Court rejected his claim. Speaking for the majority, Justice Marshall interpreted *Robinson* as invalidating only punishment for a mere status:

> *Robinson* so viewed brings this Court but a very small way into the substantive criminal law. And unless *Robinson* is so viewed it is difficult to see any limiting principle that would serve to prevent this Court from becoming, under the aegis of the cruel and unusual punishment clause, the ultimate arbiter of the standards of criminal responsibility, in diverse areas of the criminal law, throughout the country.

> It is suggested in dissent that *Robinson* stands for the "simple" but "subtle" principle that "[c]riminal penalties may not be inflicted upon a person for being in a condition he is powerless to change." ... In that view, appellant's "condition" of public intoxi-

cation was "occasioned by a compulsion symptomatic of the disease" of chronic alcoholism. . . . Whatever may be the merits of such a doctrine of criminal responsibility, it surely cannot be said to follow from *Robinson*. The entire thrust of *Robinson*'s interpretation of the cruel and unusual punishment clause is that criminal penalties may be inflicted only if the accused has committed some act, has engaged in some behavior, which society has an interest in preventing, or perhaps in historical common law terms, has committed some actus reus. It thus does not deal with the question of whether certain conduct cannot constitutionally be punished because it is, in some sense, "involuntary" or "occasioned by a compulsion."

The upshot of *Robinson* and *Powell* is, as Justice Marshall said, that the federal Constitution goes only "a very small way into the substantive criminal law." Notions of voluntariness are left to the state legislatures and courts, and though there is some disagreement on these issues, the requirement of a voluntary act has not generally been taken to disable prosecution for drug or alcohol use, even by persons who might plausibly be described as addicted to those substances.

**8. Relation to Other Doctrines.** Finally, it must be emphasized that the voluntary-act requirement is not the only exculpatory doctrine of the criminal law that is animated by concerns about voluntariness. As explained in Chapter V, a person whose capacity for choice is constrained by external circumstances beyond his or her control may be excused from criminal liability. The prototypical case is duress, where—as illustrated in Note 1 above—an otherwise criminal act may be excused because it resulted from threats by another person. Also, in many jurisdictions a person whose capacity to conform behavior to societal norms is compromised by mental illness may be relieved from criminal liability on grounds of insanity. See Chapter VI.

The analytical boundaries separating these doctrines from the voluntary-act requirement are not always well marked. It is important, however, to remember that specifying the "minimum link between mind and body" of the act requirement does not exhaust the law's receptivity to claims turning on lack of free choice. Finding an act to be "voluntary" for purposes of the act requirement does not lead inexorably to liability; it merely forecloses one of several potential grounds of exculpation.

---

## SECTION 2: THE REQUIREMENT THAT OFFENSES BE PREVIOUSLY DEFINED

### Rex v. Manley

Court of Criminal Appeal, 1932.
[1933] 1 K.B. 529.

Appeal against conviction, a certificate of fitness for appeal having been granted by the Recorder of London.

On November 18, 1932, the appellant, Elizabeth Manley, was charged at the Central Criminal Court on an indictment containing two counts, the first count being that she "on September 10, 1932, did, by means of certain false statements, to wit that on that day a man whose description she then gave had hit her with his fist and taken from her handbag, six 10s. notes, nine 1l. notes, 15s. in silver, and a receipt, cause officers of the metropolitan police maintained at public expense for the public benefit to devote their time and services to the investigation of false allegations, thereby temporarily depriving the public of the services of these public officers, and rendering liege subjects of the king liable to suspicion, accusation and arrest, and in so doing did unlawfully effect a public mischief"; and the second count being that on September 15, 1932, she made a statement that on September 10, 1932, a man whose description she gave came up behind her and that she then felt a blow in the back and that her bag containing 12l. 12s. 6d. had been taken from under her arm.

The appellant pleaded not guilty.

On behalf of the prosecution evidence was called to support the allegations in the indictment.

On behalf of the appellant these allegations were not denied and no evidence was called, but the submission was made that the indictment disclosed no offence known to the law, and that there was no cause to go to the jury.

In giving judgment on that submission the Recorder said: "It is my clear view that this act is one which may tend to a public mischief. It would be intolerable that our police force, already hard pressed to preserve law and order in a time of increasing lawlessness, should have their services deflected in order to follow up charges which are entirely bogus to the knowledge of those making them. In my view, taking the times—you must consider the times in which we live—such an act may distinctly tend to the public mischief. . . . I hold as a matter of law that this indictment discloses a common-law misdemeanour."

The jury found on the evidence that the appellant had done the acts which she was alleged to have done and that she was guilty of the offence with which she was charged.

The Recorder postponed sentence, and granted a certificate that the case was fit for an appeal to the Court of Criminal Appeal on the question whether he was right in holding that the indictment disclosed a common-law misdemeanour; and he bound the appellant over to come up for judgment when the Court of Criminal Appeal had decided the question of law. . . .

■ LORD HEWART, C.J. The appellant in this case was indicted at the Central Criminal Court before the learned Recorder of London for having effected a public mischief. [His Lordship read the counts of the indictment, and continued:] The appellant was convicted, and was bound over to come up for judgment when called upon to do so after this court had decided the question of law now raised. It was then submitted on her behalf, as it is submitted now, that she had committed no offence; but before that proposition can be assented to it is necessary, as counsel for the prosecution has indicated, to consider two questions.

The first is whether it is true at the present day to say that there is a misdemeanour of committing an act tending to the public mischief. In our opinion that question ought to be answered in the affirmative. We think that the law remains as it was stated to be by Lawrence, J., in Rex v. Higgins, [1801] 2 East 5, 21: "All offences of a public nature, that is, all such acts or attempts as tend to the prejudice of the community, are indictable." That case was referred to with approval in the case of Rex v. Brailsford, [1905] 2 K.B. 730, and in the still more recent case of Rex v. Porter, [1910] 1 K.B. 369, 372, where Lord Alverstone, C.J., in delivering the judgment of the court, said: "We are of opinion that it is for the court to direct the jury as to whether such an act may tend to the public mischief, and that it is not in such a case an issue of fact upon which evidence can be given."

The second question is whether the appellant did acts which constitute a public mischief. As counsel has said, the facts stated in the indictment are not in dispute, and it is admitted that what is there alleged to have been done by the appellant was done by her. In the opinion of the Court the indictment aptly describes two ingredients of public mischief or prejudice to the community, one of these being that officers of the metropolitan police were led to devote their time and services to the investigation of an idle charge, and the other being that members of the public, or at any rate those of them who answered a certain description, were put in peril of suspicion and arrest.

For these reasons the court is of opinion that the conviction should stand and that the appeal should be dismissed.

Appeal dismissed.

----

## NOTES ON *MANLEY* AND THE COMMON LAW

**1. Introduction to the Common Law.** *Manley* illustrates the methodology of the "common law." That phrase has a variety of meanings but is used chiefly to refer to judge-made law. Most of the ancient English offenses were judicial in origin. By the accession of Elizabeth I (1558), the English courts had created and defined felonies of murder, suicide,[a] manslaughter, arson, burglary, robbery, mayhem, larceny, sodomy, and rape. Various lesser wrongs were punished as misdemeanors. Offenses in both categories were created by judges who acted without aid of statute to protect societal interests as they saw them. The legacy of the common law, therefore, was a judicial assumption of authority to adapt broad principles to new situations as the occasion arose.

[a] Actually, it is unclear whether suicide was an independent offense or a species of murder. See ALI, Model Penal Code and Commentaries § 210.5, pp. 90–91 (1980).

Over time, the exercise of this authority became more constrained. For one thing, with the evolution of the idea of precedent, the common-law tradition bred its own limitation. As an ever more elaborate body of precedent built up, opportunities for judicial innovation were reduced. Moreover, increasing activity by parliament lessened the need for activism by the courts. The earliest legislative efforts were usually addressed to gaps in the common law. As parliament met more often and grew in power and prestige, more and more statutes were enacted to supplement or correct the law as declared by judges. Gradually, the locus of crime creation shifted from the courts to the legislature. As early as 1600, judicial creation of new felonies was already a thing of the past. New misdemeanors, on the other hand, continued to be recognized, albeit infrequently, throughout the 17th and 18th centuries. The judges who decided these cases often spoke of the residual authority of courts to punish as criminal any conduct contra bonos mores et decorum—in more modern phrasing, any conduct tending to outrage decency or to corrupt public morals.

A famous early assertion of this power was Rex v. Sidley, 82 E.R. 1036 (1663), where Sir Charles Sidley was found guilty of a common-law misdemeanor for standing naked on a balcony at Covent Garden. Others were held liable for such things as blasphemy, publication of an obscene book, undressing on a public beach, and digging up corpses for anatomical inspection. Decisions of this sort were made sporadically at least through 1774, when the underlying claim of continuing common-law authority was endorsed by the great Lord Mansfield. "Whatever is contra bonos mores et decorum," said Mansfield, "the principles of our law prohibit, and the king's court, as the general censor and guardian of the public manners, is bound to restrain and punish." Jones v. Randall, [1774] 98 E.R. 706, 707.

By the late 19th century, the power of the courts to punish all conduct tending to corrupt morals or to create public mischief had fallen into disuse and apparent disrepute. In 1883 the common-law authority to create new crimes was denounced by no less an authority than Sir James Fitzjames Stephen, a successor to Mansfield on the Queen's Bench and pre-eminent Victorian historian of the criminal law: "Though the existence of this power as inherent in the judges has been asserted by several high authorities for a great length of time, it is hardly probable that any attempt would be made to exercise it at the present day; and any such attempt would be received with great opposition, and would place the bench in an invidious position." 3 James Stephen, A History of the Criminal Law of England 359–60 (1883). The result was that *Manley*, decided half a century after Stephen's pronouncement, came as a surprise and provoked something of a furor in English legal circles.[b]

**2.  Later English Cases.** In Shaw v. Director of Public Prosecutions, [1961] 2 All E.R. 446, the defendant was convicted of the common-law

[b] For criticism of *Manley* and a discussion of its aftermath in England and other Commonwealth jurisdictions, see Glanville Williams, Criminal Law: The General Part 596–600 (2d ed. 1961), and the authorities cited in id. at 596 n.2. See also Director of Public Prosecutions v. Withers, [1975] A.C. 842, in which *Manley* is expressly repudiated.

misdemeanor of conspiracy to corrupt public morals. Viscount Simonds stated the facts as follows:

> When the Street Offences Act, 1959, came into operation, it was no longer possible for prostitutes to ply their trade by soliciting in the streets, and it became necessary for them to find some other means of advertising the services that they were prepared to render. It occurred to [Shaw] that he could with advantage to himself assist them to this end. The device that he adopted was to publish on divers days . . . a magazine or booklet which was called "Ladies Directory." It contained the names, addresses and telephone numbers of prostitutes with photographs of nude female figures, and in some cases details which conveyed to initiates willingness to indulge not only in ordinary sexual intercourse but also in various perverse practices.

Shaw appealed his conviction on the ground that the law of England no longer recognized a generic offense of conspiracy to corrupt public morals. Alternatively, he argued that if such a crime did exist, it should be limited to factual circumstances previously declared to fall within its scope. The House of Lords rejected both contentions and upheld the conviction. Viscount Simonds restated judicial authority to declare the law in terms as broad as those used two centuries before:

> . . . In the sphere of criminal law, I entertain no doubt that there remains in the courts of law a residual power to enforce the supreme and fundamental purpose of the law, to conserve not only the safety and order but also the moral welfare of the state, and that it is their duty to guard it against attacks which may be the more insidious because they are novel and unprepared for. . . . When Lord Mansfield . . . said that the Court of King's Bench was the custos morum of the people and had the superintendency of offences contra bonos mores, he was asserting, as I now assert, that there is in that court a residual power, where no statute has yet intervened to supersede the common law, to superintend those offences which are prejudicial to the public welfare.[c]

A similar decision was reached in Knuller v. Director of Public Prosecutions, [1972] 2 All E.R. 898. In *Knuller* the publishers of a "progressive" magazine were convicted of conspiracy to corrupt public morals for running classified ads by male homosexuals. Relying on the authority of *Shaw*, the House of Lords sustained this charge despite an act of parliament decriminalizing private homosexual acts between consenting adults.[d]

---

[c] For criticism of *Shaw*, see Wolfgang Friedmann, Law in a Changing Society 54–62 (2d ed. 1972); H.L.A. Hart, Law, Liberty and Morality 7–12 (1963); David Seaborne Davies, The House of Lords and the Criminal Law, 6 J. Soc. Pub. Tchrs. Law 104 (1961). For a favorable reaction by Arthur Goodhart, see The *Shaw* Case: The Law and Public Morals, 77 L.Q.Rev. 560 (1961).

[d] Like *Shaw* and *Manley*, *Knuller* quickly became subject to academic criticism. See, e.g., John Finch, Stare Decisis and Changing Standards in English Law, 51 Can. B. Rev. 523 (1973); Comment, Conspiracies Contra Bonos Mores, 19 McGill L.J. 136 (1973). For

**3.  Questions and Comments on Judicial Crime Creation.** What, exactly, is wrong with the decision in *Manley*? Is there reason to doubt that the defendant should have been punished? Would it have objectionable if the defendant had been convicted of violating a statute such as § 241.5 of the Model Penal Code?

————

NOTES ON THE PRINCIPLE OF LEGALITY

**1.  Introduction.** The "principle of legality" is not in any ordinary sense a rule of law. It is more nearly a statement of an ideal. That is not to say that the principle has no practical application. It is a very widely accepted ideal, and familiarity with it is essential to understanding the criminal law.

Put simply, the principle of legality forbids the retroactive crime definition. Often reduced to the maxim, nulla poena (or nullum crimen) sine lege, this construct condemns judicial crime creation of the sort involved in *Manley* and *Shaw*. The essential idea is that no one should be punished for a crime that has not been so defined in advance by the appropriate authority. Generally speaking, the appropriate institution for crime definition is the legislature. For most purposes, therefore, the principle of legality may be taken to signify *the desirability in principle of advance legislative specification of criminal conduct*.

Note that the insistence on advance crime definition has no necessary relation to the content of the offenses so defined. The principle of legality does not speak to the question of what conduct should be declared criminal. Rather, it states a normative expectation regarding how that decision should be made. In other words, the principle concerns the *process* of crime definition rather than the *content* of specific offenses.

Today, few would dispute the desirability of advance legislative specification of criminal conduct. This precept is widely recognized as a cornerstone of the penal law. Yet while the idea of nulla poena sine lege is undoubtedly of long standing, its significance has changed over time. This discussion begins, therefore, with a look at the history of the principle of legality and its evolving role in American penal law.[a]

**2.  European Origins.** Although there may have been ancient antecedents, the categorical insistence on advance legislative crime definition began in late 18th-century Europe. The idea sprang from the intellectual movement known as the Enlightenment, and its origins are deeply embedded in the premises and purposes of Enlightenment thought.

a more favorable view, see Comment, 19 McGill L.J. 130 (1973).

[a] For an examination of the philosophical underpinnings of legality, see Bostjan Zupan-cic, On Legal Formalism: The Principle of Legality in Criminal Law, 27 Loy. L. Rev. 369 (1981).

At the level of individual behavior, Enlightenment thinkers viewed humans as rational and hedonistic. Since individual conduct presumably was based on a utilitarian calculation of pain and pleasure, criminal acts could be deterred by a credible threat of a penalty sufficient to outweigh the expected gain from wrongdoing. In order for this scheme to work, crimes and punishments had to be spelled out in advance.

At the level of societal organization, Enlightenment thought emphasized contractarian notions of the legitimacy of government. The state owed its authority to the aggregate surrenders of individual freedom necessary to the formation of the social compact. Everyone gave up some freedom in order to secure the benefits of an ordered society, and the punishment of individuals was legitimate if based on laws established for the protection of society as a whole. Implicit in this conception is a commitment to representative government. Accordingly, Enlightenment thinkers identified the legislature as the only legitimate institution for assessing the needs of society and for implementing those judgments through penal laws. Thus, Enlightenment ideology insisted not only that crime definition be prospective in nature but also that it be legislative in origin.

Enlightenment thinkers who proved specially influential in the development of criminal law were Montesquieu and Cesare Beccaria. In a republic, according to Montesquieu, "the people should have the sole power to enact laws." Montesquieu, The Spirit of the Laws 13 (T. Nugent, trans., 1897). As the branch of government most directly responsive to the popular will, the legislature had the power to define crimes. Judges were to enforce statutes, not to make law. Beccaria emphasized the notion that advance definition of offenses was essential to crime control. He argued that crime was actually caused, in part, by the obscurity and irrationality of the penal law. By creating clear, precise, and reasonable laws, with penalties proportionate to the gravity of the offense and sufficiently harsh to offset any gain to the offender, the legislature could attack the problem of crime. In Beccaria's view, judicial innovation would lead to arbitrariness and inconsistency. Results would depend on "the good or bad logic of the judge; and this will depend on his good or bad digestion; on the violence of his passion; on the rank and condition of the accused, or on his connections with the judge...." Cesare Beccaria, On Crimes and Punishments 23–24 (E. Ingraham, trans., 1819). The upshot of such disarray would be impairment of the law's capacity to exert a restraining influence on human passions.

**3. The American Experience: Encounter with the Common Law.** In many ways the newly independent American nation was fertile soil for the doctrine of nulla poena sine lege. For one thing, there was the pervasive influence of Enlightenment thought generally.[b] There was also specific familiarity with the principal works on penal law. Montesquieu and Beccaria were widely read, and their ideas were a prominent feature of the American intellectual landscape at the time of the Revolution. Their insistence on a sharp differentiation of legislative, executive, and judicial

---

[b] See generally Bernard Bailyn, The Ideological Origins of the American Revolution (1967), and Peter Gay, America The Paradoxical, 62 Va. L. Rev. 843 (1976).

functions found practical expression in the American scheme of separation of powers. That concept called for a division of responsibilities among three branches of government. The power to make laws was assigned to the legislature. Perhaps most importantly, the insistence on legislative action as essential to the political legitimacy of crime definition was a natural corollary of the American ideal of popular sovereignty through republican government.

In light of these factors, one might have expected nulla poena sine lege quickly to take its place as the first principle of American criminal law. In fact, the story is much more complicated. "English law—as authority, as legitimizing precedent, as embodied principle, and as the framework of historical understanding—stood side by side with Enlightenment rationalism" in influencing the American revolutionaries. Bernard Bailyn, The Ideological Origins of the American Revolution 31 (1967). In the United States, unlike Europe, the theoretical insistence on legislative crime definition ran up against the ancient, familiar, and entrenched tradition of the English common law.

The conflict between the common-law heritage and Enlightenment ideals of political organization was nowhere more apparent than in the debate whether to allow criminal prosecution for non-statutory offenses. At the federal level, the answer was "no." There is no federal common law of crimes.[c] At the state level, the story was entirely different. Despite the efforts of early law reformers, all of the original states, and most of the later ones, adopted English common law insofar as it was deemed applicable to local conditions.

This "reception" of the common law, as it came to be called, usually included English law of a general nature as of a certain date. Many states used 1607, when the first colony was founded, while others used 1775 or 1776, when the break with England occurred. Whatever the date used, the reception of English common law included not only the roster of offenses previously defined by the English courts, but also the familiar and intimately related assumption that the courts had residual authority to adapt old principles to new situations should the need arise. See generally Ford W. Hall, The Common Law: An Account of Its Reception in the United States, 4 Vand. L. Rev. 791 (1951).

An early example of the exercise of this power is Pennsylvania v. Gillespie, 1 Add. 267 (1795), where the defendant was indicted for "unlawfully, forcibly and contemptuously tearing down" an advertisement for a tax sale. This act was held criminal despite the absence of any statute against it. In State v. Buckman, 8 N.H. 203 (1836), the defendant was indicted for putting a dead animal into a well. The court upheld the conviction on the ground that the act was analogous to selling unwhole-

---

[c] See United States v. Hudson and Goodwin, 11 U.S. (7 Cranch) 32 (1812); United States v. Coolidge, 14 U.S. (1 Wheat.) 415 (1816). But see Dan M. Kahan, Lenity and Federal Common Law Crimes, 1994 Sup. Ct. Rev. 345 (arguing that "federal criminal law, no less than other statutory domains, is dominated by judge-made law crafted to fill the interstices of open-textured statutory provisions").

some food and to poisoning food or drink intended for human consumption, both of which were indictable at common law. The rationale for such innovations was explained by the Supreme Court of Pennsylvania in Commonwealth v. Taylor, 5 Binn. 277, 281 (Pa.1812):

> It is impossible to find precedents for all offenses. The malicious ingenuity of mankind is constantly producing new inventions in the art of disturbing their neighbors. To this invention must be opposed general principles, calculated to meet and punish them.

Respected commentators also endorsed this approach. See Joel Bishop, Commentaries on the Criminal Law 18 (8th ed. 1892).

4.   **Recent Experience.** In the United States, judicial crime creation is increasingly hard to find. The most nearly modern example is Commonwealth v. Mochan, 177 Pa.Super. 454, 110 A.2d 788 (1955). The defendant was indicted for making obscene telephone calls, despite the absence of either statute or precedent specifically proscribing such conduct. The Superior Court of Pennsylvania nevertheless affirmed a misdemeanor conviction, noting that "[a]ny act is indictable at common law which from its nature scandalously affects the morals or health of the community."

Today, decisions such as *Mochan* are widely viewed as relics. Judges no longer feel free to respond to new situations as the occasion demands. They increasingly regard themselves as bound to enforce only those offenses previously declared to exist. In part, this development is due to the consensus that judicial crime creation is in principle unacceptable. In part, however, the decline in such activity is due simply to the fact that legislatures sit more frequently and for longer sessions than ever before. Penal statutes accumulate over time, and there seems to be little difficulty in focusing legislative sentiment on the need to prohibit anti-social conduct. It is a rare legislative session that does not add to the list of offenses, often by proscribing more specifically misconduct already covered by existing statutes. The result is such a comprehensiveness, not to say redundancy, of penal legislation that judicial crime creation is rendered unnecessary as well as objectionable.

5.   **Growing Acceptance and Evolving Meaning.** As the legality concept has won increasing acceptance, its meaning has evolved. Today, few would take seriously Beccaria's idea that advance legislative crime definition plays a crucial role in the practical business of controlling criminal conduct. It seems far-fetched to believe that the social problem of crime results in significant degree from the failure of citizens to know what is forbidden. Of much greater importance are the actor's assessment of the probability that punishment will actually be imposed and the magnitude of the penalty expected. Most criminals know their conduct is illegal but believe they will not be caught. For these reasons, the principle of legality today is seldom advanced as an aid to deterrence. Instead, it is defended chiefly as a normative proposition, essential to the ethical integrity of the criminal law, but not to its efficiency.

In contrast, the political-legitimacy rationale for insisting on advance legislative crime definition survives, though perhaps with somewhat diminished force. Separation of powers remains a fundamental principle of American government, and lawmaking continues to be primarily the responsibility of the legislative branch. To this extent, Montesquieu's ideas endure.

It is clear, however, that the political-legitimacy rationale for preferring legislative to judicial crime creation does not tell the whole story behind the contemporary commitment to legality. Modern explanations of that ideal also emphasize fairness to the individual defendant as a central goal of the legality construct. In particular, modern theorists view the principle of legality as an important prophylaxis against the arbitrary and abusive exercise of discretion in the enforcement of the penal law.

The connection between this evil and an insistence on advance legislative crime definition is a matter of some subtlety. The best articulation comes from Herbert Packer, The Limits of the Criminal Sanction 88–91 (1968):*

> It is plain, then, that the objectives of criminal law ... require a set of institutions for detecting the commission of offenses, apprehending offenders, and determining whether they should be held for the adjudicative process. In short, it is essential to have police and prosecutors. But it is also essential to have checks on the exercise of discretion in the initiating phase of criminal prosecution.... And it is here that we can see the real importance of the principle of legality in the criminal law today; for this principle operates primarily to control the discretion of the police and of prosecutors rather than that of judges.
>
> In the judicial process the principle of legality is not essential to guarding against abuses of discretion because other checks accomplish the same thing. Courts operate in the open through what has been described as a process of reasoned elaboration. They have to justify their decisions. It is not enough to say: this man goes to jail because he did something bad. There is an obligation to relate the particular bad thing that this man did to other bad things that have been treated as criminal in the past. The system of analogical reasoning that we call the common-law method is a very substantial impediment to arbitrary decision-making. The fact that courts operate in the open according to a system of reasoning that is subjected to the scrutiny of an interested audience, both professional and lay, militates against any but the most marginal invasions of the values represented by the principle of legality.

* Reprinted from The Limits of the Criminal Sanction by Herbert L. Packer, with the permission of the publishers, Stanford University Press. © 1968 by Herbert L. Packer.

By contrast, the police and the official prosecutors operate in a setting of secrecy and informality. Their processes are subjected to public scrutiny in only the most sporadic and cursory ways. Although some courts (particularly low-level courts in large cities faced with the necessity for dispensing assembly-line justice) at times behave with the informality and lack of articulation that [characterize] the police and prosecutors, no one has ever discovered a police or prosecutorial organization that behaves like a court. When judges deviate from the model of openness, evenhandedness, and rationality, it is recognized and deplored as a deviation from their ideal role. But no one expects the police or the prosecutors to behave the way a court is supposed to behave; that is simply not their role, and they are not subjected to even the minimal psychological constraints that flow from self-perceived deviation from an acknowledged role.

The principle of legality, then, is important for the allocation of competences not between the legislative and judicial branches, but among those who initiate the criminal process through the largely informal methods of investigation, arrest, interrogation, and charge that characterize the operation of criminal justice. [The existence of these largely informal decisions] poses problems in the exercise of power to which the principle of legality is an important response.

Does this mean, then, that the conventional focus of the principle of legality, which is on defining the respective roles of legislatures and courts, is distorted? Does it really make no difference whether the operative law is "made" by legislatures, declaring certain kinds of conduct criminal before they occur, or by courts, looking backward at the conduct whose criminality they are called upon to adjudicate? Not at all. The conventional focus is perfectly correct although not, as we have seen, for conventional reasons. It is correct because in a system that lodges the all-important initiating power in the hands of officials who operate, as they must, through informal and secret processes, there must be some devices to insure that the initiating decisions are, to the greatest extent possible, fair, evenhanded, and rational. Most of these devices ... are in the nature of post-audits on the decisions taken by the police and prosecutors. But the most important single device is the requirement ... that the police and prosecutors confine their attention to the catalogue of what has already been defined as criminal....

If criminal law can be made a posteriori by judges, rather than a priori, by legislatures, then the enforcement officials are under strong temptation to guess what the judges will do in a particular case. This temptation cannot be eliminated ..., but it can be minimized through the habits of thought acquired by enforcement officials who work under the principle of legality. To take a modern [1968] instance, consider the problem of dangerous drugs such as LSD. If judges had as broad a lawmaking power as legislatures do, any policeman who thought that taking LSD was a bad thing that should be treated as criminal and any prosecutor who agreed with him could combine to put the criminal process in motion against people who took LSD. And if they could find one judge (among hundreds in a jurisdiction) who agreed with them, they could obtain a criminal conviction. And if a majority of the members of the appellate court in the jurisdiction agreed with them, they would carry the day.

In fact, nothing of the sort has occurred, despite the sentiment, probably greater among law enforcement officials than among the public at large, for the suppression of LSD. Aside from a little informal harassment of the kind that no legal system can effectively preclude, members of the deviant subculture composed of LSD takers remained free to follow their bent until legislative bodies began declaring, according to their mode of operation that, henceforth or from a certain day forward, anyone who takes LSD will be committing a crime. This kind of certainty and regularity is particularly to be prized....

Note the centrality to Packer's argument of his belief that it is desirable to protect the "deviant subculture" of LSD users from discretionary repression by law enforcement. The particular example may be dated, but modern America continues to spawn "subcultures" that contravene, and sometimes openly flout, community standards of morals or behavior. Factors such as race, ethnic identity, religious practice, and sexual orientation may place one or another group of citizens outside the mainstream of the culture in which they live. That the institutions of law should be arrayed to protect such diversity may seem obvious in a liberal democracy, but it is far from commonplace, either historically or among contemporary cultures. Would a Puritan theocracy or an Islamic state or a Marxist dictatorship have a comparable commitment to protecting "deviant subcultures"? That is not to say, of course, that other cultures and other ideologies are inferior, but only that the principle of legality as a fundamental ideal of the penal law is especially compatible with liberal democracy and its underlying assumptions about the relation of the state to individual citizens.

**6.   The Continuing Significance of the Common Law.** Despite the fact that judicial crime creation is largely a thing of the past, the common law of crimes remains significant. Rejection of the methodology of the common law does not necessarily mean that the results of that tradition have also been abandoned. Several states occasionally enforce previously recognized non-statutory offenses, even though they do not assert the authority to create new ones.[d] Such prosecutions are not widely

---

[d] As of 1947, fully 31 American jurisdictions recognized the continued viability of the common law insofar as it had not been superseded by legislation. Note, Common Law

perceived as violations of the principle of legality, so long as they are adequately based on prior precedents defining the specific conduct as an offense at common law.

Of far greater consequence than the occasional prosecution for a non-statutory offense is the pervasive role of the common law as an aid to statutory construction. A few jurisdictions expressly adopt the common law as the background for interpreting penal legislation. Kansas, for example, provides that "where a crime is denounced by any statute of this state, but not defined, the definition of such crime at common law shall be applied." Kan. Stat. Ann. § 21–3102 (1988). More often, the point is left to implication, as in the common legislative practice of assigning penalties for "manslaughter" without defining that crime. In such instances, courts must resort to the common law in order to ascertain the meaning of the legislative enactment. Even when a statute purports to define a crime, it often does no more than ·memorialize the common-law definition. In such cases, gaps or ambiguities in the statutory formulation are often filled in by reference to the common-law understanding. Thus, the common law of crimes, although rarely enforced as such, remains vitally important to the student of the criminal law.

---

## Kolender v. Lawson

Supreme Court of the United States, 1983.
461 U.S. 352.

■ JUSTICE O'CONNOR delivered the opinion of the Court.

This appeal presents a facial challenge to a criminal statute that requires persons who loiter or wander on the streets to provide a "credible and reliable" identification and to account for their presence when requested by a peace officer under circumstances that would justify a stop under the standards of Terry v. Ohio, 392 U.S. 1 (1968).[1] We conclude that the

---

Crimes in the United States, 47 Colum. L. Rev. 1332 (1947). In succeeding decades, the number of states taking this position declined sharply. The greatest single factor was the widespread adoption of revised criminal codes, virtually all of which follow Section 1.05 of the Model Penal Code in eliminating non-statutory crimes. Nevertheless, in 1995, at least 15 states continued to allow prosecution for non-statutory offenses. See Fla. Stat. Ann. § 775.01 (West 1992); Md. Const. Code Ann. art. 5 (Supp. 1994); Mass. Gen. Laws Ann. Const. pt. 2, ch. 6, art. 6 (West 1978); Mich. Comp. Laws Ann. Const. art. 3, § 7 (West 1985); Miss. Code Ann. § 99–1–3 (1972); N.M. Stat. Ann. § 30–1–3 (Michie 1978); N.C. Gen. Stat. § 4–1 (1986); R.I. Gen. Laws § 11–1–1 (1994); S.C. Code Ann. § 14–

1–50 (Law Co-op 1976); Vt. Stat. Ann. tit. 1, § 271 (1985); Va. Code Ann. § 1–10 (Michie 1995); Wash. Rev. Code Ann. § 9A.04.060 (West 1988); W.Va. Code § 2–1–1 (1994); Wyo. Stat. § 8–1–101 (1989). In Tennessee there is no express statute but case law indicates that prosecution for common-law crimes continues. E.g., Gervin v. State, 212 Tenn. 653, 371 S.W.2d 449 (1963).

[1] California Penal Code § 647(e) provides:

Every person who commits any of the following acts is guilty of disorderly conduct, a misdemeanor:

* * *

(e) Who loiters or wanders upon the streets or from place to place without

statute as it has been construed is unconstitutionally vague within the meaning of the due process clause of the 14th Amendment[a] by failing to clarify what is contemplated by the requirement that a suspect provide a "credible and reliable" identification. Accordingly, we affirm the judgment of the court below.

I

Appellee Edward Lawson was detained or arrested on approximately 15 occasions between March 1975 and January 1977 pursuant to Cal. Pen. Code § 647(e).[2] Lawson was prosecuted only twice, and was convicted once. The second charge was dismissed.

Lawson then brought a civil action in the District Court for the Southern District of California seeking a declaratory judgment that § 647(e) is unconstitutional.... [The District Court granted relief, and the Court of Appeals affirmed, holding the statute] unconstitutional in that ... it contains a vague enforcement standard that is susceptible to arbitrary enforcement, and it fails to give fair and adequate notice of the type of conduct prohibited....

II

In the courts below, Lawson mounted an attack on the facial validity of § 647(e). "In evaluating a facial challenge to a state law, a federal court must, of course, consider any limiting construction that a state court or enforcement agency has proffered." Hoffman Estates v. Flipside, Hoffman Estates, Inc., 455 U.S. 489, 494 n.5 (1982). As construed by the California Court of Appeal, § 647(e) requires that an individual provide "credible and reliable" identification when requested by a police officer who has reasonable suspicion of criminal activity sufficient to justify a *Terry* detention.[5] People v. Solomon, 33 Cal. App. 3d 429 (1973). "Credible and reliable" identification is defined by the state Court of Appeal as identification

apparent reason or business and who refuses to identify himself and to account for his presence when requested by any peace officer so to do, if the surrounding circumstances are such as to indicate to a reasonable man that the public safety demands such identification.

[a] Section 1 of the 14th Amendment provides that no state shall "deprive any person of life, liberty, or property, without due process of law...."—[Footnote by eds.]

[2] The District Court failed to find facts concerning the particular occasions on which Lawson was detained or arrested under § 647(e). However, the trial transcript contains numerous descriptions of the stops given both by Lawson and by the police officers who detained him. For example, one police officer testified that he stopped Lawson while walking on an otherwise vacant street be-cause it was late at night, the area was isolated, and the area was located close to a high crime area. Another officer testified that he detained Lawson, who was walking at a late hour in a business area where some businesses were still open, and asked for identification because burglaries had been committed by unknown persons in the general area. The appellee states that he has never been stopped by police for any reason apart from his detentions under § 647(e).

[5] [A]ccording to *Terry*, the applicable test under the Fourth Amendment requires that the police officer making a detention "be able to point to specific and articulable facts which, taken together with rational inferences from those facts, reasonably warrant that intrusion." 392 U.S., at 21....

"carrying reasonable assurance that the identification is authentic and providing means for later getting in touch with the person who has identified himself." In addition, a suspect may be required to "account for his presence . . . to the extent that it assists in producing credible and reliable identification. . . ." Under the terms of the statute, failure of the individual to provide "credible and reliable" identification permits the arrest.

## III

. . . As generally stated, the void-for-vagueness doctrine requires that a penal statute define the criminal offense with sufficient definiteness that ordinary people can understand what conduct is prohibited and in a manner that does not encourage arbitrary and discriminatory enforcement. Papachristou v. City of Jacksonville, 405 U.S. 156 (1972) [and other cases]. Although the doctrine focuses on actual notice to citizens and arbitrary enforcement, we have recognized recently that the more important aspect of the vagueness doctrine "is not actual notice, but the other principal element of the doctrine—the requirement that a legislature establish minimal guidelines to govern law enforcement." Smith v. Goguen, 415 U.S. 566, 574 (1974). Where the legislature fails to provide such minimal guidelines, a criminal statute may permit "a standardless sweep [that] allows policemen, prosecutors, and juries to pursue their personal predilections." Id., at 575.[7]

Section 647(e), as presently drafted and as construed by the state courts, contains no standard for determining what a suspect has to do in order to satisfy the requirement to provide a "credible and reliable" identification. As such, the statute vests virtually complete discretion in the hands of the police to determine whether the suspect has satisfied the statute and must be permitted to go on his way in the absence of probable cause to arrest. An individual, whom police may think is suspicious but do not have probable cause to believe has committed a crime, is entitled to continue to walk the public streets "only at the whim of any police officer" who happens to stop that individual under § 647(e). Shuttlesworth v. City of Birmingham, 382 U.S. 87, 90 (1965). Our concern here is based upon the "potential for arbitrarily suppressing first amendment liberties. . . ." Id., at 91. In addition, § 647(e) implicates consideration of the constitutional right to freedom of movement. See Kent v. Dulles, 357 U.S. 116, 126 (1958); Aptheker v. Secretary of State, 378 U.S. 500, 505–06 (1964).

Section 647(e) is not simply a "stop-and-identify" statute. Rather, the statute requires that the individual provide a "credible and reliable" identification that carries a "reasonable assurance" of its authenticity, and

---

[7] Our concern for minimal guidelines finds its roots as far back as our decision in United States v. Reese, 92 U.S. 214, 221 (1875): "It would certainly be dangerous if the legislature could set a net large enough to catch all possible offenders, and leave it to the courts to step inside and say who could be rightfully detained, and who should be set at large. This would, to some extent, substitute the judicial for the legislative department of government."

that provides "means for later getting in touch with the person who has identified himself." *Solomon*, supra, at 438, 108 Cal.Rptr. 867. In addition, the suspect may also have to account for his presence "to the extent it assists in producing credible and reliable information." Id.

At oral argument, the appellants confirmed that a suspect violates § 647(e) unless "the officer [is] satisfied that the identification is reliable." In giving examples of how suspects would satisfy the requirement, appellants explained that a jogger, who was not carrying identification, could, depending on the particular officer, be required to answer a series of questions concerning the route that he followed to arrive at the place where the officers detained him,[9] or could satisfy the identification requirement simply by reciting his name and address.

It is clear that the full discretion accorded to the police to determine whether the suspect has provided a "credible and reliable" identification necessarily "entrust[s] law-making 'to the moment-to-moment judgment of the policeman on his beat.'" *Smith*, supra, at 575. Section 647(e) "furnishes a convenient tool for 'harsh and discriminatory enforcement by local prosecuting officials against particular groups deemed to merit their displeasure,'" *Papachristou*, supra, at 170, and "confers on police a virtually unrestrained power to arrest and charge persons with a violation." Lewis v. City of New Orleans, 415 U.S. 130, 135 (1974) (Powell, J., concurring in result). In providing that a detention under § 647(e) may occur only where there is the level of suspicion sufficient to justify a *Terry* stop, the state ensures the existence of "neutral limitations on the conduct of individual officers." Brown v. Texas, 443 U.S. 47, 51 (1979). Although the initial detention is justified, the state fails to establish standards by which the officers may determine whether the suspect has complied with the subsequent identification requirement.

Appellants stress the need for strengthened law enforcement tools to combat the epidemic of crime that plagues our nation. The concern of our citizens with curbing criminal activity is certainly a matter requiring the attention of all branches of government. As weighty as this concern is, however, it cannot justify legislation that would otherwise fail to meet constitutional standards for definiteness and clarity. Section 647(e), as presently construed, requires that "suspicious" persons satisfy some undefined identification requirement, or face criminal punishment. Although due process does not require "impossible standards" of clarity, see United States v. Petrillo, 332 U.S. 1, 7–8 (1947), this is not a case where further precision in the statutory language is either impossible or impractical.

## IV

We conclude that § 647(e) is unconstitutionally vague on its face because it encourages arbitrary enforcement by failing to describe with

---

[9] To the extent that § 647(e) criminalizes a suspect's failure to answer such questions put to him by police officers, Fifth Amendment concerns are implicated. It is a "settled principle that while police have the right to request citizens to answer voluntarily questions concerning unsolved crimes they have no right to compel them to answer." Davis v. Mississippi, 394 U.S. 721, 727, n.6 (1969).

sufficient particularity what a suspect must do in order to satisfy the statute. Accordingly, the judgment of the Court of Appeals is affirmed....

■ JUSTICE BRENNAN, concurring.

I join the Court's opinion; it demonstrates convincingly that the California statute at issue in this case, as interpreted by California courts, is unconstitutionally vague. Even if the defect identified by the Court were cured, however, I would hold that this statute violates the Fourth Amendment.[b] Merely to facilitate the general law enforcement objectives of investigating and preventing unspecified crimes, states may not authorize the arrest and criminal prosecution of an individual for failing to produce identification or further information on demand by a police officer.

It has long been settled that the Fourth Amendment prohibits the seizure and detention or search of an individual's person unless there is probable cause to believe that he has committed a crime, except under certain conditions strictly defined by the legitimate requirements of law enforcement and by the limited extent of the resulting intrusion on individual liberty and privacy. The scope of that exception to the probable cause requirement for seizures of the person has been defined by a series of cases, beginning with Terry v. Ohio, 392 U.S. 1 (1968), holding that a police officer with reasonable suspicion of criminal activity, based on articulable facts, may detain a suspect briefly for purposes of limited questioning and, in so doing, may conduct a brief "frisk" of the suspect to protect himself from concealed weapons....

Terry and the cases following it give full recognition to law enforcement officers' need for an "intermediate" response, short of arrest, to suspicious circumstances; the power to effect a brief detention for the purpose of questioning is a powerful tool for the investigation and prevention of crimes. Any person may, of course, direct a question to another person in passing. The Terry doctrine permits police officers to do far more: If they have the requisite reasonable suspicion, they may use a number of devices with substantial coercive impact on the person to whom they direct their attention, including an official "show of authority," the use of physical force to restrain him, and a search of the person for weapons.

[T]he scope of seizures of the person on less than probable cause that Terry permits is strictly circumscribed, to limit the degree of intrusion they cause. Terry encounters must be brief; the suspect must not be moved or asked to move more than a short distance; physical searches are permitted only to the extent necessary to protect the police officers involved during the encounter; and, most importantly, the suspect must be free to leave after a short time and to decline to answer the questions put to him.... Failure to observe these limitations converts a Terry encounter into the

---

[b] The Fourth Amendment provides: "The right of the people to be secure in their persons, houses, papers, and effects, against unreasonable searches and seizures, shall not be violated, and no Warrants shall issue, but upon probable cause, supported by Oath or affirmation, and particularly describing the place to be searched, and the persons or things to be seized."—[Footnote by eds.]

sort of detention that can be justified only by probable cause to believe that a crime has been committed.

... Detention beyond the limits of *Terry* without probable cause would improve the effectiveness of legitimate police investigations by only a small margin, but it would expose individual members of the public to exponential increases in both the intrusiveness of the encounter and the risk that police officers would abuse their discretion for improper ends. Furthermore, regular expansion of *Terry* encounters into more intrusive detentions, without a clear connection to any specific underlying crimes, is likely to exacerbate ongoing tensions, where they exist, between the police and the public. [A]ppellants do not claim that § 647(e) advances any interest other than general facilitation of police investigation and preservation of public order.... Nor do appellants show that the power to arrest and to impose a criminal sanction, in addition to the power to detain and to pose questions under the aegis of state authority, is so necessary in pursuit of the state's legitimate interests as to justify the substantial additional intrusion on individuals' rights....

■ Justice White, with whom Justice Rehnquist joins, dissenting.

The usual rule is that the alleged vagueness of a criminal statute must be judged in light of the conduct that is charged to be violative of the statute. If the actor is given sufficient notice that his conduct is within the proscription of the statute, his conviction is not vulnerable on vagueness grounds, even if as applied to other conduct, the law would be unconstitutionally vague. None of our cases "suggests that one who has received fair warning of the criminality of his own conduct from the statute in question is nonetheless entitled to attack it because the language would not give similar fair warning with respect to other conduct which might be within its broad and literal ambit. One to whose conduct a statute clearly applies may not successfully challenge it for vagueness." Parker v. Levy, 417 U.S. 733, 756 (1974). The correlative rule is that a criminal statute is not unconstitutionally vague on its face unless it is "impermissibly vague in all of its applications." Hoffman Estates v. Flipside, 455 U.S. 489, 497 (1982).... Of course, if his own actions are themselves protected by the First Amendment or other constitutional provision, or if the statute does not fairly warn that it is proscribed, he may not be convicted. But it would be unavailing for him to claim that although he knew his own conduct was unprotected and was plainly enough forbidden by the statute, others may be in doubt as to whether their acts are banned by the law.

The upshot of our cases, therefore, is that ... a statute ... should not be held unconstitutionally vague on its face unless it is vague in all of its possible applications. If any fool would know that a particular category of conduct would be within the reach of the statute, if there is an unmistakable core that a reasonable person would know is forbidden by the law, the enactment is not unconstitutional on its face and should not be vulnerable to a facial attack in a declaratory judgment action such as is involved in this case. Under our cases, this would be true, even though as applied to other conduct the provision would fail to give the constitutionally required notice of illegality. . . .

The Court says that its decision "rests on our concern for arbitrary law enforcement, and not on the concern for lack of actual notice." But if there is a range of conduct that is clearly within the reach of the statute, law enforcement personnel, as well as putative arrestees, are clearly on notice that arrests for such conduct are authorized by the law. There would be nothing arbitrary or discretionary about such arrests. If the officer arrests for an act that both he and the law breaker know is clearly barred by the statute, it seems to me an untenable exercise of judicial review to invalidate a state conviction because in some other circumstance the officer may arbitrarily misapply the statute. That the law might not give sufficient guidance to arresting officers with respect to other conduct should be dealt with in those situations. It is no basis for . . . invalidating the statute on its face, thus forbidding its application to identifiable conduct that is within the state's power to sanction.

I would agree with the majority in this case if it made at least some sense to conclude that the requirement to provide "credible and reliable identification" after a valid stop on reasonable suspicion of criminal conduct is "impermissibly vague in all of its applications." *Hoffman Estates v. Flipside*, supra, at 495. But the statute is not vulnerable on this ground; and the majority, it seems to me, fails to demonstrate that it is. Suppose, for example, an officer requests identification information from a suspect during a valid *Terry* stop and the suspect answers: "Who I am is just none of your business." Surely the suspect would know from the statute that a refusal to provide any information at all would constitute a violation. It would be absurd to suggest that in such a situation only the unfettered discretion of a police officer, who has legally stopped a person on reasonable suspicion, would serve to determine whether a violation of the statute has occurred.

"It is self-evident that there is a whole range of conduct that anyone with at least a semblance of common sense would know is [a failure to provide credible and reliable identification] and that would be covered by the statute. . . . In these instances there would be ample notice to the actor and no room for undue discretion by enforcement officers. There may be a variety of other conduct that might or might not be claimed [to have failed to meet the statute's requirements] by the state, but unpredictability in those situations does not change the certainty in others." Smith v. Goguen, 415 U.S. 566, 584 (1974) (White, J., concurring in the judgment). . . . The judgment below should therefore not be affirmed but reversed and appellee Lawson remitted to challenging the statute as it has been or will be applied to him.

The majority finds that the statute "contains no standard for determining what a suspect has to do in order to satisfy the requirement to provide a 'credible and reliable' identification." At the same time, the majority concedes that "credible and reliable" has been defined by the state court to mean identification that carries reasonable assurance that the identification is authentic and that provides means for later getting in touch with the person. The narrowing construction given this statute by the state court cannot be likened to the "standardless" statutes involved in the cases cited by the majority. For example, Papachristou v. City of Jacksonville, 405 U.S. 156 (1972), involved a statute that made it a crime to be a "vagrant." The statute provided: "Rogues and vagabonds, or dissolute persons who go about begging, common gamblers, ... common drunkards, common night walkers, ... lewd, wanton and lascivious persons, ... common railers and brawlers, persons wandering or strolling around from place to place without any lawful purpose or object, habitual loafers, ... shall be deemed vagrants." ... The present statute, as construed by the state courts, does not fall in the same category.

[T]he majority makes a vague reference to potential suppression of First Amendment liberties, but the precise nature of the liberties threatened are never mentioned. Shuttlesworth v. City of Birmingham, 382 U.S. 87 (1965), is cited, but that case dealt with an ordinance making it a crime to "stand or loiter upon any street or sidewalk ... after having been requested by an police officer to move on," and the first amendment concerns implicated by the statute ... dealt with the ... right to distribute leaflets on city streets and sidewalks. There are no such concerns in the present case.

Of course, if the statute on its face violates the Fourth or Fifth Amendment—and I express no views about that question—the Court would be justified in striking it down. But the majority apparently cannot bring itself to take this course. It resorts instead to the vagueness doctrine to invalidate a statute that is clear in many of its applications but which is somehow distasteful to the majority. As here construed and applied, the doctrine serves as an open-ended authority to oversee the states' legislative choices in the criminal-law area and in this case leaves the state in a quandary as to how to draft a statute that will pass constitutional muster.

I would reverse the judgment of the Court of Appeals.

———

## NOTES ON THE VAGUENESS DOCTRINE

**1. Rationales of the Vagueness Doctrine.** As Justice O'Connor noted in *Kolender*, a vague statute has at least two flaws. First, it fails to give adequate notice of what is prohibited. The lack of fair warning is a recurrent theme in vagueness decisions. As the Court said in Lanzetta v. New Jersey, 306 U.S. 451, 453 (1939), "[n]o one may be required at peril of life, liberty or property to speculate as to the meaning of penal statutes." Similarly, in Connally v. General Construction Co., 269 U.S. 385, 391 (1926), the Court said that, "a statute which either forbids or requires the doing of an act in terms so vague that men of common intelligence must necessarily guess at its meaning and differ as to its application, violates the first essential of due process of law."

A second problem is that an indefinite law invites arbitrary and discriminatory enforcement. In essence, the power to define a vague statute is left to those who enforce it. The fear is that the penal law will be unfairly applied. As the Supreme Court noted over a century ago, "[i]t would certainly be dangerous if the legislature could set a net large enough to catch all possible offenders, and leave it to the courts to step inside and say who could be rightfully detained, and who should be set at large." United States v. Reese, 92 U.S. 214, 221 (1875). A vague law leaves police and prosecutors similarly unconstrained in the performance of their duties. The result is a drift toward arbitrariness in the administration of justice.

**2.   Limits of the Vagueness Rationales.** Modern decisions focus on fair warning and non-discriminatory enforcement as rationales for invalidating vague laws, but neither justification can be accepted at face value. Consider fair warning. Invalidating some laws because they do not give adequate notice presupposes that other laws provide effective notice. Yet there is something inescapably fictive in the notion that potential criminals learn what is forbidden from the words of a statute. That assumption may hold true for those who seek advice of counsel, but the ordinary citizen is not likely to have such resources. Most people do not have access to the statute books or the skill to unravel the legislative language should they find it.

The rationale of fair warning is further compromised by the rule that the precision required of a penal statute need not appear on its face. Facial uncertainty can be cured by judicial construction. Thus, review of a state statute for unconstitutional vagueness often turns not on the text of the law as it stands on the books but on its meaning as construed by the courts. In *Kolender*, for example, the dispute turned on the definiteness or indefiniteness of a state-court decision requiring "credible and reliable" identification. Where the meaning of a statute depends on prior judicial construction, ascertaining the content of the law becomes even more difficult.

The concern for non-discriminatory enforcement of the penal law also has difficulties. It is true that the vagueness doctrine invalidates laws that are especially susceptible to arbitrary enforcement and contributes to evenhandedness in the administration of justice. Yet it is revealing to note how imperfect is the law's commitment to that goal. A vague statute may *invite* arbitrary enforcement, but virtually any law *allows* it. The difference may not be all that great. Even an ideally precise statute is subject to discretionary, and hence potentially discriminatory, administration. The police decide which laws to enforce and whom to arrest. Prosecutors decide whether to bring charges and for which offenses. Prosecutors may accept or reject guilty pleas and make or withhold recommendations of sentence. In all these decisions, the exercise of discretion is virtually uncontrolled. Only in the truly exceptional case where the defendant can prove that the prosecutorial decision was made on some plainly illegitimate basis—such as race or religion—can a prosecution be defeated on grounds of arbitrary or selective enforcement. Otherwise, discretion prevails.[a]

What, if anything, does the prevalence of discretionary authority throughout the criminal justice system say about the non-discriminatory enforcement rationale of the vagueness doctrine? Does the pervasive potential for ad hoc and arbitrary enforcement of any penal statute mean that invalidating some laws for failure to provide determinate standards is essentially fraudulent? Or is the vagueness doctrine justified as an important, though insufficient, corollary of the rule of law?[b]

**3.** *Papachristou v. City of Jacksonville.* The *Kolender* majority relied on, and the dissent distinguished, Papachristou v. City of Jacksonville, 405 U.S. 156 (1972). The ordinance there considered is so extravagant and yet so typical of the municipal legislation of a certain era that it merits reprinting in full:

> Rogues and vagabonds, or dissolute persons who go about begging, common gamblers, persons who use juggling or unlawful games or plays, common drunkards, common night walkers, thieves, pilferers or pickpockets, traders in stolen property, lewd, wanton and lascivious persons, keepers of gambling places, common railers and brawlers, persons wandering or strolling around from place to place without any lawful purpose or object, habitual loafers, disorderly persons, persons neglecting all lawful business and habitually spending their time by frequenting houses of ill fame, gaming houses, or places where alcoholic beverages are sold or served, persons able to work but habitually living upon the earnings of their wives or minor children shall be deemed vagrants and, upon conviction in the Municipal Court shall be punished as provided. . . .

This ordinance was invoked against two white women and two black men who were arrested while driving on the main thoroughfare of Jackson-

---

[a] For discussion of the exercise of discretion by prosecutors in charging, and in negotiating and accepting guilty pleas, see James Vorenberg, Decent Restraint of Prosecutorial Power, 94 Harv. L. Rev. 1521 (1981). For an informative study of federal prosecutorial discretion, see Richard S. Frase, The Decision to File Federal Criminal Charges: A Quantitative Study of Prosecutorial Discretion, 47 U. Chi. L. Rev. 246 (1980). And for description of the sometimes extraordinary powers enjoyed by federal prosecutors, see John C. Jeffries, Jr., and John Gleeson, The Federalization of Organized Crime: The Advantages of Federal Prosecution, 46 Hastings L.J. 1095 (1995).

To sample the rich literature on police discretion, see Kenneth Culp Davis, Police Discretion (1975); Jerome H. Skolnick, Justice Without Trial: Law Enforcement in Dem-

ocratic Society (2d ed. 1975); Ronald J. Allen, The Police and Substantive Rule–Making: Reconciling Principle and Expediency, 125 U.Pa.L.Rev. 62 (1976); Joseph Goldstein, Police Discretion Not to Invoke the Criminal Process: Low–Visibility Decisions in the Administration of Justice, 69 Yale L.J. 543 (1960).

[b] For a critical account of the vagueness doctrine as a "conscious interpretive construct" used to mask or avoid political choices in the application of the criminal law, see Mark Kelman, Interpretive Construction in the Substantive Criminal Law, 33 Stan. L. Rev. 591, 652–62 (1981). For a more favorable view of the contribution of the vagueness doctrine to the rule of law, see John C. Jeffries, Jr., Legality, Vagueness, and the Construction of Penal Statutes, 71 Va.L.Rev. 189, 201–19 (1985).

ville. The arresting officers denied that race played any part in their decision to arrest, but the Court was plainly worried:

> Those generally implicated by the imprecise terms of the ordinance—poor people, non-conformists, dissenters, idlers—may be required to comport themselves according to the lifestyle deemed appropriate by the Jacksonville police and the courts. Where, as here, there are no standards governing the exercise of the discretion granted by the ordinance, the scheme permits and encourages an arbitrary and discriminatory enforcement of the law. It furnishes a convenient tool for "harsh and discriminatory enforcement by local prosecuting officials, against particular groups deemed to merit their displeasure." ... It results in a regime in which the poor and the unpopular are permitted to "stand on a public sidewalk ... only at the whim of any police officer." ... Under this ordinance, "[I]f some carefree type of fellow is satisfied to work just so much, and no more, as will pay for one square meal, some wine, and a flophouse daily, but a court thinks this kind of living subhuman, the fellow can be forced to raise his sights or go to jail as a vagrant." Anthony Amsterdam, Federal Constitutional Restrictions on the Punishment of Crimes of Status, Crimes of General Obnoxiousness, Crimes of Displeasing Police Officers, and the Like, 3 Crim.L.Bull. 205, 226 (1967).

> ... Of course, vagrancy statutes are useful to the police. Of course, they are nets making easy the roundup of so-called undesirables. But the rule of law implies equality and justice in its application. Vagrancy laws of the Jacksonville type teach that the scales of justice are so tipped that even-handed administration of the law is not possible. The rule of law, evenly applied to minorities as well as majorities, to the poor as well as the rich, is the great mucilage that holds society together.

**4.  Tolerable Vagueness and the Demands of Necessity.** When *Papachristou* struck down traditional vagrancy laws, legislatures responded with more refined attempts to allow police to deal with incipient criminality. *Kolender* involved one such attempt. Obviously, the California statute was an improvement over the older laws; equally obviously, it still had some of the same problems.

One factor in evaluating such statutes is the feasibility of being more precise. Imprecision is an inevitable feature of generality. Laws drawn to regulate future conduct necessarily speak in abstract terms, and the reduction of general language to specific results is often uncertain. Indeed, nothing is more common than a statutory standard that is intelligible in concept though unclear in its application to particular facts. Yet the courts are reluctant to invalidate for vagueness laws that cannot reasonably be made more precise. To do so would be to render legislatures incapable of dealing with the problem at hand. This is drastic medicine, and the courts are unwilling to administer it in any doubtful case. Thus, the demands of necessity often move the courts to accept in some contexts a degree of indeterminacy that might not be permitted elsewhere.

An example of such reasoning comes from United States v. Petrillo, 332 U.S. 1 (1947). A provision of the Federal Communications Act made it criminal to use any means to coerce or compel a broadcast licensee to employ "any person or persons in excess of the number of employees needed by such licensee...." The defendant challenged the law for vagueness, and the trial court agreed that the reference to "number of employees needed" was too indefinite to give fair warning of the meaning of the law. The Supreme Court reversed:

> Clearer and more precise language might have been framed by Congress to express what it meant by "number of employees needed." But none occurs to us, nor has any better language been suggested, effectively to carry out what appears to have been the congressional purpose. The argument really seems to be that it is impossible for a jury or court ever to determine how many employees a business needs, and that, therefore, no statutory language could meet the problem Congress had in mind. If this argument should be accepted, the result would be that no legislature could make it an offense for a person to compel another to hire employees, no matter how unnecessary they were, and however desirable a legislature might consider suppression of the practice to be.

> The Constitution presents no such insuperable obstacle to legislation. We think that the language Congress used provides an adequate warning as to what conduct falls under its ban, and marks boundaries sufficiently distinct for judges and juries fairly to administer the law in accordance with the will of Congress. That there may be marginal cases in which it is difficult to determine the side of the line on which a particular fact situation falls is no sufficient reason to hold the language too ambiguous to define a criminal offense.... [T]he Constitution does not require impossible standards.

**5.    *Nash v. United States* and Questions of Degree.** The concern that legislatures not be required to meet "impossible standards" of precision comes directly into play for questions of degree. The most famous example is Nash v. United States, 229 U.S. 373 (1913). *Nash* involved a vagueness challenge to criminal prosecution under the Sherman Antitrust Act, which had been interpreted to forbid an *"undue* restraint of trade."[c]

---

[c] Section 1 of the Sherman Antitrust Act declared illegal "[e]very contract, combination in the form of trust or otherwise, or conspiracy in restraint of trade or commerce...." Of course, it is the essence of contract to restrain future choice. If read literally, the Sherman Act would forbid any commercial agreement. The Supreme Court avoided this absurdity by declaring, in the context of civil antitrust litigation, that the Sherman Act should be interpreted according to a "rule of reason." See Standard Oil Co. v. United States, 221 U.S. 1 (1911), and United States v. American Tobacco Co., 221 U.S. 106 (1911). By this construction, the Court transformed the condemnation of "every" restraint of trade to one that reached only an *undue* restraint of trade.

The defendant argued that the question of degree involved in the term "undue" rendered the statute unconstitutionally vague, but Justice Holmes responded as follows:

> [T]he law is full of instances where a man's fate depends on his estimating rightly, that is, as the jury subsequently estimates it, some matter of degree. If his judgment is wrong, not only may he incur a fine or a short imprisonment, as here; he may incur the penalty of death.... "The criterion in such cases is to examine whether common social duty would, under the circumstances, have suggested a more circumspect conduct."

The Sherman Act is still on the books and occasionally is enforced by criminal prosecution. Is it sufficiently precise to survive vagueness review? Should it matter that an antitrust statute is likely to be applied against persons who have the means and opportunity to seek advice of counsel?

Whatever one's views on the merits of these questions, it is clear that Justice Holmes' remarks on the prevalence of distinctions of degree remain accurate. Today, as in 1913, the law is full of instances where the fact or grade of criminal liability turns on an estimate of degree. Following another may be punished as stalking, for example, if it causes that person "reasonably" to fear for her safety.[d] Assault may be a felony or a misdemeanor depending on whether the attack caused "serious" bodily harm.[e] Even the imposition of the death penalty may depend on whether the accused had a "significant" history of prior criminal activity[f] or whether the circumstances of his crime were "especially" heinous.[g]

In all of these cases and a great many others besides, the law requires that a line be drawn somewhere along a spectrum of infinite gradation. The exact location of that line cannot be known until, as Holmes said, "the jury subsequently estimates it." And jury evaluations of this sort are inevitably somewhat ad hoc. Although the indefiniteness of distinctions of degree seems to implicate both of the underlying concerns of the vagueness doctrine, such uncertainty is nonetheless widely tolerated in the law.

---

[d] Conn. Gen. Stat. § 53a–181d declares that a person is guilty of stalking "when, with intent to cause another person to fear for his physical safety, he willfully and repeatedly follows or lies in wait for such other person and causes such other person to reasonably fear for his physical safety." This provision was upheld against a void-for-vagueness challenge in State v. Culmo, 642 A.2d 90 (Conn. Super. 1993).

[e] See, e.g., N.H.Rev.Stat.Ann. §§ 631:1 and 631:2 (1994). The concept of "serious bodily harm" is defined under New Hampshire law to include "harm to the body which causes severe, permanent, or protracted loss of or impairment to the health or the func-

tion of any part of the body." N.H.Rev.Stat. Ann. § 625:11(VI) (1986).

[f] The Arkansas, Florida, and Utah death penalty statutes list among relevant mitigating circumstances the fact that the "defendant has no significant history of prior criminal activity." Ark. Code Ann. § 5–4–605(6) (Michie 1993); Fla.Stat.Ann. § 921.141(6)(a) (West 1995); Utah Code Ann. § 76–3–207(3)(a) (1995).

[g] See, e.g., Fla.Stat. Ann. § 921.141(5)(h) (West 1995) (identifying as an aggravating circumstance for determination of sentence that the "capital felony was especially heinous, atrocious or cruel"), upheld in Proffitt v. Florida, 428 U.S. 242 (1976).

**6. Intolerable Vagueness and Protected Freedoms.** As the preceding discussion indicates, the difficulty of being more precise is an important factor favoring judicial acceptance of statutory indeterminacy. An equally significant factor cutting the other way is the impact of indefinite laws on constitutionally protected rights. Judicial scrutiny under the vagueness doctrine is most rigorous when the law in question impinges on first-amendment freedoms of speech and press.

The rationale for heightened scrutiny of laws touching first-amendment freedoms is that vagueness in this context is especially costly. It is costly not merely in terms of the usual concerns of the vagueness doctrine—lack of fair notice and the prospect of arbitrary enforcement—but also in terms of the unwanted deterrence of constitutionally protected activities. A prohibition of uncertain scope may cast a shadow over actions that may be constitutionally protected. In the traditional terminology of the First Amendment, an imprecise law may have a "chilling effect" on the exercise of protected rights. Thus, the requirement of specificity in the penal law is enforced with special rigor where it also serves to avoid incidental impairment of first-amendment freedoms.

This point was explained by the Supreme Court in N.A.A.C.P. v. Button, 371 U.S. 415 (1963). After noting that the "standards of permissible statutory vagueness are strict in the area of free expression," the Court gave the following justification for this special version of vagueness review:

> The objectionable quality of vagueness ... does not depend upon absence of fair notice to a criminally accused or upon unchanneled delegation of legislative powers, but upon the danger of tolerating, in the area of first-amendment freedoms, the existence of a penal statute susceptible of sweeping and improper application. These freedoms are delicate and vulnerable, as well as supremely precious in our society. The threat of sanctions may deter their exercise almost as potently as the actual application of sanctions. Because first-amendment freedoms need breathing space to survive, government may regulate in the area only with narrow specificity....[h]

**7. Questions and Comments on *Kolender v. Lawson*.** In striking down Cal. Penal Code § 647(e), Justice O'Connor asserted that "this is not a case where further precision in the statutory language is either impossible or impractical," but she did not spell out what the statute should have said. What would you suggest? Can you think of language to resolve the problem, or is the difficulty more fundamental than sloppy draftsmanship?

In this connection, consider the Model Penal Code version of a loitering statute. Section 250.6 provides:

> A person commits a violation if he loiters or prowls in a place, at a time, or in a manner not usual for law-abiding individuals

---

[h] Of special relevance to this discussion is Anthony G. Amsterdam, The Void-for-Vagueness Doctrine in the Supreme Court, 109 U.Pa.L.Rev. 67 (1960). Though dated, Amsterdam's article remains a classic analysis of the vagueness doctrine.

under circumstances that warrant alarm for the safety of persons or property in the vicinity. Among the circumstances which may be considered in determining whether such alarm is warranted is the fact that the actor takes flight upon appearance of a peace officer, refuses to identify himself, or manifestly endeavors to conceal himself or any object. Unless flight by the actor or other circumstance makes it impracticable, a peace officer shall prior to any arrest for an offense under this section afford the actor an opportunity to dispel any alarm which would otherwise be warranted, by requesting him to identify himself and explain his presence and conduct. No person shall be convicted of an offense under this section if the peace officer did not comply with the preceding sentence, or if it appears at trial that the explanation given by the actor was true and, if believed by the peace officer at the time, would have dispelled the alarm.

Is this proposal better than Cal. Penal Code § 647(e)? The courts have split on this question, striking down several statutes based on this provision but upholding other, very similar laws.[i]

---

OPTIONAL PROBLEM: OBSCENITY, A CASE STUDY IN VAGUENESS

**1.   The Obscenity Problem.** The First Amendment to the Constitution of the United States says that "Congress shall make no law ... abridging the freedom of speech...." The 14th Amendment applies the same limitation to states and localities. One might assume that the effect of these provisions is to invalidate any legislative restraint on expression. It has long been settled, however, that certain kinds of "speech" fall outside the protections of the First Amendment and are subject to legislative regulation. Obscenity is one such category. According to the Supreme Court, obscenity is not constitutionally protected speech and may be suppressed by appropriate legislation.

Of course, the exclusion of obscenity from the protections of the First Amendment is not beyond debate. On the contrary, it is enduringly controversial. Even if that debate is laid to one side, however, there remain

[i] For decisions invalidating statutes based on the Model Code provision, see State v. Bitt, 118 Idaho 584, 798 P.2d 43 (1990); City of Bellevue v. Miler, 85 Wash.2d 539, 536 P.2d 603 (1975); Newsome v. Malcolm, 492 F.2d 1166 (2d Cir. 1974); City of Portland v. White, 495 P.2d 778 (Ore. Ct. App. 1972); State v. Starks, 51 Wis.2d 256, 186 N.W.2d 245 (1971).

For decisions upholding such statutes, see City of Milwaukee v. Nelson, 149 Wis.2d 434, 439 N.W.2d 562 (1989); People v. Superior Court of Santa Clara County, 46 Cal.3d 381. 250 Cal.Rptr. 515, 758 P.2d 1046 (1988); Porta v. Mayor, City of Omaha, 593 F.Supp. 863 (D.Neb. 1984); Bell v. State, 252 Ga. 267, 313 S.E.2d 678 (1984); Florida v. Ecker, 311 So.2d 104 (Fla.1975); Seattle v. Jones, 79 Wash.2d 626, 488 P.2d 750 (1971); Carmarco v. City of Orange, 111 N.J.Super. 400, 268 A.2d 354 (1970).

And for a comparable split on another version of a loitering law, see Salt Lake City v. Savage, 541 P.2d 1035 (Utah 1975), and People v. Berck, 32 N.Y.2d 567, 300 N.E.2d 411 (1973).

imposing difficulties in the use of the criminal law to regulate obscenity. If obscenity is to be excluded from the realm of constitutionally protected speech, it is necessary to define what "obscenity" is. And if the criminal law is to be used to suppress obscenity, the vagueness doctrine comes into play. The history of the Supreme Court's consideration of the obscenity question centers on the continuing search for definiteness in laws against obscenity.

**2.  The *Roth–Memoirs* Test.** The Supreme Court's effort to define obscenity began in Roth v. United States, 354 U.S. 476 (1957). The California statute at issue in *Roth* provided misdemeanor sanctions for "every person who, wilfully and lewdly, ... writes, composes, stereotypes, prints, publishes, sells, distributes, keeps for sale, or exhibits any obscene or indecent writing, paper, or book; or designs, copies, draws, engraves, paints, or otherwise prepares any obscene or indecent picture or print; or molds, cuts, casts, or otherwise makes any obscene or indecent figure." A companion case involved a federal statute that declared non-mailable, and hence punishable by criminal penalties, "[e]very obscene, lewd, lascivious, or filthy book, pamphlet, picture, paper, letter, writing, print, or other publication of an indecent character...." These statutes were attacked on the claim that reliance on such words as "obscene" and "indecent" rendered the laws unconstitutionally vague.

The *Roth* Court upheld both statutes. Having determined that "obscenity is not within the area of constitutionally protected speech," the Court undertook to formulate a constitutional definition of "obscenity." The test ultimately adopted was this: "whether to the average person, applying contemporary community standards, the dominant theme of the material taken as a whole appeals to the prurient interest." This concept was elaborated by a dictionary definition of "prurient" as meaning "[i]tching; longing; uneasy with desire or longing; of persons having itching, morbid or lascivious longings; of desire, curiosity, or propensity, lewd."

Finally, the *Roth* Court specifically rejected the claim that this standard was impermissibly vague:

> Many decisions have recognized that these terms of obscenity statutes are not precise. This Court, however, has consistently held that lack of precision is not itself offensive to the requirements of due process. "[T]he Constitution does not require impossible standards"; all that is required is that the language "conveys sufficiently definite warning as to the proscribed conduct when measured by common understanding and practices...." United States v. Petrillo, 332 U.S. 1, 7–8 (1947). These words, applied according to the proper standard for judging obscenity, already discussed, give adequate warning of the conduct proscribed and mark "... boundaries sufficiently distinct for judges and juries fairly to administer the law.... That there may be marginal cases in which it is difficult to determine the side of the line on which a particular fact situation falls is no sufficient reason to hold the language too ambiguous to define a criminal offense."

The *Roth* test was restated and expanded in Memoirs v. Massachusetts, 383 U.S. 413 (1966), to require the coalescence of three elements:

[I]t must be established that (i) the dominant theme of the material taken as a whole appeals to a prurient interest in sex; (ii) the material is patently offensive because it affronts contemporary community standards relating to the description or representation of sexual matters; and (iii) the material is utterly without redeeming social value.

This formulation became known as the *Roth-Memoirs* test and governed obscenity litigation for the next several years. Its application caused notable difficulties, especially (but not only) in determining whether pornographic material was "utterly without redeeming social value."

**3. Redefining Obscenity: *Miller v. California*.** In 1973 the Supreme Court undertook a full scale re-examination of the obscenity area. The lead case was Miller v. California, 413 U.S. 15 (1973). The new California obscenity statute punished criminally anyone who "knowingly sends ... into this state for sale or distribution, or in this state prepares, publishes, prints, exhibits, distributes, or offers to distribute ... any obscene matter." "Obscene" was defined according to the *Roth-Memoirs* test:

As used in this chapter:

(a) "Obscene" means that to the average person, applying contemporary standards, the predominant appeal of the matter, taken as a whole, is to prurient interest, i. e., a shameful or morbid interest in nudity, sex, or excretion, which goes substantially beyond customary limits of candor in description or representation of such matters and is matter which is utterly without redeeming social importance.

The defendant in *Miller* was convicted for mass-mailing advertisements for "adult" books bearing such titles as "Intercourse," "Sex Orgies Illustrated," and "An Illustrated History of Pornography." Illustrated brochures advertising these products were mailed, unsolicited, to the homes of California residents. The brochures themselves were found to constitute "obscene matter" within the meaning of the statute.

The Supreme Court affirmed in an opinion by Chief Justice Burger:

This much has been categorically settled by the Court, that obscene material is unprotected by the First Amendment.... We acknowledge, however, the inherent dangers of undertaking to regulate any form of expression. State statutes designed to regulate obscene materials must be carefully limited. As a result, we now confine the permissible scope of such regulation to works which depict or describe sexual conduct. That conduct must be specifically defined by the applicable state law, as written or authoritatively construed. A state offense must also be limited to works which, taken as a whole, appeal to the prurient interest in sex, which portray sexual conduct in a patently offensive way, and which, taken as a whole, do not have serious literary, artistic, political, or scientific value.

The basic guidelines for the trier of fact must be: (i) whether "the average person, applying contemporary community standards" would find that the work, taken as a whole, appeals to the prurient interest; (ii) whether the work depicts or describes, in a patently offensive way, sexual conduct specifically defined by the applicable state law; and (iii) whether the work, taken as a whole, lacks serious literary, artistic, political, or scientific value.…

We emphasize that it is not our function to propose regulatory schemes for the states. That must await their concrete legislative efforts. It is possible, however, to give a few plain examples of what a state statute could define for regulation under part (ii) of the standard announced in this opinion, supra:

(a) Patently offensive representations or descriptions of ultimate sexual acts, normal or perverted, actual or simulated.

(b) Patently offensive representations or descriptions of masturbation, excretory functions, and lewd exhibition of the genitals.

Sex and nudity may not be exploited without limit by films or pictures exhibited or sold in places of public accommodation any more than live sex and nudity can be exhibited or sold without limit in such public places. At a minimum, prurient, patently offensive depiction or description of sexual conduct must have serious literary, artistic, political, or scientific value to merit first-amendment protection. For example, medical books for the education of physicians and related personnel necessarily use graphic illustrations and descriptions of human anatomy. In resolving the inevitably sensitive questions of fact and law, we must continue to rely on the jury system, accompanied by the safeguards that judges, rules of evidence, presumption of innocence, and other protective features provide, as we do with rape, murder, and a host of other offenses against society and its individual members.…

Additional portions of the *Miller* opinion dealt with "contemporary community standards." The majority rejected the contention that there had to be a fixed, national standard for determining what is obscene. In the course of this discussion, the Court threw additional light on the kinds of judgments it expected jurors to make in obscenity cases:

Under a national Constitution, fundamental first-amendment limitations on the powers of the states do not vary from community to community, but this does not mean that there are, or should or can be, fixed, uniform national standards of precisely what appeals to the "prurient interest" or is "patently offensive." These are essentially questions of fact, and our nation is simply too big and too diverse for this Court to reasonably expect that such standards could be articulated for all 50 states in a single formulation, even assuming the prerequisite consensus exists. When triers of fact are asked to decide whether "the average person, applying contemporary community standards" would consider certain materials "prurient," it would be unrealistic to require that the answer be based on some abstract formulation. The adversary system, with lay jurors as the usual ultimate factfinders in criminal prosecutions, has historically permitted triers of fact to draw on the standards of their community, guided always by limiting instructions on the law. . . .

A companion case was decided on the same day. In Paris Adult Theatre I v. Slaton, 413 U.S. 49 (1973), a local district attorney filed a civil complaint seeking injunctive relief against the showing of two movies said to violate the Georgia criminal obscenity statute. The Georgia statute was similar to the *Miller* law. The defendants claimed that the cases should be treated differently because the movie theaters were open only to consenting adults (recall that *Miller* involved unsolicited mailings), but the Supreme Court found this difference immaterial and remanded the case for proceedings not inconsistent with *Miller*.

**4.   The Brennan Dissent.** In *Paris Adult Theatre*, Justice Brennan filed a 41–page dissent calling for a new approach to the law of obscenity. Brennan argued that all general obscenity statutes should be held unconstitutional. He left open the question whether narrower statutes dealing with the distribution of obscenity to juveniles or exhibition to unconsenting adults could be sustained. Significantly, Brennan did not say that obscenity is constitutionally protected speech. He indicated in a footnote that he found that view plausible, at least as to consenting adults, but he expressly disclaimed reliance on this rationale:

> Whether or not a class of "obscene" and thus entirely unprotected speech does exist, I am forced to conclude that the class is incapable of definition with sufficient clarity to withstand attack on vagueness grounds. Accordingly, it is on principles of the void-for-vagueness doctrine that this opinion exclusively relies.

Brennan then recounted the history of *Roth* and *Memoirs*. He described the *Miller* Court's redefinition of obscenity as "a slightly altered formulation of the basic *Roth* test" and launched an attack on the entire approach:

> [A]fter 16 years of experimentation and debate I am reluctantly forced to the conclusion that none of the available formulas, including the one announced today, can reduce the vagueness to a tolerable level. . . . Any effort to draw a constitutionally acceptable boundary on state power must resort to such indefinite concepts as "prurient interest," "patent offensiveness," "serious literary value," and the like. The meaning of these concepts necessarily varies with the experience, outlook, and even idiosyncrasies of the person defining them. Although we have assumed that obscenity does exist and that we "know it when [we] see it," Jacobellis v. Ohio, 378 U.S. 184, 197 (1964) (Stewart, J., concurring), we are manifestly unable to describe it in advance except by reference to

concepts so elusive that they fail to distinguish clearly between protected and unprotected speech....

The vagueness of the standards in the obscenity area produces a number of separate problems, and any improvement must rest on an understanding that the problems are to some extent distinct. First, a vague statute fails to provide adequate notice to persons who are engaged in the type of conduct that the statute could be thought to proscribe.... In this context, even the most painstaking efforts to determine in advance whether certain sexually oriented expression is obscene must inevitably prove unavailing. For the insufficiency of the notice compels persons to guess not only whether their conduct is covered by a criminal statute, but also whether their conduct falls within the constitutionally permissible reach of the statute. The resulting level of uncertainty is utterly intolerable, not alone because it makes "[b]ookselling ... a hazardous profession," but as well because it invites arbitrary and erratic enforcement of the law.

In addition to problems that arise when any criminal statute fails to afford fair notice of what it forbids, a vague statute in the areas of speech and press creates a second level of difficulty. We have indicated that "stricter standards of permissible statutory vagueness may be applied to a statute having a potentially inhibiting effect on speech; a man may the less be required to act at his peril here, because the free dissemination of ideas may be the loser." ...

The problems of fair notice and chilling protected speech are very grave standing alone. But it does not detract from their importance to recognize that a vague statute in this area creates a third, although admittedly more subtle, set of problems. These problems concern the institutional stress that inevitably results where the line separating protected from unprotected speech is excessively vague. In *Roth* we conceded that "there may be marginal cases in which it is difficult to determine the side of the line on which a particular fact situation falls...." Our subsequent experience demonstrates that almost every case is "marginal." And since the "margin" marks the point of separation between protected and unprotected speech, we are left with a system in which almost every obscenity case presents a constitutional question of exceptional difficulty.

On the basis of these difficulties, Justice Brennan concluded that the approach initiated in *Roth* should be abandoned:

I would hold, therefore, that at least in the absence of distribution to juveniles or obtrusive exposure to unconsenting adults, the First and 14th Amendments prohibit the state and federal governments from attempting wholly to suppress sexually oriented materials on the basis of their allegedly "obscene" contents.... Difficult questions must still be faced, notably in the areas of distribution to juveniles and offensive exposure to unconsenting adults. Whatever the extent of state power to regulate in those areas, it should be clear that the view I espouse today would introduce a large measure of clarity to this troubled area, would reduce the institutional pressure on this Court and the rest of the state and federal judiciary, and would guarantee fuller freedom of expression while leaving room for the protection of legitimate governmental interests. . . .

If Brennan's position would achieve "a large measure of clarity" in the context of consenting adults, it would do so at the cost of largely negating legislative authority to suppress obscene matter. And Brennan admits, at least for purposes of this opinion, that legislative action to achieve that end is constitutionally permissible. Thus, the upshot of Brennan's approach would be to deny legislative authority to control obscenity because of a lack of acceptable means to accomplish its purpose. Is this justified? Should the vagueness doctrine be invoked where there is no reasonable prospect of greater precision? Is the majority position in *Miller* defensible on this basis? Recall the discussion of questions of degree in *Nash* v. *United States*. Does Justice Brennan's analysis suggest that *Nash* was wrong? Or is obscenity importantly different?

**5.   Pornography as a Violation of Women's Rights.** In the years after *Miller*, the attack on pornography took a new direction. Traditionalists concerned to defend standards of decency were joined by feminists eager to combat the subordination of women. Most influential were Catharine MacKinnon and Andrea Dworkin, who drafted for the city of Minneapolis an ordinance punishing pornography (whether or not legally obscene) as "a form of discrimination on the basis of sex."[a] The Minneapolis proposal was vetoed by the mayor, but a modified version was enacted in Indianapolis. It defined pornography as "the graphic sexually explicit subordination of women" involving one or more of the following:

(1) Women are presented as sexual objects who enjoy pain or humiliation; or

(2) Women are presented as sexual objects who experience sexual pleasure in being raped; or

[a] See Catharine MacKinnon, Not a Moral Issue, 2 Yale L. & Policy Rev. 321 (1984); Catharine MacKinnon, Pornography, Civil Rights, and Speech, 20 Harv. C.R.-C.L.L. Rev. 1 (1985); Andrea Dworkin, Pornography: Men Possessing Women (1981). The proposed Minneapolis ordinance is reprinted in 2 Const. Com. 181–89 (1985), and in 11 Wm. Mitch. L. Rev. 119–25 (1985). Prominent among the flood of commentary provoked by this approach are David Bryden, Between Two Constitutions: Feminism and Pornography, 2 Const. Com. 147 (1985); Nadine Strossen, A Feminist Critique of "The" Feminist Critique of Pornography, 79 Va. L. Rev. 1099 (1993); and Cass R. Sunstein, Pornography and the First Amendment, 1986 Duke L.J. 589. The political background and context of the Minneapolis experience are recounted in Paul Brest and Ann Vandenberg, Politics, Feminism, and the Constitution: The Anti–Pornography Movement in Minneapolis, 39 Stan. L. Rev. 607 (1987).

(3) Women are presented as sexual objects tied up or cut up or mutilated or bruised or physically hurt, or as dismembered or truncated or fragmented or severed into body parts; or

(4) Women are presented as being penetrated by objects or animals; or

(5) Women are presented in scenarios of degradation, injury, abasement, torture, shown as filthy or inferior, bleeding, bruised, or hurt in a context that makes these conditions sexual; or

(6) Women are presented as sexual objects for domination, conquest, violation, exploitation, possession, or use, or through postures or positions of servility or submission or display.

This law was struck down in American Booksellers Ass'n, Inc. v. Hudnut, 771 F.2d 323 (7th Cir. 1985), on the ground that it violated the First Amendment by attempting "to ordain preferred viewpoints."[b] Suppose that problem were overcome. Suppose that combating the subordination of women were found to be a sufficiently compelling interest to justify restricting free speech. Could the Indianapolis statute, or some parts of it, survive a vagueness challenge? Are the key terms appreciably less definite than those used in *Miller*? Is it possible to frame any law against obscenity or pornography that is not significantly vague? If not, must all such publications be permitted?

## SECTION 3: OMISSIONS

## Billingslea v. State

Court of Criminal Appeals of Texas, 1989.
780 S.W.2d 271.

■ DUNCAN, JUDGE.

Appellant was charged with the offense of injury to an elderly individual pursuant to V.T.C.A. Penal Code, § 22.04(a)(1). A jury found the appellant guilty as charged and assessed his punishment at 99 years in the Texas Department of Corrections. The appellant's conviction was subsequently reversed and his acquittal ordered. We affirm the judgment of the court of appeals.

---

[b] "Under the ordinance graphic sexually explicit speech is 'pornography' or not depending on the perspective the author adopts. Speech that 'subordinates' women and also, for example, presents women as enjoying pain, humiliation, or rape, or even simply presents women in 'positions of servility or submission or display' is forbidden, no matter how great the literary or political value of the work taken as a whole. Speech that portrays women in positions of equality is lawful, no matter how graphic the sexual content. This is thought control. It establishes an 'approved' view of women, of how they may react to sexual encounters, of how the sexes may relate to each other. Those who espouse the approved view may use sexual images; those who do not, may not." 771 F.2d, at 328.

The State's petition for discretionary review was granted to consider the following grounds: First, whether the court of appeals erred in holding that the indictment charging the appellant was defective because it did not allege a statutory duty to act; and, second, whether the court of appeals erred in finding the evidence insufficient to support appellant's conviction because he had no statutory duty to act.

We note at the outset that the Legislature recently amended the statute under which the appellant was charged and initially convicted. The amended version . . . is set forth fully in [the appendix to this opinion]. We are compelled, however, to review this case in light of the statute as it existed at the time of this offense.

I.

Since the State assails the court of appeals' ruling on the sufficiency of the evidence, a brief review of the facts is in order. Appellant, his wife, and son lived with Hazel Billingslea (also referred to as the decedent), appellant's 94–year-old mother, in a small two-story frame house in Dallas. Hazel Billingslea's home had been her son's residence since approximately 1964. Appellant's only sibling was his sister, Katherine Jefferson, a resident of New Mexico. Virginia Billingslea (the decedent's granddaughter), Katherine Jefferson's daughter, lived approximately 15 blocks from her grandmother's Dallas' home. Virginia Billingslea was raised by Hazel Billingslea and had a close relationship with her. Accordingly, she kept in regular contact by telephone and by occasional visits to her grandmother's house.

Unspecified frailties of old age affecting the elder Mrs. Billingslea forced her to become bedridden in March, 1984. Granddaughter Virginia, unaware of her grandmother's condition, made several attempts to visit her during the ensuing weeks. On each occasion her uncle (appellant) "testily" informed her that her grandmother was "asleep." Undaunted, Virginia attempted to reach her grandmother by telephone, only to be threatened by her uncle on at least two occasions to "keep [her] goddamned motherfucking ass out of him and his mother's business or he would kill [her]."

After all attempts to visit her grandmother failed, Virginia contacted her mother (appellant's sister), Katherine Jefferson, in New Mexico. Mrs. Jefferson in turn contacted the Dallas Social Security Office and requested a formal inquiry into her mother's welfare.

Velma Mosley with the Adult Protective Services section of the Texas Department of Human Resources testified that she received a report from the Social Security Office on April 20, 1984, requesting that she check on the elder Mrs. Billingslea. A few days later, Ms. Mosley, accompanied by two Dallas police officers and a police social service employee, proceeded to Mrs. Billingslea's house.

They came upon the appellant in the front yard. After some discussion, he reluctantly allowed them to enter the premises. Upon entering, they were assailed by the strong, offensive odor of rotting flesh permeating the household. While one of the police officers remained downstairs with the appellant, who wanted to know "what these motherfuckers were doing in his house," the social worker and police officer made their way upstairs. Upon entering the bedroom, they found Hazel Billingslea lying in bed, moaning and asking for help. Ms. Mosley testified that the stench was so overwhelming that she was forced to cover her face. Ms. Mosley pulled back the sheets to examine Mrs. Billingslea. Nude from the waist down, Mrs. Billingslea appeared weak and in a great deal of pain.

Ms. Mosley discovered that part of Mrs. Billingslea's heel was eaten away by a large decubitus (bedsore). Other decubiti on her hip and back appeared to have eaten through to the bone. When Ms. Mosley attempted to raise Mrs. Billingslea from the bed to continue her physical examination, "she moaned so much till I didn't look any further." Mrs. Billingslea was immediately transported to Parkland Hospital in Dallas.

Dr. Frase, at that time Chief Medical Resident at Parkland Hospital, examined Mrs. Billingslea. He testified that she was severely cachectic, i.e., that she had suffered severe muscle loss. Her mental state was one of near-total disorientation, and she had apparently been unable to feed herself for some time. In addition to the decubiti, second degree burns and blisters were found on her inner thighs, caused by lying in pools of her own urine. Maggots were festering in her open bedsores.

Dr. Frase testified that weeping bedsores as severe as those he found on Hazel Billingslea would have taken anywhere from four to six weeks to develop. He further testified that until her death Mrs. Billingslea required large dosages of narcotics to relieve her pain. In his opinion, the bedsores, burns, blisters, and loss of muscle resulted in serious bodily injury indicative of overall neglect of Mrs. Billingslea in the months prior to her death.

II.

The question of whether criminal liability may be imposed for omissions against elderly individuals is one of first impression in Texas.

The defendant was charged under V.T.C.A. Penal Code, § 22.04. Until September 1, 1981, § 22.04 covered only offenses against children 14 years of age or younger. That year, the Legislature added "elderly individuals 65 years of age or older" to the definition of those protected by § 22.04:

Injury to a Child or Elderly Individual.

(a) A person commits an offense if he intentionally, knowingly, recklessly, or with criminal negligence, by act or omission, engages in conduct that causes to a child who is 14 years of age or younger or to an individual who is 65 years of age or older:

   (1) serious bodily injury;

   (2) serious physical or mental deficiency or impairment;

   (3) disfigurement or deformity; or

   (4) bodily injury.

Deleting the formal requisites, the indictment is as follows:

[That the defendant did] then and there intentionally and knowingly engage in conduct that caused serious bodily injury to

Hazel Billingslea, an individual over 65 years of age, said conduct being by the following act and omission, to wit: the said defendant failed to obtain medical care for Hazel Billingslea, the natural mother of the said defendant, who lived in the same house as the defendant, and the said Hazel Billingslea was at said time physically unable to secure medical care for herself.[2]

In its petition, the State contends that a duty to act need not be embodied in a statute for § 22.04 to apply. Instead, the State argues that the duty to act in behalf of an elderly person may be derived from legal or common law duties as would arise from the factual, not necessarily familial, relationship of the parties. Limiting § 22.04 to explicit statutory duties, according to the State, "would vitiate the intent of the statute." Relative to the present case, the State contends that the appellant owed a duty of care to the decedent because he voluntarily assumed primary responsibility for caring for his mother who was unable to care for herself and, by assuming that responsibility, prevented others from coming to her aid. According to the State, the indictment is legally sufficient because it alleges facts giving rise to appellant's duty and failure to act pursuant to that duty. Consequently, the State argues that the court of appeals erred in holding that the indictment was fundamentally defective.

While we agree with the State that the 1981 amendments to § 22.04 reflect the Legislature's intention to penalize omissions toward elderly persons, the indictment is nevertheless fundamentally defective for failing to include a statutory duty imposing a punishable omission.

An "omission" is defined in the Penal Code as a failure to act. V.T.C.A. Penal Code, § 1.07(a)(23). The Penal Code's foundation for criminal omissions may be found in § 6.01, which states that a person commits an offense if he "voluntarily engages in conduct, including an act, omission, or possession." Subsection (c) provides that "a person who omits to perform an act does not commit an offense unless a statute provides that the omission is an offense or otherwise provides that he has a duty to perform the act." Stated another way, (1) a statute must provide that an omission is an offense, or (2) a statute otherwise prescribes a duty to act, and a subsequent failure to act pursuant to that duty is an offense. Since § 6.01(c) is stated in the disjunctive, it appears to provide alternative grounds for finding a criminally punishable omission. In reality, however, only the second clause is substantive.

The first ground is obscure because it purports to allow a penal statute to make an omission an offense merely by stating that "an omission is an offense." This simply begs the question of what constitutes an omission. Logic dictates that in order for there to be an omission, there must be a corresponding duty to act. As one commentator noted, "giving legal effect

---

[2] Although the indictment was couched in terms of an "act or omission" on the part of the defendant, the offensive conduct was recited as omission: "The defendant failed to obtain medical care [for the decedent]." While § 22.04 unquestionably imposes criminal liability for acts committed against elderly individuals, the allegation that a punishable "act" occurred is absent from this indictment.

to [the first] portion of § 6.01(c) would abolish the requirement of a legal duty altogether."

The Practice Commentary to V.T.C.A. Penal Code, § 6.01(c), offers the following interpretation of the first clause of Subsection (c): "many offenses proscribe omissions to act, and when they do the first branch of the rule permits the imposition of criminal responsibility for the omission. Examples of such offenses include Sections 25.03 (interference with child custody), 25.05 (criminal nonsupport), [and] 38.08 (permitting or facilitating escape)."

Notably, each of these provisions provides the duty to act and the omission within the parameters of the specific penal proscription. For example, § 38.08, Permitting or Facilitating Escape, provides that "an official or an employee that is responsible for maintaining persons in custody commits an offense if he intentionally, knowingly, or recklessly permits or facilitates the escape of a person in custody." Similarly, § 25.05, Criminal Nonsupport, provides that "an individual commits an offense if he intentionally or knowingly fails to provide support for his child younger than 18 years of age or for his child who is the subject of a court order requiring the individual to support the child." Thus, each omission is predicated upon a duty to act; both elements of which are found within the same statute.

In neglect cases, the focus has been upon the second ground, which must be read in conjunction with a corresponding statute specifying a duty to act. Since no provisions of the Penal Code at the time of this offense included a duty to provide care for another person, the duties were typically derived from other statutes outside of the Penal Code. The Practice Commentary offers the following illustration:

> If the offense itself does not penalize an omission, "there must be a violation of some duty [to perform the omitted act] imposed by law, directly or impliedly, and with which duty the defendant is especially charged...." The second branch codifies the common law rule, but narrows it to encompass only duties imposed by statute.... [A] niece's failure to feed her invalid aunt, who starves to death as a result, is not guilty of criminal homicide because the niece has no statutory duty of support. Contractual duties, or those arising from a special relationship, or fact situation, are thus excluded and will not support the imposition of criminal responsibility.

Analogous to the offense of injury to an elderly person, child abuse and neglect cases demonstrate how the second branch of § 6.01(c) has been applied. For example, in Ronk v. State, 544 S.W.2d 123 (Tex.Cr.App. 1976), this Court held that an indictment charging injury to a child was fundamentally defective because it failed to allege a necessary element to the offense, i.e., it failed to allege a relationship between the defendants and child which would have placed the defendants under a statutory duty to secure medical treatment for the child. The corresponding duty to act was found in V.T.C.A. Family Code, § 12.04(3), which imposes a duty on parents "to support the child, including providing the child with clothing, food, shelter, medical care, and education;..."

Similarly, in Smith v. State, 603 S.W.2d 846 (Tex.Cr.App. 1980), the mother and the stepfather were charged under § 22.04 with burning, striking, and denying adequate food and medical care to a young boy. This Court agreed that the allegation "by then and there denying the said Michael Franks of food and nourishment and adequate medical attention" should be construed as alleging omissions, but held the "omissions" portion of the indictment defective in that it failed to allege a statutory duty to act pursuant to the Family Code. As to the allegations of conduct of burning and striking the child, however, the indictment was sufficient because they constituted acts, not omissions. Criminal responsibility for acts does not require an underlying duty of any kind. The Court noted that "parents and non-parents alike may commit the offense of injury to a child by such acts as striking and burning."

And, in Lang v. State, 586 S.W.2d 532 (Tex.Cr.App. 1979), we reversed the defendant's conviction based upon a fundamentally defective indictment because it failed to state, pursuant to § 22.04, that the victim was a child 14 years or younger. The appellant's conviction was overturned on this basis in spite of the defendant's guilty plea and judicial confession. Although §§ 12.04 and 4.02 of the Family Code require parents to care for their minor children, Penal Code § 22.04 limits that duty to children 14 years old or younger.

While the above cases seem to have allowed reprehensible conduct to go unpunished on the basis of a defective indictment, it is indisputable that those accused of an offense are entitled to sufficient notice of the charges against them. While other States may imply duties or derive them from the common law,[5] under the laws of this State notice of an offense must invariably rest on a specific statute. This notion is firmly rooted in the evolution of Texas criminal jurisprudence. Since the days of the Republic and early statehood, Texas courts have been prohibited from allowing common law duties to form the basis of criminal sanctions. That longstanding prohibition is specifically embodied in our Penal Code, which provides that "conduct does not constitute an offense unless it is defined as an offense by statute, municipal ordinance, order of a county commissioners court, or rule authorized by and lawfully adopted under a statute." V.T.C.A. Penal Code, § 1.03(a).

Moreover, penal provisions which criminalize a failure to act without informing those subject to prosecution that they must perform a duty to avoid punishment are unconstitutionally vague.[6] Where an indictment in

---

[5] [For example], in State v. Mason, 18 N.C.App. 433, 197 S.E.2d 79 (1973), the North Carolina Court of Appeals upheld the manslaughter conviction of parents charged with failing to provide proper care for their child, basing their decision on the ground that the defendants omitted to perform a legal duty owed their child based on a common law relationship.

[6] See, e.g., Kolender v. Lawson, 461 U.S. 352 (1983) (California statute requiring loiterers to carry "credible and reliable" identification or be subject to penalty unconstitu-

Texas fails to allege the deceased child's age, or fails to allege a parent-child relationship, thereby invoking a concomitant statutory duty to act in behalf of the child, a conviction based on that indictment is void. Similarly, although the indictment herein alleged sufficient facts to imply both a duty to act and an omission under the common law, the indictment is fundamentally defective in the absence of an allegation reciting a concomitant statutory duty to care for an elderly person. Accordingly, the indictment could not have alleged a statutory duty for the appellant to act in behalf of his ailing parent because no such duty existed.

As one commentator noted:

> If no one is under a statutory duty to act toward an elderly person, then how can a court choose to prosecute B for the death of A instead of prosecuting X, a neighbor, or Y, A's sister, or Z, the Governor? In a jurisdiction like Texas which does not allow common law duties to form the basis for criminal actions, the duty to care for A must therefore rest either on all persons alive at her death or on no one, since the duty has not been statutorily assigned to any particular person.

While children may have a moral duty to care for their elderly parents, moral imperatives are not the functional equivalent of legal duties. Since we do not recognize legal duties derived from the common law and since no one was assigned a statutory duty to care for an elderly person, the version of § 22.04 relative to omissions toward elderly individuals under which the appellant was indicted is unenforceable. Consequently, the indictment charging the appellant with "failure to obtain medical care" for his mother is fundamentally defective. The State's first ground for review is overruled.

III.

The State's second ground for review contends that the court of appeals erred in holding the evidence insufficient to support the appellant's conviction. In light of the foregoing discussion, it is axiomatic that the State failed to establish an essential element of the offense, namely, the duty to act, because no such duty existed. Accordingly, the State's second ground for review is overruled.

IV.

Fortuitously, the Legislature identified the problematical application of § 22.04 as applied to omissions toward elderly persons and recently amended the statute. [See appendix.] If anything, the amendments to § 22.04 clearly suggest that the Legislature perceived the paradoxical futility of applying the former law: there could never be a failure to perform that which no one had a statutory duty to perform in the first place. The recent action taken by the Legislature in amending the statute to correct the

tionally vague for failure to clarify meaning of "credible and reliable"); Lambert v. California, 355 U.S. 225 (1957) (Los Angeles city ordinance requiring those convicted of felony to register with the city held unconstitutionally vague; due process allowed defendant to plead ignorance of the law as a defense where "circumstances which might move one to inquire as to the necessity of [taking affirmative action] are completely lacking.").

previous statute's defect further underscores our conclusion that the version of § 22.04 under which the appellant was convicted was unenforceable. Nevertheless, we must adhere to the law as it existed at the time of the offense. Accordingly, we affirm the judgment of the court of appeals.

APPENDIX

V.T.C.A. Penal Code, § 22.04, as amended May 29, 1989, S.B. 1154, effective Sept. 1, 1989, is as follows:

Section 22.04. Injury to a Child, Elderly Individual, or Invalid.

(a) A person commits an offense if he intentionally, knowingly, recklessly, or with criminal negligence, by act or intentionally, knowingly, or recklessly by omission, engages in conduct that causes to a child, elderly individual, or invalid individual:

(1) serious bodily injury;

(2) serious physical or mental deficiency or impairment;

(3) disfigurement or deformity; or

(4) bodily injury.

(b) An omission that causes a condition described by Subsections (a)(1) through (a)(4) of this section is conduct constituting an offense under this section if:

(1) the actor has a legal or statutory duty to act; or

(2) the actor has assumed care, custody or control of a child, elderly individual, or invalid individual.

(c) In this section:

(1) "Child" means a person 14 years of age or younger;

(2) "Elderly individual" means a person 65 years of age or older;

(3) "Invalid individual" means a person older than 14 years of age who by reason of age or physical or mental disease, defect, or injury is substantially unable to protect himself from harm or to provide food, shelter, or medical care for himself.

(d) The actor has assumed care, custody, or control if he has by act, words, or course of conduct acted so as to cause a reasonable person to conclude that he has accepted responsibility for protection, food, shelter, and medical care for a child, elderly individual, or invalid individual. . . .

(i) It is an affirmative defense to the prosecution under Subsection (b)(2) of this section that before the offense the actor:

(1) notified in person the child, elderly individual, or invalid individual that he would no longer provide any of the care described by Subsection (d) of this section; and

(2) notified in writing the parents or person other than himself acting in loco parentis to the child, elderly individual, or invalid individual that he would no longer provide any of the care described by Subsection (d) of this section; or

(3) notified in writing the Texas Department of Human Services that he would no longer provide any of the care set forth in Subsection (d) of this section. . . .

(k)(1) It is a defense to prosecution under this section that the conduct engaged in by act or omission consisted of:

(A) reasonable medical care occurring under the direction of or by a licensed physician; or

(B) emergency medical care administered in good faith and with reasonable care by a person not licensed in the healing arts.

(2) It is an affirmative defense to prosecution under this section that the act or omission was based on treatment in accordance with the tenets and practices of a recognized religious method of healing with a generally accepted record of efficacy.

---

## NOTES ON OMISSIONS

**1. The Necessity of a Duty to Act**. *Billingslea* starkly illustrates the distinction between the law's treatment of "acts," on the one hand, and "omissions" or "failures to act," on the other. As the court remarked when discussing the *Smith* case, a prosecution based on acts, such as "striking and burning," does not require proof of "an underlying duty of any kind." By contrast, a prosecution based on an omission may proceed only where the accused had a duty to perform the omitted act. Moreover, a moral obligation to perform the act will not do; in the words of *Billingslea*, "moral imperatives are not the functional equivalent of legal duties." In the absence of a legal duty to act, the accused may not be held criminally liable no matter how morally reprehensible the failure to act or how serious the consequences of such failure.

Of course, many criminal statutes expressly punish failures to act. In addition to the examples of such statutes mentioned in *Billingslea*, there are other familiar examples, such as laws punishing failure to stop at a red light, failure to file a tax return, failure (by men) to register for the draft, etc. In such cases, the statute defining the crime creates the legal duty to act. The same may be said of the host of penal statutes proscribing some combination of act and omission—e.g., driving without a license. Enforcement of such offenses yields no special difficulty.

Problems arise where the offense in question does not expressly proscribe a particular omission or, for that matter, a particular act, but covers any conduct that causes a forbidden result. The classic example is homicide. Typically, criminal homicide statutes punish one who "causes death of another." A more elaborate formulation might provide that a person is guilty if he or she "does or omits to do anything that causes death of another." Despite the potential breadth of such statutory language, criminal liability for causing the forbidden result is importantly constrained by the rule that an omission suffices only when it breaches a legal duty to act. In other words, courts will interpret statutory language such as "omits to do anything" as if it stated "omits to do anything that the actor has a legal duty to do." Where the legal duty is not found on the face of the statute defining the offense, as is the case with homicide statutes, it must be found in some other source of law, either statutory or decisional, that specifies legal obligations among citizens.

Unlike Texas, most jurisdictions recognize that legal duties to act may be rooted in a contract or in a common-law source, as well as in a statute. The chief categories of legal duty are summarized in Jones v. United States, 308 F.2d 307 (D.C. Cir. 1962). They include:

— duties based on statute, such as the common provision that a driver involved in an automobile accident must stop and render assistance to injured persons;

— duties based on relationship, such as that between a parent and a minor child;

— duties based on contract, such as the employment responsibilities of a lifeguard; and

— duties based on voluntary assumption of responsibility that effectively precludes aid from others, such as the person who takes a foundling home and thus secretes it from the agencies of public assistance.

In some circumstances, legal duties may also be based on control over the conduct of another, as in the obligation of an employer to oversee employees, and sometimes on the existence of a peril for which the actor was in some way responsible. Finally, a landowner or businessman may be found to have a legal duty to provide for the safety of persons invited onto the property. A survey of recognized legal duties may be found in Paul H. Robinson, Criminal Liability for Omissions: A Brief Summary and Critique of the Law in the United States, 29 N.Y.L.S.L.Rev. 101 (1984).

**2. Questions and Comments on *Billingslea*.** As *Billingslea* explains, Texas criminal jurisprudence authorizes liability for omissions only in cases where a statute explicitly imposes a duty to perform the omitted act. On what grounds does the court justify this apparently grudging approach to omissions liability? By its verdict, the jury found that Billingslea's neglect had caused his mother to suffer serious bodily injury. And, as the court acknowledged, the Texas legislature intended to penalize omissions committed against elderly persons. Nonetheless, the court throws out Billingslea's conviction. Does the court identify compelling reasons for doing so?

Notice too that everyone agrees that, if Billingslea had caused his mother's "second-degree burns" by "acts of burning," rather than by neglect, his conviction would have been upheld. Is it true that Billingslea committed no "acts" at all that contributed to his mother's injuries? Was the prosecution compelled to pursue this case only on the basis of culpable omissions, or might the state have alleged that Billingslea engaged in culpable actions as well?

Consider the amended version of the "elder abuse" statute set forth in the *Billingslea* appendix. If that statute has been in effect at the time of Billingslea's failure to care for his mother, could the state have successfully prosecuted him? Is there any other actor in the case who might have been held liable thereunder?

**3.  Failure to Provide Sustenance.** Many omission cases involve failure to provide sustenance to a person who dies of starvation and neglect. Consider two examples, neither of which would appear to provide the basis for a conviction under *Billingslea*:

(i) ***Regina v. Instan.*** A famous case is Regina v. Instan, [1893] Cox C.C. 602. The defendant lived with, and was supported by, her aunt. Some 10 days before her death, the aunt contracted gangrene. The defendant continued to live in the aunt's house and to take in food supplied by tradespeople, but she neither procured medical attention nor notified anyone of the aunt's condition. The aunt died of gangrene and neglect, and defendant was found guilty of manslaughter. The court upheld the conviction:

> It is not correct to say that every moral obligation is a legal duty, but every legal duty is founded upon a moral obligation. In this case, as in most cases, the legal duty can be nothing else than taking upon oneself the performance of the moral obligation. There is no question whatever that it was this woman's clear duty to impart to the deceased so much of that food which was taken into the house and paid for by the deceased as was necessary to sustain her life.

Is *Instan* correct? Does it matter that the defendant was supported by the deceased? Would the case have been different if the defendant had had her own income? Would liability have attached merely because the defendant was the only person who knew of the aunt's condition? If so, would the same rule apply to a neighbor who happened to discover the situation but did nothing to help?

(ii) ***Jones v. United States.*** The defendant was entrusted with the care of two children, Robert Lee Green and Anthony Lee Green. Initially, the mother agreed to pay for the care of the elder child, but the payments stopped after a few months. It was disputed whether any such arrangement was made for the younger child.

Collectors for the local gas company discovered the two children in the defendant's basement. Three days later the police removed the children to the hospital, where Anthony Lee was found to be suffering from malnutrition and lesions caused by diaper rash. He was fed repeatedly but died of malnutrition less than 34 hours after being admitted to the hospital. At birth, he had weighed six pounds, 15 ounces. At his death, 10 months later, he weighed seven pounds, 13 ounces. Normal weight would have been approximately double that figure.

A jury found the defendant guilty of involuntary manslaughter, but the appeals court reversed. Jones v. United States, 308 F.2d 307 (D.C. Cir. 1962). The trial court had erred by failing to require the jury to find that defendant had a legal duty to care for Anthony Lee. The appeals court found that the failure to on the necessity of a legal duty left critical factual issues unresolved—specifically, "whether appellant had entered into a contract with the mother for the care of Anthony Lee or, alternatively, whether she assumed the care of the child and secluded him from the care of his mother, his natural protector." The evidence might have been sufficient to support a finding of legal duty on these grounds, but since no such finding had been made, the conviction was reversed.

**4. Failure to Summon Medical Assistance for Drug Overdose.** What duties do people owe to companions who need emergency medical care for a drug or alcohol overdose? To say the least, these cases raise difficult ethical and practical dilemmas for the people involved in them. What role should the criminal law play in creating incentives for behavior in this context or in providing the occasion for the expression of community condemnation? Over the years, courts have struggled with these questions, and they will continue to do so. Consider the following cases:

**(i) *People v. Beardsley.*** A famous old chestnut is People v. Beardsley, 150 Mich. 206, 113 N.W. 1128 (1907). Defendant arranged with one Blanche Burns to spend the weekend in his rooms. They drank more or less steadily for two days. Additionally, without his consent and, indeed, over his objections, she obtained and took some morphine. When defendant began to expect the return of his wife, he arranged for Blanche to be moved to the room of a friend, whom he asked to look after her and to let her out the back way when she awoke. Some hours later she died.

Defendant was convicted of manslaughter for failure to render reasonable care, but the Supreme Court of Michigan reversed:

> It is urged by the prosecutor that the [defendant] "stood towards this woman for the time being in the place of her natural guardian and protector, and as such owed her a clear legal duty which he completely failed to perform." The cases cited and digested establish that no such legal duty is created based upon a mere moral obligation. The fact that this woman was in his house created no such legal duty as exists in law and is due from a husband towards his wife, as seems to be intimated by the prosecutor's brief. Such an inference would be very repugnant to our moral sense.... Had this been a case where two men under like circumstances had voluntarily gone on a debauch together, and one had attempted suicide, no one would claim that this doctrine of legal duty could be invoked to hold the other criminally respon-

sible for omitting to make effort to rescue his companion. How can the fact that in this case one of the parties was a woman change the principle of law applicable to it?

Around the middle of the last century, one commentator condemned *Beardsley* as a "savage proclamation that the wages of sin is death." Graham Hughes, Criminal Omissions, 67 Yale L.J. 590, 624 (1958). Do you agree? Is it, as Hughes continued, reflective of a morality which is "smug, ignorant, and vindictive," or is there some other justification for the result?

The quoted passage from *Beardsley* implies that, unlike mere social acquaintances or friends, husbands and wives owe each other duties of care, whose omission may provide the basis for criminal liability. Yet, litigation over the appropriate scope of any such spousal duties can raise questions of considerable difficulty. It might seem obvious, as the passage from *Beardsley* suggests, that spouses are legally obliged to rescue each other in medical emergencies. But what if one spouse wants to use drugs or drink excessively? Must the other, on pain of criminal punishment, intervene? If so, under what precise circumstances and to what extent? Complicated questions also arise when a spouse decides to forgo medical treatment for a serious health condition or elects one course of treatment rather than another. Does the other spouse have the obligation to question and, possibly, to override that decision? If such an obligation exists, when is it triggered, and how is it satisfied? Some of these questions have been litigated in homicide prosecutions of spouses whose partners have died after choosing to rely on prayer, rather than medicine, to treat their illnesses. See People v. Robbins, 443 N.Y.S.2d 1016 (App. Div. 1981); Commonwealth v. Konz, 265 Pa.Super. 570, 402 A.2d 692 (1979), rev'd, 498 Pa. 639, 450 A.2d 638 (1982).

**(ii) *People v. Oliver.*** A modern variation on *Beardsley* arose in People v. Oliver, 210 Cal.App.3d 138, 258 Cal.Rptr. 138 (1989). The defendant returned to her apartment with Carlos Cornejo, whom she had met in a bar. Although already extremely drunk, Cornejo asked for a spoon, which the defendant provided. She then remained in the living room while he "shot up" in the bathroom. Afterward, he collapsed, and she returned to the bar. Later, the defendant's daughter and a friend returned home to find the unconscious Cornejo. On defendant's instructions, they dragged him outside "in case he woke up and became violent" and put him behind a shed so that the neighbors would not see. By the next morning, he had died of heroin overdose.

Defendant moved to dismiss an indictment for involuntary manslaughter on the ground that she owed no legal duty to the deceased, but the court disagreed:

> At the time [defendant] left the bar with Cornejo, she observed that he was extremely drunk, and drove him to her home. In so doing, she took him from a public place where others might have taken care to prevent him from injuring himself, to a private place—her home—where she alone could provide such care. To a certain, if limited, extent, therefore, she took charge of a person

unable to prevent harm to himself. She then allowed Cornejo to use her bathroom, without any objection on her part, to inject himself with narcotics, an act involving the definite potential for fatal consequences. When Cornejo collapsed to the floor, [defendant] should have known that her conduct had contributed to creating an unreasonable risk of harm for Cornejo—death. At that point, she owed Cornejo a duty to prevent that risk from occurring by summoning aid. . . .

**5.  A General Duty to Rescue?** An underlying issue in all these cases is whether there should be a general duty to rescue. Rather than focusing on particular legal duties based on contract or status, why should not the law simply recognize that each of us has a duty to give reasonable assistance to a person in peril?

Consider, for example, the facts of *Jones*. Why should it be necessary to prove that the defendant had contracted with the boy's mother for maintenance or that she had acted to seclude him from his mother's protection? Why isn't it enough that the defendant, at no special cost or danger to herself, could have saved the life of a child and that she chose not to do so?

A defense of the traditional view against a general duty to rescue was attempted by Lord Macaulay. In his notes on a proposed Indian penal code, Macaulay undertook to assess the extent to which omissions productive of evil consequences should be punished on the same footing as affirmative misconduct leading to those results. After rejecting the categorical alternatives of "always" and "never," Macaulay explained the drafters' choice of a "middle course":

> What we propose is this: that where acts are made punishable on the ground that they have caused, or have been intended to cause, or have been known to be likely to cause, a certain evil effect, omissions which have caused, which have been intended to cause, or which have been known to be likely to cause the same effect, shall be punishable in the same manner, provided that such omissions were, on other grounds, illegal. An omission is illegal if it be an offense, if it be a breach of some direction of law, or if it be such a wrong as would be a good ground for a civil action.
>
> We cannot defend this rule better than by giving a few illustrations of the way in which it will operate. *A* omits to give *Z* food, and by that omission voluntarily causes *Z*'s death. Is this murder? Under our rule it is murder if *A* was *Z*'s jailer, directed by the law to furnish *Z* with food. It is murder if *Z* was the infant child of *A*, and had, therefore, a legal right to sustenance, which right a civil court would enforce against *A*. It is murder if *Z* was a bedridden invalid, and *A* a nurse hired to feed *Z*. . . . It is not murder if *Z* is a beggar, who has no other claim on *A* than that of humanity. . . .
>
> We are sensible that in some of the cases which we have put, our rule may appear too lenient; but we do not think that it can be

made more severe without disturbing the whole order of society. It is true that the man who, having abundance of wealth, suffers a fellow-creature to die of hunger at his feet is a bad man—a worse man, probably, than many of those for whom we have provided very severe punishment. But we are unable to see where, if we make such a man legally punishable, we can draw the line. If the rich man who refuses to save a beggar's life at the cost of a little copper is a murderer, is the poor man just one degree above beggary also to be a murderer if he omits to invite the beggar to partake his hard-earned rice? Again, if the rich man is a murderer for refusing to save the beggar's life at the cost of a little copper, is he also to be a murderer if he refuses to save the beggar's life at the cost of a thousand rupees? . . . The distinction between a legal and an illegal omission is perfectly plain and intelligible; but the distinction between a large and a small sum of money is very far from being so, not to say that a sum which is small to one man is large to another. . . .

It is, indeed, most highly desirable that men should not merely abstain from doing harm to their neighbors, but should render active services to their neighbors. In general, however, the penal law must content itself with keeping men from doing positive harm, and must leave to public opinion, and to the teachers of morality and religion, the office of furnishing men with motives for doing positive good. . . .

Thomas Macaulay, Notes on the Indian Penal Code, in 4 Miscellaneous Works 251–56 (1880).

Is Macaulay's argument persuasive? Are the line-drawing problems so intractable as to preclude recognition of a general duty to rescue? Might this difficulty be alleviated by drawing the line very far to one side—as, for example, in a rule imposing a duty to rescue only where there is no appreciable risk or expense to the actor? For trenchant criticism of the traditional view, see Daniel B. Yeager, A Radical Community of Aid: A Rejoinder to Opponents of Affirmative Duties to Help Strangers, 71 Wash. U.L.Q. 1 (1993). See also A.D. Woozley, A Duty to Rescue: Some Thoughts on Criminal Liability, 69 Va. L. Rev. 1273 (1983).

For the most sophisticated and sustained philosophic analysis of the significance of action or omission in the criminal law, see Michael S. Moore, Act and Crime (1993). Moore's views have been subject to equally sophisticated and multi-faceted criticism in a symposium devoted to his book. See 142 U. Penn. L. Rev. 1443 (1994).

———

## NOTES ON THE OMISSION OF LIFE–SUSTAINING TREATMENT

**1. *Barber v. Superior Court*.** Barber v. Superior Court of Los Angeles County, 147 Cal.App.3d 1006, 195 Cal.Rptr. 484 (1983), is a very rare reported prosecution of medical personnel for conduct that occurs with some frequency, namely, the removal of a deeply comatose patient from life-sustaining equipment. In *Barber*, a patient went into cardio-respiratory arrest after undergoing routine surgery. The medical staff revived him and placed him on life-support equipment. Within several days, medical specialists concluded that he had suffered severe brain damage and that his vegetative state was likely to be permanent. Following consultation with the patient's family, the doctors removed him from all life-support equipment, including a respirator and the intravenous tubes that had provided hydration and nourishment. After the patient died, the doctors were prosecuted for murder and conspiracy to commit murder. The California Court of Appeals relied on the distinction between omission and act in throwing out the criminal complaint:

> As a predicate to our analysis of whether the petitioners' conduct amounted to an "unlawful killing," we conclude that the cessation of "heroic" life support measures is not an affirmative act but rather a withdrawal or omission of further treatment.

> Even though these life support devices are, to a degree, "self-propelled," each pulsation of the respirator or each drop of fluid introduced into the patient's body by intravenous feeding devices is comparable to a manually administered injection or item of medication. Hence "disconnecting" of the mechanical devices is comparable to withholding the manually administered injection or medication. . . .

> In the final analysis, since we view petitioners' conduct as that of omission rather than affirmative action, the resolution of this case turns on whether petitioners had a duty to continue to provide life sustaining treatment.

> There is no criminal liability for failure to act unless there is a legal duty to act. Thus the critical issue becomes one of determining the duties owed by a physician to a patient who has been reliably diagnosed as in a comatose state from which any meaningful recovery of cognitive brain function is exceedingly unlikely. . . .

> A physician has no duty to continue treatment, once it has proved to be ineffective. Although there may be a duty to provide life-sustaining machinery in the *immediate* aftermath of a cardio-respiratory arrest, there is no duty to continue its use once it has become futile in the opinion of qualified medical personnel. . . .

As for the question of "who should make these vital decisions," the court concluded that, "whenever possible, the patient himself should . . . be the ultimate decision-maker." In cases where patients are incapable of deciding for themselves, family members ordinarily should be authorized to make the decision for them.

*Barber* accords with prevailing medical practice, both in upholding the acceptability of terminating life-sustaining treatment and in grounding that result in a distinction between act and omission.[a] But does the distinction make sense? If the physician and/or the patient's family are competent to decide when the duty to treat has ended, why are they not equally competent to decide whether there should be an affirmative action to end the patient's suffering? Do the considerations at stake really depend on the distinction between act and omission?

**2.  Report of the President's Commission.** In connection with the above questions, consider the views of the President's Commission for the Study of Ethical Problems in Medicine and Biomedical and Behavioral Research. The significance of the act/omission distinction was extensively discussed in a report entitled "Deciding to Forego Life–Sustaining Treatment." The Commission began with the observation that a distinction between act and omission is widely followed by medical personnel dealing with the irreversibly ill:

> Physicians commonly acquiesce in the wishes of competent patients not to receive specified treatments, even when failure to provide those treatments will increase the chance—or make certain—that the patient will die soon. When some patients are dying of a disease process that cannot be arrested, physicians may, for example, write orders not to provide resuscitation if the heart should stop, forego antibiotic treatment of pneumonia and other infections, cease use of respirators, or withhold aggressive therapy from overwhelmingly burned patients. Courts have sanctioned such decisions by guardians for incompetent patients, as well as by competent patients who might have lived for an indefinite period if treated. Although declining to start or continue life-sustaining treatment is often acceptable, health care providers properly refuse to honor a patient's request to be directly killed. Not only would killing, as by violence or strychnine, be outside the bounds of accepted medical practice, but as murder it would be subject to a range of criminal sanctions, regardless of the provider's motives.

The Commission then undertook to identify the possible grounds for differentiating between acts and omissions:

> Usually, one or more of several factors make fatal actions worse than fatal omissions:
>
> (i) The motives of an agent who acts to cause death are usually worse (for example, self-interest or malice) than those of someone who omits to act and lets another die.
>
> (ii) A person who is barred from acting to cause another's death is usually thereby placed at no personal risk of harm;

---

[a] See, e.g., § 2.11 of the Opinions of the Judicial Council of the American Medical Association (1982), where it is stated: "For humane reasons, with informed consent a physician may do what is medically necessary to alleviate severe pain, or cease or omit treatment to let a terminally ill patient die, but he should not intentionally cause death." For a comprehensive but economical treatment of the "right to stop treatment" of incompetent patients, see John A. Robertson, The Rights of the Critically Ill 49–70 (1983).

whereas, especially outside the medical context, if a person were forced to intercede to save another's life (instead of standing by and omitting to act), he or she would often be put at substantial risk.

(iii) The nature and duration of future life denied to a person whose life is ended by another's act is usually much greater than that denied to a dying person whose death comes slightly more quickly due to an omission of treatment.

(iv) A person, especially a patient, may still have some possibility of surviving if one omits to act, while survival is more often foreclosed by actions that lead to death.

Each of these factors—or several in combination—can make a significant moral difference in the evaluation of any particular instance of acting and omitting to act. Together they help explain why most actions leading to death are correctly considered morally worse than most omissions leading to death.

The Commission recognized, however, that not all of these factors can plausibly be invoked in the medical context. Specifically, (I) health care professionals could be "equally merciful" in acting or omitting; (ii) medical personnel usually act at no personal risk to themselves and indeed have a "special role-related duty" to act on behalf of their patients; and (iii) they often face special situations concerning the "nature and duration of future life." "Only the final factor," therefore, "can apply as much in medical settings as elsewhere":

Indeed, this factor has particular relevance here since the element of uncertainty—whether a patient really will die if treatment is ceased—is sometimes unavoidable in the medical setting. A valid distinction may therefore arise between an act causing certain death (for example, a poisoning) and an omission that hastens or risks death (such as not amputating a gangrenous limb). But sometimes death is as certain following withdrawal of a treatment as following a particular action that is reliably expected to lead to death.

Consequently, merely determining whether what was done involved a fatal act or omission does not establish whether it was morally acceptable. Some actions that lead to death can be acceptable: very dangerous but potentially beneficial surgery or the use of hazardous doses of morphine for severe pain are examples. Some omissions that lead to death are very serious wrongs: deliberately failing to treat an ordinary patient's bacterial pneumonia or ignoring a bleeding patient's pleas for help would be totally unacceptable conduct for that patient's physician.

In view of this reasoning, one might have thought that the Commission would recommend abandoning the act/omission distinction. But that was not the case:

Although there are some cases in which the acting-omitting distinction is difficult to make and although its moral importance originates in other considerations, the commonly accepted prohibition of active killing helps to produce the correct decision in the great majority of cases. Furthermore, weakening the legal prohibition to allow a deliberate taking of life in extreme circumstances would risk allowing wholly unjustified taking of life in less extreme circumstances.... Thus, the Commission concludes that the current interpretation of the legal prohibition of active killing should be sustained.

Is this conclusion sound? Is it defensible on the ground stated? On any other ground?

**3.   Differentiating Acts From Omissions.** Even if one accepts that there is a difference in principle between acting and omitting to act in this context, there remains the difficulty of differentiating between them. The tendency in medical practice is to demark that difference with terms that are both descriptive and conclusory. Thus, unacceptable conduct leading to death of a patient is often identified as "killing," a word that connotes both the affirmative act and its unacceptability. Acceptable conduct, by contrast, is usually described as "allowing to die."

In some cases the distinction seems clear. If a terminally ill patient experiences spontaneous cardio-respiratory arrest, the physician who foregoes heroic attempts at resuscitation has, whatever the moral or legal import of this conclusion, omitted to act. Less clear is the termination of a treatment already underway. Is turning off the respirator an act or an omission? Many physicians, who are ready to *withhold* treatment in appropriate cases, are nevertheless reluctant to *withdraw* treatment once begun. The former conduct seems an acceptable omission, while the latter comes dangerously close to an act.[b]

The *Barber* court obviated this difficulty by construing turning off the respirator and withdrawing intravenous feeding as omissions rather than acts. Is this characterization persuasive? Is there a meaningful distinction to be made between not turning on a respirator and later turning it off? Between turning off the respirator and withdrawing sustenance? Between

---

[b] Ironically, the distinction between withholding and withdrawing treatment may sometimes be medically perverse. The President's Commission received testimony that the fear that a therapy once begun could not be discontinued has "unduly raised the threshold" for vigorous intervention on behalf of defective newborns. The Commission's view was that, contrary to the usual formulation, the decision to withhold treatment should actually require a *greater* justification than the decision to withdraw treatment. "Whether a particular treatment will have positive effects is often highly uncertain before the therapy has been tried. If a trial of therapy makes clear that it is not helpful to the patient, this is actual evidence (rather than mere surmise) to support stopping because the therapeutic benefit that earlier was a possibility has been found to be clearly unobtainable." The President's Commission for the Study of Ethical Problems in Medicine and Biomedical and Behavioral Research, Deciding to Forego Life–Sustaining Treatment 75–76 (1983).

any of these "omissions" and the "act" of injecting a lethal dose of morphine?

**4.   Legislative Solutions.** Increasingly, situations such as that presented in *Barber* are handled under special legislation. Most common is the statutory provision for a "living will," an advance declaration of the patient's wishes regarding the withdrawal of life-sustaining treatment. Such laws are variously entitled "Death with Dignity" or "Natural Death" acts, and they differ in detail. The common theme is to enable a patient to direct that medical treatment be stopped under specified circumstances even though the patient is at that point incompetent to address the issue. Under the terms of these statutes, physicians who follow such directives are protected from civil or criminal liability for doing so. If Mr. Herbert had executed a "living will" in accordance with California's Natural Death Act, the prosecution in *Barber* would never have occurred.

There is support for the view that a "living will" may be legally valid even where it is not specially authorized by statute. The argument seems to be that the physician's obligation is only to treat the patient to the extent of his or her consent. If the patient directs that medical care be stopped in certain circumstances, the physician is then free, or perhaps required, to withhold treatment should those circumstances arise. Of course, this argument is necessarily based on the distinction between act and omission, as there is no suggestion that a patient may validly consent to being actively killed by his or her physician. And there is also tension between this conclusion and the traditional doctrine that consent of the victim is not a defense to murder.[c]

Less widespread are legislative provisions for designation of a proxy to speak on the patient's behalf in the event that he or she becomes incompetent. This may be accomplished as part of the "living will" legislation or as an amendment to a "durable" power-of-attorney statute. The idea is that the proxy will make the critical decision regarding continuation of life-sustaining care in light of the patient's wishes and the medical situation. Without explicit legislative authorization, however, the legal status of such arrangements may well be doubted.

**5.   Assisted Suicide.** The preceding notes have focused on the question of whether criminal charges should be brought in connection with the death of comatose patients whose potential for cognitive recovery was found to be highly unlikely. There continues to be litigation in such cases, particularly where patients have not specified in advance their wishes concerning the appropriate level of medical intervention should they become incompetent. Indeed, state governors and legislatures occasionally have tried to block efforts by family members to authorize the removal of life-support from comatose patients.[d] Speaking generally, however, physicians no longer are likely to face criminal liability for removal of life-

[c] See, e.g., § 2.11(2) of the Model Penal Code, which, because of the definition of "conduct" in § 1.13(5), applies both to acts and to omissions.

[d] See Irvin Molotsky, Wife Wins Right-to-Die Case; Then a Governor Challenges It, New York Times, Oct. 2, 1998, A26; Sean Mussenden & Maya Bell, Guardian Ok'd for Woman on Life Support, Orlando Sentinel, Oct. 23, 2003, A1.

support equipment, provided that they follow appropriate medical protocol and available legal procedures.

Not so for physicians who assist competent persons who are gravely ill to commit suicide. Of course, one's choice of rhetoric to describe this conduct—"assisted suicide" as opposed to the "cessation of heroic life-support"—begs the difficult questions that medical and legal practitioners must resolve in this arena. While one state has enacted legislation that authorizes physicians to aid competent, terminally-ill adults in taking their own lives, see Ore. Rev. Stat. § 127.800 et seq. (1996), other states have refused to follow suit and, indeed, have continued to authorize severe criminal penalties against doctors who provide such aid to competent patients whose illnesses cause them to suffer debilitating pain, see People v. Kevorkian, 248 Mich.App. 373, 639 N.W.2d 291 (2001); People v. Kevorkian, 447 Mich. 436, 527 N.W.2d 714 (1994).

Recently, the United States Supreme Court rejected several constitutional challenges to state criminal prohibitions on physician-assisted suicide. See Washington v. Glucksberg, 521 U.S. 702 (1997). In Vacco v. Quill, 521 U.S. 793 (1997), the Court leaned heavily on the distinction between omissions and acts in holding that New York did not violate the Equal Protection Clause of the 14th Amendment by simultaneously forbidding assisted-suicide while allowing patients to refuse life-saving medical treatment. Speaking through Chief Justice Rehnquist, the Court reasoned that "the distinction between assisting suicide and withdrawing life-sustaining treatment" is "rational," indeed, "important and logical." The distinction is "widely recognized and endorsed in the medical profession." More crucially, the distinction plays a significant role in criminal jurisprudence because it "comports with fundamental legal principles of causation and intent." As the Court explained:

> ... First, when a patient refuses life-sustaining medical treatment, he dies from an underlying fatal disease or pathology; but if a patient ingests lethal medication prescribed by a physician, he is killed by that medication....
>
> Furthermore, a physician who withdraws, or honors a patient's refusal to begin, life-sustaining medical treatment purposefully intends, or may so intend, only to respect his patient's wishes and "to cease doing useless and futile or degrading things to the patient when [the patient] no longer stands to benefit from them." ... The same is true when a doctor provides aggressive palliative care; in some cases, painkilling drugs may hasten a patient's death, but the physician's purpose and intent is, or may be, only to ease his patient's pain. A doctor who assists a suicide, however, "must, necessarily and indubitably, intend primarily that the patient be made dead." Similarly, a patient who commits suicide with a doctor's aid necessarily has the specific intent to end his or her own life, while a patient who refuses or discontinues treatment might not....

The law has long used actors' intent or purpose to distinguish between two acts that may have the same result. . . . See, e.g., . . . M. Hale, 1 Pleas of the Crown 412 (1847) ("If A. with an intent to prevent a gangrene beginning in his hand doth without any advice cut off his hand, by which he dies, he is not thereby felo de se for tho it was a voluntary act, yet it was not with an intent to kill himself"). Put differently, the law distinguishes actions taken "because of" a given end from actions taken "in spite of" their unintended but foreseen consequences. . . . Compassion in Dying v. Washington, 79 F.3d 790, 858 (CA9 1996) (Kleinfeld, J., dissenting) ("When General Eisenhower ordered American soldiers onto the beaches of Normandy, he knew that he was sending many American soldiers to certain death. . . . His purpose, though, was to . . . liberate Europe from the Nazis.").

--------

## NOTE ON POSSESSION

As the preceding materials indicate, criminal liability may be based either on an affirmative act proscribed by law or on failure to perform an act required by law. There is also a third possibility—liability for possession. Possession may be thought of as a status that begins with the act of acquisition and that is continued by a failure to divest. Alternatively, possession may be viewed simply as an indirect way of proving the act of acquisition. In any event, possession is widely employed as a basis of criminal liability. The Model Penal Code merely confirms existing law when it identifies possession, along with acts and omissions, as possible grounds for criminal liability. Section 2.01(4) provides that, "[p]ossession is an act . . . if the possessor knowingly procured or received the thing possessed or was aware of his control thereof for a sufficient period to have been able to terminate his possession." At least as so defined, there seems to be no objection in principle to punishing crimes of possession. In other words, there seems to be no reason to regard possession as an inherently inappropriate basis for imposing penal sanctions, although problems can and do arise in the administration of such offenses. See Charles H. Whitebread and Ronald Stevens, Constructive Possession in Narcotics Cases: To Have and Have Not, 58 Va. L. Rev. 751 (1972).

--------

## SECTION 4: INTERPRETATION OF CONDUCT ELEMENTS

## Keeler v. Superior Court of Amador County

Supreme Court of California, 1970.
2 Cal.3d 619, 87 Cal.Rptr. 481, 470 P.2d 617.

■ MOSK, J. In this proceeding for [a] writ of prohibition we are called upon to decide whether an unborn but viable fetus is a "human being" within the meaning of the California statute defining murder, Cal.Penal Code § 187. We conclude that the legislature did not intend such a meaning, and that for us to construe the statute to the contrary and apply it to this petitioner would exceed our judicial power and deny petitioner due process of law.

The evidence received at the preliminary examination may be summarized as follows: Petitioner and Teresa Keeler obtained an interlocutory decree of divorce on September 27, 1968. They had been married for 16 years. Unknown to petitioner, Mrs. Keeler was then pregnant by one Ernest Vogt, whom she had met earlier that summer. She subsequently began living with Vogt in Stockton, but concealed the fact from petitioner. Petitioner was given custody of their two daughters, aged 12 and 13 years, and under the decree Mrs. Keeler had the right to take the girls on alternate weekends.

On February 23, 1969, Mrs. Keeler was driving on a narrow mountain road in Amador County after delivering the girls to their home. She met petitioner driving in the opposite direction; he blocked the road with his car, and she pulled over to the side. He walked to her vehicle and began speaking to her. He seemed calm, and she rolled down her window to hear him. He said, "I hear you're pregnant. If you are you had better stay away from the girls and from here." She did not reply, and he opened the car door; as she later testified, "He assisted me out of the car.... [I]t wasn't roughly at this time." Petitioner then looked at her abdomen and became "extremely upset." He said, "You sure are. I'm going to stomp it out of you." He pushed her against the car, shoved his knee into her abdomen, and struck her in the face with several blows. She fainted, and when she regained consciousness petitioner had departed.

Mrs. Keeler drove back to Stockton, and the police and medical assistance were summoned. She had suffered substantial facial injuries, as well as extensive bruising of the abdominal wall. A caesarian section was performed and the fetus was examined in utero. Its head was found to be severely fractured, and it was delivered stillborn. The pathologist gave as his opinion that the cause of death was skull fracture with consequent cerebral hemorrhaging, that death would have been immediate, and that the injury could have been the result of force applied to the mother's abdomen. There was no air in the fetus' lungs, and the umbilical cord was intact.

Upon delivery the fetus weighed five pounds and was 18 inches in length. Both Mrs. Keeler and her obstetrician testified that fetal movements had been observed prior to February 23, 1969. The evidence was in conflict as to the estimated age of the fetus; the expert testimony on the point, however, concluded "with reasonable medical certainty" that the fetus had developed to the stage of viability, i.e., that in the event of premature birth on the date in question it would have had a 75 per cent to 96 per cent chance of survival.

An information was filed charging petitioner, in count I, with committing the crime of murder in that he did "unlawfully kill a human being, to wit Baby Girl Vogt, with malice aforethought." . . . His motion to set aside the information for lack of probable cause was denied, and he now seeks a writ of prohibition. . . .

Penal Code Section 187 provides: "Murder is the unlawful killing of a human being, with malice aforethought." The dispositive question is whether the fetus which petitioner is accused of killing was, on February 23, 1969, a "human being" within the meaning of the statute. If it was not, petitioner cannot be charged with its "murder" and prohibition will lie.

Section 187 was enacted as part of the Penal Code of 1872. Inasmuch as the provision has not been amended since that date, we must determine the intent of the legislature at the time of its enactment. But Section 187 was, in turn, taken verbatim from the first California statute defining murder, part of the Crimes and Punishments Act of 1850. Penal Code Section 5 (also enacted in 1872) declares: "The provisions of this code, so far as they are substantially the same as existing statutes, must be construed as continuations thereof, and not as new enactments." We begin, accordingly, by inquiring into the intent of the legislature in 1850 when it first defined a murder as the unlawful and malicious killing of a "human being."

It will be presumed, of course, that in enacting a statute the legislature was familiar with the relevant rules of the common law, and, when it couches its enactment in common-law language, that its intent was to continue those rules in statutory form. This is particularly appropriate in considering the work of the first session of our legislature: its precedents were necessarily drawn from the common law, as modified in certain respects by the Constitution and by legislation of our sister states.

We therefore undertake a brief review of the origins and development of the common law of abortional homicide. [An extensive review of English cases and authorities revealed that an infant could not be the subject of criminal homicide at common law unless it had been born alive.]

By the year 1850 this rule of the common law had long been accepted in the United States. As early as 1797 it was held that proof the child was born alive is necessary to support an indictment for murder. . . .

While it was thus "well settled" in American case law that the killing of an unborn child was not homicide, a number of state legislatures in the first half of the 19th century undertook to modify the common law in this respect. [The court then discussed the enactment in New York and in a few other states, but not in California, of statutes specially directed against feticide.]

We conclude that in declaring murder to be the unlawful and malicious killing of a "human being" the legislature of 1850 intended that term to have the settled common-law meaning of a person who had been born alive, and did not intend the act of feticide—as distinguished from abortion—to be an offense under the laws of California.

Nothing occurred between the years 1850 and 1872 to suggest that in adopting the new penal code on the latter date the legislature entertained any different intent. The case law of our sister states, for example, remained consonant with the common law....

Any lingering doubt on this subject must be laid to rest by a consideration of the legislative history of the Penal Code of 1872. The act establishing the California Code Commission required the commissioners to revise all statutes then in force, correct errors and omissions, and "recommend all such enactments as shall, in the judgment of the commission, be necessary to supply the defects of and give completeness to the existing legislation of the state...." In discharging this duty the statutory schemes of our sister states were carefully examined, and we must assume the commissioners had knowledge of the feticide laws noted hereinabove. Yet the commissioners proposed no such law for California, and none has been adopted to this day....

It is the policy of this state to construe a penal statute as favorably to the defendant as its language and the circumstances of its application may reasonably permit; just as in the case of a question of fact, the defendant is entitled to the benefit of every reasonable doubt as to the true interpretation of words or the construction of language used in a statute. We hold that in adopting the definition of murder in Penal Code Section 187 the legislature intended to exclude from its reach the act of killing an unborn fetus.

The People urge, however, that the sciences of obstetrics and pediatrics have greatly progressed since 1872, to the point where with proper medical care a normally developed fetus prematurely born at 28 weeks or more has an excellent chance of survival, i.e., is "viable"; that the common-law requirement of live birth to prove the fetus had become a "human being" who may be the victim of murder is no longer in accord with scientific fact, since an unborn but viable fetus is now fully capable of independent life; and that one who unlawfully and maliciously terminated such a life should therefore be liable to prosecution for murder under Section 187. We may grant the premises of this argument; indeed, we neither deny nor denigrate the vast progress of medicine in the century since the enactment of the Penal Code. But we cannot join in the conclusion sought to be deduced: we cannot hold this petitioner to answer for murder by reason of his alleged act of killing an unborn—even though viable—fetus. To such a charge there are two insuperable obstacles, one "jurisdictional" and the other constitutional.

Penal Code Section 6 declares in relevant part that "[n]o act or omission" accomplished after the code has taken effect "is criminal or punishable, except as prescribed or authorized by this code, or by some of the statutes which it specifies as continuing in force and as not affected by its provisions, or by some ordinance, municipal, county, or township regulation...." This section embodies a fundamental principle of our tripartite form of government, i.e., that subject to the constitutional prohibition against cruel and unusual punishment, the power to define crimes and fix penalties is vested exclusively in the legislative branch. Stated differently, there are no common-law crimes in California....

Settled rules of construction implement this principle. Although the Penal Code commands us to construe its provisions "according to the fair import of their terms, with a view to effect its objects and to promote justice," Cal.Penal Code § 4, it is clear the courts cannot go so far as to create an offense by enlarging a statute, by inserting or deleting words, or by giving the terms used false or unusual meanings. Penal statutes will not be made to reach beyond their plain intent; they include only those offenses coming clearly within the import of their language. . . .

Applying these rules to the case at bar, we would undoubtedly act in excess of the judicial power if we were to adopt the People's proposed construction of Section 187. As we have shown, the legislature has defined the crime of murder in California to apply only to the unlawful and malicious killing of one who has been born alive. We recognize that the killing of an unborn but viable fetus may be deemed by some to be an offense of similar nature and gravity; but as Chief Justice Marshall warned long ago, "[i]t would be dangerous, indeed, to carry the principle, that a case which is within the reason or mischief of a statute, is within its provisions, so far as to punish a crime not enumerated in the statute, because it is of equal atrocity, or of kindred character, with those which are enumerated." Whether to thus extend liability for murder in California is a determination solely within the province of the legislature. For a court to simply declare, by judicial fiat, that the time has now come to prosecute under Section 187 one who kills an unborn but viable fetus would indeed be to rewrite the statute under the guise of construing it. Nor does a need to fill an asserted "gap" in the law between abortion and homicide—as will appear, no such gap in fact exists—justify judicial legislation of this nature: to make it a "judicial function" to explore such new fields of crime as they may appear from time to time "is wholly foreign to the American concept of criminal justice" and "raises very serious questions concerning the principle of separation of powers."

The second obstacle to the proposed judicial enlargement of Section 187 is the guarantee of due process of law. Assuming arguendo that we have the power to adopt the new construction of this statute as the law of California, such a ruling, by constitutional command, could operate only prospectively, and thus could not in any event reach the conduct of petitioner on February 23, 1969.

The first essential of due process is fair warning of the act which is made punishable as a crime. "That the terms of a penal statute creating a new offense must be sufficiently explicit to inform those who are subject to it what conduct on their part will render them liable to its penalties, is a well-recognized requirement, consonant alike with ordinary notions of fair play and the settled rules of law." Connally v. Gen. Constr. Co., 269 U.S. 385, 391 (1926). "No one may be required at peril of life, liberty or property to speculate as to the meaning of penal statutes. All are entitled to be informed as to what the state commands or forbids." Lanzetta v. New Jersey, 306 U.S. 451, 453 (1939). . . .

This requirement of fair warning is reflected in the constitutional prohibition against the enactment of ex post facto laws, U.S.Const. art. I, §§ 9, 10; Cal.Const. art. I, § 16. When a new penal statute is applied retrospectively to make punishable an act which was not criminal at the time it was performed, the defendant has been given no advance notice consistent with due process. And precisely the same effect occurs when such an act is made punishable under a pre-existing statute but by means of an unforeseeable *judicial* enlargement thereof. Bouie v. City of Columbia, 378 U.S. 347 (1964).

In *Bouie* two Negroes took seats in the restaurant section of a South Carolina drugstore; no notices were posted restricting the area to whites only. When the defendants refused to leave upon demand, they were arrested and convicted of violating a criminal trespass statute which prohibited entry on the property of another "after notice" forbidding such conduct. Prior South Carolina decisions had emphasized the necessity of proving such notice to support a conviction under the statute. The South Carolina Supreme Court nevertheless affirmed the convictions, construing the statute to prohibit not only the act of entering after notice not to do so but also the wholly different act of remaining on the property after receiving notice to leave.

The United States Supreme Court reversed the convictions, holding that the South Carolina court's ruling was "unforeseeable" and when an "unforeseeable state-court construction of a criminal statute is applied retroactively to subject a person to criminal liability for past conduct, the effect is to deprive him of due process of law in the sense of fair warning that his contemplated conduct constitutes a crime." Analogizing to the prohibition against retrospective penal legislation, the high court reasoned

> Indeed, an unforeseeable judicial enlargement of a criminal statute, applied retroactively, operates precisely like an ex post facto law, such as Art. I, § 10, of the Constitution forbids. An ex post facto law has been defined by this Court as one "that makes an action done before the passing of the law, and which was *innocent* when done, criminal; and punishes such action," or "that *aggravates* a *crime*, or makes it *greater* than it was, when committed." If a state legislature is barred by the ex post facto clause from passing such a law, it must follow that a state supreme court is barred by the due process clause from achieving precisely the same result by judicial construction. The fundamental principle that "the required criminal law must have existed when the conduct in issue occurred," must apply to bar retroactive criminal prohibitions emanating from courts as well as from legislatures. If a judicial construction of a criminal statute is "unexpected and indefensible by reference to the law which had been expressed prior to the conduct in issue," it must not be given retroactive effect....

It is true that Section 187, on its face, is not as "narrow and precise" as the South Carolina statute involved in *Bouie*; on the other hand, neither is it as vague as the statutes struck down in *Connally* and *Lanzetta*. Rather, Section 187 bears a plain, common-sense meaning, well settled in the common law and fortified by its legislative history in California. In *Bouie*, moreover, the Court stressed that a breach of the peace statute was also in force in South Carolina at the time of the events, and that the defendants were in fact arrested on that ground and prosecuted (but not convicted) for that offense. Here, too, there was another statute on the books which petitioner could well have believed he was violating: Penal Code Section 274 defines the crime of abortion, in relevant part, as the act of "[e]very person who ... uses or employs any instrument *or any other means whatever*, with intent thereby to procure the miscarriage" of any woman, and does not come within the exceptions provided by law. The gist of the crime is the performance, with the requisite intent, of any of the acts enumerated in the statute. It is therefore no defense to a charge of violating Section 274 that the act was committed unusually late in the woman's pregnancy or by a method not commonly employed for that purpose....

Turning to the case law, we find no reported decisions of the California courts which should have given petitioner notice that the killing of an unborn but viable fetus was prohibited by Section 187....

Properly understood, the often cited case of People v. Chavez, 77 Cal.App.2d 621, 176 P.2d 92 (1947), does not derogate from this rule. There the defendant was charged with the murder of her newborn child, and convicted of manslaughter. She testified that the baby dropped from her womb into the toilet bowl; that she picked it up two or three minutes later, and cut but did not tie the umbilical cord; that the baby was limp and made no cry; and that after 15 minutes she wrapped it in a newspaper and concealed it, where it was found dead the next day. The autopsy surgeon testified that the baby was a full-term, nine-month child, weighing six and one-half pounds and appearing normal in every respect; that the body had very little blood in it, indicating the child had bled to death through the untied umbilical cord; that such a process would have taken about an hour; and that in his opinion "the child was born alive, based on conditions he found and the fact that the lungs contained air and the blood was extravasated or pushed back into the tissues, indicating heart action."

On appeal, the defendant emphasized that a doctor called by the defense had suggested other tests which the autopsy surgeon could have performed to determine the matter of live birth; on this basis, it was contended that the question of whether the infant was born alive "rests entirely on pure speculation." The Court of Appeals found only an insignificant conflict in that regard, and focused its attention instead on testimony of the autopsy surgeon admitting the possibility that the evidence of heart and lung action could have resulted from the child's breathing "after presentation of the head but before the birth was completed."

The court cited [various] mid–19th century English infanticide cases ... and noted that the decisions had not reached uniformity on whether breathing, heart action, severance of the umbilical cord, or some combination of these or other factors established the status of "human being" for the purposes of the law of homicide. The court then adverted to the state of modern medical knowledge, discussed the phenomenon of viability, and held that "a viable child *in the process of being born* is a human being within the meaning of the homicide statutes, whether or not the process has been fully completed. It should at least be considered a human being where it is a living baby and where in the natural course of events *a birth which is already started* would naturally be successfully completed." (Italics added.) Since the testimony of the autopsy surgeon left no doubt in that case that a live birth had at least begun, the court found "the evidence is sufficient here to support the implied finding of the jury that this child *was born alive and became a human being within the meaning of the homicide statutes*." (Italics added.)

*Chavez* thus stands for the proposition—to which we adhere—that a viable fetus "in the process of being born" is a human being within the meaning of the homicide statutes. But it stands for no more; in particular it does not hold that a fetus, however viable, which is *not* "in the process of being born" is nevertheless a "human being" in the law of homicide. On the contrary, the opinion is replete with references to the common-law requirement that the child be "born alive," however that term is defined, and must accordingly be deemed to reaffirm that requirement as part of the law of California. . . .

We conclude that the judicial enlargement of Section 187 now urged upon us by the People would not have been foreseeable to this petitioner, and hence that its adoption at this time would deny him due process of law.

Let a peremptory writ of prohibition issue restraining respondent court from taking any further proceedings on Count I of the information, charging petitioner with the crime of murder.

■ BURKE, ACTING C.J. [dissenting]. The majority hold that "Baby Girl" Vogt, who, according to medical testimony, had reached the 35th week of development, had a 96 percent chance of survival, and was "definitely" alive and viable at the time of her death, nevertheless was not a "human being" under California's homicide statutes. In my view, in so holding, the majority ignore significant common-law precedents, frustrate the express intent of the legislature, and defy reason, logic and common sense. . . .

The majority opinion suggests that we are confined to common-law concepts, and to the common-law definition of murder or manslaughter. However, the legislature, in Penal Code Sections 187 and 192, has defined those offenses: homicide is the unlawful killing of a "human being." These words need not be frozen in place as of any particular time, but must be fairly and reasonably interpreted by this court to promote justice and to carry out the purposes of the legislature in adopting a homicide statute. Thus, Penal Code Section 4, which was enacted in 1872 along with Sections 187 and 192, provides: "The rule of the common law, that penal statutes are to be strictly construed, has no application to this code. All its provisions are to be construed according to the fair import of their terms, with a view to effect its objects and to promote justice." . . . .

Penal Code Section 4, which abolishes the common-law principle of the strict construction of penal statutes, ... permits this court fairly to construe the terms of those statutes to serve the ends of justice. Consequently, nothing should prevent this court from holding that Baby Girl Vogt was a human ("belonging or relating to man; characteristic of man")[4] being ("existence, as opp. to nonexistence; specif. life")[5] under California's homicide statutes.

We commonly conceive of human existence as a spectrum stretching from birth to death. However, if this court properly might expand the definition of "human being" at one end of that spectrum, we may do so at the other end. Consider the following examples: All would agree that "shooting or otherwise damaging a corpse is not homicide...." In other words, a corpse is not considered to be a "human being" and thus cannot be the subject of a "killing" as those terms are used in the homicide statutes. However, it is readily apparent that our concepts of what constitutes a "corpse" have been and are being continually modified by advances in the field of medicine, including new techniques for life revival, restoration and resuscitation such as artificial respiration, open heart massage, transfusions, transplants and a variety of life-restoring stimulants, drugs and new surgical methods. Would this court ignore these developments and exonerate the killer of an apparently "drowned" child merely because that child would have been pronounced dead in 1648 or 1850? Obviously not. Whether a homicide occurred in that case would be determined by medical testimony regarding capability of the child to have survived prior to the defendant's act. And that is precisely the test which this court should adopt in the instant case.

The common-law reluctance to characterize the killing of a quickened fetus as a homicide was based solely upon a presumption that the fetus would have been born dead. This presumption seems to have persisted in this country at least as late as 1876. Based upon the state of the medical art in the 17th, 18th and 19th centuries, that presumption may have been well-founded. However, as we approach the 21st century, it has been apparent that "This presumption is not only contrary to common experience and the ordinary course of nature, but it is contrary to the usual rule with respect to presumptions followed in this state." *People* v. *Chavez*, supra.

There are no accurate statistics disclosing fetal death rates in "common-law England," although the foregoing presumption of death indicates a significantly high death experience. On the other hand, in California the fetal death rate[6] in 1968 is estimated to be 12 deaths in 1,000, a ratio which would have given Baby Girl Vogt a 98.8 per cent chance of survival. If, as I have contended, the term "human being" in our homicide statutes is a

---

[4] Webster's New International Dictionary (2d ed. 1959), page 1211, column 3.

[5] Id. at 247.

[6] I.e., fetal deaths of 20 weeks or more gestation.

fluid concept to be defined in accordance with present conditions, then there can be no question that the term should include the fully viable fetus.

The majority suggests that to do so would improperly create some new offense. However, the offense of murder is no new offense. Contrary to the majority opinion, the legislature has not "defined the crime of murder in California to apply only to the unlawful and malicious killing of one who has been born alive." Instead, the legislature simply used the term "human being" and directed the courts to construe that term according to its "fair import" with a view to effect the objects of the homicide statutes and promote justice. Cal.Penal Code § 4. What justice will be promoted, what objects effectuated, by construing "human being" as excluding Baby Girl Vogt and her unfortunate successors? Was defendant's brutal act of stomping her to death any less an act of homicide than the murder of a newly born baby? No one doubts that the term "human being" would include the elderly or dying persons whose potential for life has nearly lapsed; their proximity to death is deemed immaterial. There is no sound reason for denying the viable fetus, with its unbounded potential for life, the same status.

The majority also suggest that such an interpretation of our homicide statutes would deny defendant "fair warning" that his act was punishable as a crime. Aside from the absurdity of the underlying premise that defendant consulted Coke, Blackstone or Hale before kicking Baby Girl Vogt to death, it is clear that defendant had adequate notice that his act could constitute homicide. Due process only precludes prosecution under a new statute insufficiently explicit regarding the specific conduct proscribed, or under a pre-existing statute "by means of an unforeseeable *judicial* enlargement thereof."

Our homicide statutes have been in effect in this state since 1850. The fact that the California courts have not been called upon to determine the precise question before us does not render "unforeseeable" a decision which determines that a viable fetus is a "human being" under those statutes. Can defendant really claim surprise that a 5–pound, 18–inch, 34–week-old, living, viable child is considered to be a human being?

The fact is that the foregoing construction of our homicide statutes easily could have been anticipated from strong dicta in *People* v. *Chavez*, supra, wherein the court reviewed common-law precedents but disapproved their requirement that the child be born alive and completely separated from its mother.... In dicta, the court discussed the question when an unborn infant becomes a human being under the homicide statutes, as follows: "... While it may not be possible to draw an exact line applicable to all cases, the rules of law should recognize and make some attempt to follow the natural and scientific facts to which they relate.... [I]t would be a mere fiction to hold that a child is not a human being because the process of birth has not been fully completed, when it has reached that state of viability when the destruction of the life of its mother would not end its existence and when, if separated from the mother naturally or by artificial means, it will live and grow in the normal manner."

Thus the *Chavez* case explodes the majority's premise that a viability test for defining the "human being" under our homicide statutes was unforeseeable.... I would conclude that defendant had sufficient notice that the words "human being" could include a viable fetus....

———

## People v. Sobiek

California Court of Appeals, 1973.
30 Cal.App.3d 458, 106 Cal.Rptr. 519.

■ BRAY, J. ... By an indictment filed in the San Mateo County Superior Court respondent was indicted for four counts of violation of Penal Code Section 487 (grand theft)[a].... He moved to quash the indictment. After a hearing, the court granted his motion.... The People appeal.

The charges arise out of a situation in San Mateo County where a group of 15 friends organized the Empire Investment Club whose purpose was to invest money in second mortgages. Respondent, an insurance and real estate field representative, was elected president. Each member originally invested $100 and paid into the club's fund $25 per month thereafter.

It is unnecessary to detail the various acts of respondent in gradually assuming practically unlimited control of the making of loans and in finally appropriating to his own use considerable sums of the group's money. The evidence on the hearing of the motion under Penal Code Section 995 to set aside the indictment clearly and amply shows reasonable cause for holding respondent to answer on all the charges unless, as contended by respondent and found by the court, Section 487 cannot apply to a member of a group such as this on the theory that a partner may not steal nor embezzle the property of his partnership.

In People v. Brody, 29 Cal.App.2d 6, 83 P.2d 952 (1938), the defendant and his friends contributed money for the purpose of operating bingo games. A partnership was formed for profit-making purposes and an agreement executed. The defendant used some of the funds for his own purposes and was charged with grand theft. The court held: "The evidence is, as defendant claims, insufficient *in law* to sustain the judgment. Viewed as a charge of embezzlement the uncontradicted evidence showed that the defendant and his associates were partners. However, it is settled law that a general partner cannot be convicted of embezzling partnership property

[a] Cal.Penal Code § 487 does not actually define grand theft. It merely differentiates grand theft from the lesser offense of petty theft. The generic crime of theft is defined in Cal.Penal Code § 484(a), which reads in pertinent part as follows:

"Every person who shall feloniously steal, take, carry, lead, or drive away the personal property of another, or who shall fraudulently appropriate property which has been entrusted to him, or who shall knowingly and designedly, by any false or fraudulent representation or pretense, defraud any other person of money, labor or real or personal property ... is guilty of theft."—[Footnote by eds.]

which comes into his possession or under his control during the course of the partnership business by reason of his being a partner." (Italics added.)

The basic thought behind the decisions sustaining the rule that a partner may not steal partnership property seems to be that as each partner is the ultimate owner of an undivided interest in all the partnership property and as no one can be guilty of stealing or embezzling what belongs to him, a general partner cannot be convicted of embezzling partnership property, i.e., the property must be "of another." This rule, when thus broadly stated, goes further than the simple statutory requirement that the property be "of another." When thus stated, the rule requires that the property be wholly that of another because a part interest by the defendant prevents a conviction. . . .

[The court then proceeded to review a number of California precedents restating the rule that a partner cannot be guilty of a theft of partnership funds. The court found that, despite the frequency with which it was repeated, the rule was based on "misinterpretation and dicta."]

The broad rule that a partner cannot embezzle from a partnership has been rejected by the American Law Institute. In Model Penal Code Section 223.0(7), "property of another" is defined to include property in which any person other than the actor has an interest which the actor is not privileged to infringe, regardless of the fact that the actor also has an interest in the property. This is the equivalent of the former, tentative definition under Section 206.1(4) (Tent.Draft No. 1, 1953), in which it is stated that the purpose of that definition is to nullify the concept that each of the joint owners has complete title to the jointly owned property so that a joint owner cannot misappropriate what already belongs to him. The draft states that, whatever might be the merits of such notions in the civil law, it is clear they have no relevance to the criminal law's effort to deter deprivations of other people's economic interests. Modern statutes, including those of Minnesota, Wisconsin, and Illinois, either expressly or impliedly reach the same result. . . .

It is both illogical and unreasonable to hold that a partner cannot steal from his partners merely because he has an undivided interest in the partnership property. Fundamentally, stealing that portion of the partners' shares which does not belong to the thief is no different from stealing the property of another person. There is nothing in Penal Code Section 484 which requires an interpretation different from that in Model Penal Code Section 223.0(7). . . .

[The court then turned to the contention that applying this new construction to the defendant would violate the federal Constitution. It reasoned as follows:]

The prohibition in the federal Constitution against ex post facto legislation was placed in Article I, Section 10, which governs legislative powers, and is not in the article relating to the judiciary, Article III. It has been held that that provision, according to the natural import of its term, is a restraint upon legislative power and concerns the making of law, not [its] construction, by the courts. However, due process does apply to the construction of statutes by the courts, and principles similar to those involved in ex post facto doctrine have evolved. Thus, in Bouie v. City of Columbia, 378 U.S. 347 (1964), which applied the lack-of-due-process rule to a prosecution of persons involved in a sit-in where no statute or ordinance prohibited such conduct, the reviewing court held that enlarging a certain statute to cover the conduct in question was an unforeseeable judicial enlargement of a criminal statute applied retroactively. That was an entirely different situation from the one at bench where not only is the interpretation of the grand theft [statute] reasonable, but the respondent must have known that his act was immoral and that he was taking the property of another.

In United States v. Rundle, 255 F.Supp. 936 (E.D.Pa.1966), [the court distinguished *Bouie* with the following remarks:]

It is not always true that where the definition of a crime is extended by judicial construction, a conviction which results therefrom is a denial of due process [and, quoting Mr. Justice Holmes], "... the law is full of instances where a man's fate depends on his estimating rightly, that is, as the jury subsequently estimates it, some matter of degree. If his judgment is wrong, not only may he incur a fine or a short imprisonment, as here; he may incur the penalty of death.... *The criterion in such cases is to examine whether common social duty would, under the circumstances, have suggested a more circumspect conduct.' Nash* v. *United States.* (Emphasis added)."

Similarly, in the case at bar, "common social duty" would have forewarned respondent that "circumspect conduct" prohibited robbing his partners and also would have told him that he was stealing "property of another."

Keeler v. Superior Court, 2 Cal.3d 619, 87 Cal.Rptr. 481, 470 P.2d 617 (1970), at first blush seems to support respondent's contention that the construction of Section 487 placed upon it by this court deprives respondent of due process. However, a study of *Keeler* shows that it is not in point. *Keeler* held that the brutal killing of a fetus did not violate Section 187 of the Penal Code, which defines murder as "the unlawful killing of a human being," because, as the court expends a number of pages to prove, a fetus is not a "human being" and "the legislature intended to exclude from its reach the act of killing an unborn fetus." The court then states that were the court to determine that an infant in utero was a human being within the meaning of the murder statute, such determination would have met jurisdictional and constitutional barriers. That this is dictum cannot be gainsaid, for once the court determined the fetus was not a human being there was nothing more that needed to be determined. Dictum is not binding on this court.

Moreover, the circumstances applying to Section 187 are entirely different from those applying to Section 487. The court in *Keeler* said that, prior to the killing, the defendant had no notice from any cause that destroying a viable fetus might be murder. As to the grand-theft statute, Section 487, there is no indication that the legislature did not intend to include in "property of another" the property of partners other than the one stealing such property, or of the partnership itself. . . .

As we have shown, respondent's defense relies upon an interpretation of the law which is improper because it is based upon mere dictum. If respondent, at the time he stole his partner's property, relied on a mistaken dictum of court, traditional notions of fair play and substantial justice are not offended by applying to his act the clear meaning of Sections 484 and 487.

The order appealed from is reversed.

————

## NOTES ON *KEELER* AND *SOBIEK*

**1. Questions on *Keeler* and *Sobiek*.** Are *Keeler* and *Sobiek* reconcilable? It is arguable that *Sobiek* involved a departure from prior understanding greater than that involved in *Keeler*. Would that necessarily mean that *Sobiek* was wrongly decided? Or was *Keeler* the case in error?

In this connection, consider the amendment to the murder statute adopted by the California legislature shortly after the *Keeler* decision:

Section 187. Murder defined; death of fetus.

(a) Murder is the unlawful killing of a human being, or a fetus, with malice aforethought.

(b) This section shall not apply to any person who commits an act which results in the death of a fetus if any of the following apply:

(1) The act complied with the Therapeutic Abortion Act. . . .

(2) The act was committed by a holder of a physician's and surgeon's certificate . . . in a case where, to a medical certainty, the result of childbirth would be death of the mother of the fetus or where her death from childbirth, although not medically certain, would be substantially certain or more likely than not.

(3) The act was solicited, aided, abetted, or consented to by the mother of the fetus.

(c) Subdivision (b) shall not be construed to prohibit the prosecution of any person under any other provision of law.

Was the effect of this statute simply to overturn *Keeler*? How does the amendment to § 187 differ from the situation that would have resulted if *Keeler* had come out the other way?

**2. Relation to *Manley*.** The fact that *Keeler* and *Sobiek* involved questions of statutory interpretation seems to differentiate these cases from *Manley*. Yet in another sense, all three courts were called upon to engage in the retrospective definition of criminal conduct. Does the fact that a statute was involved make a difference? Is the process of judicial decision-making illustrated in *Sobiek* and endorsed by the *Keeler* dissent really any different from that adopted in *Manley*?[a]

**3.  *Bouie*: Background of a Constitutional Precedent.** The Supreme Court's opinion in *Bouie* is featured prominently in both *Keeler* and *Sobiek*. That case arose during the "sit-in" demonstrations of the early 1960s, the object of which was to secure equal access to places of public accommodation for blacks. Throughout the South blacks were refused service in many restaurants, lunch counters, hotels, motels, and similar establishments.

The fight for equal access was waged on two fronts. First, the courts were asked to recognize a constitutional right based on the equal protection clause of the 14th Amendment. There was, however, a formidable obstacle to this line of attack. The equal protection clause applies only to actions by a "state"—i.e., to actions in some way commanded or authorized by government. Racial discrimination in privately owned places of public accommodation falls outside the traditional conception of "state action." Whether that concept could be stretched to encompass such discrimination presented a difficult and unresolved question of constitutional law.

The second arena of battle was the Congress of the United States. As early (or as late) as 1946, President Truman initiated an unsuccessful effort to deal legislatively with some aspects of racial discrimination. In 1957 and again in 1960, civil-rights proposals were threatened by filibuster and were enacted only in compromise versions. As passed, neither statute prohibited racial discrimination in privately owned places of public accommodation.

While the legislative effort remained stalled, resort to the courts accelerated. In the years 1960–1963, the Supreme Court decided some 33 cases involving essentially similar facts. A group of blacks would seek service at a "white" lunch counter or other place of public accommodation and, when denied service, would refuse to leave. The management would call the police, who would arrest the demonstrators for criminal trespass, breach of the peace, or disorderly conduct. In the resulting prosecutions, the defendants would renew the claim to a constitutional right to equal treatment. In each of these 33 cases, the Supreme Court reversed the criminal convictions but never reached the equal protection claim pressed by the protestors. Instead, the Court came up with a series of ingenious, if not disingenuous, reasons for holding the convictions invalid. It seemed clear that sit-in cases were being subjected to far more rigorous scrutiny than would be applied in ordinary criminal prosecutions.

[a] For review of *Keeler* and *Sobiek* and an argument that these cases are in fact importantly different from *Manley*, see John C. Jeffries, Jr., Legality, Vagueness, and the Construction of Penal Statutes, 71 Va.L.Rev. 189, 223–34 (1985). For a thoughtful analysis of these issues from a British perspective, see A.T.H. Smith, Judicial Law Making in the Criminal Law, 100 Law Q.R. 46 (1984).

On June 10, 1963, the Court granted certiorari in an additional four sit-in cases, including *Bouie*, which were argued in October of that year. On November 18, 1963, the Solicitor General of the United States, who had appeared as an amicus supporting reversal of the convictions on various narrow grounds, was invited, by a five-to-four vote, "to file a brief ... expressing the views of the United States ... [on] the broader constitutional issues which have been mooted." This extremely unusual invitation was accepted by the Solicitor General, who on January 7, 1964, filed a brief supporting the protestors' claim of a constitutional right of equal access.

Meanwhile, events were also progressing on the legislative front. On February 28, 1963, President Kennedy transmitted recommendations to the House pertaining to civil-rights legislation he intended to propose, and the resulting bill, including a public-accommodations provision, finally reached the floor of the Senate on March 9, 1964. The traditional filibuster then began, and on May 12 became the longest in Senate history. Finally, on June 18, 1964, the filibuster ended after 82 days, 6,300 pages in the Congressional Record, and 10 million words. Enactment followed on July 3, 1964. The law provided, in substance, that "[a]ll persons shall be entitled to the full and equal enjoyment of the goods, services, facilities, privileges, advantages, and accommodations of any place of public accommodation [defined to include inns, motels, hotels, restaurants, lunch counters, gas stations, theaters, sports arenas, etc.] without discrimination or segregation on the ground of race, color, religion, or national origin." 42 U.S.C. § 2000a. By creating a statutory right of equal access to public accommodations, this legislation obviated any practical necessity for a constitutional pronouncement to that effect.

The Supreme Court may have had its eye on events across the street in Congress. Four days after the filibuster was broken, on June 22, 1964, the five sit-in cases which had been pending since October were decided. All convictions were reversed, in each case on grounds that did not address the merits of the equal-protection claim[b] and in several cases, including *Bouie*, on grounds that had not even been argued. During the Court's next term, the public-accommodations provision of the 1964 Civil Rights Act was upheld as constitutional[c] and also was found to be retroactive in effect,[d] so that it voided all pending sit-in prosecutions based on events that occurred prior to the passage of the statute. The constitutional question raised by *Bouie* remained unanswered.

---

[b] In fact, six of the justices addressed the equal-protection question, three on each side. Chief Justice Warren and Justices Douglas and Goldberg voted to uphold the constitutional claim, and Justices Black, Harlan, and White voted to reject it. Justices Brennan, Stewart, and Clark took no view on these questions, but confined their votes to reverse to other "narrower" grounds. For a discussion of the views expressed in these five cases, see Monrad Paulsen, The Sit-in Cases of 1964, But Answer Came There None, 1964 Sup.Ct.Rev. 137.

[c] See Heart of Atlanta Motel v. United States, 379 U.S. 241 (1964); Katzenbach v. McClung, 379 U.S. 294 (1964).

[d] Hamm v. City of Rock Hill, 379 U.S. 306 (1964).

## NOTES ON THE DOCTRINE OF STRICT CONSTRUCTION

**1.  Origin of the Doctrine.** Recall the statement of the *Keeler* court that "[i]t is the policy of this state to construe a penal statute as favorably to the defendant as its language and the circumstances of its application may reasonably permit...." This is the doctrine of strict construction. It requires that ambiguity in the interpretation of criminal statutes be resolved in favor of the accused. The history of this doctrine is described in Livingston Hall, Strict or Liberal Construction of Penal Statutes, 48 Harv.L.Rev. 748, 749–51 (1935):*

> "The rule that penal laws are to be construed strictly, is perhaps not much less old than construction itself." [United States v. Wiltberger, 5 Wheat. 76, 95 (U.S. 1820).] Thus did Chief Justice Marshall pay his respects more than 100 years ago to the antiquity of this rule. It did not spring into existence as soon as there were any statutes to construe. It arose to meet a very definite situation, and for a very definite purpose.

> Some history of benefit of clergy is necessary for a proper understanding of the growth of the rule. Benefit of clergy (freedom from the usual death penalty for common-law felonies) did not become really important until the growing literacy among laymen in the latter part of the 14th century made a considerable number of them eligible to claim it under the literacy test adopted some years earlier. A century later the number of successful claimants became so large that the first of many statutes ousting benefit of clergy in specified crimes was passed, applying to a lay person murdering his lord or master.

> In the reign of Henry VIII, who is said to have executed 72,000 of his subjects, numerous statutes were passed to exclude from benefit of clergy persons convicted as principals or accessories before the fact in a number of specified felonies. These statutes were repealed by Edward VI in 1547 except as to principals in five named felonies, to which accessories were added in 1557. A few other felonies were made non-clergyable by Elizabeth and James I.

> It was against this background of unmitigated severity in serious crimes that the doctrine of strict construction emerged. Prior to the 17th century there were only a few cases where it was employed, and there were others where it was rejected. It did not become a general rule of conscious application until the growing humanitarianism of 17th century England came into serious conflict with the older laws of the preceding century. During this period there seems to have been no further non-clergyable offenses created. But from 1691 to 1765 benefit of clergy was ousted in

various forms of fraud, embezzlement, and aggravated larceny, and a conflict ensued between the legislature on the one hand and courts, juries, and even prosecutors on the other. The former was committed by inertia, or pressure from property owners, to a policy of deterrence through severity, while the latter tempered this severity with strict construction carried to its most absurd limits, verdicts contrary to the evidence, and waiver of the non-clergyable charge in return for a plea of guilty to a lesser offense. It was from cases and text writers in the England of this period that the doctrine of strict construction was brought to this country.

The 19th century, both here and in England, marked the end of the death penalty as the chief mode of punishment for serious crimes. And with its passing, the factor which had brought the doctrine of strict construction into existence as literally in favorem vitae disappeared—yet the doctrine itself lived, the sole relic of what had once been a veritable conspiracy for administrative nullification.

**2. The Legislative Response.** Faced with this persistent frustration of statutory purpose, 19th-century legislatures tried to overrule the doctrine of strict construction. The original suggestion came from the Field Code proposed for New York:

> The rule of the common law that penal statutes are to be strictly construed has no application to this Code. All its provisions are to be construed according to the fair import of their terms, with a view to effect its objects and to promote justice.

David Field, William Noyes and Alexander Bradford, Draft of a Penal Code for the State of New York § 10 (1864). As *Keeler* reveals, this proposal was adopted verbatim as § 4 of the California Code of 1872. Additionally, some 18 other states, most of them west of the Mississippi, passed similar statutes in the years before World War I. In a few cases, the enactment of such laws seems immediately to have altered the terms of judicial construction, but in other jurisdictions the courts continued to invoke the doctrine of strict construction despite the contrary legislative command.

Modern penal codes typically include some statement on statutory construction. Often, they simply carry forward a variant of the Field Code proposal quoted above. See, e.g., N.Y. Penal Law § 5.00 (McKinney 1987). Other states have followed the more elaborate formulation in § 1.02 of the Model Penal Code:

> (1) The general purposes of the provisions governing the definition of offenses are:
>
> (a) to forbid and prevent conduct that unjustifiably and inexcusably inflicts or threatens substantial harm to individual or public interests;
>
> (b) to subject to public control persons whose conduct indicates that they are disposed to commit crimes;

(c) to safeguard conduct that is without fault from condemnation as criminal;

(d) to give fair warning of the nature of the conduct declared to constitute an offense;

(e) to differentiate on reasonable grounds between serious and minor offenses....

(3) The provisions of the Code shall be construed according to the fair import of their terms but when the language is susceptible of differing constructions it shall be interpreted to further the general purposes stated in this Section and the special purposes of the particular provision involved....

**3.  *McBoyle* v. *United States*.** As *Keeler* and *Sobiek* suggest, the doctrine of strict construction continues to be invoked, albeit selectively,[a] as an aid in the interpretation of penal statutes. Today, however, the policy most often advanced to support this approach is not aversion to the severity of penal sanctions but rather the concern for fair notice of what is proscribed. In the words of one scholar, the modern principle of strict construction "may perhaps be viewed as something of a junior version of the vagueness doctrine." Herbert Packer, The Limits of the Criminal Sanction 95 (1968).

An early illustration of this approach is McBoyle v. United States, 283 U.S. 25 (1931). McBoyle was convicted of interstate transportation of a stolen "motor vehicle." The statute defined that term to include "an automobile, automobile truck, automobile wagon, motor cycle, or any other self-propelled vehicle not designed for running on rails." Speaking through Justice Holmes, the Supreme Court found that a stolen airplane did not qualify:

The question is the meaning of the word "vehicle" in the phrase, "any other self-propelled vehicle not designed for running on rails." No doubt etymologically it is possible to use the word to signify a conveyance working on land, water or air, and sometimes legislation extends the use in that direction.... But in everyday speech "vehicle" calls up the picture of a thing moving on land.... Airplanes were well known in 1919 when this statute was passed; but it is admitted that they were not mentioned in the reports or in the debates in Congress. It is impossible to read words that so carefully enumerate the different forms of motor vehicles and have no reference to any kind of aircraft, as including airplanes under a term that usage more and more precisely confines to a different class....

Although it is not likely that a criminal will carefully consider the text of the law before he murders or steals, it is reasonable

---

[a] See Dan M. Kahan, Lenity and Federal Common Law Crimes, 1994 Sup. Ct. Rev. 345 (arguing that judicial enforcement of the rule of strict construction is "notoriously sporadic and unpredictable").

that a fair warning should be given to the world in language that the common world will understand, of what the law intends to do if a certain line is passed. To make the warning fair, so far as possible the line should be clear. When a rule of conduct is laid down in words that evoke in the common mind only the picture of vehicles moving on land, the statute should not be extended to aircraft simply because it may seem to us that a similar policy applies, or upon the speculation that, if the legislature had thought of it, very likely broader words would have been used.

Justice Holmes' speculation as to what the legislature would have done had it thought of the situation was confirmed when Congress amended the law to cover interstate transportation of a stolen motor vehicle "or aircraft." 59 Stat. 536 (1945). "Aircraft" was defined to include "any contrivance now known or hereafter invented, used, or designed for navigation of or for flight in the air."

What should the Supreme Court do if this statute, now codified as 18 U.S.C. § 2312 (1988 and Supp. V 1993), were invoked against the interstate transportation of a stolen boat?

**4. Strict Construction of Federal Statutes: *United States* v. *Bass*.** United States v. Bass, 404 U.S. 336 (1971), illustrates an aspect of strict construction peculiar to federal law. Under the Constitution, the federal government has certain enumerated powers. An example is the power "to regulate Commerce with foreign Nations, and among the several States." No federal statute may be enacted unless it pertains to one or another of these enumerated powers. In practice, the powers of Congress have been expansively construed, but it remains true, at least theoretically, that every attempt by the federal government to punish criminal misconduct must be related to a federal interest within the enumerated powers.

The limitation of the national government to the enumerated powers affects the way federal crimes are defined. Most federal offenses include components specifically addressed to the underlying federal power being exercised. These are called "jurisdictional" elements, and they are distinctive features of federal crimes. For example, federal law does not directly punish incitement to riot; it punishes travel in interstate or foreign commerce, or use of any facility of interstate or foreign commerce with intent to incite a riot. 18 U.S.C. § 2101 (1988). Among the common jurisdictional bases (in addition to those dealing with interstate commerce) are use of the mails; the status of the offender or victim as a federal employee; and involvement of property owned, licensed, or insured by the federal government. Under current law, these jurisdictional components are part of the definition of federal crimes and must be proved to the jury beyond a reasonable doubt just as any other element of the offense charged.

*United States v. Bass* involved one of the many federal criminal statutes based on the power over interstate commerce. Specifically, 18 U.S.C. App. § 1202(a) (subsequently repealed as part of new legislation on this subject) punished anyone previously convicted of a felony "who receives, possesses, or transports in commerce or affecting commerce" any firearm. The issue before the Supreme Court was whether the phrase "in commerce or affecting commerce" applied only to transporting or whether it also limited the scope of the receiving and possessing offenses.

The Court held that the phrase "in commerce or affecting commerce" should be read to apply to all three aspects of the offense. The Court did not base its decision on the face of the statute or on the legislative history. Instead, it adopted the "narrower reading" in recognition of "two wise principles this Court has long followed." The first was that "ambiguity concerning the ambit of criminal statutes should be resolved in favor of lenity." This "strict construction" was defended in terms of fair warning and economy in the use of penal sanctions, both concerns applicable to all criminal laws. The second principle applied only to federal criminal law. It was that "unless Congress conveys its purpose clearly, it will not be deemed to have significantly changed the federal-state balance":

> Congress has traditionally been reluctant to define as a federal crime conduct readily denounced as criminal by the states.... In traditionally sensitive areas, such as legislation affecting the federal balance, the requirement of clear statement assures that the legislature has in fact faced, and intended to bring into issue, the critical matters involved in the judicial decision.... In the instant case, the broad construction urged by the government renders traditionally local criminal conduct a matter for federal enforcement and would also involve a substantial extension of federal police resources. Absent proof of some interstate-commerce nexus in each case, § 1202(a) dramatically intrudes upon traditional state criminal jurisdiction. [T]he legislative history provides scanty basis for concluding that Congress faced these serious questions and meant to affect the federal-state balance in the way now claimed by the government. Absent a clearer statement of intention from Congress than is present here, we do not interpret § 1202(a) to reach the "mere possession" of firearms.

Is the Court's second (or "federalism") principle applicable only to "jurisdictional" elements of federal offenses? Could it have been applied with equal force in *McBoyle*?

With respect to the Court's first (or "strict construction") rationale, note that in *Bass* and *McBoyle* the question was not whether the underlying conduct was criminal but whether state or federal authorities would prosecute. Should the courts be especially concerned about fair notice that certain misconduct violates a federal statute if it is in any event prohibited by state law? Are there other reasons to support "strict construction," even in the context of federal jurisdictional provisions?

---

## SECTION 5:  OPTIONAL CONCLUDING PROBLEM

### INTRODUCTORY NOTE

The United States Supreme Court decision reproduced below offers an opportunity to consider the material covered in this Chapter in a different context. It tests a Tennessee Supreme Court interpretation of the Tennessee murder statute against the federal Constitution. On the dissenting view, the Tennessee Court retroactively expanded the coverage of the murder statute in an unwarranted manner. The majority thought the interpretation well within the authority of the state Supreme Court.

# Rogers v. Tennessee

United States Supreme Court, 2001.
532 U.S. 451.

■ JUSTICE O'CONNOR delivered the opinion of the Court.

This case concerns the constitutionality of the retroactive application of a judicial decision abolishing the common law "year and a day rule." At common law, the year and a day rule provided that no defendant could be convicted of murder unless his victim had died by the defendant's act within a year and a day of the act. The Supreme Court of Tennessee abolished the rule as it had existed at common law in Tennessee and applied its decision to petitioner to uphold his conviction. The question before us is whether, in doing so, the Court denied petitioner due process of law in violation of the 14th Amendment.

I

Petitioner Wilbert K. Rogers was convicted in Tennessee state court of second degree murder. According to the undisputed facts, petitioner stabbed his victim, James Bowdery, with a butcher knife on May 6, 1994. One of the stab wounds penetrated Bowdery's heart. During surgery to repair the wound to his heart, Bowdery went into cardiac arrest, but was resuscitated and survived the procedure. As a result, however, he had developed a condition known as "cerebral hypoxia," which results from a loss of oxygen to the brain. Bowdery's higher brain functions had ceased, and he slipped into and remained in a coma until August 7, 1995, when he died from a kidney infection (a common complication experienced by comatose patients). Approximately 15 months had passed between the stabbing and Bowdery's death which, according to the undisputed testimony of the county medical examiner, was caused by cerebral hypoxia " 'secondary to a stab wound to the heart.' "

Based on this evidence, the jury found petitioner guilty under Tennessee's criminal homicide statute. The statute, which makes no mention of the year and a day rule, defines criminal homicide simply as "the unlawful killing of another person which may be first degree murder, second degree murder, voluntary manslaughter, criminally negligent homicide or vehicular homicide." Tenn.Code Ann. § 39–13–201 (1997). Petitioner appealed his conviction to the Tennessee Court of Criminal Appeals, arguing that, despite its absence from the statute, the year and a day rule persisted as part of the common law of Tennessee and, as such, precluded his conviction. The Court of Criminal Appeals rejected that argument and affirmed the conviction. . . .

The Supreme Court of Tennessee affirmed.... The Court observed that it had recognized the viability of the year and a day rule in Tennessee in Percer v. State, 118 Tenn. 765, 103 S.W. 780 (1907), and that, "[d]espite the paucity of case law" on the rule in Tennessee, "both parties ... agree that the ... rule was a part of the common law of this State." Turning to the rule's present status, the Court noted that the rule has been legislatively or judicially abolished by the "vast majority" of jurisdictions recently to have considered the issue.... After reviewing the justifications for the rule at common law ... the Court found that the original reasons for recognizing the rule no longer exist. Accordingly, the Court abolished the rule as it had existed at common law in Tennessee.

The Court disagreed with petitioner's contention that application of its decision abolishing the rule to his case would violate the Ex Post Facto Clauses of the State and Federal Constitutions. Those constitutional provisions, the Court observed, refer only to legislative Acts. The Court then noted that in Bouie v. City of Columbia, 378 U.S. 347 (1964), this Court held that due process prohibits retroactive application of any " 'judicial construction of a criminal statute [that] is unexpected and indefensible by reference to the law which has been expressed prior to the conduct in issue.' " The Court concluded, however, that application of its decision to petitioner would not offend this principle. We granted certiorari and we now affirm.

## II

Although petitioner's claim is one of due process, the Constitution's Ex Post Facto Clause figures prominently in his argument. The Clause provides simply that "[n]o State shall ... pass any ... ex post facto Law." Art. I, § 10, cl. 1. The most well-known and oft-repeated explanation of the scope of the Clause's protection was given by Justice Chase, who long ago identified, in dictum, four types of laws to which the Clause extends:

> 1st. Every law that makes an action done before the passing of the law, and which was innocent when done, criminal; and punishes such action. 2d. Every law that aggravates a crime, or makes it greater than it was, when committed. 3d. Every law that changes the punishment, and inflicts a greater punishment, than the law annexed to the crime, when committed. 4th. Every law that alters the legal rules of evidence, and receives less, or different, testimony, than the law required at the time of the commission of the offense, in order to convict the offender. Calder v. Bull, 3 U.S. (3 Dall.) 386, 390 (1798).

As the text of the Clause makes clear, it "is a limitation upon the powers of the Legislature, and does not of its own force apply to the Judicial Branch of government." Marks v. United States, 430 U.S. 188, 191 (1977).

We have observed, however, that limitations on ex post facto judicial decisionmaking are inherent in the notion of due process. In *Bouie v. City of Columbia,* we considered the South Carolina Supreme Court's retroactive application of its construction of the State's criminal trespass statute to the petitioners in that case. The statute prohibited "entry upon the lands of another ... after notice from the owner or tenant prohibiting such entry...." The South Carolina Court construed the statute to extend to patrons of a drug store who had received no notice prohibiting their entry into the store, but had refused to leave the store when asked. Prior to the Court's decision, South Carolina cases construing the statute had uniformly held that conviction under the statute required proof of notice before entry. None of those cases, moreover, had given the "slightest indication that that requirement could be satisfied by proof of the different act of remaining on the land after being told to leave."

We held that the South Carolina Court's retroactive application of its construction to the store patrons violated due process. Reviewing decisions in which we had held criminal statutes "void for vagueness" under the Due Process Clause, we noted that this Court has often recognized the "basic principle that a criminal statute must give fair warning of the conduct that it makes a crime." Deprivation of the right to fair warning, we continued, can result both from vague statutory language and from an unforeseeable and retroactive judicial expansion of statutory language that appears narrow and precise on its face. For that reason, we concluded that "[i]f a judicial construction of a criminal statute is 'unexpected and indefensible by reference to the law which had been expressed prior to the conduct in issue,' [the construction] must not be given retroactive effect." We found that the South Carolina Court's construction of the statute violated this principle because it was so clearly at odds with the statute's plain language and had no support in prior South Carolina decisions.

Relying largely upon *Bouie,* petitioner argues that the Tennessee Court erred in rejecting his claim that the retroactive application of its decision to his case violates due process. Petitioner contends that the Ex Post Facto Clause would prohibit the retroactive application of a decision abolishing the year and a day rule if accomplished by the Tennessee Legislature. He claims that the purposes behind the Clause are so fundamental that due process should prevent the Supreme Court of Tennessee from accomplishing the same result by judicial decree. In support of this claim, petitioner takes *Bouie* to stand for the proposition that "[i]n evaluating whether the retroactive application of a judicial decree violates Due Process, a critical question is whether the Constitution would prohibit the same result attained by the exercise of the state's legislative power."

To the extent petitioner argues that the Due Process Clause incorporates the specific prohibitions of the Ex Post Facto Clause as identified in *Calder,* petitioner misreads *Bouie.* To be sure, our opinion in *Bouie* does contain some expansive language that is suggestive of the broad interpretation for which petitioner argues. Most prominent is our statement that "[i]f a state legislature is barred by the Ex Post Facto Clause from passing ... a law, it must follow that a State Supreme Court is barred by the Due Process Clause from achieving precisely the same result by judicial construction." 378 U.S., at 353–54; see also id., at 353 ("[A]n unforeseeable judicial enlargement of a criminal statute, applied retroactively, operates precisely like an ex post facto law''); id., at 362, 84 S.Ct. 1697 (''The Due Process Clause compels the same result'' as would the constitutional proscription against ex post facto laws ''where the State has sought to achieve precisely the same [impermissible] effect by judicial construction of the statute''). This language, however, was dicta. Our decision in *Bouie* was rooted firmly in well established notions of *due process*. Its rationale rested on core due process concepts of notice, foreseeability, and, in particular, the right to fair warning as those concepts bear on the constitutionality of attaching criminal penalties to what previously had been innocent conduct. And we couched its holding squarely in terms of that established due process right, and not in terms of the ex post facto-related dicta to which petitioner points. Id., at 355 (concluding that ''the South Carolina Code did not give [the petitioners] fair warning, at the time of their conduct . . ., that the act for which they now stand convicted was rendered criminal by the statute''). Contrary to petitioner's suggestion, nowhere in the opinion did we go so far as to incorporate jot-for-jot the specific categories of *Calder* into due process limitations on the retroactive application of judicial decisions.

Nor have any of our subsequent decisions addressing *Bouie*-type claims interpreted *Bouie* as extending so far. Those decisions instead have uniformly viewed *Bouie* as restricted to its traditional due process roots. In doing so, they have applied *Bouie*'s check on retroactive judicial decisionmaking not by reference to the ex post facto categories set out in *Calder,* but, rather, in accordance with the more basic and general principle of fair warning that *Bouie* so clearly articulated.

Petitioner observes that the Due Process and Ex Post Facto Clauses safeguard common interests—in particular, the interests in fundamental fairness (through notice and fair warning) and the prevention of the arbitrary and vindictive use of the laws. While this is undoubtedly correct, petitioner is mistaken to suggest that these considerations compel extending the strictures of the Ex Post Facto Clause to the context of common law judging. The Ex Post Facto Clause, by its own terms, does not apply to courts. Extending the Clause to courts through the rubric of due process thus would circumvent the clear constitutional text. It also would evince too little regard for the important institutional and contextual differences between legislating, on the one hand, and common law decisionmaking, on the other.

Petitioner contends that state courts acting in their common law capacity act much like legislatures in the exercise of their lawmaking function, and indeed may in some cases even be subject to the same kinds of political influences and pressures that justify ex post facto limitations upon legislatures. A court's ''opportunity for discrimination,'' however, ''is more limited than [a] legislature's, in that [it] can only act in construing existing law in actual litigation.'' James v. United States, 366 U.S. 213, 247, n. 3 (1961) (Harlan, J., concurring in part and dissenting in part). Moreover, ''[g]iven the divergent pulls of flexibility and precedent in our case law system,'' ibid., incorporation of the *Calder* categories into due process limitations on judicial decisionmaking would place an unworkable and unacceptable restraint on normal judicial processes and would be incompatible with the resolution of uncertainty that marks any evolving legal system.

That is particularly so where, as here, the allegedly impermissible judicial application of a rule of law involves not the interpretation of a statute but an act of common law judging. In the context of common law doctrines (such as the year and a day rule), there often arises a need to clarify or even to reevaluate prior opinions as new circumstances and fact patterns present themselves. Such judicial acts, whether they be characterized as "making" or "finding" the law, are a necessary part of the judicial business in States in which the criminal law retains some of its common law elements. Strict application of ex post facto principles in that context would unduly impair the incremental and reasoned development of precedent that is the foundation of the common law system. The common law, in short, presupposes a measure of evolution that is incompatible with stringent application of ex post facto principles. It was on account of concerns such as these that *Bouie* restricted due process limitations on the retroactive application of judicial interpretations of criminal statutes to those that are "unexpected and indefensible by reference to the law which had been expressed prior to the conduct in issue." *Bouie v. City of Columbia*, 378 U.S., at 354.

We believe this limitation adequately serves the common law context as well. It accords common law courts the substantial leeway they must enjoy as they engage in the daily task of formulating and passing upon criminal defenses and interpreting such doctrines as causation and intent, reevaluating and refining them as may be necessary to bring the common law into conformity with logic and common sense. It also adequately respects the due process concern with fundamental fairness and protects against vindictive or arbitrary judicial lawmaking by safeguarding defendants against unjustified and unpredictable breaks with prior law. Accordingly, we conclude that a judicial alteration of a common law doctrine of criminal law violates the principle of fair warning, and hence must not be given retroactive effect, only where it is "unexpected and indefensible by reference to the law which had been expressed prior to the conduct in issue." Ibid.

Justice Scalia makes much of the fact that, at the time of the framing of the Constitution, it was widely accepted that courts could not "change" the law and that (according to Justice Scalia) there is no doubt that the Ex Post Facto Clause would have prohibited a legislative decision identical to the Tennessee Court's decision here. This latter argument seeks at bottom merely to reopen what has long been settled by the constitutional text and our own decisions: that the Ex Post Facto Clause does not apply to judicial decisionmaking. The former argument is beside the point. Common law courts at the time of the framing undoubtedly believed that they were finding rather than making law. But, however one characterizes their actions, the fact of the matter is that common law courts then, as now, were deciding cases, and in doing so were fashioning and refining the law as it then existed in light of reason and experience. Due process clearly did not prohibit this process of judicial evolution at the time of the framing, and it does not do so today.

### III

Turning to the particular facts of the instant case, the Tennessee Court's abolition of the year and a day rule was not unexpected and indefensible. The year and a day rule is widely viewed as an outdated relic of the common law. Petitioner does not even so much as hint that good reasons exist for retaining the rule, and so we need not delve too deeply into the rule and its history here. Suffice it to say that the rule is generally believed to date back to the 13th century, when it served as a statute of limitations governing the time in which an individual might initiate a private action for murder known as an "appeal of death"; that by the 18th century the rule had been extended to the law governing public prosecutions for murder; that the primary and most frequently cited justification for the rule is that 13th century medical science was incapable of establishing causation beyond a reasonable doubt when a great deal of time had elapsed between the injury to the victim and his death; and that, as practically every court recently to have considered the rule has noted, advances in medical and related science have so undermined the usefulness of the rule as to render it without question obsolete.

For this reason, the year and a day rule has been legislatively or judicially abolished in the vast majority of jurisdictions recently to have addressed the issue. Citing *Bouie,* petitioner contends that the judicial abolition of the rule in other jurisdictions is irrelevant to whether he had fair warning that the rule in Tennessee might similarly be abolished and, hence, to whether the Tennessee Court's decision was unexpected and indefensible as applied to him. In discussing the apparent meaning of the South Carolina statute in *Bouie,* we noted that "[i]t would be a rare situation in which the meaning of a statute of another State sufficed to afford a person 'fair warning' that his own State's statute meant something quite different from what its words said." This case, however, involves not the precise meaning of the words of a particular statute, but rather the continuing viability of a common law rule. Common law courts frequently look to the decisions of other jurisdictions in determining whether to alter or modify a common law rule in light of changed circumstances, increased knowledge, and general logic and experience. Due process, of course, does not require a person to apprise himself of the common law of all 50 States in order to guarantee that his actions will not subject him to punishment in light of a developing trend in the law that has not yet made its way to his State. At the same time, however, the fact that a vast number of jurisdictions have abolished a rule that has so clearly outlived its purpose is surely relevant to whether the abolition of the rule in a particular case can be said to be unexpected and indefensible by reference to the law as it then existed.

Finally, and perhaps most importantly, at the time of petitioner's crime the year and a day rule had only the most tenuous foothold as part of the criminal law of the State of Tennessee. The rule did not exist as part of Tennessee's statutory criminal code. And while the Supreme Court of Tennessee concluded that the rule persisted at common law, it also pointedly observed that the rule had never once served as a ground of decision in any prosecution for murder in the State. Indeed, in all the reported Tennessee cases, the rule has been mentioned only three times, and each time in dicta.

The first mention of the rule in Tennessee, and the only mention of it by the Supreme Court of that State, was in 1907 in *Percer v. State.* In *Percer,* the Court reversed the defendant's conviction for second degree murder because the defendant was not present in court when the verdict was announced and because the proof failed to show that the murder occurred prior to the finding of the indictment. . . . The Court . . . quoted the rule that "[i]n murder, the death must be proven to have taken place within a year and a day from the date of the injury received." [But the] Court made no mention of the year and a day rule anywhere in its legal analysis or, for that matter, anywhere else in its opinion. Thus, whatever the import of the Court's earlier quoting of the rule, it is clear that the rule did not serve as the basis for the *Percer* Court's decision.

The next two references to the rule both were by the Tennessee Court of Criminal Appeals in cases [decided in 1974 and 1995, respectively] in which the date of the victim's death was not even in issue. . . .

These cases hardly suggest that the Tennessee Court's decision was "unexpected and indefensible" such that it offended the due process principle of fair warning articulated in *Bouie* and its progeny. This is so despite the fact that, as Justice Scalia correctly points out, the Court viewed the year and a day rule as a "substantive principle" of the common law of Tennessee. As such, however, it was a principle in name only, having never once been enforced in the State. The Supreme Court of Tennessee also emphasized this fact in its opinion, and rightly so, for it is surely relevant to whether the Court's abolition of the rule in petitioner's case violated due process limitations on retroactive judicial decisionmaking. And while we readily agree with Justice Scalia that fundamental due process prohibits the punishment of conduct that cannot fairly be said to have been criminal at the time the conduct occurred, nothing suggests that is what took place here.

There is, in short, nothing to indicate that the Tennessee Court's abolition of the rule in petitioner's case represented an exercise of the sort of unfair and arbitrary judicial action against which the Due Process Clause aims to protect. Far from a marked and unpredictable departure from prior precedent, the Court's decision was a routine exercise of common law decisionmaking in which the Court brought the law into conformity with reason and common sense. It did so by laying to rest an archaic and outdated rule that had never been relied upon as a ground of decision in any reported Tennessee case.

The judgment of the Supreme Court of Tennessee is accordingly affirmed.

It is so ordered.

■ JUSTICE STEVENS, dissenting.

While I have joined Justice Scalia's entire dissent, I must add this brief caveat. The perception that common law judges had no power to change the law was unquestionably an important aspect of our judicial heritage in the 17th century but, as he has explained, that perception has played a role of diminishing importance in later years. Whether the most significant changes in that perception occurred before the end of the 18th century or early in the 19th century is, in my judgment, a tangential question that need not be resolved in order to decide this case correctly. For me, far more important than the historical issue is the fact that the majority has undervalued the threat to liberty that is posed whenever the criminal law is changed retroactively.

■ JUSTICE SCALIA, with whom JUSTICE STEVENS and JUSTICE THOMAS join, and with whom JUSTICE BREYER joins as to Part II, dissenting.

The Court today approves the conviction of a man for a murder that was not murder (but only manslaughter) when the offense was committed. It thus violates a principle—encapsulated in the maxim nulla poena sine lege—which "dates from the ancient Greeks" and has been described as one of the most "widely held value-judgment[s] in the entire history of human thought." J. Hall, General Principles of Criminal Law 59 (2d ed. 1960). Today's opinion produces, moreover, a curious constitution that only a judge could love. One in which (by virtue of the Ex Post Facto Clause) the elected representatives of all the people cannot retroactively make murder what was not murder when the act was committed; but in which unelected judges can do precisely that. One in which the predictability of parliamentary lawmaking cannot validate the retroactive creation of crimes, but the predictability of judicial lawmaking can do so. I do not believe this is the system that the Framers envisioned—or, for that matter, that any reasonable person would imagine.

### I.A.

To begin with, let us be clear that the law here was altered after the fact. Petitioner, whatever else he was guilty of, was innocent of murder under the law as it stood at the time of the stabbing, because the victim did not die until after a year and a day had passed.... Though the Court spends some time questioning whether the year-and-a-day rule was ever truly established in Tennessee, the Supreme Court of Tennessee said it was, and this reasonable reading of state law by the State's highest court is binding upon us.

Petitioner's claim is that his conviction violated the Due Process Clause of the 14th Amendment, insofar as that Clause contains the principle applied against the legislature by the Ex Post Facto Clause of Article I.

We first discussed the relationship between these two Clauses in Bouie v. City of Columbia, 378 U.S. 347 (1964). There, we considered Justice Chase to have spoken for the Court in Calder v. Bull, 3 U.S. (3 Dall.) 386, 390 (1798), when he defined an ex post facto law as, inter alia, one that "aggravates a crime, or makes it greater than it was, when committed." We concluded that, "[i]f a state legislature is barred by the Ex Post Facto Clause from passing such a law, it must follow that a State Supreme Court is barred by the Due Process Clause from achieving precisely the same result by judicial construction." The Court seeks to avoid the obvious import of this language by characterizing it as mere dicta. Only a concept of dictum that includes the very reasoning of the opinion could support this characterization. The ratio decidendi of *Bouie* was that the principle applied to the legislature though the Ex Post Facto Clause was contained in the Due Process Clause insofar as judicial action is concerned. I cannot understand why the Court derives such comfort from the fact that later opinions applying *Bouie* have referred to the Due Process Clause rather than the Ex Post Facto Clause; that is entirely in accord with the rationale of the case, which I follow and which the Court discards.

The Court attempts to cabin *Bouie* by reading it to prohibit only " 'unexpected and indefensible' " judicial law revision, and to permit retroactive judicial changes so long as the defendant has had "fair warning" that the changes might occur. This reading seems plausible because *Bouie* does indeed use those quoted terms; but they have been wrenched entirely out of context. The "fair warning" to which *Bouie* and subsequent cases referred was not "fair warning that the law might be changed," but fair warning *of what constituted the crime at the time of the offense.* And *Bouie* did not express disapproval of "unexpected and indefensible changes in the law" (and thus implicitly approve "expected or defensible changes"). It expressed disapproval of "*judicial construction* of a criminal statute" that is "unexpected and indefensible *by reference to the law which had been expressed prior to the conduct in issue.*" It thus implicitly approved only a judicial construction that was an expected or defensible application of prior cases interpreting the statute. Extending this principle from statutory crimes to common-law crimes would result in the approval of retroactive holdings that accord with prior cases expounding the common law, and the disapproval of retroactive holdings that clearly depart from prior cases expounding the common law. According to *Bouie,* not just "unexpected and indefensible" retroactive changes in the common law of crimes are bad, but *all* retroactive changes.

*Bouie* rested squarely upon "[t]he fundamental principle that 'the required criminal law must have existed when the conduct in issue occurred,' " (Nulla poena sine lege.) Proceeding from that principle, *Bouie* said that "a State Supreme Court is barred by the Due Process Clause from achieving precisely the same result [prohibited by the Ex Post Facto Clause] by judicial construction." There is no doubt that "fair warning" of the legislature's intent to change the law does not insulate retroactive *legislative* criminalization. Such a statute violates the Ex Post Facto Clause, no matter that, at the time the offense was committed, the bill enacting the change was pending and assured of passage—or indeed, had already been passed but not yet signed by the President whose administration had proposed it. It follows from the analysis of *Bouie* that "fair warning" of impending change cannot insulate retroactive *judicial* criminalization either.

Nor is there any reason in the nature of things why it should. According to the Court, the exception is necessary because prohibiting retroactive judicial criminalization would "place an unworkable and unacceptable restraint on normal judicial processes," would be "incompatible with the resolution of uncertainty that marks any evolving legal system," and would "unduly impair the incremental and reasoned development of precedent that is the foundation of the common law system." That assessment ignores the crucial difference between simply applying a law to a new set of circumstances and changing the law that has previously been applied to the very circumstances before the court. Many criminal cases present some factual nuance that arguably distinguishes them from cases that have come before; a court applying the penal statute to the new fact pattern does not purport to *change* the law. That, however, is not the action before us here, but rather, a square, head-on *overruling* of prior law—or, more accurately, something even more extreme than that: a judicial opinion acknowledging that under prior law, for reasons that used to be valid, the accused could not be convicted, but decreeing that, because of changed circumstances, "we hereby abolish the common law rule," 992 S.W.2d, at 401, and upholding the conviction by applying the new rule to conduct that occurred before the change in law was announced. Even in civil cases, and even in modern times, such retroactive revision of a concededly valid legal rule is extremely rare. With regard to criminal cases, I have no hesitation in affirming that it was unheard-of at the time the original Due Process Clause was adopted. As I discuss in detail in the following section, proceeding in that fashion would have been regarded as contrary to the judicial traditions embraced within the concept of due process of law.

**B.**

The Court's opinion considers the judgment at issue here "a routine exercise of common law decisionmaking," whereby the Tennessee Court "brought the law into conformity with reason and common sense," by "laying to rest an archaic and outdated rule." This is an accurate enough description of what modern "common law decisionmaking" consists of—but it is not an accurate description of the theoretical model of common-law decisionmaking accepted by those who adopted the Due Process Clause. At the time of the framing, common-law jurists believed (in the words of Sir Francis Bacon) that the judge's "office is jus dicere, and not jus dare; to interpret law, and not to make law, or give law." Bacon, Essays, Civil and Moral, in 3 Harvard Classics 130 (C. Eliot ed.1909) (1625). Or as described by Blackstone, whose Commentaries were widely read and "accepted [by the framing generation] as the most satisfactory exposition of the common law of England," "judicial decisions are the principal and most authoritative *evidence,* that can be given, of the existence of such a custom as shall form a part of the common law." 1 W. Blackstone, Commentaries on the Laws of England *69 (1765) (hereinafter Blackstone) (emphasis added).

Blackstone acknowledged that the courts' exposition of what the law was could change. Stare decisis, he said, "admits of exception, where the former determination is most evidently contrary to reason...." But "in such cases the subsequent judges do not pretend to make a new law, but to vindicate the old one from misrepresentation." To fit within this category of bad law, a law must be "manifestly absurd or unjust." It would not suffice, he said, that "the particular reason [for the law] can at this distance of time [not be] precisely assigned." "For though [its] reason be not obvious at first view, yet we owe such a deference to former times as not to suppose they acted wholly without consideration."[1] ....

There are, of course, stray statements and doctrines found in the historical record that—read out of context—could be thought to support the modern-day proposition that the common law was always meant to evolve. Take, for instance, Lord Coke's statement in the Institutes that "the reason of the law ceasing, the law itself ceases." This maxim is often cited by modern devotees of a turbulently changing common law—often in its Latin form (cessante ratione legis, cessat ipse lex) to create the impression of great venerability. [But this principle] had to do, not with a changing of the common-law rule, but with a change of circumstances that rendered the common-law rule no longer applicable to the case....

It is true that framing-era judges in this country considered themselves authorized to reject English common-law precedent they found "barbarous" and "ignorant," see 1 Z. Swift, A System of the Laws of the State of Connecticut 46 (1795) (hereinafter Swift); N. Chipman, A Dissertation on the Act Adopting the Common and Statute Laws of England, in Reports and Dissertations 117, 128 (1793) (hereinafter Chipman). That, however, was not an assertion of *judges'* power to *change* the common law. For, as Blackstone wrote, the common law was a law for England, and did not automatically transfer to the American Colonies; rather, it had to be adopted. See 1 Blackstone * 107–08 (observing that "the common law of England, as such, has no allowance or authority" in "[o]ur American plantations"). In short, the colonial courts felt themselves perfectly free to pick and choose which parts of the English common law they would adopt.[3] ... This discretion not to adopt would not presuppose, or even support, the power of colonial courts subsequently to change the accumulated colonial common law....

---

[1] Inquiring into a law's original reasonableness was perhaps tantamount to questioning whether it existed at all. "In holding the origin to have been unreasonable, the Court nearly always doubts or denies the actual origin and continuance of the custom in fact." C. Allen, Law in the Making 140 (3d ed.1939) (hereinafter Allen).

[3] In fact, however, "most of the basic departures [from English common law] were accomplished not by judicial decision but by local statute, so that by the time of the American Revolution one hears less and less about the unsuitability of common law principles to the American environment." 1 M. Horwitz, Transformation of American Law 1780–1860, p. 5 (1977).

Nor is the framing era's acceptance of common-law crimes support for the proposition that the Framers accepted an evolving common law. The acknowledgment of a new crime, not thitherto rejected by judicial decision, was not a *changing* of the common law, but an *application* of it. At the time of the framing, common-law crimes were considered unobjectionable, for " 'a law founded on the law of nature may be retrospective, because it always existed,' " Horwitz, at 7, quoting Blackwell v. Wilkinson, Jefferson's Rep. 73, 77 (Va.1768) (argument of then-Attorney General John Randolph). Of course, the notion of a common-law crime is utterly anathema today, which leads one to wonder why that is so. The obvious answer is that we now agree with the perceptive chief justice of Connecticut, who wrote in 1796 that common-law crimes "partak[e] of the odious nature of an ex post facto law." 2 Swift 365–66. But, as Horwitz makes clear, a widespread sharing of Swift's "preoccupation with the unfairness of administering a system of judge-made criminal law was a distinctly *post-revolutionary* phenomenon, reflecting a profound change in sensibility. For the inarticulate premise that lay behind Swift's warnings against the danger of judicial discretion was *a growing perception that judges no longer merely discovered law; they also made it.*" Horwitz 14–15 (emphases added). In other words, the connection between ex post facto lawmaking and common-law judging would not have become widely apparent *until* common-law judging *became* lawmaking, not (as it had been) law declaring. This did not happen, until the 19th century, *after* the framing.

What occurred in the present case, then, is precisely what Blackstone said—and the Framers believed—would not suffice. The Tennessee Supreme Court made no pretense that the year-and-a-day rule was "bad" law from the outset; rather, it asserted, the need for the rule, as a means of assuring causality of the death, had disappeared with time. Blackstone—and the Framers who were formed by Blackstone—would clearly have regarded that *change* in law as a matter for the legislature, beyond the *power* of the court. It may well be that some common-law decisions of the era in fact changed the law while purporting not to. But that is beside the point. What is important here is that it was an undoubted point of principle, at the time the Due Process Clause was adopted, that courts could not "change" the law. That explains why the Constitution restricted only the legislature from enacting ex post facto laws. Under accepted norms of judicial process, an ex post facto law (in the sense of a judicial holding, not that a prior decision was erroneous, but that the prior valid law is hereby retroactively *changed*) was simply not an option for the courts. . . .

It is not a matter, therefore, of "[e]xtending the [Ex Post Facto] Clause to courts through the rubric of due process," and thereby "circumvent [ing] the clear constitutional text." It is simply a matter of determining what due judicial process consists of—and it does not consist of retroactive creation of crimes. The Ex Post Facto Clause is relevant only because it demonstrates beyond doubt that, however much the acknowledged and accepted role of common-law courts could evolve (as it has) in other respects, retroactive revision of the criminal law was regarded as so fundamentally unfair that an alteration of the judicial role which permits *that* will be a denial of due process. Madison wrote that "ex-post-facto laws ... are contrary to the first principles of the social compact, and to every principle of social legislation." The Federalist No. 44, p. 282 (C. Rossiter ed.1961). I find it impossible to believe, as the Court does, that this strong sentiment attached only to retroactive laws passed by the legislature, and would not apply equally (or indeed with even greater force) to a court's production of the same result through disregard of the traditional limits upon judicial power. Insofar as the "first principles of the social compact" are concerned, what possible difference does it make that "[a] court's opportunity for discrimination" by retroactively changing a law "is more limited than a legislature's, in that it can only act in construing existing law in actual litigation"? The injustice to the individuals affected is no less.

## II

Even if I agreed with the Court that the Due Process Clause is violated only when there is lack of "fair warning" of the impending retroactive change, I would not find such fair warning here. It is not clear to me, in fact, what the Court believes the fair warning consisted of. Was it the mere fact that "[t]he year and a day rule is widely viewed as an outdated relic of the common law"? So are many of the elements of common-law crimes, such as "breaking the close" as an element of burglary, or "asportation" as an element of larceny. Are all of these "outdated relics" subject to retroactive judicial rescission? Or perhaps the fair warning consisted of the fact that "the year and a day rule has been legislatively or judicially abolished in the vast majority of jurisdictions recently to have addressed the issue." But why not count in petitioner's favor (as giving him no reason to expect a change in law) those even more numerous jurisdictions that have chosen *not* "recently to have addressed the issue"? And why not also count in petitioner's favor (rather than *against* him) those jurisdictions that have abolished the rule *legislatively,* and those jurisdictions that have abolished it through *prospective* rather than *retroactive* judicial rulings (together, a large majority of the abolitions)? That is to say, even if it was predictable that the rule would be changed, it was *not* predictable that it would be changed *retroactively,* rather than in the *prospective* manner to which legislatures are restricted by the Ex Post Facto Clause, or in the *prospective* manner that most other courts have employed.

In any event, as the Court itself acknowledges, "[d]ue process ... does not require a person to apprise himself of the common law of all 50 States in order to guarantee that his actions will not subject him to punishment in light of a developing trend in the law that has not yet made its way to his State." The Court tries to counter this self-evident point with the statement that "[a]t the same time, however, the fact that a vast number of jurisdictions have abolished a rule that has so clearly outlived its purpose is surely relevant to whether the abolition of the rule in a particular case can be said to be unexpected and indefensible by reference to the law as it then existed." This retort rests upon the fallacy that I discussed earlier: that "expected or defensible" "abolition" of prior law was approved by *Bouie.* It was not—and according such conclusive effect to the "defensibility" (by which I presume the Court means the "reasonableness") of the change in law will validate the retroactive creation of many new crimes.

Finally, the Court seeks to establish fair warning by discussing at great length how unclear it was that the year-and-a-day rule was ever the law in Tennessee. As I have already observed, the Supreme Court of Tennessee is the authoritative expositor of Tennessee law, and has said categorically that the year-and-a-day rule was the law. Does the Court mean to establish the principle that fair warning of impending change exists—or perhaps fair warning can be dispensed with—when the prior law is not crystal clear? Yet another boon for retroactively created crimes.

I reiterate that the only "fair warning" discussed in our precedents, and the only "fair warning" relevant to the issue before us here, is fair warning *of what the law is*. That warning, unlike the new one that today's opinion invents, goes well beyond merely "safeguarding defendants against *unjustified* and *unpredictable* breaks with prior law." It safeguards them against *changes in the law after the fact*. But even accepting the Court's novel substitute, the opinion's conclusion that this watered-down standard has been met seems to me to proceed on the principle that a large number of almost-valid arguments makes a solid case. As far as I can tell, petitioner had nothing that could fairly be called a "warning" that the Supreme Court of Tennessee would retroactively eliminate one of the elements of the crime of murder.

* * *

To decide this case, we need only conclude that due process prevents a court from (1) acknowledging the validity, when they were rendered, of prior decisions establishing a particular element of a crime; (2) changing the prior law so as to eliminate that element; and (3) applying that change to conduct that occurred under the prior regime. A court would remain free to apply common-law criminal rules to new fact patterns so long as that application is consistent with a fair reading of prior cases. It would remain free to conclude that a prior decision or series of decisions establishing a particular element of a crime was in error, and to apply that conclusion retroactively (so long as the "fair notice" requirement of *Bouie* is satisfied). It would even remain free, insofar as the ex post facto element of the Due Process Clause is concerned, to "reevaluat[e] and refin[e]" the elements of common-law crimes to its heart's content, so long as it does so prospectively. (The majority of state courts that have abolished the year-and-a-day rule have done so in this fashion.) And, of course (as Blackstone and the Framers envisioned), legislatures would be free to eliminate outmoded elements of common-law crimes for the future *by law*. But what a court cannot do, consistent with due process, is what the Tennessee Supreme Court did here: avowedly *change* (to the defendant's disadvantage) the criminal law governing past acts.

For these reasons, I would reverse the judgment of the Supreme Court of Tennessee.

■ JUSTICE BREYER, dissenting.

I agree with the Court's basic approach. Justice Cardozo pointed out that retroactivity should be determined "not by metaphysical conceptions of the nature of judge-made law, . . . but by considerations of convenience, of utility, and of the deepest sentiments of justice." The Nature of the Judicial Process 148–49 (1921). Similarly, the Due Process Clause asks us to consider the basic fairness or unfairness of retroactive application of the Tennessee Court's change in the law. That Clause provides protection against after-the-fact changes in criminal law that deprive defendants of fair warning of the nature and consequences of their actions. It does not enshrine Blackstone's "ancient dogma that the law declared by . . . courts had a Platonic or ideal existence before the act of declaration," Great Northern R. Co. v. Sunburst Oil & Refining Co., 287 U.S. 358, 365 (1932) (Cardozo, J.).

I also agree with the Court that, in applying the Due Process Clause, we must ask whether the judicial ruling in question was "unexpected and indefensible by reference to the law which had been expressed prior to the conduct in issue." Bouie v. City of Columbia, 378 U.S. 347, 354 (1964).

I cannot agree, however, with the majority's application of that due process principle to this case. As Justice Scalia well explains, Rogers did not have fair warning that the Tennessee courts would abolish the year and a day rule or that they would retroactively apply the new law to the circumstances of his case, thereby upgrading the crime those circumstances revealed from attempted murder to murder. I therefore join Part II of Justice Scalia's dissenting opinion.

———

# CHAPTER II

# THE CRIMINAL MIND

---

## SECTION 1: THE FOUNDATIONS OF MENS REA

---

## SUBSECTION A: HISTORICAL ORIGINS OF MENS REA

---

### INTRODUCTORY NOTES ON THE REQUIREMENT OF MENS REA

**1. The History.** A "guilty mind" or "mens rea" is generally regarded as an essential requirement for the imposition of criminal liability. It is captured in the ancient maxim "actus reus non facit reum nisi mens sit rea," which means "the act is not guilty unless the mind is guilty." The origins of this requirement are obscure. It is clear, however, that for most offenses some requirement of mens rea has existed for many centuries. The early development of this concept is admirably treated in Francis Bowes Sayre, Mens Rea, 45 Harv. L. Rev. 974 (1932), on which the following summary is based.[a]

With respect to some offenses, early criminal law apparently focused on harms caused and not on the motive or intent of the actor. Liability was, in modern parlance, "absolute" or "strict." By the 12th century, the influence of Roman and canon law led to what Sayre calls an inquiry into "general moral blameworthiness." The next stage of development consisted of the conversion of this requirement into more specific questions about the defendant's state of mind that varied with the particular crime involved. In larceny, for example, Sayre observed three stages of evolution: (i) an initial formulation (prior to the legal separation of crime and tort) permitting an action against one in possession of stolen goods without regard to wrongful intent and whether or not that person was the thief; (ii) the later idea that the proper inquiry for the criminal law was whether the actor was morally blameworthy in the sense that the conduct was wicked or evil; (iii) and finally, the modern concept that the mens rea for larceny should focus more precisely on the defendant's state of mind at the time of the taking, as reflected in what became the traditional common-law definition of the

---

[a] For a more recent review of the history, see Martin R. Gardner, The Mens Rea Enigma: Observations on the Role of Motive in the Criminal Law Past and Present, 1993 Utah L. Rev. 635.

offense: "taking and carrying away the personal property of another with intent permanently to deprive the other of the property."

Sayre's general conclusion was that the concept of mens rea "has no fixed continuing meaning" over time. Instead:

> The conception of mens rea has varied with the changing underlying conceptions and objectives of criminal justice.... Under the dominating influence of the canon law and the penitential books the underlying objective of criminal justice gradually came to be the punishment of evil-doing; as a result the mental factors necessary for criminality were based upon a mind bent on evil-doing in the sense of moral wrong. Our modern objective tends more and more in the direction, not of awarding adequate punishment for moral wrong-doing, but of protecting social and public interests. To the extent that this objective prevails, the mental element requisite for criminality ... is coming to mean, not so much a mind bent on evil-doing as an intent to do that which unduly endangers social or public interests.

**2. *Morissette v. United States*.** The commitment of modern criminal law to the mens rea requirement was summarized by Justice Robert Jackson in a well known opinion in Morissette v. United States, 342 U.S. 246 (1952):

> ... The contention that an injury can amount to a crime only when inflicted by intention is no provincial or transient notion. It is as universal and persistent in mature systems of law as belief in freedom of the human will and a consequent ability and duty of the normal individual to choose between good and evil.[4] A relation between some mental element and punishment for a harmful act is almost as instinctive as the child's familiar exculpatory "But I didn't mean to," and has afforded the rational basis for a tardy and unfinished substitution of deterrence and reformation in place of retaliation and vengeance as the motivation for public prosecution. Unqualified acceptance of this doctrine by English common law in the 18th century was indicated by Blackstone's sweeping statement that to constitute any crime there must first be a "vicious will.".....
>
> Crime, as a compound concept, generally constituted only from concurrence of an evil-meaning mind with an evil-doing hand, was congenial to an intense individualism and took deep and early root in American soil. As the state codified the common law of crimes, even if their enactments were silent on the subject, their courts assumed that the omission did not signify disapproval of the principle but merely recognized that intent was so inherent in the

---

[4] ... "Historically, our substantive criminal law is based upon a theory of punishing the vicious will. It postulates a free agent confronted with a choice between doing right and doing wrong and choosing freely to do wrong." Ezra Pound, Introduction to Sayre, Cases on Criminal Law (1927).

idea of the offense that it required no statutory affirmation. Courts, with little hesitation or division, found an implication of the requirement as to offenses that were taken over from the common law. The unanimity with which they have adhered to the central thought that wrongdoing must be conscious to be criminal is emphasized by the variety, disparity and confusion of their definitions of the requisite but elusive mental element. However, courts of various jurisdictions, and for the purposes of different offenses, have devised working formulae, if not scientific ones, for the instruction of juries around such terms as "felonious intent," "criminal intent," "malice aforethought," "guilty knowledge," "fraudulent intent," "wilfulness," "scienter," to denote guilty knowledge, or "mens rea," to signify an evil purpose or mental culpability. By use or combination of these various tokens, they have sought to protect those who were not blameworthy in mind from conviction of infamous common-law crimes. . . .

Stealing, larceny, and its variants and equivalents, were among the earliest offenses known to the law that existed before legislation; they are invasions of rights of property which stir a sense of insecurity in the whole community and arouse public demand for retribution, the penalty is high and, when a sufficient amount is involved, the infamy is that of a felony, which, says Maitland, is ". . . . as bad a word as you can give to man or thing." . . . . The purpose and obvious effect of doing away with the requirement of a guilty intent [would be] to ease the prosecution's path to conviction, to strip the defendant of such benefit as he derived at common law from innocence of evil purpose, and to circumscribe the freedom heretofore allowed juries. Such a manifest impairment of the immunities of the individual should not be extended to common-law crimes on judicial initiative. [W]here Congress borrows terms of art in which are accumulated the legal tradition and meaning of centuries of practice, it presumably knows and adopts the cluster of ideas that were attached to each borrowed word in the body of learning from which it was taken and the meaning its use will convey to the judicial mind unless otherwise instructed. In such case, absence of contrary direction may be taken as satisfaction with widely accepted definitions, not as a departure from them.

**3. The Implications of Prevention; Oliver Wendell Holmes.** In *The Rationale of Punishment*, published in 1830, Jeremy Bentham took the position that "[g]eneral prevention ought to be the chief end of punishment, as it is its real justification." In comments first published in *The Common Law* in 1881, Oliver Wendell Holmes explained why this view was consistent with a general requirement of mens rea in the criminal law:

> . . . No society has ever admitted that it could not sacrifice individual welfare for its own existence. If conscripts are necessary for its army, it seizes them, and marches them, with bayonets in

their rear, to death. It runs highways and railroads through old family places in spite of the owner's protest, paying in this instance the market value, to be sure, because no civilized government sacrifices the citizen more than it can help, but still sacrificing his will and his welfare to that of the rest.

[T]here can be no case in which the law-maker makes certain conduct criminal without his thereby showing a wish and purpose to prevent that conduct. Prevention would accordingly seem to be the chief and only universal purpose of punishment. The law threatens certain pains if you do certain things, intending thereby to give you a new motive for not doing them. If you persist in doing them, it has to inflict the pains in order that its threats may continue to be believed.

If this is a true account of the law as it stands, the law does undoubtedly treat the individual as a means to an end, and uses him as a tool to increase the general welfare at his own expense. It has been suggested above, that this course is perfectly proper; but even if it is wrong, our criminal law follows it, and the theory of our criminal law must be shaped accordingly. . . .

If the foregoing arguments are sound, it is already manifest that liability to punishment cannot be finally and absolutely determined by considering the actual personal unworthiness of the criminal alone. That consideration will govern only so far as the public welfare permits or demands.[b] And if we take into account the general result which the criminal law is intended to bring about, we shall see that the actual state of mind accompanying a criminal act plays a different part from what is commonly supposed.

For the most part, the purpose of the criminal law is only to induce external conformity to rule. All law is directed to conditions of things manifest to the senses. And whether it brings those conditions to pass immediately by the use of force, as when it protects a house from a mob by soldiers, or appropriates private property to public use, or hangs a man in pursuance of a judicial sentence, or whether it brings them about mediately through men's fears, its object is equally an external result. In directing itself against robbery or murder, for instance, its purpose is to put a stop to the actual physical taking and keeping of other men's goods, or the actual poisoning, shooting, stabbing, and otherwise putting to death of other men. If those things are not done, the law forbidding them is equally satisfied, whatever the motive.

---

[b] Holmes had earlier observed that "[i]f punishment stood on the moral grounds which are proposed for it, the first thing to be considered would be those limitations in the capacity for choosing rightly which arise from abnormal instincts, want of education, lack of intelligence, and all the other defects which are most marked" in the vast majority of criminals. Yet, he continued, the criminal law has never been structured to take these elements into account.—[Footnote by eds.]

Considering this purely external purpose of the law together with the fact that it is ready to sacrifice the individual so far as necessary in order to accomplish that purpose, we can see more readily than before that the actual degree of personal guilt involved in any particular transgression cannot be the only element, if it is an element at all, in the liability incurred. . . .

It is not intended to deny that criminal liability . . . is founded on blameworthiness. Such a denial would shock the moral sense of any civilized community; or, to put it another way, a law which punished conduct which would not be blameworthy in the average member of the community would be too severe for that community to bear. It is only intended to point out that, when we are dealing with that part of the law which aims more directly than any other at establishing standards of conduct, we should expect there more than elsewhere to find that the tests of liability are external, and independent of the degree of evil in the particular person's motives or intentions. The conclusion follows directly from the nature of the standards to which conformity is required. These are not only external, as was shown above, but they are of general application. They do not merely require that every man should get as near as he can to the best conduct possible for him. They require him at his own peril to come up to a certain height. They take no account of incapacities, unless the weakness is so marked as to fall into well-known exceptions, such as infancy or madness. They assume that every man is as able as every other to behave as they command. If they fall on any one class harder than on another, it is on the weakest. For it is precisely to those who are most likely to err by temperament, ignorance, or folly, that the threats of the law are the most dangerous.

The reconciliation of the doctrine that liability is founded on blameworthiness with the existence of liability where the party is not to blame . . . is found in the conception of the average man, the man of ordinary intelligence and reasonable prudence. Liability is said to arise out of such conduct as would be blameworthy in him. But he is an ideal being, represented by the jury when they are appealed to, and his conduct is an external or objective standard when applied to any given individual. That individual may be morally without stain, because he has less than ordinary intelligence or prudence. But he is required to have those qualities at his peril. If he has them, he will not, as a general rule, incur liability without blameworthiness.

Holmes meant in this passage to be describing the minimum level of mens rea that ought to be required. Higher levels of mens rea were appropriate, he thought, in other contexts. One example was the law of theft. Generally speaking, larceny and other theft crimes require an "intent to steal," that is, an intent to effect a permanent deprivation of property. Holmes defended this result:

In larceny the consequences immediately flowing from the act are generally exhausted with little or no harm to the owner. Goods are removed from his possession by trespass, and that is all, when the crime is complete. But they must be permanently kept from him before the harm is done which the law seeks to prevent. A momentary loss of possession is not what has been guarded against with such severe penalties. What the law means to prevent is the loss of it wholly and forever, as is shown by the fact that it is not larceny to take for a temporary use without intending to deprive the owner of his property. If then the law punishes the mere act of taking, it punishes an act which will not of itself produce the evil effect sought to be prevented, and punishes it before that effect has in any way come to pass.

The reason is plain enough. The law cannot wait until the property has been used up or destroyed in other hands than the owner's, or until the owner has died, in order to make sure that the harm which it seeks to prevent has been done. And for the same reason it cannot confine itself to acts likely to do that harm. For the harm of permanent loss of property will not follow from the act of taking, but only from the series of acts which constitute removing and keeping the property after it has been taken. After these preliminaries, the bearing of intent upon the crime is easily seen.

According to Mr. Bishop, larceny is "the taking and removing, by trespass, of personal property which the trespasser knows to belong either generally or specially to another, with the intent to deprive such owner of his ownership therein...."

There must be an intent to deprive such owner of his owner-ship therein, it is said. But why? ... The true answer is, that the intent is an index to the external event which probably would have happened, and that, if the law is to punish at all, it must, in this case, go on probabilities, not on accomplished facts. The analogy to the manner of dealing with attempts is plain. Theft may be called an attempt to permanently deprive a man of his property, which is punished with the same severity whether successful or not. If theft can rightly be considered in this way, intent must play the same part as in other attempts. An act which does not fully accomplish the prohibited result may be made wrongful by evidence that but for some interference it would have been followed by other acts coordinated with it to produce that result. This can only be shown by showing intent. In theft the intent to deprive the owner of his property establishes that the thief would have retained, or would not have taken steps to restore, the stolen goods....

**4.   Questions and Comments.** Is it clear that the criminal law, as a general proposition, ought to focus on the defendant's state of mind when actions are taken? What policies support that result? What consequences would ensue if mens rea in the criminal law was abandoned?

As the content of mens rea in the criminal law is explored below, a better foundation for consideration of these questions will emerge. The point of raising them now is that they should remain near the surface as the later materials are examined.

———

## Regina v. Faulkner

Ireland, Court of Crown Cases Reserved, 1877.
13 Cox C.C. 550.

[The defendant was a seaman on a ship carrying a cargo of rum, sugar, and cotton. He was not permitted in the cargo area where the rum was stored, but ignoring the prohibition in order to satisfy his thirst, he entered the storage hold, poked a hole in a rum cask, and helped himself. In order to plug the hole after he was finished, he lit a match to see. The rum caught fire, which injured him and destroyed the ship. He was indicted for arson, on the charge that he "feloniously, unlawfully, and maliciously did set fire to the said ship, with intent thereby to prejudice" the owners of the ship. It was conceded that he had no actual intention to set fire to the vessel, and no instruction was requested as to his awareness of the probable consequences of his act.

[The prosecutor's theory was that since the defendant was stealing rum when he started the fire, his felonious intent with respect to the arson was established by his intent with respect to the theft. The trial judge accepted this theory in the instructions, and the jury convicted. On appeal, the prosecutor argued that " 'the terms malice and malicious are used in a general sense, as denoting a wicked, perverse, and incorrigible disposition.' Here the felonious act of the prisoner showing a wicked, perverse, and incorrigible disposition supplies the malice required...." One member of the court, Justice Keogh, accepted the theory, noting that he was of the opinion "that the conviction should stand, as I consider all questions of intention and malice are closed by the finding of the jury, that the prisoner committed the act with which he was charged whilst engaged in the commission of a substantive felony. On this broad ground, irrespective of all refinements as to 'recklessness' and 'wilfulness,' I think the conviction is sustained."

[The majority of the appellate court, however, voted to quash the conviction. Excerpts from some of their opinions follow.]

■ FITZGERALD, J. ... I am ... of opinion that in order to establish the charge ..., the intention of the accused forms an element in the crime to the extent that it should appear that the defendant intended to do the very act with which he is charged, or that it was the necessary consequence of some other felonious or criminal act in which he was engaged, or that having a probable result which the defendant foresaw, or ought to have foreseen, he, nevertheless, persevered in such other felonious or criminal act. The prisoner did not intend to set fire to the ship—the fire was not the necessary result of the felony he was attempting; and if it was a probable result, which he ought to have foreseen, of the felonious transaction on which he was engaged, and from which a malicious design to commit the injurious act with which he is charged might have been fairly imputed to him, that view of the case was not submitted to the jury. On the contrary, it was excluded from their consideration on the requisition of the counsel for the prosecution. Counsel for the prosecution in effect insisted that the defendant, being engaged in the commission of, or in an attempt to commit a felony, was criminally responsible for every result that was occasioned thereby, even though it was not a probable consequence of his act or such as he could have reasonably foreseen or intended. No authority has been cited for a proposition so extensive, and I am of opinion that it is not warranted by law. . . .

■ FITZGERALD, B. . . . The utmost which I can conceive the jury to have found over and above the facts stated is, that at the time when the prisoner set fire to this ship he was actuated by a felonious intent, which no doubt is malice; but I must take this not to have been the particular malicious intent of burning the vessel, but the particular felonious intent, which is an element of larceny. Its whole force, therefore, in the present case (if any) is as evidence of malice in general. . . In my opinion, this general malice might have been sufficiently connected with the overt act in this case, from which the injury resulted, if the jury had found that the injury was a reasonable consequence—that is to say, a consequence which any man of reason might have anticipated as probable of an act or acts. . . . Now, however clearly I may be satisfied that the jury ought, as a matter of fact, if the question had been left to it, to have found that injury was the reasonable consequence of an act or acts done with a felonious intent, I cannot draw the conclusion as a matter of law. . . . I am quite satisfied that in cases like the present, if the overt act from which injury resulted be actuated by any malice, and the injury is the reasonable consequence of such overt act so actuated, malice would be sufficiently established. . . . I am clearly of opinion that there was evidence on which the jury might have found the malice necessary to sustain the indictment . . . , yet I think the question of malice was not left to the jury at all—the conviction cannot be sustained.

■ PALLES, C.B. I concur in the opinion of the majority of the Court. . . . I agree with my brother Keogh that from the facts proved the inference might have been legitimately drawn that the setting fire to the ship was malicious. . . . I am of opinion that that inference was one of fact for the jury, and not a conclusion of law at which we can arrive upon the case before us. There is one fact from which, if found, that inference would, in my opinion, have arisen as matter of law, as that the setting fire to the ship was the probable result of the prisoner's act in having a lighted match in the place in question; and if that had been found I should have concurred in the conclusion at which Mr. Justice Keogh has arrived. In my judgment the law imputes to a person who wilfully commits a criminal act an intention to do everything which is the probable consequence of the act constituting the corpus delicti which actually ensues. In my opinion this inference arises irrespective of the particular consequence which ensued being or not being foreseen by the criminal, and whether his conduct is reckless or the reverse. . . .

———

## NOTES ON THE EVOLUTION OF MENS REA

**1. The Language of Mens Rea.** The first lesson to be learned about common law mens rea terminology is that the words usually do not mean what one would expect. There is often little correlation between the legal meaning and the ordinary language meaning of words used by the common law to describe the required state of mind for a criminal offense. Before mens rea terms can be understood in their special legal sense, therefore, one must face the problem of translation. Just as one begins the study of a foreign language by learning the English equivalent of the words to be used, and gradually learns to use the foreign vocabulary without the intermediate step of constant translation, it is useful to treat common law mens rea terms, and indeed much of the language of the law, as words that must be translated into ordinary language before one can learn how to use them.

The difficulty of the terminology is compounded by the colorful variety of mens-rea terms in common usage. They include "corruptly," "scienter," "wilfully," "maliciously," "fraudulently," "wantonly," "feloniously," "wilful neglect," "recklessly," "negligently," "wanton and wilful," and many more. Learning to use these words would not be too problematic if their meanings were settled. Unfortunately, this is not the case. To return to the foreign language analogy, there are no accepted meanings into which these terms invariably can be translated. Different courts translate them differently, and the same court will use them differently for different crimes. What is required of the student, therefore, is not memorization of accepted definitions, but sensitive assessment and analysis, informed by the realization that context is essential to understanding.

There is at least one further difficulty. It is typical in American legislation based on common law terminology for a collection of mens rea terms to be strung together, without attention to what they mean or how they relate to each other. An example of the origins of the practice is the phrase "feloniously, unlawfully, and maliciously" in the indictment in *Faulkner*. A study of modern federal criminal legislation is also instructive:

> . . . The "mental element" of federal crimes is specified in the definitions of the crimes, which definitions are frequently modified, if not indeed distorted, in judicial decisions. If one looks to the statutes alone, the specifications of mental states form a staggering array: [Here some 78 different combinations of words are extracted from various federal statutes. Examples are "willfully and corruptly," "willfully and maliciously," "willfully or maliciously," "willfully and unlawfully," "willfully and knowingly," "willfully, deliberate, malicious, and premeditated," "unlawfully

and willfully," "knowingly and willfully," "knowingly or willfully," "fraudulently or wrongfully," "from a premeditated design
unlawfully and maliciously to," "knowingly, willfully, and corruptly," "willfully neglects," and "improperly."]

Unsurprisingly, the courts have been unable to find substantive correlates for all these varied descriptions of mental states,
and, in fact, the opinions display far fewer mental states than the
statutory language. Not only does the statutory language not
reflect accurately or consistently what are the mental elements of
the various crimes; there is no discernible pattern or consistent
rationale which explains why one crime is defined or understood to
require one mental state and another crime another mental state
or indeed no mental state at all.

1 National Commission on Reform of Federal Criminal Laws, Working
Papers 119–20 (1970). The same study concludes with respect to the word
"willfully" that "the courts, including the Supreme Court, have endowed
the requirement of willfulness with the capacity to take on whatever
meaning seems appropriate in the statutory context." The same comment
could be made about many other common-law mens-rea terms.

**2. Mens Rea and General Malevolence.** Sayre described the
emerging notion of mens rea in the 13th century as a concept of "general
moral blameworthiness." By that he appears to have meant an unfocused
judgment about the general character and disposition of the actor. The
argument advanced by the prosecutor in *Faulkner* was similar: " '[T]he
terms malice and malicious are used in a general sense, as denoting a
wicked, perverse, and incorrigible disposition.' Here the felonious act of the
prisoner [stealing rum] showing a wicked, perverse, and incorrigible disposition supplies the malice required...." The word "malice" is not being
used by the prosecutor in *Faulkner* in an artificial sense. In common usage
it means "badness," "wickedness," "active ill-will," or the like. Yet the
appellate court, reflecting changes in the law that Sayre recounted, rejected
this common sense definition and substituted a different measure of the
defendant's blameworthiness.

What exactly is the appellate court's definition of "malice"? Assume
that Faulkner was a seaman whose job it was periodically to inspect the
hold in which the rum was kept. Could he have been convicted if, while
performing that duty, he lit a match in order to see and carelessly caused
the same destruction? Whatever the answer to this question, it is clear that
the judges are using the string of mens rea words in the indictment in a
way that is foreign to their ordinary-language meaning. Do the opinions by
Fitzgerald, Fitzgerald, and Palles reflect serious disagreement about the
mens rea that should be required? On what elements of the context and the
defendant's behavior do they focus?

Use of the vocabulary of general moral blameworthiness is not confined to 19th century English courts. In United States v. Bishop, 412 U.S.
346, 360 (1973), for example, the United States Supreme Court said that
"the requirement of willfulness [has been held to mean] 'bad faith or evil

intent,' . . . or 'evil motive and want of justification'. . .'' In State v. Dunn, 199 N.W.2d 104, 107 (Iowa 1972), the court said that "the word 'maliciously,' when used in a legislative enactment pertaining to the crime of arson, denotes that malice which characterizes all acts done with an evil disposition, a wrong and unlawful motive or purpose." Similarly, the court in Wilson v. State, 303 A.2d 638, 640–41 (Del.1973), said that "a felony requires the existence of felonious intent; stated conversely, without a felonious intent there is no felony. [A]n act feloniously done proceeds from an evil heart or purpose." It seems likely that the reason such language persists in appellate opinions and, significantly, in modern jury instructions is that judges have failed to adjust their vocabulary as the law of mens rea has evolved toward a more focused state of mind.

One of the major contributions of the American Law Institute's Model Penal Code is that it has been the catalyst for important changes in the vocabulary of mens rea. As illustrated below and as inspired by the Model Code, most modern legislation and many modern courts—supported by modern academic commentary—reject the common law language and describe mens rea concepts in more readily accessible language.

   **3.  *Regina v. Cunningham*.** In Regina v. Cunningham, 41 Crim. App. 155 (1957), the defendant was convicted and sentenced to five years' imprisonment under the following statute:

> Whosoever shall unlawfully and maliciously administer to or cause to be administered to or taken by any other person any poison or other destructive or noxious thing, so as thereby to endanger the life of such person, or so as thereby to inflict upon such person any grievous bodily harm, shall be guilty of felony.

The facts, as recited by the appellate court, were that:

> [T]he appellant was engaged to be married and his prospective mother-in-law was the tenant of a house, No. 7a, Bakes Street, Bradford, which was unoccupied but which was to be occupied by the appellant after his marriage. Mrs. Wade and her husband, an elderly couple, lived in the house next door. At one time the two houses had been one, but when the building was converted into two houses a wall had been erected to divide the cellars of the two houses, and that wall was composed of rubble loosely cemented. On the evening of January 17 last the appellant went to the cellar of No. 7a, Bakes Street, wrenched the gas meter from the gas pipes and stole it, together with its contents, and in a second indictment he was charged with the larceny of the gas meter and its contents. To that indictment he pleaded guilty and was sentenced to six months' imprisonment. In respect of that matter he does not appeal. The facts were not really in dispute, and in a statement to a police officer the appellant said: "All right I will tell you. I was short of money, I had been off work for three days, I got eight shillings from the gas meter. I tore it off the wall and threw it away." Although there was a stop tap within two feet of the meter, the appellant did not turn off the gas, with the result that a very

considerable volume of gas escaped, some of which seeped through the wall of the cellar and partially asphyxiated Mrs. Wade, who was asleep in her bedroom next door, with the result that her life was endangered.

The trial judge instructed the jury as follows:

You will observe that there is nothing [in the statute] about "with intention that that person should take [the noxious substance]." He has not got to intend that it should be taken; it is sufficient that by his unlawful and malicious act he causes it to be taken. What you have to decide here, then, is whether, when he loosed that frightful cloud of coal gas into the house which he shared with this old lady, he caused her to take it by his unlawful and malicious action. "Unlawful" does not need any definition. It is something forbidden by law. What about "malicious"? "Malicious" for this purpose means wicked—something which he has no business to do and perfectly well knows it. "Wicked" is as good a definition as any other which you would get. The facts ... are these. [T]he prisoner quite deliberately, intending to steal the money that was in the meter, ... broke the gas mains away from the supply pipes and thus released the main supply of gas at large into that house. When he did that he knew that this old lady and her husband were living next door to him. The gas meter was in a cellar. The wall which divided his cellar from the cellar next door was a kind of honeycomb wall through which gas could very well go, so that when he loosed that cloud of gas into that place he must have known perfectly well that gas would percolate all over the house. If it were part of this offence—which it is not—that he intended to poison the old lady, I should have left it to you to decide, and I should have told you that there was evidence on which you could find that he intended that, since he did an action which he must have known would result in that. As I have already told you, it is not necessary to prove that he intended to do it; it is quite enough that what he did was done unlawfully and maliciously.

The appellate court quashed the conviction. Excerpts from the opinion follow:

"In any statutory definition of a crime, malice must be taken not in the old vague sense of wickedness in general but as requiring either (i) an actual intention to do the particular kind of harm that in fact was done; or (ii) recklessness as to whether such harm should occur or not (i.e., the accused has foreseen that the particular kind of harm might be done and yet has gone on to take the risk of it). It is neither limited to nor does it indeed require any ill will towards the person injured." ... We think that this is an accurate statement of the law.... In our opinion, the word "maliciously" in a statutory crime postulates foresight of consequence....

With the utmost respect to the learned judge, we think it is incorrect to say that the word "malicious" in a statutory offence merely means wicked. We think the learned judge was in effect telling the jury that if they were satisfied that the appellant acted wickedly—and he had clearly acted wickedly in stealing the gas meter and its contents—they ought to find that he had acted maliciously in causing the gas to be taken by Mrs. Wade so as thereby to endanger her life.

In our view, it should have been left to the jury to decide whether, even if the appellant did not intend the injury to Mrs. Wade, he foresaw that the removal of the gas meter might cause injury to someone but nevertheless removed it. We are unable to say that a reasonable jury, properly directed as to the meaning of the word "maliciously" in the [statute], would without doubt have convicted.

In these circumstances this court has no alternative but to allow the appeal and quash the conviction.

4.  *Faulkner* **and** *Cunningham* **Compared.** There are important differences between the mental state required by the Irish Court of Crown Cases Reserved in *Cunningham* and the English Court of Criminal Appeals in *Faulkner*, differences that would appear to have little to do with the language used in the definition of the respective offenses. Both courts appear to have been concerned to state the minimum conditions of criminal liability in general terms—terms likely to be applied to other offenses as well as the ones before the court. What accounts for the disagreement between the two courts? What practical differences are there between the two positions? What philosophical differences might account for the different results?

Assume that Cunningham had been a meter repairman who allowed the gas to escape and endanger Mrs. Wade when he dismantled the meter and returned to his shop to get a spare part. Could he then have been convicted under the approach taken by the *Cunningham* court? How do *Faulkner* and *Cunningham* fit within the evolution of mens rea described by Sayre?

———

NOTES ON MISTAKE OF FACT AND THE COMMON LAW

1.  **"Specific" and "General" Intent.** Common law courts divided crimes into two categories for purposes of determining the relevance of certain defenses, among them the defense of mistake of fact. The easiest to understand consisted of crimes that required a "specific intent." The other category, basically, was "everything else." Crimes that did not fit into the "specific intent" category were called crimes that required only "general intent."

There is, however, an initial difficulty. Crimes do not come with a "specific" or a "general" intent label, nor are they printed in different colors so one can tell into which category they fall. Often, crimes are completely silent as to whether the defendant's conduct must be accompanied by a particular state of mind. The rule normally is that such a crime will require mens rea anyway, although silence in the definition does not automatically signal whether the offense fits into the "specific" or the "general" intent category.

Moreover, when a crime does include a specified state of mind requirement, often it is stated in a murky manner that—to borrow a phrase from Justice Cardozo from another context—can only be characterized as a "mystifying cloud of words."[a] *Faulkner* and *Cunningham* are examples. In neither case did the mens rea required by the court have anything to do with the words used in the definition of the offense.

But this is not the only confusion to be found in mens rea words. A crime may have a perfectly understandable mens rea term in its definition—"knowingly," for example—but the meaning of the mens rea term may have nothing to do with what the word ordinarily connotes.

Illustrations of these complexities are given in the Notes to follow.

**(i) Specific Intent Crimes.** Holmes illustrated the specific intent category in an excerpt reproduced above.[b] As he explained, "taking and carrying away the personal property of another," even without permission, does not warrant the severe sanctions of theft—unless the defendant intends to keep the property. Rather than wait until a permanent deprivation of the property has occurred, the criminal law intervenes at a point where possession has been obtained accompanied by the intent to effect a permanent deprivation. It is this additional "specific" intent that makes the offense serious enough to be classified as theft.

The "specific intent" to steal, to illustrate, is the difference between car theft and joyriding. The "specific intent" required for larceny is an essential part of the definition of the offense. The punitive objectives of the law of theft are not implicated unless the offender has the particular state of mind required by the definition of the offense. The offense requires that the defendant engage in specified conduct, with the intent to bring about a specified result that will occur in the future. The law intervenes before that result occurs, and convicts based on the combination of conduct and intent specified in the definition of the offense.

Burglary is another example of a "specific intent" crime. The common law definition of burglary ran something like this: "breaking and entering the dwelling house of another at night with the intent to commit a crime therein." Here the defendant engages in specified conduct (breaking and

---

[a] Benjamin Cardozo, Law and Literature 101 (1931), quoted in context in the discussion of the Pennsylvania deliberation and premeditation formula for murder in Chapter 8. Sometimes, it must be noted, the "mystify-ing cloud of words" might be held to signal a specific intent. Often, however, they will be held to imply only "general" criminal intent.

[b] See Note 3 in the Introductory Notes preceding *Regina v. Faulkner.*

entering the dwelling house of another at night), with the "specific" intent to engage in further conduct (with the intent to commit a crime therein). The law chooses to intervene before that additional conduct has occurred, and measures its likelihood by asking whether the defendant intended its occurrence. Better not to wait until the additional crime is committed, the reasoning goes, but to punish based on the commission of a threatening act in a context where the defendant intends further criminal behavior.[c]

The paradigm example of a specific intent crime, then, is an offense where the definition describes specific behavior in which the defendant must engage, and further specifies a particular state of mind which must accompany that behavior. Examples would be an intention to cause a harmful result in the future (larceny), or an intention to engage in further criminal behavior (burglary).[d] The defendant who engages in the specified behavior is guilty if that state of mind exists. The defendant is not guilty if that state of mind is absent.

**(ii) General Intent Crimes.** It is much more difficult to summarize the meaning of "general intent." The mens rea required for general intent offenses is not spelled out at all, much less with any clarity, in the definition of a "general intent" offense or in any widely applied rule. The mens rea in general intent offenses also has chameleon-like characteristics. Its content is usually explicated when specific exculpatory defenses are raised, and that content tends to change based on policies that govern the availability and scope of the different defenses. The best that can be said by way of generalization has been said above. Some crimes require a specific intent. General intent crimes are "everything else."

**(iii) The Mistake of Fact Rules.** A common defense raised in criminal cases has to do with the defendant's perception of external circumstances that are encompassed within the definition of the crime. These circumstances may be part of the actus reus of the offense, that is, the circumstances must actually exist in order for the crime to be committed. Or they may be a required part of a specific intent, that is, they must be thought to exist in order for a required specific intent to be carried out. The question to be considered is what happens if the defendant is mistaken about one or more of these circumstances. The defendant thinks they do not exist, but they do. The defendant gets the facts wrong.

Over time, the common law developed two default rules for dealing with the defense of mistake of fact. The specific intent rule is simple and logical. A specific intent is a special intent required for the commission of an offense. A mistake of fact is a defense if it shows that the required special intent did not exist. As the common law put it, a mistake of fact is a

[c] It is likely that a given jurisdiction will have one or more lesser offenses (e.g., trespass, breaking and entering a building, breaking and entering a dwelling at night) that are committed if the defendant does not have the additional specific intent. These offenses will then be "graded" along a spectrum of potential punishments with burglary the most severe.

[d] As Note 4, below, illustrates, this is not the only form that a "specific intent" can take.

defense to a specific intent crime if it is honestly (that is, actually) made. A lie won't do, in other words, but if the defendant claims not to have had the intent because of a mistake of fact and the jury believes the defendant's assertion, then the mistake is a defense.

The general intent rule can be stated simply, but is subject to a number of qualifications. The rule says that a mistake of fact is a defense to a general intent crime if it is "honest and reasonable," that is, if the defendant actually made the mistake *and* if the mistake was reasonable under the circumstances. This imposes a form of liability for negligence, and would be fairly simple to administer if consistently applied. But as illustrated below, the general intent rule needs to be studied in the context of different kinds of mistakes of fact in order to appreciate some subtleties in its application.

**2.   Specific Intent Crimes;** *Green v. State.* In Green v. State, 153 Tex.Cr.R. 442, 221 S.W.2d 612 (1949), the defendant drove into a woodland and killed several hogs. He loaded them into his car and took them home. The police arrived, identified the hogs as belonging to someone else, and returned them to their owner. The defendant was prosecuted for stealing the hogs. His defense was that he had hogs running on the range at the time and thought the hogs he killed were his own.

Larceny was defined, in effect, as "taking and carrying away the personal property of another with intent permanently to deprive the other of the property." The defendant in *Green* unquestionably committed the actus reus of this offense—he clearly "took and carried away the personal property of another." But his testimony raised the question whether he had the required "intent permanently to deprive the other of the property." At common law, the question to be put to the jury was one of fact: did Green actually have the intent to appropriate someone else's property? If he honestly thought the hogs were his, he did not have this intent and would be entitled to acquittal. An honest mistake of fact is a defense to a specific intent crime.

**3.   General Intent Crimes;** *State v. Walker.* In State v. Walker, 35 N.C.App. 182, 241 S.E.2d 89 (1978), the defendant was charged with child abduction. It was established in prior cases that the statute was violated only if neither parent consented to the abduction.

The defendant and his son abducted a seven-year-old boy and a five-year-old girl as the children were leaving a school bus in front of the school building. About five minutes later, the girl was found walking back to the school. The boy was still missing at the time of trial. The boy was the defendant's grandson. The appellate court dismissed the case as to his abduction on the ground that the father of the boy had participated in the abduction and had thereby given his consent. The girl, however, was unrelated to the two men. The defendant's contention as to her is revealed in the following excerpt from the court's opinion:

> [D]efendant contends that the trial judge erred in failing to instruct the jury on the defense of mistake of fact. In support of

this argument defendant cites evidence tending to show that defendant and his son were operating under the mistaken belief that the female child whom they allegedly abducted was Joy Walker, the granddaughter of defendant.

It is an elementary principle that general criminal intent is an essential component of every malum-in-se criminal offense. [A]n inference of general criminal intent is raised by evidence tending to show that the defendant committed the acts comprising the elements of the offense charged. [But if] an inference that the defendant committed the act without criminal intent is raised by the evidence then the [defendant is entitled to a jury instruction on mistake of fact.]

An examination of the evidence presented by the defendant reveals that the general principles recited above are applicable to the present case. The defendant testified that when he took the little girl, Vickie Irby, he believed that she was his granddaughter, Joy Walker; that he discerned the true identity of the child after he and his son had driven one-half mile from the school; that upon realizing that the child was not his granddaughter, he returned to the school and let the child out of the automobile. According to this evidence, if the facts had been as the defendant supposed, he would have committed no crime in taking Joy Walker since he was acting under the authority and with the consent of her father. The evidence viewed in this light obviously permits the inference that defendant in taking Vickie Irby was laboring under a mistake as to the identity of the little girl which could negate any criminal intent. In appropriate cases, culpable negligence has been considered the equivalent of criminal intent. Accordingly, in order to negate criminal intent, the mistake under which the defendant was acting must have been made in good faith and with due care.

In accordance with the principles set forth, we hold that the trial judge erred in not declaring and explaining the law on a substantial feature of the case arising from the evidence that the defendant believed that he and his son were taking the latter's daughter, Joy Walker, when they were in fact taking Vickie Irby. . . .

The statute at issue in *Walker* punished a person who abducted a child without the consent of either parent. There was no special mens rea requirement in the definition of the offense, indeed no mens rea requirement at all. As the North Carolina courts had interpreted the statute, the crime of child abduction required only a general intent, which meant that an honest and reasonable mistake of fact was a defense. Since the defendant offered evidence that he had made such a mistake, he was entitled to a jury instruction on the issue. In the court's language, he was entitled to a defense if the mistake was "made in good faith and with due care."

The concept of general intent and its corresponding common law mistake-of-fact doctrine reflect the default rule of the culpability required for crime. Any given offense might require more culpability (a specific intent) or less culpability (strict liability) depending on its definition and the interpretational policies the courts think applicable. But the requirement of a general criminal intent was the customary starting point for reasoning about the appropriate mens rea for all serious crimes at common law.

**4. "Know" as a Mens Rea Requirement.** Variants of the word "know" will frequently be encountered in crime definition.[e] Several points need to be understood about what they might mean.

Of course, they might mean the defendant needs to know. That is, they might be meant to carry the meaning that could be found by looking the word up in a dictionary, something like "general awareness or possession of information." This is not problematic. The problem comes when they mean something else.

As is the case with all mens rea words used by the common law, "know" or some variant of the word could be an artificial token that stands for a completely different concept. An example is provided by Pereira v. United States, 347 U.S. 1 (1954). In that case, the United States Supreme Court read the words "knowingly causes to be delivered by mail" in the federal mail fraud statute, 18 U.S.C. § 1341, to mean "where such use can reasonably be foreseen, even though not actually intended." There need be no concern now with *why* "knowingly" was read that way in that case. The lessons now are that "know" and its variants *are* read that way from time to time, and that there is no a priori way of figuring out whether they *will* be read that way (or some other way) by a particular court interpreting a particular crime. The beginning of wisdom on this point is to be alert to the possibility of differing interpretations, and not to be fooled by the automatic assumption that lawyers speak English. Only by being alert to such possibilities can one learn in time when and why the law will mean what it says, and when and why it will mean something else.

The complexity does not end here. Sometimes "know" (whatever it means) is an express mens rea term included in the definition of an offense. *Pereira* is an example. Another example is given in the next Note. Sometimes, however, "know" (whatever it means) will be the mens rea even though the definition of the offense says nothing at all about the topic. An example of the latter is the crime involved in Staples v. United States, 511 U.S. 600 (1994).[f] The statute in that case, silent on mens rea, punished possession of certain unregistered weapons. The weapon involved in the case was a machine gun. The Court held that the defendant had to know (in the sense of actually being aware) that the possessed weapon had the characteristics that made it a machine gun, that is, that it would fire repeatedly with a single pull of the trigger.

So "know" might or might not mean "know," and it might or might not be a mens rea element of an offense even though the statute says

---

[e] E.g., "knowing," "knowingly," "with knowledge that," etc.

[f] *Staples* is discussed in the Notes below following *United States v. Freed.*

nothing. What can be said to a fair degree of certainty is that when it does mean "know" in the ordinary English sense of the word, the mistake of fact defense will be handled by applying the "specific intent" rule. When "know" is an element of an offense and is to be taken literally, in other words, it will be characterized as a "specific intent." In the context under discussion here, the offense will mean, in effect, that the defendant must "know" that certain circumstances exist, and it will be a defense if the defendant lacks such "knowledge" due to a mistake of fact. The next Note provides an illustration.

**5. Further Illustration of Specific and General Intent Crimes; *United States v. Oglivie*.** In United States v. Oglivie, 29 M.J. 1069 (1990), the United States Army Court of Military Review faced a situation that further illustrates the operation of the common law rules on mistake of fact for specific and general intent crimes. The Court recited the facts as follows:

> The appellant married his first wife, Amparo, in December 1986, while stationed in Panama. In January 1987, the appellant was reassigned from Panama to Germany, but his wife remained in Panama. While in Germany, the appellant did not know Amparo's address or telephone number, but sent letters to a friend, who passed them on to her. The appellant returned from Germany in March 1988 and was reassigned to Fort Sill, Oklahoma. In August 1988, the appellant sent his wife a money order with his telephone number written on it. The appellant filed for divorce in Oklahoma and sent a copy of the petition to a friend's post office box in Panama for delivery to his wife. In September or October 1988, Amparo called the appellant from Panama and informed him that she had filed for divorce in Panama, that there was "nothing between the two of us" and that he "didn't have to worry about her anymore." The appellant testified that he thought he was divorced at that point. In November 1988, the Red Cross notified the appellant that Amparo had been hospitalized. The Red Cross referred to Amparo as his "ex-wife." On 9 November 1988, the appellant requested that his basic allowance for quarters (BAQ) at the "with dependents" rate be terminated because he was divorced.... In December 1988, the appellant married Jackline, and requested that his BAQ at the "with dependents" rate be reinstated.

Oglivie was convicted of bigamy. He was also convicted on two counts of making a false official statement. The first statement was on November 9 when he told military officials that he was divorced from Amparo. The second was in December when he told officials that he was married to Jackline. He defended on the ground that he honestly believed that he was divorced from Amparo.

The Court addressed the false statement offenses first:

Making a false official statement in violation of UCMJ, Article 107, 10 U.S.C. § 907 (1982),[g] is a specific intent crime. An honest mistake of fact regarding the truth of the statement made is a defense. The evidence establishes that Amparo told the appellant she had filed for divorce, that the appellant received correspondence from the Red Cross referring to Amparo as his "ex-wife," and that he attempted to terminate his entitlement to BAQ, on the ground that he was divorced. He then participated in a marriage ceremony and received a marriage certificate indicating that he was married to Jackline. Based upon the entire record, we find that the defense of an honest mistake of fact was raised and not overcome by the government's evidence. Accordingly, we find that the evidence is insufficient to prove appellant's guilt of making false official statements. . . .

But as to the bigamy charge, the result was different:

Bigamy is a general intent crime.[h] To constitute a defense to bigamy, a mistake of fact must be both honest and reasonable. While the appellant may have honestly believed that he was divorced from Amparo, we find that he did not take the steps which a reasonable man would have taken to determine the validity of his honest belief. He was not reasonable in assuming that he was divorced. . . . Accordingly, we find that the evidence is sufficient to prove bigamy.

**6. General Intent Elements of Specific Intent Crimes; *United States v. Yermian*.** An additional wrinkle to the "specific intent" rule was the following: If a common law crime required a specific intent but the mistake of fact was relevant to an element of the offense other than the specific intent, the courts followed the general intent rule. The specific intent mistake-of-fact rule, in other words, applied only to the specific intent.

For an example, consider United States v. Yermian, 468 U.S. 63 (1984). That case concerned the federal "false statements" offense, defined as follows:

[g] "Any person subject to this chapter who, with intent to deceive, signs any false record, return, regulation, order, or other official document, knowing it to be false, or makes any other false official statement knowing it to be false, shall be punished as a court-martial may direct."—[Footnote by eds.]

[h] The Court added the following footnote on the definition of bigamy:

Regarding the definition of bigamy, the Court of Military Appeals noted in Unit-

ed States v. Patrick, 7 C.M.R. 65, 67, 2 USCMA 189, 191, 1953 WL 1518 (1953): "There is no definition of bigamy in the punitive articles of the Uniform Code of Military Justice. However, the section on forms contained in the Manual for Courts–Martial, United States, 1951, describes the offense in terms substantially in accord with those of the common law—that is, that the accused entered into marriage, having at the time a lawful spouse then living."—

[Footnote by eds.]

> Whoever, in any matter within the jurisdiction of any department or agency of the United States knowingly and willfully ... makes any false ... statements ... shall be fined not more than $10,000 or imprisoned not more than five years, or both.

Everyone agreed that "knowingly and willfully" in this statute meant, in ordinary language, that defendants had to know that the statements were false. The offense therefore required a "specific intent."

Yermian knowingly made false statements on a security clearance form so that his answers would be consistent with false statements he had made in his application for employment. His defense was that he did not realize that his lies on the security clearance form related to a matter "within the jurisdiction of [a] department or agency of the United States." The District Court responded to the asserted defense by instructing the jury that it should convict if it found that the defendant "knew or should have known that the information was to be submitted to a government agency."

One could apply the common law terminology to this result in the following manner. The false statements offense required a specific intent ("knowingly ... makes any false ... statements"). But the mistake of fact offered as a defense was not relevant to the specific intent—the defendant admitted that he knowingly made false statements. The mistake was offered with regard to an element of the offense that was not part of the specific intent, i.e., that the false statement involved a "matter within the jurisdiction of" the United States. The general intent rules therefore apply, and the question accordingly was whether the defendant "honestly and reasonably" believed that the lies did not implicate the interests of the federal government. This question, in turn, translates into the District Court's instruction that the issue was whether the defendant "knew or should have known" that the answers were relevant to the federal government's concerns.[i]

**7. Strict Liability for Grading Elements.** The common law formulation of the mistake of fact rule applicable to general intent crimes was usually qualified in the following manner:

> If an actor honestly and reasonably, although mistakenly, believed the facts to be other than they were, and if his conduct would not have been criminal had the facts been as he believed them to be, then his mistake is a defense if he is charged with a crime which requires "mens rea". . . .

Jerome Michael and Herbert Wechsler, Criminal Law and Its Administration 756 (1940).[j]

---

[i] Yermian appealed on the ground that the jury should have been told that "knowledge" (in the sense of "actually being aware of") was the required mens rea. The Supreme Court affirmed the conviction. The District Court's instruction was sufficient, the Court held, but may not have been necessary. This aspect of the case is considered when *Yermian* is revisited in Section 2(C) below.

[j] Compare the statement in *State v. Walker* (quoted in context in Note 3 above) that "[a]ccording to [the] evidence, if the facts had been as the defendant supposed, he would have committed no crime in taking Joy

Consider the following hypothetical. Defendant commits a theft of jewelry actually valued at $10,000. Defendant thinks the item stolen was merely elaborate costume jewelry and therefore fenced it for $50. Assume that the defendant's belief was reasonable under the circumstances. In a common law jurisdiction, if the dividing line between grand larceny and petty larceny is $500, should evidence of the defendant's "honest and reasonable" mistake of fact be admissible as a basis for reducing the conviction from grand to petty larceny?

The answer at common law was "no," by the following reasoning. Even though larceny is a "specific intent" offense, the value of the property relates to elements not included in the specific intent. Therefore the "general intent" rules apply. See the discussion of *Yermian* in the preceding note.

The general intent rule, as formulated by Michael and Wechsler, would permit a mistake "honestly and reasonably made" to be a defense if, but only if, on the facts as the defendant believed them to be, no crime would have been committed. Here on the facts as the defendant believed them to be, at least petty larceny was being committed. For that reason, the mistake of fact defense as to the value of the property will be denied. In effect, strict liability is applied to the "grading" element of the offense— that is, to an element that differentiates one level of criminality from another. The defendant is graded on the basis of what was done, not what was thought to have been done.

**8. Strict Liability for Independent Moral Wrongs; *Regina v. Prince*.** There was also a category of common law crimes that applied strict liability to elements that did not differentiate one grade of offense from another, but in which an independent moral wrong would have been committed had the facts been as the defendant believed them to be. The most famous early example is Regina v. Prince, L.R. 2 C.C.R. 154 (1875).

The defendant in *Prince* was indicted under a statute that read:

> Whosoever shall unlawfully take ... any unmarried girl, being under the age of 16 years, out of the possession and against the will of her father ... shall be guilty of a misdemeanor....

The defendant committed the acts proscribed by this statute, but believed that the girl was 18 years old. In fact she was 14, but the jury determined that the defendant's mistaken belief was honest and reasonable. The question was whether such a mistake should be a defense.

Conviction of the defendant was affirmed in four separate opinions. The one of relevance now[k] was written by Judge Bramwell, who reasoned that the conviction should be affirmed because Prince's conduct would have been morally wrong even if the girl had been 18. He explained:

Walker since he was acting under the authority and with the consent of her father."

[k] For a thorough consideration of the various opinions in *Prince*, see Glanville

Williams, Criminal Law: The General Part 185–99 (2d ed. 1961).

The act forbidden is wrong in itself, if without lawful cause; I do not say illegal, but wrong.... The legislature has enacted that if anyone does this wrong act, he does it at the risk of her turning out to be under 16. This opinion gives full scope to the doctrine of the mens rea. If the taker believed he had the father's consent, though wrongly, he would have no mens rea; so if he did not know she was in anyone's possession, nor in the care or charge of anyone. In those cases he would not know he was doing the *act* forbidden by the statute—an act which, if he knew she was in possession and in care or charge of anyone, he would know was a crime or not, according as she was under 16 or not.

Judge Bramwell's position was that since Prince knew enough about his conduct to make it a morally wrong act, his mistake about the age of the girl should be irrelevant. To put the point another way, mens rea should be required as to those elements central to the wrongfulness of the act. Liability should be strict as to the remaining elements of the offense.

The context of *Prince* is dated, to be sure, but the principle on which Judge Bramwell relies seems clear enough and is still applied in some contexts. In Ignorance and Mistake in Criminal Law, 88 U. Pa. L. Rev. 35, 62–65 (1939), Rollin Perkins argued that Judge Bramwell's view in *Prince* is reflected in the early common law development of a number of other crimes:*

In certain very extreme situations one may be convicted of a true crime although at the time of his deed he was laboring under a mistake of fact based upon reasonable grounds, and of such a nature that the thing done would not have been a crime had the facts been as he reasonably supposed them to be. These are cases in which the deed would have involved a high degree of moral delinquency even under the supposed facts, and the claim for acquittal is based, not upon the ground that defendant thought his deed was proper or lawful but only that he thought it was a type of wrongful conduct for which no criminal penalty had been provided. The common examples fall within the fields of statutory rape, abduction and adultery.

A man who has illicit sexual intercourse with a girl under the age of consent is guilty of statutory rape although she consented and he mistakenly believed she was older than the limit thus established. This is true no matter how reasonable his mistaken belief may have been, as in cases in which both her appearance and her positive statement indicated she was older than she was in fact, or in which he had exercised considerable pains in the effort to ascertain her age. One who has illicit intercourse with a married person is guilty of adultery even if he has no idea that the other is married....

* Reprinted by permission of the University of Pennsylvania Law Review and Fred B. Rothman Company from the University of Pennsylvania Law Review, vol. 88, pp. 62–65.

It has sometimes been suggested that the reason for this result in such cases is that these are crimes which have no mens rea requirement. This is quite unsound and should be avoided because it will lead to very unsatisfactory results in certain cases, such as those of *innocent* mistake of fact. The latter problem has arisen most frequently in the adultery cases. If the intercourse is obviously illicit, the mistaken belief in the unmarried status of the other party is not an *innocent* mistake, however well grounded it may be, since the conduct falls far below the line of social acceptability even under the supposed facts. "In such a case there is a measure of wrong in the act as the defendant understands it, and his ignorance of the fact that makes it a greater wrong will not relieve him from the legal penalty." On the other hand, in spite of some indication to the contrary, it is clearly established that if the intercourse follows a marriage ceremony entered into in good faith, with no thought or reason to believe that the other party is already married, it does not constitute the crime of adultery if it does not occur after the mistake has been discovered.

**9.  Questions and Comments.** When summed up, do the various common law positions on mistake of fact make sense? Do they follow a coherent set of policies? An appropriate set of policies?

Note that each of the mistake of fact situations described above relates to the defendant's perception of the external circumstances in which the alleged offense was committed. That is, Green's mistake was as to who owned the hogs, Walker's was as to the identity of his granddaughter, Yermian's was as to whether the federal government was interested in his truth-telling, etc. Mistake of fact defenses, in other words, arise in situations where the defendant admittedly engaged in the behavior defined as part of the offense, but claims to have been mistaken about the context in which that behavior occurred.

As subsequent materials illustrate, the mens rea applicable at common law to other types of offense elements will not necessarily be controlled by the mistake of fact rules. Criminal homicide, for example, is graded into different categories based on the defendant's mens rea as to the death. Convictions for different levels of criminal homicide will turn on whether the defendant negligently, recklessly, or intentionally caused a death.[1] The same point needs to be made about other types of defenses. The mistake of fact rules may or may not apply when the defendant's mistake is one of law, or when the defendant claims a mistake based on intoxication or mental disease, or when the defendant is mistaken about the need to act in self defense. Each defense must be studied in context in order to discern the relevant mens rea rules and policies. The occasion for this study is provided in subsequent materials.

---

[1] Chapter 8 is devoted to these issues.

## SUBSECTION B: THE MODEL PENAL CODE

---

### INTRODUCTORY NOTES ON THE MODEL PENAL CODE

The Model Penal Code introduced a new vocabulary and a new approach to mens rea. The approach is new both in analytical structure and in judgments of policy. It builds, however, on the common law tradition and works a skillful blending of the old and the new. As many as half of the states have adopted culpability provisions derived from the analytical structure of the Model Code. The remainder of the states still base the culpability inquiry on the common law, but even in these states the Model Code is having an important impact on decisional law.

The Model Code abandons much of the terminology of the common law. It proposes instead a tightly integrated structure built on definitions that are more faithful to the ordinary sense of language. That structure is difficult, at first imposingly so, and requires careful and repeated study.

**1. The Actus Reus.** The starting point is the criminal act. The required criminal act is determined by careful reading of the definition of the offense. Elements of the offense that describe state of mind should temporarily be set aside. The act elements of the offense are characterized as "conduct," "circumstances," and "results."

"Conduct" elements describe the acts or omissions required to commit an offense. Examples are "taking and carrying away" in larceny, "breaking and entering" in burglary, and the like. Every offense must contain some "conduct" as so defined, although sometimes the exact nature of the conduct is not described. For example, the act component of murder is any conduct (or omission in the face of a legal duty to act) that causes the death of another person. For murder, some "conduct" by the defendant must occur, and the total universe of behavior that causes the death of another is included in the offense because the definition is not more specific. For offenses such as larceny or burglary, by contrast, only conduct properly described as "taking," "breaking," etc., suffices. In cases where conduct elements are specifically designated in the definition of the offense, nice questions can arise as to whether they are satisfied. For example, does reaching through an open window (and breaking the plane fixed by the window) constitute a "breaking" for purposes of burglary?

"Circumstance" elements consist of external facts that must exist in order for the crime to be committed. Larceny, for example, typically requires the taking and carrying away "of the personal property of another." The circumstance elements are that the object taken must be "personal property" (do growing crops count?) of "another" (is partnership property included?). Other examples of circumstance elements are "the dwelling of another at night" (is an occupied tent a dwelling? when does "night" begin?) that may be included in the crime of burglary, the status of a person as an FBI agent in the federal crime of killing an FBI agent, the age of the victim where made relevant by the definition of the crime, and so on.

"Result" elements are any consequences of the defendant's conduct that are incorporated in the definition of the offense. The obvious example is "the death of another" in murder. Other results that may be required include "serious bodily injury" in an assault-and-battery statute, "fear of bodily injury" induced in an assault victim, and the like. Note that most offenses are defined only in terms of conduct and circumstances, with no required result. For example, only conduct and circumstance actus reus elements are contained in the common law definition of larceny as "taking and carrying away the personal property of another with intent to effect a permanent deprivation." Note also that in cases where results are specified, an additional element of a causal relation between the defendant's conduct and the prohibited result is necessarily implied.

These three categories are somewhat arbitrary. It would be relatively easy to develop a different terminology. Moreover, it is not always clear how a particular element should be classified. For example, in rape as defined in § 213.1(1)(a) of the Model Penal Code, the actor is guilty if "he compels [the victim] to submit by force." Is it intuitively clear how each of these elements should be classified? Does the quoted phrase describe conduct or a result?

Fortunately, in most situations nothing turns on an improper classification of a given element. The principal purpose of adopting this structure is satisfied by the exercise of focusing separately on each component of the offense rather than treating the actus reus as an undifferentiated whole. Separating the actus-reus elements in this manner is an essential analytical step in approaching *every* criminal offense under the Model Code or any statute based upon it.

There are some cases, however, (the crime of attempt provides an example), where proper categorization of some elements is crucial. These are considered in due course below. For now, it would be wise to experiment with the classification scheme, and be aware of the ambiguities and difficulties that a given classification entails. To this end, a useful exercise would be to select a variety of substantive offenses defined by the Model Code and, before reading on, to classify each "act" element (that is, those elements that do not deal with a required state of mind) as conduct, circumstance, or result. This should be done enough times so that it becomes an automatic first step in *every* analysis of a problem to be dealt with under the Model Code or a similar statute.

**2.   The Mens Rea.** The next step in the Model Penal Code analysis is to ascertain the required mens rea. The Model Code is based on the proposition that four culpability concepts are both necessary and sufficient to define criminal offenses. They are "purpose," "knowledge," "recklessness," and "negligence." Each of these terms is carefully defined. The mens rea elements of a given crime are determined by ascertaining which of these four terms applies to *each* of the actus-reus components of the offense and by adding any other specifically defined mens rea requirement.

Thus, once the crime is broken down into its conduct, circumstance, and result components, one of the four culpability concepts will be applied to each component in order to determine the level of mens rea required for that offense. And there may be yet additional mens rea components required by the definition of the offense.

To illustrate, larceny was defined above as "taking and carrying away the personal property of another with intent to effect a permanent deprivation." One would first classify "taking" and "carrying away" as conduct elements, and ask whether that conduct has occurred. One would then ask which of the four culpability terms applies to each element. The same analysis would then be followed for the circumstance elements "personal property" and "of another." One could then describe the mens rea for larceny as consisting of the applicable culpability term applied to each actus-reus element of the offense *in addition to* the specified intent to effect a permanent deprivation.

At this point, careful study of the provisions of § 2.02 is required. The notes following the text of the Code explicate their meaning.

––––––––

## MODEL PENAL CODE CULPABILITY PROVISIONS

### Section 2.02. General Requirements of Culpability

(1) <u>Minimum Requirements of Culpability.</u> Except as provided in Section 2.05, a person is not guilty of an offense unless he acted purposely, knowingly, recklessly or negligently, as the law may require, with respect to each material element of the offense.

(2) <u>Kinds of Culpability Defined.</u>

(a) <u>Purposely.</u>

A person acts purposely with respect to a material element of an offense when:

(i) if the element involves the nature of his conduct or a result thereof, it is his conscious object to engage in conduct of that nature or to cause such a result; and

(ii) if the element involves the attendant circumstances, he is aware of the existence of such circumstances or he believes or hopes that they exist.

(b) <u>Knowingly.</u>

A person acts knowingly with respect to a material element of an offense when:

(i) if the element involves the nature of his conduct or the attendant circumstances, he is aware that his conduct is of that nature or that such circumstances exist; and

(ii) if the element involves a result of his conduct, he is aware that it is practically certain that his conduct will cause such a result.

(c) Recklessly.

A person acts recklessly with respect to a material element of an offense when he consciously disregards a substantial and un-justifiable risk that the material element exists or will result from his conduct. The risk must be of such a nature and degree that, considering the nature and purpose of the actor's conduct and the circumstances known to him, its disregard involves a gross devia-tion from the standard of conduct that a law-abiding person would observe in the actor's situation.

(d) Negligently.

A person acts negligently with respect to a material element of an offense when he should be aware of a substantial and unjustifi-able risk that the material element exists or will result from his conduct. The risk must be of such a nature and degree that the actor's failure to perceive it, considering the nature and purpose of his conduct and the circumstances known to him, involves a gross deviation from the standard of care that a reasonable person would observe in the actor's situation.

(3) Culpability Required Unless Otherwise Provided. When the culpa-bility sufficient to establish a material element of an offense is not pre-scribed by law, such element is established if a person acts purposely, knowingly or recklessly with respect thereto.

(4) Prescribed Culpability Requirement Applies to All Material Ele-ments. When the law defining an offense prescribes the kind of culpability that is sufficient for the commission of an offense, without distinguishing among the material elements thereof, such provision shall apply to all the material elements of the offense, unless a contrary purpose plainly appears.

(5) Substitutes for Negligence, Recklessness and Knowledge. When the law provides that negligence suffices to establish an element of an offense, such element also is established if a person acts purposely, knowingly or recklessly. When recklessness suffices to establish an element, such ele-ment also is established if a person acts purposely or knowingly. When acting knowingly suffices to establish an element, such element also is established if a person acts purposely . . . .

(7) Requirement of Knowledge Satisfied by Knowledge of High Proba-bility. When knowledge of the existence of a particular fact is an element of an offense, such knowledge is established if a person is aware of a high probability of its existence, unless he actually believes that it does not exist . . . .

## Section 2.04. Ignorance or Mistake

(1) Ignorance or mistake as to a matter of fact or law is a defense if:

(a) the ignorance or mistake negatives the purpose, knowledge, belief, recklessness or negligence required to establish a material element of the offense; or

(b) the law provides that the state of mind established by such ignorance or mistake constitutes a defense....

———

## NOTES ON THE MODEL PENAL CODE CULPABILITY STRUCTURE

**1. Minimum Requirements of Culpability.** There are several points to be noted about § 2.02(1):

**(i) Strict Liability.** Section 2.05, to which reference is made in the opening phrase, is the Model Penal Code's response to the "public welfare" offenses described by Justice Jackson in *Morissette*. The Model Code calls these offenses "violations." Under § 1.04, violations are not "crimes" and carry only fines, forfeitures, or other civil penalties. The culpability structure does not apply to violations.

**(ii) Types of Culpability.** Section 2.02(1) introduces the four mainstays of the culpability structure—purpose, knowledge, recklessness, and negligence. Each of these terms is defined in § 2.02(2). Common law mens rea terms are discarded.

The provision of only four basic levels of culpability—five if you count strict liability—represents an important insight. The Model Code position is that these concepts are both necessary and sufficient—necessary because the distinctions among them are required as a basis for crime definition and grading, and sufficient because additional generalized discriminations would be superfluous. This proposition can be tested by asking whether all of the concepts encountered in previously studied cases can be translated into one or more of these ideas.

**(iii) "As the Law May Require."** The phrase "as the law may require" refers to the analytical process for determining which mens rea elements are to be applied to each actus reus element. This process is described in detail below.

**(iv) Material Element.** The term "material element" is defined in § 1.13(9) and § 1.13(10). The important point for present purposes is that the definition explicitly includes "(i) such conduct or (ii) such attendant circumstances or (iii) such a result of conduct as ... is included ... in the definition of the offense." Section 1.13 thus establishes the basic division of the actus reus of an offense into its conduct, circumstance, and result components. As has been said, application of § 2.02 to an offense requires the allocation of each of the actus-reus elements of an offense to one of these three categories.

**(v) "Each" Material Element.** "Each" may be the most important word in § 2.02(1). It requires that a level of mens rea—purpose, knowledge, recklessness, or negligence[a]—be applied to "each" conduct, circumstance, and result element of the actus reus of an offense. Thus every actus reus element of an offense has its own mens rea requirement.

As an analytical matter, this provision represents one of the most important contributions of the Model Code. Thinking about mens rea separately for each element of an offense permits far more precision than was achieved by the common law. This is true both for legislatures as they specify what the law should be and for courts and juries as they implement legislative decisions. Note that this analytical insight does not require the legislature to select any particular mens rea requirement for a given element of an offense. The legislature is completely free to set the mens rea at any one of the four levels it chooses, or indeed to impose strict liability. The structure simply requires that the mens rea question be asked for each element; it does not itself give the answer to that question. The answer is provided by the interaction of § 2.02 with the definition of the individual offense.

**2. "Purpose."** "Purpose" is defined in the ordinary-language sense of conscious objective or desire. Many enactments based on the Model Code have used the word "intent" to mean the same thing.

Why has the Model Code defined the term differently for conduct and result elements on the one hand and circumstance elements on the other? The answer lies in common sense. Circumstances cannot be "intended." They concern matters external to the actor that either exist or do not exist (property does or does not belong to another; it is or is not night; the victim is or is not a specified age; the victim is or is not a public officer). The actor can, of course, *believe* or *hope* that property belongs to another, that it is night, or that the victim is a certain age. And the actor can make a mistake—i.e., can believe or hope for that which is not true. But it is strained in terms of the ordinary use of language, the Model Code drafters thought, to say that a defendant has a purpose that it now be nighttime.

**3. "Knowledge."** "Knowledge" is defined as awareness. Why in this case are conduct and circumstances distinguished from results? The answer is that one cannot "know" with certainty that results will flow from conduct. Common experience will indicate a degree of likelihood, but cause and effect are always matters of probability.

"Knowledge" under the Model Code scheme is satisfied if the actor is "practically certain" that the result will follow. Whether the result is desired is irrelevant to such knowledge, though of course it would be relevant to whether there was a purpose to cause the result. For most offenses, it can be said, this subtle difference between "purpose" and

---

[a] Occasionally, but only occasionally, the Model Penal Code will impose strict liability for an element, that is, will not require any mens rea for a particular element of an offense. In the rare cases where this is done, the definition of the offense is explicit that no mens rea is required. For an example, see § 213.6(1) (age below 10 in sex offenses). This, then, is "as the law may require" for this particular offense.

"knowledge" is unimportant. It is rare for the definition of an offense to distinguish between them.

**4. "Recklessness."** Application of the Model Code concept of recklessness requires careful dissection of the definition in § 2.02(2)(c). Unlike "purpose" and "knowledge," "recklessness" applies in the same terms to conduct, circumstances, and results. It is also unlike "purpose" and "knowledge" in a more important respect. Deciding whether the defendant had a purpose to do something or knew that an external circumstance existed requires the jury to make a finding of fact—the defendant either had the required purpose or knowledge or did not. Asking a jury to determine whether a defendant was "reckless," by contrast, requires it to make a judgment. In this case, the jury is asked to apply a set of criteria to the defendant's beliefs and actions, and to make a judgment whether the defendant fell sufficiently below community standards of behavior to warrant criminal punishment.

Section 2.02(2)(c) requires that the risk that an element of the offense will occur be "substantial" and "unjustifiable." Obviously relevant to a judgment that a risk should not have been taken are the likelihood or predictability that the risk will be realized and the justifications one might have for taking it. Physicians, for example, are frequently called upon to take very substantial risks, but such risks can be entirely justifiable given the alternatives. What the jury must decide is how "substantial" the risk was and how "justifiable" it might have been to take the risk in the context of the defendant's behavior. To be guilty of an offense that requires recklessness, the defendant must be aware of the facts that make the risk substantial and the facts that make it unjustifiable.

But this is not the end of the inquiry. In effect, the jury must decide that given the context, the defendant should not have taken the risk and should be subject to criminal punishment for having done so. This it does by applying the criteria in the second sentence of the definition. It must consider "the nature and purpose of the actor's conduct and the circumstances known to him," and in that light decide whether disregarding the risk "involves a gross deviation from the standard of conduct that a law-abiding person would observe in the actor's situation."

The word "situation" contains an important and deliberate ambiguity. Suppose, for example, the defendant has a physical condition that impairs perception or judgment. Should that be relevant in deciding whether taking the risk was a "gross deviation" from law-abiding behavior? The drafters of the Model Code decided not to resolve this question in advance, but to leave the matter to judicial evolution. The function of the word "situation" is to permit the courts to personalize the standard where mitigation or exoneration based on individual characteristics of the offender would not undermine the functions of the criminal law. This problem surfaces in numerous places and raises policy questions of the most fundamental kind.

Some final observations should be added about the relationship between the definitions of knowledge and recklessness. For result elements, there is a fine line between being "practically certain" (knowledge) and a "substantial and unjustifiable risk" (recklessness). Does this draw too fine a line? The answer is that maybe it does, but it makes little practical difference. Most cases turning on the occurrence of results involve one or another form of criminal homicide. There are special rules to deal with this problem in the law of homicide, even under the Model Penal Code.[b] Few offenses other than homicide turn on results actually caused, and even fewer turn on the difference between results caused knowingly and results caused recklessly. The issue can arise, however, as in the provisions of § 211.1(2)(b) of the Model Code, which defines aggravated assault as occurring, inter alia, when one "knowingly causes bodily injury to another with a deadly weapon."

Another subtlety in the relationship between knowledge and recklessness is raised by § 2.02(7). It is there stated that when knowledge "of the existence of a particular fact" (as opposed to knowledge that a result will follow) is an element of an offense, such knowledge is established if the defendant "is aware of a high probability of its existence, unless he actually believes that it does not exist." This language incorporates the notion of "wilful blindness," originally developed in English law. The issue would arise, for example, in a case where the defendant was offered $5,000 to drive a car across the Mexican–American border. If the car is found to contain illegal drugs, the defendant may not be heard to complain that she or he was ignorant of that fact.

**5. "Negligence."** The major difference between recklessness and negligence is that negligence is based on inattention to risk. The defendant must be "consciously aware" of the risk to be reckless. To be negligent, it is enough that the defendant "should have been aware" of the risk. Otherwise, the analysis is the same. The jury decides whether the risks were substantial and unjustifiable and whether the defendant should have been aware of them. And considering "the nature and purpose of the actor's conduct and the circumstances known to him," the jury must decide whether disregarding the risk "involves a gross deviation from the standard of care that a reasonable person would observe in the actor's situation."[c]

**6. Hierarchy of Model Penal Code Culpability Terms.** Section 2.02(5) ranks the four Model Code culpability terms. If negligence is the mens rea required for a given element the prosecution can establish its case by proving purpose, knowledge, recklessness, or negligence. Plainly, if negligence is sufficient, the defendant is *more* culpable, not less, if purpose, knowledge, or recklessness can be proved. Similarly, if recklessness is required by the definition of a particular offense, proof of knowledge or purpose should also suffice. Section 2.02(5) thus stands for the common-

---

[b] These special rules need not be of concern now. They are dealt with briefly in connection with the next main case and more extensively in the homicide chapter.

[c] No explanation has been offered for why "reasonable person" is used for negli-gence and "law-abiding person" for recklessness. Nor has one been offered to explain why the words "standard of conduct" are used in the definition of recklessness as opposed to "standard of care" in the definition of negligence.

sense proposition that if the prosecutor proves the defendant more blame-worthy than is required by the offense charged, the defendant should be convicted.

**7. Offense Silent as to Mens Rea.** Section 2.02(3) establishes a drafting convention and an important substantive conclusion. These two points deserve separate consideration.

Section 2.02(3) states that recklessness is the minimum culpability required for every element of every offense, absent specific provision to the contrary in a particular definition. As a drafting matter, such a provision is a great convenience. It eliminates the necessity to spell out the culpability requirement for each separate actus-reus element of an offense and thus makes the defining process less cumbersome. It permits implementation of an important analytical insight of the Model Code—that culpability should be established in advance for each element of an offense—without unnecessary verbiage in the definitions themselves.

Section 2.02(3) also expresses an important substantive judgment by providing that the default standard of liability for each element of a criminal offense is recklessness. The conclusion of the Model Penal Code drafters was that liability based on negligence should be exceptional and that, if negligence is to be used, the decision to do so should be based on judgments made in defining particular offenses and not on a general principle that negligence is appropriate.[d]

It should be added that § 2.02(3) is defended by its drafters as a statement of the usual common law position. Whether this assertion is descriptively accurate can be doubted and is called into question in some of the materials that follow. In any event, § 2.02(3) expresses an important normative proposition, the correctness of which can be debated independently of the analytical structure established by the Model Code culpability provisions.

**8. Ambiguous Mens Rea Provisions.** A second drafting convention is established by § 2.02(4). It is intended merely to resolve grammatical ambiguities, but its application is sometimes confusing. Four illustrations are given below: the first two are cases where the application of § 2.02(4) presents little difficulty; the third is a straightforward application of § 2.02(3); the last raises a common point of confusion between § 2.02(3) and § 2.02(4), where the answer intended by the drafters of the Model Code is clear but the text of § 2.02(4) is not.

**(i) False Imprisonment.** Consider the facts of State v. Walker, 35 N.C.App. 182, 241 S.E.2d 89 (1978), previously mentioned in the notes on Mistake of Fact and the Common Law. The defendant and his son abducted a seven-year-old boy and a five-year-old girl as they were leaving a

---

[d] "Negligence" is rarely used in the Model Penal Code. The most important use is in negligent homicide (§ 210.4), and there are few others (e.g., § 211.1(1)(b)). As subsequent materials illustrate, one major differ-ence between the Model Code and the common law is the extent to which negligence suffices for certain aspects of criminal liability.

school bus in front of their school. About five minutes later the girl was found walking back to the school. The boy was still missing at the time of trial. The boy, it turned out, was the defendant's grandson. The court held that his abduction was "lawful" because the boy's father participated in the affair and, as the father, was entitled to take custody of his own son. But the girl was unrelated to the two men. The defense in *Walker* was that the two men also thought it was "lawful" to take the girl because they thought she was the boy's sister. When they found out that she was not, they let her go.

What result if the father and grandfather are prosecuted under § 212.3 of the Model Penal Code, which punishes one who "knowingly restrains another unlawfully so as to interfere substantially with his liberty"? Would they be able to defend on the ground that they thought the girl was their daughter and granddaughter, respectively? The answer, if the jury believes the defendants, is "yes."

The first step in reaching this result is to apply § 2.02(4) to the definition of the offense. The key to understanding § 2.02(4) is to begin by breaking the offense into its actus reus components. Here, there are four: "restrains," "another [person]," "unlawfully," and "so as to interfere substantially with his liberty." The next step is to ask why the word "knowingly" is included in the definition of the offense. The answer is that it *at least* establishes that the defendant must *know* that one of the actus reus elements (the restraint) has occurred.

With respect to the other actus reus elements, § 212.3 is grammatically ambiguous. One cannot tell whether the word "knowingly" modifies only the word "restrains" or whether it also modifies the remaining words in the sentence. Section 2.02(4) was included for the purpose of resolving such a grammatical ambiguity, *and only for that purpose*. It applies *only when* a mens rea term establishes the mens rea for one actus reus element and it is not clear from the wording whether it applies to all of them. Section 2.02(4) says that "unless a contrary purpose plainly appears" from the definition of the offense, a culpability term that provides the mens rea for one actus reus element also provides the mens rea for all of the other actus reus elements. Since it is not clear from reading the definition in § 212.3 whether "knowingly" applies only to "restrains" or whether it also applies to the other actus reus elements of the offense, the mens rea of "knowingly" should be applied to all of them.

Under § 2.04, therefore, the mens rea for "unlawfully" is "knowledge." To be guilty in the *Walker* situation posed above, the defendants must "know" the facts that make it "unlawful" for the restraint to occur. They must have known, in other words, that the girl was not, respectively, their daughter and granddaughter. If the jury believes the defendants, they must be acquitted.

The provisions of § 2.04(1)(a) should also be examined in connection with this hypothetical. Notice that § 2.04(1)(a) in effect states the reciprocal of § 2.02. If § 2.02 requires knowledge for a certain element, then § 2.04(1)(a) gives a defense if the defendant does not know. In the *Walker* hypothetical, § 2.04(1)(a) gives the defense because the application of § 2.02(4) establishes "knowledge" as the applicable mens rea for the actus reus element "unlawfully."

Is there another defense these defendants might be able to assert to a charge of violating § 212.3 if the jury disbelieves them on this one?

**(ii) Reckless Burning.** Section 220.1(2)(a) punishes one who "purposely starts a fire . . . and thereby recklessly places another person in danger of death or bodily injury." If Faulkner were charged with this offense, could he defend on the ground that it was not his objective to place other persons in danger of death or bodily injury? Does § 2.02(4) mean that the defendant must "purposely" create the danger of death or bodily injury to another? Plainly not. Here the definition of the offense is clear that "recklessly" modifies the element "places another person in danger of death or bodily injury," and there is no ambiguity for § 2.02(4) to resolve. As applied to the facts of *Faulkner*, the mens rea question under § 220.1(2)(a) would be whether Faulkner was reckless in placing others in danger of death or injury.

Is there another defense that Faulkner might be able to assert if charged with a violation of § 220.1(2)(a)?

**(iii) Escape.** Section 242.6(1) covers one who "fails to return to official detention following temporary leave granted for a . . . limited period." What is the mens rea for the "limited period" component of the offense? Must the defendant know that the length of time for which leave was granted has expired? The answer is that "recklessness" is the mens rea as to this element. No mens rea term is included in the definition of the offense, and § 2.02(3) provides that recklessness is required as to all actus reus elements in such a case.

**(iv) Hindering Prosecution.** Section 242.3(5) provides that a person commits an offense "if, with purpose to hinder the apprehension, prosecution, conviction or punishment of another for crime, he . . . volunteers false information to a law enforcement officer." Consider a situation where, in order to prevent the apprehension of a fugitive, the defendant tells everyone who asks that he was seen in California last week. In fact, the defendant knows that the fugitive is still in Chicago. If the defendant said this to a plainclothes police officer, could the defense to a charge under § 242.3(5) be that the defendant did not know that the person lied to was "a law enforcement officer"? The answer is "no." Recklessness, not knowledge, is the mens rea for this actus reus element. The issue would be whether the defendant was reckless as to whether the person lied to was a law enforcement officer.

How is this answer derived? Section 2.02(4) might be read to say that if a culpability term is used anywhere in the definition of the offense, it applies to every element of the offense "unless a contrary purpose plainly appears." Under this reading, purpose would apply to all elements of § 242.3(5) since the defendant must have a "purpose to hinder" and since there is no indication that this purpose need not accompany the commission of each element of the offense. Since "purpose" is the same as "knowledge" when applied to circumstance elements (see § 2.02(2)(a)(ii)), "knowledge" would be required for the circumstance element "law enforcement officer" under this reading of § 2.02(4).

Although this is certainly a plausible reading of § 2.02(4), it is not the reading the drafters intended. The intended reading can be derived from the following reasoning. Again, the first step is to isolate the actus reus elements of the offense. Here they are "volunteers," "false," "information," and "law enforcement officer." These are events that must happen in order for this crime to occur. The next step is to ask whether there are any words in the offense providing that purpose, knowledge, recklessness, or negligence applies to any one of these events. *There are no such words in the definition of this offense.* Here the purpose of including the mens rea phrase in the definition of the offense is not to designate the mens rea required for any component of the actus reus of the offense, but to describe an additional objective or motive that must accompany the defendant's conduct. The defendant must, in effect, hope that the conduct will have the described impact on law enforcement. That impact need not in fact occur; the defendant is still guilty even if the officer disbelieves the defendant and does nothing in response to the false information. The desire to hinder must exist independently of any mens rea that may or may not be required for each of the actus reus elements of the offense.

The intent of the drafters of § 2.02(4) is that additional motives or purposes of this sort should be ignored in applying the drafting conventions of § 2.02. Such motives or purposes are additional mental states required by the offense. They do not supply the mens rea for the actus reus elements of the offense. Instead, one must ask whether the offense contains any mens rea words that are intended to describe the mental state the defendant must have for any actus reus element of the offense. Section 242.3(5) has no such mens rea words, and hence the mens rea for "law enforcement officer" would be "reckless" under § 2.02(3).

Contrast the situation that would occur if the definition of the offense were "if, with purpose to hinder the apprehension, prosecution, conviction or punishment of another for crime, he knowingly volunteers false information to a law enforcement officer." In that case, the function of the word "knowingly" would be at least to describe the mens rea for the actus reus element "volunteers." If this were the definition of the offense, the mens rea for "law enforcement officer" would be "knowledge," derived from the provisions of § 2.02(4) as in the false imprisonment example given above.

Compare the definition of falsely incriminating another in § 241.5. The crime is committed if one "knowingly gives false information to any law enforcement officer with purpose to implicate another." Applying § 2.02(4), the mens rea for the element "law enforcement officer" would be "knowledge."

If the word "knowingly" were omitted from the definition and it was otherwise worded the same way, the mens rea for "law enforcement officer" would be "recklessness." Section 2.02(4) would not apply, and the answer would be derived from § 2.02(3). But suppose the offense definition were changed to read "with purpose to implicate another, gives false information to any law enforcement officer." Does that change anything? What mens rea for "law enforcement officer" then? The answer is that it still would be "recklessness," based on the reasoning outlined above in connection with the hindering prosecution example. Moving the "with purpose to" clause around in the sentence does not change the analysis. It still has the function of describing what the common law would call a "specific intent." There is no work for § 2.02(4) to do, and the mens rea for this element would be derived from the default provisions in § 2.02(3). If the legislative objective were to make "knowledge" the mens rea for "law enforcement officer," one way to do so would be to word the offense "with purpose to implicate another, knowingly gives false information to any law enforcement officer." And it still would not matter whether the "with purpose to" clause were at the beginning or the end of the sentence. The offense as worded this way would have the same actus reus and mens rea elements as the offense defined by § 241.5.

Two final twists. What mens rea for "false information" if the offense reads "with purpose to implicate another, knowingly gives false information to any law enforcement officer"? If it reads "with purpose to implicate another, gives false information to a person known to be a law enforcement officer"? The answer is "knowledge" in the first case and "recklessness" in the second. You ought by now to be able to spell out the reasoning.

**9.   Mistake of Fact.** As illustrated by the false imprisonment example given above, § 2.04(1)(a) states a tautology. If an offense requires a prescribed mental state for a given element, it is a defense if the defendant did not have that mental state.ᵉ If knowledge is the mens rea for a given element, it is a defense if the defendant did not know. If recklessness is the mens rea, it is a defense if the defendant was not reckless. And so on.

The application of § 2.04(1)(a) is therefore totally dependent on an accurate determination of the mens rea for the element at issue. If the mens rea is properly derived from the definition of the offense and the rules stated in § 2.02, the significance of a mistake of fact automatically follows. Section 2.04(1)(a) merely confirms what logic would dictate.

Notice another aspect of the Model Penal Code treatment of mistakes of fact. The common law default for general intent crimes provides a defense if the mistake is "honest and reasonable." The standard here is an ordinary form of negligence. By contrast, the Model Penal Code default for mistakes of fact—established by the application of § 2.02(3)—is that recklessness is the standard for the typical mistake. Recklessness, moreover, not only requires that the defendant actually be aware of the risk that the relevant element exists, but requires the jury to conclude that ignoring the risk involved "a gross deviation from the standard of conduct that a law-

---

ᵉ There are exceptions to this statement, most notably in some cases where the defendant is intoxicated by drink or drugs. These situations are dealt with below, and need not be of concern now.

abiding person would observe in the actor's situation." This is by any measure a much higher standard of culpability for mistakes of fact than its common law counterpart. What accounts for the difference? Which level of culpability is more appropriate for the ordinary mistake of fact?

**10. Grading.** Most modern statutes are ambiguous on the effect of mistakes of fact that relate only to grading elements. A new federal code proposed but not enacted by the Congress explicitly embraced the common law rule: "Except as otherwise expressly provided, culpability is not required with respect to any fact which is solely a basis ... for grading." Final Report of the National Commission on Reform of Federal Criminal Laws § 302(3)(c) (1971).

Notice that the Model Penal Code disagrees. Section 2.04(2) provides:

> Although ignorance or mistake would otherwise afford a defense to the offense charged, the defense is not available if the defendant would be guilty of another offense had the situation been as he supposed. In such case, however, the ignorance or mistake of the defendant shall reduce the grade and degree of the offense of which he may be convicted to those of the offense of which he would be guilty had the situation been as he supposed.

Application of the mens rea structure to grading elements is meant to be confirmed in § 2.02(1). The culpability structure established by § 2.02 applies to "each material element of the offense." Section 1.13(9) defines "element" to include all of the conduct, result, and circumstance components "included in the description of the forbidden conduct in the definition of the offense." A "material" element, as provided in § 1.13(10), is any element having to do with "the harm or evil, incident to conduct, sought to be prevented by the law defining the offense." There is, to be sure, some ambiguity in these provisions. It is not entirely clear, for example, whether § 223.1(2) is part of "the description of the forbidden conduct in the definition of the offense" punished by § 223.2. But there is no doubt that it was the intention of the drafters of the Model Code to apply ordinary culpability rules to the grading elements of crimes.[f]

This point can be tested by reconsideration of the theft example posited in Note 7 in the Notes on Mistake of Fact and the Common Law. The defendant committed a theft of jewelry actually valued at $10,000, but thought the item stolen was merely elaborate costume jewelry and therefore fenced it for $50. By what mens rea is the defendant's mistake to be judged if prosecuted under § 223.2 of the Model Penal Code? The answer is "recklessness." Section 223.1(2) establishes $500 as the dividing line between felony and misdemeanor theft. No mens rea is provided for this element, so the default of "recklessness" would be applied under § 2.02(3). If the defendant was not reckless in the belief that the jewelry was worth less than $500, the conviction would be for the misdemeanor not the felony.

---

[f] See American Law Institute, Model Penal Code and Commentaries § 2.04, pp. 272–74 (1985).

At common law on the same facts, the conviction would be for the felony. How can this difference be explained? Which solution is right?

**11.   Lesser Moral Wrong.** Judge Bramwell's opinion in *Regina v. Prince*[g] describes, in effect, a rule of statutory construction. Elements of an offense that are an essential part of the community ethic as measured by current societal standards should require some form of mens rea. But if the defendant would be violating accepted social standards even on a mistaken view of a given element of an offense, strict liability should be imposed for that element and the mistake should not be a defense. This principle is not universally followed, but it has been used by the common law in several contexts.

It is irrelevant under the Model Penal Code—except perhaps on credibility—that a lesser moral wrong was committed on the facts as the defendant believed them to be. But consider § 213.1(1)(d), which provides that a "male who has sexual intercourse with a female not his wife is guilty of rape if . . . the female is less than 10 years old." Section 213.6(1) imposes strict liability on the age element of this offense. It denies a defense if the claim is "I thought she was 11," even if the belief was entirely reasonable on the facts. On what rationale might this provision be defended? Why might it be wrong?

———

## SUBSECTION C: IGNORANCE OR MISTAKE OF LAW

———

## State v. Fox

Supreme Court of Idaho, 1993.
124 Idaho 924, 866 P.2d 181.

■ MCDEVITT, CHIEF JUSTICE.

On January 11, 1991, appellant Milton Fox was charged with . . . possession of ephedrine, a controlled substance. As far as the Court can tell from the record, Fox ordered and received 100,000 tablets of ephedrine from an out-of-state mail order distributor. According to the Physician's Desk Reference, ephedrine has a stimulative effect on the central nervous system and is used to treat asthma symptoms. In some states, ephedrine is a legal over-the-counter drug. In Idaho, ephedrine was listed as a Schedule II substance in the Uniform Controlled Substances Act in 1988. I.C. § 37–2707(g)(1)(b). Compounds containing ephedrine could be sold over-the-counter until November 1990, when the Idaho Board of Pharmacy designated ephedrine as a prescription drug.

[g] See the discussion of *Prince* in the Notes on Mistake of Fact and the Common Law.

... During the trial ..., Fox attempted to introduce [as defense exhibits] magazines carrying mail order advertisements for ephedrine from out-of-state suppliers. The state objected to the exhibits as cumulative (apparently the state introduced a magazine with a similar advertisement) and the court sustained the state's objection. The court then held a hearing outside the presence of the jury. During this hearing, the court held that the proffered exhibits were not relevant because knowledge that possession of ephedrine was illegal was not an element of the offense.

The next day, Fox renewed his argument that the exhibits were relevant. He pointed out that the state's proposed jury instruction required that it prove that "Milton Fox had knowledge of its [i.e., the ephedrine's] presence and nature as a controlled substance." The court responded by ruling that it would not give that instruction, or the similar one which the defense proposed, because these instructions did not accurately state the law.

After that ruling, Fox entered a conditional plea of guilty pursuant to I.C.R. 11(a)(2) which preserved his right to appeal the trial court's rulings. On appeal, Fox states the issues as follows:

> Did the District Court err in holding that intent, general intent or specific intent, "is not a required element for guilt in possession of a controlled substance" and, further, "that mistakes of law or fact are not defenses to the crime of possession of a controlled substance[?]"

We will address each contention in turn.

1.   THE MENS REA ELEMENT OF THE OFFENSE OF POSSESSION OF A CONTROLLED SUBSTANCE IS KNOWLEDGE OF POSSESSION, NOT KNOWLEDGE THAT THE SUBSTANCE POSSESSED IS A CONTROLLED SUBSTANCE.

The Uniform Controlled Substances Act, in I.C. § 37–2732(c), states that:

> It is unlawful for any person to possess a controlled substance unless the substance was obtained directly from, or pursuant to, a valid prescription or order of a practitioner while acting in the course of his professional practice, or except as otherwise authorized by this chapter.

The text of the possession statute does not set forth any mental state as an element of the offense. This Court has previously ruled that "whether a criminal intent is a necessary element of a statutory offense is a matter of construction, to be determined from the language of the statute in view of its manifest purpose and design, and where such intent is not made an ingredient of the offense, the intention with which the act is done, or the lack of any criminal intent in the premises, is immaterial." State v. Sterrett, 35 Idaho 580, 583, 207 P. 1071, 1072 (1922).

Fox therefore turns to I.C. § 18–114, which provides that "[i]n every crime or public offense there must exist a union, or joint operation, of act and intent, or criminal negligence." Fox argues that this statute means that conviction under the possession statute requires specific intent. The state argues that only a general intent is required. This Court has explained the difference between specific and general intent as follows: A general criminal intent requirement is satisfied if it is shown that the defendant knowingly performed the proscribed acts, but a specific intent requirement refers to that state of mind which in part defines the crime and is an element thereof.

This Court has previously determined, however, that the intent required by I.C. § 18–114 is "not the intent to commit a crime, but is merely the intent to knowingly perform the interdicted act, or by criminal negligence the failure to perform the required act." State v. Parish, 79 Idaho 75, 78, 310 P.2d 1082, 1083 (1957).

Fox then argues that a mistake of fact is available to him, pursuant to I.C. § 18–201. Idaho Code § 18–201 provides a defense for "[p]ersons who committed the act or made the omission charged, under an ignorance or mistake of fact which disproves any criminal intent." Our review of the record does not support this contention. Fox does not claim that he did not know he possessed ephedrine. His claim is that he did not know ephedrine was illegal. In short, Fox asserts a mistake of law claim rather than a mistake of fact claim.

Thus, as I.C. § 37–2732(c) does not expressly require any mental element and I.C. § 18–114 only requires a general intent, we conclude that the offense only requires a general intent, that is, the knowledge that one is in possession of the substance. Consequently, we also conclude that the trial court was correct in refusing Fox's proffered exhibits because any evidence tending to establish Fox's lack of knowledge that ephedrine was illegal is irrelevant. Evidence that is not relevant is not admissible. I.R.E. 402. We also affirm the district court's refusal to give the proposed jury instructions because they were not accurate statements of the law.

2. FOX CANNOT CLAIM A GOOD FAITH MISTAKE OF LAW DEFENSE UPON THE RECORD IN THIS CASE.

Fox also argues that a good faith mistake of law excuses his possession of the ephedrine. As far as we can tell, Fox's attempted defense at trial on this issue was that he did not know or reasonably could not have known that ephedrine was a controlled substance.

Ignorance of the law is not a defense. See e.g., Hale v. Morgan, 22 Cal.3d 388, 149 Cal.Rptr. 375, 380, 584 P.2d 512, 517 (1978) ("[I]n the absence of specific language to the contrary, ignorance of a law is not a defense to a charge of its violation"); State v. Einhorn, 213 Kan. 271, 515 P.2d 1036, 1039 (1973) ("The general rule is that ignorance of the law does not disprove criminal intent"). There is no indication in the record, nor is any argument made, that the defendant could not have discovered what substances were listed in the schedules of controlled substances. Ephedrine had in fact been added to the list in 1988, several years prior to Fox's possession of the substance in 1991.

This is simply a case where Fox possessed a substance, knowing full well what the substance was, but claiming now that he did not know it was listed in the statutes as a controlled substance. There is nothing in that argument which would rise to the level of a viable defense.

The district court is affirmed.

■ JOHNSON, TROUT and SILAK, JJ., concur.

■ BISTLINE, JUSTICE, conceding that the applicable statute is controlling as the state contends, but dissenting from the result.

That the other members of the Court have readily joined an opinion which affirms the trial court is not a great surprise. As the brief prepared in the office of the Attorney General of the State of Idaho informs its readers, the law as presently structured makes it impossible to do other than affirm the trial court; the hands of the trial judge were equally tied. Reluctantly I concede that convicting Fox under I.C. § 37–2732(c) was the correct procedure in this case. I write separately to register my concerns regarding the potential application of I.C. § 37–2732(c) to other Idaho citizens who possess far smaller amounts of ephedrine than did Fox, who purchase [the] ephedrine validly, but who may subsequently be convicted as felons.

Fox ordered the ephedrine by calling the toll-free number of a national outlet. Apparently, some of the ephedrine advertisements that are available to Idaho citizens contain warnings that the offer is void where prohibited by law, but some do not; ordering from the wrong catalog may therefore be a defendant's biggest mistake. In another potential scenario, an Idaho citizen might travel to another state for business or pleasure, purchase ephedrine while there to alleviate his or her bronchial or other health-related symptoms, and return home again, bearing the ephedrine, only to be possibly convicted under I.C. § 37–2732(c).

Ephedrine is a drug used for medical purposes. Surely persons who make out-of-state purchases of ephedrine for medical reasons pose no more of a threat to Idaho's safety and freedom from drug traffickers than persons who purchase ephedrine pursuant to a valid prescription or practitioner order while in Idaho. The Idaho Legislature is to be commended in its effort to reduce the trade of drugs, but I.C. § 37–2732(c) is truly too blunt an instrument. Moreover, at the least, the statute should provide a defense to Idaho citizens who did not know about the statute, did not comprehend its import, and were not alert enough to see that they should comply, even though they knew naught.

It is often stated that ignorance of the law is no excuse. The responsibility of the legislative branch in drafting the laws that govern society, then, is weighty. A law that imposes a felony for potentially very innocent behavior must be carefully worded; I.C. § 37–2732 is not.

## NOTES ON IGNORANCE OR MISTAKE OF CRIMINALITY

**1. The Model Penal Code.** *Fox* illustrates the maxim, ignorantia juris neminem excusat.[a] As will be seen, the maxim is susceptible to misapplication and increasingly subject to exceptions. It is nevertheless descriptive of the dominant policy of the penal law with respect to awareness of illegality. Generally speaking, criminal liability does not depend on the actor's awareness of the criminality of conduct. Thus, ignorance or mistake regarding the criminality of one's act is no defense to criminal prosecution. In more familiar phrasing, "ignorance of the law is no excuse."

Section 2.02(9) of the Model Code continues this tradition:

> Neither knowledge or recklessness or negligence as to whether conduct constitutes an offense or as to the existence, meaning or application of the law determining the elements of an offense is an element of such offense, unless the definition of the offense or the Code so provides.

**2. Application of the Maxim.** The idea that mistake or ignorance as to criminality should not have defensive significance is deeply embedded in the law. Some idea of the law's commitment to this policy may be illustrated by the following cases:

**(i) *People v. Marrero*.** The problem in *People v. Marrero* was stated by an intermediate appellate court:

> Defendant, employed as a federal corrections officer in Danbury, Connecticut, was found to be in possession of a loaded .38 caliber pistol on December 19, 1977, while in a social club located at 207 Madison Street, New York City. This resulted in an indictment charging defendant with criminal possession of a weapon in the third degree pursuant to Penal Law § 265.02. The sole issue on appeal is whether the defendant is exempt from prosecution pursuant to Penal Law § 265.20(a)(1)(a) which in pertinent part provides that the offense for which defendant was indicted shall not apply to "... peace officers as defined in ... section 1.20 of the criminal procedure law." Relevant to defendant's status, CPL § 1.20 enumerates as being peace officers "[a]n attendant, or an official, or guard of any state prison or of any penal correctional institution." In dismissing the indictment on defendant's motion to dismiss, the [trial court] found CPL § 1.20 to be ambiguous in that the adjective "state" may be construed as modifying only the term "prison" and not the term "any penal correctional institution." Having found such ambiguity, the court chose to resolve it in defendant's favor by concluding that as defendant was a federal corrections officer, he was entitled to the statutory exemption.

[a] Sometimes given as ignorantia legis neminem excusat or as ignorantia juris non excusat.

A divided (three-to-two) intermediate appellate court read the statute differently, holding "that the clear intent of Penal Law § 265.20 [when other provisions were taken into account] was to provide persons in the service of the United States (as is defendant) immunity from prosecution for weapon possession [only] when that possession is duty-related or duly authorized by federal law, regulation or order." It accordingly reversed the dismissal of the indictment and remanded the case for trial.

At trial, the defendant argued that his "personal misunderstanding of the statutory definition of a peace officer is enough to excuse him from criminal liability." Evidence was offered that other federal officers had so construed the statute, as had the merchant who sold defendant the gun. The trial judge refused to charge the jury on this defense, and the resulting conviction was affirmed by the intermediate appellate court. In People v. Marrero, 69 N.Y.2d 382, 507 N.E.2d 1068 (1987), the New York Court of Appeals affirmed.

**(ii) *Hopkins v. State.*** The Reverend William F. Hopkins specialized in weddings. In an apparent attempt to discourage this enterprise, the legislature made it unlawful to erect or maintain any sign intended to aid in the solicitation or performance of marriages. Hopkins then sought the advice of the local state's attorney as to the legality of certain signs he proposed to erect. After receiving assurances that they would not violate the law, Hopkins put up one sign with the words, "Rev. W. F. Hopkins" and another with the legend, "W. F. Hopkins, Notary Public, Information."

Three years later, Hopkins was indicted for violating the anti-sign law. His offer of proof regarding the assurances by the state's attorney was excluded from evidence, and conviction resulted. In Hopkins v. State, 193 Md. 489, 499, 69 A.2d 456, 460 (1949), the state supreme court affirmed:

> If the right of a person to erect a sign of a certain type and size depends upon the construction and application of a penal statute, and the right is somewhat doubtful, he erects the sign at his peril. In other words, a person who commits an act which the law declares to be criminal cannot be excused from punishment upon the theory that he misconstrued or misapplied the law.

The fact that the misconstruction was confirmed by the state's attorney was thought inconsequential.

**(iii) *State v. Striggles.*** The facts of State v. Striggles, 202 Iowa 1318, 210 N.W. 137 (1926), were stated by the court as follows:

> On August 1, 1923, in several proceedings then pending in the municipal court of the city of Des Moines, a decision was rendered holding that [a particular] machine was not a gambling device. The distributors of the machine in question thereupon secured a certified copy of said decree, and equipped themselves with a letter from the county attorney, and also one from the mayor of the city, stating that such machine was not a gambling device. Thus equipped they presented themselves to appellant, Striggles, who

conducted a restaurant in the city of Des Moines, and induced him
to allow them to install a machine in his place of business.

Two years later, the Supreme Court of Iowa held that the machine in
question was indeed a gambling device. Striggles was convicted for permitting such a machine to be used for gambling on his premises. The Iowa
Supreme Court upheld his conviction:

> There is no case cited, nor can we find one on diligent search,
> holding that the decision of an inferior court can be relied upon to
> justify the defendant in a criminal case in the commission of the
> act which is alleged to be a crime. We are disposed to hold ...
> that, when the highest court of a jurisdiction passes on any given
> proposition, all citizens are entitled to rely upon such decision; but
> we refuse to hold that the decisions of any court below, inferior to
> the supreme court, are available as a defense under similar cir-
> cumstances.

The letters from the county attorney and the mayor were given no further
mention.

**3.  Problems With the Maxim.** Is it obvious that the claims of Fox,
Marrero, Hopkins, and Striggles should have been rejected? Or is there
something wrong with criminal conviction in some or all of these cases?

Some have argued that criminal punishment without regard to awareness of illegality is objectionable because it is ineffective. See Ron Cass,
Ignorance of the Law: A Maxim Reexamined, 17 Wm & M.L. Rev. 671, 684–
85 (1976). The argument seems to be that the threat of penal sanctions can
have no deterrent effect if the actor reasonably believes conduct to be
lawful. The infliction of punishment in such cases is therefore seen as
gratuitous and hence unjustified. Is this a correct analysis? Does a reasonable belief in the legality of one's conduct vitiate the deterrent function of
the law? Consider in this connection the following observations by Livingston Hall and Selig J. Seligman, in Mistake of Law and Mens Rea, 8 U. Chi.
L. Rev. 641, 648 (1941):

> This problem of educating the community by law is a practical
> one. A conviction for doing that which violates a new law, although
> not regarded as wrong in the community, is a matter of considera-
> ble interest and does a great deal to educate the community; an
> acquittal for violation of such a law, on the ground of a mistake of
> law, would scarcely cause a ripple in the current of community
> thought. As de Saint–Exupery has his airline manager say, to
> justify cutting pilots' punctuality bonuses whenever their planes
> started late, even where it was due to the weather and was not
> their fault: "If you only punish men enough, the weather will
> improve." It is a hard doctrine, but an effective one.

A different contention is that punishment on these facts is objectionable because it is unfair. In what sense might it be unfair to punish without
regard to awareness of illegality? Is any element of unfairness the same in
each of the cases referred to above? In connection with these questions,

consider the following possible justifications for adherence to the traditional policy regarding ignorance of the law.

**4. Justifications for the Maxim.** Ignorantia juris neminem excusat is often associated with the statement that "everyone is presumed to know the law." At one time this "presumption" may have been a fair approximation of reality. Certainly, awareness of illegality would be likely in a legal system where the penal law was used almost exclusively to redress depredations against the person or property of another. It was with respect to such offenses, sometimes called mala in se, that one court commented that "every one has an innate sense of right and wrong, which enables him to know when he violates the law, and it is of no consequence, if he be not able to give the name, by which the offence is known in the law books, or to point out the nice distinctions between the different grades of offence." State v. Boyett, 32 N.C. 336, 343–44 (1849).

However plausible this view may have been at one time, the situation today is hardly comparable. Modern laws define a great many crimes that are not mala in se but only mala prohibita. For such offenses, no "innate sense of right and wrong" suffices, and the presumption that everyone knows the law seems an obvious fiction. Not surprisingly, it is precisely in the context of modern regulatory offenses that plausible claims of ignorance of the law most commonly arise. In such cases, the policy of ignorantia legis must be explained as something other than an attempt to describe reality. Consider the following efforts to provide a rationale for the ignorantia-legis concept:

(i) 1 J. Austin, Lectures on Jurisprudence 498–99 (3d ed. 1869):

The only *sufficient* reason for the rule in question, seems to be this: that if ignorance of law were admitted as a ground of exemption, the courts would be involved in questions which it were scarcely possible to solve, and which would render the administration of justice next to impracticable. If ignorance of law were admitted as a ground of exemption, ignorance of law would always be alleged by the party, and the court, in every case, would be bound to decide the point.

But, in order that the court might decide the point, it [is] incumbent upon the court to examine the following questions of fact: First, was the party ignorant of the law at the time of the alleged wrong? Second, assuming that he was ignorant of the law at the time of the wrong alleged, was his ignorance of the law *inevitable* ignorance, or had he been previously placed in such a position that he might have known the law, if he had duly tried?

It is manifest that the latter question is not less material than the former. If he might have known the law in case he had duly tried ... the conduct in question [is] imputable, in the last result, to his *negligence*.

Now either of these questions [is] next to insoluble. Whether the party was *really* ignorant of the law, and was *so* ignorant of the law that he had no *surmise* of its provisions, could scarcely be determined by any evidence accessible to others. And for the purpose of determining the *cause* of his ignorance (its *reality* being ascertained), it [would be] incumbent upon the tribunal to unravel his previous history, and to search his whole life for the elements of a just solution.

(ii)  O. Holmes, The Common Law 47–48 (1881):

Ignorance of the law is no excuse for breaking it. This substantive principle is sometimes put in the form of a rule of evidence, that every one is presumed to know the law. It has accordingly been defended by Austin and others, on the ground of difficulty of proof. If justice requires the fact to be ascertained, the difficulty of doing so is no ground for refusing to try. But every one must feel that ignorance of the law could never be admitted as an excuse, even if the fact could be proved by sight and hearing in every case. Furthermore, now that parties can testify, it may be doubted whether a man's knowledge of the law is any harder to investigate than many questions which are gone into. The difficulty, such as it is, would be met by throwing the burden of proving ignorance on the law-breaker.

The principle cannot be explained by saying that we are not only commanded to abstain from certain acts, but also to find out that we are commanded. For if there were such a second command, it is very clear that the guilt of failing to obey it would bear no proportion to that of disobeying the principal command if known, yet the failure to know would receive the same punishment as the failure to obey the principal law.

The true explanation of the rule is the same as that which accounts for the law's indifference to a man's particular temperament, faculties, and so forth. Public policy sacrifices the individual to the general good. It is desirable that the burden of all should be equal, but it is still more desirable to put an end to robbery and murder. It is no doubt true that there are many cases in which the criminal could not have known that he was breaking the law, but to admit the excuse at all would be to encourage ignorance where the law-maker has determined to make men know and obey, and justice to the individual is rightly outweighed by the larger interests on the other side of the scale.

(iii)  J. Hall, General Principles of Criminal Law 380–83 (2d ed. 1960):[a]

Holmes' thesis, that to allow the defense would "encourage ignorance where the lawmaker has determined to make men know and obey," is surely questionable. [P]enal policy is not to make men know the law, as such, but to help them inhibit harmful conduct. The influence of penal law results not from men's learn-

[a] Reprinted with the permission of the author and Bobbs–Merrill Co., Inc.

ing criminal law as amateur lawyers, but from the significance of the public condemnation of, and imposition of punishment for, certain highly immoral acts....

A defensible theory of ignorantia juris must, it is suggested, find its origin in the central fact ... that the meaning of the rules of substantive penal law is unavoidably vague, the degree of vagueness increasing as one proceeds from the core of the rules to their periphery. It is therefore possible to disagree indefinitely regarding the meaning of these words. But in adjudication, such indefinite disputation is barred because that is opposed to the character and requirements of a legal order, as is implied in the principle of legality. Accordingly, a basic axiom of legal semantics is that legal rules do or do not include certain behavior; and the linguistic problem must be definitely solved one way or the other, on that premise. These characteristics of legal adjudication imply a degree of necessary reliance upon authority. The debate must end and the court must decide one way or the other within a reasonable time. The various needs are met by prescribing a rational procedure and acceptance of the decisions of the "competent" officials as authoritative. Such official declaration of the meaning of a law is what the law is, however circuitously that is determined.

Now comes a defendant who truthfully pleads that he did not know that his conduct was criminal, implying that he thought it was legal. This may be because he did not know that any relevant legal prohibition existed (ignorance) or, if he did know any potentially relevant rule, that he decided it did not include his intended situation or conduct (mistake). In either case, such defenses always imply that the defendant thought he was acting legally. If that plea were valid, the consequence would be: Whenever a defendant in a criminal case thought the law was thus and so, he is to be treated as though the law were thus and so, i.e., *the law actually is thus and so*. But such a doctrine would contradict the essential requisites of a legal system, the implications of the principle of legality.

To permit an individual to plead successfully that he had a different opinion or interpretation of the law would contradict the ... postulates of a legal order. For there is a basic incompatibility between asserting that the law is what certain officials declare it to be after a prescribed analysis, and asserting also, that those officials *must* declare it to be, i.e. that the law is, what defendants or their lawyers believed it to be. A legal order implies the rejection of such contradiction. It opposes objectivity to subjectivity, judicial process to individual opinion, official to lay, and authoritative to non-authoritative declarations of what the law is. This is the rationale of ignorantia juris neminem excusat.

**5. Proposals for Reform.** There have been occasional proposals to ameliorate the ignorantia juris concept. The revised New Jersey penal code, for example, provides that a belief that one's conduct does not constitute a crime is a defense if the mistake is reasonable and if the actor "diligently pursues all means available to ascertain the meaning and application of the offense to his conduct and honestly and in good faith concludes his conduct is not an offense in circumstances in which a law-abiding and prudent person would also so conclude." N.J.Stat.Ann. § 2C:2–4(c)(3). A similar proposal was advanced earlier in Rollin M. Perkins, Ignorance and Mistake in Criminal Law, 88 U. Pa. L. Rev. 35, 45 (1939):

> If the meaning of a statute is not clear, and has not been judicially determined, one who has acted in "good faith" should not be held guilty of crime if his conduct would have been proper had the statute meant what he "reasonably believed" it to mean, even if the court should decide later that the proper construction is otherwise.

Do these provisions address the most sympathetic cases for granting a defense? One could argue that a defendant who knows that a statute *might* be applicable has a fair opportunity to avoid breaking the law simply by not engaging in the conduct. But what of the defendant who has no idea that proposed conduct might violate the criminal law? In contrast to the New Jersey provision quoted above, would it be rational to deny a defense for a reasonable *mistake* about the meaning of the criminal law but grant it for reasonable *ignorance* that proposed conduct might be punished as a crime? Is it a sufficient response that if a court can be persuaded in the face of "legality" and "fair warning" arguments that a statute should be construed to include particular conduct, the defendant should not be permitted to argue to a jury that it was reasonable to believe that no crime was being committed?

**6. *Lambert v. California.*** Consider Justice Bistline's dissent in *Fox* in connection with the preceding questions. What was his concern with the Idaho statute?

The Supreme Court addressed a comparable situation in Lambert v. California, 355 U.S. 225 (1957). Ms. Lambert had been convicted in Los Angeles of forgery. Unknown to her, Los Angeles had a city ordinance that required all convicted felons to register if they remained in Los Angeles for a period longer than five days. Another ordinance made each day's failure to register a misdemeanor, punishable by a fine of up to $500 and/or up to six months in jail. She lived in Los Angeles. She was arrested on suspicion of committing another offense, but was convicted of violating the registration law, was fined $250, and was placed on probation for three years. She argued that not allowing her a defense that she was unaware of the registration requirement violated her rights under the due process clause of the 14th Amendment to the federal Constitution.[d]

---

[d] Section 1 of the 14th Amendment provides that no state shall "deprive any person of life, liberty, or property, without due process of law...."

The Supreme Court reversed her conviction in an opinion by Justice Douglas:

> Registration laws are common and their range is wide. Many such laws are akin to licensing statutes in that they pertain to the regulation of business activities. But the present ordinance is entirely different. Violation of its provisions is unaccompanied by any activity whatever, mere presence in the city being the test. Moreover, circumstances which might move one to inquire as to the necessity of registration are completely lacking. At most the ordinance is but a law-enforcement technique designed for the convenience of law-enforcement agencies through which a list of the names and addresses of felons then residing in a given community is compiled. The disclosure is merely a compilation of former convictions already publicly recorded in the jurisdiction where obtained. Nevertheless, this appellant on first becoming aware of her duty to register was given no opportunity to comply with the law and avoid its penalty, even though her default was entirely innocent. She could but suffer the consequences of the ordinance, namely, conviction with the imposition of heavy criminal penalties thereunder. We believe that actual knowledge of the duty to register or proof of the probability of such knowledge and subsequent failure to comply are necessary before a conviction under the ordinance can stand. As Holmes wrote in The Common Law, "A law which punished conduct which would not be blameworthy in the average member of the community would be too severe for that community to bear." Its severity lies in the absence of an opportunity either to avoid the consequences of the law or to defend any prosecution brought under it. Where a person did not know of the duty to register and where there was no proof of the probability of such knowledge, he may not be convicted consistently with due process. Were it otherwise, the evil would be as great as it is when the law is written in print too fine to read or in a language foreign to the community.

In Mens Rea and the Supreme Court, [1962] Sup.Ct.Rev. 107, Herbert Packer summarizes *Lambert* by saying that the mental element of crime "is an important requirement, but it is not a constitutional requirement, except sometimes." Is it possible to be more specific? Is *Lambert* merely an exception to the ignoranti legis principle, or does it address a more fundamental concern about the minimum acceptable conditions for the imposition of criminal liability? Consider the following hypotheticals in connection with these questions:

(i) Defendant is prosecuted for murder. He deliberately allowed his infant son to starve to death, and defends on the ground that he did not know of his duty of care in such a situation or that such behavior could be murder.

(ii) Defendant, a manufacturer of sulphuric acid, shipped its product by common carrier. Federal regulations require such shipments to be labeled "Corrosive Liquid." Defendant did not so label the shipment, and defends prosecution for violation of the regulation on the ground that it did not know of its existence.

(iii) Defendant purchased a bottle labeled "aspirin" in a drug store and she believed the label. She is arrested as she leaves the store and is prosecuted for possession of narcotics, which tests prove the bottle contained.

Would *Lambert* forbid prosecution in any of these cases? Would it forbid prosecution in *Fox*? In the variation of *Fox* suggested in Justice Bistline's dissent? In any of the other cases in the notes following *Fox*?

**7. Official Misstatement of Criminal Law.** There is one situation in which there is emerging statutory agreement that an exception to *ignoranti legis* is warranted. Section 2.04 of the Model Penal Code is illustrative:

(3) A belief that conduct does not legally constitute an offense is a defense to a prosecution for that offense based upon such conduct when:

(a) the statute or other enactment defining the offense is not known to the actor and has not been published or otherwise reasonably made available prior to the conduct alleged; or

(b) he acts in reasonable reliance upon an official statement of the law, afterward determined to be invalid or erroneous, contained in (i) a statute or other enactment; (ii) a judicial decision, opinion or judgment; (iii) an administrative order or grant of permission; or (iv) an official interpretation of the public officer or body charged by law with responsibility for the interpretation, administration or enforcement of the law defining the offense.

(4) The defendant must prove a defense arising under Subsection (3) of this Section by a preponderance of the evidence.

This provision may be defended on several grounds. First, persons who fall within the exception will have engaged in behavior that is consistent with a law-abiding character, the likelihood of collusion between the defendant and those upon whom she or he might rely is small, and it will not be difficult in such a context to determine whether the statute has "reasonably [been] made available" or whether the defendant acted "in reasonable reliance" upon the named official sources. Second, and more broadly, the exception is most likely to apply in regulatory contexts, where there are no significant moral overtones to the defendant's conduct. In such cases, only deliberate and repeated violations are appropriately punished by criminal sanctions.

Provisions based on the Model Code proposal have been enacted in at least 17 states, though several restrict the defense even more than does the Model Code. An example is Article 8.03 of the Texas Penal Code:

(a) It is no defense to prosecution that the actor was ignorant of the provisions of any law after the law has taken effect.

(b) It is an affirmative defense to prosecution that the actor reasonably believed the conduct charged did not constitute a crime and that he acted in reasonable reliance upon:

(1) an official statement of the law contained in a written order or grant of permission by an administrative agency charged by law with responsibility for interpreting the law in question; or

(2) a written interpretation of the law contained in an opinion of a court of record or made by a public official charged by law with responsibility for interpreting the law in question.

(c) Although an actor's mistake of law may constitute a defense to the offense charged, he may nevertheless be convicted of a lesser included offense of which he would be guilty if the law were as he believed.

**8. _Cox v. Louisiana._** In Cox v. Louisiana, 379 U.S. 559 (1965), the defendant was convicted of violating a statute punishing one who "pickets or parades . . . near a building housing a [state] court." The defendant's contention is revealed in the following excerpt from the decision reversing the conviction:

Thus, the highest police officials of the city, in the presence of the sheriff and mayor, in effect told the demonstrators that they could meet where they did, 101 feet from the courthouse steps, but could not meet closer to the courthouse. In effect, appellant was advised that a demonstration at the place it was held would not be one "near" the courthouse within the terms of the statute.

In Raley v. Ohio, 360 U.S. 423 (1959), this Court held that the due process clause prevented conviction of persons refusing to answer questions of a state investigating commission when they relied upon assurances of the commission, either express or implied, that they had a privilege under state law to refuse to answer, though in fact this privilege was not available to them. The situation presented here is analogous to that in _Raley_, which we deem to be controlling. As in _Raley_, under all the circumstances of this case, after the public officials acted as they did, to sustain appellant's later conviction for demonstrating where they told him he could "would be to sanction an indefensible sort of entrapment by the state—convicting a citizen for exercising a privilege which the state had clearly told him was available to him." The due-process clause does not permit convictions to be obtained under such circumstances.[e]

---

[e] For general discussion of _Cox_ and related cases, see Sean Connelly, Bad Advice: The Entrapment by Estoppel Doctrine in Criminal Law, 48 U. Miami L. Rev. 627 (1994).

## NOTES ON IGNORANCE OR MISTAKE OF NON–CRIMINAL LAW

**1. Introduction.** The materials studied thus far support two broad generalizations. First, ignorance or mistake as to the existence, scope, or meaning of the criminal law is not a defense. Second, a mistake of fact that negates a required element of mens rea is a defense. The issue now to be considered concerns a third kind of mistake.

The situation arises when the defendant makes a mistake of non-criminal law relevant to the criminality of conduct. Many crimes—larceny and burglary, for example—involve invasions of the property rights of others. The criminal law is not the source of property rights. These rights are created by a body of private law that defines the extent to which ordinary civil remedies can be invoked for their protection. The question to be considered is this: If the defendant makes a mistake as to the relevant law of property and wrongly comes to the conclusion that she or he "owns" certain property, is it a defense if the actor then does things with or to the property that would otherwise constitute larceny or burglary? The problem is a pervasive one. Can a mistake as to the validity of a divorce be offered as a defense to a charge of adultery or bigamy? Can a mistake as to child-custody rights be a defense to abduction? The following notes deal with the response of the criminal law to these questions.

**2. The Common Law.** The common law, at least as it has emerged in modern times, was very clear on one aspect of this problem. If the offense required a specific intent or some other special mental element, a mistake of the non-criminal law that negated the required mens rea was a defense. Thus, for example, a mistake as to ownership of property resulting from an error of property law was a defense to larceny because the requisite intent to deprive another would be lacking. It follows that in a prosecution for larceny, it does not matter whether a mistake as to ownership is a mistake of fact or a mistake of property law.

The offense of persistent non-support as defined in § 230.5 of the Model Penal Code provides another illustration: "A person commits a misdemeanor if he persistently fails to provide support which he can provide and which he knows he is legally obliged to provide to a spouse, child or other dependent." The legal obligation to provide support arises from the general provisions of family law and, in particular cases, may be governed by a support decree or some other specific court order. Since the offense as defined requires that one "know" of the legal obligation to provide support, any mistake as to the scope of the legal duty would be a defense under the common law rule summarized above, as it would be under the Model Penal Code itself.

General intent crimes, however, were sometimes treated differently. The usual rule was that no mistakes of law were exculpatory. Rarely were the reasons for this conclusion explained. Sometimes the result was said to be required by the policies underlying the particular offense. More often, it was explained by a reflexive invocation of the principle that "ignorance of the law is no excuse."

**3. General Intent Rule in Operation; *Long v. State*.** Operation of the general intent rule is illustrated by Long v. State, 44 Del. 262, 65 A.2d 489 (1949). The defendant, a resident of Delaware, obtained a divorce in Arkansas and moved back to Delaware. He subsequently wished to remarry, but was concerned about whether he was free to do so. He had consulted a Delaware attorney before he obtained the divorce and was assured that it would be valid. He consulted again with the same attorney before he remarried, and again was assured that his divorce was valid and he was free to marry again. He made arrangements with a minister to perform the ceremony. The minister was concerned about the legal situation, so he too went to the defendant's lawyer to make sure the divorce was valid. He was assured that it was. The defendant then returned to the attorney one more time to make sure, after which he went through with the second marriage.

He was subsequently prosecuted for bigamy. The court held that the prior divorce was invalid in Delaware, and that he was therefore in fact not free to remarry. Among his defenses was the argument that he had been assured that the applicable family law rules in Delaware recognized the dissolution of his first marriage, that he honestly believed he was free to marry again, that his belief was reasonable, and that his belief should afford him a defense even if mistaken. The court began its analysis of this issue by resolving a debate in other jurisdictions about whether bigamy was a strict liability crime that did not recognize a mistake of fact defense:[f]

> Of course, the mere specification of certain defenses in [the bigamy statute] does not exclude all other defenses. We can think of no sound reason why defenses of coercion and insanity, for instance, should not be available. A recognition of mistake of fact as a defense is found in Regina v. Tolson, 23 Q.B.D. 168 (1889). There, the defense of absence of a spouse for seven years, specified in a bigamy statute, was held not to exclude a defense of reasonable mistake of fact where the accused, believing erroneously but on reasonable grounds that her husband was dead, had remarried after his absence for less than seven years. The defense of mistake of fact is important only because it negatives a "criminal mind," general criminal intent. Upon considering the particular behavior defined as criminal . . . , the specified defenses themselves, and the seriousness of the punishment provided, we accept the view that the [bigamy] statute does not exclude as a defense the absence of general criminal intent. . . .

[f] Most bigamy statutes of the day (including Delaware's) listed a series of available defenses, none of which were applicable to the defendant's behavior. Many courts held that this list was exclusive, and no other defenses should be permitted. The *Long* court adopted the minority view that the list was not exclusive, and that the elements of bigamy should be treated under the ordinary general intent rules.

The question then was whether the defendant's mistake was a defense to a crime of general criminal intent. The court summarized the applicable rules as follows:

> We turn now to the ground that this is a case to which the ignorance of law maxim applies. In many crimes involving a *specific* criminal intent, an honest mistake of law constitutes a defense if it negatives the specific intent. [Citing cases involving larceny and embezzlement]. As to crimes not involving a specific intent, an honest mistake of law is usually ... held not to excuse conduct otherwise criminal.

Without more, therefore, the defense was to be denied.

**4.   The Model Penal Code.** Re-examine § 2.04(1)(a) of the Model Penal Code. Notice that it reads "[i]gnorance or mistake as to a matter of fact *or law* is a defense if ..." What is the function of the words "or law" in this formulation?

This provision must be read in conjunction with § 2.02(9), the effect of which—as explained above—is to deny a defense for ignorance or mistake of the criminal law. In order to give effect to both provisions, it would seem to follow—and it was so intended by the Model Penal Code drafters—that the "or law" provision in § 2.04(1)(a) would apply to ignorance or mistakes of non-criminal law. The Model Penal Code, therefore, treats mistakes of non-criminal law the same as mistakes of fact. Both are a defense if they show that a required mens rea element is missing. It does not matter whether the crime would have been characterized at common law as a crime of general or specific intent. On the facts of *Long*, therefore, the Model Penal Code would recognize a defense if the mistake disproved the required mens rea for bigamy.

Consider an example. Assume that *A* lived with *B* long enough and under such conditions that under the law of the relevant jurisdiction their relationship amounted to a common-law marriage. *A*, unaware that the law has attached this conclusion to her relationship with *B*, marries *C*. *B* complains to the police and *A* is prosecuted for bigamy under § 230.1 of the Model Code. Is *A*'s evidence of ignorance of law admissible, and if so, under what jury instruction?

**5.   Categorization of Mistakes of Fact and Law.** Can it be argued that the defendant's mistake in *Long* was one of fact? Can the same argument be made in the common-law marriage example in the previous note? What is the difference between a mistake of law and a mistake of fact in situations like these?

**(i)** *State v. Long* **Revisited.** In the end, the *Long* court recognized the asserted defense. It began with a comment:

> A mistake of law, where not a defense, may nevertheless negative a general criminal intent as effectively as would an exculpatory mistake of fact. Thus, mistake of law is disallowed as a defense in spite of the fact that it may show an absence of the criminal mind.

Having recognized that *functionally* a mistake of law and a mistake of fact in the *Long* situation can have the same effect on the defendant's underlying culpability, the court turned to the underlying rationale for the common law rule that nonetheless denied the defense. The reasons for the rule, the court noted, "are practical considerations dictated by deterrent effects upon the administration and enforcement of the criminal law, which are deemed likely to result if it were allowed as a general defense." The court then rehearsed the reasons, discussed above, for why ignorance or mistake of the criminal law is generally not recognized as a defense. In the end, it adopted an exception to the ignoranti juris concept similar to the statute later enacted in New Jersey:[g]

> Any deterrent effects upon the administration of the criminal law which might result from allowing [the] defense seem greatly outweighed by considerations which favor allowing it. To hold a person punishable as a criminal transgressor where the conditions of [this case] are present would be palpably unjust and arbitrary. Most of the important reasons which support the prohibition of ex post facto legislation are opposed to such a holding. It is difficult to conceive what more could be reasonably expected of a "model citizen" than that he guide his conduct by "the law" ascertained in good faith, not merely by efforts which might seem adequate to a person in his situation, but by efforts as well designed to accomplish ascertainment as any available under our system. We are not impressed with the suggestion that a mistake under such circumstances should aid the defendant only in inducing more lenient punishment by a court, or executive clemency after conviction. The circumstances seem so directly related to the defendant's behavior upon which the criminal charge is based as to constitute an integral part of that behavior, for purposes of evaluating it. No excuse appears for dealing with it piecemeal. We think such circumstances should entitle a defendant to full exoneration as a matter of right, rather than to something less, as a matter of grace.

**(ii) *People v. Bray.*** In People v. Bray, 52 Cal.App.3d 494, 124 Cal.Rptr. 913 (1975), the defendant was convicted on two counts of being a felon in possession of a concealable firearm. There was no doubt that he had possessed two concealable firearms. The question was whether he knew he was a convicted felon. His only prior conviction had occurred in Kansas some years before, where he had pleaded guilty to being an accessory after the fact and had been sentenced to, and successfully served, a period of probation. Even the prosecutor was not sure that the offense involved was a felony under Kansas law. He sought to introduce expert testimony at the trial to the effect that it was. On numerous occasions, the defendant had been required to fill out forms asking if he had a prior felony conviction. On most, he had answered that he did not know and made full disclosure of the situation. California officials had permitted him to vote in the face of such disclosures.

[g] See Note 5, Proposals for Reform, in the Notes following *State v. Fox*, above.

The court reversed Bray's conviction on the ground that the jury had not been properly instructed on the doctrine of mistake of fact:

> Although the district attorney had great difficulty in determining whether the Kansas offense was a felony or a misdemeanor, he expects the layman Bray to know his status easily. There was no doubt Bray knew he had committed an offense; there was, however, evidence to the effect he did not know the offense was a felony. Without this knowledge Bray would be ignorant of the facts necessary for him to come within the proscription of [the statute]. Under these circumstances the requested instructions on mistake or ignorance of fact and knowledge of the facts which make the act unlawful should have been given.

Presumably the instruction to which Bray was entitled would state the typical common law rule on mistake of fact for general intent offenses.

**(iii) Questions and Comments.** The court in *Long* treated the issue before it as though it involved a mistake of the criminal law. That is, it treated mistakes of the criminal law and non-criminal law alike, and reasoned on the facts before it to an exception to the general principle that ignorance of the law should not be an excuse. Is the premise of the court's reasoning correct? Should mistakes of criminal law and mistakes of non-criminal law be treated the same way? Or, in terms of the policies that should control, are mistakes of the non-criminal law more like mistakes of fact?

Compare the reasoning in *Long* to the reasoning in *Oglivie*, summarized in Note 5 of the Notes on Mistakes of Fact, above. Oglivie was convicted of bigamy because his mistake of "fact" concerning whether he was divorced was unreasonable. Is it clear why Oglivie made a mistake of "fact" and Long made a mistake of "law"? Now consider *Bray*. The California court never mentioned the possibility that Bray made a mistake of law. Is that right? How could a mistake about whether a crime is a felony *not* be a mistake of law? If the mistake was one of law, was it a mistake of criminal law or non-criminal law? How can the result in *Bray* be explained?

The Model Penal Code does not contain an offense comparable to the one charged in *Bray*. If it did, how would the *Bray* situation be analyzed? Is this a case for application of § 2.02(9) or § 2.04(1)(a)? How is one to decide which provision applies?

---

# SECTION 2: APPLICATION OF THE MENS REA STRUCTURE

---

## SUBSECTION A: NEGLIGENCE

---

# Director of Public Prosecutions v. Smith

House of Lords, 1960.
[1960] 3 All.E.R. 161, [1961] A.C. 290.

■ VISCOUNT KILMUIR, L.C.: My Lords, the respondent, Jim Smith, was convicted on April 7, 1960, of the wilful murder on March 2, 1960, of Leslie Edward Vincent Meehan, a police officer acting in the execution of his duty. Such a crime constitutes capital murder under § 5 of the Homicide Act, 1957, and, accordingly, the respondent was sentenced to death. [The conviction was set aside by the Court of Criminal Appeal and the case was then brought by the prosecution to the House of Lords.] There was never any suggestion that the respondent meant to kill the police officer, but it was contended by the prosecution that he intended to do the officer grievous bodily harm as a result of which the officer died. . . .

The facts can be summarised as follows: At about 7:30 p.m. on March 2, 1960, the respondent, accompanied by a man named Artus, was driving a Ford Prefect motor car through Woolwich. In the boot and the back of the car were sacks containing scaffolding clips that they had just stolen. The car was stopped in Beresford Square by the police officer on point duty in the normal course of traffic control and, while so stopped, P[olice] C[onstable] Meehan, who was acquainted with the respondent, came to the driver's window and spoke to him. No doubt as a result of what P.C. Meehan saw in the back of the car, he told the respondent when the traffic was released to draw in to his near-side. The respondent began to do so, and P.C. Meehan walked beside the car. Suddenly, however, the respondent accelerated along Plumstead Road and P.C. Meehan began to run with the car shouting to the officer on point duty to get on to the police station. Despite the fact that the respondent's car had no running board, P.C. Meehan succeeded in hanging on and never let go until some 130 yards up Plumstead Road when he was thrown off the car and under a bubble car coming in the opposite direction, suffering a crushed skull and other injuries from which he died.

What happened during the time the car travelled that 130 yards was the subject of considerable evidence. The police officer on traffic duty, P. C. Baker, said that he last saw the car doing what he thought was about 20 miles per hour which P. C. Meehan running and holding on to it. Mr. Doran, a bus driver, whose vehicle had also been held up in Berestford Square, said that the respondent's car suddenly accelerated with P. C. Meehan holding on to it; that it started to zigzag; and that the police officer appeared to be thrown across the bonnet of the car. Mr. Lynch, who was standing in the centre of the square, said that the car suddenly accelerated, zigzagging all the time, the police officer holding on, his feet hanging on the ground; that it kept on accelerating and he thought he saw the right hand of someone in the car trying to push the officer off. He thought that the car reached a speed of 30 to 60 miles per hour.

Four cars were coming in the opposite direction. The driver of the first car, a Mr. Gill, said that the respondent's car appeared to come at him at a fast to medium speed. There appeared to be someone on the car either falling from the driver's seat or picked up on the bonnet. He felt a slight bump on the rear of his car but sufficient to make him stop. The driver of the second car, a Mr. Mills, said that he saw the respondent's car gathering speed and swerving towards him. The side of his car was struck. The driver of the third car, a Mr. Eldridge, thought that the respondent's car was travelling at about 40 to 50 miles per hour; he saw what he could only describe as an object hanging on below the driver's window. His car was struck violently, the off-side front mudguard being bashed in. Having regard to the fact that there were no marks on the respondent's car the inevitable conclusion is that the contact of all three cars was with P. C. Meehan. Mr. Rollingson, the driver of the fourth car, a bubble car, said that the respondent's car was going very fast and swerving. He saw something coming towards him; there was a terrific crash and he stopped and P. C. Meehan was underneath his car. The respondent's car went tearing up the road.

Mr. Heywood, a cyclist, who was ahead of the respondent's car and was passed by the car just after P. C. Meehan was thrown off, described the car as going fast. Finally, Artus, the passenger in the respondent's car, described how the officer was holding on to the door by the driver's window with his left hand and was banging the windscreen with his right hand. He said that the respondent said: "Let go, Bert."

After P.C. Meehan had been thrown off, the respondent drove his car a little further up Plumstead Road and into a side turning where he and Artus threw the sacks of clips out of the car. Artus then went off but the respondent returned to the scene. According to P.C. Weatherill, the respondent first asked: "Is he dead?" and then, on being told that it was believed so, he said: "I knew the man, I wouldn't do it for the world. I only wanted to shake him off." The respondent, however, denied that he had spoken the last few words. The respondent was taken to the police station. On being arrested and cautioned, he said: "I didn't mean to kill him but I didn't want him to find the gear." The respondent then made and signed a statement in which, inter alia, he said:

> P.C. Meehan jumped on the side of the car and I got frightened. I don't know what I got frightened about. I don't think I thought of the stolen gear I had on board. I don't know what I did next in respect of driving the car. All I know is when he fell off he must have been hurt. I knew he fell off, and I then took a turning off the Plumstead Road. I drove up this turning some way and turned right down a back street.

> I stopped the car in the back street, as George wanted to get out of it. I got out too and chucked the gear out of the car on to the pavement. I got rid of it, because I was scared the police would find it in my motor.

The respondent gave evidence at the trial. He said that, when P.C. Meehan jumped on the side of the car, his foot went down on the accelerator and he was scared. "I was scared very much. I was very much frightened." He agreed that he did not take his foot off the accelerator.

I never thought of it, sir. I was frightened. I was up in the traffic. I never thought of it. It happened too quick.

Asked why he did not take his foot off the accelerator, he said: "I would have done, but when he jumped on the side he took my mind off what I was doing." "When he jumped on I was frightened. I was up the road before it happened. It all happened in a matter of seconds." He further said that, when going up Plumstead Road, he didn't realise that the officer was still hanging on to the car. Asked about his car swerving, he said: "My motor was swaying because of the load in the back."

. . . It is said that the jury were misdirected as to the intent which has to be proved in order to constitute the necessary ingredient of malice. The passages complained of are these:

> The intention with which a man did something can usually be determined by a jury only by inference from the surrounding circumstances. . . . If you feel yourselves bound to conclude from the evidence that the accused's purpose was to dislodge the officer, then you ask yourselves this question: Could any reasonable person fail to appreciate that the likely result would be at least serious harm to the officer? If you answer that question by saying that the reasonable person would certainly appreciate that, then you may infer that that was the accused's intention, and that would lead to a verdict of guilty on the charge of capital murder. . . .

> Now the only part of that evidence of P.C. Weatherill which the accused challenges is the part that incriminates him, namely, "I only wanted to shake him off." He says he did not say that. Well, you may think it is a curious thing to imagine, and further it may well be the truth—he did only want to shake him off; but if the reasonable man would realise that the effect of doing that might well be to cause serious harm to this officer, then, as I say, you would be entitled to impute such an intent to the accused, and, therefore, to sum up the matter as between murder and manslaughter, if you are satisfied that when he drove his car erratically up the street, close to the traffic on the other side, he must as a reasonable man have contemplated that grievous bodily harm was likely to result to that officer still clinging on, and that such harm did happen and the officer died in consequence, then the accused is guilty of capital murder, and you should not shrink from such a verdict because of its possible consequences.

> On the other hand, if you are not satisfied that he intended to inflict grievous bodily harm upon the officer—in other words, if you think he could not as a reasonable man have contemplated that grievous bodily harm would result to the officer in consequence of his actions—well, then, the verdict would be guilty of manslaughter.

The main complaint is that the learned judge was there applying what is referred to as an objective test, namely, the test of what a reasonable man would contemplate as the probable result of his acts, and therefore, would intend, whereas the question for the jury, it is said, was what the respondent himself intended. This, indeed, was the view of the Court of Criminal Appeal who said:

> [T]he present case [is] one in which the degree of likelihood of serious injury to the police officer depended on which of the not always consistent versions of the facts given by witnesses for the prosecution was accepted. It was one in which it could not be said that there was a certainty that such injury would result; and it was one in which there always remained the question whether the appellant really did during the relevant 10 seconds realise what was the degree of likelihood of serious injury. If the jury took the view that the appellant [the present respondent] deliberately tried to drive the body of the police officer against oncoming cars, the obvious inference was open to them that the appellant intended serious injury to result; if, however, they concluded he merely swerved or zigzagged to shake off the officer, or if they concluded that for any reason he may not have realised the degree of danger to which he was exposing the officer, a different situation would arise with regard to the inferences to be drawn.

[T]he Court of Criminal Appeal ... were saying that it was for the jury to decide, whether, having regard to the panic in which he said he was, the respondent in fact at the time contemplated that grievous bodily harm would result from his actions or, indeed, whether he contemplated anything at all. Unless the jury were satisfied that he in fact had such contemplation, the necessary intent to constitute malice would not, in their view, have been proved. This purely subjective approach involves this, that, if an accused said that he did not in fact think of the consequences and the jury considered that that might well be true, he would be entitled to be acquitted of murder.

My Lords, the proposition has only to be stated thus to make one realise what a departure it is from that on which the courts have always acted. The jury must of course in such a case as the present make up their minds on the evidence whether the accused was unlawfully and voluntarily doing something to someone. The unlawful and voluntary act must clearly be aimed at someone in order to eliminate cases of negligence or of careless or dangerous driving. Once, however, the jury are satisfied as to that, it matters not what the accused in fact contemplated as the probable result, or whether he ever contemplated at all, provided he was in law responsible and accountable for his actions.... On the assumption that he is accountable for his actions, the sole question is whether the unlawful and voluntary act was of such a kind that grievous bodily harm was the natural and probable result. The only test available for this is what the ordinary responsible man would, in all the circumstances of the case, have contemplated as the natural and probable result. That, indeed, has always been the law and I would only make a few citations.

The true principle is well set out in that persuasive authority The Common Law by Holmes, J. After referring to Stephens' Digest of the Criminal Law and the statement that foresight of the consequences of the act is enough, he says:

> But again, what is foresight of consequence? It is a picture of a future state of things called up by knowledge of the present state of things, the future being viewed as standing to the present in the relation of effect to cause. Again, we must seek a reduction to lower terms. If the known present state of things is such that the act done will very certainly cause death, and the probability is a matter of common knowledge, one who does the act, knowing the present state of things, is guilty of murder, and the law will not inquire whether he did actually foresee the consequence or not. The test of foresight is not what this very criminal foresaw, but what a man of reasonable prudence would have foreseen.

And again:

> But furthermore, on the same principle, the danger which in fact exists under the known circumstances ought to be of a class which a man of reasonable prudence could foresee. Ignorance of a fact and inability to foresee a consequence have the same effect on blameworthiness. If a consequence cannot be foreseen, it cannot be avoided. But there is this practical difference, that whereas, in most cases, the question of knowledge is a question of the actual condition of the defendant's consciousness, the question of what he might have foreseen is determined by the standard of the prudent man, that is, by general experience.

In Regina v. Faulkner, 13 Cox C.C. 550 (1877), the Court of Crown Cases Reserved for Ireland [on grounds immaterial to this case quashed a conviction] for arson of a sailor who with intent to steal tapped a cask of rum. He was holding a lighted match and the rum caught fire and the vessel was destroyed. Palles, C.B., said:

> In my judgment the law imputes to a person who willfully commits a criminal act an intention to do everything which is the probable consequence of the act constituting the corpus delicti which actually ensues. In my opinion this inference arises irrespective of the particular consequences which ensured being or not being foreseen by the criminal, and whether his conduct is reckless or the reverse. . . .

My Lords, the law being as I have endeavoured to define it, there seems to be no ground on which the approach by the trial judge in the present case can be criticised. [H]e asked the jury to consider what were the exact circumstances at the time as known to the respondent and what were the unlawful and voluntary acts which he did towards the police officer. The learned judge then prefaced the passages of which complaint is made by saying, in effect, that if, in doing what he did, he must as a reasonable man have contemplated that serious harm was likely to occur then he was guilty of murder. My only doubt concerns the use of the expression "a reasonable man," since this to lawyers connotes the man on the Clapham omnibus by reference to whom a standard of care in civil cases is acertained. In judging of intent, however, it really denotes an ordinary man capable of reasoning who is responsible and accountable for his actions, and this would be the sense in which it would be understood by a jury. [O]nce the accused's knowledge of the circumstances and the nature of his acts have been ascertained, [absent] proof of incapacity to form an intent[, the defendant is responsible for] the natural and probable consequences of his acts. [T]he test of the reasonable man, properly understood, . . . should present no difficulty to a jury and contains all the necessary ingredients of malice aforethought. . . .

In the result, the appeal should, in my opinion, be allowed and the conviction of capital murder restored.

---

## NOTES ON THE MEANING OF NEGLIGENCE IN THE CRIMINAL LAW

**1.   Background on the Law of Criminal Homicide.** One of the major functions of the mental element in crime is to draw the line between criminal and non-criminal behavior. Another involves the grading of criminal offenses, that is, determining the relative seriousness of different versions of the same general type of behavior. Nowhere are these functions better illustrated than in the law of criminal homicide, which must deal with a spectrum that ranges from no crime at all to the most serious offenses known to the law. The killing of one person by another is in some circumstances justifiable and therefore not a crime. In others, it is accidental (the law would say "excusable") and not a crime. And in the typical American jurisdiction there ordinarily are three or four grades of criminal homicide, culminating in forms of murder that warrant the most severe sanctions used for any crime.

From a modern perspective, the most important aspect of the early English law on criminal homicide was the development of the separate offenses of murder and manslaughter. In time, murder came to include all homicides committed with "malice aforethought," and manslaughter all criminal homicides committed without "malice aforethought." As the law evolved, to paraphrase Stephen, the judges allocated criminal homicides between murder and manslaughter—and gave meaning to the determinative term "malice aforethought"—according to which offenders deserved to be hanged.[a] This initial effort at grading criminal homicide offenses used

---

[a] See Royal Comm'n on Capital Punishment, CMND. No. 8932, at 28 (1953). What Stephen actually said (in 1866), was that "the loose term 'malice' was used, and then when a particular state of mind came to their notice the judges called it 'malice' or not

the definition of murder as the device for isolating those homicides for which the death penalty was to be imposed.[b]

The remaining common-law history of murder and manslaughter principally concerns the content of the two categories.[c] *Smith* involves one of the traditional types of murder, namely a case where the actor caused a death while intending to inflict grievous bodily harm or knowing that such harm would result.

**2. The Meaning of "Negligence" in the Criminal Law.** What were the analytic steps used by the Court to determine whether Smith was culpable? Compare the Model Penal Code definition of negligence in § 2.02(2)(d):

> A person acts negligently with respect to a material element of an offense when he should be aware of a substantial and unjustifiable risk that the material element exists or will result from his conduct. The risk must be of such a nature and degree that the actor's failure to perceive it, considering the nature and purpose of his conduct and the circumstances known to him, involves a gross deviation from the standard of care that a reasonable person would observe in the actor's situation.

Are there substantial differences?

**3. Language and Content in Common Law Mens Rea.** *Smith* provides another occasion to comment on the unique vocabulary of the common law. As *Smith* illustrates, it is not uncommon for courts to talk in terms of "intention" but in the end to rely on a concept more like negligence. Smith was charged with "wilful murder" in that he "intended to do the officer grievous bodily harm as a result of which the officer died." And the court concluded that he acted with "malice aforethought." But the standard of liability to which he was held looked more like ordinary negligence. Consider also the quotation in *Smith* from *Faulkner*. What does it mean to say that the law "imputes" an "intention" to someone? How many layers of translation are required before one gets to the bottom of the matter? Only in jurisdictions that have adopted the Model Penal Code vocabulary has American criminal law escaped such talk.

"Criminal negligence" is frequently defined by the courts as an especially egregious sort of callousness that is different in kind or degree from the "ordinary" negligence that will warrant recovery in a civil suit for

---

according to their view of the propriety of hanging particular people. That is, in two words, the history of the definition of murder."

[b] The traditional definition of murder, as paraphrased from Coke's rendition in the 17th century, was: "When a man of sound memory and of the age of discretion unlawfully kills any reasonable creature in being

and under the King's peace, with malice aforethought, either express or implied by the law, the death taking place within a year and a day." See 3 Coke, Institutes * 47; Royal Comm'n on Capital Punishment, CMND. No. 8932, at 28 (1953).

[c] The topic of criminal homicide is further developed in Chapter 8.

damages. In General Principles of Criminal Law 124 (2d ed. 1960), Jerome Hall summarized early English efforts to define criminal negligence:

> For many years [the judges] relied on adjectives qualifying "negligence" to carry their meaning; and they continued to do this long after the adjectives were regarded as mere "vituperative epithets." Nor has so-called "criminal negligence" been clarified by judicial efforts to distinguish it from civil negligence. The opinions run in terms of "wanton and wilful negligence," "gross negligence," and more illuminating yet, "that degree of negligence that is more than the negligence required to impose tort liability." The apex of this infelicity is "wilful, wanton negligence," which suggests a triple contradiction—"negligence" implying inadvertence; "wilful," intention; and "wanton," recklessness.

Notice that the Court in *Smith* did not rely on such language in describing the applicable standard of liability. Instead, it invoked a standard more akin to the "honest and reasonable" language used for a mistake of fact defense to a general intent crime. Did the Court get the right answer? Should it have used words more like those employed by Hall? Should it have used a different culpability standard altogether?

**4.  Oliver Wendell Holmes.** The Court relied in *Smith* on comments by Oliver Wendell Holmes in The Common Law, first published in 1881. In the law of murder, said Holmes, "malice" obviously does not mean ill will, for "[it is just as much murder to shoot a sentry for the purpose of releasing a friend, as to shoot him because you hate him." Rather, the term "malice" is used to signify the mens rea required by the law. The test for mens rea, according to Holmes, should be not whether the actor actually desired or foresaw the death of another, but whether "a man of reasonable prudence" would have anticipated that consequence and would therefore have refrained from acting. The key, said Holmes, is that the actor be aware of the existence of those circumstances that render conduct dangerous and that would put the reasonably prudent person on notice to desist:

> It is enough that such circumstances were actually known as would have led a man of common understanding to infer from them the rest of the group making up the present state of things. For instance, if a workman on a housetop at mid-day knows that the space below him is a street in a great city, he knows facts from which a man of common understanding would infer that there were people passing below. He is therefore bound to draw that inference, or, in other words, is chargeable with knowledge of that fact also, whether he draws the inference or not. If then, he throws down a heavy beam into the street, he does an act which a person of ordinary prudence would foresee is likely to cause death, or grievous bodily harm, and he is dealt with as if he foresaw it, whether he does so in fact or not. If a death is caused by the act, he is guilty of murder. But if the workman has reasonable cause to believe that the space below is a private yard from which every one

is excluded, and which is used as a rubbish-heap, his act is not blameworthy, and the homicide is a mere misadventure. . . .

But furthermore, on the same principle, the danger which in fact exists under the known circumstances ought to be of a class which a man of reasonable prudence could foresee. Ignorance of a fact and inability to foresee a consequence have the same effect on blameworthiness. If a consequence cannot be foreseen, it cannot be avoided. But there is this practical difference, that whereas, in most cases, the question of knowledge is a question of the actual condition of the defendant's consciousness, the question of what he might have foreseen is determined by the standard of the prudent man, that is, by general experience. For it is to be remembered that the object of the law is to prevent human life being endangered or taken; and that, although it so far considers blameworthiness in punishing as not to hold a man responsible for consequences which no one, or only some exceptional specialist, could have foreseen, still the reason for this limitation is simply to make a rule which is not too hard for the average member of the community. As the purpose is to compel men to abstain from dangerous conduct, and not merely to restrain them from evil inclinations, the law requires them at their peril to know the teachings of common experience, just as it requires them to know the law. Subject to these explanations, it may be said that the test of murder is the degree of danger to life attending the act under the known circumstances of the case.

Does the result in *Smith* follow? Should it?

**5. Negligence as a Basis for Criminal Liability.** There is disagreement in the literature about whether negligence can ever be a proper basis for criminal liability.[d] The argument against the use of negligence proceeds from the premise that personal blameworthiness is the essential ethical predicate for the criminal sanction. The question is whether criminal sanctions are ever appropriate for inadvertence.

H.L.A. Hart discusses this question in Punishment and Responsibility (1968). He starts by observing:

"I didn't *mean* to do it: I just didn't think." "But you should have thought." Such an exchange, perhaps over the fragments of a broken vase destroyed by some careless action, is not uncommon; and most people would think that, in ordinary circumstances, such a rejection of "I didn't think" as an excuse is quite justified. No doubt many of us have our moments of scepticism about both the

---

[d] In contrast to Holmes, see, e.g., Richard A. Wasserstrom, H.L.A. Hart and the Doctrine of Mens Rea and Criminal Responsibility, 35 U.Chi.L.Rev. 92 (1967); Jerome Hall, Negligent Behavior Should be Excluded from Penal Liability, 63 Colum.L.Rev. 632 (1963). But see James B. Brady, Punishment for Negligence: A Reply to Professor Hall, 22 Buff.L.Rev. 107 (1972). See also Rebecca Dresser, Culpability and Other Minds, 2 So. Cal. Interdisc. L.J. 41 (1993); Kenneth W. Simons, Culpability and Retributive Theory: The Problem of Criminal Negligence, 5 J. Contemp. Legal Issues 365 (1994).

justice and the efficacy of the whole business of blaming and punishment; but, if we are going in for the business at all, it does not appear unduly harsh, or a sign of archaic or unenlightened conceptions of responsibility, to include gross, unthinking carelessness among the things for which we blame and punish.... There seems a world of difference between punishing people for the harm they unintentionally but carelessly cause, and punishing them for the harm which no exercise of reasonable care on their part could have avoided.

Most opponents of negligence as a basis for criminal liability concede this much, and respond with a point anticipated in Hart's next paragraph:

So "I just didn't think" is not in ordinary life, in ordinary circumstances, an excuse; nonetheless it has its place in the rough assessments which we make, outside the law, of the gravity of different offences which cause the same harm. To break your Ming china, deliberately or intentionally, is worse than to knock it over while waltzing wildly round the room and not thinking of what might get knocked over. Hence, showing that the damage was not intentional, but the upshot of thoughtlessness or carelessness, has its relevance as a mitigating factor affecting the quantum of blame or punishment.

The question then becomes whether the "quantum of blame or punishment" for thoughtlessness or carelessness is sufficient to justify use of the criminal sanction. This is the fighting issue.

The argument in favor of negligence as an appropriate basis for criminal liability can proceed from two sorts of premises. The first, illustrated by Holmes, is essentially utilitarian, based on the need for effective social control tempered by limitations based on blameworthiness. The second is that liability for negligence is consistent with other forms of liability based on blame. The argument is that the central characteristic that justifies blame in any case is present when liability is based on negligence. Hart also takes this position. Criminal liability is appropriate in cases where the actor intended the harm caused or where there was foresight of consequences and the actor nonetheless took the risk that they would occur. Hart asks whether negligence is importantly different:

[Consider] the case of a signalman whose duty it is to signal a train.... He may say after the disaster, "Yes, I went off to play a game of cards. I just didn't stop to think about the 10:15 when I was asked to play." [I]f anyone is *ever* responsible for *anything*, there is no general reason why men should not be responsible for such omissions to think, or to consider the situation and its dangers before acting.

Hart sees analytical similarities between liability for negligence and liability where there is foresight of consequences. He concludes that it is appropriate in both cases to blame the defendant because she or he knew enough about the context to have behaved differently.

How should all of this be applied to Smith? Would it have been appropriate to convict him of negligent homicide under the Model Penal Code? Manslaughter? Murder? Was the "quantum of blame" attributable to his behavior sufficient to justify the death penalty?[e]

---

## SUBSECTION B: INTOXICATION

---

## Director of Public Prosecutions v. Majewski

House of Lords, 1976.
[1976] 2 All E.R. 142.

■ LORD ELWYN-JONES, L.C. My Lords, Robert Stefan Majewski appeals against his conviction [for] assault occasioning actual bodily harm. [H]e was placed on probation for three years....

The appellant's case was that when the assaults were committed he was acting under the influence of a combination of drugs (not medically prescribed) and alcohol, to such an extent that he did not know what he was doing and that he remembered nothing of the incidents that had occurred. After medical evidence had been called by the defence as to the effect of the drugs and drink the appellant had taken, the learned judge ... ruled that he would direct the jury in due course that ... the question whether [the defendant] had taken drink or drugs was immaterial. The learned judge directed the jury that in relation to an offence not requiring a specific intent, the fact that a man has induced in himself a state in which he is under the influence of drink and drugs, is no defence....

In view of the conclusion to which I have come that the appeal should be dismissed ..., it is desirable that I should refer in some detail to the facts, which were largely undisputed. During the evening of 19th February 1973 the appellant and his friend, Leonard Stace, who had also taken drugs and drink, went to the Bull public house in Basildon. The appellant obtained a drink and sat down in the lounge bar at a table by the door. Stace became involved in a disturbance. Glasses were broken. The landlord asked Stace to leave and escorted him to the door. As he did so, Stace called to the appellant: "He's putting me out." The appellant got up and prevented the landlord from getting Stace out and abused him. The landlord told them both to go. They refused. The appellant butted the landlord in the

---

[e] Professor Rhoda Berkowitz of the University of Toledo College of Law informed the editors that, in response to the curiosity of her students, she checked with the Home Office in England to find out whether Smith was actually executed. He was not, she learned; his sentence was commuted to life imprisonment. Did that solve the problem? It should be added that a statute was enacted in England that purported to overrule *Smith,* Criminal Justice Act of 1967, c. 80, pt. I, § 8, although there was debate at the time over whether it successfully did so. See J.C. Smith and Brian Hogan, Criminal Law 285–91 (4th ed. 1978).

face and bruised it, and punched a customer. The customers in the bar and the landlord forced the two out through the bar doors. They re-entered by forcing the outer door, a glass panel of which was broken by Stace. The appellant punched the landlord and pulled a piece of broken glass from the frame and started swinging it at the landlord and a customer, cutting the landlord slightly on his arm. The appellant then burst through the inner door of the bar with such force that he fell on the floor. The landlord held him there until the police arrived. The appellant was violent and abusive and spat in the landlord's face. When the police came, a fierce struggle took place to get him out. He shouted at the police: "You pigs, I'll kill you all, you f . . . pigs, you bastards." P.C. Barkway said the appellant looked at him and kicked him deliberately. . . .

Cross-examined as to the appellant's condition that evening the publican said he seemed to have gone berserk, his eyes were a bit glazed and protruding. A customer said he was "glary-eyed," and went "berserk" when the publican asked Stace to leave. He was screaming and shouting. A policeman said he was in a fearful temper.

The appellant gave evidence and said that on Saturday, 17th February 1973, he bought, not on prescription, about 440 Dexadrine tablets ("speeds") and early on Sunday morning consumed about half of them. That gave him plenty of energy until he "started coming down." He did not sleep throughout Sunday. On Monday evening at about 6:00 p.m. he acquired a bottle full of sodium nembutal tablets which he said were tranquillisers—"downers," "barbs"—and took about eight of them at about 6:30 p.m. He and his friends went to the Bull. He said he could remember nothing of what took place there save for a flash of recollection of Stace kicking a window. All he recollected of the police cell was asking the police to remove his handcuffs and then being injected.

In cross-examination he admitted he had been taking amphetamines and barbiturates, not on prescription, for two years, in large quantities. On occasions he drank barley wine or Scotch. He had sometimes "gone paranoid." This was the first time he had "completely blanked out."

Dr. Bird, called for the defence, said that the appellant had been treated for drug addiction since November 1971. There was no history in his case of psychiatric disorder or diagnosable mental illness, but the appellant had a personality disorder. Dr. Bird said that barbiturates and alcohol are known to potentiate each other and to produce rapid intoxication and affect a person's awareness of what was going on. In the last analysis one could be rendered unconscious and a condition known as pathological intoxication can occur, but it is uncommon and there are usually well-marked episodes. It would be possible, but unlikely, to achieve a state of automatism as a result of intoxication with barbiturates and alcohol or amphetamines and alcohol. Aggressive behavior is greater. After a concentration of alcohol and barbiturates it was not uncommon for "an amnesic patch" to ensue.

In cross-examination, Dr. Bird said he had never in practice come across a case of "pathological intoxication" and it is an unusual condition.

It is quite possible that a person under the influence of barbiturates, amphetamines or alcohol or all three in combination may be able to form certain intentions and execute them, punching and kicking people, and yet afterwards be unable to remember anything about it. During such "disinhibited behaviour" he may do things which he would not do if he was not under the influence of the various sorts of drink and drugs about which evidence has been given.

In a statement Dr. Mitchell expressed the opinion that at the police station on the morning of 20th February, the appellant was completely out of control mentally and physically, which might have been due to "withdrawal symptoms."

The Court of Appeal dismissed the appeal against conviction but granted leave to appeal to your Lordships' House.... The appeal raises issues of considerable public importance.... Self-induced alcoholic intoxication has been a factor in crimes of violence, like assault, throughout the history of crime in this country. But voluntary drug taking with the potential and actual dangers to others it may cause has added a new dimension to the old problem with which the courts have had to deal in their endeavour to maintain order and to keep public and private violence under control. To achieve this is the prime purpose of the criminal law. I have said "the courts," for most of the relevant law has been made by the judges. A good deal of the argument in the hearing of this appeal turned on that judicial history, for the crux of the case for the Crown was that, illogical as the outcome may be said to be, the judges have evolved for the purpose of protecting the community a substantive rule of law that, in crimes of basic intent as distinct from crimes of specific intent, self-induced intoxication provides no defence and is irrelevant to offences of basic intent, such as assault.

The case of counsel for the appellant was that there was no such substantive rule of law and that if there was, it did violence to logic and ethics and to fundamental principles of the criminal law which had been evolved to determine when and where criminal responsibility should arise. [Lord Elwyn–Jones began his consideration of this argument with a general discussion of the meaning of mens rea and the definition of assault. He concluded that assault was a crime of "basic intent" and that recklessness was the minimum culpability ordinarily required. He then continued by asking:]

How does the factor of self-induced intoxication fit into [this] analysis? If a man consciously and deliberately takes alcohol and drugs not on medical prescription, but in order to escape from reality, to go "on a trip," to become hallucinated, whatever the description may be, and thereby disables himself from taking the care he might otherwise take and as a result by his subsequent actions causes injury to another—does our criminal law enable him to say that because he did not know what he was doing he lacked both intention and recklessness and accordingly is entitled to an acquittal?

Originally the common law would not and did not recognise self-induced intoxication as an excuse.... The authority which for the last half century has been relied on in this context has been the speech of Lord Birkenhead, L.C. in Director of Public Prosecutions v. Beard, [1920] A.C. 479, 494, [1920] All E.R. 21, 25:

> Under the law of England as it prevailed until early in the 19th century voluntary drunkenness was never an excuse for criminal misconduct; and indeed the classic authorities broadly assert that voluntary drunkenness must be considered rather an aggravation than a defence. This view was in terms based upon the principle that a man who by his own voluntary act debauches and destroys his will power shall be no better situated in regard to criminal acts than a sober man.

Lord Birkenhead, L.C. made an historical survey of the way the common law from the 16th century on dealt with the effect of self-induced intoxication on criminal responsibility. [He] concluded that ... the decisions....

> establish where a specific intent is an essential element in the offence, evidence of a state of drunkenness rendering the accused incapable of forming such an intent should be taken into consideration in order to determine whether he had in fact formed the intent necessary to constitute the particular crime. If he was so drunk that he was incapable of forming the intent required he could not be convicted of a crime which was committed only if the intent was proved....

From this it seemed clear—and this is the interpretation which the judges have placed on the decision during the ensuing half-century—that it is only in the limited class of cases requiring proof of specific intent that drunkenness can exculpate. Otherwise in no case can it exempt completely from criminal liability....

I do not for my part regard that general principle as either unethical or contrary to the principles of natural justice. If a man of his own volition takes a substance which causes him to cast off the restraints of reason and conscience, no wrong is done to him by holding him answerable criminally for any injury he may do while in that condition. His course of conduct in reducing himself by drugs and drink to that condition in my view supplies the evidence of mens rea, of guilty mind certainly sufficient for crimes of basic intent. It is a reckless course of conduct and recklessness is enough to constitute the necessary mens rea in assault cases.... The drunkenness is itself an intrinsic, an integral part of the crime, the other part being the evidence of the unlawful use of force against the victim. Together they add up to criminal recklessness.... This approach is in line with the American Model Code [Section 2.08(2)]:

> When recklessness establishes an element of the offence, if the actor, due to self-induced intoxication, is unaware of a risk of which he would have been aware had he been sober, such unawareness is immaterial.

Acceptance generally of intoxication as a defence (as distinct from the exceptional cases where some additional mental element above that of ordinary mens rea has to be proved) would in my view undermine the criminal law and I do not think that it is enough to say, as did counsel for the appellant, that we can rely on the good sense of the jury ... to ensure that the guilty are convicted....

■ LORD SIMON OF GLAISDALE.... One of the prime purposes of the criminal law, with its penal sanctions, is the protection from certain proscribed conduct of persons who are pursuing their lawful lives. Unprovoked violence has, from time immemorial, been a significant part of such proscribed conduct. To accede to the argument on behalf of the appellant would leave the citizen legally unprotected from unprovoked violence, where such violence was the consequence of drink or drugs having obliterated the capacity of the perpetrator to know what he was doing or what were its consequences.

... Though the problem of violent conduct by intoxicated persons is not new to society, it has been rendered more acute and menacing by the more widespread use of hallucinatory drugs. For example, in Regina v. Lipman, [1969] All E.R. 410, [1970] 1 Q.B. 152, the accused committed his act of mortal violence under the hallucination (induced by drugs) that he was wrestling with serpents.[1] He was convicted of manslaughter. But, on the logic of the appellant's argument, he was innocent of any crime.

[T]here is nothing unreasonable or illogical in the law holding that a mind rendered self-inducedly insensible ..., through drink or drugs, to the nature of a prohibited act or to its probable consequences is as wrongful a mind as one which consciously contemplates the prohibited act and foresees its probable consequences (or is reckless whether they ensue). The latter is all that is required by way of mens rea in a crime of basic intent. But a crime of specific intent requires something more than contemplation of the prohibited act and foresight of its probable consequences. The mens rea in a crime of specific intent requires proof of a purposive element. This purposive element either exists or not; it cannot be supplied by saying that the impairment of mental powers by self-induced intoxication is its equivalent, for it is not. So ... the 19th century development of the law as to the effect of self-induced intoxication on criminal responsibility is juristically entirely acceptable....

■ LORD SALMON.... A number of distinguished academic writers support [the defendant's] contention on the ground of logic. As I understand it, the argument runs like this. Intention, whether special or basic (or whatever fancy name you choose to give it), is still intention. If voluntary intoxication by drink or drugs can, as it admittedly can, negative the special or specific intention necessary for the commission of crimes such as murder and theft, how can you justify in strict logic the view that it cannot

---

[1] Lipman killed his companion by stuffing bedclothes down her throat under the delusion, induced by hallucinatory drugs, that he was fighting for his life against snakes.—[Footnote by eds.]

negative a basic intention, e.g., the intention to commit offences such as assault and unlawful wounding? The answer is that in strict logic this view cannot be justified. But this is the view that has been adopted by the common law of England, which is founded on common sense and experience rather than strict logic. There is no case in the 19th century when the courts were relaxing the harshness of the law in relation to the effect of drunkenness on criminal liability in which the courts ever went so far as to suggest that drunkenness, short of drunkenness producing insanity, could ever exculpate a man from any offence other than one which required some special or specific intent to be proved.

. . . I accept that there is a degree of illogicality in the rule that intoxication may excuse or expunge one type of intention and not another. This illogicality is, however, acceptable to me because the benevolent part of the rule removes undue harshness without imperilling safety and the stricter part of the rule works without imperilling justice. It would be just as ridiculous to remove the benevolent part of the rule (which no one suggests) as it would be to adopt the alternative of removing the stricter part of [the] rule for the sake of preserving absolute logic. . . .

■ LORD EDMUND-DAVIES. . . . Illogical though the present law may be, it represents a compromise between the imposition of liability on inebriates in complete disregard of their condition (on the alleged ground that it was brought on voluntarily), and the total exculpation required by the defendant's actual state of mind at the time he committed the harm in issue. . . . As to the complaint that it is unethical to punish a man for a crime when his physical behaviour was not controlled by a conscious mind, I have long regarded as a convincing theory in support of penal liability for harms committed by voluntary inebriates, the view of Austin, who argued that a person who voluntarily became intoxicated is to be regarded as acting recklessly, for he made himself dangerous in disregard of public safety. . . . It may be that Parliament should look at [the situation], and devise a new way of dealing with drunken or drugged offenders. But, until it does, the continued application of the existing law is far better calculated to preserve order than [acceptance of the argument] that he and all who act similarly should leave the dock as free men. . . .

■ LORD RUSSELL OF KILLOWEN. . . . That the facts of the case give rise to the question [raised], I doubt. The appellant's participation in the events of the evening begin when he is told by the other man that the latter is to be ejected: whereupon the appellant stationed himself before the door to prevent that, which shows comprehension and intention on his part. When the police arrived the appellant called them adjectival pigs, a word which has of recent years been revived as a reference to law enforcement officers, having been current in the early 19th century. . . . This . . . negatives lack of understanding. Nevertheless, the question requires to be answered, and I agree with the answer proposed. . . .

Appeal dismissed.

———

NOTES ON MENS REA AND INTOXICATION

**1. Introduction.** In *Majewski* the House of Lords considers the significance of a claim that the defendant's conscious mental functioning at the time of the offense was impaired as a result of intoxication. In rare cases, a defendant might claim, as Majewski did, that he or she was so intoxicated as to lack any conscious awareness of, or control over, behavior. This claim may be thought to be legally significant because it shows that the defendant's conduct was not produced by a "voluntary act." More typically, a defendant who was consciously aware of some aspects of conduct may claim to have lacked the mens rea required for conviction because of unawareness or misperception of legally pertinent circumstances or risks, or may claim to have lacked the type of conscious objective (e.g., purpose to kill) prescribed by the offense. All of these claims may be logically relevant to the elements of the offense. However, as the *Majewski* opinions indicate, there has been broad consensus that evidence of voluntary intoxication should be restricted considerably short of its logical import.[a] How far short has been the question on which the authorities disagree.

**2. General Intent Crimes.** There is a consensus in American law that the result in *Majewski* is correct, i.e., that intoxication evidence is inadmissible to negate mens rea for general or "basic" intent offenses. If "general intent" is equated to negligence, this result is not surprising. It is clear enough that the standard for negligence should not be the "reasonable intoxicated" person, clear enough that it is never "reasonable" for a mistake to be induced by intoxication. But even the Model Penal Code modifies the rule of logical relevance when the actual awareness of risk required for recklessness is sought to be rebutted by evidence of intoxication.

The Model Code position has been defended on four grounds: (i) the weight of authority, which is virtually unanimous; (ii) the fairness of postulating a moral equivalence between the act of getting drunk as a risk-taking venture and the risks subsequently created by drunken conduct; (iii) the difficulty of measuring actual foresight when the actor is drunk; and (iv) the rarity of cases in which drunkenness leads to unawareness as opposed to imprudence.[b] Are these reasons persuasive as applied to alcohol?

---

[a] As *Majewski* indicates, the law does not distinguish between drugs and alcohol in this context. It should also be noted that the doctrine applied in *Majewski* pertains only to voluntary ingestion of intoxicating substances; involuntary or otherwise non-culpable intoxication is governed by other doctrines, considered elsewhere in these materials. Finally, the restrictive doctrine illustrated by *Majewski* and the notes to follow is qualified by the possibility that a person who ingests alcohol or drugs may become legally insane. The relation between intoxi-

cation and the insanity defense is also considered elsewhere in these materials.

[b] Compare Monrad Paulsen, Intoxication as a Defense to Crime, 1961 U.Ill.L.F. 1: "Drinking alcohol impairs judgment, releases inhibitions, and thus permits the drinker to engage in behavior quite different from the normal pattern. 'Alcohol is an anesthetic or depressant, and its action is approximately the same on all human central nervous systems: it is usually described as reducing the speed and accuracy of perception, slowing down reaction time, and diminishing ten-

As applied to the types of substances ingested by Majewski? As applied to all drugs? What of Glanville Williams' point, in Criminal Law: The General Part 564 (2d ed. 1961), that "[i]f a man is punished for doing something when drunk that he would not have done when sober, is he not in plain truth punished for getting drunk?"

**3.   Specific Intent Crimes.** There is disagreement in American law on the proposition advanced in *Majewski* that evidence of intoxication is admissible to negate a specific intent. The cases fall into three groups.

**(i) Restrictive Positions.** In at least 11 states, evidence of intoxication is not admissible in any (or most) specific intent crimes. Virginia is an example.[c] In Chittum v. Commonwealth, 211 Va. 12, 174 S.E.2d 779 (1970), the defendant was convicted of attempted rape. The defendant's argument on appeal, and the terms in which it was rejected, are revealed in the following excerpt from the affirmance of his conviction:

> The issue presented . . . is whether a defendant is entitled to have the jury instructed to the effect that when a specific intent is a necessary element of the crime charged, the drunkenness of defendant, although voluntary, may be considered in determining whether he was capable of forming or entertaining that requisite intent.

> Although a majority of jurisdictions would allow such an instruction, we have held . . . that "[v]oluntary drunkenness, where it has not produced permanent insanity, is *never* an excuse for crime; *except,* where a party is charged with murder, if it appear that the accused was too drunk to be capable of deliberating and premeditating, then he can be convicted only of murder in the second degree." . . . We think this to be the better rule.

> In [another case involving] a prosecution for robbery, an instruction was offered on the theory that if defendant was too drunk to entertain the specific intent to rob he could not be found guilty. We agreed with the trial court that there was no evidence to support the instruction and said, "Even if there had been evidence of drunkenness, under the decisions of this court, it would have been no excuse for the crime."

If it is right to reject evidence of intoxication offered to negate the awareness required for recklessness, why is it not also right to reject its use in all cases? Consider in this connection the following excerpt from Monrad Paulsen, Intoxication as a Defense to Crime, 1961 U.Ill.L.F. 1, 11:

sions, anxieties and inhibitions.' Drinking 'stimulates' the drinker, but does so by 'loosening the brakes,' not by 'stepping on the gas.' "

[c] Citations to cases and statutes in 10 other states that adopt a version of the Virginia position are contained in Montana v. Egelhoff, 518 U.S. 37, 48 n.2 (1996). *Egelhoff* upheld the constitutionality over four dissents of a Montana rule that excluded evidence of intoxication offered to show that the defendant lacked "purpose" or "knowledge" (both defined similarly to the Model Penal Code) in a murder prosecution.

The present policy of the law which permits the disproof of knowledge or purpose by evidence of extreme intoxication is sound enough. If a crime (or a degree of crime) requires a showing of one of these elements, it is because the conduct involved presents a special danger, if done with purpose or knowledge or the actor presents a special cause for alarm. A burglar, one who breaks in with a purpose to commit a felony, is more dangerous than the simple housebreaker. The aggravated assaults are punished more severely precisely because of the danger presented by the actor's state of mind. He who passes counterfeit money with knowledge is a greater threat than the actor who transfers it without understanding. If purpose or knowledge are not present, the cause for the lack is not important. The policy served by requiring these elements of culpability will obtain whether or not their absence is established by proof of extreme intoxication or any other evidence.

Contrast to this line of argument the following comments from Montana v. Egelhoff, 518 U.S. 37 (1996), where the Supreme Court upheld the constitutionality of a Montana rule excluding evidence of intoxication on the issues of "purpose" and "knowledge" in a murder prosecution. Writing for a plurality of the Court, Justice Scalia reviewed the history, noting that initially the common law embodied a "stern rejection of inebriation as a defense" in all cases, but that "by the end of the 19th century, in most American jurisdictions, intoxication could be considered in determining whether a defendant was capable of forming the specific intent necessary to commit the crime charged." Nonetheless, he upheld the restrictive Montana rule, in part because it conformed to "a lengthy common-law tradition which remains supported by valid justifications today." He added:

It is not surprising that many states have held fast to or resurrected the common-law rule prohibiting consideration of voluntary intoxication in the determination of mens rea, because that rule has considerable justification.... A large number of crimes, especially violent crimes, are committed by intoxicated offenders; modern studies put the numbers as high as half of all homicides, for example. Disallowing consideration of voluntary intoxication has the effect of increasing the punishment for all unlawful acts committed in that state, and thereby deters drunkenness or irresponsible behavior while drunk. The rule also serves as a specific deterrent, ensuring that those who prove incapable of controlling violent impulses while voluntarily intoxicated go to prison. And finally, the rule comports with and implements society's moral perception that one who has voluntarily impaired his own faculties should be responsible for the consequences.

There is, in modern times, even more justification for [such] laws ... than there used to be. Some recent studies suggest that the connection between drunkenness and crime is as much cultural as pharmacological—that is, that drunks are violent not simply because alcohol makes them that way, but because they are behaving in accord with their learned belief that drunks are violent. See, e.g., James J. Collins, Suggested Explanatory Frameworks to Clarify the Alcohol Use/Violence Relationship, 15 Contemp. Drug Prob. 107, 115 (1988); Barbara Critchlow, The Powers of John Barleycorn, 41 Am. Psychologist 751, 754–55 (July 1986). This not only adds additional support to the traditional view that an intoxicated criminal is not deserving of exoneration, but it suggests that juries—who possess the same learned belief as the intoxicated offender—will be too quick to accept the claim that the defendant was biologically incapable of forming the requisite mens rea. Treating the matter as one of excluding misleading evidence therefore makes some sense.

**(ii) Lack of Capacity vs. Factual Relevance.** Modern cases also reflect a division—originating in 19th century English decisions—as to how the rule relating to specific intent should be stated. The dispute is illustrated by two hypothetical instructions drafted for a proposed charge of larceny of a radio by a defendant who was "quite drunk" and based on form instructions for the two states involved. The hypotheticals are contained in Arthur A. Murphy, The Intoxication Defense: An Introduction to Mr. Smith's Article, 76 Dick. L. Rev. 1, 10 (1971–72):*

Early in his charge the court would instruct on the elements of larceny, including the intent element and make it clear that the jury cannot convict unless satisfied beyond [a] reasonable doubt as to all elements. If the judge were to use the California form of intoxication charge, he might proceed in this fashion:

In the crime of larceny a necessary element is the existence in the mind of the defendant of the specific intent to deprive the owner permanently of his radio.

If the evidence shows that the defendant was intoxicated at the time of the alleged offense you should consider his state of intoxication in determining if the defendant had that specific intent.

Were the judge to use the Ohio form he might instruct as follows:

Intoxication is not an excuse for a crime. However, such evidence is admissible for the purpose of showing that the defendant was so intoxicated he was incapable of forming the intent to deprive the owner permanently of his radio. On this issue, the burden of proof is upon the defendant to establish by a greater weight of the evidence that his mind did not form that intent. If you find by a greater weight of the evidence that the defendant was incapable of forming an intent to deprive the owner permanently of his property then you must find the defendant not guilty.

* The excerpts below are reprinted with permission of Professor Murphy of the Dick-      inson School of Law and the Dickinson Law Review.

What is there to be said for these two formulations? Which one does the Model Penal Code adopt? Consider also Murphy's comments:

> If given no further guidance than the California charge, a juror might believe that an inebriate who acts on impulse never acts with specific intent or that specific intent requires relatively clearheaded thought processes. When the proof shows that a defendant was even moderately drunk, he might feel bound by the accused's testimony that "I didn't mean to do it" or "I didn't know what I was doing." The juror would in effect be insisting on a higher quality of specific intent—a more culpable state of mind—than required by generally accepted legal doctrine.

> The Ohio charge includes a verbal formula which conveys the idea that only extreme intoxication precludes intent. It focuses the inquiry on the defendant's *potential* for forming the required intent and implies that any intent will serve (impulsive or at a low level of awareness?) so long as the defendant is *capable* of the kind of intent required by law. If we accept the premises that the criminal law should treat most people alike, that specific-intent crimes can be committed by stupid, unstable and quite peculiar people and that intent or conscious purpose does not require a cool head, clear thinking or, indeed, very much in the way of mental activity, the Ohio charge seems more likely to avoid improper verdicts than the California form.

**(iii) Burden of Persuasion.** Perhaps as many as half of the states adopt the Ohio version of the specific-intent rule as stated by Murphy. Typically, these states also follow the practice of placing the burden of persuasion on the defendant. Notice the anomaly created by Murphy's Ohio instruction and consider his comments thereon:

> The California charge avoids a problem of conflicting burdens of persuasion that is inherent in any instruction which, like the Ohio form, makes incapacity a true affirmative defense. Looking back at our sample Ohio charge, we see that the accused has the burden of persuading the jury that he was so drunk he was unable to form the intent to steal, while the state retains the burden of proving beyond reasonable doubt that the accused had that intent. If the jurors have even a reasonable doubt of the defendant's capacity to form an intent to steal, how can they be convinced beyond reasonable doubt that he did in fact intend to steal? The Ohio charge appears to reconcile the conflicting burdens in the only way it can logically be done—by conceiving the capacity defense as working a partial exception to the prosecutor's normal burden of proving the intent element. The jury is told that on the capacity issue the defendant has the burden of proving "that his mind did not form the intent." In many courts, however, which treat incapacity as a true affirmative defense, the jurors are left to resolve the anomaly for themselves.

Is this a serious problem? What is the jury to do?

———

## NOTE ON MENTAL ABNORMALITY AND MENS REA

Evidence of mental abnormality can be relevant to the mens rea determinations previously explored. As in the case of intoxication, however, the law has always treated a claim of ignorance or mistake based on mental abnormality as presenting a special problem. The long-standing tradition has been to recognize a separate defense of insanity which, if established, excuses the actor even though the formal elements of actus reus and mens rea have been proved. Whether evidence of mental abnormality can also be considered on mens-rea issues is a question of considerable difficulty and debate.

It is helpful in understanding why this is so to recognize that the common law courts saw sanity and insanity as categorical concepts. Insane persons—those who acted in a frenzy induced by madness, in the language of the early days—were said to lack the capacity to entertain a "criminal intent." They were incapable of having "guilty minds." However, a defendant who did not claim to be insane was conclusively presumed to have the capacity to form a criminal intent. There was no middle ground. As a result, evidence of mental abnormality was inadmissible unless it was offered in support of an insanity defense.

This categorical approach to evidence of mental abnormality began to break down during the late 19th and early 20th centuries. One important factor was the emergence of psychiatry as a recognized scientific discipline, a development which was accompanied by efforts to relate advances in psychological understanding to the doctrines of the criminal law. A central theme in the forensic literature of the period was the variety and complexity of mental dysfunction and the difficulty of relating emerging psychiatric concepts to the sane-insane model of the law. Another important influence was the emergence during the same period of integrated approaches to the culpability requirements of the criminal law, including an increased focus on subjective components of mens rea.

Today there is considerable support for the proposition that evidence of mental abnormality, including expert testimony, should be admissible whenever it is relevant to any issue of culpability in the criminal law. However, some jurisdictions adhere rigorously to the notion that evidence of mental abnormality may be considered only in connection with the insanity defense. Others admit the evidence only on some mens rea issues, and still others admit it whenever relevant to any mens rea issue. There is disagreement too—as in the case of intoxication—on how its relevance should be stated in cases where it is admissible. Some jurisdictions, for example, insist that evidence of mental abnormality must show lack of capacity to formulate the required mens rea and that such evidence must be confined to cases where the defendant was afflicted with some recognized disease or illness.

Full explication and evaluation of these issues cannot usefully be undertaken until the separate defense of insanity is considered, an enterprise that is postponed to Chapter VI in these materials. Chapter VI deals with insanity and then returns to the problems of mens rea and evidence of mental abnormality. Additionally, Chapter VIII explores some related problems in the law of criminal homicide.

———

## SUBSECTION C: ESTABLISHING THE APPROPRIATE MENS REA STANDARD

———

## Morissette v. United States

Supreme Court of United States, 1952.
342 U.S. 246.

■ MR. JUSTICE JACKSON delivered the opinion of the Court.

This would have remained a profoundly insignificant case to all except its immediate parties had it not been so tried and submitted to the jury as to raise questions both fundamental and far-reaching in federal criminal law, for which reason we granted certiorari.

On a large tract of uninhabited and untilled land in a wooded and sparsely populated area of Michigan, the government established a practice bombing range over which the Air Force dropped simulated bombs at ground targets. These bombs consisted of a metal cylinder about 40 inches long and eight inches across, filled with sand and enough black powder to cause a smoke puff by which the strike could be located. At various places about the range signs read "Danger—Keep Out—Bombing Range." Nevertheless, the range was known as good deer country and was extensively hunted.

Spent bomb casings were cleared from the targets and thrown into piles "so that they will be out of the way." They were not stacked or piled in any order but were dumped in heaps, some of which had been accumulating for four years or upwards, were exposed to the weather and rusting away.

Morissette, in December of 1948, went hunting in this area but did not get a deer. He thought to meet expenses of the trip by salvaging some of these casings. He loaded three tons of them on his truck and took them to a nearby farm, where they were flattened by driving a tractor over them. After expending this labor and trucking them to market in Flint, he realized $84.

Morissette, by occupation, is a fruit stand operator in summer and a trucker and scrap iron collector in winter. An honorably discharged veteran of World War II, he enjoys a good name among his neighbors and has had no blemish on his record more disreputable than a conviction for reckless driving.

The loading, crushing and transporting of these casings were all in broad daylight, in full view of passers-by, without the slightest effort at concealment. When an investigation was started, Morissette voluntarily, promptly and candidly told the whole story to the authorities, saying that he had no intention of stealing but thought the property was abandoned, unwanted and considered of no value to the government. He was indicted, however, on the charge that he "did unlawfully, wilfully and knowingly steal and convert" property of the United States of the value of $84, in violation of 18 U.S.C. § 641[2].... Morissette was convicted and sentenced to imprisonment for two months or to pay a fine of $200. The Court of Appeals affirmed, one judge dissenting.

On his trial, Morissette, as he had at all times told investigating officers, testified that from appearances he believed the casings were cast-off and abandoned, that he did not intend to steal the property, and took it with no wrongful or criminal intent. The trial court, however, was unimpressed, and ruled:

> [H]e took it because he thought it was abandoned and he knew he was on government property.... That is no defense.... I don't think anybody can have the defense [that] they thought the property was abandoned on another man's piece of property.

The court stated:

> I will not permit you to show this man thought it was abandoned.... I hold in this case that there is no question of abandoned property.

The court refused to submit or to allow counsel to argue to the jury whether Morissette acted with innocent intention. It charged:

> And I instruct you that if you believe the testimony of the government in this case, he intended to take it.... He had no right to take this property. [A]nd it is no defense to claim that it was abandoned, because it was on private property.... And I instruct you to this effect: That if this young man took this property (and he says he did), without any permission (he says he did), that was on the property of the United States Government (he says it was), that it was of the value of one cent or more (and evidently it was), that he is guilty of the offense charged here. If you believe the government, he is guilty.... The question on intent is whether or not he intended to take the property. He says he did. Therefore, if you believe either side, he is guilty.

---

[2] Section 641, so far as pertinent, reads:

Whoever embezzles, steals, purloins, or knowingly converts to his use or the use of another ... any ... thing of value of the United States [s]hall be fined not more than $10,000 or imprisoned not more than ten years, or both; but if the value of such property does not exceed the sum of $100, he shall be fined not more than $1,000 or imprisoned not more than one year, or both.

Petitioner's counsel contended, "But the taking must have been with a felonious intent." The court ruled, however: "That is presumed by his own act."

The Court of Appeals suggested that "greater restraint in expression should have been exercised," but affirmed the conviction because, "[a]s we have interpreted the statute, appellant was guilty of its violation beyond a shadow of doubt, as evidenced even by his own admissions." Its construction of the statute is that it creates several separate and distinct offenses, one being knowing conversion of government property. The court ruled that this particular offense requires no element of criminal intent. This conclusion was thought to be required by the failure of Congress to express such a requisite and this Court's decisions in United States v. Behrman, 258 U.S. 280 (1922), and United States v. Balint, 258 U.S. 250 (1922).

I.

In those cases this Court did construe mere omission from a criminal enactment of any mention of criminal intent as dispensing with it. If they be deemed precedents for principles of construction generally applicable to federal penal statutes, they authorize this conviction. Indeed, such adoption of the literal reasoning announced in those cases would do this and more— it would sweep out of all federal crimes, except when expressly preserved, the ancient requirement of a culpable state of mind. We think a resume of their historical background is convincing that an effect has been ascribed to them more comprehensive than was contemplated and one inconsistent with our philosophy of criminal law.

The contention that an injury can amount to a crime only when inflicted by intention is no provincial or transient notion. It is as universal and persistent in mature systems of law as belief in freedom of the human will and a consequent ability and duty of the normal individual to choose between good and evil. A relation between some mental element and punishment for a harmful act is almost as instinctive as the child's familiar exculpatory "But I didn't mean to," and has afforded the rational basis for a tardy and unfinished substitution of deterrence and reformation in place of retaliation and vengeance as the motivation for public prosecution. Unqualified acceptance of this doctrine by English common law in the eighteenth century was indicated by Blackstone's sweeping statement that to constitute any crime there must first be a "vicious will." . . .

Crime, as a compound concept, generally constituted only from concurrence of an evil-meaning mind with an evil-doing hand, was congenial to an intense individualism and took deep and early root in American soil.[9] As the states codified the common law of crimes, even if their enactments were silent on the subject, their courts assumed that the omission did not signify disapproval of the principle but merely recognized that intent was so inherent in the idea of the offense that it required no statutory affirmation.

[9] Holmes, The Common Law, considers intent in the chapter on The Criminal Law, and earlier makes the pithy observation: "Even a dog distinguishes between being stumbled over and being kicked."

Courts, with little hesitation or division, found an implication of the requirement as to offenses that were taken over from the common law. The unanimity with which they have adhered to the central thought that wrongdoing must be conscious to be criminal is emphasized by the variety, disparity and confusion of their definitions of the requisite but elusive mental element. However, courts of various jurisdictions, and for the purposes of different offenses, have devised working formulae, if not scientific ones, for the instruction of juries around such terms as "felonious intent," "criminal intent," "malice aforethought," "guilty knowledge," "fraudulent intent," "wilfulness," "scienter," to denote guilty knowledge, or "mens rea," to signify an evil purpose or mental culpability. By use or combination of these various tokens, they have sought to protect those who were not blameworthy in mind from conviction of infamous common-law crimes.

However, the *Balint* and *Behrman* offenses belong to a category of another character, with very different antecedents and origins. The crimes there involved depend on no mental element but consist only of forbidden acts or omissions. This . . . is made clear from examination of a century-old but accelerating tendency, discernible both here and in England,[11] to call into existence new duties and crimes which disregard any ingredient of intent. The industrial revolution multiplied the number of workmen exposed to injury from increasingly powerful and complex mechanisms, driven by freshly discovered sources of energy, requiring higher precautions by employers. Traffic of velocities, volumes and varieties unheard of came to subject the wayfarer to intolerable casualty risks if owners and drivers were not to observe new cares and uniformities of conduct. Congestion of cities and crowding of quarters called for health and welfare regulations undreamed of in simpler times. Wide distribution of goods became an

---

[11] The changes in English law are illustrated by 19th Century English cases. In 1814, it was held that one could not be convicted of selling impure foods unless he was aware of the impurities. Rex v. Dixon, 3 M. & S. 11 (K.B.1814). However, 32 years later, in an action to enforce a statutory forfeiture for possession of adulterated tobacco, the respondent was held liable even though he had no knowledge of, or cause to suspect, the adulteration. Countering respondent's arguments, Baron Parke said, "It is very true that in particular instances it may produce mischief, because an innocent man may suffer from his want of care in not examining the tobacco he has received, and not taking a warranty; but the public inconvenience would be much greater, if in every case the officers were obliged to prove knowledge. They would be very seldom able to do so." Regina v. Woodrow, 15 M. & W. 404, 417 (Exch. 1846). Convenience of the prosecution thus emerged as a rationale. In 1866, a quarry owner was held liable for the nuisance caused by his workmen dumping refuse into a river, in spite of his plea that he played no active part in the management of the business and knew nothing about the dumping involved. His knowledge or lack of it was deemed irrelevant. Regina v. Stephens, L.R. 1 Q.B. 702 (1866). . . . After these decisions, statutes prohibiting the sale of impure or adulterated food were enacted. Adulteration of Food Act (35 & 36 Vict. c. 74, s 2 (1872)); Sale of Food and Drugs Act of 1875 (38 & 39 Vict. c. 63). A conviction under the former was sustained in a holding that no guilty knowledge or intent need be proved in a prosecution for the sale of adulterated butter, Fitzpatrick v. Kelly, L.R. 8 Q.B. 337 (1873), and in Betts v. Armstead, L.R. 20 Q.B.D. 771 (1888), involving the latter statute, it was held that there was no need for a showing that the accused had knowledge that his product did not measure up to the statutory specifications.

instrument of wide distribution of harm when those who dispersed food, drink, drugs, and even securities, did not comply with reasonable standards of quality, integrity, disclosure and care. Such dangers have engendered increasingly numerous and detailed regulations which heighten the duties of those in control of particular industries, trades, properties or activities that affect public health, safety or welfare.

While many of these duties are sanctioned by a more strict civil liability, lawmakers, whether wisely or not, have sought to make such regulations more effective by invoking criminal sanctions to be applied by the familiar technique of criminal prosecutions and convictions. This has confronted the courts with a multitude of prosecutions, for what have been aptly called "public welfare offenses." These cases do not fit neatly into any of such accepted classifications of common-law offenses, such as those against the state, the person, property, or public morals. Many of these offenses are not in the nature of positive aggressions or invasions, with which the common law so often dealt, but are in the nature of neglect where the law requires care, or inaction where it imposes a duty. Many violations of such regulations result in no direct or immediate injury to person or property but merely create the danger or probability of it which the law seeks to minimize. While such offenses do not threaten the security of the state in the manner of treason, they may be regarded as offenses against its authority, for their occurrence impairs the efficiency of controls deemed essential to the social order as presently constituted. In this respect, whatever the intent of the violator, the injury is the same, and the consequences are injurious or not according to fortuity. Hence, legislation applicable to such offenses, as a matter of policy, does not specify intent as a necessary element. The accused, if he does not will the violation, usually is in a position to prevent it with no more care than society might reasonably expect and no more exertion than it might reasonably exact from one who assumed his responsibilities. Also, penalties commonly are relatively small, and conviction does no grave damage to an offender's reputation. Under such considerations, courts have turned to construing statutes and regulations which make no mention of intent as dispensing with it and holding that the guilty act alone makes out the crime. This has not, however, been without expressions of misgiving.

The pilot of the movement in this country appears to be a holding that a tavernkeeper could be convicted for selling liquor to an habitual drunkard even if he did not know the buyer to be such. Barnes v. State, 19 Conn. 398 (1849). Later came Massachusetts holdings that convictions for selling adulterated milk in violation of statutes forbidding such sales require no allegation or proof that defendant knew of the adulteration. Commonwealth v. Farren, 9 Allen 489 (1864); Commonwealth v. Nichols, 10 Allen 199 (1865); Commonwealth v. Waite, 11 Allen 264 (1865). Departures from the common-law tradition, mainly of these general classes, were reviewed and their rationale appraised by Chief Justice Cooley, as follows: "I agree that as a rule there can be no crime without a criminal intent, but this is not by any means a universal rule.... Many statutes which are in the nature of police regulations, as this is, impose criminal penalties irrespective of any intent to violate them, the purpose being to require a degree of diligence for the protection of the public which shall render violation impossible." People v. Roby, 52 Mich. 577, 579, 18 N.W. 365, 366 (1884).

After the turn of the Century, a new use for crimes without intent appeared when New York enacted numerous and novel regulations of tenement houses, sanctioned by money penalties. Landlords contended that a guilty intent was essential to establish a violation. Judge Cardozo wrote the answer: "The defendant asks us to test the meaning of this statute by standards applicable to statutes that govern infamous crimes. The analogy, however, is deceptive. The element of conscious wrongdoing, the guilty mind accompanying the guilty act, is associated with the concept of crimes that are punished as infamous.... Even there it is not an invariable element. But in the prosecution of minor offenses there is a wider range of practice and of power. Prosecutions for petty penalties have always constituted in our law a class by themselves.... That is true, though the prosecution is criminal in form." Tenement House Department of City of New York v. McDevitt, 215 N.Y. 160, 168, 109 N.E. 88, 90 (1915).

Soon, employers advanced the same contention as to violations of regulations prescribed by a new labor law. Judge Cardozo, again for the court, pointed out, as a basis for penalizing violations whether intentional or not, that they were punishable only by fine "moderate in amount," but cautiously added that in sustaining the power so to fine unintended violations "we are not to be understood as sustaining to a like length the power to imprison. We leave that question open." People ex rel. Price v. Sheffield Farms–Slawson-Decker Co., 225 N.Y. 25, 32–33, 121 N.E. 474, 476, 477 (1918).

Thus, for diverse but reconcilable reasons, state courts converged on the same result, discontinuing inquiry into intent in a limited class of offenses against such statutory regulations.

Before long, similar questions growing out of federal legislation reached this Court. Its judgments were in harmony with this consensus of state judicial opinion, the existence of which may have led the Court to overlook the need for full exposition of their rationale in the context of federal law. In overruling a contention that there can be no conviction on an indictment which makes no charge of criminal intent but alleges only making of a sale of a narcotic forbidden by law, Chief Justice Taft, wrote: "While the general rule at common law was that the scienter was a necessary element in the indictment and proof of every crime, and this was followed in regard to statutory crimes even where the statutory definition did not in terms include it ..., there has been a modification of this view in respect to prosecutions under statutes the purpose of which would be obstructed by such a requirement. It is a question of legislative intent to be construed by the court...." *United States v. Balint*, supra, 258 U.S. at 251–52.

He referred, however, to "regulatory measures in the exercise of what is called the police power where the emphasis of the statute is evidently upon achievement of some social betterment rather than the punishment of the crimes as in cases of mala in se," and drew his citation of supporting authority chiefly from state court cases dealing with regulatory offenses.

On the same day, the Court determined that an offense under the Narcotic Drug Act does not require intent, saying, "If the offense be a statutory one, and intent or knowledge is not made an element of it, the indictment need not charge such knowledge or intent." *United States v. Behrman*, supra, 258 U.S. at 288.

Of course, the purpose of every statute would be "obstructed" by requiring a finding of intent, if we assume that it had a purpose to convict without it. Therefore, the obstruction rationale does not help us to learn the purpose of the omission by Congress. And since no federal crime can exist except by force of statute, the reasoning of the *Behrman* opinion, if read literally, would work far-reaching changes in the composition of all federal crimes. Had such a result been contemplated, it could hardly have escaped mention by a Court which numbered among its members [Justice Holmes] one especially interested and informed concerning the importance of intent in common-law crimes. This might be the more expected since the *Behrman* holding did call forth his dissent, in which Mr. Justice McReynolds and Mr. Justice Brandeis joined, omitting any such mention.

It was not until recently that the Court took occasion more explicitly to relate abandonment of the ingredient of intent, not merely with considerations of expediency in obtaining convictions, nor with the malum prohibitum classification of the crime, but with the peculiar nature and quality of the offense. We referred to ". . . a now familiar type of legislation whereby penalties serve as effective means of regulation," and continued, "such legislation dispenses with the conventional requirement for criminal conduct—awareness of some wrongdoing. In the interest of the larger good it puts the burden of acting at hazard upon a person otherwise innocent but standing in responsible relation to a public danger." But we warned: "Hardship there doubtless may be under a statute which thus penalizes the transaction though consciousness of wrongdoing be totally wanting." United States v. Dotterweich, 320 U.S. 277, 280–81, 284 (1943)

Neither this Court nor, so far as we are aware, any other has undertaken to delineate a precise line or set forth comprehensive criteria for distinguishing between crimes that require a mental element and crimes that do not. We attempt no closed definition, for the law on the subject is neither settled nor static. The conclusion reached in the *Balint* and *Behrman* cases has our approval and adherence for the circumstances to which it was there applied. A quite different question here is whether we will expand the doctrine of crimes without intent to include those charged here.

Stealing, larceny, and its variants and equivalents, were among the earliest offenses known to the law that existed before legislation; they are invasions of rights of property which stir a sense of insecurity in the whole community and arouse public demand for retribution, the penalty is high and, when a sufficient amount is involved, the infamy is that of a felony, which, says Maitland, is ". . . as bad a word as you can give to man or thing." State courts of last resort, on whom fall the heaviest burden of interpreting criminal law in this country, have consistently retained the requirement of intent in larceny-type offenses. If any state has deviated, the exception has neither been called to our attention nor disclosed by our research.

Congress, therefore, omitted any express prescription of criminal intent from the enactment before us in the light of an unbroken course of judicial decision in all constituent states of the Union holding intent inherent in this class of offense, even when not expressed in a statute. Congressional silence as to mental elements in an Act merely adopting into federal statutory law a concept of crime already so well defined in common law and statutory interpretation by the states may warrant quite contrary inferences than the same silence in creating an offense new to general law, for whose definition the courts have no guidance except the Act. Because the offenses before this Court in the *Balint* and *Behrman* cases were of this latter class, we cannot accept them as authority for eliminating intent from offenses incorporated from the common law. Nor do exhaustive studies of state court cases disclose any well-considered decisions applying the doctrine of crime without intent to such enacted common-law offenses[20] . . . .

The Government asks us by a feat of construction radically to change the weights and balances in the scales of justice. The purpose and obvious effect of doing away with the requirement of a guilty intent is to ease the prosecution's path to conviction, to strip the defendant of such benefit as he derived at common law from innocence of evil purpose, and to circumscribe the freedom heretofore allowed juries. Such a manifest impairment of the immunities of the individual should not be extended to common-law crimes on judicial initiative.

The spirit of the doctrine which denies to the federal judiciary power to create crimes forthrightly admonishes that we should not enlarge the reach of enacted crimes by constituting them from anything less than the incriminating components contemplated by the words used in the statute. And where Congress borrows terms of art in which are accumulated the legal tradition and meaning of centuries of practice, it presumably knows and adopts the cluster of ideas that were attached to each borrowed word in the body of learning from which it was taken and the meaning its use will convey to the judicial mind unless otherwise instructed. In such case, absence of contrary direction may be taken as satisfaction with widely accepted definitions, not as a departure from them.

We hold that mere omission from § 641 of any mention of intent will not be construed as eliminating that element from the crimes denounced.

---

[20] Francis Bowes Sayre, Public Welfare Offenses, 33 Colum. L. Rev. 55, 73, 84 (1933), cites and classifies a large number of cases and concludes that they fall roughly into subdivisions of (1) illegal sales of intoxicating liquor, (2) sales of impure or adulterated food or drugs, (3) sales of misbranded articles, (4) violations of anti-narcotic Acts, (5) criminal nuisances, (6) violations of traffic regulations, (7) violations of motor-vehicle laws, and (8) violations of general police regulations, passed for the safety, health or well-being of the community.

II.

It is suggested, however, that the history and purposes of § 641 imply something more affirmative as to elimination of intent from at least one of the offenses charged under it in this case. The argument does not contest that criminal intent is retained in the offenses of embezzlement, stealing and purloining, as incorporated into this section. But it is urged that Congress joined with those, as a new, separate and distinct offense, knowingly to convert government property, under circumstances which imply that it is an offense in which the mental element of intent is not necessary.

Congress has been alert to what often is a decisive function of some mental element in crime. It has seen fit to prescribe that an evil state of mind, described variously in one or more such terms as "intentional," "wilful," "knowing," "fraudulent" or "malicious," will make criminal an otherwise indifferent act, or increase the degree of the offense or its punishment. Also, it has at times required a specific intent or purpose which will require some specialized knowledge or design for some evil beyond the common-law intent to do injury.... In view of the care that has been bestowed upon the subject, it is significant that we have not found, nor has our attention been directed to, any instance in which Congress has expressly eliminated the mental element from a crime taken over from the common law.

The section with which we are here concerned was enacted in 1948, as a consolidation of four former sections of Title 18.... We find no other purpose in the 1948 re-enactment than to collect from scattered sources crimes so kindred as to belong in one category. Not one of these had been interpreted to be a crime without intention and no purpose to differentiate between them in the matter of intent is disclosed. No inference that some were and some were not crimes of intention can be drawn from any difference in classification or punishment. [E]ach is, at its least, a misdemeanor, and if the amount involved is $100 or more each is a felony. If one crime without intent has been smuggled into a section whose dominant offenses do require intent, it was put in ill-fitting and compromising company. The government apparently did not believe that conversion stood so alone when it drew this one-count indictment to charge that Morissette "did unlawfully, wilfully and knowingly steal and convert to his own use."

Congress, by the language of this section, has been at pains to incriminate only "knowing" conversions. But, at common law, there are unwitting acts which constitute conversions. In the civil tort, except for recovery of exemplary damages, the defendant's knowledge, intent, motive, mistake, and good faith are generally irrelevant.[31] If one takes property

---

[31] The rationale underlying [this rule] is that when one clearly assumes the rights of ownership over property of another no proof of intent to convert is necessary. It has even been held that one may be held liable in conversion even though he reasonably supposed that he had a legal right to the property in question. [Such cases] leave no doubt that Morissette could be held liable for a civil conversion for his taking of the property here involved, and the instructions to the jury might have been appropriate in such a civil action. This assumes of course that actual abandonment was not proven, a matter which petitioner should be allowed to prove if he can.

which turns out to belong to another, his innocent intent will not shield him from making restitution or indemnity, for his well-meaning may not be allowed to deprive another of his own.

Had the statute applied to conversions without qualification, it would have made crimes of all unwitting, inadvertent and unintended conversions. Knowledge, of course, is not identical with intent and may not have been the most apt words of limitation. But knowing conversion requires more than knowledge that defendant was taking the property into his possession. He must have had knowledge of the facts, though not necessarily the law, that made the taking a conversion. In the case before us, whether the mental element that Congress required be spoken of as knowledge or as intent, would not seem to alter its bearing on guilt. For it is not apparent how Morissette could have knowingly or intentionally converted property that he did not know could be converted, as would be the case if it was in fact abandoned or if he truly believed it to be abandoned and unwanted property.

It is said, and at first blush the claim has plausibility, that, if we construe the statute to require a mental element as part of criminal conversion, it becomes a meaningless duplication of the offense of stealing, and that conversion can be given meaning only by interpreting it to disregard intention. But here again a broader view of the evolution of these crimes throws a different light on the legislation.

It is not surprising if there is considerable overlapping in the embezzlement, stealing, purloining and knowing conversion grouped in this statute. What has concerned codifiers of the larceny-type offense is that gaps or crevices have separated particular crimes of this general class and guilty men have escaped through the breaches. The books contain a surfeit of cases drawing fine distinctions between slightly different circumstances under which one may obtain wrongful advantages from another's property. The codifiers wanted to reach all such instances. Probably every stealing is a conversion, but certainly not every knowing conversion is a stealing. "To steal means to take away from one in lawful possession without right with the intention to keep wrongfully." Conversion, however, may be consummated without any intent to keep and without any wrongful taking, where the initial possession by the converter was entirely lawful. Conversion may include misuse or abuse of property. It may reach use in an unauthorized manner or to an unauthorized extent of property placed in one's custody for limited use. Money rightfully taken into one's custody may be converted without any intent to keep or embezzle it merely by commingling it with the custodian's own, if he was under a duty to keep it separate and intact. It is not difficult to think of intentional and knowing abuses and unauthorized uses of government property that might be knowing conversions but which could not be reached as embezzlement, stealing or purloining. Knowing conversion adds significantly to the range of protection of government property without interpreting it to punish unwitting conversions.

The purpose which we here attribute to Congress parallels that of codifiers of common law in England and in the states and demonstrates that the serious problem in drafting such a statute is to avoid gaps and loopholes between offenses. It is significant that the English and state codifiers have tried to cover the same type of conduct that we are suggesting as the purpose of Congress here, without, however, departing from the common-law tradition that these are crimes of intendment.

We find no grounds for inferring any affirmative instruction from Congress to eliminate intent from any offense with which this defendant was charged.

III.

As we read the record, this case was tried on the theory that even if criminal intent were essential its presence (a) should be decided by the court (b) as a presumption of law, apparently conclusive, (c) predicated upon the isolated act of taking rather than upon all of the circumstances. In each of these respects we believe the trial court was in error.

Where intent of the accused is an ingredient of the crime charged, its existence is a question of fact which must be submitted to the jury. State court authorities cited to the effect that intent is relevant in larcenous crimes are equally emphatic and uniform that it is a jury issue. The settled practice and its reason are well stated by Judge Andrews in People v. Flack, 125 N.Y. 324, 334, 26 N.E. 267, 270 (1891):

> It is alike the general rule of law and the dictate of natural justice that to constitute guilt there must be not only a wrongful act, but a criminal intention. Under our system (unless in exceptional cases), both must be found by the jury to justify a conviction for crime. However clear the proof may be, or however incontrovertible may seem to the judge to be the inference of a criminal intention, the question of intent can never be ruled as a question of law, but must always be submitted to the jury. Jurors may be perverse; the ends of justice may be defeated by unrighteous verdicts, but so long as the functions of the judge and jury are distinct, the one responding to the law, the other to the facts, neither can invade the province of the other without destroying the significance of trial by court and jury. . . .

It follows that the trial court may not withdraw or prejudge the issue by instruction that the law raises a presumption of intent from an act. It often is tempting to cast in terms of a "presumption" a conclusion which a court thinks probable from given facts. . . .

We think presumptive intent has no place in this case. A conclusive presumption which testimony could not overthrow would effectively eliminate intent as an ingredient of the offense. A presumption which would permit but not require the jury to assume intent from an isolated fact would prejudge a conclusion which the jury should reach of its own volition. A presumption which would permit the jury to make an assumption which all the evidence considered together does not logically establish would give to a proven fact an artificial and fictional effect. In either case, this presumption would conflict with the overriding presumption of innocence with which the law endows the accused and which extends to every element of the crime.

Moreover, the conclusion supplied by presumption in this instance was one of intent to steal the casings, and it was based on the mere fact that defendant took them. The court thought the only question was, "Did he intend to take the property?" That the removal of them was a conscious and intentional act was admitted. But that isolated fact is not an adequate basis on which the jury should find the criminal intent to steal or knowingly convert, that is, wrongfully to deprive another of possession of property. Whether that intent existed, the jury must determine, not only from the act of taking, but from that together with defendant's testimony and all of the surrounding circumstances.

Of course, the jury, considering Morissette's awareness that these casings were on government property, his failure to seek any permission for their removal and his self-interest as a witness, might have disbelieved his profession of innocent intent and concluded that his assertion of a belief that the casings were abandoned was an afterthought. Had the jury convicted on proper instructions it would be the end of the matter. But juries are not bound by what seems inescapable logic to judges. They might have concluded that the heaps of spent casings left in the hinterland to rust away presented an appearance of unwanted and abandoned junk, and that lack of any conscious deprivation of property or intentional injury was indicated by Morissette's good character, the openness of the taking, crushing and transporting of the casings, and the candor with which it was all admitted. They might have refused to brand Morissette as a thief. Had they done so, that too would have been the end of the matter.

Reversed.

■ MR. JUSTICE DOUGLAS concurs in the result.

■ MR. JUSTICE MINTON took no part in the consideration or decision of this case.

———

## NOTES ON PUBLIC WELFARE OFFENSES

**1. Introduction.** Justice Jackson set out to reconcile two lines of cases in his *Morissette* opinion. One, traditionally called "regulatory" or "public welfare" offenses, typically dispensed with the common law mens rea tradition by employing strict liability on a central element, and sometimes vicarious liability as well. Often, though not always, these were not offenses of high moral stigma, and generally they did not result in significant imprisonment. The other line of cases involved the traditional common law crimes that initially emerged from judicial development but increasingly, over the years, were statutory in origin. Typically they concerned offenses such as murder, rape, arson, burglary, robbery, larceny, embezzlement, extortion, bribery, blackmail, and additional serious offenses which carried high moral stigma and high penalties. The tradition here, reflecting the common law focus on personal responsibility and blame, was to require significant mens rea elements along lines previously studied in this Chapter. As Jackson framed the question in *Morissette*, his task was to ascertain which of the two lines of cases controlled the issue before the Court.

Jackson discussed three Supreme Court cases in the "public welfare" line of decisions. Each is described below.

**2.  *United States v. Behrman.*** United States v. Behrman, 258 U.S. 280 (1922), involved a federal statute which the Court summarized as follows:

> The statute ... makes it an offense to sell, barter, exchange, or give away any of the narcotic drugs named in the act except in pursuance of a written order of the person to whom such article is sold, bartered, exchanged, or given, on a form to be issued in blank for that purpose by the Commissioner of Internal Revenue. It is further provided that nothing in the section shall apply to the dispensing or distribution of any of the drugs to a patient of a registered physician in the course of his professional practice....

The indictment charged that Dr. Behrman was a physician who wrote three prescriptions to one Willie King for 150 grains of heroin, 360 grains of morphine, and 210 grains of cocaine. It further charged that King was known by Dr. Behrman to be an addict who used all three drugs, and that here was no medical reason, other than addiction, for which the drugs were prescribed. And it charged that once the drugs were in King's possession, what he did with them was up to him. The District Court dismissed the indictment, but the Supreme Court held that an offense was properly charged:

> The question is: Do the acts charged in this indictment constitute an offense within the meaning of the statute. As we have seen, the statute contains an exception to the effect that it shall not apply to the dispensing or distribution of such drugs to a patient by a registered physician in the course of his professional practice.... The rule applicable to such statutes is that it is enough to charge facts sufficient to show that the accused is not within the exception....
>
> Former decisions of this court have held that the purpose of the exception is to confine the distribution of these drugs to the regular and lawful course of professional practice, and that not everything called a prescription is necessarily such....
>
> It is enough to sustain an indictment that the offense be described with sufficient clearness to show a violation of law, and to enable the accused to know the nature and cause of the accusation and to plead the judgment, if one be rendered, in bar of

further prosecution for the same offense. If the offense be a statutory one, and intent or knowledge is not made an element of it, the indictment need not charge such knowledge or intent.

It may be admitted that to prescribe a single dose, or even a number of doses, may not bring a physician within the penalties of the act; but what is here charged is that the defendant physician by means of prescriptions has enabled one, known by him to be an addict, to obtain from a pharmacist the enormous number of doses contained in 150 grains of heroin, 360 grains of morphine, and 210 grains of cocaine. As shown by Wood's United States Dispensatory, a standard work in general use, the ordinary dose of morphine is one-fifth of a grain, of cocaine one-eighth to one-fourth of a grain, of heroin one-sixteenth to one-eighth of a grain. By these standards more than 3,000 ordinary doses were placed in the control of King. Undoubtedly doses may be varied to suit different cases as determined by the judgment of a physician. But the quantities named in the indictment are charged to have been intrusted to a person known by the physician to be an addict without restraint upon him in its administration or disposition by anything more than his own weakened and perverted will. Such so-called prescriptions could only result in the gratification of a diseased appetite for these pernicious drugs or result in an unlawful parting with them to others. . . .

We hold that the acts charged in the indictment constituted an offense within the terms and meaning of the act. The judgment of the District Court to the contrary should be reversed.

Joined by Justices McReynolds and Brandeis, Justice Holmes dissented:

. . . The defendant was a licensed physician and his part in the sale was the giving of prescriptions for the drugs. In view of . . . the absence of any charge to the contrary it must be assumed that he gave them in the regular course of his practice and in good faith. Whatever ground for skepticism we may find in the facts we are bound to accept the position knowingly and deliberately taken by the pleader and evidently accepted by the Court below.

It seems to me impossible to construe the statute as tacitly making such acts, however foolish, crimes, by saying that what is in form a prescription and is given honestly in the course of a doctor's practice, and therefore, so far as the words of the statute go, is allowed in terms, is not within the words, is not a prescription and is not given in the course of practice, if the Court deems the doctor's faith in his patient manifestly unwarranted. It seems to me wrong to construe the statute as creating a crime in this way without a word of warning.

**3. The Historical Context of *Behrman*.** Full understanding of *Behrman* requires additional information about its historical context. When the statute under which Dr. Berhman was prosecuted (The Harrison

Narcotics Act) was enacted in 1914, a large number of people addicted to drugs (opiates and cocaine) were being treated by physicians who dispensed the drugs to help addicts avoid withdrawal and satisfy their craving—so-called maintenance treatment.[a] Soon after the Harrison Act was passed, a controversy arose within the medical profession regarding the medical acceptability of maintenance treatment, although a substantial body of medical opinion supported the practice. Notwithstanding the difference of opinion among physicians, federal enforcement authorities sought to bring maintenance treatment to an end through a campaign of intimidation and prosecution against physicians who provided such maintenance. The agency also shut down in several major cities so-called "maintenance clinics" that had been created to treat addicted patients who had no access to private physicians.[b]

Although the government's anti-maintenance position was challenged in court, it was eventually upheld. Whether maintenance treatment was within the scope of medical practice within the meaning of the Act was initially addressed by the Supreme Court in Webb v. United States, 249 U.S. 96 (1919). In that case, a retail druggist and a practicing physician had been indicted for conspiracy to violate the Act by providing maintenance supplies to an addict with no intention to cure but rather "for the sake of continuing his accustomed use." In a 5–4 decision, the Court upheld the sufficiency of the indictment, saying that calling "such an order a physician's prescription would be so plain a perversion of meaning that no discussion of the subject is required."

Three years after *Berhman* was decided, another case reached the Supreme Court testing the reach of *Webb* and *Berhman*. In Linder v. United States, 268 U.S. 5 (1925), Linder was a Spokane physician who dispensed three tablets of cocaine and one tablet of morphine to a narcotics agency informant. He said the informant told him that she had severe abdominal pains such as might be symptomatic of an ulcer or cancer, while the government claimed that the physician knew the informant was an addict and needed the drugs to avoid withdrawal. A unanimous Supreme Court reversed Linder's conviction:

> [*Berhman*] cannot be accepted as authority for holding that a physician who acts bona fide and according to fair medical standards may never give an addict moderate amounts of drugs for self-administration in order to relieve conditions incident to addiction. Enforcement [of the Act] demands no such drastic rule....[c]

[a] It is also noteworthy that a significant proportion of people addicted to these drugs at this time had actually become addicted "accidentally" though over-prescribing by physicians who were unaware of the addictive properties of the drugs.

[b] For extensive discussion on the history of narcotic drug control in the United States, see David Musto, The American Disease (3d ed. 1999).

[c] The Harrison Act has since been repealed, and replaced by a complex series of federal laws regulating prescription and use of psychoactive drugs. The history recited above is offered for whatever light it sheds on the meaning of *Berhman* as a decision. It has no relevance to the meaning of modern laws on this or similar topics.

**4.  *United States v. Balint.*** United States v. Balint, 258 U.S. 250 (1922), involved the same statute as *Behrman* and was decided on the same day. It concerned a prosecution for selling a derivative of opium without using a written order on a form supplied by federal taxing authorities. Again, the indictment had been dismissed by the District Court. This time the Court was unanimous, one Justice not participating:

> The defendants demurred to the indictment on the ground that it failed to charge that they had sold the inhibited drugs knowing them to be such. The statute does not make such knowledge an element of the offense. The District Court sustained the demurrer and quashed the indictment. The correctness of this ruling is the question before us.
>
> While the general rule at common law was that the scienter was a necessary element in the indictment and proof of every crime, and this was followed in regard to statutory crimes even where the statutory definition did not in terms include it, there has been a modification of this view in respect to prosecutions under statutes the purpose of which would be obstructed by such a requirement. It is a question of legislative intent to be construed by the court. It has been objected that punishment of a person for an act in violation of law when ignorant of the facts making it so, is an absence of due process of law. But that objection is considered and overruled in Shevlin–Carpenter Co. v. Minnesota, 218 U.S. 57, 69, 70 (1910),[a] in which it was held that in the prohibition or punishment of particular acts, the state may in the maintenance of a public policy provide "that he who shall do them shall do them at his peril and will not be heard to plead in defense good faith or ignorance." Many instances of this are to be found in regulatory measures in the exercise of what is called the police power where the emphasis of the statute is evidently upon achievement of some social betterment rather than the punishment of the crimes as in cases of mala in se. So, too, in the collection of taxes, the importance to the public of their collection leads the Legislature to impose on the taxpayer the burden of finding out the facts upon which his liability to pay depends and meeting it at the peril of punishment. Again where one deals with others and his mere negligence may be dangerous to them, as in selling diseased food or poison, the policy of the law may, in order to stimulate proper care, require the punishment of the negligent person though he be ignorant of the noxious character of what he sells.
>
> The question before us, therefore, is one of the construction of the statute and of inference of the intent of Congress. The Narcotic Act has been held by this court to be a taxing act with the incidental purpose of minimizing the spread of addiction to the use

of poisonous and demoralizing drugs.... It is very evident from a reading of it that the emphasis of the section is in securing a close supervision of the business of dealing in these dangerous drugs by the taxing officers of the Government and that it merely uses a criminal penalty to secure recorded evidence of the disposition of such drugs as a means of taxing and restraining the traffic. Its manifest purpose is to require every person dealing in drugs to ascertain at his peril whether that which he sells comes within the inhibition of the statute, and if he sells the inhibited drug in ignorance of its character, to penalize him. Congress weighed the possible injustice of subjecting an innocent seller to a penalty against the evil of exposing innocent purchasers to danger from the drug, and concluded that the latter was the result preferably to be avoided. Doubtless considerations as to the opportunity of the seller to find out the fact and the difficulty of proof of knowledge contributed to this conclusion. We think the demurrer to the indictment should have been overruled.

Conviction for the offense involved in *Behrman* and *Balint* carried a maximum prison sentence of five years.

**5.  *United States v. Dotterweich.*** Dotterweich was president and general manager of a company that purchased drugs from a manufacturer, repackaged them, and shipped them under a new label. He was convicted of a misdemeanor for company shipments of adulterated and misbranded drugs in interstate commerce. He had no personal involvement in the shipments on which the prosecution was based. He was sentenced to pay a fine and to 60 days on probation. In United States v. Dotterweich, 320 U.S. 277 (1943), the Supreme Court upheld his conviction. For the Court, Justice Frankfurter wrote:

The Food and Drugs Act of 1906 was an exertion by Congress of its power to keep impure and adulterated food and drugs out of the channels of commerce. By the Act of 1938, Congress extended the range of its control over illicit and noxious articles and stiffened the penalties for disobedience. The purposes of this legislation thus touch phases of the lives and health of people which, in the circumstances of modern industrialism, are largely beyond self-protection. Regard for these purposes should infuse construction of the legislation if it is to be treated as a working instrument of government and not merely as a collection of English words. The prosecution to which Dotterweich was subjected is based on a now familiar type of legislation whereby penalties serve as effective means of regulation. Such legislation dispenses with the conventional requirement for criminal conduct—awareness of some wrongdoing. In the interest of the larger good it puts the burden of acting at hazard upon a person otherwise innocent but standing in responsible relation to a public danger. United States v. Balint, 258 U.S. 250 (1922)....

Whether an accused shares responsibility in the business process resulting in unlawful distribution depends on the evidence produced at the trial and its submission—assuming the evidence warrants it—to the jury under appropriate guidance. The offense is committed, unless the enterprise which they are serving enjoys the immunity of a guaranty, by all who do have such a responsible share in the furtherance of the transaction which the statute outlaws, namely, to put into the stream of interstate commerce adulterated or misbranded drugs. Hardship there doubtless may be under a statute which thus penalizes the transaction though consciousness of wrongdoing be totally wanting. Balancing relative hardships, Congress has preferred to place it upon those who have at least the opportunity of informing themselves of the existence of conditions imposed for the protection of consumers before sharing in illicit commerce, rather than to throw the hazard on the innocent public who are wholly helpless.

It would be too treacherous to define or even to indicate by way of illustration the class of employees which stands in such a responsible relation. To attempt a formula embracing the variety of conduct whereby persons may responsibly contribute in furthering a transaction forbidden by an Act of Congress, to wit, to send illicit goods across state lines, would be mischievous futility. In such matters the good sense of prosecutors, the wise guidance of trial judges, and the ultimate judgment of juries must be trusted. Our system of criminal justice necessarily depends on "conscience and circumspection in prosecuting officers," Nash v. United States, 229 U.S. 373, 378 (1913), even when the consequences are far more drastic than they are under the provision of law before us. See *United States v. Balint*, supra (involving a maximum sentence of five years). For present purpose it suffices to say that in what the defense characterized as "a very fair charge" the District Court properly left the question of the responsibility of Dotterweich for the shipment to the jury, and there was sufficient evidence to support its verdict.

**6. Questions and Comments.** Rather plainly, *Dotterweich* is an example of a public welfare offense in the classic sense. Dotterweich was convicted even though he did not personally participate in the transactions on which the prosecution was based. His liability was both strict and vicarious. His conviction was for a misdemeanor, and his penalty was minor.

*Behrman* and *Balint* are a different story. In those cases, indictments were upheld for offenses that carried potential five-year maximum prison sentences. Consider both cases from two perspectives.

First, if exceptions from normal common law mens rea requirements are to be made in prosecutions such as these, was it appropriate to hold that this should be so because the statutes fit the mold of the "public welfare" offense as described by Justice Jackson in *Morissette*? Do they satisfy the criteria identified by Jackson for public welfare offenses? If not, why did Jackson decline the opportunity to disavow them?

Second, do the two cases in fact involve exceptions from the common law mens rea tradition? In particular, what mistake does it appear that Balint may be seeking to raise as a defense? Would the common law ordinarily permit such a defense? Same questions for *Behrman*. Do they both fit within the traditional mens rea structure applicable to common law crimes? If so, why did the Court invoke the public welfare analogy, and more particularly, why did Jackson treat them as public welfare cases in *Morissette*?

Quite apart from how *Balint* and *Behrman* should be regarded, there is no doubt, as Jackson recounts in *Morissette*, that there is a long tradition— beginning in the mid 1800s—of using the criminal law to prosecute offenses under a different set of assumptions than is normally associated with ordinary criminal cases. The next note provides a modern example.

**7.  *United States v. Park*.** Park was the chief executive officer of Acme Markets, a national retain food chain with 874 retail outlets, 16 warehouses, and 36,000 employees. He was charged with five violations of the Federal Food, Drug, and Cosmetic Act based on shipments of food that had been exposed to contamination by rodents in an Acme warehouse. The company had been repeatedly warned that FDA inspections had discovered evidence of rodent infestation and other insanitary conditions in specified Acme warehouses. A subsequent inspection of one of the warehouses found that "there was still evidence of rodent activity in the building and in the warehouses and . . . some rodent-contaminated lots of food items."

Park maintained in his defense that he had been assured that appropriate company officials responsible for sanitation were dealing with the problems and that he did not "believe there was anything [he] could have done more constructively than what [he] found was being done." On cross examination he admitted that "providing sanitary conditions for food offered for sale to the public was something that he was 'responsible for in the entire operation of the company.' " He also admitted that the repeat offenses "indicated the system for handling sanitation 'wasn't working perfectly' and that as Acme's chief executive officer he was responsible for 'any result which occurs in our company.' " Park was convicted and sentenced to pay a fine of $50 for each of the five offenses.[b] In United States v. Park, 421 U.S. 658 (1975), the Supreme Court affirmed.

Chief Justice Burger wrote the opinion for the Court. He said:

> The rule that corporate employees who have "a responsible share in the furtherance of the transaction which the statute outlaws" are subject to the criminal provisions of the Act was not formulated in a vacuum. Cf. Morissette v. United States, 342 U.S. 246, 258 (1952). Cases under the Federal Food and Drugs Act of

---

[b] The maximum penalty for a first violation of the statute under which Park was convicted was one year and/or a fine of not more than $1,000. A second or subsequent offense carried a maximum of three years and/or a fine of $10,000.

1906 reflected the view both that knowledge or intent were not required to be proved in prosecutions under its criminal provisions, and that responsible corporate agents could be subjected to the liability thereby imposed. Moreover, the principle had been recognized that a corporate agent, through whose act, default, or omission the corporation committed a crime, was himself guilty individually of that crime. The principle had been applied whether or not the crime required "consciousness of wrongdoing," and it had been applied not only to those corporate agents who themselves committed the criminal act, but also to those who by virtue of their managerial positions or other similar relation to the actor could be deemed responsible for its commission.

In the latter class of cases, the liability of managerial officers did not depend on their knowledge of, or personal participation in, the act made criminal by the statute. Rather, where the statute under which they were prosecuted dispensed with "consciousness of wrongdoing," an omission or failure to act was deemed a sufficient basis for a responsible corporate agent's liability. It was enough in such cases that, by virtue of the relationship he bore to the corporation, the agent had the power to prevent the act complained of.

The rationale of the interpretation given the Act in *Dotterweich*, as holding criminally accountable the persons whose failure to exercise the authority and supervisory responsibility reposed in them by the business organization resulted in the violation complained of, has been confirmed in our subsequent cases. Thus, the Court has reaffirmed the proposition that "the public interest in the purity of its food is so great as to warrant the imposition of the highest standard of care on distributors." Smith v. California, 361 U.S. 147, 152 (1959). In order to make "distributors of food the strictest censors of their merchandise," ibid., the Act punishes "neglect where the law requires care, or inaction where it imposes a duty." *Morissette v. United States*, supra, at 255. "The accused, if he does not will the violation, usually is in a position to prevent it with no more care than society might reasonably expect and no more exertion than it might reasonably exact from one who assumed his responsibilities." Id., at 256. Similarly, in cases decided after *Dotterweich*, the Courts of Appeals have recognized that those corporate agents vested with the responsibility, and power commensurate with that responsibility, to devise whatever measures are necessary to ensure compliance with the Act bear a "responsible relationship" to, or have a "responsible share" in, violations.

Thus *Dotterweich* and the cases which have followed reveal that in providing sanctions which reach and touch the individuals who execute the corporate mission—and this is by no means necessarily confined to a single corporate agent or employee—the

Act imposes not only a positive duty to seek out and remedy violations when they occur but also, and primarily, a duty to implement measures that will insure that violations will not occur. The requirements of foresight and vigilance imposed on responsible corporate agents are beyond question demanding, and perhaps onerous, but they are no more stringent than the public has a right to expect of those who voluntarily assume positions of authority in business enterprises whose services and products affect the health and well-being of the public that supports them.

The Act does not, as we observed in *Dotterweich*, make criminal liability turn on "awareness of some wrongdoing" or "conscious fraud." The duty imposed by Congress on responsible corporate agents is, we emphasize, one that requires the highest standard of foresight and vigilance, but the Act, in its criminal aspect, does not require that which is objectively impossible. The theory upon which responsible corporate agents are held criminally accountable for "causing" violations of the Act permits a claim that a defendant was "powerless" to prevent or correct the violation to "be raised defensively at a trial on the merits." United States v. Wiesenfeld Warehouse Co., 376 U.S. 86, 91 (1964). If such a claim is made, the defendant has the burden of coming forward with evidence, but this does not alter the Government's ultimate burden of proving beyond a reasonable doubt the defendant's guilt, including his power, in light of the duty imposed by the Act, to prevent or correct the prohibited condition. Congress has seen fit to enforce the accountability of responsible corporate agents dealing with products which may affect the health of consumers by penal sanctions cast in rigorous terms, and the obligation of the courts is to give them effect so long as they do not violate the Constitution.

**8. Questions and Comments on *Park*.** Liability for Park, as it was for Dotterwiech, was both vicarious and strict. Park did not personally participate in the violations, nor was he aware of them when they occurred. What he did was fail to prevent them after warnings that they had occurred in the past. The Court gave him a potential defense, to be sure, if he could offer evidence that he was "powerless" to prevent or correct the violation, something the CEO of a company would be loathe to admit and that Park himself was not prepared to take advantage of.

Is this an appropriate use of the "public welfare" concept? How important were the prior warnings? Prior warnings were not required by the statute under which Park was prosecuted. Suppose there had been no warnings and that Park had been prosecuted after problems were revealed by the first inspection. Would the conviction then have been appropriate? If not, should the Court have upheld the conviction on the record as presented?

––––––––

NOTES ON *MORISSETTE*

**1. Background on the Law of Theft.** The common-law crime of larceny required a trespassory taking of the personal property of another with intent to appropriate. The taking was said to be "trespassory" when the initial acquisition of the property violated rights of possession. For this reason, larceny was often said to be an offense against possession.

It is plain, however, that theft can occur in contexts where the actor does not "trespass" on the possessory rights of others to obtain the property. Bank tellers, servants, and agents, for example, lawfully possess property that belongs to others; for many purposes they are lawful custodians of other people's property. They are not, however, entitled to treat such property as their own. When they deprive owners of their property, such persons should be as guilty of theft as the person who acquires the property without permission.

The Anglo–American legal system reached this conclusion only very slowly. The earliest forms of larceny were concerned with misappropriations by violence or stealth. Over the years, and often through legal fictions, the concept of trespassory taking was expanded to encompass a variety of means by which one can misappropriate property of another. For example, "larceny by trick" covered cases where a "constructive" trespass was said to have occurred if the property was obtained under specified fraudulent circumstances. Generally speaking, "larceny by trick" occurred when the actor had the intent to steal property at the time its temporary use was lawfully obtained from the owner. Thus, for example, one who intended to steal a car at the time it was rented would be guilty of larceny by trick. On the other hand, if one rented a car and decided to steal it after the rental agreement was consummated, the law's ability to perceive a fictional trespass would have been exceeded, and no larceny would have occurred. Indeed, for a substantial period of common-law history, no crime at all would have been committed if property had been obtained under such circumstances.

The most important effort to close this gap was begun in England in 1799 by the enactment of the statutory offense of embezzlement. Originally, embezzlement was designed to deal with situations where a master's property was received from a third person by a servant who proceeded to steal it. Subsequently the offense was expanded by additional statutes, both in this country and in England, to cover most variations of the situation where a lawful custodian misappropriates custodial property. In separate developments, offenses also emerged to deal with obtaining property by false pretenses, extortion, and the like.[a]

The technical distinctions among these various theft offenses were extremely complicated. Moreover, the procedures of the early common law

---

[a] For a more detailed review of the history of larceny, embezzlement, and related offenses, see Jerome Hall, Theft, Law and Society (2d ed. 1952); Wayne LaFave & Austin Scott, Criminal Law 618–712 (1972); Rollin Perkins & Ronald Boyce, Criminal Law 292–452 (3d ed. 1982).

were such that it mattered a great deal that the prosecutor charged the right offense at the outset of the case. If the prosecutor charged larceny by trick, the defendant could defend successfully on the ground that what really happened was embezzlement. The defendant might then be charged with embezzlement, but could defend the second charge on the ground that the crime really was larceny by trick.[b]

Statutes such as the one in *Morissette* were enacted to avoid such technicalities and to make sure, as the Court says, that gaps between the various theft offenses were filled. More comprehensive consolidation of theft offenses was suggested by the Model Penal Code, and most modern statutes have followed its approach. The provisions of article 223 of the Model Code consolidate the law of theft into a single, comprehensive offense.[c] The principal thrust of these provisions is to eliminate technical distinctions between separately defined crimes that turn on how the property was acquired. As can be seen from the detail of article 223, however, this approach does not eliminate the need to draft limitations, many of which could be found in the common law, designed to describe the appropriate reach of each aspect of the crime of theft.

**2. Questions and Comments.** There was no doubt on the facts that Morissette meant permanently to appropriate to himself the value of the bomb casings. He sold them and pocketed the money. Assume, however, a different scenario. Suppose he spotted an Army truck on the property, used it to take the casings home, and then returned it. Or suppose he was a government employee who, in violation of office policy, took an office computer home for the weekend and brought it back on Monday. Would he be guilty of "knowing conversion" of the truck or the computer in these situations? Is the Court reading Congress as having significantly extended the crime of theft? If so, is the extension justified?

Jackson said at one point in his opinion that "Congressional silence as to mental elements in an act merely adopting into federal statutory law a concept of crime already so well defined in common law and statutory interpretation by the states may warrant quite contrary inferences than the same silence in creating an offense new to general law, for whose definition the courts have no guidance except the act." Does this mean that different mens rea principles ought to apply to offenses that are not derived

---

[b] The example may sound fanciful but, as reported in Jerome Michael & Herbert Wechsler, Criminal Law and Its Administration 545 (1940), the "books are replete with dismissals and reversals on the ground that the indictment or the conviction was for the wrong crime." They cite Commonwealth v. O'Malley, 97 Mass. 584 (1867), as an illustration. In that case the defendant was acquitted of larceny and later convicted of embezzlement. The conviction was then set aside on the ground that the evidence proved larceny.

[c] For a general discussion of the purpose of consolidation and some of the problems of implementation, see ALI, Model Penal Code and Commentaries § 223.1, pp. 127–38 (1980). At least 30 states have adopted consolidated theft provisions since the promulgation of the Model Penal Code in 1962. The Model Code was not the first effort at consolidation, though it has been by far the most influential. An earlier treatment of the consolidation issue can be found in Jerome Michael & Herbert Wechsler, Criminal Law and Its Administration 545–52 (1940).

from common law antecedents but are "new to general law"? Consider the next case and its notes in connection with this question.

---

## United States v. Freed

Supreme Court of the United States, 1971.
401 U.S. 601.

■ MR. JUSTICE DOUGLAS delivered the opinion of the Court.

[The defendants were indicted for possession of unregistered hand grenades in violation of a federal statute that carried a 10–year maximum sentence. The district court dismissed the indictments on the ground, inter alia, that due process was violated by the failure to allege mens rea. The government appealed.]

We . . . conclude that the district court erred in dismissing the indictment for absence of an allegation of scienter.

The act requires no specific intent or knowledge that the hand grenades were unregistered. It makes it unlawful for any person "to receive or possess a firearm which is not registered to him." . . .

The presence of a "vicious will" or mens rea was long a requirement of criminal responsibility. But the list of exceptions grew, especially in the expanding regulatory area involving activities affecting public health, safety, and welfare. The statutory offense of embezzlement, borrowed from the common law where scienter was historically required, was in a different category:

> [W]here Congress borrows terms of art in which are accumulated the legal tradition and meaning of centuries of practice, it presumably knows and adopts the cluster of ideas that were attached to each borrowed word in the body of learning from which it was taken and the meaning its use will convey to the judicial mind unless otherwise instructed.

Morissette v. United States, 342 U.S. 246, 263 (1952).

At the other extreme is Lambert v. California, 355 U.S. 225 (1957), in which a municipal code made it a crime to remain in Los Angeles for more than five days without registering if a person had been convicted of a felony. Being in Los Angeles is not per se blameworthy. The mere failure to register, we held, was quite "unlike the commission of acts, or the failure to act under circumstances that should alert the doer to the consequences of his deed." The fact that the ordinance was a convenient law enforcement technique did not save it:

> Where a person did not know of the duty to register and where there was no proof of the probability of such knowledge, he may not be convicted consistently with due process. Were it otherwise, the evil would be as great as it is when the law is

written in print too fine to read or in a language foreign to the community.

In United States v. Dotterweich, 320 U.S. 277 (1943), a case dealing with the imposition of a penalty on a corporate officer whose firm shipped adulterated and misbranded drugs in violation of the Food and Drug Act, we approved the penalty "though consciousness of wrongdoing be totally wanting."

The present case is in the category neither of *Lambert* nor *Morissette*, but is closer to *Dotterweich*. This is a regulatory measure in the interest of the public safety, which may well be premised on the theory that one would hardly be surprised to learn that possession of hand grenades is not an innocent act. They are highly dangerous offensive weapons, no less dangerous than the narcotics involved in United States v. Balint, 258 U.S. 250 (1922), where a defendant was convicted of sale of narcotics against his claim that he did not know the drugs were covered by a federal act. We say with Chief Justice Taft in that case:

> It is very evident from a reading of it that the emphasis of the section is in securing a close supervision of the business of dealing in these dangerous drugs by the taxing officers of the government and that it merely uses a criminal penalty to secure recorded evidence of the disposition of such drugs as a means of taxing and restraining the traffic. Its manifest purpose is to require every person dealing in drugs to ascertain at his peril whether that which he sells comes within the inhibition of the statute, and if he sells the inhibited drug in ignorance of its character, to penalize him. Congress weighed the possible injustice of subjecting an innocent seller to a penalty against the evil of exposing innocent purchasers to danger from the drug, and concluded that the latter was the result preferably to be avoided.

Reversed.

■ MR. JUSTICE BRENNAN, concurring in the judgment of reversal.

[A]lthough I reach the same result as the Court on the intent the government must prove to convict, I do so by another route....

The Court's discussion of the intent the government must prove ... does not dispel the confusion surrounding a difficult, but vitally important, area of the law. This case does not raise questions of "consciousness of wrongdoing" or "blameworthiness." If the ancient maxim that "ignorance of the law is no excuse" has any residual validity, it indicates that the ordinary intent requirement—mens rea—of the criminal law does not require knowledge that an act is illegal, wrong, or blameworthy. Nor is it possible to decide this case by a simple process of classifying the statute involved as a "regulatory" or a "public welfare" measure. To convict appellees of possession of unregistered hand grenades, the government must prove three material elements: (i) that appellees possessed certain items; (ii) that the items possessed were hand grenades; and (iii) that the hand grenades were not registered. The government and the Court agree that the prosecutor must prove knowing possession of the items and also knowledge that the items possessed were hand grenades. Thus, while the Court does hold that no intent at all need be proved in regard to one element of the offense—the unregistered status of the grenades—knowledge must still be proved as to the other two elements. Consequently, the National Firearms Act does not create a crime of strict liability as to all its elements. It is no help in deciding what level of intent must be proved as to the third element to declare that the offense falls within the "regulatory" category.

Following the analysis of the Model Penal Code, I think we must recognize, first, that "[t]he existence of a mens rea is the rule of, rather than the exception to, the principles of Anglo–American criminal jurisprudence;" second, that mens rea is not a unitary concept, but may vary as to each element of a crime; and third, that Anglo–American law has developed several identifiable and analytically distinct levels of intent, e.g., negligence, recklessness, knowledge, and purpose. To determine the mental element required for conviction, each material element of the offense must be examined and the determination made what level of intent Congress intended the government to prove, taking into account constitutional considerations, ... as well as the common-law background, if any, of the crime involved. See Morissette v. United States, 342 U.S. 246 (1952).

Although the legislative history of the amendments to the National Firearms Act is silent on the level of intent to be proved in connection with each element of the offense, we are not without some guideposts. I begin with the proposition stated in *Morissette* that the requirement of mens rea "is no provincial or transient notion. It is as universal and persistent in mature systems of law as belief in freedom of the human will and a consequent ability and duty of the normal individual to choose between good and evil." In regard to the first two elements of the offense, (i) possession of items that (ii) are hand grenades, the general rule in favor of some intent requirement finds confirmation in the case law.... [W]e may therefore properly infer that Congress meant that the government must prove knowledge with regard to the first two elements of the offense under the amended statute.

The third element—the unregistered status of the grenades—presents more difficulty. Proof of intent with regard to this element would require the government to show that the appellees knew that the grenades were unregistered or negligently or recklessly failed to ascertain whether the weapons were registered. It is true that such a requirement would involve knowledge of law, but it does *not* involve "consciousness of wrongdoing" in the sense of knowledge that one's actions were prohibited or illegal. Rather, the definition of the crime, as written by Congress, requires proof of circumstances that involve a legal element, namely whether the grenades were registered in accordance with federal law. The knowledge involved is solely knowledge of the circumstances that the law has defined as material to the offense....

Therefore, as with the first two elements, the question is solely one of congressional intent. And while the question is not an easy one, two factors persuade me that proof of mens rea as to the unregistered status of the grenades is not required. First, ... the case law under the provisions replaced by the current law dispensed with proof of intent in connection with this element. Second, the firearms covered by the act are major weapons such as machine guns and sawed-off shotguns; deceptive weapons such as flashlight guns and fountain-pen guns; and major destructive devices such as bombs, grenades, mines, rockets, and large caliber weapons including mortars, anti-tank guns, and bazookas. Without exception, the likelihood of governmental regulation of the distribution of such weapons is so great that anyone must be presumed to be aware of it. In the context of a ... registration scheme, I therefore think it reasonable to conclude that Congress dispensed with the requirement of intent in regard to the unregistered status of the weapon, as necessary to effective administration of the statute.

---

## NOTES ON ESTABLISHING THE APPROPRIATE MENS REA STANDARD

**1.** ***Staples v. United States.*** Staples v. United States, 511 U.S. 600 (1994), involved the failure to register a machine gun under the same statute that was at issue in *Freed*. The Court held that the defendant had to know of the characteristics of the weapon he possessed that required its classification as a machine gun, namely that it was capable of being fired repeatedly with a single pull of the trigger.

For the Court, Justice Thomas began his reasoning as follows:

> Whether or not § 5861(d) requires proof that a defendant knew of the characteristics of his weapon that made it a "firearm" under the Act is a question of statutory construction.... The language of the statute, the starting place in our inquiry, provides little explicit guidance in this case. Section 5861(d) is silent concerning the mens rea required for a violation. It states simply that "[i]t shall be unlawful for any person ... to receive or possess a firearm which is not registered to him in the National Firearms Registration and Transfer Record." 26 U.S.C. § 5861(d). Nevertheless, silence on this point by itself does not necessarily suggest that Congress intended to dispense with a conventional mens rea element, which would require that the defendant know the facts that make his conduct illegal.... On the contrary, we must construe the statute in light of the background rules of the common law, in which the requirement of some mens rea for a crime is firmly embedded.... See ... Morissette v. United States, 342 U.S. 246, 250 (1952).... Relying on the strength of the traditional rule, we have stated that offenses that require no mens rea generally are disfavored, and have suggested that some indica-

tion of congressional intent, express or implied, is required to dispense with mens rea as an element of a crime.

As to the relevance of *Freed*, Thomas added:

> *Freed* did not address the issue presented here. In *Freed*, we decided only that § 5861(d) does not require proof of knowledge that a firearm is *unregistered*. The question presented by a defendant who possesses a weapon that is a "firearm" for purposes of the Act, but who knows only that he has a "firearm" in the general sense of the term, was not raised or considered. And our determination that a defendant need not know that his weapon is unregistered suggests no conclusion concerning whether § 5861(d) requires the defendant to know of the features that make his weapon a statutory "firearm"; different elements of the same offense can require different mental states. Moreover, our analysis in *Freed* likening the Act to the public welfare statute in *Balint* rested entirely on the assumption that the defendant knew that he was dealing with hand grenades—that is, that he knew he possessed a particularly dangerous type of weapon (one within the statutory definition of a "firearm"), possession of which was not entirely "innocent" in and of itself. The predicate for that analysis is eliminated when, as in this case, the very question to be decided is *whether* the defendant must know of the particular characteristics that make his weapon a statutory firearm....
>
> [D]espite their potential for harm, guns generally can be owned in perfect innocence. Of course, we might surely classify certain categories of guns—no doubt including the machineguns, sawed-off shotguns, and artillery pieces that Congress has subjected to regulation—as items the ownership of which would have the same quasi-suspect character we attributed to owning hand grenades in *Freed*. But precisely because guns falling outside those categories traditionally have been widely accepted as lawful possessions, their destructive potential ... cannot be said to put gun owners sufficiently on notice of the likelihood of regulation to justify interpreting § 5861(d) as not requiring proof of knowledge of a weapon's characteristics.

Justice Thomas also made the following general comments about the category of public welfare offenses:

> The potentially harsh penalty attached to violation of [the registration statute]—up to 10 years' imprisonment—confirms our reading of the act. Historically, the penalty imposed under a statute has been a significant consideration in determining whether the statute should be construed as dispensing with mens rea. Certainly, the cases that first defined the concept of the public welfare offense almost uniformly involved statutes that provided for only light penalties such as fines or short jail sentences, not imprisonment in the state penitentiary.

As commentators have pointed out, the small penalties attached to such offenses logically complemented the absence of a mens rea requirement: in a system that generally requires a "vicious will" to establish a crime, 4 William Blackstone, Commentaries *21, imposing severe punishments for offenses that require no mens rea would seem incongruous. See Francis Bowes Sayre, Public Welfare Offenses, 33 Colum.L.Rev. 55, 70 (1933). Indeed, some courts justified the absence of mens rea in part on the basis that the offenses did not bear the same punishments as "infamous crimes," Tenement House Dept. v. McDevitt, 215 N.Y. 160, 168, 109 N.E. 88, 90 (1915) (Cardozo, J.), and questioned whether imprisonment was compatible with the reduced culpability required for such regulatory offenses. See, e.g., People ex rel. Price v. Sheffield Farms–Slawson–Decker Co., 225 N.Y. 25, 32–33, 121 N.E. 474, 477 (1918) (Cardozo, J.). Similarly, commentators collecting the early cases have argued that offenses punishable by imprisonment cannot be understood to be public welfare offenses, but must require mens rea. See Rollin Perkins, Criminal Law 793–98 (2d ed. 1969) (suggesting that the penalty should be the starting point in determining whether a statute describes a public welfare offense); Sayre, supra, at 72 ("Crimes punishable with prison sentences ... ordinarily require proof of a guilty intent").

In rehearsing the characteristics of the public welfare offense, we, too, have included in our consideration the punishments imposed and have noted that "penalties commonly are relatively small, and conviction does no grave damage to an offender's reputation." Morissette v. United States, 342 U.S. 246, 256 (1952)....

Our characterization of the public welfare offense in *Morissette* hardly seems apt, however, for a crime that is a felony, as is violation of [this statute.] After all, "felony" is, as we noted in distinguishing certain common law crimes from public welfare offenses, " 'as bad a word as you can give to man or thing.' " *Morissette*, supra, at 260. Close adherence to the early cases described above might suggest that punishing a violation as a felony is simply incompatible with the theory of the public welfare offense. In this view, absent a clear statement from Congress that mens rea is not required, we should not apply the public welfare offense rationale to interpret any statute defining a felony offense as dispensing with mens rea....

The Court declined, however, to "adopt such a definitive rule of construction to decide this case...." It held instead that "a severe penalty is a further factor tending to suggest that Congress did not intend to eliminate a mens rea requirement" in the case before the Court. Therefore, "the usual presumption that a defendant must know the facts that make his conduct illegal should apply."

**2.   Questions and Comments on *Freed*.** Strict liability promotes preventive goals at the expense of culpability limitations on the criminal law. Another way of putting the argument in favor of the *Freed* result is that it is appropriate to use strict liability where the potential social harm is very great and where it can at least be said that the known context gives adequate notice that the behavior is clearly wrong. Is this a persuasive rationale for the imposition of strict liability? Was the result in *Freed* correct? Of what relevance is *Lambert v. California* in this situation?[a]

A similar strain of reasoning can be found even in public welfare offenses. Consider the following comments by Justice Thomas in *Staples*:

> [P]ublic welfare offenses have been created by Congress, and recognized by this Court, in "limited circumstances." United States v. United States Gypsum, 438 U.S. 422, 437 (1978). Typically, our cases recognizing such offenses involve statutes that regulate potentially harmful or injurious items. Cf. United States v. International Minerals & Chemical Corp., 402 U.S. 558, 564–65 (1971) (characterizing [such] cases as involving statutes regulating "dangerous or deleterious devices or products or obnoxious waste materials"). In such situations, we have reasoned that as long as a defendant knows that he is dealing with a dangerous device of a character that places him "in responsible relation to a public danger," United States v. Dotterweich, 320 U.S. 277, 281 (1943), he should be alerted to the probability of strict regulation, and we have assumed that in such cases Congress intended to place the burden on the defendant to "ascertain at his peril whether [his conduct] comes within the inhibition of the statute." United States v. Balint, 258 U.S. 250, 254 (1922). Thus, we essentially have relied on the nature of the statute and the particular character of the items regulated to determine whether congressional silence concerning the mental element of the offense should be interpreted as dispensing with conventional mens rea requirements.[3]

**3.   *United States v. Yermian*.** Contrast United States v. Yermian, 468 U.S. 63 (1984), to the cases considered above. Yermian lied about his

---

[a] *Lambert* is discussed in the Notes following *Fox* in Section 1, Subsection C, above.

[3] By interpreting such public welfare offenses to require at least that the defendant know that he is dealing with some dangerous or deleterious substance, we have avoided construing criminal statutes to impose a rigorous form of strict liability. See, e.g., United States v. International Minerals & Chemical Corp., 402 U.S. 558, 563–64 (1971) (suggesting that if a person shipping acid mistakenly thought that he was shipping distilled water, he would not violate a statute criminalizing undocumented shipping of acids). True strict liability might suggest that the defendant need not know even that he was dealing with

a dangerous item. Nevertheless, we have referred to public welfare offenses as "dispensing with" or "eliminating" a mens rea requirement or "mental element" and have described them as strict liability crimes. While use of the term "strict liability" is really a misnomer, we have interpreted statutes defining public welfare offenses to eliminate the requirement of mens rea; that is, the requirement of a "guilty mind" with respect to an element of a crime. Under such statutes we have not required that the defendant know the facts that make his conduct fit the definition of the offense. Generally speaking, such knowledge is necessary to establish mens rea....

employment history and criminal record on a security questionnaire[b] which his employer, a defense contractor, required him to complete because he would have access to classified information on the job. He was convicted of violating 18 U.S.C. § 1001, which provides:

> Whoever, in any matter within the jurisdiction of any department or agency of the United States knowingly and willfully ... makes any false ... statements ... shall be fined not more than $10,000 or imprisoned not more than five years, or both.

Yermian admitted at his trial that he had intentionally made false statements on the form so that the information it contained would be consistent with similar false statements he had made on his employment application. His sole defense was that he had no knowledge that his false statements would be transmitted to a federal agency. His attorney requested an instruction to the effect that the jury could not convict unless it found that he knew that the statements were made in a matter within the jurisdiction of a federal agency. The trial judge rejected this request, but instructed the jury that it should convict if it found that the defendant "knew or should have known that the information was to be submitted to a government agency."

The Court of Appeals reversed, but the Supreme Court reinstated the conviction. Justice Powell's opinion for the Court classified the language "in any matter within the jurisdiction of any department or agency of the United States" as a "jurisdictional element," that is, an element "whose primary purpose is to identify the factor that makes the false statement an appropriate subject for federal concern." "Jurisdictional language," Justice Powell continued, "need not contain the same culpability requirement as other elements of the offense." He then noted that the statutory language was clear in this case, since the

> jurisdictional language appears in a phrase separate from the prohibited conduct modified by the terms "knowingly and willfully." Any natural reading of § 1001, therefore, establishes that the terms "knowingly and willfully" modify only the making of "false ... statements" and not the predicate circumstance that those statements be made in a matter within the jurisdiction of a federal agency. Once this is clear, there is no basis for requiring proof that the defendant had actual knowledge of federal agency jurisdiction. The statute contains no language suggesting any additional element of intent.... On its face, therefore, § 1001 requires that the government prove that false statements were made knowingly and willfully, and it unambiguously dispenses with any requirement

---

[b] The form was entitled "Department of Defense Personnel Security Questionnaire." The document contained a reference to the "Defense Industrial Security Clearance Office," stated that Yermian's work would require access to "secret" material, and stated explicitly that signing it would grant the "Department of Defense" permission to conduct an investigation. A warning that any false answers would subject him to prosecution under "§ 1001 of the United States Criminal Code" was printed right above the place where Yermian signed the form.

that the government also prove that those statements were made with actual knowledge of federal agency jurisdiction.

Justice Powell's reading of the legislative history of the statute confirmed this conclusion. He then turned to the defendant's argument that construed in this manner § 1001 becomes a " 'trap for the unwary' imposing criminal sanctions on 'wholly innocent conduct.' " Justice Powell responded:

> Whether or not respondent fairly may characterize the intentional and deliberate lies prohibited by the statute (and manifest in this case) as "wholly innocent conduct," this argument is not sufficient to overcome the express statutory language of § 1001. Respondent does not argue that Congress lacks the power to impose criminal sanctions for deliberately false statements submitted to a federal agency, regardless whether the person who made such statements actually knew that they were being submitted to the federal government. That is precisely what Congress has done here. In the unlikely event that § 1001 could be the basis for imposing an unduly harsh result on those who intentionally make false statements to the federal government, it is for Congress and not this Court to amend the criminal statute.[14]

Justice Rehnquist dissented, joined by Justices Brennan, Stevens, and O'Connor. He argued that the statute was ambiguous and that the legislative history confirmed that actual knowledge as to the jurisdictional element should be required. He also argued that it should not lightly be inferred that Congress

> intended to criminalize the making of even the most casual false statements so long as they turned out, unbeknownst to their maker, to be material to some federal agency function. The latter interpretation would substantially extend the scope of the statute even to reach, for example, false statements privately made to a neighbor if the neighbor then uses those statements in connection with his work for a federal agency.

He also criticized the Court for not resolving the question whether some lesser culpability was required for the jurisdictional element.

[14] In the context of this case, respondent's argument that § 1001 is a 'trap for the unwary' is particularly misplaced. It is worth noting that the jury was instructed, without objection from the prosecution, that the government must prove that respondent 'knew or should have known' that his false statements were made within the jurisdiction of a federal agency.

As the government did not object to the reasonable foreseeability instruction, it is unnecessary for us to decide whether that instruction erroneously read a culpability requirement into the jurisdictional phrase. Moreover, the only question presented in this case is whether the government must prove that the false statement was made with *actual* knowledge of federal agency jurisdiction. The jury's finding that federal agency jurisdiction was reasonably foreseeable by the defendant, combined with the requirement that the defendant had actual knowledge of the falsity of those statements, precludes the possibility that criminal penalties were imposed on the basis of innocent conduct.

Was *Yermian* correctly decided? When the issue returns, should the Court hold that negligence or strict liability is the operative mens rea for the jurisdictional element? Or should it opt for a higher standard?

---

## SUBSECTION D: OPTIONAL CONCLUDING PROBLEM

---

### NOTE ON THE CONSTITUTIONAL BACKGROUND

The next main case, *United States v. X–Citement Video*, involves many of the themes developed above. It also concerns the relationship between constitutionally protected freedom of speech and crimes prohibiting obscenity. The following description by no means exhausts the ways in which pornographic speech can be regulated by the government, but it does provide the necessary backdrop for the issues of criminal law presented by the case.

The First Amendment to the federal Constitution provides that "Congress shall make no law ... abridging the freedom of speech." The traditional definition of speech is very broad—it goes well beyond oral statements to include books, movies, videos, photographs, paintings, sculpture, and indeed virtually any form of verbal or visual communication. But it has long been settled that the First Amendment does not protect from government regulation all activity that might be classified as "speech." There are numerous pockets of unprotected speech that can be regulated or even prohibited by criminal prosecution. Among the more common illustrations are "fighting words" and incitement to riot (words designed to provoke the listener into a violent response), defamation, and conversation leading to a conspiracy to commit a crime (e.g., conversation preceding an agreement to commit a murder). Another well-known example is Justice Holmes' comment in Schenck v. United States, 249 U.S. 47, 52 (1919), that "the character of every act depends upon the circumstances in which it is done. The most stringent protection of free speech would not protect a man in falsely shouting fire in a theatre and causing a panic."

Obscenity is another well-accepted category of unprotected speech. As elaborated at the end of Chapter I, section 1, supra, the line between sexually explicit protected speech and legally obscene unprotected speech is fuzzy and, to say the least, hard to draw in particular cases. But once speech has been properly classified as obscene, it is clear that it can be regulated by government and punished as a crime.

It was established in New York v. Ferber, 458 U.S. 747 (1982), moreover, that government can punish child pornography in situations where it could not were only adults involved. Other cases have held that speech can be regulated or prohibited in ways to keep it from the eyes and ears of children that could not be employed to shield it from consenting adults. What this means is that speech that is not legally obscene can nonetheless be prohibited in order to keep it from children or to keep children from being exploited.

The result is that there are three layers of speech that are relevant to the Court's decision in *X-Citement Video*, each of which shades imperceptibly into its neighbor. They can perhaps best be thought of as three concentric circles. The smallest circle at the center is unprotected hard-core obscenity. It can be prohibited no matter who is the subject and no matter who is the audience. The second, significantly larger circle, consists of sexually explicit pornographic material that is constitutionally protected if only adults are involved, but that can be prohibited if children are its subjects or its audience. And the third still larger circle consists of speech that may be regarded as more mildly pornographic or that is somehow related to sex but that is constitutionally protected and that cannot therefore be prohibited by the state.

---

## United States v. X–Citement Video, Inc.

Supreme Court of the United States, 1994.
513 U.S. 64.

■ CHIEF JUSTICE REHNQUIST delivered the opinion of the Court.

The Protection of Children Against Sexual Exploitation Act of 1977 . . . prohibits the interstate transportation, shipping, receipt, distribution or reproduction of visual depictions of minors engaged in sexually explicit conduct. The Court of Appeals . . . reversed the conviction of respondents for violation of this act. It held that the act did not require that the defendant know that one of the performers was a minor, and that it was therefore facially unconstitutional. We conclude that the act is properly read to include such a requirement.

Rubin Gottesman owned and operated X–Citement Video, Inc. Undercover police posed as pornography retailers and targeted X–Citement Video for investigation. During the course of the sting operation, the media exposed Traci Lords for her roles in pornographic films while under the age of 18. Police Officer Steven Takeshita expressed an interest in obtaining Traci Lords tapes. Gottesman complied, selling Takeshita 49 videotapes featuring Lords before her 18th birthday. Two months later, Gottesman shipped eight tapes of the underage Traci Lords to Takeshita in Hawaii.

These two transactions formed the basis for a federal indictment under the child pornography statute. . . . Evidence at trial suggested that Gottesman had full awareness of Lords' underage performances. The District Court convicted respondents. . . . [B]y a divided vote, [the Court of Appeals held] that the first amendment requires that the defendant possess knowledge of the particular fact that one performer had not reached the age of majority at the time the visual depiction was produced. Because the court found the statute did not require such a showing, it reversed respondents' convictions. We granted certiorari and now reverse.

Title 18 U.S.C. § 2252 provides, in relevant part:

(a) Any person who—

    (1) knowingly transports or ships in interstate or foreign commerce by any means including by computer or mails, any visual depiction, if—

        (A) the producing of such visual depiction involves the use of a minor engaging in sexually explicit conduct; and

        (B) such visual depiction is of such conduct;

    (2) knowingly receives, or distributes, any visual depiction that has been mailed, or has been shipped or transported in interstate or foreign commerce, or which contains materials which have been mailed or so shipped or transported, by any means including by computer, or knowingly reproduces any visual depiction for distribution in interstate or foreign commerce or through the mails, if—

        (A) the producing of such visual depiction involves the use of a minor engaging in sexually explicit conduct; and

        (B) such visual depiction is of such conduct; . . .

shall be punished as provided in subsection (b) of this section.

The critical determination which we must make is whether the term "knowingly" in subsections (1) and (2) modifies the phrase "the use of a minor" in subsections (1)(A) and (2)(A). The most natural grammatical reading, adopted by the [Court of Appeals], suggests that the term "knowingly" modifies only the surrounding verbs: transports, ships, receives, distributes, or reproduces. Under this construction, the word "knowingly" would not modify the elements of the minority of the performers, or the sexually explicit nature of the material, because they are set forth in independent clauses separated by interruptive punctuation. But we do not think this is the end of the matter, both because of anomalies which result from this construction, and because of the respective presumptions that some form of scienter is to be implied in a criminal statute even if not expressed, and that a statute is to be construed where fairly possible so as to avoid substantial constitutional questions.

If the term "knowingly" applies only to the relevant verbs in § 2252— transporting, shipping, receiving, distributing and reproducing—we would have to conclude that Congress wished to distinguish between someone who knowingly transported a particular package of film whose contents were unknown to him, and someone who unknowingly transported that package. It would seem odd, to say the least, that Congress distinguished between someone who inadvertently dropped an item into the mail without realizing it, and someone who consciously placed the same item in the mail, but was nonetheless unconcerned about whether the person had any knowledge of the prohibited contents of the package.

Some applications of respondents' position would produce results that were not merely odd, but positively absurd. If we were to conclude that "knowingly" only modifies the relevant verbs in § 2252, we would sweep within the ambit of the statute actors who had no idea that they were even dealing with sexually explicit material. For instance, a retail druggist who returns an uninspected roll of developed film to a customer "knowingly distributes" a visual depiction and would be criminally liable if it were later discovered that the visual depiction contained images of children engaged in sexually explicit conduct. Or, a new resident of an apartment might receive mail for the prior resident and store the mail unopened. If the prior tenant had requested delivery of materials covered by § 2252, his residential successor could be prosecuted for "knowing receipt" of such materials. Similarly, a Federal Express courier who delivers a box in which the shipper has declared the contents to be "film" "knowingly transports" such film. We do not assume that Congress, in passing laws, intended such results.

Our reluctance to simply follow the most grammatical reading of the statute is heightened by our cases interpreting criminal statutes to include broadly applicable scienter requirements, even where the statute by its terms does not contain them. The landmark opinion in Morissette v. United States, 342 U.S. 246 (1952), discussed the common law history of mens rea as applied to the elements of the federal embezzlement statute. That statute read: "Whoever embezzles, steals, purloins, or knowingly converts to his use or the use of another, or without authority, sells, conveys or disposes of any record, voucher, money, or thing of value of the United States ... [s]hall be fined." 18 U.S.C. § 641. Perhaps even more obviously than in the statute presently before us, the word "knowingly" in its isolated position suggested that it only attached to the verb "converts," and required only that the defendant intentionally assume dominion over the property. But the Court used the background presumption of evil intent to conclude that the term "knowingly" also required that the defendant have knowledge of the facts that made the taking a conversion—i.e., that the property belonged to the United States.

Liparota v. United States, 471 U.S. 419 (1985), posed a challenge to a federal statute prohibiting certain actions with respect to food stamps. The statute's use of "knowingly" could be read only to modify "uses, transfers, acquires, alters, or possesses" or it could be read also to modify "in any manner not authorized by [the statute]." Noting that neither interpretation posed constitutional problems, the Court held the scienter requirement applied to both elements by invoking the background principle set forth in *Morissette*. In addition, the Court was concerned with the broader reading which would "criminalize a broad range of apparently innocent conduct." Imposing criminal liability on an unwitting food stamp recipient who purchased groceries at a store that inflated its prices to such purchasers struck the Court as beyond the intended reach of the statute.

The same analysis drove the recent conclusion in Staples v. United States, 511 U.S. 600 (1994), that to be criminally liable a defendant must know that his weapon possessed automatic firing capability so as to make it a machine gun as defined by the National Firearms Act. Congress had not expressly imposed any mens rea requirement in the provision criminalizing the possession of a firearm in the absence of proper registration. The Court first rejected the argument that the statute described a public welfare offense, traditionally excepted from the background principle favoring scienter. The Court then expressed concern with a statutory reading that would criminalize behavior that a defendant believed fell within "a long tradition of widespread lawful gun ownership by private individuals." The Court also emphasized the harsh penalties attaching to violations of the statute as a "significant consideration in determining whether the statute should be construed as dispensing with mens rea."

Applying these principles, we think the [Court of Appeals'] plain language reading of § 2252 is not so plain. First, § 2252 is not a public welfare offense. Persons do not harbor settled expectations that the contents of magazines and film are generally subject to stringent public regulation. In fact, first amendment constraints presuppose the opposite view. Rather, the statute is more akin to the common law offenses against the "state, person, property, or public morals," *Morissette*, supra, 342 U.S., at 255, that presume a scienter requirement in the absence of express contrary intent.[2] Second, *Staples'* concern with harsh penalties looms equally large respecting § 2252: violations are punishable by up to 10 years in prison as well as substantial fines and forfeiture.

*Morissette*, reinforced by *Staples*, instructs that the presumption in favor of a scienter requirement should apply to each of the statutory elements which criminalize otherwise innocent conduct. *Staples* held that the features of a gun as technically described by the firearm registration act was such an element. Its holding rested upon "the nature of the particular device or substance Congress has subjected to regulation and the expectations that individuals may legitimately have in dealing with the regulated items." Age of minority in § 2252 indisputably possesses the same status as an elemental fact because non-obscene, sexually explicit materials involving persons over the age of 17 are protected by the first amendment. [Citations omitted.][3] In the light of these decisions, one would

---

[2] *Morissette*'s treatment of the common law presumption of mens rea recognized that the presumption expressly excepted "sex offenses, such as rape, in which the victim's actual age was determinative despite defendant's reasonable belief that the girl had reached the age of consent." But as in the criminalization of pornography production at 18 U.S.C. § 2251, see infra, at n.5, the perpetrator confronts the underage victim personally and may reasonably be required to ascertain that victim's age. The opportunity for reasonable mistake as to age increases significantly once the victim is reduced to a visual depiction, unavailable for questioning by the distributor or receiver. Thus we do not think the common law treatment of sex offenses militates against our construction of the present statute. [The quotation from *Morissette* at the beginning of this footnote was from a portion of the opinion omitted in the earlier rendition of that case in this Chapter.—Addition to footnote by eds.]

[3] In this regard, age of minority is not a "jurisdictional fact" that enhances an offense otherwise committed with an evil intent. See,

reasonably expect to be free from regulation when trafficking in sexually explicit, though not obscene, materials involving adults. Therefore, the age of the performers is the crucial element separating legal innocence from wrongful conduct.

The legislative history of the statute evolved over a period of years, and perhaps for that reason speaks somewhat indistinctly to the question whether "knowingly" in the statute modifies the elements of (1)(A) and (2)(A)—that the visual depiction involves the use of a minor engaging in sexually explicit conduct—or merely the verbs "transport or ship" in (1) and "receive or distribute ... [or] reproduce" in (2). [At this point the Court examined the complex and convoluted legislative history of the statute. It continued:]

[I]mportantly, the [House] bill retained the adverb "knowingly" in § 2252 while simultaneously deleting the word "knowingly" from § 2251(a).[a] The Conference Committee explained the deletion in § 2251(a) as reflecting an "intent that it is not a necessary element of a prosecution that the defendant knew the actual age of the child."[5] [We reject the argument] that § 2252 ought to be read like § 2251....

The legislative history can be summarized by saying that it persuasively indicates that Congress intended that the term "knowingly" apply to the requirement that the depiction be of sexually explicit conduct; it is a good deal less clear from the Committee Reports and floor debates that Congress intended that the requirement extend also to the age of the performers. But, turning once again to the statute itself, if the term "knowingly" applies to the sexually explicit conduct depicted, it is emancipated from merely modifying the verbs in subsections (1) and (2). And as a matter of grammar it is difficult to conclude that the word "knowingly" modifies one of the elements in (1)(A) and (2)(A), but not the other.

e.g., United States v. Feola, 420 U.S. 671 (1975). There, the Court did not require knowledge of "jurisdictional facts"—that the target of an assault was a federal officer. Criminal intent serves to separate those who understand the wrongful nature of their act from those who do not, but does not require knowledge of the precise consequences that may flow from that act once aware that the act is wrongful.

[a] Section 2251(a) punishes "[a]ny person who employs, uses, persuades, induces, entices, or coerces any minor to engage in, or who has a minor assist any other person to engage in, or who transports any minor in interstate or foreign commerce, or in any Territory or Possession of the United States, with the intent that such minor engage in any sexually explicit conduct for the purpose of producing any visual depiction of such conduct, ... if such person knows or has reason to know that such visual depiction will be transported in interstate or foreign commerce or mailed, or if such visual depiction has actually been transported in interstate or foreign commerce or mailed."—[Footnote by eds.]

[5] The difference in congressional intent with respect to § 2251 versus § 2252 reflects the reality that producers are more conveniently able to ascertain the age of performers. It thus makes sense to impose the risk of error on producers. Although producers may be convicted under § 2251(a) without proof they had knowledge of age, Congress has independently required both primary and secondary producers to record the ages of performers with independent penalties for failure to comply.

A final canon of statutory construction supports the reading that the term "knowingly" applies to both elements. [Our cases] suggest that a statute completely bereft of a scienter requirement as to the age of the performers would raise serious constitutional doubts. It is therefore incumbent upon us to read the statute to eliminate those doubts so long as such a reading is not plainly contrary to the intent of Congress.

For all of the foregoing reasons, we conclude that the term "knowingly" in § 2252 extends both to the sexually explicit nature of the material and to the age of the performers.... The judgment of the Court of Appeals is

Reversed.

■ JUSTICE STEVENS, concurring.

In my opinion, the normal, commonsense reading of a subsection of a criminal statute introduced by the word "knowingly" is to treat that adverb as modifying each of the elements of the offense identified in the remainder of the subsection.... Surely reading this provision to require proof of scienter for each fact that must be proved is far more reasonable than adding such a requirement to a statutory offense that contains no scienter requirement whatsoever. Cf. Staples v. United States, 511 U.S. 600 (1994) (Stevens, J., dissenting). Indeed, as the Court demonstrates, to give the statute its most grammatically correct reading, and merely require knowledge that a "visual depiction" has been shipped in interstate commerce, would be ridiculous. Accordingly, I join the Court's opinion without qualification.

■ JUSTICE SCALIA, with whom JUSTICE THOMAS joins, dissenting.

Today's opinion is without antecedent. None of the decisions cited as authority support interpreting an explicit statutory scienter requirement in a manner that its language simply will not bear. Staples v. United States, 511 U.S. 600 (1994), applied the background common law rule of scienter to a statute that said nothing about the matter. Morissette v. United States, 342 U.S. 246 (1952), applied that same background rule to a statute that did contain the word "knowingly," in order to conclude that "knowingly converts" requires knowledge not merely of the fact of one's assertion of dominion over property, but also knowledge of the fact that that assertion is a conversion, i.e., is wrongful.* Liparota v. United States, 471 U.S. 419 (1985), again involved a statute that did contain the word " 'knowingly,' " used in such a fashion that it could reasonably and grammatically be thought to apply (1) only to the phrase " 'uses, transfers, acquires, alters, or possesses' " (which would cause a defendant to be liable without wrongful intent), or (2) also to the later phrase " 'in any manner not authorized by [the statute].' " Once again applying the background rule of scienter, the latter reasonable and permissible reading was preferred.

---

* The case did not involve, as the Court claims, a situation in which, "even more obviously than in the statute presently before us, the word 'knowingly' in its isolated position suggested that it only attached to the verb 'converts,' " and we nonetheless applied it as well to another word. The issue was simply the meaning of "knowingly converts."

There is no way in which any of these cases, or all of them in combination, can be read to stand for the sweeping proposition that "the presumption in favor of a scienter requirement should apply to each of the statutory elements which criminalize otherwise innocent conduct," *even when the plain text of the statute says otherwise*. All those earlier cases employ the presumption as a rule of interpretation which applies when Congress has not addressed the question of criminal intent (*Staples*), or when the import of what it has said on that subject is ambiguous (*Morissette* and *Liparota*). Today's opinion converts the rule of interpretation into a rule of law, contradicting the plain import of what Congress has specifically prescribed regarding criminal intent.

... To say, as the Court does, that [the Court of Appeals'] interpretation is "the most grammatical reading" or "[t]he most natural grammatical reading" is understatement to the point of distortion—rather like saying that the ordinarily preferred total for 2 plus 2 is 4. The [Court of Appeals] interpretation is in fact and quite obviously the only grammatical reading. If one were to rack his brains for a way to express the thought that the knowledge requirement in subsection (a)(1) applied only to the transportation or shipment of visual depiction in interstate or foreign commerce, and not to the fact that that depiction was produced by use of a minor engaging in sexually explicit conduct, and was a depiction of that conduct, it would be impossible to construct a sentence structure that more clearly conveys that thought, and that thought alone. The word "knowingly" is contained, not merely in a distant phrase, but in an entirely separate clause from the one into which today's opinion inserts it. The equivalent, in expressing a simpler thought, would be the following: "Anyone who knowingly double-parks will be subject to a $200 fine if that conduct occurs during the 4:30–to–6:30 rush hour." It could not be clearer that the scienter requirement applies only to the double-parking, and not to the time of day. So also here, it could not be clearer that it applies only to the transportation or shipment of visual depiction in interstate or foreign commerce. There is no doubt. There is no ambiguity. There is no possible "less natural" but nonetheless permissible reading....

The Court acknowledges that "it is a good deal less clear from the Committee Reports and floor debates that Congress intended that the requirement [of scienter] extend ... to the age of the performers." That is surely so. In fact it seems to me that the dominant (if not entirely uncontradicted) view expressed in the legislative history is that ... the scienter requirement applies to the element of the crime that the depiction be of "sexually explicit conduct," but not to the element that the depiction "involv[e] the use of a minor engaging" in such conduct....

The Court rejects this construction of the statute for two reasons: First, because "as a matter of grammar it is difficult to conclude that the word 'knowingly' modifies one of the elements in (1)(A) and (2)(A), but not the other." But as I have described, "as a matter of grammar" it is also difficult (nay, impossible) to conclude that the word "knowingly" modifies *both* of those elements. It is really quite extraordinary for the Court, fresh from having, as it says, "emancipated" the adverb from the grammatical restriction that renders it inapplicable to the entire conditional clause, suddenly to insist that the demands of syntax must prevail over legislative intent—thus producing an end result that accords *neither* with syntax *nor* with supposed intent. If what the statute says must be ignored, one would think we might settle at least for what the statute was meant to say; but alas, we are told, what the statute says prevents this.

The Court's second reason is even worse: "[A] statute completely bereft of a scienter requirement as to the age of the performers would raise serious constitutional doubts." In my view . . . that is not true. The Court derives its "serious constitutional doubts" from the fact that "sexually explicit materials involving persons over the age of 18 are protected by the first amendment." We have made it entirely clear, however, that the first amendment protection accorded to such materials is not as extensive as that accorded to other speech. "[T]here is surely a less vital interest in the uninhibited exhibition of material that is on the borderline between pornography and artistic expression than in the free dissemination of ideas of social and political significance." Young v. American Mini Theatres, Inc., 427 U.S. 50, 61 (1976). . . . Let us be clear about what sort of pictures are at issue here. They are not the sort that will likely be found in a catalog of the National Gallery or the Metropolitan Museum of Art. " '[S]exually explicit conduct,' " as defined in the statute, does not include mere nudity, but only *conduct* that consists of "sexual intercourse . . . between persons of the same or opposite sex," "bestiality," "masturbation," "sadistic or masochistic abuse," and "lascivious exhibition of the genitals or pubic area." See 18 U.S.C. § 2256(2). What is involved, in other words, is not the clinical, the artistic, nor even the risqué, but hard-core pornography. Indeed, I think it entirely clear that all of what is involved constitutes not merely pornography but fully proscribable obscenity. . . .

I am not concerned that holding the purveyors and receivers of this material absolutely liable for supporting the exploitation of minors will deter any activity the United States Constitution was designed to protect. But I am concerned that the Court's suggestion of the unconstitutionality of such absolute liability will cause Congress to leave the world's children inadequately protected against the depredations of the pornography trade. As we recognized in [another case], the producers of these materials are not always readily found, and are often located abroad; and knowledge of the performers' age by the dealers who specialize in child pornography, and by the purchasers who sustain that market, is obviously hard to prove. The first amendment will lose none of its value to a free society if those who knowingly place themselves in the stream of pornographic commerce are obliged to make sure that they are not subsidizing child abuse. It is no more unconstitutional to make persons who knowingly deal in hard-core pornography criminally liable for the underage character of their entertainers than it is to make men who engage in consensual fornication criminally liable (in statutory rape) for the underage character of their partners.

I would dispose of the present case ... by reading the statute as it is written: to provide criminal penalties for the knowing transportation or shipment of a visual depiction in interstate or foreign commerce, and for the knowing receipt or distribution of a visual depiction so transported or shipped, if that depiction was (whether the defendant knew it or not) a portrayal of a minor engaging in sexually explicit conduct. I would find the statute, as so interpreted, to be unconstitutional since, by imposing criminal liability upon those not knowingly dealing in pornography, it establishes a severe deterrent, not narrowly tailored to its purposes, upon fully protected first amendment activities. This conclusion of unconstitutionality is of course no ground for going back to reinterpret the statute, making it say something that it does not say, but that is constitutional. Not every construction, but only " 'every *reasonable* construction must be resorted to, in order to save a statute from unconstitutionality.' " Edward J. DeBartolo Corp. v. Florida Gulf Coast Building & Construction Trades Council, 485 U.S. 568, 575 (1988) (emphasis added). Otherwise, there would be no such thing as an unconstitutional statute. As I have earlier discussed, in the present case no reasonable alternative construction exists.... I therefore agree with the [Court of Appeals] that respondent's conviction cannot stand.

I could understand (though I would not approve of) a disposition which, in order to uphold this statute, departed from its text as little as possible in order to sustain its constitutionality—i.e., a disposition applying the scienter requirement to the pornographic nature of the materials, but not to the age of the performers. I can neither understand nor approve of the disposition urged by the United States before this Court and adopted today, which not only rewrites the statute, but (1) rewrites it more radically than its constitutional survival demands, and (2) raises baseless constitutional doubts that will impede congressional enactment of a law providing greater protection for the child-victims of the pornography industry. The Court today saves a single conviction by putting in place a relatively toothless child-pornography law that Congress did not enact, and by rendering congressional strengthening of that new law more difficult. I respectfully dissent.

———

# CHAPTER III

# ATTEMPT

---

### INTRODUCTORY NOTE ON THE CRIME OF ATTEMPT

Rex v. Scofield, Cald. 397 (1784), written by Lord Mansfield, was the seminal decision in the evolution of the crime of attempt. It involved an attempt to commit arson and conviction was based on the doctrine, as subsequently reformulated in Rex v. Higgins, 2 East 5, 102 Eng. Rep. 269 (1801), that "all offenses of a public nature, that is, all such acts or attempts as tend to the prejudice of the community, are indictable."[1] This development occurred too late to be received as part of the common law in the United States. But in both England (by decision) and America (by statute), it had become settled by the mid–1830s that an attempt to commit any offense was punishable as a separate crime.[2]

There were crimes in the early law covering certain forms of analytically similar conduct. Indeed, it seems clear that the pressure to create a generic attempt offense emerged so late because many of the more serious forms of attempt had already been recognized as substantive crimes. Larceny, for example, was defined in terms that fell short of requiring a permanent deprivation of property. Assault, defined as an attempt to commit a battery, dealt with efforts to attack a person. Robbery in effect was an aggravated combination of the two—an effort to obtain property by means of assault. Burglary combined an attempt to commit a felony with trespass in a dwelling. Early American statutes supplemented these offenses with many crimes of the "assault with intent" variety, as in "assault with intent to kill," "assault with intent to rape," etc.

The crime of attempt punishes conduct preliminary to other crimes, including those that themselves address inchoate behavior. Thus, for example, it is a crime to attempt to commit larceny, which is itself defined in inchoate terms. The effect is to push back toward more preliminary conduct the point at which criminal liability attaches.

---

[1] Compare *Rex v. Manley* in Chapter I.

[2] The history is summarized in Jerome Hall, General Principles of the Criminal Law 558–74 (2d ed. 1960), and in Francis Bowes Sayre, Criminal Attempts, 41 Harv. L. Rev. 821 (1928). Attempts carry penalties that are usually a proportion of the penalty for the completed offense. For a discussion of American grading patterns, see ALI, Model Penal Code and Commentaries § 5.05, pp. 485–87 (1985); Herbert Wechsler, William Kenneth Jones & Harold L. Korn, The Treatment of Inchoate Crimes in the Model Penal Code of the American Law Institute: Attempt, Solicitation, and Conspiracy II, 61 Colum. L. Rev. 957, 1022–24 (1961).

## SECTION 1: THE REQUIRED CONDUCT

INTRODUCTORY NOTES ON THE CONDUCT REQUIRED FOR
ATTEMPT

**1.   The Act Requirement.** It would be appropriate at this point to
revisit the discussion in Chapter I, Section 1, addressing the conduct
requirement in the criminal law. As the following materials demonstrate,
the law of attempt tests the rationale for the conduct requirement. One
question in every attempt case is whether there has been enough conduct
to justify criminal punishment. Thinking about that question must begin
with why the criminal law requires conduct in the first place.

**2.   Minimum Conduct and the Law of Attempt.** Although minimum conduct requirements are a matter of pervasive importance in the
penal law, the issue has received doctrinal attention primarily in the law of
attempt. Attempt is defined chiefly by reference to the object offense. Thus,
there can be no attempt standing alone. There must be an attempt to
commit murder, rape, larceny, or some other substantive offense. In each
instance, the actor takes steps toward completion of the underlying crime.
The question is: How many steps are enough? How far must the actor
proceed towards completion of the underlying offense for attempt liability
to attach? Doctrinally, this question is put as the distinction between
attempt and preparation. The former is punishable, the latter is not. The
line between preparation and attempt marks the point at which the actor's
conduct triggers criminal liability.

In order to isolate the question of how much conduct is enough, it is
necessary to assume that all other requirements of the law of attempt have
been met. In particular, one must take as given that the actor has been
shown to have the state of mind required for the crime of attempt. For
present purposes, one should assume (and this turns out to be very nearly
correct) that the state of mind required for attempt is purpose. The actor
must have a conscious objective or desire to complete a course of conduct
proscribed as criminal. In each of the situations discussed below, the trier
of fact is prepared to conclude, beyond a reasonable doubt, that the actor
had such a purpose. The question is whether actions toward fulfilling that
purpose were sufficient to support criminal liability.

---

## People v. Bowen and Rouse

Court of Appeals of Michigan, 1968.
10 Mich.App. 1, 158 N.W.2d 794.

■ LEVIN, JUDGE. Defendants, Sherrel Bowen and William Rouse, appeal their
convictions of attempted larceny in a building.

On January 19, 1965, at approximately eight o'clock p.m., the defendants and two female companions were admitted to the home of one Matilda Gatzmeyer, an 80–year-old woman. The defendants' car was observed parked in front of Miss Gatzmeyer's residence and a neighbor, believing the defendants to have designs upon her property, called the police. Two police officers arrived and entered the home along with the neighbor. The defendants were found in the rear of the house near or on the basement steps. The two female companions were seated on either side of Miss Gatzmeyer, apparently engaged with her in conversation. The bedroom of the house was in a state of disarray.

The police ordered defendants to come to the front of the house and sit in the living room. Defendant Rouse seated himself within a foot of the TV, and some time thereafter one of the police officers spotted under the TV set two rings belonging to Miss Gatzmeyer. The neighbor testified she found a necklace on the staircase near where defendant Bowen had been standing when he was first sighted by the police. When the neighbor's discovery was called to the attention of one of the police officers, he and Miss Gatzmeyer went to the staircase and found the necklace in that location.

After interrogation, the defendants were arrested and charged with larceny of "rings and necklace" in a building in violation of Mich. Comp. Laws Ann. § 28.592.[a]

Bowen had been to the Gatzmeyer home on a number of prior occasions, ostensibly as a handyman, the same reason he gave Miss Gatzmeyer for appearing on the night in question. Miss Gatzmeyer testified that on this occasion the defendants sought to hire themselves out to clean and to do some masonry work on the chimney. She complained about the high prices charged by Bowen and his failure to do work as agreed, and that Bowen's helper (the role allegedly filled by Rouse at the time of the incident) generally helped himself to things that belonged to her.

The neighbor testified that she had met Bowen on three occasions prior to the one in question and that on one occasion Bowen had induced Miss Gatzmeyer to go with him to the bank, but it was not clear whether the visit to the bank was to withdraw money to pay Bowen that which was due him or unlawfully to separate Miss Gatzmeyer from her money.

The neighbor testified that she visited with Miss Gatzmeyer daily and assisted her in various chores and generally in getting around. She stated that when she and the police officers arrived on the night in question the dresser drawers in the bedroom were all pulled out and everything thrown all over the bed. This was not the way Miss Gatzmeyer generally kept the house according to the neighbor: "she has a very neat house, everything is in its place." The neighbor further testified that "after Miss Gatzmeyer cleaned up (presumably after the police left) she found more jewelry back of

---

[a] The statute provides, in pertinent part, that "[a]ny person who shall commit the crime of larceny by stealing in any dwelling house . . . or any building used by the public shall be guilty of a felony."—[Footnote by eds.]

the pillows" on the couch Bowen sat on during his interrogation by the police.

Miss Gatzmeyer testified that the defendants removed the jewelry from her bedroom without her consent.

At the beginning of his charge to the jury, the trial judge stated that because he doubted whether the case properly could be submitted to the jury on the original charge of larceny in a building he had decided to submit it to the jury solely on the included offense of attempt to commit larceny in a building.

## I

There was sufficient evidence to support the defendants' conviction of attempt to commit larceny. The jury could properly infer from the testimony that the defendants did in fact ransack Miss Gatzmeyer's bedroom and furniture without her permission, remove the two rings which were found under the TV set and the necklace found on the staircase. Such a finding would justify conviction of attempted larceny, the elements of which are a felonious intent to commit larceny and an overt act going beyond mere preparation towards the commission of the crime. It is the jury's function to weigh the evidence and to determine therefrom whether such intent is manifest and in doing so the jury may draw reasonable inferences from the facts.

## II

We do find error in the judge's failure properly to charge the jury on the necessity of finding an overt act [towards commission of larceny in a building]. It has been said that the overt act "is the essence of the offense" or the "gravamen of the offense." Not only did the trial judge fail to charge the jury at all concerning the necessity of finding an overt act, but he also incorrectly charged that the jury could convict if it found that the defendants came to or entered Miss Gatzmeyer's house with the intention of committing larceny.

During the charge, the trial judge stated:

> The theory of the People is that the evidence in this case, that is, the age of the complainant, Mrs. Gatzmeyer, the lateness of the visit to the house, the presence of two women to talk to the complainant, and the condition of the bedroom which it is claimed indicated ransacking and the attempt of the defendants to hide when the police were called, bear upon and indicate that the two defendants *came there with the intention* of committing larceny in the dwelling. The offense of larceny isn't clear but the attempt to commit larceny it is charged by the People . . . is clear.

> Now, the defense is rather brief and that is that the testimony given here does not tend to prove beyond a reasonable doubt that the defendants *entered the place with the intent* or for the purpose of attempting to commit larceny. In other words, the defense is

that the testimony that is shown here is not sufficient to convict the defendants beyond a reasonable doubt of *coming* into that building or *going into the building* on the night in question *with the intent* to commit larceny. (Emphasis supplied.)

There was ample evidence from which the jury could have found felonious intent. There are the circumstances related by the judge in his charge, as well as the other evidence previously set forth in this opinion. We must assume that, in convicting the defendants, the jury followed the judge's instructions and found the requisite felonious intent.

[T]he trial judge's failure to charge the jury on the necessity of finding commission of an overt act, as a separate ingredient or element, might not be error if he were correct in charging the jury that if it found defendants "came" to or "entered" Miss Gatzmeyer's house with intent to commit larceny it could bring in a verdict of guilty. If defendants' coming to, or entering, Miss Gatzmeyer's house with felonious intent was an "overt act", the jury verdict of guilty could be viewed as a finding of the requisite overt act.

Thus, the narrow question before us is whether the defendants when they came to or entered Miss Gatzmeyer's house with the intent to commit larceny committed an overt act that would support their conviction of attempted larceny. In our opinion, their mere coming to or entry of Miss Gatzmeyer's house was not an overt act, under the circumstances that Mr. Bowen and other helpers had rightfully been in the house on prior occasions and were admitted to the house by Miss Gatzmeyer on the night in question....

In People v. Coleman, 350 Mich. 268, 86 N.W.2d 281 (1957), the Supreme Court stated that a defendant may not be convicted of an attempt unless he has "gone beyond acts of an ambiguous nature" or those that are "equivocal,"[7] and that a "thoughtful test" for the resolution of the equivocal act has been phrased by Turner in his article, Attempts to Commit Crimes in 5 Camb. L.J. 230, 237–38 (1933), in these words:

> If the acts of the accused, taken by themselves, are unambiguous, and cannot, in reason, be regarded as pointing to any other end than the commission of the specific crime in question, then they constitute a sufficient actus reus. In other words, his acts must be *unequivocally referable* to the commission of the specific

---

[7] ... Other courts have said much the same thing in describing the overt act as one that can have "no other purpose" or "apparent result" than the commission of the principal crime—the "natural and probable" effect test is of the same genre; and then there are the judicial and text statements which speak of the overt act as an act that "commences" or has a "direct tendency" or "sufficient proximity" or "sufficient nearness" to the commission of the principal offense that (some add, having in mind the seriousness and enormity of the principal offense), in the opinion of the court, the actor's purpose is clear. Whether the differences in language used by the courts bring about different results or merely permit the courts that speak in terms of proximity or nearness or the like to explain their results with greater ease is beyond the scope of this opinion. On the question before us, we found substantial uniformity in results, if not in their explanation.

crime. They must, as the late Sir John Salmond said, "speak for themselves." If the example may be permitted, it is as though a cinematograph film, which has so far depicted merely the accused person's acts without stating what was his intention, had been suddenly stopped, and the audience were asked to say to what end those acts were directed. If there is only one reasonable answer to this question then the accused has done what amounts to an "attempt" to attain that end. If there is more than one reasonably possible answer, then the accused has not yet done enough. . . .

It has been suggested that the basic function of the overt act is corroboration of the felonious intent. However, that analysis can become somewhat circular if we permit intent to be gleaned from the overt act itself.

The testimony in this case was that defendant Bowen had, on a number of prior occasions, been in Miss Gatzmeyer's house with helpers. With that in mind and even if it be assumed (on the basis of the jury finding) that the defendants entered her house with a felonious intent, their mere presence there did not indicate, let alone "corroborate," that intention. The defendants did not break into Miss Gatzmeyer's house— they were voluntarily admitted by her. At the time of defendants' admission to Miss Gatzmeyer's house their *acts* were entirely "ambiguous" and "equivocal." It is the acts thereafter allegedly committed (but as to which we have no finding from the jury)[10] that were neither ambiguous nor equivocal.

Our analysis of the authorities convinces us that the function of the overt act is not to "corroborate," but rather to demonstrate that the defendant has converted resolution into action. Man being what he is, evil thoughts and intentions are easily formed. Fortunately, for society, most felonious thoughts are not fulfilled. The law does not punish evil intent or even every act done with the intent to commit a crime. The requirement that the jury find an overt act proceeds on the assumption that the devil may lose the contest, albeit late in the hour.

The overt act is not any act. In this connection, "overt" is used in the sense of "manifest" or symbolic. The act must manifest, or be symbolic of, the crime. Considering that Bowen and helpers had been in Miss Gatzmeyer's house on previous occasions (and, whatever her differences with Bowen may have been, she nevertheless admitted him on the night in question), the fact that the defendants came to and entered Miss Gatzmeyer's house

---

[10] The only jury finding before us is a finding that the defendants came to Miss Gatzmeyer's house with a felonious intent. While we proceed on the assumption that in convicting the defendants the jury concluded that the defendants came to or entered Miss Gatzmeyer's house with a felonious intent, we cannot similarly assume that the jury found that the defendant ransacked Miss Gatzmeyer's room or removed her personal belongings from her bedroom or were responsible for the fact that they were found under the TV set or on the staircase, where the only issue submitted to the jury was whether the "defendants *came there* with intention of committing larceny." The jury could have found such *intention* on the basis of evidence other than the ransacking and the atypical locations of her personal belongings.

would not manifest or symbolize the crime ... which they were convicted of attempting to commit....

Attempt patterns vary widely. No rule can be laid down applicable to all cases. Most cases will in the end turn on their own facts.

> It is a question of degree.... [T]he degree of proximity held sufficient may vary with the circumstances, including among other things the apprehension which the particular crime is calculated to excite.

Commonwealth v. Peaslee, 177 Mass. 267, 272, 59 N.E. 55, 56 (1901) [per Holmes, J.].

In the last cited case the defendant arranged combustibles in a building, then left the building. Later he set out for the building with the intention of lighting it, but changed his mind and turned back. Held not to be an attempt.

In People v. Pippin, 316 Mich. 191, 25 N.W.2d 164 (1946), defendant, who had on a prior occasion been convicted of gross indecency, was found guilty of parole violation on evidence that he had invited a 13-year-old boy to enter his automobile. The Supreme Court said the question was whether the defendant could be convicted of attempt to commit the crime of gross indecency. The court assumed arguendo that intent had been established (just as we assume in this case that the jury found the defendants here before us harbored a felonious intent) but ruled that an overt act had not been established—"the act [committed by Pippin], at most can be considered no more than preparation for the attempt."

In People v. Youngs, 122 Mich. 292, 81 N.W. 114 (1899), the defendant armed himself with a revolver, purchased cartridges, obtained an armed accomplice, carried slippers to perpetrate a silent entry of the intended victim's house, purchased chloroform to be used in the commission of the crime, and had already set out for the selected scene of the crime when he was arrested. Our Supreme Court reversed the conviction, holding that the defendant had not gone beyond preparation....

Where entry or attempted entry upon the victim's premises has been held in itself sufficient to constitute an overt act, such entry or attempted entry has been without permission, or the defendant came armed or with burglary tools or other means of committing the crime....

Reversed and remanded for a new trial.

---

## NOTES ON PREPARATION AND ATTEMPT

**1. Proximity Tests.** The drafters of the Model Penal Code referred to the distinction between preparation and attempt as "the most difficult problem in defining criminal attempt." Model Penal Code and Commentaries § 5.01, at 321 (1985). This judgment is confirmed by the cases.

Many courts have emphasized the physical proximity of the actor's conduct to the completed offense. The focus here is not on what has already been done but on what yet remains to be done to complete the crime. Under this view, the actor's separation from the criminal objective—whether in terms of time, distance, or necessary steps not yet taken—becomes the critical factor.

The physical-proximity test is illustrated by the well known case of People v. Rizzo, 246 N.Y. 334, 158 N.E. 888 (1927). Defendant and three others planned to rob Charles Rao, a payroll clerk for a construction company. The men armed themselves and set off in a car to find their intended victim. They went to the bank from which he was supposed to draw the money and to the company's construction sites, but they located neither the clerk nor the money. They succeeded, however, in attracting the attention of the police, with the result that the defendants were convicted of attempt to commit robbery. The courts construed New York law to require that the actor come "*very near* to the accomplishment of the crime" in order to be liable for attempt. Applying this standard, the Court of Appeals reversed the convictions:

> To constitute the crime of robbery, the money must have been taken from Rao by means of force or violence, or through fear. The crime of attempt to commit robbery was committed, if these defendants did an act tending to the commission of this robbery. Did the acts above described come dangerously near to the taking of Rao's property? Did the acts come so near the commission of robbery that there was reasonable likelihood of its accomplishment but for the interference [of the police]? Rao was not found; the defendants were still looking for him; no attempt to rob him could be made, at least until he came in sight. . . . Men would not be guilty of an attempt at burglary if they had planned to break into a building and were arrested while they were hunting about the streets for the building not knowing where it was. Neither would a man be guilty of an attempt to commit murder if he armed himself and started out to find the person whom he had planned to kill but could not find him. So here these defendants were not guilty of an attempt to commit robbery . . . when they had not found or reached the presence of the person they intended to rob.

An expanded version of the proximity test was advanced by Justice Holmes. Under his approach the issue of the actor's nearness to completion of the offense is subsumed in a broader inquiry that also encompasses the gravity of the harm threatened, the degree of apprehension aroused, and the probability that the conduct would result in the intended offense. Evaluating all these factors, the courts should ask whether there was a "dangerous proximity to success" in the actor's conduct. Hyde v. United States, 225 U.S. 347, 388 (1912) (Holmes, J., dissenting). See also Commonwealth v. Peaslee, 177 Mass. 267, 59 N.E. 55 (1901).

This approach—in common with other variations on the proximity doctrine—reflects the view that the essential purpose of the law of attempt is to punish dangerous conduct. The ultimate harms to be avoided are those identified by substantive crimes. Where the substantive offense is complete, the danger has been realized and punishment is warranted. Where the offense is not complete, the danger has not been realized and the case for punishment is weaker. Only where the anticipatory conduct comes dangerously close to accomplishing the harm ultimately feared is there sufficient justification for punishment of the actor, even though best efforts may have been made to commit the completed crime.

**2. Res Ipsa Loquitur.** An entirely different approach was first suggested by Justice Salmond of New Zealand in King v. Barker, [1924] N.Z.L.R. 865, 874:

> An act done with intent to commit a crime is not a criminal attempt unless it is of such a nature as to be in itself sufficient evidence of the criminal intent with which it is done. A criminal attempt is an act which shows criminal intent on the face of it. The case must be one in which res ipsa loquitur.

See also J. Salmond, Jurisprudence 350–52 (3d ed. 1910).

Unlike the various proximity doctrines, Salmond's inquiry looks to what the actor has already done rather than to what remains to be done. The object of this inquiry is not to assess the dangerousness of the anticipatory conduct itself, but to focus on the dangerousness of the actor who engaged in it. The premise is that the individual who has demonstrated a resolute commitment to a criminal endeavor poses a threat to the social order and therefore may properly be subject to criminal punishment. The argument is that the objectives of the criminal law are well served by focusing on the actor's demonstrated propensity toward criminal misbehavior rather than solely on the dangerousness of completed conduct.

The difficulty with this view is that it calls for a prediction. Where an individual is judged dangerous on some basis other than the demonstrated dangerousness of completed conduct (as the proximity tests would require), the possibility of error seems great. The problem is the potential for overprediction, and the question is whether a focus on the dangerous propensities of individuals can separate those who are truly intent on criminal misconduct from those who may not complete the offense.

The res ipsa loquitur test responds to these concerns in two ways. First, the requirement that the actor's criminal purpose be evident on the face of the conduct precludes criminal liability based solely on confessions or other representations of purpose. In other words, the requirement of unequivocal conduct demands manifest evidence of the actor's blameworthiness. It protects against conviction based on inadequate or unreliable proof of criminal purpose. Second, the res ipsa loquitur test may also be justified on the closely related ground of ensuring adequate evidence of the actor's commitment to the criminal purpose. Requiring conduct that speaks for itself differentiates daydream from fixed intention and limits liability for attempt to persons firmly resolved to violate societal interests.

Critics of the res ipsa test question its feasibility. Does any conduct truly speak for itself? Consider, for example, the hypotheticals offered in Salmond's *Barker* opinion, [1924] N.Z.L.R. at 875–76:

> To buy a box of matches with intent to use them in burning a haystack is not an attempt to commit arson, for it is in itself and in appearance an innocent act, there being many other reasons than arson for buying matches. The act does not speak for itself of any guilty design. The criminal intent is not manifested by any overt act sufficient for that purpose. But he who takes matches to a haystack and there lights one of them, and blows it out on finding that he is observed, has done an act which speaks for itself, and he is guilty of a criminal attempt accordingly.

Does the latter conduct really speak for itself? Does it show criminal intent on the face of it, or are there other possible explanations for lighting a match near a haystack? Strict adherence to the res ipsa loquitur test would disable the law in cases where liability should obtain. Glanville Williams used a variation of Salmond's hypothetical in support of his view that conviction should be permitted in at least some instances where unequivocality cannot be shown:

> D goes up to a haystack, fills his pipe, and lights a match. The act of lighting the match, even to a suspicious-minded person, is ambiguous. It may indicate only that *D* is going to light his pipe; but perhaps, on the other hand, the pipe is only a "blind" and *D* is really bent on setting fire to the stack. We do not know. Therefore, on the equivocality test, the act is not proximate. But suppose that as a matter of actual fact *D*, after his arrest, confesses to the guilty intent, and suppose that that confession is believed. We are now certain of the intent and the only question is as to proximity. It becomes clear that the act satisfies all the requirements for a criminal attempt.

Glanville Williams, Criminal Law: The General Part 630 (2d ed. 1961). Is Williams right in relying on subjective indicia of intent? Or is Salmond is right in insisting on conduct which is "in itself sufficient evidence of the intent with which it is done"?

**3.  The Model Penal Code.** The Model Penal Code standard for distinguishing preparation from attempt is stated in § 5.01(1)(c). Conviction for attempt is allowed where the actor engages in "an act or omission constituting a substantial step in a course of conduct planned to culminate in his commission of the crime." Section 5.01(2) elaborates on the meaning of "substantial step":

> Conduct shall not be held to constitute a substantial step under Subsection (1)(c) of this Section unless it is strongly corroborative of the actor's criminal purpose. Without negativing the sufficiency of other conduct, the following, if strongly corroborative of the actor's criminal purpose, shall not be held insufficient as a matter of law:

(a) lying in wait, searching for or following the contemplated victim of the crime;

(b) enticing or seeking to entice the contemplated victim of the crime to go to the place contemplated for its commission;

(c) reconnoitering the place contemplated for the commission of the crime;

(d) unlawful entry of a structure, vehicle or enclosure in which it is contemplated that the crime will be committed;

(e) possession of materials to be employed in the commission of the crime, which are specially designed for such unlawful use or which can serve no lawful purpose of the actor under the circumstances;

(f) possession, collection or fabrication of materials to be employed in the commission of the crime, at or near the place contemplated for its commission, where such possession, collection or fabrication serves no lawful purpose of the actor under the circumstances;

(g) soliciting an innocent agent to engage in conduct constituting an element of the crime.

The Model Code significantly broadens liability for attempt. The fact that the actor has not come dangerously close to completing the crime would not bar conviction—provided that the completed conduct constitutes a substantial step strongly corroborative of criminal purpose. In focusing on what has been done rather than on what remains to be done, the Model Code reflects the conclusion that the proximity tests unduly compromise the social control function of the penal law. The rationales for the Model Code conduct requirement are the same as for the res ipsa loquitur test. Both standards seek to avoid speculative and undisciplined inquiry into state of mind, both seek to ensure that the existence and firmness of the actor's criminal purpose are substantiated by objectively demonstrable conduct. Unlike the res ipsa test, however, the Model Code does not demand that the actor's conduct be *in itself* sufficient evidence of criminal purpose. Instead, it demands only that the actor's conduct *strongly corroborate* the existence of a criminal purpose that may be shown by other means. In essence, therefore, the Model Code recasts the conceptual focus of the res ipsa loquitur test into a more manageable standard for imposing liability. The ultimate objectives are to protect individuals against freewheeling inquiries into criminal purpose and at the same time to broaden the scope of attempt so as to facilitate early police intervention and the effective neutralization of dangerous persons.

**4. Testing Cases: *United States v. Harper.*** *Rizzo* provides a testing case for how one should approach the sufficiency of acts to support an attempt conviction. Consider the factual variations on this theme discussed in United States v. Harper, 33 F.3d 1143 (9th Cir. 1994). *Harper* itself involved the following situation:

Police officers in Buena Park, California, found [Harper and two other defendants] sitting in a rented car in the parking lot of the Home Savings Bank shortly after 10:00 p.m. on the evening of September 21, 1992. The officers searched the defendants, the vehicle and the surrounding area. They found two loaded handguns—a .44 caliber Charter Arms Bulldog and a .357 magnum Smith and Wesson—under a bush located five or six feet from the car, where a witness had earlier seen one of the car's occupants bending over. In the car, the police discovered a roll of duct tape in a plastic bag, a stun gun, and a pair of latex surgical gloves. They found another pair of latex surgical gloves in the pocket of [one of the defendant's] sweat pants. They also found six rounds of .357 magnum ammunition in the pocket of his shorts, which he wore under his sweat pants. Some of this ammunition came from either the same box or the same lot as the ammunition in the loaded .357 magnum handgun. The defendants had a total of approximately $182 in cash among them and [another defendant] was carrying an automated teller machine (ATM) card which bore the name of Kimberly Ellis.

Harper had used the ATM card belonging to Kimberly Ellis shortly before 9:00 p.m. that evening in an ATM at the Buena Park branch of the Bank of America, which was located adjacent to the Home Savings parking lot in which the defendants were parked. The ATM's camera photographed Harper. Harper had requested a $20 withdrawal from the ATM, but had not removed the cash from the cash drawer. This omission had created what is known as a "bill trap." When a bill trap occurs, the ATM shuts itself down and the ATM supply company that monitors the ATM contacts its ATM service technicians to come and repair the ATM. These facts were known to Harper, who had previously worked for both Bank of America and one of its ATM service companies. . . . The prosecution's theory was that Harper had intentionally caused the bill trap to summon the ATM service technicians who would have to open the ATM vault to clear the trap. At that time, the theory went, the defendants planned to rob the technicians of the money in the ATM.

The three defendants were convicted of attempted bank robbery. The Circuit Court agreed that there was sufficient evidence to find that the defendants intended to rob the Bank of America. But it concluded that they had not taken a "substantial step" towards commission of the offense:

> Our primary authorities are United States v. Buffington, 815 F.2d 1292, 1301 (9th Cir.1987), and United States v. Still, 850 F.2d 607, 608 (9th Cir.1988). In *Buffington*, the defendants had driven past the supposed target bank twice. One of the three male defendants then entered a store near the bank and observed the bank. The two other defendants, one dressed as a woman, exited their vehicle in the bank parking lot, stood near the vehicle and

focused their attention on the bank. They were armed. We held that the evidence was insufficient ... as to the existence of conduct constituting a substantial step towards the commission of the crime. With regard to the latter element, we observed:

> Not only did appellants not take a single step toward the bank, they displayed no weapons and no indication that they were about to make an entry. Standing alone, their conduct did not constitute that requisite "appreciable fragment" of a bank robbery, nor a step toward commission of the crime of such substantiality that, unless frustrated, the crime would have occurred.

The same may be said of the defendants in this case. True, Harper had left money in the ATM, causing a bill trap that would eventually bring service personnel to the ATM. That act, however, is equivocal in itself. The robbery was in the future and, like the defendants in *Buffington*, the defendants never made a move toward the victims or the Bank to accomplish the criminal portion of their intended mission. They had not taken a step of "such substantiality that, unless frustrated, the crime would have occurred." Id. Their situation is therefore distinguishable from that of the defendant in United States v. Moore, 921 F.2d 207 (9th Cir.1990), upon which the government relies. In *Moore*, the defendant was apprehended "walking toward the bank, wearing a ski mask, and carrying gloves, pillowcases and a concealed, loaded gun." These actions were a true commitment toward the robbery, which would be in progress the moment the would-be robber entered the bank thus attired and equipped. That stage of the crime had not been reached by [the defendants here]; their actual embarkation on the robbery lay as much as 90 minutes [the normal response time for the ATM service technicians] away from the time when Harper left money in the ATM, and that time had not expired when they were apprehended.

*Still* provides further support for our conclusion. There, we relied upon *Buffington* to reverse a similar conviction for attempted bank robbery. The defendant in that case was seen sitting in a van approximately 200 feet from the supposed target bank. In the van he had a fake bomb, a red pouch with note demanding money attached to it, a police scanner, and a notebook containing drafts of the note. He also had been seen putting on a blonde wig while sitting in the van. The defendant's intent was clear; he told police that he had been about to rob the bank and "[t]hat's what [he] was putting the wig on for." We concluded, however, that the evidence was insufficient to establish that the defendant had taken a substantial step toward commission of the offense. "Our facts do not establish either actual movement toward the bank or actions that are analytically similar to such movement." Defendant Still, like the defendants here, was sitting in his vehicle when the police approached. As in *Still*, we conclude that the crime was too inchoate to constitute an attempt.

When criminal intent is clear, identifying the point at which the defendants' activities ripen into an attempt is not an analytically satisfying enterprise. There is, however, a substantial difference between causing a bill trap, which will result in the appearance of potential victims, and moving toward such victims with gun and mask, as in *Moore*. Making an appointment with a potential victim is not of itself such a commitment to an intended crime as to constitute an attempt, even though it may make a later attempt possible. Little more happened here; this case is more like *Buffington* and *Still* than it is like *Moore*. Accordingly, we reverse the appellants' convictions for attempted bank robbery.

In how many of these cases did the court get the right answer? How would the cases have been decided under the Model Penal Code? Under the approach of *Bowen and Rouse*?

**5.   Testing Case: *State v. Mettetal*.**[a] In 1995, prosecutors in Nashville, Tennessee, charged Ray Wallace Mettetal with the attempted murder of Dr. George Allen. On August 22, 1995, Mettetal was arrested as he was walking on a sidewalk near the Vanderbilt Medical Center. The police approached him after receiving a tip from a Medical Center employee who had observed him in the Medical Center parking garage. The employee became suspicious because Mettetal was "looking around at cars" and was wearing a fake beard, a wig, as well as a hat and a three-piece suit on a hot (90 degrees) morning. As the employee put it when testifying at Mettetal's preliminary hearing, "The hair was definitely fake, and the beard was obviously fake.... The man looked like a weirdo."[b] When the officers spotted Mettetal on the street, they too noticed that he was wearing an "obvious fake Afro wig and a fake beard that looked like Abraham Lincoln." The officers stopped him and asked him "his business." Mettetal replied that "he had a girlfriend that he was trying to—he thought she was seeing someone else and he was watching her." One of the officers accused Mettetal of stalking, and he asked for the woman's name, but Mettetal said that he would prefer not to identify her. The officers also asked Mettetal to produce his own identification. At first he said he had none, but, eventually, he handed over an identification card from the British West Indies, which bore the name of Stephen Ray Maupin. From its appearance, the officers suspected that the card was a fake, and they later determined that the card, indeed, was false. During the encounter with the police, Mettetal was perspiring heavily, and his fake beard and moustache began to peel off. Eventually, the officers arrested him for criminal trespass and stalking.

[a] The following description is taken from United States v. Mettetal, 213 F.3d 634 (4th Cir.2000), as well as from the news stories cited below.

[b] Glenn Henderson, Mettetal Case Evidence Handled with Care, The Nashville Banner, Sept. 4, 1995, at B3.

Incident to the arrest, the officers searched a bag Mettetal was carrying. There, they found fake tattoos, nonprescription glasses, mustache glue, sketches of the Vanderbilt Medical Center parking garage, sketches of an automobile, and a large hypodermic syringe. The syringe was inscribed "super-vet" and was filled with a clear liquid. (At first, police chemists stated that they could not conclusively identify the contents of the syringe, but subsequent tests disclosed that it contained a saline solution.) But Mettetal refused to answer questions or even to disclose his name. On the following day, FBI agents informed the Nashville police that their suspect was Ray Mettetal, a neurologist from Harrisonburg, Virginia. Information about Mettetal's true identity came from, among other sources, one of his neighbors. On the night of Mettetal's arrest, the neighbor was watching a TV news program, and she saw a video-tape of Mettetal being taken from a squad car to the police station. She told reporters that she was stunned to see Mettetal's outfit. "I told my husband, Charles, 'good grief, he's wearing Little Ray's Halloween wig! How strange!'" (Little Ray is Mettetal's son.)[c]

Three days later, Virginia police searched Mettetal's home and office. The search warrants were based on the circumstances surrounding the arrest and on information obtained from family members, friends, and neighbors. These witnesses reported that Mettetal owned several high-powered firearms and that he had a long-standing grudge against Dr. George Allen, who is the chairman of the Vanderbilt Neurosurgery Department. In 1984, Mettetal was a resident in that Department, and he assisted Allen in performing an operation. At the conclusion of the operation, Allen criticized Mettetal's technical skills, and Mettetal abruptly resigned from the Vanderbilt program. A few weeks later, Mettetal petitioned for readmission, but Allen denied that request. Allen also refused to write letters supporting Mettetal's applications to other medical schools. When he described these developments to family and friends, Mettetal raged about Allen and blamed Allen for stalling his career. Mettetal then applied for a residency in the Neurosurgery Department at the University of Virginia Medical Center in Charlottesville. This application was rejected, but the school did admit him as a neurology fellow. Upon learning that he would not be permitted to study neurosurgery at Virginia, Mettetal told his ex-wife that Allen had "blackballed [him] all over the world." In 1994, he completed the neurology program and began working in the office of a Harrisonburg neurosurgeon.[d]

The search of Mettetal's home turned up a number of books with titles such as *Kill Without Joy: The Complete How-to-Kill Book*, *The Death Dealer's Manual*, *Silent Death*, and *Disguise Techniques*, as well as more bogus identification documents, fake hair, moustaches, make-up, and a hospital uniform from the Vanderbilt Medical Center. The police also found notes that described the home, cars, movements, and personal history of Dr. Allen, and they found photos of Allen, Allen's house, his cars, and the

[c] See Jim East, Looking Behind Disguise of Dr. Mettetal, The Tennessean, Sept. 1, 1995, at A1.

[d] See id.

parking garage at Vanderbilt Medical Center, together with a map of the garage surveillance cameras. Later, police searched a storage unit in Harrisonburg that had been rented by a man calling himself Stephen Ray Maupin. There, the police found a large jar of ricin, which is a deadly toxin whose possession is closely regulated, and they also found various kinds of explosives. The Nashville police later determined that Mettetal had used his fake identification to purchase the ricin and the explosives, and that he had used it to rent a post-office box.

The attempted murder prosecution fell apart when a Tennessee court granted Mettetal's motion to suppress most of the evidence on the ground that it was the fruit of the illegal seizure that occurred when the police stopped him outside the Vanderbilt Medical Center. What would have been the result if the judge had denied Mettetal's suppression motion and the case had proceeded to trial? Might additional facts be available upon investigation that would help the determination? If so, what facts and why might they matter?

_____

## NOTES ON MINIMUM CONDUCT REQUIREMENTS FOR OTHER OFFENSES

**1. _People v. Adami._** People v. Adami, 36 Cal.App.3d 452, 111 Cal. Rptr. 544 (1973), involved the following situation:

> Defendant was under investigation for sales of narcotics. Agent Thomas Dell'Ergo, who was conducting the undercover investigation, made several purchases of cocaine from defendant. During the course of their dealings, defendant mentioned to Dell'Ergo that he was having marital problems with his wife, and he was interested in getting rid of her. He expressed concern that his wife would inform the local authorities of his drug dealings. This conversation took place on November 1, 1972, over the telephone. Later that day Dell'Ergo met with defendant to negotiate the purchase of cocaine, and once again defendant mentioned that he wanted to get rid of his wife. He suggested arranging a fatal automobile accident.

> On the following day Dell'Ergo telephoned defendant regarding the purchase of cocaine, and defendant said he really wanted to have something done about his wife because she had stolen $5,000 in cash from him. Defendant said that he was interested in having Dell'Ergo be the one to do something about it.

> On the evening of November 6, 1972, Dell'Ergo contacted defendant and advised him that he had been in touch with an individual who would be willing to kill defendant's wife for a price. Dell'Ergo advised defendant that a $500 deposit was required, and it would be necessary for the defendant to furnish a photograph of

his wife. Defendant agreed, and Dell'Ergo advised him that he would set up a meeting for the following day.

Dell'Ergo met with defendant at a restaurant parking lot on November 7, 1972, in the afternoon, and drove him to the Laurel Motor Inn, where Inspector King of the San Francisco Police Department was waiting in the room. Dell'Ergo introduced King to defendant as the would-be assassin. Defendant gave King $500 and furnished him with a photograph of his wife. Defendant then wrote her description out in detail and told King of her possible whereabouts.

King testified that defendant told him that he wanted to get rid of his wife, that there was some talk about an insurance policy with a double indemnity clause that defendant had on his wife, and that they discussed the most profitable way of killing her. King then asked defendant to write out his wife's name, her physical description, where she was living (defendant and his wife were separated), the description of any cars she might be driving, and anything else that might come to defendant's mind. Defendant wrote this information on Laurel Motor Inn stationery. King told defendant the price would be $2,000 and that he wanted $500 as a down-payment with the balance to be paid upon completion of the agreement. King then asked defendant if he was going to change his mind. Defendant replied that he was not going to change his mind and when King asked him if he was sure he wanted his wife dead, defendant replied "yes". Defendant then left.

Of course, Inspector King did not carry out the plan but instead had the defendant arrested. He was indicted for attempt to commit murder, but the court refused to allow that charge to go forward. The defect, said the court, was that since neither the defendant nor the undercover agent had taken direct steps coming dangerously close to the commission of the contemplated crime, there was at most mere preparation, not a criminal attempt. Apparently, the defendant's liability for attempt required actual participation by the person solicited to commit the crime.

**2.  Solicitation as an Independent Offense.** In many American jurisdictions, prosecution on the facts of *Adami* would have to go forward under a charge of attempt. The difficulty of securing conviction for attempt in this situation, however, has led to the fairly widespread enactment of independent crimes of criminal solicitation. The prototype is § 5.02 of the Model Penal Code:

> A person is guilty of solicitation to commit a crime if with the purpose of promoting or facilitating its commission he commands, encourages or requests another to engage in specific conduct which would constitute such crime or an attempt to commit such crime....

Such provisions are based on the conclusion that purposeful solicitation of criminal conduct by another warrants preventive intervention by the police and is sufficiently indicative of criminality to support penal sanctions. Recognizing solicitation as an independent offense renders immaterial the fact that the person solicited may not actually intend to commit the crime. The guilt or innocence of the person solicited has no bearing on the liability of the initiating party.[a]

Should there be an independent offense of criminal solicitation? If so, is the Model Code definition successful? Does every solicitation involve sufficient conduct to justify penal liability?[b]

**3. Footnote on Conspiracy.** A third inchoate offense is criminal conspiracy. Traditionally, conspiracy is defined as an agreement between two or more persons to do an unlawful act or to do a lawful act by an unlawful means. The offense is inchoate or anticipatory in nature because liability is based on the preliminary step of agreement rather than on completed misconduct. The question therefore arises whether the act of agreement is a sufficient basis in conduct to support the imposition of penal sanctions. This and other aspects of the law of conspiracy are examined in detail in Chapter VIII.

**4. Completed Offenses.** The minimum conduct sufficient for criminal liability has received scant theoretical attention outside the law of attempt. Indeed, the distinction between criminal attempt and mere preparation may be the only established doctrine that squarely addresses the issue. Yet the problem arises with some frequency.

Of course, some crimes require that the actor's conduct be complete in the sense that it actually causes the ultimate harm sought to be prevented by the law. Murder is the premier example. Many crimes, however, do not require fully completed harm as a condition of liability. A false statement may be punished as perjury, even though the trial outcome is not affected. Bribery of a public servant is a crime, even though no official action is influenced. Larceny can be committed even though the property is ultimately returned. And various kinds of risk creation may be criminal, even where no injury results. In all of these cases, the law proscribes conduct preliminary to the harm ultimately feared. The issue therefore arises: How early in a course of conduct leading to actual harm should liability attach? This is exactly the same question posed by the distinction between attempt and preparation, but here it is considered in the context of defining substantive crimes.

The issue is most obvious in offenses, such as burglary, that punish some form of inchoate wrongdoing as a completed crime. The traditional

---

[a] For a more detailed exposition of this view, along with a useful review of the common law history of criminal solicitation, see Herbert Wechsler, William Kenneth Jones & Harold L. Korn, The Treatment of Inchoate Crimes in the Model Penal Code of the American Law Institute: Attempt, Solicitation, and Conspiracy, Part I, 61 Colum. L. Rev. 571, 621–28 (1961).

[b] For a discussion of some of these issues and an argument that solicitation should be limited to cases where the underlying offense is serious, see Note, Reforming the Law of Inchoate Crimes, 59 Va. L. Rev. 1235, 1260–68 (1973).

common law definition of burglary required breaking and entering the dwelling of another in the nighttime with intent to commit a felony therein. Since burglary is a more serious crime than breaking and entering without such intent, the grade of liability turns on having a purpose to engage in conduct that need not actually take place. In that respect, the offense reaches inchoate or anticipatory behavior, even though it is formally a completed crime. Moreover, some modern statutes exaggerate the inchoate aspect of the offense by diluting the actus reus to require only unauthorized entry rather than breaking and entering. Obviously, enforcement of such provisions may raise difficult questions about the sufficiency of the actor's conduct to support a finding of intent to commit a felony. Conceptually, this is the same issue as the sufficiency of the actor's conduct to support a finding of criminal purpose in the law of attempt. And in light of the conflicting resolutions of this issue in the law of attempt, it should not be surprising that the courts have also made differing interpretations of the minimum conduct requirements of modern burglary statutes.[c] The same issue arises in prosecutions for perjury, bribery, larceny, robbery, assault, and indeed virtually every other offense whose definition contains an inchoate component.

**5.  Possession.** As was noted in Chapter I, possession is a common basis of criminal liability. Generally, the term denotes exclusive dominion and control over the thing possessed. It is typically punished as a proxy for use, distribution, or sale of the item possessed. Focusing on possession greatly simplifies the practical and evidentiary burdens of law enforcement, and for that reason is a popular strategy in dealing with controlled substances and unauthorized weapons, as well as in other contexts.

Crimes of possession allow police to intervene in a course of criminal conduct at an earlier stage than might otherwise be possible. For example, the police do not need to wait until actual use of narcotics is at hand; instead they can arrest for the completed and continuing offense of possession whenever and wherever it occurs. Similarly, offenses such as possession of burglar's tools allow police to arrest and prosecute suspected burglars in the preparation stage, before conduct that would constitute attempted burglary.

In the usual run of cases, punishing possession as a legislative shortcut to proscribing use presents no serious problem. At least in the context of contraband, such as narcotics, where there is no occasion for legitimate possession, exclusive dominion and control over the forbidden item is a sufficient basis for imposing penal sanctions.

Difficulty arises, however, when the concept of possession is stretched to include borderline situations. Often the result is called *constructive* possession, presumably to indicate that liability is to be imposed even though actual possession or exclusive control cannot be proved. In some

---

[c] Compare, for example, State v. Rood, 11 Ariz.App. 102, 462 P.2d 399 (1969), where unauthorized but non-forcible entry of another's home was found inadequate to support a finding of intent to steal, with Ealey v. State, 139 Ga.App. 604, 229 S.E.2d 86 (1976), where the opposite conclusion was reached on similar facts.

cases, the courts have emphasized presence plus a proprietary interest in the premises as the basis of liability for possession. Thus, the owner or lessee of a dwelling might be convicted of possessing contraband found there. The problem is especially acute in group arrests. Several persons may be found in a single room or apartment that contains an illegal drug. Does a proprietary or possessory interest in the premises justify distinguishing one person from the others present? Does the answer depend on where within the premises the contraband was found? What if it is found in the owner's bedroom or in some other location to which guests ordinarily would not have access? What if the owner is married and the contraband is found in the marital bedroom? Are both parties to the marriage guilty of possession? Neither? Obviously, such problems are resolved, at least in part, if the courts stick to actual, personal dominion and control and do not venture into the uncertainties of so-called constructive possession.

---

## SECTION 2:  MENS REA

## People v. Thomas

Supreme Court of Colorado, 1986.
729 P.2d 972.

■ LOHR, JUSTICE. The defendant, John Leago Thomas, Jr., was convicted of attempted reckless manslaughter and first degree assault as the result of a jury trial in Adams County District Court. On appeal, the defendant argued, among other things, that attempted reckless manslaughter is not a cognizable crime in Colorado. The court of appeals agreed with the defendant's argument and reversed the conviction for attempted reckless manslaughter, but affirmed the conviction for first degree assault. We granted certiorari to determine whether attempted reckless manslaughter is a cognizable crime in the state of Colorado. We conclude that it is, and hold that the court of appeals erred in reversing the defendant's conviction for that crime.

I.

On the evening of February 4, 1981, the defendant received a telephone call from a former girlfriend informing him that she had been raped in her apartment by a man who lived in an apartment upstairs. The defendant arrived at the woman's apartment shortly thereafter, armed with a pistol. He went upstairs and gained entrance into the apartment occupied by the alleged assailant by identifying himself as a policeman. The defendant pointed his gun at the man who, believing the defendant was a police officer, accompanied him back down to the woman's apartment. The woman identified the man as the rapist, and the defendant instructed her to call the police. At that time, the man started to flee to his own apartment, and the <u>defendant gave chase</u>. The <u>defendant fired three shots,</u> <u>two of which struck the fleeing man.</u> The defendant testified that he fired the first shot as a warning when the man was going up the stairs, that he fired a second shot accidentally when the man kicked him while on the stairs, and that the third shot was also a warning shot, fired from the outside of the building near the window of the apartment occupied by the alleged rapist. When the police arrived, they found the defendant still waiting outside, holding the gun.

The jury was instructed on the crimes of attempted first degree murder, first degree assault, and the lesser included offenses of attempted second degree murder, attempted reckless manslaughter, attempted heat of passion manslaughter, and second degree assault.[a] The <u>jury returned</u> <u>verdicts of guilty to the charges of first degree assault and attempted</u> <u>reckless manslaughter, and the trial court entered judgment accordingly.</u>

<u>Upon appeal, the court of appeals sustained the conviction for first</u> <u>degree assault, but reversed the attempted</u> reckless manslaughter conviction on the basis that attempted reckless manslaughter is not a legally <u>cognizable offense in Colorado.</u> We granted certiorari to review that latter conclusion and the resulting reversal of the defendant's conviction for attempted reckless manslaughter.

II.A.

The language of the relevant statutes provides the framework for our analysis. The crime of reckless manslaughter is defined in § 18–3–104(1)(a), 8B C.R.S. (1986), as follows:

> (1) <u>A person commits the crime of manslaughter if:</u> (a) He reckless<u>ly causes the death of another person;</u> . . . .

"Recklessly," the relevant culpable mental state for this crime, is defined in § 18–1–501(8):

> A person <u>acts recklessly when he consciously disregards a</u> substantial and u<u>njustifiable risk that a result will occur or that a</u> <u>circumstance exists.</u>

As applied to the offense of reckless manslaughter, the requisite conscious disregard of a substantial and unjustifiable risk relates to a result, the death of another person.

The inchoate offense of criminal attempt is defined as follows in § 18–2–101(1):

> <u>A person commits</u> criminal attempt if, acting with the kind of culpability otherwise required for commission of an offense, he engages <u>in conduct constituting a substantial step toward the</u> commission of the offense. A substantial step is <u>any conduct,</u> <u>whether act, omission, or possession, which is strongly corrobora-</u>

---

[a] The relevant Colorado statutes are reproduced in Appendix B.—[Footnote by eds.]

tive of the firmness of the actor's purpose to complete the commission of the offense. . . .

The court of appeals held that "[r]ecklessness is . . . a mental culpability which is incompatible with the concept of an intentional act." This is so, the court held, because the "conscious disregard" with respect to risk of death that is essential to reckless manslaughter cannot be equated with the conscious intent to cause death which the court of appeals implicitly determined to be a necessary element of the offense of criminal attempt in this context. On certiorari review, the defendant supports this analysis, contending that "[o]ne cannot intend to cause a specific result . . . by consciously disregarding the risk that the result will occur." A careful analysis of the elements of criminal attempt and of reckless manslaughter demonstrates, however, that the court of appeals' analysis and the defendant's supporting arguments are misconceived.

In People v. Frysig, 628 P.2d 1004 (Colo.1981), we construed the criminal attempt statute in the context of a charge of attempted first degree sexual assault. We held that the intent to commit the underlying offense is an essential element of the crime. More precisely, in order to be guilty of criminal attempt, the actor must act with the kind of culpability otherwise required for commission of the underlying offense and must engage in the conduct which constitutes the substantial step with the further intent to perform acts which, if completed, would constitute the underlying offense. In order to complete the offense of reckless manslaughter, it is necessary that the actor cause the death of another person by acting in a manner that involves a substantial and unjustifiable risk of death of that other person and that the actor be conscious of that risk and of its nature when electing to act. Attempted reckless manslaughter requires that the accused have the intent to commit the underlying offense of reckless manslaughter. The "intent to commit the underlying offense" of which People v. Frysig speaks is the intent to engage in and complete the risk-producing act or conduct. It does not include an intent that death occur even though the underlying crime, reckless manslaughter, has death as an essential element.

The crime of attempted reckless manslaughter also requires that the risk-producing act or conduct be commenced and sufficiently pursued to constitute a "substantial step toward the commission of the offense." § 18–2–101(1). That is, the act or conduct must proceed far enough to be "strongly corroborative of the firmness of the actor's purpose" to complete those acts that will produce a substantial and unjustifiable risk of death of another.

Finally, in order to be guilty of attempted reckless manslaughter the actor must engage in the requisite acts or conduct "with the kind of culpability otherwise required for the commission of the underlying offense," that is, with a conscious disregard of a substantial and unjustifiable risk that the acts or conduct will cause the death of another person. Based upon this analysis, and contrary to the defendant's argument, there is no logical or legal inconsistency involved in the recognition of attempted reckless manslaughter as a crime under the Colorado Criminal Code.

Our analysis of the crime of attempted reckless manslaughter is buttressed by the case of People v. Castro, 657 P.2d 932 (Colo. 1983), in which we held that attempted extreme indifference murder is a cognizable crime under the Colorado Criminal Code. In that case, the defendant urged that extreme indifference murder involves an unintentional and inchoate act—apparently referring to the required element of the death of another, which can more accurately be characterized as a result than as an act—and that criminal attempt requires an intent to complete the underlying offense. The latter intent, the argument proceeded, necessarily involves an intent that the death of another result from the actor's conduct. The defendant argued that to intend an unintentional and inchoate act defies logic, so there can be no such crime as attempted extreme indifference murder. We concluded that an essential premise of this argument was fatally flawed. [W]e noted that "[t]he crime of extreme indifference murder, . . . while not requiring a conscious object to kill, necessitates a conscious object to engage in conduct that creates a grave risk of death to another. . . . In this sense the culpability element of extreme indifference murder is akin to what traditionally has been known as 'general intent.' " Therefore, since the intentional state of mind required by the crime of attempted extreme indifference murder relates to the proscribed conduct and not the proscribed result, death of another person, we concluded that there is no logical inconsistency inherent in charging an attempt to commit extreme indifference murder. This parallels the foregoing analysis and conclusion with respect to the crime of attempted reckless manslaughter to which the present case relates.

Stated somewhat differently, *People v. Castro* makes clear that the intent requirement for extreme indifference murder does not involve a conscious object to kill, but instead necessitates a conscious object to engage in conduct that in fact creates a grave risk of death to another. This is not the specific intent encompassed within the Colorado Criminal Code's definition of the terms "intentionally" or "with intent" which requires a conscious object to cause a proscribed result. Rather, it is "akin to what traditionally has been known as 'general intent,' " which is described by the terms "knowingly" or "willfully," defined in § 18–1–501(6) as those terms relate to conduct. Therefore, since the underlying crime of extreme indifference murder does not involve unintentional conduct, the attempt to commit that crime does not involve an attempt to commit an unintentional act. So it is as well with the crime of reckless manslaughter.

B.

In People v. Krovarz, 697 P.2d 378 (Colo. 1985), we employed a new mode of analysis to determine whether a particular substantive crime can provide a foundation for criminal attempt liability. There, we examined the rationale for imposition of criminal penalties for attempts falling short of accomplishment of a completed substantive crime. We concluded that "culpability for criminal attempt rests primarily upon the actor's purpose to cause harmful consequences," and that "[p]unishment is justified where the actor intends harm because there exists a high likelihood that his 'unspent' intent will flower into harmful conduct at any moment." We held, however, that our criminal attempt statute does not require a conscious purpose to achieve proscribed results as a condition to criminal liability. That is, criminal attempt is not a specific intent offense.... Rather, the probability of future dangerousness that has given rise to the justified legislative judgment that criminal attempt liability should be imposed "is equally present when one acts knowingly."....

One acts recklessly with respect to result when he consciously disregards a substantial and unjustified risk that a result will occur. When one engages in conduct that involves a risk of death that is both substantial and unjustified, and is conscious of the nature and extent of the risk, the actor demonstrates such a disregard for the likelihood that another will die as to evince a degree of dangerousness hardly less threatening to society than if the actor had chosen to cause death.....[5]

... The critical inquiry under *Krovarz* is potential for future danger. For this purpose, the awareness of a practical certainty of the prohibited result that is required for knowing conduct cannot be viewed as more dangerous, in any important degree, than the conscious disregard of a substantial and unjustifiable risk that the proscribed result will occur—the hallmark of reckless action. Although a difference in the degree of moral culpability of the actor might be perceived between knowingly achieving a proscribed result and recklessly accomplishing it, we now conclude that the difference in potential for future danger inherent in those two culpable mental states is not significant enough to justify a different result under the *Krovarz* test.

We conclude that the index of dangerousness analysis utilized in *People v. Krovarz* leads to the same result achieved by examining and construing the statutory language under the standards of *People v. Castro* and *People v. Frysig*. Accordingly, we hold that attempted reckless manslaughter is a crime proscribed by the Colorado Criminal Code.

We reverse that part of the court of appeals' judgment overturning the defendant's conviction for attempted reckless manslaughter.

■ DUBOFSKY, J., specially concurs. I join the majority opinion under the facts of this case. People v. Krovarz, 697 P.2d 378, 381 n.9 (Colo. 1985), suggests that the analysis employed in that case should not be extended to attempted reckless conduct. The footnote in Krovarz reflected the concern of a commentator who observed that allowing one to be charged with attempted murder under the wide range of conduct encompassed within "reckless,"

---

[5] In People v. Hernandez, 44 Colo.App. 161, 614 P.2d 900 (1980), the court of appeals held that attempted criminally negligent homicide is not a cognizable crime. The analysis in that case parallels that of the court of appeals in the present case. Although we have rejected this analysis, we express no opinion concerning the correctness of the result reached by the court of appeals in *People v. Hernandez*.

without a resulting death, may extend criminal liability for harmful conduct to situations such as driving very fast on the wrong side of the road while going around a curve. Arnold Enker, Mens Rea and Criminal Attempt, 1977 Am.Bar Found.Res.J. 845, 854. The conduct is not in fact harmful if there is no traffic coming in the opposite direction. The commentator suggested that where the actor risks harm, rather than intending harm, the conduct should be penalized under a legislative definition of a substantive crime instead of the common law definition of attempt. Given the facts in this case, however, I am convinced that the defendant came close enough to intending harm that he can be convicted of attempted reckless manslaughter.

---

## NOTES ON THE MENS REA OF ATTEMPT

**1. The Traditional View:** *Thacker v. Commonwealth.* The result in *Thomas* is unusual.[a] The traditional view is that attempt requires a specific intent "to do the entire evil thing. The intent in the mind covers the thing in full; the act covers it only in part." Merritt v. Commonwealth, 164 Va. 653, 661, 180 S.E. 395, 399 (1935). Thacker v. Commonwealth, 134 Va. 767, 114 S.E. 504 (1922), illustrates the traditional approach. The facts were:

> The accused, in company with two other young men, ... was attending a church festival in Allegheny County, at which all three became intoxicated. They left the church between 10 and 11 o'clock at night, and walked down the country road about one and one-half miles, when they came to a sharp curve. Located in this curve was a tent in which ... Mrs. J.A. Ratrie, her husband, four children, and a servant were camping for the summer. The husband, though absent, was expected home that night, and Mrs. Ratrie, upon retiring, had placed a lighted lamp on a trunk by the head of her bed. After 11 o'clock she was awakened by the shots of a pistol and loud talking in the road near by, and heard a man say, "I am going to shoot that Goddamned light out"; and another voice said, "Don't shoot the light out." The accused and his friends then appeared at the back of the tent, where the flaps of the tent were open, and said they were from Bath County and had lost

---

[a] But it is not unique. Compare Gentry v. State, 437 So.2d 1097 (Fla. 1983):

> In the instant case, the appellant ... swore at his father, choked him, snapped a pistol several times to his head and when the weapon failed to fire, struck his father in the head with the gun. Had a homicide occurred, there can be no doubt that the appellant could have been successfully prosecuted for second-degree murder without the state adducing proof

of a specific intent to kill. The fact that the father survived was not the result of any design on the part of the appellant not to effect death but was simply fortuitous. We can think of no good reason to reward the appellant for such fortuity by imposing upon the state the added burden of showing a specific intent to kill in order to successfully prosecute the attempted offense.

their way, and asked Mrs. Ratrie if she could take care of them all night. She informed them she was camping for the summer, and had no room for them. One of the three thanked her, and they turned away, but after passing around the tent the accused used some vulgar language and did some cursing and singing. When they got back in the road, the accused said again he was going to shoot the light out, and fired three shots, two of which went through the tent, one passing through the head of the bed in which Mrs. Ratrie was lying, just missing her head and the head of her baby, who was sleeping with her. The accused did not know Mrs. Ratrie, and had never seen her before. He testified he did not know any of the parties in the tent, and had no ill will against either of them; that he simply shot at the light, without any intent to harm Mrs. Ratrie or any one else; that he would not have shot had he been sober, and regretted his action.

The defendant was convicted of attempted murder, but the Supreme Court of Appeals of Virginia reversed:

In discussing the law of attempts, W. Clark, Criminal Law 111–12 (1894), says:

The act must be done with the specific intent to commit a particular crime. This specific intent at the time the act is done is essential. To do an act from general malevolence is not an attempt to commit a crime because there is no specific intent, though the act according to its consequences may amount to a substantive crime.... A man actuated by general malevolence may commit murder, though there is not actual intention to kill; to be guilty of an attempt to murder there must be a specific intent to kill.

1 J. Bishop, Criminal Law 731–36 (8th ed. 1892), says:

... When we say that a man attempted to do a given wrong, we mean that he intended to do specifically it, and proceeded a certain way in the doing. The intent in the mind covers the thing in full; the act covers it only in part. Thus to commit murder, one need not intend to take life, but to be guilty of an attempt to murder, he must so intend. It is not sufficient that his act, had it proved fatal, would have been murder. We have seen that the unintended taking of life may be murder, yet there can be no attempt to murder without the specific intent to commit it.... For example, if one from a housetop recklessly throws down a billet of wood upon the sidewalk where persons are constantly passing, and it falls upon a person passing by and kills him, this would be common law murder, but if, instead of killing, it inflicts only a slight injury, the party could not be convicted of an assault with intent to commit murder since, in fact, the murder was not intended.

The application of the foregoing principles to the facts of the instant case shows clearly, as we think, that the judgment complained of is erroneous. While it might possibly be said that the firing of the shot into the head of Mrs. Ratrie's bed was an act done towards the commission of the offense charged, the evidence falls far short of proving that it was fired with the intent to murder her . . . .[b]

**2. The Model Penal Code.** The Model Penal Code accepts the *Thacker* result, but departs from the common law position that a specific intent is required as to *all* elements of the offense attempted. Section 5.01 of the Model Code provides:

> (1) . . . A person is guilty of an attempt to commit a crime if, acting with the kind of culpability otherwise required for commission of the crime, he:

> > (a) purposely engages in conduct which would constitute the crime if the attendant circumstances were as he believes them to be; or

> > (b) when causing a particular result is an element of the crime, does or omits to do anything with the purpose of causing or with the belief that it will cause such result without further conduct on his part; or

> > (c) purposely does or omits to do anything which, under the circumstances as he believes them to be, is an act or omission constituting a substantial step in a course of conduct planned to culminate in his commission of the crime.

This is one of the more inartfully drafted provisions of the Model Code. Its intended meaning is clear, although how one gets there from the statutory language is uncharacteristically obscure. The intended meaning is explained in elaborate commentary by its drafters in Herbert Wechsler, William Kenneth Jones & Harold L. Korn, The Treatment of Inchoate Crimes in the Model Penal Code of the American Law Institute: Attempt, Solicitation, and Conspiracy, 61 Colum. L. Rev. 571, 957 (1961). The Model Code means to require a purpose to engage in the conduct and result

---

[b] People v. Acevedo, 32 N.Y.2d 807, 345 N.Y.S.2d 555 (1973), reached the same result. The defendant fired a rifle from a rooftop and seriously wounded several people. The applicable murder statute covered "[t]he killing of a human being [by] an act imminently dangerous to others, and evincing a depraved mind, regardless of human life, although without a premeditated design to effect the death of any individual." Acevedo's conviction of attempted murder was reversed because the jury instruction did not require the finding of a specific intent to kill.

A situation comparable to *Thacker* and *Acevedo* arose under the revised Oregon statutes reproduced in Appendix B. In State v. Smith, 21 Or.App. 270, 534 P.2d 1180 (1975), the court held that a charge of attempted reckless murder could not be sustained. For discussion of an interesting series of Illinois decisions coming eventually to the same result, see People v. Harris, 72 Ill.2d 16, 17 Ill.Dec. 838, 377 N.E.2d 28 (1978).—[Footnote by eds.]

elements of the object offense,[c] but the mens rea for the circumstance elements of the attempt would be the same as would be required were the offense completed.[d] The Model Code does, however, add an offense designed to cover the *Thomas* and *Thacker* situations. Section 211.2 (recklessly endangering another person) provides:

> A person commits a misdemeanor if he recklessly engages in conduct which places or may place another person in danger of death or serious bodily injury. Recklessness and danger shall be presumed where a person knowingly points a firearm at or in the direction of another, whether or not the actor believed the firearm to be loaded.

**3.   Rationale for Specific Intent Requirement.** One frequently given reason to require a specific intent for attempts was described in Oliver Wendell Holmes, The Common Law as etymological in origin. It is illustrated by the following passage from Smith, Two Problems in Criminal Attempts, 70 Harv. L. Rev. 422, 434 (1957):

> The conception of attempt seems necessarily to involve the notion of an intended consequence. Thus the word "attempt" is defined in the Shorter Oxford English Dictionary as "a putting forth of effort to accomplish what is uncertain or difficult." When a man attempts to do something he is "endeavoring" or "trying" to do it. All these ways of describing an attempt seem to require a desired, or at least an intended, consequence. Recklessness and negligence are incompatible with desire or intention. [T]herefore, in a crime which by definition may be committed recklessly or negligently . . . , it is impossible to conceive of an attempt.[e]

Holmes himself preferred a different rationale. He argued:

> There is [a] class of cases in which intent plays an important part. . . . The most obvious examples of this class are criminal attempts. . . .
>
> Some acts may be attempts . . . which could not have effected the crime unless followed by other acts on the part of the wrong-

[c] There is a minor exception for result elements intended by the language "or with the belief that it will cause such result without further conduct on his part" in subsection (1)(b). These words are designed to permit an attempt charge against actors who believe that a forbidden result will occur, though they may be indifferent to its occurrence. An example would be a case where a business rival rigs a competitor's airplane so that it will crash, in order to cause a prospective customer to believe that it is defectively designed. The actor in such a case may believe that the pilot will be killed, but either not care or hope that the pilot is skillful enough to escape in some manner. Such a case, in the view of the Model Code drafters, should be assimilated to one where the actor intends to kill.

[d] Section 5.01 thus is one of the rare instances under the Model Code where proper classification of an element as a "circumstance" as opposed to "conduct" or "result" is crucial.

[e] Cf. Rollin Perkins & Ronald Boyce, Criminal Law 637 (3d ed. 1982): "The word 'attempt' means to try; it implies an effort to bring about a desired result. Hence an attempt to commit any crime requires a specific intent to commit that particular offense."

doer. For instance, lighting a match with intent to set fire to a haystack has been held to amount to a criminal attempt to burn it, although the defendant blew out the match on seeing that he was watched. . . .

In such cases the law goes on a new principle, different from that governing most substantive crimes. The reason for punishing any act must generally be to prevent some harm which is foreseen as likely to follow that act under the circumstances in which it is done. In most substantive crimes the ground on which that likelihood stands is the common working of natural causes as shown by experience. But when an act is punished the natural effect of which is not harmful under the circumstances, that ground alone will not suffice. The probability does not exist unless there are grounds for expecting that the act done will be followed by other acts in connection with which its effect will be harmful, although not so otherwise. But as in fact no such acts have followed, it cannot, in general, be assumed, from the mere doing of what has been done, that they would have followed if the actor had not been interrupted. They would not have followed it unless the actor had chosen, and the only way generally available to show that he would have chosen to do them is by showing that he intended to do them when he did what he did. The accompanying intent in that case renders the otherwise innocent act harmful, because it raises a probability that it will be followed by such other acts and events as will all together result in harm. The importance of the intent is not to show that the act was wicked, but to show that it was likely to be followed by hurtful consequences. . . .

Are there other reasons for the specific intent requirement? Should the specific intent apply to all elements of the object offense? The next two notes explore these questions in more detail.

**4.  Circumstance Elements.** Consider the following hypotheticals:

The crime of statutory rape is usually defined as sexual intercourse with a person below a certain age, irrespective of consent. Typically, liability is strict as to the age of the victim. A mistake by the defendant as to age, no matter how reasonable, is not a defense. Assume that the age of consent is 16 and that the defendant has passed beyond mere preparation and is interrupted just prior to actual intercourse. Assume further that the defendant intended intercourse, that the defendant's conduct fully corroborates this intent, and that the victim was 15. Should a belief that the victim was 17 be a defense? The answer would be "yes" if specific intent is required for *all* of the elements of the completed offense—if, indeed, the defendant must intend "to do the entire evil thing." Is this the right answer? How would the *Thomas* court analyze this problem?

Assume that burglary is defined in the traditional common law manner as breaking and entering the dwelling house of another at night with the intent to commit a felony therein. Assume that 7 p.m. is when "night" begins. If the defendant completed the offense at 7:30 p.m., the defendant's belief that it was only 6:30 would not be a valid defense. If the defendant was caught before the offense was completed, would the belief that it was only 6:30 constitute a defense to attempted burglary? Should it?

J.C. Smith has argued that no special policy of the law of attempt should displace the mens rea otherwise required for the completed offense in the situation illustrated by these two hypotheticals. He believes that the mens rea as to circumstance elements should be the same for the attempt as it would be for the completed offense. In Two Problems in Criminal Attempts, 70 Harv. L. Rev. 422, 434–35 (1957),* he explains:

> [A]n attempt is so essentially connected with consequences— with that event or series of events which is the principal constituent of the crime—that the only essential intention is an intention to bring about those consequences; and ... if recklessness, or negligence, or even blameless inadvertence with respect to the remaining constituents of the crime (the ... circumstances) will suffice for the substantive crime, it will suffice also for the attempt. It must be admitted that there appears to be no authority in support of these propositions,[f] but there appears to be no authority against them and it is submitted that they achieve a common-sense result and are in accordance with principle....
>
> Since the consequence which is involved in the complete crime must be intended, the emphasis in attempts is naturally on intention. But where D intends to produce a consequence which in the actual existing circumstances will constitute the actus reus of a substantive crime, and he does so with the mens rea of that same crime (being reckless or negligent or blamelessly inadvertent, as the case may be, as to a ... circumstance), is there any reason why he should not be convicted of an attempt if he fails to accomplish his intention? It is submitted that there is not. If D's state of mind

[f] The English Court of Appeal subsequently adopted Smith's view in Regina v. Pigg, [1982] 2 All. E.R. 591, holding that recklessness was sufficient for the "consent" element in a charge of attempted rape. See also Glanville Williams, The Problem of Reckless Attempts, [1983] Crim. L. Rev. 365, which defends *Pigg* as the right result even under the subsequently enacted English attempt statute that requires an "intent to commit an offence" without differentiating among the elements thereof.

There seem to be few American authorities that speak to this point. But see State v. Davis, 108 N.H. 158, 160–61, 229 A.2d 842, 844 (1967), where the court said without elaboration: "The fact that defendant was ignorant of the age of the female or that he did not intend the intercourse to be with a girl of non-age would not prevent his act from constituting [statutory] rape if completed, or an attempt, if it failed." In People v. Krovarz, 697 P.2d 378, 383 n.11 (Colo.1985), the court adverted to the issue but found it not presented by the facts of the case.—[Footnote by eds.]

is sufficiently blameworthy to ground liability for the complete crime, it is surely sufficiently blameworthy to ground liability for the attempt; and if *D* had done all that he intended to do, his act would have constituted the actus reus of that same crime. He has attempted to produce a consequence which in the existing circumstances is, if accompanied by a particular state of mind, forbidden by law and he has that state of mind which the law prescribes as a condition of guilt.

Is Smith right? In Mens Rea and Criminal Attempt, 1977 A.B.F. Res. J. 845, 866–78, Arnold Enker argues that Smith's distinction between results and circumstances "seems to be justified in terms of policy" in cases where the object offense and the attempt require recklessness as to a circumstance element. In cases where negligence or strict liability suffices for the completed offense, however, he argues that there may be a problem of insufficient warning from the conduct of which the actor is aware that a criminal offense is being attempted. If this were so, he concludes, a mens rea of at least recklessness should be required for that element.

**5. Completed Conduct But No Result.** Does *Thomas* likewise present a situation where no special policy of the law of attempt should elevate the mens rea above what would be required for the completed offense? Consider the following line of argument.

The law of attempt proceeds on the premise that the deterrent or social control functions of the criminal law require punishment of those who come dangerously close to the commission of crime or who manifest a dangerous propensity to engage in criminal behavior. Thomas completed conduct that created a serious risk of fatality and, for all that appears, was saved from a manslaughter conviction only by fortuitous circumstances. He appears to have been no less culpable and no less dangerous than he would have been had a death occurred.

Consider also the arguments in favor of requiring a specific intent for attempts. Holmes contended that specific intent is required in attempt offenses in order to show that the defendant was likely to engage in additional conduct that would complete the crime. This rationale explains some cases, but seems clearly inapplicable to situations like that presented in *Thomas*. Thomas completed his planned course of behavior, and no further conduct would have been required to justify convicting him of manslaughter had a death resulted.

If a specific intent is to be required in the *Thomas* situation, therefore, some other rationale must be advanced. One possibility is that the requirement of specific intent serves the function of protecting the innocent from unwarranted conviction. However, this interest, which arises frequently in attempt prosecutions, is of serious concern only when the defendant's conduct is ambiguous and there is genuine doubt whether the defendant actually presented the dangers at which the law of attempt is aimed. There is little basis for such concern on the facts of *Thomas*.

How, then, can one explain the traditional view to the contrary and its endorsement in the Model Penal Code? How would one answer the line of argument recited above?

**6.   Questions and Comments on *Thomas*.** Thomas was convicted of assault in the first degree (a class 3 felony) and attempted reckless manslaughter (manslaughter is a class 4 felony; an attempt to commit a class 4 felony is a class 5 felony).[g] Consider the following provisions of Colorado law in connection with *Thomas*:

> § 18–3–206. Menacing. A person commits the crime of menacing if, by any threat or physical action, he knowingly places or attempts to place another person in fear of imminent serious bodily injury. Menacing is a class 3 misdemeanor, but, if committed by the use of a deadly weapon, it is a class 5 felony.

> § 18–3–208. Reckless endangerment. A person who recklessly engages in conduct which creates a substantial risk of serious bodily injury to another person commits reckless endangerment, which is a class 3 misdemeanor.

What is the function in Colorado of the offense of attempted reckless manslaughter? More specifically, is there any violation of § 18–3–206 or § 18–3–208 that would not also be an attempted manslaughter? Has the court in *Thomas* undermined the grading structure adopted by the Colorado legislature? On what principles does that grading structure appear to be based? Compare *People v. Castro* (described in *Thomas*). Does that case present the same problems?

Notice that there is no offense of "negligent endangering" in the Model Penal Code or in Colorado law. Should there be one? When the question decided in *People v. Hernandez* (described in a footnote in *Thomas*) reaches the Colorado Supreme Court, how should it be decided?

# Section 3:  Impossibility

## People v. Dlugash

Court of Appeals of New York, 1977.
41 N.Y.2d 725, 363 N.E.2d 1155, 395 N.Y.S.2d 419.

■ Jasen, Judge.

The criminal law is of ancient origin, but criminal liability for attempt to commit a crime is comparatively recent. At the root of the concept of attempt liability are the very aims and purposes of penal law. The ultimate issue is whether an individual's intentions and actions, though failing to

---

[g] The sentencing provisions of Colorado law are complex, but in rough terms the maxima in 1995 were 16 years for a class 3 felony, eight years for a class 4 felony, and four years for a class 5 felony. The maximum penalties in effect at the time of Thomas' offense for each class were half of the 1995 levels.

achieve a manifest and malevolent criminal purpose, constitute a danger to organized society of sufficient magnitude to warrant the imposition of criminal sanctions. Difficulties in theoretical analysis and concomitant debate over very pragmatic questions of blameworthiness appear dramatically in reference to situations where the criminal attempt failed to achieve its purpose solely because the factual or legal context in which the individual acted was not as the actor supposed them to be. Phrased somewhat differently, the concern centers on whether an individual should be liable for an attempt to commit a crime when, unknown to him, it was impossible to successfully complete the crime attempted. For years, serious studies have been made on the subject in an effort to resolve the continuing controversy when, if at all, the impossibility of successfully completing the criminal act should preclude liability for even making the futile attempt. The 1967 revision of the Penal Law approached the impossibility defense to the inchoate crime of attempt in a novel fashion. The statute provides that, if a person engages in conduct which would otherwise constitute an attempt to commit a crime, "it is no defense to a prosecution for such attempt that the crime charged to have been attempted was, under the attendant circumstances, factually or legally impossible of commission, if such crime could have been committed had the attendant circumstances been as such person believed them to be." (Penal Law, § 110.10.) This appeal presents to us, for the first time, a case involving the application of the modern statute. We hold that, under the proof presented by the People at trial, defendant Melvin Dlugash may be held for attempted murder, though the target of the attempt may have already been slain, by the hand of another, when Dlugash made his felonious attempt.

On December 22, 1973, Michael Geller, 25 years old, was found shot to death in the bedroom of his Brooklyn apartment. The body, which had literally been riddled by bullets, was found lying face up on the floor. An autopsy revealed that the victim had been shot in the face and head no less than seven times. Powder burns on the face indicated that the shots had been fired from within one foot of the victim. Four small caliber bullets were recovered from the victim's skull. The victim had also been critically wounded in the chest. One heavy caliber bullet passed through the left lung, penetrated the heart chamber, pierced the left ventricle of the heart upon entrance and again upon exit, and lodged in the victim's torso. A second bullet entered the left lung and passed through to the chest, but without reaching the heart area. Although the second bullet was damaged beyond identification, the bullet tracks indicated that these wounds were also inflicted by a bullet of heavy caliber. A tenth bullet, of unknown caliber, passed through the thumb of the victim's left hand. The autopsy report listed the cause of death as "[m]ultiple bullet wounds of head and chest with brain injury and massive bilateral hemothorax with penetration of [the] heart." Subsequent ballistics examination established that the four bullets recovered from the victim's head were .25 caliber bullets and that the heart-piercing bullet was of .38 caliber. [The evidence revealed that Joe Bush had fired as many as five shots with a .38 caliber weapon and that "a few minutes [later], perhaps two, perhaps as much as five," the defendant "walked over to the fallen Geller, drew his .25 caliber pistol, and fired approximately five shots in the victim's head and face."]

Defendant was indicted by the Grand Jury of Kings County on a single count of murder in that, acting in concert with another person actually present, he intentionally caused the death of Michael Geller.... From [two] physicians, the prosecution sought to establish that Geller was still alive at the time defendant shot at him. Both physicians testified that each of the two chest wounds, for which defendant alleged Bush to be responsible, would have caused death without prompt medical attention. Moreover, the victim would have remained alive until such time as his chest cavity became fully filled with blood. Depending on the circumstances, it might take five to 10 minutes for the chest cavity to fill. Neither prosecution witness could state, with medical certainty, that the victim was still alive when, perhaps five minutes after the initial chest wounds were inflicted, the defendant fired at the victim's head.

The defense produced but a single witness, the former Chief Medical Examiner of New York City. This expert stated that, in his view, Geller might have died of the chest wounds "very rapidly" since, in addition to the bleeding, a large bullet going through a lung and the heart would have other adverse medical effects. "Those wounds can be almost immediately or rapidly fatal or they may be delayed in there, in the time it would take for death to occur. But I would say that wounds like that which are described here as having gone through the lungs and the heart would be fatal wounds and in most cases they're rapidly fatal."

The trial court ... submitted ... two theories to the jury: that defendant had either intentionally murdered Geller or had attempted to murder Geller. The jury found the defendant guilty of murder.... [8] On appeal, the Appellate Division reversed.... The court ruled that "the People failed to prove beyond a reasonable doubt that Geller had been alive at the time he was shot by defendant; defendant's conviction of murder thus cannot stand." Further, the court held that the judgment could not be modified to reflect a conviction for attempted murder because "the uncontradicted evidence is that the defendant, at the time that he fired the five shots into the body of the decedent, believed him to be dead...."

Preliminarily, we state our agreement with the Appellate Division that the evidence did not establish, beyond a reasonable doubt, that Geller was alive at the time defendant fired into his body. To sustain a homicide conviction, it must be established, beyond a reasonable doubt, that the defendant caused the death of another person. The People were required to

---

[8] It should be noted that Joe Bush pleaded guilty to a charge of manslaughter in the first degree. At the time he entered his plea, Bush detailed his version of the homicide. According to Bush, defendant Dlugash was a dealer in narcotic drugs and Dlugash claimed that Geller owed him a large sum of money from drug purchases. Bush was in the kitchen alone when Geller entered and threatened him with a shotgun. Bush pulled out his .38 caliber pistol and fired five times at Geller. Geller slumped to the floor. Dlugash then entered, withdrew his .25 caliber pistol and fired five shots into the deceased's face. Bush, however, never testified at Dlugash's trial.

establish that the shots fired by defendant Dlugash were a sufficiently direct cause of Geller's death. While the defendant admitted firing five shots at the victim approximately two to five minutes after Bush had fired three times, all three medical expert witnesses testified that they could not, with any degree of medical certainty, state whether the victim had been alive at the time the latter shots were fired by the defendant. Thus, the People failed to prove beyond a reasonable doubt that the victim had been alive at the time he was shot by the defendant. Whatever else it may be, it is not murder to shoot a dead body. Man dies but once.

. . . The most intriguing attempt cases are those where the attempt to commit a crime was unsuccessful due to mistakes of fact or law on the part of the would-be criminal. A general rule developed in most American jurisdictions that legal impossibility is a good defense but factual impossibility is not. Thus, for example, it was held that defendants who shot at a stuffed deer did not attempt to take a deer out of season, even though they believed the dummy to be a live animal. The court stated that there was no criminal attempt because it was no crime to "take" a stuffed deer, and it is no crime to attempt to do that which is legal. (State v. Guffey, 262 S.W.2d 152 (Mo. App. 1953); see, also, State v. Taylor, 345 Mo. 325, 133 S.W.2d 336 (1939)(no liability for attempt to bribe a juror where person bribed was not, in fact, a juror).) These cases are illustrative of legal impossibility. A further example is Francis Wharton's classic hypothetical involving Lady Eldon and her French lace. Lady Eldon, traveling in Europe, purchased a quantity of French lace at a high price, intending to smuggle it into England without payment of the duty. When discovered in a customs search, the lace turned out to be of English origin, of little value and not subject to duty. The traditional view is that Lady Eldon is not liable for an attempt to smuggle. (1 F. Wharton, Criminal Law (12th ed.), § 225, p. 304, n.9 (1932); for variations on the hypothetical see Graham Hughes, One Further Footnote on Attempting the Impossible, 42 N.Y.U.L. Rev. 1005 (1967).)

On the other hand, factual impossibility was no defense. For example, a man was held liable for attempted murder when he shot into the room in which his target usually slept and, fortuitously, the target was sleeping elsewhere in the house that night. (State v. Mitchell, 170 Mo. 633, 71 S.W. 175 (1902)) Although one bullet struck the target's customary pillow, attainment of the criminal objective was factually impossible. State v. Moretti, 52 N.J. 182, 244 A.2d 499 (1968) presents a similar instance of factual impossibility. The defendant agreed to perform an abortion, then a criminal act, upon a female undercover police investigator who was not, in fact, pregnant. The court sustained the conviction, ruling that "when the consequences sought by a defendant are forbidden by the law as criminal, it is no defense that the defendant could not succeed in reaching his goal because of circumstances unknown to him." On the same view, it was held that men who had sexual intercourse with a woman, with the belief that she was alive and did not consent to the intercourse, could be charged for attempted rape when the woman had, in fact, died from an unrelated ailment prior to the acts of intercourse. (United States v. Thomas, 13 U.S.C.M.A. 278 (1962))

The New York cases can be parsed out along similar lines. One of the leading cases on legal impossibility is People v. Jaffe, 185 N.Y. 497, 78 N.E. 169 (1906), in which we held that there was no liability for the attempted receipt of stolen property when the property received by the defendant in the belief that it was stolen was, in fact under the control of the true owner. Similarly, in People v. Teal, 196 N.Y. 372, 89 N.E. 1086 (1909), a conviction for attempted subornation of perjury was overturned on the theory that the testimony attempted to be suborned was irrelevant to the merits of the case. Since it was not subornation of perjury to solicit false, but irrelevant, testimony, "the person through whose procuration the testimony is given cannot be guilty of subornation of perjury and, by the same rule, an unsuccessful attempt to that which is not a crime when effectuated, cannot be held to be an attempt to commit the crime specified." Factual impossibility, however, was no defense. Thus, a man could be held for attempted grand larceny when he picked an empty pocket. (People v. Moran, 123 N.Y. 254, 25 N.E. 412 (1890)).

As can be seen from even this abbreviated discussion, the distinction between "factual" and "legal" impossibility was a nice one indeed and the courts tended to place a greater value on legal form than on any substantive danger the defendant's actions posed for society. The approach of the draftsmen of the Model Penal Code was to eliminate the defense of impossibility in virtually all situations. Under the [Model Penal Code] provision, to constitute an attempt, it is still necessary that the result intended or desired by the actor constitute a crime. However, the [Model Penal Code] suggested a fundamental change to shift the locus of analysis to the actor's mental frame of reference and away from undue dependence upon external considerations. The basic premise of the [Model Penal Code] provision is that what was in the actor's own mind should be the standard for determining his dangerousness to society and, hence, his liability for attempted criminal conduct.

In the belief that neither of the two branches of the traditional impossibility arguments detracts from the offender's moral culpability, the Legislature substantially carried the [Model Penal Code's] treatment of impossibility into the 1967 revision of the Penal Law. Thus, a person is guilty of an attempt when, with intent to commit a crime, he engages in conduct which tends to effect the commission of such crime. (Penal Law, § 110.00.) It is no defense that, under the attendant circumstances, the crime was factually or legally impossible of commission, "if such crime could have been committed had the attendant circumstances been as such person believed them to be." (Penal Law, § 110.10.) Thus, if defendant believed the victim to be alive at the time of the shooting, it is no defense to the charge of attempted murder that the victim may have been dead.

Turning to the facts of the case before us, we believe that there is sufficient evidence in the record from which the jury could conclude that the defendant believed Geller to be alive at the time defendant fired shots into Geller's head. Defendant admitted firing five shots at a most vital part of the victim's anatomy from virtually point blank range. Although defendant contended that the victim had already been grievously wounded by another, from the defendant's admitted actions, the jury could conclude that the defendant's purpose and intention was to administer the coup de grace. . . .

Defendant argues that the jury was bound to accept, at face value, . . . indications in his admissions [to the police] that he believed Geller dead [when he shot him.] Certainly, it is true that the defendant was entitled to have the entirety of the admissions, both the inculpatory and the exculpatory portions, placed in evidence before the trier of facts. . . . However, the jury was not required to automatically credit the exculpatory portions of the admissions. . . . In this case, there is ample other evidence to contradict the defendant's assertion that he believed Geller dead. There were five bullet wounds inflicted with stunning accuracy in a vital part of the victim's anatomy. The medical testimony indicated that Geller may have been alive at the time defendant fired at him. The defendant voluntarily left the jurisdiction immediately after the crime with his coperpetrator. Defendant did not report the crime to the police when left on his own by Bush. Instead, he attempted to conceal his and Bush's involvement with the homicide. In addition, the other portions of defendant's admissions make his contended belief that Geller was dead extremely improbable. Defendant, without a word of instruction from Bush, voluntarily got up from his seat after the passage of just a few minutes and fired five times point blank into the victim's face, snuffing out any remaining chance of life that Geller possessed. Certainly, this alone indicates a callous indifference to the taking of a human life. His admissions are barren of any claim of duress and reflect, instead, an unstinting co-operation in [subsequent] efforts to dispose of vital incriminating evidence [the guns]. Indeed, defendant maintained a false version of the occurrence until such time as the police informed him that they had evidence that he lately possessed a gun of the same caliber as one of the weapons involved in the shooting. From all of this, the jury was certainly warranted in concluding that the defendant acted in the belief that Geller was yet alive when shot by defendant.

The jury convicted the defendant of murder. Necessarily, they found that defendant intended to kill a live human being. Subsumed within this finding is the conclusion that defendant acted in the belief that Geller was alive. . . . Although it was not established beyond a reasonable doubt that Geller was, in fact, alive, such is no defense to attempted murder since a murder would have been committed "had the attendant circumstances been as (defendant) believed them to be." (Penal Law, § 110.10.) The jury necessarily found that defendant believed Geller to be alive when defendant shot at him.

The Appellate Division erred in not modifying the judgment to reflect a conviction for the lesser included offense of attempted murder. An attempt to commit a murder is a lesser included offense of murder and the Appellate Division has the authority, where the trial evidence is not legally sufficient to establish the offense of which the defendant was convicted, to modify the judgment to one of conviction for a lesser included offense which is legally established by the evidence. . . .

———

## NOTES ON IMPOSSIBILITY AND ATTEMPT

**1. "Legal" and "Factual" Impossibility.** Cases such as *Dlugash* have bedeviled the courts throughout the history of the law of attempt. Indeed, the "impossibility" problem is more widely discussed in the cases and the literature than any other aspect of the offense.

*Dlugash* describes the traditional approach. Situations are classified as involving "legal" or "factual" impossibility. "Factual" impossibility cases can be prosecuted as attempts. "Legal" impossibility cases cannot. How can one tell the difference?

In Booth v. State, 398 P.2d 863, 870–71 (Okla. Crim. App.1964), the distinction was defined as follows:

> The reason for the "impossibility" of completing the substantive crime ordinarily falls into one of two categories: (i) where the act if completed would not be criminal, a situation which is usually described as a "legal impossibility," and (ii) where the basic or substantive crime is impossible of completion, simply because of some physical or factual condition unknown to the defendant, a situation which is usually described as a "factual impossibility."

Does this help?

**2. An Alternative Common–Law Approach.** Rollin Perkins and Ronald Boyce, in Criminal Law 624 (2d ed. 1982),* have argued that in at least some of the situations illustrated in *Dlugash*, the actor properly can be viewed as having passed beyond preparation and completed an attempt before any impossibility problem arose. Thus, as to *People v. Jaffe* (discussed in *Dlugash*), they reasoned:

> [M]uch could be said for [acquittal] if nothing was involved except the purchase of property under such circumstances that the buyer firmly, but mistakenly, believed it to be stolen. More was involved, however. . . . Property had in fact been stolen, the thief and [the defendant] had made arrangements for [the defendant] to receive it and [the defendant] did receive it. In the meantime the thief had been apprehended and the property recovered. After it had thus lost its stolen character it was returned to the thief to carry out the original plan [and it was then sold to the defendant for about half its value]. The courts overlooked everything except the very last step by which the property was actually handed over.

* Copyright © 1982 by The Foundation Press. The two excerpts below are reprinted with permission.

[The defendant] had gone beyond preparation and moved in the direction of receiving stolen property before that last step and should have been convicted. . . .

Other factual patterns, Perkins and Boyce continue, should be analyzed differently:

> Deeply intrenched in the common law is the principle that conviction of crime cannot be based upon intent alone. . . . This raises the question of "inconsistent intents." At times one has two different intents which seem only one to him but are so inconsistent that only one is possible of achievement. . . . In such a situation the law regards one intent as primary and the other as secondary and only the primary intent controls[a]. . . .
>
> It has been said that if *D* takes his own umbrella, thinking it belongs to another and with intent to steal, this does not constitute an attempt to commit larceny. Here . . . we find utterly inconsistent intents unrealized by the actor. He intends to take a particular umbrella (which actually belongs to him). He also has in mind the intent to steal the umbrella of another. His primary intent is to take the umbrella he actually seizes and hence there is nothing wrongful in what is actually done but only in his secondary, inconsistent intent. Hence in such a situation, if there is nothing in his conduct either preceding or following the taking, which manifests a criminal purpose he should not be held guilty of attempted larceny. To convict him merely because he admitted his mistaken notion at a later time would be to convict him on intent alone. But this does not mean that he should not be convicted of attempt to steal if his conduct at the time of the transaction clearly manifested a criminal purpose.

How helpful is the primary-secondary intent distinction? Does it aid analysis, or does it rationalize a result reached for other reasons? Could the same analysis proceed in terms that do not rely on distinguishing between two kinds of intents?

Suppose *A* aims a gun at *B* and pulls the trigger with intent to kill. If the bullet misses, what is *A*'s primary intent? Is this case different from the umbrella situation? From *Jaffe*?

**3. Policy.** Francis Beale Sayre, in Criminal Attempts, 41 Harv. L. Rev. 821, 849–51 (1928),* argued that the key to understanding the impossibility cases lies in the underlying purposes of the criminal law:

> Under the retributive or expiative theory, the object of criminal justice is conceived to be punishment qua punishment, and the

---

[a] For more elaborate statements of this position, see Edwin R. Keedy, Criminal Attempts at Common Law, 102 U. Pa. L. Rev. 464 (1954); Rollin Perkins, Criminal Attempt and Related Problems, 2 U.C.L.A.L. Rev. 319 (1955).—[Footnote by eds.]

aim is to make the defendant suffer in exact proportion to his guilt. Since the proportionment of an individual's guilt cannot be divorced from moral and psychological considerations, punishment for a criminal attempt under this theory must be determined from an essentially subjective viewpoint, i.e., a defendant will deserve punishment if he actually intended to consummate a crime and committed such acts as *from his viewpoint* would be effective in achieving the crime, quite regardless of whether in the world of fact his acts could or could not cause the criminal consummation desired. If, on the other hand, one follows the more modern utilitarian theory of criminal justice, i.e., that the end of criminal law is to protect public and social interests, and that criminality should depend primarily, therefore, not on moral guilt but on whether or not social or public interests are unduly injured or endangered, then it follows that the question of punishment for a criminal attempt must be determined from an *objective* viewpoint. Under this view the question of the criminality of an attempt will depend primarily not on what may have been passing through the mind of the individual defendant, but on the degree of actual danger to social or public interests arising from his acts.

At this point many of the followers of the utilitarian theory of criminal justice fall into the error of arguing that if, because of some misconception of fact, the defendant's act in the light of the actual circumstances could not possibly achieve the criminal objective desired, it follows that since there is no actual endangering of social or public interests, the acts of the defendant should not be made punishable. In truth, however, the allowing of such acts to go unpunished might very seriously endanger social interests by encouraging repetition on the part of the defendant or others; the real danger lies in future similar acts when the actor may have learned to guard against his mistakes.

Whenever a gunman fires to kill and misses, all possible danger from that particular attempt has passed; yet surely even the staunchest adherent of the objective theory would convict such a gunman for a criminal attempt. Even under the objective viewpoint, therefore, when a defendant to achieve some crime commits an act which because of his mistake could not possibly cause the desired criminal consequence, he should be convicted if allowing him to go free would menace social interests through the danger of repetition.... A defendant who endeavors to kill his enemies with a toy pistol or by incantations may safely be allowed freely to continue making such attempts. As long as he abstains from acts reasonably adapted to the attainment of the desired criminal consequence, no social or public interests are endangered nor is any sense of social security violated. On the other hand, the gunman who shoots to kill his victim but fails because, unknown to him, a detective had previously slipped a blank cartridge into his gun, is no more able to kill his victim than the man who seeks to kill with a toy pistol or an incantation, but his conduct endangers public and social interests to a far greater degree. . . .

**4. The Model Penal Code.** The Model Penal Code approach to impossibility cases can be extracted from three separate sources.

First, § 5.01(1) is based on the premise that criminality should be judged from the circumstances as the defendant viewed them. This is accomplished in Subsection (1)(a) by the language "if the attendant circumstances were as he believes them to be." Thus, the defendant would be guilty in the umbrella case hypothesized by Perkins. Similar language in Subsection (1)(c) applies where the actor's conduct is incomplete but has passed beyond mere preparation. And the same result would also follow under Subsection (1)(b) in the case where the defendant shot a stuffed deer believing it to be alive. The actor in that case would have fired at the dummy "with the purpose of causing [the death of the deer] without further conduct on his part."

Second, the provisions of §§ 5.05(2) and 2.12 permit the grade of the offense to be reduced, or in extreme cases the prosecution to be dismissed, when the actor's conduct "is so inherently unlikely to result or culminate in the commission of a crime that neither such conduct nor the actor presents a public danger" or where the actor's conduct "did not actually cause or threaten the harm or evil sought to be prevented by the law defining the offense or did so only to an extent too trivial to warrant the condemnation of conviction." Thus, in a case involving a toy pistol, incantation, or voodoo, the court would have the authority to decide that the actor should be convicted of a lesser offense or no offense at all, based on its evaluation of the dangers presented by the defendant.

Third, certain substantive offenses, most particularly § 223.6 (receiving stolen property), have been defined so as to eliminate the possibility of acquittal on the basis of an impossibility argument. Section 223.6 provides that an actor is guilty who has received property "believing that it has probably been stolen." On the facts of *Jaffe*, it is likely that the defendant would be guilty of the completed substantive offense and resort to a charge of attempt would be unnecessary.

These results are defended[b] on the rationale that most defendants in impossibility situations have demonstrated their readiness to violate the criminal law, have manifested the required culpability, and have posed sufficient social danger to justify the invocation of criminal sanctions. Three functions are seen to have been served by the impossibility defense. First, it has functioned as a surrogate for uncertainties on the facts about whether the defendant had the required criminal purpose. Second, it similarly has functioned as a surrogate for the entrapment defense and has thus allowed the courts to express their displeasure at certain law enforce-

---

[b] See Herbert Wechsler, William Kenneth Jones & Harold L. Korn, The Treatment of Inchoate Crimes in the Model Penal Code of the American Law Institute: Attempt, Solicitation, and Conspiracy, 61 Colum. L. Rev. 571, 578–84 (1961). See also ALI, Model Penal Code and Commentaries § 5.01, pp. 315–17 (1985).

ment techniques involving the use of traps or decoys. Third, the impossibility defense has eliminated from the ambit of the criminal law certain cases where the defendant does not threaten the interests the law is designed to serve. Each of these functions is said to have been sufficiently taken into account elsewhere in the Model Code provisions, and accordingly impossibility as such is no defense.

**5. The Importance of the Actus Reus.** Arnold Enker, in Impossibility in Criminal Attempts—Legality and the Legal Process, 53 Minn. L. Rev. 665 (1969),* argued that it is important to retain the impossibility defense in certain situations because it reinforces the act requirement. He observed that criminal convictions based on equivocal conduct—conduct that does not corroborate the inferences of intent sought to be drawn—create an unacceptable risk of extending the criminal law to innocent behavior:

> [P]rosecution for attempt contains potential for arbitrary ex post facto judgments. But in large measure this danger is mitigated by the following factors: (i) The requirement that the defendant intend to commit the substantive crime . . . (ii) The requirement that the act evidence commitment to the criminal venture and corroborate the mens rea . . . (iii) The use of the technique of analogy whereby the decision in each case must be rationalized in comparison with other more or less similar cases which presumably were decided neutrally. (iv) Finally, the alternative to running the risk of occasional erroneous or arbitrary judgment is to prosecute only those attempts which can be carefully defined in advance, a rather intolerable option at least in the case of the more serious crimes.

> Though it does not ordinarily occur to us, our legal system could have adopted a completely different technique for distinguishing culpable attempts from those which are not culpable but are rather, in the conventional terminology, preparations. It would have been possible to eliminate the preparation-attempt dichotomy, thereby eliminating any notion of particular indispensable acts, and simply approach each case in terms of whether the evidence at hand is sufficient to prove the necessary intent, encompassing intent and commitment to the venture, or will. But even the Model Penal Code resolution of the issue does not rely solely on the sufficiency of the evidence to prove intent and will. It, too, requires that the act itself be "a substantial step" toward completion of the crime and that the act corroborate "the actor's criminal purpose."

> There are several reasons justifying our reluctance to substitute a sufficiency-of-the-evidence test for the act requirement.

---

* The three excerpts below are reprinted with permission of the author and the Minnesota Law Review.

Degrees of commitment vary so that we would again lack an objective criterion in cases falling short of consummation. Accomplice testimony and alleged confessions would ordinarily meet the sufficiency hurdles so that this would be an inadequate technique for controlling the jury unless corroboration standards were tightened. Defendants with prior criminal records for similar crimes would be particularly vulnerable under such an approach. And the technique of analogy would be considerably less significant, possibly resulting in less judicial objectivity.

Enker argued that the actual existence of required actus reus elements of crime, especially circumstance elements, provides important corroboration of criminal intent that would be lost if the impossibility defense were totally abandoned. He then criticized the Model Code solution:

> The draftsmen of the Model Penal Code have argued that while eliminating legal impossibility as a defense, the Code adequately takes care of these problems by its separate provision requiring that the defendant's act corroborate his mens rea. But the Model Penal Code's requirement that the act corroborate the mens rea applies only to cases in the preparation-attempt continuum. Cases such as *Jaffe* and Lady Eldon are covered by a separate provision which provides that where the defendant does any act which would constitute a crime under the circumstances as he thought them to be, he is guilty of an attempt. The corroboration requirement of § 5.01(2) does not apply to this section.[40] Perhaps the draftsmen assumed that doing the act defined in the substantive crime will always supply at least as much corroboration of mens rea as is present in the substantive crime itself. If so, what they have failed to see is that the act in its narrow sense of the defendant's physical movements can be perfectly innocent in itself—possession of goods, bringing goods into the country—and that what gives the act character as corroborative of mens rea is often the objective element or the attendant circumstances that the goods possessed are in fact stolen, or that the goods brought into the country are in fact dutiable, or that the goods possessed are in fact narcotics.

The Model Code is defended in the face of these criticisms in ALI, Model Penal Code and Commentaries § 5.01, pp. 319–20 (1985). Three reasons are advanced in support of the Model Code as drafted: (i) the issue is "more theoretical than practical" because it is unlikely that persons will be prosecuted for innocuous behavior solely on the basis of their admis-

---

[40] "Impossibility cases are dealt with in Subsections (1)(a) ... and (1)(b) ... of Section 5.01. Subsection (1)(c) deals with attempt-preparation cases. The corroboration requirement is contained in the first sentence of Section 5.01(2) which is limited to defining the term 'substantial step' under Subsection (1)(c). Indeed, Subsections (1)(a) and (1)(b) do not require a 'substantial step.' And while some impossibility cases will fit under Section (1)(c), the requirement of substantiality is judged there, too, by reference to 'the circumstances as [the defendant] believes them to be....' "

sions; (ii) a requirement of corroboration in the context of completed conduct may lead to the acquittal of persons whose behavior alone is insufficiently corroborative, but whose behavior in light of contemporaneous statements and later admissions provides a sufficient case for guilt; and (iii) contemporaneous statements and later admissions might be thought to be a more reliable indicator of guilt in a case of completed conduct than in a case where the actor has yet to complete proposed behavior. Is this persuasive? Or is Enker right that the Model Code does not adequately protect against the risk of convicting innocent persons?

**6. True Legal Impossibility.** There is one variation of the impossibility situation on which everyone agrees. Consider the following case. The defendant smokes one marijuana cigarette, believing that it is a crime to do so. If such behavior is not a crime in the jurisdiction in question, and if the Model Penal Code approach to impossibility were to be taken, could this person be convicted of attempting to violate the law? The answer is "no." A defendant cannot be convicted of an attempt if, on the facts as they were believed to be, no crime would have been committed. As the court said in *Dlugash*, "it is still necessary that the result intended or desired by the actor constitute a crime."

**7. Completed Offenses: *Bronston v. United States*.** To what extent should the proper analysis of impossibility cases in the law of attempt apply to "completed" crimes? Consider, in this connection, Bronston v. United States, 409 U.S. 352 (1973). Bronston was the president and sole owner of Bronston Productions. The company petitioned for an arrangement with creditors under the federal Bankruptcy Act. At a hearing to determine the extent and location of the company's assets, Bronston gave the following testimony:

Q. Do you have any bank accounts in Swiss banks, Mr. Bronston?

A. No, sir.

Q. Have you ever?

A. The company had an account there for about six months, in Zurich.

Q. Have you any nominees who have bank accounts in Swiss banks?

A. No, sir.

Q. Have you ever?

A. No, sir.

The facts, as described by the Court, were as follows:

It is undisputed that for a period of nearly five years, between October 1959 and June 1964, petitioner had a personal bank account at the International Credit Bank in Geneva, Switzerland, into which he made deposits and upon which he drew checks totaling more than $180,000. It is likewise undisputed that petitioner's answers were literally truthful. (i) Petitioner did not at the time of questioning have a Swiss bank account. (ii) Bronston Productions, Inc., did have the account in Zurich described by petitioner. (iii) Neither at the time of questioning nor before did petitioner have nominees who had Swiss accounts. The government's prosecution for perjury went forward on the theory that in order to mislead his questioner, petitioner answered the second question with literal truthfulness but unresponsively addressed his answer to the company's assets and not to his own—thereby implying that he had no personal Swiss bank account at the relevant time.

Bronston was convicted of perjury, but the Supreme Court unanimously reversed. It reasoned:

> Beyond question, petitioner's answer to the crucial question was not responsive if we assume, as we do, that the first question was directed at personal bank accounts. There is, indeed, an implication in the answer to the second question that there was never a personal bank account; in casual conversation this interpretation might reasonably be drawn. But we are not dealing with casual conversation.... [W]e perceive no reason why Congress would intend the drastic sanction of a perjury prosecution to cure a testimonial mishap that could readily have been reached with a single additional question by counsel alert—as every examiner ought to be—to the incongruity of petitioner's unresponsive answer. Under the pressures and tensions of interrogation, it is not uncommon for the most earnest witnesses to give answers that are not entirely responsive. Sometimes the witness does not understand the question, or may in an excess of caution or apprehension read too much or too little into it. It should come as no surprise that a participant in a bankruptcy proceeding may have something to conceal and consciously tries to do so, or that a debtor may be embarrassed at his plight and yield information reluctantly. It is the responsibility of the lawyer to probe; testimonial interrogation, and cross-examination in particular, is a probing, prying, pressing form of inquiry. If a witness evades, it is the lawyer's responsibility to recognize the evasion and to bring the witness back to the mark, to flush out the whole truth with the tools of adversary examination.

> It is no answer to say that here the jury found that petitioner intended to mislead his examiner. A jury should not be permitted to engage in conjecture whether an unresponsive answer, true and complete on its face, was intended to mislead or divert the examiner.... It may well be that petitioner's answers were not guileless but were shrewdly calculated to evade. Nevertheless, we [conclude] that any special problems arising from the literally true but unresponsive answer are to be remedied through the "questioner's acuity" and not by a federal perjury prosecution.

What was the basis for the reversal of Bronston's conviction? Should the result be the same if Bronston had been charged with perjury under § 241.1 of the Model Penal Code? Would the situation be any different if he was charged with attempted perjury? More broadly, is the impossibility-attempt situation symptomatic of a larger and more pervasive problem in the criminal law, one that really has little to do with "impossibility" as a concept or even the crime of attempt?

## SECTION 4: ABANDONMENT IN ATTEMPT AND OTHER OFFENSES

### Ross v. Mississippi
Supreme Court of Mississippi, 1992.
601 So.2d 872.

■ PRATHER, JUSTICE, for the Court....

This attempted-rape case arose on the appeal of Sammy Joe Ross from the 10–year sentence imposed ... by the Circuit Court of Union County. The appellant timely filed a notice of appeal and dispositively raises the issue: Whether the trial court erred in denying the defendant's motion for directed verdict on the charge of attempted rape. This Court reverses ... the conviction for attempted rape....

On September 16, 1987, sometime around 2:15 in the afternoon, Deputy Sheriff Edwards of the Union County Sheriff's Department was driving on Highway 30 heading east. Before he turned south onto Highway 9, he saw an oncoming truck, a white, late-model Ford pickup, turn left onto the first gravel road. Because the truck had out-of-county tags and turned down a road on which several crimes had occurred, Edwards jotted down the tag number, which action he described as routine practice.

Dorothy Henley[1] and her seven-year-old daughter lived in a trailer on the gravel road. Henley was alone at home and answered a knock at the door to find Sammy Joe Ross asking directions. Henley had never seen Ross before. She stepped out of the house and pointed out the house of a neighbor who might be able help him. When she turned back around, Ross pointed a handgun at her. He ordered her into the house, told her to undress, and shoved her onto the couch. Three or four times Ross ordered Henley to undress and once threatened to kill her. Henley described herself as frightened and crying. She attempted to escape from Ross and told him that her daughter would be home from school at any time. She testified: "I started crying and talking about my daughter, that I was all she had because her daddy was dead, and he said if I had a little girl he wouldn't do anything, for me just to go outside and turn my back." As instructed by Ross, Henley walked outside behind her trailer. Ross followed and told her to keep her back to the road until he had departed. She complied....

On December 21, 1987, a Union County grand jury indicted Sammy Joe Ross for the attempted rape of Henley, charging that Ross "did

---

[1] The complainant's name has been changed.

unlawfully and feloniously attempt to rape and forcibly ravish" the complaining witness, an adult female. On January 25, 1988, Ross waived arraignment and pled not guilty.

On June 23, 1988, the jury found Ross guilty. On July 7, the court sentenced Ross to a 10–year term. When Ross moved for a judgment notwithstanding the verdict or, in the alternative, for a new trial, the court denied the motion. Ross timely filed a notice of appeal.

[T]he ... issue ... is whether sufficient evidence presents a question of fact as to whether Ross abandoned his attack as a result of outside intervention.... Ross asserts that "it was not ... Henley's resistance that prevented her rape nor any independent intervening cause or third person, but the voluntary and independent decision by her assailant to abandon his attack." The state, on the other hand, claims that Ross "panicked" and "drove away hastily."

As recited above, Henley told Ross that her daughter would soon be home from school. She also testified that Ross stated if Henley had a little girl, he wouldn't do anything to her and to go outside [the house] and turn her back [to him]. Ross moved that the court direct a verdict in his favor on the charge of attempted rape, which motion the court denied.

The trial court instructed the jury that if it found that Ross did "any overt act with the intent to have unlawful sexual relations with [the complainant] without her consent and against her will" then the jury should find Ross guilty of attempted rape. The court further instructed the jury that:

> before you can return a verdict against the defendant for attempted rape, that you must be convinced from the evidence and beyond a reasonable doubt, that the defendant was prevented from completing the act of rape or failed to complete the act of rape by intervening, extraneous causes. If you find that the act of rape was not completed due to a voluntary stopping short of the act, then you must find the defendant not guilty.

Ross did not request, and the court did not give, any lesser included offense instructions.

Review of a directed verdict made at the close of the defendant's case consists of this court's applying a reasonable doubt standard to the verdict, while viewing the evidence in a light most favorable to the verdict. Stever v. State, 503 So.2d 227, 230 (Miss.1987). This court may not then discharge the defendant unless the court concludes that no reasonable, hypothetical juror could have found the defendant guilty. Pearson v. State, 428 So.2d 1361, 1364 (Miss.1983)....

The crime of attempt to commit an offense occurs when a person "shall design and endeavor to commit an offense, and shall do any overt act toward the commission thereof, but shall fail therein, or shall be prevented from committing the same." Miss. Code Ann. § 97–1–7 (1972). Put otherwise, attempt consists of "1) an intent to commit a particular crime; 2) a direct ineffectual act done toward its commission; and 3) failure to consummate its commission." Pruitt v. State, 528 So.2d 828, 830 (Miss.1988) (attempted rape was voluntarily abandoned by defendant when he told victim she was free to leave).

The Mississippi attempt statute requires that the third element, failure to consummate, result from extraneous causes. Thus, a defendant's voluntary abandonment may negate a crime of attempt. Where a defendant, with no other impetus but the victim's urging, voluntarily ceases his assault, he has not committed attempted rape. In *Pruitt*, where the assailant released his throathold on the unresisting victim and told her she could go, after which a third party happened on the scene, the court held that the jury could not have reasonably ruled out abandonment.

In comparison, this court has held that where the appellant's rape attempt failed because of the victim's resistance and ability to sound the alarm, the appellant cannot establish an abandonment defense. Alexander v. State, 520 So.2d 127, 130 (Miss.1988). In the *Alexander* case, the evidence sufficiently established a question of attempt for the jury. The defendant did not voluntarily abandon his attempt, but instead fled after the victim, a hospital patient, pressed the nurse's buzzer; a nurse responded and the victim spoke the word "help." The court concluded, "[T]he appellant ceased his actions only after the victim managed to press the buzzer alerting the nurse." In another case, the court properly sent the issue of attempt to the jury where the attacker failed because the victim resisted and freed herself. Harden v. State, 465 So.2d 321, 325 (Miss.1985).

Thus, abandonment occurs where, through the verbal urging of the victim, but with no physical resistance or external intervention, the perpetrator changes his mind. At the other end of the scale, a perpetrator cannot claim that he abandoned his attempt when, in fact, he ceased his efforts because the victim or a third party intervened or prevented him from furthering the attempt. Somewhere in the middle lies a case such as *Alexander*, where the victim successfully sounded an alarm, presenting no immediate physical obstacle to the perpetrator's continuing the attack, but sufficiently intervening to cause the perpetrator to cease his attack.

In this case, Ross appeals the denial of his motion for directed verdict; thus, he challenges only the sufficiency of the evidence, that is, whether it raised a sufficient factual issue to warrant a jury determination. Even under this rigorous standard of review, Ross's appeal should succeed on this issue. The evidence does not sufficiently raise a fact question as to whether he attempted rape. The evidence uncontrovertibly shows that he did not, but instead abandoned the attempt.

The key inquiry is a subjective one: what made Ross leave? According to the undisputed evidence, he left because he responded sympathetically to the victim's statement that she had a little girl. He did not fail in his attack. No one prevented him from completing it. Henley did not sound an alarm. She successfully persuaded Ross, of his own free will, to abandon his attempt. No evidence shows that Ross panicked and hastily drove away, but rather, the record shows that he walked the complainant out to the back of her trailer before he left. Thus, the trial court's failure to grant a directed verdict on the attempted rape charge constituted reversible error. As this court stated in *Pruitt*, this is not to say that Ross committed no criminal act, but "our only inquiry is whether there was sufficient evidence to support a jury finding that [Ross] did not abandon his attempt to rape [Henley]." This Court holds that there was not....

Reversed and appellant discharged.

———

## NOTES ON ABANDONMENT IN ATTEMPT AND OTHER OFFENSES

**1.   The Traditional Position on Abandonment.** Analytically, *Ross* presents two distinct questions. The first is whether the defendant progressed sufficiently beyond "mere preparation" to attempted rape. The second is whether, if he did (and did so with the required specific intent), he is nevertheless entitled to acquittal if he "voluntarily" abandoned his criminal plan. How should the second issue be treated? Should it matter whether Ross changed his mind and relinquished his criminal purpose before he completed the crime?

In Criminal Attempts, 41 Harv. L. Rev. 821, 847 (1928), Francis Beale Sayre states the usual position of the courts on this question:

> So far as the defendant's criminality is concerned, it would seem to make little or no difference whether the interruption of the defendant's intended acts is due to another's interference or to his own repentance or change of mind. Once the defendant's acts have gone far enough to make him liable for a criminal attempt, no subsequent repentance or change of mind or abstention from further crime can possibly wipe away liability for the crime already committed. Genuine repentance may cause a reduction of sentence, but it cannot free from criminal liability. In the cases where the defendant voluntarily abandons his intended course of conduct, therefore, the problem reduces itself to whether or not the defendant's conduct before the abandonment had gone so far as to constitute an indictable attempt. The burglar who, while trying to force the lock on the front door, decides to abandon the attempt is equally guilty whether his change of mind is due to the voice of his own conscience or the voice of an approaching policeman. Present virtue never wipes away past crimes.

**2.   Comments and Questions on the Traditional Position.** What purposes are served by punishing a person who abandons a criminal intention before committing a completed offense? Does the abandonment raise doubt about the firmness of the actor's original criminal purpose, suggesting that it was only "half-formed or provisional"?[a] Does a voluntary change of mind suggest that the defendant has not, in fact, "gone far enough to show that he has broken through the psychological barrier to

———

[a] G. Williams, Criminal Law: The General Part 620–21 (2d ed. 1961).

crime?"[b] In this sense, is an abandonment defense a desirable complement to a modern reformulation of the actus reus of attempt?

It has been argued that a voluntary renunciation of criminal intentions should be regarded as a praiseworthy act that erases the defendant's original blameworthiness and therefore removes the ethical predicate for criminal liability.[c] Others have claimed that recognition of an abandonment defense would offer an incentive to inchoate offenders to desist from their plan to commit a criminal offense.[d] Are these plausible hypotheses?[e]

**3. The Model Penal Code.** Section 5.01(4) of the Model Penal Code reads as follows:

> When the actor's conduct would otherwise constitute an attempt under Subsection (1)(b) or (1)(c) of this Section, it is an affirmative defense that he abandoned his effort to commit the crime or otherwise prevented its commission, under circumstances manifesting a complete and voluntary renunciation of his criminal purpose. . . .
>
> Within the meaning of this Article, renunciation of criminal purpose is not voluntary if it is motivated, in whole or in part, by circumstances, not present or apparent at the inception of the actor's course of conduct, which increase the probability of detection or apprehension or which make more difficult the accomplishment of the criminal purpose. Renunciation is not complete if it is motivated by a decision to postpone the criminal conduct until a more advantageous time or to transfer the criminal effort to another but similar objective or victim.

Although the Model Code proposal has been adopted in several states, it has not met with widespread approval in recent American penal code revisions. Why might this be so? Is there a relationship between the grading of attempt and the case for an abandonment defense?

---

[b] Id. at 379–80.

[c] G. Fletcher, Rethinking the Criminal Law 190 (1978).

[d] "In our view, the most persuasive argument in favour of the provision of a withdrawal defence is that, since the object of the criminal law is to prevent crime, it is equally important to give reasonable encouragement to a conspirator, attempter or inciter to withdraw before a substantive offence is committed as it is to encourage an accomplice to end his participation in that offence. The absence of such a defence may operate to dissuade an individual who might otherwise decide to cease participating in the planning of a crime from taking that decision, since, having become a party to the inchoate offence, there is no inducement for him to cease his activities before commission of the substantive offence takes place. It may well be that the type of criminal who is liable to change his mind in this way is a relative newcomer to crime and would, in any event, be given the opportunity to give evidence for the prosecution. But provision of the defence would make it quite clear that the criminal in these circumstances would not be liable to be charged at all." The Law Commission, Working Paper No. 50, Inchoate Offences 102 (1973).

[e] "How likely is it that a man who is sufficiently far along the path towards committing a criminal offense, that he would be guilty of an attempt if he stopped, and who then decided not to commit it, would change his mind again and decide to carry on, since he realizes he is guilty of the attempt anyway? The argument is farfetched." M. Wasik, Abandoning Criminal Intent, [1980] Crim. L. Rev. 785, 793.

**4. Scope of the Defense.** If provision of an abandonment defense is sound for attempts, are there other offenses to which it should also be applicable? Note that the Model Code includes a comparable defense for solicitation (§ 5.02(3)), conspiracy (§ 5.03(6)), and perjury (§ 241.1(4)). No similar provision is made, however, for larceny or burglary. Are these offenses distinguishable either analytically or as a policy matter? If the actor "exercise[d] unlawful control over ... property of another with purpose to deprive" (§ 223.2(1)) and at the next instant had a change of heart, would the situation be any different from a case where the actor tried to exercise unlawful control and voluntarily desisted after committing an attempt? Should the abandonment defense be applicable, if it is to be recognized at all, to all offenses defined in terms that fall short of ultimate harm? If not, by what criteria should offenses be distinguished?[f]

---

[f] For discussion of these issues, see Paul R. Hoeber, The Abandonment Defense to Criminal Attempt and Other Problems of Temporal Individuation, 74 Calif. L. Rev. 377 (1986).

# CHAPTER IV

# SEXUAL OFFENSES

---

## SECTION 1: RAPE

### INTRODUCTORY NOTE

Within contemporary culture, the tasks of defining and enforcing the law of rape and other sexual offenses are complicated and contentious. Much of the controversy is exacerbated, if not directly produced, by gender politics. During the past several decades, feminist commentators have made the elimination of violence against women a central focus of their campaign for social justice. As part of this agenda, a number of feminists are seeking to expand the definition of rape. Other feminists approach this project cautiously since they believe that legal intervention in sexual matters largely has served to constrain the sexual activity of women, not that of men. Like other strategists for political change, feminists have injected these issues into mainstream discourse, where they have provoked an energetic and, at times, angry debate. The popular debate often divides along gender lines, and sophisticated feminist arguments sometimes degenerate into simple claims that represent women and men as opponents: women are raped and thus share the victim's interests; men rape and thus share the perpetrator's interests. While it is difficult to foresee the long-term implications of these claims for rape doctrine and for gender relations, they have produced a level of antagonism between some of the disputants that is unusual even within an adversarial legal culture.

Of course, for the participants in individual rape prosecutions, long-term developments are eclipsed by the judgment in their own case. As Catharine MacKinnon has remarked, the debate over competing sexual norms abruptly loses its abstract quality when the conduct of a real defendant is at stake: "someone either is or is not going to jail." Catharine A. MacKinnon, Toward Feminist Jurisprudence, 34 Stan. L. Rev. 703, 728 (1982). The integrity of the criminal process demands that punishment be imposed or withheld in individual cases; with each conviction or acquittal, the criminal process resolves the contest over the underlying social norms, at least for purposes of the actors in that case. Moreover, since so many people regularly have and/or want to have sex, legislators and courts must weigh the policies favoring stable criminal norms (e.g., providing notice that certain conduct is a crime) against arguments that support redefining the crime of rape in accordance with evolving norms about sexuality and gender equality.

According to contemporary wisdom, rape accusations involve two different kinds of sexual encounter, each of which presents distinct challenges to law enforcement. Susan Estrich was one of the first commentators to identify these different categories of rape and their legal significance. See Susan Estrich, Real Rape (1987). Like any other generalization, this one does not wholly withstand close scrutiny, but a brief description of these categories provides a useful way of distinguishing the issues that will be emphasized in this chapter from those that will be given passing treatment.

In the first type of case, the alleged rapist and victim are strangers to each other. In these cases, there often is no reasonable doubt that a crime occurred, particularly where the victim was physically injured. Professor Estrich calls this "real rape." Here, the difficult task for law enforcement personnel is identifying the perpetrator. Often, the victim is the only witness to the crime and the events leading up to it. Because the attacker is a stranger and his conduct so traumatic, the victim may have trouble describing him. Depending on the physical evidence connecting the perpetrator to the victim and to the crime scene, police officers may be unable to locate and apprehend him. If they do make an arrest and the case is strong enough to proceed to trial, the most hotly contested issue likely will be the identity of the rapist. The suspect may offer a variety of arguments (e.g., alibi, mistaken eyewitness identification, mishandling of physical evidence) designed to persuade jurors that, though a crime occurred, some other person committed it. These cases raise problems that are of great importance in the enforcement of rape laws, but the problems usually implicate investigatory procedures and evidence rules. In other words, these cases tend not to raise difficult substantive questions. Once jurors are convinced that the accused is the person who had sex with the victim, they often are ready to agree that the elements of the offense are satisfied.

By contrast, the second category of cases presents difficult questions about the substantive definition of rape. Here, accuser and suspect are acquaintances, and, in the most vexing cases, they are dating or are married to or sexually involved with each other. These cases raise few of the investigatory problems mentioned above. The accuser can identify the suspect by name, as well as provide an accurate physical description, and the police usually are able promptly to arrest him. In these cases, the suspect often concedes that he is the person who had sex with the accuser on the occasion she claims she was raped. However, he sharply disputes her characterization of their encounter as a rape; instead, he takes the position that the encounter was an ordinary act of sexual intercourse. Most of the materials in this chapter will focus on the substantive issues that legislators, courts, and jurors must resolve in order to adjudicate between these competing accounts.

———

## Subsection A:  The Traditional Approach to Rape

———

### INTRODUCTORY NOTE

The common law defined rape as "the carnal knowledge of a woman forcibly and against her will." 4 William Blackstone, Commentaries *210.

This concise prohibition remains influential today. The durability of this particular definition is itself noteworthy: cultural attitudes towards sexuality have changed, possibly radically, over the course of this century, and rape has been the topic of law reform projects for the past several decades. Yet, as the following materials reflect, contemporary rape doctrine resembles the common-law prohibition in important respects.

Many aspects of rape are not in dispute. By now, almost every state has departed from the common-law approach by defining rape in gender-neutral terms. That is, most statutory formulations now provide that the crime occurs whenever a "person" (rather than "man") forces another "person" (rather than "woman") to have sex. However, in the vast majority of cases, rape remains a crime that men perpetrate against women, though men do rape other men with some frequency. The psychological literature contains several accounts of women forcibly raping adult men, but the case reporters mention no prosecutions of women for this crime. Usually, both rapist and victim are young. Children and adolescents are the most frequent victims of sexual assault, and most rapists are under the age of 30. Many rape victims are well-acquainted with, if not related by blood or marriage to, their attackers. In most cases, victim and perpetrator are members of the same race. Finally, rape is one of the most, if not the most, underreported violent crimes.

The actus reus of rape is some form of sexual physical touching. At common law, the requisite touching was "carnal knowledge." While modern courts treat this phrase as a synonym for "sexual intercourse," Perkins and Boyce explain that the phrase also conveyed the requirement that the sexual connection be "unlawful." Rollin M. Perkins and Ronald N. Boyce, Criminal Law 202–03 (1982). Until very recently, sexual intercourse was unlawful when the participants were not married to each other.[a] While the requirement that the intercourse be "unlawful" had a number of implications for rape doctrine, the most significant practical implication was that a man could not be convicted for raping his wife since sex within marriage was not unlawful. At early common law, there was a conflict in authority over whether the completed crime required *both* penetration of the vagina by the penis *and* emission of semen, or whether penetration alone was enough. A consensus soon emerged that the slightest penetration sufficed.

Contemporary statutes define the actus reus of rape in various ways. A significant minority of statutes continue to define the sexual act as vaginal intercourse. One statute retains the phrase "carnal knowledge." In recent years, many states have expanded this definition to include penetration of mouth or anus, as well as vagina. Another legislative innovation treats

[a] Today, states rarely, if ever, bring prosecutions for adultery or fornication, but a number of state statutes still criminalize extramarital intercourse, and military courts continue to convict military personnel for these crimes in some circumstances.

different types of sexual touching as distinct offenses with different penalties. These statutory variations reflect a disagreement over what kinds of physical touching should be classified as sexual and over how they should be ranked for grading. For the most part, however, once a given state's legislators have resolved these disagreements to their satisfaction, the definitions do not raise significant difficulties in application.

The common law also required that the intercourse be done "forcibly" and "against [the woman's] will." These elements have been much more difficult for modern lawmakers to define and apply. Accordingly, the materials in this section largely will focus on the meaning of these elements. For purposes of clarity, many of the notes treat these elements, just as judicial opinions and statutes frequently do, as if they are distinct. Yet, as the following case reflects, the nature of that distinction and, indeed, the question of whether it should be abandoned altogether are among the most difficult unresolved issues in rape law today.

————

# State v. Rusk

Court of Appeals of Maryland, 1981.
289 Md. 230, 424 A.2d 720.

■ MURPHY, CHIEF JUDGE. Edward Rusk was found guilty by a jury in the Criminal Court of Baltimore of second degree rape in violation of Maryland Code art. 27, § 463(a)(1), which provides in pertinent part:

> A person is guilty of rape in the second degree if the person engages in vaginal intercourse with another person:
>
> > (1) By force or threat of force against the will and without the consent of the other person....

On appeal, the Court of Special Appeals, sitting en banc, reversed the conviction; it concluded by an eight-five majority that in view of the prevailing law as set forth in Hazel v. State, 221 Md. 464, 157 A.2d 922 (1960), insufficient evidence of Rusk's guilt had been adduced at the trial to permit the case to go to the jury. We granted certiorari to consider whether the Court of Special Appeals properly applied the principles of *Hazel* in determining that insufficient evidence had been produced to support Rusk's conviction.

At the trial, the 21–year-old prosecuting witness, Pat, testified that on the evening of September 21, 1977, she attended a high school alumnae meeting where she met a girl friend, Terry. After the meeting, Terry and Pat agreed to drive in their respective cars to Fells Point to have a few drinks. On the way, Pat stopped to telephone her mother, who was baby sitting for Pat's two-year-old son; she told her mother that she was going with Terry to Fells Point and would not be late in arriving home.

The women arrived in Fells Point about 9:45 p.m. They went to a bar where each had one drink. After staying approximately one hour, Pat and

Terry walked several blocks to a second bar, where each of them had another drink. After about 30 minutes, they walked two blocks to a third bar known as E.J. Buggs. The bar was crowded and a band was playing in the back. Pat ordered another drink and as she and Terry were leaning against the wall, Rusk approached and said "hello" to Terry. Terry, who was then conversing with another individual, momentarily interrupted her conversation and said "Hi, Eddie." Rusk then began talking with Pat and during their conversation both of them acknowledged being separated from their respective spouses and having a child. Pat told Rusk that she had to go home because it was a week-night and she had to wake up with her baby early in the morning.

Rusk asked Pat the direction in which she was driving and after she responded, Rusk requested a ride to his apartment. Although Pat did not know Rusk, she thought that Terry knew him. She thereafter agreed to give him a ride. Pat cautioned Rusk on the way to the car that "I'm just giving a ride home, you know, as a friend, not anything to be, you know, thought of other than a ride;" and he said, "Oh, okay." They left the bar between 12:00 and 12:20 a.m.

Pat testified that on the way to Rusk's apartment, they continued the general conversation that they had started in the bar. After a 20–minute drive, they arrived at Rusk's apartment in the 3100 block of Guilford Avenue. Pat testified that she was totally unfamiliar with the neighborhood. She parked the car at the curb on the opposite side of the street from Rusk's apartment but left the engine running. Rusk asked Pat to come in, but she refused. He invited her again, and she again declined. She told Rusk that she could not go into his apartment even if she wanted to because she was separated from her husband and a detective could be observing her movements. Pat said that Rusk was fully aware that she did not want to accompany him to his room. Notwithstanding her repeated refusals, Pat testified that Rusk reached over and turned off the ignition to her car and took her car keys. He got out of the car, walked over to her side, opened the door and said, "Now, will you come up?" Pat explained her subsequent actions:

> At that point, because I was scared, because he had my car keys, I didn't know what to do. I was someplace I didn't even know where I was. It was in the city. I didn't know whether to run. I really didn't think, at that point, what to do.

> Now, I know that I should have blown the horn. I should have run. There were a million things I could have done. I was scared, at that point, and I didn't do any of them.

Pat testified that at this moment she feared that Rusk would rape her. She said: "[I]t was the way he looked at me, and said 'Come on up, come on up;' and when he took the keys, I knew that was wrong." It was then about 1 a.m. Pat accompanied Rusk across the street into a totally dark house. She followed him up two flights of stairs. She neither saw nor heard anyone in the building. Once they ascended the stairs, Rusk unlocked the door to his one-room apartment, and turned on the light. According to Pat, he told her to sit down. She sat in a chair beside the bed. Rusk sat on the bed. After Rusk talked for a few minutes, he left the room for about one to five minutes. Pat remained seated in the chair. She made no noise and did not attempt to leave. She said that she did not notice a telephone in the room. When Rusk returned, he turned off the light and sat down on the bed. Pat asked if she could leave; she told him that she wanted to go home and "didn't want to come up." She said, "Now, [that] I came up, can I go?" Rusk, who was still in possession of her car keys, said he wanted her to stay.

Rusk then asked Pat to get on the bed with him. He pulled her by the arms to the bed and began to undress her, removing her blouse and bra. He unzipped her slacks and she took them off after he told her to do so. Pat removed the rest of her clothing, and then removed Rusk's pants because "he asked me to do it." After they were both undressed Rusk started kissing Pat as she was lying on her back. Pat explained what happened next:

> I was still begging him to please let, you know, let me leave. I said, "you can get a lot of other girls down there, for what you want," and he just kept saying, "no"; and then I was really scared, because I can't describe, you know, what was said. It was more the look in his eyes; and I said, at that point—I didn't know what to say; and I said, "If I do what you want, will you let me go without killing me?" Because I didn't know, at that point, what he was going to do; and I started to cry; and when I did, he put his hands on my throat, and started lightly to choke me; and I said, "If I do what you want, will you let me go?" And he said, yes, and at that time, I proceeded to do what he wanted me to.

Pat testified that Rusk made her perform oral sex and then vaginal intercourse.

Immediately after the intercourse, Pat asked if she could leave. She testified that Rusk said, "Yes," after which she got up and got dressed and Rusk returned her car keys. She said that Rusk then "walked me to my car, and asked if he could see me again; and I said, 'Yes'; and he asked me for my telephone number; and I said, 'No, I'll see you down Fells Point sometime,' just so I could leave." Pat testified that she "had no intention of meeting him again." She asked him for directions out of the neighborhood and left.

On her way home, Pat stopped at a gas station, went to the ladies room, and then drove "pretty much straight home and pulled up and parked the car." At first she was not going to say anything about the incident. She explained her initial reaction not to report the incident: "I didn't want to go through what I'm going through now [at the trial]." As she sat in her car reflecting on the incident, Pat said she began to "wonder what would happen if I hadn't of done what he wanted me to do. So I thought the right thing to do was to go report it, and I went from there to Hillendale to find a police car." She reported the incident to the police at about 3:15 a.m. Subsequently, Pat took the police to Rusk's apartment, which she located without any great difficulty....

Rusk and two of his friends, Michael Trimp and David Carroll, testified on his behalf. According to Trimp, they went ... to Buggs' bar to dance, drink and "tr[y] to pick up some ladies." Rusk stayed at the bar, while the others went to get something to eat.

... Trimp testified that at about 2:00–2:30 a.m. he returned to the room he rented with Rusk on Guilford Avenue and found Rusk to be the only person present. Trimp said that ... the room he rented with Rusk was referred to as their "pit stop." Both Rusk and Trimp actually resided at places other than the Guilford Avenue room....

Rusk, the 31–year-old defendant, testified that he was in the Buggs Tavern for about 30 minutes when he noticed Pat standing at the bar. Rusk said: "She looked at me, and she smiled. I walked over and said, hi, and started talking to her." He did not remember either knowing or speaking to Terry. When Pat mentioned that she was about to leave, Rusk asked her if she wanted to go home with him. In response, Pat said that she would like to, but could not because she had her car. Rusk then suggested that they take her car. Pat agreed and they left the bar arm-in-arm.

Rusk testified that during the drive to her apartment, he discussed with Pat their similar marital situations and talked about their children. He said that Pat asked him if he was going to rape her. When he inquired why she was asking, Pat said that she had been raped once before. Rusk expressed his sympathy for her. Pat then asked him if he planned to beat her. He inquired why she was asking and Pat explained that her husband used to beat her. Rusk again expressed his sympathy. He testified that at no time did Pat express a fear that she was being followed by her separated husband.

According to Rusk, when they arrived in front of his apartment Pat parked the car and turned the engine off. They sat for several minutes "petting each other." Rusk denied switching off the ignition and removing the keys. He said that they walked to the apartment house and proceeded up the stairs to his room. Rusk testified that Pat came willingly to his room and that at no time did he make threatening facial expressions. Once inside his room, Rusk left Pat alone for several minutes while he used the bathroom down the hall. Upon his return, he switched the light on but immediately turned it off because Pat, who was seated in the dark in a chair next to the bed, complained it was too bright. Rusk said that he sat on the bed across from Pat and reached out

> and started to put my arms around her, and started kissing her; and we fell back into the bed, and she—we were petting, kissing, and she stuck her hand down in my pants and started playing with me; and I undid her blouse, and took off her bra; and then I sat up and I said "Let's take our clothes off;" and she said, "Okay"; and I

took my clothes off, and she took her clothes off; and then we proceeded to have intercourse.

Rusk explained that after the intercourse, Pat "got uptight."

> Well, she started to cry. She said that—she said, "You guys are all alike," she says, "just out for," you know, "one thing."

> She started talking about—I don't know, she was crying and all. I tried to calm her down and all; and I said, "What's the matter?" And she said, that she just wanted to leave; and I said, "Well, okay"; and she walked out to the car. I walked out to the car. She got in the car and left.

Rusk denied placing his hands on Pat's throat or attempting to strangle her. He also denied using force or threats of force to get Pat to have intercourse with him. . . .

The vaginal intercourse once being established, the remaining elements of rape in the second degree under § 463(a)(1) are, as in a prosecution for common law rape (1) force—actual or constructive, and (2) lack of consent. . . .

*Hazel*, which was decided in 1960, long before the enactment of § 463(a)(1), involved a prosecution for common law rape, there defined as "the act of a man having unlawful carnal knowledge of a female over the age of ten years by force without the consent and against the will of the victim." [The defendant in *Hazel* argued that the sexual encounter was consensual and, therefore, not a rape because the victim failed to resist his sexual advances. In rejecting this claim the court] recognized that force and lack of consent are distinct elements of the crime of rape. It said:

> Force is an essential element of the crime and to justify a conviction, the evidence must warrant a conclusion either that the victim resisted and her resistance was overcome by force or that she was prevented from resisting by threats to her safety. But no particular amount of force, either actual or constructive, is required to constitute rape. Necessarily that fact must depend upon the prevailing circumstances. As in this case force may exist without violence. If the acts and threats of the defendant were reasonably calculated to create in the mind of the victim—having regard to the circumstances in which she was placed—a real apprehension, due to fear, of imminent bodily harm, serious enough to impair or overcome her will to resist, then such acts and threats are the equivalent of force.

As to the element of lack of consent, the Court said in *Hazel*:

> [I]t is true, of course, that however reluctantly given, consent to the act at any time prior to penetration deprives the subsequent intercourse of its criminal character. There is, however, a wide difference between consent and a submission to the act. Consent may involve submission, but submission does not necessarily imply

consent. Furthermore, submission to a compelling force, or as a result of being put in fear, is not consent.

The Court noted that lack of consent is generally established through proof of resistance or by proof that the victim failed to resist because of fear. The degree of fear necessary to obviate the need to prove resistance, and thereby establish lack of consent, was defined in the following manner:

> The kind of fear which would render resistance by a woman unnecessary to support a conviction of rape includes, but is not necessarily limited to, a fear of death or serious bodily harm, or a fear so extreme as to preclude resistance, or a fear which would well nigh render her mind incapable of continuing to resist, or a fear that so overpowers her that she does not dare resist.

*Hazel* thus made it clear that lack of consent could be established through proof that the victim submitted as a result of fear of imminent death or serious bodily harm. In addition, if the actions and conduct of the defendant were reasonably calculated to induce this fear in the victim's mind, then the element of force is present. *Hazel* recognized, therefore, that the same kind of evidence may be used in establishing both force and nonconsent, particularly when a threat rather than actual force is involved....

*Hazel* did not expressly determine whether the victim's fear must be "reasonable." Its only reference to reasonableness related to whether "the acts and threats of the defendant were reasonably calculated to create in the mind of the victim ... a real apprehension, due to fear, of imminent bodily harm...." Manifestly, the Court was there referring to the calculations of the accused, not to the fear of the victim. While *Hazel* made it clear that the victim's fear had to be genuine, it did not pass upon whether a real but unreasonable fear of imminent death or serious bodily harm would suffice. The vast majority of jurisdictions have required that the victim's fear be reasonably grounded in order to obviate the need for either proof of actual force on the part of the assailant or physical resistance on the part of the victim. We think that, generally, this is the correct standard.

[T]he Court of Special Appeals held that a showing of a reasonable apprehension of fear was essential under *Hazel* to establish the elements of the offense where the victim did not resist. The Court did not believe, however, that the evidence was legally sufficient to demonstrate the existence of "a reasonable fear" which overcame Pat's ability to resist. In support of the Court's conclusion, Rusk maintains that the evidence showed that Pat voluntarily entered his apartment without being subjected to a "single threat nor a scintilla of force"; that she made no effort to run away nor did she scream for help; that she never exhibited a will to resist; and that her subjective reaction of fear to the situation in which she had voluntarily placed herself was unreasonable and exaggerated. Rusk claims that his acts were not reasonably calculated to overcome a will to resist; that Pat's verbal resistance was not resistance within the contemplation of *Hazel*; that his alleged menacing look did not constitute a threat of force; and that even had he pulled Pat to the bed, and lightly choked her, as she claimed, these actions, viewed in the context of the entire incident—no prior threats having been made—would be insufficient to constitute force or a threat of force or render the intercourse nonconsensual.

We think the reversal of Rusk's conviction by the Court of Special Appeals was in error for the fundamental reason so well expressed in the dissenting opinion by Judge Wilner when he observed that the majority had "trampled upon the first principle of appellate restraint ... [because it had] substituted [its] own view of the evidence (and the inferences that may fairly be drawn from it) for that of the judge and jury [and had thereby] improperly invaded the province allotted to those tribunals." In view of the evidence adduced at the trial, the reasonableness of Pat's apprehension of fear was plainly a question of fact for the jury to determine.... Applying the constitutional standard of review ..., i.e.—whether after considering the evidence in the light most favorable to the prosecution, any rational trier of fact could have found the essential elements of the crime beyond a reasonable doubt—it is readily apparent to us that the trier of fact could rationally find that the elements of force and non-consent had been established.... Quite obviously, the jury disbelieved Rusk and believed Pat's testimony. From her testimony, the jury could have reasonably concluded that the taking of her car keys was intended by Rusk to immobilize her alone, late at night, in a neighborhood with which she was not familiar; that after Pat had repeatedly refused to enter his apartment, Rusk commanded in firm tones that she do so; that Pat was badly frightened and feared that Rusk intended to rape her; that unable to think clearly and believing that she had no other choice in the circumstances, Pat entered Rusk's apartment; that once inside Pat asked permission to leave but Rusk told her to stay; that he then pulled Pat by the arms to the bed and undressed her; that Pat was afraid that Rusk would kill her unless she submitted; that she began to cry and Rusk then put his hands on her throat and began "lightly to choke" her; that Pat asked him if he would let her go without killing her if she complied with his demands; that Rusk gave an affirmative response, after which she finally submitted.

Just where persuasion ends and force begins in cases like the present is essentially a factual issue, to be resolved in light of the controlling legal precepts. That threats of force need not be made in any particular manner in order to put a person in fear of bodily harm is well established. Indeed, conduct, rather than words, may convey the threat. That a victim did not scream out for help or attempt to escape, while bearing on the question of consent, is unnecessary where she is restrained by fear of violence.

Considering all of the evidence in the case, with particular focus upon the actual force applied by Rusk to Pat's neck, we conclude that the jury could rationally find that the essential elements of second degree rape had been established and that Rusk was guilty of that offense beyond a reasonable doubt.

Judgment of the Court of Special Appeals reversed; case remanded to that court with directions that it affirm the judgment of the Criminal Court of Baltimore; costs to be paid by the appellee.

■ COLE, JUDGE, dissenting.

... The majority ... concludes that "[i]n view of the evidence adduced at the trial, the reasonableness of Pat's apprehension of fear was plainly a question of fact for the jury to determine." In so concluding, the majority has skipped over the crucial issue. It seems to me that whether the prosecutrix's fear is reasonable becomes a question only after the court determines that the defendant's conduct under the circumstances was reasonably calculated to give rise to a fear on her part to the extent that she was unable to resist. In other words, the fear must stem from his articulable conduct, and equally, if not more importantly, cannot be inconsistent with her own contemporaneous reaction to that conduct. The conduct of the defendant, in and of itself, must clearly indicate force or the threat of force such as to overpower the prosecutrix's ability to resist or will to resist. In my view, there is no evidence to support the majority's conclusion that the prosecutrix was forced to submit to sexual intercourse, certainly not fellatio. . . .

While courts no longer require a female to resist to the utmost or to resist where resistance would be foolhardy, they do require her acquiescence in the act of intercourse to stem from fear generated by something of substance. She may not simply say, "I was really scared," and thereby transform consent or mere unwillingness into submission by force. These words do not transform a seducer into a rapist. She must follow the natural instinct of every proud female to resist, by more than mere words, the violation of her person by a stranger or an unwelcomed friend. She must make it plain that she regards such sexual acts as abhorrent and repugnant to her natural sense of pride. She must resist unless the defendant has objectively manifested his intent to use physical force to accomplish his purpose. The law regards rape as a crime of violence. The majority today attenuates this proposition. It declares the innocence of an at best distraught young woman. It does not demonstrate the defendant's guilt of the crime of rape.

My examination of the evidence in a light most favorable to the state reveals no conduct by the defendant reasonably calculated to cause the prosecutrix to be so fearful that she should fail to resist and, thus, the element of force is lacking in the state's proof.

Here we have a full grown married woman who meets the defendant in a bar under friendly circumstances. They drink and talk together. She agrees to give him a ride home in her car. When they arrive at his house, located in an area with which she was unfamiliar but which was certainly not isolated, he invites her to come up to his apartment and she refuses. According to her testimony he takes her keys, walks around to her side of the car, and says "Now will you come up?" She answers, "yes." The majority suggests that "from her testimony the jury could have reasonably concluded that the taking of her keys was intended by Rusk to immobilize her alone, late at night, in a neighborhood with which she was unfamiliar. . . ." But on what facts does the majority so conclude? There is no evidence descriptive of the tone of his voice; her testimony indicates only the bare statement quoted above. How can the majority extract from this conduct a threat reasonably calculated to create a fear of imminent bodily harm? There was no weapon, no threat to inflict physical injury.

She also testified that she was afraid of "the way he looked," and afraid of his statement, "come on up, come on up." But what can the majority conclude from this statement coupled with a "look" that remained undescribed? There is no evidence whatsoever to suggest that this was anything other than a pattern of conduct consistent with the ordinary seduction of a female acquaintance who at first suggests her disinclination....

The majority relies on the trial court's statement that the defendant responded affirmatively to her question "If I do what you want, will you let me go without killing me?" The majority further suggests that the jury could infer the defendant's affirmative response. The facts belie such inference since by the prosecutrix's own testimony the defendant made no response. He said nothing!

She then testified that she started to cry and he "started lightly to choke" her, whatever that means. Obviously, the choking was not of any persuasive significance. During this "choking" she was able to talk. She said "If I do what you want will you let me go?" It was at this point that the defendant said yes.

I find it incredible for the majority to conclude that on these facts, without more, a woman was forced to commit oral sex upon the defendant and then to engage in vaginal intercourse. In the absence of any verbal threat to do her grievous bodily harm or the display of any weapon and threat to use it, I find it difficult to understand how a victim could participate in these sexual activities and not be willing.

What was the nature and extent of her fear anyhow? She herself testified she was "fearful that maybe I had someone following me." She was afraid because she didn't know him and she was afraid he was going to "rape" her. But there are no acts or conduct on the part of the defendant to suggest that these fears were created by the defendant or that he made any objective, identifiable threats to her which would give rise to this woman's failure to flee, summon help, scream, or make physical resistance.

As the defendant well knew, this was not a child. This was a married woman with children, a woman familiar with the social setting in which these two actors met. It was an ordinary city street, not an isolated spot. He had not forced his way into her car; he had not taken advantage of a difference in years or any state of intoxication or mental or physical incapacity on her part. He did not grapple with her. She got out of the car, walked with him across the street and followed him up the stairs to his room. She certainly had to realize that they were not going upstairs to play Scrabble....

The record does not disclose the basis for this young woman's misgivings about her experience with the defendant. The only substantive fear she had was that she would be late arriving home. The objective facts make it inherently improbable that the defendant's conduct generated any fear for her physical well-being.

In my judgment the state failed to prove the essential element of force beyond a reasonable doubt and, therefore, the judgment of conviction should be reversed. . . .

————

## NOTES ON RESISTANCE AND THE ELEMENTS OF RAPE

**1.  Questions and Comments on *Rusk*.** The court in *Rusk* states that the elements of second-degree rape are "vaginal intercourse[,] . . . force—actual or constructive, and . . . lack of consent." Is this a fair interpretation of the language of the statute? The court also states that "force and lack of consent are distinct elements of the crime of rape." Does the court's subsequent comment that the "same kind of evidence may be used in establishing both force and nonconsent" undercut this assertion?

In finding the evidence sufficient to sustain Rusk's conviction for rape, the court places special emphasis "upon the actual force applied by Rusk to Pat's neck." If that fact (the "light choking") were eliminated from the case, would the result be the same?

The term "resistance" does not appear in either the statute under which Rusk was charged or the common-law definition that the court cites. Yet, as the case makes clear, resistance by the victim is a central preoccupation of rape law. Among other things, Rusk asserted that "Pat's verbal resistance was not resistance." Did the court disagree? If not, why did the court reinstate the conviction? What is resistance? How, if at all, does *Rusk* revise the role that *Hazel* assigned to resistance?

As *Rusk* illustrates, courts do not require proof of resistance in some cases where the prosecution claims that the woman submitted out of fear. *Rusk* suggests that this claim succeeds only where the woman's fear is attributed to a particular source and reaches a specific level. What does the source of the woman's apprehension have to be? How frightened must she be? Assuming satisfactory answers to these two questions, why do courts also require, as does *Rusk*, that the woman's fear be "reasonable"? Why is it not sufficient that she submitted because she was afraid?

After describing his view that the court had misapplied the resistance requirement, the dissenting judge remarks that the majority "declares the innocence of an at best distraught young woman." What does the dissenting judge have in mind when he uses the word "innocence"? In his view, of what has Pat been "declared innocent"?

**2.  Resistance at Common Law.** At common law and under early rape statutes, the courts treated proof of resistance by the victim as a necessary component of rape, although, as *Rusk* explains, this "require-ment" was subject to significant exceptions. The common law defined "resistance" as physical opposition by the woman to the man's sexual advances. Verbal resistance did not suffice, since courts took the view that the woman who offered verbal, but not physical, opposition in fact had consented. "[T]hough she object verbally, if she make no outcry and no resistance, she by her conduct consents, and the act is not rape in the man." Mills v. United States, 164 U.S. 644 (1897). Although every jurisdiction agreed that resistance was required, the decisions disagreed over the degree of resistance the victim must offer. Many courts demanded "earnest" or "utmost" resistance, which required the victim to do all that she was physically capable of doing to repel the man and to "resist until exhausted or overpowered." People v. Dohring, 59 N.Y. 374 (1874). By contrast, some courts rejected the "utmost" resistance requirement and held that the resistance must only be sufficient to establish that the woman's lack of consent was "honest and real." See Commonwealth v. McDonald, 110 Mass. 405 (1872).

Some early codifications explicitly included resistance as an element of the crime. For example, a 19th-century California provision defined rape as "sexual intercourse accomplished with a female, not the wife of the perpetrator ... where she resists, but her resistance was overcome by force or violence." See People v. Fleming, 94 Cal. 308, 29 P. 647 (1892). As *Rusk* indicates, even where the definition of rape made no reference to resistance, courts defined the two most contested elements in terms of the victim's resistance. By her physical resistance, the woman established that she did not consent to the encounter, and for sexual intercourse to occur despite the woman's resistance, the man must have used force.

Early opinions do not identify clearly the cultural values underlying the resistance requirement. One intriguing and, to modern lawyers, annoying feature of these opinions is most judges' refusal to narrate facts they deemed unsavory, let alone describe their understanding of human sexuality. A comment by the Supreme Court of Pennsylvania is representative: "This case discloses an amount of social and moral degradation that is not pleasant to contemplate. Its discussion will be confined within the narrowest possible bounds." Commonwealth v. Allen, 135 Pa. 483, 19 A. 957 (1890). From the few remarks that judges ventured, they apparently believed that the resistance requirement was the product of "common sense applied to the nature of a virtuous woman." Hollis v. State, 27 Fla. 387, 9 So. 67 (1891).

> Can the mind conceive of a woman, in the possession of her faculties and powers, revoltingly unwilling that this deed should be done upon her, who would not resist so hard and so long as she was able? And if a woman, aware that it will be done unless she does resist, does not resist to the extent of her ability on the occasion, must it not be that she is not entirely reluctant?

People v. Dohring, 59 N.Y. 374, 384 (1874). These and similar comments also reveal why the courts believed that women would be "revoltingly unwilling" to submit. Utmost resistance was expected because "a woman jealous of her chastity, shuddering at the bare thought of dishonor, and flying from pollution" would not adopt a "passive policy" or engage in "half-way" measures. State v. Burgdorf, 53 Mo. 65 (1873).

**3.  Reform of the Resistance Requirement.** The resistance requirement is a favorite target of the rape reform movement.

First, the resistance requirement may expose victims to increased risk of physical harm. Empirical studies report that some rapists become "more violent in response to victim resistance." People v. Barnes, 42 Cal.3d 284, 721 P.2d 110, 228 Cal.Rptr. 228 (1986). While other studies indicate that resistance deters rapists in some circumstances, it may be difficult to determine whether resistance will thwart, rather than incite, a particular rapist. If the best that can be said is that resistance may prevent the rape or "prove an invitation to death or serious harm," the law should not prescribe resistance as the only appropriate response by victims. ALI, Model Penal Code and Commentaries § 213.1, pp. 304–05 (1980).

Second, resistance may be an imprecise proxy for nonconsent. Although the courts believed that women naturally resist unwanted sexual attention, the reformers offer recent studies that contradict this assumption. Rather than fighting their attackers, "many women demonstrate 'psychological infantilism'—a frozen fright response." *People v. Barnes*, supra. In some cases, "the 'frozen fright' response resembles cooperative behavior," but the response is not evidence of consent because it is produced by a "profound primal terror," not by willingness to have sexual intercourse. In short, "while the presence of resistance may well be probative on the issue of force or nonconsent, its absence may not."

Third, by imposing a "duty" to resist, the law puts the crime victim, rather than the perpetrator, on trial. Jurors are instructed to scrutinize the victim's behavior, and, if they find her opposition to be insufficiently "earnest," they are advised to acquit the defendant, notwithstanding evidence of his culpability. Reformers have pointed out that victims of other crimes, such as robbery, kidnaping, and assault, are not required to resist physically even though nonconsent is also an element of those crimes. Reformers attribute this unique feature of rape trials to misogynistic attitudes. By refusing to credit women's verbal objections to intercourse, the law denies women rights of sexual self-determination and confers on men broad sexual access to women. It is not enough for women to "just say no." If they do no more, men are free to have sex with them. Accordingly, one of the most vehement messages of feminist reformers is that the resistance standard should be eliminated and jurors admonished that "no means no." Susan Estrich, Real Rape 102 (1987).

**4.  The Current Status of the Resistance Requirement.** In response to the reformers' arguments, most jurisdictions have relaxed the requirement. The "earnest" or "utmost" resistance standard has been all but abolished. Only Alabama continues to define the force element as "physical force that overcomes earnest resistance...." Ala. Crim. Code Ann. § 13A–6–60(8) (Michie 1994). Some statutory provisions purport to reject the resistance requirement altogether. However, as *Rusk* reflects, a substantial number of jurisdictions require the woman to do more than say "no." Media stories about the rape trial of Mike Tyson educated the public about the victim's duty to resist. During jury selection, a deputy prosecutor informed members of the venire that Indiana law did not require the woman to offer any physical resistance. Tyson's lawyers objected to these comments, and the trial judge advised the venire that the prosecutor was wrong. As the judge put it, the victim is "not required to have a knock-down, drag-out, but she is required to resist." E.R. Shipp, "Notes from Tyson Trial: Many Say It Ain't So," N.Y. Times, Feb. 3, 1992.

As these comments suggest, in most jurisdictions the crime of rape does not occur merely because a man sexually penetrates a woman who verbally opposes his advances. A rape conviction requires something more than nonconsensual sexual intercourse. A recent decision by the Supreme Court of Pennsylvania is illustrative. In Commonwealth v. Berkowitz, 537 Pa. 143, 641 A.2d 1161 (1994), the defendant was convicted of rape, a first-degree felony, and indecent assault, a second-degree misdemeanor. The rape statute defined the crime as "sexual intercourse with another person ... by forcible compulsion." The indecent assault statute defined the offense as "indecent contact with another ... without the consent of the other person." The court reversed the rape conviction on the ground that the record contained insufficient evidence of "forcible compulsion." The fact that the complainant had "stated 'no' throughout the encounter" was "relevant to the issue of consent," but did not establish that the intercourse was "forcible." The court acknowledged that the defendant "penetrated [the complainant's] vagina with his penis," but, in the court's view, "the weight of his body on top of her was the only force applied." Under the court's holding, such "force" does not satisfy the "forcible compulsion" element of rape. On the other hand, the court decided that the evidence was sufficient to support the conviction for indecent assault, which required proof of victim nonconsent but not proof of forcible compulsion. Since "[t]he victim testified that she repeatedly said 'no' throughout the encounter, ... the jury reasonably could have inferred that the victim did not consent to the indecent contact." If the complainant in *Berkowitz* had pushed against the defendant's shoulders as he lay on top of her and penetrated her, would he be guilty of rape? If so, why is that fact determinative of the outcome?

**5.   A Feminist Critique of the Requirement of Force.** In *Berkowitz*, "forcible compulsion" was the line that divided the felony of rape from the misdemeanor of indecent assault. The trial judge sentenced Berkowitz to concurrent terms of one to four years on the rape count and six to 12 months on the indecent assault count. With the rape conviction reversed on appeal, Berkowitz served six months in county jail. Under the traditional definition of rape illustrated by *Rusk* and still applied in most states, force is the line that divides the crime of rape from noncriminal sexual intercourse. These grading schemes appear to rest, in part, on a judgment that "forcible" intercourse inflicts injuries more serious than those imposed by intercourse that is only "nonconsensual."

According to Donald Dripps, this judgment is sound because "people generally, male and female, would rather be subjected to unwanted sex than be shot, slashed, or beaten with a tire iron.... [A]s a general matter unwanted sex is not as bad as violence. I think it follows that those who press sexual advances in the face of refusal act less wickedly [and should be punished less severely] than those who shoot, slash, or batter." Donald A. Dripps, Beyond Rape: An Essay on the Difference Between the Presence of Force and the Absence of Consent, 92 Colum. L. Rev. 1780, 1801 (1992).

Many feminist commentators reject this conclusion. For example, Robin West argues that the distinction between "forcible" and "nonconsensual" intercourse is illusory. West explains that the distinction ignores "the violence, and hence the injury, of the penetration itself. From the victim's perspective, unwanted sexual penetration involves unwanted force, and unwanted force is violent—it is physically painful, sometimes resulting in internal tearing and often leaving scars." Robin L. West, Legitimating the Illegitimate: A Comment on Beyond Rape, 93 Colum. L. Rev. 1442, 1448 (1993). The distinction also ignores the psychological injuries imposed by nonconsensual intercourse. As West remarks, "[r]ape accompanied by additional acts of violence is no doubt a worse experience than what we misleadingly think of as 'nonviolent' rape. [But both] involve violent assaults upon the body. Both are experienced, and typically described, as . . . spiritual murder."

Catharine MacKinnon criticizes feminists and other commentators who argue that rape should be understood as a violent (rather than sexual) act against women. According to MacKinnon, those who assert that rape is a crime of violence, not sex, are attempting to characterize sexuality as "a preexisting natural sphere to which domination is alien." MacKinnon argues that such characterization is mistaken because in our culture there is no "uncoerced context for sexual expression." Rather, "sexuality [is] a social sphere of male power to which forced sex is paradigmatic." In a culture in which normal men are expected to be dominant and sexually aggressive, normal "sex, in the legal perspective, can entail a lot of force." Moreover, since "coercion has become integral to [normal] male sexuality," rape cases find high levels of force to be unobjectionable because judges interpret sexual encounters from the perspective of "normal male sexual behavior, rather than [from] the victim's, or women's, point of violation." MacKinnon insists that, if feminists intend to dismantle "male supremacy," they must persuade lawmakers that "the elements 'with force and without consent' [are] redundant. Force is present because consent is absent." She continues:

> The deeper problem is that women are socialized to passive receptivity; may have or perceive no alternative to acquiescence; may prefer it to the escalated risk of injury and the humiliation of a lost fight; submit to survive. . . . Sexual intercourse may be deeply unwanted, the woman would never have initiated it, yet no force may be present. . . . Force may be used, yet the woman may prefer the sex—to avoid more force or because she, too, eroticizes dominance. Women and men know this. Considering rape as violence not sex evades, at the moment it most seems to confront,

the issue of who controls woman's sexuality and the domi-
nance/submission dynamic that has defined it.

Catharine A. MacKinnon, Toward a Feminist Theory of the State 172–74
(1989). While these objections are provocative, their practical value is
difficult to assess in the abstract, and MacKinnon does not pursue their
doctrinal implications.

**6. Rape as the Woman's Excuse for Committing Fornication
or Adultery.** Anne Coughlin argues that one of the primary functions of
the traditional elements of rape was to provide an excuse for women who
would otherwise be guilty of fornication or adultery. Most contemporary
critics of rape law hold that the parties' "consent" is the line that divides
lawful from unlawful sexual intercourse. Where the sex is consensual, no
crime is committed; where it is non-consensual, one of the parties (invariably, the male) is guilty of rape. However, Coughlin points out that the
understanding that consensual sexual intercourse is lawful "is in conflict
with the fundamental moral and legal premises of the culture from which
the rape prohibition emerged and even with a basic ingredient of the
traditional rape crime." Anne M. Coughlin, Sex and Guilt, 84 Va. L. Rev. 1,
20 (1998). According to the traditional morés that shaped the rape crime,
the line between lawful and unlawful sex was not the parties' consent, but
their marriage. In that world, all marital sex was lawful, all nonmarital sex
was unlawful, and, depending on their marital status and that of their
sexual partners, males and females who engaged in nonmarital sex would
be punished for fornication or adultery. Coughlin argues that the prohibitions on fornication and adultery could be expected to and did exert a
powerful influence on the substantive definition of rape:

> ... How would judges who believed that consensual nonmari-
> tal intercourse was a crime define rape? ... By unearthing our
> ancestors' belief that *all* nonmarital intercourse should be crimi-
> nalized, we may begin to understand, even as we reject, the
> inclination of courts to approach rape complaints with deep suspi-
> cion. Since, under our ancestors' system, the underlying sexual
> activity in which a rape complainant engaged (albeit, by her own
> testimony, unwillingly) was criminal misconduct, her complaint
> logically could be construed as a plea to be relieved of responsibili-
> ty for committing that crime. A court would be receptive to such a
> plea only if the woman could establish that, although she had
> participated in a sexual transgression, she did so under circum-
> stances that afforded her a defense to criminal liability. Signifi-
> cantly, careful examination of rape doctrine reveals that the ele-
> ments of the rape offense (almost) are a mirror image of the
> defenses we would expect from women accused of fornication or
> adultery. Such traditional defensive strategies would include the
> claim that the woman had committed no actus reus, that she
> lacked the mens rea for fornication or adultery, or that she had
> submitted to the intercourse under duress. For example, just as
> courts allowed perpetrators of nonsexual crimes to interpose a

duress defense, so we must assume that they would be willing to excuse those women suspected of fornication or adultery who could prove that their accomplices had forced them to offend under threat of death or grievous bodily harm. According to this account, the features of rape law to which the critics most strenuously object—namely, the peculiar definitions of the nonconsent and force elements of the crime—are better understood as criteria that excuse the woman for committing an illegal sexual infraction, than as ingredients of the man's offense. Curiously, when we acknowledge, rather than ignore or minimize the long-standing and explicit connection our culture has made between sexual intercourse and criminal guilt, we produce a description of rape law that incorporates a justification for thorough doctrinal reform. That is, if we now are prepared to agree that fornication and adultery should no longer be criminalized—whether because those offenses violate contemporary constitutional guarantees or contemporary moral and political judgments (to the extent that such judgments differ from constitutional guarantees)—then there appears to be no justification for adhering to a definition of rape that treats the rapist's victim as a lawbreaker who must plead for an excuse from criminal responsibility.

**7.   M.T.S.** The Supreme Court of New Jersey adopted a definition of "force" that appears to endorse MacKinnon's perspective. In State ex rel. M.T.S., 129 N.J. 422, 609 A.2d 1266 (1992), the court upheld a delinquency adjudication based on the commission of sexual assault. The victim of the assault was a 15–year-old girl, who was a "good friend[]" of the 17–year-old male defendant. At the time of the alleged assault, the victim and the defendant were engaged in a "heavy petting" session, as they had done several times before. The trial judge found that they "had been kissing and petting, had undressed and had gotten into the victim's bed...." The defendant penetrated the victim's vagina with his penis. The victim slapped the defendant on the face and pushed him off her. The defendant immediately got dressed and left the victim's room. In a delinquency hearing, the defendant was charged with "second-degree sexual assault" under a statute that defined the crime "as an act of sexual penetration with another person [by the use of] physical force or coercion." The trial judge concluded that the crime had occurred. Although "the victim had consented to a session of kissing and heavy petting with [the defendant,] she had not consented to the actual sexual act." On appeal, the intermediate appellate court reversed. The only evidence of force was the act of sexual penetration, which by itself was insufficient to satisfy the "physical force" element. The state appealed, and the Supreme Court of New Jersey reversed and reinstated the delinquency judgment. As that court explained, since 1978 the New Jersey penal code "has referred to the crime that was once known as 'rape' as 'sexual assault.'" In part through this change in nomenclature, the New Jersey legislature manifested its intention to redefine rape "consistent with the law of assault and battery." Significantly, under the law of assault and battery, "any unauthorized touching of another" is a crime. The court then explained how this definition applies in the context of "sexual assault":

> [A]ny act of sexual penetration engaged in by the defendant without the affirmative and freely-given permission of the victim to the specific act of penetration constitutes the offense of sexual assault. Therefore, physical force in excess of that inherent in the act of sexual penetration is not required for such penetration to be unlawful. The definition of "physical force" is satisfied ... if the defendant applies any amount of force against another person in the absence of what a reasonable person would believe to be affirmative and freely-given permission to the act of sexual penetration.
>
> Under the reformed statute, permission to engage in sexual penetration must be affirmative and it must be given freely, but that permission may be inferred either from acts or statements reasonably viewed in light of the surrounding circumstances. Persons need not, of course, expressly announce their consent to engage in intercourse for there to be affirmative permission. Permission to engage in an act of sexual penetration can be and indeed often is indicated through physical actions rather than words. Permission is demonstrated when the evidence, in whatever form, is sufficient to demonstrate that a reasonable person would have believed that the alleged victim had affirmatively and freely given authorization to the act.

Applying this standard to the facts of the case, the court found no reason to disturb the trial court's finding that "the victim had not expressed consent to the act of intercourse, either through her words or actions."

Under *M.T.S.*, what kinds of "physical actions" express affirmative permission to engage in sexual intercourse? The New Jersey Supreme Court deferred to, but did not analyze, the trial court's finding that the victim did not give permission, notwithstanding her consensual participation in "heavy petting." Rather, the court chose to emphasize that the New Jersey statute "places no burden on the alleged victim to have expressed non-consent or to have denied permission, and no inquiry is made into what he or she thought or desired or why he or she did not resist or protest." According to Donald Dripps, the court misallocated the burden:

> The burden of asking permission can be placed on the man, or the burden of expressing refusal can be placed on the woman. Granting that gender prejudice is implicated by either choice, I think the second alternative is superior, because sexual encounters ought not to be lived or analyzed as sequences of particular touchings. In practice couples do not discuss in advance each specific sex act that one or another might initiate, and there is no strong reason why the law should encourage them to do so. Suppose, for example, the victim in *M.T.S.* had begun to perform fellatio on the defendant without asking permission. Suppose, further, that he has religious or other scruples about oral sex. He

protests as soon as he knows what she is doing, and she stops as soon as he protests. Still, under the court's opinion, she is guilty of sexual assault. If uncertainty and spontaneity can enhance the pleasures of love-making, people of either sex might prefer not being asked—so long as they can be sure that behavior they don't like will be stopped on demand. The interest in freedom from wrong guesses by one's bedmates is not so great as to call the criminal law into play.

Donald A. Dripps, Beyond Rape: An Essay on the Difference Between the Presence of Force and the Absence of Nonconsent, 92 Colum. L. Rev. 1780, 1793 n.41 (1992).

Douglas Husak and George Thomas acknowledge that an approach to rape like that endorsed by *M.T.S.* would eliminate the "potential for error" in sexual encounters and the pain that such errors inflict. However, since social norms about sexual intercourse do not currently demand explicit affirmations of consent, they argue that punishing a defendant merely for departing from the *M.T.S.* model

> can be justified only on Holmes's view that "[p]ublic policy sacrifices the individual to the general good," and that it is more important to encourage the social convention to change or to vindicate a particular view of women's autonomy than to do justice in an individual case. But if the law should deal justly with each individual defendant, it is objectionable to punish someone to promote an ideology or to effect a change in societal views.

Douglas N. Husak & George C. Thomas III, Date Rape, Social Convention, and Reasonable Mistakes, 11 Law & Phil. 95, 108–09, 112 (1992). Does the law ever punish or, for that matter, refuse to punish someone without promoting an ideology?

**8. Grading.** As the drafters of the Model Penal Code observed, the common law placed "different forms of rape . . . in a single category for grading purposes. The effect of [such definition] was to authorize grave sanctions for a range of conduct that included offenses plainly less serious than the most aggravated forms of rape." ALI, Model Penal Code and Commentaries § 213.1, at p. 278 (1980). By the time the Model Code was being drafted, "there was . . . an emerging consensus that departure from the single-category approach to the punishment of rape was appropriate and that legislative attention should be addressed to the creation of meaningful grading distinctions among the different forms of the offenses." However, there was and continues to be little agreement as to what these grading distinctions should be.

The sexual assault statute at issue in *M.T.S.* represents one approach to grading.[a] As the court in *M.T.S.* explained, the New Jersey legislature replaced the common-law "rape" crime with an offense known as "sexual

---

[a] The relevant New Jersey statutes are reproduced in Appendix B, together with "rape" statutes from Michigan and Virginia.

assault." The statute divides sexual assault into two categories, namely, "aggravated sexual assault" and "sexual assault." "Aggravated sexual assault" occurs when an actor sexually penetrates the body of another person under specified aggravating circumstances. Such circumstances include the sexual penetration of a victim who is under age 13, commission of the sexual penetration during the perpetration of another serious felony, the threatened use of a weapon, the presence of several attackers, and the use of physical force or coercion accompanied by the infliction of "severe personal injury" on the victim. "Aggravated sexual assault" is punishable by 10 to 20 years in prison.

By contrast, an actor commits the crime of "sexual assault" when he or she sexually penetrates another under circumstances that are blameworthy, but less serious than those involved in aggravated sexual assault. For example, as was found to be the case in *M.T.S.*, an actor is guilty of "sexual assault" when he sexually penetrates another person by the use of "physical force or coercion," but he does not severely injure the other person. "Sexual assault" is punishable by five to 10 years in prison.

The New Jersey Penal Code also includes the offense of "criminal sexual contact." The actus reus of this offense is sexual touching not amounting to sexual penetration. This offense also is divided into two categories for grading purposes, namely, "aggravated criminal sexual contact" and "criminal sexual contact," and these categories are distinguished by the presence or absence of aggravating factors similar to those enumerated in the sexual assault provisions. "Aggravated criminal sexual contact" is punishable by three to five years in prison, while "criminal sexual contact" is punishable by up to 18 months in prison.

*M.T.S.* involved a juvenile delinquency proceeding, and the reported opinions do not reflect what penalty the judge imposed on M.T.S. for the sexual assault. Is the penalty (five to 10 years in prison) authorized by the statute an appropriate one?

---

## NOTES ON THE CRIMINALIZATION OF SEX OBTAINED BY COERCION OR FRAUD

**1. Introduction.** Should the law punish people who obtain sex by threats of harm other than physical injury or who obtain sex by deception?[a]

[a] Stephen Schulhofer argues that rape statutes that require proof of violence fail to protect women's sexual freedom, and he provides a definition of "sexual autonomy" designed to assist lawmakers in identifying forms of nonviolent sexual misconduct that warrant criminal punishment. See Stephen J. Schulhofer, Taking Sexual Autonomy Seriously: Rape Law and Beyond, 11 L. & Phil. 35 (1992). Similarly, Donald Dripps argues that lawmakers should replace rape with a variety of offenses that differentiate between the violent and nonviolent expropriation of sexual favors. See Donald A. Dripps, Beyond Rape: An Essay on the Difference Between the Presence of Force and the Absence of Consent, 92 Colum. L. Rev. 1780 (1992).

The following notes identify several different kinds of nonviolent practices that have formed the basis for criminal prosecutions.

**2. Psychological Coercion.** In Commonwealth v. Mlinarich, 518 Pa. 247, 542 A.2d 1335 (1988), the defendant was convicted of rape and attempted rape for his sexual contacts with a 14–year-old girl. Mlinarich was the girl's guardian. Prior to going to live in his home, the girl had been committed to a juvenile detention facility for stealing her brother's ring. Mlinarich and his wife requested custody of the girl, and a court released her into their care. Soon thereafter, Mlinarich began to fondle her. She told him that "he shouldn't do that," but he ignored her "protestations, desisting only if she began to cry." During several of these encounters, Mlinarich attempted and, on one occasion, achieved intercourse with the girl. Each time, she "insisted that she 'did not want to do anything,'" and, during the first unsuccessful attempt, she "experienced pain and 'scream[ed], holler[ed]' and cried." However, Mlinarich persisted, and she submitted to the activity after he "threatened to send her back to the detention home" if she refused him.

On appeal, the intermediate appellate court reversed the rape and attempted rape convictions on the ground that these crimes require "forcible compulsion," which is not satisfied by "threats to do non-violent acts." Commonwealth v. Mlinarich, 345 Pa.Super. 269, 498 A.2d 395 (1985).[b] The Supreme Court of Pennsylvania affirmed by an equally divided court. 518 Pa. 247, 542 A.2d 1335. All of the Justices agreed that the term "forcible compulsion" is not limited to physical violence, but also includes "psychological duress." They divided over the question of whether Mlinarich's threat rose to that level. According to the three Justices who voted to affirm, a threat inflicts psychological duress only where it attacks the victim's will rather than her intellect. They explained:

> The critical distinction is where the compulsion overwhelms the will of the victim in contrast to a situation where the victim can make a deliberate choice to avoid the encounter even though the alternative may be an undesirable one. Indeed, the victim in this instance apparently found the prospect of being returned to the detention home a repugnant one. Notwithstanding, she was left with a choice and therefore the submission was the result of a deliberate choice and was not an involuntary act. . . .

> . . . The purpose of [the forcible compulsion element is] to distinguish between assault upon the will and the forcing of the victim to make a choice regardless how repugnant. Certainly

[b] In addition to the rape and attempted rape counts, Mlinarich was convicted of involuntary deviate sexual intercourse and corrupting the morals of a child. The trial court had imposed "an aggregate term of three to eight years imprisonment in the county jail." With the rape and attempted rape convictions reversed on appeal, Mlinarich's sentence was reduced to a term of two to five years in prison. The state could not try Mlinarich for statutory rape because the girl was over the age of consent. In Pennsylvania, the age of consent for purposes of statutory rape is 14, and Mlinarich began sexually molesting her on her 14th birthday.

difficult choices have a coercive effect but the result is the product of the reason, albeit unpleasant and reluctantly made. . . .

For the three Justices who voted to reverse and reinstate the convictions, the threat of incarceration constituted forcible compulsion. As Justice McDermott put it, "all threats, however compelling in the mind of the actor, leave a choice in the victim. . . . The question is not whether she could make a choice to yield or be confined, but whether the law should allow such a choice at all. The purpose of law is to narrow the choices that may be offered to compel others in order to gain an end of one's own." Thus, the magnitude of the threat, the dread it inspired in the girl, and whether it overcame her reasonable resolve were questions for the jury to weigh in light of all the circumstances in the case.

*Mlinarich* was a divisive opinion for the Justices who decided it, and it proved to be a controversial one for commentators and members of the popular press. In 1995, the Pennsylvania legislature responded to criticisms of *Mlinarich* and cases that followed it by enacting this definition of "forcible compulsion" for purposes of the rape statute: "Compulsion by use of physical, intellectual, moral, emotional, or psychological force, either express or implied." 18 Pa. Cons. Stat. Ann. § 3101 (2000). If a case similar to *Mlinarich* were to be tried under this definition, what would the result be? Assuming that *Mlinarich* was a "problem," as many commentators argued, is this revision an appropriate "fix"? Does the revision go far enough? Too far?

   **3.   Extortion.** In some jurisdictions, the sexual offenses chapter of the penal code punishes the extortion of sexual relations. A dearth of reported cases of sex by extortion suggests that this theory is rarely invoked by prosecutors. In jurisdictions whose penal codes do not specifically prohibit sex by extortion, the question is whether such activity may be prosecuted under a general extortion statute, as in the following case.

   **(i)  Is Sex a Thing of Value?** In United States v. Hicks, 24 M.J. 3 (1987), the victim, a woman named Julie, was visiting her boyfriend at his military base. Sergeant Hicks was the leader of the section to which Julie's boyfriend was assigned. When Hicks learned that Julie was staying in the barracks in violation of a regulation, he advised her boyfriend to bring her to Hicks's room where she would not be detected by the staff duty officer. Soon after the boyfriend followed this advice, Hicks returned to his room. He informed "Julie that he was preparing a charge sheet," under which her boyfriend would "lose his pay and privileges" and "probably get thrown in the brig." Hicks then told Julie that "if she 'wanted to get . . . [her boyfriend] out of that trouble,' " she should have sex with him. After a further exchange during which Hicks' made additional threatening comments, Julie submitted to sexual intercourse with him. Based on this episode, Hicks was convicted of rape[c] and extortion of sexual favors, and sentenced to confinement for 30 years.

---

   [c] Hicks was convicted of rape under a statute that required proof that the sexual intercourse was accomplished "by force and without [the victim's] consent." The court

Hicks appealed, and the United States Court of Military Appeals affirmed. To convict Hicks for extortion, the prosecution had to prove two elements: "(1) communication of a threat; (2) 'with the intention thereby to obtain anything of value or any acquittance, advantage, or immunity.'" Hicks attacked only the second element, arguing that it did not encompass "sexual favors or the fulfillment of subjective desires." The court disagreed, holding that "[i]t is sufficient if there is some 'value' or 'advantage' to the accused in the thing sought. 'Value' and 'advantage' are broad concepts and are not limited to pecuniary or material gain." Accordingly, "[t]he extortion offense was complete upon communication of the threat to report [the boyfriend] with the requisite intent."

Not all courts have been receptive to the claim that "sexual favors" satisfy the second element of extortion. In State v. Stockton, 97 Wash.2d 528, 647 P.2d 21 (1982), the Supreme Court of Washington reversed an extortion conviction based on letters threatening to kill a woman and her husband if she did not agree to have sex with the defendant. Extortion was defined as "knowingly to obtain or attempt to obtain by threats property or services." After examining the definition of services provided in the statute, as well as the language of predecessor statutes, the court held that the only "services" contemplated were "those for which compensation is usually received ... and not the sexual favors which defendant was asking to be freely given to him." The court implied that the defendant could have been tried under a "coercion" statute, which punished threats uttered to "induce[] a person to engage in conduct which [she] has a legal right to abstain from." Noting that coercion is only a misdemeanor, the court conceded that it was anomalous to punish as a felony threats to obtain commercial services, while a threat to obtain sexual favors was punished less severely. However, the legislature had created, and was the appropriate body to resolve, that anomaly.

**(ii) Nature of the Threat.** If sexual contacts satisfy the second element of extortion, the nature of the threat determines whether a crime occurred. Not surprisingly, threats of serious violence suffice for an extortion conviction, but so do other threats. Threats to injure the victim

held that there was sufficient evidence to support the rape conviction, relying in part on Julie's testimony that, after threatening to report her boyfriend, Hicks took her hand and stated, "It doesn't matter if you cooperate or not, I'm going to give it to you anyway." According to the court, this testimony established that Hicks intended "to use whatever force was necessary to accomplish intercourse." The court also concluded that Julie "was placed in fear of bodily harm; she remembered being advised by various articles and television programs [primarily, talk shows] that it was better not to resist unless you are sure you can hurt your assailant to such an extent as to make good your escape."

The court also decided that convicting Hicks for both rape and extortion did not violate the double jeopardy clause, which provides that no person "shall be subject for the same offence to be twice put in jeopardy of life or limb." In this case, rape and extortion were not the "same offense" for double jeopardy purposes because "[t]here are elements in each offense which are not contained within the other, and neither offense is a lesser-included offense of the other. The extortion offense was complete upon communication of the threat to report [the boyfriend] with the requisite intent; the rape was accomplished by means of placing the victim in fear of bodily harm."

financially, to harm the victim's reputation, and to confine the victim all have been held sufficient in cases involving the extortion of pecuniary assets. While the threat element of extortion thus encompasses a wider variety of coercive pressures than does the traditional definition of rape, extortion does not prohibit inducements to behavior that fall short of a threat to cause an injury. In State v. Hilton, 1991 WL 168608 (Tenn. Crim. App., Sept 4, 1991), a man who had sexual intercourse with his 17–year-old stepdaughter was convicted of incest and rape. To support the rape conviction, the prosecutor argued that the defendant had extorted the sexual contacts because he demanded that the girl have sex with him "for permission to go places, do things, or get things." While sex by extortion is a form of rape under the Tennessee penal code,[d] the appellate court found that there was insufficient evidence of a threat to injure the girl. Rather than being coerced by a threat, she agreed to engage in sexual intercourse "because she wanted the defendant to buy her something. [S]ex was the price she paid for receiving things which her sisters did not have." How clear is the line between a threat to injure someone if they refuse to submit and a promise to compensate them if they acquiesce?

The drafters of the Model Penal Code sought to define that line and to explain its normative significance. Under the Model Code, the most serious form of rape involves "force" or threats of serious bodily harm. See MPC § 213.1(1)(a). However, the Code also punishes, as a lesser crime, sexual intercourse obtained by non-violent threats. Thus, § 213.1(2)(a) provides that a male commits the offense of "gross sexual imposition" where he "has sexual intercourse with a female ... if he compels her to submit by any threat that would prevent resistance by a woman of ordinary resolution." According to the drafters, this crime occurs where the woman submits because of "coercion rather than bargain." Endeavoring to explain the distinction between "coercion" and "bargain," the drafters remarked that "the man who 'threatens' to withhold an expensive present unless his girlfriend permits his advances is plainly not a fit subject for punishment under the law of rape." The drafters continued:

> ... Examples [of threats that might suffice include a] threat to cause her to lose her job or to deprive her of a valued possession.... Although threat of economic injury may be deemed less serious than threat of physical attack, threat of either description may be sufficient to deny the freedom of choice that the law of rape ... seeks to protect and to subject a woman to unwanted and degrading sexual intimacy....
>
> [By requiring a "threat that would prevent resistance by a woman of ordinary resolution," the Code eliminates] cases of

[d] The Tennessee statute construed in *Hilton* provides that rape is "unlawful sexual penetration of another [where] force or coercion is used to accomplish the act." Tenn. Code Ann. § 39–2–604(a)(1) (1982). Under the statute, the term "coercion" is defined, among other things, as "extortion." § 39–2–602(1). A subsequent revision of the Tennessee sex offenses retains these provisions. See Tenn. Code Ann. §§ 39–13–501(1), 39–13–503(a)(1) (1991).

intimidation by threat of remote or trivial harm. Thus, for example, the policeman who persuades a woman to submit to intercourse rather than to accept a parking ticket may be guilty of some minor abuse of office, but he should not be subject to felony sanctions.... Similarly, a man who threatens to destroy an inexpensive object unless its owner agrees to sexual relations should not be guilty of this offense. [I]t is virtually impossible to find genuine coercion in such situations. The absence of coercion arises not from the nature of the threat but simply from its triviality. In each of the hypotheticals, the male may make the plausible assumption that the woman's acquiescence has as much to do with his own attractiveness as with the prospect of threatened harm. In terms of blameworthiness and of dangerousness ..., he is not comparable to the male who compels submission by some threat generally sufficient to overcome the resistance of a woman of ordinary resolution....

[Moreover, the] threat must be such that submission by the female results from coercion rather than bargain.... Thus, if a wealthy man were to threaten to withdraw financial support from his unemployed girlfriend, it is at least arguable under the circumstances that he is making a threat "that would prevent resistance by a woman of ordinary resolution." The reason why this case is excluded from liability ... is not the gravity of the harm threatened—it may be quite substantial—but its essential character as part of a process of bargain. He is not guilty of compulsion overwhelming the will of his victim but only of offering her an unattractive choice to avoid some unwanted alternative....

... Guidance may be derived from other contexts in which the penal law must distinguish illegitimate threat from the process of bargain.... So, for example, a son may threaten to desert his filial duties unless his aged mother agrees to include him in her inheritance. This conduct is unattractive but plainly outside the appropriate reach of criminal sanctions....

ALI, Model Penal Code and Commentaries § 213.1, pp. 312–14 (1980).

**(iii) Should Sexual Harassment Be a Form of Rape?** A threat by a supervisor to fire or fail to promote an employee unless the employee has sex with the supervisor is known as "quid pro quo" sexual harassment. Title VII of the Civil Rights Act of 1964, 42 U.S.C. § 2000e, and state tort law provide civil remedies to victims of such harassment. By uttering a quid pro quo threat, would the supervisor also commit the crime of extortion under *Hicks*? If the employee acquiesced and had sex with the supervisor, would the supervisor be guilty of rape under *Hilton* or of "gross sexual imposition" under § 213.1(2)(a) of the Model Penal Code?

The military justice system has taken some tentative steps in the direction of criminalizing quid pro quo sexual harassment. Military courts have recognized that the element of "force" for purposes of rape law includes not only the application of actual, physical force, but also "constructive force." Thus, like courts in other jurisdictions, military tribunals hold that the force element may be satisfied "by proof of a coercive atmosphere that includes, for example, threats to injure others or statements that resistance would be futile." United States v. Simpson, 58 M.J. 368, 377 (Ct. App. Armed Forces 2003). Moreover, when deciding whether the alleged perpetrator used constructive force, it is proper for the members of the court-martial to consider the disparity between his rank and that of the complaining witness. In *Simpson*, the Court of Appeals for the Armed Forces cautioned that constructive force requires more than proof of rank disparity. Still, the fact that the accused was the victim's superior officer may go a long way towards satisfying the force element. As *Simpson* observed, for example, there is a "special relationship between non-commissioned officers and trainees" such that the non-commissioned officer:

> cannot create by his own actions an environment of isolation and fear and then seek excusal from the crime of rape by claiming the absence of force especially where, as here, passive acquiescence is prompted by the unique situation of dominance and control presented by appellant's superior rank and position.

4.  **Sex by Fraud.** A number of state statutes punish as rape sexual intercourse or penetration accomplished "by fraud." The scope of this prohibition is determined by the meaning of the term "fraud." Traditionally, the courts have construed the term narrowly by holding that sexual intercourse procured by fraud is a rape in cases of "fraud in the factum" but not in cases of "fraud in the inducement." As the United States Court of Military Appeals has explained, "fraud in the factum" is a "deception [that] causes a misunderstanding as to the fact itself." United States v. Booker, 25 M.J. 114 (1987). The most common perpetrator of rape by fraud in the factum is the doctor who sexually penetrates the body of a patient who is unaware that the act is occurring because she believes she is submitting to a routine medical examination or procedure. E.g., McNair v. State, 108 Nev. 53, 825 P.2d 571 (1992); People v. Ogunmola, 193 Cal. App.3d 274, 238 Cal.Rptr. 300 (1987). By contrast, "fraud in the inducement" is a "deception [that] relate[s] not to the thing done but merely to some collateral matter." *United States v. Booker* elaborates the distinction:

> Clearly, fraud in the inducement includes such general knavery as: "No, I'm not married"; "Of course I'll respect you in the morning"; "We'll get married as soon as ..."; "I'll pay you [ ] dollars"; and so on. Whatever else such tactics amount to, they are not rape.
>
> The question is—what is fraud in the factum in the context of consensual intercourse? The better view is that the "factum" involves both the nature of the act and the identity of the participant. Thus in the "doctor" cases, consent would not be present unless the patient realized that the "procedure" being employed was not medical, but sexual. Further while it is arguable that there may be people who are willing to hop into bed with absolutely anyone, we take it that even the most uninhibited people

ordinarily make some assessment of a potential sex partner and exercise some modicum of discretion before consenting to sexual intercourse. Thus, consent to the act is based on the identity of the prospective partner.[2]

Under *Booker*, what kinds of misrepresentations about the "identity" of one's sexual partner constitute fraud in the factum?[e]

The traditional distinction between fraud in the factum and fraud in the inducement may be eroding. At least one court has stated that "fraud" in this context is not limited to fraud in the factum. In State v. Tizard, 897 S.W.2d 732 (Tenn. Crim. App. 1994), the victim was a 17–year-old male high school student who approached the defendant, a physician, and requested steroids to enhance his athletic performance. During the victim's third appointment, Dr. Tizard physically examined the victim as he had on past visits. Towards the end of the examination, the doctor "rubbed the shaft of the [victim's] penis with his hand for a couple of minutes until it was erect." The victim testified that "he was embarrassed and thought that what the defendant did . . . was not right, but he returned for . . . two [more] visits because he wanted steroids." During two subsequent examinations, Dr. Tizard again rubbed the victim's penis until it was erect. On their last appointment, Dr. Tizard continued this activity "for five to ten minutes" until the victim ejaculated. Dr. Tizard was convicted of two counts of sexual battery by fraud. On appeal, the defense argued that the crime required fraud in the factum and that the prosecution had failed to prove such fraud because the victim was not under any misunderstanding as to the act itself. To the contrary, "the victim was completely aware of what was happening and indicated a belief that the defendant's conduct was improper, but returned to obtain steroids while allowing the defendant to commit the act upon which the convictions are based." The Tennessee Court of Criminal Appeals rejected this argument, holding that "the definition of fraud . . . is not limited to any particular type of fraud. [F]raud comprises 'anything calculated to deceive, including all acts, omissions, and concealments involving a breach of legal or equitable duty, trust, or confidence justly reposed, resulting in damage to another, or by which an undue and unconscientious [sic] advantage is taken of another.'"

Why is *Tizard* an example of sexual battery by fraud? Assuming that the case does involve fraud, did Dr. Tizard commit fraud in the factum or

---

[2] . . . To be more basic, for there to be actual consent, a woman must be agreeable to the penetration of her body by a particular "membrum virile": it is quite irrelevant whether she knows the "real" identity of the owner thereof.

[e] The Model Penal Code punishes some instances of sex by fraud in the factum. Section 213.1(2)(c) provides that "a male who has sexual intercourse with a female not his wife commits a felony of the third degree if . . . he knows that she is unaware that a

sexual act is being committed upon her or that she submits because she mistakenly supposes that he is her husband." The drafters concluded that it was generally undesirable to criminalize sex by fraud in the inducement. However, the Code does impose misdemeanor liability for "seduction," a form of sex by fraud in the inducement. Under § 213.3(1)(d), seduction occurs when a male induces a female to participate in sexual intercourse "by a promise of marriage which the actor does not mean to perform."

fraud in the inducement? Boro v. Superior Court, 163 Cal.App.3d 1224, 210 Cal.Rptr. 122 (1985), is often cited as an example of sex by fraud in the inducement, which the court there held was not punishable as rape. The defendant in *Boro* telephoned a woman, represented that he was a doctor, and told her that "she had contracted a dangerous, highly infectious and perhaps fatal disease." He further advised her that, happily, there were two available cures: the first was a painful form of surgery, which cost $9,000.00, and the second was sexual intercourse with "an anonymous donor" who had been injected with a special serum, which cost only $4,500.00. The woman chose the second alternative, met the defendant at a hotel, and had intercourse with him. The court in *Boro* issued a writ of prohibition, restraining prosecution of the defendant on charges of rape.[f] Although the woman had "succumbed to [the defendant's] fraudulent blandishments" because she was afraid that otherwise she might die, she "precisely understood the 'nature of the act' " to which she was submitting and thus was merely the victim of noncriminal sex by fraud in the inducement.

Under the definition of fraud quoted by the *Tizard* court, would the examples of sex by fraud in the inducement that *Booker* viewed as "general knavery" be rape? Should those incidents be punishable as rape?

Richard Posner provides the following explanation for why the law might be reluctant to punish the actor who obtains sex, rather than money, by fraud in the inducement:[*]

> ... The law usually treats force and fraud symmetrically in the sense of punishing both, though the latter more leniently. It is a crime to take money at gunpoint. It is also a crime, though normally a lesser one, to take it by false pretenses. But generally it is not a crime to use false pretenses to entice a person into a sexual relationship. Seduction, even when honeycombed with lies that would convict the man of fraud if he were merely trying to obtain money, is not rape. The thinking may be that if the woman is not averse to having sex with a particular man, the wrong if any is in the lies (and we usually do not think of lying in social settings as a crime) rather than in an invasion of her bodily integrity. It is otherwise if the man is impersonating the woman's husband or claims to be administering medical treatment to the woman rather than to be inserting his penis in her. In both cases the act itself, were the true facts known to the woman, would be disgusting as well as humiliating, rather than merely humiliating as in the case of the common misrepresentations of dating and courtship.
>
> How to explain the difference in offensiveness? Girls are taught by their parents to be suspicious of the blandishments of

---

[f] Based on this episode, the defendant also was charged with attempted grand theft and burglary. He did not challenge those counts of the information.

suitors.... Ordinarily, to be sure, the law does not place the burden of preventing fraud on the victim; it is cheaper for the potential injurer not to commit fraud than for the victim to take measures of self-protection against it. Nevertheless, a person who has acted the fool is likely to feel slightly less offended at having been fleeced. The problems of proof of seduction by false pretenses—in particular the problem of distinguishing by the methods of litigation between a false statement of one's feelings and a change in those feelings—are exquisitely difficult and argue for making a difference in degree a difference in legal kind, substituting victim self-protection for legal remedies. It is a plausible substitution in a society such as ours in which (adult) virginity is for the most part no longer a highly valued good....

Richard A. Posner, Sex and Reason 392–93 (1992).

According to Anne Coughlin, courts recognized the crime of rape "by fraud in the factum" but not by "fraud in the inducement" because, in the former cases, the woman lacked the mens rea necessary to convict her for fornication or adultery, and, hence, it was appropriate to convict only the man for the illegal sex act:

[T]he rule that sex by fraud constitutes rape only in the context of "fraud in the factum" singles out for prosecution as rape the few cases in which a woman engaged in fornication or adultery only through an exculpatory mistake of fact. The argument proceeds as follows: Though the woman in fact had participated in an act of nonmarital intercourse, she was innocent because she neither knew nor should have known that her conduct was of the forbidden character. This argument would be successful in only two types of cases. First, the argument would be accepted in cases were the woman showed that she reasonably believed that her conduct was nonsexual, such as participating in a routine medical procedure, but the man had used the procedure as a subterfuge to perpetrate sexual intercourse. Second, a mistake of fact argument might prevail where the woman believed that the sex act constituted marital (i.e., lawful) intercourse because she believed that she was having sex with her husband, when in fact the paramour was someone else. That the woman was induced to engage in sexual intercourse based on some other mistaken belief that she held, even if such belief was created by active deception on the man's part, would be irrelevant to her mental state and, ultimately, to her guilt. In such cases, standard mistake of fact analysis instructs that the woman knew or should have known that she was engaging in nonmarital intercourse, and therefore she, as well as her partner, deserved to be punished for that crime.

Anne M. Coughlin, Sex and Guilt, 84 Va. L. Rev. 1, 32–33 (1998).

———

## SUBSECTION B: NONCONSENT AND MENS REA

---

## State v. Smith

Supreme Court of Connecticut, 1989.
210 Conn. 132, 554 A.2d 713.

■ SHEA, JUDGE. After a jury trial the defendant was convicted of sexual assault in the first degree. [On appeal he claims that evidence of the victim's nonconsent was insufficient and that the first degree sexual assault statute is unconstitutionally vague, as applied to the facts of this case.] We find no error.

... On March 18, 1987, the victim, *T*, a 26–year old woman, and her girlfriend, *A*, a visitor from Idaho, went to a bar in West Haven. *T* was introduced by a friend to the defendant, who bought her a drink. The defendant invited her and *A*, together with a male acquaintance *A* had met at the bar, to dinner at a restaurant across the street. After dinner, the defendant having paid for *T's* share, the four left the restaurant. The defendant proposed that they all go to his apartment in West Haven. Because *A's* acquaintance had a motorcycle, the defendant gave them directions to the apartment so that they could ride there, while he and *T* walked.

After a 20 minute walk, the defendant and *T* arrived at the apartment at about 10 p.m. *A* and her acquaintance were not there and never arrived at the apartment. When *T* and the defendant had entered the apartment they sat on the couch in the living room to watch television. After a while the defendant put his arm around *T* and told her he wanted a kiss. She gave him a kiss. She testified that "He wouldn't back off. He wouldn't let go of me. So I said, look, I am not kidding. I really don't want to do anything. I don't know you and whatnot." The defendant still held onto *T*. She testified that he was "still right in my face wanting to kiss me. You know, saying so, saying that you don't think I paid for dinner for nothing, do you."

*T* testified that she was scared: "At first I didn't know what to do. I did spit in his face and he didn't even take it seriously. Then I tried kicking him off, which was to no avail. He was way too big for me." *T* described the defendant as "at least six foot two" and "at least two hundred pounds." She testified: "He told me he could make it hard on me or I could make it easy on myself, which I finally decided was probably my best bet." *T* understood that the defendant was determined to "have sex" with her and that either he would hurt her or she "was going to go along with it." At the point where *T* ceased resistance, she was "down on the couch" and the defendant was "on top of" her.

*T* testified that she had informed the defendant that she had to pick up her daughter, had insulted him, and had told him that he was "a big man to have to force a woman." She testified, however, that after she decided to "give in," she tried to convince the defendant that she was not going to fight and "was going to go along with him and enjoy it."

The defendant removed *T's* clothing as she remained on the couch and led her into the bedroom. When she declined his request for oral sex, he did not insist upon it, but proceeded to engage in vaginal intercourse with her. After completion of the act, the defendant said that he knew the victim felt that she had been raped, but that she could not prove it and had really enjoyed herself.

After they both had dressed, the defendant requested *T's* telephone number, but she gave him a number she concocted as a pretense. He also offered her some sherbet, which she accepted and ate while she waited for a cab that the defendant had called. *T*, however, placed her pink cigarette lighter underneath the couch, so that she would be able to prove she had been in the apartment. When the cab arrived, she left the apartment. She told the cab driver to take her to the police station because she had been raped. At the station she gave her account of the event to the police. The defendant was arrested. The police found *T's* lighter under the couch in his living room, where *T* had informed them it was located.

I

Although the defendant claims insufficiency of the evidence as the basis for his claim that he was entitled to an acquittal, he actually seeks to have this court impose a requirement of mens rea, or guilty intent, as an essential element of the crime of sexual assault in the first degree. In fact, he concedes in his reply brief that, if conviction for sexual assault in the first degree requires only a general intent, he cannot prevail on his claim that the evidence was insufficient to support his conviction. This court has held that our [sexual assault] statute requires proof of only a general intent to perform the physical acts that constitute that crime. "No specific intent is made an element of the crime of first degree sexual assault.... It is well settled that first degree sexual assault is a general intent crime."

The defendant, nevertheless, urges that we adopt a construction ... making the mental state of the defendant the touchstone for the resolution of the issue of consent when presented in a prosecution for first degree sexual assault. He refers to this mental state as a mens rea, a guilty mind, and describes it as an awareness on the part of a man that he is forcing sex upon a woman against her will and that he intends to do so. In the context of the evidence in this case, the defendant claims, though he did not testify at trial, that he honestly believed that at the time the sexual act occurred that *T* had consented to it. He bases this claim upon her testimony that, after their preliminary encounter on the couch, and his remark that he could "make it hard" for her or she could "make it easy" on herself, she ceased resisting his advances and decided to "go along with it." *T* also testified that, once she decided to "give in," she acted as if she were "going to go along with him and enjoy it."

The position advocated by the defendant that the requisite mens rea should be an element of the crime of sexual assault in the first degree is supported by a widely publicized decision of the British House of Lords in 1975, Director of Public Prosecutions v. Morgan, 1976 App. Cas. 182, 205, 2 W.L.R. 913, 2 All E.R. 347 (H.L. 1975).[a] A majority of the court held that a defendant cannot properly be convicted of rape if he in fact believed that the woman had consented, even though the basis for his belief may not have been reasonable. Lord Hailsham expressed the view that, for the crime of rape at common law, "the prohibited act is and always has been intercourse without the consent of the victim and the mental element is and always has been the intention to commit that act, or the equivalent intention to have intercourse willy-nilly, not caring whether the victim consents or no." A similar position has been adopted in Alaska, where it is held that the state has the burden of proving at least "that the defendant acted 'recklessly' regarding his putative victim's lack of consent." The Supreme Court of California has concluded that a wrongful intent is an element of a rape offense, but, contrary to *Morgan*, has held that this element would be negated if a defendant entertained a "reasonable and bona fide belief" that the complainant had consented. . . .

Most courts have rejected the proposition that a specific intention to have intercourse without the consent of the victim is an element of the crime of rape or sexual assault. . . . One of the complications that might arise, if such a mental element were required, involves the problem of intoxication, which is generally held to be relevant to negate a crime of specific intent but not a crime of general intent. The difficulty of convicting a thoroughly intoxicated person of rape, if awareness of lack of consent were an element of the crime, would diminish the protection that our statutes presently afford to potential victims from lustful drunkards. Another related problem would be the admissibility of evidence of other similar behavior of a defendant charged with rape to prove his intent to disregard any lack of consent. Such evidence is now usually excluded as more prejudicial than probative, because only a general intent is necessary to constitute the offense. . . .

While the word "consent" is commonly regarded as referring to the state of mind of the complainant in a sexual assault case, it cannot be viewed as a wholly subjective concept. Although the actual state of mind of the actor in a criminal case may in many instances be the issue upon which culpability depends, a defendant is not chargeable with knowledge of the

---

[a] In *Morgan*, a woman was in bed sleeping when her husband and his three drinking companions entered the room. "[S]he was aroused from her sleep, . . . held by each of her limbs, . . . while [her husband's companions] in turn had intercourse with her in front of the others." The woman testified that she "made her opposition to what was being done very plain indeed." Nonetheless, the three men claimed that they believed she was consenting. According to their testimony, the woman's husband had suggested that they have intercourse with her, and he also had "told them that they must not be surprised if his wife struggled a bit, since she was 'kinky' and this was the only way in which she could get 'turned on.' " The House of Lords agreed with the defendants that the trial judge erred by failing to charge the jury that an honest belief that the woman was consenting negated the mental state for rape. However, the Lords refused to overturn the convictions on the ground that, despite the erroneous instruction, "no miscarriage of justice has or conceivably could have occurred."—[Footnote by eds.]

internal workings of the minds of others except to the extent that he should reasonably have gained such knowledge from his observations of their conduct. The law of contract has come to recognize that a true "meeting of the minds" is no longer essential to the formation of a contract and that rights and obligations may arise from acts of the parties, usually their words, upon which a reasonable person would rely. Similarly, whether a complainant has consented to intercourse depends upon her manifestations of such consent as reasonably construed. If the conduct of the complainant under all the circumstances should reasonably be viewed as indicating consent to the act of intercourse, a defendant should not be found guilty because of some undisclosed mental reservation on the part of the complainant. Reasonable conduct ought not to be deemed criminal. . . .

Thus we adhere to the view expressed in our earlier decisions that no specific intent, but only a general intent to perform the physical acts constituting the crime, is necessary for the crime of first degree sexual assault. We reject the position of the British courts, as well as that adopted in Alaska, that the state must prove either an actual awareness on the part of the defendant that the complainant had not consented or a reckless disregard of her nonconsenting status. We agree, however, with the California courts that a defendant is entitled to a jury instruction that a defendant may not be convicted of this crime if the words or conduct of the complainant under all the circumstances would justify a reasonable belief that she had consented.

[I]t is clear that the jury could properly have found beyond a reasonable doubt that *T's* words and actions could not reasonably be viewed to indicate her consent to intercourse with the defendant. According to her uncontradicted testimony, she expressly declined his advances, explaining that she did not know him and wanted to pick up her child. She spat in his face and "tried kicking him off." She "gave in" only after the defendant declared that "he could make it hard" for her if she continued to resist. This statement she could reasonably have regarded as a threat of physical injury. Only by entertaining the fantasy that "no" meant "yes," and that a display of distaste meant affection, could the defendant have believed that *T's* behavior toward him indicated consent. Such a distorted view of her conduct would not have been reasonable. The evidence was more than sufficient to support the verdict.

II

The defendant's second claim, that our first degree sexual assault statute, is unconstitutionally vague, is closely related to the first. He contends that, unless the statute is construed to require proof of a guilty mind, "every act of sexual intercourse can be punishable as a class B felony regardless of the mind set of the accused, because all that would be required to establish guilt is the act of sexual intercourse coupled with the statement of the victim that she felt threatened." He suggests that the reasonableness of the complainant's fear of physical injury generated by the threat "could readily be established simply by the differences in size between the man and the woman or the strangeness to the victim of the place she had gone to."

The horrendous scenario postulated by the defendant that a sexual assault conviction may be based wholly upon a statement by the complainant of feeling threatened because of the greater size of the person accused, combined with the strangeness of the surroundings, is contrary to the conclusion we have reached in Part I. There we held that the crux of the inquiry on the issue of consent was not the subjective state of mind of the complainant but rather her manifestations of lack of consent by words or conduct as reasonably construed. Further, since [the sexual assault statute] requires that one compel another person to engage in sexual intercourse "by the use of force ... or by the threat of use of force ... which reasonably causes such person to fear physical injury," it is clear that a defendant must either use force or threaten its use by words or conduct that would reasonably generate fear of physical injury.

"[A] penal statute must be sufficiently definite to enable a person to know what conduct he must avoid." When first amendment freedoms are not involved, a claim that a statute is void for vagueness is determined by its applicability to the particular facts presented. "Hence, that a statutory provision may be of questionable applicability in speculative situations is usually immaterial if the challenged provision applies to the conduct of the defendant in the case at issue." The hypothetical put forth by the defendant of the wholly passive sexual assault victim intimidated solely by the size of the accused and the unfamiliarity of her surroundings, rather than by the use of force or threats, is far removed from the facts that the jury could reasonably have found in support of the verdict in this case. We conclude that the defendant's claim that the [sexual assault statute] is void for vagueness is without merit in the context of the circumstances of this case.

---

## NOTES ON NONCONSENT AND MENS REA

**1.   Availability of the Mistake of Fact Defense.** Notably, *Smith* fails to mention that a few courts have held that even an honest and reasonable mistake as to nonconsent is not exculpatory. See, e.g., Commonwealth v. Ascolillo, 405 Mass. 456, 541 N.E.2d 570 (1989). Under these decisions, nonconsent apparently is treated as a strict liability element. In one such case, the court claimed that this treatment is "in harmony with the analogous rule" in "statutory rape" cases. Commonwealth v. Simcock, 31 Mass. App. Ct. 184, 575 N.E.2d 1137 (1991). Statutory rape provisions criminalize sex with children and adolescents who are below the age at which persons are deemed competent to consent to sexual activity. A majority of jurisdictions treat the age of the victim as a strict liability element. Is the statutory rape analogy cited by *Simcock* persuasive?

In jurisdictions in which a mistaken belief as to consent is exculpatory, trial courts must identify the cases in which a jury instruction concerning mistake is required. The Supreme Court of California decided that trial judges are not required to give such an instruction whenever a defendant claims that the encounter was consensual. Rather, the instruction is required only where the record contains "substantial evidence of equivocal conduct that would have led a defendant to reasonably and in good faith believe consent existed where it did not." People v. Williams, 4 Cal.4th 354, 841 P.2d 961, 14 Cal.Rptr.2d 441 (1992). In *Williams*, there was no such evidence. Rather, the victim and the defendant provided dramatically different versions of the victim's behavior, neither of which was equivocal. The victim claimed that she submitted to sexual intercourse only after the defendant punched and threatened to harm her, while the defendant asserted that the victim initiated and participated aggressively in the intercourse. According to the court, the jurors had to identify the credible account, and, once they did, they could find only the presence or absence of "actual consent.... These wholly divergent accounts create no middle ground from which Williams could argue he reasonably misinterpreted Deborah's conduct."

   **2.   Resolving the Facts.** In rape prosecutions, as in every other trial, the adversaries usually offer conflicting stories about the underlying events. Date rape trials often present poignant conflicts of this kind. See Kate E. Bloch, A Rape Law Pedagogy, 7 Yale J.L. & Feminism 307 (1995). In the most difficult cases, the parties' factual accounts are substantially similar: they agree that the intercourse occurred, and they even agree as to what each participant said and did before, during, and after the sexual encounter. The dispute arises because each actor offers a different interpretation of the same events, and its resolution depends on whose perspective—the victim's or the defendant's—the court adopts. For example, it is not uncommon for the question of what conduct constitutes "force" to receive different answers, depending on the perspective invoked. In *Rusk*, Pat testified that Rusk put his hands on her throat and "started lightly to choke" her. The Maryland Court of Appeals accepted Pat's interpretation in finding that the evidence of force was sufficient. By contrast, the intermediate appellate court interpreted this behavior as amorous; it endorsed defense counsel's characterization of Rusk's hands on Pat's throat as a "heavy caress." One of the most frequently recurring and divisive issues in date rape cases is the interpretation to be given the word "no." In *Smith*, the court dismisses as a "fantasy" the notion that a woman who says "no" to a sexual invitation may mean "yes." Fantasy or not, rape defendants continue to testify to precisely this understanding. The defendant in *Berkowitz* testified that the victim said "no, no, no," when he "started massaging her breasts with [his] mouth," but he understood those words to be "passionate no's" and a "positive response" to his sexual advances. Commonwealth v. Berkowitz, Record at 134–35, 141 (Ct. Common Pleas, Monroe County, No. 241–1988); see also, e.g., United States v. Johnson, 25 M.J. 691 (1987).

   Some empirical reports suggest that misunderstandings like that between victim and defendant in *Berkowitz* are not uncommon. One researcher who studied college students claims that often it is difficult for people "to decide whether certain words or actions are signs of platonic friendliness or of sexual attraction" because there is an "overlap in the cues used to convey friendliness and seduction," particularly in the early stages of a relationship. Antonia Abbey, Misperception as an Antecedent of Acquaintance Rape: A Consequence of Ambiguity in Communication Between Men and Women, in Acquaintance Rape: The Hidden Crime 96 (Andrea Parrot & Laurie Bechhofer eds. 1991). The study also found that men tend to mistake friendly overtures for sexual ones more often than women do. The potential for misunderstanding is exacerbated by the reluctance of men and women to express their sexual intentions directly. "When people become used to 'yes' being conveyed through subtle hints, it is not surprising that they frequently mistake a 'no' for a 'yes' and feel that it is appropriate to persist after being rebuffed." Worse complications will arise if some women sometimes say "no" to a sexual overture when they mean "yes," as several studies have found. For example, in a study of 610 female undergraduates at Texas A & M University, 39.3% of the respondents "reported saying no to sexual intercourse" even though they *had every intention to and were willing to engage in sexual intercourse.*" Charlene L. Muehlenhard & Lisa C. Hollabaugh, Do Women Sometimes Say No When They Mean Yes? The Prevalence and Correlates of Women's Token Resistance to Sex, 54 J. Person. & Soc. Psychol. 872, 874 (1988). If women engage in such indirection—and if men understand that women do so—then men may tend to interpret "no" as a token form of resistance, which they feel safe to ignore, even when the word is uttered by a woman who means it.

Other empirical data suggest that men and women perceive differently the kind of "heavy petting" that occurred in *M.T.S.* A study of self-disclosed date rapists suggests that men tend to view heavy petting as foreplay that culminates in intercourse. By contrast, women may see petting as a sexual end in itself, rather than as a prelude to vaginal penetration. One study showed:*

> [All] of the rape events ... were preceded by some consensual sexual activity. Approximately 84 percent of these rapes followed some sort of genital play. This activity was largely reciprocal, 68 percent of the cases, and in those pairings where only one party was active it was, surprisingly, almost equally apt to be either sex. These contacts were overwhelmingly orogenital. The remaining cases involved lesser erotic intimacies beyond the level of kissing. . . .
>
> [I]mplicit "promises," those male imputations of their companions' imminent sexual capitulation, run rampant as a factor contributing to these episodes. . . . Attempting to explain why they raped ... over 90 percent [of the men] dwelled upon their perception of their companions' extreme sexual arousal which, in turn, intensified their own sexual arousal to the extent that they experi-

enced a rather exaggerated selective perception of the female's receptivity.... The typical explanation offered by these respondents [was] that it was difficult to take [the women's] rejections seriously considering the advanced intimacy already achieved....

At this point it is important to view these situations from the perspective of the victim. One might point out that the female did play a part in her victimization by instituting high levels of exposure to risk. On the other hand, many of these women did make efforts to evoke agreements and promises regarding the limits of sexual involvement. In 68 percent of the cases of consensual genital play the female was reported to have stipulated or made an effort to stipulate that this was to be her maximum level of sexual activity.... These delimiting pronouncements were not taken seriously since they were viewed to be the usual show of reticence that respectable females demonstrate in order to ward off the impression of being "easy." The perpetuation of this classic stereotype inevitably leads to a frustration of female sexual self-determination.

Eugene J. Kanin, Date Rape: Unofficial Criminals and Victims, 9 Victimology 95, 99–104 (1984).

**3.   The Relationship Between Mens Rea and Actus Reus.** Some commentators have expressed the view that the mens rea for rape and related offenses must be recalibrated to take account of new definitions of "force" that have been proposed by reformers and endorsed by legislators. For example, the members of the Criminal Instructions Subcommittee of the Pennsylvania Supreme Court Committee suggest that, in some date rape cases (those not involving high levels of physical violence), the mens rea should not be gross negligence, but recklessness or, even, knowledge:

> In the opinion of the Subcommittee there may be cases, especially now that [the legislature] has extended the definition of force to psychological, moral and intellectual force, where a defendant might non-recklessly or even reasonably, but wrongly, believe that his words and conduct do not constitute force or the threat of force and that a non-resisting female is consenting. An example might be "date rape" resulting from mutual misunderstanding. The boy does not intend or suspect the intimidating potential of his vigorous wooing. The girl, misjudging the boy's character, believes he will become violent if thwarted; she feigns willingness, even some pleasure. In our opinion the defendant in such a case ought not to be convicted of rape.

Pennsylvania Suggested Standard Criminal Jury Instructions, Subcommittee Note, at 15.3121A. Why should the girl, and not the boy, have to bear the risk of their "mutual misunderstanding"? Is there some other doctrinal revision that might resolve this situation?

**4.   Feminist Perspectives on the Mistake Defense.** Although feminists are determined to vindicate women's perspectives on sexuality and sexual violence, feminist legal scholars do not necessarily agree on how the criminal law should incorporate those perspectives. Susan Estrich endorses the majority approach to the mens rea requirement, under which reasonable mistakes as to consent are exculpatory. According to Estrich, strict liability will disadvantage rape victims, even though it appears to simplify the prosecution's case. By eschewing any inquiry into the defendant's culpability, strict liability invites jurors to scrutinize the victim's actions and attitude. A negligence standard is preferable because it assures that the trial remains focused on "the man's blameworthiness instead of the woman's." Susan Estrich, Real Rape 94–100 (1987).

Catharine MacKinnon argues that, in societies in which the sexes are unequal, the mistake-of-fact defense inevitably validates male perspectives and experiences:*

> ... The problem is this: the injury of rape lies in the meaning of the act to its victims, but the standard for its criminality lies in the meaning of the same act to the assailants. Rape is only an injury from the woman's point of view. It is only a crime from the male point of view, explicitly including that of the accused....
>
> ... To [men, rape] accusations are false because, to them, the facts describe sex. To interpret such events as rapes distorts their experience. Since they seldom consider that their experience of the real is anything other than reality, they can only explain the woman's version as maliciously invented. Similarly, the male anxiety that rape is easy to charge and difficult to disprove (also widely believed in the face of overwhelming evidence to the contrary) arises because rape accusations express one thing that men cannot seem to control: the meaning to women of sexual encounters.
>
> [W]hen an accused wrongly but sincerely believes that a woman he sexually forced consented, he may have a defense of mistaken belief or fail to satisfy the mental requirement of knowingly proceeding against her will.... Now reconsider to what extent the man's perceptions should determine whether a rape occurred. From whose standpoint, and in whose interest, is a law that allows one person's conditioned unconsciousness to contraindicate another's experienced violation? This aspect of the rape law reflects the sex inequality of the society not only in conceiving a cognizable injury from the viewpoint of the reasonable rapist, but in affirmatively rewarding men with acquittals for not comprehending women's point of view on sexual encounters.
>
> [T]he deeper problem is the rape law's assumption that a single, objective state of affairs existed, one which merely needs to be determined by evidence, when many (maybe even most) rapes involve honest men and violated women. When the reality is

split—a woman is raped, but not by a rapist?—the law tends to conclude that a rape did not happen. [Thus, the reasonable mistake standard] is one-sided: male-sided.

Catharine A. MacKinnon, Feminism, Marxism, Method, and the State: Toward Feminist Jurisprudence, 8 Signs 635, 654 (1983).

**5. The Relevance of Prior Sexual Activity.** Before the 1970s, rape prosecutions routinely included an extensive airing of the victim's past sexual conduct and her reputation for chastity or unchastity. There were several theories for allowing the defense to explore these matters, including the notion that an unchaste woman did not suffer the injury that rape laws were intended to prevent and avenge. The dominant rationale was that evidence of a woman's prior unchaste behavior was probative of her consent to the intercourse for which the defendant was on trial. See, e.g., People v. Abbot, 19 Wend. 192 (N.Y. 1838).

Starting in the mid–1970s, American jurisdictions began enacting "rape shield laws," which sharply curtail admission of evidence of the victim's prior sexual conduct. As Richard Posner has explained:

> The essential insight behind the rape shield statute is that in an age of post-Victorian sexual practice, in which most unmarried young women are sexually active, the fact that a woman has voluntarily engaged in a particular sexual activity on previous occasions does not provide appreciable support for an inference that she consented to engage in this activity with the defendant on the occasion on which she claims that she was raped. And allowing defense counsel to spread the details of a woman's sex life on the public record not only causes embarrassment to the woman but by doing so makes it less likely that victims of rape will press charges.

Sandoval v. Acevedo, 996 F.2d 145 (7th Cir.1993). Although rape shield provisions vary from jurisdiction to jurisdiction, many resemble Federal Rule of Evidence 412, which limits admission of evidence of the victim's prior sexual behavior to the following categories: (a) "evidence of specific instances of sexual behavior by the alleged victim offered to prove that a person other than the accused was the source of semen, injury or other physical evidence;" (b) "evidence of specific instances of sexual behavior by the alleged victim with respect to the person accused of the sexual misconduct offered by the accused to prove consent or by the prosecution;" and (c) "evidence the exclusion of which would violate the constitutional rights of the defendant."

Rape shield statutes raise a number of significant questions, which are covered in evidence courses. For purposes of the criminal process, key issues are whether evidence of the victim's prior sexual conduct creates a doubt about the accused's culpability and, if so, whether the evidence nonetheless should be excluded in order to prevent embarrassment of the victim and reinforcement of sexist stereotypes.

Assume that a defendant claims that he reasonably believed that the woman had consented, and he wants to testify that (a) before their encounter, he learned that she had consensual intercourse with other men in the past and (b) he selected her to be the recipient of his attentions with that understanding in mind. Notice that the defendant is not asking the jury to believe that the woman willingly had sex with him merely because she previously had consented to have sex with other men. Rather, his claim is that going into the particular encounter, *his purpose* was to have *consensual* sexual intercourse. To insure that the connection was consensual, he selected a prospective partner based on his assessment that she would consent, which rested on, among other things, his knowledge of her sexual history. That knowledge also influenced his perception of her attitude during the encounter. Does this testimony tend to show that the defendant's mistake of fact was honest and reasonable? If so, are there policies that nonetheless require that the testimony be excluded? Is the woman prejudiced by admission of this testimony? Does the testimony reinforce misogynist stereotypes about women of "easy virtue"? Should the testimony be admitted in some cases, but not in others? Under Federal Rule of Evidence 412, would the evidence be admissible?

**6. Withdrawal of Consent**. Is rape committed if a woman who initially consented to intercourse then withdraws her consent, but the male continues to have sex with her? This contentious issue was considered by the California Supreme Court in In re John Z., 29 Cal.4th 756, 60 P.3d 183, 128 Cal.Rptr.2d 783 (2003). The court took the case to resolve questions created by People v. Vela, 172 Cal.App.3d 237, 218 Cal.Rptr. 161 (1985), in which the California Court of Appeal had held that "the presence or absence of consent at the moment of initial penetration appears to be the crucial point in the crime of rape." According to *Vela*, "the essence of the crime of rape is the outrage to the person and feelings of the female resulting from the nonconsensual violation of her womanhood." Although a woman who withdraws her consent may feel outraged if the man ignores her wishes, "the sense of outrage . . . could hardly be of the same magnitude" as that in cases where the woman initially refused consent. Hence, *Vela* reasoned, "the essential guilt of rape . . . is lacking in the withdrawn consent scenario."

The Supreme Court of California was not persuaded:

> With due respect to *Vela* and the two sister state cases on which it relied, we found their reasoning unsound. First, contrary to *Vela's* assumption, we have no way of accurately measuring the level of outrage the victim suffers from being subjected to continued sexual intercourse following withdrawal of her consent. We must assume that the sense of outrage is substantial. [More important, the California rape statute does not provide, nor any California case hold] that the victim's outrage is an element of the crime of rape. . . .

> *Vela* appears to assume that, to constitute rape, the victim's objections must be raised, or a defendant's use of force must be applied, before intercourse commences, but that argument is clearly flawed. One can readily imagine situations in which the defen-

dant is able to obtain penetration before the victim can express an objection or attempt to resist. Surely, if the defendant thereafter ignores the victim's objections and forcibly continues the act, he has committed "an act of sexual intercourse accomplished ... against a person's will by means of force...."

Defendant, candidly acknowledging *Vela*'s flawed reasoning, contends that, in cases involving an initial consent to intercourse, the male should be permitted a "reasonable amount of time" in which to withdraw, once the female raises an objection to further intercourse. As defendant argues, "By essence of the act of sexual intercourse, a male's primal urge to reproduce is aroused. It is therefore unreasonable for a female and the law to expect a male to cease having sexual intercourse immediately upon her withdrawal of consent. It is only natural, fair and just that a male be given a reasonable amount of time in which to quell his primal urge...."

We disagree with defendant's argument. Aside from the apparent lack of supporting authority for defendant's "primal urge" theory, the principal problem with his argument is that it is contrary to the language of [the rape statute. Nothing in the statutory language] or the case law suggests that the defendant is entitled to persist in intercourse once his victim withdraws her consent.

In any event, even were we to accept defendant's "reasonable time" argument, in the present case he clearly was given ample time to withdraw but refused to do so despite Laura's resistance and objections. Although defendant testified he withdrew as soon as Laura objected, for purposes of appeal we need not accept this testimony as true in light of Laura's contrary testimony. As noted above, Laura testified that she struggled to get away when she was on top of defendant, but that he grabbed her waist and pushed her down onto him. At this point, Laura told defendant that if he really cared about her, he would respect her wishes and stop. Thereafter, she told defendant three times that she needed to go home and that she did not accept his protestations he just needed a "minute." Defendant continued the sex act for at least four or five minutes after Laura first told him she had to go home. According to Laura, after the third time she asked to leave, defendant continued to insist that he needed more time and "just stayed inside of me and kept like basically forcing it on me," for about a "minute, minute and [a] half." Contrary to the dissent's concerns the force defendant exerted in resisting Laura's attempts to stop the act was clearly ample to satisfy [the requirement that the defendant use "force" above and beyond that necessary for the sex act itself].

Although the dissent ... would prefer more guidance for future cases, this is an appeal from a juvenile court adjudication rather than a jury trial, and the briefing does not address what pinpoint instructions, if any, might be appropriate in these withdrawn consent cases. Accordingly, we do not explore or recommend instructional language governing such matters as the defendant's knowledge of the victim's withdrawal of consent, the possibly equivocal nature of that withdrawal, or the point in time at which defendant must cease intercourse once consent is withdrawn.

**7. Competence to Consent and Intoxication.** Sexual intercourse with a person who is incompetent to consent to the act has long been punished as a form of rape. This crime requires no increment of force beyond that required to achieve penetration. Incompetent actors include persons who are unconscious or asleep, as well as persons who lack the mental capacity to consent to sexual relations. One substantive issue over which jurisdictions disagree is the level of culpability required. Must the defendant know that the victim was incompetent, or should punishment be imposed for negligence or even on the basis of strict liability?

Another difficult issue is the standard to be used to evaluate mental competence to consent to sexual intercourse. In many jurisdictions, the competence standard requires the person to possess sufficient mental capacity to understand the "nature and consequences" of sexual intercourse. However, courts have disagreed over the scope of the "nature and consequences" test. For example, some courts require only that the person understand the physiological nature and consequences of intercourse, while others also require some understanding of its moral status and social consequences. See State v. Olivio, 123 N.J. 550, 589 A.2d 597 (1991).

When the complainant was intoxicated at the time of the intercourse, the prosecution may proceed on the theory that she was incompetent to consent. Cultural norms regarding alcohol consumption and sexuality make such cases difficult to resolve. The most common and least controversial cases involve victims who had imbibed to the point of unconsciousness and thus were physically incapable of consenting. There is widespread agreement that intercourse with an unconscious person should be a crime. The more difficult cases are those in which the prosecution contends that the complainant, though conscious, was so drunk that she temporarily lacked mental capacity to consent. The accused will argue that the complainant may have been feeling the effects of the alcohol, but that she remained capable of consenting. The accused also will invoke pervasive views about alcohol's sexually disinhibiting effects: because the woman was drinking, she was more likely to and, in fact, did desire to engage in sexual intercourse. See William H. George et al., Perceptions of Postdrinking Female Sexuality: Effects of Gender, Beverage Choice, and Drink Payment, 18 J. Applied Soc. Psychol. 1295 (1988).

In date rape cases where both participants have been drinking and thus experiencing alcohol's sexually disinhibiting effects, how should the law distinguish the perpetrator from the victim? Probably, such cases occur frequently, since empirical studies suggest that "one third to two thirds of rapists, and many rape victims, are intoxicated." Charlene L. Muehlenhard and Melaney A. Linton, Date Rape and Sexual Aggression in Dating Situations: Incidence and Risk Factors, 34 J. Counseling Psychol. 186, 187 (1987). Moreover, depending on the standard used to evaluate capacity to consent to sex, it is possible for both participants to be so intoxicated as to lack such capacity. In such a case, may one of them be held responsible for raping the other, and if so, what grounds should be used to identify the responsible actor?

The Model Code resolves these difficult questions by limiting liability to cases where a man has sex with a woman who is so drunk that she "is unconscious" or where he "substantially impaired her power to appraise or control her conduct by administering ... without her knowledge ... intoxicants ... for the purpose of preventing resistance." ALI, Model Penal Code § 213.1(1)(b), (c). Where the woman is intoxicated but conscious and she became intoxicated voluntarily, the drafters concluded that it would be "extravagant" to impose on the man a "duty to make exceedingly fine, but inevitably uncertain, distinctions" about her capacity to consent. In the view of the drafters, such a duty

> fails to take into account the social context of romance and seduction. Liquor and drugs may be potent agents of incapacitation, but they are also common ingredients of the ritual of courtship. The traditional routine of soft music and wine or the modern variant of loud music and marijuana implies some relaxation of inhibition. With continued consumption, relaxation blurs into intoxication and insensibility. Where this progression occurs in a course of mutual and voluntary behavior, it would be unrealistic and unfair to assign to the male total responsibility for the end result.

ALI, Model Penal Code and Commentaries § 213.01, pp. 315–20.

University sexual assault counselors frequently argue that liquor and drugs are not appropriate ingredients of courtship, even when they are imbibed voluntarily. Moreover, some counselors appear to take the position that it is fair to hold men, but not women, responsible for what they do when they are drunk. Counselors at one college explain that "any drinking by the assailant is always irrelevant because alcohol use does not diminish one's responsibility for one's actions. The victim's voluntary drinking is only relevant when the victim has expressed consent and there is no coercion. Then ... the issue is whether the voluntary drinking rendered the victim 'unable to understand' and therefore unable to truly consent." In other words, if the "victim" is so drunk that she is "unable to understand," the man who has sex with her is guilty of rape even if he too is very drunk. Lawrence A. Tucker and Mary Crozier, Alcohol and Sexual Assault: Personal and Judicial Perspectives on Impairment (The College of William & Mary Counseling Center). This response is helpful to the extent that it suggests that the standard for judging responsibility for criminal misconduct apparently is not the same as the standard for judging capacity to consent to sexual intercourse. However, the response fails to explain whether and, if so, why, men are inevitably the "assailants" in these situations and women inevitably the "victims."

––––––

## NOTE ON MARITAL RAPE

For the better part of the 20th century, most states recognized some form of "marital exemption" for rape. Under the marital exemption, a married man who raped his wife was not subject to criminal liability. In the closing decades of the century, the marital exemption was widely (but by no means completely) abrogated as a result of legislative and judicial action.

The defendant in People v. Liberta, 64 N.Y.2d 152, 485 N.Y.S.2d 207 (1984), was convicted of forcibly raping his wife. At the time of the rape, the defendant and his wife were separated, and he was under court order to stay away from her. Although the New York rape statute codified the marital exemption, the statute treated the defendant as an unmarried man since he was living apart from his wife pursuant to a court order. The defendant argued that the rape statute violated the equal protection clause because it burdened "some, but not all males (all but those within the 'marital exemption')." The New York Court of Appeals agreed that the marital exemption constituted a violation of equal protection. *Liberta* is widely cited for its concise summary of the policies offered to support the marital exemption and its reasons for finding those polices irrational:

> ... The assumption ... that a man could not be guilty of raping his wife is traceable to a statement made by the 17th century English jurist Lord Hale, who wrote: "[The] husband cannot be guilty of a rape committed by himself upon his lawful wife, for by their mutual matrimonial consent and contract the wife hath given up herself in this kind unto her husband, which she cannot retract." Although Hale cited no authority for his statement it was relied on by state legislatures which enacted rape statutes with a marital exemption and by courts which established a common-law exemption for husbands....

> Presently, over 40 states still retain some form of marital exemption for rape. While the marital exemption is subject to an equal protection challenge, because it classifies unmarried men differently than married men, the equal protection clause does not prohibit a state from making classifications, provided the statute does not arbitrarily burden a particular group of individuals. Where a statute draws a distinction based upon marital status, the classification must be reasonable and must be based upon "some ground of difference that rationally explains the different treatment." ...

> We find that there is no rational basis for distinguishing between marital rape and nonmarital rape. The various rationales which have been asserted in defense of the exemption are either

based upon archaic notions about the consent and property rights incident to marriage or are simply unable to withstand even the slightest scrutiny. . . .

Lord Hale's notion of an irrevocable implied consent by a married woman to sexual intercourse has been cited most frequently in support of the marital exemption. Any argument based on a supposed consent, however, is untenable. Rape is not simply a sexual act to which one party does not consent. Rather, it is a degrading, violent act which violates the bodily integrity of the victim and frequently causes severe, long-lasting physical and psychic harm. To ever imply consent to such an act is irrational and absurd. . . . Certainly, then, a marriage license should not be viewed as a license for a husband to forcibly rape his wife with impunity. A married woman has the same right to control her own body as does an unmarried woman. If a husband feels "aggrieved" by his wife's refusal to engage in sexual intercourse, he should seek relief in the courts governing domestic relations, not in "violent or forceful self-help."

The other traditional justifications for the marital exemption were the common-law doctrines that a woman was the property of her husband and that the legal existence of the woman was "incorporated and consolidated into that of the husband." Both these doctrines, of course, have long been rejected in this state. . . .

Because the traditional justifications for the marital exemption no longer have any validity, other arguments have been advanced in its defense. The first of these recent rationales . . . is that the marital exemption protects against governmental intrusion into marital privacy and promotes reconciliation of the spouses, and thus that elimination of the exemption would be disruptive to marriages. While protecting marital privacy and encouraging reconciliation are legitimate state interests, there is no rational relation between allowing a husband to forcibly rape his wife and these interests. The marital exemption simply does not further marital privacy because this right of privacy protects consensual acts, not violent sexual assaults. Just as a husband cannot invoke a right of marital privacy to escape liability for beating his wife, he cannot justifiably rape his wife under the guise of a right to privacy.

Similarly, it is not tenable to argue that elimination of the marital exemption would disrupt marriages because it would discourage reconciliation. Clearly, it is the violent act of rape and not the subsequent attempt of the wife to seek protection through the criminal justice system which "disrupts" a marriage. Moreover, if the marriage has already reached the point where intercourse is accomplished by violent assault it is doubtful that there is anything left to reconcile. This, of course, is particularly true if the wife is willing to bring criminal charges against her husband which could result in a lengthy jail sentence.

Another rationale sometimes advanced in support of the marital exemption is that marital rape would be a difficult crime to prove. A related argument is that allowing such prosecutions could lead to fabricated complaints by "vindictive" wives. The difficulty of proof argument is based on the problem of showing lack of consent. Proving lack of consent, however, is often the most difficult part of any rape prosecution, particularly where the rapist and the victim had a prior relationship. Similarly, the possibility that married women will fabricate complaints would seem to be no greater than the possibility of unmarried women doing so. The criminal justice system, with all of its built-in safeguards, is presumed to be capable of handling any false complaints. Indeed, if the possibility of fabricated complaints were a basis for not criminalizing behavior which would otherwise be sanctioned, virtually all crimes other than homicides would go unpunished.

The final argument in defense of the marital exemption is that marital rape is not as serious an offense as other rape and is thus adequately dealt with by the possibility of prosecution under criminal statutes, such as assault statutes, which provide for less severe punishment. The fact that rape statutes exist, however, is a recognition that the harm caused by a forcible rape is different, and more severe, than the harm caused by an ordinary assault. "Short of homicide, [rape] is the ultimate violation of self." . . .

Moreover, there is no evidence to support the argument that marital rape has less severe consequences than other rape. On the contrary, numerous studies have shown that marital rape is frequently quite violent and generally has *more* severe, traumatic effects on the victim than other rape.

Among the recent decisions in this country addressing the marital exemption, only one court has concluded that there is a rational basis for it. See People v. Brown, 632 P.2d 1025 (Colo. 1981). We agree with the other courts which have analyzed the exemption, which have been unable to find any present justification for it. Justice Holmes wrote: "It is revolting to have no better reason for a rule of law than that so it was laid down in the time of Henry IV. It is still more revolting if the grounds upon which it was laid down have vanished long since, and the rule simply persists from blind imitation of the past." This statement is an apt characterization of the marital exemption; it lacks a rational basis, and therefore violates the equal protection clauses of both the federal and state constitutions.

After declaring the marital exemption unconstitutional, the court considered what the remedy should be. The court rejected the defendant's invitation to invalidate the rape statute in its entirety because the effect of invalidation "would have a disastrous effect on the public interest and safety." Rather, the court concluded that the marital exemption "must be read out of the statutes prohibiting forcible rape," and, therefore, it affirmed the defendant's conviction.

Do any of the policy arguments supporting the marital exemption retain vitality today? This question is important because the marital exemption, albeit in an attenuated form, continues its influence. The law of marital rape is difficult to summarize concisely because a variety of approaches exist.[a] As *Liberta* illustrates, a number of states have eliminated the marital rape exemption completely. In these states, the fact that the participants in the sexual encounter are married is of no relevance in a rape prosecution. However, many rape statutes draw some distinctions between marital and nonmarital rape. Some states have replaced the marital exemption with a distinct crime of marital rape, which usually is graded less severely than a rape that occurs between persons who are not married to each other. In other states, marital rape is a crime, but only when the rapist uses a degree of force greater than that required to establish nonmarital rape. Under yet another approach, the marital exemption is not a defense to a first-degree rape charge, but the exemption continues to bar prosecution of husbands who perpetrate lesser sexual assaults against their wives.

## SECTION 2: STATUTORY RAPE

### INTRODUCTORY NOTE

The phrase "statutory rape" originally was used to distinguish sexual intercourse with a minor, an offense created by statute, from rape, the common law crime requiring force and nonconsent. Under one of the earliest statutes of this kind, which was enacted in 1576, the crime was committed if the "woman child was under the age of 10 years; in which case the consent or non-consent is immaterial, as by reason of her tender years she is incapable of judgment and discretion." 4 William Blackstone, Commentaries *212. Over the course of the 19th and 20th centuries, state legislatures gradually raised the age of consent. Modern penal codes are in conflict over the age at which people are mature enough to have sex. The age ranges from 12 to 18, with most states fixing the age of consent at 13 or 14. Today, the most difficult questions posed by these laws involve sexual activity by adolescents.

————

### Garnett v. State

Court of Appeals of Maryland, 1993.
332 Md. 571, 632 A.2d 797.

■ MURPHY, JUDGE. Maryland's "statutory rape" law prohibiting sexual intercourse with an underage person is codified in Maryland Code Art. 27, § 463, which reads in [part]:

[a] For a summary of the law of marital rape, see Jaye Sitton, Old Wine in New Bottles: The "Marital" Rape Allowance, 72 N.C. L. Rev. 261 (1993).

Second degree rape.

(a) What constitutes.—A person is guilty of rape in the second degree if the person engages in vaginal intercourse with another person:

. . .

(3) Who is under 14 years of age and the person performing the act is at least four years older than the victim.

(b) Penalty.—Any person violating the provisions of this section is guilty of a felony and upon conviction is subject to imprisonment for a period of not more than 20 years.

Subsection (a)(3) represents the current version of a statutory provision dating back to the first comprehensive codification of the criminal law by the Legislature in 1809.[6] Now we consider whether under the present statute, the state must prove that a defendant knew the complaining witness was younger than 14 and, in a related question, whether it was error at trial to exclude evidence that he had been told, and believed, that she was 16 years old.

## I

Raymond Lennard Garnett is a young retarded man. At the time of the incident in question he was 20 years old. He has an I.Q. of 52. His [school] guidance counselor . . . described him as a mildly retarded person who read on the third-grade level, did arithmetic on the fifth-grade level, and interacted with others socially at school at the level of someone 11 or 12 years of age.... Raymond attended special education classes and for at least one period of time was educated at home when he was afraid to return to school due to his classmates' taunting. Because he could not understand the duties of the jobs given him, he failed to complete vocational assignments; he sometimes lost his way to work. As Raymond was unable to pass any of the state's functional tests required for graduation, he received only a certificate of attendance rather than a high-school diploma.

In November or December 1990, a friend introduced Raymond to Erica Frazier, then aged 13; the two subsequently talked occasionally by telephone. On February 28, 1991, Raymond, apparently wishing to call for a ride home, approached the girl's house at about nine o'clock in the evening. Erica opened her bedroom window, through which Raymond entered; he testified that "she just told me to get a ladder and climb up her window." The two talked, and later engaged in sexual intercourse. Raymond left at about 4:30 a.m. the following morning. On November 19, 1991, Erica gave birth to a baby, of which Raymond is the biological father.

[6] "If any person shall carnally know and abuse any woman-child under the age of 10 years, every such carnal knowledge shall be deemed felony, and the offender, being convicted thereof, shall, at the discretion of the court, suffer death by hanging . . . or undergo a confinement in the penitentiary for a period not less than one year nor more than 21 years." . . . The minimum age of the child was raised from 10 years to 14 years in Chapter 410 of the Acts of 1890.

Raymond was tried before the Circuit Court for Montgomery County on one count of second degree rape under § 463(a)(3).... At trial, the defense twice proffered evidence to the effect that Erica herself and her friends had previously told Raymond that she was 16 years old, and that he had acted with that belief. The trial court excluded such evidence as immaterial, explaining [that statutory rape is a strict liability offense]. The court found Raymond guilty. It sentenced him to a term of five years in prison, suspended the sentence and imposed five years of probation, and ordered that he pay restitution to Erica and the Frazier family....

## II

... Section 463(a)(3) does not expressly set forth a requirement that the accused have acted with a criminal state of mind, or mens rea. The state insists that the statute, by design, defines a strict liability offense, and that its essential elements were met in the instant case when Raymond, age 20, engaged in vaginal intercourse with Erica, a girl under 14 and more than 4 years his junior. Raymond replies that the criminal law exists to assess and punish morally culpable behavior. He says such culpability was absent here. He asks us either to engraft onto subsection (a)(3) an implicit mens rea requirement, or to recognize an affirmative defense of reasonable mistake as to the complainant's age. Raymond argues that it is unjust, under the circumstances of this case which led him to think his conduct lawful, to brand him a felon and rapist.

## III

Raymond asserts that the events of this case were inconsistent with the criminal sexual exploitation of a minor by an adult. As earlier observed, Raymond entered Erica's bedroom at the girl's invitation; she directed him to use a ladder to reach her window. They engaged voluntarily in sexual intercourse. They remained together in the room for more than seven hours before Raymond departed at dawn. With an I.Q. of 52, Raymond functioned at approximately the same level as the 13–year-old Erica; he was mentally an adolescent in an adult's body. Arguably, had Raymond's chronological age, 20, matched his socio-intellectual age, about 12, he and Erica would have fallen well within the four-year age difference obviating a violation of the statute, and Raymond would not have been charged with any crime at all.

The precise legal issue here rests on [the trial court's refusal to entertain] a defense of reasonable mistake of Erica's age, by which defense Raymond would have asserted that he acted innocently without a criminal design. At common law, a crime occurred only upon the concurrence of an individual's act and his guilty state of mind.... The requirement that an accused have acted with a culpable mental state is an axiom of criminal jurisprudence....

To be sure, legislative bodies since the mid–19th century have created strict liability criminal offenses requiring no mens rea. Almost all such statutes responded to the demands of public health and welfare arising from the complexities of society after the Industrial Revolution. Typically misdemeanors involving only fines or other light penalties, these strict liability laws regulated food, milk, liquor, medicines and drugs, securities, motor vehicles and traffic, the labeling of goods for sale, and the like. Statutory rape, carrying the stigma of felony as well as a potential sentence of 20 years in prison, contrasts markedly with the other strict liability regulatory offenses and their light penalties.

Modern scholars generally reject the concept of strict criminal liability. Professors LaFave and Scott summarize the consensus that punishing conduct without reference to the actor's state of mind fails to reach the desired end and is unjust:

> "It is inefficacious because conduct unaccompanied by an awareness of the factors making it criminal does not mark the actor as one who needs to be subjected to punishment in order to deter him or others from behaving similarly in the future, nor does it single him out as a socially dangerous individual who needs to be incapacitated or reformed. It is unjust because the actor is subjected to the stigma of a criminal conviction without being morally blameworthy. Consequently, on either a preventive or retributive theory of criminal punishment, the criminal sanction is inappropriate in the absence of mens rea." ...

The commentators similarly disapprove of statutory rape as a strict liability crime. [T]hey observe that statutory rape prosecutions often proceed even when the defendant's judgment as to the age of the complainant is warranted by her appearance, her sexual sophistication, her verbal misrepresentations, and the defendant's careful attempts to ascertain her true age. Voluntary intercourse with a sexually mature teenager lacks the features of psychic abnormality, exploitation, or physical danger that accompanies such conduct with children.

Two sub-parts of the rationale underlying strict criminal liability require further analysis at this point. Statutory rape laws are often justified on the "lesser legal wrong" theory or the "moral wrong" theory; by such reasoning, the defendant acting without mens rea nonetheless deserves punishment for having committed a lesser crime, fornication, or for having violated moral teachings that prohibit sex outside of marriage. Maryland has no law against fornication. It is not a crime in this state. Moreover, the criminalization of an act, performed without a guilty mind, deemed immoral by some members of the community rests uneasily on subjective and shifting norms. "[D]etermining precisely what the 'community ethic' actually is [is] not an easy task in a heterogeneous society in which our public pronouncements about morality often are not synonymous with our private conduct." The drafters of the Model Penal Code remarked:

> [T]he actor who reasonably believes that his partner is above that age [of consent] lacks culpability with respect to the factor deemed critical to liability. Punishing him anyway simply because his intended conduct would have been immoral under the facts as he supposed them to be postulates a relation between criminality

and immorality that is inaccurate on both descriptive and normative grounds. The penal law does not try to enforce all aspects of
community morality, and any thoroughgoing attempt to do so
would extend the prospect of criminal sanctions far into the sphere
of individual liberty and create a regime too demanding for all save
the best among us.

We acknowledge here that it is uncertain to what extent Raymond's
intellectual and social retardation may have impaired his ability to comprehend imperatives of sexual morality in any case.

### IV

The legislatures of 17 states have enacted laws permitting a mistake of
age defense in some form in cases of sexual offenses with underage
persons. . . . In some states, the defense is available in instances where the
complainant's age rises above a statutorily prescribed level, but is not
available when the complainant falls below the defining age. In other
states, the availability of the defense depends on the severity of the sex
offense charged to the accused.

In addition, the highest appellate courts of four states have determined
that statutory rape laws by implication required an element of mens rea as
to the complainant's age. In the landmark case of People v. Hernandez, 61
Cal.2d 529, 39 Cal.Rptr. 361, 393 P.2d 673 (1964), the California Supreme
Court . . . questioned the assumption that age alone confers a sophistication sufficient to create legitimate consent to sexual relations: "the sexually
experienced 15–year-old may be far more acutely aware of the implications
of sexual intercourse than her sheltered cousin who is beyond the age of
consent." The court then rejected the traditional view that those who
engage in sex with young persons do so at their peril, assuming the risk
that their partners are underage:

> [If the perpetrator] participates in a mutual act of sexual
> intercourse, believing his partner to be beyond the age of consent,
> with reasonable grounds for such belief, where is his criminal
> intent? In such circumstances he has not consciously taken any
> risk. Instead he has subjectively eliminated the risk by satisfying
> himself on reasonable evidence that the crime cannot be commit-
> ted. If it occurs that he has been misled, we cannot realistically
> conclude for such reason alone the intent with which he undertook
> the act suddenly becomes more heinous. . . .

### V

We think it sufficiently clear, however, that Maryland's second-degree
rape statute defines a strict liability offense that does not require the state
to prove mens rea; it makes no allowance for a mistake-of-age defense. The
plain language of § 463, viewed in its entirety, and the legislative history of
its creation lead to this conclusion.

It is well settled that in interpreting a statute to ascertain and
effectuate its goal, our first recourse is to the words of the statute, giving

them their ordinary and natural import. While penal statutes are to be strictly construed in favor of the defendant, the construction must ultimately depend upon discerning the intention of the legislature when it drafted and enacted the law in question. . . .

Section 463(a)(3) prohibiting sexual intercourse with underage persons makes no reference to the actor's knowledge, belief, or other state of mind. As we see it, this silence as to mens rea results from legislative design. First, subsection (a)(3) stands in stark contrast to the provision immediately before it, [which prohibits] vaginal intercourse with incapacitated or helpless persons. In subsection (a)(2), the legislature expressly provided as an element of the offense that "the person performing the act knows or should reasonably know the other person is mentally defective, mentally incapacitated, or physically helpless." In drafting this subsection, the legislature showed itself perfectly capable of recognizing and allowing for a defense that obviates criminal intent; if the defendant objectively did not understand that the sex partner was impaired, there is no crime. That it chose not to include similar language in subsection (a)(3) indicates that the legislature aimed to make statutory rape with underage persons a more severe prohibition based on strict criminal liability.

Second, an examination of the drafting history of § 463 during the 1976 revision of Maryland's sexual offense laws reveals that the statute was viewed as one of strict liability from its inception and throughout the amendment process. . . .

This interpretation is consistent with the traditional view of statutory rape as a strict liability crime designed to protect young persons from the dangers of sexual exploitation by adults, loss of chastity, physical injury, and, in the case of girls, pregnancy. The majority of states retain statutes which impose strict liability for sexual acts with underage complainants. We observe again, as earlier, that even among those states providing for a mistake-of-age defense in some instances, the defense often is not available where the sex partner is 14 years old or less; the complaining witness in the instant case was only 13. The majority of appellate courts . . . have held statutory rape to be a strict liability crime.

## VI

Maryland's second degree rape statute is by nature a creature of legislation. Any new provision introducing an element of mens rea, or permitting a defense of reasonable mistake of age, with respect to the offense of sexual intercourse with a person less than 14, should properly result from an act of the legislature itself, rather than judicial fiat. Until then, defendants in extraordinary cases, like Raymond, will rely upon the tempering discretion of the trial court at sentencing.

■ ELDRIDGE, JUDGE, dissenting: Both the majority opinion and Judge Bell's dissenting opinion view the question in this case to be whether, on the one hand, § 463(a)(3), is entirely a strict liability statute without any mens rea requirement or, on the other hand, contains the requirement that the defendant knew that the person with whom he or she was having sexual relations was under 14 years of age....

In my view, the [mens rea] issue is not limited to a choice between one of these extremes.... I agree with the majority that an ordinary defendant's mistake about the age of his or her sexual partner is not a defense to [statutory rape. Moreover, I am not persuaded by the argument made by Judge Bell that the federal and state constitutions require that a defendant's honest mistake as to the victim's age be a defense.] This does not mean, however, that the statute contains no mens rea requirement at all....

... In enacting [§ 463(a)(3)], the General Assembly assumed that a defendant is able to appreciate the risk involved by intentionally and knowingly engaging in sexual activities with a young person. There is no indication that the General Assembly intended that criminal liability attach to one who, because of his or her mental impairment, was unable to appreciate that risk.

It is unreasonable to assume that the legislature intended for one to be convicted under § 463(a)(3), ... regardless of his or her mental state. Suppose, for example, that Raymond Garnett had not had an I.Q. of 52, but rather, had ... an I.Q. of 25–30, was physiologically capable of [fathering] a child, but was unable to comprehend the act of sexual intercourse, or even to understand the difference between the sexes. If someone so disabled, having reached Raymond's chronological age, then had "consensual" sexual intercourse with a person younger than 14 years of age, I do not believe that he or she would have violated § 463(a)(3). Under the view that [the statute defines] pure strict liability offenses without any regard for the defendant's mental state, presumably a 20–year-old, who passes out because of drinking too many alcoholic beverages, would be guilty of a sexual offense if a 13–year-old engages in various sexual activities with the 20–year-old while the latter is unconscious. I cannot imagine that the General Assembly intended any such result....

■ [The dissenting opinion of Judge Bell is omitted.]

---

## NOTES ON STATUTORY RAPE

**1. Questions and Comments on *Garnett*.** As the court in *Garnett* explains, a majority of jurisdictions treat statutory rape as a strict liability offense. Courts and commentators approach this instance of strict liability as one that requires careful justification because conviction exposes the accused to significant criminal penalties. *Garnett* describes and criticizes two theories that have been offered to support strict liability in this context, namely, the "lesser legal wrong" and "moral wrong" theories. The court rejects the "lesser legal wrong" theory on the ground that "Maryland has no law against fornication." In states that continue to criminalize fornication (assuming that such laws do not violate any constitutional guarantees), does the "lesser legal wrong" theory support the classification of statutory rape as a strict liability offense?

The court in *Garnett* also criticizes the "moral wrong" theory on the ground that such theory requires judges to identify and enforce community norms, which are "subjective and shifting." In the court's view, what is the problem with imposing punishment on one who may be unaware that he is violating the criminal law, but whose conduct violates a moral norm? Peter Brett argues that the "moral wrong" theory is "clearly in accord with principle. It reflects the view that we learn our duties, not by studying the statute book, but by living in a community. [Therefore, a] defense of mistake rests ultimately on the defendant's being able to say that he has observed the community ethic. . . ." Peter Brett, An Inquiry into Criminal Guilt 149 (1963). Can a defendant who has sex with an adolescent "say that he has observed the community ethic"? If not, why is it unfair to punish him?

Richard Posner argues that strict liability may promote efficiency in the context of statutory rape:

> . . . The girl may look 16 (let us assume 16 is the age of consent), but if she is younger, a reasonable mistake will not excuse the male. Another example is felony murder: if death occurs in the course of a felony through no fault of the felon's, still he is liable as a murderer. [In these cases,] we do not care about deterring activity bordering on the activity that the basic criminal prohibition is aimed at. Because we do not count the avoidance of that activity as a social cost, it pays to reduce the costs of prosecution by eliminating the issue of intent (more precisely, an issue of intent). The male can avoid liability for statutory rape by keeping away from young girls, and the robber can avoid liability for felony murder by not robbing, or by not carrying a weapon. In effect we introduce a degree of strict liability into criminal law as into tort law when a change in activity level is an efficient method of avoiding a social cost.

Richard A. Posner, An Economic Theory of the Criminal Law, 85 Colum. L. Rev. 1193, 1222 (1985). Is Posner's argument a version of the "moral wrong" theory criticized by the court in *Garnett*?

**2. Statutory Rape Under the Model Code.** Statutory rape is the one crime for which the Model Code sometimes imposes punishment without proof of culpability. The Code includes two different provisions that proscribe sexual intercourse with minors. Section 213.1(1)(d) states that a male "is guilty of rape," which is a second-degree felony, if he has sexual intercourse with a female "less than 10 years old." Under § 213.3(1)(a), the offense of "corruption of minors" occurs where a man has sexual intercourse with a woman who is "less than [16] years old" and the man "is at least [4] years older than" the woman. Corruption of minors is graded as a third-degree felony. Consistent with its rejection of strict liability crimes, the Code allows a person accused of corruption of minors to interpose a "mistake of age" defense. In connection with this defense, the

Code departs from its ordinary requirement that the prosecution prove that the defendant acted "recklessly." Rather, § 213.6(1) places the burden on the accused "to prove by a preponderance of the evidence that he reasonably believed the [victim] to be above the critical age." By contrast, when a man is charged with the crime of rape for having intercourse with a girl less than 10 years old, § 213.6(1) entirely disallows a mistake of age defense. The drafters justified this provision by invoking the "moral wrong" theory: "no credible error regarding the age of a child in fact less than 10 years old would render the actor's conduct anything less than a dramatic departure from societal norms." ALI, Model Penal Code & Commentaries § 213.6, p. 414 (1980).

**3. Harm.** What policies are served by laws forbidding adults to have sex with children and adolescents? Are those policies implicated in cases where an adolescent previously has engaged in sexual activity? In the past, many courts held that consensual sex with a minor was a crime only if the minor was "of previously chaste character." Today, only one or two states retain the "unchaste victim exception" to statutory rape. See McBrayer v. State, 467 So.2d 647 (Miss. 1985). What policies support the unchaste victim exception? Does a sexual experience confer on children the wisdom or maturity necessary to give meaningful consent to future sexual activity? Or does the exception suggest that the sole purpose of the statutory rape law is to protect minors from loss of chastity?

In most jurisdictions today, lawmakers assert that sex between a minor and an adult subjects the minor, whether chaste or unchaste, to a range of injuries. Moreover, minors are said to incur these injuries even when they claim that they desired the sexual contact and do not perceive that they have been harmed. For example, in Jones v. State, 640 So.2d 1084 (Fla. 1994), two men, one 19 and the other 20 years old, were convicted for having sexual intercourse with girls under the age of 16. "The parties stipulated at trial that the girls with whom the defendants had sexual intercourse were 14 years of age and consented to having intercourse. Neither girl desired to prosecute and the charges were instituted by" the girls' relatives. On appeal, defense counsel "argue[d] that the statute is unconstitutional as applied because the girls in this case have not been harmed; they wanted to have the personal relationships they entered into with these men; and, they do not want the 'protections' advanced by the state." The Supreme Court of Florida rebuffed these claims:

> ... We are of the opinion that sexual activity with a child opens the door to sexual exploitation, physical harm, and sometimes psychological damage, regardless of the child's maturity or lack of chastity. [N]either the level of intimacy nor the degree of harm are relevant when an adult and a child under the age of 16 engage in sexual intercourse. The statutory protection ... assures that, to the extent the law can prevent such activity, minors will not be sexually harmed. "Sexual exploitation of children is a particularly pernicious evil that sometimes may be concealed behind the zone of privacy that normally shields the home. The state

unquestionably has a very compelling interest in preventing such conduct."

... The legislature enacted [the statutory rape provision] based on a "morally neutral judgment" that sexual intercourse with a child under the age of 16, with or without consent, is potentially harmful to the child. Although the right to be let alone protects adults from government intrusion into matters relating to marriage, contraception, and abortion, the state "may exercise control over the sexual conduct of children beyond the scope of its authority to control adults."

The Supreme Court of Florida has held that this reasoning does not apply where a minor is prosecuted for having sex with another minor. In B.B. v. State, 659 So.2d 256 (Fla. 1995), a 16–year-old boy was charged with "unlawful carnal intercourse," a felony, for having consensual sex with a 16–year-old girl, who was "of previous chaste character." The court decided that, as applied to this activity, the statute violated the defendant's state constitutional right to privacy:

While we do recognize that Florida does have an obligation and a compelling interest in protecting children from sexual activity before their minds and bodies have sufficiently matured to make it appropriate, safe, and healthy for them and that this interest pertains to one minor engaging in carnal intercourse with another, the crux of the state's interest in an adult-minor situation is the prevention of exploitation of the minor by the adult. Whereas in this minor-minor situation, the crux of the state's interest is in protecting the minor from the sexual activity itself for reasons of health and quality of life. Having distinguished between the state's interest in the adult-minor situation and in the minor-minor situation, we conclude that the state has failed to demonstrate ... that the adjudication of B.B. as a delinquent ... is the least intrusive means of furthering what we have determined to be the state's compelling interest....

At present, we will not debate morality in respect to the statute or debate whether this century-old statute fits within the contemporary "facts of life." We do say that if our decision was what should be taught and reasoned to minors, the unequivocal text of our message would be abstinence. We are all too aware of the real-life crisis of children having children.... We recognize the plague of AIDS and the evidence that this epidemic and the rampant spread of serious communicative disease are the sad product of sexual promiscuity. However, our decision is not about what should be taught but about what can be adjudicated to be delinquency as a second-degree felony.

Many states' penal codes no longer criminalize consensual sex between adolescents. These provisions are similar to the statute at issue in *Garnett*, under which the crime occurs only when the minor has sex with an actor who is a specified number of years older than the minor. What policy choices support these provisions?

**4. Harm and Gender Differences.** Are boys and girls similarly situated with respect to loss of chastity and other injuries these laws were designed to prevent? In Michael M. v. Superior Court of Sonoma County, 450 U.S. 464 (1981), the Supreme Court concluded that there were important reasons why a state legislature might answer this question in the negative. There, the Court decided that California's statutory rape law, which imposed criminal liability only on men, did not violate the equal protection clause of the 14th amendment.[a] The following excerpt is from the plurality opinion authored by Justice Rehnquist:

> We need not be medical doctors to discern that young men and young women are not similarly situated with respect to the problems and risks of sexual intercourse. Only women may become pregnant, and they suffer disproportionately the profound physical, emotional, and psychological consequences of sexual activity. The statute at issue here protects women from sexual intercourse at an age when those consequences are particularly severe....
>
> Because virtually all of the significant harmful and inescapably identifiable consequences of teenage pregnancy fall on the young female, a legislature acts well within its authority when it elects to punish only the participant who, by nature, suffers few of the consequences of his conduct. It is hardly unreasonable for a legislature acting to protect minor females to exclude them from punishment. Moreover, the risk of pregnancy itself constitutes a substantial deterrence to young females. No similar natural sanctions deter males. A criminal sanction imposed solely on males thus serves to roughly "equalize" the deterrents on the sexes....

*Michael M.* tends to provide the focal point for feminist criticism of statutory rape laws. Today, the vast majority of these laws are neutral with respect to the gender of potential offender and victim.[b] Statutes in a few states continue to define the crime as one that is perpetrated by a male against a female. See, e.g., Ga. Code Ann. § 16–6–3 (1992); Idaho Code § 18–6101(1) (Supp. 1994). However, as they are applied in actual prosecutions, these laws generally assign responsibility for the sexual encounter based on gender: males are perpetrators, and females are victims. Accord-

---

[a] The provision at issue in *Michael M.* defined "unlawful sexual intercourse as 'an act of sexual intercourse accomplished with a female not the wife of the perpetrator, where the female is under the age of 18 years.'" At the time of the incident that gave rise to his prosecution under this statute, the defendant in *Michael M.* was 17½ years old, and the young woman with whom he had intercourse was 16½.

[b] In 1993, the California legislature revised that state's statutory rape provision so that it punishes "[a]ny person" who has sexual intercourse with a "person under the age of 18 years." Cal. Penal Code § 261.5 (West Supp. 1995). This change in the law reportedly was prompted by two cases in which prosecutors were unable to bring statutory rape charges against adult women who had sex with underage boys. See Mark Gladstone and Daniel M. Weintraub, "New Law Broadens the Provisions of Statutory Rape," L.A. Times, Oct. 2, 1993.

ing to some feminists, statutory rape laws thus operate to reinforce invidious stereotypes, under which "men are always responsible for initiating sexual intercourse and females must always be protected against their aggression." Nadine Taub & Elizabeth M. Schneider, Women's Subordination and the Role of Law 170, in The Politics of Law (David Kairys ed., 1990). Arguments by other feminists suggest that it is difficult to decide how the criminal law should participate in breaking down these stereotypes. As Frances Olsen remarks, the "double standard of sexual morality" assumes that "[f]or males, sex is an accomplishment; they gain something through intercourse. For women, sex entails giving something up." Frances Olsen, Statutory Rape: A Feminist Critique of Rights Analysis, 63 Tex. L. Rev. 387, 405 (1984). The problem for feminists who reject these assumptions as archaic stereotypes is that the stereotypes may influence the ways in which people actually experience sex. That is, young women may experience their first sexual encounter as a stigmatizing loss, while young men experience it as an honorable acquisition. If so, should those who make and enforce statutory rape laws ignore these different experiences and perspectives? Should the law treat adolescent boys, as well as girls, as if they require protection from sexual activity? Should it punish adolescent girls, as well as boys, for having sex?

**5. Extending Statutory Rape Laws.** In 1996, the Governor of New York signed into law a bill criminalizing all sexual intercourse, whether coerced or consensual, between prison employees and prison inmates. See N.Y. Penal Law § 130.05(3)(3) (Consol. 2003). The theory underlying this statute is that "the imbalance of power between inmates and officers" is so great that it "negates the possibility of true consent." Monte Williams, Bill Seeks to Protect Inmates From Guards Who Seek Sex, N.Y. Times, Apr. 23, 1996, at A1. Under the statute, therefore, the inmate is defined as a "person deemed incapable of consent" to sex, so that liability for any intercourse between guard and inmate is thrown entirely on the guard. According to the law's proponents, it is difficult to prosecute guards under forcible rape statutes because guards rarely resort to the kind of physical force that such statutes require. Yet, the proponents claimed, sexual intercourse in this context inevitably is coercive. "Female inmates have no capacity to say, 'No'" to sexual advances from corrections officers because the officers have the power to penalize inmates in a variety of formal and informal ways. Opponents of the bill argued that women prisoners sometimes initiate sexual encounters because they "just want the sex," and they contended that the population of female inmates includes many litigious persons who are likely to file false accusations. Notice that both sides of this debate seem to have assumed that the guard-perpetrators in these cases inevitably would be male and the inmate-victims would be female. Is that a fair assumption? Do male inmates not need protection from female guards?

Is it fair to assume that all sexual intercourse between guards and inmates is so inherently coercive that it should be criminalized and the guards (alone) held liable for it? If so, this type of statutory rape law might be extended to other relationships in which the participants do not possess equivalent power. Lawmakers could identify such relationships and simply outlaw all sexual intercourse between the parties thereto. Possible candidates include relationships between teachers and students, employers and employees, and superior officers and their military subordinates. Are there other relationships that "negate the possibility of true consent"? What kind of "power" over the life of another person has that effect? Does this approach provide a desirable way to resolve some of the enforcement problems encountered under forcible rape statutes? Are such laws likely to have any adverse consequences?

———

# CHAPTER V

# JUSTIFICATION AND EXCUSE

---

## INTRODUCTORY NOTE ON JUSTIFICATION AND EXCUSE

The preceding chapters cover the central doctrines that shape the definition of criminal offenses. This chapter explores a body of defenses that are extrinsic to the definitions of specific crimes but that further elaborate the conditions of criminal liability. These defenses are usually grouped into the two general categories of justification and excuse.[a]

Justification defenses state exceptions to the prohibitions laid down by specific offenses. Thus, for example, an intentional homicide that would otherwise be murder is no crime at all if committed in self-defense. Similarly, conduct that would otherwise constitute criminal assault may be justified by a policeman's obligation to enforce the law. Self-defense and law enforcement are typical defenses of justification. They qualify and refine the proscriptions of the penal law. The considerations determining the scope of justification defenses are essentially the same as those governing the contours of particular offenses; both define the prohibitory content of the criminal law. Section 1 of this chapter elaborates the concept of justification, both generally and in selected specific contexts.

The law also includes doctrines of excuse. These defenses recognize claims that particular individuals cannot fairly be blamed for admittedly wrongful conduct. The defendant is excused not because his or her conduct was socially desirable, but rather because the circumstances of the offense evoke the societal judgment that criminal conviction and punishment would be morally inappropriate. As Francis Bowes Sayre explained in Mens Rea, 45 Harv.L.Rev. 974, 1021 (1932), doctrines of excuse were a natural outgrowth of the early common-law insistence on moral guilt as the basis of criminal liability:

---

[a] For analysis of the doctrinal structure of exculpatory defenses, see Paul Robinson, Criminal Law Defenses: A Systematic Analysis, 83 Colum.L.Rev. 199 (1982), and Glanville Williams, Offences and Defences, 2 Leg. Stud. 233 (1982). For specific coverage of defensive doctrines, see Paul Robinson, Criminal Law Defenses (1984) (2 vols.). For discussion of the significance of the distinction between justification and situational excuse, see Mitchell N. Berman, Justification and Excuse, Law and Morality, 53 Duke L.J. 1 (2003); George P. Fletcher, Rethinking the Criminal Law, 759 et seq. (1978); Joshua Dressler, New Thoughts About the Concept of Justification in the Criminal Law: A Critique of Fletcher's Thinking and Rethinking, 32 UCLA L.Rev. 61 (1984); Kent Greenawalt, The Perplexing Borders of Justification and Excuse, 84 Colum.L.Rev. 1897 (1984); Glanville Williams, The Theory of Excuses, [1982] Crim.L.Rev. 732.

[T]he strong tendency of the early days to link criminal liability with moral guilt made it necessary to free from punishment those who perhaps satisfied the requirements of specific intent for particular crimes but who, because of some personal mental defect or restraint, should not be convicted of any crime. The person who lacked a normal intelligence because of mental disease, or who lacked discretion because of tender years, or who through fear of death lacked the power to choose his conduct—all these must escape punishment if criminality was to be based upon moral guilt. Thus, there developed certain well-recognized defenses in criminal law, affecting one's general capacity to commit crime. . . .

At one time, theoretical coherence was attempted by characterizing all the various doctrines of excuse as defects of capacity. Insane persons, infants, and those acting under duress were all said to lack the capacity for criminal mens rea. Today, this unifying rubric has dissolved in the face of recognition that the various defects of "capacity" raise very different kinds of issues. In these materials, therefore, the topics of excuse are sorted into two categories. Section 2 of this chapter explores "situational excuse." This label is designed to suggest that offenders may be excused if the situations in which they find themselves overbear their otherwise normal abilities to conform their conduct to the requirements of law. In other words, the doctrines of situational excuse make allowance for abnormal situations, not abnormal persons. In such cases, the focus, as in the defenses of justification, is on the external realities of the actor's situation and the attitude of the actor concerning those realities. The problems of abnormal individuals—most notably immaturity and insanity—are covered in Chapter VI under the rubric of "criminal responsibility."

---

## SECTION 1: JUSTIFICATION

### SUBSECTION A: THE GENERAL PRINCIPLE OF JUSTIFICATION

----

## Commonwealth v. Markum

Superior Court of Pennsylvania, 1988.
373 Pa.Super. 341, 541 A.2d 347.

■ CIRILLO, PRESIDENT JUDGE. Appellants take this appeal from a judgment of sentence of one day to three months imprisonment imposed by . . . the Court of Common Pleas of Philadelphia County following their conviction for defiant trespass. We affirm.

On August 10, 1985, as part of an anti-abortion demonstration, appellants pushed their way into the Northeast Women's Center on Roosevelt Boulevard in Philadelphia, and occupied several rooms there. Once inside, they damaged two aspirator machines and other medical instruments, threw equipment out of a third floor window, and placed "pro-life" stickers on the doors, walls, and ceilings. Appellants refused to leave, even after several requests by the Center's staff, and were ultimately removed when police arrived and carried them from the scene. . . .

During a hearing on a motion in limine, appellants made an offer of proof in support of . . . a defense of justification. [The trial judge] ruled that justification did not lie. [The jury convicted all appellants.] . . .

Following sentencing, the appellants were immediately paroled on the condition that they each perform fifty hours of community service, not to be served in any pro-life agencies, and refrain from trespassing on medical facilities that perform abortions. . . .

Appellants raise one issue on appeal: whether the trial judge erred in not allowing appellants to present the defense of justification to the jury. . . .

[In Pennsylvania, the defense of justification is recognized by statute.] Section 503 states:

(a) General rule.—Conduct which the actor believes to be necessary to avoid a harm or evil to himself or to another is justifiable if:

(1) the harm or evil sought to be avoided by such conduct is greater than that sought to be prevented by the law defining the offense charged;

(2) neither this title nor other law defining the offense provides exceptions or defenses dealing with the specific situation involved; and

(3) a legislative purpose to exclude the justification claimed does not otherwise plainly appear.

(b) Choice of evils.—When the actor was reckless or negligent in bringing about the situation requiring a choice of harms or evils or in appraising the necessity for his conduct, the justification afforded by this section is unavailable in a prosecution for any offense for which recklessness or negligence, as the case may be, suffices to establish culpability. . . .

The Pennsylvania Supreme Court, in Commonwealth v. Capitolo, 508 Pa. 372, 498 A.2d 806 (1985), and Commonwealth v. Berrigan, 509 Pa. 118, 501 A.2d 226 (1985), addressed the applicability of the justification provisions. . . .

In *Capitolo*, Patricia Capitolo and four others crept under a fence enclosing the Shippingsport Nuclear Power Plant. Once through, they sat down about ten to twelve feet inside of the fence and held hands. They were placed under arrest after refusing requests of plant representatives that they leave the premises. The five sought to present a justification defense under § 503, . . . but . . . the trial judge [rejected the defense on the ground that the defendants] would not have been able to prove that their trespass was justified. They were subsequently convicted of trespass. . . .

On appeal, a majority of this court reversed the decision of the trial court, concluding that appellants' offer of proof met the requirements of § 503 and that they should have been able to present to the jury evidence in support of the defense.

Our supreme court reversed and reinstated the convictions, holding that the defense of justification is available only when the [defendant] is able to make an offer of proof which establishes:

(1) that the actor was faced with a clear and imminent harm, not one which is debatable or speculative;

(2) that the actor could reasonably expect that the actor's actions would be effective in avoiding this greater harm;

(3) there was no legal alternative which will be effective in abating the harm; and

(4) the legislature had not acted to preclude the defense by a clear and deliberate choice regarding the matter at issue. . . .

After applying these basic principles, [the *Capitolo*] court concluded that the danger at the nuclear plant was not imminent and that the appellees "could not establish that their criminal conduct was necessary to avoid harm or evil to themselves or others."

In *Berrigan*, the Berrigan brothers and six others entered the General Electric plant in King of Prussia, Pennsylvania, where they damaged hydrogen bomb missile components and poured human blood on the premises. Property damage exceeded $28,000. The eight involved were charged and convicted of burglary, criminal mischief, and criminal conspiracy. An offer of proof was made . . . to present the defense of justification. The trial judge permitted them to offer their own testimony in support of the defense, but refused to permit them to present expert testimony.

On appeal, this court held that appellants should have been able to present the defense, and present expert testimony in support of the defense.

Once again, our supreme court reversed. . . . The court . . . reiterated the four-part test used in *Capitolo* and determined that the trial court had properly ruled that the offer of proof was insufficient to establish that the nuclear holocaust that appellees sought to avert was a clear and imminent public disaster.

The court in *Berrigan* went even further, however, and held additionally that the defense of justification was not available "in situations where the conduct some perceive to engender public disaster has been specifically approved of by legislation making it legal conduct . . .".

Abortion has been specifically approved by the Pennsylvania legislature in the Abortion Control Act. . . . Were it not protected by such legislation, the justification defense would continue to remain unavailable because a woman's right to abortion is protected by the Constitution of the United States. Roe v. Wade, 410 U.S. 113 (1973). The *Berrigan* mandate that a justification defense may not be raised if the asserted "harm" is legal is not dependent upon whether such conduct has been made legal through legislative choice or judicial fiat.... We are each bound by the law no matter what its source. Were we free to pick and choose which laws we wished to obey, the result would be a society of strife and chaos.... Democracy allows the citizenry to protest laws of which they disapprove. But they must nonetheless obey such laws or face the legal consequences. To allow the defense of justification to those who willingly and intentionally break the law would encourage criminality cloaked in the guise of conscience....

Appellants wish to produce testimony to establish that life begins at conception. They wish to show scientifically that a fetus as young as eight weeks of age has measurable brain-wave activity. Because Pennsylvania's Determination of Death Act, provides that death occurs when all brain activity ceases, appellants assert that their evidence would demonstrate that abortion is the taking of a human life, and hence, a "public disaster." They also claim that the disaster was imminent, not speculative, and that their actions were effective in averting the disaster. Finally, they assert that there was no legal alternative for their actions.

Appellants' first argument, that abortion constitutes a public disaster, fails. As we have noted, pre-viability abortion is lawful by virtue of state statute and federal constitutional law. The United States Supreme Court has consistently held that the state's interest in protecting fetal life does not become compelling, and cannot infringe on a woman's right to choose abortion, until the fetus is viable. Appellants do not suggest that viability and conception are simultaneous occurrences. We find that a legally sanctioned activity cannot be termed a public disaster.

Appellants' second argument, that the disaster was imminent and that their actions were effective in averting it, similarly must fail. It is unreasonable for appellants to believe that their brief occupation of one center would effectively put an end to the practice of abortion. Appellants' occupation of the Women's Center did not stop its operation. Legal abortions continued to be performed in the Center and were available in other medical facilities throughout Pennsylvania.

Appellants' third contention, that there was no legal alternative to their actions, is misguided. As [the trial court] noted, "[t]here are obviously numerous means in a democratic society to express a point of view or to attempt to prevent a perceived harm without resorting to criminal behavior." Appellants were free to peacefully demonstrate outside of the center in an effort to prevent the harm that they perceived from occurring.

Finally, appellants' offer of proof was insufficient to show that no legislative purpose exists to exclude the justification defense, nor could they, because Pennsylvania law is to the contrary.... Clearly, to permit private citizens the right to prevent women from exercising their right to abortion would be a violation of both state statute and federal constitutional law....

The appellants are actually requesting that this court countenance civil disobedience, which is defined as: A form of lawbreaking employed to demonstrate the injustice or unfairness of a particular law and indulged in deliberately to focus attention on the allegedly undesirable law.

Though our nation has a long and proud history of civil disobedience, appellants are not in that tradition. From the Boston Tea Party to the abolitionists to conscientious objectors to the sit-ins of Martin Luther King, civil disobedience has often stirred our nation's collective conscience and spurred us to change or repeal unjust laws. Often, juries refused to convict good men of conscience whose love of justice had motivated them to violate the law. On some occasions, a jury would convict but the judge in recognition of the righteousness of the underlying cause would suspend sentence or issue a nominal fine. Abortion demonstrators argue that they are in this tradition and should be treated accordingly. They overlook the key distinction between their actions and the behavior of those cited above.

The true conscientious objector refuses to obey the very law which he claims is unjust. Rosa Parks refused to sit in the back of the bus and "draft dodgers" refused to register for the draft. When prosecuted, they challenged the wisdom, morality and constitutionality of the law in question.[2] They did not employ their objections to that law as an excuse to engage in general or targeted violence. But that is what the demonstrators in this case have done. On this appeal, the demonstrators challenge the applicability of our criminal trespass laws to their activities. But they do not assert that those laws are unconstitutional or unjust. Rather they believe that because they disagree with the practice of abortion they are entitled to deface and occupy property belonging to other persons. How sad that their sense of justice and outrage is so narrowly focused. . . .

■ McEWEN, JUDGE, concurring and dissenting. . . . I write . . . to express the view that appellants have surmounted three of the four obstacles to presentation of the defense. . . .

While the defense of justification has a number of synonyms, it is " 'often expressed in terms of choice of evils: When the pressure of circumstances presents one with a choice of evils, the law prefers that he avoid the greater evil by bringing about the lesser evil.' " "Determination of the issues of competing values and, therefore, the availability of the defense of necessity is precluded, however, when there has been a deliberate legislative choice as to the values at issue." . . .

The disaster which appellants sought to prevent was the abortions that would be completed in a very brief time after the women entered the building. . . . The danger perceived by appellants was, therefore, clear and imminent. Further, were appellants able to prevent the women from entering into the building, their action would have been quite effective in

[2] Of course, some civil disobedience such as the Boston Tea Party or the work of the abolitionists calls into question the very moral authority of the government. Obviously, this is not what the appellants intended as on this appeal they seek the protection of a statutory defense promulgated by our government.

thwarting the immediate disaster appellants perceived as awaiting the women and their unborn children in the clinic. And, of course, appellants had no legal alternative available. Therefore, I conclude that appellants complied with three of the conditions precedent to presentation of the defense of justification.

[However, I agree with the majority that] the appellants here did not—in fact, could not—establish the absence of a legislative purpose to exclude the defense of justification....

■ TAMILIA, JUDGE, dissenting. I follow and support the reasoning of the majority in its analysis of the justification defense to the point where it holds that [the] defense ... is precluded by legislative and constitutional protection. Abortion is constitutionally protected but it [receives] qualified protection. The significant distinction between this case and [*Berrigan*] is that there was no imminent danger in constructing atomic warheads. Abortion stands on an entirely different footing. I believe the defense is available in two respects despite statutory and constitutional limitations. First, if the clinic was processing abortions beyond the time of viability, as established by *Roe*, the right to protect the life of a fetus in those circumstances would exist within the present legislative and constitutional parameters. [Second,] the Supreme Court, in fixing viability at a point supported by medical knowledge as it existed at [the time *Roe* was decided], has left open the question of when the state may intervene, [and the answer to that question is] dependent on medical evidence as to viability at the time at issue. *Roe v. Wade* was promulgated in 1973. In the intervening years, enormous strides have been made in sustaining [fetal] life outside the womb....

[In *Roe*, the Supreme Court observed that medical experts accepted a fetal age of 28 weeks as the appropriate criterion of viability at that time. In subsequent cases, the Supreme Court acknowledged that *Roe* left the point of viability "flexible for anticipated advancements in medical skill." Today, viability has been reduced to below 24 weeks. Thus, while viability, and not conception, determines when the state interest may be invoked on behalf of the fetus, the viability criterion of 28 weeks applied in *Roe* is no longer valid given the developments in medical technology. Indeed, fetal viability in the first trimester of pregnancy may be possible in the not too distant future.]

If viability has significantly been advanced and abortion services continue to apply the *Roe* standards, then a state interest in protecting fetal life is likely implicated in some cases. Fetal life is, therefore, protected in those instances and the defense of justification would be available to persons attempting to protect or save a fetus capable of surviving under the advanced medical standards. Unquestionably, clinics and hospitals can and do establish standards and controls to assure that no abortions are performed except in cases in which the fetus could not be viable under advanced medical technology. This may not, however, be presumed in the face of an offer of proof on the defense of justification....

In this case, the appellants conceivably could have produced evidence that ... a viable fetus, who would survive under the advanced medical technology available, would be terminated and that the actions of the appellants would be effective in avoiding the greater harm.... It is also clear that no legal alternative would have been effective in abating the harm. Thus, the denial of the right to pursue the justification defense precluded the appellants from attempting to establish the proof of viability and the inherent right to protect life under the circumstances of this case....

---

## NOTES ON THE DEFENSE OF NECESSITY

**1. Common–Law Necessity.** In his concurring and dissenting opinion, Judge McEwen notes that the "general defense of justification" is a codification of the common law defense of necessity. At one level, the proposition that the common law recognized a general defense of necessity is unexceptional, for the unifying theme of the specific defenses of justification is the necessity for making a choice among evils. Defense of self and others, defense of property, the exercise of public authority, and law enforcement are doctrinal particularizations of the necessity principle.

Whether there remains a residual and otherwise undefined defense of necessity apart from such specific doctrines is not entirely clear. Most courts and commentators seem to agree that a general necessity defense did exist at common law.[a] The uncertainty is no doubt due to the infrequency with which the issue is presented. Most claims of justification are handled under the more specific doctrines of self-defense, defense of others, etc. Only rarely is there need to consider whether any more general doctrine should be recognized. *Markum* provides an unusual occasion for exploring necessity and its place in the structure of justification defenses.

In jurisdictions that have not codified a general defense of justification or necessity, modern decisions tend to assume the existence of such defense at common law, often while holding that the defendant's evidence is legally insufficient to raise it. As *Markum* illustrates, claims of necessity or choice of evils have often been raised, almost always unsuccessfully, by persons protesting politically controversial issues, including U.S. participation in the Vietnam War,[b] the construction or operation of nuclear power plants,[c] and abortion.[d]

[a] See, e.g., 2 Wayne R. LaFave, Substantive Criminal Law 121–24 (2003), and the authorities cited therein.

[b] See, e.g., United States v. Simpson, 460 F.2d 515 (9th Cir.1972); United States v. Kroncke, 459 F.2d 697 (8th Cir.1972).

[c] See, e.g., Commonwealth v. Capitolo, 508 Pa. 372, 498 A.2d 806 (1985); State v. Warshow, 138 Vt. 22, 410 A.2d 1000 (1979);

State v. Dorsey, 118 N.H. 844, 395 A.2d 855 (1978).

[d] See, e.g., State v. O'Brien, 784 S.W.2d 187 (Mo.App.1989); Sigma Reproductive Health Center v. State, 297 Md. 660, 467 A.2d 483 (1983); Cleveland v. Municipality of Anchorage, 631 P.2d 1073 (Alaska 1981); People v. Krizka, 92 Ill.App.3d 288, 48 Ill. Dec. 141, 416 N.E.2d 36 (1980); Gaetano v. United States, 406 A.2d 1291 (D.C.App.1979).

**2. Modern Statutory Formulations.** The Pennsylvania justification statute applied in *Markum* is identical to the general choice-of-evils defense in the Model Penal Code. This provision was one of the significant innovations of the Model Code, and it has been adopted in substance by approximately 10 American jurisdictions.

New York also has codified the defense of justification, and its provision has served as the model for legislation in about 10 additional states. Section 35.05 of the New York Penal Code states, in pertinent part:

> Unless otherwise limited by the ensuing provisions of this article defining justifiable use of physical force, conduct which would otherwise constitute an offense is justifiable and not criminal when....
>
> > (2) Such conduct is necessary as an emergency measure to avoid an imminent public or private injury which is about to occur by reason of a situation occasioned or developed through no fault of the actor, and which is of such gravity that, according to ordinary standards of intelligence and morality, the desirability and urgency of avoiding such injury clearly outweigh the desirability of avoiding the injury sought to be prevented by the statute defining the offense in issue. The necessity and justifiability of such conduct may not rest upon considerations pertaining only to the morality and advisability of the statute, either in its general application or with respect to its application to a particular class of cases arising thereunder. Whenever evidence relating to the defense of justification under this [provision] is offered by the defendant, the court shall rule as a matter of law whether the claimed facts and circumstances would, if established, constitute a defense.

On facts similar to those of *Markum*, a New York court concluded that the New York provision and the Model Penal Code section embody different definitions of what constitutes an evil or "injury to be avoided" for purposes of the necessity defense. In People v. Archer, 537 N.Y.S.2d 726 (1988), the City Court of Rochester compared the alternative approaches:

> [The Model Penal Code eliminates the necessity defense whenever the legislature has specifically spoken on the topic.] Under the Model Penal Code, whatever [is] legal, therefore, could not be evil. The Model Code, in other words, precluded the necessity defense whenever the legislature had legalized conduct.
>
> But what this court must observe is that [New York adopted] a different standard. [The New York statute provides] that the "injury ... to be avoided must ... *according to ordinary standards of intelligence and morality*, clearly outweigh the injury" the criminal law(s) in question were designed to prevent. The [legisla-

ture] deliberately chose to enlarge the categories of possible evils to include not simply illegal behavior, but any injury which existed "according to ordinary standards of intelligence and morality." . . .

What is obvious here is that [the New York legislature has recognized] a different standard of judgment for determining what is an "injury to be avoided," which standard is broader, and more encompassing, than the legal/illegal classifications within the Penal Law itself. Granted what is criminally illegal is, *ipso facto*, an injury to be avoided. But the contrary of that proposition—namely, "what is legal is therefore *not* an injury to be avoided" does not follow. In the former case, behavior which is criminally forbidden always violates "ordinary standards of intelligence and morality." But in the latter case, behavior which is permissively legal, does not always comport with ordinary standards of intelligence and morality.

In Nevada, for example, prostitution is legal, but still, immoral. Some type of gambling is almost everywhere legal, but many persons of ordinary intelligence and morality still consider it immoral. Traffic in alcoholic beverages is legal, but its byproduct, drunkenness, remains immoral. Divorce is legal, but, in many cases, it is immoral, especially when it affects innocent children of the marriage. Thus . . . morality and legality . . . are not the same. Morality is the standard of conduct to which, as good and decent people, we all aspire. Legality is the standard of conduct to which, as members of a civilized society, and under penalty of the criminal sanction, we must all adhere. . . .

Thus, in cases of moral indignation, the flexibility of the New York statute avoids the chafing attrition of the eternal struggle between what is legal and what is moral. The statute allows a jury to ventilate its displeasure at morally reprehensible conduct regardless of its legality by approving, in a verdict of not guilty, the behavior of those who try, even illegally, to prevent that conduct from happening.

According to *Archer*, the New York justification defense authorizes jurors to reject the legislative "choice among evils," embodied in a statute legalizing abortions, and to decide that abortions inflict injuries that outweigh those sought to be prevented by the trespass laws. However, the court also concluded that first-trimester abortions do not qualify as "injuries to be avoided" for purposes of this defense. Since such abortions are constitutionally protected under *Roe v. Wade*, "neither the [justification] statute, nor the Court, nor the Jury itself, can intrude upon that constitutionally protected area of privacy."

Does *Archer* properly construe the New York justification statute? Why does a judicial choice of evils, such as that endorsed by *Roe v. Wade*, preclude the necessity defense if a legislative choice of evils does not?

**3.  Economic Necessity.** An often cited choice-of-evils case is State
v. Moe, 174 Wash. 303, 24 P.2d 638 (1933), which arose during the
Depression. The defendants tried, unsuccessfully, to persuade the chairman
of the local Red Cross relief committee to increase their allowance of flour.
Having been advised that their demands would not be met, the defendants
entered a local grocery store and helped themselves. The Washington
Supreme Court affirmed their convictions for grand larceny and riot and
upheld the trial court's rejection of defendants' offer to prove their poverty
in justification of their actions. The court stated:

> Economic necessity has never been accepted as a defense to a
> criminal charge. The reason is that, were it ever countenanced, it
> would leave to the individual the right to take the law into his own
> hands. In larceny cases, economic necessity is frequently invoked
> in mitigation of punishment, but has never been recognized as a
> defense.

The reach of this language has frequently been criticized on the ground
that a defense might be appropriate in a case involving theft by a mother to
feed her starving child, but no such case appears in the books. However, an
analogous claim of economic necessity was raised in Mayfield v. State, 585
S.W.2d 693 (Tex. Crim. App. 1979).[e] Mayfield was charged with fraudulently obtaining welfare assistance. She admitted that she had falsely stated
that she was unemployed and that she had failed to report her earned
income to her caseworker as she was legally required to do. She claimed
that she needed the additional money to prevent irreparable harm to her
children. In support of her claim, she proffered the testimony of a physician
and nurse who testified that the Mayfield children were suffering from
nutritional deficiencies amounting to "starvation" in the medical sense.
Welfare department employees testified that the level of benefits granted to
recipients was only 75 percent of that computed in 1969 to be needed by a
family of her size for a subsistence level of living. She also proffered
testimony by an economist who stated that the failure of the welfare
department to adjust benefit levels between 1969 and 1974 (when the
offenses occurred) had resulted in a 30 per cent loss of purchasing power. Is
this evidence legally sufficient to raise a necessity defense at common law?
Would Mayfield be entitled to a jury instruction under the Model Code?
Under the New York statute?

**4.  Medical Necessity.** One of the issues discussed in *Markum* is the
effect of prior judicial and legislative resolution of the abortion issue. A
comparable issue arises in cases where an accused argues that a violation of
the drug laws is justifiable by reason of medical necessity.

Medical necessity sometimes is used to defend against marijuana
possession charges. In such cases, the accused claims that he or she suffers
from a physical infirmity for which there is no effective conventional

---

[e] *Mayfield* is discussed in J. Thomas Sullivan, The Defense of Necessity in Texas:
Legislative Invention Comes of Age, 16 Houston L.Rev. 333 (1979). Mayfield's conviction
was reversed on other grounds in Mayfield v.
State, 585 S.W.2d 693 (Tex.Crim.App.1979).

treatment, but for which ingestion of marijuana provides relief. These claims have met with varying success in the courts. State v. Tate, 102 N.J. 64 (1986), represents one reaction. The defendant in *Tate* was a quadriplegic. According to the Supreme Court of New Jersey, "[t]he spasticity associated with that condition is sometimes so severe as to render defendant completely disabled." When he was charged with unlawful possession of marijuana, defendant argued that his conduct was justified because, unlike conventional treatments, marijuana eased the spastic contractions. The court held that the legislature intended to preclude such a defense. In particular, the court pointed out that the legislature had passed a Therapeutic Research Act, which authorized the study of medical uses of controlled substances and allowed marijuana to be prescribed to patients in some circumstances. By making available this "specific exception," the legislature intended to exclude claims based on medical necessity in all other cases of marijuana possession. Should the outcome be different in states whose legislatures have not enacted laws allowing the use of controlled substances in therapeutic research? What if a federal therapeutic research program is available?

Other courts have allowed defendants to defend drug possession charges on grounds of medical necessity. For example, in State v. Diana, 24 Wash.App. 908, 604 P.2d 1312 (1979), the defendant suffered from multiple sclerosis, and he claimed that marijuana relieved disabling symptoms for which lawful treatments were ineffective. Although the defendant had not offered a medical necessity defense at trial, the Court of Appeals of Washington concluded that the interests of justice required that the case be remanded for the trial court to consider such defense. The state legislature recently had enacted a Controlled Substances Therapeutic Act, which authorized the dispensing of marijuana to persons suffering from the effects of glaucoma and cancer chemotherapy. According to the court, the legislature thus had recognized that in some cases marijuana possesses medicinal benefits that outweigh any harms its use inflicts, and the defendant should be given the opportunity to demonstrate that multiple sclerosis is another such case:

> ... To summarize, medical necessity exists in this case if the court finds that (1) the defendant reasonably believed his use of marijuana was necessary to minimize the effects of multiple sclerosis; (2) the benefits derived from its use are greater than the harm sought to be prevented by the controlled substances law; and (3) no drug is as effective in minimizing the effects of the disease. [C]orroborating medical testimony is required. In reaching this decision, the court must balance the defendant's interest in preserving his health against the state's interest in regulating the drug involved. Defendant bears the burden of proving the existence of necessity, an affirmative defense, by a preponderance of the evidence....

Finally, consider the recent threat by the federal Food and Drug Administration to crack down on illegal sales of thalidomide. Thalidomide was first produced and widely marketed in Europe in the late 1950's. At that time, the drug was prescribed for pregnant women as a medication to relieve morning sickness. The consequences were tragic: in the early 1960's, researchers discovered that thalidomide caused severe birth defects. Thousands of the women who took thalidomide gave birth to babies with missing or deformed limbs, or damaged internal organs; some of the babies were born dead. The drug was banned worldwide in 1962.[f] However, in recent years, some scientists have concluded that thalidomide may be beneficial to persons afflicted with serious illnesses, including AIDS, cancer, leprosy, and tuberculosis. In 1995, the FDA approved the experimental use of thalidomide in clinical studies involving persons suffering from severe AIDS-related maladies, but the agency continues to prohibit broader distribution of the drug. Because some early studies suggest that thalidomide may prolong the lives of persons in the late stages of AIDS, the drug is being sold illegally by AIDS activists. Could the sale of thalidomide be justified by medical necessity? Does such sale raise the same issues as *Markum* or the marijuana possession cases?

**5. Necessity as a Justification for Homicide: *Dudley and Stephens*.** The claim of necessity as a justification for intentional homicide arguably presents a special case. At common law, self-defense and other specific doctrines of justification authorized the necessary use of deadly force against a wrongdoer. The common law did not, however, permit a general plea of necessity to justify killing an innocent person in order to avoid some other evil. In contrast, most modern statutes, including both the Model Penal Code and the New York provision, seem to contemplate that a defense of necessity or choice of evils may be raised where one innocent person is killed in order to save others. This position was defended by the drafters of the Model Penal Code on the ground that "[i]t would be particularly unfortunate to exclude homicidal conduct from the scope of the defense," because "recognizing that the sanctity of life has a supreme place in the hierarchy of values, it is nonetheless true that conduct that results in taking life may promote the very value sought to be protected by the law of homicide."[g]

The question of whether necessity may justify intentional homicide is considered in the famous case of Regina v. Dudley and Stephens, 14 Q.B.D. 273 (1884).[h] The facts were found by the jury in a special verdict:

> [T]hat on July 5, 1884, the prisoners, Thomas Dudley and Edward Stephens, with one Brooks, all able-bodied English seamen, and the deceased also an English boy between 17 and 18

[f] Sale of thalidomide never has been lawful in the United States because the FDA refused to approve the drug until research demonstrated that it was safe and effective. To date, in the view of the FDA, such research has not been forthcoming.

[g] ALI, Model Penal Code and Commentaries, § 3.02, p. 14 (1985). Several jurisdictions reject this position and withdraw the necessity defense in murder cases. See 2 Paul H. Robinson, Criminal Law Defenses 63 (1984).

[h] For a superb historical account of this case, see A.W.B. Simpson, Cannibalism and the Common Law: The Story of the Tragic Last Voyage of the *Mignonette* and the Strange Legal Proceedings to Which It Gave Rise (1984).

years of age, the crew of an English yacht, a registered English vessel, were cast away in a storm on the high seas 1600 miles from the Cape of Good Hope, and were compelled to put into an open boat belonging to the said yacht. That in this boat they had no supply of water and no supply of food, except two one lb. tins of turnips, and for three days they had nothing else to subsist upon. That on the fourth day they caught a small turtle, upon which they subsided for a few days, and this was the only food they had up to the 20th day when the act now in question was committed. That on the 12th day the remains of the turtle were entirely consumed, and for the next eight days they had nothing to eat. That they had no fresh water, except such rain as they from time to time caught in their oilskin capes. That the boat was drifting on the ocean, and was probably more than 1000 miles away from land. That on the 18th day, when they had been seven days without food and five without water, the prisoners spoke to Brooks as to what should be done if no succour came, and suggested that some one should be sacrificed to save the rest, but Brooks dissented, and the boy, to whom they were understood to refer, was not consulted. That on the 24th of July, the day before the act now in question, the prisoner Dudley proposed to Stephens and Brooks that lots should be cast who should be put to death to save the rest, but Brooks refused to consent, and it was not put to the boy, and in point of fact there was no drawing of lots. That on that day the prisoners spoke of their having families, and suggested it would be better to kill the boy that their lives should be saved, and Dudley proposed that if there was no vessel in sight by the morrow morning the boy should be killed. That next day, the 25th of July, no vessel appearing, Dudley told Brooks that he had better go and have a sleep, and made signs to Stephens and Brooks that the boy had better be killed. The prisoner Stephens agreed to the act, but Brooks dissented from it. That the boy was then lying at the bottom of the boat quite helpless, and extremely weakened by famine and by drinking sea water, and unable to make any resistance, nor did he ever assent to his being killed. The prisoner Dudley offered a prayer asking forgiveness for them all if either of them should be tempted to commit a rash act, and that their souls might be saved. That Dudley, with the assent of Stephens, went to the boy, and telling him that his time was come, put a knife into his throat and killed him then and there; that the three fed upon the body and blood of the boy for four days; that on the fourth day after the act had been committed the boat was picked up by a passing vessel, and the prisoners were rescued, still alive, but in the lowest state of prostration. That they were carried to the port of Falmouth, and committed for trial at Exeter. That if the men had not fed upon the body of the boy they would probably not have survived to be so picked up and rescued, but would within the four days have died of famine. That the boy, being in a much weaker condition, was likely to have died before them. That at the time of the act in question there was no sail in sight, nor any reasonable prospect of relief. That under these circumstances there appeared to the prisoners every probability that unless they then fed or very soon fed upon the boy or one of themselves they would die of starvation. That there was no appreciable chance of saving life except by killing someone for the others to eat. That assuming any necessity to kill anybody, there was no greater necessity for killing the boy than any of the other three men.

On these facts, the court found the defendants guilty of murder. The court rejected the defendants' necessity defense. The following excerpt from the opinion of Lord Coleridge explains why:

... Now, it is admitted that the deliberate killing of this unoffending and unresisting boy was clearly murder, unless the killing can be justified by some well-recognised excuse admitted by the law. It is further admitted that there was in this case no such excuse, unless the killing was justified by what has been called "necessity." But the temptation to the act which existed here was not what the law has ever called necessity. Nor is this to be regretted. Though law and morality are not the same, and many things may be immoral which are not necessarily illegal, yet the absolute divorce of law from morality would be of fatal consequence; and such divorce would follow if the temptation to murder in this case were to be held by law an absolute defence of it. It is not so. To preserve one's life is generally speaking a duty, but it may be the plainest and the highest duty to sacrifice it. War is full of instances in which it is a man's duty not to live, but to die. The duty, in case of shipwreck, of a captain to his crew, of the crew to the passengers, of soldiers to women and children, ... these duties impose on men the moral necessity, not of the preservation, but of the sacrifice of their lives for others, from which in no country, least of all, it is to be hoped, in England, will men ever shrink, as indeed, they have not shrunk. It is not correct, therefore, to say that there is any absolute or unqualified necessity to preserve one's life.... It would be a very easy and cheap display of commonplace learning to quote from Greek and Latin authors, from Horace, from Juvenal, from Cicero, from Euripides, passage after passage, in which the duty of dying for others has been laid down in glowing and emphatic language as resulting from the principles of heathen ethics; it is enough in a Christian country to remind ourselves of the Great Example whom we profess to follow. It is not needful to point out the awful danger of admitting the principle which has been contended for. Who is to be the judge of this sort of necessity? By what measure is the comparative value of lives to be measured? Is it to be strength, or intellect, or what? It is plain that the principle leaves to him who is to profit by it to determine the necessity which will justify him in deliberately taking another's life to save his own. In this case the weakest, the youngest, the most unresisting, was chosen. Was it more necessary to kill him than one of the grown men? The answer must be "No"— ... It is not suggested that in this particular case the deeds were "devilish," but it is quite plain that such a principle once admitted might be made the legal cloak for unbridled passion and atrocious crime. There is no safe path for judges to tread but to ascertain the law to the best of their ability and to declare it according to their judgment; and if in any case the law appears to be too severe on individuals, to leave it to the sovereign to exercise that prerogative of mercy which the constitution has intrusted to the hands fittest to dispense it.

It must not be supposed that in refusing to admit temptation to be an excuse for crime it is forgotten how terrible the temptation was; how awful the suffering; how hard in such trials to keep the judgment straight and the conduct pure. We are often compelled to set up standards we cannot reach ourselves, and to lay down rules which we could not ourselves satisfy. But a man has no right to declare temptation to be an excuse, though he might himself have yielded to it, nor allow compassion for the criminal to change or weaken in any manner the legal definition of the crime. It is therefore our duty to declare that the prisoners' act in this case was wilful murder, that the facts as stated in the verdict are no legal justification of the homicide; and to say that in our unanimous opinion the prisoners are upon this special verdict guilty of murder.[i]

Should choice of evils never be allowed to justify intentional homicide, or is there some narrower principle on which the result in *Dudley and Stephens* can be defended?

**6. Necessity Created by Fault of the Actor.** The New York statute construed in *Archer* expressly limits the choice-of-evils defense to cases where the necessity is "occasioned or developed through no fault of the actor." Most state statutes on the subject impose a similar limitation, as does the Model Penal Code.[j] The application of this limitation is typically illustrated by the following hypothetical: *A* becomes voluntarily intoxicated and, in an impaired condition, seriously injures *B*. Because *B* needs immediate medical assistance, *A* drives *B* to the hospital. If *A* is arrested for driving while intoxicated, *A* could not justify doing so by the necessity to seek help for *B*. The defect in the claim is that the situation requiring a choice of evils arose from *A*'s own fault. Is there logic to this position? Might there be cases in which denial of a necessity defense on this ground (assuming that the actor was aware of the law and acted accordingly) would encourage socially undesirable behavior? If there is to be a middle ground,

[i] The court sentenced the defendants to death; however, this sentence was afterwards commuted by the Crown to six months' imprisonment.—[Footnote by eds.]

[j] For a thorough discussion of this limitation, see Paul H. Robinson, Causing the Conditions of One's Own Defense: A Study in the Limits of Theory in Criminal Law Doctrine, 71 Va.L.Rev. 1 (1985).

in what kinds of situations should the necessity defense be denied because of the actor's fault in creating the occasion for his conduct?

_____

## Subsection B: Defense Against Aggression

_____

## People v. Goetz

Court of Appeals of New York, 1986.
68 N.Y.2d 96, 497 N.E.2d 41, 506 N.Y.S.2d 18.

■ Wachtler, Chief Judge. A grand jury has indicted defendant on attempted murder, assault, and other charges for having shot and wounded four youths on a New York City subway train after one or two of the youths approached him and asked for $5. The lower courts, concluding that the prosecutor's charge to the grand jury on the defense of justification was erroneous, have dismissed the attempted murder, assault and weapons possession charges. We now reverse and reinstate all counts of the indictment.

I.

The precise circumstances of the incident giving rise to the charges against defendant are disputed, and ultimately it will be for a trial jury to determine what occurred. We feel it necessary, however, to provide some factual background to properly frame the legal issues before us. Accordingly, we have summarized the facts as they appear from the evidence before the grand jury. We stress, however, that we do not purport to reach any conclusions or holding as to exactly what transpired or whether defendant is blameworthy. The credibility of witnesses and the reasonableness of defendant's conduct are to be resolved by the trial jury.

On Saturday afternoon, December 22, 1984, Troy Canty, Darryl Cabey, James Ramseur, and Barry Allen boarded an IRT express subway train in the Bronx and headed south toward lower Manhattan. The four youths rode together in the rear portion of the seventh car of the train. Two of the four, Ramseur and Cabey, had screwdrivers inside their coats, which they said were to be used to break into the coin boxes of video machines.

Defendant Bernhard Goetz boarded this subway train at 14th Street in Manhattan and sat down on a bench towards the rear section of the same car occupied by the four youths. Goetz was carrying an unlicensed .38 caliber pistol loaded with five rounds of ammunition in a waistband holster. The train left the 14th Street station and headed towards Chambers Street.

It appears from the evidence before the Grand Jury that Canty approached Goetz, possibly with Allen beside him, and stated "give me five dollars." Neither Canty nor any of the other youths displayed a weapon. Goetz responded by standing up, pulling out his handgun and firing four shots in rapid succession. The first shot hit Canty in the chest; the second struck Allen in the back; the third went through Ramseur's arm and into his left side; the fourth was fired at Cabey, who apparently was then standing in the corner of the car, but missed, deflecting instead off of a wall of the conductor's cab. After Goetz briefly surveyed the scene around him, he fired another shot at Cabey, who then was sitting on the end bench of the car. The bullet entered the rear of Cabey's side and severed his spinal cord.

. . . The conductor, who had been in the next car, heard the shots and instructed the motorman to radio for emergency assistance. The conductor then went into the car where the shooting occurred and saw Goetz sitting on a bench, the injured youths lying on the floor or slumped against a seat, and two women who had apparently taken cover, also lying on the floor. Goetz told the conductor that the four youths had tried to rob him.

While the conductor was aiding the youths, Goetz headed towards the front of the car. The train had stopped just before the Chambers Street station and Goetz went between two of the cars, jumped onto the tracks and fled. Police and ambulance crews arrived at the scene shortly thereafter. Ramseur and Canty, initially listed in critical condition, have fully recovered. Cabey remains paralyzed, and has suffered some degree of brain damage.

On December 31, 1984, Goetz surrendered to police. . . . Later that day, after receiving *Miranda* warnings, he made two lengthy statements, both of which were tape recorded with his permission. In the statements, . . . Goetz admitted that he had been illegally carrying a handgun in New York City for three years. He stated that he had first purchased a gun in 1981 after he had been injured in a mugging. Goetz also revealed that twice . . . he had successfully warded off assailants simply by displaying the pistol.

[T]he first contact [Goetz] had with the four youths came when Canty, sitting or lying on the bench across from him, asked "how are you," to which he replied "fine." Shortly thereafter, Canty, followed by one of the other youths, walked over to the defendant and stood to his left, while the other two youths remained to his right, in the corner of the subway car. Canty then said "give me five dollars." Goetz stated that he knew from the smile on Canty's face that they wanted to "play with me." Although he was certain that none of the youths had a gun, he had a fear, based on prior experiences, of being "maimed."

Goetz then established "a pattern of fire," deciding specifically to fire from left to right. His stated intention at that point was to "murder [the four youths], to hurt them, to make them suffer as much as possible." When Canty again requested money, Goetz stood up, drew his weapon, and began firing, aiming for the center of the body of each of the four. Goetz recalled that the first two he shot "tried to run through the crowd [but] they had nowhere to run." Goetz then turned to his right to "go after the other two." One of these two "tried to run through the wall of the train, but . . . he had nowhere to go." The other youth (Cabey) "tried pretending that he wasn't with [the others]" by standing still, holding on to one of the subway hand straps, and not looking at Goetz. Goetz nonetheless fired his fourth shot at him. He then ran back to the first two youths to make sure they had been "taken care of." Seeing that they had both been shot, he spun back to check on the latter two. Goetz noticed that the youth who had been standing still was now sitting on a bench and seemed unhurt. As Goetz told the police, "I said '[you] seem to be all right, here's another,'" and he then fired the shot which severed Cabey's spinal cord. Goetz added that "if I was a little more under self-control ... I would have put the barrel against his forehead and fired." He also admitted that "if I had had more [bullets], I would have shot them again, and again, and again."

II.

On March 27, 1985, the ... grand jury filed a 10–count indictment, containing four charges of attempted murder, four charges of assault in the first degree, one charge of reckless endangerment in the first degree, and one charge of criminal possession of a weapon in the second degree....

... Goetz moved to dismiss the charges ... alleging, among other things, that the evidence before the ... grand jury was not legally sufficient to establish the offenses charged, and that the prosecutor's instructions to [the] grand jury on the defense of justification were erroneous and prejudicial to the defendant so as to render its proceedings defective.

[W]hile the motion to dismiss was pending ... the New York Daily News [published a column in] which the columnist ... claimed that Cabey had told him ... that the other three youths had all approached Goetz with the intention of robbing him. The day after the column was published, a ... police officer informed the prosecutor that he had been one of the first police officers to enter the subway car after the shootings, and that Canty had said to him "we were going to rob [Goetz]." ...

[The] Criminal Term ... dismissed all counts of the ... indictment, other than the reckless endangerment charge.... The court ... rejected Goetz's contention that there was not legally sufficient evidence to support the charges. It held, however, that the prosecutor, in a supplemental charge elaborating upon the justification defense, had erroneously introduced an objective element into this defense by instructing the grand jurors to consider whether Goetz's conduct was that of a "reasonable man in [Goetz's] situation." The court ... concluded that the statutory test for whether the use of deadly force is justified to protect a person should be wholly subjective, focusing entirely on the defendant's state of mind when he used such force. It concluded that dismissal was required for this error because the justification issue was at the heart of the case....

On appeal by the People, a divided Appellate Division affirmed Criminal Term's dismissal of the charges....

III.

Penal Law article 35 recognizes the defense of justification, which "permits the use of force under certain circumstances." One such set of circumstances pertains to the use of force in defense of a person, encompassing both self-defense and defense of a third person. Penal Law § 35.15(1) sets forth the general principles governing all such uses of force: "[a] person may ... use physical force upon another person when and to the extent he reasonably believes such to be necessary to defend himself or a third person from what he reasonably believes to be the use or imminent use of unlawful physical force by such other person."[3]

Section 35.15(2) sets forth further limitations on these general principles with respect to the use of "deadly physical force:" "A person may not use deadly physical force upon another person under circumstances specified in subdivision one unless (a) He reasonably believes that such other person is using or about to use deadly physical force ...[4] or (b) He reasonably believes that such other person is committing or attempting to commit a kidnapping, forcible rape, forcible sodomy or robbery."

Thus, ... Penal Law § 35.15 permits the use of deadly physical force only where requirements as to triggering conditions and the necessity of a particular response are met. As to the triggering conditions, the statute requires that the actor "reasonably believes" that another person either is using or about to use deadly physical force or is committing or attempting to commit one of certain enumerated felonies, including robbery. As to the need for the use of deadly physical force as a response, the statute requires that the actor "reasonably believes" that such force is necessary to avert the perceived threat.[5]

Because the evidence before the ... grand jury included statements by Goetz that he acted to protect himself from being maimed or to avert a robbery, the prosecutor correctly chose to charge the justification defense.... The prosecutor properly instructed the grand jurors to consider whether the use of deadly physical force was justified to prevent either serious physical injury or a robbery, and, in doing so, to separately analyze the defense with respect to each of the charges. He elaborated ... by ... paraphrasing ... Penal Law § 35.15....

When the prosecutor had completed his charge, one of the grand jurors asked for clarification of the term "reasonably believes." The prosecutor responded by instructing the grand jurors that they were to consider the circumstances of the incident and determine "whether the defendant's conduct was that of a reasonable man in the defendant's situation." It is this response by the prosecutor—and specifically his use of "a reasonable man"—which is the basis for the dismissal of the charges by the lower

---

[3] Subdivision (1) contains certain exceptions to this general authorization to use force, such as where the actor himself was the initial aggressor.

[4] Section 35.15(2)(a) further provides, however, that even under these circumstances a person ordinarily must retreat "if he knows that he can with complete safety as to himself and others avoid the necessity of [using deadly physical force] by retreating."

[5] While the [provision] pertaining to the use of deadly physical force to avert a felony such as robbery does not contain a separate "retreat" requirement, it is clear from reading subdivisions (1) and (2) of § 35.15 together, as the statute requires, that the general "necessity" requirement in subdivision (1) applies to all uses of force under § 35.15, including the use of deadly physical force under subdivision (2)(b).

courts. As expressed repeatedly in the Appellate Division's plurality opinion, because § 35.15 uses the term "he reasonably believes," the appropriate test, according to that court, is whether a defendant's beliefs and reactions were "reasonable to him." Under that reading of the statute, a jury which believed a defendant's testimony that he felt that his own actions were warranted and were reasonable would have to acquit him, regardless of what anyone else in defendant's situation might have concluded. . . .

Penal statutes in New York have long codified the right recognized at common law to use deadly physical force, under appropriate circumstances, in self-defense. These provisions have never required that an actor's belief as to the intention of another person to inflict serious injury be correct in order for the use of deadly force to be justified, but they have uniformly required that the belief comport with an objective notion of reasonableness. . . .

In Shorter v. People, 2 N.Y. 193 (1849), we emphasized that deadly force could be justified . . . even if the actor's beliefs as to the intentions of another turned out to be wrong, but noted there had to be a reasonable basis, viewed objectively, for the beliefs. We explicitly rejected the position that the defendant's own belief that the use of deadly force was necessary sufficed to justify such force regardless of the reasonableness of the beliefs. . . .

In 1961 the Legislature established a Commission to undertake a complete revision of the Penal Law. . . . The impetus for the decision to update the Penal Law came in part from the drafting of the Model Penal Code by the American Law Institute, as well as from the fact that the existing law was poorly organized and in many aspects antiquated. . . . The drafting of the general provisions of the new Penal Law, including the article on justification, was particularly influenced by the Model Penal Code. While using the Model Penal Code provisions on justification as general guidelines, however, the drafters of the new Penal Law did not simply adopt them verbatim.

The provisions of the Model Penal Code with respect to the use of deadly force in self-defense reflect the position of its drafters that any culpability which arises from a mistaken belief in the need to use such force should be no greater than the culpability such a mistake would give rise to if it were made with respect to an element of a crime. Accordingly, under Model Penal Code § 3.04(2)(b), a defendant charged with murder (or attempted murder) need only show that he "[believed] that [the use of deadly force] was necessary to protect himself against death, serious bodily injury, kidnapping or [forcible] sexual intercourse" to prevail on a self-defense claim. If the defendant's belief was wrong, and was recklessly, or negligently formed, however, he may be convicted of the type of homicide charge requiring only a reckless or negligent, as the case may be, criminal intent.

The drafters of the Model Penal Code recognized that the wholly subjective test set forth in § 3.04 differed from the existing law in most states by its omission of any requirement of reasonableness. The drafters were also keenly aware that requiring that the actor have a "reasonable belief" rather than just a "belief" would alter the wholly subjective test. . . .

New York did not follow the Model Penal Code's equation of a mistake as to the need to use deadly force with a mistake negating an element of a crime, choosing instead to use a single statutory section which would provide either a complete defense or no defense at all to a defendant charged with any crime involving the use of deadly force. The drafters of the new Penal Law adopted in large part the structure and content of Model Penal Code § 3.04, but, crucially, inserted the word "reasonably" before "believes."

The plurality below [held] that the change in the statutory language from "reasonable ground," used prior to 1965, to "he reasonably believes" in Penal Law § 35.15 evinced a legislative intent to conform to the subjective standard contained in Model Penal Code § 3.04. This argument, however, ignores the plain significance of the insertion of "reasonably." Had the drafters of § 35.15 wanted to adopt a subjective standard, they could have simply used the language of § 3.04. "Believes" by itself requires an honest or genuine belief by a defendant as to the need to use deadly force. Interpreting the statute to require only that the defendant's belief was "reasonable to him," as done by the plurality below, would hardly be different from requiring only a genuine belief; in either case, the defendant's own perceptions could completely exonerate him from any criminal liability.

We cannot lightly impute to the legislature an intent to fundamentally alter the principles of justification to allow the perpetrator of a serious crime to go free simply because that person believed his actions were reasonable and necessary to prevent some perceived harm. To completely exonerate such an individual, no matter how aberrational or bizarre his thought patterns, would allow citizens to set their own standards for the permissible use of force. It would also allow a legally competent defendant suffering from delusions to kill or perform acts of violence with impunity, contrary to fundamental principles of justice and criminal law.

We can only conclude that the legislature retained a reasonableness requirement to avoid giving a license for such actions. The plurality's interpretation, as the dissenters below recognized, excises the impact of the word "reasonably." . . .

Goetz also argues that the introduction of an objective element will preclude a jury from considering factors such as the prior experiences of a given actor and thus, require it to make a determination of "reasonableness" without regard to the actual circumstances of a particular incident. This argument, however, falsely presupposes that an objective standard means that the background and other relevant characteristics of a particular actor must be ignored. To the contrary, . . . a determination of reasonableness must be based on the "circumstances" facing a defendant or his "situation." Such terms encompass more than the physical movements of the potential assailant. [T]hese terms include any relevant knowledge the defendant had about that person. They also necessarily bring in the physical attributes of all persons involved, including the defendant. Furthermore, the defendant's circumstances encompass any prior experiences he had which could provide a reasonable basis for a belief that another person's intentions were to injure or rob him or that the use of deadly force was necessary under the circumstances....

... The grand jury has indicted Goetz. It will now be for the petit jury to decide whether the prosecutor can prove beyond a reasonable doubt that Goetz's reactions were unreasonable and therefore excessive....

Accordingly, the order of the Appellate Division should be reversed, and the dismissed counts of the indictment reinstated.

---

## NOTES ON DEADLY FORCE IN DEFENSE OF SELF AND PROPERTY

**1. Introduction.** In general, one who is free from fault may use force to defend his or her person or property against harm threatened by the unlawful act of another if: (i) the person cannot avoid the threatened harm without using defensive force or giving up some right or privilege; and (ii) the force used for this purpose is not excessive in view of the harm which it is intended to prevent. This general principle has acquired contextual specificity through centuries of judicial development. Separate defenses are usually provided for use of force in defense of person, habitation, and property, and in aid of law enforcement. Cutting across these doctrines is a set of limitations regarding the use of deadly force (force intended or likely to cause death or great bodily harm) as distinguished from non-deadly, or moderate, force. It is in this context, where one person kills another in defense of his or her own interests, that the most controversial issues arise.

The common law and many codes recognize several situations in which the use of deadly force might be privileged. Each of these privileges implicates difficult questions. What are the permissible occasions for defensive use of deadly force? What interests (if any) other than the preservation of life should justify killing an aggressor?

According to Sanford Kadish, the doctrines governing the use of deadly force represent an evolving accommodation of values of personal autonomy and proportionality. Kadish argues that personal autonomy presupposes that "no one may be used as the mere instrument of another." Sanford L. Kadish, Respect for Life and Regard for Rights in the Criminal Law, 64 Cal.L.Rev. 871, 886–88 (1976). Therefore, people have the "right to resist threats to [themselves] or interests closely identified therewith." As Kadish emphasizes, an autonomy-based right to resist aggression has no intrinsic limitation; the victim of aggression may use whatever force is necessary, including deadly force, to protect any of his or her "interests of personality." However, he argues, the principle of autonomy is limited by a concept of proportionality: "[T]he moral right to resist threats is subject to the qualification that the actions necessary to resist the threat must not be out of proportion to the nature of the threat." It is the tension between these two principles, Kadish concludes, that "underlies the perennial controversy and changing shape of the law with respect to defining the interests for whose protection one may kill." He explains:*

> ... The proportionality principle is widely in evidence. It is strongly seen in the reform efforts of recent years ... to confine the right to kill generally to cases where killing is necessary to avoid a danger to life. It is also evidenced in more settled provisions of the law which, while not so strictly defining proportionality, draw the line at some point on what interests deadly force may be used to protect—for example, the various restraints on killing to protect property ... and even the denial of a right to kill to prevent an unaggravated battery. At the same time, however, the autonomy principle [continues to have] its influence. Even under recent statutes one may kill to protect one's property where the threat occurs through a forcible entry of one's dwelling.... Moreover, despite efforts to confine the use of deadly force to prevent felonies threatening the life of the person, the law of most states continues to permit its use in a much wider range of situations, such as whenever any degree of force is used by the aggressor.
>
> Now it may be argued that these latter rules are reflections not of the autonomy principle, but of varying judgments of what interests are proportional to taking the life of the aggressor. The argument has force in cases of killing to prevent crimes like kidnapping and rape, for one may plausibly argue that the interests protected are comparable to that of the victim's life. But one cannot say the same of the interest in remaining where one is, or in protecting one's property from an intruder into one's home, or in preventing any felony whenever some force is used. The strong current of sentiment behind such rules can be understood best as a reflection of the autonomy principle, which extends the right to resist aggression broadly to cover threats to the personality of the victim. It is hard to see from where the force behind the elevation of these distinctly lesser interests can come other than from the moral claim of the person to autonomy over his life.

**2.   Self–Defense.** As the New York Court of Appeals observed in *Goetz*, the prosecutor properly instructed on the justification defense because the evidence before the grand jury "included statements by Goetz that he acted to protect himself from being maimed." All jurisdictions and commentators agree that an actor's interest in preserving his life or protecting himself from serious bodily harm justifies the use of deadly force to repel an aggressor. If the self-defense privilege rests on a balance of the competing harms, why does the preservation of one life (that of Goetz) outweigh the (potential) loss of four lives? Does the balance of evils take account of some interests or values other than the protection of life and physical integrity?

**3.   Prevention of Dangerous Felonies.** Goetz's statement to the police also suggested that he shot the youths "to avert a robbery." At common law, every citizen was entitled to prevent any felony from being committed, regardless of whether he or she was the intended victim. Today, for several reasons, the privilege of crime-prevention has an uncertain status. First, many of the situations covered by this common-law defense are now covered by separate privileges concerning defense of person, habitation, and property against unprovoked attack. Second, the penal law now punishes as felonies a range of misconduct far wider than the major predatory crimes so classified at common law. Third, at common law all felonies were punishable by death; today only the most serious homicides are subject to the capital sanction. Where crime prevention is still recognized as a separate defense, it usually justifies deadly force only to prevent "dangerous" felonies. Statutory formulations typically provide that innocent victims may use deadly force to protect against forcible sexual assault, kidnapping, or robbery.

Media reports about the *Goetz* case suggest that the public is ambivalent about the status of the crime prevention privilege. At the time of the subway shootings, many people apparently believed that the shootings were justified even if Goetz's life was not in danger. Assuming that Goetz was confronted with a demand that he hand over his money—but not with a threat of death or serious bodily harm—should his use of lethal force nonetheless be justified? If justification defenses require that the actor avoid the greater evil, what arguments might Goetz's lawyers offer to suggest that the shootings averted a more serious injury than they inflicted?

**4.   Prevention of Escape.** Consider the following variation of the facts of *Goetz*. Suppose that after Goetz entered the subway car, the four men robbed him and exited the subway at the next stop, threatening to kill him if he went to the police. Suppose further that Goetz followed them onto the subway platform and shouted at them to stop. When they failed to comply, Goetz shot one of the men as he ran away.

On these facts, the use of force would no longer be necessary for Goetz to defend himself or his property against any present threat, since the harm already would have occurred. Although Goetz would be privileged to use reasonable force to recapture his property in fresh pursuit of the thief, it is clear that he would not be justified in using deadly force merely to recover his property. Nor would the assailant's threat to harm him in the future create a present necessity to defend himself.

However, another justification might be available in this situation. Although deadly force was never permitted for the purpose of apprehending a misdemeanant or preventing his escape from custody, the common law was clearly otherwise for fleeing felons:

> If a felony be committed and the felon fly from justice . . . it is the duty of every man to use his best endeavours for preventing an escape; and if in the pursuit the felon be killed, where he cannot otherwise be overtaken, the homicide is justifiable.

1 E. East, Pleas of the Crown 298 (1806). Although some states continue to authorize private citizens to use deadly force to prevent the escape of a person believed to have committed a violent felony, the modern trend is to permit deadly force to be used in such circumstances only by law-enforcement officers and those aiding them. Moreover, police department regulations permit officers to use deadly force only when apprehending offenders who pose a threat of serious harm to others.[a]

Should this hypothetical use of deadly force be justified on the ground that it was necessary to arrest the attackers or to prevent their escape? If not, should the victim ever be permitted to use deadly force to prevent the escape of a felonious attacker? What if the attacker had just killed or raped a family member?

How would this hypothetical be analyzed under the Model Penal Code? Would Goetz be entitled to acquittal under § 3.07(1) and (2), governing use of deadly force to effect an arrest? Under § 3.07(5), governing use of deadly force to prevent the "consummation" of a crime? Under § 3.06(3)(d), governing use of deadly force to prevent "consummation" of robbery? Are the Model Penal Code provisions consistent?

**5. Defense of Habitation.** Under another traditional common-law doctrine, a person was permitted to use deadly force to prevent an entry into his or her home based on the reasonable belief that such force was necessary to prevent robbery, burglary, arson, or felonious assault. This defense applied even if the actor did not fear death or great bodily injury. As a practical matter, of course, circumstances that would arouse a reasonable fear of such dangers often would also arouse fear of death or serious injury. The trend appears to be in the direction of reaffirming a distinct "defense of habitation," which is available even where the fact-finder concludes that deadly force was not reasonably necessary to defend life. See Rollin M. Perkins and Ronald N. Boyce, Criminal Law 1148–54 (3d ed.1982). For example, although most jurisdictions disallow the use of deadly force to prevent a mere trespass or non-felonious attack, the Colorado legislature recently proclaimed that "citizens . . . have a right to expect absolute safety within their own homes," and it enacted a law known as the "make my day statute." Section 18–1–704.5(2) of the Colorado Revised Statutes provides:

> [A]ny occupant of a dwelling is justified in using any degree of physical force, including deadly physical force, against another person when that other person has made an unlawful entry into

---

[a] This policy judgment represents a constitutional limitation. In Tennessee v. Garner, 471 U.S. 1 (1985), the Supreme Court held that the Fourth Amendment limits police officers' use of deadly force in making arrests to those cases where the force is necessary to prevent the escape of one who poses a threat of death or serious bodily harm.

the dwelling, and when the occupant has a reasonable belief that such other person has committed a crime in the dwelling in addition to the uninvited entry, or is committing or intends to commit a crime against a person or property in addition to the uninvited entry, and when the occupant reasonably believes that such other person might use any physical force, no matter how slight, against any occupant.

————

## NOTES ON THE REQUIREMENT OF RETREAT

**1. The Retreat Rule.** Suppose *A*, who is free from fault, is placed in actual peril of deadly attack by *B*, who is wielding a knife. Should *A* be privileged "to stand his ground and resort to deadly force *there* merely because he is where he has a right to be, or must he take advantage of an obviously safe retreat if one is available"? Rollin Perkins, Self–Defense Re-examined, 1 U.C.L.A.L.Rev. 133, 145 (1954). This has been one of the most hotly contested questions in the law of self-defense.

The dispute regarding the "retreat rule" was summarized by the New Jersey Supreme Court in State v. Abbott, 36 N.J. 63, 69–72, 174 A.2d 881, 884–86 (1961):

> The question whether one who is neither the aggressor nor a party to a mutual combat must retreat has divided the authorities. Self-defense is measured against necessity. From that premise one could readily say there was no necessity to kill in self-defense if the use of deadly force could have been avoided by retreat. The critics of the retreat rule do not quarrel with the theoretical validity of this conclusion, but rather condemn it as unrealistic. The law of course should not denounce conduct as criminal when it accords with the behavior of reasonable men. Upon this level, the advocates of no-retreat say the manly thing is to hold one's ground, and hence society should not demand what smacks of cowardice. Adherents of the retreat rule reply it is better that the assailed shall retreat than that the life of another be needlessly spent. They add that not only do right-thinking men agree, but further a rule so requiring may well induce others to adhere to that worthy standard of behavior. There is much dispute as to which view commands the support of ancient precedents. . . .

> Other jurisdictions are closely divided upon the retreat doctrine. . . . The Model Penal Code embraces the retreat rule while acknowledging that on numerical balance a majority of the precedents oppose it.

> We are not persuaded to depart from the principle of retreat. We think it salutary if reasonably limited. Much of the criticism goes not to its inherent validity but rather to unwarranted applications of the rule. For example, it is correctly observed that one can

hardly retreat from a rifle shot at close range. But if the weapon were a knife, a lead of a city block might be well enough. Again, the rule cannot be stated baldly, with indifference to the excitement of the occasion. As Mr. Justice Holmes cryptically put it, "[d]etached reflection cannot be demanded in the presence of an uplifted knife." Brown v. United States, 256 U.S. 335, 343 (1921). Such considerations, however, do not demand that a man should have the absolute right to stand his ground and kill in any and all situations. Rather, they call for a fair and guarded statement of appropriate principles....

We believe the following principles are sound:

1.   The issue of retreat arises only if the defendant resorted to a deadly force. It is deadly force which is not justifiable when an opportunity to retreat is at hand....

Hence it is not the nature of the force defended against which raises the issue of retreat, but rather the nature of the force which the accused employed in his defense. If he does not resort to a deadly force, one who is assailed may hold his ground whether the attack upon him be of a deadly or some lesser character.

2.   What constitutes an opportunity to retreat which will defeat the right of self-defense? As [§ 3.04(2)(b)(ii)] of the Model Penal Code states, deadly force is not justifiable "if the actor *knows* that he can avoid the necessity of using such force *with complete safety* by retreating. ..." We emphasize "knows" and "with complete safety." One who is wrongfully attacked need not risk injury by retreating, even though he could escape with something less than serious bodily injury. It would be unreal to require nice calculations as to the amount of hurt, or to ask him to endure any at all. And the issue is not whether in retrospect it can be found the defendant could have retreated unharmed. Rather the question is whether he knew the opportunity was there, and of course in that inquiry the total circumstances including the attendant excitement must be considered....

Glanville Williams has argued, contrary to the view taken in *Abbott* and the Model Penal Code, that the retreat rule should be abolished. Glanville Williams, Textbook of Criminal Law 462–63 (1978). Although Williams concedes that the privilege of self defense should ordinarily be "limited to circumstances of necessity," he argues that the requirement of necessity is not unqualified. He illustrates his point with the following hypothetical: If *A* says to *B*, "If you don't do as I tell you, I will kill you," *B* is entitled to refuse to obey the order and to resist any attack thereafter initiated by *A* even though *B* could have avoided the necessity of self-defense by complying with the order in the first instance. Similarly, Williams argues, the requirement of necessity should "not generally imply a duty to run away." Even though "many courageous people would rather run away than shed blood," the law should not impose such a duty. To the contrary, he concludes, "one who prefers to stand his ground and then act in necessary self-defence should be allowed to do so, unless he was the initial aggressor."

Which approach is preferable, that proposed by Williams or that endorsed by *Abbott* and the Model Penal Code? Is there a middle ground?

**2. The Wisdom of Rules.** As the *Abbott* court notes, the majority of states reject the retreat rule. However, they also reject the "right to stand one's ground" preferred by Professor Williams. Instead, the preponderant view seems to be the one endorsed by the United States Supreme Court in Brown v. United States, 256 U.S. 335, 343 (1921), that "the failure to retreat is a circumstance to be considered with all the others in order to determine whether the defendant went farther than he was justified in doing; not a categorical proof of guilt."

The debate regarding the retreat rule illustrates one of the generic issues in the formulation of doctrines of personal defense: To what extent should the norms governing the use of defensive force, especially deadly force, be specified by rule rather than be left to particularized applications of standards of "reasonableness" and "necessity." The typical formulation of the retreat rule has been criticized because of its inflexibility: "For the law to attempt a detailed formulation of rights and duties in cases of self-defence would be both futile and unjust—futile because no one can foresee all the possible circumstances in which self-defence might be raised, and unjust insofar as the result of failure to legislate for a particular type of situation might be the absence of rights on a most worthy occasion." A.J. Ashworth, Self–Defence and the Right to Life, 34 Camb.L.J. 282, 292 (1975). On the other hand, the "open-textured" standard of reasonableness—reflected in the majority view that the availability of an avenue of retreat is merely one of the circumstances taken into account in assessing the reasonableness of the defendant's use of deadly force—may be criticized on the grounds that it gives inadequate protection to human life and that it leaves too much room for inconsistent administration of the law.

What are the operational differences—in ruling on sufficiency of the evidence, in framing jury instructions, and in the role of appellate courts—between these two approaches to the retreat problem? Are the outcomes of jury deliberations on self-defense claims likely to depend on which of these instructions is given?

**3. The "Castle" Exception.** Even jurisdictions that have adopted the requirement of retreat recognize an exception for a person attacked in his or her own home. As the court observed in Crawford v. State, 231 Md. 354, 190 A.2d 538 (1963), "a man faced with the danger of an attack upon his dwelling need not retreat ... but ... if necessary to repel the attack, may kill the attacker." The rationale for the so-called "castle" doctrine was reviewed by Judge Cardozo in People v. Tomlins, 213 N.Y. 240, 243–44, 107 N.E. 496, 497–98 (1914), a case in which a father killed his 22–year-old son, who had attacked him in the family home:

> It is not now and never has been the law that a man assailed in his own dwelling, is bound to retreat. If assailed there, he may

stand his ground and resist the attack. He is under no duty to take to the fields and the highways, a fugitive from his own home. More than 200 years ago it was said by Lord Chief Justice Hale (1 M. Hale, Pleas of the Crown 486): In case a man is assailed in his own house, he "need not flee as far as he can as in other cases of se defendendo, for he hath the protection of his house to excuse him from flying, as that would be to give up the protection of his house to his adversary by his flight." Flight is for sanctuary and shelter, and shelter, if not sanctuary, is in the home. That there is, in such a situation, no duty to retreat is, we think, the settled law in the United States as in England. . . . The rule is the same whether the attack proceeds from some other occupant or from an intruder. It was so adjudged in Jones v. State, 76 Ala. 8, 14 (1884). "Why," it was there inquired, "should one retreat from his own house, when assailed by a partner or cotenant, any more than when assailed by a stranger who is lawfully upon the premises? Whither shall he flee, and how far, and when may he be permitted to return?" We think that the conclusion there reached is sustained by principle, and we have not been referred to any decision to the contrary. . . .

If such a doctrine is to be embraced, questions obviously will arise as to what constitutes a "castle" and whether any other places aside from a dwelling should qualify. The Model Penal Code, which requires retreat if it can be accomplished "with complete safety," incorporates the traditional exception and does not require retreat from a person's "dwelling or place of work, unless [the actor] was the initial aggressor or is assailed in his place of work by another person whose place of work the actor knows it to be." Section 3.04(2)(b)(ii)(1). Are these exceptions to the retreat rule appropriate? Why did the drafters fail to require retreat in the workplace if it can be accomplished with complete safety? Why should it make any difference that the assailant and the victim work in the same place? If this makes a difference, why did the drafters fail to require a person to retreat from his home when the assailant also lives there? Can rules of this detail sensibly be prescribed in legislation?

———

## NOTES ON THE EFFECT OF MISTAKE IN CLAIMS OF SELF-DEFENSE

**1. Introduction.** The court in *Goetz* emphasized that the self-defense statute does not require that the "actor's belief as to the intention of another person to inflict serious injury be correct in order for the use of deadly force to be justified." Rather, deadly force may be "justified" even if the actor's beliefs as to the need for lethal force "turned out to be wrong." As the discussion in *Goetz* reflects, courts assume that juries are capable of predicting what the alleged attacker ultimately would have done had the defendant not resisted. Assuming that a jury engages in this predictive exercise and concludes that the defendant's belief in the need to use deadly force was wrong, the question arises: Under what circumstances, if any, should such mistaken belief support a self-defense claim?

**2. Reasonable Mistake.** Under *Goetz*, the right to kill another in self-defense is triggered in cases where the actor honestly and reasonably believes in the need to use deadly force, even if hindsight reveals that such belief was not correct. The common law and modern statutes concur in this view. An honest and reasonable belief in the existence of justificatory facts is ordinarily a defense, even if the belief turns to have been mistaken.[a] Since one of the most crucial and difficult issues in the law of self-defense is the meaning of the term "reasonable belief," that issue is discussed in separate notes below.

**3. Unreasonable Mistake.** Assume that jurors determined that Goetz's apprehension of harm was unreasonable. The youths did not display a weapon, and their conduct—asking Goetz "how are you" and requesting that he give them five dollars—was not life-threatening. Even if Goetz genuinely feared that they planned to maim him, he was wrong, and his fear was not reasonable. What would be the effect of such a mistake under the New York self-defense provision?

**4. Mistake and the Model Penal Code.** In *Goetz*, the New York Court of Appeals contrasts New York's approach to the use of defensive force—which "provide[s] either a complete defense or no defense at all"— to the approach offered by the drafters of the Model Penal Code. The Model Code endorses the doctrine of "imperfect justification." The common law developed this doctrine in response to the following problem. A person who intentionally kills another ordinarily is guilty of murder. If an actor intentionally kills another in the honest and reasonable, but mistaken, belief that deadly force is essential to the actor's self-defense, the actor is guilty of no crime. But if the actor's belief in the necessity of deadly force is unreasonable, the actor has no defense and is guilty of murder, even though liability for murder generally requires more than negligence. Under the doctrine of "imperfect justification," an unreasonable belief in the existence of justificatory facts negates the mens rea required for murder. The unreasonable mistake, however, provides no defense to the lesser charge of manslaughter. The effect is that unreasonable mistake is a mitigation but not a complete defense.

The Model Penal Code generalizes the idea of imperfect justification. This is done by linking the kind of mistake deemed exculpatory with the kind of culpability required by the definition of the offense. Conceptually, the scheme is quite simple. A person who believes, however unreasonably, in the existence of justificatory facts has a defense to any crime requiring a culpability of purpose or knowledge. For a crime requiring recklessness, the mistaken belief must be not only sincere but also non-reckless. And for a

[a] It is not clear that the common law uniformly recognized reasonable mistake as a defense for all doctrines of justification. The position stated above seems to have been firmly established for self defense, however, which is the paradigm doctrine of justifica-tion and the principal context for litigation of such questions. For an illuminating descrip-tion and criticism of the literature on mistak-en justification, see Mitchell N. Berman, Jus-tification and Excuse, Law and Morality, 53 Duke L.J. 1, 39–58 (2003).

crime requiring only negligence, the mistaken belief is exculpatory if non-negligent.

Implementation of this scheme is technically elaborate. It is accomplished in two steps. First, each of the several justification defenses is defined in purely subjective terms. For example, § 3.04(1) provides that "the use of force upon or toward another person is justifiable when the actor *believes* that such force is immediately necessary for the purpose of protecting himself against the use of unlawful force by such other person on the present occasion" (emphasis added). Section 3.04(2)(b) provides that the use of deadly force in self-defense is not justified "unless the actor *believes* that such force is necessary to protect himself against death, serious bodily harm, kidnapping or sexual intercourse compelled by force or threat ..." (emphasis added). If these provisions were left unqualified, an honest belief in the necessity of using deadly force would be a defense to any charge of assault or homicide, no matter how reckless or negligent the actor might have been in forming that belief.

Section 3.09(2) provides the second step:

> When the actor believes that the use of force upon or toward the person of another is necessary for any of the purposes for which such belief would establish a justification ... but the actor is reckless or negligent in having such belief or in acquiring or failing to acquire any knowledge or belief which is material to the justifiability of his use of force, the justification ... is unavailable in a prosecution for an offense for which recklessness or negligence, as the case may be, suffices to establish culpability.

This scheme achieves a symmetry between the kind of belief recognized as a defense and the kind of culpability required by the definition of the crime. The rationale for this approach, however, is not merely aesthetic. The Model Code treatment of mistaken belief in the existence of justificatory facts is an essential feature of its general commitment to the proposition that criminal punishment should be proportional to the culpability manifested by the defendant.

**5. Excessive Use of Defensive Force.** In general, a person who responds to unlawful aggression with excessive force is guilty of the assaultive offense applicable to his or her conduct. Although the provoking circumstances undoubtedly will influence prosecutorial charging and plea-bargaining decisions, the fact that a person who uses excessive force was defending against unlawful aggression is technically immaterial to the grade of the offense. However, a person who kills an aggressor whose conduct justified only moderate force would not be liable for murder in most jurisdictions. Instead, the conviction would be for manslaughter. In most cases, this would be because the actor responded in the "heat of passion" to the aggressor's provocation and therefore would be said to lack the "malice aforethought" required for a murder conviction.[b]

---

[b] The concept of provocation is explored in Chapter 8.

## NOTES ON THE MEANING OF "REASONABLE" BELIEF

**1.  Objective Reasonableness.** In *Goetz*, the New York Court of Appeals rejected the standard employed by the intermediate appellate court for evaluating whether the accused had a reasonable belief in the need to use deadly force. The courts disagreed over the perspective to be used to evaluate the reasonableness of the defendant's belief.

The intermediate appellate court concluded that the test "is whether a defendant's beliefs and reactions were 'reasonable to him.' " The New York Court of Appeals rejected this standard on the ground that it was "wholly subjective," effectively requiring jurors to acquit a defendant who honestly believed "that his own actions were warranted and were reasonable ..., regardless of what anyone else in defendant's situation might have concluded." According to the Court of Appeals, the defendant's belief must comport with an "objective" standard of reasonableness. Under this "objective" inquiry, jurors must decide whether the defendant's beliefs would be held by a reasonable person in the defendant's "situation." This standard depends on precisely what factors or circumstances are encompassed by the defendant's "situation." What factors does the Court of Appeals mention?

From the time of the subway shooting through the trial and its aftermath, the *Goetz* case has raised explosive questions concerning racism in the criminal justice system. Goetz is white, and the four men he shot are black. For purposes of the present discussion, the question is whether race should have any bearing on the reasonableness of Goetz's belief that the men intended to maim or rob him. Although the Court of Appeals did not mention this issue, its description of the defendant's "situation" might be interpreted to include inferences about a person's dangerousness arising from his or her race. Is the race of the alleged attackers "relevant knowledge" that Goetz possessed "which could provide a reasonable basis" for a belief that their intentions were to injure or rob him?

When the case went to trial, the evidence included statements Goetz made to police and prosecutors in which he mentioned that in 1981 he had been mugged and seriously injured by three men. As George Fletcher explains, Goetz's defense did not bring out the fact that the men who attacked Goetz in 1981 were black or otherwise explicitly appeal to racist bias. However, Fletcher contends that Goetz's defense team made a powerful indirect appeal to racist assumptions:*

> This silence about the race of the prior muggers is particularly striking, for a good case can be made for the legal relevance of all of Goetz's prior experiences that shaped his fears and his violent reaction [on the subway.] Does it not bear upon the reasonableness of his response that he was once mugged by youths who conformed in age, gender, and race to those whom he confronted the second time? Some judges interviewed respond that they would have

* Reprinted with the permission of The Free Press, a division of Simon & Schuster from A Crime of Self–Defense: Bernhard Goetz and the Law on Trial by George P. Fletcher. Copyright © 1988 by George P. Fletcher.

regarded it as permissible for the witness to the prior mugging to disclose the race of the assailants to the jury. Other lawyers active in civil rights causes insist that ... the principle of color-blind justice would require suppression of all racial factors bearing on Goetz's acts.

The question whether a reasonable person considers race in assessing the danger that four youths on the subway might represent goes to the heart of what the law demands of us. The statistically ordinary New Yorker would be more apprehensive of the "kind of people" who mugged him once, and it is difficult to expect the ordinary person in our time not to perceive race as one—just one—of the factors defining the "kind" of person who poses a danger. The law, however, may demand that we surmount racially based intuitions of danger. Though ... there is no settled law on this issue, the standard of reasonableness may require us to be better than we really are.

Reading the record of the *Goetz* case, one hardly finds an explicit reference to the race of anyone. But indirectly and covertly, the defense played on the racial factor. [Defense counsel's] strategy of relentlessly attacking the "gang of four," "the predators" on society, calling them "vultures" and "savages," carried undeniable racial overtones....

George P. Fletcher, A Crime of Self Defense: Bernhard Goetz and the Law on Trial 206 (1988).

Fletcher concludes that the defense strategy was effective precisely because it "remained hidden behind innuendo and suggestion." An open conversation about racial fear might have assisted the jurors to consider rationally and to reject their own racial biases. In any event, the petit jury acquitted Goetz on all four charges of attempted murder, and, as Fletcher points out, many members of the public seem to have interpreted the verdict as a declaration that Goetz's use of deadly force was reasonable.

State v. Brown, 91 N.M. 320, 573 P.2d 675 (1977), raises additional questions about the relationship between race and the reasonableness of an actor's belief that he needs to use deadly force. Brown was a black man who was convicted of two counts of assault upon a police officer with intent to kill. Brown conceded that he shot the officers, but he argued that he did so in self-defense. At trial, Brown testified that he feared the officers because the police "hassled" him and other black persons in his neighborhood. The trial court allowed Brown and other defense witnesses to describe specific encounters between Brown and police officers, in which the officers harassed and threatened Brown. However, the trial court refused the defense's proffer of testimony by a social psychologist concerning "police conduct toward minority groups and the perception by minority groups, particularly blacks, that the police are a threat to minority group members." On appeal, the Court of Appeals of New Mexico held that exclusion of the expert's testimony was reversible error. Such testimony was relevant to an element of self-defense, namely, whether Brown feared that he was in immediate danger of bodily harm. Moreover, the psychologist's testimony may have rebutted an inference that Brown acted not out of fear, but out "of anger and ... rejection of authority." Does the expert testimony also support the conclusion that Brown's fear was "objectively" reasonable under the *Goetz* standard? Do Fletcher's concerns about the invidious implications of the defense strategy in *Goetz* apply with equal force to the defense theory in *Brown*?

**2. Subjective Reasonableness.** The court in *Goetz* remarked that some states apply a subjective standard of reasonableness " 'and judge from the standpoint of the very defendant concerned.' "[a] In State v. Leidholm, 334 N.W.2d 811 (1983), the Supreme Court of North Dakota adopted a subjective definition of reasonableness and endeavored to explain the distinction between the objective and subjective approaches:

> Courts have traditionally distinguished between standards of reasonableness by characterizing them as either "objective" or "subjective." An objective standard of reasonableness requires the factfinder to view the circumstances surrounding the accused at the time he used force from the standpoint of a hypothetical reasonable and prudent person. Ordinarily, under such a view, the unique physical and psychological characteristics of the accused are not taken into consideration in judging the reasonableness of the accused's belief.

> This is not the case, however, where a subjective standard of reasonableness is employed. Under the subjective standard the issue is not whether the circumstances attending the accused's use of force would be sufficient to create in the mind of a reasonable and prudent person the belief that the use of force is necessary ..., but rather whether the circumstances are sufficient to induce in *the accused* an honest and reasonable belief that he must use force to defend himself against imminent harm....

> Because ... we agree ... that a subjective standard is the more just, we [adopt such standard.]

> The practical and logical consequence of this interpretation is that an accused's actions are to be viewed from the standpoint of a person whose mental and physical characteristics are like the accused's and who sees what the accused sees and knows what the accused knows. For example, if the accused is a timid, diminutive male, the factfinder must consider these characteristics in assessing the reasonableness of his belief. If, on the other hand, the accused is a strong, courageous, and capable female, the factfinder must consider these characteristics in judging the reasonableness of her belief.

[a] Ohio appears to employ a purely subjective perspective. See Nelson v. State, 42 Ohio App. 252, 181 N.E. 448 (1932).

Is the standard endorsed by the New York Court of Appeals in *Goetz* all that different from the "subjective standard of reasonableness" adopted in *Leidholm*? Is *Leidholm* a wholly "subjective" standard? What is the difference between (a) a standard that asks whether the reasonable person in the defendant's situation would have believed deadly force was necessary and (b) a standard that asks whether the accused reasonably believed that deadly force was necessary?

The court in *Leidholm* asserts that a subjective standard of reasonableness is "more just" than an objective standard.[b] Perhaps the judges believed that individuals differ markedly in their reactions to stress and in their susceptibility to panic. If that is the case, it may be difficult, if not impossible, to identify a community standard to which actors who subjectively perceive a deadly peril should be required to conform. Glanville Williams defends a subjective approach in his Textbook of Criminal Law 452 (1978). He argues that the reasonableness requirement is designed to encourage people to verify their beliefs before acting and to compel compliance with well-known rules of prudence. However, persons who are convinced they are about to be attacked tend to act instantly and instinctively. In such cases, he argues, punishment serves no utilitarian purpose:

> ... No rule of prudence decides the question whether another person is about to launch a fierce attack on you. Generally there will be no way in which the defender can check the validity of his belief, and such a situation is so unlikely to be repeated that he will probably not benefit from experience. Also, a defender is subject to the strong emotion of fear, which may well warp his judgment. If the law is to allow self-defence at all, must it now allow it on the facts as they appear to the defender whether reasonably or unreasonably?

**3. What Difference Does It Make?** In order to identify and evaluate the difference between the objective and subjective standards, consider the following case.[c]

In June 1994 in Nashville, Tennessee, Charles Langley shot and killed Harry Woods. At his trial for first-degree murder, Langley argued that the killing was justified because he had acted in self-defense. Just before the killing, Langley and his father were refinishing hardwood floors at a mansion that was undergoing renovation. Woods arrived at the mansion to fix the plumbing; he was accompanied by his son and nephew. Ignoring signs warning them to stay off the floors, the three plumbers walked across

---

[b] For an illuminating discussion of why a self-defense theory that incorporates some subjective criteria is preferable for purposes of both moral philosophy and criminal law, see Russell Christopher, Self-Defense and Defense of Others, 27 Phil. & Pub. Affairs 123 (1998).

[c] The following description of the *Langley* case is based on Kirk Loggins, Suspect

"Scared to Death" Doctor Says, The Tennessean, Sept. 28, 1995, at B1; Kirk Loggins, Floor Finisher Found Not Guilty of Murder, The Tennessean, Sept. 29, 1995, at A1; Toni Dew, Self–Defense, Not Murder Verdict, For Man Who Shot, Killed Plumber, The Nashville Banner, Sept. 29, 1995, at B3.

a floor that Langley had just finished sanding. Woods's son and Langley exchanged harsh words. Langley picked up a linoleum knife and said that he would cut the plumber's throat if he walked on the floor again. Upon hearing about Langley's threat, Woods became very angry and tried to hit Langley with a lead pipe. The job foreman intervened and separated the men, but Woods managed to kick Langley in the side. Langley went outside the mansion to his truck, retrieved a semiautomatic pistol, and placed the gun in the back of his waistband. He then stood in the yard talking with the job foreman. At this point, Woods came running towards them. Woods was not armed, but he shoved the foreman out of the way in an attempt to get at Langley. Langley opened fire and shot Woods four or five times, with two shots hitting Woods in the back. Langley was 30 years old, stood five feet, six inches tall, and weighed 130 pounds. Woods was 48 years old, six feet tall, and 220 pounds.

Before the trial, Langley was examined by a clinical psychologist and a psychiatrist. The experts concluded that Langley was an insecure and usually passive man. He was much more likely than the average person to become frightened quickly when he felt threatened. He felt vulnerable because of his small size and because he was tormented by bullies when he was in school. Langley was not an angry person; if given the chance, he would run away from confrontations. At the time he shot Woods, Langley was scared to death.

What would the result be under the "objective" standard employed by *Goetz*? Under the "objective" standard described and rejected by the court in *Leidholm*? Under the "subjective" standard endorsed by *Leidholm*? In applying these standards, which of the foregoing facts about the confrontation, about Langley, and about Woods would jurors be permitted to consider?

————

# State v. Kelly

Supreme Court of New Jersey, 1984.
97 N.J. 178, 478 A.2d 364.

■ WILENTZ, C.J. . . . On May 24, 1980, defendant, Gladys Kelly, stabbed her husband, Ernest, with a pair of scissors. He died shortly thereafter. . . .

Ms. Kelly was indicted for murder. At trial, she did not deny stabbing her husband, but asserted that her action was in self-defense. To establish the requisite state of mind for her self-defense claim, Ms. Kelly called Dr. Lois Veronen as an expert witness to testify about the battered-woman's syndrome. After hearing a lengthy voir dire examination of Dr. Veronen, the trial court ruled that expert testimony concerning the syndrome was inadmissible on the self-defense issue. . . . Apparently the court believed that the sole purpose of this testimony was to explain and justify defendant's perception of the danger rather than to show the objective reasonableness of that perception. Ms. Kelly was convicted of reckless manslaughter....

The Kellys had a stormy [seven-year] marriage. Some of the details of their relationship, especially the stabbing, are disputed. The following is Ms. Kelly's version of what happened—a version that the jury could have accepted and, if they had, a version that would make the proffered expert testimony not only relevant, but critical.

The day after the marriage, Mr. Kelly got drunk and knocked Ms. Kelly down. Although a period of calm followed the initial attack, the next seven years were accompanied by periodic and frequent beatings, sometimes as often as once a week. During the attacks, which generally occurred when Mr. Kelly was drunk, he threatened to kill Ms. Kelly and to cut off parts of her body if she tried to leave him. Mr. Kelly often moved out of the house after an attack, later returning with a promise that he would change his ways. Until the day of the homicide, only one of the attacks had taken place in public.

[On the morning of the stabbing, Mr. Kelly] left for work. Ms. Kelly next saw her husband late that afternoon at a friend's house. She had gone there with her daughter, Annette, to ask Ernest for money to buy food. He told her to wait until they got home, and shortly thereafter the Kellys left. After walking past several houses, Mr. Kelly, who was drunk, angrily asked "What the hell did you come around here for?" He then grabbed the collar of her dress, and the two fell to the ground. He choked her by pushing his fingers against her throat, punched or hit her face, and bit her leg.

A crowd gathered on the street. Two men from the crowd separated them, just as Gladys felt that she was "passing out" from being choked. Fearing that Annette had been pushed around in the crowd, Gladys then left to look for her....

After finding her daughter, Ms. Kelly then observed Mr. Kelly running toward her with his hands raised. Within seconds he was right next to her. Unsure of whether he had armed himself while she was looking for their daughter, and thinking that he had come back to kill her, she grabbed a pair of scissors from her pocketbook. She tried to scare him away, but instead stabbed him.[1] ...

In the past decade social scientists and the legal community began to examine the forces that generate and perpetuate wife beating and violence in the family.[2] What has been revealed is that the problem affects many more people than had been thought....

---

[1] This version of the homicide—with a drunk Mr. Kelly as the aggressor both in pushing Ms. Kelly to the ground and again in rushing at her with his hands in a threatening position after the two had been separated—is sharply disputed by the state. The prosecution presented testimony intended to show that the initial scuffle was started by Gladys; that upon disentanglement, while she was restrained by bystanders, she stated that she intended to kill Ernest; that she then chased after him, and upon catching up with him stabbed him....

[2] The works that comprise the basic study of the problem of battered women are all relatively recent. See, e.g., Roger Langley

Due to the high incidence of unreported abuse (the FBI and other law enforcement experts believe that wife abuse is the most unreported crime in the United States), estimates vary of the number of American women who are beaten regularly by their husband, boyfriend, or the dominant male figure in their lives. One recent estimate puts the number of women beaten yearly at over one million. The state police statistics show more than 18,000 *reported* cases of domestic violence in New Jersey during the first nine months of 1983, in 83% of which the victim was female. It is clear that the American home, once assumed to be the cornerstone of our society, is often a violent place.

While common-law notions that assigned an inferior status to women, and to wives in particular, no longer represent the state of the law as reflected in statutes and cases, many commentators assert that a bias against battered women still exists, institutionalized in the attitudes of law enforcement agencies unwilling to pursue or uninterested in pursuing wife-beating cases. See Comment, The Battered Wife's Dilemma: Kill or be Killed, 32 Hastings L.J., 895, 897–911 (1981)....

As the problem of battered women has begun to receive more attention, sociologists and psychologists have begun to focus on the effects a sustained pattern of physical and psychological abuse can have on a woman. The effects of such abuse are what some scientific observers have termed "the battered-woman's syndrome," a series of common characteristics that appear in women who are abused physically and psychologically over an extended period of time by the dominant male figure in their lives....

According to Dr. [Lenore] Walker, relationships characterized by physical abuse tend to develop battering cycles. Violent behavior directed at the woman occurs in three distinct and repetitive stages that vary both in duration and intensity depending on the individuals involved.

Phase one of the battering cycle is referred to as the "tension-building stage," during which the battering male engages in minor battering incidents and verbal abuse while the woman, beset by fear and tension, attempts to be as placating and passive as possible in order to stave off more serious violence.

Phase two of the battering cycle is the "acute battering incident." At some point during phase one, the tension between the battered woman and the batterer becomes intolerable and more serious violence inevitable. The triggering event that initiates phase two is most often an internal or external event in the life of the battering male, but provocation for more severe violence is sometimes provided by the woman who can no longer tolerate or control her phase-one anger and anxiety.

& Richard C. Levy, Wife Beating: The Silent Crisis (1979); Del Martin, Battered Wives (1976); Lenore E. Walker, The Battered Woman (1979); Richard J. Gelles, The Violent Home: A Study of Physical Aggression Between Husbands and Wives (1971); Battered Women: A Psychosociological Study of Domestic Violence (Maria Roy ed. 1977).

Phase three of the battering cycle is characterized by extreme contrition and loving behavior on the part of the battering male. During this period the man will often mix his pleas for forgiveness and protestations of devotion with promises to seek professional help, to stop drinking,[5] and to refrain from further violence. For some couples, this period of relative calm may last as long as several months, but in a battering relationship the affection and contrition of the man will eventually fade and phase one of the cycle will start anew.

The cyclical nature of battering behavior helps explain why more women simply do not leave their abusers. The loving behavior demonstrated by the batterer during phase three reinforces whatever hopes these women might have for their mate's reform and keeps them bound to the relationship. Roger Langley & Richard C. Levy, Wife Beating: The Silent Crisis 112–14 (1977).

Some women may even perceive the battering cycle as normal, especially if they grew up in a violent household. Battered Women, A Psychosociological Study of Domestic Violence 60 (Maria Roy ed. 1977); Del Martin, Battered Wives, 60 (1981). Or they may simply not wish to acknowledge the reality of their situation. Terry Davidson, Conjugal Crime, at 50 (1978) ("The middle-class battered wife's response to her situation tends to be withdrawal, silence and denial. . . .").

Other women, however, become so demoralized and degraded by the fact that they cannot predict or control the violence that they sink into a state of psychological paralysis and become unable to take any action at all to improve or alter the situation. There is a tendency in battered women to believe in the omnipotence or strength of their battering husbands and thus to feel that any attempt to resist them is hopeless.

In addition to these psychological impacts, external social and economic factors often make it difficult for some women to extricate themselves from battering relationships. A woman without independent financial resources who wishes to leave her husband often finds it difficult to do so because of a lack of material and social resources.

Even with the progress of the last decade, women typically make less money and hold less prestigious jobs than men, and are more responsible for child care. Thus, in a violent confrontation where the first reaction might be to flee, women realize soon that there may be no place to go. Moreover, the stigma that attaches to a woman who leaves the family unit without her children undoubtedly acts as a further deterrent to moving out.

In addition, battered women, when they want to leave the relationship, are typically unwilling to reach out and confide in their friends, family, or

---

[5] Alcohol is often an important component of violence toward women. Evidence points to a correlation between alcohol and violent acts between family members. In one British study, 44 of 100 cases of wife abuse occurred when the husband was drunk. John J. Gayford, Wife Battering: A Preliminary Survey of 100 Cases, 1 Brit. Med. J. 194–97 (1975). . . .

the police, either out of shame and humiliation, fear of reprisal by their husband, or the feeling they will not be believed.

Dr. Walker and other commentators have identified several common personality traits of the battered woman: low self-esteem, traditional beliefs about the home, the family, and the female sex role, tremendous feelings of guilt that their marriages are failing, and the tendency to accept responsibility for the batterer's actions.

Finally, battered women are often hesitant to leave a battering relationship because, in addition to their hope of reform on the part of their spouse, they harbor a deep concern about the possible response leaving might provoke in their mates. They literally become trapped by their own fear. Case histories are replete with instances in which a battered wife left her husband only to have him pursue her and subject her to an even more brutal attack.

The combination of all these symptoms—resulting from sustained psychological and physical trauma compounded by aggravating social and economic factors—constitutes the battered-woman's syndrome. Only by understanding these unique pressures that force battered women to remain with their mates, despite their long-standing and reasonable fear of severe bodily harm and the isolation that being a battered woman creates, can a battered woman's state of mind be accurately and fairly understood.

The voir dire testimony of Dr. Veronen ... conformed essentially to this outline of the battered-woman's syndrome. Dr. Veronen ... documented, based on her own considerable experience in counseling, treating, and studying battered women, and her familiarity with the work of others in the field, the feelings of anxiety, self-blame, isolation, and, above all, fear that plagues these women and leaves them prey to a psychological paralysis that hinders their ability to break free or seek help. . . .

Dr. Veronen described the various psychological tests and examinations she had performed in connection with her independent research. These tests and their methodology, including their interpretation, are, according to Dr. Veronen, widely accepted by clinical psychologists. Applying this methodology to defendant (who was subjected to all of the tests, including a five-hour interview), Dr. Veronen concluded that defendant was a battered woman and subject to the battered-woman's syndrome.

In addition, Dr. Veronen was prepared to testify as to how, as a battered woman, Gladys Kelly perceived her situation at the time of the stabbing, and why, in her opinion, defendant did not leave her husband despite the constant beatings she endured.

Whether expert testimony on the battered-woman's syndrome should be admitted in this case depends on whether it is relevant to defendant's claim of self-defense, and, in any event, on whether the proffer meets the standards for admission of expert testimony in this state. We examine first the law of self-defense and consider whether the expert testimony is relevant. . . .

While it is not imperative that *actual* necessity exist, a valid plea of self-defense will not lie absent an actual (that is, honest) belief on the part of the defendant in the necessity of using force. [Further,] even when the defendant's belief in the need to kill in self-defense is conceded to be sincere, if it is found to have been unreasonable under the circumstances, such a belief cannot be held to constitute complete justification for a homicide. As with the determination of the existence of the defendant's belief, the question of the reasonableness of this belief "is to be determined by the jury, not the defendant, in light of the circumstances existing at the time of the homicide." . . .

Gladys Kelly claims that she stabbed her husband in self-defense, believing he was about to kill her. The gist of the state's case was that Gladys Kelly was the aggressor, that she consciously intended to kill her husband, and that she certainly was not acting in self-defense.

The credibility of Gladys Kelly is a critical issue in this case. If the jury does not believe Gladys Kelly's account, it cannot find she acted in self-defense. The expert testimony offered was directly relevant to one of the critical elements of that account, namely, what Gladys Kelly believed at the time of the stabbing, and was thus material to establish the honesty of her stated belief that she was in imminent danger of death.[10] . . .

As can be seen from our discussion of the expert testimony, Dr. Veronen would have bolstered Gladys Kelly's credibility. Specifically, by showing that her experience, although concededly difficult to comprehend, was common to that of other women who had been in similarly abusive relationships, Dr. Veronen would have helped the jury understand that Gladys Kelly could have honestly feared that she would suffer serious bodily harm from her husband's attacks, yet still remain with him. This, in turn, would support Ms. Kelly's testimony about her state of mind (that is, that she honestly feared serious bodily harm) at the time of the stabbing. . . .

We also find the expert testimony relevant to the reasonableness of defendant's belief that she was in imminent danger of death or serious injury. We do not mean that the expert's testimony could be used to show that it was understandable that a battered woman might believe that her life was in danger when indeed it was not and when a reasonable person would not have so believed. . . . Expert testimony in that direction would be relevant solely to the honesty of defendant's belief, not its objective reasonableness. Rather, our conclusion is that the expert's testimony, if

[10] The factual contentions of the parties eliminated any issue concerning the duty to retreat. If the state's version is accepted, defendant is the aggressor; if defendant's version is accepted, the possibility of retreat is excluded by virtue of the nature of the attack that defendant claims took place. We do not understand that the state claims defendant breached that duty under any version of the facts. If, however, the duty becomes an issue on retrial, the trial court will have to determine the relevancy of the battered-woman's syndrome to that issue. Without passing on that question, it appears to us to be a different question from whether the syndrome is relevant to defendant's failure to leave her husband in the past.

accepted by the jury, would have aided it in determining whether, under the circumstances, a reasonable person would have believed there was imminent danger to her life.

At the heart of the claim of self-defense was defendant's story that she had been repeatedly subjected to "beatings" over the course of her marriage. While defendant's testimony was somewhat lacking in detail, a juror could infer from the use of the word "beatings," as well as the detail given concerning some of these events (the choking, the biting, the use of fists), that these physical assaults posed a risk of serious injury or death. When that regular pattern of serious physical abuse is combined with defendant's claim that the decedent sometimes threatened to kill her, defendant's statement that on this occasion she thought she might be killed when she saw Mr. Kelly running toward her could be found to reflect a reasonable fear; that is, it could so be found if the jury believed Gladys Kelly's story of the prior beatings, if it believed her story of the prior threats, and, of course, if it believed her story of the events of that particular day.

The crucial issue of fact on which this expert's testimony would bear is why, given such allegedly severe and constant beatings, combined with threats to kill, defendant had not long ago left decedent. Whether raised by the prosecutor as a factual issue or not, our own common knowledge tells us that most of us, including the ordinary juror, would ask himself or herself just such a question. And our knowledge is bolstered by the experts' knowledge, for the experts point out that one of the common myths, apparently believed by most people, is that battered wives are free to leave. To some, this misconception is followed by the observation that the battered wife is masochistic, proven by her refusal to leave despite the severe beatings; to others, however, the fact that the battered wife stays on unquestionably suggests that the "beatings" could not have been too bad for if they had been, she certainly would have left. The expert could clear up these myths, by explaining that one of the common characteristics of a battered wife is her *inability* to leave despite such constant beatings; her "learned helplessness"; her lack of anywhere to go; her feeling that if she tried to leave, she would be subjected to even more merciless treatment; her belief in the omnipotence of her battering husband; and sometimes her hope that her husband will change his ways.

Unfortunately, in this case the state reinforced the myths about battered women. On cross-examination, when discussing an occasion when Mr. Kelly temporarily moved out of the house, the state repeatedly asked Ms. Kelly: "You wanted him back, didn't you?" The implication was clear: domestic life could not have been too bad if she wanted him back. In its closing argument, the state trivialized the severity of the beatings, saying:

> I'm not going to say they happened or they didn't happen, but life isn't pretty. Life is not a bowl of cherries. [E]ach and every person who takes a breath has problems. Defense counsel says bruised and battered. Is there any one of us who hasn't been battered by life in some manner or means?

Even had the state not taken this approach, however, expert testimony would be essential to rebut the general misconceptions regarding battered women. . . .

Since a retrial is necessary, we think it advisable to indicate the limit of the expert's testimony on this issue of reasonableness. It would not be proper for the expert to express the opinion that defendant's belief on that day was reasonable, not because this is the ultimate issue, but because the area of *expert* knowledge relates, in this regard, to the reasons for defendant's failure to leave her husband. Either the jury accepts or rejects that explanation and, based on that, credits defendant's stories about the beatings she suffered. No expert is needed, however, once the jury has made up its mind on those issues, to tell the jury the logical conclusion, namely, that a person who has in fact been severely and continuously beaten might very well reasonably fear that the imminent beating she was about to suffer could be either life-threatening or pose a risk of serious injury. What the expert could state was that defendant had the battered-woman's syndrome, and could explain that syndrome in detail, relating its characteristics to defendant, but only to enable the jury better to determine the honesty and reasonableness of defendant's belief. Depending on its content, the expert's testimony might also enable the jury to find that the battered wife, because of the prior beatings, numerous beatings, as often as once a week, for seven years, from the day they were married to the day he died, is particularly able to predict accurately the likely extent of violence in any attack on her. That conclusion could significantly affect the jury's evaluation of the reasonableness of defendant's fear for her life.[13]

Having determined that testimony about the battered-woman's syndrome is relevant, we now consider whether Dr. Veronen's testimony satisfies the limitations placed on expert testimony by Evidence Rule 56(2) and by applicable case law. . . .

As previously discussed, a battering relationship embodies psychological and societal features that are not well understood by lay observers.

---

[13] At least two other courts agree that expert testimony about the battered-woman's syndrome is relevant to show the reasonableness as well as the honesty of defendant's fear of serious bodily harm. . . .

Defendant's counsel at oral argument made it clear that defendant's basic contention was that her belief in the immediate need to use deadly force was both honest and reasonable; and that the evidence concerning the battered-woman's syndrome was being offered solely on that issue. We therefore are not faced with any claim that a battered woman's honest belief in the need to use deadly force, even if objectively unreasonable, constitutes justification so long as its unreasonableness results from the psychological impact of the beatings. The effect of cases like State v. Sikora, 44 N.J. 453, 210 A.2d 193 (1965) (opinion of psychiatrist that acts of defendant, admittedly sane, were predetermined by interaction of events and his abnormal character held inadmissible on issue of premeditation), and State v. Bess, 53 N.J. 10, 247 A.2d 669 (1968) (reasonableness of belief in need for deadly force not measured by what would appear "reasonable" to abnormal defendant) is not before us. Nor is there any claim that the battering provocation might have some legal effect beyond the potential reduction of defendant's culpability to manslaughter, or that something other than an "immediate" need for deadly force will suffice. See State v. Felton, 110 Wis.2d 485, 329 N.W.2d 161 (1983) (battered wife stabs sleeping husband).

Indeed, these features are subject to a large group of myths and stereotypes. It is clear that this subject is beyond the ken of the average juror and thus is suitable for explanation through expert testimony.

The second requirement that must be met before expert testimony is permitted is a showing that the proposed expert's testimony would be reliable. The rationale for this requirement is that expert testimony seeks to assist the trier of fact. An expert opinion that is not reliable is of no assistance to anyone.

[J]udicial opinions thus far have been split concerning the scientific acceptability of the syndrome and the methodology used by the researchers in this area. [T]he record before us reveals that the battered woman's syndrome has a sufficient scientific basis to produce uniform and reasonably reliable results.... The numerous books, articles and papers referred to earlier indicate the presence of a growing field of study and research about the battered woman's syndrome and recognition of the syndrome in the scientific field. However, while the record before us could require such a ruling, we refrain from conclusively ruling that Dr. Veronen's proffered testimony about the battered-woman's syndrome would satisfy New Jersey's standard of acceptability for scientific evidence. This is because the state was not given a full opportunity in the trial court to question Dr. Veronen's methodology in studying battered women or her implicit assertion that the battered-woman's syndrome has been accepted by the relevant scientific community....[23]

[The Court reversed the conviction and remanded for a new trial.]

■ HANDLER, J., concurring in part and dissenting in part.... The court in this case takes a major stride in recognizing the scientific authenticity of battered women's syndrome and its legal and factual significance in the trial of certain criminal cases. My difference with the court is quite narrow. I believe that defendant Gladys Kelly has demonstrated at her trial by sufficient expert evidence her entitlement to the use of the battered women's syndrome in connection with her defense of self-defense. I would

---

[23] We note that under the Code even if it is certain that the actor's life will soon be threatened, the actor may not use deadly defensive force until that threat is imminent.... The requirement that the use of deadly force, in order to be justifiable, must be immediately necessary, has as its purpose the preservation of life by preventing the use of deadly force except when its need is beyond debate. The rule's presumed effect on an actor who reasonably fears that her life will soon be endangered by an imminent threat is to cause her to leave the danger zone, especially if, because of the circumstances, she knows she will be defenseless when that threat becomes imminent. The rule, in effect, tends to protect the life of both the potential aggressor and victim. If, however-

er, the actor is unable to remove herself from the zone of danger (a psychological phenomenon common to battered women, according to the literature), the effect of the rule may be to prevent her from exercising the right of self-defense at the only time it would be effective. Instead she is required by the rule to wait until the threat against her life is imminent before she responds, at which time she may be completely defenseless.

There is, of course, some danger that any attempt to mitigate what may be undeserved punishment in these cases (by some further statutory differentiation of criminal responsibility) might weaken the general deterrent effect of our homicide laws. That is a matter the legislature might wish to examine.

therefore not require this issue—the admissibility of the battered women's syndrome—to be tried again. . . .

———

## NOTES ON DOMESTIC VIOLENCE AND THE LAW OF SELF–DEFENSE

**1.   Questions and Comments on *Kelly*.** The issue raised in *Kelly* has been widely litigated in the last two decades. Most courts have allowed testimony concerning the battered woman syndrome to be admitted in this context if offered by a qualified expert. See Laurie Kratky Dore, Downward Adjustment and the Slippery Slope: The Use of Duress in Defense of Battered Offenders, 56 Ohio St. L. J. 665, 683–84 n.77 (1995) ("Today, courts uniformly regard the battered woman syndrome as generally accepted scientific evidence, and, subject to case-specific relevance and expert qualifications, admissible in support of self-defense."). Recently, the Court of Criminal Appeals of Oklahoma remarked, "[t]o date, 31 states and the District of Columbia allow the use of expert testimony on the subject. Five states [have] acknowledged its validity, but held the testimony inadmissible based on the facts of the particular case." Bechtel v. State, 840 P.2d 1 (Okla.Crim.App.1992).

One of the disputes regarding testimony on the battered woman syndrome has focused on its scientific merit.[a] Once that debate is resolved in favor of the scientific validity of such evidence, the critical question is whether the testimony is relevant to a self-defense claim. According to *Kelly*, the syndrome describes "a series of common characteristics that appear in women" who are the victims of domestic abuse. What are those characteristics? To which elements of the self-defense claim are the characteristics relevant? Why does the expert testimony (assuming that the jury accepts it) tend to support a finding that Kelly's fear of her husband was "objectively reasonable," as the court asserts?

James Acker and Hans Toch argue that the probative value of testimony concerning battered woman syndrome is outweighed by its tendency to expand the scope of self-defense beyond the bounds of lawful justification:

> When the prior bad acts (the repeated beatings) and the bad character ("battering husband") of the deceased are made principal issues, this through the supportive testimony of an expert witness, the classic defense stratagem of "blaming the victim" for his own demise has been interjected before the jury. This "defense" has been dignified by the "syndrome" concept which draws attention to the prevalence of domestic victimization in society, and which makes the victim and the deceased examples of this problem. The killing of a battering husband could be "justified" in

[a] See generally John Monahan & Laurens Walker, Social Science in Law: Cases and Materials 465–73 (2002).

the jurors' minds not because it was necessary that a battered woman act with responsive deadly force when she was threatened with death or serious bodily injury by her mate but because it was a fitting act of retribution directed at a member of a sadistic fraternity who had finally reaped his just deserts.

James Acker and Hans Toch, Battered Women, Straw Men, and Expert Testimony: A Comment on State v. Kelly, 21 Crim.L.Bull. 125 (1985). Is this argument persuasive? The risk of distortion described by Acker and Toch appears to exist even without the expert testimony. Kelly was entitled to testify, and introduce corroborative evidence, about her husband's prior acts of violence against her. Moreover, on the facts presented, she was entitled to an instruction on self-defense. Does the expert testimony enhance the risk of distortion?

**2. Battered Woman Syndrome and Imminence.** Unlike Acker and Toch, some commentators argue that the battered woman syndrome is valuable precisely because it may lead lawmakers to relax the requirements of self-defense. One such requirement is that the threat of harm confronting the actor be "imminent." In *Kelly*, the court mentioned that this requirement might not be satisfied in some cases where women kill abusive men. As the court explained, the imminence requirement is designed to protect both "the potential aggressor and victim" from deadly harm: "The rule's presumed effect on an actor who reasonably fears that her life will soon be endangered by an imminent threat is to cause her to leave the danger zone...." However, the court questioned whether the imminence requirement achieves a just result in cases involving battered women. "If ... the actor is unable to remove herself from the zone of danger (a psychological phenomenon common to battered women, according to the literature), the effect of the rule may be to prevent her from exercising the right of self-defense at the only time it would be effective. Instead she is required by the rule to wait until the threat against her life is imminent before she responds, at which time she may be completely defenseless."

Responding to these concerns, some commentators have asserted that it may be necessary for a woman to kill her abuser even though at the time she does so he presents no imminent harm because "he has already finished beating her, has only threatened to attack her at some time in the future, or has even fallen asleep." Kit Kinports, Defending Battered Women's Self–Defense Claims, 67 Or. L. Rev. 393, 425 (1988). Kinports argues:

> [T]he battered woman may reasonably believe that any other efforts to avoid her husband's violence are futile. For a variety of reasons, she may reasonably feel that she cannot escape from her husband and that she cannot rely on the police for meaningful help. Moreover, any attempt to defend herself while her husband is beating her is likely to be useless because of the substantial disparity in their size and strength and because efforts to resist typically further infuriate the attacker. Thus, the battered woman may come to believe that her only options are killing herself,

letting her husband kill her, or killing him—and, in addition, that her only opportunity to kill him is in a nonconfrontational setting.

According to one psychologist, battered women sometimes perceive that they must use deadly force to repel threats of future harm:[*]

> [B]ecause of her extensive experience with her abuser's violence, [the battered woman] can detect changes or signs of novelty in the pattern of normal violence that connote increased danger. . . .
>
> [C]onsider the case of Madelyn Diaz, a 24–year-old . . . woman, who [killed] her husband as he slept. . . . Her husband was a police officer who frequently used his gun to get her to comply with his wishes. He had beaten her frequently during the course of their marriage. . . . He had also used his gun to force her to have sexual intercourse with a stranger. . . .
>
> The night before she killed him, Madelyn and her husband had an argument. He was drunk and wanted to have sex with her. She refused. . . . He said that if she did not change [her attitude] by the following day, he would "blow the baby's brains out." He took his gun and placed it against the head of their six month old daughter as he made this threat. . . . Following this exchange, they both went to sleep. In the morning, Madelyn woke up before her husband. She dressed her children and took them outside to the car to go grocery shopping. She then realized she had forgotten her money. She went back into the apartment and went to the drawer where they kept their money. Her husband's gun was in the same drawer. She took the gun from the drawer; as she did, she relived the moment of his threat against their daughter. She later reported that she could see him holding his gun to the baby's head—something he had never done before, a novel form of violence for him. She fired twice into his sleeping body. . . .

Julie Blackman, Potential Uses for Expert Testimony: Ideas Toward the Representation of Battered Women Who Kill, 9 Women's Rts. L. Rptr. 227, 236–37 (1986). At Diaz's trial for second-degree murder, Blackman provided expert testimony on behalf of the defense, and Diaz "was acquitted on the grounds of self-defense." In Blackman's estimation, the verdict reflected the jurors' "acceptance . . . of the idea that a perception of future, inescapable danger could provide sufficient grounds for reasonable, self-defensive, life-taking action—even when the source of the danger was asleep."

Should the imminence requirement be replaced by a standard that authorizes the use of deadly force to repel a "future, inescapable danger"? Under what circumstances is a future danger "inescapable"? Was the danger "inescapable" in *Diaz*?

---

[*] Reprinted with permission of the author and the Women's Rights Law Reporter.

By contrast, some courts have ruled that a woman who kills her husband when he is asleep may not interpose a self-defense claim. According to the Kansas Supreme Court, "a battered woman cannot reasonably fear imminent life-threatening danger from her sleeping spouse." State v. Stewart, 243 Kan. 639, 763 P.2d 572 (1988). *Stewart* emphasized that "the existence of the battered woman syndrome in and of itself" does not provide a defense to murder, and it refused to relax the imminence requirement in the context of domestic abuse. Similarly, in State v. Norman, 324 N.C. 253, 378 S.E.2d 8 (1989), the court held that self-defense was not available to a woman who shot and killed her sleeping husband. The court in *Norman* acknowledged that the defendant had been subjected to years of "physical and mental abuse" by her husband. However, the court explained that a decision to relax the imminence requirement

> could not be limited to a few cases decided on evidence as poignant as this. [A relaxed imminence requirement] would tend to categorically legalize the opportune killing of abusive husbands by their wives solely on the basis of the wives' testimony concerning their subjective speculation as to the probability of future felonious assaults by their husbands. Homicidal self-help would then become a lawful solution, and perhaps the easiest and most effective solution to this problem.

Martha Mahoney criticizes *Stewart* and *Norman* for ignoring the fact that both defendants attempted to leave their violent marriages and that their husbands responded by escalating the abuse. Rather than engaging in vigilante action, as the courts implied, the women were "hostages" who resisted death at their "captors'" hands. Mahoney concludes, "We believe the danger to a hostage is imminent *both* because the force used to hold them there is apparent *and* because our cultural knowledge includes the memory of the many hostages who have been harmed in the past." Martha R. Mahoney, Legal Images of Battered Women: Redefining the Issue of Separation, 90 Mich. L. Rev. 1, 92–93 (1991).

Does Mahoney's "hostage" metaphor answer the concerns raised by *Stewart* and *Norman*? Consider a hypothetical offered by Paul Robinson:

> Suppose *A* kidnaps and confines *D* with the announced intention of killing him one week later. *D* has an opportunity to kill *A* and escape each morning as *A* brings him his daily ration. Taken literally, the imminence requirement would prevent *D* from using deadly force in self-defense until *A* is standing over him with a knife, but that outcome seems inappropriate.... The proper inquiry is not the immediacy of the threat but the immediacy of the response necessary in defense. If a threatened harm is such that it cannot be avoided if the intended victim waits until the last moment, the principle of self-defense must permit him to act earlier—as early as is required to defend himself effectively.

2 Paul H. Robinson, Criminal Law Defenses 78 (1984). Is the battered woman's predicament analogous to the case Robinson describes?

### 3. Feminist Perspectives on the Battered Woman Syndrome.

As *Kelly* recounts, commentators from a variety of disciplines claim that testimony concerning battered woman syndrome assists in rebutting sexist "myths and misconceptions" about women who are victims of domestic abuse. Feminist lawyers first encountered these "myths and misconceptions" when defending women charged with murdering abusive men. According to Elizabeth Schneider and Susan Jordan, the law of self-defense developed in response to male experiences and perceptions of violence and, therefore, fails to reflect the circumstances under which women resort to lethal force:*

> Standards of justifiable homicide have been based on male models and expectations. Familiar images of self-defense are a soldier, a man protecting his home, family, or the chastity of his wife, or a man fighting off an assailant.... The man's ... motivation is understood by those sitting in judgment upon his act, since his conduct conforms to the expectation that a real man would fight to the death to protect his pride and property....

> Sex bias permeates [self-defense] doctrine regarding the perception of imminent and lethal danger.... While a man is assumed to have the ability to perceive danger accurately and respond appropriately, a woman is viewed as responding hysterically and inappropriately to physical threat....

> [Society] has relegated women to a position of second-class status with respect to their abilities to defend themselves. Women have been ... discouraged from learning how to defend themselves physically because such behavior would be "unfeminine." Women are socialized to be less active physically, not to display physical aggression, and to be more afraid of physical pain than men. These problems are exacerbated by the fact that most women are physically smaller than men.

> Women who have learned to associate femininity with being weak and helpless experience great anxiety when confronted with a situation where they must display aggression.... These circumstances must be included ... within the standard of self-defense....

> [Moreover], the special circumstances which may require a woman to use a weapon must be fully explained in the trial, [namely, that women perceive the male's fist or body to be a deadly weapon]. The jury must be allowed to consider the [woman's] possible need to resort to a weapon when faced with an unarmed assailant. This approach equalizes the application of the law to women by incorporating the woman's perspective into the deadly force standard and other standards of self-defense.

---

\* Reprinted with permission of the authors and the Women's Rights Law Reporter.

Elizabeth M. Schneider and Susan B. Jordan, Representation of Women Who Defend Themselves in Response to Physical or Sexual Assault, 4 Women's Rts. L. Rptr. 149, 153–57 (1978). Building on these observations, feminist lawyers began to promote the syndrome testimony as one method for educating judges and jurors about women's perceptions and experiences of violence.

For example, Kit Kinports asserts that the syndrome testimony helps jurors to understand that the woman's lethal conduct was "reasonable" because the expert witness "describes the emotions and reactions that any woman who has experienced spousal abuse for an extended period of time is likely to exhibit." Kit Kinports, Defending Battered Women's Self–Defense Claims, 67 Or. L. Rev. 393, 417 (1988). Kinports also argues that the testimony establishes that the "emotions and reactions" that prompt the woman to kill do not support the imposition of criminal blame:

> ... Unlike traits such as hotheadedness, drunkenness, or cowardice, the traits characteristic of the battered woman are not attributes that the woman can reasonably be expected to control, that evidence some sort of moral failure for which she can fairly be blamed, or that the criminal law is designed to alter. The battered woman typically has done nothing to bring on her husband's abuse. Therefore, she cannot justly be blamed for her status as a battered woman.

Other feminists point out that appellate opinions authorizing admission of the syndrome testimony tend to "resonate with familiar stereotypes of female incapacity." Elizabeth M. Schneider, Describing and Changing: Women's Self–Defense Work and the Problem of Expert Testimony on Battering, 9 Women's Rts. L. Rptr. 195, 199 (1986). Schneider argues that judges have misinterpreted the syndrome testimony. While the testimony describes a context within which the woman's acts are reasonable, the courts tend to represent battered women as "suffering from a psychological disability [that] prevents them from acting normally." Mahoney agrees that the courts primarily focus on those aspects of the testimony that suggest that battered women are "dysfunctional." Martha R. Mahoney, Legal Images of Battered Women: Redefining the Issue of Separation, 90 Mich. L. Rev. 1, 38–43 (1991). Thus, Mahoney argues that defense lawyers should supplement the syndrome testimony with evidence that the woman was barred from leaving the abusive relationship by a lack of resources, by the apathetic responses of the police, and/or by increased violence by the man.

**4. Self–Defense by a Battered Child.** Analogous issues have been raised in cases involving defendants charged with patricide who seek to introduce expert testimony regarding "battered child syndrome." The relation between this evidentiary question and the substantive doctrine of self-defense was discussed at length in Jahnke v. State, 682 P.2d 991 (Wyo.1984). Richard John Jahnke, then 16, killed his father with a shotgun in the driveway of their home as his mother and father were returning from dinner. The court described the killing as follows:

[Earlier in the evening defendant] had been involved in a violent altercation with his father, and he had been warned not to be at the home when the father and mother returned. During the absence of his parents the [defendant] made elaborate preparation for the final confrontation with his father. He changed into dark clothing and prepared a number of weapons which he positioned at various places throughout the family home that he selected to serve as "backup" positions in case he was not successful in his first effort to kill his father. These weapons included two shotguns, three rifles, a .38 caliber pistol and a Marine knife. In addition, he armed his sister, Deborah, with a .30 caliber M–1 carbine which he taught her how to operate so that she could protect herself in the event that he failed in his efforts.... He then waited inside the darkened garage in a position where he could not be seen but which permitted him to view the lighted driveway on the other side of the garage door. Shortly before 6:30 p.m. the parents returned, and the [defendant's] father got out of the vehicle and came to the garage door. The [defendant] was armed with a 12–gauge shotgun loaded with slugs, and when he could see the head and shoulders of his father through the spacing of the slats of the shade covering the windows of the garage door, he blew his R.O.T.C. command-sergeant-major's whistle for courage, and he opened fire. All six cartridges in the shotgun were expended, and four of them in one way or another struck the father....

Jahnke was charged with first-degree murder. In support of his self-defense plea, he sought to introduce evidence that his father had beaten him, his sister, and his mother over many years, and proffered psychiatric testimony that he was a battered child who believed himself to be in immediate danger of death or serious harm when he shot his father. Although the jury was instructed on the law of self-defense, the expert testimony was excluded. Jahnke was convicted of voluntary manslaughter and sentenced to a 5–to–15 year term of imprisonment. The Wyoming Supreme Court affirmed the conviction and sentence. The majority explained its ruling on the evidentiary issue as follows:

It is clear that self-defense is circumscribed by circumstances involving a confrontation, usually encompassing some overt act or acts by the deceased, which would induce a reasonable person to fear that his life was in danger or that at least he was threatened with great bodily harm.... Although many people, and the public media, seem to be prepared to espouse the notion that a victim of abuse is entitled to kill the abuser, that special justification defense is antithetical to the mores of modern civilized society. It is difficult enough to justify capital punishment as an appropriate response of society to criminal acts even after the circumstances have been carefully evaluated by a number of people. To permit capital punishment to be imposed upon the subjective conclusion of the individual that prior acts and conduct of the deceased justified the killing would amount to a leap into the abyss of anarchy. [If expert testimony] has any role at all, it is in assisting the jury to evaluate the reasonableness of the defendant's fear in a case involving the recognized circumstances of self-defense which include a confrontation or conflict with the deceased not of the defendant's instigation. . . .

[The] record contained no evidence that [defendant] was under either actual or threatened assault by his father at the time of the shooting. Reliance upon the justification of self-defense requires a showing of an actual or threatened imminent attack by the deceased. Absent [such a showing] the reasonableness of [the defendant's] conduct at the time was not an issue in the case, and the trial court, at the time it made its ruling, properly excluded the testimony sought to be elicited from the forensic psychiatrist.

On facts similar to those of *Jahnke*, the Court of Appeals of Washington reversed the conviction of a man who, at age 17, shot and killed his stepfather as the stepfather was returning home from work. See State v. Janes, 64 Wash.App. 134, 822 P.2d 1238 (1992). The court concluded that the trial court erred by excluding expert testimony concerning the "battered child syndrome":

> While the "imminent danger" prong requires the jury to find that the victim honestly and reasonably believed that the aggressor intended to inflict serious bodily injury in the near future, there need be no evidence of an actual physical assault to demonstrate the immediacy of the danger. . . .

> . . . Washington uses a subjective standard to evaluate the imminence of the danger a defendant faced at the time of the act. This requires the court and the jury to evaluate the reasonableness of the defendant's perception of the imminence of that danger in light of all the facts and circumstances known to the defendant at the time he acted, including the facts and circumstances as he perceived them before the crime. Because battering itself can alter the defendant's perceptions, Washington courts have held that expert testimony with respect to the battered woman syndrome is admissible to explain a woman's perception that she had no alternative but to act in the manner that she did. . . .

> Neither law nor logic suggests any reason to limit to women recognition of the impact a battering relationship may have on the victim's actions or perceptions. [C]hildren are both objectively and subjectively more vulnerable to the effects of violence than are adults. For that reason, the rationale underlying the admissibility of testimony regarding the battered woman syndrome is at least as compelling, if not more so, when applied to children. [Until they reach the age of majority, children] have virtually no independent ability to support themselves, thus preventing them from escaping the abusive atmosphere. Further, unlike an adult who may come into a battering relationship with at least some basis on which to make comparisons between current and past experiences, a child

has no such equivalent life experience on which to draw to put the battering into perspective. There is therefore every reason to believe that a child's entire world view and sense of self may be conditioned by reaction to that abuse.

Which of these analyses is preferable? By emphasizing children's unique vulnerability to domestic violence, does the court in *Janes* undercut the rationale supporting the battered woman syndrome?

------

## NOTE ON THE URBAN SURVIVAL SYNDROME

The success of the battered woman syndrome has encouraged defense lawyers to offer testimony concerning other kinds of syndromes in an effort to bolster self-defense claims. One such syndrome is known as "urban survival syndrome." The following case describes the theory underlying urban survival syndrome, as well as one context in which the syndrome is likely to be raised.[a]

On April 18, 1993, Daimian Osby, an 18–year-old black man, shot and killed Willie and Marcus Brooks, who also were black men. The shootings took place in Fort Worth, Texas. Both victims were shot in the side of the head. At his trial on two counts of first-degree murder, Osby claimed that his use of deadly force was justifiable self-defense. According to Osby, during the year that preceded the shootings, the two men had harassed him repeatedly for payment of a gambling debt. The harassment included threats of violence against Osby and members of his family. On at least one occasion, the two men had stalked Osby and threatened him with shotguns. At the time that Osby shot the men, they were unarmed, but Osby believed that the only way for him to avoid death or serious bodily injury at their hands was for him to kill them first. A sociologist testifying on behalf of the defense explained to the jury that Osby lived in an inner city neighborhood with one of the highest rates of violent crime in the country, and he explained that young men raised in these neighborhoods quickly learn that the greatest danger they face is being killed "by one of their own." Based on this testimony, defense counsel argued that Osby's belief that he needed to use lethal force was reasonable. The jury deadlocked eleven to one in favor of conviction. According to defense counsel, the one juror who held out for acquittal was a black man from Osby's neighborhood who agreed that the neighborhood was a "war zone." When Osby was tried a second time on murder charges, his attorneys sought to introduce testimony from a psychologist, as well as the sociologist, concerning the psychological characteristics of persons who live in violent, poor, urban neighborhoods. The trial judge refused to allow the psychologist to testify. Osby was convicted of two counts of murder and sentenced to life in prison.

------

[a] The following description of the *Osby* case is based on Jacquielynn Floyd, Double–Murder Case Is Declared Mistrial, The Dallas Morning News, April 21, 1994, at A25; Selwyn Crawford, Teen Guilty in Slayings of Two in Fort Worth, The Dallas Morning News, Nov. 11, 1994, at A29.

Should the trial court have excluded the psychologist's testimony concerning urban survival syndrome? Does the answer depend on the standard of reasonableness (objective or subjective) employed by Texas in evaluating claims of self-defense? Recall the arguments offered to support admission of testimony concerning the battered woman syndrome. Can the same kinds of arguments be made to support admission of urban survival syndrome? Do blacks and whites have different perceptions of confrontational situations? If so, must evidence of those differences nonetheless be excluded in order to avoid reinforcing racist stereotypes concerning black men and violence?

In this connection, consider again the facts of State v. Brown, 91 N.M. 320, 573 P.2d 675 (1977). Brown was convicted of two counts of assault upon a police officer with intent to kill. Brown was a black man who lived in an inner-city neighborhood, and he claimed that he "feared the officers and shot them in self-defense." Defense witnesses were permitted to describe instances in which police officers physically and verbally harassed Brown and other black persons from his neighborhood. However, the trial court refused to allow a social psychologist to testify about "police conduct toward minority groups and the perception by minority groups, particularly blacks, that the police are a threat to minority group members." Nor did the court allow the psychologist to testify that, in his opinion, Brown "would be likely to fear the police" if he encountered them on the street. The Court of Appeals of New Mexico decided that exclusion of the expert's testimony was erroneous, and it reversed and remanded for a new trial. Such testimony supported Brown's claim that he feared he was in immediate danger of bodily harm when he shot the officers, and it may have rebutted an inference created by other evidence that Brown acted out "of anger and ... rejection of authority." Did Brown (or, for that matter, Osby) suffer from a "syndrome" in the sense that term is employed by the court in *Kelly*? Is Brown's predicament factually and ethically distinguishable from that of Osby? From that of Kelly?

---

# People v. Young

New York Supreme Court, Appellate Division, 1961.
12 A.D.2d 262, 210 N.Y.S.2d 358.

■ BREITEL, JUSTICE. The question is whether one is criminally liable for assault in the third degree[a] if he goes to the aid of another who he

---

[a] At the time of the *Young* case, the New York penal law defined three degrees of assault. According to § 240, a person "who, with an intent to kill a human being or to commit a felony upon the person or property of the one assaulted, or of another, assaults another with [deadly force] is guilty of assault in the first degree." According to § 242, a person who "wilfully and wrongfully wounds or inflicts grievous bodily harm upon another, either with or without a weapon" or who "wilfully and wrongfully assaults another by the use of a weapon or other instrument or thing likely to produce grievous bodily harm ... is guilty of assault in the second degree." Finally, § 244 provided that a per-

mistakenly, but reasonably, believes is being unlawfully beaten, and thereby injures one of the apparent assaulters. In truth, the seeming victim was being lawfully arrested by two police officers in plain clothes. Defendant stands convicted of such a criminal assault, for which he received a sentence of 60 days in the workhouse, the execution of such sentence being suspended.

Defendant, aged 40, regularly employed, and with a clean record except for an $8 fine in connection with a disorderly conduct charge 19 years before in Birmingham, Alabama, observed two middle-aged men beating and struggling with a youth of 18. This was at 3:40 p. m. on October 17, 1958 in front of 64 West 64th Street in Manhattan. Defendant was acquainted with none of the persons involved; but believing that the youth was being unlawfully assaulted, and this is not disputed by the other participants, defendant went to his rescue, pulling on or punching at the seeming assailants. In the ensuing affray one of the older men got his leg locked with that of defendant and when defendant fell the man's leg was broken at the kneecap. The injured man then pulled out a revolver, announced to defendant that he was a police officer, and that defendant was under arrest. It appears that the youth in question had played some part in a street incident which resulted in the two men, who were detectives in plain clothes, seeking to arrest him for disorderly conduct. The youth had resisted, and it was in the midst of this resistance that defendant came upon the scene.

At the trial the defendant testified that he had known nothing about what had happened before he came upon the scene; that he had gone to his aid because the youth was crying and trying to pull away from the middle-aged men; and that the older men had almost pulled the trousers off the youth. The only detective who testified stated, in response to a question from the court, that defendant did not know and had no way of knowing, so far as he knew, that they were police officers or that they were making an arrest.

Two things are to be kept sharply in mind in considering the problem at hand. The first is that all that is involved here is a criminal prosecution for simple assault, and that the court is not concerned with the incidence of civil liability in the law of torts as a result of what happened on the street. Second, there is not here involved any question of criminal responsibility for interfering with an arrest where it is known to the actor that police officers are making an arrest, but he mistakenly believes that the arrest is unlawful.

Assault and battery is an ancient crime cognizable at the common law. It is a crime in which an essential element is intent. Of course, in this state the criminal law is entirely statutory. But, because assault and battery is a "common-law" crime, the statutory provisions, as in the case of most of the

son who "commits an assault, or an assault and battery" that is not specified in Sections 240 or 242 "is guilty of assault in the third degree." In its opinion, the court occasionally refers to assault in the third degree as "simple assault."—[Footnote by eds.]

common-law crimes, do not purport to define the crime with the same particularity as those crimes which have a statutory origin initially. One of the consequences, therefore, is that while the provisions governing assault, contained in the Penal Law, refer to various kinds of intent, in most instances the intent is related to a supplemental intent, in addition to the unspecified general intent to commit an assault, in order to impose more serious consequences upon the actor. In some instances, of course, the intent is spelled out to distinguish the prohibited activity from what might otherwise be an innocent act or merely an accidental wrong.

It is in this statutory context that it was held in People v. Katz, 290 N.Y. 361, 49 N.E.2d 482 (1943), that in order to sustain a charge of assault in the second degree, based upon the infliction of grievous bodily harm, not only must there be a general intent to commit unlawful bodily harm but there must be a "specific intent," i.e., a supplemental intent to inflict grievous bodily harm. The case therefore does provide an interesting parallel analysis forwarding the idea that assault is always an intent crime even when the statute omits to provide expressly for such general intent, as is the case with regard to assault in the third degree. . . .

With respect to intent crimes, under general principles, a mistake of fact relates as a defense to an essential element of the crime, namely, to the mens rea. The development of the excuse of mistake is a relatively modern one and is of expanding growth. . . .

Mistake of fact, under our statutes, is a species of excuse rather than a matter of justification. Consequently, reliance on § 42[1] of the Penal Law which relates exclusively to justification is misplaced. Section 42 would be applicable only to justify a third party's intervention on behalf of a victim of an unlawful assault, but this does not preclude the defense of mistake which is related to subjective intent rather than to the objective ground for action. . . . While the distinctions between excuse and justification are often fuzzy, and more often fudged, in the instance of § 42 its limited application is clear from its language.

It is in the homicide statutes in which the occasions for excuse or justification are made somewhat clearer; but the distinction is still relevant with respect to most crimes. In homicide it is made explicitly plain that the actor's state of mind, if reasonable, is material and controlling.[b] It does not

---

[1] The section reads as follows:

§ 42.   Rule when act done in defense of self or another.

An act, otherwise criminal, is justifiable when it is done to protect the person committing it, or another whom he is bound to protect, from inevitable and irreparable personal injury, and the injury could only be prevented by the act, nothing more being done than is necessary to prevent the injury.

[b] Section 1055 provided, in relevant part, as follows:

Homicide is . . . justifiable when committed:

1.   In the lawful defense of the slayer, or of his or her husband, wife, parent, child, brother, sister, master or servant, or of any person in his presence or company, when there is reasonable ground to apprehend a design on the part of the person slain to commit a felony, or to do some great personal injury to the slayer, or to any such person, and there is imminent danger of such design being accomplished. . . .—[Footnote by eds.]

seem rational that the same reasonable misapprehension of fact should excuse a killing in seeming proper defense of a third person in one's presence but that it should not excuse a lesser personal injury.

In this state there are no discoverable precedents involving mistake of fact when one intervenes on behalf of another person and the prosecution has been for assault, rather than homicide. (The absence of precedents in this state and many others may simply mean that no enforcement agency would prosecute in the situations that must have occurred.) No one would dispute, however, that a mistake of fact would provide a defense if the prosecution were for homicide. This divided approach is sometimes based on the untenable distinction that mistake of fact may negative a "specific" intent required in the degrees of homicide but is irrelevant to the general intent required in simple assault, or, on the even less likely distinction, that the only intent involved in assault is the intent to touch without consent or legal justification (omitting the qualification of unlawfulness)....

There have been precedents elsewhere among the states. There is a split among the cases and in the jurisdictions. Most hold that the rescuer intervenes at his own peril, but others hold that he is excused if he acts under mistaken but reasonable belief that he is protecting a victim from unlawful attack. Many of the cases which hold that the actor proceeds at his peril involve situations where the actor was present throughout, or through most, or through enough of the transaction and, therefore, was in no position to claim a mistake of fact. Others arise in rough situations in which the feud or enmity generally to the peace officer is a significant factor. Almost all apply unanalytically the rubric that the right to intervene on behalf of another is no greater than the other's right to self-defense, a phrasing of ancient but questionable lineage going back to when crime and tort were not yet divided in the common law—indeed, when the right to private redress was not easily distinguishable from the sanction for the public wrong....

The modern view, as already noted, is not to impose criminal responsibility in connection with intent crimes for those who act with good motivation, in mistaken but reasonable misapprehension of the facts....

More recently in the field of criminal law the American Law Institute in drafting a model penal code has concerned itself with the question in this case. Under § 3.05 of the Model Penal Code the use of force for the protection of others is excused if the actor behaves under a mistaken belief.

The comments by the reporters on the Model Penal Code are quite appropriate. After stating that the defense of strangers should be assimilated to the defense of oneself the following is said:

> In support of such a ruling, it may perhaps be said that the potentiality for deterring the actor from the use of force is greater where he is protecting a stranger than where he is protecting himself or a loved one, because in the former case the interest protected is of relatively less importance to him; moreover the

potential incidence of mistake in estimating fault or the need for action on his part is increased where the defendant is protecting a stranger, because in such circumstances he is less likely to know which party to the quarrel is in the right. These arguments may be said to lead to the conclusion that, in order to minimize the area for error or mistake, the defendant should act at his peril when he is protecting a stranger. This emasculates the privilege of protection of much of its content, introducing a liability without fault which is indefensible in principle. The cautious potential actor who knows the law will, in the vast majority of cases, refrain from acting at all. The result may well be that an innocent person is injured without receiving assistance from bystanders. It seems far preferable, therefore, to predicate the justification upon the actor's belief, safeguarding if thought necessary against abuse of the privilege by the imposition of a requirement of proper care in evolving the belief. Here, as elsewhere, the latter problem is dealt with by the general provision in § 3.09.

Apart from history, precedents, and the language distinctions that may be found in the statutes, it stands to reason that a man should not be punished criminally for an intent crime unless he, indeed, has the intent. Where a mistake of relevant facts is involved the premises for such intent are absent. . . .

It is a sterile and desolate legal system that would exact punishment for an intentional assault from one like this defendant, who acted from the most commendable motives and without excessive force. Had the facts been as he thought them, he would have been a hero and not condemned as a criminal actor. The dearth of applicable precedents—as distinguished from theoretical generalizations never, or rarely, applied—in England and in most of the states demonstrates that the benevolent intervenor has not been cast as a pariah. It is no answer to say that the policeman should be called when one sees an injustice. Even in the most populous centers, policemen are not that common or that available. Also, it ignores the peremptory response to injustice that the good man has ingrained. Again, it is to be noted, in a criminal proceeding one is concerned with the act against society, not with the wrong between individuals and the right to reparation, which is the province of tort.

Accordingly, the judgment of conviction should be reversed, on the law, and the information dismissed. . . .

■ VALENTE, JUSTICE (dissenting) . . . I dissent and would affirm the conviction because the intent to commit a battery was unquestionably proven; and, since there was no relationship between defendant and the person whom the police officers were arresting, defendant acted at his peril in intervening and striking the officer. Under well established law, defendant's rights were no greater than those of the person whom he sought to protect; and since the arrest was lawful, defendant was no more privileged to assault the police officer than the person being arrested.

Under our statutes a *specific* intent is necessary for the crimes of assault in the first and second degrees. Generally, the assaults contemplated by those sections were known as "aggravated" assaults under the common law. However, assault in the third degree is defined by § 244 of the Penal Law as an assault and battery not such as is specified in Sections 240 and 242. No specific intent is required under § 244. All that is required is the knowledgeable doing of the act. "It is sufficient that the defendant voluntarily intended to commit the unlawful act of touching."

In the instant case, had the defendant assaulted the officer with the specific intent of preventing the lawful apprehension of the other person he would have been subject to indictment [for] assault in the second degree. But the inability to prove a specific intent does not preclude the People from establishing the lesser crime of assault in the third degree which requires proof only of the general intent "to commit the unlawful act of touching," if such exists.

There is evidently no New York law on the precise issue on this appeal. However, certain of our statutes point to the proper direction for solution of the problem. Section 42 of the Penal Law provides:

> An act, otherwise criminal, is justifiable when it is done to protect the person committing it, or another whom he is bound to protect, from inevitable and irreparable personal injury. . . .

Similarly, § 246, so far as here pertinent, provides:

> To use or attempt, or offer to use, force or violence upon or towards the person of another is not unlawful in the following cases: . . .
>
> > 3. When committed either by the party about to be injured or by another person in his aid or defense, in preventing or attempting to prevent an offense against his person, or a trespass or other unlawful interference with real or personal property in his lawful possession, if the force or violence used is not more than sufficient to prevent such offense.

These statutes represent the public policy of this state regarding the areas in which an assault will be excused or rendered "not unlawful" where one goes to the assistance of another. They include only those cases in which the other person is one whom the defendant "is bound to protect" or where the defendant is "preventing or attempting to prevent an offense against" such other person. Neither statute applies to the instant case since the other person herein was one unlawfully resisting a legal arrest—and hence no offense was being committed against his person by the officer—and he was not an individual whom defendant was "bound to protect."

It has been held in other states that one who goes to the aid of a third person acts at his peril, and his rights to interfere do not exceed the rights of the person whom he seeks to protect. We need not consider to what extent that rule is modified by § 42 of the Penal Law since there is no question here but that the person being arrested was not in any special relation to defendant so that he was a person whom defendant was "bound to protect." It follows then that there being no right on the part of the person, to whose aid defendant came, to assault the officer—the arrest being legal—defendant had no greater right or privilege to assault the officer.

The conclusion that defendant was properly convicted in this case comports with sound public policy. It would be a dangerous precedent for courts to announce that plain-clothes police officers attempting lawful arrests over wrongful resistance are subject to violent interference by strangers ignorant of the facts, who may attack the officers with impunity so long as their ignorance forms a reasonable basis for a snap judgment of the situation unfavorable to the officers. Although the actions of such a defendant, who acts on appearances, may eliminate the specific intent required to convict him of a felony assault, it should not exculpate him from the act of aggressive assistance to a law breaker in the process of wrongfully resisting a proper arrest.

I do not detract from the majority's views regarding commendation of the acts of a good Samaritan, although it may be difficult in some cases to distinguish such activities from those of an officious intermeddler. But opposed to the encouragement of the "benevolent intervenor" is the conflicting and more compelling interest of protection of police officers. In a city like New York, where it becomes necessary to utilize the services of a great number of plain-clothes officers, the efficacy of their continuing struggle against crime should not be impaired by the possibility of interference by citizens who may be acting from commendable motives. It is more desirable—and evidently up to this point the legislature has so deemed it—that in such cases the intervening citizen be held to act at his peril when he assaults a stranger, who unknown to him is a police officer legally performing his duty. In this conflict of interests, the balance preponderates in favor of the protection of the police rather than the misguided intervenor.

The majority points to the recommendations of the American Law Institute in drafting a Model Penal Code which make the use of force justifiable to protect a third person when the actor believes his intervention is necessary for the protection of such third person. Obviously these are recommendations which properly are to be addressed to a legislature and not to courts. The comments of the reporters on the Model Penal Code, from which the majority quotes, indicate that in the United States the view is preserved in much state legislation that force may not be used to defend others unless they stand in a special relationship to their protector. The reporters state: "The simple solution of the whole problem is to assimilate the defense of strangers to the defense of oneself, and this the present section does." If this be so, then even under the Model Penal Code, since the stranger, who is being lawfully arrested, may not assault the officers a third person coming to his defense may not do so. In any event, the Model Penal Code recognizes that the law as it now stands requires the conviction of the defendant herein. Until the legislature acts, the courts should adhere to the well-established rules applicable in such cases. Such adherence demands the affirmance of the conviction herein.

————

## People v. Young

Court of Appeals of New York, 1962.
11 N.Y.2d 274, 183 N.E.2d 319.

■ PER CURIAM.

Whether one, who in good faith aggressively intervenes in a struggle between another person and a police officer in civilian dress attempting to effect the lawful arrest of the third person, may be properly convicted of assault in the third degree is a question of law of first impression here.

The opinions in the court below in the absence of precedents in this state carefully expound the opposing views found in other jurisdictions. The majority in the Appellate Division have adopted the minority rule in the other states that one who intervenes in a struggle between strangers under the mistaken but reasonable belief that he is protecting another who he assumes is being unlawfully beaten is thereby exonerated from criminal liability. The weight of authority holds with the dissenters below that one who goes to the aid of a third person does so at his own peril.

While the doctrine espoused by the majority of the court below may have support in some states, we feel that such a policy would not be conducive to an orderly society. We agree with the settled policy of law in most jurisdictions that the right of a person to defend another ordinarily should not be greater than such person's right to defend himself. Subdivision 3 of § 246 of the Penal Law does not apply as no offense was being committed on the person of the one resisting the lawful arrest. Whatever may be the public policy where the felony charged requires proof of a specific intent and the issue is justifiable homicide, it is not relevant in a prosecution for assault in the third degree where it is only necessary to show that the defendant knowingly struck a blow.

In this case there can be no doubt that the defendant intended to assault the police officer in civilian dress. The resulting assault was forceful. Hence motive or mistake of fact is of no significance as the defendant was not charged with a crime requiring such intent or knowledge. To be guilty of third-degree assault "[i]t is sufficient that the defendant voluntarily intended to commit the unlawful act of touching." Since in these circumstances the aggression was inexcusable the defendant was properly convicted.

Accordingly, the order of the Appellate Division should be reversed and the information reinstated.

■ [The dissenting opinion of Judge Froessel is omitted.]

————

## NOTE ON DEFENSE OF OTHERS

The opinions in the *Young* litigation adequately canvass the policy arguments usually made on both sides of the question raised. How should that question be resolved?

How is the distinction between general and specific intent relevant to the reasoning in *Young*? Why is Young not equally guilty of aggravated assault if he seriously injures the victim?

———

## SUBSECTION C:  PUBLIC AUTHORITY

———

## INTRODUCTORY NOTE ON PUBLIC AUTHORITY

From the earliest times, the common law regarded as justifiable otherwise criminal acts, including homicide, which were performed in execution of the law or in furtherance of justice. By the 13th century, according to Pollock and Maitland, some homicides were regarded as "absolutely justifiable." They offer two examples: "One such case is the execution of a lawful sentence of death. Another—and this is regarded as a very similar case—is the slaying of an outlaw or a hand-having thief or other manifest felon who resists capture." 2 Frederick Pollock and Frederic W. Maitland, The History of English Law 478 (2d ed. 1899).

This subsection is devoted to an issue that cuts across all public-authority justifications—the problem of mistake regarding the existence of the claimed authority, either by a public official or by a private citizen who complies with an official request for assistance. The problem is illustrated in an unusual and controversial substantive context—the scope of the president's authority to authorize warrantless searches and seizures in the interests of "national security."

———

## Problem Based on United States v. Ehrlichman

United States Court of Appeals for the District of Columbia Circuit, 1976.
546 F.2d 910.

[This problem and the following one are based on the facts of a prosecution associated with the Watergate scandal. In the actual case, John Ehrlichman was convicted of conspiring to violate the civil rights of Dr. Louis J. Fielding in violation of § 241 of Title 18 of the United States Code. However, it will simplify the issues to assume instead that Ehrlichman was convicted, as in fact he might have been, of conspiracy to commit burglary.[a]

---

[a] Assume that the offenses are defined as they are in Sections 5.03 and 221.1 of the Model Penal Code. Assume further that the unauthorized copying of confidential patient information from a psychiatrist's file is a criminal offense.

[The material reproduced below is excerpted from the unanimous decision affirming Ehrlichman's conviction. It has been modified only to take into account the assumption just made regarding the offense charged.]

■ WILKEY, CIRCUIT JUDGE. . . . The publication of the "Pentagon Papers" in the summer of 1971 spurred the President to form a "Special Investigations" or "Room 16" unit within the White House, whose purpose was to investigate the theft of the Pentagon Papers and prevent other such security leaks. Defendant Ehrlichman, who was the Assistant to the President for Domestic Affairs, exercised general supervision over the unit; Egil Krogh and David Young were charged with its operation. At the time, Krogh was an assistant to Ehrlichman; Young worked with the National Security Council. They sought, and received, Ehrlichman's approval to add G. Gordon Liddy, a former F.B.I. agent, and E. Howard Hunt, a former C.I.A. agent, to the unit.

. . . The unit's principal enterprise seemed to be the acquisition of all files and source material on Daniel Ellsberg. There was a generalized concern over his motives for releasing classified materials (the Pentagon Papers). Young and Krogh instructed the CIA to do a psychological profile on Ellsberg. Since Dr. Fielding had refused an interview by the FBI on the ground of doctor/patient confidentiality, Hunt suggested examining Dr. Fielding's file on Ellsberg, and further suggested a "black bag job" (surreptitious entry) while noting that the FBI no longer engaged in such activities. When Young reviewed the psychological assessment on Ellsberg prepared by the CIA, he determined that it was superficial, and recommended that a "covert operation be undertaken to examine all the medical files held by Ellsberg's psychoanalyst." The exhibit reflects Ehrlichman's approval of the recommendation with his addition: "Provided that it is not traceable back to the White House."

The members of the unit were clear that the "covert operation" in question would be a surreptitious entry into Dr. Fielding's office. Ehrlichman's primary defense at trial, however, was that he was not apprised of, and thus did not authorize, such an entry. He testified that he thought he had approved only a conventional private investigation, involving no surreptitious search of Dr. Fielding's office. Considerable evidence was introduced on both sides of the question. The jury's guilty verdict . . . reflected a finding that Ehrlichman had in fact authorized the search.

Krogh and Young insisted that no one employed by the White House was to effect the actual entry into Fielding's office. Hunt traveled to Miami in mid-August 1971 to enlist the assistance of Bernard Barker, who had worked under Hunt during the Bay of Pigs operation. Hunt was widely known and respected in Miami's Cuban–American community as a government agent who had been a leader in the fight to liberate Cuba. He did not identify the object of the search, but told Barker only that the operation involved a traitor who had been passing information to the Soviet Embassy.

On the basis of this information Barker recruited two men, Eugenio Martinez and Felipe de Diego, for the operation.

Hunt and Liddy met Barker, Martinez, and de Diego in Los Angeles on 2 September 1971. The Miamians were informed their mission was to enter Dr. Fielding's office, that Dr. Fielding was not himself the subject of the investigation, but that they were to photograph the file of one of his patients (they were not told Ellsberg's name until minutes before the break-in) and return the file to its place. On 3 September Barker and de Diego, dressed as deliverymen, delivered a valise containing photographic equipment to Dr. Fielding's office, enabling them at the same time to unlock the door to facilitate subsequent entry. Later that evening they and Martinez, contrary to expectations, found both the building and Dr. Fielding's office locked. The Miamians forced their way into the building, broke the lock on the office door, and used a crowbar on Dr. Fielding's file cabinets. As instructed if this became necessary, they spilled pills and materials about the office to make it appear that the break-in was the work of a drug addict. Throughout the operation surgical gloves were used to avoid fingerprint detection. In spite of all efforts, Ellsberg's records eluded them.

After relating the details of the entry and their lack of success to Hunt, Barker, Martinez, and de Diego returned to Miami. Hunt and Liddy returned to Washington, where they reported the failure of the operation to Krogh and Young. Krogh relayed that information to Ehrlichman.

White House involvement in the break-in remained unknown for almost two years. When the facts about the operation began to surface, however, on 14 March 1973 Ehrlichman was called before the grand jury to testify about his knowledge of the affair. He stated that he had not been aware prior to the break-in that the Room 16 unit was looking for information with which to compose a psychological profile of Ellsberg, and had had no advance knowledge that an effort was to be made to get such information from Dr. Fielding. One year later he was indicted, subsequently tried and convicted, for his role in authorizing the break-in and for his efforts to conceal his involvement by lying to the grand jury.

[Ehrlichman challenged his conspiracy conviction on two grounds. First, he claimed that the break-in was justified because it was undertaken pursuant to the president's constitutional prerogative to authorize such a search, for national-security reasons, without first obtaining a judicial warrant. Thus, since the burglary itself was justified, he could not be guilty of conspiracy to commit it. Second, he claimed that even if the warrantless search was unconstitutional—and the burglary was therefore unjustified— his reasonable belief to the contrary should excuse him from criminal liability.

[The question of actual authority requires an interpretation of the fourth amendment.[b] According to settled construction, this constitutional

---

[b] The fourth amendment provides that "the right of the people to be secure in their persons, houses, papers, and effects, against unreasonable searches and seizures, shall not

provision bars warrantless searches of private property "except in certain carefully defined classes of cases." Camara v. Municipal Court, 387 U.S. 523 (1967). Ehrlichman sought to rely on a so-called "national-security" exception to the warrant requirement. The court rejected his claim as follows:]

Ehrlichman claimed that the . . . entry was undertaken pursuant to an authorized "foreign-affairs" or "national-security" operation. Since 1940 the "foreign-affairs" exception to the prohibition against wiretapping has been espoused by the executive branch as a necessary concomitant to the president's constitutional power over the exercise of this country's foreign affairs, and warrantless electronic surveillance has been upheld by lower federal courts on a number of occasions. No court has ruled that the president does not have this prerogative in a case involving foreign agents or collaborators with a foreign power. The Supreme Court, in a number of decisions requiring officials to obtain a warrant before engaging in electronic surveillance, has been careful to note that its rulings do not reach such cases.

Hoping to fall within this as yet not fully defined exception, Ehrlichman urges that in September 1971 "in a matter affecting national security and foreign-intelligence gathering" the absence of a judicially approved warrant did not render unlawful "a search and seizure authorized by a presidential delegate pursuant to a broad presidential mandate of power given to that delegate."

Ehrlichman further argues [in his brief] that no specific authorization by the president or the attorney general was required:

Implicitly, an instruction to accomplish an end carries with it the duty of performing all lawful acts necessary to accomplish that end. In the instant case, the president delegated the power, to sworn officials of the executive branch, including Ehrlichman, to prevent and halt leaks of vital security information. To contend that the president must specifically chart out the methods of employing the power each and every time he delegates power is absurd.

The district court ruled as a matter of law that the national security exemption did not excuse the failure to obtain a judicial warrant for a physical search of Dr. Fielding's office either because there is no exemption for physical searches or because the exemption can only be invoked by the president or the attorney general in a particular case. . . .

[Whether or not the national-security exemption extends beyond wiretapping to physical searches] the district court was unquestionably correct in its ruling that in any event the "national-security" exemption can only be invoked if there has been a specific authorization by the president, or by the attorney general as his chief legal advisor, for the particular case.

be violated; and no warrants shall issue, but upon probable cause, supported by oath or affirmation, and particularly describing the place to be searched, and the persons or things to be seized."

Neither Ehrlichman nor any of his co-defendants [has] alleged that the attorney general gave his approval to the Fielding operation; and none has attempted to refute former President Nixon's assertion that he had no prior knowledge of the break-in and, therefore, could not and did not authorize the search.[66] . . . No court has ever in any way indicated, nor has any presidential administration or attorney general claimed, that any executive officer acting under an inexplicit presidential mandate may authorize warrantless searches of foreign agents or collaborators, much less the warrantless search of the offices of an American citizen not himself suspected of collaboration. . . .

As a constitutional matter, if presidential approval is to replace judicial approval for foreign intelligence gathering, the personal authorization of the President—or his alter ego for these matters, the attorney general—is necessary to fix accountability and centralize responsibility for insuring the least intrusive surveillance necessary and preventing zealous officials from misusing the presidential prerogative.

[The court then concluded that "under the circumstances of this case, the law is clear" that the warrantless burglary of Dr. Fielding's office exceeded Ehrlichman's constitutional authority and was therefore unjustified. The court then considered Ehrlichman's contention that his reasonable belief in the legality of the search of Dr. Fielding's office should defeat criminal liability. Noting that mistake of law is generally no excuse, the court found "no support for Ehrlichman's position in any of the recognized common-law exceptions to the mistake-of-law doctrine." In particular, the court observed, "Ehrlichman cannot and does not argue that he should be allowed a defense based upon his reasonable reliance on an apparently valid statute or judicial decision. . . ." Nor, the court concluded, was he relying on a misleading assertion of authority by the president or the attorney general, even if that would establish an excuse. "He simply asserts that it was his belief that the break-in was lawful notwithstanding the absence of any such specific defense."]

For the foregoing reasons, the district-court judgment is

Affirmed.

———

## NOTES ON MISTAKES BY PUBLIC OFFICIALS REGARDING THEIR OWN AUTHORITY

**1. *Ehrlichman* and Ignorantia Juris.** A mistake regarding the justifiability of otherwise criminal conduct ordinarily comes within the

[66] Indeed, for Ehrlichman to argue that the President gave his express authorization to a surreptitious entry and search of Dr. Fielding's office would have been patently inconsistent with Ehrlichman's primary defense at trial. Such authorization would have been transmitted to the "Room 16" unit through Ehrlichman, and he claimed not to have known the unit planned a surreptitious entry and search. The trial judge, however, put the question of Ehrlichman's prior knowledge of the break-in squarely to the jury and they found him guilty as charged.

traditional principle of ignorantia juris. Applying this principle, the *Ehrlichman* court concluded that the defendant's mistake regarding the scope of his constitutional authority, however reasonable, was without exculpatory significance. Was this a correct application of the ignorantia-juris principle? Ehrlichman's mistake concerned the meaning of the fourth amendment rather than the meaning of the conspiracy or burglary statutes. Is it clear that his mistake pertained, in the language of § 2.02(9) of the Model Penal Code, to the "existence, meaning or application of the law determining the elements of an offense"?

**2.  Special Rules for Official Mistakes of Law.** Many modern criminal codes expressly provide a defense, under some circumstances, for officials who exceed their authority. For example, § 939.45 of the Wisconsin Penal Code affords a "defense of privilege . . . when the actor's conduct is in good faith and is an apparently authorized and reasonable fulfillment of any duties of a public office." Section 35.05 of the New York Penal Code, which has been the model for many other states, provides that "conduct which would otherwise constitute an offense is justifiable [if] such conduct is required or authorized by law or by a judicial decree or is performed by a public servant in the reasonable exercise of his official powers, duties or functions." Do these provisions differ in important respects? Would the evidence in *Ehrlichman* support a jury instruction under either statute? Would Ehrlichman have a defense under § 3.03 of the Model Penal Code?

**3.  The Debate on Official Mistake.** In 1973, the Judiciary Committee of the United States Senate considered two proposed federal criminal code bills. Each of the bills included an official mistake provision. One of the bills provided a defense if "the defendant reasonably believed that the conduct charged was required or authorized by law . . . to carry out his duty as a public servant." Inclusion of this provision was vigorously criticized by the American Civil Liberties Union and other witnesses on the ground that it would encourage official abuses of power. One witness summarized the argument in the following terms:[a]

> [I]f enacted, this section would seriously dilute the power of the law to deal with criminal conduct on the part of federal officers. The public-duty defense would permit federal officials to use their position of public trust to defend against criminal prosecutions brought against them for violating that trust. Rather than focusing on the legality of specific actions, rather than considering whether those actions were in fact called for by the individual's public duty, this section would focus the court's attention on whether the official reasonably believed his conduct was legal. If an official simply convinces a jury that he reasonably believed his actions were authorized or required by law, his crime would be excused. . . .

[a] Reform of the Federal Criminal Laws, Hearings on S. 1 and S. 1400 before the Subcommittee on Criminal Laws and Procedures of the Committee on the Judiciary, United States Senate, 94th Cong., 1st Sess., Part XI, 8018–19 (Statement of Gregory Craig) (1974).

Whenever a federal official believes he can convince a jury that his conduct, though perhaps unlawful in retrospect, was guided by honest and praiseworthy motives and therefore reasonable, he will not be deterred from engaging in that conduct. The public servant is thereby given a free rein in the shadowy no-man's land of activities which are on the borderline of illegality. Rather than steering clear of the legally dubious, the public servant can chart a course significantly nearer criminal conduct with the assurance that his only burden is to persuade a jury that it was a gray area, that the lawfulness of his conduct was in his eyes, unclear, and that he was motivated by a sense of public duty rather than criminal malice. . . .

Proponents of such a provision claim that a general mistake defense is necessary to take into account the uncertain scope of many official duties and obligations. It is said that "public officials . . . who act in accordance with a reasonable belief that their actions are lawful should not be treated as criminals and cannot be so treated if we expect our laws to be enforced with the vigor required for successful implementation."[b] One opponent responded to these contentions as follows:[c]

[T]he public servant should not be protected from legal consequences of acts which are in the twilight zone of legality. Because the public servant exercises individual discretion, because he can always refuse or resign, because he carries with his office substantial social responsibility and public trust, because the public servant invokes all the might and majesty of the state when he acts, the public servant should, at the very least, be held to the same standard of conduct applied to the ordinary citizen. One would hope, if anything, that a higher standard would be expected in the conduct of a public official.

Which is the better position? Should public officials such as Ehrlichman be acquitted if they persuade a jury that they "reasonably believed" that their criminal conduct was authorized by law? Would recognition of such a defense encourage abuse of official authority? Alternatively, would application of the ignorantia-juris principle in this context make public officials unduly timid? Even apart from the impact of the alternative approaches on official behavior, should a public servant's "good motives" be irrelevant to the question of penal liability?

———

## Problem Based on United States v. Barker

United States Court of Appeals for the District of Columbia Circuit, 1976.
546 F.2d 940.

■ WILKEY, CIRCUIT JUDGE. Two of the "footsoldiers" of the Watergate affair, Bernard Barker and Eugenio Martinez, are with us again.[a] They haven't been promoted, they are still footsoldiers. They come before us this time to

[b] Id. at 8053 (Statement of John C. Kenney).

[c] Id. at 8020 (Statement of Gregory Craig).

challenge their convictions ... for their parts in the 1971 burglary of the office of Dr. Lewis J. Fielding.

[As in *United States* v. *Ehrlichman,* the defendants were convicted under 18 U.S.C. § 241 of conspiracy to violate Dr. Fielding's civil rights. For purposes of this problem, assume instead that they were convicted of burglary as defined in § 221.1 of the Model Penal Code. After describing the circumstances surrounding the creation of the "Room 16" unit, detailed in *United States* v. *Ehrlichman,* Judge Wilkey summarized the evidence concerning the recruitment of Barker and Martinez by Howard Hunt:]

Hunt had been a career agent in the CIA before his employment by the White House. One of his assignments was as a supervising agent for the CIA in connection with the Bay of Pigs invasion, and as "Eduardo," he was well known and respected in Miami's Cuban–American community. A fact destined to be of considerable importance later, he had been Bernard Barker's immediate supervisor in that operation. When the "Room 16" unit determined that it would be best if the actual entry into Dr. Fielding's office were made by individuals not in the employ of the White House, Hunt recommended enlisting the assistance of some of his former associates in Miami.

Hunt had previously re-established contact with Barker in Miami in late April 1971, and he met Martinez at the same time. He gave Barker an unlisted White House number where he could be reached by phone and wrote to Barker on White House stationery. On one occasion Barker met with Hunt in the Executive Office Building. By August 1971 Hunt returned to Miami and informed Barker that he was working for an organization at the White House level with greater jurisdiction than the FBI and the CIA. He asked Barker if he would become "operational" again and help conduct a surreptitious entry to obtain national-security information on "a traitor to this country who was passing ... classified information to the Soviet Embassy." He stated further that "the man in question ... was being considered as a possible Soviet agent himself."

Barker agreed to take part in the operation and to recruit two additional people. He contacted Martinez and Felipe de Diego. Barker conveyed to Martinez the same information Hunt had given him, and Martinez agreed to participate. Like Barker, Martinez had begun working as a covert agent for the CIA after Castro came to power in Cuba. Although Barker's formal relationship with the CIA had ended in 1966, Martinez was still on CIA retainer when he was contacted.

Both testified at trial that they had no reason to question Hunt's credentials. He clearly worked for the White House and had a well-known

a Judge Wilkey was referring to the efforts of Barker and Martinez to withdraw their guilty pleas in the case involving the burglary of the Democratic National Committee headquarters in the Watergate Office Building.—[Footnote by eds.]

background with the CIA. During the entire time they worked for the CIA, neither Barker nor Martinez was ever shown any credentials by their superiors. Not once did they receive written instructions to engage in the operations they were ordered to perform. Nevertheless, they testified, their understanding was always that those operations had been authorized by the government of the United States. That they did not receive more detail on the purpose of the Fielding operation or its target was not surprising to them; Hunt's instructions and actions were in complete accord with what their previous experience had taught them to expect. They were trained agents, accustomed to rely on the discretion of their superiors and to operate entirely on a "need-to-know" basis.

On 2 September 1971 Hunt and Liddy met Barker, Martinez and de Diego at a hotel in Beverly Hills, California. Hunt informed the defendants that they were to enter an office, search for a particular file, photograph it, and replace it. The following day the group met again. Hunt showed Barker and Martinez identification papers and disguises he had obtained from the CIA. That evening the defendants entered Dr. Fielding's office. Contrary to plan, it was necessary for them to use force to effect the break-in. As instructed in this event, the defendants spilled pills on the floor to make it appear the break-in had been a search for drugs. No file with the name Ellsberg was found.

The next day Barker and Martinez returned to Miami. The only funds they received from Hunt in connection with the entry of Dr. Fielding's office were reimbursement for their living expenses, the costs of travel, and $100.00 for lost income. . . .

[At their trial, the district court refused proffered jury instructions setting forth the defendants' theory of the case—that they should be found not guilty if they reasonably relied on Hunt's apparent authority. Instead the court specifically instructed the jury that a mistake as to the legality of the operation was *not* a defense.]

The primary ground upon which defendants Barker and Martinez rest their appeal is the refusal of the district court to allow them a defense based upon their good faith, reasonable reliance on Hunt's apparent authority.

. . . A defendant's error as to his *authority* to engage in particular activity, if based upon a mistaken view of legal requirements (or ignorance thereof), is a mistake of *law*. Typically, the fact that he relied upon the erroneous advice of another is not an exculpatory circumstance.

[A]lthough the basic policy behind the mistake-of-law doctrine is that, at their peril, all men should know and obey the law, in certain situations there is an overriding societal interest in having individuals rely on the authoritative pronouncements of officials whose decisions we wish to see respected.

For this reason, a number of exceptions to the mistake-of-law doctrine have developed where its application would be peculiarly unjust or counterproductive. Their recognition in a particular case should give the defendant a defense [if his mistake] is *objectively reasonable* under the circumstances. The mistake of a government agent in relying on a magistrate's approval of a search can be considered virtually per se reasonable.... Similarly, if a private person is summoned by a police officer to assist in effecting an unlawful arrest, his reliance on the officer's authority to make the arrest may be considered reasonable as a matter of law. The citizen is under a legal obligation to respond to a proper summons and is in no position to second-guess the officer's determination that an arrest is proper. Indeed, it is society's hope in recognizing the reasonableness of a citizen's mistake in this situation to encourage unhesitating compliance with a police officer's call.[25]

Other situations in which a government official enlists the aid of a private citizen to help him perform a governmental task are not so obviously reasonable on their face. If the official does not *order* the citizen to assist him, but simply asks for such assistance, the citizen is not under a legal compulsion to comply. Also, if the circumstances do not require immediate action, the citizen may have time to question the lawfulness of the planned endeavor. Nevertheless, the public policy of encouraging citizens to respond ungrudgingly to the request of officials for help in the performance of their duties remains quite strong. Moreover, the gap (both real and perceived) between a private citizen and a government official with regard to their ability and authority to judge the lawfulness of a particular governmental activity is great. It would appear to serve both justice and public policy in a situation where an individual acted at the behest of a government official to allow the individual a defense based upon his reliance on the official's authority—*if* he can show that his reliance was *objectively reasonable* under the particular circumstances of his case.

... I think it plain that a citizen should have a legal defense to a criminal charge arising out of an unlawful arrest or search which he has aided in the reasonable belief that the individual who solicited his assistance was a duly authorized officer of the law. It was error for the trial court to bar this defense in the admission of evidence and instructions to the jury, and the convictions must accordingly be

Reversed.

■ LEVENTHAL, CIRCUIT JUDGE (dissenting).... This [case] calls, I think, for an opening exclamation of puzzlement and wonder. Is this judicial novelty, a bold injection of mistake of law as a valid defense to criminal liability, really being wrought in a case where defendants are charged with combining to violate civil and constitutional rights? Can this extension be justified where there was a deliberate forcible entry, indeed a burglary, into the office of a doctor who was in no way suspected of any illegality or even impropriety, with the force compounded by subterfuge, dark of night, and

---

[25] This common-law exception to the mistake-of-law doctrine is codified in § 3.07(4)(a) of the Model Penal Code....

the derring-do of "salting" the office with nuggets to create suspicion that the deed was done by addicts looking for narcotics?

Judge Wilkey begins to cast his spell by describing Barker and Martinez as "footsoldiers" here in court again. Of course, they are here this time for an offense that took place the year before the notorious 1972 Watergate entry that led them to enter pleas of guilty to burglary. Every violation of civil rights depends not only on those who initiate, often unhappily with an official orientation of sorts, but also on those whose active effort is necessary to bring the project to fruition. To the extent appellants are deemed worthy of sympathy, that has been provided by the probation. To give them not only sympathy but exoneration, and absolution, is to stand the law upside down, in my view, and to sack legal principle instead of relying on the elements of humane administration that are available to buffer any grinding edge of law. That this tolerance of unlawful official action is a defense available for selective undermining of civil-rights laws leads me to shake my head both in wonder and despair....

I do not discount defendants' claims that their background, and particularly their previous relations with the CIA and Hunt explain their good-faith reliance on Hunt's apparent authority and their consequent failure to inquire about the legality of the activities they were to undertake on his request. I feel compassion for men who were simultaneously offenders and victims, and so did the trial judge when it came to sentencing. But testing their special circumstances against analogies they rely on to project a mistake-of-law defense, leads me to reject their claim to be relieved of personal accountability for their acts.

Appellants invoke the acceptance of good-faith reliance defenses in the Model Penal Code. However, the American Law Institute carefully limited the sections cited to persons responding to a call for aid from a police officer making an unlawful arrest,[34] and to obeying unlawful military orders,[35] and specifically rejected the defense for other mistake-of-law contexts.[36] In both instances, the A.L.I. recognizes limited curtailment of the doctrine excluding a mistake-of-law defense on the ground that the actor is under a duty to act—to help a police officer in distress to make an arrest when called upon, or to obey military orders. In each case, society has no alternative means available to protect its interest short of imposing a duty to act without a correlative duty to inquire about the legality of the act.[38] Punishing an individual for failure to inquire as to the lawful basis

[34] See, e.g., Model Penal Code § 3.07(4)....

[35] See Model Penal Code § 2.10....

[36] When § 3.07(4) does not specifically apply, § 3.09(1) withdraws any justification defense to the use of improper force where the actor's "error is due to ignorance or mistake as to the provisions of the Code, any other provision of the criminal law or the law governing the legality of an arrest or search." The commentary explained that provision as dealing with a "body of law [which] is not stated in the Code and may not appear in the form of penal law at all. It seems clear, however, that the policy which holds mistake of penal law to be immaterial applies with no less force to the law of arrest or search." ...

[38] A similar rationale underlies the exception for reliance on government authority when acting under a public duty. See Model Penal Code § 3.03.

for the officer's request would frustrate the effective functioning of the duly constituted police (and military) forces and in its operation on the individual would compel a choice between the whirlpool and the rock. . . .

Barker and Martinez were under no tension of conflicting duties comparable to that experienced by a soldier or citizen responding to orders. They had and claim no obligation to aid Hunt. Nor did they have a belief of fact rendering their voluntary assistance lawful within § 3.07(4). . . . Nor is there a compelling social interest to be served in allowing private citizens to undertake extra-legal activities, acting simply on the word of a government official. The purposes of the law in rejecting such a defense are underscored by the very kinds of extra-governmental, outside-normal-channels conduct that Barker and Martinez engaged in here. Government officials who claim to be seeking to implement the ends of government by bypassing the agencies and personnel normally responsible and accountable to the public transmit a danger signal. Barker and Martinez acted to help Hunt on his explanation that he sought their recruitment because the FBI's "hands were tied by Supreme Court decisions and the Central Intelligence Agency didn't have jurisdiction in certain matters." There is reason for the law to carve out limited exceptions to the doctrine negating defenses rooted in mistake of law, but the pertinent reasons have minimal weight, and face countervailing policies, when they are invoked for situations that on their face are outside the basic channels of law and government—in this case, requests for surreptitious or, if necessary, forcible entry and clandestine files search. These are plainly crimes, malum in se, unless there is legal authority. Citizens may take action in such circumstances out of emotions and motives that they deem lofty, but they must take the risk that their trust was misplaced, and that they will have no absolution when there was no authority for the request and their response. If they are later to avoid the consequences of criminal responsibility, it must be as a matter of discretion. To make the defense a matter of right would enhance the resources available to individual officials bent on extra-legal government behavior. The purpose of the criminal law is to serve and not to distort the fundamental values of the society. . . .

The ultimate point is that appellants' mistake of law, whether or not it is classified as reasonable, does not negative legal responsibility, but at best provides a reason for clemency on the ground that the strict rules of law bind too tight for the overall public good. . . .

But sympathy for defendants, or the possibility that their mistake might be considered "reasonable" given their unique circumstances, must not override a pragmatic view of what the law requires of persons taking this kind of action. I come back—again and again, in my mind—to the stark fact that we are dealing with a breaking and entering in the dead of night, both surreptitious and forcible, and a violation of civil-rights statutes. This is simply light years away from the kinds of situations where the law has gingerly carved out exceptions permitting reasonable mistake of law as a defense—cases like entering a business transaction on the erroneous advice of a high responsible official or district attorney, or like responding to an urgent call for aid from a police officer. I dissent.

———

## NOTES ON CITIZEN RELIANCE ON APPARENT OFFICIAL AUTHORITY

**1. Introduction.** Barker and Martinez did not claim that they believed that the search of Dr. Fielding's office had been authorized by a magistrate pursuant to normal procedures for obtaining a warrant. Nor did they claim that they had been misled into believing that the president or the attorney general had personally authorized the break-in. Instead, they testified that they believed that some White House official—Hunt, Krogh or, at best, Ehrlichman—had authorized it. Their mistake was in assuming that this constituted lawful authority; and, as Judges Wilkey and Leventhal seem to agree, this is a mistake of law regarding the justifiability of the defendants' conduct. The question is whether, and under what circumstances, a citizen's otherwise criminal conduct should be excused because he or she acted at the request or direction of a public official who exceeded his or her authority. Should a mistake regarding the lawfulness of the request or direction exculpate the citizen even though it would be insufficient to exculpate the public official?

**2. Compliance With Official Orders or Requests.** In ordinary social relationships there is no overriding societal interest in reflexive obedience to, and respect for, authority. Thus, suppose A orders a business subordinate, B, to do an illegal act. If B subsequently claims that she did not know it was illegal, the mistake is no defense; or if B subsequently claims she had no choice but to comply because she was pressured, afraid, or fearful of losing her job, her fear of the consequences will be ignored. The subordinate is expected to retain the capacity for free and independent judgment.

In some situations, however, there is a societal interest in unquestioning obedience. This is most obviously true in the military setting, and the common law has long recognized a defense for soldiers who obey superior orders, so long as they are not "palpably illegal."[a] Section 2.10 of the Model

---

[a] See, e.g., United States v. Calley, 46 C.M.R. 1131, 1179–84 (1973); United States v. Kinder, 14 C.M.R. 742 (1954). In the *Calley* case, the defendant, a platoon leader, was convicted of three counts of murder arising out of a military operation in the Vietnamese hamlet of My Lai. During this operation, Calley directed and participated in the killing of approximately 70 unarmed villagers. He claimed, inter alia, that he did so in obedience to the orders of his superiors. The members of the court martial considered this claim under the following instruction, which was subsequently upheld by the Court of Military Review:

A determination that an order is illegal does not, of itself, assign criminal responsibility to the person following the order for acts done in compliance with it. Soldiers are taught to follow orders, and special attention is given to obedience of orders on the battlefield. Military effectiveness depends upon obedience to others. On the other hand, the obedience of a soldier is not the obedience of an au-

Penal Code codifies this defense. (It should be emphasized that the "superior-orders" defense has not been applied outside the military context.) Common-law precedents also afford a defense to citizens who assist the police to make arrests that turn out to be unlawful.[b] This rule is codified in § 3.07(4)(a) of the Model Penal Code and appears in most modern statutes.

The relationship between Hunt and the Cuban defendants resembles the relationship between police officers and ordinary citizens. Judge Wilkey concluded that the similarity was close enough to warrant a defense for reasonable reliance on Hunt's apparent authority. Judge Leventhal disagreed. Who is right? Should a defense be available to citizens who assist public officials in reasonable reliance on their apparent authority? Would recognition of such a defense increase the likelihood of official abuse of power? On the other hand, is it just to punish a person who comes to the aid of a public official who appears to be acting within his or her authority?

Judge Leventhal points out that the *Barker* defendants invoked the "good-faith-reliance defenses" of the Model Penal Code. In response, he says that the defenses in the Code are "carefully limited ... to persons responding to a call for aid from a police officer making an unlawful arrest and to obeying unlawful military orders." Is he right?

Examine § 3.03(3)(b) of the Model Code. Does Barker's claim raise a defense under this section?[c]

---

## SECTION 2: SITUATIONAL EXCUSE

### INTRODUCTORY NOTE ON THE DEFENSE OF DURESS

The law has traditionally recognized a defense of duress, as in a case where A commits a crime because B holds a gun to A's head and forces A to do so. Usually, this defense has been restrictively defined. Moreover, the defendant typically bears the burden of proving the elements of the defense to the satisfaction of the jury.

---

tomaton. A soldier is a reasoning agent, obliged to respond, not as a machine, but as a person. The law takes these factors into account in assessing criminal responsibility for acts done in compliance with illegal orders.

The acts of a subordinate done in compliance with an unlawful order given him by his superior are excused and impose no criminal liability upon him unless the superior's order is one which a man of ordinary sense and understanding would, under the circumstances, know to be unlawful, or if the order in question is actually known to the accused to be unlawful.

[b] Some statutes impose a duty on the citizen to aid a police officer under some circumstances; failure to obey would itself be a criminal offense. In these situations, the citizen has a public duty that justifies otherwise criminal conduct. See Model Penal Code § 3.03(1)(a).

[c] For discussions of *Barker*, see Comment, United States v. Barker: Misapplication of the Reliance on an Official Interpretation of the Law Defense, 66 Calif.L.Rev. 809 (1978); Note, Reliance on Apparent Authority as a Defense to Criminal Prosecution, 77 Colum.L.Rev. 775 (1977).

The materials in this section explore the nature of the duress defense. At the outset, it is helpful to note the analytical distinction between the defense of duress and the "voluntary act" doctrine considered in Chapter II. It would do no violence to the English language to characterize as "involuntary" *A*'s act of committing a crime under duress. Indeed, *A*'s claim might appear, at first blush, to be functionally similar to the claim that could be raised by *A* if, with intent to injure *C*, *B* shoved *A* into *C*, thereby knocking *C* into the path of an oncoming car. However, the law draws a distinction between bodily movements that are within the conscious control of the actor and those that are not.

In 2 A History of the Criminal Law of England 102 (1883), Sir James Fitzjames Stephen described this distinction as follows:

> A criminal walking to execution is under compulsion if any man can be said to be so, but his motions are just as much voluntary actions as if he [were] going to leave his place of confinement and regain his liberty. He walks to his death because he prefers it to being carried.

As a matter of legal definition, an act which the actor feels constrained to commit is regarded as "voluntary" for purposes of establishing that the actus reus of the offense has been committed. The involuntary-act doctrine covers cases where the actor makes no choice at all, not those where he or she is forced by circumstances to make a "hard choice."

Traditionally, the duress defense has been the main device by which the law takes into account external constraints on a person's capacity to choose to comply with the law.[a] Of course, the task of determining when a "hard choice" should have exculpatory significance requires a judgment of degree. As Glanville Williams has noted, "[f]ear of violence does not differ in kind from fear of economic ills, fear of displeasing others, or any other determinant of choice." Criminal Law: The General Part 751 (2d ed. 1961). Under what circumstances should it be said that a person was "compelled" to commit a crime, that he or she should not be punished for failing to do otherwise? Stephen concluded that the law should never give exculpatory significance to hard choices, even those produced by threats of death. In a famous passage opposing the duress defense, 2 A History of the Criminal Law of England 107–08 (1883), Stephen argued as follows:

> Criminal law is itself a system of compulsion on the widest scale. It is a collection of threats of injury to life, liberty, and property if people do commit crimes. Are such threats to be withdrawn as soon as they are encountered by opposing threats? The law says to a man intending to commit murder, if you do it I will hang you. Is the law to withdraw its threat if someone else says, if you do not do it, I will shoot you?
>
> Surely it is at the moment when temptation to crime is strongest that the law should speak most clearly and emphatically

---

[a] The impact of a person's abnormal mental condition on his or her capacity to conform to the law is explored in connection with the insanity defense in Chapter VI.

to the contrary. It is, of course, a misfortune for a man that he should be placed between two fires, but it would be a much greater misfortune for society at large if criminals could confer impunity upon their agents by threatening them with death or violence if they refused to execute their commands. If impunity could be so secured a wide door would be opened to collusion, and encouragement would be given to associations of malefactors, secret or otherwise. No doubt the moral guilt of a person who commits a crime under compulsion is less than that of a person who commits it freely, but any effect which is thought proper may be given to this circumstance by a proportional mitigation of the offender's punishment.

These reasons lead me to think that compulsion by threats ought in no case whatever to be admitted as an excuse for crime, though it may and ought to operate in mitigation of punishment in most though not in all cases. . . .

Glanville Williams has observed that Stephen's view "would now be regarded as over-severe." In some cases, he continues, "justice demand[s] not merely a mitigation of punishment but no punishment at all. . . ." Glanville Williams, Criminal Law: The General Part 755 (2d ed. 1961). The drafters of the Model Penal Code responded to Stephen's argument as follows:

[L]aw is ineffective in the deepest sense, indeed ... it is hypocritical, if it imposes on the actor who has the misfortune to confront a dilemmatic choice, a standard that his judges are not prepared to affirm that they should and could comply with if their turn to face the problem should arise. Condemnation in such a case is bound to be an ineffective threat; what is, however, more significant is that it is divorced from any moral base and is unjust. Where it would be both "personally and socially debilitating" to accept the actor's cowardice as a defense, it would be equally debilitating to demand that heroism should be the standard of legality.[b]

Other authors have criticized Stephen's opposition to the duress defense, and a few have suggested that it is a fundamental mistake to characterize duress as an "excuse" rather than as a "justification." Most courts and commentators treat duress as a species of excuse, "rather than a justification, because the community prefers that actors not offend, even under the pressure of serious threats, but will withhold blame where the threats are sufficiently grievous."[c] Still, as the United States Supreme Court has observed, the distinction between duress and necessity is a

---

[b] ALI, Model Penal Code and Commentaries, § 2.09, pp. 374–75 (1985).

[c] Anne M. Coughlin, Excusing Women, 82 Cal. L. Rev. 1, 29–30 & n.143 (1994); see also Mitchell N. Berman, Justification and Excuse, Law and Morality, 53 Duke L.J. 1, 69–73 (2003).

blurry one.[d] In connection with these observations, consider the following case.

————

# United States v. Haney

United States Court of Appeals, Tenth Circuit, 2002.
287 F.3d 1266.

■ HENRY, CIRCUIT JUDGE. Robert M. Haney appeals his conviction and sentence for violation of 18 U.S.C. § 1791(a)(2) (possession of escape paraphernalia in prison). Mr. Haney asserts that the district court erred in ... not permitting him to raise a defense of duress, a defense the jury accepted, on a related count, as to Mr. Haney's co-defendant. [We] vacate Mr. Haney's conviction for possession of escape paraphernalia....

## I.  BACKGROUND

Following his escape from prison, the television show "America's Most Wanted" incorrectly described Tony S. Francis, friend and co-defendant of Mr. Haney, as a leader of the Aryan Brotherhood, a prison gang preaching white supremacy. Once recaptured, Mr. Francis found himself housed in the federal penitentiary in Florence, Colorado; Mr. Francis developed anxiety about his incarceration in this facility for at least two reasons. First, Mr. Francis feared the reaction of African–American prisoners because at least some of those prisoners had, in all likelihood, heard the claim of Aryan Brotherhood membership made by "America's Most Wanted." Second, Mr. Francis feared the reaction of members of the Aryan Brotherhood because, in reality, Mr. Francis was not a member of that prison gang.

In 1997, prison authorities became concerned about growing racial tension in the Florence penitentiary; beginning on September 3, 1997, prison authorities "locked down" the penitentiary for ten days. Immediately after prison authorities lifted the lock-down, three African–American inmates threatened Mr. Francis. The inmates approached Mr. Francis, told him that they had seen him on "America's Most Wanted," and offered a warning to the effect that: "When the shit jumps off, you know what time it is"—i.e., a race war was brewing and Mr. Francis was a target.

Mr. Francis concluded that his only option was to attempt a prison escape. In their respective testimonies, Mr. Francis and Mr. Haney each explained this implicit decision not to seek the aid of the prison authorities as resting on the alleged fact that seeking such aid did not constitute a reasonable alternative. Mr. Francis and Mr. Haney testified that, had Mr. Francis sought such assistance, Mr. Francis and Mr. Haney's fellow inmates would have labeled Mr. Francis a snitch, thereby placing Mr. Francis in further danger. Additionally, according to the testimony of Mr. Francis and Mr. Haney, because the special housing units were far from free from

---

[d] See United States v. Bailey, 444 U.S. 394 (1980)

violence, placing Mr. Francis in protective custody would also have proven of limited benefit.

Mr. Haney agreed to help Mr. Francis in Mr. Francis' attempted escape. Mr. Haney used his position as an employee in the prison laundry to collect a variety of escape paraphernalia. On September 26, 1997— approximately two weeks after the initial threat—Mr. Francis was shown a "kite" (a note) in which an inmate commented that Mr. Francis was still considered a target. This threat provided renewed impetus for the escape attempt.

On the night of October 3, 1997, Mr. Francis and Mr. Haney gathered the collected escape paraphernalia and hid in the prison yard. As they hid, however, Mr. Haney endeavored to convince Mr. Francis that an escape attempt was, in fact, imprudent; Mr. Haney argued, in effect: "The best possible solution would be to get caught trying to escape, thereby getting placed into disciplinary segregation without having to report the death threats to prison officials." Mr. Francis ultimately agreed. After two hours of strewing the yard with the escape paraphernalia, the two inmates were finally caught.

The United States charged both Mr. Francis and Mr. Haney with (1) violation of 18 U.S.C. § 1791(a)(2) (possession of escape paraphernalia in prison) and (2) violation of 18 U.S.C. § 751(a) (attempted escape). As to Mr. Francis, the district court instructed the jury on the duress defense in regard to both counts; as to Mr. Haney, however, the court refused to give a duress instruction on either count. The jury convicted both Mr. Francis and Mr. Haney of possessing escape paraphernalia but acquitted both Mr. Francis and Mr. Haney of attempting to escape. In acquitting Mr. Francis of the attempted escape, the jury expressly invoked the duress defense.

II.  DISCUSSION: Applicability of the Duress Defense

Mr. Haney argues that he was entitled to present a duress defense to the jury.[3] In order to have a theory of defense submitted to the jury, a defendant must present sufficient evidence, on each element of the defense, by which the jury could find in the defendant's favor. Indeed, a "defendant is entitled to jury instructions on any theory of defense finding support in the evidence and the law. Failure to so instruct is reversible error." . . . The district court concluded that Mr. Haney failed to present sufficient evidence as to the elements of the duress defense and thus that the duress defense was, as a matter of law, inapplicable to Mr. Haney.

[The] duress defense typically consists of three elements:

> (1) The threat of immediate infliction, upon the defendant, of death or bodily harm;

---

[3] Interestingly, Mr. Haney's counsel offered, at least once, to abandon pursuit of the duress defense if the government would agree not to pursue an "aiding and abetting" theory as to the charged attempted escape; the government, however, declined to accept the offer.

(2) The defendant's well-grounded fear that the threat will be carried out; and

(3) The defendant's lack of a reasonable opportunity to otherwise avert the threatened harm.

By his own admission, Mr. Haney cannot meet the elements of the duress defense, as described above. Quite basically, Mr. Haney makes no allegation that he ever feared for his own safety. Mr. Haney seeks to overcome this obstacle by proposing an extension of the duress defense; Mr. Haney argues that the duress defense should encompass defendants who correctly recognize that another individual's safety is at risk. Thus, Mr. Haney would describe the elements of the duress defense as requiring:[4]

(1) The threat of immediate infliction, upon the defendant or a third person, of death or bodily harm;

(2) The defendant's well-grounded fear that the threat will be carried out; and

(3) The defendant's, and third person's, lack of a reasonable opportunity to otherwise avert the threatened harm.

The government presents no argument that the duress defense should not extend, in at least certain circumstances, to third parties, thereby essentially conceding the point. Rather, the government presses two grounds on which we might nevertheless conclude, as a matter of law, that the duress defense is here unavailable to Mr. Haney. The government first suggests that the duress defense should be extended to third parties only where the defendant enjoys a familial relationship with the threatened individual. Second, the government suggests that Mr. Haney produced inadequate evidence to create a jury question as to either the first or third element of the duress defense. We address these arguments in turn.

A.  Third Party Duress

1.  Whether the duress defense should ever extend to third parties

Despite the fact that the government essentially abandons this position (presenting no argument and citing no cases or other legal authority), we begin our discussion of third party duress by considering whether the duress defense should ever be available when a third party (a party other than the defendant) is threatened with death or bodily harm. Logic and overwhelming legal authority conjoin in establishing that the duress defense should, indeed, extend to third parties.

The principle underlying the duress defense is one of hard-nosed practicality: sometimes social welfare is maximized by forgiving a relatively minor offense in order to avoid a greater social harm.... Where *A*, with apparent credibility, threatens to shoot *B* unless *B* jaywalks (and where *B*, in fear of the threat, possesses no reasonable opportunity to otherwise

---

[4] The defense of duress, as formulated by Mr. Haney, remains distinct from the "defense of another" in that "defense of another" scenarios feature the defendant taking action directly against the threatening individual(s), while a "third party duress" scenario would involve the defendant taking any other course of action.

avert the shooting), the law excuses $B$'s relatively minor offense in order to avoid the greater social harm threatened by $A$. The same logic dictates that so, too, where $A$, again with apparent credibility, threatens to shoot $B$ unless $C$ jaywalks, the defense of third party duress should excuse $C$'s relatively minor offense (at least so long as (1) $C$ actually feared that $A$ would execute the shooting and (2) neither $B$ nor $C$ possessed a reasonable alternative to otherwise avert the shooting).

Commentators and the case law agree that the duress defense should extend to the defense of third parties. . . .

2.   Whether the duress defense, once extended to third parties, should be limited to third parties with a familial relationship to the defendant

It is true that, as the government observes, most cases of third-party duress involve familial relationships between the defendant and the threatened individual; however, neither logic nor practicality supports such a "family relationship" limitation. Returning to our basic illustration of the duress defense above, why should it matter whether $C$ (who jaywalks in order to prevent $A$ from shooting $B$) enjoys a family relationship with $B$; in either case, permitting $C$ to jaywalk avoids the greater social harm. Professors Scott and LaFave agree: "As a matter of principle, the threatened harm need not be directed at the defendant himself; it may be aimed at a member of his family or a friend (or, it would seem, even a stranger)." 1 Wayne R. LaFave & Austin W. Scott, Jr., Substantive Criminal Law § 5.3, at 624 (1986); see also, e.g., Model Penal Code § 2.09(1) (declining to limit the duress defense to parties enjoying a familial relationship: "It is an affirmative defense that the actor engaged in the conduct charged to constitute an offense because he was coerced to do so by the use of, or a threat to use, unlawful force against his person or the person of another."); cf. LaFave & Scott, supra, § 5.08(a), at 664 (noting, in the context of the "defense of another" defense, that, while "some early English cases suggested that force may not be used in defense of another unless the defender stands in some personal relationship to the one in need of protection[,] . . . the modern and better rule is that there need be no such relationship").

Indeed, as Professor Hill has written, the applicability of the duress defense may be particularly important precisely where $B$ and $C$ are not related because it is in this circumstance that $C$ may need greater reassurance before risking criminal punishment in order to improve the well-being of $B$.

> Third parties are in special need of protection in situations where the defendant may have no great incentive to protect the third party [i.e., where the defendant and the threatened party are not bonded by familial ties]. Permitting the defense [of duress] in these situations allows the defendant to succumb to the threat without fear of punishment, rather than risk the safety of the third party. In sum, the law should extend the defense to this situation precisely because the actor might not be sufficiently coerced to act in a situation where we should encourage such an act.

John Lawrence Hill, A Utilitarian Theory of Duress, 84 Iowa L. Rev. 275, 325 (1999).

Not only is the government's "family members only" limitation unprincipled, it is unworkable. Under the government's proposed limitation, the duress defense would presumably remain available where $B$ and $C$ enjoy a mother-son or husband-wife relationship but not where $B$ and $C$ merely find themselves seated next to each other on a public bus. A family relationship, however, is somewhat difficult to identify: what of a couple engaged to be married, an aunt and nephew, in-laws, distant cousins who know each other well, siblings who have never met, unmarried co-habitants, etc.?[5] The government's failure to offer guidance on these issues is surely a product of the unprincipled line drawn by the "family relationship" test.

It is, then, hardly surprising that, in the only federal case ... to explicitly address the duress defense in the context of an unrelated defendant and threatened party, the Ninth Circuit did not even pause to consider whether the duress defense might not apply in such a situation. United States v. Lopez, 885 F.2d 1428 (9th Cir.1989), involved a defendant invoking the duress defense after flying a helicopter into a federal prison in order to avert a threatened harm to his "girlfriend," an inmate in that prison. Rather than struggle over whether a non-marital romantic attachment may constitute a "family relationship," the Ninth Circuit moved directly to consideration of whether the defendant had established the substantive elements of the duress defense. Just as we know of no federal case categorically declining to apply the duress defense in the third-party context, we know of no federal case categorically limiting the third party duress defense to defendants who happen to enjoy a family relationship to the threatened individual.

In sum, we see no principled justification for limiting the duress defense to defendants whose own safety is threatened. Nor do we see any justification for limiting the duress defense to defendants in a familial relationship with the threatened individual. Such distinctions would be arbitrary and unjust. As Mr. Haney correctly observes, the duress defense is appropriately defined not by "the nature of the relationship between the alleged law-breaker and the beneficiary third party" but by the "nature of the crime committed and the benefit conferred upon the third party."[6]

---

[5] And, again, how are any of these relationships meaningfully distinct, for purposes of application of the duress defense, from the relationship between two close friends, long-time roommates, work colleagues, a teacher and student, etc.?

[6] While the government has not explicitly argued the point, we briefly consider, and reject, the notion that the prison context ... should control the applicability of the duress defense. The prison environment does present unique circumstances; these unique circumstances, however, have never before justified a departure from general legal principles. The defenses of insanity and self-defense, for instance, apply both inside and outside the prison walls ... ; indeed, we know of no defense made unavailable by the fact that the alleged crime occurred within a prison. The same principles that ordinarily underlie the duress defense persist within the prison context: there will be some circumstances, even within a prison, where social utility is maximized by the commission of a relatively minor offense....

### B. Sufficiency of the Evidence

Nor can we accept the government's argument that Mr. Haney failed to produce adequate evidence to create a jury issue on either the first or third element of the duress defense. Here, of course, the government's position is weakened (though not logically foreclosed) by the fact that the jury explicitly invoked the duress defense to acquit Mr. Francis of the charged attempted escape. The fact that the jury, hearing much of the same evidence that Mr. Haney would have applied toward his own duress defense, accepted the duress defense in a related context suggests that Mr. Haney did, indeed, offer sufficient evidence.

### 1. Whether Mr. Haney presented sufficient evidence as to the first element of the duress defense

The first element of the duress defense requires a threat of immediate infliction of death or bodily harm. The government argues that Mr. Haney's testimony that he was "not a hundred percent sure that [Mr. Francis] was going to try to follow through" with the escape, establishes, as a matter of law, that the relevant threat could not have been an immediate one. We reject this notion. Mr. Francis testified to racially motivated threats upon his life in the context of simmering racial tension. [As he stated], "Most everyone in the joint and even in the staff ... believed that there was going to be a racial war on a riot type of scale. . . . I was going to be one of the first ones hit, killed." Numerous witnesses substantiated the severe racial tension in the prison and the fact that, as a consequence of that tension, Mr. Francis had received a specific and credible threat upon his life. . . .

Certainly the testimony of Mr. Francis, Mr. Haney, prison officials, and fellow inmates created a jury issue regarding the imminence of the threat against Mr. Francis' life. Mr. Haney's admission of some degree of uncertainty regarding whether Mr. Francis would execute the escape attempt creates, at best, some doubt regarding that imminence; Mr. Haney's admission in no way establishes, as a matter of law, that Mr. Francis faced no immediate threat of death or bodily harm.

### 2. Whether Mr. Haney presented sufficient evidence as to the third element of the duress defense

The third element of the duress defense requires that Mr. Haney and Mr. Francis have each lacked a reasonable legal opportunity to avert the threatened harm. The government notes that "evidence was presented that an inmate could get placed in protective custody through a variety of means, including with the assistance of another inmate." The government points to the testimony of Mr. Francis and Paul Chartier, another inmate at the Florence Penitentiary. On cross-examination and re-cross-examination, respectively, both Mr. Francis and Mr. Chartier answered "yeah" in regard to a question as to whether Mr. Haney might have passed an anonymous note to the prison guards in order to have Mr. Francis involuntarily isolated. In the government's view, Mr. Haney's exercise of that alternative would have averted the threatened harm to Mr. Francis (while also avoiding adverse collateral consequences [inmate-on-inmate violence]); thus, the proposed course of action was a reasonable alternative to the possession of escape paraphernalia.

Again, however, the government confuses evidence that suggests the existence of such a reasonable alternative with evidence establishing, as a matter of law, the existence of such a reasonable alternative. Mr. Francis testified extensively regarding the risks inherent in engineering one's own check-in. [Indeed, he put it bluntly,] "You can be killed when you're labeled [as a check-in]." Further, immediately following Mr. Chartier's "yeah" response noted above, Mr. Chartier added: "It's not an option, though, when you live that life." Other inmates testified along similar lines....

Given the opportunity, a jury certainly might have concluded that Mr. Haney could not claim the duress defense because either he or Mr. Francis possessed a reasonable alternative to the possession of escape paraphernalia. On the other hand, however, a jury could also have concluded that (1) if Mr. Francis had simply checked himself in, he would have exposed himself to an unreasonable risk and likewise (2) if Mr. Haney were to have engineered Mr. Francis' check-in, Mr. Haney would have exposed Mr. Francis to an unreasonable risk that fellow inmates would perceive Mr. Haney's actions to be at the behest of his friend Mr. Francis. In short, the jury could have concluded that neither Mr. Haney nor Mr. Francis in fact possessed any reasonable alternative to the possession of escape paraphernalia.

Because a jury could have concluded (1) that the threat against Mr. Francis was immediate in nature, (2) that Mr. Haney actually possessed a well-grounded fear that the threat would be executed, and (3) that neither Mr. Haney nor Mr. Francis, in order to avert the threatened harm, maintained any reasonable alternative to possessing escape paraphernalia, the district court should have granted Mr. Haney's request for jury instructions on the duress defense.

## III. CONCLUSION

For the reasons set forth above, we decline to limit the duress defense to defendants related by familial ties to a threatened individual and we further conclude that Mr. Haney presented adequate evidence to create a jury issue as to the applicability of that defense to his alleged possession of escape paraphernalia. Obviously we express no further opinion as to the likely merits of Mr. Haney's duress defense. Should the government choose to retry this case, the government, with the duress issue now in play, may well produce overwhelming evidence as to either the non-immediacy of the threat against Mr. Francis or the existence of reasonable alternatives to the possession of escape paraphernalia. These, however, are considerations for a jury: we vacate Mr. Haney's conviction and sentence and remand for further proceedings consistent with this opinion.

## NOTES ON DURESS AND SITUATIONAL EXCUSE

**1. Questions and Comments on *Haney*.** *Haney* offers a description of duress doctrine with which the vast majority of jurisdictions would agree. Some courts may provide a somewhat more elaborate treatment of the defense, but most statements of doctrine resemble closely the three elements cited in *Haney*. But *Haney*'s account of the principles underlying duress is controversial. According to *Haney*, the theoretical basis for the defense "is one of hard-nosed practicality: sometimes social welfare is maximized by forgiving a relatively minor offense in order to avoid a greater social harm." Here, the court invokes the rhetoric of necessity rather than that of excuse. With this rhetoric, together with its illustrative "jaywalking" example, the court implies that a properly instructed jury might have acquitted Haney on the ground that he did the right thing. It was proper for him to commit a trivial wrong in order to save his friend's life; indeed, because he correctly balanced the evils confronting him, he committed no crime at all. By contrast, if the court had treated duress as an excuse, it would have valued Haney's conduct quite differently. According to the theoretical rationale for excuse, it is unjust to punish a person who committed his crime under the compulsion of threats that other members of the community would not have had the fortitude to resist. On this theory, a jury might have acquitted Haney, but not on the ground that he did the right thing. Rather, the judgment would be that he did the wrong thing, but he should not be punished for it because his options were so excruciating.

Does Haney or any other defendant care if the jury decides that his or her crime should merely be excused rather than justified? In either case, the accused is spared the pain of punishment, and it may be that he or she never notices the normative nuances implied by one judgment as opposed to the other. But, as the Introductory chapter shows when describing the purposes of punishment, the criminal law speaks to more than one audience. Actual offenders are far from the only, or even the principal, targets of the messages that criminal punishment is designed to convey. So it is that commentators and lawmakers continue to believe that members of the community, including the law-abiding as well as potential wrongdoers, do hear and respond to the different evaluative judgements conveyed by the doctrines of excuse and of justification. As Anne Coughlin observes, the community is encouraged to emulate actors whose conduct is justified but not those who are excused: "By finding that a defendant's conduct was justified, the decisionmaker not only announces that no wrong was committed, it also expresses its confidence in the actor's capacity to behave responsibly in the future. In sharp contrast to the justified actor, who is adjudged to have governed himself in an exemplary fashion, the excused defendant achieves leniency only by showing that, at the time he offended, his capacity to choose lawful over unlawful conduct was grossly distorted."[a] Of course, these nuances may not be lost on individual offenders, but even if they are, the system remains committed to making them.

[a] Anne M. Coughlin, Excusing Women, 82 Cal. L. Rev. 1, 14 (1994).

In *Haney*, the court decided that the duress defense should be extended to cases where the target of the threat was not the offender himself, but a third party. The court concluded that there was no principled basis for refusing to allow the defense in such cases. Indeed, the court argued that extending the defense to cases involving threats against third parties would create good incentives for behavior, as actors otherwise might hesitate to violate the law in order to protect the safety of others. If the court's analysis had been informed by principles of excuse rather than necessity, would it have reached the same outcome? If duress is an excuse, is there a principled reason to refuse to allow the defense in cases involving threats against others? To limit it to cases involving threats against family members?

**2.  Elements of Duress.** As *Haney* reports, the duress defense requires the defendant to show that he was under a "threat of immediate infliction ... of death or bodily harm" and that he lacked "a reasonable legal opportunity to avert the threatened harm." The court does not explain why, if the defense indeed is a species of necessity, it is defined so narrowly. Why would threats to destroy property or reputation not suffice, as long as the actor correctly chose the lesser of two evils? Does the grudging scope of the defense suggest that it is an excuse, rather than a justification?

A frequently litigated aspect of duress is the requirement that the death threat be "imminent" or "immediate." An example is State v. Toscano, 74 N.J. 421, 378 A.2d 755 (1977). Dr. Toscano, a chiropractor, was convicted of conspiring with one William Leonardo and others to obtain money by false pretenses. Specifically, Toscano signed a false medical report for use by Leonardo in an insurance fraud scheme. Toscano claimed that he "just had to do it" in order to protect himself and his family from bodily harm threatened by Leonardo. Leonardo allegedly made several phone calls insisting that Toscano file the false report and sounded "vicious" and "desperate." Leonardo said, among other things: "Remember you just moved into a place that has a very dark entrance and you live there with your wife.... You and your wife are going to jump at shadows when you leave that dark entrance." Defendant finally agreed to Leonardo's demand and made out a single false medical report. He later moved to another house and changed his telephone number to avoid future contact with Leonardo. What he did not do was call the police.

The trial court refused to instruct on duress. The court reasoned that defendant's evidence, even if believed, would not show a "present, imminent and impending" threat of harm. Because Leonardo was not in a position to act immediately, Toscano had ample opportunity to call the police.

The Supreme Court of New Jersey held the evidence of duress sufficient to go to the jury and reversed Toscano's conviction. That court relied on § 2.09 of the Model Penal Code and the then proposed (and subsequently enacted) New Jersey statute, both of which explicitly reject the common-law requirement of a threat of imminent harm. Under these provisions, the immediacy of the danger is merely one of the circumstances to be considered in determining whether the threatened use of force was such that "a person of reasonable firmness in [the defendant's] situation would have been unable to resist."

Which approach is preferable? Is it fair to expect a person in Toscano's situation to contact the police rather than commit the crime? Even if he or she believes the police will be unable to provide effective protection? Does the Model Penal Code approach unduly compromise the deterrent effect of the law? Does it permit a terrorist to confer standing immunity on others to do his or her bidding?

**3. Duress and Battered Woman Syndrome.** The elements of duress bear more than a superficial resemblance to those of self-defense. For either defense to succeed, the actor must establish that she faced an "imminent" or "immediate" threat of serious bodily harm and that she lacked other "reasonable legal alternatives." Over the past decade, defense lawyers have started to argue that evidence that the actor suffered from battered woman syndrome should be admissible to help support a claim of duress, just as it is allowed to establish self-defense.

In United States v. Willis, 38 F.3d 170 (1994), the United States Court of Appeals for the Fifth Circuit upheld a trial judge's decision to exclude evidence of battered woman syndrome to support a female defendant's claim that she committed her crime under duress from her male partner. Willis was arrested for selling marijuana to an undercover cop. During the search incident to her arrest, officers found a loaded semi-automatic pistol in her handbag. Willis was "indicted for carrying a firearm during, and in relation to, the commission of a drug trafficking crime," and, at trial, she claimed that the gun belonged to her boyfriend and that he had placed it in her purse because, as a convicted felon, it was a crime for him to possess it. Willis explained that her boyfriend was very violent, that he had beaten her up badly in the past, and that she believed that he would beat her if she refused to hide the gun for him. To support her claim that she was actually in fear for her life at the time she came into possession of the gun, Willis sought to introduce testimony by an expert that she was suffering from battered woman syndrome. The trial court excluded this testimony, and the jury convicted Willis, rejecting her claim that she had committed her crime under duress. The Fifth Circuit affirmed, reasoning as follows:

> The argument made by Willis herein compels this court to consider the place of battered woman syndrome evidence [in] a duress defense to criminal liability. The duress defense is a common law concept that federal criminal law has incorporated. Under this defense, otherwise criminal behavior may be excused under narrow circumstances. To succeed with this defense, the defendant must show:
>
> > 1.   that the defendant was under an unlawful and present, imminent, and impending threat of such a nature as to induce a well-grounded apprehension of death or serious bodily injury;

2.   that the defendant had not recklessly or negligently placed herself in a situation in which it was probable that she would be forced to choose the criminal conduct;

3.   that the defendant had no reasonable legal alternative to violating the law; a chance both to refuse to do the criminal act and also to avoid the threatened harm, and

4.   that a direct causal relationship may be reasonably anticipated between the criminal action taken and the avoidance of the threatened harm.

These requirements are addressed to the impact of a threat on a reasonable person. The fear of death or serious bodily injury must be "well-grounded." There must be no "reasonable" alternative to violating the law. This objective formulation is in harmony with the analysis of duress in the Model Penal Code which recognizes duress as a defense if the threat of the use of unlawful force is such "that a person of reasonable firmness in his [or her] situation would have been unable to resist." ALI, Model Penal Code § 2.09(I) (1985).

Evidence that the defendant is suffering from the battered woman's syndrome is inherently subjective, however. Such evidence is not addressed to whether a person of reasonable firmness would have succumbed to the level of coercion present in a given set of circumstances. Quite the contrary, such evidence is usually consulted to explain why this particular defendant succumbed when a reasonable person without a background of being battered might not have. Specifically, battered woman's syndrome evidence seeks to establish that, because of her psychological condition, the defendant is unusually susceptible to the coercion. Thus, the issue we face today is whether it was error to exclude such subjective evidence.

This issue was thoroughly explored by the Ninth Circuit in the case of United States v. Johnson, 956 F.2d 894 (9th Cir. 1992). In *Johnson*, several women were convicted for functioning as low-level operatives in a large drug operation. They appealed arguing that the evidence that they were battered women was not properly taken into account as to both their convictions and their sentences. The appellate court upheld all of their convictions, however. In so doing, the court recognized that the classical elements of duress are stated in objective terms. Further, the court noted that, as a defense to a charge of criminal conduct, claims of subjective vulnerability have not been taken into account. Accordingly, the *Johnson* court found that subjective evidence of the battered woman's syndrome could not be taken into account in determining criminal liability and thus could not upset the convictions.

[However, the *Johnson* court found] that such evidence could be taken into account for purposes of criminal sentencing. For support, the court looked to the Federal Sentencing Guidelines which specifically provide for the possibility of [mitigation] if the defendant committed the offense because of "serious coercion, blackmail or duress, under circumstances not amounting to a complete defense.... The extent of the [mitigation] ordinarily should depend on the reasonableness of the defendant's actions and on the extent to which the conduct would have been less harmful under the circumstances as the defendant believed them to be." ... Therefore, the *Johnson* court remanded the sentences ... for reconsideration in light of those subjective factors....

Like the *Johnson* [court], we hold that evidence [that the accused was a battered woman] is not relevant [to her duress defense]. This is because in order for a duress defense to criminal liability to succeed, the coercive force of the threat must be sufficient such that a person of ordinary firmness would succumb. Additionally, there must be no reasonable legal alternative to violating the law. These requirements set out an objective test. To consider battered woman's syndrome evidence in applying that test, however, would be to turn the objective inquiry that duress has always required into a subjective one. The question would no longer be whether a person of ordinary firmness could have resisted. Instead, the question would [be] whether this individual woman, in light of the psychological condition from which she suffers, could have resisted. In addition to being contrary to settled duress law, we conclude that such a change would be unwise. Accordingly, while evidence that a defendant is suffering from the battered woman's syndrome provokes our sympathy, it is not relevant, for purposes of determining criminal responsibility, to whether the defendant acted under duress.

Turning to the facts of the instant case, we note that the district court [admitted] all of the objective evidence of Willis' fear of Perez, including testimony as to Perez's violent nature and all of the specific instances of abuse she had suffered at Perez's hands. By contrast, the expert testimony that was excluded dealt with Willis' subjective perceptions stemming from the battered woman's syndrome. As we have concluded that such subjective evidence is irrelevant, there was no abuse of discretion in excluding that evidence....

Can *Willis* be reconciled with *Kelly*? According to *Kelly*, testimony regarding the battered woman syndrome may tend to prove not only that the abused woman feared for her life, but also that her fear was "objectively reasonable." Would the *Willis* court necessarily disagree? Does the mental health condition known as "battered woman syndrome" provide a less convincing psychological explanation for the conduct of Willis than for that of Kelly? Are there policy reasons that support a decision to allow battered woman syndrome to buttress a claim of self-defense but not a claim of duress?

In *Willis*, the court argues that its "objective formulation" of the duress defense "is in harmony with the analysis of duress in the Model Penal Code." According to § 2.09(1) of the Code, the jury is to evaluate the compelling character of the alleged unlawful threat of force from the perspective of "a person of reasonable firmness in [the actor's] situation." Why does Willis's "situation" encompass evidence of her history with her violent boyfriend, but not evidence that she is suffering from a syndrome that may affect any person who is subjected to domestic abuse?

**4. Duress as a Defense to Murder.** A controversial issue is whether duress should be recognized as a defense to intentional homicide. The common law rejected such a claim, and many modern codes adhere to this common law position. The drafters of the Model Penal Code, on the other hand, swept away this limitation. Which position should the law favor?[b]

For a brief period, British authorities supported the proposition that the duress defense should be available to a person charged with being an accomplice to murder but not to the principal actor in the homicide. In Director of Public Prosecutions for Northern Ireland v. Lynch, [1975] A.C. 653, the defendant drove several members of the Irish Republican Army on an expedition in which they shot and killed a Belfast policeman. In his defense, he claimed that he was not a member of the I.R.A. and that he drove the vehicle only because he feared that the leader of the group would shoot him if he disobeyed. The Appellate Committee of the House of Lords held, by a three-to-two majority, that an accomplice to murder could rely on a duress defense. However, in Abbott v. The Queen, [1976] 3 All E.R. 140, the Judicial Committee of the Privy Council, sitting on an appeal from Trinidad, refused to extend *Lynch* to a "principal in the first degree."

The defendant in *Abbott* was pressed into the service of a man named Malik who had a reputation for violence. Malik had established a commune in Trinidad and insisted that Abbott join it. A week later, Malik directed Abbott and others to kill the mistress of another member of the commune and outlined the plan for doing so. When Abbott objected, Malik said that if he did anything to endanger the others, Abbott and his mother would be killed. After Malik left, Abbott and the others began to dig a hole as they had been instructed. When the victim arrived, appellant pushed her into the hole and held her while another person stabbed her. Because she was struggling, only minor wounds were inflicted and Abbott called to another of the group for help. This person jumped into the hole and inflicted a major wound in the victim's lung. The four men, including Abbott, then buried her while she was still alive and struggling. The Lords sitting in *Abbott* distinguished *Lynch* on the ground that this evidence supported the conclusion that Abbott was guilty as "a principal in the first degree in that he took an active and indeed leading part in the killing."

---

[b] In some jurisdictions an otherwise valid duress claim can reduce murder to manslaughter.

In Regina v. Howe, [1987] 1 All ER 771, the House of Lords revisited this question and decided that the duress defense should be available to neither accomplices nor principals to murder. The facts of *Howe* suggest that the line between accomplice and principal is not a clear one. The appellants in *Howe* were two young men (aged 19 and 20) who assisted two other men in committing two homicides. One of the other men was the "dominant figure" in the group. He was 35 years old and "was dishonest, powerful, violent and sadistic. Through acts of actual violence or threats of violence, [he] gained control of each of the appellants, who became fearful of him." On successive days in October 1983, the four men kidnapped a man and killed him, after raping and torturing him. The appellants participated in beating the first victim, but the "coup de grace was delivered by" one of the other men. The second victim died when the appellants "strangl[ed] him with [a] shoelace, each holding one end." The appellants alleged that they committed these acts "in fear of their own lives;" indeed, they claimed that they believed that their companion "would treat them in the same way as [the victims] had been treated if they did not comply with his directions." Concluding that the appellants had acted as accomplices to the first homicide and as principals to the second, the trial court instructed the jury that the defense of duress was available in connection with the first, but not the second, murder.

The appellants challenged their convictions on the ground that, among other things, the trial court erred in charging the jurors that duress could not be raised by a principal to murder. The House of Lords rejected this argument and took the occasion to overrule *Lynch*. As Lord Mackay remarked in his opinion:

> The argument for the appellants essentially is that, . . . there being no practical distinction available between *Lynch's* case and the present case, this case should be decided in the same way. The opposite point of view is that, since *Lynch's* case was concerned not with the actual killer but with a person who was made guilty . . . by the doctrine of accession, the correct starting point for this matter is the case of the actual killer. In my opinion this latter is the correct approach. The law has extended the liability to trial and punishment faced by the actual killer to those who are participants with him in the crime and it seems to me, therefore, that, where there is a question as important as this in issue, the correct starting point is the case of the actual killer. [W]riters of authority [have long agreed] that the defence of duress was not available in a charge of murder . . . because of the supreme importance that the law afforded to the protection of human life and . . . .it seemed repugnant that the law should recognize in any individual in any circumstances, however extreme, the right to choose that one innocent person should be killed rather than another. In my opinion that is the question which we still must face. Is it right that the law should confer this right in any circumstances, however extreme? [The House should return to the

answer that Hale gave to this question, namely, that a person "ought rather to die himself than kill an innocent."]

The Lords agreed with the proposition that different killers might bear different levels of culpability, but they concluded that the distinction between accomplice and principal did not provide a principled way to distinguish between those who should be permitted to plead duress and those who should not. Lord Brandon explained the dilemma:

> [A]s a matter of common sense one participant in a murder may be considered less morally at fault than another. The youth who hero-worships the gang leader and acts as a look-out man whilst the gang enter a jeweller's shop and kill the owner in order to steal is an obvious example. In the eyes of the law they are all guilty of murder, but justice will be served by requiring those who did the killing to serve a longer period in prison before being released ... than the youth who acted as look-out. However, it is not difficult to give examples where more moral fault may be thought to attach to a participant in murder who was not the actual killer; I have already mentioned the example of a contract killing.... Another example would be an intelligent man goading a weak-minded individual into a killing he would not otherwise commit.
>
> It is therefore neither rational nor fair to make the defence dependent on whether the accused is the actual killer or took some other part in the murder. I have toyed with the idea that it might be possible to leave it to the discretion of the trial judge to decide whether the defence should be available to one who was not the killer, but I have rejected this as introducing too great a degree of uncertainty into the availability of the defence. I am not troubled by some of the extreme examples cited in favour of allowing the defence to those who are not the killer, such as a woman motorist being highjacked and forced to act as getaway driver, or a pedestrian being forced to give misleading information to the police to protect robbery and murder in a shop. The short, practical answer is that it is inconceivable that such persons would be prosecuted; they would be called as the principal witnesses for the prosecution.

**5. Contributory Actions by the Defendant.** *Willis* recognizes another important limitation on the availability of the duress defense. As one of the elements of the defense, the defendant must show that she "had not recklessly or negligently placed herself in a situation in which it was probable that she would be forced to choose the criminal conduct." Section 2.09(2) of the Model Penal Code recognizes a version of this limitation, by providing that the duress defense "is unavailable if the actor recklessly placed himself in a situation in which it was probable that he would be subjected to duress." What policy judgments support this provision? Is the provision consistent with the general grading principles underlying the Model Code? Recall, for example, that a person who mistakenly believes in the necessity of self-defense can be convicted only of an offense for which recklessness is the required culpability if the mistake was made recklessly, and only of an offense for which negligence is the required culpability if the mistake was made negligently.[c] Compare also § 3.02(2). Does the duress defense present a special situation justifying departure from this principle?

Williams v. State, 101 Md.App. 408, 646 A.2d 1101 (1994), presents one context in which this limitation on the defense may apply. In *Williams*, the Court of Special Appeals of Maryland concluded that the duress defense was not available because the "compulsion arose by the defendant's own fault." Williams was convicted for attempted robbery and other crimes after he and three other men pushed their way into the home of Reverend Hale, threatened Hale with a gun, and searched Hale's home for money and "dope." Testifying at trial, Williams explained how he came to participate in this episode:

> [Williams stated] that he was abducted by the three men because they believed that he knew the whereabouts of the drug stash of one Chuckie Eubanks, a reputed drug dealer. Williams had borrowed money from Chuckie's brother . . . and had been induced to make a drug run to New York in order to help repay his debt. The Eubanks organization required Williams to make a second trip to New York, during which Williams cooperated with the police. . . . Apparently, the three abductors, who were former members of Eubanks's drug organization, knew of Williams's relationship with Eubanks and believed that he would know the location of the stash house. When Williams was abducted by the men, he told them that he did not know its location. Williams led the men to Hale's apartment, told them it was the stash house, and knocked on the door. Once inside Hale's apartment, Williams testified that he pretended to participate in the search of the premises.

After surveying the authorities, the court decided to endorse the Model Code's approach, under which the duress defense is not available to an accused who "recklessly . . . places himself or herself in a situation where it is probable that he or she would be subjected to duress." The court also adopted the reasoning articulated by the drafters of the Model Code in support of this approach. Although this limitation "may have the effect of sanctioning conviction of a crime of purpose when the actor's culpability was limited to recklessness, we think the substitution is permissible in view of the exceptional nature of the defense. The [limitation] will have its main room for operation in the case of persons who connect themselves with criminal activities, in which case too fine a line need not be drawn." Finally, the court concluded that the duress defense was not available to Williams because "his prior conduct contributed mightily to the predicament in which he later found himself:"

---

[c] The Model Code provides in § 2.09(2) that the defense "is also unavailable if he was negligent in placing himself in such a situation, whenever negligence suffices to establish culpability for the offense charged." Section 2.09(2) is thus consistent with the grading judgments expressed elsewhere in the Model Code.

... Williams voluntarily became involved with the Eubanks's drug organization.... Williams borrowed money from Rodney Eubanks. Because of his inability to repay promptly, Williams [made two drug runs.] [T]he evidence does not suggest that he was forced to make these runs[;] he did this of his own volition to help pay off his debt. By becoming involved with this drug ring, Williams through his own recklessness made others aware of his connection with Eubanks, including his abductors.... This was a situation that would not have occurred but for Williams's association with the drug organization.

Paul Robinson has criticized the Model Code approach on the ground that it "simply does not generate liability proportionate to the actor's culpability." For example, "[o]ne who is reckless as to placing himself in a situation where he will be subjected to coercion is not necessarily reckless as to being coerced *into injuring another*." Paul H. Robinson, Causing the Conditions of One's Own Defense: A Study in the Limits of Theory in Criminal Law Doctrine, 71 Va. L. Rev. 1, 20 (1985). Accordingly, Robinson argues that an actor such as Williams should be punished where he "is not only culpable as to causing the defense conditions, but also has a culpable state of mind *as to causing himself to engage in the conduct constituting the offense*." Would the defendant in *Williams* be liable under Robinson's proposal? Is Robinson's approach preferable to the Model Code's position?

**6. Brainwashing or Coercive Persuasion.** Patricia Hearst was kidnapped and held in captivity by the Symbionese Liberation Army. She reported that she was confined in a closet—tied and blindfolded—for almost two months, and was subjected to persistent interrogation, and to physical, emotional, and sexual abuse, by her captors. See United States v. Hearst, 563 F.2d 1331 (9th Cir. 1977). Two-and-one-half months after her capture, she participated in a bank robbery with her abductors and was subsequently arrested and charged with bank robbery and weapons offenses. She raised two related defensive claims. On the one hand, she claimed that she was forced to participate in the robbery by threats of death—a traditional duress claim; on the other hand, she claimed that after the robbery, her involvement in other criminal activity and her continuing relationship with her captors was attributable to the "brainwashing" or "coercive persuasion" to which she had been subjected. In essence, her claim was that her captors had succeeded in inducing a profound alteration in her character, displacing her attitudes, beliefs, and values with their own.

"Coercive persuasion" was first raised as a defense, unsuccessfully, by American prisoners of war in Korea who were charged in the 1950's with collaborating with the enemy. See, e.g., United States v. Batchelor, 19 C.M.R. 452 (1955). The phenomenon attracted considerable clinical and scientific interest, which was revived in the wake of the Hearst trial. Legal scholars have disagreed over whether the law should recognize "coercive persuasion" as a ground of exculpation. Compare Richard Delgado, Assumption of Criminal States of Mind: Towards a Defense Theory for the

Coercively Persuaded ("Brainwashed") Defendant, 63 Minn. L. Rev. 1 (1978), with Joshua Dressler, Professor Delgado's "Brainwashing" Defense: Courting a Determinist Legal System, 63 Minn. L. Rev. 335 (1979). Assuming that sensory deprivation, social isolation, and persistent indoctrination actually can induce a drastic alteration of a captive's character and values, is it morally appropriate to punish the defendant for conduct engaged in while "brainwashed?" Would recognition of the defense undermine the social control functions of the law? Consider, in this connection, the argument that the brainwashed individual's claim is morally indistinguishable from that of a defendant whose attitudes and values were shaped by the experience of growing up in a deviant subculture. If the two claims are morally indistinguishable, should both or neither be recognized as excuses for criminal misconduct? Should one claim be allowed, but not the other?

**7. A General Principle of Situational Compulsion?** There appears to be a moral gap between the traditional defenses of duress and necessity. Neither the common law nor most modern codes provide a defense in situations where the defendant's choice is constrained, however severely, by circumstances other than personal threats of harm—unless the harm caused by the offense is less than that which would have occurred in its absence. It has been suggested that the law should close this gap by recognizing a general principle of situational compulsion. The notion is that the law should afford an excuse to defendants whose conduct was responsive to coercive situational pressures rather than to defects of character.

Would such an excuse be appropriate in *Regina* v. *Dudley and Stephens*? In that case two members of a starving, shipwrecked crew were charged with murder for killing and eating a dying cabin boy in order to preserve their own lives. Assuming that the killing of an innocent person under these circumstances is not morally justified as a choice of evils, is it nonetheless appropriate to recognize that the homicide should be excused? Even if Dudley and Stephens acted wrongfully, can they fairly be blamed for having succumbed to the overwhelming pressures that confronted them? Surely, the threshold for giving in to the pressure—and taking an innocent life—should be high, but is it fair to say that there is no point at which such action should be excused? How much fortitude can fairly be demanded of persons in that situation?

Should the principle of situational compulsion be generalized beyond coercive circumstances involving demonstrable threats to the actor's life and safety? Are there other unusual circumstances that can propel the ordinary person toward criminal conduct, even though they may not be as coercive as those involved in *Dudley and Stephens*?

Consider, for example, the recurrent cases of mercy killings. In one publicized case, a 23–year-old man shot his dearly-loved elder brother who had been paralyzed, irreversibly, below the neck in a motorcycle accident. The victim, who was in severe pain, begged his brother to kill him. Three days after the accident, the defendant walked into the hospital and asked his brother if he was still in pain, and his brother nodded that he was. The defendant then said: "Well, I'm here today to end your pain. Is that all right with you?" His brother nodded and the defendant said: "Close your eyes, George. I'm going to kill you." He then placed his shotgun against his brother's temple and pulled the trigger.[d] Should the law recognize a claim of situational excuse in such a case?

———————

## NOTES ON THE DEFENSE OF ENTRAPMENT

**1. The Entrapment Defense.** The defense of entrapment, which is recognized in every United States jurisdiction, usually is covered in courses in criminal procedure. The theory for studying the defense under the rubric of criminal procedure is that the defense functions as a limitation on police investigative practices. The idea is that, by making such a defense available, the criminal law will discourage the police from using tactics that improperly induce citizens to commit crimes for which they are then arrested. Under this view, the defense of entrapment, though it is not constitutionally based, is similar to other rules—many of them constitutional in origin—that are designed to limit the zeal with which the police enforce the law. However, there is a competing view of entrapment that holds that the scope of the defense should be determined in part by principles of situational excuse. The two approaches are explored in the following case.

**(i)** ***People v. Barraza.*** In People v. Barraza, 23 Cal.3d 675, 153 Cal.Rptr. 459, 591 P.2d 947 (1979), the defendant was charged with two counts of selling heroin to a female undercover agent. He denied that the first sale had occurred and claimed he had been entrapped into committing the second. The court summarized the evidence concerning the second transaction:

> [Both the] agent and the defendant testified that the agent tried to contact defendant by telephoning the [drug abuse detoxification center] where he worked as a patient-care technician, several times during the three weeks between the dates of the two alleged heroin sale transactions. On September 11, the agent finally succeeded in speaking to defendant and asked him if he had "anything"; defendant asked her to come to the detoxification center. The two then met at the center and talked for some time— a few minutes according to the agent, more than an hour by the defendant's account.

> The agent's version of this encounter described defendant as hesitant to deal because "he had done a lot of time in jail and he couldn't afford to go back to jail and . . . he had to be careful about what he was doing." She further testified that after she convinced defendant she "wasn't a cop," he gave her a note, to present to a

[d] This case is described in Paige Mitchell, Act of Love: The Killing of George Zygmanik (1976).

woman named Stella, which read: "Saw Cheryl [the agent]. Give her a pair of pants [argot for heroin]. [signed] Cal." The agent concluded her testimony by stating that she then left defendant, used the note to introduce herself to the dealer Stella, and purchased an orange balloon containing heroin.

Defendant described a somewhat different pattern of interaction with the agent at their September 11th meeting. He related that he had asked her to come and see him because he was "fed up with her" and wanted her to quit calling him at the hospital where he worked because he was afraid she would cause him to lose his job. He insisted he told her during their conversation that he did not have anything; that he had spent more than 23 years in prison but now he had held a job at the detoxification center for four years, was on methadone and was clean, and wanted the agent to stop "bugging" him. He testified that the agent persisted in her efforts to enlist his aid in purchasing heroin, and that finally—after more than an hour of conversation—when the agent asked for a note to introduce her to a source of heroin he agreed to give her a note to "get her off . . . [his] back." According to the defendant, he told the agent that he did not know if Stella had anything, and gave her a note which read: "Saw Cheryl. If you have a pair of pants, let her have them." . . .

The trial judge refused to instruct the jury on entrapment, and Barraza was convicted. His conviction was reversed by the California Supreme Court.

**(ii) Approaches to the Defense.** The *Barraza* court's opinion summarized the competing approaches to the entrapment defense as follows:

> Though long recognized by the courts of almost every United States jurisdiction,[1] the defense of entrapment has produced a deep schism concerning its proper theoretical basis and mode of application. The opposing views have been delineated in a series of United States Supreme Court decisions. The Court first considered the entrapment defense in Sorrells v. United States, 287 U.S. 435 (1932). The majority held that entrapment tended to establish innocence, reasoning that Congress in enacting the criminal statute there at issue could not have intended to punish persons otherwise innocent who were lured into committing the proscribed conduct by governmental instigation. This focus on whether persons were "otherwise innocent" led the majority to adopt what has become known as the subjective or origin-of-intent test under

[1] "The defense appears to have first been asserted by Eve, who complained, when charged with eating fruit of the tree of knowledge of good and evil: 'The serpent beguiled me, and I did eat.' Genesis 3:13. Though Eve was unsuccessful in asserting the defense, it has been suggested that the defense was unavailable to her because the entrapping party was not an agent of the punishing authority. Roger D. Groot, The Serpent Beguiled Me and I (Without Scienter) Did Eat—Denial of Crime and the Entrapment Defense, 1973 U.Ill.L.F. 254."

which entrapment is established only if (i) governmental instigation and inducement overstep the bounds of permissibility, and
(ii) the defendant did not harbor a pre-existing criminal intent.
Under the subjective test a finding that the defendant was predisposed to commit the offense would negate innocence and therefore
defeat the defense. Finally, because entrapment was viewed as
bearing on the guilt or innocence of the accused, the issue was
deemed proper for submission to the jury.

Justice Roberts wrote an eloquent concurring opinion, joined
by Justices Brandeis and Stone, in which he argued that the
purpose of the entrapment defense is to deter police misconduct.
He emphatically rejected the notion that the defendant's conduct
or predisposition had any relevance: "The applicable principle is
that courts must be closed to the trial of a crime instigated by the
government's own agents. No other issue, no comparison of equi-
ties as between the guilty official and the guilty defendant, has any
place in the enforcement of this overruling principle of public
policy." Because he viewed deterrence of impermissible law enforcement activity as the proper rationale for the entrapment
defense, Justice Roberts concluded that the defense was inappropriate for jury consideration: "It is the province of the court and of
the court alone to protect itself and the government from such
prostitution of the criminal law."

In Sherman v. United States, 356 U.S. 369 (1958), the majority refused to adopt the "objective" theory of entrapment urged by
Justice Roberts, choosing rather to continue recognizing as relevant the defendant's own conduct and predisposition. The court
held that "a line must be drawn between the trap for the unwary
innocent and the trap for the unwary criminal." Justice Frankfurter, writing for four members of the Court in a concurring
opinion, argued forcefully for Justice Roberts' objective theory:
"The courts refuse to convict an entrapped defendant, not because
his conduct falls outside the proscription of the statute, but
because, even if his guilt be admitted, the methods employed on
behalf of the government to bring about conviction cannot be
countenanced." He reasoned that "a test that looks to the character and predisposition of the defendant rather than the conduct of
the police loses sight of the underlying reason for the defense of
entrapment. No matter what the defendant's past record and
present inclinations to criminality, or the depths to which he has
sunk in the estimation of society, certain police conduct to ensnare
him into further crime is not to be tolerated by an advanced
society.... Permissible police activity does not vary according to
the particular defendant concerned...." "Human nature is weak
enough," he wrote, "and sufficiently beset by temptations without
government adding to them and generating crime." Justice Frankfurter concluded that guidance as to appropriate official conduct
could only be provided if the court reviewed police conduct and
decided the entrapment issue.

The United States Supreme Court recently reviewed the theoretical basis of the entrapment defense in United States v. Russell, 411 U.S. 423 (1973), and once again the court split five votes to four in declining to overrule the subjective theory adopted in *Sorrells*.

A dissenting opinion in *Barraza* noted that the test in the federal courts and in all but seven states is the "predisposition" or subjective standard. The *Barraza* court nonetheless adopted the minority view on the ground that the defense should be granted in order to deter objectionable police behavior even if the defendant was predisposed to commit the crime. This is also the approach codified in § 2.13 of the Model Penal Code.[a]

**(iii) Questions on the Defense.** Traditionally, the entrapment defense has been limited to cases involving inducements by the police. In other words, there is no defense of "private entrapment." To the extent that entrapment implies a lack of blameworthiness, why should it matter whether the defendant was entrapped by the police? On the other hand, the law's failure to recognize private entrapment tends to confirm the idea that the defense is designed mainly to deter unacceptable police behavior. If so, does it follow that the subjective test should be abandoned in favor of a test focusing squarely on the propriety of the official conduct? Does it follow, in other words, that considerations of individual blameworthiness should be irrelevant to the application of the defense? If so, why should a defendant who was predisposed to commit the crime be acquitted simply because the "ordinary" law-abiding person would also have been induced by the police tactics? Conversely, should a defendant who proves that *he or she* was induced by the police, and would not otherwise have committed the crime, be deprived of the defense because the jury concludes that a hypothetical law-abiding person would not have been induced?

On the other hand, is the entrapment defense consistent with the substantive policies of the penal law? Can it be sensibly argued that the ordinary law-abiding citizen should have the fortitude to resist inducements to criminal behavior, whether by the police or by anyone else? Is a person induced to commit a criminal act by the clever manipulations of undercover agents or informants any less blameworthy than a person who is induced to provide criminal assistance to an employer who threatens to fire him or disclose a sorry episode from his past? Or a person who is induced to provide illegal aid to a loved one who has become enmeshed in criminal activity? Short of duress, does sympathy, friendship, or fear provide an excuse for criminal behavior? Even if a jury were to find that Barraza was not otherwise predisposed to deal heroin and wanted to return to a law-abiding path, is it unfair to hold him criminally liable for giving in to Cheryl's persistent entreaties? Laying aside the question of deterring undesirable police practices, would it be sensible to abolish the entrapment defense?

**2. *Cox v. Louisiana.*** In Cox v. Louisiana, 379 U.S. 559 (1965), the defendant was convicted of violating a statute punishing one who "pickets

---

[a] The two approaches to entrapment are skillfully contrasted in Roger Park, The Entrapment Controversy, 60 Minn.L.Rev. 163 (1976).

or parades ... near a building housing a [state] court." The defendant's contention is revealed in the following excerpt from the decision reversing the conviction:

> Thus, the highest police officials of the city, in the presence of the sheriff and mayor, in effect told the demonstrators that they could meet where they did, 101 feet from the courthouse steps, but could not meet closer to the courthouse. In effect, appellant was advised that a demonstration at the place it was held would not be one "near" the courthouse within the terms of the statute.
>
> In Raley v. Ohio, 360 U.S. 423 (1959), this Court held that the due process clause prevented conviction of persons refusing to answer questions of a state investigating commission when they relied upon assurances of the commission, either express or implied, that they had a privilege under state law to refuse to answer, though in fact this privilege was not available to them. The situation presented here is analogous to that in *Raley*, which we deem to be controlling. As in *Raley*, under all the circumstances of this case, after the public officials acted as they did, to sustain appellant's later conviction for demonstrating where they told him he could "would be to sanction an indefensible sort of entrapment by the state—convicting a citizen for exercising a privilege which the state had clearly told him was available to him." The due-process clause does not permit convictions to be obtained under such circumstances.

What was the basis for the *Cox* decision? Is "entrapment" the best description for the idea the Court had in mind? Was the Court aiming to deter objectionable police behavior? Or did the Court conclude that the defendants could not fairly be blamed for violating the law under these circumstances? On the other hand, if *Cox* is a case of situational excuse, is it consistent with the ignorantia-juris principle studied in Chapter II?

How would *Cox* be decided under the Model Penal Code? Would the defendants be entitled to a defense based on official misstatement of the law under § 2.04(3)(b)(iv)? Should the existence of the defense depend upon whether the "highest police officials" were present? Consider also § 2.13(1)(a). Should the existence of the defense depend upon whether the police made "knowingly false" statements designed to induce the defendants to violate the law?

In connection with *Cox*, consider *United States* v. *Barker*. That case involved the "foot-soldiers" of the burglary of the office of Daniel Ellsberg's psychiatrist. The defendants claimed that they believed the break-in had been legally authorized by top White House aides. It turned out, however, that the aides did not have the authority to order a warrantless search. Can the defendants fairly be blamed for unquestioning obedience in this situation? Should a citizen's reasonable reliance on apparent official authority constitute a defense when it turns out that the officials exceeded their authority? Does *Cox* have any bearing on these questions?

---

## CHAPTER VI

# CRIMINAL RESPONSIBILITY

### INTRODUCTORY NOTE ON CRIMINAL RESPONSIBILITY

In contemporary usage, the term "mens rea" usually denotes the specific states of mind defined as "elements" of particular criminal offenses. The language is no longer meant to convey the idea of general malevolence characteristic of early common-law usage. However, the idea of a "guilty mind," in a more generalized moral sense, has continuing significance in relation to what the commentators have called "the general conditions of criminal responsibility." The two most important of these conditions are maturity and sanity. Early on, the common-law courts developed the "defenses" of infancy and insanity (including "idiocy" and "lunacy") to exclude from criminal punishment those who lacked the "capacity" to have a "morally accountable and punishable mind."[a]

This concept of "responsibility" is not congruent with the technical requirements of culpability studied in Chapter II. As Sanford Kadish has noted:[b]

> In requiring mens rea in [its] special sense the law [absolves a person who] has shown himself . . . to be no different than the rest of us, or not different enough to justify the criminal sanction. In requiring . . . legal responsibility, the law absolves a person precisely because his deficiencies of temperament, personality or maturity distinguish him so utterly from the rest of us to whom the law's threats are addressed that we do not expect him to comply.

It is sometimes said that the "tests" of responsibility aim to identify those persons whose immaturity or mental aberration deprives them of the capacity to have criminal intent or mens rea. However, this is not accurate. It is true, of course, that small infants lack the capacity to form a conscious purpose, to have a conscious awareness of the environment, or even to be conscious of making any choices at all. Elderly adults suffering from severe deterioration of brain function also might lack such capacities. However, the defenses of infancy and insanity have never been limited to such persons; the law has also withheld criminal liability from children and mentally disordered adults who clearly had the capacity to entertain the purposes, intentions, beliefs, or perceptions that would establish mens rea

---

[a] Henry W. Ballentine, Criminal Responsibility of the Insane and Feebleminded, 9 J.Crim.L. & Criminology 485, 493 (1919).

[b] Sanford Kadish, The Decline of Innocence, 26 Camb.L.J. 273, 275 (1968).

in its technical sense. As one commentator observed, "insane persons ... may have intent to kill, to set fire to houses, to steal, to rape, to defraud; but the great question is whether [such a person] is a responsible moral agent."[c]

The materials in this chapter explore the factors that determine whether children and mentally disordered adults are "responsible moral agents" subject to criminal liability and punishment. Section 1 covers the common-law defense of infancy and its contemporary applications in the context of juvenile justice. Section 2 covers the defense of insanity and other doctrines dealing with mental abnormality.

## SECTION 1: IMMATURITY

### INTRODUCTORY NOTES ON THE INFANCY DEFENSE AND THE JUVENILE COURT

**1. The Common–Law Presumptions.** As the requirement of blameworthiness began to take shape in the criminal law, the idea soon developed—by the end of the 13th century—that children of tender years could not have a guilty mind and, accordingly, were not punishable. Although older children could be convicted if the circumstances of the offense demonstrated an "understanding discretion," royal pardons apparently spared many such children from execution. Sayre notes that the defense of infancy had "taken definite form" by the 16th century:

> ... An infant's guilt depended upon his mental state; but in a day when the defendant accused of felony was not allowed to take the stand, the determination of his mental capacity and discretion was naturally sought through legal presumptions and through the consequent drawing of somewhat arbitrary age lines when infants would be conclusively presumed to possess or to lack the necessary "discretion."[a]

The lines marking the operation of these presumptions were somewhat unsettled until the 17th century, when the works of Coke and Hale fixed seven and 14 as the critical ages for determining the criminal responsibility of children. According to Lord Matthew Hale,[b] an infant younger than seven could not "be guilty of felony" because "for them a felonious discretion is almost an impossibility in nature"; the presumption of incapacity was irrebuttable. However, adolescents older than 14 were subject to criminal liability on the same terms as adults, for it was presumed that

---

[c] Henry W. Ballentine, Criminal Responsibility of the Insane and Feebleminded, 9 J.Crim.L. & Criminology 485, 492 (1919).

[a] Francis Bowes Sayre, Mens Rea, 45 Harv.L.Rev. 974, 1009 (1932).

[b] Matthew Hale, The History of the Pleas of the Crown 25–27 (Philadelphia 1847) (1st ed. 1736). On the development of the common-law presumptions, see generally A.W.G. Kean, The History of the Criminal Liability of Children, 53 L.Q.Rev. 364 (1937).

"they are doli capaces and can discern between good and evil." A child between seven and 14 could be convicted only if it was proved by "strong and pregnant evidence" that "he understood what he did." In these cases the presumption of incapacity applied, but it was rebuttable. These common-law presumptions were received intact in the United States.

**2.   Antecedents of the Juvenile Court.** The determination that a youth was criminally liable did not necessarily mean that she or he was punished on the same terms as an adult. Historians who have researched early English records and colonial American practices have concluded that the death penalty generally was not imposed on youthful offenders. Also, during the colonial and post-colonial era, convicted children often were bound to masters for lengthy apprenticeships instead of suffering the normal penal consequences of conviction. Nonetheless, many youthful offenders were confined with adults in local jails or almshouses and, eventually, in the penitentiaries that most states established during the first half of the 19th century.

A major 19th-century development was the creation of separate "houses of refuge," or reformatories, for children charged with, or convicted of, criminal offenses. One of the first such institutions was established in Pennsylvania in 1826 with statutory authority to "receive ... such children who shall be taken up or committed as vagrants, or upon any criminal charge, or duly convicted of criminal offenses, as may ... be deemed proper objects."[c] By the turn of the century, most states had established such institutions. Although some states prohibited confinement of youthful offenders in penitentiaries, assignment to the reformatories usually was discretionary. As a result, juvenile offenders frequently were confined in local jails with adults, both before trial and after conviction. Also, juveniles convicted of serious crimes—usually those punishable by life imprisonment—customarily were regarded as unfit subjects for correction in the houses of refuge and were imprisoned in the penitentiary.

The placement of juvenile offenders in reformatories was an important dispositional reform, but it left the substantive criminal law unchanged. Children older than seven were still subject to conviction and punishment for criminal offenses. However, a concurrent statutory development had more far-reaching substantive significance. Nine years after establishing its House of Refuge, the Pennsylvania legislature authorized the institution to admit children who had not been charged with or convicted of crime, but who had been found by justices of the peace to be incorrigible or beyond parental authority.[d] In so doing, the state was invoking its power as parens patriae or "common guardian of the community." The opinion of the Supreme Court of Pennsylvania rejecting a constitutional challenge to the commitment procedure reveals the animating spirit of these early laws:

> The House of Refuge is not a prison, but a school. Where reformation, and not punishment, is the end, it may indeed be

---

[c] Act of March 23, 1826, quoted in Ex parte Crouse, 4 Whart. 9, 10 (Pa.1839).

[d] Act of April 10, 1835, quoted in Ex parte Crouse, 4 Whart. 9, 10 (Pa.1839).

used as a prison for juvenile convicts who would else be committed to a common gaol; and in respect to these, the constitutionality of the act which incorporated it, stands clear of controversy. It is only in respect of the application of its discipline to subjects admitted on the order of the court, a magistrate or the managers of the Almshouse, that a doubt is entertained. The object of the charity is reformation, by training its inmates to industry; by imbuing their minds with principles of morality and religion; by furnishing them with means to earn a living; and, above all, by separating them from the corrupting influence of improper associates. To this end may not the natural parents, when unequal to the task of education, or unworthy of it, be superseded by the parens patriae, or common guardian of the community? It is to be remembered that the public has a paramount interest in the virtue and knowledge of its members, and that of strict right, the business of education belongs to it. That parents are ordinarily intrusted with it is because it can seldom be put into better hands; but where they are incompetent or corrupt, what is there to prevent the public from withdrawing their faculties, held, as they obviously are, at its sufferance? ... As to abridgment of indefeasible rights by confinement of the person, it is no more than what is borne, to a greater or less extent, in every school; and we know of no natural right to exemption from restraints which conduce to an infant's welfare. Nor is there a doubt of the propriety of their application in the particular instance. The infant has been snatched from a course which must have ended in confirmed depravity; and, not only is the restraint of her person lawful, but it would be an act of extreme cruelty to release her from it.[e]

Following Pennsylvania's lead, most states authorized summary commitment of incorrigible, ungovernable, or neglected children to the reformatories, and this practice was routinely upheld by the courts. Although data are not available, it seems likely that those youths who lacked criminal responsibility for otherwise criminal acts by operation of the common-law infancy defense were committed to reformatories through this separate "civil" process.[f]

    **3.   The Juvenile–Court Movement.** The next step was the creation of the juvenile court, a reform reflecting a wholesale repudiation of the premises and methods of the criminal law and an equally sweeping assertion of the state's parens-patriae authority. Jurisdiction over "delinquent" children below a designated age—usually 16 or 18—was vested exclusively in the juvenile court. The declared purpose of the intervention was therapeutic rather than punitive; the judge's task was to diagnose the child's problem and to order appropriate treatment. Illinois generally is credited with enacting the first juvenile-court law in 1899, and by 1917 all but three

[e] Ex parte Crouse, 4 Whart. 9, 11 (Pa. 1839).

[f] The development of the juvenile court is traced in Anthony M. Platt, The Child Savers (1960).

states had passed such laws. The attitudes and beliefs leading to creation of the juvenile court have been much discussed by legal and social historians. It "represents the most important and ambitious effort yet undertaken by our law to give practical expression to the rehabilitative ideal."[g] The philosophy underlying the new court is captured in the following excerpt from Herbert H. Lou, Juvenile Courts in the United States 2 (1927):[*]

> [The] principles upon which the juvenile court acts are radically different from those of the criminal courts. In place of judicial tribunals, restrained by antiquated procedure, saturated in an atmosphere of hostility, trying cases for determining guilt and inflicting punishment according to inflexible rules of law, we have now juvenile courts, in which the relations of the child to his parents or other adults and to the state or society are defined and are adjusted summarily according to the scientific findings about the child and his environments. In place of magistrates, limited by the outgrown custom and compelled to walk in the paths fixed by the law of the realm, we have now socially-minded judges, who hear and adjust cases according not to rigid rules of law but to what the interests of society and the interests of the child or good conscience demand. In place of juries, prosecutors, and lawyers, trained in the old conception of law and staging dramatically, but often amusingly, legal battles, as the necessary paraphernalia of a criminal court, we have now probation officers, physicians, psychologists and psychiatrists, who search for the social, physiological, psychological, and mental backgrounds of the child in order to arrive at reasonable and just solutions of individual cases. In other words, in this new court we tear down primitive prejudice, hatred, and hostility toward the lawbreaker in that most hidebound of all human institutions, the court of law, and we attempt, as far as possible, to administer justice in the name of truth, love, and understanding.

Challenges to the constitutionality of the procedures employed in juvenile proceedings were quickly and uniformly rejected. The courts typically emphasized the benevolent purposes of the intervention, as did the Supreme Court of Pennsylvania in 1905:

> To save a child from becoming a criminal, or from continuing in a career of crime, to end in maturer years in public punishment and disgrace, the legislature surely may provide for the salvation of such a child ... by bringing it into one of the courts of the state without any process at all....
>
> [T]he act is not for the trial of a child charged with a crime but is mercifully to save it from such an ordeal, with the prison or

[g] Francis Allen, The Borderland of Criminal Justice 48–49 (1964).

[*] From Juvenile Courts in the United States by Herbert H. Lou. Copyright 1927

The University of North Carolina press. Reprinted by permission of the publisher.

penitentiary in its wake, if the child's own good and the best interests of the state justify such salvation. . . .

The design is not punishment nor the restraint imprisonment any more than is the wholesome restraint which a parent exercises over his child.[h]

**4. Contemporary Reform of Juvenile Justice.** By the 1960s, it was widely recognized that the juvenile-justice system had fallen far short of the aspirations of the child-savers described by Lou. The criticisms, which extended both to the premises and methods of the juvenile court, were summarized in 1967 by an influential government report from which the following excerpts are taken.

————

## The President's Commission on Law Enforcement and Administration of Justice, Task Force Report: Juvenile Delinquency and Youth Crime

Pages 7–9 (1967).

[T]he great hopes originally held for the juvenile court have not been fulfilled. It has not succeeded significantly in rehabilitating delinquent youth, in reducing or even stemming the tide of juvenile criminality, or in bringing justice and compassion to the child offender. . . .

One reason for the failure of the juvenile courts has been the community's continuing unwillingness to provide the resources—the people and facilities and concern—necessary to permit them to realize their potential and prevent them from taking on some of the undesirable features typical of lower criminal courts in this country. In few jurisdictions, for example, does the juvenile-court judgeship enjoy high status in the eyes of the bar, and while there are many juvenile-court judges of outstanding ability and devotion, many are not. One crucial presupposition of the juvenile-court philosophy—a mature and sophisticated judge, wise and well versed in law and the science of human behavior—has proved in fact too often unattainable. A recent study of juvenile-court judges . . . revealed that half had not received undergraduate degrees; . . . a fifth were not members of the bar. [J]udicial hearings often are little more than attenuated interviews of 10 or 15 minutes' duration. . . .

Other resources are equally lacking. The survey of juvenile-court judges reveals the scarcity of psychologists and psychiatrists—over half a century after the juvenile-court movement set out to achieve the coordinated application of the behavioral and social sciences to the misbehaving child. Where clinics exist, their waiting lists usually are months long and frequently they provide no treatment but only diagnosis. And treatment,

[h] Commonwealth v. Fisher, 213 Pa. 48, 53–56, 62 A. 198, 200–01 (1905). For a review of the early judicial decisions upholding the juvenile court procedures, see Julian Mack, The Juvenile Court, 23 Harv.L.Rev. 104 (1909).—[Footnote by eds.]

even when prescribed, is often impossible to carry out because of the unavailability of adequate individual and family casework, foster-home placement, treatment in youth institutions. . . .

The dispositional alternatives available even to the better endowed juvenile courts fall far short of the richness and the relevance to individual needs envisioned by the court's founders. In most places, indeed, the only alternatives are release outright, probation, and institutionalization. Probation means minimal supervision at best. A large percentage of juvenile courts have no probation services at all, and in those that do, caseloads typically are so high that counseling and supervision take the form of occasional phone calls and perfunctory visits instead of the careful, individualized service that was intended. Institutionalization too often means storage—isolation from the outside world—in an overcrowded, understaffed, high-security institution with little education, little vocational training, little counseling or job placement or other guidance upon release. Programs are subordinated to everyday control and maintenance. . . .

But it is of great importance to emphasize that a simple infusion of resources into juvenile courts and attendant institutions would by no means fulfill the expectations that accompanied the court's birth and development. There are problems that go much deeper. The failure of the juvenile court to fulfill its rehabilitative and preventive promise stems in important measure from a grossly over-optimistic view of what is known about the phenomenon of juvenile criminality and of what even a fully equipped juvenile court could do about it. Experts in the field agree that it is extremely difficult to develop successful methods for preventing serious delinquent acts through rehabilitative programs for the child.

[O]fficial action . . . may do more harm than good. Official action may actually help to fix and perpetuate delinquency in the child through a process in which the individual begins to think of himself as delinquent and organizes his behavior accordingly. The process itself is further reinforced by the effect of the labeling upon the child's family, neighbors, teachers, and peers, whose reactions communicate to the child in subtle ways a kind of expectation of delinquent conduct. The undesirable consequences of official treatment are heightened in programs that rely on institutionalizing the child. The most informed and benign institutional treatment of the child, even in well designed and staffed reformatories and training schools, thus may contain within it the seeds of its own frustration and itself may often feed the very disorder it is designed to cure.

. . . While statutes, judges, and commentators still talk the language of compassion, help, and treatment, it has become clear that in fact the same purposes that characterize the use of the criminal law for adult offenders—retribution, condemnation, deterrence, incapacitation—are involved in the disposition of juvenile offenders too. These are society's ultimate techniques for protection against threatening conduct; it is inevitable that they should be used against threats from the young as well as the old when other resources appear unavailing. As Professor Francis Allen has acutely observed:

In a great many cases the juvenile court must perform functions essentially similar to those exercised by any court adjudicating cases of persons charged with dangerous and disturbing behavior. It must reassert the norms and standards of the community when confronted by seriously deviant conduct, and it must protect the security of the community by such measures as it has at its disposal, even though the available means may be unsatisfactory when viewed either from the standpoint of the community interest or of the welfare of the delinquent child.

The difficulty is not that this compromise with the rehabilitative ideal has occurred, but that it has not been acknowledged. Juvenile-court laws and procedures that can be defended and rationalized solely on the basis of the original optimistic theories endure as if the vitality of those theories were undiluted. Thus, for example, juvenile courts retain expansive grounds of jurisdiction authorizing judicial intervention in relatively minor matters of morals and misbehavior, on the ground that subsequent delinquent conduct may be indicated, as if there were reliable ways of predicting delinquency in a given child and reliable ways of redirecting children's lives. Delinquency is adjudicated in informal proceedings that often lack safeguards fundamental for protecting the individual and for assuring reliable determinations, as if the court were a hospital clinic and its only objective were to discover the child's malady and to cure him. As observed by Mr. Justice Fortas, speaking for the Supreme Court in Kent v. United States, 383 U.S. 541, 546 (1966), "there may be grounds for concern that the child receives the worst of both worlds: that he gets neither the protections accorded to adults nor the solicitous care and regenerative treatment postulated for children."

What emerges then, is this: In theory the juvenile court was to be helpful and rehabilitative rather than punitive. In fact the distinction often disappears, not only because of the absence of facilities and personnel but also because of the limits of knowledge and technique. In theory the court's action was to affix no stigmatizing label. In fact a delinquent is generally viewed by employers, schools, the armed services—by society generally—as a criminal. In theory the court was to treat children guilty of criminal acts in non-criminal ways. In fact it labels truants and runaways as junior criminals.

In theory the court's operations could justifiably be informal, its findings and decisions made without observing ordinary procedural safeguards, because it would act only in the best interest of the child. In fact it frequently does nothing more nor less than deprive a child of liberty without due process of law—knowing not what else to do and needing, whether admittedly or not, to act in the community's interest even more imperatively than the child's. In theory it was to exercise its protective powers to bring an errant child back into the fold. In fact there is increasing reason to believe that its intervention reinforces the juvenile's unlawful impulses.

... What is required is ... a revised philosophy of the juvenile court based on the recognition that in the past our reach exceeded our grasp. The spirit that animated the juvenile-court movement was fed in part by a humanitarian compassion for offenders who were children. That willingness to understand and treat people who threaten public safety and security should be nurtured, not turned aside as hopeless sentimentality, both because it is civilized and because social protection itself demands constant search for alternatives to the crude and limited expedient of condemnation and punishment. But neither should it be allowed to outrun reality. The juvenile court is a court of law, charged like other agencies of criminal justice with protecting the community against threatening conduct. Rehabilitating offenders through individualized handling is one way of providing protection, and appropriately the primary way in dealing with children. But the guiding consideration for a court of law that deals with threatening conduct is nonetheless protection of the community. The juvenile court, like other courts, is therefore obliged to employ all the means at hand, not excluding incapacitation, for achieving that protection. What should distinguish the juvenile from the criminal courts is greater emphasis on rehabilitation, not exclusive preoccupation with it.

----

## NOTE ON CONTEMPORARY REFORM OF JUVENILE JUSTICE

Doubts about the benevolent purposes and effects of delinquency adjudication have led to sweeping contemporary reforms designed to conform the juvenile-justice process more closely to the criminal process. Generally speaking, the doctrines governing the definition of criminal conduct and the procedures required for its proof now apply fully to the definition and proof of delinquent acts. In a series of decisions beginning with In re Gault, 387 U.S. 1 (1967), the Supreme Court of the United States held that, aside from trial by jury, a juvenile charged with a delinquent act is constitutionally entitled to virtually all of the procedural protections afforded to a defendant in a criminal prosecution.

The administration of juvenile justice has been reshaped. As the following materials make apparent, however, no consensus has emerged regarding the theoretical underpinnings of delinquency adjudication. Ultimately, the question is whether juvenile justice should be framed on a model of control and treatment or on a model of punishment.

----

## In re Tyvonne

Supreme Court of Connecticut, 1989.
211 Conn. 151, 558 A.2d 661.

■ GLASS, ASSOCIATE JUSTICE. In this case we decide whether the common law defense of infancy applies to juvenile delinquency proceedings....

The relevant facts are not in dispute. The respondent was born on July 28, 1978. He lived with his mother, grandmother and two younger siblings in Hartford and attended the Clark Street School. On March 1, 1987, the respondent, who was eight years old, found a small pistol while he was playing in the school yard. He took the pistol and hid it under some papers in a hallway in building 38 of Bellevue Square. The following day he took the pistol to school and put it by a fence. He then went into the school and told another child about the pistol. Other children, including the victim, heard about the pistol. The victim told Tyvonne that she thought the pistol was a fake. After school, the respondent and the victim began arguing over whether the pistol was real. Several children examined the pistol and decided that it was a toy. The victim challenged the respondent again by saying, "Shoot me, shoot me." The respondent exclaimed, "I'll show you it's real." He then pointed the pistol at the victim, pulled the trigger, and fired one shot, which struck and injured her. The respondent then swore at the victim, shouted that he had been telling the truth, and ran from the scene. Shortly thereafter he was apprehended and taken into police custody.

[T]he state filed a petition alleging five counts of delinquent[1] behavior arising from the shooting. The trial court found that Tyvonne had committed assault in the second degree in violation of General Statutes § 53a–60(a)(2)[3] . . . . It dismissed the other counts [and] committed the respondent to the department of children and youth services (DCYS) for a period not to exceed four years.[4]

On appeal, the respondent assigns as error the trial court's denial of his motion for judgment of acquittal. He asserts that Connecticut's juvenile justice legislation does not expressly or implicitly eliminate the common law infancy defense from delinquency proceedings. He further argues that because the original goals of rehabilitation and remediation in the juvenile justice system have not been attained, there is no justification for excluding the infancy defense from juvenile delinquency proceedings. Consequently, he claims, the trial court erred in not requiring the state to rebut the

---

[1] General Statutes § 46b–120 provides in pertinent part: "[A] child may be found 'delinquent' (1) who has violated any . . . state law. . . ."

[3] General Statutes § 53a–60(a)(2) provides in pertinent part: "A person is guilty of assault in the second degree when . . . (2) with intent to cause physical injury to another person, he causes such injury to such person . . . by means of a deadly weapon or a dangerous instrument." Under General Statutes § 46b–120, assault in the second degree in violation of § 53a–60 is included in the category of offenses designated as a "serious juvenile offense."

[4] The respondent's attorney filed a petition with the trial court seeking an adjudication that the respondent was an "uncared for" child. See General Statutes § 46b–120 (uncared for child defined as one "who is homeless or whose home cannot provide the specialized care which his physical, emotional or mental condition requires"). The trial court found that the respondent was an uncared for child. In addition to the four year commitment based on the delinquency adjudication, the trial court ordered a commitment of eighteen months based on the adjudication that the respondent was an uncared for child.

presumption that he was incapable of committing the offense underlying the delinquency adjudication. We are not persuaded.

## I

The respondent argues that ... because the juvenile justice legislation is silent with respect to the common-law infancy defense, the common law presumptions must apply to delinquency proceedings. The state argues, however, that Connecticut's juvenile justice legislation implicitly abolishes the defense and, further, that application of the defense in delinquency proceedings would frustrate the legislation's remedial objectives....

The common-law defense of infancy, like the defense of insanity, differs from the criminal law's requirement of "mens rea" or criminal intent. The law recognized that while a child may have actually intended to perform a criminal act, children in general could not reasonably be presumed capable of differentiating right from wrong. The presumptions of incapacity were created to avoid punishing those who, because of age, could not appreciate the moral dimensions of their behavior, and for whom the threat of punishment would not act as a deterrent....

The concept of juvenile delinquency did not exist at common law. In most states, including Connecticut, legislation was enacted that rendered children under a certain age liable as "delinquents" for committing acts that, if committed by an adult, would be criminal....

Shortly after the creation of the juvenile justice system, we addressed the issue whether a delinquency proceeding is tantamount to a criminal prosecution. Cinque v. Boyd, 99 Conn. 70, 121 A. 678 (1923). In that case, we stated that "the Act [creating the juvenile justice system] ... is not of a criminal nature...." "The Act is but an exercise by the state of its ... power over the welfare of its children," and a juvenile subjected to delinquency proceedings "[is] tried for no offense," but "[comes] under the operation of the law in order that he might not be tried for any offense." ...

The rehabilitative nature of our juvenile justice system is most saliently evidenced by the statutory provisions pertaining to the disposition of delinquent juveniles. Under General Statutes § 46b–134, the trial court may not render a disposition of the case of any delinquent child until the trial court receives from the probation officer assigned to the case a comprehensive background report on the child's characteristics, history and home life. The disposition of a child found delinquent for a serious juvenile offense may be made only after the court receives a complete evaluation of the child's physical and psychological health....

Significantly, commitment of the child to DCYS may be made only if the court finds that "its probation services or other services available to the court are not adequate for such child...." Prior to any such commitment, however, the court must "consult with [DCYS] to determine the placement which will be in the best interest of such child." When the trial court determines that a commitment must be made, it may commit the child to

DCYS for an indeterminate period not to exceed two years, or in the case of a child found delinquent for committing a serious juvenile offense, for an indeterminate period not to exceed four years. General Statutes § 46b–141(a).[7] DCYS may petition for an extension of the commitment of a child originally committed for two years. An extension may not exceed an additional two years, and may only be ordered when, after a hearing, it is found to be in the best interests of the child. . . .

It is clear from our analysis that the purpose of the comprehensive statutory treatment of "juvenile delinquents" is clinical and rehabilitative, rather than retributive or punitive. As we recently observed, "[t]he objective of juvenile court proceedings is to 'determin[e] the needs of the child and of society rather than adjudicat[e] criminal conduct. The objectives are to provide measures of guidance and rehabilitation . . . not to fix criminal responsibility, guilt and punishment.' Thus the child found delinquent is not perceived as a criminal guilty of one or more offenses, but rather as a child in need of guidance and rehabilitative services." In effect, the statutes regulating juvenile misconduct represent a system-wide displacement of the common law.

With the enactment of juvenile justice legislation nationwide, several courts have addressed the issue whether the infancy defense applies to delinquency proceedings. Most have held that, in the absence of legislation codifying or adopting the defense, incapacity is not a defense in delinquency proceedings. These courts observe that because a delinquency adjudication is not a criminal conviction, it is unnecessary to determine whether the juvenile understood the moral implications of his or her behavior. In addition, some decisions recognize that the defense would frustrate the remedial purposes of juvenile justice legislation.

Because Connecticut's juvenile justice system is designed to provide delinquent minors with guidance and rehabilitation; we agree with the courts that hold that the common-law infancy defense, created to protect children from being punished as criminals, has no place in delinquency proceedings. We also agree that the legislature could decide that the infancy defense would unnecessarily interfere with the state's legitimate efforts to provide structured forms of guidance for children who have committed acts of delinquency. It could conclude that the defense inevitably would exclude those children most in need of guidance from a system designed to instill socially responsible behavior. To construe the legislature's silence as indicating an intent to preserve the infancy defense in delinquency proceedings is unwarranted in light of the legislation's obvious and singular remedial objectives. We are not persuaded that recognition of the defense would advance the interests of either child or society.[9]

---

[7] In the present case, the respondent has not challenged the trial court's factual basis for committing the respondent to DCYS for four years.

[9] Nothing in this opinion should be construed to deter the legislature from consider-

ing the desirability of a floor for such juvenile proceedings in recognition of the fact that the clinical and rehabilitative needs of a four or eight year old are different from those of a fourteen or fifteen year old.

## II

Relying on a number of decisions in other states, however, the respondent argues that the rehabilitative objectives of juvenile justice have become defunct, and cannot justify excluding the infancy defense from delinquency proceedings. . . .

We acknowledge that the United States Supreme Court has opined that the rehabilitative goals of the various state juvenile courts have often not been attained. The Court has made it quite clear that states may not deny juveniles fundamental due process rights simply by labeling delinquency proceedings "civil," or by asserting that the purpose of delinquency proceedings is rehabilitative. *In re Gault.* Thus, the parens patriae doctrine does not support inroads on basic constitutional guarantees simply because a state claims that its juvenile justice system is "rehabilitative" rather than "punitive." The United States Supreme Court, however, has expressly refused to hold that the rehabilitative goals of the various systems of juvenile justice may under no circumstances justify appropriate differential treatment of a child adjudicated a delinquent. . . .

We do not discern in [the Court's decisions] an abandonment of the rehabilitative focus of juvenile justice. The respondent has not presented us with any grounds for concluding that the rehabilitative objectives of Connecticut's juvenile justice system are contradicted in practice. We therefore decline to adopt the somewhat cynical view expressed by some writers that the ideals of the juvenile justice system are now bankrupt, and have necessarily succumbed to the corrosive effects of institutionalization.

Further, we are not persuaded by the respondent's argument that the statutory treatment of juveniles who commit "serious juvenile offenses" requires a conclusion that there is no genuine difference between juvenile and criminal proceedings. The four-year maximum commitment term for serious juvenile offenders certainly contemplates the possibility of a serious restriction on the juvenile's liberty. But as we have already observed, any commitment order must be predicated on a determination that other options not involving commitment are inadequate to address the child's needs. In addition, placement of the child in a program or facility must be based on the child's best interests. We cannot infer from these provisions a legislative intent to inflict retribution on the serious juvenile offender.

Finally, we reject the respondent's argument that the common-law presumption should apply in this case because the offense charged was a serious juvenile offense. We acknowledge that the commission of a serious juvenile offense is a prerequisite to the transfer of a juvenile case to the superior court criminal docket. Another prerequisite to such a transfer, however, is that the child must have committed the offense after attaining the age of fourteen. In the present case, the respondent was eight years of age at the time of the predicate offense.

There is no error.

————

## NOTES ON RESPONSIBILITY IN DELINQUENCY PROCEEDINGS

**1. The Relevance of Statutory Purpose.** *Tyvonne* states the prevailing view that the common-law infancy defense does not apply to delinquency proceedings. Should delinquency adjudication require proof that the offender appreciated the wrongfulness of his or her conduct? Do the benevolent purposes of the juvenile-justice system provide a persuasive rationale for not doing so?

Consider whether the result would be different if the Connecticut legislature had explicitly abandoned the rehabilitative model of juvenile justice. In Minnesota, for example, the juvenile-court legislation provides that "[t]he purpose of the laws relating to children alleged or adjudicated to be delinquent is to promote the public safety and reduce juvenile delinquency by maintaining the integrity of the substantive law prohibiting certain behavior and by developing individual responsibility for lawful behavior."[a] Similarly the Washington legislature declared that the purposes of delinquency adjudication included "mak[ing] the juvenile offender accountable for his or her criminal behavior; [and] provid[ing] for punishment commensurate with the age, crime, and criminal history of the juvenile offender."[b] How should *Tyvonne* be decided by a judge in Minnesota or Washington?[c]

**2. *In re Gladys R.*** In recent years, several courts have held that the infancy defense applies in delinquency adjudication, emphasizing the changing character of juvenile justice. One of the first of these decisions was In re Gladys R., 1 Cal.3d 855, 83 Cal.Rptr. 671, 464 P.2d 127 (1970).[d] In that case a juvenile court found that Gladys R., a 12–year-old girl, had committed an act proscribed by the penal code (annoying or molesting a child under 18) and declared her to be a ward of the court under the delinquency provision (§ 602) of the juvenile-court law. The Supreme Court of California reversed the decision, holding that "in order to become a ward of the court under [the delinquency provision], clear proof must show that a child under the age of 14 years at the time of committing the act appreciated its wrongfulness." The court explained that the common-law infancy defense, which had been codified in Section 26 of the California Penal Code, "provides the kind of fundamental protection to children

---

[a] Minn.Stat.Ann. § 260.011. Before the amendment the sole declared purpose of the juvenile code had been to secure "for each minor ... the care and guidance, preferably in his own home, as will serve the ... welfare of the minor and the best interests of the state ... and when the minor is removed from his own family, to secure for him custody, care and discipline as nearly as possible equivalent to that which should have been given by his parents." No distinction in purpose was drawn before the amendment between delinquency proceedings and "dependency-and-neglect" proceedings. As a result of the 1980 amendment, the declaration of exclusively benevolent purposes applies only to dependency-and-neglect jurisdiction.

[b] Rev.Wash.Code Ann. § 13.40.010(2)(c), (d).

[c] See Rev.Wash.Code Ann § 9A.04.050, interpreted and applied in State v. J.P.S., 135 Wash.2d 34, 954 P.2d 894 (1998).

[d] See also In re William A., 313 Md. 690, 548 A.2d 130 (1988).

charged under Section 602 which this court should not lightly discard.'' The court continued:

> If a juvenile court finds a lack of clear proof that a child under 14 years at the time of committing the act possessed knowledge of its wrongfulness . . . the court might well declare the child a ward under § 600 [dependent children] or 601 [ungovernable children]. These latter provisions carry far less severe consequences for the liberty and life of the child. After all, it is the purpose of the Welfare and Institutions Code to ''insure that the rights or physical, mental or moral welfare of children are not violated or threatened by their present circumstances or environment.'' Strong policy reasons cast doubt upon the placement of a child who is unable to appreciate the wrongfulness of his conduct [in] an institution where he will come into contact with many youths who are well versed in criminality. . . . We cannot condone a decision which would expose the child to consequences possibly disastrous to himself and society as a whole.
>
> Other sections may possibly be invoked to provide for a wardship for this child with no injurious potentials. Section 601 provides that a child who disobeys the lawful orders of his parents or school authorities, who is beyond the control of such persons, or who is in danger of leading an immoral life may be adjudged a ward of the court. Section 601 might clearly cover younger children who lacked the age or experience to understand the wrongfulness of their conduct. If the juvenile court considers § 601 inappropriate for the particular child, he may be covered by the even broader provisions of § 600.
>
> Section 602 should apply only to those who are over 14 and may be presumed to understand the wrongfulness of their acts and to those under the age of 14 who clearly appreciate the wrongfulness of their conduct. In the instant case we are confronted with a 12–year-old girl of the social and mental age of a seven-year-old. Section 26 stands to protect her and other young people like her from the harsh strictures of § 602. Only if the age, experience, knowledge, and conduct of the child demonstrate by clear proof that he has violated a criminal law should he be declared a ward of the court under § 602.

Although Gladys R. may not be subject to control as a delinquent, the court strongly hints that she would be committable under the less precise dependency and ungovernability provisions. How would the Supreme Court of California characterize the justifying purposes of intervention under §§ 600 and 601 on the one hand and § 602 on the other? Is it likely to matter to Gladys R. whether she was committed under one section or another? Does anything turn on the distinction?

**3.   Minimum Age for Delinquency Jurisdiction.** Even if the common-law infancy presumptions do not apply to delinquency proceedings, should there be a minimum age for delinquency jurisdiction? A few states specify minimum ages ranging from seven to 10 years of age. However, one commentator has noted that "even in the absence of a minimum age in the statute, there are no reported cases involving an attempt to charge delinquency against a child under the common-law immunity age of seven."[e] The Juvenile Justice Standards promulgated by the Institute of Judicial Administration and the American Bar Association recommend that delinquency liability be precluded for children younger than 10.[f]

The designation of a minimum age for delinquency intervention could be based on a utilitarian judgment that any of the available dispositions would be more detrimental to the child's development than leaving his or her discipline and care to parents, schools, and other non-governmental institutions of social control. However, the rationale for the common-law immunity, which is endorsed by the IJA–ABA standards, is that children below some level of maturity cannot fairly be blamed for their wrongful acts. What hypotheses about cognitive, social, and moral development underlie this judgment? Would it be important to know when children conform to social norms because they understand the reasons for the norms rather than because they fear the hand of authority figures? Researchers appear to agree that this phase of moral development does not ordinarily occur until at least six.[g] What other factors should be taken into account in determining when a person is sufficiently mature to be held responsible as a delinquent for wrongful acts?

---

## INTRODUCTORY NOTE ON TRANSFER OF JUVENILES TO CRIMINAL COURT

*In re Tyvonne* and the previous notes dealt with the minimum level of maturity necessary for the imposition of delinquency liability. As *In re Gladys R.* suggests, the issue may also be characterized as the definition of the boundary between delinquency liability and "non-punitive" methods of coercive intervention for children. The following materials address the other boundary of juvenile-court jurisdiction—the boundary between juvenile delinquency and criminal conviction.

At the extremes, the offender's age is the sole determinant of the jurisdictional question.[a] On the one hand, criminal prosecution of a person younger than 14 is absolutely barred in a substantial majority of states; the juvenile court's jurisdiction over such offenders is exclusive regardless of the offense charged. On the other hand, most states set the outer limit of

---

[e] Sanford Fox, Juvenile Courts in a Nutshell 29 (1984).

[f] IJA–ABA, Standards Relating to Juvenile Delinquency and Sanctions § 2.1(A) (1980).

[g] See generally Moral Development and Behavior: Theory, Research and Social Issues (T. Lickona ed., 1976).

[a] The statutes are summarized in Richard Redding, Adjudicatory and Dispositional Decision Making in Juvenile Justice. In Current Perspectives on Delinquency: Prevention, Assessment, and Intervention (K. Heilbrun, N. Goldstein, & R. Redding eds., 2004).

juvenile-court jurisdiction at the 18th birthday; if the act charged occurred after that date, the criminal court's jurisdiction is exclusive.

The offender's age is not the sole jurisdictional criterion if the offender was older than the minimum (usually 14 or 15) and younger than the maximum (usually 18) at the time of the alleged offense. If the older adolescent is charged with a serious offense, the juvenile court is permitted or required in most states to waive its jurisdiction and to transfer the case to the criminal court. The statutes reflect three general approaches to transfer. Under the individualized approach, the juvenile-court judge retains or waives jurisdiction according to whether, after a transfer hearing, the offender is found "amenable to treatment" in the juvenile system or presents a danger to the community. A second approach is a statute requiring transfer of a juvenile older than the designated age if the court finds probable cause to believe that the offender committed one of several specified serious offenses (or that the offender had a prior record of serious delinquency). These statutes are sometimes characterized as "legislative-waiver" provisions, as contrasted with the "judicial-waiver" provisions described above. It should be noted, however, that even in "legislative-waiver" states, the prosecutor's charging decision may determine which court has jurisdiction. In fact, there has been a recent trend towards implementing a third approach to transfer, which is explicitly to repose discretionary authority in the prosecutor to initiate either juvenile or criminal proceedings. This approach, which is predicated upon conferring concurrent jurisdiction on juvenile and criminal courts, is known as "prosecutorial waiver."

Various arguments have been made supporting and criticizing the "prosecutorial waiver" approach, also known as "direct file." Its supporters argue that some discretion is needed (as opposed to a categorical legislative offense classification), but that giving such discretion to prosecutors is preferable to giving it to juvenile judges, who tend to be have a bias in favor of retaining jurisdiction. Critics argue that prosecutors tend to be biased toward criminal prosecution, and also that vesting transfer power in prosecutors eventually leads to more subjective and inconsistent transfer decisions than under the judicial transfer process. Proponents of "prosecutorial waiver" also argue that under the approach, transfer determinations are made more quickly and efficiently than under "judicial waiver" because the decision is not subject to the traditional routes of review that could elongate the "judicial waiver" process, and that efficiency leads to more effective justice. But many opponents of "prosecutorial waiver" criticize the approach precisely because the prosecutor's decisions are essentially unreviewable. Some states are considering whether prosecutorial transfer decisions should remain unreviewable, or if they should be subject to the same appellate scrutiny as "judicial waiver" decisions.

At least one state supreme court has declared the "prosecutorial waiver" approach unconstitutional. In large part because of the unbridled discretion given to prosecutors, the Utah Supreme Court found that the state's "direct file" statute denied juvenile defendants equal protection in

State v. Mohi, 901 P.2d 991 (Utah 1995), because individual offenders accused of the same offenses were treated differently. However, most state courts have upheld the constitutionality of "prosecutorial waiver," stating that the power to make the transfer decision rests firmly within the charging authority of the executive branch and that such prosecutorial power does not usurp any exclusively judicial power. See, e.g., Manduley v. Superior Court, 27 Cal.4th 537, 41 P.3d 3, 117 Cal.Rptr.2d 168 (2002); People v. Conat, 238 Mich.App. 134, 605 N.W.2d 49 (Mich.App. 1999).

The individualized judicial approach to transfer has also been subject to many criticisms. Some critics say that 15-, 16-, or 17–year-olds who commit serious offenses are no less deserving of punishment than older offenders; the transfer decision, they argue, should be governed by the policies of the criminal law rather than the therapeutic assumptions of the juvenile court. Other critics argue that the individualized approach is objectionable on practical grounds. The problem, they argue, is that the question whether a particular juvenile is dangerous or amenable to treatment cannot be answered reliably. The jurisdictional decision, therefore, should be based on the application of more objective criteria. Another common concern in cases involving serious offenses is that the gap between the sanctions available to the juvenile court and those available in the criminal court is often very large, thereby exacerbating the problems of discretionary decisionmaking.

Despite these objections, the traditional individualized approach was endorsed by the Joint Commission on Juvenile Justice Standards of the Institute of Judicial Administration and the American Bar Association.[b] The Commission took the position that persons under 18 should be presumptively subject to juvenile-court jurisdiction; transfer is appropriate, the Commission said, only when a juvenile charged with a serious "class one" juvenile offense[c] "has demonstrated a propensity for violent attacks against other persons and, on the basis of personal background, appears unlikely to benefit from any disposition available in juvenile court." The Commission did not endorse any single rationale in support of its presumption in favor of juvenile-court jurisdiction. While it claimed that the "rehabilitative argument for the juvenile court" has "great moral force," the Commission nonetheless acknowledged that "recent research urges skepticism about the efficacy of existing rehabilitative methods." The Commission also noted the argument that persons below 18 are "in some moral sense less responsible for their acts and more deserving of compassion than are adults." In the final analysis, however, the Commission relied on the argument that delinquency intervention represents the lesser of two evils:

> [T]he criminal justice system is so inhumane, so poorly financed and staffed and so generally destructive that the juvenile

[b] IJA–ABA, Standards Relating to Transfer Between Courts 3–7, 37 (1980).

[c] The Commission defined a class one juvenile offense as:

"Those criminal offenses for which the maximum sentence for adults would be death or imprisonment for life or a term in excess of 20 years."

court cannot do worse. Perhaps it can do better.[d]

Since the mid 1980s, a strong trend has favored displacing juvenile court jurisdiction in the most serious cases involving older adolescents. Evidence of this can be seen in the tendency of legislatures to embrace legislative and prosecutorial waiver statutes, both of which aim to curtail juvenile court jurisdiction. However, because the decision to proceed against the offender as an adult carries such significant sentencing consequences, the longstanding debate about waiver, and about juvenile justice in general, has intensified.[e] Key themes in the controversy are revealed in the sequence of Minnesota cases that follows.

---

# In re Dahl

Supreme Court of Minnesota, 1979.
278 N.W.2d 316.

■ Scott, Justice. This is an appeal from an order of a three-judge panel of the Ninth Judicial District affirming the Beltrami County Court's referral of a juvenile to district court for adult prosecution. . . .

On April 8, 1978, the dead body of Ricky Alan McGuire, who had been missing since November 17, 1977, was found in a remote area of Beltrami County. A witness described the frontal section of his head as "just disappeared, gone." A cap found near the body had a hole in it about the size of a half dollar. Three expended shotgun cartridges were also found lying near the body. In a petition filed on April 10, 1978, in Beltrami County Court, appellant was charged with delinquency for the first-degree murder of Ricky Alan McGuire. The petition alleged that appellant admitted that he shot McGuire on November 17, 1977, and planned to return to the scene in the spring to conceal the body; that witnesses are fearful of their safety and lives if appellant is freed during the pendency of the proceedings; that appellant was using a considerable amount of marijuana; and that appellant had recently authored a note stating that certain local persons must be "terminated." In addition, the petition requested that the court enter an order referring appellant for prosecution as an adult pursuant to Minn.Stat.Ann. § 260.125.[a]

---

[d] For a criticism of the Commission's position, see In Re Seven Minors, 664 P.2d 947 (Nev.1983).—[Footnote by eds.]

[e] See generally Elizabeth S. Scott and Laurence Steinberg, Essay—Blaming Youth, 81 Texas L Rev. 799 (2003); Thomas Grisso and Robert G. Schwartz, eds., Youth on Trial (2000); Jeffrey Fagan and Franklin E. Zimring, eds., The Changing Borders of Juvenile Justice (2000); Darnell Hawkins and Kimberly Kempf–Leonard, eds., Race, Development and Juvenile Justice (2002); Lisa S. Beresford, Is Lowering The Age At Which Juveniles Can Be Transferred To Adult Criminal Court The Answer To Juvenile Crime? A State–By–State Assessment, 37 San Diego L. Rev. 783 (2000).

[a] Section 260.125 then provided:

"(1) When a child is alleged to have violated a state or local law or ordinance after becoming 14 years of age the juvenile court may enter an order referring the alleged violation to the appropriate prosecuting authority for action under laws in force gov-

Appellant was born on March 2, 1960, and therefore was 17 years old at the time of the alleged offense and 18 years old at the time the delinquency petition was filed. His parents described him as a respectful, obedient, and trustworthy child. Appellant stated that he had good relationships with his parents and younger brothers, and denied that he had any emotional problems.

At the time of the alleged wrongful conduct, appellant was a senior in high school, maintaining about a B average. He plans to attend Bemidji State University upon his graduation from high school. He participated in interscholastic track and cross-country running and in intramural basketball. He once received a two day in-school suspension for swearing and kicking his locker. This conduct apparently occurred upon appellant's discovery that his expensive watch had been stolen. Appellant was employed since the fall of 1976 by a local restaurant. Prior to that time he worked as a stock boy and carryout boy at a local grocery store and as a trap setter at a local gun club. He was a steady and industrious worker.

Appellant's only prior contact with the juvenile court involved a charge of reckless driving which was eventually dismissed at the completion of a 45–day suspension of his driver's license. Accordingly, the county court observed that:

> [It is clearly apparent that the juvenile is not the typical delinquent seen by the juvenile court. This offense [first-degree murder], if he is guilty of it, appears to be an isolated delinquent act rather than an outcropping pattern of behavior normally associated with the classification of juvenile delinquent.

... A reference study by the county probation officer at the order of the court ... recommended that appellant be referred for prosecution as an adult because of the lack of treatment programs for the serious juvenile offender who has reached the age of 18, and because the public safety is not served by the security measures taken at juvenile treatment centers. No psychological or psychiatric information concerning appellant was obtained.

[After a hearing] the [juvenile] court rendered its decision, referring appellant for prosecution as an adult for both non-amenability to treatment and public safety grounds. [A] three-judge panel of the Ninth Judicial District Court affirmed the decision of the [juvenile] court....

The question before us is whether the ... juvenile court, has met the required standards in ordering this juvenile referred to the adult authorities for prosecution.... Since § 2(d) is phrased in the alternative, a finding of either non-amenability to treatment or harm to public safety is sufficient

erning the commission of and punishment for violations of statutes or local laws or ordinances....

"(2) The juvenile court may order a reference only if

(a) A petition has been filed ....

(b) Notice has been given ....

(c) A hearing has been held ....

(d) The court finds that the child is not suitable to treatment or that the public safety is not served under the provisions of the law relating to juvenile courts."—[Footnote by eds.]

to refer a juvenile for prosecution as an adult. . . . In the instant case, the juvenile court found that both criteria . . . were satisfied, and thus referred appellant for prosecution as an adult.

The decision to refer a juvenile for prosecution as an adult, of course, is of tremendous consequence to both the involved juvenile and society in general. Unfortunately, the standards for referral adopted by present legislation are not very effective in making this important determination. . . .

[The opinion at this point refers to studies indicating that behavioral scientists are unable to predict future behavior and tend to over-predict future violence. It continues:]

Due to these difficulties in making the waiver decision, many juvenile-court judges have tended to be over-cautious, resulting in the referral of delinquent children for criminal prosecution on the erroneous, albeit good-faith, belief that the juveniles pose a danger to the public. Accordingly, a re-evaluation of the existing certification process may be in order. . . .

[However,] until changed, the statutory scheme for reference must be followed.

In this case, appellant was referred for prosecution as an adult primarily because the juvenile court determined that appellant could not be successfully treated within the period of time remaining before the juvenile court's jurisdiction of this matter is terminated.[2] This is a proper basis for concluding that a juvenile is unsuitable for treatment; however, the court's finding is not reasonably supported by the evidence. Although requested by the juvenile, no mental testing of appellant was performed, and consequently the record is devoid of any psychological or psychiatric data which could conceivably support the juvenile court's observation. Nor does the evidence disclose any negative information regarding the juvenile's background prior to the present act. On the contrary, the record shows that appellant has an exemplary background and is not the typical chronic offender who is usually subject to reference. In making its decision the juvenile court relied on the serious nature of the offense involved, appellant's age, "social adjustment," and maturity level. These considerations, in the absence of supporting psychological data or a history of misconduct, are insufficient to support the court's finding that appellant could not be successfully treated within the remaining three years the juvenile could be under the control of the juvenile-court system.

. . . The [juvenile and district] courts, in making their decisions, may very well have been using equitable reasoning and common sense based upon complete and sound logic in viewing a factual situation where an individual shot another three times, killing him; where . . . an adult jury would probably convict; and where in the eyes of the public, if he is

---

[2] Minn.Stat.Ann. § 260.181(4) states that the juvenile court's jurisdiction continues until the child reaches the age of 21, unless the court terminates its jurisdiction before that time. Thus, at the time of the court's decision, appellant could have been under the jurisdiction of the juvenile court for a little less than three years.

convicted, a sentence for more than three years should be served. This attitude seems to be reflected by the record. But no matter how pragmatic such reasoning may be, it is a mistaken interpretation of the statutory intent of the legislature.

The legislature did not single out certain crimes for reference to adult prosecution, although it had that specific opportunity. The law does not say that all petitions filed in juvenile court alleging first-degree murder are automatically subject to certification, nor does the statute provide that 17–year-old violators are automatically referred for adult prosecution.... It appears in this case that reference was made because of age and seriousness of the crime, neither of which meets the statutory requirements.

The state argues that the juvenile court's determination, relative to public safety, is reasonable when the considerations set out in State v. Hogan, 297 Minn. 430, 438, 212 N.W.2d 664, 669 (1973),[6] are applied to the facts of this case. Although this contention has some superficial appeal, when we apply all of the relevant evidence there is nothing in the record to show that the public safety will suffer in the future, or has done so in the time between the act and the arrest. No psychological information is contained in the record which might support this finding, nor does the juvenile's exemplary background indicate that he is a threat to the public safety. The record must reflect more reasons portending future danger; otherwise appellant would be referred solely on the basis of the offense in question. As discussed above, the existing statutory framework does not authorize referral based on the specific crime charged. Accordingly, this court did not intend the application of the *Hogan* factors to result in the referral of a juvenile solely because of the alleged offense. Rather, as stated in *Hogan*, the criteria we listed in that decision are only "*among* the relevant factors to be considered." ... The record must contain direct evidence that the juvenile endangers the public safety for the statutory reference standard to be satisfied.

The present [delinquency] petition may make one shudder in reflecting upon the alleged event, but the record fails to show that this juvenile is "not suitable" to treatment or that the "public safety" will suffer. We therefore remand to the [juvenile] court with instructions to examine properly admissible evidence to be submitted at a further hearing for the purpose of determining whether, in light of this opinion, the statutory reference criteria are satisfied. If the record's substance is not materially altered as a result of this additional evidence, reference to adult court is not justified and thus the proceedings should continue in juvenile court.

---

[6] In *Hogan*, we stated that: "[I]n determining if the public safety would be threatened, among the relevant factors to be considered are: (i) the seriousness of the offense in terms of community protection; (ii) the circumstances surrounding the offense; (iii) whether the offense was committed in an aggressive, violent, premeditated, or willful manner; (iv) whether the offense was directed against persons or property; (v) the reasonably foreseeable consequences of the act; and (vi) the absence of adequate protective and security facilities available to the juvenile treatment system."

The reference order is vacated and the matter is remanded for further proceedings consistent with this opinion.

———

NOTES ON *IN RE DAHL*

**1. Questions on *In re Dahl*.** The *Dahl* court noted its uneasiness with the individualized predictive approach to the transfer decision and invited the Minnesota legislature to reconsider the statutory criteria for transfer. What are the proper criteria for determining the boundary between delinquency and criminal liability? Should jurisdiction be based on age alone? On some combination of age, offense charged, and prior record of delinquency? Or on the traditional individualized assessment of amenability to treatment? To what extent does the choice depend upon ideological assumptions about the respective purposes of juvenile and criminal processes? Or on dispositional considerations?

**2. The Legislative Response.** Consider the Minnesota legislature's response to *In re Dahl*. Although the legislature retained the criteria specified in § 260.125(2)(d) to govern the transfer decision, a 1980 amendment provided that the prosecutor establishes a "prima-facie case that the public safety is not served or that the child is not suitable for treatment" if the child was at least 16 years of age at the time of the alleged offense and if the child:

(1) Is alleged by delinquency petition to have committed an aggravated felony against the person and (a) in committing the offense, the child acted with particular cruelty or disregard for the life or safety of another; or (b) the offense involved a high degree of sophistication or planning by the juvenile; or

(2) Is alleged by delinquency petition to have committed murder in the first degree; or

(3) Has been found by the court ... to have committed an offense within the preceding 24 months, which would be a felony if committed by an adult, and is alleged by delinquency petition to have committed murder in the second or third degree, manslaughter in the first degree, criminal sexual conduct in the first degree or assault in the first degree; or

(4) Has been found by the court ... to have committed two offenses, not in the same behavioral incident, within the preceding 24 months which would be felonies if committed by an adult, and is alleged by delinquency petition to have committed manslaughter in the second degree, kidnapping, criminal sexual conduct in the second degree, arson in the first degree, aggravated robbery, or assault in the second degree; or

(5) Has been found by the court ... to have committed two offenses, not in the same behavioral incident, within the preceding 24 months, one or both of which would be the felony of burglary of

a dwelling if committed by an adult, and the child is alleged by the delinquency petition to have committed another burglary of a dwelling . . . ; or

(6) Has been found by the court . . . to have committed three offenses, none in the same behavioral incident, within the preceding 24 months which would be felonies if committed by an adult, and is alleged by delinquency petition to have committed any felony other than those described in clauses (2), (3) or (4).

Is this a better approach? What is its underlying rationale concerning the respective purposes of the juvenile and criminal processes? Is it likely that transfer practices would change?[a] Would the 1980 amendment have required a different result in *Dahl*?

---

## In re D.F.B.

Supreme Court of Minnesota, 1988.
433 N.W.2d 79.

[Sixteen-year-old D.F.B. was a high-school sophomore with a B+ average who appeared to his peers and teachers to be a well-adjusted teenager. He had no history of illegal misconduct, drug abuse, or aggressive behavior. However, on February 18, 1988, D.F.B. killed both of his parents and younger brother and sister with an axe. According to extensive psychiatric testimony (by a court-appointed expert and by a psychiatrist retained by the defense) at the waiver hearing, D.F.B. was experiencing a severe depressive disorder arising out of persistent conflict with his parents. This progressively worsening problem was manifested by several undetected suicide attempts and eventually led to the homicides. On the basis of this evidence, the trial judge concluded that the state had not proven, by clear and convincing evidence either that D.F.B. posed a threat to public safety[a] or that he "cannot be successfully treated by his 19th birthday."[b] He further commented that, although "it does not make much sense" that a person "convicted of the crime alleged in this case should serve a sentence of less than three years," he was not authorized to decide the case based on his own "feeling of justice." After the court of appeals reversed and ordered

---

[a] For an empirical study of the impact of these amendments on transfer practices, see Lee Ann Osbun and Peter A. Rode, Prosecuting Juveniles as Adults: The Quest for Objective Decisions, 22 Criminology 187 (1984).

[a] The trial judge relied on undisputed clinical opinion that the offense arose out of an explosive family situation and that D.F.B. did not present a risk to the general public.— [Footnote by eds.]

[b] The judge observed that placement of the burden of proof was significant:

I do not believe the child could prove suitability for treatment if the burden were placed on him. However, the prosecution has been unable to prove the contrary. Each of the experts [said] that it is possible to complete the treatment in the time available; certainly no one said he could not. Since the evidence cannot be said to be clear and convincing proof that he cannot be treated, the [state] has failed to carry the burden of proof on this issue.—[Footnote by eds.]

the case to be certified to the criminal court, the Minnesota Supreme Court granted D.F.B.'s petition for review.]

■ OPINION BY THE COURT. [T]he court of appeals reversed a decision of the district court denying a motion by the state pursuant to Minn. Stat. § 260.125 (1986) to refer D.F.B., a juvenile, for prosecution as an adult. We granted D.F.B.'s petition for review not because we disagree with the ultimate decision of the court of appeals but in order to provide a different analysis as to why reference is required.

D.F.B., age 16, used an axe to kill his parents and a younger brother and younger sister. The experts seem to agree that D.F.B. had been depressed for a number of years, that he was experiencing severe depression at the time he committed the murders, and that his feeling that he was trapped in a family situation not to his liking somehow led him to the conclusion that the only remedy was to kill the parents. (D.F.B. has said that he killed the younger siblings not because he was angry with them but to spare them further pain.) The experts, however, disagree over the ultimate issue of whether D.F.B. is unamenable to treatment in the juvenile court system consistent with the public safety. Dr. Carl Malmquist, the psychiatrist consulted by the court, reported to the court that he has "serious reservations" as to whether D.F.B. can be treated appropriately and effectively in the juvenile court system before he reaches age 19. He recommended "long term" treatment with the aim of "a whole reconstruction of how [D.F.B.] deals with aggression." James Gilbertson, Ph.D., opined that D.F.B. can be treated successfully in 2-1/2 years, and probably in considerably less time. However, he acknowledged that many such depressed people fail in treatment and/or have recurrences after treatment. It appears that the treatment programs for depression available in Minnesota generally provide security only as an initial component of the program.

After thoughtful and careful consideration, the district court concluded that the facts were analogous to those in Matter of Welfare of Dahl, 278 N.W.2d 316 (Minn. 1979), and that—given its conclusion that *Dahl* is still good law in a case such as this where the juvenile has produced substantial evidence of amenability to treatment in the juvenile court system consistent with the public safety—it had no choice but to deny the reference petition, much as it was otherwise inclined to grant the petition.

The court of appeals in a thoughtful opinion concluded that the district court misinterpreted the effect and the intent of the 1980 legislation enacted in response to our decision in *Dahl*. It concluded that keeping D.F.B. in the juvenile court system is inconsistent with the intent of the legislature expressed in those amendments and it therefore reversed the district court....ᶜ

---

ᶜ The court of appeals reasoned that the language of the waiver provision should be interpreted in light of the legislature's simultaneous amendment of the purpose clause of the juvenile code, declaring that the purpose of delinquency adjudication is "to promote the public safety by maintaining the integrity of the substantive law prohibiting certain behavior and by developing individual responsibility for lawful behavior." According to the

We have decided a number of post-amendment reference cases. For example, we have made it clear that when the defendant produces "significant" or "substantial" evidence rebutting a prima facie case for reference under the statute, then the role for the juvenile court is to decide on the basis of the entire record, without reference to the prima facie case, whether the state has met its burden of proving by clear and convincing evidence that the juvenile is unamenable to treatment in the juvenile court system consistent with the public safety. Matter of Welfare of J.F.K., 316 N.W.2d 563, 564 (Minn. 1982); Matter of Welfare of Givens, 307 N.W.2d 489, 490 (Minn. 1981). We used the word "substantial" evidence in *J.F.K.* and the word "significant" in *Givens*. We regard the words to be interchangeable. Furthermore, it was our intent that the quantum of evidence connoted by these terms is that which is required to rebut a prima facie case in other civil matters. See Barry C. Feld, Juvenile Court Legislative Reform and the Serious Young Offender: Dismantling the "Rehabilitative Ideal", 65 Minn. L. Rev. 167, 209–10 (1981). Minn. R. Juv. Ct. 32.05, subdivision 2, adopts the prima facie standard of the statute and uses the phrase "rebutted by significant evidence."

In this case the juvenile, D.F.B., came forward with evidence bearing both on amenability to treatment and on public safety. At least, in our opinion, the clear implication of the testimony of the defense expert, Gilbertson, is that he was not just of the opinion that D.F.B. could be treated successfully but was also of the opinion that he could be treated in the juvenile court system consistent with the public safety.

The issue then becomes whether it can be said that the state met its burden of proof without regard to the presumption. In our view, once the district court concludes that the juvenile has rebutted the presumption, then the district court has to analyze the entire record, using the same basic multi-factor analysis discussed in *Dahl*, to see if it may be said that the state has proved by clear and convincing evidence that the juvenile is unamenable to treatment in the juvenile court system consistent with the public safety. Minn. R. Juv. Ct. 32.05, which sets forth the various circumstances that may be involved in the totality of the circumstances, supports this conclusion. Employing the multi-factor analysis in this case—which is what the trial court in *Dahl* was directed to do on remand—would justify a reference decision in this case even if the legislature's 1980 amendment of the purpose section was without significance. While we agree with the court of appeals' conclusion that the amendment of the purpose section makes it easier to conclude that reference is justified in this case, we do not agree with the implication that reference is justified any time a juvenile commits a heinous offense. Rather, reference in this case is justified because—

court of appeals, the legislature intended to prevent "an excessively minimal response to an offense which had a major impact on society" and "to protect the strong and legitimate interest of the public in a fair response by the criminal justice system to a heinous crime." As a result, the "state's interest in the integrity of the substantive law, under the facts of this case, overcomes any consideration, however weighty, given by the trial court to the absence of anti-social or violent behavior in D.F.B.'s past."—[Footnote by eds.]

bearing in mind the legislature's revised statement of purpose and looking at all the factors listed in R. 32.05, including the offense with which D.F.B. is charged, the manner in which he committed the offense, the interests of society in the outcome of this case, the testimony of Dr. Malmquist suggesting that treatment of D.F.B. might be unsuccessful, and the weakness of Dr. Gilbertson's testimony—the state met its burden of proving by clear and convincing evidence that D.F.B. is unamenable to treatment in the juvenile court system consistent with the public safety....

In summary, we affirm the decision of the court of appeals reversing the decision of the district court denying the motion to refer D.F.B. for prosecution as an adult.

Affirmed.

---

NOTES ON *IN RE D.F.B.*

1. **Questions and Comments on *In re D.F.B.*** As the Minnesota Supreme Court acknowledged, the 1980 amendment to the waiver provision did not alter the clinical certification criteria. Moreover, the Supreme Court agreed with the trial judge that the prima facie case favoring certification (based on the murder charges and D.F.B.'s age) had been rebutted by the psychiatric evidence offered in D.F.B.'s behalf. As a result, the criteria governing D.F.B's case were the same as those applied in Dahl's case. Is *D.F.B.* distinguishable from *Dahl*? Did the court offer a persuasive reason for displacing the trial court's findings with its own? In connection with these questions, consider the following critique of *D.F.B.* by Barry Feld, Bad Law Makes Hard Cases: Reflections on Teen Aged Axe–Murderers, Judicial Activism, and Legislative Default, 8 Law and Inequality 1, 85–86 (1989):

> The [court] confronted the problem posed by the legislature's continued emphasis on the characteristics of the offender coupled with the trial courts' virtually unrestricted discretion to make waiver decisions. The problem became critical when a conscientious trial judge followed the legislature's mandate in an extraordinarily difficult and troubling case. *D.F.B.* laid bare the fundamental tension between the principle of individualized justice and the principle of offense. Unfortunately, the supreme court's resolution of *D.F.B.* undermined the integrity of the trial process and did violence to its own appellate function. Although the court may be satisfied that it reached the "right result," it did so by misrepresenting the trial court factual record and the legal issues before it.

> In reaching its result, the supreme court may have concluded that it was preferable for one case—*D.F.B.*—to be decided "wrongly", i.e. contrary to the offender-oriented legislative mandate, in order to avoid a precedent, such as that of the court of appeals, that would create more problems for juveniles and for the adminis-

tration of the waiver process. Assuring that [D.F.B.] was tried as an adult would provide juvenile courts with the political elbow room to continue exercising sentencing discretion for more routine cases. Thus, the court's strategy supports discretionary, offender-oriented sentencing over retributive, offense-based sentencing, albeit at [D.F.B.'s] expense. As a matter of sentencing policy, the court may have concluded that, despite substantial individual variations, the indeterminacy of discretionary sentencing is likely to result in shorter sentences for most offenders, even though occasional highly visible or career offenders may receive disproportionately severe sentences. This trade-off between discretionary leniency for most juveniles, coupled with severity for a few, is consistent with the view of the waiver process as a "symbolic gesture" which requires occasional "sacrificial lambs" as a strategy for maintaining juvenile court jurisdiction over the vast majority of youths and deflecting more fundamental critiques of juvenile justice administration.

**2.  The Legislative Response.** In 1994, the Minnesota legislature substantially revised the waiver statute in several respects. First, it required certification of any case involving a child 16 or older charged with first-degree murder. Second, it eliminated the "amenability to treatment" prong of the certification criteria, leaving as the exclusive standard whether "retaining the proceeding in juvenile court serves the public safety." Third, in determining whether the public safety is served, the court is directed "to give greater weight to the seriousness of the alleged offense and the child's prior record of delinquency than to" the other factors specified as being relevant. Finally, the statute establishes a presumption in favor of certification in cases involving children 16 or older alleged to have committed "an offense that would result in a presumptive commitment to prison under the sentencing guidelines and applicable statutes" or a felony involving a firearm. When the presumption applies, the case must be certified unless the child proves by clear and convincing evidence that retaining the case in the juvenile court would serve the public safety. Was this a satisfactory response to the problems revealed by *Dahl* and *D.F.B.*?

## SECTION 2:  MENTAL ABNORMALITY

INTRODUCTORY NOTES ON THE INSANITY DEFENSE

**1.  Introduction.** No area of the substantive criminal law has received more scholarly attention during the 20th century than the relation between mental abnormality and criminal responsibility. Although insanity has been an acknowledged ground of acquittal for several centuries, contemporary opinion reflects continuing disagreement about the type of mental incapacity that should suffice and, indeed, about the desirability of any insanity defense at all. The dimensions of the dispute can readily be seen in any representative sample of commentary on the subject.[a] The reader will find proposals to broaden the exculpatory reach of the defense side-by-side with proposals to abolish it. While proponents of the defense argue that humanitarian morality demands exculpation of the mentally ill, abolitionists assert that a decent respect for the dignity of such persons requires that they be held accountable for their wrongdoing.

The insanity defense is a difficult subject. In large measure this is because the causal links between body, mind, and behavior continue to defy scientific understanding. Most of the clinician's operating assumptions about mental abnormality are not susceptible to empirical validation. Moreover, the prevailing clinical understanding is not easily translated into concepts of interest to the criminal law, mainly because scientific study of the human mind is fundamentally unconcerned with questions of blameworthiness and responsibility.

Another difficulty arises from the diversity of perspectives employed by the mental health disciplines in the study of human behavior and in the treatment of mental, emotional, and behavioral problems. One draws on the traditional medical concept of "disease" to describe and explain abnormal mental phenomena. This view rests on the assumption that there are categorical differences, with probable biological underpinnings, between individuals having and not having the "disease." Another approach is taken by behavioral scientists who have tried to identify and measure various dimensions of the human personality that differentiate one person from another—features that fall along a spectrum of degree and, at some point, can be characterized as abnormal. Yet another approach is taken by clinicians who study human motivation, aiming to identify the biological, psychological, and social forces that shape behavior, both normal and abnormal.

Although each of these three perspectives is undoubtedly required for a complete understanding of abnormal behavior, the heterogeneous and often conflicting approaches employed by mental health practitioners can befuddle the law's efforts to shape and administer a doctrine of responsibility. Of particular concern are fluid and often imprecise clinical concepts of abnormality. Lines are not easily drawn between mental "illness" or "disease" and other conditions characterized by maladaptive behavior or emotional distress. Yet the law is in an important sense faced with an either/or choice. Questions of degree can be taken into account in grading and sentencing, but the defendant either is guilty or is not guilty of committing a crime.

There is yet another overarching problem. The criminal law's response to the mentally disordered offender is shaped by preventive concerns as well as retributive ones. The imposition of criminal punishment on culpable

---

[a] E.g., Abraham Goldstein, The Insanity Defense (1967); Joel Feinberg, Doing and Deserving: Essays in the Theory of Responsibility (1970); Herbert Fingarette and Ann F. Hasse, Mental Disabilities and Criminal Responsibility (1979); Norval Morris, Madness and the Criminal Law (1982); Donald H.J. Hermann, The Insanity Defense: Philosophical, Historical and Legal Perspectives (1983); Michael Moore, Law and Psychiatry: Rethinking the Relationship (1984).

offenders serves the preventive ends of the penal law, including incapacitation of the dangerous. If abnormal offenders are beyond the reach of the penal law, the preventive function must be performed by alternative mechanisms of social control, such as civil commitment.

The subject of mental abnormality and criminal responsibility is further complicated by questions of implementation. In much of the contemporary commentary, evidentiary questions about the proper scope of expert testimony by psychiatrists and other mental-health professionals[b] are superimposed on the substantive questions regarding the legal significance of mental abnormality. Although the limits of psychiatric expertise and the special risks associated with expert testimony merit independent attention, the materials in this book focus primarily on the substantive issues concerning the exculpatory or mitigating significance of mental abnormality rather than on the evidentiary questions associated with the proof of such conditions.

Despite these many difficulties, the criminal law traditionally has included special doctrines for mentally disordered offenders. From the earliest times, the courts and legislatures have coupled unique dispositional provisions with exculpatory "tests" of criminal responsibility. The following notes introduce the major tests of responsibility. They focus on the criteria of responsibility stated by various "tests" and ask: (i) how the specified criteria relate to other doctrines of exculpation previously studied; (ii) whether it seems appropriate to exculpate mentally disordered offenders who fit these criteria; and (iii) why it seems appropriate to do so. These notes are followed by a series of problems, notes, and cases designed to highlight the clinical realities of mental disorder and to identify the major policy questions that must be addressed by contemporary courts and legislators.

**2. Early History.** Before the 12th century, mental disease, as such, apparently had no legal significance.[c] However, as criminal liability came to be predicated upon general notions of moral blameworthiness, "madness" was recognized as an excusing condition. At first, insanity (like self-defense) was not a bar to criminal liability but only a recognized ground for granting a royal pardon; while the records are fragmentary, it appears that the king would remand the person to some form of indefinite custody in lieu of execution. The first recorded case of outright acquittal by reason of insanity occurred in 1505.[d]

[b] In most jurisdictions, opinion testimony concerning a person's mental condition may be offered by psychologists as well as psychiatrists. For convenience of reference, these materials will use "psychiatric testimony" to refer to testimony by any qualified mental-health professional.

[c] For general background on the common-law history of the insanity defense, see Nigel Walker, Crime and Insanity in England (1968); Homer Crotty, The History of Insanity as a Defense to Crime in English Criminal Law, 12 Calif.L.Rev. 105 (1924); Anthony Platt and Bernard Diamond, The Origins of the "Right and Wrong" Test of Criminal Responsibility and Its Subsequent Development in the United States: An Historical Survey, 54 Calif.L.Rev. 1227 (1966).

[d] Nigel Walker, Crime and Insanity in England 26 (1968). Apparently the offender was set free.

The only early commentator to give sustained attention to the subject was Lord Hale, whose treatise was published posthumously in 1736. According to Hale:[e]

> Man is naturally endowed with these two great faculties, understanding and liberty of will.... The consent of the will is that which renders human actions either commendable or culpable.... And because the liberty or choice of the will presupposeth an act of understanding to know the thing or action chosen by the will, it follows that, where there is a total defect of the understanding, there is no free act of the will....

Hale distinguished between "total defect of understanding" due to insanity and partial madness involving those who "discover their defect in excessive fears and griefs and yet are not wholly destitute of the use of reason." Conceding that "it is very difficult to define the indivisible line that divides perfect and partial insanity," Hale sought to identify that level of "understanding" necessary for criminal liability by assimilating insanity to infancy: "Such a person as labouring under melancholy distempers hath yet ordinarily as great understanding, as ordinarily a child of 14 years hath, is such a person as may be guilty of ... felony."

Hale's approach failed to take hold.[f] Instead, as Sayre notes, 18th century courts "hark[ed] back strongly to the old ethical basis of criminal responsibility and [made] the test one of capacity to intend evil. Could the defendant at the time of the offense 'distinguish good from evil'?"[g] An often-cited example is Justice Tracy's charge to the jury in Arnold's Case, 16 How.St.Tr. 695, 764 (1724), which involved a known madman who killed a nobleman in the delusion that the victim had "bewitched him" and was "the occasion of all the troubles in the nation." After summarizing the evidence, Justice Tracy said that the only question was "whether this man had the use of his reason and senses." He continued:

> [It is not every kind of frantic humour or something unaccountable in a man's actions, that points him out to be such a madman as is to be exempted from punishment; it must be a man that is totally deprived of his understanding and memory, and doth not know what he is doing, no more than an infant, than a brute, or a wild beast, such a one is never the object of punishment; therefore I must leave it to your consideration, whether the condition this man was in ... doth shew a man, who knew what he was doing, and was able to distinguish whether he was doing good or evil, and understood what he did....

[e] Matthew Hale, The History of Pleas of the Crown 14–15 (Philadelphia 1847) (1st ed. 1736).

[f] Sir James Stephen criticized Hale's comparison of infancy and insanity: "The one is healthy immaturity, the other diseased maturity and between these there is no sort of resemblance." 2 A History of the Criminal Law of England 150–51 (1883).

[g] Francis Bowes Sayre, Mens Rea, 45 Harv.L.Rev. 974, 1006 (1932).

As late as 1840, no appellate court in England or the United States had occasion to state the law on the defense of insanity. However, the subject received a great deal of attention on both sides of the Atlantic during the middle third of the century. One important development was the publication of Isaac Ray's treatise on the Medical Jurisprudence of Insanity in 1838, signifying the first efforts of the infant science of psychiatry to influence the development of the law. Another major development was the trial, in 1843, of Daniel M'Naghten.

**3. _M'Naghten's_ Case.** The modern formulations of the insanity defense derive from the "rules" stated by the House of Lords in Daniel M'Naghten's Case, 10 Cl. & F. 200, 8 Eng. Rep. 718 (H.L.1843).[h] M'Naghten was indicted for shooting Edward Drummond, secretary to Robert Peel, the Prime Minister of England. According to M'Naghten's statements to the police, he came to London for the purpose of shooting Peel. However, Drummond was riding in Peel's carriage that day, and M'Naghten shot Drummond in error. M'Naghten described his motive as follows:

> The tories in my native city have compelled me to do this. They follow and persecute me wherever I go, and have entirely destroyed my peace of mind.... I cannot sleep at night in consequence of the course they pursue towards me.... They have accused me of crimes of which I am not guilty; they do everything in their power to harass and persecute me; in fact they wish to murder me.

The thrust of the medical testimony was that M'Naghten was suffering from what would today be described as delusions of persecution symptomatic of paranoid schizophrenia. One of the medical witnesses concluded that:

> The act with which he is charged, coupled with the history of his past life, leaves not the remotest doubt on my mind of the presence of insanity sufficient to deprive the prisoner of all self-control. I consider the act of the prisoner in killing Mr. Drummond to have been committed whilst under a delusion; the act itself I look upon as the crowning act of the whole matter—as the climax—as a carrying out of the pre-existing idea which had haunted him for years.

The expert testimony was summarized in the official reports as follows:

> That persons of otherwise sound mind, might be affected by morbid delusions; that the prisoner was in that condition; that a

[h] The history of the _M'Naghten_ case is reviewed, and the relevant documents collected, in Donald West and Andrew Walk, Daniel McNaughton: His Trial and the Aftermath (1977), and Richard Moran, Knowing Right from Wrong (1981).

M'Naghten's name has been spelled at least 12 different ways. Apparently, the traditional spelling—the one used in this book—is the only one that cannot be reconciled with the defendant's own signature. See Bernard Diamond, On the Spelling of Daniel M'Naghten's Name, 25 Ohio St. L.J. 84 (1964). According to Moran, the correct spelling is probably "McNaughtan."

person so labouring under a morbid delusion might have a moral perception of right and wrong, but that in the case of the prisoner it was a delusion which carried him away beyond the power of his own control, and left him no such perception; and that he was not capable of exercising any control over acts which had connexion with his delusion; that it was of the nature of the disease with which the prisoner was affected, to go on gradually until it had reached a climax, when it burst forth with irresistible intensity; that a man might go on for years quietly, though at the same time under its influence, but would all at once break out into the most extravagant and violent paroxysms.

In his charge to the jury, Chief Justice Tindal practically directed a verdict of not guilty by reason of insanity. He observed "that the whole of the medical evidence is on one side and that there is no part of it which leaves any doubt on the mind," and then instructed the jury that the verdict should turn on the answer to the following question:

> [W]hether ... at the time the act was committed [M'Naghten] had that competent use of his understanding as that he knew that he was doing, by the very act itself, a wicked and a wrong thing. If he was not sensible at the time he committed that act, that it was a violation of the law of God or of man, undoubtedly he was not responsible for that act, or liable to any punishment whatever flowing from that act.... But if ... you think the prisoner capable of distinguishing between right and wrong, then he was a responsible agent....

The jury returned a verdict of not guilty by reason of insanity.[i] This verdict became the subject of "popular alarm," and was regarded with particular concern by Queen Victoria.[j] As a result, the House of Lords asked the judges of that body to give an advisory opinion regarding the answers to five questions "on the law governing such cases." The combined answers to two of these questions have come to be known as *M'Naghten's* rules:

> [E]very man is to be presumed to be sane.... [T]o establish a defence on the ground of insanity, it must be clearly proved that, at the time of the committing of the act, the party accused was labouring under such a defect of reason, from disease of the mind, as not to know the nature and quality of the act he was doing; or if he did know it, that he did not know he was doing what was wrong.

[i] Most commentary on the *M'Naghten* case proceeds on the assumption that he was mentally ill and that his crime was related to his delusions. However, a recent book by Richard Moran presents strong evidence in support of the proposition that M'Naghten was not delusional and that his attempt to assassinate the Tory Prime Minister was "a purposeful act of political criminality." Richard Moran, Knowing Right From Wrong (1981).

[j] She had been the target of assassination attempts three times in the preceding two years, and one of her attackers, Oxford, had also had won an insanity acquittal.

**4. Other Common–Law Formulations.** *M'Naghten* quickly became the prevailing approach to the insanity defense in England and in the United States. However, the test was criticized almost as soon as it was uttered. Nineteenth-century critics offered two alternative formulations:

**(i) The Product Test.** The "intellectualist" approach of the 18th-and 19th-century English judges was criticized by Isaac Ray[k] and his followers because it failed to comprehend the more subtle forms of mental illness. The prevailing judicial ideas about idiocy and lunacy were derived, Ray argued, from "those wretched inmates of the madhouses whom chains and stripes, cold and filth, had reduced to the stupidity of the idiot or exasperated to the fury of a demon." The law failed to recognize "those nice shades of the disease" which can influence behavior and ought to have exculpatory significance. Accordingly, Ray argued, the insanity defense should turn on whether "the mental unsoundness ... embraced the act within the sphere of its influence."

The New Hampshire Supreme Court accepted Ray's view. In State v. Pike, 49 N.H. 399 (1870), the court severely criticized the *M'Naghten* rules; the next year, in State v. Jones, 50 N.H. 369 (1871), the court stated its own rule, commonly known as the "product" test:

> No man shall be held accountable, criminally, for an act which was the offspring and product of mental disease. Of the soundness of this proposition there can be no doubt.... No argument is needed to show that to hold that a man may be punished for what is the offspring of disease would be to hold that he may be punished for disease. Any rule which makes that possible cannot be law.

Although the New Hampshire formulation was applauded by many medical and legal commentators during the early 20th century, it failed to win support in the courts.[l]

**(ii) The Control Test.** Although the notion of "irresistible impulse" was much discussed during the decades after the *M'Naghten* rules were announced,[m] it is not altogether clear whether the early proponents viewed it as an elaboration of *M'Naghten* or as an independent ground of exculpation. Some state courts employed the concept simply to acknowledge that an "insane impulse" could be so strong as to "dethrone reason" and thereby deprive the offender of the capacity to know right from wrong.[n]

[k] Isaac Ray, A Treatise on the Medical Jurisprudence of Insanity (1838).

[l] The product test was adopted by the United States Court of Appeals for the D.C. Circuit in Durham v. United States, 214 F.2d 862 (D.C. Cir. 1954), but was abandoned in favor of the Model Penal Code test in United States v. Brawner, 471 F.2d 969 (D.C. Cir. 1972).

[m] See generally Sheldon Glueck, Mental Disorder and the Criminal Law (1925); John Barker Waite, Irresistible Impulse and Criminal Liability, 23 Mich.L.Rev. 443 (1925).

[n] See, e.g., Commonwealth v. Rogers, 48 Mass. (7 Metc.) 500, 41 Am.Dec. 458 (1844). For a review of the early decisions, see Jerome Hall, Psychiatry and Criminal Responsibility, 65 Yale L.J. 761 (1956); Edwin Keedy, Irresistible Impulse as a Defense in the Criminal Law, 100 U.Pa.L.Rev. 956 (1952).

However, the phrase ultimately came to denote an independent exculpatory doctrine. The central proposition was that a person's inability to control behavior as a result of mental disease ought to be exculpatory even though the offender might be aware that the act was wrong. The focus of this doctrine is on mental disease that deprives the individual of the capacity to exercise will, the capacity to choose whether or not to engage in proscribed behavior. It is therefore frequently referred to as a "volitional" or "control" inquiry, in contrast to the focus of the *M'Naghten* rules on the "cognitive" capacities of the defendant.

Sir James Stephen became a leading proponent of a control test. In 1883 he stated: "If it is not, it ought to be the law of England that no act is a crime if the person who does it is at the time . . . prevented either by defective mental power or by any disease affecting his mind from controlling his own conduct, unless the absence of the power of control has been produced by his own default."[o] The first unequivocal appellate endorsement of the control formulation as a supplement to *M'Naghten* is found in Parsons v. State, 81 Ala. 577, 596, 2 So. 854 (1886):

> [D]id he know right from wrong, as applied to the particular act in question? . . . If he did have such knowledge, he may nevertheless not be legally responsible if the two following conditions concur: (i) If, by reason of the duress of such mental disease, he had so far lost the *power to choose* between the right and wrong, and to avoid doing the act in question, as that his free agency was at the time destroyed; (ii) and if, at the same time, the alleged crime was so connected with such mental disease, in the relation of cause and effect, as to have been the product of it *solely*.

Although several other courts endorsed this view during the next decade, most states rejected it. The predominant attitude of the common-law judges was graphically stated by a Canadian judge in 1908:

> The law says to men who say they are afflicted with irresistible impulses: "If you cannot resist an impulse in any other way, we will hang a rope in front of your eyes, and perhaps that will help." No man has a right under our law to come before a jury and say to them, "I did commit that act, but I did it under an uncontrollable impulse," leave it at that and then say, "now acquit me."[p]

The formative era of the modern insanity defense was completed by the end of the 19th century. Notwithstanding the persistent barrage of unfavorable commentary by forensic psychiatrists and academic lawyers, the law remained essentially unchanged for the first half of the 20th century. At the time the Model Penal Code was being drafted in 1955, the *M'Naghten* test still constituted the exclusive criterion of exculpation on ground of insanity in about two-thirds of the states.

**5.   The Model Penal Code.** Section 4.01 of the Model Code provides:

> A person is not responsible for criminal conduct if at the time of such conduct as a result of mental disease or defect he lacks

---

[o] 2 James F. Stephen, A History of the Criminal Law of England 168 (1883).

[p] King v. Creighton, 14 Can. Cr. Cases 349, 350 (1908) (Riddell, J.).

substantial capacity either to appreciate the criminality [wrongfulness] of his conduct or to conform his conduct to the requirements of law.

Two points should be noted about this formulation of the insanity defense. First, in its joint focus on the capacity to appreciate criminality and the capacity to conform one's conduct to the requirements of law, the Model Code formulation includes both cognitive and volitional criteria. The drafters thus accepted the major criticism of *M'Naghten* that the exclusive focus on cognitive capacity was too narrow. The Model Code formulation accords *independent* exculpatory significance to volitional impairment.[q] Second, the Model Code "substantial capacity" formulation explicitly acknowledges that there is no bright line between the sane and the insane. Herbert Wechsler, who inspired the Model Code language, explained:[*]

> [O]ur judgment was that no test is workable that calls for the complete impairment of ability to know or to control; and that the extremity of these conceptions, as applied in court, posed the largest difficulty.... Disorientation, we were told, might be extreme and still might not be total; what clinical experience revealed was closer to a graded scale with marks along the way. Hence, an examiner confronting a person who had performed a seemingly purposive act might helpfully address himself to the extent of awareness, understanding and control. If, on the other hand, he must speak to utter incapacity vel non, he could testify meaningfully only as to delusional psychosis, when the act would not be criminal if the facts were as they deludedly were thought to be, although he knew that there were other situations in which the disorder was extreme. To meet this aspect of the difficulty, it was thought that the criterion should ask if there was, as a result of disease or defect, a deprivation of "substantial capacity" to know or to control, meaning thereby the reduction of capacity to the vagrant and trivial dimensions characteristic of the most severe afflictions of the mind.[r]

[q] It should also be noted that the cognitive branch of the Model Code formulation asks only one of the *M'Naghten* questions. Section 4.01 omits reference to the capacity of the defendant to "know the nature and quality" of the act. One reason is that the significance of a person's mistake regarding the nature of an act lies, ultimately, in the fact that it prevents knowledge that it was wrong. Thus, this prong of the test is theoretically superfluous. Another reason is that this aspect of the *M'Naghten* formula is primarily directed to the capacity of the defendant to form mens rea. As addressed in Subsection E below, the admissibility of evidence of mental abnormality on mens rea issues is itself a controversial question. Since the Model Code resolves the controversy in § 4.02 in favor of admissibility, there is no need to include cognition as to the nature of the defendant's behavior as part of the insanity formulation. The effect of Section 4.01, therefore, is to supplement what remains of the *M'Naghten* formula with the volitional or control inquiry.

[*] Reprinted with the permission of the author and the Columbia Law Review.

[r] Herbert Wechsler, Codification of the Criminal Law in the United States: The Mod-

The Model Penal Code test was very influential. By 1980, it had been adopted—by legislation or judicial ruling—in more than half the states. In the absence of congressional action, formulations based on the Model Code were also adopted by all the federal courts of appeal.

**6.  The Hinckley Case.** Signs of dissatisfaction with the prevailing approach to insanity began to emerge in the late 1970s. One major factor was public concern about premature release of dangerous defendants acquitted by reason of insanity. During this period, several states narrowed the insanity criteria or introduced a new verdict of "guilty but mentally ill" to supplement the traditional alternatives of conviction or acquittal. One state, Montana, abolished the insanity defense in 1979. The simmering debate about the law of insanity took on national proportions in the aftermath of the trial of John W. Hinckley, Jr.

On March 30, 1981, Hinckley shot and wounded President Ronald Reagan and three other people as the President was walking from the Washington Hilton to his waiting limousine. The shooting was observed by scores of eyewitnesses and seen by millions on television. Hinckley was indicted for 13 offenses, including an attempt to assassinate the President. His claim of insanity was adjudicated under the Model Penal Code test then used in the federal courts for the District of Columbia. Hinckley's trial began on May 4, 1982, and lasted seven weeks. The prosecution and defense experts disagreed on the nature and severity of Hinckley's mental disorder and on his ability to appreciate the wrongfulness of his behavior and conform to the requirements of the law. On June 21, after deliberating for three days, the jury returned a verdict of not guilty by reason of insanity on each of the 13 counts.[s]

According to media accounts and opinion surveys, the Hinckley acquittal shocked and angered the American public. Three days after the verdict, the New York Times referred to a "national reaction of stunned surprise" and a "cascade of public outrage." The verdict catalyzed latent public discomfort with the insanity defense and its administration, and triggered legislative activity throughout the country. The American Bar Association, the American Psychiatric Association, and the National Conference of Commissioners on Uniform State Laws recommended a narrowing of the insanity defense by eliminating its volitional prong. The American Medical Association recommended abolition of the defense entirely. During the ensuing three years, Congress and half of the states modified the law of insanity in some significant respect.

**7.  Current Law.** As a result of the post-*Hinckley* reforms, the Model Code no longer represents the prevailing approach in the United States. The sole criterion in about half the states is whether the defendant was unable to "know" or "appreciate" the nature or wrongfulness of the conduct. In these states volitional impairment is not an independent basis of exculpation. About 20 states retain the Model Code formula, and a few

el Penal Code, 68 Colum.L.Rev. 1425, 1443 (1968).

[s] See Richard J. Bonnie, Peter W. Low, and John C. Jeffries, Jr., The Trial of John W. Hinckley, Jr.: A Case Study in the Insanity Defense (2d. ed. 2000).

states use *M'Naghten* together with some variation of the "irresistible impulse" test. Only New Hampshire uses the "product" test. Four states— Montana, Idaho, Kansas, and Utah—have abolished the insanity defense.[t]

Another feature of the law of insanity prominently featured in public discussion after *Hinckley* was the burden of proof. All states place the burden of producing sufficient evidence to raise the defense on the defendant. In two-thirds of the states, the defendant also bears the burden of persuasion, usually by a preponderance of the evidence.[u] In the remaining states, the prosecution bears the burden of disproving the defendant's claim of insanity beyond a reasonable doubt.[v]

Moreover, Congress has modified the federal law on the insanity defense. Until 1984, no statute governed the subject. Although the Supreme Court had ruled in 1895 that the government bore the burden of persuasion on insanity claims in federal prosecutions, the Court had never prescribed a substantive test of insanity for the federal courts. As noted above, each of the federal circuits had adopted tests based on the Model Penal Code. The 1984 legislation eliminated the volitional prong of the defense and required the defendant to establish an insanity claim by clear and convincing evidence. The new federal statute, codified at 18 U.S.C. § 20, provides:

> (a) Affirmative Defense.—It is an affirmative defense to a prosecution under any federal statute that, at the time of the commission of the acts constituting the offense, the defendant as a result of a severe mental disease or defect, was unable to appreciate the nature and quality or the wrongfulness of his acts. Mental disease or defect does not otherwise constitute a defense.[w]

> (b) Burden of Proof.—The defendant has the burden of proving the defense of insanity by clear and convincing evidence.

---

## SUBSECTION A:    THE INSANITY DEFENSE AND MAJOR MENTAL DISORDER

---

### The Case of Joy Baker

[The following material presents the facts from a real case involving Joy Baker, a 31–year-old woman who was indicted for the murder of her

---

[t] The statutes in these states are discussed in the notes on abolition of the insanity defense at the end of this Chapter. Twelve states have supplemented the insanity defense with a separate verdict of "guilty but mentally ill." These statutes are considered in notes at the end of Subsection D.

[u] The constitutionality of placing the burden of persuasion on the defendant has been upheld in Leland v. Oregon, 343 U.S. 790 (1952), and Rivera v. Delaware, 429 U.S. 877 (1976). The constitutionality of burden-shifting defenses is considered in Chapter IX.

[v] For empirical assessments of the impact of the post-*Hinckley* changes, see Henry J. Steadman et al, Before and After Hinckley (1993); and Rita J. Simon and David J. Aaronson, The Insanity Defense: A Critical Assessment of Law and Policy in the Post–Hinckley Era (1988).

[w] In United States v. Lyons, 731 F.2d 243, 739 F.2d 994 (5th Cir. 1984) (en banc), the Fifth Circuit anticipated the eventual congressional action by abandoning the volitional prong of the Model Penal Code test.

aunt (Trevah) and pleaded not guilty by reason of insanity. It is designed to provide a basis for exploring the relationship between criminal responsibility and major mental disorder and for analyzing the meanings of the various "tests" of insanity reviewed in the preceding notes. After a summary of Joy Baker's testimony concerning her background, the material includes a transcript of her own statements concerning the offense. As this material is read, consider how the various tests of insanity could be applied to her case. The notes following the case will explore the issues raised and will include relevant excerpts from expert testimony supporting her insanity claim.]

Mrs. Baker testified that her mother had a history of psychiatric hospitalization and that, due to her mother's emotional instability, she was raised by her grandparents until the age of 10. She then lived with her mother for three years and with Aunt Trevah for two. After an unsuccessful attempt to rejoin her mother, she lived briefly in a foster home before returning to her grandparents.

Upon graduation from high school at 18, Mrs. Baker married. The marriage ended in divorce six years later with Mrs. Baker retaining custody of the two children. A year later she married her present husband, Curtis Baker. According to Mrs. Baker's account, the marriage was a stressful one from the outset. Her husband was often violent, especially when he had been drinking, and frequently assaulted her; the most recent episode was about a month before the offense. She stated that her husband told her that she was "jinxed" and that she brought him bad luck. He also frequently accused her of having extramarital affairs, allegations that she denied.

Mrs. Baker's description of the offense and the preceding three-day period is excerpted below. A transcription of her words obviously cannot convey the intensity with which she delivered this account; however, the transcript does fairly reflect the coherence and detail of her presentation, qualities which are atypical in such cases. During the course of this testimony, Mrs. Baker refers to her two children—Danny (age 11) and Betty (age 9).

Q:   What do you remember about the night of the shooting?

A:   I know that about three days before that ... I had gone out to take care of my cats and I noticed that the dog outside had a rope wrapped around her paw, and her paw was swollen and out like this and I put her on the back porch. I took the kitten that had an infected ear to the vet and I drove back.... When I got home, for some reason I felt ... I had to dump all the dirty things in the house outside the house—anything that was bad, like alcohol, or stale food, leftover foods. I put it all in garbage bags and I got rid of the garbage and—

Q:   You said you felt you had to do that?

A: I felt like I *had* to, that I *had* to get these things out because something bad was going to happen.

Q: If you didn't take them out.

A: Yes, take all these things out. And I felt like I had to get the house clean, the house had to be very, very clean. Then—I can't keep the days straight, I think it was the next day—my husband decided to stay home, was going to stay home with me for a while.

Q: Why was he going to stay home?

A: He was just going to go in to work late that day for some reason. And over a long period of time—we've been living there about five and one-half years—he'd been asking me who I'd been with, who'd I seen, and where did I go, what did I do. He would accuse me of running around and I went ahead and told him about this one guy that I have talked to before, gave him his name, where he worked and he got angry; he said to write his name down. I wrote his name down on a card and he stormed out of the house. He said he was going to find him and he was going to kill him.

Q: Do you remember when that happened in relationship to the night of the shooting.

A: I think that was the day before the shooting. . . .

Q: Let me repeat this and correct me if I'm wrong. It's my understanding that you had had feelings that something bad was going to happen to you that day. That's why you didn't want to go down the highway [to pick the children up at school]. Is that right?

A: I went down. . . .

Q: But you went anyway.

A: Yes. Well I left the dog out at the school grounds and then I felt like if I leave the dog there she's going to bite the children. I was trying to get the dog in, but I didn't want to put the dog back in the car because I was afraid she'd bite me, but my son started hollering and crying that he wanted his dog Brownie.

Q: Does the dog bite?

A: No, but she didn't want to come to me and I had trouble getting her in so I drove on up the road. I thought that maybe if I drove slow she would follow us.

Q: You say she didn't want to come to you? Is that not like her, or usually she comes to you?

A: Usually she comes to me, but she didn't want to come to me that day.

Q: Wonder why that was?

A: I don't know, but I drove on down to the main highway and I parked the car and I told the children to stay in the car and I felt like that I had to walk down the highway. I felt that sometime during my walk through that field Brownie was going to come up behind me or in front of me and just grab me around the throat and kill me and I stood out there waiting for her to do this and she never came and I turned around for her to do this and she never came and I turned around and started walking back. I remember I was scared and I started walking back to the car and when I got to the door I just jerked the door real quick and jumped in and I started taking off. Danny started hollering that he wanted Brownie and sometime on the way down the road towards the house, Brownie was following us, so I let Brownie in the car from the other side and I told Betty to hold her. I didn't want her near me because I was afraid she'd bite me.

I got home. That afternoon the children were upstairs in their room playing checkers and I was up there and Curtis came up there and he was angry and he had a gun in his hand and he said, "Come with me," and I said, "Well, what about the children?" He said "Leave the children here, they'll be all right." He told me to get in the truck and it was about 4:30, sometime in the afternoon. And I said "Where will we be going?" He says "We're going for a drive."

We drove all over the place, Centerville and everywhere possible. We went to that man's mother's house and several other places. Somebody else's house, I don't know whose and everytime we stopped somewhere he'd say "I want you to meet my wife, the adultress." And we stopped at this store. Curtis got out and was talking to this elderly man who ran the store and when he got ready to get back into the truck I asked the man if he had a telephone. I wanted to call somebody and tell them that Curtis was acting silly, you know, because he kept the gun between us on the truck seat and kept screaming at me about who I went with and what I had done, that I should be ashamed of myself and God is going to get me for this. He demanded I throw my rings out of the window and I threw them out because he was getting angry.

It was late when I got home and we had to knock on the door several times and my daughter came to the door and opened it. The whole time that I was riding around in the truck I thought the dog was going to bite my kids before I could get back home. When I got home I felt sick. I was tired, I hadn't eaten, the children hadn't eaten. I had to get them up at three and I was trying to fix something for them to eat at three o'clock in the morning.

And Brownie was in the house and it looked like everywhere I went, that dog was following me. If I had any food in my hand, she kept trying to get it out of my hands. Then, I fixed bacon. I figured I would throw the bacon real quick to the dog so she'd eat that and be busy eating that so I could give my children something to eat because I felt that she was going to bother them.

And that black dog of Curtis'—when we got back from the ride, that truck ride, he sat down at the table and we were arguing and I saw Curtis make sort of a sneer with his mouth and when he did that then that dog of his growled each time he pulled his lip up. The dog would growl, the black dog. And then Curtis got up, he kind of kicked the chair over and he says, "Make up the bed, I'm going to bed." And he made up the bed. He put the gun on the nightstand and that worried me. I took the gun. He asked me where I was going with it and I put it under the bed. I couldn't sleep. I was upset. I felt like if I went to sleep he was going to kill me. That night I just felt like Curtis didn't act right and I thought well I can't trust him and nobody. So I stayed up and it was about 7:30 when I went to bed because I was just too tired.

Q:   7:30?

A:   The next morning. And I guess I slept 'til around 10.

Q:   That was the morning of the shooting, is that right?

A:   Yes.

Q:   What happened that day. You got up?

A:   I had a headache again. I felt bad, I was tired and when I got up Curtis wasn't there. I didn't see Curtis and I walked around the house three times and I called him three times and I didn't get any answer. The last time, after I walked through the bedroom and I got right into the living room, he says, "Yeah, what do you want?" I turned around and he was sitting on the bed. That kind of scared me because I hadn't seen him.

And I went ahead and took a bath. I thought maybe that would make me feel better. And I took a bath and then I tried to fix breakfast and everything I did that morning went wrong. I burned the bacon. I tried to clean the house. It seemed like when I cleaned the house I was making more of a mess than I was doing anything else. I tried to wash the dishes and I didn't feel like washing dishes cause when I did it, it just looked like there were that many more dishes to wash.

I tried to clean out my rabbit cage and I felt like if I put my hand in there that rabbit's going to bite me. I felt like my rabbit and my dog had rabies and my yellow cat. As I was putting the dog outside later that morning, she had, well, I don't know, she just looked like she had foam all around her mouth and when I saw that I thought "Oh my God, that dog's got rabies," and I wouldn't let her in and I looked at my yellow cat and he was panting and I said, well the dog has probably bitten the cat and I can't let him in.

Q: Were they vaccinated?

A: Yes.

Q: So even though they were vaccinated you had that feeling they had rabies.

A: Then, Curtis said he was going to the grocery store. I asked him not to leave me in the house in the first place because I was scared and that I was afraid something was going to happen, and he said nothing is going to happen.

Q: What did you think was going to happen?

A: I just felt like somebody was out to get me or those animals were going to attack me or something. When he left I shut the doors and well, really, I thought that the neighborhood—what they call it is God's country, they call that area God's country and for some reason I kind of thought it was funny because I thought to myself this is not God's country, this is Devil's land or something—and I thought like those people round there are witches and I felt like sooner or later they're going to get me. They're either going to kill me or they're going to do something to me and if they don't get to me, my dogs are going to break into the house and they are going to tear me to pieces and for a few minutes, I even thought my children were possessed by demons or a devil, or something.

Q: Had you ever had feelings like this before that day?

A: No, I have never been through anything like this before. I have never felt like I was going to be—[pause]—"slaughtered" is the word for it. I just felt like they were going to do anything and everything they could to destroy me. And my animals—I've never been afraid of my animals except for Midnight. Now I don't particularly like Midnight, the black dog.

Q: That's Curtis' dog.

A: Yeah, he has taught her to jump up and she'd put her teeth around your arm, like this, and she plays rough and when I came back from that ride the day I went to the school, I heard her barking on the back porch and she started growling. Well I was scared to go in there . . . but I had to in order to get in the house because the front door was shut. And to keep the dog from biting me I kept watching her and holding my pocketbook in front of her face because I just felt like she would bite me. And I even asked Curtis several times to get her off the back porch and take and put her back outside because I couldn't get out on the back porch to hang up clothes or anything else because she was out there.

Q: So then what happened?

A: So anyway, sometime or other I found the gun under the bed where I had laid it.

Q: Whose gun was it?

A: It's Curtis' gun.

Q: Does he have a lot of guns at home?

A: Well, he had another one that was hidden, that my aunt had hidden in the trunk, and he wanted that back so I got it back and gave it to him. He used to have a German type gun and he's bought another one since then, I don't know what type it is, it's a smaller one, and this one is a Western style. It's about so long and got a handle on it like this.

Q: Are you experienced with firearms? Do you shoot a lot?

A: No, he said sometime before this happened he said I ought to learn how to load a gun, and he had loaded it and then he says, "Now you try it." And I put the bullet in the slot but I was afraid to push this thing that slides out because I was afraid if I pushed it in and then turned it I might go too far and it might go off or something, so he said, "Well, here let me do it and I'll do it." So he put the two bullets back in the gun.

Q: So there were only the two bullets in the gun?

A: That's all he put in there.

Q: Was there anything special about keeping two bullets in the gun?

A: No, it was just bullets and . . .

Q: So he had that loaded, that gun was loaded then all the time in the house with the two bullets.

A: Yes, it was loaded with those two and he had mentioned something about he had ordered me a gun cause he thought I needed one to protect myself at the house at night and I might need it, being there by myself. Well I don't know anything about guns. The only gun I ever shot was a .22 rifle of my brother's when I was 17 and I just took two shots at a target out on the farm and from then on I had never bothered with guns.

Q: So this day you said you found the gun. It was under the bed. Is that right? You had put it under—

A: It's where I put it the night before and I got scared and I ran into the bedroom and I pulled the gun out and my children, I don't know, I kept telling my children that I felt something was going to happen. Something was wrong and that somebody was going to kill me and I upset them and they were sitting on the couch and I kept thinking "Are you against me too?"

Q: These feelings that everyone was against you were stronger as the day went on; they got worse?

A:   Yes, I even demanded my children to tell me which one was against me and if they knew what was going on, that they better tell me. And finally I felt upset because I felt like I was getting so close to shooting my children—you know, I felt that I was going to kill my children—that I told both of them to get up real quick and go in the other room and get a Bible apiece and then go back to the sofa and sit down and turn to the 23rd Psalm and just keep reading it and reading it and not stop reading, because I felt like as long as they were reading that Bible—I said, "God would protect you from me because I am sick and I'm scared and I don't know what's going on and somebody is going to hurt me."

And I held that gun just like this because I didn't want to use it on my children. And I was just like this and while I was standing there I could see through my living room curtains and my aunt's car came flying down the hill. She looked like she was speeding. Well I didn't expect Trevah. I hadn't even called Trevah and she came up to the front porch and started knocking and calling me and I didn't answer her. I just figured she would go away and she'll leave me alone. But I felt like somebody was going to kill me, or was trying to hurt me and I wouldn't answer that door for her because I felt like, well, she's the one, it's going to be her. So she left the steps and she went around the house and I went through the living room to the back.

Q:   Did you see her physically?

A:   I could see her shadow through the curtains and I could hear her voice.

Q:   You couldn't see her face clearly or you could see her face clearly?

A:   Not at the front door.

Q:   Not at the front. Okay.

A:   And she went around the back and I had to go out and that black dog was there and that dog bothered me cause I thought, "Well if I get out there that thing is going to jump on me." So I took my foot and was kind of kicking the dog away and pushing the dog away with my other hand, and Trevah came around the corner of the back screen door and I told her to stay away and just stay right where she was and to leave me alone, that I didn't want to be bothered.

Q:   When you said that to her through the screen door did you see her?

A:   I could see her face.

Q:   You could see her, and did it look like her or did it look different?

A:   She didn't look happy. I mean she looked angry, was how she looked to me. She just looked angry and I said "Trevah get away from me and leave me alone." I said, "You're not going to hurt me, you're the devil, you're a demon or something is wrong, but you stay away from me and don't you come near me."

Q: Have you ever seen her look like that before?

A: Yes, when she's been angry.

Q: Does she look exactly like she looks when she looked angry or did she look different?

A: She looked angry. The expression on her face looked like she was angry and yet I kept telling her to leave me alone. I thought she'd just go on and leave me alone, get away from me.

Q: Were you hearing voices at this time, do you remember?

A: I wasn't hearing any voices. I felt like, right then I felt like "Okay, you're here and if you get your hands on me, you're going to kill me, or those kids are going to kill me, or that dog in front of me is going to jump me," and I was worried about Midnight and my aunt. I had my aunt over there and this black dog over here, and both of them were bothering me and I didn't know what to do with either one of them and I thought well maybe if I could holler at Trevah or get her away from me, she'd leave me alone, and she said, "No, I'm not leaving you alone." She says, "I'm coming in that door," and I said, "You better not, you better get away from me" and she says, "No, I'm not," and she took her hands and she started opening the door knobs off the screen, I think. She took her hands to get the edge of the door and started opening it, and that got on my nerves because I told her to leave me alone. And then I had that black dog in front of me and she turned around and I was trying to kick the dog and Trevah was coming in the door and I just took my hands and I just went like this—right through the screen.

Q: What happened?

A: I shot her.

Q: Then what happened after you shot her?

A: When I shot her she went backwards and she fell in the mud on her back and the dog kept coming near me and I pushed the door open real quick and got the dog out of the way and I, just—I don't know—I just stood there. I started crying and I felt like tearing up, I felt like tearing up everything in that back porch. I felt like taking something heavy and just smashing that red washing machine all to pieces. That's how I felt like. I just felt like I hated everybody and everything that minute, and I was hurting and I was mixed up and I felt sick and I was angry at Curtis for leaving me and I was angry because I had shot my aunt and I just felt like—

Q: Did you know that was your aunt when she came?

A: I know it was Trevah.

Q: Other times, you have said you had feelings that it was something else.

A:   No, I knew that that was Trevah, but I felt like she and Curtis, and several of the people in the neighborhood were witches or had given their souls to the devil and they were all out to do some harm to me because they were against me. I just, that's how I felt and I felt like if Trevah got hold of me she was going to kill me because she was with everybody else. And I felt like Curtis was against me because he told me himself when he started taking me around in that truck ride—he says "I'm going to teach you a lesson you'll never forget." And . . .

Q:   It was a pretty upsetting experience. . . .

A:   So, I talked to my aunt a few minutes, right after I shot her and she said "Joy why?" and I said, "Trevah," I said, "You're the devil," and I said, "You came here to hurt me didn't you?" and she said, "Honey, no, I came to help you." And I started crying and then she said she was hurting and I don't know why I did this— but I guess because I felt that I was the reason for her bleeding to death—I took the gun and shot her again just to relieve the pain she was having because she said she hurt. And that was it. [Witness cries]

Q:   What are you feeling now, Mrs. Baker?

A:   Hurt. [Witness cries] [Long pause]

You know, sometimes you wonder, I've wondered, if I was going to do something like that, why did I have to hit her to kill her? You know, some people you read about, they shoot people and they hurt them in the arm. I feel like why in the world couldn't I have hit her in the arm and I know I hit her here [in the head] because I saw all that blood coming out of her chest.

Mrs. Baker's husband and children corroborated those portions of her account about which they had direct knowledge.

―――――

## NOTES ON THE INSANITY DEFENSE AND MAJOR MENTAL DISORDER

**1.  Joy Baker's Credibility.** Because an insanity claim is based largely on what a defendant says was going on in his or her mind—mental events that cannot be verified by, or tested against, the experiences of ordinary people in the same circumstances—administration of the defense involves a considerable risk of fabrication. Does Joy Baker's testimony give you any reason to doubt the veracity of her account of her feelings and thoughts at the time of the offense? Is it relevant that she had no previous history of disordered behavior or psychiatric treatment? Would your assessment of her credibility depend on whether the prosecution introduced any evidence suggesting a "motive" for the killing other than the one described by the defendant? Would your assessment be different if she had shot her husband instead of her aunt?

**2. The Existence of Mental Disease.** Assume that the defendant's testimony is credible and that she has accurately described the feelings and thoughts that she experienced before and during the shooting. (In fact, everyone who interviewed her or heard her testimony believed she was telling the truth.) Does this evidence demonstrate that she had a "defect of reason from disease of the mind," as *M'Naghten* requires, or the "mental disease or defect" required under the Model Penal Code formulation?

The purpose and scope of the "mental-disease" requirement is explored in some detail in the materials that follow; however, several points should be noted here. First, the concept of mental disease is a threshold condition; abnormal psychological functioning at the time of a crime has exculpatory significance only if it can be attributed to the effects of a "mental disease." Obviously this excludes those aberrations in human behavior that are attributable to defects of character, intoxication, or emotional upheaval due to anger, panic, or grief. Second, while the boundaries of the concept are unclear, it plainly comprehends "psychotic" conditions, i.e., those abnormal mental conditions involving "gross impairment of reality testing" and often evidenced by hallucinations or delusions.[a] Indeed, a psychosis is widely regarded as the only manifestation of mental disorder that can have exculpatory significance under *M'Naghten*.[b] Third, mental disease is *not* confined to those abnormalities associated with injured brain tissue, customarily labeled organic brain syndromes—for example, dementia attributable to trauma, cerebrovascular disease or Alzheimer's disease. If the concept were restricted to "organic" disorders, it would exclude a substantial proportion of persons whose contact with reality is severely impaired by what clinicians have traditionally called "functional" psychoses—those for which the presence of a specific organic cause has not yet been established, but which are associated with abnormal functioning of the brain. The major types of "functional" psychoses are the

[a] According to the glossary of the fourth edition of the Diagnostic and Statistical Manual of the American Psychiatric Association (DSM–IV) the meaning of the term "psychotic" varies somewhat in relation to particular disorders. However, the "narrowest definition" is restricted to delusions or prominent hallucinations in the absence of insight into their pathological nature. Conceptually, the term refers to a "gross impairment in reality testing":

> When there is gross impairment in reality testing, the individual incorrectly evaluates the accuracy of his or her perceptions and thoughts and makes incorrect inferences about external reality, even in the face of contrary evidence. The term psychotic does not apply to minor distortions of reality that involve matters of relative judgment. For example, a depressed person who underestimated his achievements would not be described as a psychotic, whereas one who believed he had caused a natural catastrophe would be so described.

[b] Many commentators—whether they support *M'Naghten* or oppose it—have taken the position that the phrase "defect of reason" is substantially equivalent to psychosis. According to Robert Waelder, for example, the threshold condition for an insanity claim is one "in which the sense of reality is crudely impaired, and inaccessible to the corrective influence of experience—for example, when people are confused or disoriented or suffer from hallucinations or delusions." Robert Waelder, Psychiatry and the Problem of Criminal Responsibility, 101 U.Pa.L.Rev. 378, 384 (1952). See also Joseph Livermore & Paul Meehl, The Virtues of *M'Naghten*, 51 Minn.L.Rev. 789, 802–04 (1967).

schizophrenic and paranoid disorders and the major affective disorders (e.g., bipolar disorder, also known as manic depressive disorder).

In Joy Baker's case, "direct evidence" of psychotic mental phenomena, including delusions, was presented in her own testimony. Should the defendant also be required to introduce expert psychiatric testimony to carry her burden of producing evidence that she was suffering from a "mental disease"? Most courts have said "no," ruling that, in a jury trial, testimony by the defendant or by lay witnesses who have observed the defendant's behavior can be sufficient to raise a jury question on the issue of insanity. In practice, of course, almost all insanity claims are predicated chiefly, if not entirely, on expert testimony. Consider the significance of the following excerpt from the expert testimony offered in Mrs. Baker's case on whether she had a "mental disease" at the time of the offense:

> Q: Doctor, in your professional opinion, was the defendant suffering from a mental disease at the time of the offense?
>
> A: When Mrs. Baker killed Trevah she was, in my professional opinion, suffering from an acute episode of paranoid schizophrenia. This is an example of a major psychotic disorder; that is, a condition during which the person loses the ability to distinguish between what is outside herself, or what is "real," and what is inside herself, and in that sense, "not real."
>
> Q: Doctor, could you explain how a person who has no previous history of mental illness would suddenly have an acute psychotic episode?
>
> A: Mrs. Baker has a predisposition for psychiatric disease not only hereditarily via her mother's history of schizophrenia, but also with the chaotic nature of her early home environment. It appears that prior to the shooting, there was a great deal of domestic stress in the Baker home. The stresses which most of us can normally tolerate may become psychologically intolerable for a person with a predisposition for psychiatric disease. The stress precipitates a disintegration of the personality, a deterioration which affects the person's thinking and emotions. Any of us could become acutely psychotic under enough stress. In Mrs. Baker's case, the stress to which she was exposed is readily apparent and this was enough to tip the psychic balance.

**3. Mental Disorder and Criminal Responsibility.** Even if Mrs. Baker was psychotic—was suffering from a major form of mental illness—at the time of the offense, she nonetheless might be found to have been criminally responsible for the homicide. This is because mental disease is a necessary condition, but not a sufficient one, for exculpation on grounds of insanity. Each of the prevailing insanity tests requires proof of two "elements": The defendant must have had (i) a mental disease (ii) that had specified incapacitating effects at the time of the offense. The various tests differ, of course, in their definitions of those incapacities that have exculpatory significance. Should the test ask simply whether the defendant was mentally ill (or "insane") at the time of the offense?

A partial answer to this question is that the criminal act may have been entirely unrelated to a person's sickness. Thus, even a psychotic person usually has some grasp of reality. For example, a person whose interactions with other people are shaped by clearly paranoid thinking and other psychotic symptoms may nonetheless take a radio known to belong to someone else simply out of a desire to have it while hoping that he or she will not be caught. The psychotic symptoms may be entirely unrelated to the "reasons" for engaging in the criminal act. It should be noted, however, that this observation does not provide a complete answer to the question posed above. It demonstrates only that the question should be reformulated to ask whether the symptoms of the defendant's mental illness (or "insanity") were related to the offense. This is precisely what the New Hampshire Supreme Court said when it endorsed the so-called "product" test in State v. Jones, 50 N.H. 369, 398 (1871):

> Whether the defendant had a mental disease . . . seems to be as much a question of fact as whether he had a bodily disease; and whether the killing of his wife was the product of that disease, [is] also as clearly a matter of fact as whether thirst and a quickened pulse are the product of fever. That it is a difficult question does not change the matter at all. [Various] symptoms, phases, or manifestations of the disease . . . are all clearly matters of evidence to be weighed by the jury upon the question whether the act was the offspring of insanity: if it was, a criminal intent did not produce it; if it was not, a criminal intent did produce it, and it was crime. . . .

Is this a sensible approach? Is it preferable to the other tests described earlier? Consider, in this connection the New Hampshire Supreme Court's criticism of the *M'Naghten* and "irresistible-impulse" tests. These tests, the court said, are misguided because they give conclusive significance to particular "symptoms, phases or manifestations of the disease," such as the capacity to distinguish right from wrong or to resist an insane impulse, instead of looking at the full impact of the disease as a clinical phenomenon. This observation was echoed 80 years later by Judge David Bazelon in a short-lived decision adopting the New Hampshire test: "In attempting to define insanity in terms of a symptom, the courts have assumed an impossible role, not merely one for which they have no special competence." Durham v. United States, 214 F.2d 862, 872 (D.C.Cir. 1954).

Do the tests of criminal responsibility purport to identify "symptoms" of insanity and therefore to establish a legal "test" for what is really a medical question? Sir James Stephen insisted, to the contrary, that definition of "[t]he mental elements of responsibility . . . is and must be a legal question. It cannot be anything else, for the meaning of responsibility is liability to punishment; and if criminal law does not determine who are to be punished under given circumstances, it determines nothing." 2 A

History of the Criminal Law of England 183 (1883). Is Stephen's response satisfactory?

**4. Applying the *M'Naghten* Test to Joy Baker.** Application of the *M'Naghten* test requires the fact-finder to reconstruct the defendant's "knowledge" at the time of the offense. The test has two prongs—knowledge of the "nature and quality" of the act and knowledge of its wrongfulness. The task of probing the defendant's psyche and applying these tests—difficult enough in any case—is complicated in Joy Baker's case by the apparent difference in her motivation for the two shots.

**(i) Knowledge of the Act.** The first prong of *M'Naghten* overlaps analytically the technical concept of mens rea. Did Mrs. Baker have the mens rea for some form of criminal homicide? It could be argued that she lacked the mens rea for murder at the time of her first shot because she did not intend to kill a "human being." At common law, this claim would probably be characterized as a mistake of fact. Since the mistake was obviously an unreasonable one, however, Mrs. Baker most likely would be guilty of some form of homicide if ordinary mens-rea principles were applied. It might also be argued that Mrs. Baker's first shot would have been justified if her delusional beliefs had been true since she would have been acting in self-defense. Again, the application of ordinary common-law culpability principles would indicate that she was unreasonably mistaken as to the existence of justificatory facts (the necessity for killing to protect herself) and her defense would fail, although the grade of the offense might be reduced to manslaughter. For present purposes, therefore, it can be assumed that Mrs. Baker would be guilty of some form of homicide—at least manslaughter—unless she is entitled to exculpation on grounds of insanity.[c]

It seems clear that Mrs. Baker was aware that she was pulling the trigger of a gun and that the bullet would kill or seriously injure the victim. But did she "know" that the intended victim was a "human being" when she fired the first shot? In this sense, did she know the nature and quality of her act?

In any event, the defendant's testimony shows that she "knew" at the time of the second shot that her aunt was not demonically possessed; her perceptual capacities appear to have been intact at this point. Remember that she observed that her aunt "hurt" and that killing her would put her out of her pain. Does this imply that she "knew" the nature and quality of the act of pulling the trigger the second time? What does "quality" mean?

**(ii) Knowledge of Wrongfulness.** Even if Joy Baker was sufficiently aware of the physical characteristics of her conduct to be said to have "known" the "nature and quality" of her act, did she "know" that it was wrong? Undoubtedly, she knew, as an abstract matter, that killing another person without justification is both legally and morally wrong.

---

[c] The general relationship between mens rea and mental abnormality is explored at the end of this section and is explored again in the specific context of homicide offenses in Chapter IX.

However, Mrs. Baker claimed to have believed at the time of the first shot that she was in imminent peril of annihilation at the hands of the devil. Would such a "defect of reason" prevent her from knowing that her act was wrong? Is it wrong, legally or morally, to shoot the devil?[d]

The second shot, unlike the first, was not motivated by Mrs. Baker's delusion. Her motive was to relieve her aunt's suffering. Was the second shot legally justified? If not, did her mental disease prevent her from "knowing" that her act was "wrong"? In what way?

The meaning of the word "wrong" in the *M'Naghten* test has often been in dispute. Some courts permit exculpation only if, as a result of mental disease, the defendant was disabled from knowing that the act was *legally* wrong. Under this approach, a defendant who knew that her conduct was a crime is legally sane regardless of her motivation or reasons for thinking it justified. The trial of Andrea Yates in Texas in 2002 is illustrative. Ms. Yates killed her 5 children, ranging in ages from six months to eight years. At her trial for killing three of the children, she presented uncontested evidence that she had experienced post-partum depression with psychotic features after the birth of her fourth child in 1999 (from which she recovered after treatment with anti-psychotic and anti-depressant medication), and that these symptoms had recurred after the birth of her fifth child but did not respond well to medication. She claimed that she believed her children were "stumbling" into the throes of the devil and were going to burn in the fires of hell for eternity, and that by killing them, she would save them from this fate, she would be executed, and Satan would be vanquished. While the prosecution conceded that she was suffering from a severe mental illness, she knew that killing her children was a crime and that she would be punished (indeed, that was part of her motivation). Her efforts to prevent anyone from finding out what she was planning to do, as well as her confession, amply showed that she knew her conduct was "wrong"—"I know what I have done," she acknowledged. The jury convicted her of murder (although it did not recommend a death sentence).[e]

[d] The *M'Naghten* decision contained another "rule" that might have been applicable to the first shot fired by Mrs. Baker. One of the questions posed by the House of Lords was: "If a person under an insane delusion as to existing facts commits an offense in consequence thereof, is he thereby excused?" The judges responded:

> [M]aking the assumption . . . that he labours under such partial delusion only, and is not in other respects insane, we think he must be considered in the same situation as to responsibility as if the facts with respect to which the delusion exists were real. For example, if, under the influence of his delusion, he supposes another man to be in the act of attempt-

ing to take away his life, and he kills that man, as he supposes, in self-defense, he would be exempt from punishment. If his delusion was that the deceased had inflicted a serious injury to his character and fortune, and he killed him in revenge for such supposed injury, he would be liable to punishment. . . .

This "insane delusion" ground of exculpation has been discarded as a separate test in modern formulations of *M'Naghten* on the theory that it is but a specific application of the "nature-and-quality" and "right-wrong" branches of the *M'Naghten* test and is thus redundant as a separate rule.

[e] State v. Kelly, 2002 WL 31730874 (Tenn. Ct. Crim. App. 2002), is very similar

Many courts take a broader view of what it means to be unable to know that one's conduct is wrong. Under this view, knowing that one's conduct is illegal does not amount to knowing that it is wrong. A famous early case setting forth this view is People v. Schmidt, 216 N.Y. 324, 110 N.E. 945 (1915), involving a defendant who claimed that he killed a woman after hearing the voice of God calling upon him to do so as a sacrifice and atonement. In an opinion by Judge Cardozo, the Court of Appeals held "that there are times and circumstances in which the word 'wrong' ... ought not to be limited to legal wrong." In particular, if a person has "an insane delusion that God has appeared to [him] and ordained the commission of a crime, we think it cannot be said of the offender that he knows the act to be wrong." More recently, the Connecticut Supreme Court took a similar view in interpreting the word "wrongfulness" to refer to the defendant's understanding of the moral wrongfulness of his actions. State v. Wilson, 242 Conn. 605, 700 A.2d 633 (1997).[f] Wilson killed a man believing that the victim was a mastermind of a large organization designed to control the minds of people worldwide, including his own. The court said that the legislature had purposely decided not to limit the insanity test to legal wrongfulness by rejecting the word "criminality" in favor of the word "wrongfulness" when it adopted the Model Code formulation of the insanity test.[g]

What is left of the right-wrong "test" under the "moral wrongfulness" approach? Does this mean that if a mentally ill person thinks, according to his own lights, that he is doing the "right" thing, then he is not criminally responsible even if he "knew" that his act was a crime and that it would be condemned by others? Courts adopting the "moral wrongfulness" position have resisted a "purely subjective" approach. In *Wilson*, for example, the Connecticut Supreme Court said that a defendant is legally insane if, as a result of mental disease, "he substantially misperceived reality and harbored a delusional belief that society, under the circumstances as the defendant honestly but mistakenly perceived them to be, would not have morally condemned his actions." How would this test apply to Joy Baker? To Andrea Yates and the other defendants mentioned above? Is there any other possible meaning of "wrong"?

to Yates. Kelley smothered his daughter because he believed God had directed him to do so in order to facilitate the second coming of Christ. He subsequently described the killing as "horrible" and told a detective that he had hoped that his wife would not enter the room during the killing. The court said that this evidence showed that he knew his conduct was wrong.

[f] See also State v. Cameron, 100 Wn.2d 520, 674 P.2d 650 (en banc 1983). Cameron stabbed and killed his stepmother, believing that she was a satanic agent and that he was doing God's will, even though he knew that he was committing a crime. The jury was instructed that "the terms 'right and wrong' refer to knowledge of a person at the time of committing an act that he was acting contrary to law." The Washington Supreme Court overturned the conviction, holding that this instruction was erroneous.

[g] The drafters of the Model Penal Code took no position on this question, leaving it to the courts and legislatures to choose whether the test should include the term "wrongfulness" or "criminality." Jurisdictions adopting the Model Code test have divided evenly on the question.

**(iii) The Value of Expert Testimony.** Is the task of applying either branch of *M'Naghten* materially aided by expert psychiatric testimony? The relevant portion of the opinion offered in Joy Baker's case is excerpted below:

Q:  At the time of the offense, did the defendant know she was shooting her aunt?

A:  In her psychotic state she was not able to draw the boundary between her internal chaotic reality (her fear of annihilation) and the external reality of her environment, and the two became fused. As she talks about that evening she states that she saw her aunt coming towards the back door and she "knew" that this person was her aunt. It is essential here to understand what the word "know" means in the context of Mrs. Baker's psychiatric illness. It is true that Mrs. Baker was able to recognize the form which approached her home as that of her aunt. This particular perceptual mechanism seemed to remain intact. However, Mrs. Baker's interpretation of this perception is what was so profoundly affected by her psychotic state. Her interpretation of her aunt approaching her home was entirely out of touch with the reality of the situation. Mrs. Baker firmly believed that her aunt was a witch and was afraid her aunt would annihilate her. It was this affective state, or emotional tone, which set the stage for Mrs. Baker's actions. She was unable at the time of the shooting, with her abnormal intellectual functions, to recognize how invalid her interpretations were. This is, of course, a result of her psychotic state. In other words, at the time of the shooting, Mrs. Baker was unable, in my professional opinion, to understand the difference between her own feelings and the events occurring in the world around her. She did not appreciate the nature and consequences of her acts and acted purely from the instinct of self-preservation.

Q:  What about the second shot, Doctor?

A:  Persons in a psychotic state have extreme polarization of emotions. One moment they may feel intense love, the next moment intense hate. One moment they may feel intensely threatened and the next moment they may feel intensely secure and so forth. In addition these polar feelings may switch very rapidly and will not appear to be connected to one another because of the chaotic state of that person's thinking. In Mrs. Baker's psychotic state she experienced these rapid disjointed changes in feelings. This enabled her to feel threatened and fearful in one moment and yet to feel concern and desire to help her wounded aunt in the next.

Thus, the first shot removed the threat of her own imminent destruction and generated feelings of relief. This, in turn "shocked" her and triggered a "jump" in her perceptual modalities. Her perceptive focus shifted from her preoccupation with the threats to herself to a recognition of her aunt's condition. Now she was preoccupied with her desire to "stop the suffering." To Mrs. Baker the immediate way to do this was to shoot her aunt again. In her "regressed" state, she was still not sufficiently in touch with reality to call into play mature, normal responses to her aunt's condition. A person in a psychotic state cannot connect logically chains of events. Hence she did not make the rational connection between the act of shooting her aunt to stop her suffering and the finality of death. Thus, it is my professional opinion that a full appreciation of the nature and consequences of the second shot could not have existed in Mrs. Baker's mind.

Does this testimony help? Should Mrs. Baker be convicted in a *M'Naghten* jurisdiction?

**5. The Meaning of "Knowing."** The *M'Naghten* formulation has been subject to the persistent criticism that it requires conviction of psychotic offenders who are not blameworthy. According to the critics, only a handful of seriously ill offenders fail to "know" in a purely intellectual sense enough about what they are doing to know that it is punishable. Yet, because a mentally ill person's "intellectual" knowledge may not be assimilated by the whole personality, such a person may lack an emotional appreciation of the significance of conduct. In other words, the term "knowledge" is clinically meaningful, the critics say, only if it is given an "affective" or emotional meaning. The expert testimony offered in Joy Baker's case illustrates this clinical interpretation of "knowledge."

Perhaps the most famous statement of the clinical objection to *M'Naghten* appeared in Gregory Zilboorg, Misconceptions of Legal Insanity, 9 Am.J. Orthopsychiat. 540, 552–53 (1939):*

The crux of the question revolves around the word "know." The law automatically assumes that a child committing a felony does not know the nature and quality of the act and does not know that it is wrong. Yet a child of moderate brightness will say that he hit his sister on the head, that she bled and then she fell; he will even admit that she died or that he killed her and will perhaps say that he was wrong to kill his sister. The criminal code does not accept this knowledge as valid; without knowing it the law itself recognizes here a fundamental medicopsychological distinction between the purely verbal knowledge which characterizes the child and the other type of knowledge which characterizes the adult. The fundamental difference between verbal or purely intellectual knowledge and the mysterious other kind of knowledge is familiar to every clinical psychiatrist; it is the difference between knowl-

---

edge divorced from affect and knowledge so fused with affect that it becomes a human reality. . . .

Therefore "defect of reason" which the law stresses may not and, with the exception of cases of mental defectives, does not lie within the field of reason at all, but within the field of emotional appreciation. This emotional appreciation is a very complex phenomenon. It is based on a series of intricate psychological mechanisms, the most potent of which is that of identification. What makes it possible for a civilized, mentally healthy human being to resist a murderous impulse is not the cold detached reasoning that it is wrong and dangerous but the automatic emotional, mostly unconscious identification with the prospective victim, an identification which automatically inhibits the impulse to kill and causes anxiety ("It is dangerous") which in turn produces the reflection: "It is wrong, the same may and should happen to me." Unless this identification is present the impulse breaks through and fear of the law and sense of wrong is paled, devoid of its affective component; it becomes a verbal, coldly intellectual, formal, childish, infantile psychological presentation.

In his definitive work on the insanity defense, Abraham Goldstein concluded that, in practice, the *M'Naghten* formula has been interpreted and applied in a much less restrictive fashion than its critics have assumed. See Abraham Goldstein, The Insanity Defense 49–51 (1967):*

The assertion that "know" is narrowly defined has been made so often and so insistently that it comes as a surprise to find that very few appellate courts have imposed the restrictive interpretation. Indeed, most of the courts which have addressed themselves to the question have favored a rather broad construction. In [many] states, the jury is told that an accused "knows" only if he "understands" enough to enable him to judge of "the nature, character and consequence of the act charged against him," or if he has the "capacity to appreciate the character and to comprehend the probable or possible consequences of his act." . . . In this view, the word "appreciate" draws most psychoses under the *M'Naghten* rules, because it addresses itself to the defendant's awareness of "the true significance of his conduct." . . .

The phrase "nature and quality of the act" is [typically] either stated to the jury without explanation or treated as adding nothing to the requirement that the accused know his act was wrong. [However, one] court has held that "nature and quality" gives "important emphasis" to the realization of the wrongfulness of an act. It marks the distinction between "vaguely [realizing] that particular conduct is forbidden" and "real insight into the conduct." This construction illustrates the close connection between the definition of "know" and that of "nature and quality." The

* Reprinted with the permission of the author and Yale University Press.

broader meaning of "nature and quality" carries with it the broader construction of "know" and vice versa. To know the quality of an act, with all its social and emotional implications, requires more than an abstract purely intellectual knowledge. Likewise, to talk of appreciating the full significance of an act means that "nature and quality" must be understood as including more than the physical nature of the act.

This broader reading of the word "knowledge" as it appears in the *M'Naghten* formulation is, as Goldstein indicated, typically achieved by emphasizing that the actor must "appreciate" the nature and quality of the conduct and that it was wrong in a moral sense. Indeed, "appreciate" has become a kind of code-word for this "affective" reading of "knowledge." The defendant must have sufficient understanding of the nature and consequences of the conduct to be said to "appreciate" its social and moral significance. Without such understanding, the defendant lacks the rudimentary tools by which "normal" responsible people govern their conduct. Use of the word "appreciate" in the reformulation of the *M'Naghten* test in Section 4.01 of the Model Penal Code is intended to embrace this broader notion of what it means to "know" something is wrong.

The trend in favor of an "affective" meaning of knowledge, however, has not been without its critics. Glanville Williams is one of them. In Criminal Law: The General Part 491–92 (2d ed. 1961), he stated:

> The tendency to widen the exemption ... by referring it to some deeper kind of metaphysical insight is ... found among American psychiatrists. The question, on this view, is not merely ... whether the accused knew he was killing a human being, but whether he had any "real appreciation" or "understanding" of his act, or of its "enormity, its significance or its implications." This is metaphysical rather than scientific language and it may be permissible to doubt whether any citizen, sane or not, can be credited with the transcendental insight of the mystic. The formula of "real nature" is used indulgently to give a general exemption on the ground of [mental illness].

Does Williams have a point? Should a mere "intellectual knowledge" be sufficient to establish criminal responsibility even if the defendant lacked a "true appreciation" of the significance of his conduct?

**6. The Significance of Cognitive Impairment.** The preceding notes have used the facts of the Joy Baker case to explore the meaning of the *M'Naghten* test and the analogous language in the Model Penal Code. Now, it is useful to return to the fundamental question raised at the outset, i.e., whether these tests identify proper criteria for assessing criminal responsibility.

To the extent that "nature and quality" of the act refers only to its physical character, the first prong of *M'Naghten* is, in the words of Lord

Patrick Devlin, "practically obsolete."[f] No one who squeezes a person's neck really thinks he is squeezing a lemon.[g] Also, as Goldstein noted, an emphasis on the moral "quality" of the act makes this prong of the test functionally equivalent to its right-wrong prong. Thus, under either *M'Naghten* or the analogous language in the Model Penal Code, the real significance of cognitive impairment lies in whether the defendant knew or appreciated the "wrongfulness" of the act. Is this the right question to ask? The liability of a sane person does not turn on having a "mind bent on wrongdoing" or full appreciation or understanding of the legal or moral significance of conduct. Why should the liability of an "insane" person turn on such an inquiry?

Glanville Williams discussed this issue in Criminal Law: The General Part 495–96 (2d ed. 1961):

> Why, precisely, does knowledge of wrong enter into a consideration of responsibility? ... The exemption ... may perhaps be regarded as dictated by the object of punishment [because] a psychotic who does not know that his act is wrong is not likely to be deterred by the legal prohibition. Yet the same is true of a sane person who does not know that his act is wrong. Why is not the rule ignorantia juris non excusat applied to the insane? Perhaps it is because the rule presupposes a mind capable of knowing right. But on this interpretation the question should be not: "Did the accused know it was wrong" but "Was he capable of knowing that it was wrong?" For if it once be admitted that some psychotics know right from wrong, it may be a mere accident of education (such as may befall a sane person) that this particular psychotic did not know the particular act to be wrong. What must be shown is that his ignorance was the result of his mental disease. . . .

Williams' point can be illustrated by the second shot in Joy Baker's case. This shot was not motivated by her delusional beliefs. Under the circumstances as she correctly perceived them, her conduct constitutes murder, for euthanasia has never been recognized as justifiable or excusable homicide under Anglo–American law. Perhaps Joy Baker did not know this, although it is more likely that she acted spontaneously and gave no thought to the legality of her conduct. Yet, if a sane person had shot an injured and suffering Aunt Trevah under similar circumstances, ignorance of (or emotional indifference to) the governing law of homicide would be legally irrelevant. Why should a different rule obtain for Joy Baker?

Questions of this nature have led some commentators to suggest that the *M'Naghten* formulation should be discarded altogether. The real basis

---

[f] Patrick Devlin, Criminal Responsibility and Punishment: Functions of Judge and Jury, [1954] Crim.L.Rev. 661, 678–79.

[g] The hypothetical case of a person who strangles someone in the mistaken belief that he is squeezing a lemon was first used in the early 1970s to illustrate the effect of abolishing the insanity defense while admitting evidence of mental abnormality to negate mens rea. See Heathcoate Wales, An Analysis of the Proposal to "Abolish" the Insanity Defense in S.1: Squeezing a Lemon, 124 U. Pa. L Rev 687 (1976).

for exculpation of the insane, they argue, lies not in a lack of a capacity to know or appreciate the wrongfulness of the conduct, but in a lack of capacity for rational control of behavior in relation to the criminal act.[h] Should irrationality be the test?

**7. Applying Control Tests to Psychotic Defendants.** The control test provides an independent basis for exculpation in more than a third of the states. Proponents of such a test traditionally have claimed that a psychotic person who is "driven" by pathological delusions or hallucinations may be unable to restrain his behavior despite knowing that it is wrong. This "loss of control" is therefore thought to be a morally relevant feature of severe mental disorder. Recall the expert testimony in *M'Naghten*'s case that "he was not capable of exercising any control over acts which had connection with his delusion" and that the natural progression of his disease was "to burst forth with irresistible intensity."

How would the control formulas apply to Joy Baker? Did she act on an "irresistible impulse"? Did she lack "substantial capacity to conform her conduct to the requirements of law"? Is further information needed to apply these tests?

Obviously, the task of applying control tests to Joy Baker requires speculation about whether she "could" have acted otherwise than she did, and whether her mental illness prevented her from having the power of choice that she "normally" would have had. Since the only evidence available is her actual behavior—the defendant shot her aunt (twice)—how can one determine whether she "could" have acted otherwise? Would expert testimony help? Consider these excerpts from the testimony offered in Mrs. Baker's case:

Q: Doesn't Mrs. Baker's effort to protect her children, only moments before the killing, indicate that she had the mental power to resist her homicidal impulses?

A: No, I don't think so. When Mrs. Baker ordered the children to read the 23rd Psalm, she was trying to assure that they would not be the ones to attack her; in this sense, putting the Bible in their hands was an act of self-defense. When the victim drove up, Mrs. Baker did everything she could to prevent her aunt from coming in the house. However, once her aunt put her hand through the door, Mrs. Baker had no options left, psychologically speaking. She was in a state of extreme anxiety and was fearful of imminent attack. The impulse for protective action was, if you will, irresistible.

Q: Defendant's own testimony would suggest that she did not feel threatened at the time of the second shot; indeed, her testimony indicates that she was acting from a rational mo-

---

[h] See, e.g., Stephen Morse, Rationality and Responsibility, 74 S. Cal. L Rev. 251 (2000); Michael Moore, Law and Psychiatry: Rethinking the Relationship (1984); Henry Fingarette and Ann F. Haase, Mental Disabilities and Criminal Responsibility (1979); Joel Feinberg, Doing and Deserving: Essays in the Theory of Responsibility 272–92 (1970).

tive—to stop her aunt's suffering. Doesn't this suggest that her capacity to make choices had returned?

A: It is probably true that she was less influenced by her delusional thinking; because her level of intense anxiety had been reduced, she was able to see the victim as her aunt. Her perceptual and interpretive capacities had been restored to some extent. But this doesn't mean her functioning was intact by any means. She still lacked insight and judgment. She saw that her aunt was in pain; the immediate issue was how to stop the pain, and she responded in a regressed, child-like way. She acted impulsively.

Q: Suppose a policeman, or perhaps the rescue squad, had pulled into the driveway after the first shot. As you understand her condition, what do you think she would have done?

A: This is speculation, of course. But I think she would have taken advantage of the alternative way to get help for her aunt. The problem, in fact, was that there were no visible options and in her compromised psychological condition she was unable to think about alternatives that were not visibly apparent.

The desirability of a control test of responsibility has been one of the most hotly debated issues in the criminal law for more than a century. In recent years the debate has focused chiefly on disorders other than psychoses. This dimension of the controversy is covered in the next section, immediately below. However, it should be emphasized that the early proponents of the "irresistible impulse" test argued that the *M'Naghten* formula was an inadequate measure of the morally significant features of psychotic deterioration. Moreover, many psychiatrists have opposed recent efforts to eliminate the volitional criterion on the same basis. In response, many of the commentators who support proposals to narrow the defense have argued that a broad, affective reading of the "knowledge" or "appreciation" test makes the control test superfluous in cases involving psychotic defendants.[i] Is this right? Is Joy Baker's case for exculpation any stronger under a test of volitional impairment than it would be if cognitive impairment were the only inquiry?

———

## SUBSECTION B: THE INSANITY DEFENSE AND THE CONTROL INQUIRY

———

### INTRODUCTORY NOTE ON VOLITIONAL CRITERIA OF RESPONSIBILITY

The central issue in the contemporary debate about the insanity defense is whether volitional incapacity should have independent exculpato-

---

[i] See, e.g., Jerome Hall, General Principles of Criminal Law 486–500 (1960).

ry significance. It is important to bear in mind that the volitional inquiry in the insanity defense intersects two other doctrines of the penal law. The first is the requirement of the voluntary act, discussed in Chapter I. According to this doctrine, some acts are regarded as involuntary because they are not within the conscious, physical control of the actor. An opportunity for choosing to act or not to act establishes the minimum link between body and mind necessary for criminal liability. Although a mentally abnormal offender may be said to be driven to act by intra-psychic forces, the technical requirement of a voluntary act is virtually always met if the person is conscious at the time of the offense.[a]

The second intersecting doctrine might be called situational compulsion. Sometimes, people may have conscious, physical control over their bodily movements, but nonetheless feel that they have no "real" choice at all. The classic case is duress: *A* takes *B*'s money because *C* holds a gun to *A*'s head and threatens to shoot if *A* does not do so. The reach of the concept of situational compulsion is explored in Chapter V. For present purposes, the important point is that a person with normal strength of character who is confronted with such coercive circumstances will not be held criminally liable for "choosing" to violate the penal law. Even if the choice is not justifiable, the actor may be excused if blame would be unfair for conduct that is, morally speaking, "beyond control."

The case for the volitional prong of the insanity defense rests on the empirical proposition that mental abnormalities can impair a person's capacity to choose to comply with the penal law and on the moral proposition that such a person cannot fairly be blamed for criminal acts that are psychologically "compelled". It should be noted, however, that acts "compelled" by internal pathology stand on a very different footing from those "compelled" by external pressure. In the latter case, the incapacity is simply the frailty of the ordinary person; in the former, the defendant's claim to exculpation is pressed precisely because the strengths of the ordinary person are lacking.

---

## ILLUSTRATIVE CASES OF VOLITIONAL IMPAIRMENT

A full appreciation of the complexities of the volitional inquiry requires familiarity with the variety of clinical explanations that can be given for

[a] Indeed, evidence of mental abnormality is routinely rejected when offered to support an involuntary-act defense. The historical reason for this result, and for the continued conceptual separation of the voluntary-act doctrine and the insanity defense, undoubtedly is closely tied to the dispositional consequences of the two doctrines. Typically, an acquittal by reason of insanity leads to some form of commitment of the defendant for treatment of the underlying mental disorder. An involuntary-act acquittal, on the other hand, has no such consequence. This factor has considerable explanatory power as to why the voluntary-act doctrine is generally conceived in relatively narrow terms.

criminal behavior. The following cases are representative of the range of claims that have been raised. The factual summaries also summarize the expert testimony presented on the defendant's behalf.

**1.  *Barnes*.**[a] James Barnes, age 18, was charged with six counts of arson and three counts of murder in connection with one of the fires, which had been set in an apartment building. He pleaded not guilty by reason of insanity. The expert witness testified that the defendant was suffering from a disorder of impulse control (pyromania) and schizoid personality disorder. According to the expert, Barnes' earliest childhood memory was watching a neighbor burn trash in the backyard. He began setting fires around his own home at the age of eight. During high school he set fires to student lockers on four occasions and periodically set fires at his part-time jobs, usually in trash containers in alleys. Despite the frequency of his firesetting, he was rarely caught and never punished for his actions.

Barnes' father was absent from home for extended periods until Barnes was 12. During adolescence, he and his father argued frequently; he felt his father viewed him as an ineffectual person, someone who "could not make it on his own."

At 16, Barnes began calling for emergency assistance from rescue squads in each of the surrounding counties by pretending to be suffocating. This practice continued for more than a year and occurred about 30 times. Barnes described a great sense of satisfaction from being cared for by the emergency crews on these occasions. Soon he became a member of his local rescue squad and felt secure as being part of a "team." He felt especially close to Carson, an older member of the squad. Along with other men of the rescue squad, Barnes and Carson spent their off-hours together.

Within a few months however, Carson married and left the rescue squad to become a fireman. During the same period, Barnes left home and moved into an apartment because of increasing tension with his father. His sense of isolation and loneliness increased soon thereafter, and he had fantasies of being rescued by Carson during a fire. In this fantasy Carson would carry him out of a burning building and would take care of him and ensure his continued safety. He also described feelings of sexual arousal in seeing firemen, particularly Carson, in their rubberized firefighting clothes.

Barnes soon began to set fires, reporting them in the hope that Carson would arrive. In this manner he would see Carson and would be either praised for his assistance in fighting the fire or would be "rescued." It was during this period that he committed the acts for which he was indicted. The last involved an apartment building.

The expert testified that, in his opinion, Barnes' drives and needs were so strong that they were able to override his generally intact judgment and

---

[a] This fact situation is based on an unreported case. For a similar case, see Briscoe v. United States, 248 F.2d 640 (D.C.Cir. 1957).

his sense of social responsibility. Acknowledging that Barnes was able to delay his impulse to start a fire until the circumstances were favorable and the likelihood of detection was reduced, the expert nonetheless concluded that Barnes exhibited an "extremely strong need to bring himself into close contact with Carson even though that required him to commit socially irresponsible and illegal actions." Moreover, the expert testified, Barnes' "need to start the fire in order to bring himself and Carson together was so strong that he unconsciously was able to keep from his awareness the possibility that others might be hurt or that extensive property damage might occur."

**2.   *Chester.*[b]** Jack Chester was charged with the murder of Beatrice Fishman and pleaded not guilty by reason of insanity. The defendant and the victim met as teenagers and became engaged while he was in the armed forces. Upon being discharged, he obtained a job in a factory in another state and plans were made for the wedding in July of that year. For a variety of reasons, the wedding was repeatedly postponed over the next four months. In October the defendant was "very perturbed" and decided that he and Beatrice "were through." He told her she could keep all that he had given her except the wedding ring.

Between October and the following April, the defendant was depressed. Although he dated other girls, none of them could replace Beatrice. He tried to bring about a reconciliation, but Beatrice seemed indifferent, although she still failed to return the wedding ring. He started to drink heavily and to use marijuana. Sometime before April, he bought a pistol.

The defendant decided to visit Beatrice one April weekend. When packing his bag for the trip he put in the pistol. Upon arriving, he went directly to the Fishman home and was told by her parents that she was "out on a date." After talking with them for a while, he left. On the following day the defendant went to the Fishman home and talked with Beatrice and her mother. Beatrice told him that he had been away so long "she didn't know [him] any more," but if he returned to Boston to live they "could get reacquainted." The defendant asked Beatrice to return the ring, and she told him it was in a safe deposit vault, and he could have it Monday. After further conversation, he became very upset; he later said that he felt that he had become entangled in an "utterly hopeless and impossible situation" and that he wanted to kill Beatrice. But he "fought this emotion down," kissed her goodbye, and walked out of the house.

The defendant, according to his testimony at the trial, went to a bar, had "two shots of bourbon," and smoked two marijuana cigarettes, becoming slightly "high." But he said that this had no effect on his behavior; he admitted that he knew what he was doing. In about half an hour he returned to the Fishman house in an angry mood. He "figured it out [that he] couldn't live with her and [he] couldn't live without her and it did not

[b] This case is based on Commonwealth v. Chester, 337 Mass. 702, 150 N.E.2d 914 (1958).

make any difference." His intent was to "blow her head off." He went to the front door with his pistol in his pocket and rang the doorbell. As Beatrice opened the door he had the pistol in his hand. Seeing it, she hesitated and then closed the door. Thereupon the defendant started pulling the trigger and kept pulling it until he had fired nine shots through the door. Three of these entered the victim's body causing wounds from which she died within an hour. Shortly thereafter the defendant asked a policeman to arrest him as he had "just murdered someone."

According to the expert testimony introduced in support of Chester's insanity defense, his father died when the defendant was about five years old. His father's death was due to a head injury caused by a fall on the ice, suffered while running after Chester after he left the house without a hat. The defendant thereafter had guilt feelings because he thought he had caused his father's death. During his boyhood, without a father, he was difficult to control and there was considerable friction between him and his mother. As a result of one dispute with his mother, the defendant, then aged 12, drank a bottle of iodine. At 15 he sustained a serious injury to his eye from an air rifle. The injury affected his appearance, and as a consequence he became self-conscious.

While in the service, the defendant became despondent because of his relations with Beatrice and at one time considered suicide. He was unusually combative and frequently got into fights with other soldiers. Because two airplane pilots lost their lives in the crash of planes on which he had done mechanical work, he felt responsible for their deaths. He felt that he was "no good," that everything he did would turn out badly, and that he would die young.

The defendant's experts concluded that defendant had suffered since the age of 12 from a "personality disorder characterized by passive obstructionism and by a tendency toward overt, aggressive, uncontrolled outbursts or giving vent to one's feelings with vigorous physical action toward others." He also had an obsession with guilt and strong feelings of worthlessness. While conceding that many people have such traits, the expert stated that Chester had them to a marked degree. "Most of the time the defendant has been able to repress his strong feelings of anger. However, when these feelings have become more intense due to an intolerably frustrating situation, he swings into impulsive violent action over which he momentarily has no conscious control." At the time of the offense, according to the expert, Chester was driven by twin motivations: uncontrollable anger at both himself and the victim, and strong feelings of guilt and worthlessness.

**3. *Ellingwood.*[c]** Sonny Ellingwood, a carpenter with no history of criminal behavior, was charged with criminal homicide in the second degree. The testimony adduced at trial revealed that the defendant shot two people with virtually no provocation and with no discernible motive. He pleaded not guilty by reason of insanity.

[c] This case is based on State v. Ellingwood, 409 A.2d 641 (Me.1979).

The evidence shows that on the day of the shooting the defendant was upset about various minor problems arising at home and on the job. During the morning he had corrected an erroneous estimate he had made on a construction project. Apparently his work had deteriorated in the weeks preceding the shooting.

At about noon of this day he returned home with two six-packs of beer. He drank some at that time. His wife chided him for drinking during the day. He complained about being pushed around by people and declared he wanted to quit his job and leave the state. Later he left his house trailer, taking with him his rifle and two bottles of beer. One of these bottles he put down and shot with his rifle. His wife came out of the trailer and reprimanded him for his action. He walked away toward a nearby gravel pit.

At the pit the defendant found James Hunter and his daughter, Jacqueline, removing some loam from the pit. The owner of the pit had requested that the defendant keep watch over it. The defendant confronted this pair demanding to know by what right they were removing soil from the pit. James Hunter countered by asking what business it was to the defendant. After this brief interchange the defendant turned his back to them, put down the remaining beer bottle, and turned again, aiming the rifle at James Hunter.

He sighted the rifle on James Hunter for a few seconds. The victim pointed at the defendant and ordered him to put down the gun. The defendant then shot, hitting James Hunter in the chest. Jacqueline Hunter heard the defendant prepare his rifle for a second shot. She looked at him and ordered him to put down the gun. He shot her in the face.

The defendant's wife drove into the pit and picked up the defendant, who then told her his life was over, that he should shoot himself because he had just killed two people. They then drove to a nearby house where the police were called at the defendant's request.

Police officers described the defendant as blubbering, babbling, and crying. Although he admitted the shooting in general terms at that time, he was never able to recall the events in detail.

The defendant introduced expert testimony to support his insanity plea. The psychiatrist testified that the defendant had an underlying obsessive-compulsive and hysterical personality disorder. Symptoms of this condition include "failure to admit feelings; being overly conscientious; being over-controlled; an inability to relax easily; a feeling of personal inadequacy; a chronic tendency to swallow difficulties without objection." The witness testified that during the days before the offense, the defendant was experiencing substantial anxiety as a result of accumulating stress and that he could not control his exaggerated retributive feelings when confronted with the intruders in the pit. According to the expert, the defendant was probably aware of his actions at the time of the shooting but probably believed, "at some primitive level of psychological functioning, that he was acting in self-defense."

**4.** *Murdock.*[d] Murdock was one of three black patrons at a hamburger shop called the Little Tavern. At about 3:00 a.m., a white woman and five white U.S. Marine lieutenants, in dress white uniforms, entered the shop and ordered food. After Murdock had walked out, an argument developed between one of the whites and Alexander, one of Murdock's associates. Apparently one of the whites used a racial epithet, and Alexander drew a gun. Murdock then came back into the shop with his own gun drawn and fired, killing several of the Marines. Alexander and Murdock were charged with murder. Murdock pleaded not guilty by reason of insanity.

Murdock testified that he pulled his gun as a reflex and fired because he thought the Marines, who he said were moving toward him, would kill him. On cross-examination, he admitted that he did not see any weapons, that he emptied his fully loaded revolver at them in the restaurant and that he fired three shots from Alexander's gun from the window of the car as they drove away. In support of his insanity claim Murdock introduced psychiatric testimony that he is "strongly delusional, though not hallucinating or psychotic." In particular, he is "greatly preoccupied with the unfair treatment of negroes in this country and believes that racial war is inevitable." The witness stated that this behavior reflects compulsiveness, emotional immaturity and some psychopathic traits, and that his emotional disorder had its roots in his childhood. His father had deserted his mother and he grew up in the Watts section of Los Angeles in a large family with little love or attention. (As his attorney put it in the closing argument, Murdock had a "rotten social background.") Since Murdock's emotional difficulties are strongly tied to his sense of racial oppression, the witness said, "it is probable that when the Marine called him a 'black bastard,' Murdock had an irresistible impulse to shoot."

————

## NOTES ON THE CONTROL INQUIRY

**1. Questions on *Barnes*, *Chester*, *Ellingwood*, and *Murdock*.** It is helpful to reflect on these cases at two levels. First, consider issues connected with applying the tests. In a jurisdiction that uses a control test, is an insanity instruction warranted or required in each case? If not, on what basis would the instruction be denied? Is there sufficient clinical information for a factfinder to decide whether any of these defendants lacked "substantial capacity" to conform his behavior to the requirements of the law? What more information would be useful?

Now consider the underlying policy issue: Does any of these cases present a morally compelling claim of non-responsibility? Should the test of

---

[d] This case is based on United States v. Alexander and Murdock, 471 F.2d 923 (D.C.Cir. 1972).

insanity include a volitional prong? Or should claims of this nature be foreclosed?

**2. The Control Tests: Criticism and Defense.** Few would dispute the moral basis for the control test—that persons who really "cannot help" doing what they did are not blameworthy. As Herbert Wechsler and Jerome Michael observed in their classic article, A Rationale of the Law of Homicide I, 37 Colum.L.Rev. 701, 754 (1937), a cognitive formulation cannot cover the whole population of those who are beyond the deterrent influence of the penal law *"if* there are persons who, even though they are aware of the potentialities of their acts and of the threat of punishment, are nevertheless incapable of choosing to avoid the act in order to avoid the punishment. There is no reason to doubt that such persons exist." Although some skeptics do, in fact, doubt that "such persons exist," most opponents of the control formulation have concentrated their criticism on the difficulty of administering such a test in light of present knowledge.

The opponents of volitional criteria of responsibility argue that there is no scientific basis for measuring a person's capacity for self-control or for calibrating the impairment of such capacity. There is, in short, no objective basis for distinguishing between offenders who were undeterrable and those who were merely undeterred, between the impulse that was irresistible and the impulse not resisted, or between substantial impairment of capacity and some lesser impairment. Whatever the precise terms of the volitional test, the critics assert that the question is unanswerable—or can be answered only by "moral guesses." To ask it at all, they say, invites fabricated claims, undermines equal administration of the penal law, and compromises its deterrent effect.

Sheldon Glueck observed in Mental Disorder and the Criminal Law 233, 430, 433 (1925), that the 19th-century effort to establish irresistible impulse as a defense met judicial resistance because "much less than we know today was known of mental disease." He predicted "that with the advent of a more scientific administration of the law—especially with the placing of expert testimony upon a neutral, unbiased basis and in the hands of well-qualified experts—much of the opposition to judicial recognition of the effect of disorders of the ... impulses should disappear." Further, he said, "expert, unbiased study of the individual case will aid judge and jury to distinguish cases of pathological irresistible impulse from those in which the impulse was merely unresisted."

Despite these optimistic sentiments, Wechsler and Michael observed, in 1937, that "except in the clearest cases, such as kleptomania, any effort to distinguish deterrable from non-deterrable persons must obviously encounter tremendous difficulty in the present state of knowledge." Advances in clinical understanding of mental illness in the 1940s inspired a new era of optimism about a "modern" doctrine of responsibility, including a control dimension. One example was the evolution of the Model Penal Code, which was drafted during the 1950s. Another was the Report of the Royal Commission on Capital Punishment, issued in 1953, which recommended that *M'Naghten* be abandoned in favor of a broadened formulation also permitting claims of volitional impairment. Many commentators, however, expressed doubt that medical science had progressed far enough to overcome the difficulties of administration. Lord Patrick Devlin observed, in Criminal Responsibility and Punishment: Functions of Judge and Jury, [1954] Crim.L.Rev. 661, 682–84:*

> If a case can be made out for saying that a man with such a disease is wholly incapable of preventing himself from committing the crime, and thus wholly irresponsible, it is prima facie a proper matter of substantive defence for the jury. The Royal Commission has come to the conclusion that medical opinion is now sufficiently certain to be able to say that there may be such cases....
>
> I think that this is a problem that ought to be solved empirically rather than theoretically. If the door is opened, a multitude will try to enter through it. Many will be cases in which men and women, abnormal, but not in any ordinary sense mad, have failed to exercise proper control over their emotions. There will be many cases of gross mental abnormality where nevertheless it cannot be said that the prisoner was wholly irresponsible. There will be some cases—and I suspect they will be in a small minority—where the disease made the accused wholly irresponsible. If a sharp dividing line could be drawn between complete and partial irresponsibility, it would be right both in theory and practice that the question should be submitted to the jury. But it does not appear at present that a sharp line can be drawn, and unless [a satisfactory rule can be framed for the jury, the doctrine cannot be accepted]. Medical science has advanced far enough to say that there ought to be an addition to the *McNaghten* rules, but not, I think, to formulate a satisfactory one. There must have been a period ... when the law fumbled over mens rea, and when conceptions of deliberate intent and recklessness and foreseeable consequences had not been worked out with sufficient detail to give the juryman of the day something he could grasp: no doubt, the new concept was introduced gradually. The wider notion of emotional irresponsibility is still, I think, as novel as mens rea was six or seven hundred years ago. I am not myself satisfied that it is yet sufficiently clarified to be delivered over to the deliberation of a jury. If this meant that prisoners who suffered from emotional disorders, must either be acquitted or hanged, there would be an urgency about it, which could not wait for careful formulation. But that is not the question. The question is simply whether the time is ripe to take the matter out of the province of sentence and let it follow mens rea into the control of the jury.

* Reprinted with the permission of Lord Devlin, the Criminal Law Review, and Sweet and Maxwell Ltd.

Lord Devlin's observations are echoed in the comments of contemporary critics of the control test.[a] Richard Bonnie's views are illustrative. In The Moral Basis of the Insanity Defense, 69 A.B.A.J. 194, 196–97 (1983), he said:

The Model Penal Code has had an extraordinary impact on criminal law. For this we should be thankful, but I believe the Code approach to criminal responsibility should be rejected. Psychiatric concepts of mental abnormality remain fluid and imprecise, and most academic commentary within the last ten years continues to question the scientific basis for assessment of volitional incapacity.

The volitional inquiry probably would be manageable if the insanity defense were permitted only in cases involving psychotic disorders. When the control test is combined with a loose or broad interpretation of the term "mental disease," however, the inevitable result is unstructured clinical speculation regarding the "causes" of criminal behavior in any case in which a defendant can be said to have a personality disorder, an impulse disorder, or any other diagnosable abnormality.

For example, it is clear enough in theory that the insanity defense is not supposed to be a ground for acquittal of persons with weak behavior controls who misbehave because of anger, jealousy, fear, or some other strong emotion. These emotions may account for a large proportion of all homicides and other assaultive crimes. Many crimes are committed by persons who are not acting "normally" and who are emotionally disturbed at the time. It is not uncommon to say that they are temporarily "out of their minds." But this is not what the law means or should mean by "insanity." Because the control test, as now construed in most states, entitles defendants to insanity instructions on the basis of these claims, I am convinced that the test involves an unacceptable risk of abuse and mistake.

It might be argued, of course, that the risk of mistake should be tolerated if the volitional prong of the defense is morally necessary. The question may be put this way: Are there clinically identifiable cases involving defendants whose behavior controls were so pathologically impaired that they ought to be acquitted although their ability to appreciate the wrongfulness of their actions was unimpaired? I do not think so. The most clinically compelling cases of volitional impairment involve the so-called impulse disorders—pyromania, kleptomania, and the like. These disorders involve severely abnormal compulsions that ought to be taken into account in sentencing, but the exculpation of pyromaniacs would be out of touch with commonly shared moral intuitions.

---

[a] See, e.g., Stephen Morse, Culpability and Control, 142 Penn. L Rev. 1587 (1994); Donald H.J. Hermann, The Insanity Defense: Philosophical, Historical and Legal Perspectives (1983).

Not surprisingly, many of the same objections have been raised against the cognitive prong of the insanity defense. However, most opponents of the volitional test do not favor abolition of the cognitive test of responsibility. They argue that the institutional risks are considerably different in the two contexts. Lady Barbara Wootton's observations are illustrative, Book Review of A. Goldstein, The Insanity Defense (1967), 77 Yale L.J. 1019, 1026–27 (1968):*

What ... has been insufficiently appreciated is that a volitional test raises practical difficulties far more formidable even than those involved in a purely cognitive formula. I am not suggesting that the *M'Naghten* test, interpreted (as most laymen would surely understand it) in strictly cognitive terms is free from ambiguities, or that it is an adequate instrument for distinguishing between the sane and the mentally disordered. But it is clear that in certain circumstances the limits of a man's knowledge and understanding can be convincingly demonstrated. Thus, if I am asked to translate a passage from Japanese into English it is indisputable that this is beyond my powers: everyone knows that merely trying harder will not make me any more successful. But if I assert that I have an uncontrollable impulse to break shop windows, in the nature of the case no proof of uncontrollability can be adduced. All that is known is that the impulse was not in fact controlled; and it is perfectly legitimate to hold the opinion that, had I tried a little harder, I might have conquered it. It is indeed apparent that some people, such as sadistic sexual perverts, suffer from temptations from which others are immune. But the fact that an impulse is unusual is no proof that it is irresistible. In short, it is not only difficult to devise a test of volitional competence the validity of which can be objectively established: it is impossible.

A similar assessment of the utility of clinical expertise was presented by the American Psychiatric Association in the course of an official statement on the insanity defense: [b]

... Many psychiatrists ... believe that psychiatric information relevant to determining whether a defendant understood the nature of his act, and whether he appreciated its wrongfulness, is more reliable and has a stronger scientific basis than, for example, does psychiatric information relevant to whether a defendant was able to control his behavior. The line between an irresistible impulse and an impulse not resisted is probably no sharper than that between twilight and dusk. Psychiatry is a deterministic discipline that views all human behavior as, to a good extent, "caused." The concept of volition is the subject of some disagreement among psychiatrists. Many psychiatrists therefore believe

* Reprinted by permission of the author, The Yale Law Journal Company, and Fred B. Rothman & Company from The Yale Law Journal, Vol. 77, pp. 1026–27.

[b] American Psychiatric Association, Statement on the Insanity Defense (December, 1982).

that psychiatric testimony (particularly that of a conclusory nature) about volition is more likely to produce confusion for jurors than is psychiatric testimony relevant to a defendant's appreciation or understanding.

Even if Lady Wootton and the other critics are right about the imprecise and speculative nature of the inquiry into volitional impairment, there is nevertheless an argument that the inquiry should be retained. In The Limits of the Criminal Sanction 132–33 (1968), Herbert Packer said:

> We must put up with the bother of the insanity defense because to exclude it is to deprive the criminal law of its chief paradigm of free will.... There must be some recognition of the generally held assumption that some people are, by reason of mental illness, significantly impaired in their volitional capacity. [I]t is not too important whether this is in fact the case. Nor is it too important how discriminating we are about drawing some kind of line to separate those suffering volitional impairment from the rest of us. The point is that some kind of line must be drawn in the face of our intuition, however wrongheaded it may be, that mental illness contributes to volitional impairment.

Should the volitional inquiry be retained? Would exclusion of claims of volitional impairment deprive the criminal law of its "chief paradigm of free will" or undermine its "moral integrity," so long as it recognizes claims of cognitive impairment? Should the difficulty of administering the control test be decisive?

**3. Responsibility and Unconscious Motivation.** The ongoing debate about the control inquiry has been carried on against the backdrop of changing scientific ideas about the human mind. One of the distinctive schools of contemporary psychology emphasizes the role of unconscious mental processes in shaping human behavior. According to the psychodynamic school of psychology, a person's behavior may "really" be explained and "caused" by unconscious processes even though the person "thinks," at a conscious level, that action is being taken for other reasons. Many examples may be drawn from normal events in everyday life—e.g., slips of the tongue, sudden lapses of memory, etc. Psychiatrists and other mental-health professionals who find clinical value in a psychodynamic perspective also believe that some types of abnormal behavior are best understood as manifestations or symptoms of unconscious mental processes.

Consider the testimony in the cases presented above. Barnes' psychiatric expert described a cluster of psychosexual motivations for his fire-setting behavior that were not accessible to Barnes on a conscious level. Similarly, Chester's homicidal conduct toward Beatrice was said to be produced by repressed feelings of anger toward himself and strong feelings of guilt and worthlessness rooted in his traumatic childhood. If the behavior of these defendants was, in fact, governed or propelled by unconscious forces, as the experts concluded, the question arises whether this explanation should have any legal significance. More generally, the question is whether psychodynamic explanations of criminal behavior should be considered in assessments of criminal responsibility.

The view that responsibility should be assessed at the conscious level was put forcefully by Chief Justice Weintraub of the New Jersey Supreme Court in State v. Sikora, 44 N.J. 453, 475–79, 210 A.2d 193, 205–07 (1965):

> [The] cause-and-effect thesis dominates the psychiatrist's view of his patient. He traces a man's every deed to some cause truly beyond the actor's own making, and says that although the man was aware of his action, he was unaware of assembled forces in his unconscious which decided his course. Thus the conscious is a puppet, and the unconscious the puppeteer....
>
> Under this psychiatric concept no man could be convicted of anything if the law were to accept the impulses of the unconscious as an excuse for conscious misbehavior....
>
> What then shall we do with our fellow automaton whose unconscious directs such anti-social deeds? For one thing, we could say it makes no difference. We could say that in punishing an evil deed accompanied by an evil-meaning mind, the law is concerned only with the existence of a will to do the evil act and it does not matter precisely where within the mind the evil drive resides.
>
> Or we could ... require an evil-meaning unconscious. The possibilities here are rich. It would be quite a thing to identify the unconscious drive and then decide whether it is evil for the purpose of criminal liability. For example, if we somehow were satisfied that a man murdered another as an alternative to an unconscious demand for suicide or because the unconscious believed it had to kill to avoid a full-blown psychosis, shall we say there was or was not a good defense? Shall we indict for murder a motorist who kills another because, although objectively he was negligent at the worst, the psychoanalyst assures us that the conscious man acted automatically to fulfill an unconscious desire for self-destruction? All of this is fascinating but much too frothy to support a structure of criminal law.
>
> Finally, we could amend our concept of criminal responsibility by eliminating the requirement of an evil-meaning mind. That is the true thrust of this psychiatric view of human behavior, for while our criminal law seeks to punish only those who act with a sense of wrongdoing and hence excuses those who because of sickness were bereft of that awareness, the psychiatrist rejects a distinction between the sick and the bad. To him no one is personally blameworthy for his make-up or for his acts. To him the law's distinction between a defect of the mind and a defect of character is an absurd invention....
>
> The subject of criminal blameworthiness is so obscure that there is an understandable disposition to let anything in for whatever use the jury may wish to make of it. But it will not do

merely to receive testimony upon the automaton thesis, for the jury must be told what its legal effect may be. Specifically, the jury must be told whether a man is chargeable with his unconscious drives.

It seems clear to me that the psychiatric view ... is simply irreconcilable with the basic thesis of our criminal law, for while the law requires proof of an evil-meaning mind, this psychiatric thesis denies there is any such thing. To grant a role in our existing structure to the theme that the conscious is just the innocent puppet of a non-culpable unconscious is to make a mishmash of the criminal law, permitting—indeed requiring—each trier of the facts to choose between the automaton thesis and the law's existing concept of criminal accountability. It would be absurd to decide criminal blameworthiness upon a psychiatric thesis which can find no basis for personal blame. [Criminal blameworthiness] must be sought and decided at the level of conscious behavior.

Chief Justice Weintraub implies that the law should take an all-or-nothing view of unconscious motivation. Is he right? Is it possible to formulate a "control" test of responsibility that would permit the fact-finder to absolve Barnes or Chester but would not open the gates to unbounded psychological determinism?

In an article on Responsibility and the Unconscious, 53 So.Cal.L.Rev. 1563 (1980), Michael Moore argues that Weintraub's concern is misplaced; the problem, he suggests, is not the deterministic premise of psychodynamic psychology but rather the meaning of the concept of compulsion, as applied to specific cases. Moore acknowledges at the outset that many psychiatrists think that "unconscious [motivations] cause bad behavior and that causation is an excuse." Moreover, he agrees with Chief Justice Weintraub that the " 'puppeteer' view of human beings" has unacceptable implications for ideas of responsibility:*

[I]f [a defendant] is to be excused simply because his behavior was caused by unconscious mental states, why are all actions not similarly excused? If all conscious mental life is determined by unconscious mental states, as many psychoanalysts believe, why is everyone not excused for all of his actions, seemingly the product of his conscious decisions but in fact determined by his unconscious mental states?

Moore's answer is that compulsion, not causation, is the legally relevant concept: an action is not "compelled" simply because it is "caused" by unconscious forces; this, he says, "makes it sound as if one's unconscious, in effect, orders one around in the same way as does a gunman with a gun

---

* The excerpts below are reprinted with the permission of the author and the Southern California Law Review.

at one's head; both compel one to do what 'they demand.' " However, the analogy is not apt, Moore says:

> Everyone is undoubtedly caused to act as they do by a myriad of environmental, physiological, or psychological factors. Yet to say that any actions are caused, for example, by an unhappy childhood, a chemical imbalance, or a belief that it is raining, is not to say the actions are compelled. One must point to something other than causation to make out the excuse of compulsion. . . .

Instead, Moore concludes, the legal significance of unconscious motivation must be determined by assessing, in each case, whether it "compelled" the criminal act:

> An unconscious emotion in general, or an unconscious but passionately felt sense of guilt in particular, can be understood in the sense in which an actor does consciously experience or feel something, but does not know the object of his emotion. One may feel angry or afraid without knowing the object of such anger or fear; one may experience the uneasy and tensed craving characteristic of compulsive desires without knowing what one craves. . . .

> The sense in which one can speak of the actor yielding to such unconscious but passionately felt desires should be evident. The kleptomaniac feels compelled and knows that he yields to compulsion when he steals; yet he does not know the object of his passionate desire. He knows only that he feels that he must steal. He is compelled by an indefinite craving for some unknown object or objective. A few thefts readily tell him it is not the stolen objects themselves.

> Moore goes on to emphasize that compulsion is a matter of degree and that a person "can be more or less compelled depending upon the severity of the constraints upon choice or upon the strength of the emotions on which one acts." Nonetheless, his argument implies that the law should recognize that pathologically strong emotions, albeit unconscious, can compromise or constrain choices. The question then becomes: "How much constraint is enough to warrant exculpation?"

> Do Moore or Weintraub make a persuasive case? Does the clinical evidence demonstrate—in Model Penal Code terms—that Barnes or Chester lacked "substantial capacity" to conform their conduct to the laws against arson and murder?

———

## NOTES ON THE BOUNDARIES OF CRIMINAL RESPONSIBILITY

**1. The Significance of Mental Disease.** The concept of "mental disease or defect" is a necessary threshold for the insanity defense under all of the existing tests. Since the concept of irresistible impulse was first recognized, the courts have said the defense is limited to persons whose volition is impaired by mental disease. It has never covered a "normal" person who acts under the influence of strong emotion, nor a person whose weakness of will is attributable to a defect of character.[a] Should a jury question be raised whenever a mental-health professional testifies that the defendant had a diagnosable mental disorder?[b] Would it make sense to rule as a matter of law that any of the defendants in the cases previously discussed did not have a "mental disease" and thereby close the door to their insanity claims? Consider the following approaches to the issue:

**(i) Restrictive Definition.** Those who are dubious about volitional impairment as an independent ground of exculpation naturally insist on a narrow definition of mental disease, one limited to psychoses. See, e.g., Joseph Livermore and Paul Meehl, The Virtues of *M'Naghten*, 51 Minn. L.Rev. 789, 831–32 (1967). However, even some advocates of the volitional inquiry have regarded a narrow definition of mental disease as an essential feature of the test. For example, the Royal Commission on Capital Punishment recommended revision of the "intellectualist" approach of *M'Naghten* in order to encompass affective and volitional considerations in a responsibility defense. The Commission also recommended that mental disease be defined restrictively, Royal Commission on Capital Punishment, Report 73 (1953):

> [M]ental disease ... broadly corresponds to what are often called major diseases of the mind, or psychoses; although it may also arise in cases, such as those of epilepsy and cerebral tumour, which are not ordinarily regarded by doctors as psychotic. Among the psychoses are the conditions known as schizophrenia, manic-depressive psychoses, and organic disease of the brain. Other conditions, not included under this term, are the minor forms of mental disorder—the neurotic reactions, such as neurasthenia, anxiety states and hysteria—and the disorders of development of the personality.

[a] E.g., Parsons v. State, 81 Ala. 577, 594, 2 So. 854, 865 (1887) ("[a] mere moral or emotional insanity, so-called, unconnected with disease of the mind, or irresistible impulse resulting from mere moral obliquity, or wicked propensities and habits, is not recognized as a defense to crime in our courts"); Bell v. State, 120 Ark. 530, 555, 180 S.W. 186, 196 (1915), ("[it] must be remembered that one who is otherwise sane will not be excused from a crime he has committed while his reason is temporarily dethroned not by disease, but by anger, jealousy, or other passion").

[b] The definition of "mental disorder" in the American Psychiatric Association's diagnostic manual, DSM–IV, provides, in part:

[A mental disorder is] ... a clinically significant behavioral or psychologic syndrome or pattern that occurs in an individual and that is associated with present distress (e.g., a painful symptom) or disability (i.e., impairment in one or more areas of functioning) or with a significantly increased risk of suffering death, pain, disability, or an important loss of freedom. In addition, this syndrome or pattern must not be merely an expectable and culturally sanctioned response to a particular event, for example, the death of a loved one. Whatever its original cause, it must currently be considered a manifestation of a behavioral, psychological or biological dysfunction in the individual. Neither deviant behavior (e.g., political, religious, or sexual) nor conflicts that are primarily between the individual and society are mental disorders unless the deviance or conflict is a symptom of a dysfunction in the individual. . . .

A similar approach has been recommended by the American Psychiatric Association:[c]

> Another major consideration in articulating standards for the insanity defense is the definition of mental disease or defect.... Allowing insanity acquittals in cases involving persons who manifest primarily "personality disorders" such as antisocial personality disorder (sociopathy) does not accord with modern psychiatric knowledge or psychiatric beliefs concerning the extent to which such persons do have control over their behavior. Persons with antisocial personality disorders should, at least for heuristic reasons, be held accountable for their behavior. The American Psychiatric Association, therefore, suggests that any revision of the insanity defense standards should indicate that mental disorders potentially leading to exculpation must be *serious*. Such disorders should usually be of the severity (if not always of the quality) of conditions that psychiatrists diagnose as psychoses.

The APA went on to endorse the definition of insanity proposed by Richard Bonnie in The Moral Basis of the Insanity Defense, 69 A.B.A.J. 194, 197 (1983). Bonnie recommended that mental disease should be defined to "include only those severely abnormal mental conditions that grossly and demonstrably impair a person's perception or understanding of reality...."[d]

**(ii) Intermediate Position.** The drafters of the Model Penal Code rejected the idea that mental disease should be limited to psychoses; they clearly intended to permit neuroses or impulse disorders (kleptomania was the example always used) to have exculpatory significance if they "substantially" affected the defendant's volitional capacity. On the other hand, the drafters contemplated that the courts would exclude some disorders of character or personality even though clinicians might regard these conditions as "mental disorders." This intention is reflected in § 4.01(2): "As used in this Article, the terms 'mental disease or defect' do not include an abnormality manifested only by repeated criminal or otherwise anti-social conduct." It is clear that the drafters meant specifically to exclude offenders who were characterized by clinicians as "psychopaths." The diagnostic label for such a condition has since been changed to "sociopathy" and later to "anti-social personality disorder."

In McDonald v. United States, 312 F.2d 847, 851 (D.C.Cir. 1962), the Court of Appeals for the District of Columbia Circuit defined mental disease or defect as "any abnormal condition of the mind which substantially affects mental or emotional processes and substantially impairs behavior controls." At the time, the court used the "product" test of insanity. However, when the court adopted the Model Penal Code test in United States v. Brawner, 471 F.2d 969 (D.C.Cir. 1972), it retained this

---

[c] American Psychiatric Association, Statement on the Insanity Defense (December, 1982).

[d] See also Stephen Morse, Excusing the Crazy: The Insanity Defense Reconsidered, 58 So.Cal.L.Rev. 777 (1985).

definition and endorsed the so-called "caveat paragraph" of Section 4.01(2) as a guideline for the judge rather than as a basis for instructing the jury.[e]

**(iii) Abandonment of the Requirement.** In a concurring opinion in *United States* v. *Brawner*, Judge Bazelon took the view that the mental-disease requirement should be abandoned:

> At no point in its opinion does the court explain why the boundary of a legal concept—criminal responsibility—should be marked by medical concepts, especially when the validity of the "medical model" is seriously questioned by some eminent psychiatrists. . . . How many psychiatrists must be convinced that a particular condition is "medical" in nature before a defendant will be permitted, within the confines of the "medical model," to predicate a responsibility defense on such a condition? . . . .

> Our instruction to the jury should provide that a defendant is not responsible *if at the time of his unlawful conduct his mental or emotional processes or behavior controls were impaired to such an extent that he cannot justly be held responsible for his act.* This test would ask the psychiatrist a single question: What is the nature of the impairment of the defendant's mental and emotional processes and behavior controls? It would leave for the jury the question whether that impairment is sufficient to relieve the defendant of responsibility for the particular act charged.

**(iv) Questions on the Mental–Disease Requirement.** Which of these is the better approach? Should the mental-disease concept be limited to psychoses? Or should the law follow Judge Bazelon's approach and abandon the requirement altogether? Does his approach invite unstructured inquiries regarding the determinants of every defendant's criminal behavior? Would the courtroom experience under the Bazelon approach differ substantially from the existing practice under the Model Penal Code or *Brawner* formulations? What is likely to happen in the federal courts under the 1984 statute, which makes the insanity defense available only if the defendant has a "severe" mental disease or defect?

**2. Compulsive Gambling.** Claims that defendants were "compelled" to commit their offenses due to disorders of volition such a pathological gambling disorder or compulsive shopping disorder have been raised with increasing frequency, not only as a basis for exculpation (under

---

[e] "The judge will be aware that the criminal and antisocial conduct of a person—on the street, in the home, in the ward—is necessarily material information for assessment by the psychiatrist. On the other hand, rarely if ever would a psychiatrist base a conclusion of mental disease solely on criminal and anti-social acts. Our pragmatic solution provides for reshaping the rule, for application by the court, as follows: The introduction or proffer of past criminal and anti-social actions is not admissible as evidence of mental disease unless accompanied by expert testimony, supported by a showing of the concordance of a responsible segment of professional opinion, that the particular characteristics of these actions constitute convincing evidence of an underlying mental disease that substantially impairs behavioral controls."

United States v. Brawner, 471 F.2d 969, 994 (D.C.Cir. 1972).

the "insanity defense"), but also as a basis for mitigation in sentencing as a form of "diminished capacity." Although courts have been skeptical about the exculpatory claims, they have been more receptive to the mitigating claims. As the following materials are read, consider whether this type of claim should have more or less legal significance.

(i) **Exculpatory Claims:** *United States v. Torniero.* Torniero, a jewelry store manager, was charged with 10 counts of interstate transportation of jewelry allegedly stolen from his employer. He filed notice of his intent to rely on the insanity defense and to introduce expert testimony showing that he suffered from "pathological gambling disorder,"[f] which led him to accumulate debts that led him to steal. The government's motion to "exclude any expert testimony regarding the defendant's alleged mental disorder 'compulsive gambling' " was granted by Judge Cabranes in United States v. Torniero, 570 F.Supp. 721 (D.Conn.1983). Judge Cabranes concluded that Torniero's compulsion to gamble, even if it existed, did not have a sufficiently "direct bearing" on the charged criminal acts to establish the legal predicate for an insanity defense.

Judge Cabranes also noted his doubts "whether compulsive gambling disorder ought even to be the basis for an insanity defense when the offense charged is gambling." He thought it "questionable whether [this] disorder, characterized more by repeated engagement in a particular activity than by any derangement of one's mental faculties, amounts to a mental disease as that concept has long been understood by the criminal law." In a more general observation, Judge Cabranes suggested that the insanity

---

[f] At the time of the *Torniero* decision, "pathological gambling disorder" was described in DSM III as follows:

> [A] chronic and progressive failure to resist impulses to gamble and gambling behavior that compromises, disrupts, or damages personal, family, or vocational pursuits. The gambling preoccupation, urge, and activity increase during periods of stress. Problems that arise as a result of the gambling lead to an intensification of the gambling behavior. Characteristic problems include loss of work due to absences in order to gamble, defaulting on debts and other financial responsibilities, disrupted family relationships, borrowing money from illegal sources, forgery, fraud, embezzlement, and income tax evasion.

> Commonly these individuals have the attitude that money causes and is also the solution to all their problems. As the gambling increases, the individual is usually forced to lie in order to obtain money and to continue gambling, but hides the extent of the gambling. There

is no serious attempt to budget or save money. When borrowing resources are strained, antisocial behavior in order to obtain money for more gambling is likely. Any criminal behavior—e.g., forgery, embezzlement, or fraud—is typically nonviolent. There is a conscious intent to return or repay the money.

DSM III also specified criteria for diagnosing pathological gambling. These included:

A. The individual is chronically and progressively unable to resist impulses to gamble.

B. Gambling compromises, disrupts, or damages family, personal, and vocational pursuits, as indicated by at least three of the following:

[Here the criteria mention seven effects of excessive gambling, including "arrest for forgery, fraud, embezzlement, or income tax evasion due to attempts to obtain money for gambling."]

C. The gambling is not due to antisocial personality disorder.

defense "can and should be limited to instances where a jury could find that the defendant's mind was truly alienated from ordinary human experience at the time of the commission of the acts with which he is charged and where that mental condition had a direct bearing on the commission of those acts."

At Torniero's subsequent trial, the government showed that he took jewelry valued at approximately $750,000 from New Haven to the "diamond district" of Manhattan and sold it for cash. Notwithstanding the exclusion of the expert testimony concerning "compulsive gambling disorder," Torniero relied on the insanity defense. In support of his claim, he presented two psychiatrists who testified that he suffered from paranoia, depression, and a narcissistic personality as a result of which he lacked responsibility under the then-applicable Model Penal Code insanity test. After deliberating for less than one hour, the jury convicted Torniero and the judge sentenced him to a three-year prison term, to be followed by five years' probation and an ongoing duty to pay restitution to his former employer.

On appeal, the Second Circuit affirmed the conviction. United States v. Torniero, 735 F.2d 725 (2d Cir.1984). After reviewing the evolution of the insanity defense in the federal courts, and taking note of the controversy aroused by the *Hinckley* acquittal two years earlier, Judge Kaufman turned to the question raised by Torniero's appeal:

> To put in issue the defense of criminal insanity under the prevailing [Model Code] test in effect in this Circuit, Torniero must make a showing that compulsive gambling is a mental disease or defect. He must also demonstrate that the infirmity could have prevented him from appreciating that theft was wrongful, or could have deprived him of the ability to restrain himself from the criminal act. Torniero does not urge that his condition could have rendered him incapable of appreciating the illegality of transporting stolen goods. He contends only that under the volitional prong of the [Model Code] test, the compulsion to gamble rendered him unable to resist becoming a thief and stealing to support his habit. . . .

> This principle on which Torniero relies is a novel one. The disorder of pathological gambling was not included in the American Psychiatric Association Diagnostic and Statistical Manual of Mental Disorders until publication in 1980 of the third edition. . . . Where, as here, a defendant contends that evidence of a newly-recognized disorder would be relevant to an insanity defense, there must be a showing that respected authorities in the field share the view that the disorder is a mental disease or defect that could have impaired the defendant's ability to desist from the offense charged or to appreciate the wrongfulness of his conduct. We state no iron-clad mathematical rule, but we do not believe that an hypothesis subscribed to by only a small number of professionals establishes that a proposed defense can carry the day on relevance.

At the same time, we recognize that unanimity on mental health issues is rare and we suggest no requirement of universal or even majority professional acceptance. In fashioning its preliminary decision on relevance, a court must make a discretionary determination that the hypotheses relied upon have substantial acceptance in the discipline, as a basis for a finding that the disorder is relevant to the insanity defense.

The first hurdle Torniero's proposed insanity defense must traverse is that the alleged disorder constitutes a mental disease or defect as the term is used in the [Model Code] definition. We are convinced that persuasive evidence was adduced at the pretrial hearing to justify a conclusion that members of the mental health profession hold seriously contradicting views in this regard. [A psychiatrist] who helped draft DSM–III testified that the clinical definition of compulsive gambling as a "failure to resist" rather than an "inability to resist" the urge to wager was a deliberate effort to distinguish this disorder from those defects of the mind appropriate for an insanity defense. Another psychiatrist testified before Judge Cabranes in support of the argument that compulsive gambling is not a mental disease or defect as defined by the [Model Code] rule. Several mental health and social work professionals testified on the debilitating effects of the compulsion to gamble and stated for the record that they believed the pathology should be considered a mental disease or defect. One of these witnesses, however, conceded that "pathological gambling has not ever been considered a serious disorder" within the profession.

The trial court stated no conclusion on the issue, nor are we called upon to rule that compulsive gambling can never constitute a mental disease or defect. We need not rest, however, on the ground that the proffered gambling defense was not shown to be a mental disease or defect. Assuming without deciding, that it did cross that threshold of the [Model Code] test, there is still ample basis for the trial court's conclusion that Torniero's compulsive gambling disorder is not relevant to the insanity defense. The trial judge correctly noted that the relevance standard requires that the pathology alleged have "a direct bearing on [the] commission of the acts with which [the defendant] is charged." In sum, a compulsion to gamble, even if a mental disease or defect, is not, ipso facto, relevant to the issue whether the defendant was unable to restrain himself from non-gambling offenses such as transporting stolen property.

Although several of Torniero's witnesses expressed the opinion that compulsive gamblers they have treated or observed were unable to resist the impulse to steal as a result of the gambling pathology, this view was vigorously contradicted by the government's experts. Moreover, not one of the experts stated that the connection between compulsive gambling and the impulse to steal for purposes of the insanity defense has substantial acceptance in the profession. While we cannot agree with the trial court that no evidence whatsoever on the volitional nexus between gambling and stealing was adduced, we are of the view that there is ample basis in the record to warrant the conclusion that the trial judge did not abuse his discretion in finding the connection between the two was not satisfactorily established. In the absence of such evidence the proffered defense cannot be deemed relevant to the insanity defense. . . .

As the psychiatric and psychological professions refine their understanding of impulse disorders such as pathological gambling, courts are called upon to make difficult and delicate decisions under the volitional prong of the insanity test. We rule today that when evidence of an impulse disorder is offered in support of an insanity defense, the trial judge must first determine that the evidence is relevant. We do not foreclose admissibility of compulsive gambling in all circumstances, nor do we speculate on the desirability of the [proposals to eliminate the volitional prong] now being considered by Congress.

The insanity defense has never been free from controversy, criticism, and revision. No rule designed to embody societal values will ever be sacrosanct. As our understanding of the intricacies of the fathomless human mind continues to evolve, legal rules must respond to changed conceptions of the nature of moral culpability, and to advances in the science of mental illness. The fundamental question will always be an inquiry into how best to embody society's sense of what conduct is appropriate for punishment by criminal sanctions. The district court's exclusion of the compulsive gambling defense proposed here accords with accepted notions of criminal responsibility. . . . Accordingly, we affirm the judgment of conviction.

Although it affirmed the district court's decision to exclude the evidence proffered by Torniero, the circuit court refused to foreclose the admissibility of such evidence "in all circumstances." Should similar evidence be admissible in a prosecution for illegal gambling? Recall that chronic and progressive inability to resist impulses to gamble was one of the diagnostic criteria under DSM III. Of what significance is that fact that the DSM IV criteria include "preoccupation" with gambling and "need" to gamble instead of "inability to resist"? If the expert testimony would be admitted in a prosecution for illegal gambling, why should it be excluded in a theft prosecution if the defendant's experts are prepared to testify that the defendant's capacity to refrain from stealing was substantially impaired? Is the circuit court decision right? Judge Kaufman's rationale?[g]

---

[g] For decisions reaching the same result on similar grounds, see United States v. Gould, 741 F.2d 45 (4th Cir.1984), and United States v. Lewellyn, 723 F.2d 615 (8th Cir.1983).

**(ii) Mitigating Claims Under the Federal Sentencing Guidelines.** Section 5K2.13 of the federal sentencing guidelines permits "downward departures" from presumptive sentences for non-violent offenses if the offender had a "significantly reduced mental capacity" at the time of the offense. In United States v. McBroom, 124 F.3d 533 (3d Cir. 1997), the court ruled that the phrase "significantly reduced mental capacity" includes a volitional component and that a defendant's "ability to control his or her own conduct is a relevant consideration when determining the defendant's eligibility for a downward departure."[h] This decision, in effect, said that defenses such as compulsive gambling, while not worthy of complete exculpation, could have a mitigating effect during sentencing.

Although the Third Circuit acknowledged that this ruling was in tension with the 1984 Insanity Defense Reform Act, through which the Congress had eliminated the volitional component of the insanity defense,[i] the court concluded that the "principles of lenity" that underlie downward departures for cognitive impairments "apply with equal force . . . to those who cannot control their behavior." In 1998, the Federal Sentencing Commission embraced the Third Circuit's view by defining the term "significantly reduced mental capacity" as follows:

> "Significantly reduced mental capacity" means the defendant, although convicted, has a significantly impaired ability to (A) understand the wrongfulness of the behavior comprising the offense or to exercise the power of reason; or (B) control behavior that the defendant knows is wrongful.

In United States v. Sandolsky, 234 F.3d 938 (6th Cir. 2000), the court applied § 5K2.13 to a claim by a defendant convicted of computer fraud that he was compelled to commit these theft offenses to pay debts incurred due to pathological gambling disorder. As in *Torniero*, the government argued that a direct causal link between the reduced capacity and the offense was required. The Sixth Circuit disagreed. In recognizing the expansion of the Federal Sentencing Guidelines to include volitional impairments such as compulsive gambling, the court explained how compulsive gambling could warrant a downgraded sentence even though the compulsive gambling did not directly constitute the offense changed:

> Section 5K2.13 does not distinguish between [significantly reduced mental capacities] that explain the behavior that *constituted* the crime charged and [significantly reduced mental capacities]

---

At least one defendant has successfully relied upon pathological gambling disorder in a theft prosecution. In State v. Lafferty, 192 Conn. 571, 472 A.2d 1275 (1984), the defendant was acquitted by reason of insanity, despite having embezzled more than $300,000 from his employer. The Connecticut General Assembly subsequently amended its insanity statute to preclude exculpation in such cases by excluding "pathological or compulsive gambling" from the definition of "mental disease or defect." Conn. Penal Code § 53a–13(c) (1994).

[h] The defendant in McBroom pled guilty to possessing child pornography, and sought a downward departure based on psychological disorders arising out of sexual abuse he suffered as a child that compelled him to commit the offenses.

[i] 18 U.S.C. § 17(a) (1994).

that explain the behavior that *motivated* the crime. In other words, § 5K2.13 does not require a direct causal link between the [significantly reduced mental capacity] and the crime charged.... Thus, because Sandolsky's gambling disorder is a likely cause of his criminal behavior, given that he had already "maxed out" his own credit line before resorting to fraud, the two-point reduction is not inconsistent with the guideline provision.

A rule distinguishing between [significantly reduced mental capacities] that *cause* the behavior that constitutes the crime and [significantly reduced mental capacities] that *motivate* the behavior that constitutes the crime could lead to arbitrary results. For example, under the Government's theory [which requires a direct causal link similar to Judge Kaufman's argument in *Torniero*], if someone with an eating disorder stole food, he or she would be entitled to a downward departure under § 5K2.13. If, however, that same person stole money to buy food, he or she would not be entitled to a downward departure. In the latter situation, the link between the crime, stealing money to buy food, and the [significantly reduced mental capacity], an eating disorder, is no longer technically direct. Nonetheless, no one can dispute that the eating disorder is the driving force behind the crime. Yet under the Government's theory, the two individuals would be treated differently based on a nebulous distinction between a volitional impairment that causes the conduct that constitutes the crime and a volitional impairment that explains the motive for the ultimate crime. This treatment is at odds with the Sentencing Guideline's goal of uniformity of sentencing. More importantly, a bright line rule would undermine not only the district court's discretion, but also the very purpose of § 5K2.13—to mitigate the sentence of one who suffers from a diminished mental capacity.

Would Torniero have been able to use his compulsive gambling to effect a downgrade in his sentence under the reasoning in *Sandolsky*?[j] Should this type of disorder be regarded as a legitimate ground for diminishing responsibility for theft offenses? If so, should it also be regarded as a legitimate basis for negating responsibility?

**3. Drug Dependence: *United States v. Moore.*** The boundaries of criminal responsibility in the related context of drug dependence were explored in United States v. Moore, 486 F.2d 1139 (D.C.Cir. 1973). Raymond Moore was charged with possession of heroin. He claimed, in defense, that he was an opiate-dependent person with an overpowering need to use heroin. He sought to introduce supporting testimony on the ground that, due to his abnormal psychological condition, he lacked substantial capacity to conform his behavior to the laws prohibiting possession of heroin. The government, though conceding that Moore was dependent on heroin, ob-

---

[j] For decisions reaching similar results, see United States v. Checoura, 176 F.Supp.2d 310 (D.N.J. 2001); United States v. Ming, 2001 WL 1631874 (N.D.Ill. 2001); United States v. Scholl, 959 F.Supp. 1189 (D.Ariz. 1997).

jected to the admissibility of this evidence on the ground that it was insufficient, as a matter of law, to establish that Moore lacked criminal responsibility for his acts. Moore was convicted and sentenced to prison. A closely divided (five to four) court of appeals, sitting en banc, affirmed the conviction, rejecting Moore's claim that he was entitled to raise a "common-law defense" of addiction. The court also rejected Moore's argument that his conviction was barred by the eighth amendment.[k]

Judge Wright's dissenting opinion observed that the eighth amendment "provides only the floor and not the ceiling for development of common-law notions of criminal responsibility" and argued that Moore's claim should be reached by evolving doctrines of volitional impairment:

> The concept of criminal responsibility is, by its very nature, "an expression of the moral sense of the community." ... [T]here has historically been a strong conviction in our jurisprudence that to hold a man criminally responsible, his actions must have been the product of a "free will." ... Thus criminal responsibility is assessed only when through "free will" a man elects to do evil, and if he is not a free agent, or is unable to choose or to act voluntarily, or to avoid the conduct which constitutes the crime, he is outside the postulate of the law of punishment.

> Despite this general principle, however, it is clear that our legal system does not exculpate all persons whose capacity for control is impaired, for whatever cause or reason. Rather, in determining responsibility for crime, the law assumes "free will" and then recognizes known deviations "where there is a broad consensus that free will does not exist" with respect to the particular condition at issue. The evolving nature of this process is amply demonstrated in the gradual development of such defenses as infancy, duress, insanity, somnambulism and other forms of automatism, epilepsy and unconsciousness, involuntary intoxication, delirium tremens, and chronic alcoholism.

> A similar consensus exists today in the area of narcotics addiction.... The World Health Organization has ranked heroin addiction as the most intensive form of drug dependence, far more severe than alcoholism. Indeed, the primary element of the most widely accepted definition of opiate addiction is "an *overpowering* desire or need to continue taking the drug," and Congress has repeatedly defined as an addict any individual who is "so far addicted to the use of narcotic drugs as to have *lost the power of self-control* with reference to his addiction." Thus it can no longer

[k] Moore's eighth amendment argument was based on *Robinson v. California*, 370 U.S. 660 (1962), which held that punishment for the status of addiction constituted "cruel and unusual punishment proscribed by the eighth amendment. He argued that punishing an addict for possessing drugs was tanta- mount to punishing him for his addiction. The court rejected the argument, relying on the Supreme Court's five-four decision in *Powell v. Texas*, 392 U.S. 514 (1968), which held that punishment of an alcoholic for public drunkenness did not violate the eighth amendment.

seriously be questioned that for at least some addicts the "overpowering" psychological and physiological need to possess and inject narcotics cannot be overcome by mere exercise of "free will." ...

The genius of the common law has long been its responsiveness to changing times, its ability to reflect new knowledge and developing social and moral values.... I conclude that imposition of criminal liability on the non-trafficking addict possessor is contrary to our historic common-law traditions of criminal responsibility. This being so, it is clear that a defense of "addiction" must exist for these individuals unless Congress has expressly and unequivocally manifested its intent to preclude such a defense. [Judge Wright concluded that recognition of the defense had not been precluded by congressional action.]

The majority of the court rejected this view. Judge Leventhal responded directly to Judge Wright in his concurring opinion:

Appellant's key defense concepts are impairment of behavioral control and loss of self-control. These have been considered by this court most fully in discussion of the insanity defense, and the philosophy of those opinions is invoked, although appellant disclaims the insanity defense as such....

Appellant's presentation rests, in essence, on the premise that the "mental disease or defect" requirement of *McDonald* and *Brawner* is superfluous. He discerns a broad principle that excuses from criminal responsibility when conduct results from a condition that impairs behavior control....

It does not follow that because one condition (mental disease) yields an exculpatory defense if it results in impairment of and lack of behavioral controls the same result follows when some other condition impairs behavior controls....

The legal conception of criminal capacity cannot be limited to those of unusual endowment or even average powers. A few may be recognized as so far from normal as to be entirely beyond the reach of criminal justice, but in general the criminal law is a means of social control that must be potentially capable of reaching the vast bulk of the population. Criminal responsibility is a concept that not only extends to the bulk of those below the median line of responsibility, but specifically extends to those who have a realistic problem of substantial impairment and lack of capacity due, say, to weakness of intellect that establishes susceptibility to suggestion; or to a loss of control of the mind as a result of passion, whether the passion is of an amorous nature or the result of hate, prejudice or vengeance; or to a depravity that blocks out conscience as an influence on conduct.

The criminal law cannot "vary legal norms with the individual's capacity to meet the standards they prescribe, absent a disability that is both gross and verifiable, such as the mental disease or defect that may establish irresponsibility. The most that it is feasible to do with lesser disabilities is to accord them proper weight in sentencing."

Only in limited areas have the courts recognized a defense to criminal responsibility, on the basis that a described condition establishes a psychic incapacity negativing free will in the broader sense. These are areas where the courts have been able to respond to a deep call on elemental justice, and to discern a demarcation of doctrine that keeps the defense within verifiable bounds that do not tear the fabric of the criminal law as an instrument of social control. . . .

[A]ppellant disclaims any direct reliance on the insanity defense. He agrees with our rulings that heroin dependence may have probative value, along with other evidence of mental disease, but is not by itself evidence of "mental disease or defect" sufficient to raise the insanity issue, unless so protracted and extensive as to result in unusual deterioration of controls.

Our opinion in *Brawner* declined to accept the suggestion that it "announce" a standard exculpating anyone whose capacity for control is insubstantial, for whatever cause or reason, and said, disclaiming an "all-embracing unified field theory," that we would discern the appropriate rule "as the cases arise in regard to other conditions."

In our view, the rule for drug addiction should not be modeled on the rule for mental disease because of crucial distinctions between conditions. The subject of mental disease, though subject to some indeterminacy, and difficulty of diagnosis when extended to volitional impairment as well as cognitive incapacity, has long been the subject of systematic study, and in that framework it is considered manageable to ask psychiatrists to address the distinction, all-important and crucial to the law, between incapacity and indisposition, between those who can't and those who won't, between the impulse irresistible and the impulse not resisted. These are matters as to which the court has accepted the analysis of medicine, medical conditions and symptoms, and on the premise that they can be considered on a verifiable basis, and with reasonable dispatch, the courts have recognized a defense even in conditions not as obvious and verifiable as those covered in the older and limited test of capacity to know right from wrong.

[T]here is considerable difficulty of verification of the claim of a drug user that he is unable to refrain from use. . . .

The difficulty of the verification problem of lack of capacity to refrain from use is sharpened on taking into account that the issue comprehends the addict's failure to participate in treatment programs. This raises problems of the addict's personal knowledge, disposition, motivation, as well as extent of community programs, that may usefully be assessed by someone considering what program to try now or next, but would irretrievably tangle a trial.

The feature that narcotic addiction is not a stable condition undercuts any approach patterned on the mental disease, where there is a reasonable projection that subsequent analysis of particular incidents over time may delineate an ascertainable condition. It is unrealistic to expect the addict himself to supply accurate information on the nature and extent of addiction at the time of the offense, particularly as to "psychic dependence."

The difficulty is sharpened by the appreciable number of narcotic "addicts" who do abandon their habits permanently, and much larger number who reflect their capacity to refrain by ceasing use for varying periods of time. The reasons are not clear but the phenomenon is indisputable....

There is need for reasonable verifiability as a condition to opening a defense to criminal responsibility. The criminal law cannot gear its standards to the individual's capacity "absent a disability that is both gross and verifiable, such as the mental disease or defect that may establish irresponsibility." ...

Reliability and validity of a legal defense require that it can be tested by criteria external to the actions which it is invoked to excuse. And so the Model Penal Code's caveat paragraph rejects an insanity defense based on an abnormality manifested only by repeated criminal or otherwise anti-social conduct. This approach was followed in *Brawner*. The defense of drug dependence to a charge of drug use cannot clear the hurdle of circularity.

Does Judge Leventhal or Judge Wright have the better view? Are the reasons given by Judge Leventhal for rejecting the addiction defense also applicable to the volitional prong of the insanity defense? Does the "mental-disease" requirement really limit the defense to conditions that are "gross and verifiable"?

---

## SUBSECTION C: THE INSANITY DEFENSE AND INTOXICATION

---

## People v. Kelly

Supreme Court of California, 1973.
10 Cal.3d 565, 111 Cal.Rptr. 171, 516 P.2d 875.

■ SULLIVAN, J. Defendant Valerie Dawn Kelly was charged in count one of an information with assault with a deadly weapon with intent to commit murder, in count two thereof with attempted murder, and in count three with assault with a deadly weapon and by means of force likely to produce great bodily injury. Defendant pleaded not guilty and not guilty by reason of insanity to all counts. Trial by jury was waived, counts one and two were dismissed by the court on the People's motion on the ground of insufficiency of evidence, and the court found defendant guilty of assault with a deadly weapon. The court thereafter found that defendant was legally sane at the time the offense was committed. Imposition of sentence was suspended and defendant was granted probation for a period of five years under specified terms and conditions. She appeals from the judgment of conviction.

Defendant has used drugs ever since she was 15 years old.[2] In the fall of 1970, when she was 18 years old, she began taking mescaline and LSD, using those drugs 50 to 100 times in the months leading up to the offense. On December 6, 1970, her parents received a telephone call that defendant was being held at the police substation located at the Los Angeles International Airport after being found wandering about the airport under the influence of drugs. In response to the call, her parents picked up defendant at the airport and drove her back to their home in San Diego. Although they recognized that she was not acting normally, at defendant's request they drove her to her own apartment where she spent the night.

On the next morning, December 7, defendant telephoned her mother and asked to be driven to her parents' home. Mrs. Kelly did so but noticed that defendant "wasn't there"; she seemed to be "[j]ust wandering" and told her mother that she heard "a lot of noises, and a lot of people talking...."[3] Mrs. Kelly made defendant change into pajamas and lie down, and then went into the kitchen to prepare defendant's breakfast. Shortly thereafter, defendant entered the kitchen and, while Mrs. Kelly was turned toward the stove, repeatedly stabbed her mother with an array of kitchen knives. The police were called, defendant was arrested, and eventually charged as already indicated.

On December 14, 1971, the case proceeded to trial before the court sitting without a jury.[4] The parties waived their right to a bifurcated trial

---

[2] In 1968, following a call by her parents to the police, defendant, then just 16 years old, was taken into custody for being under the influence of drugs. She spent three weeks in a ward of the county mental-health clinic for abuse of habit-forming drugs and was released on two-years' probation. In December 1968, she voluntarily entered Patton State Hospital, after again being found under the influence of drugs. Two months later, she ran away from the hospital but refrained from using drugs until the period preceding the instant offense. In November 1970, about a month before the offense here involved, defendant was again taken into custody for drug abuse and spent several days in the

county mental health clinic after which she was released.

[3] In a psychiatric report made after the attack and introduced into evidence, defendant described her hallucinations at this time. She thought that her parents "were with the devils." She would talk to her parents "but not out loud." Her mother "told" her that "they had devils," and defendant "realized that something was going to die— that they were going to kill me."

[4] Before defendant could be tried, the trial court, doubting her competency, ordered a hearing to determine whether she was presently sane. The court found that defendant was insane and ordered her committed to

on the separate issues of guilt and insanity and agreed that the court upon receiving evidence at a single trial, could separately decide the two issues after allowing counsel to argue as to each. . . .[a]

Much of the evidence presented at the trial consisted of the reports and testimony of seven psychiatrists. Since there was substantial agreement among them, we briefly summarize their testimony. . . .

Defendant suffered from personality problems—according to one witness an underlying schizophrenia—but was normally a sane person.[5] However, her voluntary and repeated ingestion of drugs over a two-month period had triggered a legitimate psychosis so that on the day of the attack, defendant was unable to distinguish right from wrong. Nevertheless, defendant was conscious in that she could perceive the events that were taking place.

The trial court heard considerable testimony that defendant was not acting simply as a person who, after ingesting drugs or alcohol, is unable to perceive reality and reason properly. Rather, the drug abuse was deemed the indirect cause of a legitimate, temporary psychosis that would remain even when defendant was temporarily off drugs. Finally, there was general agreement that defendant, although still a "brittle" person with latent schizophrenic tendencies, was sane at the time of trial.

At the conclusion of all the evidence, the prosecutor and defense counsel presented their arguments to the court on the guilt phase of the case. The court then in essence found that defendant did the acts constituting an assault with a deadly weapon, that at such time she was not in a state of unconsciousness, and that defendant was "guilty as charged."

After a recess, counsel for both parties then presented their arguments on the sanity phase of the case. At the conclusion of the arguments the court found that while defendant was indeed psychotic both before and after the attack, and "was not capable of understanding that her act was wrong," her insanity was no defense because it "was not of a settled and permanent nature, and, in addition, was produced by the voluntary in-

---

Patton State Hospital. . . . She remained there for nine months and was released in September 1971, after being certified as sane and able to stand trial. . . .

[a] A defendant in California may plead both "not guilty" and "not guilty by reason of insanity." When a defendant enters both pleas, the case is tried in two phases. During the first phase of the bifurcated trial, the defendant is presumed to be sane, and the issue of "guilt or innocence" of the crime is decided. If the defendant is convicted, the trial moves into a second phase, during which the defendant's "legal sanity" at the time of the crime is adjudicated. Although one of the objectives of the bifurcated trial is to defer

evidence of mental abnormality to the second phase, this aim may be frustrated if the defendant is permitted to introduce such evidence to disprove mens rea during the first phase.—[Footnote by eds.]

[5] The testimony of several psychiatrists showed that defendant had underlying personality defects accompanied by a "schizoid personality," which denotes a tendency to withdraw from reality but is not as severe as schizophrenia. "She was not overtly schizophrenic. . . . Normally sane, but she did have a character disorder [even before her period of drug abuse]."

gestion of hallucinatory drugs." Accordingly the court found that defendant was legally sane at the time the offense was committed.

Defendant contends (i) that the evidence before the court established a defense of unconsciousness and (ii) that insanity, however caused, was a defense to [assault with a deadly weapon], a general-intent crime.

In support of her first contention, defendant argues that the evidence showed her to be psychotic at the time of her actions. She relies on the court's findings that there was no evidence she was fully aware of what she was doing on the day of the assault but was shown to have been intermittently aware of her actions. . . . She urges that the only determination to be made by the trial court was whether she was in fact unconscious at the time of her acts and that the fact that such unconsciousness was the product of drug intoxication voluntarily induced should not negate the defense.

[U]nconsciousness caused by voluntary intoxication is only a partial defense to a criminal charge—that is, it may serve to negate the specific intent or state of mind requisite to the offense. . . . It follows, therefore, that unconsciousness caused by voluntary intoxication is *no* defense to a general-intent crime—by definition a crime in which no specific intent is required. Assault with a deadly weapon is such a crime, and we have held that the requisite general intent therefor may not be negated through a showing of voluntary intoxication. Thus, if there was substantial evidence to support the trial court's conclusion, defendant's argument that she was not guilty because of unconsciousness must fail. . . .

We turn to defendant's second contention which relates to the sanity phase of her trial. She claims that the court erred in finding her legally sane at the time of the offense on the basis that, although she did not know that what she was doing was wrong, her insanity was drug-induced and not of a settled and permanent nature. . . . She argues that insanity, however caused, is a defense to a criminal charge.

It is fundamental to our system of jurisprudence that a person cannot be convicted for acts performed while insane. . . . Insanity, under the California *M'Naghten* test, denotes a mental condition which renders a person incapable of knowing or understanding the nature and quality of his act, or incapable of distinguishing right from wrong in relation to that act.[b] . . . This is a factual question to be decided by the trier of fact. . . .

In this case the trial court found that defendant "was not capable of understanding that her act was wrong." We can only construe this finding to mean that defendant was insane under the aforementioned test. Despite this finding, the trial court adjudged defendant legally sane because her psychosis was "not of a settled and permanent nature, and, in addition, was produced by the voluntary ingestion of hallucinatory drugs." In so ruling,

---

[b] The California Supreme Court subsequently abandoned the *M'Naghten* test and adopted the Model Penal Code formulation in People v. Drew, 22 Cal.3d 333, 149 Cal.Rptr. 275, 583 P.2d 1318 (1978). A popular initiative restored the *M'Naghten* test in 1982.—[Footnote by eds.]

the trial court misinterpreted the rules regarding the defense of insanity and committed prejudicial error.

As we have already stated, voluntary intoxication by itself is no defense to a crime of general intent such as assault with a deadly weapon.... However, we have repeatedly held that "when insanity is the result of long continued intoxication, it affects responsibility in the same way as insanity which has been produced by any other cause." ...

Policy considerations support this distinction in treatment between voluntary intoxication resulting in unconsciousness and voluntary intoxication which causes insanity. The former encompasses those situations in which mental impairment does not extend beyond the period of intoxication....

When long-continued intoxication results in insanity, however, the mental disorder remains even after the effects of the drug or alcohol have worn off. The actor is "legally insane," and the traditional justifications for criminal punishment are inapplicable because of his inability to conform, intoxicated or not, to accepted social behavior.... He is, of course, subject to commitment in a mental institution. In the instant case, the trial court appears to have confused these separate rules. The proper rule of law was early established.... "[S]ettled insanity produced by a long-continued intoxication affects responsibility in the same way as insanity produced by any other cause. *But it must be 'settled insanity,' and not merely a temporary mental condition produced by recent use of intoxicating liquor.*" Thus it is immaterial that voluntary intoxication may have caused the insanity, as long as the insanity was of a settled nature and qualifies under the *M'Naghten* test as a defense.

The trial court carried this distinction too far, however, for it required proof that defendant's insanity was both settled and *permanent*. Such a requirement violates the rule that "[t]emporary insanity, as a defense to crime, is as fully recognized by law as is permanent insanity." ... Thus, if defendant at the time of the offense was insane under the California *M'Naghten* test, it makes no difference whether the period of insanity lasted several months, as in this case, or merely a period of hours....

We have reviewed the record in the instant case and we find substantial evidence to support the trial court's finding that defendant was psychotic at the time of the offense. This finding is amply supported by the testimony of psychiatrists. Substantial evidence also supports the finding that the psychosis was a product of voluntary ingestion of drugs. Finally, the trial court found that defendant "was not capable of understanding that her act was wrong," a finding supported by considerable psychiatric testimony that defendant could not distinguish right from wrong at the time of her offense.

As already pointed out, if defendant was insane at the time of the offense, it is immaterial that her insanity resulted from repeated voluntary intoxication, as long as her insanity was of a settled nature. The trial court made a compound finding that defendant's insanity "was not of a settled and permanent nature"; however, we have pointed out that insanity need not be permanent in order to establish a defense. The trial court also found that defendant suffered from a "temporary psychosis" that "was operating on this defendant from some time in November, at least through December and beyond the date of December 7." We hold that such a temporary psychosis which was not limited merely to periods of intoxication ... and which rendered defendant insane under the *M'Naghten* test constitutes a settled insanity that is a complete defense to the offense here charged.

The judgment is reversed and the cause is remanded to the trial court with directions to enter a judgment of not guilty by reason of insanity and to take such further proceedings as are required by law.

------

## NOTES ON THE INSANITY DEFENSE AND INTOXICATION

**1. Introduction.** It is often said that voluntary intoxication is not a defense to criminal liability. This position is reflected in both the voluntary-act doctrine and the insanity defense: Voluntary intoxication is not an excuse even if the defendant's mental functioning was so impaired by the acute effects of alcohol or other drugs as to establish what otherwise would be a defense of "unconsciousness" or insanity. In cases of incapacitating voluntary intoxication, the law finds the governing moral criterion in the culpable origin of the incapacity rather than in its severity. As Lord Matthew Hale said, a person who commits a crime while drunk "shall have no privilege by this voluntary contracted madness, but shall have the same judgment as if he were in his right senses."[a] However, Hale identified two situations in which the madness induced by intoxication would not be contracted voluntarily and therefore would have exculpatory significance:

> [First,] if a person by the unskillfulness of his physician, or by the contrivance of his enemies, eat or drink such a thing as causeth such a temporary or permanent phrenzy, ... this puts him into the same condition, in reference to crimes, as any other phrenzy, and equally excuseth him. [Second,] although the *simplex* phrenzy occasioned immediately by drunkenness excuses not in criminals, yet if by one or more such practices, an *habitual* or fixed phrenzy be caused, though this madness was contracted by the vice and will of the party, yet this habitual and fixed phrenzy thereby caused puts the man into the same condition in relation to crimes, as if the same were contracted involuntarily at first.

Each of these two propositions now represents settled law in the United States.

**2. Non–Culpable Intoxication.** The first of the principles mentioned by Hale, typically labeled "involuntary intoxication," covers a vari-

[a] 1 Matthew Hale, The History of the Pleas of the Crown 32 (Philadelphia 1847) (1st ed. 1736).

ety of cases in which the person cannot fairly be blamed for becoming intoxicated. Cases of intoxication under duress or by contrivance (*A* puts LSD in *B*'s coffee) simply do not appear in the books. Most of the reported cases involve psychoactive side effects of medically-prescribed substances, typically arising in connection with automobile offenses.

The leading case is Minneapolis v. Altimus, 306 Minn. 462, 238 N.W.2d 851 (1976). The defendant was charged with careless driving and a "hit and run" offense. The evidence showed that he made an illegal left turn from a right-hand lane, crashed into another vehicle, and then continued driving. He was arrested by a policeman who had observed the accident. In his defense, he testified that three days before the incident he started taking Valium (a psychoactive, anti-anxiety drug with muscle-relaxing effects) for back pain pursuant to a physician's prescription. He said that he began experiencing mental confusion and disorientation while driving and remembered nothing about either the accident or the arrest. He also introduced expert testimony regarding the effects of Valium. The court instructed the jury on voluntary intoxication but refused to instruct on "involuntary intoxication." The Minnesota Supreme Court reversed, holding that defendant's evidence that "at the time he committed the acts in question he was intoxicated and unaware of what he was doing due to an unusual and unexpected reaction to drugs prescribed by a physician" was sufficient "to raise the defense of temporary insanity due to involuntary intoxication."

How should the jury be instructed on remand? The court's language suggests that the test has two elements: first, the intoxication must be "involuntary," which means the effect must have been both atypical and "unexpected" by Altimus; and the unexpected impairment must amount to "insanity," which in Minnesota is defined according to the *M'Naghten* test. Are these the correct criteria? Compare § 2.08 of the Model Penal Code. Does the Model Penal Code formulation differ from the court's test in *Altimus*? How? Is the Model Code approach sound?

**3. Alcohol–Related Insanity.** The second principle to which Hale referred was the exculpatory effect of the "fixed phrenzy" produced by chronic intoxication. The clinical predicate for this universally recognized doctrine is that chronic use of alcohol can result in organic brain pathology. Although chronic alcohol use can contribute to the development of "dementia,"[b] a condition sometimes associated with aging, the most relevant disorder for present purposes is "alcohol withdrawal delirium" (also called delirium tremens, or "DT's"), which is precipitated by a cessation or reduction of alcohol consumption after heavy use for many years. This condition usually involves delusions, vivid hallucinations, and agitated behavior. A related condition is alcoholic hallucinosis, involving vivid and usually unpleasant auditory hallucinations without the clouding of consciousness characteristic of delirium. Usually this disorder lasts only a few hours or days but can involve significant danger if the individual responds

---

[b] Dementia is the general term for an organic brain syndrome characterized by intellectual deficits and impaired memory and often by impaired judgment and impulse control.

to hallucinatory threats. This condition can occur after a long period of "spree" drinking.

A famous case involving delirium tremens is Beasley v. State, 50 Ala. 149 (1874). Beasley was charged with murder. The evidence showed that the defendant had shot himself in the head, partially paralyzing his left side, 19 years before the offense, and had been chronically drunk for several years before the killing. He frequently experienced hallucinations and had an attack of delirium tremens three weeks before the killing. He testified that he was seeing devils and witches before and during the day of the shooting and that he "imagined that men were after him to kill him." Prosecution evidence showed that the killing was brutal and unprovoked. The trial court refused to instruct on insanity saying, instead, that "drunkenness, in itself, was no palliation or excuse." Beasley was convicted of second-degree murder. On appeal the conviction was reversed because the intoxication charge failed to distinguish between the "immediate effects of the defendant's drunkenness" and the effects of "mental unsoundness brought on by excessive drinking which remains after the intoxication has subsided." The appellate court held that the jury should have been instructed on insanity.

It is often said that delirium tremens and alcoholic hallucinosis exculpate to the same degree as any other psychotic disorder, notwithstanding the fact that these conditions were "caused" by the defendant's own excessive drinking. In these situations, the law looks not to the original source of the impairment but to its effect. In sum, the defendant's pattern of voluntary decisions loses its moral significance when behavior "ripens" into a pathological condition no longer subject to voluntary control.

What is the basis for this distinction? Why does the idiom of moral discourse shift from voluntariness to involuntariness when one moves from the unanticipated and uncontrollable effects of an acute episode of intoxication to the unanticipated and uncontrollable effects of a pattern of intoxication? What is the crucial moral variable? The chronicity of the condition? The psychotic character of the impairment? The remote connection between a psychotic condition and individual instances of intoxication? Consider the suggestion of Monrad Paulsen in Intoxication as a Defense to Crime, 1961 U.Ill.L.F. 1, 22–23:

> ... In a sense it is true that an actor, who by drinking destroys his powers of perception or self-control, bears responsibility for his ultimate state. Does it follow that mental disorder produced by long-term alcoholic behavior should be given a different effect in the law from insanity not produced by "voluntary" behavior? The law is clear. Lack of responsibility can be shown by "settled" insanity without regard to the chain of causation. To give the genesis of mental disorder a legal effect is to put upon the processes of litigation an impossible task. If the full exculpatory effect of mental disease were denied to those illnesses which are related to unwise choices in life, many cases other than those of the alcoholics would be involved. We need only recall that general

paresis [a type of dementia] was a not-uncommon consequence of syphilis.

Is this persuasive? Is it really an "impossible" task to determine whether the defendant's disorder is attributable to once voluntary choices? Or does the law rest on a moral judgment that a person cannot fairly be said to have voluntarily assumed the risk of becoming "mentally ill"?

Hale emphasized the "fixed" nature of the "phrenzy" and, as *Kelly* demonstrates, the courts have typically said that an alcohol-related condition must be "settled" to have exculpatory significance. However, recent commentary has taken note of the clinical reality that both delirium and hallucinosis linked to cessation of drinking usually involve temporary impairment incidental to chronic and heavy use. Although the person's heavy drinking has probably caused organic brain damage, the "phrenzy" is in fact not "fixed." This has led one court to note that "the distinction, notwithstanding the language of the cases, is not so much between temporary and permanent insanity as it is one between the direct results of drinking, which are voluntarily sought after, and its remote and undesired consequences." Parker v. State, 7 Md.App. 167, 179, 254 A.2d 381, 388 (1969). Should this be the governing principle? Is there not an increased risk of fabrication associated with claims of "temporary" insanity due to drinking? Does this concern you?

**4.   Insanity Related to Use of Other Drugs.** It is well known, of course, that alcohol intoxication impairs perception and judgment and, in doing so, loosens behavioral controls. However, alcohol use is not generally associated with psychotic symptoms, such as delusions or hallucinations, except in relation to the two "withdrawal syndromes" described above. Thus, to the extent that the law's conception of insanity requires psychotic symptoms, the distinction reflected in *Beasley* between the effects of intoxication and the effects of "disease" conforms to clinical realities.

This doctrinal picture became considerably blurred by the patterns of psychoactive drug use that emerged in the 1960's. Many of these drugs can affect cognitive functioning in profound ways that bear no resemblance to the effects of alcohol. As one court noted in 1968, "we anticipate ... that the demands of due process may require adjustment and refinement in traditional and 'stock' instructions on the subject of criminal responsibility in view of the frightening effects of the hallucinatory drugs."[c] Three distinct clinical situations are explored below.

**(i)   Psychoactive Effects of Intoxication.** Hallucinogenic drugs such as LSD have sometimes been called "psychotomimetic" drugs because the acute effects of ordinary doses "mimic" psychotic symptoms. The perceptual changes include subjective intensification of perceptions, depersonalization, illusion, and visual hallucinations. The direct effects of the intoxication usually last about six hours. Users of high doses of amphetamines and other stimulant drugs may experience delusions or hallucina-

[c] Pierce v. Turner, 402 F.2d 109, 112 (10th Cir. 1968).

tions; and users of phencyclidine (PCP) and related substances may experience hallucinations and paranoid ideation.

The question is whether the hallucinogenic effects of these drugs warrant any qualification of the rule that voluntary intoxication is no defense regardless of the nature and severity of the impairment. The courts have uniformly rejected this claim. Consider, for example, State v. Hall, 214 N.W.2d 205 (Iowa 1974). Hall was charged with the fatal shooting of his driving companion during the course of a trip from Oregon to Chicago. He testified that before the shooting he had taken a pill (presumably LSD) which he had been told was a "little sunshine" and would make him feel "groovy." He said he drove all the way to Iowa without rest, took the pill at Des Moines and began experiencing hallucinations. The victim, who was sleeping, appeared to make growling sounds and turn into a rabid dog like one he saw his father kill when he was a child. In panic, he seized the victim's gun and shot him three times. The trial court refused an insanity instruction, and the jury convicted defendant of first-degree murder despite an instruction that his intoxication could be considered in connection with the issue of intent. The appellate court affirmed, holding that the acute, psychotomimetic effects of LSD do not justify a departure from the traditional rule that "a temporary mental condition caused by voluntary intoxication ... does not constitute a complete defense." Three judges dissented, arguing, inter alia:

> ... The fallacy in the majority's position is that it puts the issue on a *time* basis rather than an *effect* basis. It says the use of drugs is no defense unless mental illness resulting from long-established use is shown because that's what we have said of alcoholic intoxication. But we have said that about alcohol because ordinarily the use of alcohol produces no mental illness except by long-continued excessive use. On the other hand, that same result can be obtained overnight by the use of modern hallucinatory drugs like LSD.

Is there merit to the view expressed in the *Hall* dissent?

**(ii) Precipitation of a "Functional" Psychosis.** As the testimony in *Kelly* indicates, use of hallucinogenic or stimulant drugs can precipitate a psychosis in a predisposed individual, even though the person has never previously had an acute psychotic episode.[d] How should a case such as *Kelly* be decided under the principles thus far reviewed? Should *Hall* or *Beasley* control? Should the applicable rule be determined by the pathological nature of the impairment or by the role of voluntary drug use in causing it?

The exculpatory approach taken by the *Kelly* court seems to represent the prevailing judicial view. In a factually similar case, State v. Maik, 60

[d] See, e.g., Michael M. Vardy and Stanley R. Kay, LSD Psychosis or LSD–Induced Schizophrenia? A Multimethod Inquiry, 40 Arch. Gen. Psychiatry 877 (1983); Beverly J. Fauman and Michael A. Fauman, Phencyclidine Abuse and Crime: A Psychiatric Perspective, 10 Bull.Amer. Acad. of Psychiatry and Law 171 (1982).

N.J. 203, 287 A.2d 715 (1972), the Supreme Court of New Jersey reached the same result. Chief Justice Weintraub wrote for a unanimous court:

> [The defendant claimed] that the drugs [LSD], acting upon [an] underlying illness, triggered or precipitated a psychotic state which continued after the direct or immediate influence of the drug had dissipated, and that it was the psychosis, rather than the drug, which rendered defendant unable to know right from wrong at the time of the killing. In other words, defendant urges that when a psychosis emerges from a fixed illness, we should not inquire into the identity of the precipitating event or action. Indeed, it may be said to be unlikely that the inquiry would be useful, for when, as here, the acute psychosis could equally be triggered by some other stress, known or unknown, which the defendant could not handle, a medical opinion as to what did in fact precipitate the psychosis is not apt to rise above a speculation among mere possibilities.

> We think it compatible with the philosophical basis of [the insanity defense] to accept the fact of a schizophrenic episode without inquiry into its etiology.

What principle emerges from these cases? Was an exculpatory defense allowed because the defendants were mentally ill *before* taking the drugs?[e] Or because they were mentally ill *after* taking the drugs? Neither court alludes to the fact that the defendant's possession and use of LSD were criminal acts. Should that make any difference?

**(iii) Toxic Psychosis.** Assume that both *Hall* and *Kelly* are correctly decided. In other words, assume (i) that a defendant is not entitled to an insanity instruction if the claimed mental impairment is directly attributable to the intoxicating effects of the drug—i.e., those effects which result from the direct action of the drug on the central nervous system during the period when it is pharmacologically active, but (ii) that a predisposed defendant who experiences a "functional" psychosis triggered by drug use may invoke the insanity defense. Which principle should control in the case of a "normal" person who uses an hallucinogenic drug and experiences a so-called "toxic psychosis"—i.e., a transient dysfunction of the brain which is directly attributable to the toxic effects of the drug but which outlasts the period of intoxication?

A toxic psychosis may vary in effect and length depending on the drug, the dose, the person's psychological status or "set," and the setting of use. For example, a single dose of PCP (phencyclidine) can cause a condition characterized by paranoid delusions and violent behavior lasting from several days to several weeks.[f] While a single dose of amphetamines would

---

[e] One court has said: "[I]f the pre-existing condition of mind of the accused is not such as would render him legally insane in and of itself, then the recent use of intoxicants causing stimulation or aggravation of the pre-existing condition to the point of in-

sanity cannot be relied upon as a defense. . . ." Evilsizer v. State, 487 S.W.2d 113, 116 (Tex.Cr.App.1972).

[f] During the 1960's, PCP was studied experimentally in "normal" volunteers. The major finding of these studies was "that PCP

be unlikely to induce a toxic psychosis, a person who has used moderate or high doses of amphetamines for a long period may develop a disorder, characterized by delusions of persecution, indistinguishable from schizophrenia.

Should a toxic psychosis be regarded as within the range of risk voluntarily assumed by a user of hallucinogenic drugs? Or should such a condition have exculpatory significance despite the fact that the "insanity" is both temporary and unrelated to any pre-existing psychopathology?

**5. Subsequent Developments in California.** In 1994, the California legislature enacted Penal Code § 25.5, which precludes an insanity defense "solely on the basis of . . . an addiction to, or abuse of, intoxicating substances." As interpreted in People v. Robinson, 72 Cal.App.4th 421 (Cal.App. 1999), this provision "erects an absolute bar prohibiting use of one's voluntary ingestion of intoxicants as the sole basis for an insanity defense, regardless whether the substances caused organic damage or a settled mental defect or disorder which persists after the immediate effects of the intoxicants have worn off."

Was this a proper interpretation of the statute? Would it alter the result in *Kelly*? Was drug abuse the *sole* basis for her insanity defense? Consider, in this connection, the definition of mental disease proposed by Richard Bonnie and endorsed by the APA—and adopted in a number of states—which includes "only those severely abnormal mental conditions that grossly and demonstrably impair a person's perception or understanding of reality and *that are not attributable primarily to the voluntary ingestion of alcohol or other psychoactive substances.*" The Moral Basis of the Insanity Defense, 69 A.B.A.J. 194, 197 (1983). What would be the result in *Kelly* under this formulation?

**6. Pathological Intoxication: The Problem of Unanticipated Effects.** Section 2.08(4) of the Model Penal Code provides that intoxication resulting in substantial cognitive or volitional incapacity is a defense if it is not self-induced or if it "is pathological." Paragraph 5(c) defines "pathological intoxication" as "intoxication grossly excessive in degree, given the amount of the intoxicant, to which the actor does not know he is susceptible."

Standing alone, this particular clinical condition is not especially important; it is extremely rare, if it exists at all,[g] and has arisen in

had no equal in its ability to produce brief psychoses nearly indistinguishable from schizophrenia." Generally, these episodes began immediately after ingestion of the drug but lasted for several hours. They were often characterized by violently paranoid behavior. Recent clinical experience with PCP users experiencing toxic psychoses indicates that they can last considerably longer and that the nature and severity of the symptoms varies widely among individuals. See generally Lui-

sada, The Phencyclidine Psychosis: Phenomenology and Treatment, in Robert C. Petersen and Richard C. Stillman (eds.), Phencyclidine (PCP) Abuse: An Appraisal 241 (1978).

[g] The 1980 edition of the psychiatric diagnostic manual, DSM–III, included a diagnosis for pathological intoxication (labeled "alcohol idiosyncratic intoxication"). The essential feature of the diagnosis was said to be "marked behavioral change—usually to aggressiveness—that is due to the recent in-

litigation only a handful of times.[h] However, it may be useful to ask whether the quoted provision in § 2.08 stands for a more general proposition. Note that pathological intoxication represents the single instance in which the drafters of the Model Code endorsed a claim of excuse based on the direct effects of intoxication by a person who knowingly and voluntarily ingests an intoxicating substance in order to experience its intoxicating properties. In this sense, the provision qualifies the definition of self-induced intoxication. Consider a general statement of this principle: "An extreme mental impairment which could not reasonably have been anticipated will not be regarded as self-induced even though the individual was aware of the tendency of the substance to cause intoxication." Is this better?

Jerome Hall made a similar proposal in General Principles of Criminal Law 554–56 (2d ed. 1966):[*]

> [T]he inexperienced inebriate ... [should not] be held criminally liable for a harm committed under gross intoxication [elsewhere defined as severe blunting of the capacity to understand the moral quality of the act in issue combined with a drastic lapse of inhibition]. For such persons, there can be no valid reliance on the drinking to support liability, because, though "voluntary," it was quite innocent....
>
> [S]ince drinking alcoholic liquor is not usually followed by gross intoxication and such intoxication does not usually lead to the commission of serious injuries, it follows that persons who commit them while grossly intoxicated should not be punished unless, at the time of sobriety and the voluntary drinking, they had such prior experience as to anticipate their intoxication and that they would become dangerous in that condition.

The commentators generally have been unenthusiastic about Hall's proposal. They have emphasized the practical difficulties involved, and have argued that awareness of the dangers of gross intoxication does not depend on personal experience. Monrad Paulsen's reaction was typical: "Our culture does not fail to give warning about drunkenness. The risks involved are so widely advertised that few can claim surprise and be believed." Does

---

gestion of alcohol insufficient to induce intoxication in most people." However, the diagnosis was omitted in the DSM–IV "because of lack of supporting evidence that it is distinct from [the diagnosis of] alcohol intoxication."

[h] For a case involving a successful claim of pathological intoxication, see Leggett v. State, 21 Tex.App. 382, 17 S.W. 159 (1886). For a recent case in which the claim was rejected, see Kane v. United States, 399 F.2d 730 (9th Cir. 1968). Kane was convicted of manslaughter in the killing of his wife. His condition was diagnosed as pathological in-

toxication by three of four expert psychiatrists and his medical history was strongly supportive of the diagnosis. Kane had suffered three head injuries, including one several months before the shooting. However, in dictum, the court observed that Kane's testimony showed that he had become aware, after the second injury, of the fact that a modest amount of alcohol would cause him to black out and experience amnesia, and that these effects intensified after the third injury.

[*] Reprinted with the permission of the author and Bobbs–Merrill Co., Inc.

the "culture" give adequate warning to naive users of the potpourri of psychoactive drugs now so widely used? The dissenting judges in the *Hall* case did not think so:

> ... There is nothing to indicate [that Hall] knew [the drug] could induce hallucinations or lead to the frightening, debilitating effects of mind and body to which the doctors testified. The majority nevertheless holds [that] the defendant's resulting drug intoxication was voluntary. I disagree....
>
> [The term] voluntary as here used should relate to acknowledgeable acceptance of the danger and risk involved....

Is this a better view? What is the Model Penal Code solution to such a case?

---

## SUBSECTION D:   MENTAL ABNORMALITY AND MENS REA

---

### INTRODUCTORY NOTES ON THE MEANING OF DIMINISHED RESPONSIBILITY

The terms "diminished capacity" and "diminished responsibility"[a] appear frequently in judicial opinions and scholarly commentary. The terms have no generally recognized meanings, however, and have been used interchangeably to refer to two distinct concepts:

**1.   Rule of Logical Relevance.** In this country, courts usually use the terms "diminished capacity" and "diminished responsibility" to refer to the following rule of evidence: "Evidence of mental abnormality is admissible whenever it is logically relevant to disprove the existence of a mental state required by the definition of an offense or by its grading." As is developed in more detail in the next two main cases and the notes accompanying them, many courts do not always follow this rule of evidence. They either exclude evidence of mental abnormality altogether or restrict its admissibility short of its full logical import, based on doubts as to its reliability and fear that its use will undermine the social-control functions of the criminal law.

The labels "diminished capacity" and "diminished responsibility" apparently have been used to refer to this evidentiary proposition because the legal effect of admitting such evidence normally is to permit a serious

---

[a] For discussion of the different meanings of diminished responsibility, see Stephen Morse, Undiminished Confusion in Diminished Capacity, 75 J.Crim.L. and Criminology 1 (1984); Susan F. Mandiberg, Protecting Society and Defendants Too: The Constitutional Dilemma of Mental Abnormality and Intoxication Defenses, 53 Ford.L.Rev. 221 (1984); Stephen Morse, Diminished Capacity: A Moral and Legal Conundrum, 2 Int'l J. of Law & Psychiatry 271 (1979); Peter Arenella, The Diminished Capacity and Diminished Responsibility Defenses: Two Children of a Doomed Marriage, 77 Colum.L.Rev. 827 (1977).

offense to be reduced in grade to a less serious offense, thereby "diminishing" the offender's legal responsibility for criminal conduct. For example, the premeditation and deliberation required for first-degree murder may be rebutted in a particular case by evidence of mental abnormality, but the defendant may still be guilty of second-degree murder or manslaughter. Use of the terms "diminished capacity" or "diminished responsibility" to describe this result is misleading, however, because the terms carry the implication that "diminished capacity" or "diminished responsibility" can be proved by showing a "partial" incapacity in contrast to the "total" incapacity of insanity. As the materials on the insanity defense have demonstrated, however, mens rea requirements in the definition of criminal offenses may not be directly related to the criteria of non-responsibility used by the insanity defense. In particular, defendants found legally insane typically have the state of mind required for conviction of the most serious offense charged. On the other hand, in some instances, a mentally abnormal person shown to lack the required mens rea may not satisfy the requirements of the insanity defense.

In any event, the question raised by American cases decided under the "diminished capacity" rubric, simply put, is whether and under what circumstances evidence of mental abnormality should be admissible on mens rea issues. This is the question to which the cases and notes in this subsection are addressed.

**2. Partial Responsibility.** The term "diminished responsibility" is sometimes—and perhaps more appropriately—used to refer to the idea that the law should recognize that some offenders are not fully responsible for their crimes even though they are not entitled to exculpation and even though they had the mens rea required for conviction. Those who are only "partly responsible" in this sense would be entitled to a formal mitigation of their crime to a lesser offense. When used in this way, "diminished responsibility" refers to a substantive limitation on criminal liability rather than an evidentiary rule. Thus, a person found to be legally sane and to have had the requisite intent might nonetheless be regarded as being only partly responsible for the crime because of the disabling effects of mental abnormality. If an intermediate or partial degree of cognitive or volitional impairment is to have independent grading significance, this will call for a "test" of diminished responsibility to supplement the test of insanity.

No American jurisdiction has explicitly adopted this approach to the grading of any criminal offense, including homicide.[b] However, it is reflected in the criteria used in several states for the verdict of "guilty but mentally ill,"[c] in the current generation of death penalty statutes,[d]and in

---

[b] In England, a finding of diminished responsibility reduces murder to manslaughter. The English doctrine and related features of the law of homicide in this country are explored in Chapter VIII.

[c] See, for example, the provisions of the GBMI statutes in Alaska and Delaware quoted in the notes on this subject in Section 3.

[d] The criteria of diminished responsibility as used in modern capital sentencing statutes are discussed in Chapter VIII.

modern sentencing statutes and guidelines.[e] It is discussed in these materials in those contexts.

———

# Regina v. Stephenson

Court of Appeal, 1979.
[1979] 1 Q.B. 695.

■ GEOFFREY LANE, LORD JUSTICE. [The] appellant was found guilty by the jury of arson, contrary to Section 1(1) and (3) of the Criminal Damage Act 1971,[a] and pleaded guilty to another count of burglary. He was made the subject of a probation order for three years with a condition of medical treatment. He now appeals against his conviction on the charge of arson....

The facts giving rise to the charge of arson were as follows. On November 28, 1977, the appellant went to a large straw stack in a field near Ampleforth, made a hollow in the side of the stack, crept into the hollow and tried to go to sleep. He felt cold, so he lit a fire of twigs and straw inside the hollow. The stack caught fire and damage of some £3,500 in all resulted. The appellant was stopped by the police soon afterwards. He first of all maintained that the fire had been caused by his smoking a cigarette. However, the next day he admitted what he had done. He said: "I kept putting bits of straw on the fire. Then the lot went up. As I ran away I looked back and saw the fire. Then getting bigger. I ran off down the road, that's when I was picked up. I'm sorry about it, it was an accident."

On those facts without more no jury would have had any difficulty in coming to the certain conclusion that the appellant had damaged the straw stack and had done so being reckless as to whether the stack would be damaged or not, whatever the true definition may be of the word "reckless."

However, the appellant did not give evidence, and the only witness called on behalf of the defence was Dr. Hawkings, a very experienced consultant psychiatrist. His evidence was to the effect that the appellant had a long history of schizophrenia. This, he said, would have the effect of making the appellant quite capable of lighting a fire to keep himself warm

[e] For example, § 5K2.13 of the United States Sentencing Guidelines authorizes a downward departure from the guideline sentence if the defendant "committed [a nonviolent] offense while suffering from a significantly reduced mental capacity" and "there was a direct causal connection" between the reduced capacity and the offense. See, e.g., United States v. Fairless, 975 F.2d 664 (9th Cir. 1992), and the related notes on the volitional inquiry in Subsection B.

[a] Criminal Damage Act 1971, § 1: "(1) A person who without lawful excuse ... damages any property belonging to another ... being reckless as to whether any such property would be ... damaged shall be guilty of an offence ... (3) An offence committed under this section by ... damaging property by fire shall be charged as arson."—[Footnote by eds.]

in dangerous proximity to a straw stack without having taken the danger into account. In other words he was saying that the appellant may not have had the same ability to foresee or appreciate risk as the mentally normal person.

The guilt or innocence of the appellant turned on the question whether the jury were satisfied so as to feel sure that he had been reckless when he lit the fire. The judge gave the following direction to the jury:

> The prosecution say to you, though, that he set fire to it in a situation and a frame of mind which amounted to recklessness as to whether the straw stack would be damaged.... [A] man is reckless if he realises that there is a risk, but nevertheless presses on regardless.... [A] man is reckless when he carried out a deliberate act knowing or closing his mind to the obvious fact that there is some risk of damage. First you perhaps want to ask yourselves whether in lighting the fire the accused carried out a deliberate act, and the answer to that one thinks must be yes, because he has said that he lit the fire. Secondly, you may want to ask yourselves whether you regard it or not as an obvious fact that there was some risk of damage and when the act is the act of lighting a fire inside a straw stack, you may have little difficulty in dealing with the question whether it is an obvious fact that there is some risk of damage. Did he then do that knowing or closing his mind to the obvious fact, in the case from which these words are taken, as I say the reason advanced or the reason found for the man closing his mind to the obvious fact was that he was so angry that he pressed on regardless, and there may be ... all kinds of reasons which make a man close his mind to the obvious fact— among them may be schizophrenia, that he is a schizophrenic....

What then must the prosecution prove in order to bring home the charge of arson in circumstances such as the present? They must prove that (i) the defendant deliberately committed some act which caused the damage to property alleged or part of such damage; (ii) the defendant had no lawful excuse for causing the damage; these two requirements will in the ordinary case not be in issue; (iii) the defendant either (a) intended to cause the damage to the property, or (b) was reckless as to whether the property was damaged or not. A man is reckless when he carries out the deliberate act appreciating that there is a risk that damage to property may result from his act. It is however not the taking of every risk which could properly be classed as reckless. The risk must be one which it is in all the circumstances unreasonable for him to take.

Proof of the requisite knowledge in the mind of the defendant will in most cases present little difficulty. The fact that the risk of some damage would have been obvious to anyone in his right mind in the position of the defendant is not conclusive proof of the defendant's knowledge, but it may well be and in many cases doubtless will be a matter which will drive the jury to the conclusion that the defendant himself must have appreciated the risk. The fact that he may have been in a temper at the time would not normally deprive him of knowledge or foresight of the risk. If he had the necessary knowledge or foresight and his bad temper merely caused him to disregard it or put it to the back of his mind not caring whether the risk materialised, or if it merely deprived him of the self-control necessary to prevent him from taking the risk of which he was aware, then his bad temper will not avail him. This was the concept which the court in Regina v. Parker, [1977] 1 W.L.R. 600, 604, was trying to express when it used the words "or closing his mind to the obvious fact that there is some risk of damage resulting from that act...." We wish to make it clear that the test remains subjective, that the knowledge or appreciation or risk of some damage must have entered the defendant's mind even though he may have suppressed it or driven it out....

How do these pronouncements affect the present appeal? The appellant, through no fault of his own, was in a mental condition which might have prevented him from appreciating the risk which would have been obvious to any normal person. When the judge said to the jury "there may be ... all kinds of reasons which make a man close his mind to the obvious fact—among them may be schizophrenia—" we think he was guilty of a misapprehension, albeit possibly an understandable misapprehension. The schizophrenia was on the evidence something which might have prevented the idea of danger entering the appellant's mind at all. If that was the truth of the matter, then the appellant was entitled to be acquitted. That was something which was never left clearly to the jury to decide.

We should add this. The mere fact that a defendant is suffering from some mental abnormality which may affect his ability to foresee consequences or may cloud his appreciation of risk does not necessarily mean that on a particular occasion his foresight or appreciation of risk was in fact absent. In the present case, for example, if the matter had been left to the jury for them to decide in the light of all the evidence, including that of the psychiatrist, whether the appellant must have appreciated the risk, it would have been open to them to decide that issue against him and to have convicted. As it is, we are of the view that, for the reasons indicated, the conviction for arson ... must be quashed....

Appeal against conviction for arson allowed.

———

## NOTES ON MENTAL ABNORMALITY AND MENS REA

**1. The Rule of Relevance.** *Stephenson* takes the position that evidence of mental abnormality should be taken into account whenever it is logically relevant to the existence of the mental state required for conviction, irrespective of whether the defendant enters an insanity plea.[a] Section

[a] The note on mens rea and mental abnormality in Chapter 2 should be re-read at this point for a summary of the historical background on this issue. The reform that led to cases like *Stephenson* was initiated in the law of homicide, where the subject still receives special attention. For that reason, this section of the book deals in general terms with mental abnormality and mens rea, and the subject is revisited in Chapter 8.

4.02(1) of the Model Penal Code adopts the same approach: "Evidence that the defendant suffered from a mental disease or defect is admissible whenever it is relevant to prove that the defendant did or did not have a state of mind which is an element of the offense."

Proponents of this position typically argue that it is illogical and unfair to define mens rea in subjective terms but then to preclude defendants from introducing otherwise competent evidence to support the claim that they in fact did not have the required state of mind. This view has been summarized by Richard Bonnie and Christopher Slobogin, The Role of Mental Health Professionals in the Criminal Process: The Case For Informed Speculation, 66 Va.L.Rev. 427, 477 (1980):

> In a criminal case involving subjective mens-rea requirements, the prosecution usually has no direct evidence concerning the defendant's state of mind; it must rely on "common sense" inferences drawn from the defendant's conduct. This has the practical effect of shifting the burden to the defendant to demonstrate that he did not perceive, believe, expect, or intend what an ordinary person would have perceived, believed, expected, or intended under the same circumstances. Restriction of clinical testimony on mens rea thus compromises the defendant's opportunity to present a defense on an issue concerning which he, in reality, bears the burden of proof. The factfinder is likely to view with considerable skepticism the defendant's claim that he did not function as would a normal person under the circumstances. The defendant must establish the plausibility of his claim of abnormality. By precluding the defendant from offering relevant expert testimony, the law unduly enhances the prosecution's advantage on this issue. For this reason, we believe the only limitations on admissibility of mens-rea testimony by mental-health professionals should be relevance and the normal requirements for expert opinion.

What reasons might justify exclusion of the type of evidence admitted in *Stephenson* even if it is relevant? Recall that all jurisdictions restrict the admissibility of intoxication evidence considerably short of its logical import, although most jurisdictions do admit such evidence to negate purpose, knowledge, or "specific intent." Would it make sense to treat evidence of intoxication and evidence of mental abnormality on the same terms, admitting the evidence to negate "specific intent" but not otherwise? Some jurisdictions that admit evidence of intoxication to negate specific intent nonetheless exclude evidence of mental abnormality in cases where evidence of intoxication would be admitted. Are there good arguments in favor of this approach?

The modern trend is clearly in the direction of the rule of relevance stated in the Model Penal Code. About one-fourth of the states have adopted a rule similar to § 4.02(1) and now admit evidence of mental abnormality in any case involving a subjective mens-rea inquiry. Another third of the states admit such evidence whenever the offense requires "specific intent." In about one-fourth of the states, however, evidence of mental abnormality is excluded altogether unless it is offered in support of an insanity plea.

   **2.   The Case for Exclusion.** In Bethea v. United States, 365 A.2d 64 (D.C.App.1976), the Court of Appeals for the District of Columbia stated the case for excluding expert psychiatric testimony on mens-rea issues. The court's argument can usefully be presented in three stages. First, the court offers a conceptual defense of the categorical approach of the common law to evidence of mental abnormality:

> In the abstract, evidence of a mental disease or defect may be as relevant to the issue of mens rea as proof of intoxication or epilepsy, and the logic of consistency could compel a similar evidentiary rule for all such incapacitating conditions. However, recognizing the unique position of the concept of insanity in the framework of criminal responsibility, and considering the substantial problems which would accrue from the adoption of the diminished-capacity doctrine, we conclude that the argument of logical relevance is insufficient to warrant [its adoption]....

> It is true, of course, that the existence of the required state of mind is to be determined subjectively in the sense that the issue must be resolved according to the particular circumstances of a given case. However, this fact may not be allowed to obscure the critical difference between the legal concepts of mens rea and insanity. The former refers to the existence in fact of a "guilty mind"; insanity, on the other hand, connotes a presumption that a particular individual lacks the capacity to possess such a state of mind. It is upon this distinction that the "logic" of the diminished-capacity doctrine founders.

> The concept of mens rea involves what is ultimately the fiction of determining the actual thoughts or mental processes of the accused. It is obvious that a certain resolution of this issue is beyond the ken of scientist and laymen alike. Only by inference can the existence of intent—or the differentiation between its forms, such as general or specific—be determined. The law presumes that all individuals are capable of the mental processes which bear the jurisprudential label "mens rea"; that is, the law presumes sanity. Moreover, for the sake of administrative efficiency and in recognition of fundamental principles of egalitarian fairness, our legal system further presumes that each person is equally capable of the same forms and degrees of intent. The concept of insanity is simply a device the law employs to define the outer limits of that segment of the general population to whom these presumptions concerning the capacity for criminal intent shall not be applied. The line between the sane and the insane for the purposes of criminal adjudication is not drawn because for one group the actual existence of the necessary mental state (or lack

thereof) can be determined with any greater certainty, but rather because those whom the law declares insane are demonstrably so aberrational in their psychiatric characteristics that we choose to make the assumption that they are incapable of possessing the specified state of mind. Within the range of individuals who are not "insane," the law does not recognize the readily demonstrable fact that as between individual criminal defendants the nature and development of their mental capabilities may vary greatly. . . .

By contradicting the presumptions inherent in the doctrine of mens rea, the theory of diminished capacity inevitably opens the door to variable or sliding scales of criminal responsibility. . . .

Next the *Bethea* court responds to the argument that restrictions on psychiatric evidence concerning mental impairment are illogical. To the contrary, the court argues, sound evidentiary policies underlie an exclusionary rule:

We recognize that there are exceptions to the basic principle that all individuals are presumed to have a similar capacity for mens rea. The rule that evidence of intoxication may be employed to demonstrate the absence of specific intent figure[s] prominently in the [argument for admissibility] of expert evidence of mental impairment. The asserted analogy is flawed, however, by the fact that there are significant evidentiary distinctions between psychiatric abnormality and the recognized incapacitating circumstances. Unlike the notion of partial or relative insanity, conditions such as intoxication, medication, epilepsy, infancy, or senility are, in varying degrees, susceptible to quantification or objective demonstration, and to lay understanding. . . .

While the rationale for . . . diminished capacity rest[s] heavily upon the concept of logical relevance, [attention must be paid] to the other general prerequisites to the admissibility of evidence, i.e., its reliability and the balance between its probative value and its potential impact upon the other interests which are critical to the adjudicatory mechanism. . . .

[T]he degree of sophistication of the psychiatric sciences and the validity and reliability of its evidentiary product are not beyond dispute. In Wahrlich v. Arizona, 479 F.2d 1137, 1138 (9th Cir. 1973), the [court] concluded:

[T]he state of the developing art of psychiatry is such that we are not convinced that psychiatric testimony directed to a retrospective analysis of the subtle gradations of specific intent has enough probative value to compel its admission. . . .

The potential impact of psychiatric evidence in an area so critically close to the ultimate issue of responsibility cannot be minimized. . . . There is no reason to suppose that the problem will be any less acute where the issue is the subtle distinction between mental states such as those reflecting specific and general intent, as opposed to the question whether there existed a mental abnormality of sufficient magnitude to be labeled insanity.  . . .

[Moreover] we are not satisfied that the rule [of admissibility can logically be limited to cases of specific intent]. Assuming the competency of experts to testify as to an accused's capacity for specific intent, we see no logical bar to their observations as to the possible existence or lack of malice or general intent. Moreover, it does not appear to us that the balance between the evidentiary value of medical testimony and its potential for improper impact upon the trier would vary sufficiently as between the various degrees of mens rea to warrant such an artificial distinction.

Finally, the court argues that the dispositional consequences of "unrestrained application" of the rule of logical relevance would be unacceptable:

While there may be superficial appeal to the idea that the standards of criminal responsibility should be applied as subjectively as possible, the overriding danger of the disputed doctrine is that it would discard the traditional presumptions concerning mens rea without providing for a corresponding adjustment in the means whereby society is enabled to protect itself from those who cannot or will not conform their conduct to the requirements of the law.

Under the present statutory scheme, a successful plea of insanity avoids a conviction, but confronts the accused with the very real possibility of prolonged therapeutic confinement. If, however, psychiatric testimony were generally admissible to cast a reasonable doubt upon whatever degree of mens rea was necessary for the charged offense, thus resulting in outright acquittal, there would be scant reason indeed for a defendant to risk such confinement by arguing the greater form of mental deficiency. Thus, quite apart from the argument that the diminished capacity doctrine would result in a considerably greater likelihood of acquittal for those who by traditional standards would be held responsible, the future safety of the offender as well as the community would be jeopardized by the possibility that one who is genuinely dangerous might obtain his complete freedom merely by applying his psychiatric evidence to the threshold issue of intent.

[It has been argued] that the statutory procedures governing civil commitment would "provide a shield against danger from persons with abnormal mental condition." We do not share [this view]. While confinement as a result of either a plea of insanity or a civil petition turns upon the existence of a similar degree of mental impairment, there exist significant procedural differences. . . . The difference between the burden and standards of proof has been justified on the quite logical ground that under normal circumstances civil commitment is directed toward a potential threat to an individual or the community, while in the context of the criminal defense, harm in fact has occurred, and the commission of the act is tacitly acknowledged. We see no justification for thwarting the legitimate policy objectives of the mandatory commitment provisions [for persons acquitted by reason of insanity] by reopening the gap between the civil and criminal structures. In our view, to do so would "tear the fabric of the criminal law as an instrument of social control.". . . .

The *Bethea* court asserts that the rule of relevance must "founder" on the conceptual distinction between insanity and mens rea. Is the court's argument persuasive? What does the court mean when it says that mens rea "ultimately [involves] the fiction of determining the actual thoughts or mental processes of the accused"? Is the court suggesting that the law is unconcerned with actual mental functioning of persons presumed to be sane and that the idea of mens rea is not as subjective as the proponents of the rule of relevance assume?

The court rejects the "asserted analogy" to intoxication on the ground that evidence of mental abnormality is less objective and reliable than evidence of "intoxication, medication, epilepsy, infancy or senility." How objective and reliable is evidence regarding the effects of intoxication, medication, etc.?

The court also asserts that the logical argument for admissibility applies to all mens-rea inquiries, including "malice or general intent," and that any distinction among specific-and general-intent offenses would be "artificial." Is the court right? Is there an acceptable ground for drawing such a distinction? Is evidence of mental abnormality relevant to general intent? Does any of the rationales offered for the traditional restriction on evidence of intoxication apply in this context?

Finally, the court observes that acquittal of a person who lacks mens rea because of mental abnormality would undermine the social-control functions of the criminal law. Is this a legitimate concern? If it is, does it suggest that the distinction between specific-and general-intent offenses would not be "artificial?" If no such line were drawn and a mentally abnormal defendant could win acquittal, what would be the appropriate disposition?

**3. *People* v. *Wetmore.*** The tension between subjective criteria of culpability and the social interest in control of dangerous persons is illustrated by the decision of the California Supreme Court in People v. Wetmore, 22 Cal.3d 318, 149 Cal.Rptr. 265, 583 P.2d 1308 (1978). Wetmore was charged with burglary. The evidence was summarized by the Supreme Court:

> [Joseph Cacciatore, the victim of the burglary] testified that he left his apartment on March 7, 1975. When he returned three days later, he discovered defendant in his apartment. Defendant was wearing Cacciatore's clothes and cooking his food. The lock on the front door had been broken; the apartment lay in a shambles. Cacciatore called the police, who arrested defendant for burglary.

Later Cacciatore discovered that a ring, a watch, a credit card, and items of clothing were missing.[1]

The psychiatric reports submitted to the court explain defendant's long history of psychotic illness, including at least 10 occasions of hospital confinement for treatment. According to the reports, defendant, shortly after his last release from [a V.A. hospital], found himself with no place to go. He began to believe that he "owned" property and was "directed" to Cacciatore's apartment. When he found the door unlocked he was sure he owned the apartment. He entered, rearranged the apartment, destroyed some advertising he felt was inappropriate, and put on Cacciatore's clothes. When the police arrived, defendant was shocked and embarrassed, and only then understood that he did not own the apartment. . . .

Wetmore argued that the psychiatric evidence showed that as a result of mental illness he lacked the specific intent required for conviction of burglary. The trial court acknowledged that the evidence might negate specific intent but concluded that, under the controlling precedents, "if a defendant's mental capacity which would preclude the forming of a specific intent is that of insanity," evidence of such a mental condition "is not admissible to establish . . . lack of specific intent due to diminished capacity." The court was also concerned that there was no lesser offense under California law for which Wetmore could be convicted if he were acquitted of burglary. It accordingly found Wetmore guilty of burglary as charged. Pursuant to California's bifurcated trial procedure, the court then considered the question of insanity and found Wetmore not guilty by reason of insanity. At a subsequent hearing, the trial court found that Wetmore "had not recovered his sanity" and ordered him committed.

The Supreme Court of California unanimously reversed the judgment:

The state bears the burden of proving every element of the offense charged; defendant cannot logically or constitutionally be denied the right to present probative evidence rebutting an element of the crime merely because such evidence also suggests insanity. Defendant's evidence established that he entered an apartment under a delusion that he owned that apartment and thus did not enter with the intent of committing a theft or felony. That evidence demonstrated that defendant lacked the specific intent required for a conviction of burglary; the trial court's refusal to consider the evidence at the guilt phase of the trial therefore constituted prejudicial error.

We reject the suggestion that we sustain the trial court by holding that a defense of diminished capacity cannot be raised whenever, owing to the lack of a lesser included offense, it might

---

[1] At the preliminary hearing defendant appeared wearing one of Cacciatore's shirts. . . .

result in the defendant's acquittal. A defendant who, because of diminished capacity, does not entertain the specific intent required for a particular crime is entitled to be acquitted of that crime. If he cannot be convicted of a lesser offense and cannot safely be released, the state's remedy is to institute civil commitment proceedings, not to convict him of a specific-intent crime which he did not commit.

The court elaborated on its rejection of the argument that civil commitment provided inadequate social protection:

A defendant whose criminal activity arises from mental disease or defect usually requires confinement and special treatment. [The penal code provides for] such confinement and treatment for persons found not guilty by reason of insanity. A defendant acquitted because, as a result of diminished capacity, he lacked the specific intent required for the crime cannot be confined pursuant to [those] sections, yet often he cannot be released without endangering the public safety.

The same danger may arise, however, when a diminished-capacity defense does not result in the defendant's acquittal, but in his conviction for a lesser-included offense. A defendant convicted of a lesser-included misdemeanor, for example, will be confined for a relatively short period in a facility which probably lacks a suitable treatment program, and may later, having served his term, be released to become a public danger. The solution to this problem thus does not lie in barring the defense of diminished capacity when the charged crime lacks a lesser included offense, but in providing for the confinement and treatment of defendants with diminished capacity arising from mental disease or defect.

[California law] provides for the civil commitment of any person who, "as a result of mental disorder, [is] a danger to others, or to himself, or gravely disabled." . . . [I]f evidence adduced in support of a successful diminished capacity defense indicates to the trial judge that the defendant is dangerous, the court is not compelled to foist the defendant upon the public; it may, instead, initiate procedures for civil commitment.

The attorney general points out that a person who commits a crime against property, such as defendant Wetmore, might not be [civilly] commitable . . . unless he were "gravely disabled." A more serious omission lies in the act's failure to provide for long-term commitment of persons dangerous to others; unless found "gravely disabled," a person "who, as a result of mental disorder, presents an imminent threat of substantial physical harm to others" cannot be confined beyond the initial 90–day post-certification treatment period unless "he has threatened, attempted, or actually inflicted physical harm to another during his period of post-certification treatment." If the [civil-commitment statute] does not adequately protect the public against crimes committed by persons with diminished mental capacity, the answer lies either in amendment to that act or in the enactment of legislation that would provide for commitment of persons acquitted by virtue of a successful diminished capacity defense in the same manner as persons acquitted by reason of insanity are presently committed. It does not lie in judicial creation of an illogical—and possibly unconstitutional—rule denying the defense of diminished capacity to persons charged with crimes lacking a lesser included offense.

Has the court properly resolved the tension between subjective criteria of culpability and the social interest in control over mentally disordered persons who have committed anti-social acts? Has the court simply shifted the tension to the civil commitment process? The *Wetmore* court rejected the "illogical" suggestion that evidence of mental abnormality should be inadmissible "whenever, owing to the lack of a lesser-included offense, it might result in the defendant's acquittal." In common-law terms, the rejected approach would preclude the use of such evidence to negate "general intent" and would also preclude its use in cases such as *Wetmore* that involve specific-intent crimes with no lesser-included general-intent offense. How should such an approach be implemented in a jurisdiction with a culpability structure based on the Model Penal Code? Would this approach be entirely illogical? Does it represent a useful compromise?

---

## United States v. Bright

United States Court of Appeals for the Second Circuit, 1975.
517 F.2d 584.

■ GURFEIN, CIRCUIT JUDGE. Catherine Bright appeals from a judgment of conviction entered on ... three counts of possession of [checks stolen from the mail].[a] [She] received a six-month suspended sentence and six-months probation.

Appellant presses two points on this appeal. First, she argues that the district court committed error in failing to permit the defense to introduce psychiatric evidence to negate her knowledge that the checks were stolen, although no insanity defense was tendered. Second, she argues that the district court committed reversible error in its charge to the jury with respect to the element of knowledge required under 18 U.S.C. § 1708. We affirm the district court on the first of these contentions, but reverse on the charge to the jury.

It is uncontested that appellant had been in possession of some nine welfare checks at various dates during 1972, and that these checks had been stolen from the mail. The checks had been in the possession of one

---

[a] The statute involved, 18 U.S.C. § 1708, provides in pertinent part: "Whoever ... unlawfully has in his possession ... any ... mail ... which has been ... stolen, ... knowing the same to have been stolen, [s]hall be fined ... or imprisoned...."—[Footnote by eds.]

Fred Scott, an acquaintance of appellant's "boyfriend" Leslie; Scott gave Bright the checks to cash for him on the pretense that he had no bank account of his own. Appellant admitted at trial that she had cashed or deposited the checks in question in the two accounts she had at her bank, but swore that she had not known that they were stolen. She testified that Scott had told her that he had received the checks in payment for debts or rent owed to him.

She testified that on one occasion, when a check she had cashed had been returned unpaid and her account charged accordingly, she confronted Scott who made good on the loss. After that incident, she cashed three more checks for Scott. The three counts of her conviction are based on her cashing the latter three checks.

At trial, the appellant's defense was based upon her purported lack of knowledge that the checks had been stolen and her naive belief that everything Scott told her was true. Appellant testified in her own behalf accordingly.

In support of her contention that she did not know the checks were stolen, appellant sought to introduce testimony by Dr. Norman Weiss, a psychiatrist who examined appellant on August 21, 1974 before trial. The trial court excluded the proffered testimony and appellant assigns the exclusion as reversible error. . . .

Though Dr. Weiss examined appellant only once, he was prepared to testify, as indicated in a letter he addressed to defense counsel, that "though I do not consider Mrs. Bright to have been suffering mental illness, I believe that her dependent, childlike character structure unconsciously 'needed' to believe that these men would never involve her in illegal activities and that Leslie [her boyfriend] could do no wrong. I believe that at the time of the alleged crime, because of this unconscious 'need,' she did not think that the checks had been stolen."

He later suggested, "I do not believe that she knew that the checks that she allegedly possessed were stolen as a result of her need to deny the possibility that the men involved would in any way take advantage of her. This passive-dependent personality disorder rendered her incapable of understanding this."

Appellant argues that the proffered psychiatric testimony should have been admitted for the purpose of showing her inability to know that the checks had been stolen, a requisite element under Section 1708. [Appellant's trial counsel] specifically disavowed the assertion of an insanity defense. . . . We hold the trial court did not err in rejecting the testimony.

The proffered testimony was a weak reed. The hurried diagnosis prepared for an advocate for purposes of trial would simply tender an opinion by the psychiatrist, not that appellant was suffering from mental disease, or that she lacked substantial capacity either to appreciate the wrongfulness of her conduct or to conform her conduct to the requirements of law, but that, on the basis of this single examination, the psychiatrist was of the opinion that appellant had a 'passive-dependent personality disorder.' " . . . Couched in simpler language he was prepared to testify that appellant was a gullible person but a person unaffected either by psychosis or neurosis.

Nor was the proffered testimony to show that appellant did not have the capacity to form a specific intent to commit the crime. Concededly she was quite capable of the mental responsibility required to cash a stolen check and to recognize circumstances that would lead to the suspicion that it was stolen. The interposition by Dr. Weiss was simply that this particular man, Leslie, was in such a relationship to the passive-dependent personality on trial that she had to believe him when he told her the checks were not stolen.

In dealing with forensic psychiatry, we must be humble rather than dogmatic. The mind and motivation of an accused who is not on the other side of the line [drawn by the insanity defense] is, by the judgment of experience, left to the jury to probe. The complexity of the fears and long-suppressed traumatic experiences of a lifetime is in the personality of all of us. All humankind is heir to defects of personality.

To transmute the effect of instability, of undue reliance on another, of unrequited love, of sudden anger, of the host of attitudes and syndromes that are a part of daily living, into opinion evidence to the jury for exculpation or condemnation is to go beyond the boundaries of current knowledge. The shallower the conception the deeper runs the danger that the jury may be misled. . . .

In short, appellant asks us to go beyond the boundaries of conventional psychiatric opinion testimony. We think the testimony offered was not sufficiently grounded in scientific support to make us reach or, indeed, cross the present frontier of admissibility. On the instant appeal we need decide no more than that [the trial judge] did not abuse her discretion in rejecting the opinion evidence.

[The court next considered the jury instruction on the meaning of knowledge. After an elaborate analysis, it concluded that the absence of several words from the instruction insufficiently emphasized the entirely subjective nature of the inquiry. It then reversed the conviction on this ground.]

---

## NOTES ON THE BOUNDARIES OF PSYCHIATRIC TESTIMONY ON MENS REA

**1. Introduction.** The *Bright* court held that the trial judge had not abused her discretion in excluding the proffered testimony by Dr. Weiss. The court does not appear to take the position that evidence of mental abnormality is categorically excluded in the absence of an insanity plea. What, then, was the ground for excluding the testimony? To what extent is the ruling based on the same substantive policies of the penal law articulated in *Bethea*? To what extent is the ruling based, instead, on general policies of the law of evidence concerning expert-opinion testimony—in this case the proper scope of opinion testimony by psychiatrists and other mental-health professionals? Three possible bases for the court's ruling are explored in the following notes.

**2.  Lack of Capacity vs. Actual State of Mind.** The *Bright* court observes that the expert testimony was not offered to show that the defendant "did not have the capacity to form a specific intent to commit the crime," but only that in fact she did not have the requisite knowledge at the time of the offense. Does this imply that expert testimony concerning mental abnormality is admissible *only* to show lack of capacity to entertain the required mental state? This approach is followed in many jurisdictions. Is this a proper basis for determining the admissibility of expert testimony and for instructing a jury on the relevance of such testimony?[a]

The capacity requirement is omitted in modern statutes and judicial decisions adopting the rule of logical relevance. The typical formulation is that of the Model Penal Code—evidence of mental disease or defect is admissible whenever it is relevant to show the absence of mens rea at the time of the offense. Would the *Bright* evidence be admissible under the Model Penal Code? Would the *Stephenson* evidence be admissible in a jurisdiction following the *Bright* court's approach?

**3.  The Significance of Mental Disease.** The *Bright* court observes that the proffered testimony did not purport to show that the defendant was "suffering from a mental disease ... but that [she] had a 'passive-dependent personality disorder.' " Clearly the defendant had no "mental disease or defect" in the sense ordinarily required for the insanity defense. But should admissibility of expert testimony concerning mens rea be dependent upon the presence of mental disease? If so, should the threshold of legal significance for clinically significant psychological "abnormalities" be the same in the mens-rea context as it is in the context of the insanity defense? Do the policies underlying the mental-disease requirement for the insanity defense apply to mens-rea inquiries?

The case against the mental-disease limitation has been made by Richard Bonnie and Christopher Slobogin in The Role of Mental Health Professionals in the Criminal Process: The Case for Informed Speculation, 66 Va.L.Rev. 427, 477–81 (1980). They argue that "the only limitations on admissibility of mens-rea testimony by mental-health professionals should be relevance and the normal requirements for expert opinion." They illustrate the theoretical bases for this position with an elaborated version of the *Bright* situation:

> The defense proffers expert testimony by a psychiatrist to the effect that Ms. *B*'s personality is marked by a high degree of passivity and dependency. Because she is highly dependent on others to satisfy her emotional needs, she is compliant and characteristically avoids situations of conflict that could threaten the stability of her emotional attachments. In this particular situation,

---

[a] Courts divide in a similar way on the significance of evidence of intoxication.

her dependence on her boyfriend and desire to please him led her to want to please his good friend Scott. As is characteristic of persons with her personality traits, Ms. *B* relies on the ego defense mechanisms of "denial" and "repression" to keep anxiety-provoking thoughts out of her consciousness, in order to maintain her emotional equilibrium. Doubts about Scott's honesty—and, by inference, about her boyfriend's character and relationship with her—would have generated intense anxiety and psychological conflict. Thus, she denied and repressed the doubts, which never rose to the level of consciousness.

This formulation, if believed, tends to support Ms. *B*'s claim that she did not "knowingly" possess stolen checks. However, it does not show that she suffered from a mental disease or defect— or even a substantial behavioral abnormality—that would deprive her of the capacity to know that the checks were stolen. Instead, it draws on theories of personality and [psychodynamic psychology] to explain the way she functions as a person, and adds some plausibility to the notion that under the described circumstances she could have been "abnormally gullible."

Let us assume that this testimony satisfies the governing evidentiary criteria for expert opinion but that it is nonetheless excluded because a claim of mental disease or defect is a prerequisite for admissibility of expert opinion testimony on mens rea. This exclusion compromises Ms. *B*'s ability to persuade the factfinder not to draw inferences about her beliefs on the basis of what a normal person would have believed under the circumstances. Because Ms. *B* carries a de-facto burden of proof on this issue, the exclusion of expert testimony in effect holds her to the standards of a normally suspicious person, selectively redefining the offense to apply objective standards to her and subjective standards to everyone else.

Why do so many courts disagree with this line of argument? Which is the best position?

**4. Proper Subjects for Expert Testimony.** As noted by Bonnie and Slobogin, otherwise relevant opinion testimony by psychiatrists and other mental-health professionals may properly be excluded if the proffered opinion fails to satisfy the normal criteria for expert testimony. In particular, the subject of the testimony must be based on the specialized knowledge of the expert. As the *Bethea* opinion suggests, the traditional exclusionary approach to evidence of mental abnormality may be linked as much to skepticism about psychiatric testimony as it is to policies of the penal law. Any residual limitations, such as the mental-disease requirement, may also be predicated on evidentiary concerns rather than substantive ones.

Doubts about the scientific basis of the proffered testimony are also reflected in the *Bright* opinion. The court observes that the expert testimony proffered by the defendant goes "beyond the boundaries of current knowledge" and is insufficiently "grounded in scientific support" to be admissible. Is the court's concern legitimate? Is psychiatric opinion about the defendant's personality traits and about the "dynamic" of her psychological functioning too speculative to warrant consideration? Insufficiently grounded in scientific support? Is there reason to be any less skeptical about the scientific basis for the testimony offered in Joy Baker's case and the other cases considered in connection with the insanity defense? Do limitations on the insanity defense, such as the allocation of the burden of proof and the dispositional consequences, justify different treatment of the issue in that context?

A final point should be made regarding expert testimony. Even if a defendant's mental functioning is a proper subject for expert-opinion testimony, the trial court must rule on the qualifications of the individual witness to offer such an opinion in the particular case. Would careful scrutiny of the training of the witness and the quality of his evaluation provide an adequate safeguard against unreliable psychiatric testimony in cases like *Bright*? Should the trial judge have admitted Dr. Weiss' testimony?

---

NOTE ON MENS REA EVIDENCE UNDER FEDERAL LAW

Section 17 (a) of The Federal Insanity Defense Reform Act, discussed in the Introductory Notes to Section 2 provides, inter alia:

> It is an affirmative defense to a prosecution under any Federal Statute that, at the time of the commission of the acts constituting the offense, the defendant, as a result of a severe mental disease or defect, was unable to appreciate the nature and quality or the wrongfulness of his acts. *Mental disease or defect does not otherwise constitute a defense.* [Emphasis added.]

Does the italicized language preclude defendants from introducing evidence of mental abnormality to negate mens rea? This issue has evoked a bewildering array of pronouncements from the federal courts. United States v. Pohlot, 827 F.2d 889 (3d Cir. 1987), sets forth the prevailing view.

After he was caught attempting to hire a hit man to kill his wife, Pohlot was found guilty of five counts of using interstate commerce facilities in the commission of a crime of violence and one count of conspiring to do the same. The pertinent evidence was summarized by the Circuit Court:

> Until the summer of 1985, Stephen Pohlot was a successful pharmacist and private investor, living with his wife, Elizabeth, and three of their children in Katonah, New York. According to Pohlot, however, beyond this façade lay a strange set of relationships, dominated by his wife. Pohlot testified, for example, that his wife had broken his thumb by crashing a coffee pot down on it; deeply gouged his face with her nails; threatened him with a hunting knife; shot him in the stomach; and often locked him out

of their house and bedroom. Pohlot also blamed his wife for the psychiatric illnesses of two of his four children, who were seriously anorexic. Illustrating her behavior, Pohlot said that she had insisted on keeping an enormous number of pets in or about the house: sixty rabbits, six goats, tanks full of fish, tanks full of snakes, a pony, six indoor cats and nine outdoor cats, numerous ducks and dogs, and a variety of birds.

In the summer of 1985, Elizabeth obtained a court order removing Pohlot from their home. In July 1985, she filed for divorce, freezing Pohlot's assets. These events, according to the government, triggered the murder plot. . . .

A defense expert witness testified that as a result of childhood experiences and his wife's abuse, Pohlot had a "compulsive personality, passive dependent personality and passive aggressive personality." Pohlot himself testified that his psychological inability to respond to his wife's abuse led to the murder plot as "a weak attempt to fight back." The expert witness further testified that Pohlot "felt as if he would hire somebody to kill [his wife] and after that happened, they would go home and live together and be happier." The court then summarized the contending positions on the admissibility of this evidence:

> The Government claims that ... the [Insanity Defense Reform] Act bars a defendant from using evidence of mental abnormality to negate mens rea. . . . We disagree. Both the wording of the statute and the legislative history leave no doubt that Congress intended, as the Senate Report stated, to bar only alternative "affirmative defenses" that "excuse" misconduct, not evidence that disproves an element of the crime itself.

> Pohlot essentially contends that mental disease or defect is admissible whenever it is relevant to prove that the defendant did or did not have a state of mind that is an element of the offense. Model Penal Code, § 4.02(1) (1962). Although this principle has sometimes been phrased as a version of the diminished capacity defense, it does not provide any grounds for acquittal not provided in the definition of the offense. Properly understood, it is therefore not a defense at all but merely a rule of evidence. As several United States Courts of Appeals have therefore stressed, [t]he use of expert testimony for this purpose is entirely distinct from the use of such testimony to relieve a defendant of criminal responsibility based on the insanity defense or one of its variants, such as diminished capacity.

The court ultimately affirmed Pohlot's conviction because the proffered testimony was not relevant to mens rea and instead was offered in support of "an unacceptable defense of diminished responsibility." Did the court correctly interpret and apply § 17(a)?[b]

---

[b] See also United States v. White, 766 F.2d 22 (1st Cir. 1985); United States v. Frisbee, 623 F.Supp. 1217 (N.D. Cal. 1985).

## NOTE ON BIFURCATION OF INSANITY AND MENS REA

Cases involving insanity pleas are sometimes tried in two phases. Under this bifurcated procedure, the issues of "guilt or innocence" and "insanity" are tried separately. Although bifurcation is permitted in many states, the procedure is required by statute only in California and a handful of others.[a]

In a jurisdiction that excludes evidence of mental abnormality from the guilt stage, the bifurcated trial can have decided advantages. By deferring psychiatric testimony to the second stage, it avoids confusing the jury and reduces the risk of compromise verdicts. Also, in many cases it helps protect the defendant's privilege against self-incrimination. If the insanity issue were tried simultaneously with the "guilt" issue, many defendants would be forced to make a strategic choice between contesting the issue of guilt or admitting the elements of the offense and attempting to prove insanity. This is because the defendant's own statements are often an integral part of a defense based on his mental condition at the time of the offense. Thus, the bifurcated trial permits the defendant to remain silent during the guilt phase, thereby assuring that the prosecution bears the burden of proving the elements of the offense without the defendant's assistance. If the prosecution is successful, the defendant is then permitted to put on an insanity defense and may choose to testify at that time.

Obviously the advantages of a bifurcated trial are diminished if the defendant is permitted to introduce evidence of mental abnormality to negate mens rea at the guilt stage while the "insanity" issue is deferred. Since this procedure bifurcates the expert testimony, the trial can become highly cumbersome and redundant. For this reason, a judge sitting in a jurisdiction which does not require bifurcation might decide to hold a unified proceeding. However, what is the correct response if bifurcation is required by statute? On the one hand, the California Supreme Court has taken the position that the defendant cannot fairly be precluded from introducing relevant evidence of mental abnormality at the guilt stage even though the insanity issue will be tried separately. This led the court to recommend that the legislature abandon the bifurcated procedure in favor of a unified trial. People v. Wetmore, 22 Cal.3d 318, 331, 149 Cal.Rptr. 265, 274, 583 P.2d 1308, 1317 (1978). On the other hand, the Wisconsin Supreme Court has concluded that the advantages of the bifurcated trial procedure provide another reason, in addition to those presented by the *Bethea* court, for excluding evidence of mental abnormality on mens-rea issues. See Steele v. State, 97 Wis.2d 72, 294 N.W.2d 2 (1980).

---

[a] In many states, the trial judge has the discretion to bifurcate the trial but is not required to do so. In some states, bifurcation is required upon the defendant's request. Some states forbid the procedure altogether.

## SUBSECTION E: ABOLITION OF THE INSANITY DEFENSE

___

### NOTES ON ABOLITION OF THE INSANITY DEFENSE

**1. Approaches to Abolition.** Proposals to abolish the insanity defense have been made since the latter 19th century. These proposals have taken two forms:

**(i) The Sentencing Approach.** Some abolitionists recommend that all evidence regarding the defendant's mental abnormality be excluded from the "guilt stage" of the criminal proceeding and that such evidence be taken into account only at the sentencing stage. This approach, which was widely discussed during the early years of this century[a] was actually enacted by the state of Washington in 1909:

> It shall be no defense to a person charged with the commission of a crime that at the time of its commission he was unable, by reason of his insanity, idiocy or imbecility, to comprehend the nature and quality of the act committed, or to understand that it was wrong; or that he was afflicted with a morbid propensity to commit prohibited acts; nor shall any testimony or other proof thereof be admitted in evidence.

The statute also provided that the trial judge could order a convicted defendant to be committed to a state hospital or confined in the psychiatric unit of the penitentiary if he determined that the defendant was insane. This scheme was declared unconstitutional by the Supreme Court of Washington in State v. Strasburg, 60 Wash. 106, 110 P. 1020 (1910). The court concluded that the statute precluded the defendant from offering evidence to negate the constitutionally required predicate for criminal liability:

> [T]he sanity of the accused, at the time of committing the act charged against him, has always been regarded as much a substantive fact, going to make up his guilt, as the fact of his physical commission of the act. It seems to us the law could as well exclude proof of any other substantive fact going to show his guilt or innocence. If he was insane at the time to the extent that he could not comprehend the nature and quality of the act—in other words, if he had no will to control the physical act of his physical body—how can it in truth be said that the act was his act? To take from the accused the opportunity to offer evidence tending to prove this fact is in our opinion as much a violation of his constitutional right of trial by jury as to take from him the right to offer evidence before the jury tending to show that he did not physically commit

___

[a] See, e.g., Curtis D. Wilbur, Should the Insanity Defense to a Criminal Charge be Abolished?, 8 A.B.A.J. 631 (1922); John R. Rood, Statutory Abolition of the Defense of Insanity in Criminal Cases, 9 Mich.L.Rev. 126 (1910). More recent endorsements include H.L.A. Hart, Punishment and Responsibility 186–205 (1968).

the act or physically set in motion a train of events resulting in the act.

**(ii) The Mens–Rea Approach.** Concerns such as those expressed by the *Strasburg* court have inspired a less sweeping abolitionist proposal. Under this approach, evidence of mental abnormality would be excluded unless relevant to the mens rea of the offense charged; criteria of criminal responsibility extrinsic to the definition of the offense would be abandoned.

The mens-rea variant of the abolitionist proposals has been especially popular in recent years. It has significant support in the academic literature[b] and has been adopted in Montana, Idaho, Utah and Kansas.[c] Section 46–14–201 of Mont.Rev.Codes Ann. provides, in relevant part:

(1) Evidence of mental disease or defect is not admissible in a trial on the merits unless the defendant ... files a written notice of his purpose to rely on a mental disease or defect to prove that he did not have a particular state of mind which is an essential element of the offense charged....

(2) When the defendant is found not guilty of the charged offense or offenses or any lesser included offense for the reason that due to a mental disease or defect, he could not have a particular state of mind that is an essential element of the offense charged, the verdict and judgment shall so state.

Assessing the merits of the mens-rea approach to mental abnormality is aided by consideration of three questions: (i) Would the outcomes of criminal cases under the mens-rea scheme differ significantly from those that would occur under the existing responsibility tests? (ii) How would the dispositional consequences of the mens-rea approach differ from those that now obtain? (iii) To the extent that some defendants now acquitted under the insanity tests would be convicted under the mens-rea approach, are these results morally acceptable? Each of these issues is addressed in the following notes.

**2. Effect on Case Outcome.** In theory, it seems clear that some claims that now fit within the various insanity tests would not be exculpatory under the mens-rea approach. First, claims of volitional impairment would have no exculpatory significance outside the narrow confines of the voluntary-act doctrine. Second, claims of cognitive impairment would have exculpatory significance only (i) if the defendant were charged with an

[b] See, e.g., Joseph Goldstein and Jay Katz, "Abolish the Insanity Defense"—Why Not?, 72 Yale L.J. 853 (1963); Norval Morris, Psychiatry and the Dangerous Criminal, 41 So.Cal.L.Rev. 514 (1968). Morris reiterated and elaborated on his views in Madness and the Criminal Law (1982). See also, Christopher Slobogin, A End to Insanity: Recasting the Role of Mental Disability in Criminal Cases, 86 Va. L Rev 1199 (2000).

[c] The insanity defense was also abolished in Nevada in favor of the mens rea approach, but the Nevada Supreme Court ruled that the legislature could not constitutionally convict a defendant who, due to mental disease, was unable the appreciate the legal wrongfulness of his acts. Finger v. State, 27 P.3d 66 (Nev. 2001).

offense requiring a subjectively defined level of culpability, and (ii) if the impairment so distorted the defendant's perceptual capacities that the physical nature and consequences of the alleged criminal acts were not perceived or foreseen. Stephenson and Wetmore might be acquitted, but Joy Baker would not.

As a practical matter, however, it is possible that case outcomes would remain much the same as they are now. If the expert testimony is admitted on mens-rea issues, judges and juries may behave as many observers believe they do now—they may ignore the technical aspects of the legal formulae and decide, very simply, whether the defendant was crazy. If judges and juries do in fact respond to psychiatric evidence in this blunt way, one might be led to expect, as Alan Dershowitz has asserted, Abolishing the Insanity Defense, 9 Crim.L.Bull. 434, 438–39 (1973), that "nothing much will change."

Empirical studies in the abolitionist states tend to support this prediction. A study in Utah showed that there were as many "mental disease/mens rea" acquittals (seven) during the two years following abolition as there had been "insanity" acquittals during the nine years preceding abolition. Moreover, the author concluded that the defendant's impaired mental functioning actually negated mens rea in only one of the seven mens rea acquittals.[d] A study of dispositions in seven Montana counties revealed a similar result, albeit by a different legal route. Unlike in Utah, Montana's abolitionist reform virtually eliminated acquittals based on mental disease: during the 3 ½ years before the change, insanity acquittals averaged about 14 per year; during the 6 ½ years following the change, there were only five acquittals altogether (and three of these occurred during the first year, when judges may have applied the pre-reform law). However, people who would have been acquitted on ground of insanity under the old law were *not* convicted under the new law:

> After the reform ... they were being found [incompetent to stand trial], their charges were dismissed or deferred, and they ended up being hospitalized in the same settings where NGRI cases had been sent. Faced with the loss of one avenue, the legal and mental health systems simply found another way to accomplish the same end. If a person's mental status was seen as sufficient to warrant reduced criminal responsibility, they were found [incompetent to stand trial] and committed to the same hospital and the same wards where they would have been confined if they had been found NGRI.[e]

**3.  Dispositional Considerations.** Concerns about the need for control of dangerous persons figure prominently in the controversies over commitment of persons acquitted by reason of insanity and the relationship between mental abnormality and mens rea. What are the dispositional implications of proposals to abolish the insanity defense in favor of a mens-

[d] Peter Heinbecker, Two Years' Experience under Utah's Mens Rea Insanity Law, 14 Bulletin of the American Academy of Psychiatry and Law 185 (1986).

[e] Henry Steadman et. al., Before and After Hinckley: Evaluating Insanity Defense Reform 136 (1993).

rea approach? Two separate issues should be considered: First, how would the abolitionists deal with mentally disordered defendants who would have been acquitted by reason of insanity but would now be convicted? Second, how would they deal with persons who are acquitted because they lack the mens rea for any form of criminal liability?

**(i) Sentencing the Mentally Disordered Offender.** Many proponents of abolition have argued that insanity tests mistakenly focus attention on backward-looking "moral guesses" about the person's blameworthiness at the time of the offense when the real issue is what ought to be done now to prevent further harm. Other abolitionists argue that considerations of responsibility are relevant but should be taken into account in mitigation of punishment rather than exculpation. Both views lead to the conclusion that evidence of mental abnormality should be taken fully into account at sentencing. Consider, in this connection, the relevant provisions of the Montana statute abolishing the insanity defense:

> Section 46–14–311. Consideration of mental disease or defect in sentencing. Whenever a defendant is convicted on a verdict or a plea of guilty and he claims that at the time of the commission of the offense . . . he was suffering from a mental disease or defect which rendered him unable to appreciate the criminality of his conduct or to conform his conduct to the requirements of law, the sentencing court shall consider any relevant evidence presented at the trial and shall require such additional evidence as it considers necessary for the determination of the issue including examination of the defendant and a report thereof. . . .

> Section 46–14–312. Sentence to be imposed. (1) If the court finds that the defendant at the time of the commission of the offense of which he was convicted did not suffer from a mental disease or defect as described in Section 46–14–311, it shall sentence him [pursuant to otherwise applicable sentencing provisions].

> (2) If the court finds that the defendant at the time of the commission of the offense suffered from a mental disease or defect as described in Section 46–14–311, any mandatory minimum sentence prescribed by law for the offense need not apply and the court shall sentence him to be committed to the custody of the director of the department of institutions to be placed in an appropriate institution for custody, care, and treatment for a definite period of time not to exceed the maximum term of imprisonment that could be imposed under Subsection (1). . . .

> (3) A defendant whose sentence has been imposed under Subsection (2) may petition the sentencing court for review of the sentence if the [responsible mental-health professional] certifies that the defendant has been cured of the mental disease or defect. The sentencing court may make any [otherwise authorized order] except that the length of confinement or supervision must be equal to that of the original sentence. The [responsible mental-health professional] shall review the defendant's status each year.

Section 46–14–313. Discharge of defendant from supervision. At the expiration of the period of commitment or period of treatment specified by the court under Section 46–14–312(2), the defendant must be discharged from custody and further supervision, subject only to the law regarding the civil commitment of persons suffering from serious mental illness.

How do the dispositional consequences of this scheme differ from those that would obtain if the insanity defense had not been "abolished"?[f]

**(ii) Disposition of Persons Lacking Mens Rea Due to Mental Disease.** One of the arguments against admitting evidence of mental abnormality whenever it is relevant to mens rea is that this could result in release of dangerous persons. The fear is that the procedures for civil commitment of the mentally ill afford inadequate social protection. Not surprisingly, proponents of the mens-rea alternative to the insanity defense usually provide for a separate commitment procedure for persons who lack mens rea due to mental disease. Thus, the same questions concerning the proper criteria for commitment of such persons that arise in a jurisdiction that admits evidence on mens rea in addition to the insanity defense would also have to be resolved under the mens-rea alternative to the defense.

Consider for example, the applicable Montana provisions.[g] After a person "is acquitted on the ground that due to a mental disease or defect he could not have a particular state of mind that is an essential element of the offense charged," the court is required to commit him to the mental-health department "for custody, care and treatment." The person is entitled to a hearing within 50 days to "determine his present mental condition and whether he may be discharged or released without danger to others." The burden of proof is placed on the defendant to prove "that he may be safely released." The person is committed indefinitely until a court finds that he "may be discharged or released on condition without danger to himself or others." Would this commitment scheme be acceptable if the subjects were persons acquitted by reason of insanity? Do they provide a more or less acceptable basis for committing persons, such as Stephenson or Wetmore, found to lack the mens rea required for criminal liability?

**4. Blameworthiness Considerations.** The proposals to abolish the insanity defense implicate fundamental moral concerns. The central question may be put as follows: To the extent that the mens-rea approach in fact would reduce the exculpatory significance of mental abnormality, would it require criminal conviction of "a class of persons who, on any

---

[f] Idaho and Utah have similar provisions. These schemes are unusual because they were adopted in lieu of an insanity defense. It should be recalled, however, that at least 12 states have *combined* a similar sentencing scheme with the insanity defense: in those states, a verdict of not guilty by reason of insanity leads to commitment while a "guilty but mentally ill" verdict leads to special sentencing procedures similar to those in Montana. See, e.g., Mich.Comp.Laws Ann. § 768.36.

[g] Mont.Rev.Stat.Ann. §§ 46–14–301, et seq. Unlike Montana, Idaho and Utah did not enact special dispositional procedures for mens-rea acquittees. In Idaho and Utah, these individuals are subject to the generally applicable civil commitment statutes.

common-sense notion of justice, are beyond blaming and ought not to be punished''?[h]

The proponents of the mens-rea approach respond that it would not. They argue that the only meaningful line between the blameless and the blameworthy is that represented by mens rea. Although they concede that responsibility may otherwise be diminished by mental disability, they argue that such factors should be taken into account in sentencing, together with other social and psychological information relevant to the offender's responsibility for his behavior. This argument was developed by Norval Morris in Psychiatry and the Dangerous Criminal, 41 So.Cal.L.Rev. 514, 520–21 (1968):*

> [T]he moral issue remains central—whether we should include as criminally responsible ... those whose freedom to choose between criminal and lawful behavior was curtailed by mental illness. It too often is overlooked that one group's exculpation from criminal responsibility confirms the inculpation of other groups. Why not permit the defense of dwelling in a Negro ghetto? Such a defense would not be morally indefensible. Adverse social and subcultural background is statistically *more* criminogenic than is psychosis; like insanity, it also severely circumscribes the freedom of choice which a non-deterministic criminal law ... attributes to accused persons. True, a defense of social adversity would politically be intolerable; but that does not vitiate the analogy for my purposes. [It will be argued] that insanity destroys, undermines, diminishes man's capacity to reject what is wrong and to adhere to what is right. So does the ghetto—more so. But surely, [it will be replied,] I would not have us punish the sick. Indeed I would, if [society insists] on punishing the grossly deprived. To the extent that criminal sanctions serve punitive purposes, I fail to see the difference between these two defenses. To the extent that they serve rehabilitative, treatment, and curative purposes I fail to see the need for the difference.
>
> ... It seems clear that there *are* different degrees of moral turpitude in criminal conduct and that the mental health or illness of an actor is relevant to an assessment of that degree—as are many other factors in a crime's social setting and historical antecedents. This does not mean, however, that we are obliged to quantify these pressures for purposes of a moral assessment ... leading to conclusions as to criminal responsibility.
>
> In a few cases moral non-responsibility is so clear that it would be purposeless to invoke the criminal process. Accident, in its purest and least subconscious, accident-prone form, is a situation where there is little utility in invoking the criminal process. The same is true where a person did not know what he was doing

[h] Sanford Kadish, The Decline of Innocence, 26 Camb.L.J. 273, 283 (1968).

* The excerpts below are reprinted with the permission of the author and the Southern California Law Review.

at the time of the alleged crime. But in these situations there is no need for [responsibility] rules, because they clearly fall within general criminal law exculpatory rules. The actor simply lacks the mens rea of the crime. It thus seems to me that, within the area of criminal responsibility and psychological disturbance, all that we need is already achieved with existing, long-established rules of intent and crime; I would allow either sane or insane mens rea to suffice for guilt.

Sanford Kadish has responded, in The Decline of Innocence, 26 Camb.L.J. 273, 284 (1968),* as follows:

> [Morris argues] that we convict and punish persons daily whose ability to conform is impaired by a variety of circumstances—by youthful neglect, by parental inadequacy, by the social and psychical deprivations of growing up in a grossly underprivileged minority subculture, or by countless other contingencies of life. This is perfectly true, but I fail to see that it supports eliminating the insanity defence. First, the argument logically is an argument for extension of the defence of lack of responsibility, not for its abolition. It is never a reason for adding to injustice that we are already guilty of some. Second, confining the defence to patent and extreme cases of irresponsibility is not a whimsical irrationality. There may well be an injustice in it, but it rests upon the practical concern to avoid vitiating the deterrent impact of the criminal law upon those who are more or less susceptible to its influences.... We may accept as a necessary evil—necessary, that is, given our commitment to a punishment system—the criminal conviction of persons whose ability to conform is somewhat impaired and still protest that it is unacceptable for a society to fail to make a distinction for those who are utterly and obviously beyond the reach of the law.

It is noteworthy that Morris and Kadish join issue most clearly on whether a qualitative line can be drawn through claims of volitional impairment. Does agreement with Morris on this issue necessarily entail abolition of the cognitive prong of the insanity defense as well?

The exchange between Morris and Kadish also highlights another dimension of the controversy. Morris argues that persons who are supposedly held blameless on grounds of insanity in fact are punished under the present system of commitment:

> [It is said that] the criminal justice system is a ... stigmatizing ... system which should not be used against the mentally ill. They are mad not bad, sick not wicked; it is important that we should not misclassify them.
>
> The rebuttal to this defense of the [insanity defense] is the fact of "double stigmatization." ... Prison authorities regard their

---

* The excerpts below are reprinted with the permission of the author and the Cambridge University Press.

inmates in the facilities for the psychologically disturbed as both criminal and insane, bad and mad; mental hospital authorities regard their inmates who have been convicted—or only arrested and charged with crime—as both insane and criminal, mad and bad. . . .

[T]he defense of insanity is neither essential to the morality of punishment nor effective at present to reduce social stigma. Nor is it a necessary or effective principle around which to mobilize clinical resources for the rational treatment of the psychologically disturbed criminal actor.

Kadish responds as follows:

The criminal law as we know it today does associate a substantial condemnatory onus with conviction for a crime. So long as this is so a just and humane legal system has an obligation to make a distinction between those who are eligible for this condemnation and those who are not. It is true, as [Morris has] argued, that a person adjudicated not guilty but insane suffers a substantial social stigma. It is also true that this is hurtful and unfortunate, and indeed, unjust. But it results from the misinterpretation placed upon the person's conduct by people in the community. It is not, like the conviction of the irresponsible, the paradigmatic affront to the sense of justice in the law which consists in the deliberative act of convicting a morally innocent person of a crime, of imposing blame when there is no occasion for it.

Kadish and Morris disagree on where the line must be drawn to separate the blameless from the blameworthy. They also disagree on the meaning of "punishment." Who is right? Should the insanity defense be abolished?[h]

---

## SECTION 3: DISPOSITION OF MENTALLY DISORDERED OFFENDERS

### INTRODUCTORY NOTES ON THE DISPOSITION OF MENTALLY DISORDERED OFFENDERS

**1. Background.** The insanity defense is raised in fewer than one per cent of all felony cases, and is successful in only a small fraction of these.

---

[h] Morris reaffirmed his position in Madness and the Criminal Law (1982). His view was endorsed by the American Medical Association in 251 J.Am.Med.Ass'n 2967 (1984). The abolitionist position is criticized in Stephen Morse, Excusing the Crazy: The Insanity Defense Reconsidered, 58 So.Cal.L.Rev. 777 (1985); Donald H.J. Hermann, Book Review: Madness and the Criminal Law, 51 G.W.L.Rev. 329 (1983); Peter Arenella, Reflections on Current Proposals to Abolish or Reform the Insanity Defense, 8 Am.J.Leg. Med. 271 (1982).

Moreover, persons acquitted by reason of insanity (NGRI's) represent a very small proportion—less than 10 per cent—of those criminal defendants who eventually are placed in institutions for mentally disordered offenders. The great majority of persons sent to such institutions either have been committed after being found incompetent to stand trial or have been placed there after conviction to serve their sentences. The latter group is by far the largest.[a]

**2.  Commitment of Persons Incompetent to Stand Trial.** Every Anglo–American jurisdiction forbids trial of a person who, as a result of mental disease or mental retardation, is incapable of understanding the proceedings or of assisting in the defense. Because this long-standing practice is regarded as "fundamental to an adversary system of justice," the United States Supreme Court has held that a judge is constitutionally required to request a competency determination whenever there is a bona fide doubt about the defendant's competency to proceed. See Drope v. Missouri, 420 U.S. 162 (1975).

If a person is found incompetent to stand trial, the criminal proceedings are suspended while he or she is committed for treatment. In the past, the incompetency commitment mooted the issue of criminal responsibility in most cases because these defendants were held indefinitely and the criminal proceedings were rarely revived. However, in Jackson v. Indiana, 406 U.S. 715 (1972), the Supreme Court held that a defendant committed solely on account of incapacity to stand trial "cannot be held more than a reasonable period of time necessary to determine whether there is a substantial probability that he will attain that capacity in the foreseeable future." If there is no substantial probability that the defendant will be restored to competency within the foreseeable future, or if the treatment provided does not succeed in advancing the defendant toward that goal, the state must either institute civil commitment proceedings or release the defendant. Most states now require such a definitive determination within 18 months. The average length of hospitalization for incompetency commitments is about six months.

The incompetency commitment still functions, in practice, as a substitute for insanity adjudication in many cases involving misdemeanors or less serious felonies. Empirical studies have shown that most persons found incompetent to stand trial are not prosecuted for the criminal offenses that triggered their commitments. The charges against these defendants are routinely dropped when they are released. Only if the charges are especially serious are they likely to be prosecuted; in many of these cases, the insanity defense is then raised.

**3.  Special Sentencing Provisions.** In the vast majority of cases, the criminal law defers consideration of the offender's mental condition until sentencing. At that time, judges in most states are empowered to take into account the defendant's dangerousness and amenability to treatment,

---

[a] See generally John Monahan and Henry Steadman (eds.), Mentally Disordered Offenders: Perspectives from Law and Social Sciences (1981).

as well as any claim of diminished responsibility, in choosing the type or severity of sentence.[b] In some states, the court's customary sentencing options are augmented by special "mentally disordered offender" provisions that permit the defendant to be confined in special institutions and that may extend the otherwise authorized period of confinement.[c] In a recent development, at least 12 states now permit or require defendants found "guilty but mentally ill" to be placed in secure psychiatric hospitals, in lieu of ordinary correctional facilities, for some portion of the term of imprisonment.[d] Finally, it should also be noted that, even without a special verdict, most states permit mentally disordered prisoners to be transferred from prisons to psychiatric hospitals while they are serving their sentences.

**4. Commitment of Persons Acquitted by Reason of Insanity.** Historically, persons acquitted by reason of insanity have been subject to special procedures requiring commitment to institutions for the "criminally insane" until such time as they "recovered their sanity." Little systematic attention was given to the procedures or criteria governing these decisions, or to the conditions in the institutions for the criminally insane, until the early 1970s, when the traditional restrictive approach was challenged on both constitutional and therapeutic grounds. It was argued that the substantial disparity between "ordinary" civil commitment procedures and the NGRI[e] procedures was constitutionally unjustified. Moreover, the mental health community argued that advances in pharmacological treatment had reduced the therapeutic need for long-term hospitalization in most cases. In response to numerous judicial rulings on the subject, every state has revised its NGRI dispositional statute. Although the initial trend was to make the NGRI statutes less restrictive, and to bring them into congruence with ordinary "civil" commitment statutes, increased public concern about premature release of dangerous insanity acquittees led to a second generation of reforms in many states.

This flurry of legislative and judicial activity has left the current generation of NGRI dispositional statutes in considerable disarray.[f] Speaking generally, the statutes fall into three categories. In some states, insanity acquittees are subject to the same criteria and procedures governing civil commitment of the mentally ill. Typically, this means that the acquittee may not be committed unless the state proves, by clear and

---

[b] The significance of mental disorder in sentencing is discussed in Norval Morris, Madness and the Criminal Law (1982), and Stephen Morse, Justice, Mercy, and Craziness, 36 Stan.L.Rev. 1485 (1984).

[c] These statutes are discussed in Thomas L. Hafemeister and John Petrila, Treating the Mentally Disordered Offender: Society's Uncertain, Conflicted and Changing Views, 21 Fla.St.U. L. Rev. 729 (1994); and George Dix, Special Dispositional Alternatives for Abnormal Offender: Developments in the Law (1981).

[d] The "guilty but mentally ill" verdict is considered at the end of this Subsection.

[e] The term "NGRI" is commonly used to refer to defendants found not guilty by reason of insanity.

[f] The statutes are surveyed and discussed in Jan Brakel, After the Verdict: Dispositional Decisions Regarding Criminal Defendants Acquitted by Reason of Insanity, 37 DePaul L. Rev. 181 (1988).

convincing evidence, that he or she is mentally ill and dangerous. The period of commitment usually does not exceed 180 days. In a second group of states, the procedures, though similar to those governing civil commitment, vary in a few significant respects. For example, while a civilly committed patient may be hospitalized for emergency evaluation for only a short period—up to one week, perhaps—NGRI's may be committed for evaluation for up to 90 days. In addition, whereas a civilly committed patient is entitled to be discharged without judicial approval whenever the medical staff determines that hospitalization is no longer necessary, statutes governing insanity acquittees typically require a judicial order authorizing discharge. Finally, in a third group of states, the procedures differ substantially from those governing civil commitment. Typically, the statutes provide for automatic, indefinite commitment of the insanity acquittee and place the burden on the acquittee to prove that he or she is no longer committable. Even in these states, however, the acquittee is usually entitled to periodic administrative and judicial review of his or her status and the burden of proof may shift to the state if the hospital authorities recommend discharge. The disposition of insanity acquittees is addressed in Subsection A.

**5.  Dangerous Sex Offender Statutes**. Some states provide for indeterminate civil commitment of persons charged with or convicted of specified sex offenses who are found, in a separate proceeding, to be "sexual psychopaths" or "mentally disordered sex offenders." Courts typically have held that these statutes are non-penal in character, the legislative purpose being to treat the person's condition rather than to punish the person for the underlying offense. See, e.g. Allen v. Illinois, 478 U.S. 364 (1986). These commitments differ somewhat from insanity commitments because they are not predicated on a finding of non-responsibility. Under some sex offender commitment laws, the prosecutor has the authority to invoke the commitment process after arrest as an alternative to criminal prosecution. In other states, the defendant is convicted of the underlying offense and then committed as an alternative to an ordinary criminal sentence. In still other states, commitment is authorized after the offender has already served his sentence. These statutes are addressed in Subsection B.

———

## SUBSECTION A:  DISPOSITION OF INSANITY ACQUITTEES

INTRODUCTORY NOTES ON *JONES v. UNITED STATES*

**1.  Introduction.** Although NGRI dispositional statutes were first exposed to intensive constitutional scrutiny in the early 1970s, the Supreme Court did not address the subject until it decided Jones v. United States, 463 U.S. 354 (1983). Michael Jones was charged with attempting to steal a jacket from a department store on September 19, 1975. He pleaded insanity and the government did not contest the plea. After the court found him not guilty by reason of insanity, Jones was automatically committed to St. Elizabeth's hospital. Under the District of Columbia NGRI commitment statute, Jones was entitled 50 or more days thereafter to request a "release hearing" at which he bore the burden of proving that he was no longer mentally ill or dangerous. At Jones' first release hearing on May 25, 1976, the court found that he was not entitled to release. A second release hearing was held on February 22, 1977. Jones' counsel requested at this hearing that he be released or civilly committed, on the ground that his cumulative hospital confinement had exceeded the one-year maximum period of incarceration for the offense charged. The court denied the request and continued Jones' commitment under the NGRI statute. The District of Columbia Court of Appeals affirmed, en banc, with three judges dissenting.

In a five-four decision, the Supreme Court affirmed. The Court addressed two questions: whether the District's automatic commitment procedure after an insanity acquittal violated the due process clause; and, if Jones' initial commitment was constitutional, whether he was entitled to be released or civilly committed upon expiration of the one-year maximum term prescribed for the offense of attempted petit larceny.

**2.  Automatic Commitment of Insanity Acquittees.** In the District of Columbia, as in most states, the defendant bears the burden of proving an insanity defense by a preponderance of the evidence. The question before the Court was whether the findings underlying Jones' insanity verdict established a constitutionally adequate basis for his commitment. Justice Powell, writing for the Court, said it did:

> [An insanity verdict] establishes two facts: (i) The defendant committed an act that constitutes a criminal offense, and (ii) he committed the act because of mental illness. Congress has determined that these findings constitute an adequate basis for hospitalizing the acquittee as a dangerous and mentally ill person.... We cannot say that it was unreasonable and therefore unconstitutional for Congress to make this determination.
>
> The fact that a person has been found, beyond a reasonable doubt, to have committed a criminal act certainly indicates dangerousness.... Indeed, the concrete evidence generally may be at least as persuasive as any predictions about dangerousness that might be made in a civil commitment proceeding....
>
> Nor can we say that it was unreasonable for Congress to determine that the insanity acquittal supports an inference of continuing mental illness. It comports with common sense to conclude that someone whose mental illness was sufficient to lead him to commit a criminal act is likely to remain ill and in need of treatment.... Because a hearing is provided within 50 days of the commitment, there is assurance that every acquittee has a prompt opportunity to obtain release if he has recovered....

We hold that when a criminal defendant establishes by a preponderance of the evidence that he is not guilty of a crime by reason of insanity, the Constitution permits the government, on the basis of the insanity judgment, to confine him to a mental institution until such time as he has regained his sanity or is no longer a danger to himself or society. This holding accords with the widely and reasonably held view that insanity acquittees constitute a special class that should be treated differently from other candidates for commitment. . . .

Justice Brennan's dissenting opinion concluded that the insanity verdict did not provide "a constitutionally adequate basis for involuntary, indefinite commitment" and that the government should be required to prove the commitment criteria, in a post-verdict hearing, by clear and convincing evidence as it is required to do in other cases of involuntary psychiatric hospitalization under Addington v. Texas, 441 U.S. 418 (1979).

Even if a state may presume that an insanity acquittee continues to be mentally ill and dangerous, shifting the burden to the acquittee to prove eligibility for release, how long may this presumption remain in force? Indefinitely? Should the state be required at some point to prove that the acquittee continues to be mentally ill and dangerous? How does this question relate to the criteria for commitment and release? How does it relate to the second issue raised in *Jones*?

**3. Commitment and Proportionality.** The Supreme Court also addressed Jones' contention "that an acquittee's hypothetical maximum sentence provides the conditional limit for his commitment." He argued that a comparison of the NGRI and civil-commitment procedures demonstrated that an NGRI commitment is inescapably based on "punitive" considerations and that, accordingly, the justification for the special procedures lapses after expiration of the maximum sentence authorized for the offense that triggered the commitment. This contention had been accepted by three judges on the District of Columbia Court of Appeals. They reasoned:

[NGRI] acquittees are not confined to mental institutions for medical reasons alone. They are confined there in part because society is unwilling to allow those who have committed crimes to escape without paying for their crimes. The intent of the statute is partially punitive, and thus the [stricter procedures governing commitment and release of NGRI's] reflect this added burden on the defendant. Because of this punitive purpose, the maximum statutory period of confinement becomes relevant, for at that point society no longer has a valid interest in continued confinement on the basis of a shortcut procedure. . . . Society's right to punish Michael Jones for his first offense, a misdemeanor—[attempting to steal] a coat—has long since expired. . . . Michael Jones should be released unless civilly committed.

The Supreme Court rejected this analysis. Writing for the majority, Justice Powell explained:

A particular sentence of incarceration is chosen to reflect society's view of the proper response to commission of a particular criminal offense, based on a variety of considerations such as retribution, deterrence, and rehabilitation. The state may punish a person convicted of a crime even if satisfied that he is unlikely to commit further crimes.

Different considerations underlie commitment of an insanity acquittee. As he was not convicted, he may not be punished. His confinement rests on his continuing illness and dangerousness. Thus, under the District of Columbia statute, no matter how serious the act committed by the acquittee, he may be released within 50 days of his acquittal if he has recovered. In contrast, one who committed a less serious act may be confined for a longer period if he remains ill and dangerous. There simply is no necessary correlation between severity of the offense and length of time necessary for recovery. The length of the acquittee's hypothetical criminal sentence therefore is irrelevant to the purposes of his commitment.

In dissent, Justice Brennan argued that since Jones' commitability had not been proved by clear and convincing evidence, he could not be held beyond the maximum sentence for attempted petit larceny. Justice Brennan did appear to concede, however, that indefinite hospitalization would be permissible if the commitment were predicated upon constitutionally adequate proof.

Did Justice Powell accurately characterize the underlying purpose of NGRI commitment? Is it so clear that an NGRI commitment does not have a "partially punitive" purpose, as claimed by the dissenting judges on the Court of Appeals? Does it have a punitive effect? Assuming that the justifying purpose is therapeutic restraint rather than punishment for an offense, does it follow that the seriousness of the triggering offense should be irrelevant in determining the length of an NGRI commitment? In determining the criteria and procedures governing release? The Supreme Court addressed some of the these questions in Foucha v. Louisiana, 504 U.S. 71 (1992), the next main case.

———

## Foucha v. Louisiana

Supreme Court of the United States, 1992.
504 U.S. 71.

■ JUSTICE WHITE delivered the opinion of the Court, except as to Part III.

When a defendant in a criminal case pending in Louisiana is found not guilty by reason of insanity, he is committed to a psychiatric hospital unless he proves that he is not dangerous. This is so whether or not he is then insane. After commitment, if the acquittee or the superintendent begins release proceedings, a review panel at the hospital makes a written report on the patient's mental condition and whether he can be released without danger to himself or others. If release is recommended, the court must hold a hearing to determine dangerousness; the acquittee has the burden of proving that he is not dangerous. If found to be dangerous, the acquittee may be returned to the mental institution whether or not he is then mentally ill. Petitioner contends that this scheme denies him due process and equal protection because it allows a person acquitted by reason of insanity to be committed to a mental institution until he is able to demonstrate that he is not dangerous to himself and others, even though he does not suffer from any mental illness.

## I

Petitioner Terry Foucha was charged by Louisiana authorities with aggravated burglary and illegal discharge of a firearm. Two medical doctors were appointed to conduct a pretrial examination of Foucha. The doctors initially reported, and the trial court initially found, that Foucha lacked mental capacity to proceed, but four months later the trial court found Foucha competent to stand trial. The doctors reported that Foucha was unable to distinguish right from wrong and was insane at the time of the offense.[1] On October 12, 1984, the trial court ruled that Foucha was not guilty by reason of insanity, finding that he "is unable to appreciate the usual, natural and probable consequences of his acts; that he is unable to distinguish right from wrong; that he is a menace to himself and others; and that he was insane at the time of the commission of the above crimes and that he is presently insane." He was committed to the East Feliciana Forensic Facility until such time as doctors recommend that he be released, and until further order of the court. In 1988, the superintendent of Feliciana recommended that Foucha be discharged or released. A three-member panel was convened at the institution to determine Foucha's current condition and whether he could be released or placed on probation without being a danger to others or himself. On March 21, 1988, the panel reported that there had been no evidence of mental illness since admission and recommended that Foucha be conditionally discharged.[2] The trial judge appointed a two-member sanity commission made up of the same two doctors who had conducted the pretrial examination. Their written report stated that Foucha "is presently in remission from mental illness [but] [w]e cannot certify that he would not constitute a menace to himself or others if released." One of the doctors testified at a hearing that upon commitment

---

[1] Louisiana law provides: "If the circumstances indicate that because of a mental disease or mental defect the offender was incapable of distinguishing between right and wrong with reference to the conduct in question, the offender shall be exempt from criminal responsibility." La.Rev.Stat.Ann. § 14:14 (West 1986)....

[2] The panel unanimously recommended that petitioner be conditionally discharged with recommendations that he (1) be placed on probation; (2) remain free from intoxicating and mind-altering substances; (3) attend a substance abuse clinic on a regular basis; (4) submit to regular and random urine drug screening; and (5) be actively employed or seeking employment. Although the panel recited that it was charged with determining dangerousness, its report did not expressly make a finding in that regard.

Foucha probably suffered from a drug-induced psychosis but that he had recovered from that temporary condition; that he evidenced no signs of psychosis or neurosis and was in "good shape" mentally; that he has, however, an antisocial personality, a condition that is not a mental disease and that is untreatable. The doctor also testified that Foucha had been involved in several altercations at Feliciana and that he, the doctor, would not "feel comfortable in certifying that [Foucha] would not be a danger to himself or to other people."

After it was stipulated that the other doctor, if he were present, would give essentially the same testimony, the court ruled that Foucha was dangerous to himself and others and ordered him returned to the mental institution. The court of appeals refused supervisory writs, and the state supreme court affirmed, holding that Foucha had not carried the burden placed upon him by statute to prove that he was not dangerous, that our decision in Jones v. United States, 463 U.S. 354 (1983), did not require Foucha's release, and that neither the due process clause nor the equal protection clause was violated by the statutory provision permitting confinement of an insanity acquittee based on dangerousness alone.

Because the case presents an important issue and was decided by the court below in a manner arguably at odds with prior decisions of this Court, we granted certiorari.

## II

Addington v. Texas, 441 U.S. 418 (1979), held that to commit an individual to a mental institution in a civil proceeding, the state is required by the due process clause to prove by clear and convincing evidence the two statutory preconditions to commitment: that the person sought to be committed is mentally ill and that he requires hospitalization for his own welfare and protection of others. Proof beyond reasonable doubt was not required, but proof by preponderance of the evidence fell short of satisfying due process.[3]

When a person charged with having committed a crime is found not guilty by reason of insanity, however, a state may commit that person without satisfying the *Addington* burden with respect to mental illness and

---

[3] Justice Thomas in dissent complains that Foucha should not be released based on psychiatric opinion that he is not mentally ill because such opinion is not sufficiently precise—because psychiatry is not an exact science and psychiatrists widely disagree on what constitutes a mental illness. That may be true, but such opinion is reliable enough to permit the courts to base civil commitments on clear and convincing medical evidence that a person is mentally ill and dangerous and to base release decisions on qualified testimony that the committee is no longer mentally ill or dangerous. It is also reliable enough for the state not to punish a person who by a preponderance of the evidence is found to have been insane at the time he committed a criminal act, to say nothing of not trying a person who is at the time found incompetent to understand the proceedings. And more to the point, medical predictions of dangerousness seem to be reliable enough for the dissent to permit the state to continue to hold Foucha in a mental institution, even where the psychiatrist would say no more than that he would hesitate to certify that Foucha would not be dangerous to himself or others.

dangerousness. Such a verdict, we observed in *Jones*, "establishes two facts: (i) the defendant committed an act that constitutes a criminal offense, and (ii) he committed the act because of mental illness," id., 463 U.S., at 363, an illness that the defendant adequately proved in this context by a preponderance of the evidence. From these two facts, it could be properly inferred that at the time of the verdict, the defendant was still mentally ill and dangerous and hence could be committed.

We held, however, that "(t)he committed acquittee is entitled to release when he has recovered his sanity or is no longer dangerous," id., at 368; i.e. the acquittee may be held as long as he is both mentally ill and dangerous, but no longer. We relied on O'Connor v. Donaldson, 422 U.S. 563 (1975), which held as a matter of due process that it was unconstitutional for a state to continue to confine a harmless, mentally ill person. Even if the initial commitment was permissible, "it could not constitutionally continue after that basis no longer existed." Id., at 575, In the summary of our holdings in our opinion we stated that "the Constitution permits the government, on the basis of the insanity judgment, to confine him to a mental institution until such time as he has regained his sanity or is no longer a danger to himself or society." Jones, 463 U.S., at 368, 370. The court below was in error in characterizing the above language from *Jones* as merely an interpretation of the pertinent statutory law in the District of Columbia and as having no constitutional significance. In this case, Louisiana does not contend that Foucha was mentally ill at the time of the trial court's hearing. Thus, the basis for holding Foucha in a psychiatric facility as an insanity acquittee has disappeared, and the state is no longer entitled to hold him on that basis. . . .

A state, pursuant to its police power, may of course imprison convicted criminals for the purposes of deterrence and retribution. . . . Here, the state has no such punitive interest. As Foucha was not convicted, he may not be punished. Jones, supra, 463 U.S., at 369. Here, Louisiana has by reason of his acquittal exempted Foucha from criminal responsibility as La.Rev.Stat. Ann. § 14:14 (West 1986) requires. See n. 1, supra.

The state may also confine a mentally ill person if it shows "by clear and convincing evidence that the individual is mentally ill and dangerous," Jones, 463 U.S., at 362. Here, the state has not carried that burden; indeed, the state does not claim that Foucha is now mentally ill.

We have also held that in certain narrow circumstances persons who pose a danger to others or to the community may be subject to limited confinement and it is on these cases, particularly United States v. Salerno, 481 U.S. 739 (1987), that the state relies in this case.

*Salerno*, unlike this case, involved pretrial detention. We observed in *Salerno* that the "government's interest in preventing crime by arrestees is both legitimate and compelling," id., 481 U.S., at 749, and that the statute involved there was a constitutional implementation of that interest. The statute carefully limited the circumstances under which detention could be sought to those involving the most serious of crimes (crimes of violence, offenses punishable by life imprisonment or death, serious drug offenses, or certain repeat offenders), and was narrowly focused on a particularly acute problem in which the government interests are overwhelming. In addition to first demonstrating probable cause, the government was required, in a "full-blown adversary hearing," to convince a neutral decisionmaker by clear and convincing evidence that no conditions of release can reasonably assure the safety of the community or any person, i.e., that the "arrestee presents an identified and articulable threat to an individual or the community." Furthermore, the duration of confinement under the act was strictly limited. The arrestee was entitled to a prompt detention hearing and the maximum length of pretrial detention was limited by the "stringent time limitations of the Speedy Trial Act." If the arrestee were convicted, he would be confined as a criminal proved guilty; if he were acquitted, he would go free. Moreover, the act required that detainees be housed, to the extent practicable, in a facility separate from persons awaiting or serving sentences or awaiting appeal.

*Salerno* does not save Louisiana's detention of insanity acquittees who are no longer mentally ill. Unlike the sharply focused scheme at issue in *Salerno,* the Louisiana scheme of confinement is not carefully limited. Under the state statute, Foucha is not now entitled to an adversary hearing at which the state must prove by clear and convincing evidence that he is demonstrably dangerous to the community. Indeed, the state need prove nothing to justify continued detention, for the statute places the burden on the detainee to prove that he is not dangerous. At the hearing which ended with Foucha's recommittal, no doctor or any other person testified positively that in his opinion Foucha would be a danger to the community, let alone gave the basis for such an opinion. There was only a description of Foucha's behavior at Feliciana and his antisocial personality, along with a refusal to certify that he would not be dangerous. When directly asked whether Foucha would be dangerous, Dr. Ritter said only "I don't think I would feel comfortable in certifying that he would not be a danger to himself or to other people." This, under the Louisiana statute, was enough to defeat Foucha's interest in physical liberty. It is not enough to defeat Foucha's liberty interest under the constitution in being freed from indefinite confinement in a mental facility.

Furthermore, if Foucha committed criminal acts while at Feliciana, such as assault, the state does not explain why its interest would not be vindicated by the ordinary criminal processes involving charge and conviction, the use of enhanced sentences for recidivists, and other permissible ways of dealing with patterns of criminal conduct. These are the normal means of dealing with persistent criminal conduct. Had they been employed against Foucha when he assaulted other inmates, there is little doubt that if then sane he could have been convicted and incarcerated in the usual way.

It was emphasized in *Salerno* that the detention we found constitutionally permissible was strictly limited in duration. 481 U.S., at 747. Here, in contrast, the state asserts that because Foucha once committed a criminal act and now has an antisocial personality that sometimes leads to aggressive conduct, a disorder for which there is no effective treatment, he may be held indefinitely. This rationale would permit the state to hold indefinitely any other insanity acquittee not mentally ill who could be shown to have a personality disorder that may lead to criminal conduct. The same would be true of any convicted criminal, even though he has completed his prison term. It would also be only a step away from substituting confinements for dangerousness for our present system which, with only narrow exceptions and aside from permissible confinements for mental illness, incarcerates only those who are proved beyond reasonable doubt to have violated a criminal law.

"In our society liberty is the norm, and detention prior to trial or without trial is the carefully limited exception." United States v. Salerno, supra, 481 U.S., at 755. The narrowly focused pretrial detention of arrestees permitted by the Bail Reform Act was found to be one of those carefully limited exceptions permitted by the due process clause. We decline to take a similar view of a law like Louisiana's, which permits the indefinite detention of insanity acquittees who are not mentally ill but who do not prove they would not be dangerous to others.[6]

## III

It should be apparent from what has been said earlier in this opinion that the Louisiana statute also discriminates against Foucha in violation of the equal protection clause of the fourteenth amendment. *Jones* established that insanity acquittees may be treated differently in some respects from those persons subject to civil commitment, but Foucha, who is not now thought to be insane, can no longer be so classified. The state nonetheless insists on holding him indefinitely because he at one time committed a criminal act and does not now prove he is not dangerous. Louisiana law, however, does not provide for similar confinement for other classes of persons who have committed criminal acts and who cannot later prove they would not be dangerous. Criminals who have completed their prison terms, or are about to do so, are an obvious and large category of such persons. Many of them will likely suffer from the same sort of personality disorder that Foucha exhibits. However, state law does not allow for their continu-

---

[6] Justice Thomas' dissent firmly embraces the view that the state may indefinitely hold an insanity acquittee who is found by a court to have been cured of his mental illness and who is unable to prove that he would not be dangerous. This would be so even though, as in this case, the court's finding of dangerousness is based solely on the detainee's antisocial personality that apparently has caused him to engage in altercations from time to time. The dissent, however, does not challenge the holding of our cases that a convicted criminal may not be held as a mentally ill person without following the requirements for civil commitment, which would not permit further detention based on dangerousness alone. Yet it is surely strange to release sane but very likely dangerous persons who have committed a crime knowing precisely what they were doing but continue to hold indefinitely an insanity detainee who committed a criminal act at a time when, as found by a court, he did not know right from wrong. The dissent's rationale for continuing to hold the insanity acquittee would surely justify treating the convicted felon in the same way, and if put to it, it appears that the dissent would permit it. But as indicated in the text, this is not consistent with our present system of justice....

ing confinement based merely on dangerousness. Instead, the state controls the behavior of these similarly situated citizens by relying on other means, such as punishment, deterrence, and supervised release. Freedom from physical restraint being a fundamental right, the state must have a particularly convincing reason, which it has not put forward, for such discrimination against insanity acquittees who are no longer mentally ill.

Furthermore, in civil commitment proceedings the state must establish the grounds of insanity and dangerousness permitting confinement by clear and convincing evidence. Addington, 441 U.S., at 425–433. Similarly, the state must establish insanity and dangerousness by clear and convincing evidence in order to confine an insane convict beyond his criminal sentence, when the basis for his original confinement no longer exists. However, the state now claims that it may continue to confine Foucha, who is not now considered to be mentally ill, solely because he is deemed dangerous, but without assuming the burden of proving even this ground for confinement by clear and convincing evidence. The court below gave no convincing reason why the procedural safeguards against unwarranted confinement which are guaranteed to insane persons and those who have been convicted may be denied to a sane acquittee, and the state has done no better in this Court.

For the foregoing reasons the judgment of the Louisiana Supreme Court is reversed.

So ordered.

■ JUSTICE O'CONNOR, concurring in part and concurring in the judgment.

Louisiana asserts that it may indefinitely confine Terry Foucha in a mental facility because, although not mentally ill, he might be dangerous to himself or to others if released. For the reasons given in Part II of the Court's opinion, this contention should be rejected. I write separately, however, to emphasize that the Court's opinion addresses only the specific statutory scheme before us, which broadly permits indefinite confinement of sane insanity acquittees in psychiatric facilities. This case does not require us to pass judgment on more narrowly drawn laws that provide for detention of insanity acquittees, or on statutes that provide for punishment of persons who commit crimes while mentally ill.

I do not understand the Court to hold that Louisiana may never confine dangerous insanity acquittees after they regain mental health. Under Louisiana law, defendants who carry the burden of proving insanity by a preponderance of the evidence will "escape punishment," but this affirmative defense becomes relevant only after the prosecution establishes beyond a reasonable doubt that the defendant committed criminal acts with the required level of criminal intent. Although insanity acquittees may not be incarcerated as criminals or penalized for asserting the insanity defense, see Jones v. United States, 463 U.S. 354 (1983), this finding of criminal conduct sets them apart from ordinary citizens.

We noted in *Jones* that a judicial determination of criminal conduct provides "concrete evidence" of dangerousness. Id., at 364. By contrast,

" '[t]he only certain thing that can be said about the present state of knowledge and therapy regarding mental disease is that science has not reached finality of judgment....' " Id., at 365, n. 13. Given this uncertainty, "courts should pay particular deference to reasonable legislative judgments" about the relationship between dangerous behavior and mental illness. Louisiana evidently has determined that the inference of dangerousness drawn from a verdict of not guilty by reason of insanity continues even after a clinical finding of sanity, and that judgment merits judicial deference.

It might therefore be permissible for Louisiana to confine an insanity acquittee who has regained sanity if, unlike the situation in this case, the nature and duration of detention were tailored to reflect pressing public safety concerns related to the acquittee's continuing dangerousness. Although the dissenters apparently disagree, I think it clear that acquittees could not be confined as mental patients absent some medical justification for doing so; in such a case the necessary connection between the nature and purposes of confinement would be absent. Nor would it be permissible to treat all acquittees alike, without regard for their particular crimes. For example, the strong interest in liberty of a person acquitted by reason of insanity but later found sane might well outweigh the governmental interest in detention where the only evidence of dangerousness is that the acquittee committed a non-violent or relatively minor crime. Cf. Salerno, supra, 481 U.S., at 750 (interest in pretrial detention is "overwhelming" where only individuals arrested for "a specific category of extremely serious offenses" are detained and "Congress specifically found that these individuals are far more likely to be responsible for dangerous acts in the community after arrest"). Equal protection principles may set additional limits on the confinement of sane but dangerous acquittees. Although I think it unnecessary to reach equal protection issues on the facts before us, the permissibility of holding an acquittee who is not mentally ill longer than a person convicted of the same crimes could be imprisoned is open to serious question.

The second point to be made about the Court's holding is that it places no new restriction on the states' freedom to determine whether and to what extent mental illness should excuse criminal behavior. The Court does not indicate that states must make the insanity defense available. See Idaho Code § 18–207(a) (1987) (mental condition not a defense to criminal charges); Mont.Code Ann. § 46–14–102 (1991) (evidence of mental illness admissible to prove absence of state of mind that is an element of the offense). It likewise casts no doubt on laws providing for prison terms after verdicts of "guilty but mentally ill." See, e.g., Del.Code Ann., Tit. 11, § 408(b) (1987); Ill.Rev.Stat., ch. 38, P 1005–2–6 (1989); Ind.Code § 35–36–2–5 (Supp.1991). If a state concludes that mental illness is best considered in the context of criminal sentencing, the holding of this case erects no bar to implementing that judgment.

Finally, it should be noted that the great majority of states have adopted policies consistent with the Court's holding....

Today's holding follows directly from our precedents and leaves the states appropriate latitude to care for insanity acquittees in a way consistent with public welfare. Accordingly, I concur in Parts I and II of the Court's opinion and in the judgment of the Court.

■ JUSTICE KENNEDY, with whom CHIEF JUSTICE REHNQUIST joins, dissenting. . . .

This is a criminal case. It began one day when petitioner, brandishing a .357 revolver, entered the home of a married couple, intending to steal. He chased them out of their home and fired on police officers who confronted him as he fled. Petitioner was apprehended and charged with aggravated burglary and the illegal use of a weapon. . . . There is no question that petitioner committed the criminal acts charged. Petitioner's response was to deny criminal responsibility based on his mental illness when he committed the acts. He contended his mental illness prevented him from distinguishing between right and wrong with regard to the conduct in question.

Mental illness may bear upon criminal responsibility, as a general rule, in either of two ways: First, it may preclude the formation of *mens rea*, if the disturbance is so profound that it prevents the defendant from forming the requisite intent as defined by state law; second, it may support an affirmative plea of legal insanity. Depending on the content of state law, the first possibility may implicate the state's initial burden, under In re Winship, 397 U.S. 358 (1970), to prove every element of the offense beyond a reasonable doubt, while the second possibility does not. Patterson v. New York, 432 U.S. 197 (1977); Leland v. Oregon, 343 U.S. 790 (1952).

The power of the states to determine the existence of criminal insanity following the establishment of the underlying offense is well established. In *Leland v. Oregon*, we upheld a state law that required the defendant to prove insanity beyond a reasonable doubt, observing that this burden had no effect on the state's initial burden to prove every element of the underlying criminal offense. . . .

Louisiana law follows the pattern in *Leland* with clarity and precision. [T]he petitioner entered a dual plea of not guilty and not guilty by reason of insanity. The dual plea, which the majority does not discuss or even mention, ensures that the *Winship* burden remains on the state prove all the elements of the crime. . . .

Compliance with the standard of proof beyond a reasonable doubt is the defining, central feature in criminal adjudication, unique to the criminal law. . . . We have often subjected to heightened due process scrutiny, with regard to both purpose and duration, deprivations of physical liberty imposed before a judgment is rendered under this standard. . . . The same heightened due process scrutiny does not obtain, though, once the state has met its burden of proof and obtained an adjudication. It is well settled that upon compliance with *In re Winship*, the state may incarcerate on any reasonable basis.

. . . A verdict of not guilty by reason of insanity is neither equivalent nor comparable to a verdict of not guilty standing alone. We would not allow a state to evade its burden of proof by replacing its criminal law with a civil system in which there is no presumption of innocence and the defendant has the burden of proof. Nor should we entertain the proposition that this case differs from a conviction of guilty because petitioner has been adjudged "not guilty by reason of insanity," rather than "guilty but insane." Petitioner has suggested no grounds on which to distinguish the liberty interests involved or procedural protections afforded as a consequence of the state's ultimate choice of nomenclature. The due process implications ought not to vary under these circumstances. This is a criminal case in which the state has complied with the rigorous demands of *In re Winship*. . . .

. . . Petitioner in *Jones* contended that *Addington* and *O'Connor* applied to criminal proceedings as well as civil, requiring the government to prove insanity and dangerousness by clear and convincing evidence before commitment. We rejected that contention. In *Jones* we distinguished criminal from civil commitment, holding that the due process clause permits automatic incarceration after a criminal adjudication and without further process. The majority today in effect overrules that holding. . . .

The majority's opinion is troubling at a further level, because it fails to recognize or account for profound differences between clinical insanity and state-law definitions of criminal insanity. It is by now well established that insanity as defined by the criminal law has no direct analog in medicine or science. . . . As provided by Louisiana law, and consistent with both federal criminal law and the law of a majority of the states, petitioner was found not guilty by reason of insanity under the traditional *M'Naghten* test. . . .

Because the *M'Naghten* test for insanity turns on a finding of criminal irresponsibility at the time of the offense, it is quite wrong to place reliance on the fact, as the majority does, that Louisiana does not contend that petitioner is now insane. This circumstance should come as no surprise, since petitioner was competent at the time of his plea, and indeed could not have entered a plea otherwise, see Drope v. Missouri, 420 U.S. 162 (1975). Present sanity would have relevance if petitioner had been committed as a consequence of civil proceedings, in which dangerous conduct in the past was used to predict similar conduct in the future. It has no relevance here, however. Petitioner has not been confined based on predictions about future behavior but rather for past criminal conduct. Unlike civil commitment proceedings, which attempt to divine the future from the past, in a criminal trial whose outcome turns on *M'Naghten*, findings of past insanity and past criminal conduct possess intrinsic and ultimate significance. . . .

The establishment of a criminal act and of insanity under the *M'Naghten* regime provides a legitimate basis for confinement. Although Louisiana has chosen not to punish insanity acquittees, the state has not surrendered its interest in incapacitative incarceration. . . . "[I]solation of the dangerous has always been considered an important function of the criminal law," Powell v. Texas, 392 U.S., at 539 (Black, J., concurring), and insanity acquittees are a special class of offenders proved dangerous beyond their own ability to comprehend. The wisdom of incarceration under these circumstances is demonstrated by its high level of acceptance. . . .

It remains to be seen whether the majority, by questioning the legitimacy of incapacitative incarceration, puts in doubt the confinement of persons other than insanity acquittees. Parole release provisions often place the burden of proof on the prisoner to prove his lack of dangerousness. . . . It is difficult for me to reconcile the rationale of incapacitative incarceration, which underlies these regimes, with the opinion of the majority, which discounts its legitimacy. . . .

I submit that today's decision is unwarranted and unwise. I share the Court's concerns about the risks inherent in requiring a committed person to prove what can often be imprecise, but as Justice Thomas observes in his dissent, this is not a case in which the period of confinement exceeds the gravity of the offense or in which there are reasons to believe the release proceedings are pointless or a sham. Petitioner has been incarcerated for less than one-third the statutory maximum for the offenses proved by the state. See La.Rev.Stat. Ann. §§ 14:60 (aggravated burglary) and 14:94 (illegal use of a weapon) (West 1986). In light of these facts, the majority's repeated reference to "indefinite detention," with apparent reference to the potential duration of confinement, and not its lack of a fixed end point, has no bearing on this case. It is also significant to observe that this is not a case in which the incarcerated subject has demonstrated his nondangerousness. Within the two months before his release hearing, petitioner had been sent to a maximum security section of the Feliciana Forensic Facility because of altercations with another patient. Further, there is evidence in the record which suggests that petitioner's initial claim of insanity may have been feigned. The medical panel that reviewed petitioner's request for release stated that "there is no evidence of mental illness," and indeed that there was "never any evidence of mental illness or disease since admission." In sum, it would be difficult to conceive of a less compelling situation for the imposition of sweeping new constitutional commands such as the majority imposes today.

Because the majority conflates the standards for civil and criminal commitment, treating this criminal case as though it were civil, it upsets a careful balance relied upon by the states, not only in determining the conditions for continuing confinement, but also in defining the defenses permitted for mental incapacity at the time of the crime in question. In my view, having adopted a traditional and well-accepted test for determining criminal insanity, and having complied with the rigorous demands of *In re Winship*, the state possesses the constitutional authority to incarcerate petitioner for the protection of society. I submit my respectful dissent.

■ JUSTICE THOMAS, with whom CHIEF JUSTICE REHNQUIST and JUSTICE SCALIA join, dissenting. . . .

The Court today attempts to circumvent Jones v. United States, 463 U.S. 354 (1983) by declaring that a state's interest in treating insanity acquittees differently from civil committees evaporates the instant an acquittee "becomes sane." I do not agree. As an initial matter, I believe that it is unwise, given our present understanding of the human mind, to suggest that a determination that a person has "regained sanity" is precise.... In this very case, the panel that evaluated Foucha in 1988 concluded that there was "never any evidence of mental illness or disease since admission," the trial court, of course, concluded that Foucha was "presently insane," at the time it accepted his plea and sent him to Feliciana.

The distinction between civil committees and insanity acquittees, after all, turns not on considerations of present sanity, but instead on the fact that the latter have "already unhappily manifested the reality of anti-social conduct...." While a state may renounce a punitive interest by offering an insanity defense, it does not follow that, once the acquittee's sanity is "restored," the state is required to ignore his criminal act, and to renounce all interest in protecting society from him.

Furthermore, the federal constitution does not require a state to "ignore the danger of 'calculated abuse of the insanity defense.'" A state that decides to offer its criminal defendants an insanity defense, which the defendant himself is given the choice of invoking, is surely allowed to attach to that defense certain consequences that prevent abuse. A state may reasonably decide that the integrity of an insanity-acquittal scheme requires the continued commitment of insanity acquittees who remain dangerous. Surely, the citizenry would not long tolerate the insanity defense if a serial killer who convinces a jury that he is not guilty by reason of insanity is returned to the streets immediately after trial by convincing a different factfinder that he is not in fact insane....

In its arguments before this Court, Louisiana chose to place primary reliance on our decision in United States v. Salerno, 481 U.S. 739 (1987) in which we upheld provisions of the Bail Reform Act of 1984 that allowed limited pretrial detention of criminal suspects. That case, as the Court notes, is readily distinguishable. Insanity acquittees, in sharp and obvious contrast to pretrial detainees, have had their day in court. Although they have not been convicted of crimes, neither have they been exonerated, as they would have been upon a determination of "not guilty" simpliciter. Insanity acquittees thus stand in a fundamentally different position from persons who have not been adjudicated to have committed criminal acts. That is what distinguishes this case (and what distinguished *Jones*) from *Salerno* and Jackson v. Indiana, 406 U.S. 715 (1972). In *Jackson*, as in *Salerno*, the state had not proven beyond a reasonable doubt that the accused had committed criminal acts or otherwise was dangerous. The Court disregards this critical distinction, and apparently deems applicable the same scrutiny to pretrial detainees as to persons determined in a judicial proceeding to have committed a criminal act.[16] ...

[16] The Court asserts that the principles set forth in this dissent necessarily apply not only to insanity acquittees, but also to con-victed prisoners. "The dissent's rationale for continuing to hold the insanity acquittee would surely justify treating the convicted

I respectfully dissent.

———

NOTES ON THE DISPOSITION OF PERSONS ACQUITTED BY
REASON OF INSANITY

**1.　Questions and Comments on *Foucha*.** *Foucha* presents many
interesting issues.[a] At the most general level, the Justices are delineating
the constitutional predicates for non-criminal confinement. Detention of
deportable aliens and quarantine of individuals with infectious diseases are
well-established cases. In *Salerno*, the Court upheld preventive definition of
dangerous defendants before trial. The Court's decisions in *Addington*,
*Jackson* and *Jones* pertain to the three usual variations of civil commitment of persons with mental illness—ordinary involuntary psychiatric
hospitalization, commitment of persons found incompetent to stand trial
and commitment of insanity acquittees. In *Foucha*, Justice White suggests
that the Louisiana statute, which dispenses with mental illness as a
predicate for civil commitment of insanity acquittees, is "only a step away
from substituting confinements for dangerousness for our present system"
of criminal punishment. Is he right?

*Foucha* also raises basic questions about the nature and meaning of the
insanity defense. Justice White, quoting *Jones*, says that "as Foucha was
convicted, he may not be punished." By contrast, Justice Kennedy argues
that the insanity verdict is equivalent to a criminal conviction, and that the
state may "incarcerate [insanity acquittees] on any reasonable basis."
Which view reflects a better understanding of the insanity defense?

Justices Kennedy and Thomas both suggest that Louisiana's statute
may have been designed in part to deter abuses of the insanity defense, and
Justice Kennedy even hints that Foucha's own insanity claim may have
been fabricated. Such an assessment of the facts strengthens the intuition
that Foucha himself should not be released, but does it provide an acceptable rationale for Louisiana's statutory scheme?

On another account of the facts, Foucha's insanity claim was predicated on a genuine drug-induced psychotic state which receded during the

felon in the same way, and, if put to it, it
appears that the dissent would permit it."
That is obviously not so. If Foucha had been
convicted of the crimes with which he was
charged and sentenced to the statutory maximum of 32 years in prison, the state would
not be entitled to extend his sentence at the
end of that period. To do so would obviously
violate the prohibition on ex post facto laws
set forth in Art. I, § 10, cl. 1. But Foucha was
not sentenced to incarceration for any definite period of time; to the contrary, he pleaded not guilty by reason of insanity and was
ordered institutionalized until he was able to

meet the conditions statutorily prescribed for
his release. To acknowledge, as I do, that it is
constitutionally permissible for a state to provide for the continued confinement of an
insanity acquittee who remains dangerous is
obviously quite different than to assert that
the state is allowed to confine anyone who is
dangerous for as long as it wishes.

[a] For analysis of *Foucha*, see James W.
Ellis, Limits on the State's Power to Confine
Dangerous Persons: Constitutional Implica-
tions of *Foucha v. Louisiana*, 15 U. of Puget
Sound L. Rev. 635 (1992).

months following the offense. Although one might have doubts about the moral basis for such insanity claim, it was apparently accepted under Louisiana law. Should the dispositional scheme for insanity acquittees be designed to prolong the hospitalization of acquittees whose mental disorders were drug-induced?

Consider finally the implications of *Foucha* for acquittees whose admittedly severe mental illnesses go into remission during hospitalization. This means that they no longer are experiencing the symptoms of the disorder, and they no longer are acutely mentally ill; from a purely clinical standpoint, they no longer need to be in the hospital. Does *Foucha* apply to these cases?

2. **Dangerousness**. As the constitutional issue was presented in *Foucha*, the Court assumes that Foucha's continued commitment was predicated on a finding of dangerousness. Note, however, that under the Louisiana statute, Foucha was not entitled to release, even on conditions, unless he could prove that he was no longer dangerous. Recall that the Feliciana psychiatrist said he would not "feel comfortable" certifying that Foucha would not be dangerous. Would you? How can an insanity acquittee prove that he will *not* be dangerous?

*Jones* held that the state is justified in presuming dangerousness based on proof of the criminal act. Does the criminal act retain its predictive value indefinitely? Should the state be required to reassume the burden of proof on the dangerousness issue at some point?

Predictive judgments of this sort are confounded by the lack of evidence about the acquittee's response to conditions outside the hospital. How should one balance the acquittee's interest in regaining freedom against the public's interest in avoiding premature release? One possibility is to provide trials of freedom with strict community supervision and expeditious rehospitalization in response to non-compliance. In recent years, a number of states have established administrative review boards to implement programs of conditional release. For an in-depth study of the operation of Oregon's "psychiatric security review board," see Joseph Bloom and Mary Williams, Management and Treatment of Insanity Acquittees: A Model for the 1990's (1994).

3. *State v. Randall.* Justice O'Connor's separate opinion in *Foucha* suggests that the Louisiana approach might have survived constitutional scrutiny if "the nature and duration of detention" had been more narrowly tailored to reflect "pressing public safety concerns." What does she have in mind? Consider in this connection the Wisconsin Supreme Court's decision in State v. Randall, 192 Wis.2d 800, 532 N.W.2d 94 (1995).

Alan Randall pleaded not guilty by reason of insanity to a variety of charges rising out of a 1976 incident in which he shot and killed two police officers and used their squad car to commit a burglary. He was found guilty, in the first stage of a bifurcated trial, of two counts of first-degree murder, one count of burglary, and one count of operating a motor vehicle without consent. In the second phase of the trial, the state entered into a stipulation agreeing that Randall was suffering from paranoid schizophrenia and that he was not guilty by reason of insanity of these offenses. Randall was then committed to a state psychiatric hospital. In January, 1990, Randall petitioned for release under Wisconsin's insanity commitment statute which authorizes discharge or conditional release "if the court is satisfied that [the acquittee] may be safely discharged or released without danger to himself or others."

At the hearing before a six-person jury, psychiatrists and mental health experts described Randall's treatment since his 1977 commitment and testified that he was no longer mentally ill. Other witnesses described his extensive experience with off-grounds privileges between 1981 until 1989 when the hospital terminated its off-grounds privilege policy. In 1986, for example, Randall "participated in numerous activities throughout Wisconsin on at least 200 different occasions." As a result of these activities, which included attendance at college and steady employment at a local business, he "functioned under normal conditions," outside the hospital for more than 1,300 hours during that year. Despite this evidence, the jury found that Randall could not be "safely discharged," and the court denied his petition for release.

In 1992, after the Supreme Court's decision in *Foucha*, Randall filed a petition seeking immediate release on the ground that Wisconsin's "dangerousness only" release criterion was unconstitutional. The Wisconsin Supreme Court held that Wisconsin's dispositional scheme was distinguishable from the Louisiana scheme struck down in *Foucha*:

> The inference of continuing dangerousness provides the basis for the acquittee's initial commitment to a mental health facility following the insanity acquittal. Under Wisconsin's statutory scheme, the acquittee, once committed, is subject to treatment programs specifically designed to treat both mental and behavioral disorders. Treatment designed to reduce those behavioral disorders which render the individual dangerous may continue even after clinical signs of mental illness are no longer apparent. Such treatment is necessary to realize the ultimate goal of safely returning the acquittee into the community. Because this state's mental health facilities provide such comprehensive treatment we cannot conclude that it is punitive to continue an acquittee's confinement based on dangerousness alone. Rather, we conclude that there is a reasonable relationship between the commitment and the purposes for which the individual is committed and, therefore, that insanity acquittees are treated in a manner consistent with the purposes of their commitment....

> Furthermore, unlike the Louisiana statutory scheme held unconstitutional in *Foucha*, we find that the Wisconsin scheme provides sufficient procedural safeguards to insure an acquittee's right to due process. Under the Louisiana statutory scheme, an insanity acquittee could be held in a mental institution for an indefinite and unlimited duration until the acquittee could prove,

by a preponderance of the evidence, that he or she was no longer dangerous. Under the Wisconsin procedure, the state, rather than the acquittee, bears the burden to prove by clear and convincing evidence that the commitment should continue because the individual is presently a danger to himself, herself or others. Moreover, commitment is not imposed for an indefinite period of time. [The] commitment may not exceed the maximum term of imprisonment which could have been imposed for the offenses charged.[a] Once the maximum period of the sentence which could have been imposed has elapsed, the court must order the discharge of the insanity acquittee subject to the state's right to commence civil commitment proceedings....

In a separate concurring opinion, Justice Abrahamson expressed doubts about whether the Wisconsin statute, as interpreted in *Randall*, is compatible with *Foucha*:

> [The statute] is silent about the relationship of mental illness, behavioral disability, medical justification, or treatment to the continued confinement of an acquittee based on dangerousness. The majority opinion appears to graft these requirements onto [the statute] because it concludes that such an interpretation ... is needed to render it constitutional. The majority is appropriately heeding a teaching of *Foucha*: 'Due process requires that the nature of commitment bear some reasonable relation to the purpose for which the individual is committed.'

> I cannot join the majority opinion, however, because I conclude that the majority's interpretation violates another teaching of *Foucha*.... *Foucha* rejected the notion that the state could confine an acquittee in a mental institution on the basis of a condition which is not a mental illness, would not have justified the insanity commitment and was not the basis of that commitment at trial. Thus a "behavioral disorder" (an important concept in the majority opinion but undefined) that renders the acquittee dangerous may be analogous to the antisocial personality condition in *Foucha*, which did not rise to the level of a mental illness or defect on which an insanity commitment could be based.

> I recognize that *Foucha* is a troublesome decision and the subject of conflicting interpretations by courts and commentators. The majority struggles to avoid the conclusion mandated by *Foucha*, that mental illness as well as dangerousness are necessary grounds to continue confinement. If I read the majority opinion correctly, the state can continue to confine an acquittee who is not mentally ill but is behaviorally disordered and dangerous if the state can treat the acquittee, but the state must release an

---

[a] Wisconsin law now limits the acquittee's confinement to two-thirds of the maximum sentence which could have been imposed.—[Footnote by eds.]

acquittee who is not mentally ill but is dangerous if no treatment is available at the institution.

Is the Wisconsin statute, as interpreted in Randall's case compatible with *Foucha*? Would it satisfy Justice O'Connor's concerns?

––––––––

## NOTE ON THE VERDICT OF GUILTY BUT MENTALLY ILL

At least 12 states have established a separate verdict of "guilty but mentally ill" (GBMI) as an optional verdict in cases in which the defendant pleads insanity.[a] The GBMI concept, as adopted in these states, should be distinguished from two other concepts to which this or similar terminology may refer. First, the GBMI verdict is available in conjunction with, rather than in lieu of, the verdict of "not guilty by reason of insanity"; this procedure should therefore be distinguished from proposals to abolish the insanity defense and to establish, in its stead, a special dispositional procedure for guilty but mentally ill defendants. Second, the consequence of a GBMI verdict is conviction and a criminal sentence; the procedure should therefore be distinguished from proposals to rename the insanity verdict ("guilty but insane" rather than "not guilty by reason of insanity") without altering its dispositional consequences—i.e., subjecting the defendant only to therapeutic restraint under a civil commitment statute.

Procedures under GBMI legislation vary significantly from state to state. However, the statutes typically provide that upon entry of the verdict, the trial judge must impose a criminal sentence. The defendant is then evaluated by correctional or mental health authorities for the purpose of determining his or her suitability for psychiatric treatment. If the evaluators conclude that psychiatric treatment is needed, the person is hospitalized and, upon discharge, is returned to prison to serve the remainder of the sentence. In effect, whether the prisoner will actually be placed in a mental health facility is typically a discretionary determination.

The GBMI verdict is predicated upon different findings in different states. Under most of the statutes, the dispositive finding is that the defendant was "mentally ill" (though not legally insane) at the time of the offense; the definition of "mental illness" is typically drawn from the state's civil commitment statute. In Michigan, for example, mental illness is defined as "a substantial disorder of thought or mood which significantly impairs judgment, behavior, capacity to recognize reality, or ability to cope with the ordinary demands of life."

––––––––

[a] For general commentary on the GBMI verdict, see Christopher Slobogin, The Guilty But Mentally Ill Verdict: An Idea Whose Time Should Not Have Come, 53 G.W.L.Rev. 494 (1985); Bradley D. McGraw, Diana Farthing–Capowich, and Ingo Keilitz, The Guilty But Mentally Ill Verdict & Current State of Knowledge, 30 Vill.L.Rev. 117 (1984); Ralph Slovenko, Commentaries on Psychiatry and Law: Guilty But Mentally Ill, 10 J.Amer.Acad.Psychiatry and L. 541 (1982).

In a few states, the required finding is linked to criteria of criminal responsibility. In Delaware, for example, the exclusive criterion of insanity is "lack of substantial capacity to appreciate wrongfulness," whereas the GBMI verdict can be based on volitional impairment (that the defendant suffered from a "psychiatric disorder" which "left [him] with insufficient will-power to choose whether he would do the act or refrain from doing it...."). In Alaska, the exclusive criterion of exculpation is that the defendant was "unable ... to appreciate the nature and quality of his conduct," whereas the criteria for the GBMI verdict are derived from the Model Penal Code insanity test.

The debate about GBMI legislation focuses in part on its dispositional consequences. Its proponents claim that it is designed to establish a procedure other than the NGRI verdict to facilitate psychiatric treatment of mentally disordered offenders who would otherwise be untreated. Critics respond that the procedure is misleading because it does not, in fact, assure treatment; further, they argue, a separate verdict is unnecessary to accomplish dispositional objectives because all states either operate psychiatric hospitals within the correctional system or have well-established procedures for transferring prisoners to secure mental health facilities. Finally, the critics say, a jury verdict based on evidence of past mental condition is an awkward device for triggering placement decisions based on the defendant's mental condition at the time of sentence.

As these observations suggest, the impact of the GBMI procedure on the sentencing and correctional process is ancillary to its effect on the adjudication of criminal responsibility. What is the intended effect of the optional verdict? Is it designed to subvert the insanity defense by offering juries a compromise verdict in cases in which an insanity acquittal would otherwise be proper? Or is it designed to establish a criterion of diminished responsibility to take into account psychological impairments that do not meet the criteria for insanity? Regardless of the legislative purpose, what is the likely effect of the GBMI procedure on the frequency of NGRI pleas and acquittals?[b]

---

## SUBSECTION B: CIVIL COMMITMENT OF DANGEROUS SEX OFFENDERS

### INTRODUCTORY NOTE ON CIVIL COMMITMENT OF DANGEROUS SEX OFFENDERS

As noted at the beginning of this Section, some states provide for indeterminate civil commitment of persons charged with or convicted of

[b] For empirical studies of the GBMI procedure, see Henry J. Steadman et al., Before and After Hinckley: Evaluating Insanity Defense Reform (1993); National Center for State Courts, The Guilty But Mentally Ill Verdict: An Empirical Study (1985); Gare A. Smith and James A. Hall, Evaluating Michigan's Guilty But Mentally Ill Verdict: An Empirical Study, 16 Mich.J.L.Reform 77 (1982).

specified sex offenses who are found, in a separate proceeding, to be "sexual psychopaths" or "mentally disordered sex offenders." Courts typically have held that these statutes are non-penal in character, the legislative purpose being to treat the person's condition rather than to punish the person for the underlying offense. See, e.g. Allen v. Illinois, 478 U.S. 364 (1986). These commitments differ somewhat from insanity commitments because they are not predicated on a finding of non-responsibility.

The first of these so-called sex psychopath laws was enacted in 1937 and by the mid-1960s about half of the states had enacted such legislation. However, in the wake of libertarian reforms of other types of civil commitment legislation and a deepening skepticism about the prospects for successful treatment of sex offenders, most states repealed their sex psychopath legislation in the 1970s and 80s.[c]

A new generation of sex offender legislation appeared in the 1990s. The first and most well-known example of this new trend was Washington's Sexually Violent Predator Law enacted in 1990.[d] Under the Washington statute, persons found to be "sexually violent predators" are subject to indeterminate commitment after they have completed serving the criminal sentence for their underlying offenses. The legislature explained the need for this approach in the preamble to the statute:

> In contrast to persons appropriate for [ordinary] civil commitment, sexually violent predators generally have antisocial personality features which are unamenable to existing mental illness treatment modalities and those features render them likely to engage in sexually violent behavior.... The legislature further finds that the prognosis for curing sexually violent offenders is poor [and] the treatment needs of this population are very long-term....

Under the statute, a "sexually violent predator" is defined as someone "who has been convicted of or charged with a crime of sexual violence and who suffers from a mental abnormality or personality disorder which makes the person likely to engage in predatory acts of sexual violence." Crimes of sexual violence include crimes not usually considered sex offenses if they are determined beyond a reasonable doubt to have been "sexually motivated." The term "personality disorder" is not defined by the statute, but the term "mental abnormality" is defined as "a congenital or acquired condition affecting the emotional or volitional capacity which predisposes the person to the commission of criminal sexual acts." "Predatory" acts are those directed at strangers or individuals groomed by the offender for the purpose of victimization.

[c] See generally, Samuel Brakel and James Cavanaugh, Jr., Of Psychopaths and Pendulums: Legal and Psychaitric Treatment of Sex Offenders in The United States, 30 N.M.L Rev. 69 (2000); American Bar Association, Criminal Justice Mental Health Standards, Std 7–8.1 (recommending repeal of sex psychopath statutes) and commentary, pages 417–25 (1986).

[d] The Washington Legislature had repealed its older sex psychopath law in 1984.

When a person's sentence for a sexually violent offense has expired or is about to expire, the state is authorized to file a petition alleging the person to be a sexually violent predator. If the state proves, beyond a reasonable doubt, that the detainee is a sexually violent predator, the detainee is committed to a facility "for control, care, and treatment" until "safe to be at large." All treatment centers in Washington are located within correctional institutions.

Over the decade after Washington enacted its Sexually Violent Predator (SVP) law, about one-third of the states enacted similar statutes. In fact, many of the legislatures copied Washington's SVP statute almost word-for-word. One of these states was Kansas. Constitutional challenges to the SVP laws have been addressed by the Supreme Court in the context of the Kansas statute in the following cases.

————

## Kansas v. Hendricks

Supreme Court of the United States, 1997.
521 U.S. 346.

■ JUSTICE THOMAS delivered the opinion of the Court.

In 1994, Kansas enacted the Sexually Violent Predator Act, which establishes procedures for the civil commitment of persons who, due to a "mental abnormality" or a "personality disorder," are likely to engage in "predatory acts of sexual violence." Kan. Stat. Ann. § 59–29a01 *et seq.* (1994). The state invoked the Act for the first time to commit Leroy Hendricks, an inmate who had a long history of sexually molesting children, and who was scheduled for release from prison shortly after the Act became law. Hendricks challenged his commitment on, inter alia, "substantive" due process, double jeopardy, and ex post facto grounds. The Kansas Supreme Court invalidated the Act, holding that its precommitment condition of a "mental abnormality" did not satisfy what the court perceived to be the "substantive" due process requirement that involuntary civil commitment must be predicated on a finding of "mental illness." ... We granted certiorari ... and now reverse the judgment below.

I.A.

The Kansas legislature enacted the Sexually Violent Predator Act (Act) in 1994 to grapple with the problem of managing repeat sexual offenders. Although Kansas already had a statute addressing the involuntary commitment of those defined as "mentally ill," the legislature determined that existing civil commitment procedures were inadequate to confront the risks presented by "sexually violent predators." In the Act's preamble, the legislature explained:

> [A] small but extremely dangerous group of sexually violent predators exist who do not have a mental disease or defect that

renders them appropriate for involuntary treatment pursuant to the [general involuntary civil commitment statute].... In contrast to persons appropriate for civil commitment under the [general involuntary civil commitment statute], sexually violent predators generally have anti-social personality features which are unamenable to existing mental illness treatment modalities and those features render them likely to engage in sexually violent behavior. The legislature further finds that sexually violent predators' likelihood of engaging in repeat acts of predatory sexual violence is high. The existing involuntary commitment procedure ... is inadequate to address the risk these sexually violent predators pose to society. The legislature further finds that the prognosis for rehabilitating sexually violent predators in a prison setting is poor, the treatment needs of this population are very long term and the treatment modalities for this population are very different than the traditional treatment modalities for people appropriate for commitment under the [general involuntary civil commitment statute].

... The Act defined a "sexually violent predator" as "any person who has been convicted of or charged with a sexually violent offense and who suffers from a mental abnormality or personality disorder which makes the person likely to engage in the predatory acts of sexual violence." A "mental abnormality" was defined, in turn, as a "congenital or acquired condition affecting the emotional or volitional capacity which predisposes the person to commit sexually violent offenses in a degree constituting such person a menace to the health and safety of others."

As originally structured, the Act's civil commitment procedures pertained to: (i) a presently confined person who, like Hendricks, "has been convicted of a sexually violent offense" and is scheduled for release; (ii) a person who has been "charged with a sexually violent offense" but has been found incompetent to stand trial; (iii) a person who has been found "not guilty by reason of insanity of a sexually violent offense"; and (iv) a person found "not guilty" of a sexually violent offense because of a mental disease or defect....

B.

In 1984, Hendricks was convicted of taking "indecent liberties" with two 13-year-old boys. After serving nearly 10 years of his sentence, he was slated for release to a halfway house. Shortly before his scheduled release, however, the state filed a petition in state court seeking Hendricks' civil confinement as a sexually violent predator.... During [the] trial, Hendricks' own testimony revealed a chilling history of repeated child sexual molestation and abuse, beginning in 1955 when he exposed his genitals to two young girls. At that time, he pleaded guilty to indecent exposure. Then, in 1957, he was convicted of lewdness involving a young girl and received a brief jail sentence. In 1960, he molested two young boys while he worked for a carnival. After serving two years in prison for that offense, he was paroled, only to be rearrested for molesting a 7-year-old girl. Attempts were made to treat him for his sexual deviance, and in 1965 he was considered "safe to be at large," and was discharged from a state psychiatric hospital.

Shortly thereafter, however, Hendricks sexually assaulted another young boy and girl—he performed oral sex on the 8–year-old girl and fondled the 11–year-old boy. He was again imprisoned in 1967, but refused to participate in a sex offender treatment program, and thus remained incarcerated until his parole in 1972. Diagnosed as a pedophile, Hendricks entered into, but then abandoned, a treatment program. He testified that despite having received professional help for his pedophilia, he continued to harbor sexual desires for children. Indeed, soon after his 1972 parole, Hendricks began to abuse his own stepdaughter and stepson. He forced the children to engage in sexual activity with him over a period of approximately four years. Then, as noted above, Hendricks was convicted of "taking indecent liberties" with two adolescent boys after he attempted to fondle them. As a result of that conviction, he was once again imprisoned, and was serving that sentence when he reached his conditional release date in September 1994.

Hendricks admitted that he had repeatedly abused children whenever he was not confined. He explained that when he "get[s] stressed out," he "can't control the urge" to molest children. Although Hendricks recognized that his behavior harms children, and he hoped he would not sexually molest children again, he stated that the only sure way he could keep from sexually abusing children in the future was "to die." Hendricks readily agreed with the state physician's diagnosis that he suffers from pedophilia and that he is not cured of the condition; indeed, he told the physician that "treatment is bull ____."

The jury unanimously found beyond a reasonable doubt that Hendricks was a sexually violent predator. The trial court subsequently determined, as a matter of state law, that pedophilia qualifies as a "mental abnormality" as defined by the Act, and thus ordered Hendricks committed to the secretary's custody.

Hendricks appealed, claiming, among other things, that application of the Act to him violated the Federal Constitution's Due Process, Double Jeopardy, and Ex Post Facto clauses. The Kansas Supreme Court accepted Hendricks' due process claim. The court declared that in order to commit a person involuntarily in a civil proceeding, a state is required by "substantive" due process to prove by clear and convincing evidence that the person is both mentally ill and a danger to himself or to others. The court then determined that the Act's definition of "mental abnormality" did not satisfy what it perceived to be this Court's "mental illness" requirement in the civil commitment context. As a result, the court held that "the Act violates Hendricks' substantive due process rights." . . .

## II.A.

Kansas argues that the Act's definition of "mental abnormality" satisfies "substantive" due process requirements. We agree. Although freedom from physical restraint "has always been at the core of the liberty protected by the due process clause from arbitrary governmental action," Foucha v. Louisiana, 504 U.S. 71 (1992), that liberty interest is not absolute. The Court has recognized that an individual's constitutionally protected interest in avoiding physical restraint may be overridden even in the civil context.... Accordingly, states have in certain narrow circumstances provided for the forcible civil detainment of people who are unable to control their behavior and who thereby pose a danger to the public health and safety. We have consistently upheld such involuntary commitment statutes provided the confinement takes place pursuant to proper procedures and evidentiary standards. It thus cannot be said that the involuntary civil confinement of a limited subclass of dangerous persons is contrary to our understanding of ordered liberty.

The challenged Act unambiguously requires a finding of dangerousness either to one's self or to others as a prerequisite to involuntary confinement. Commitment proceedings can be initiated only when a person "has been convicted of or charged with a sexually violent offense," and "suffers from a mental abnormality or personality disorder which makes the person likely to engage in the predatory acts of sexual violence." The statute thus requires proof of more than a mere predisposition to violence; rather, it requires evidence of past sexually violent behavior and a present mental condition that creates a likelihood of such conduct in the future if the person is not incapacitated. As we have recognized, "[p]revious instances of violent behavior are an important indicator of future violent tendencies," Heller v. Doe, 509 U.S. 312, 323 (1993).

A finding of dangerousness, standing alone, is ordinarily not a sufficient ground upon which to justify indefinite involuntary commitment. We have sustained civil commitment statutes when they have coupled proof of dangerousness with the proof of some additional factor, such as a "mental illness" or "mental abnormality." See e.g., *Heller v. Doe*, at 314–15 (Kentucky statute permitting commitment of mentally retarded or mentally ill and dangerous individuals); Allen v. Illinois, 478 U.S. 364, 366 (1986) (Illinois statute permitting commitment of "mentally ill" and dangerous individual).... These added statutory requirements serve to limit involuntary civil confinement to those who suffer from a volitional impairment rendering them dangerous beyond their control. The Kansas Act is plainly of a kind with these other civil commitment statutes: It requires a finding of future dangerousness, and then links that finding to the existence of a "mental abnormality" or "personality disorder" that makes it difficult, if not impossible, for the person to control his dangerous behavior. The precommitment requirement of a "mental abnormality" or "personality disorder" is consistent with the requirements of these other statutes that we have upheld in that it narrows the class of persons eligible for confinement to those who are unable to control their dangerousness.

Hendricks nonetheless argues that our earlier cases dictate a finding of "mental illness" as a prerequisite for civil commitment, citing *Foucha*.... He then asserts that a "mental abnormality" is *not* equivalent to a "mental illness" because it is a term coined by the Kansas legislature, rather than by the psychiatric community. Contrary to Hendricks' assertion, the term "mental illness" is devoid of any talismanic significance. Not only do "psychiatrists disagree widely and frequently on what constitutes mental illness," but the Court itself has used a variety of expressions to describe the mental condition of those properly subject to civil confinement. Indeed, we have never required state legislatures to adopt any particular nomenclature in drafting civil commitment statutes. Rather, we have traditionally left to legislators the task of defining terms of a medical nature that have legal significance. As a consequence, the states have, over the years, developed numerous specialized terms to define mental health concepts. Often, those definitions do not fit precisely with the definitions employed by the medical community. The legal definitions of "insanity" and "competency," for example, vary substantially from their psychiatric counterparts. See, *e.g.,* Jules Gerard, The Usefulness of the Medical Model to the Legal System, 39 Rutgers L.Rev. 377, 391–394 (1987) (discussing differing purposes of legal system and the medical profession in recognizing mental illness). Legal definitions, however, which must "take into account such issues as individual responsibility ... and competency," need not mirror those advanced by the medical profession. American Psychiatric Association, Diagnostic and Statistical Manual of Mental Disorders xxiii, xxvii (4th ed.1994).

To the extent that the civil commitment statutes we have considered set forth criteria relating to an individual's inability to control his dangerousness, the Kansas Act sets forth comparable criteria and Hendricks' condition doubtless satisfies those criteria. The mental health professionals who evaluated Hendricks diagnosed him as suffering from pedophilia, a condition the psychiatric profession itself classifies as a serious mental disorder. Hendricks even conceded that, when he becomes "stressed out," he cannot "control the urge" to molest children. This admitted lack of volitional control, coupled with a prediction of future dangerousness, adequately distinguishes Hendricks from other dangerous persons who are perhaps more properly dealt with exclusively through criminal proceedings. Hendricks' diagnosis as a pedophile, which qualifies as a "mental abnormality" under the Act, thus plainly suffices for due process purposes.

B.

[The Court then addressed Hendricks' argument that the Act violates the constitution's Double Jeopardy prohibition and its ban on Ex Post Facto lawmaking:]

The thrust of Hendricks' argument is that the Act establishes criminal proceedings; hence confinement under it necessarily constitutes punishment. He contends that where, as here, newly enacted "punishment" is predicated upon past conduct for which he has already been convicted and forced to serve a prison sentence, the constitution's Double Jeopardy and Ex Post Facto clauses are violated. We are unpersuaded by Hendricks' argument that Kansas has established criminal proceedings.

The categorization of a particular proceeding as civil or criminal "is first of all a question of statutory construction." *Allen,* supra, 478 U.S., at 368. We must initially ascertain whether the legislature meant the statute to establish "civil" proceedings. If so, we ordinarily defer to the legislature's stated intent. Here, Kansas' objective to create a civil proceeding is evidenced by its placement of the Act within the Kansas probate code, instead of the criminal code, Kan. Stat. Ann., Article 29 (1994) ("Care and Treatment for Mentally Ill Persons"), as well as its description of the Act as creating a *"civil commitment procedure"* (emphasis added). Nothing on the face of the statute suggests that the legislature sought to create anything other than a civil commitment scheme designed to protect the public from harm.

Although we recognize that a "civil label is not always dispositive," *Allen,* supra, at 369, we will reject the legislature's manifest intent only where a party challenging the statute provides "the clearest proof" that "the statutory scheme [is] so punitive either in purpose or effect as to negate [the State's] intention" to deem it "civil," United States v. Ward, 448 U.S. 242, 248–49 (1980). In those limited circumstances, we will consider the statute to have established criminal proceedings for constitutional purposes. Hendricks, however, has failed to satisfy this heavy burden.

As a threshold matter, commitment under the Act does not implicate either of the two primary objectives of criminal punishment: retribution or deterrence. The Act's purpose is not retributive because it does not affix culpability for prior criminal conduct. Instead, such conduct is used solely for evidentiary purposes, either to demonstrate that a "mental abnormality" exists or to support a finding of future dangerousness. We have previously concluded that an Illinois statute was nonpunitive even though it was triggered by the commission of a sexual assault, explaining that evidence of the prior criminal conduct was "received not to punish past misdeeds, but primarily to show the accused's mental condition and to predict future behavior." *Allen,* supra, at 371. In addition, the Kansas Act does not make a criminal conviction a prerequisite for commitment— persons absolved of criminal responsibility may nonetheless be subject to confinement under the Act. An absence of the necessary criminal responsibility suggests that the state is not seeking retribution for a past misdeed. Thus, the fact that the Act may be "tied to criminal activity" is "insufficient to render the statut[e] punitive." United States v. Ursery, 518 U.S. 267 (1996).

Moreover, unlike a criminal statute, no finding of scienter is required to commit an individual who is found to be a sexually violent predator; instead, the commitment determination is made based on a "mental abnormality" or "personality disorder" rather than on one's criminal intent. The existence of a scienter requirement is customarily an important element in distinguishing criminal from civil statutes. See Kennedy v. Mendoza-Martinez, 372 U.S. 144, 168 (1963). The absence of such a requirement here is evidence that confinement under the statute is not intended to be retributive.

Nor can it be said that the legislature intended the Act to function as a deterrent. Those persons committed under the Act are, by definition, suffering from a "mental abnormality" or a "personality disorder" that prevents them from exercising adequate control over their behavior. Such persons are therefore unlikely to be deterred by the threat of confinement. And the conditions surrounding that confinement do not suggest a punitive purpose on the state's part. The State has represented that an individual confined under the Act is not subject to the more restrictive conditions placed on state prisoners, but instead experiences essentially the same conditions as any involuntarily committed patient in the state mental institution. Because none of the parties argues that people institutionalized under the Kansas general civil commitment statute are subject to punitive conditions, even though they may be involuntarily confined, it is difficult to conclude that persons confined under this Act are being "punished."

Although the civil commitment scheme at issue here does involve an affirmative restraint, "the mere fact that a person is detained does not inexorably lead to the conclusion that the government has imposed punishment." United States v. Salerno, 481 U.S. 739, 746 (1987). The state may take measures to restrict the freedom of the dangerously mentally ill. This is a legitimate nonpunitive governmental objective and has been historically so regarded. The Court has, in fact, cited the confinement of "mentally unstable individuals who present a danger to the public" as one classic example of nonpunitive detention. Id., at 748–49. If detention for the purpose of protecting the community from harm *necessarily* constituted punishment, then all involuntary civil commitments would have to be considered punishment. But we have never so held.

Hendricks focuses on his confinement's potentially indefinite duration as evidence of the state's punitive intent. That focus, however, is misplaced. Far from any punitive objective, the confinement's duration is instead linked to the stated purposes of the commitment, namely, to hold the person until his mental abnormality no longer causes him to be a threat to others. Cf. *Jones v. United States*, 463 U.S., at 368 (noting with approval that "because it is impossible to predict how long it will take for any given individual to recover [from insanity] or indeed whether he will ever recover—Congress has chosen ... to leave the length of commitment indeterminate, subject to periodic review of the patients' suitability for release"). If, at any time, the confined person is adjudged "safe to be at large," he is statutorily entitled to immediate release.

Furthermore, commitment under the Act is only *potentially* indefinite. The maximum amount of time an individual can be incapacitated pursuant to a single judicial proceeding is one year. If Kansas seeks to continue the detention beyond that year, a court must once again determine beyond a reasonable doubt that the detainee satisfies the same standards as required for the initial confinement. This requirement again demonstrates that Kansas does not intend an individual committed pursuant to the Act to remain confined any longer than he suffers from a mental abnormality rendering him unable to control his dangerousness.

Hendricks next contends that the state's use of procedural safeguards traditionally found in criminal trials makes the proceedings here criminal rather than civil. In *Allen,* we confronted a similar argument. There, the petitioner "place[d] great reliance on the fact that proceedings under the Act are accompanied by procedural safeguards usually found in criminal trials" to argue that the proceedings were civil in name only. We rejected that argument, however, explaining that the state's decision "to provide some of the safeguards applicable in criminal trials cannot itself turn these proceedings into criminal prosecutions." The numerous procedural and evidentiary protections afforded here demonstrate that the Kansas legislature has taken great care to confine only a narrow class of particularly dangerous individuals, and then only after meeting the strictest procedural standards. That Kansas chose to afford such procedural protections does not transform a civil commitment proceeding into a criminal prosecution.

Finally, Hendricks argues that the Act is necessarily punitive because it fails to offer any legitimate "treatment." Without such treatment, Hendricks asserts, confinement under the Act amounts to little more than disguised punishment. Hendricks' argument assumes that treatment for his condition is available, but that the state has failed (or refused) to provide it. The Kansas Supreme Court, however, apparently rejected this assumption, explaining:

> It is clear that the overriding concern of the legislature is to continue the segregation of sexually violent offenders from the public. Treatment with the goal of reintegrating them into society is incidental, at best. The record reflects that treatment for sexually violent predators is all but nonexistent. The legislature concedes that sexually violent predators are not amenable to treatment under [the existing Kansas involuntary commitment statute]. If there is nothing to treat under [that statute], then there is no mental illness. In that light, the provisions of the Act for treatment appear somewhat disingenuous.

It is possible to read this passage as a determination that Hendricks' condition was *untreatable* under the existing Kansas civil commitment statute, and thus the Act's sole purpose was incapacitation. Absent a treatable mental illness, the Kansas court concluded, Hendricks could not be detained against his will.

Accepting the Kansas court's apparent determination that treatment is not possible for this category of individuals does not obligate us to adopt its legal conclusions. We have already observed that, under the appropriate circumstances and when accompanied by proper procedures, incapacitation may be a legitimate end of the civil law. See *Allen*, supra, at 373; *Salerno*, 481 U.S., at 748–49. Accordingly, the Kansas court's determination that the Act's "overriding concern" was the continued "segregation of sexually violent offenders" is consistent with our conclusion that the Act establishes civil proceedings, especially when that concern is coupled with the state's ancillary goal of providing treatment to those offenders, if such is possible. While we have upheld state civil commitment statutes that aim both to incapacitate and to treat, see *Allen*, supra, we have never held that the constitution prevents a state from civilly detaining those for whom no treatment is available, but who nevertheless pose a danger to others. A state could hardly be seen as furthering a "punitive" purpose by involuntarily confining persons afflicted with an untreatable, highly contagious disease. Accord, Compagnie Francaise de Navigation a Vapeur v. Louisiana Bd. of Health, 186 U.S. 380 (1902) (permitting involuntary quarantine of persons suffering from communicable diseases). Similarly, it would be of little value to require treatment as a precondition for civil confinement of the dangerously insane when no acceptable treatment existed. To conclude otherwise would obligate a state to release certain confined individuals who were both mentally ill and dangerous simply because they could not be successfully treated for their afflictions.

Alternatively, the Kansas Supreme Court's opinion can be read to conclude that Hendricks' condition is treatable, but that treatment was not the state's "overriding concern," and that no treatment was being provided (at least at the time Hendricks was committed). Even if we accept this determination that the provision of treatment was not the Kansas Legislature's "overriding" or "primary" purpose in passing the Act, this does not rule out the possibility that an ancillary purpose of the Act was to provide treatment, and it does not require us to conclude that the Act is punitive. Indeed, critical language in the Act itself demonstrates that the Secretary, under whose custody sexually violent predators are committed, has an obligation to provide treatment to individuals like Hendricks. ("If the court or jury determines that the person is a sexually violent predator, the person shall be committed to the custody of the secretary of social and rehabilitation services for *control, care and treatment* until such time as the person's mental abnormality or personality disorder has so changed that the person is safe to be at large" (emphasis added)). Other of the Act's sections echo this obligation to provide treatment for committed persons.

Although the treatment program initially offered Hendricks may have seemed somewhat meager, it must be remembered that he was the first person committed under the Act. That the state did not have all of its treatment procedures in place is thus not surprising. What is significant, however, is that Hendricks was placed under the supervision of the Kansas Department of Health and Social and Rehabilitative Services, housed in a unit segregated from the general prison population and operated not by employees of the Department of Corrections, but by other trained individuals. And, before this Court, Kansas declared "[a]bsolutely" that persons committed under the Act are now receiving in the neighborhood of "31½ hours of treatment per week."

Where the state has "disavowed any punitive intent;" limited confinement to a small segment of particularly dangerous individuals; provided strict procedural safeguards; directed that confined persons be segregated from the general prison population and afforded the same status as others who have been civilly committed; recommended treatment if such is possible; and permitted immediate release upon a showing that the individual is no longer dangerous or mentally impaired, we cannot say that it acted with punitive intent. We therefore hold that the Act does not establish criminal proceedings and that involuntary confinement pursuant to the Act is not punitive. Our conclusion that the Act is nonpunitive thus removes an essential prerequisite for both Hendricks' double jeopardy and ex post facto claims.

1

The Double Jeopardy clause provides: "[N]or shall any person be subject for the same offence to be twice put in jeopardy of life or limb." . . . Hendricks argues that, as applied to him, the Act violates double jeopardy principles because his confinement under the Act, imposed after a conviction and a term of incarceration, amounted to both a second prosecution and a second punishment for the same offense. We disagree.

Because we have determined that the Kansas Act is civil in nature, initiation of its commitment proceedings does not constitute a second prosecution. Cf. Jones v. United States, 463 U.S. 354 (1983) (permitting involuntary civil commitment after verdict of not guilty by reason of insanity). Moreover, as commitment under the Act is not tantamount to "punishment," Hendricks' involuntary detention does not violate the Double Jeopardy clause, even though that confinement may follow a prison term. Indeed, in Baxstrom v. Herold, 383 U.S. 107 (1966), we expressly recognized that civil commitment could follow the expiration of a prison term without offending double jeopardy principles. We reasoned that "there is no conceivable basis for distinguishing the commitment of a person who is nearing the end of a penal term from all other civil commitments." If an individual otherwise meets the requirements for involuntary civil commitment, the state is under no obligation to release that individual simply because the detention would follow a period of incarceration. . . .

2

Hendricks' ex post facto claim is similarly flawed. The Ex Post Facto clause, which " 'forbids the application of any new punitive measure to a crime already consummated,' " has been interpreted to pertain exclusively to penal statutes. California Dept. of Corrections v. Morales, 514 U.S. 499, 505 (1995). As we have previously determined, the Act does not impose punishment; thus, its application does not raise ex post facto concerns. Moreover, the Act clearly does not have retroactive effect. Rather, the Act permits involuntary confinement based upon a determination that the person *currently* both suffers from a "mental abnormality" or "personality disorder" and is likely to pose a future danger to the public. To the extent that past behavior is taken into account, it is used, as noted above, solely for evidentiary purposes. Because the Act does not criminalize conduct legal before its enactment, nor deprive Hendricks of any defense that was available to him at the time of his crimes, the Act does not violate the ex post facto clause.

III.

We hold that the Kansas Sexually Violent Predator Act comports with due process requirements and neither runs afoul of double jeopardy principles nor constitutes an exercise in impermissible ex post facto lawmaking. Accordingly, the judgment of the Kansas Supreme Court is reversed.

It is so ordered.

■ JUSTICE KENNEDY, concurring.

I join the opinion of the Court in full and add these additional comments.

Though other issues were argued to us, as the action has matured it turns on whether the Kansas statute is an ex post facto law. A law enacted after commission of the offense and which punishes the offense by extending the term of confinement is a textbook example of an ex post facto law. If the object or purpose of the Kansas law had been to provide treatment but the treatment provisions were adopted as a sham or mere pretext, there would have been an indication of the forbidden purpose to punish. The Court's opinion gives a full and complete explanation why an ex post facto challenge based on this contention cannot succeed in the action before us. All this, however, concerns Hendricks alone. My brief, further comment is to caution against dangers inherent when a civil confinement law is used in conjunction with the criminal process, whether or not the law is given retroactive application.

It seems the dissent, too, would validate the Kansas statute as to persons who committed the crime after its enactment, and it might even validate the statute as to Hendricks, assuming a reasonable level of treatment. As all members of the Court seem to agree, then, the power of the state to confine persons who, by reason of a mental disease or mental abnormality, constitute a real, continuing, and serious danger to society is well established. Confinement of such individuals is permitted even if it is pursuant to a statute enacted after the crime has been committed and the offender has begun serving, or has all but completed serving, a penal sentence, provided there is no object or purpose to punish. See Baxstrom v. Herold, 383 U.S. 107, 111–12 (1966). The Kansas law, with its attendant protections, including yearly review and review at any time at the instance of the person confined, is within this pattern and tradition of civil confinement. In this action, the mental abnormality—pedophilia—is at least described in the DSM–IV. American Psychiatric Association, Diagnostic and Statistical Manual of Mental Disorders 524–525, 527–28 (4th ed. 1994).

Notwithstanding its civil attributes, the practical effect of the Kansas law may be to impose confinement for life. At this stage of medical knowledge, although future treatments cannot be predicted, psychiatrists or other professionals engaged in treating pedophilia may be reluctant to find measurable success in treatment even after a long period and may be unable to predict that no serious danger will come from release of the detainee.

A common response to this may be, "A life term is exactly what the sentence should have been anyway".... The point, however, is not how long Hendricks and others like him should serve a criminal sentence. With his criminal record, after all, a life term may well have been the only sentence appropriate to protect society and vindicate the wrong. The concern instead is whether it is the criminal system or the civil system which should make the decision in the first place. If the civil system is used simply to impose punishment after the state makes an improvident plea bargain on the criminal side, then it is not performing its proper function. These concerns persist whether the civil confinement statute is put on the books before or after the offense. We should bear in mind that while incapacitation is a goal common to both the criminal and civil systems of confinement, retribution and general deterrence are reserved for the criminal system alone.

On the record before us, the Kansas civil statute conforms to our precedents. If, however, civil confinement were to become a mechanism for retribution or general deterrence, or if it were shown that mental abnormality is too imprecise a category to offer a solid basis for concluding that civil detention is justified, our precedents would not suffice to validate it.

■ JUSTICE BREYER, with whom JUSTICE STEVENS and JUSTICE SOUTER join, and with whom JUSTICE GINSBURG joins as to Parts II and III, dissenting.

I agree with the majority that the Kansas Sexually Violent Predator Act's "definition of 'mental abnormality'" satisfies the "substantive" requirements of the Due Process clause. Kansas, however, concedes that Hendricks' condition is treatable; yet the Act did not provide Hendricks (or others like him) with any treatment until after his release date from prison and only inadequate treatment thereafter. These, and certain other, special features of the Act convince me that it was not simply an effort to commit Hendricks civilly, but rather an effort to inflict further punishment upon him. The Ex Post Facto clause therefore prohibits the Act's application to Hendricks, who committed his crimes prior to its enactment.

I.

I begin with the area of agreement. This Court has held that the civil commitment of a "mentally ill" and "dangerous" person does not automatically violate the due process clause provided that the commitment takes place pursuant to proper procedures and evidentiary standards. See *Foucha v. Louisiana.* The Kansas Supreme Court, however, held that the due process clause forbids application of the Act to Hendricks for "substantive" reasons, i.e., irrespective of the procedures or evidentiary standards used. The court reasoned that Kansas had not satisfied the "mentally ill" requirement of the Due Process clause because Hendricks was not "mentally ill." Moreover, Kansas had not satisfied what the court believed was an additional "substantive due process" requirement, namely, the provision of treatment. I shall consider each of these matters briefly.

A.

In my view, the due process clause permits Kansas to classify Hendricks as a mentally ill and dangerous person for civil commitment purposes. *Allen v. Illinois*. I agree with the majority that the constitution gives states a degree of leeway in making this kind of determination. But, because I do not subscribe to all of its reasoning, I shall set forth three sets of circumstances that, taken together, convince me that Kansas has acted within the limits that the due process clause substantively sets.

First, the psychiatric profession itself classifies the kind of problem from which Hendricks suffers as a serious mental disorder. E.g., American Psychiatric Assn., Diagnostic and Statistical Manual of Mental Disorders 524–525, 527–28 (4th ed. 1994) (describing range of paraphilias and discussing how stress aggravates pedophilic behavior).... I concede that professionals also debate whether or not this disorder should be called a mental "illness." But the very presence and vigor of this debate is important. The constitution permits a state to follow one reasonable professional view, while rejecting another. The psychiatric debate, therefore, helps to inform the law by setting the bounds of what is reasonable, but it cannot here decide just how states must write their laws within those bounds.

Second, Hendricks' abnormality does not consist simply of a long course of antisocial behavior, but rather it includes a specific serious, and highly unusual inability to control his actions. (For example, Hendricks testified that, when he gets "stressed out," he cannot "control the urge" to molest children.) The law traditionally has considered this kind of abnormality akin to insanity for purposes of confinement. See, e. g., Minnesota ex rel. Pearson v. Probate Court of Ramsey Cty., 309 U.S. 270, 274 (1940) (upholding against a due process challenge the civil confinement of a dangerous person where the danger flowed from an " 'utter lack of power to control ... sexual impulses' ").... Indeed, the notion of an "irresistible impulse" often has helped to shape criminal law's insanity defense and to inform the related recommendations of legal experts as they seek to translate the insights of mental health professionals into workable legal rules. See also American Law Institute, Model Penal Code § 4.01 (insanity defense, in part, rests on inability "to conform ... conduct to the requirements of law"); Abraham Goldstein, The Insanity Defense 67–79 (1967) (describing "irresistible impulse" test).

Third, Hendricks' mental abnormality also makes him dangerous. Hendricks "has been convicted of ... a sexually violent offense," and a jury found that he "suffers from a mental abnormality ... which makes" him "likely to engage" in similar "acts of sexual violence" in the future. The evidence at trial favored the state. Dr. Befort, for example, explained why Hendricks was likely to commit further acts of sexual violence if released. And Hendricks' own testimony about what happens when he gets "stressed out" confirmed Dr. Befort's diagnosis.

Because (i) many mental health professionals consider pedophilia a serious mental disorder; and (ii) Hendricks suffers from a classic case of irresistible impulse, namely, he is so afflicted with pedophilia that he cannot "control the urge" to molest children; and (iii) his pedophilia presents a serious danger to those children, I believe that Kansas can classify Hendricks as "mentally ill" and "dangerous" as this Court used those terms in *Foucha*. . . .

The Kansas Supreme Court also held that the Due Process clause requires a state to provide treatment to those whom it civilly confines (as "mentally ill" and "dangerous"). It found that Kansas did not provide Hendricks with significant treatment. And it concluded that Hendricks' confinement violated the Due Process clause for this reason as well.

This case does not require us to consider whether the due process clause *always* requires treatment—whether, for example, it would forbid civil confinement of an *untreatable* mentally ill, dangerous person. To the contrary, Kansas argues that pedophilia is an "abnormality" or "illness" that can be treated. Two groups of mental health professionals agree [citing amicus briefs]. Indeed, no one argues the contrary. Hence the legal question before us is whether the clause forbids Hendricks' confinement unless Kansas provides him with treatment *that it concedes is available.*

Nor does anyone argue that Kansas somehow could have violated the Due Process clause's *treatment* concerns had it provided Hendricks with the treatment that is potentially available (and I do not see how any such argument could succeed). Rather, the basic substantive due process treatment question is whether that clause requires Kansas to provide treatment that it concedes is potentially available to a person whom it concedes is treatable. This same question is at the heart of my discussion of whether Hendricks' confinement violates the Constitution's Ex Post Facto clause. For that reason, I shall not consider the substantive due process treatment question separately, but instead shall simply turn to the Ex Post Facto clause discussion. As Justice Kennedy points out some of the matters there discussed may later prove relevant to substantive due process analysis.

II.

Kansas' 1994 Act violates the federal constitution's prohibition of "any . . . ex post facto Law" if it "inflicts" upon Hendricks "a greater punishment" than did the law "annexed to" his "crime[s]" when he "committed" those crimes in 1984. Calder v. Bull, 3 Dall. 386, 390 (1798) (opinion of Chase, J.); U.S. Const., Art. I, § 10. The majority agrees that the clause " 'forbids the application of any *new punitive measure* to a crime already consummated.' " California Dept. of Corrections v. Morales, 514 U.S. 499, 505 (1995). But it finds the Act is not "punitive." With respect to that basic question, I disagree with the majority.

Certain resemblances between the Act's "civil commitment" and traditional criminal punishments are obvious. Like criminal imprisonment, the Act's civil commitment amounts to "secure" confinement and "incarceration against one's will," In re Gault, 387 U.S. 1 (1967). In addition, a basic objective of the Act is incapacitation, which, as Blackstone said in describing an objective of criminal law, is to "depriv[e] the party injuring of the power to do future mischief." 4 W. Blackstone, Commentaries *11–*12 (incapacitation is one important purpose of criminal punishment).... Moreover, the Act, like criminal punishment, imposes its confinement (or sanction) only upon an individual who has previously committed a criminal offense. And the Act imposes that confinement through the use of persons (county prosecutors), procedural guarantees (trial by jury, assistance of counsel, psychiatric evaluations), and standards ("beyond a reasonable doubt") traditionally associated with the criminal law.

These obvious resemblances by themselves, however, are not legally sufficient to transform what the Act calls "civil commitment" into a criminal punishment. Civil commitment of dangerous, mentally ill individuals by its very nature involves confinement and incapacitation. Yet "civil commitment," from a constitutional perspective, nonetheless remains civil. *Allen v. Illinois*. Nor does the fact that criminal behavior triggers the Act make the critical difference. The Act's insistence upon a prior crime, by screening out those whose past behavior does not concretely demonstrate the existence of a mental problem or potential future danger, may serve an important noncriminal evidentiary purpose. Neither is the presence of criminal law-type procedures determinative. Those procedures can serve an important purpose that in this context one might consider noncriminal, namely, helping to prevent judgmental mistakes that would wrongly deprive a person of important liberty.

If these obvious similarities cannot by themselves prove that Kansas' "civil commitment" statute is criminal, neither can the word "civil" written into the statute by itself prove the contrary....

In this circumstance, with important features of the Act pointing in opposite directions, I would place particular importance upon those features that would likely distinguish between a basically punitive and a basically nonpunitive purpose. And I note that the Court, in an earlier civil commitment case, *Allen v. Illinois* looked primarily to the law's concern for treatment as an important distinguishing feature. I do not believe that *Allen* means that a particular law's lack of concern for treatment, by itself, is enough to make an incapacitative law punitive. But, for reasons I will point out, when a state believes that treatment does exist, and then couples that admission with a legislatively required delay of such treatment until a person is at the end of his jail term (so that further incapacitation is therefore necessary), such a legislative scheme begins to look punitive....

The *Allen* Court's focus upon treatment, as a kind of touchstone helping to distinguish civil from punitive purposes, is not surprising, for one would expect a nonpunitive statutory scheme to confine, not simply in order to protect, but also in order to cure. That is to say, one would expect a nonpunitively motivated legislature that confines *because of* a dangerous mental abnormality to seek to help the individual himself overcome that abnormality (at least insofar as professional treatment for the abnormality exists and is potentially helpful, as Kansas, supported by some groups of mental health professionals, argues is the case here). Conversely, a statutory scheme that provides confinement that does not reasonably fit a practically available, medically oriented treatment objective, more likely reflects a primarily punitive legislative purpose.

Several important treatment-related factors—factors of a kind that led the five-member *Allen* majority to conclude that the Illinois legislature's purpose was primarily civil, not punitive—in this action suggest precisely the opposite. First, the state supreme court here, unlike the state court in *Allen*, has held that treatment is not a significant objective of the Act. The Kansas court wrote that the Act's purpose is "segregation of sexually violent offenders," with "treatment" a matter that was "incidental at best...."

Second, the Kansas statute, insofar as it applies to previously convicted offenders such as Hendricks, commits, confines, and treats those offenders *after* they have served virtually their entire criminal sentence. That time-related circumstance seems deliberate. The Act explicitly defers diagnosis, evaluation, and commitment proceedings until a few weeks prior to the "anticipated release" of a previously convicted offender from prison. But why, one might ask, does the Act not commit and require treatment of sex offenders sooner, say, soon after they begin to serve their sentences? ... [T]he timing provisions of the statute confirm the Kansas Supreme Court's view that treatment was not a particularly important legislative objective....

Third, the statute, at least as of the time Kansas applied it to Hendricks, did not require the committing authority to consider the possibility of using less restrictive alternatives, such as postrelease supervision, halfway houses, or other methods.... This Court has said that a failure to consider, or to use, "alternative and less harsh methods" to achieve a nonpunitive objective can help to show that legislature's "purpose ... was to punish." Bell v. Wolfish, 441 U.S. 520, 539, n.20 (1979)....

Fourth, the laws of other states confirm, through comparison, that Kansas' "civil commitment" objectives do not require the statutory features that indicate a punitive purpose. I have found 17 States with laws that seek to protect the public from mentally abnormal, sexually dangerous individuals through civil commitment or other mandatory treatment programs. Ten of those statutes, unlike the Kansas statute, begin treatment of an offender soon after he has been apprehended and charged with a serious sex offense. Only seven, like Kansas, delay "civil" commitment (and treatment) until the offender has served his criminal sentence (and this figure includes the Acts of Minnesota and New Jersey, both of which generally do not delay treatment). Of these seven, however, six (unlike Kansas) require consideration of less restrictive alternatives....

The majority suggests in the alternative that recent evidence shows that Kansas is now providing treatment. That evidence comes from two sources: First, a statement by the Kansas Attorney General at oral argument that those committed under the Act are now receiving treatment; and second, in a footnote, a Kansas trial judge's statement, in a state habeas proceeding nearly one year after Hendricks was committed, that Kansas is providing treatment. I do not see how either of these statements can be used to justify the validity of the Act's application to Hendricks at the time he filed suit. . . .

. . . Kansas points to United States v. Salerno, 481 U.S. 739 (1987), a case in which this Court held preventive detention of a dangerous accused person pending trial constitutionally permissible. *Salerno,* however, involved the brief detention of that person, after a finding of "probable cause" that he had committed a crime that would justify further imprisonment, and only pending a speedy judicial determination of guilt or innocence. This Court, in *Foucha,* emphasized the fact that the confinement at issue in *Salerno* was "strictly limited in duration." It described that "pretrial detention of arrestees" as "one of those carefully limited exceptions permitted by the due process clause." And it held that *Salerno* did not authorize the indefinite detention, on grounds of dangerousness, of "insanity acquittees who are not mentally ill but who do not prove they would not be dangerous to others." 504 U.S., at 83. Whatever *Salerno*'s "due process" implications may be, it does not focus upon, nor control, the question at issue here, the question of "punishment" for purposes of the ex post facto clause. . . .

## III.

To find that the confinement the Act imposes upon Hendricks is "punishment" is to find a violation of the ex post facto clause. Kansas does not deny that the 1994 Act changed the legal consequences that attached to Hendricks' earlier crimes, and in a way that significantly "disadvantage[d] the offender."

To find a violation of that clause here, however, is not to hold that the clause prevents Kansas, or other states, from enacting dangerous sexual offender statutes. A statute that operates prospectively, for example, does not offend the ex post facto clause. Neither does it offend the ex post facto clause for a state to sentence offenders to the fully authorized sentence, to seek consecutive, rather than concurrent, sentences, or to invoke recidivism statutes to lengthen imprisonment. Moreover, a statute that operates retroactively, like Kansas' statute, nonetheless does not offend the clause *if the confinement that it imposes is not punishment*—if, that is to say, the legislature does not simply add a later criminal punishment to an earlier one.

The statutory provisions before us do amount to punishment primarily because, as I have said, the legislature did not tailor the statute to fit the nonpunitive civil aim of treatment, which it concedes exists in Hendricks' case. The clause in these circumstances does not stand as an obstacle to achieving important protections for the public's safety; rather it provides an assurance that, where so significant a restriction of an individual's basic freedoms is at issue, a state cannot cut corners. Rather, the legislature must hew to the constitution's liberty-protecting line. See The Federalist No. 78, p. 466 (C. Rossiter ed. 1961) (A. Hamilton).

I therefore would affirm the judgment below.

———

## Kansas v. Crane

Supreme Court of the United States, 2002.
534 U.S. 407.

■ Justice Breyer delivered the opinion of the Court.

This case concerns the constitutional requirements substantively limiting the civil commitment of a dangerous sexual offender—a matter that this Court considered in Kansas v. Hendricks, 521 U.S. 346 (1997). The State of Kansas argues that the Kansas Supreme Court has interpreted our decision in *Hendricks* in an overly restrictive manner. We agree and vacate the Kansas court's judgment. . . .

II

. . . The state here seeks the civil commitment of Michael Crane, a previously convicted sexual offender who, according to at least one of the state's psychiatric witnesses, suffers from both exhibitionism and antisocial personality disorder. . . . After a jury trial, the Kansas district court ordered Crane's civil commitment. But the Kansas Supreme Court reversed. In that court's view, the Federal Constitution as interpreted in *Hendricks* insists upon "a finding that the defendant cannot control his dangerous behavior"—even if (as provided by Kansas law) problems of "emotional capacity" and not "volitional capacity" prove the "source of bad behavior" warranting commitment. And the trial court had made no such finding.

Kansas now argues that the Kansas Supreme Court wrongly read *Hendricks* as requiring the state *always* to prove that a dangerous individual is *completely* unable to control his behavior. That reading, says Kansas, is far too rigid.

III

We agree with Kansas insofar as it argues that *Hendricks* set forth no requirement of *total* or *complete* lack of control. *Hendricks* referred to the Kansas Act as requiring a "mental abnormality" or "personality disorder" that makes it *"difficult,* if not impossible, for the [dangerous] person to control his dangerous behavior." The word "difficult" indicates that the lack of control to which this Court referred was not absolute. Indeed, as different amici on opposite sides of this case agree, an absolutist approach is unworkable. Cf. Brief for American Psychiatric Association et al. as Amici Curiae; cf.also American Psychiatric Association, Statement on the Insanity Defense (1982) (" 'The line between an irresistible impulse and an impulse not resisted is probably no sharper than that between twilight and dusk' "). Moreover, most severely ill people—even those commonly termed "psychopaths"—retain some ability to control their behavior. See Stephen Morse, Culpability and Control, 142 U. Pa. L.Rev. 1587, 1634–35 (1994); cf.

Bruce Winick, Sex Offender Law in the 1990s: A Therapeutic Jurisprudence Analysis, 4 Psychol. Pub. Pol'y & L. 505, 520–25 (1998). Insistence upon absolute lack of control would risk barring the civil commitment of highly dangerous persons suffering severe mental abnormalities.

We do not agree with the state, however, insofar as it seeks to claim that the constitution permits commitment of the type of dangerous sexual offender considered in *Hendricks* without *any* lack-of-control determination. *Hendricks* underscored the constitutional importance of distinguishing a dangerous sexual offender subject to civil commitment "from other dangerous persons who are perhaps more properly dealt with exclusively through criminal proceedings." That distinction is necessary lest "civil commitment" become a "mechanism for retribution or general deterrence"—functions properly those of criminal law, not civil commitment. The presence of what the "psychiatric profession itself classifie[d] ... as a serious mental disorder" helped to make that distinction in *Hendricks*. And a critical distinguishing feature of that "serious ... disorder" there consisted of a special and serious lack of ability to control behavior.

In recognizing that fact, we did not give to the phrase "lack of control" a particularly narrow or technical meaning. And we recognize that in cases where lack of control is at issue, "inability to control behavior" will not be demonstrable with mathematical precision. It is enough to say that there must be proof of serious difficulty in controlling behavior. And this, when viewed in light of such features of the case as the nature of the psychiatric diagnosis, and the severity of the mental abnormality itself, must be sufficient to distinguish the dangerous sexual offender whose serious mental illness, abnormality, or disorder subjects him to civil commitment from the dangerous but typical recidivist convicted in an ordinary criminal case. See Foucha v. Louisiana, 504 U.S. 71 (1992) (rejecting an approach to civil commitment that would permit the indefinite confinement "of any convicted criminal" after completion of a prison term).

We recognize that *Hendricks* as so read provides a less precise constitutional standard than would those more definite rules for which the parties have argued. But the constitution's safeguards of human liberty in the area of mental illness and the law are not always best enforced through precise bright-line rules. For one thing, the States retain considerable leeway in defining the mental abnormalities and personality disorders that make an individual eligible for commitment. For another, the science of psychiatry, which informs but does not control ultimate legal determinations, is an ever-advancing science, whose distinctions do not seek precisely to mirror those of the law. See also, e.g., DSM–IV xxx ("concept of mental disorder ... lacks a consistent operational definition"); id., at xxxii–xxxiii (noting the "imperfect fit between the questions of ultimate concern to the law and the information contained in [the DSM's] clinical diagnosis"). Consequently, we have sought to provide constitutional guidance in this area by proceeding deliberately and contextually, elaborating generally stated constitutional standards and objectives as specific circumstances require. *Hendricks* embodied that approach.

## IV

The State also questions how often a volitional problem lies at the heart of a dangerous sexual offender's serious mental abnormality or disorder. It points out that the Kansas Supreme Court characterized its state statute as permitting commitment of dangerous sexual offenders who suffered from a mental abnormality properly characterized by an "emotional" impairment and suffered no "volitional" impairment. It adds that, in the Kansas court's view, *Hendricks* absolutely forbids the commitment of any such person. And the State argues that it was wrong to read *Hendricks* in this way.

We agree that *Hendricks* limited its discussion to volitional disabilities. And that fact is not surprising. The case involved an individual suffering from pedophilia—a mental abnormality that critically involves what a lay person might describe as a lack of control. DSM–IV 571–572 (listing as a diagnostic criterion for pedophilia that an individual have acted on, or been affected by, "sexual urges" toward children). Hendricks himself stated that he could not " 'control the urge' " to molest children. In addition, our cases suggest that civil commitment of dangerous sexual offenders will normally involve individuals who find it particularly difficult to control their behavior—in the general sense described above. And it is often appropriate to say of such individuals, in ordinary English, that they are "unable to control their dangerousness."

Regardless, *Hendricks* must be read in context. The Court did not draw a clear distinction between the purely "emotional" sexually related mental abnormality and the "volitional." Here, as in other areas of psychiatry, there may be "considerable overlap between a ... defective understanding or appreciation and ... [an] ability to control ... behavior." American Psychiatric Association Statement on the Insanity Defense, 140 Am. J. Psychiatry 681, 685 (1983) (discussing "psychotic" individuals). Nor, when considering civil commitment, have we ordinarily distinguished for constitutional purposes among volitional, emotional, and cognitive impairments. See, e.g., Jones v. United States, 463 U.S. 354 (1983). The Court in *Hendricks* had no occasion to consider whether confinement based solely on "emotional" abnormality would be constitutional, and we likewise have no occasion to do so in the present case.

\* \* \*

For these reasons, the judgment of the Kansas Supreme Court is vacated, and the case is remanded for further proceedings not inconsistent with this opinion.

It is so ordered.

■ Justice Scalia, with whom Justice Thomas joins, dissenting. . . .

## I

Respondent was convicted of lewd and lascivious behavior and pleaded guilty to aggravated sexual battery for two incidents that took place on the same day in 1993. In the first, respondent exposed himself to a tanning salon attendant. In the second, 30 minutes later, respondent entered a video store, waited until he was the only customer present, and then exposed himself to the clerk. Not stopping there, he grabbed the clerk by the neck, demanded she perform oral sex on him, and threatened to rape her, before running out of the store. Following respondent's plea to aggravated sexual battery, the State filed a petition in state district court to have respondent evaluated and adjudicated a sexual predator under the SVPA. That Act permits the civil detention of a person convicted of any of several enumerated sexual offenses, if it is proven beyond a reasonable doubt that he suffers from a "mental abnormality"—a disorder affecting his "emotional or volitional capacity which predisposes the person to commit sexually violent offenses"—or a "personality disorder," either of "which makes the person likely to engage in repeat acts of sexual violence."

Several psychologists examined respondent and determined he suffers from exhibitionism and antisocial personality disorder. Though exhibitionism alone would not support classification as a sexual predator, a psychologist concluded that the two in combination did place respondent's condition within the range of disorders covered by the SVPA, "cit[ing] the increasing frequency of incidents involving [respondent], increasing intensity of the incidents, [respondent's] increasing disregard for the rights of others, and his increasing daring and aggressiveness." Another psychologist testified that respondent's behavior was marked by "impulsivity or failure to plan ahead," indicating his unlawfulness "was a combination of willful and uncontrollable behavior." The state's experts agreed, however, that " '[r]espondent's mental disorder does not impair his volitional control to the degree he cannot control his dangerous behavior.' "

Respondent moved for summary judgment, arguing that for his detention to comport with substantive due process the State was required to prove not merely what the statute requires—that by reason of his mental disorder he is "likely to engage in repeat acts of sexual violence"—but also that he is unable to control his violent behavior. The trial court denied this motion, and instructed the jury pursuant to the terms of the statute. The jury found, beyond a reasonable doubt, that respondent was a sexual predator as defined by the SVPA. The Kansas Supreme Court reversed, holding the SVPA unconstitutional as applied to someone, like respondent, who has only an emotional or personality disorder within the meaning of the Act, rather than a volitional impairment. For such a person, it held, the state must show not merely a likelihood that the defendant would engage in repeat acts of sexual violence, but also an inability to control violent behavior. It based this holding solely on our decision in *Hendricks*.

## II

... The first words of [*Hendricks*] dealing with the merits of the case were as follows: "Kansas argues that the Act's definition of 'mental abnormality' satisfies 'substantive' due process requirements. We agree."

And the *reason* it found substantive due process satisfied was clearly stated:

> The Kansas Act is plainly of a kind with these other civil commitment statutes [that we have approved]: It requires a finding of future dangerousness [viz., that the person committed is "likely to engage in repeat acts of sexual violence"], and then links that finding to the existence of a "mental abnormality" or "personality disorder" *that makes it difficult, if not impossible, for the person to control his dangerous behavior.* (Emphasis added.)

It is the italicized language in the foregoing excerpt that today's majority relies upon as establishing the requirement of a separate *finding* of inability to control behavior.

That is simply not a permissible reading of the passage, for several reasons. First, because the authority cited for the statement ... is the section of the SVPA that defines "mental abnormality," *which contains no requirement of inability to control.* What the opinion was obviously saying was that the SVPA's required finding of a *causal connection* between the likelihood of repeat acts of sexual violence and the existence of a "mental abnormality" or "personality disorder" *necessarily* establishes "difficulty if not impossibility" in controlling behavior. . . .

The Court relies upon the fact that "*Hendricks* underscored the constitutional importance of distinguishing a dangerous sexual offender subject to civil commitment 'from other dangerous persons who are perhaps more properly dealt with exclusively through criminal proceedings.' " But the SVPA as written—without benefit of a supplemental control finding—already achieves that objective. It conditions civil commitment not upon a mere finding that the sex offender is likely to reoffend, but only upon the additional finding (beyond a reasonable doubt) that the *cause* of the likelihood of recidivism is a "mental abnormality or personality disorder." Ordinary recidivists *choose* to reoffend and are therefore amenable to deterrence through the criminal law; those subject to civil commitment under the SVPA, because their mental illness is an affliction and not a choice, are unlikely to be deterred. We specifically pointed this out in *Hendricks.* "Those persons committed under the Act," we said, "are, by definition, suffering from a 'mental abnormality' or a 'personality disorder' that prevents them from exercising adequate control over their behavior. Such persons are therefore unlikely to be deterred by the threat of confinement."

III

. . . I cannot resist observing that the distinctive status of volitional impairment which the Court mangles *Hendricks* to preserve would not even be worth preserving by more legitimate means. There is good reason why, as the Court accurately says, "when considering civil commitment ... we [have not] ordinarily distinguished for constitutional purposes among volitional, emotional, and cognitive impairments." We have not done so because it makes no sense. It is obvious that a person may be able to exercise volition and yet be unfit to turn loose upon society. The man who has a will of steel, but who delusionally believes that every woman he meets is inviting crude sexual advances, is surely a dangerous sexual predator.

## IV

I not only disagree with the Court's gutting of our holding in *Hendricks;* I also doubt the desirability, and indeed even the coherence, of the new constitutional test which (on the basis of no analysis except a misreading of *Hendricks*) it substitutes. Under our holding in *Hendricks,* a jury in an SVPA commitment case would be required to find, beyond a reasonable doubt, that the person previously convicted of one of the enumerated sexual offenses is suffering from a mental abnormality or personality disorder, and that this condition renders him likely to commit future acts of sexual violence. Both of these findings are coherent, and (with the assistance of expert testimony) well within the capacity of a normal jury. Today's opinion says that the constitution requires the addition of a third finding: that the subject suffers from an inability to control behavior—not utter inability, and not even inability in a particular constant degree, but rather inability in a degree that will vary "in light of such features of the case as the nature of the psychiatric diagnosis, and the severity of the mental abnormality itself."

This formulation of the new requirement certainly displays an elegant subtlety of mind. Unfortunately, it gives trial courts, in future cases under the many commitment statutes similar to Kansas's SVPA, *not a clue* as to how they are supposed to charge the jury! Indeed, it does not even provide a clue to the trial court, on remand, *in this very case.* What is the judge to ask the jury to find? It is fine and good to talk about the desirability of our "proceeding deliberately and contextually, elaborating generally stated constitutional standards and objectives as specific circumstances require," but one would think that this plan would at least produce the "elaboration" of what the jury charge should be in the "specific circumstances" of the present case. "[P]roceeding deliberately" is not synonymous with not proceeding at all.

I suspect that the reason the Court avoids any elaboration is that elaboration which passes the laugh test is impossible. How *is* one to frame for a jury the degree of "inability to control" which, in the particular case, "the nature of the psychiatric diagnosis, and the severity of the mental abnormality" require? Will it be a percentage ("Ladies and gentlemen of the jury, you may commit Mr. Crane under the SVPA only if you find, beyond a reasonable doubt, that he is 42% unable to control his penchant for sexual violence")? Or a frequency ratio ("Ladies and gentlemen of the jury, you may commit Mr. Crane under the SVPA only if you find, beyond a reasonable doubt, that he is unable to control his penchant for sexual violence 3 times out of 10")? Or merely an adverb ("Ladies and gentlemen of the jury, you may commit Mr. Crane under the SVPA only if you find, beyond a reasonable doubt, that he is appreciably—or moderately, or substantially, or almost totally–unable to control his penchant for sexual violence")? None of these seems to me satisfactory.

But if it is indeed possible to "elaborate" upon the Court's novel test, surely the Court has an obligation to do so in the "specific circumstances" of the present case, so that the trial court will know what is expected of it on remand. It is irresponsible to leave the law in such a state of utter indeterminacy. . . .

———

## NOTES ON *HENDRICKS* AND *CRANE*

1. **Legislative Purpose or Justification.** Judging from the Court's opinion in *Hendricks*, the constitutionality of the SVP law depends heavily on how its underlying purpose or justification is characterized. How should it be characterized?

(i) **Punishment.** The threshold issue in resolving Hendricks' ex post facto and double jeopardy claims is whether his detention under the SVP law amounts to punishment for constitutional purposes. Obviously the label deployed in the statute can not be determinative. What factors were determinative in the majority judgment? In that of the dissent? The dissenters concluded that the SVP law imposed additional punishment on offenders who had committed their predicate sex offenses before the law was enacted and had already served the terms for which they had been sentenced. Does it follow that post-sentence commitment would also violate the double jeopardy provision even if it were applied prospectively?

(ii) **Treatment.** In *Allen*, the Court found that treatment was one of the legislative goals. The majority equivocates on this issue in *Hendricks*, while the dissent regards the absence of a therapeutic objective as evidence that the goal is punitive. Exactly what is the constitutional significance of treatment? On the one hand, could the legislative purpose be both punitive and therapeutic? On the other, could it be neither? Regardless of declared purpose, does it matter whether treatment is provided? Whether it is efficacious?

(iii) **Incapacitation.** If incapacitation were the *sole* purpose of SVP commitment, does that mean it is not punitive for constitutional purposes? Assuming that a commitment law with an exclusively incapacitative objective would pass muster under the double jeopardy and ex post facto provisions, would it be permissible under the due process clause? Does *Foucha* have any bearing on the answer?

2. **The Significance of Mental Disorder.** How does the SVP requirement of a "mental abnormality or personality disorder" relate to the questions about legislative purpose raised in the previous note? To what extent does this requirement support Kansas' argument that the legislative purpose is not punitive? That it is partly therapeutic?

Assuming again that the statutory purpose of SVP laws is primarily or exclusively incapacitative, is some sort of mental disorder constitutionally required under *Foucha*? If so, what type of mental disorder is necessary? Some critics of the SVP laws object to the statutory definition of "mental abnormality" on the ground that it is essentially a legal definition, not a clinical or scientific one. Is that right? Recall the debate over the criteria for the insanity defense. Clearly these are legal criteria, not medical ones. What bearing, if any, does that have on the propriety of the definition of "mental abnormality" in the SVP statutes?

**3.   The Relationship Between Mental Disorder and Dangerous Conduct.** In the SVP commitment proceedings against Hendricks and Crane, the juries were apparently instructed in the bare language of the statute. In *Hendricks*, the Court upheld the statute on its face and as applied. However, in *Crane*, the Court held that the law had been unconstitutionally applied. Why? How do the cases differ? How should the jury be instructed on remand in *Crane*?

**4.   Volitional and Emotional Impairment.** Is a finding of volitional impairment the only constitutionally permissible basis for commitment under an SVP statute? If so, does this imply that NGRI commitments must be predicated on a similar finding? If not, what alternative predicate could support civil commitment? Would such a finding be supportable in *Crane*?[e]

---

[e] For analysis of *Hendricks* and *Crane* and further reading on SVP laws, see Stephen Morse, Uncontrollable Urges and Irrational People, 88 Va. L. Rev 1025 (2002); Eric S. Janus, *Hendricks* and the Moral Terrain of Police Power Civil Commitment, 4 Psychol. Pub Pol'y & L. 505 (1998); Bruce J. Winick and John Q. LaFond (eds), Protecting Society from Sexually Dangerous Offenders (2003).

# CHAPTER VII

# LIABILITY FOR THE CONDUCT OF ANOTHER

## SECTION 1: COMPLICITY

### INTRODUCTORY NOTES ON PARTIES TO CRIME

1. **The Common Law.** At common law, parties to a felony were differentiated as principals in the first and second degree and accessories before and after the fact. The principal in the first degree was normally the primary actor, the person who personally engaged in criminal conduct. A principal in the second degree aided or abetted the primary actor in the commission of a felony and was present at the perpetration thereof. Presence was essential, but it could be constructive in nature. A typical example was the lookout who was posted some distance from a robbery in order to stand guard. In general, a person was constructively present at a felony whenever he or she was situated to assist the primary actor during commission of the crime. One who aided, counseled, commanded, or encouraged the commission of a felony but who was not present at its perpetration, became an accessory before the fact. Finally, one who assisted a known felon to avoid apprehension, trial, or punishment became an accessory after the fact.

Even at common law, the distinction among principals rarely mattered. Principals in the first and second degree received the same punishment. Since both had to be "present" at the scene of the crime, both were subject to the jurisdiction of the same court. Furthermore, it was not necessary, as a matter of pleading, to specify the degree of a principal's participation; conviction in either capacity could be had upon the same indictment. Finally, liability of one principal did not depend upon the liability of the other. A principal in the second degree could be tried before or after the principal in the first degree and could be convicted even following acquittal of the primary actor.

In contrast, the distinction between principals and accessories was critically important. Jurisdiction over principals lay where the crime was committed, but an accessory could be tried only where the act of assistance was performed. Moreover, the indictment had to specify the defendant's role as principal or accessory. A person charged as an accessory before the fact could not be convicted if the evidence demonstrated liability as a principal, or vice versa. Most striking of all was the requirement of conviction of the principal as a prerequisite to liability of an accessory.

Anything that defeated conviction of the primary actor also barred punishment of an accessory. Thus, if the principal escaped apprehension, or died
before trial, or for any reason was found not guilty, the accessory had to go
free.

This scheme invited evasion of justice. One person might induce
another to perform criminal conduct for which that person could not be
held liable. For example, the infancy, insanity, or innocent mistake of one
who actually administered a lethal poison might bar conviction for murder
of the person who tricked him or her into doing so. The common-law
answer to this problem was the doctrine of innocent agency. Under this
view, the guiltless actor was deemed a mere instrumentality of the ultimate
wrongdoer. Thus, a person apparently in the posture of an accessory before
the fact could be tried and convicted as a principal in the first degree for
acting through an innocent agent. Where the immediate actor was less than
"innocent," however, his or her conviction remained an essential prerequisite for punishment of any secondary party.

**2.  Abrogation of the Common Law.** The common law regarded
accessorial liability as derivative in nature. Since the liability of an accessory derived from that of the principal offender, establishing the guilt of the
latter was an indispensable precondition to punishing the former. Today,
virtually every American jurisdiction has modified this scheme by legislation. The essential features of these statutes are to abrogate procedural
distinctions between principals and accessories before the fact and to allow
prosecution of all such parties as principals. The statutes specifically reject
the rule that conviction of the principal is a precondition for conviction of
an accessory. The California provision is fairly typical in providing that,
"An accessory to the commission of a felony may be prosecuted, tried, and
punished, though the principal may be neither prosecuted nor tried, and
though the principal may have been acquitted." Cal. Penal Code § 972.
Since it is no longer necessary to distinguish between principals and
accessories before the fact, all such parties may be designated by the
generic term "accomplice." (Accessories after the fact continue to be
treated separately, as is described in a subsequent note.)

It must not be supposed, however, that the statutory abrogation of the
common law has rendered that tradition entirely irrelevant. In many
jurisdictions, common-law terminology is still used. And even though the
common law has been everywhere curtailed, bits and pieces of that legacy
continue to turn up. Most importantly, the concept of derivative liability
continues to influence judicial articulation of the substantive requirements
for liability as an accomplice. Thus, although conviction of the principal is
no longer a procedural prerequisite to trial of an accessory, it may continue
to be necessary to prove, in the prosecution of a secondary party, that the
activity of the primary actor amounted to a "crime."

**3.  Accessories After the Fact.** Despite the widespread abrogation
of distinctions between principals and accessories before the fact, accessories after the fact continue to be dealt with separately. For one thing, they
are punished differently. The common law made all parties to crime equally

liable. One who helped a murderer escape became subject to the penalties for murder. Today, the liability of an accessory after the fact is fixed, usually at the level of a misdemeanor or junior felony. More radically, many modern statutes abandon altogether the fiction that one who aids a felon to avoid justice somehow becomes a retroactive participant in the original crime. These statutes punish such misconduct as a form of obstruction of justice.

Section 242.3 of the Model Penal Code is illustrative. It does not deal with parties to crime but defines an independent substantive offense of hindering apprehension of another. The gist of the offense is the purposeful hindering of the apprehension, prosecution, conviction, or punishment of another by any of a number of specified activities—e.g., harboring a fugitive; providing a weapon, transportation, disguise, or other means of effecting escape; or concealing evidence. The focus of this offense is on interference with law enforcement rather than on the obvious fiction that one who aids a fugitive thereby becomes a party to the original crime. In line with this approach, the Model Code provision is not limited to aiding persons known to be guilty of crime; it also applies to persons merely charged with, or sought for, criminal activity. The core of the offense is obstructive conduct done with the purpose "to hinder the apprehension, prosecution, conviction or punishment of another for crime." Penalties for this offense are similar to those assigned to other forms of obstruction of justice and in no case approach the very serious sanctions provided for major felonies.

---

## SUBSECTION A: THE CONDUCT REQUIRED FOR COMPLICITY

---

## Rex v. Russell

Supreme Court of Victoria, 1932.
[1933] Vict. L.R. 59.

■ CUSSEN, ACTING CHIEF JUSTICE. In this case the accused was charged on the first count of the presentment with having at Sunshine in Victoria on the 11th day of June 1932 murdered Ivy Letitia Russell; on the second count with having at the same time and place murdered Harold George Russell; and on the third count with having at the same time and place murdered Eric Russell. Ivy Letitia Russell was the accused's wife, and the others mentioned their two children, aged three-and-a-half and one-and-a-half years respectively, and the deaths of all were due to drowning. After a trial beginning on Monday the 26th September 1932 and lasting several days, the presiding judge opened his charge to the jury by saying:

> Gentlemen, the prisoner is presented on three counts charging
> him for that he severally murdered his wife and his two chil-

dren. . . . These three persons came to their deaths by drowning, and the Crown case is that the prisoner drowned them. If the evidence satisfies you of the truth of that charge, then he was guilty of murder. The opposing theory—and it seems to be the only possible opposing theory—is that they drowned themselves; that is, that the mother destroyed her children and committed suicide. . . .

His Honour having completed his charge, the jury at 1:10 p.m. on the 30th September, retired to consider its verdict; and at 4:25 returned into court to ask a question. What then took place is as follows:

The Foreman: "Assuming that the woman took the children into the water without the assistance of putting them in the water by the man, but that he stood by, conniving to the act, what is the position from the standpoint of the law?"

His Honour: "One has to be very careful about the facts that you are supposing. As I understand your question, he is looking on?"

The Foreman: "Yes."

His Honour: "Are you supposing a case where he is offering no encouragement or persuasion to her to do it, but simply standing by and watching his wife drown the children? Is that the case?"

The Foreman: "That is the position."

His Honour: "It is a question upon which, before I answer it, I should like to hear some argument from counsel, because the circumstances are very special, having regard to the relationship of these parties; and I will ask you to return to your room, and I will bring you in again and answer it as I understand the law to be."

At 4:28 p.m. the jury again retired, and His Honour discussed with counsel matters arising out of the jury's question. . . . At 4:50 p.m. the jury again returned into court, and His Honour addressed them as follows:

Mr. Foreman and gentlemen, you have raised a case of some nicety, and I will do my best to put the position clearly before you. On the bare facts as you have stated them to me, and I repeated them to you, the position is that the accused man, being under a duty by reason of his parenthood of caring for the safety of children in his charge and in his power, would come under a duty to take steps to prevent the commission of that crime by his wife, and his failure to discharge that duty—standing by, as you put it, and doing nothing—would make him guilty of the crime of manslaughter. . . .

[The jury subsequently returned a verdict of guilty of manslaughter on all three counts.]

In my view, which I shall elaborate later, the jury must be taken to have found that though the act immediately resulting in all three deaths was that of the accused's wife, the accused was present "conniving to" the act; and the legal result of such finding was, in the circumstances, that the accused was guilty as a participator or principal or, as it is sometimes called, a principal in the second degree. In these circumstances I think it will be convenient in the first place to cite some authorities relating to the principles of criminal law with regard to the liability of principals in the second degree....

In Lord Mohun's Case, [1692] 12 How.St.Tr. 949, it was said if the person present "doth neither aid nor abet, nor any ways agree to the doing of the thing," i.e., the killing, "it will neither be murder nor manslaughter"; and later it was stated: "for if he never engaged or agreed to the killing of him, nor was there for that purpose, nor at the time did any way act, or join, or assist, in the doing of it; in those cases he is certainly not guilty"....

In 2 W. Hawkins, Pleas of the Crown, ch. 19, § 10 (1716), it is stated: "Also those who by accident are barely present when a felony is committed, and are merely passive, and neither any way encourage it, nor endeavor to hinder it, nor to apprehend the offenders, shall neither be adjudged principals, or accessories...."

In M. Dalton, Justice of the Peace 527 (1727), it is stated: "But he that is present at the time of the felony committed (be it in case of murder, robbery, burglary or larceny) is a principal at this day, if he were either a procurer, or mover or aider, comforter or consenter thereto, although at that present he doth nothing." ... In M. Foster, Crown Law 350 (3d ed. 1809) (originally published in 1762), it is stated: "In order to render a person an accomplice and a principal in a felony, he must be aiding and abetting at the fact, or ready to afford assistance, if necessary: and therefore if A happeneth to be present at a murder for instance, and taketh no part in it, nor endeavoureth to prevent it, nor apprehendeth the murderer, nor levyeth hue and cry after him; this strange behaviour of his, though highly criminal, will not of itself render him either principal or accessory...." In Regina v. Coney, [1882] 8 Q.B.D. 534, 539–40, Cave, J. says: "Now it is a general rule in the case of principals in the second degree that there must be participation in the act, and that, although a man is present whilst a felony is being committed, if he takes no part in it, and does not act in concert with those who commit it, he will not be a principal in the second degree merely because he does not endeavour to prevent the felony, or apprehend the felon".... In the same case, Hawkins, J. says:

> In my opinion, to constitute an aider and abettor some active steps must be taken by word, or action, with the intent to instigate the principal, or principals.... It is no criminal offense to stand by, a mere passive spectator of a crime, even of a murder. Non-interference to prevent a crime is not itself a crime. But the fact that a person was voluntarily and purposely present witnessing the commission of a crime, and offered no opposition to it, though he might reasonably be expected to prevent and had the power so to do, or at least to express his dissent, might under some

circumstances afford cogent evidence upon which a jury would be justified in finding that he wilfully encouraged and so aided and abetted. . . .

Taking these authorities as a whole, I am of the opinion (i) that if a person present at the commission of a crime in the opinion of the jury on sufficient evidence shows his assent to such commission, he is guilty as a principal, and (ii) that assent may in some cases be properly found by the jury to be shown by the absence of dissent, or in the absence of what may be called an effective dissent. Various words, such as "aiding," "abetting," "comforting," "concurring," "approbating," "encouraging," "consenting," "assenting," "countenancing," are to be found in the authorities. . . . All the words abovementioned are, I think, instances of one general idea, that the person charged as a principal in the second degree is in some way linked in purpose with the person actually committing the crime, and is by his words or conduct doing something to bring about, or rendering more likely, such commission. . . . Now in the circumstances of this case I think that an absence of dissent or of a real dissent by the accused might well "show assent" to the wife's action in drowning herself and their children. The jury may well have considered the woman was desperate and distracted or angry and thought that there was no way but this to end her troubles. One of the influences which would lead her to this would be the fact that her husband did not care what became of her or of her and the children, and that this was shown by his non-interference. In such a case a husband and father doing nothing, or nothing effective, to prevent a tragedy may well be taken as showing his assent to what he contemplated as likely to happen. . . .

For the reasons I have given, I think the verdicts on all three counts should stand. . . .

---

## NOTES ON THE CONDUCT REQUIRED FOR COMPLICITY

**1. Questions and Comments on *Russell*.** The liability of a secondary participant in criminal activity is determined by the conduct and culpability required for complicity. The actus reus of complicity raises the familiar question of how much conduct is enough. How much aid or encouragement must the accomplice give? How much must the accomplice's conduct contribute to the perpetration of the crime? Think about this issue as you study the *Russell* opinion and consider the following questions and comments.

**(i) Accomplice Liability.** How important is it to the result in *Russell* that the defendant was husband and father to the deceased? Would the same rule of assent by silence apply to someone who had no legal responsibility towards the persons involved? At one point, the opinion seems to emphasize the defendant's familial relationship as the basis of his duty to take steps to prevent the suicide[a] of the wife and the murder of the children. Would a relationship of this sort would be necessary for an on-looker's silence to "show assent" to the criminal scheme? Might a lover or friend, or even the wife's lawyer, also be found to be "comforting," "encouraging," or "countenancing" the wife's scheme by standing by and doing nothing? Should such a person be held guilty of complicity in a homicide?

**(ii) Independent Liability.** Could the defendant in *Russell* could have been convicted as a principal in the first degree rather than as a secondary party? Given that he had a legal duty to care for his wife and children, could his failure to do so be an independent basis of liability for homicide? This possibility was considered but rejected in an opinion in the same case by Justice Mann. After citing cases involving starvation of a child or ward through neglect of a parent or guardian, he said:

> These cases may be regarded as defining the legal sanctions which the law attaches to the moral duty of a parent to protect his children of tender years from physical harm. If applicable to the present case, those authorities would point to the accused's being guilty of what I may call an independent crime of murder. The outstanding difference between the facts of such cases as I have cited and the facts of the present case is the interposition in the latter of a criminal act of a third person which is the immediate cause of death, and the difficulty in such a case is in saying, in the absence of express authority, that the inaction of the accused has caused the death of the children, within the meaning of the criminal law.

Causation in the criminal law is covered in Chapter VIII. It is important to note here, however, that many secondary participants in homicide cases might plausibly be said to have "caused" the forbidden result of death of another by aiding or encouraging the primary actor. In such cases the secondary participant arguably could be held directly and independently liable for criminal homicide. The law, however, has not developed in this way. Traditionally, the courts have refused to find a remote actor liable for "causing" death of another where the chain of causation involves independent criminal participation by a responsible person. Justice Mann's argument against independent liability for criminal homicide on the facts of *Russell* reflects the settled understanding on this point.

There is one situation, however, in which the liability of a secondary participant for the primary actor's conduct or the result of that conduct is measured by the concept of causation. Where the remote actor acts through an "innocent agent," i.e., a duped or irresponsible participant, he or she may be held liable as a principal in the first degree for "causing" the conduct of the agent. Thus, for example, if Russell had tricked his wife into

---

[a] At common law, suicide was a felony leading to forfeiture of goods and ignominious burial. It followed that one who aided and abetted a successful suicide could be punished as a party to that crime.

administering poison to their children, he could have been punished for "causing" their deaths by means of an innocent agent.

Given that Russell's wife was apparently a responsible (if distraught) agent in the deaths, the issue was whether the defendant "aided or abetted" his wife in causing the deaths and thereby became liable as an accomplice. And the answer to this question depends on how much conduct is required to support liability for aiding, abetting, or encouraging another to commit a crime.

**2. *State v. Walden*.** Compare with *Russell* the very similar facts presented in State v. Walden, 306 N.C. 466, 293 S.E.2d 780 (1982). The defendant was charged with aiding and abetting a felonious assault on her one-year-old son. The child was beaten with a leather belt by "Bishop" Hoskins. The belt had a metal buckle, and the child was seriously injured. The mother was present during the beating. She did not participate, but neither did she do anything to prevent the assault. The trial court ruled that no affirmative action by the mother was necessary to her liability. Specifically, the jury was instructed that the defendant should be found guilty if she "was present with the reasonable opportunity and duty to prevent the crime and failed to take reasonable steps to do so." The resulting conviction was affirmed by the North Carolina Supreme Court, which stated:

> It remains the law that one may not be found to be an aider and abettor, and thus guilty as a principal, solely because he is present when a crime is committed. It will still be necessary, in order to have that effect, that it be shown that the defendant said or did something showing his consent to the criminal purpose and contribution to its execution. But we hold that the failure of a parent who is present to take all steps reasonably possible to protect the parent's child from an attack by another person constitutes an act of omission by the parent showing the parent's consent and contribution to the crime being committed.

Is the decision correct? Does it rest on the same ground as the result in *Russell,* or are the two cases distinguishable?

**3. *McGhee v. Virginia*.** In McGhee v. Virginia, 221 Va. 422, 270 S.E.2d 729 (1980), the defendant was convicted as an accessory before the fact to the murder of her husband, and sentenced to a term of 20 years. The husband and two co-workers were killed by defendant's lover and his brother. The evidence showed that the defendant had urged the lover to kill her husband and had informed him of the logging site where the husband could be found. There was no evidence that the defendant was involved in planning the details of the killings or that she knew the precise date.

The Supreme Court of Virginia affirmed the conviction. The court noted that Virginia law defined an accessory as "one not present at the commission of the offense, but who is in some way concerned therein, either before or after, as [a] contriver, instigator or advisor, or as a receiver or protector of the perpetrator." Applying this definition, the court said:

In the trial of an accessory before the fact, the Commonwealth must establish the accused was a "contriver, instigator *or* advisor" of the crime committed by the principal. An instigator of a crime is an accessory before the fact even though he or she did not participate in the planning of the crime or even though unaware of the precise time or place of the crime's commission or of the precise method employed by the principal. A contrary holding would allow instigators to escape liability for their actions by removing themselves from the planning of crimes they have incited.

One justice dissented.

Is this result sound? Is the court's standard for imposing accessorial liability satisfactory?

**4. *State v. Tally.*** In this connection consider the famous old case of State ex rel. Attorney General v. Tally, Judge, 102 Ala. 25, 15 So. 722 (1894). An impeachment proceeding was brought against Judge Tally for his role in the murder of one Ross. Ross had seduced Tally's sister-in-law, Annie Skelton. Fearing retaliation by her kinsmen, Ross set out from Scottsboro to Stevenson, where he meant to catch a train to Chattanooga. A group of Skeltons followed Ross to Stevenson, where they ambushed and killed him.

Judge Tally remained in Scottsboro. After the Skeltons left town, he stationed himself at the telegraph office to prevent any warning to Ross. When a relative of Ross did send a warning, Judge Tally wired to his friend Huddleston, the telegraph operator in Stevenson, the following message: "Do not let the party warned get away.... Say nothing." Huddleston received both messages and immediately went to look for Ross. Not finding him, Huddleston returned to his office. He then saw a hack coming from the direction of Scottsboro with a man whom he correctly supposed to be Ross. This time, however, Huddleston made no effort to deliver the warning, and Ross was killed shortly thereafter.

The court found that these facts made Tally an accomplice in the murder of Ross:

> [B]efore Judge Tally can be found guilty of aiding and abetting the Skeltons to kill Ross, it must appear that his vigil at Scottsboro to prevent Ross from being warned of his danger was by preconcert with them, or at least known to them, whereby they would naturally be incited, encouraged, and emboldened—given confidence—to the deed, or that he aided them to kill Ross, contributed to Ross' death, in point of physical fact, by means of the telegram he sent to Huddleston. The assistance given, however, need not contribute to the criminal result in the sense that but for it the result would not have ensued. It is quite sufficient if it facilitated a result that would have transpired without it. It is quite enough if the aid merely rendered it easier for the principal actor to accomplish the end intended by him and the aider and

abettor, though in all human probability the end would have been attained without it. If the aid in homicide can be shown to have put the deceased at a disadvantage, to have deprived him of a single chance of life which but for it he would have had, he who furnishes such aid is guilty, though it cannot be known or shown that the dead man, in the absence thereof, would have availed himself of that chance; as, where one counsels murder, he is guilty as an accessory before the fact, though it appears to be probable that murder would have been done without his counsel....

[The evidence shows] that Tally's standing guard at the telegraph office in Scottsboro to prevent Ross being warned of the pursuit of the Skeltons was not by preconcert with them, and was not known to them. It is even clear and more certain that they knew neither of the occasion nor the fact of the sending of the message by him to Huddleston; and hence they were not, and could not have been, aided in the execution of their purpose to kill by the keeping of this vigil, or by the mere fact of the forwarding of the message to Stevenson, since these facts in and of themselves could not have given them any actual, substantial help, as distinguished from incitement and encouragement, and they could not have aided them by way of incitement and encouragement, because they were ignorant of them; and so we are come to a consideration of the effect, if any, produced upon the situation at Stevenson by the message of Judge Tally to Huddleston....

It is inconceivable to us after the maturest consideration, reflection, and discussion, but that Ross' predicament was rendered infinitely more desperate, his escape more difficult, and his death of much more easy and certain accomplishment by the withholding from him of the message [of warning]....

Is *Tally* a difficult case? As the court saw it, Tally made the killing of Ross "of much more easy and certain accomplishment." Given this conclusion, should it matter that the primary actors did not know of Tally's assistance?

A more difficult issue is posed where the accomplice's "aid" is entirely ineffective. Suppose, for example, that Tally had posted himself at the telegraph office in order to intercept a warning to Ross, but no such warning had ever been sent. In such a case his conduct, although intended to assist the Skeltons, would have had no impact on the course of events. Would Tally properly have been liable on those facts?

**5. Describing the Proscribed Conduct: Modern Statutes and the Common Law.** The opinion in *Russell* is typical of the common-law tradition in the profusion of terms defining (or describing) the actus reus of complicity. Modern statutes tend to pare the verbiage of the common law, but one may doubt whether they achieve any great advance in specificity. Many states simply substitute a somewhat shortened list of verbs. The New York statute, for example, provides that one person is criminally liable for the conduct of another when, acting with the required culpability, he or she "solicits, requests, commands, importunes, or intentionally aids such person to engage in such conduct." N.Y. Penal Code § 20.00. The Model Penal Code formulation is more elaborate. Section 2.06(3)(a) declares that a person is liable as an accomplice of another person if:

> with the purpose of promoting or facilitating the commission of the offense, he
>
> > (i) solicits such other person to commit it; or
> >
> > (ii) aids or agrees or attempts to aid such other person in planning or committing it; or
> >
> > (iii) having a legal duty to prevent the commission of the offense, fails to make proper effort so to do....

The Model Code formulation has the advantage of making clear what the drafters envisioned for a case such as *Russell*. Inaction is a basis for accomplice liability, but only for persons having a legal duty to act. For others, some affirmative aid or assistance would be required. Would the same conclusion be reached under the New York statute?

In this connection, reconsider the hypothetical at end of the preceding note. If the actor attempted to aid another in a criminal endeavor but in fact made absolutely no contribution to the outcome of events, what would be the standard of liability under the Model Penal Code? Under the New York law?

**6. A Problem and an Analogy.** As the preceding note illustrates, the Model Penal Code proposes an exceedingly broad formulation of the conduct necessary for liability as an accomplice. The provision covers not only one who aids another in the commission of an offense, but also one who "agrees or attempts to aid such other person in planning or committing it." The drafters justified the reach of this proposal on the grounds that there is no risk to the innocent where a purpose to further or facilitate is required and that there is thereafter no reason, therefore, to make liability turn on the impact of the actor's conduct. MPC § 2.04, Comment at 26 (Tent.Draft No. 1, 1953). Is this persuasive? Are you satisfied that so long as proof of a purpose to facilitate is required, there is no risk of convicting the innocent?

Compare the law of attempt. Attempt requires proof of the actor's purpose to complete the underlying offense. Yet the law does not rest liability entirely on proof of purpose. It also mandates an independent inquiry into the sufficiency of the actor's conduct. In the phraseology of the common law, this is the distinction between a criminal attempt and mere preparation. Under the Model Penal Code and derivative statutes, this issue is addressed through the requirement of "an act or omission constituting a substantial step in a course of conduct planned to culminate in [the] commission of the crime." MPC § 5.01(1)(c). This standard is elaborated further by examples and by the general specification that it must be conduct "strongly corroborative of the actor's criminal purpose." MPC § 5.01(2). Why is not the same concern present in the context of accomplice liability? Indeed, why should not the Model Code approach to this question in the law of attempt be adapted for inclusion in the law of complicity? Might it not be profitable to inquire, for example, whether the actor's "aid," or, as in *Russell* and *Walden*, inaction in the face of a duty to act, was sufficiently corroborative of culpability to support liability as an accomplice?

One answer might be that the Model Code formulation ("aids . . . or attempts to aid") requires either actual aid, in which case the actor's culpability is corroborated by the fact of assistance in a criminal endeavor, or an attempt to aid, in which case the standards of § 5.01 apply. Is this a sufficient response?

---

## SUBSECTION B: THE CULPABILITY REQUIRED FOR COMPLICITY

---

## United States v. Peoni

United States Court of Appeals for the Second Circuit, 1938.
100 F.2d 401.

■ L. HAND, CIRCUIT JUDGE. Peoni was indicted in the Eastern District of New York upon three counts for possessing counterfeit money. . . . The jury convicted him on all counts, and the only question we need consider is whether the evidence was enough to sustain the verdict. It was this. In the Borough of the Bronx Peoni sold counterfeit bills to one, Regno; and Regno sold the same bills to one, Dorsey, also in the Bronx. All three knew the bills were counterfeit, and Dorsey was arrested while trying to pass them in the Borough of Brooklyn. The question is whether Peoni was guilty as an accessory to Dorsey's possession. . . .

The prosecution's argument is that, as Peoni put the bills in circulation and knew that Regno would be likely, not to pass them himself, but to sell them to another guilty possessor, the possession of the second buyer was a natural consequence of Peoni's original act, with which he might be charged. If this were a civil case, that would be true; an innocent buyer from Dorsey could sue Peoni and get judgment against him for his loss. But the rule of criminal liability is not the same; since Dorsey's possession was not de facto Peoni's, and since Dorsey was not Peoni's agent, Peoni can be liable only as an accessory to Dorsey's act of possession. The test of that must be found in the appropriate federal statute. [Title 18, § 550, predecessor of the current 18 U.S.C. § 2, provided punishment as a principal for anyone who "aids, abets, counsels, commands, induces, or procures" the commission of any offense against the United States.]

It will be observed that all these definitions have nothing whatever to do with the probability that the forbidden result would follow upon the accessory's conduct; and that they all demand that he in some sort associate himself with the venture, that he participate in it as in something that he wishes to bring about, that he seek by his action to make it succeed. All the words used—even the most colorless, "abet"—carry an implication of purposive attitude towards it. So understood, Peoni was not an accessory to Dorsey's possession; his connection with the business ended when he got his money from Regno, who might dispose of the bills as he chose; it was of no moment to him whether Regno sold them to a second possible passer. His utterance of the bills was indeed a step in the causal chain which ended in Dorsey's possession, but that was all. . . .

Conviction reversed; accused discharged.

---

## Backun v. United States

United States Court of Appeals for the Fourth Circuit, 1940.
112 F.2d 635.

■ PARKER, CIRCUIT JUDGE. This is an appeal from a conviction and sentence under an indictment charging the appellant Backun and one Zucker with the crime of transporting stolen merchandise of a value in excess of $5,000 in interstate commerce, knowing it to have been stolen, in violation of the National Stolen Property Act, 18 U.S.C. § 415. Zucker pleaded guilty and testified for the prosecution. There was evidence to the effect that he was apprehended at a pawnshop in Charlotte, N.C. in possession of a large quantity of silverware, a portion of which was shown to have been stolen a short while before. He testified that he purchased all of the silverware from Backun in New York; that the purchase was partly on credit; that Backun had the silverware concealed in a closet and in the cellar of his residence; that there was no sale for second-hand silverware in New York but a good market for it in the South; that Backun knew of Zucker's custom to travel in the South and was told by Zucker that he wished to take the silverware on the road with him; and that Backun sold to him for $1,400 silverware which was shown by other witnesses to be of a much greater value. A part of the silverware was wrapped in a laundry bag which was identified by means of a laundry ticket as having been in the possession of Backun. . . .

There is no serious controversy as to the evidence being sufficient to show that Backun sold the property to Zucker knowing it to have been stolen. It is contended, however . . . that there is no evidence that Backun had anything to do with the transportation in interstate commerce.

. . . [I]t is to be noted that the case presented is not that of a mere seller of merchandise, who knows that the buyer intends to put it to an unlawful use, but who cannot be said in anywise to will the unlawful use by the buyer. It is the case of a sale of stolen property by a guilty possessor who knows that the buyer will transport it in interstate commerce in violation of law and who desires to sell it to him for that reason. The stolen property was not salable in New York. Backun knew that Zucker could dispose of it on his visits to the Southern pawnbrokers and would take it with him on his trips to the South. The sale was made at a grossly inadequate price and Zucker was credited for a part even of that. While there was no express contract that Zucker was to carry the property out of the state, Backun knew that he would do so; and, by making the sale to him, caused the transportation in interstate commerce just as certainly as if that transportation had been a term of the contract of sale. As his will thus contributed to the commission of the felony by Zucker, he would have been guilty at common law as an accessory before the fact to the commission of the felony. His guilt as a principal is fixed by 18 U.S.C. § 550, which provides that one who "aids, abets, counsels, commands, induces, or procures" the commission of an offense is guilty as a principal....

Whether one who sells property to another knowing that the buyer intends to use it for the commission of a felony renders himself criminally liable as aiding and abetting in its commission, is a question as to which there is some conflict of authority. It must be remembered, however, that guilt as accessory before the fact has application only in cases of felony; and since it is elementary that every citizen is under moral obligation to prevent the commission of felony, if possible, and has the legal right to use force to prevent its commission and to arrest the perpetrator without warrant, it is difficult to see why, in selling goods which he knows will make its perpetration possible with knowledge that they are to be used for that purpose, he is not aiding and abetting in its commission within any fair meaning of those terms. Undoubtedly he would be guilty, were he to give to the felon the goods which make the perpetration of the felony possible with knowledge that they would be used for that purpose; and we cannot see that his guilt is purged or his breach of social duty excused because he receives a price for them. In either case, he knowingly aids and assists in the perpetration of the felony.

Guilt as an accessory depends, not on "having a stake" in the outcome of the crime ... but on aiding and assisting the perpetrators; and those who make a profit by furnishing to criminals, whether by sale or otherwise, the means to carry on their nefarious undertakings aid them just as truly as if they were actual partners with them, having a stake in the fruits of their enterprise. To say that the sale of goods is a normally lawful transaction is beside the point. The seller may not ignore the purpose for which the purchase is made if he is advised of that purpose, or wash his hands of the aid that he has given the perpetrator of a felony by the plea that he has merely made a sale of merchandise. One who sells a gun to another knowing that he is buying it to commit a murder, would hardly escape conviction as an accessory to the murder by showing that he received full price for the gun; and no difference in principle can be drawn between such a case and any other case of a seller who knows that the purchaser intends to use the goods which he is purchasing in the commission of felony. In any such case, not only does the act of the seller assist in the commission of the felony, but his will assents to its commission, since he could refuse to give the assistance by refusing to make the sale....

But even if the view be taken that aiding and abetting is not to be predicated [on] an ordinary sale made with knowledge that the purchaser intends to use the goods purchased in the commission of felony, we think that the circumstances relied on by the government here are sufficient to establish the guilt of Backun. The sale here was not of a mere instrumentality to be used in the commission of felony, but of the very goods which were to be feloniously transported. Backun knew not only that the commission of felony was contemplated by Zucker with respect to such goods, but also that the felony could not be committed by Zucker unless the sale were made to him. The sale thus made possible the commission of the felony by Zucker; and, if Zucker is to be believed, the commission of the felony was one of the purposes which Backun had in mind in making the sale. After testifying that he had told Backun that he wished to go on the road with the silverware (i.e., transport it in interstate commerce), he says "He (Backun) knew that. That is the reason he wanted to sell it to me." There can be no question, therefore, but that the evidence sustains the view that the felony committed by Zucker flowed from the will of Backun as well as from his own will, and that Backun aided its commission by making the sale. There was thus evidence of direct participation of Backun in the criminal purpose of Zucker; and whatever view be taken as to the case of a mere sale, certainly such evidence is sufficient to establish guilt. . . .

[Conviction reversed on other grounds.]

———

## NOTES ON THE CULPABILITY REQUIRED FOR COMPLICITY

**1.   Knowledge vs. Stake in the Venture.** *Peoni* and *Backun* are the most famous entries in the continuing debate on the culpability required for complicity. Of course, everyone agrees that the accomplice must have some culpability (probably knowledge) with respect to the conduct that constitutes aid or assistance. That is to say, the accomplice must be aware of his or her own conduct. Not surprisingly, that aspect of the required culpability is so rarely put in issue that it is virtually never discussed.

The issue that sparks dispute is the accomplice's required culpability with respect to the conduct of the primary actor. Must the accomplice must actually intend to promote the criminal venture in the sense of being interested in its success? Or does it suffice that the accomplice knowingly assist criminal activity by another? The distinction matters, for example, when a vendor sells some thing with knowledge that it will be used in the commission of a crime, or when a landlord leases premises with knowledge that they will be used for illegal activity, or when a utility provides telephone service with knowledge that it will be used for bookmaking.

How should these situations be resolved? Should sellers of goods or services be liable as accomplices whenever they know of a customer's criminal purpose? Should the sale of bongs be punished on this ground? On the other hand, might it go too far to require that an accomplice actually be interested in the success of the crime? Would you allow one who knowingly aided a would-be assassin simply to ignore the consequences of that act?

The drafters of the Model Penal Code had trouble coming to rest on this point. The tentative draft provision on complicity included the following language:

> A person is an accomplice of another person in commission of a crime if ... acting with knowledge that such other person was committing or had the purpose of committing the crime, he knowingly, substantially facilitated its commission.

MPC § 2.04 (Tent. Draft No. 1, 1953). The drafters defended this proposal on the ground that knowing assistance should suffice for liability whenever such assistance *substantially* facilitated the criminal scheme. A vendor in the ordinary course of business probably would not be liable as an accomplice to a customer's crime, even if the criminal purpose were known at the time of sale. On the other hand, a vendor of highly specialized goods (e.g., unregistered firearms or an obscure poison) or one who sells outside the ordinary course of business (e.g., through special credit arrangements to an otherwise uncreditworthy purchaser) perhaps would be covered. Evidently, the wisdom of this approach came to be doubted, for the quoted provisions were deleted by vote of the American Law Institute after a floor debate in which both Judge Hand and Judge Parker participated. As finally approved, the Model Penal Code imposes liability as an accomplice only where the aider has "the purpose of promoting or facilitating the commission of the offense." Is the change justified?[a]

**2. Compromise Solutions and the Offense of Facilitation.** Some have sought to compromise the choice between knowledge and a stake in the venture. One such effort was the original Model Penal Code proposal to punish knowing assistance as complicity, but only where it substantially facilitated commission of the offense. Another idea is to punish knowing assistance for serious offenses, but to require a stake in the venture for minor crimes. Although the courts seldom articulate a distinction of this sort, a review of the cases suggests that the gravity of the offense affects the readiness to base accomplice liability on knowing aid.

The most interesting compromise comes from the revised penal code of New York. The New York provision on complicity requires that the accomplice "intentionally aid" the criminal conduct of another. N.Y. Penal Code § 20.00. As the accompanying commentary explains, this formulation was intended to preclude liability as an accomplice for knowing aid rendered "without having any specific intent ... to commit or profit from the crime." N.Y. Penal Code § 20.00, Practice Commentaries at 44. Additionally, however, the New York Code includes an entirely new offense called "criminal facilitation":

[a] For a general treatment of this issue, see Louis Westerfield, The Mens Rea Requirement of Accomplice Liability in American Criminal Law—Knowledge or Intent, 51 Miss.L.J. 155 (1980). The involved but interesting history of the issue in California is analyzed in Catherine L. Carpenter, Should the Court Aid and Abet the Unintending Accomplice: The Status of Complicity in California, 24 Santa Clara L.Rev. 343 (1984).

> A person is guilty of criminal facilitation . . . when, believing it probable that he is rendering aid to a person who intends to commit a crime, he engages in conduct which provides such person with means or opportunity for the commission thereof and which in fact aids such person to commit a felony.

N.Y. Penal Code § 115.00. Although this provision punishes some instances of knowing assistance to criminal activity by another, it does not always do so. For one thing, the facilitation offense requires that the aid or assistance provide the principal actor "with means or opportunity for the commission" of the crime. This specification of the quantum of assistance required has no parallel in the New York complicity provision. It is reminiscent of the original Model Code proposal, which emphasized the substantiality of facilitation as a criterion of liability. Moreover, the New York facilitation offense is limited to conduct which in fact aids another to commit a *felony*. By this limitation, knowing assistance to minor offenses is excluded. Finally, facilitation is graded less severely than the underlying offense.

For an argument in favor of a facilitation offense and analysis of its application in particular cases, see Catherine L. Carpenter, Should the Court Aid and Abet the Unintending Accomplice: The Status of Complicity in California, 24 Santa Clara L. Rev. 353, 363–70 (1984).

**3. Culpability Required for Results.** It seems clear, although the cases seldom so state, that the entire debate between intent to promote and knowing assistance is directed to the accomplice's state of mind with respect to the *conduct* elements of the underlying offense. In other words, the debates concerns what mental attitude the accomplice must have with respect to the criminal acts done by the principal.

A different approach has been used for assessing the accomplice's culpability with respect to the *results* of that conduct. The following hypothetical presents the issue:

> A entertains B in her home. A has promised to drive B home but at the end of the evening she is too tired. A therefore lends B her car, even though she knows that B is quite drunk and unable to drive safely. On his way home, B veers onto the wrong side of the road and crashes into another driver, who dies instantly.[b]

Clearly B is liable for some form of criminal homicide. The question is whether A is liable as an accomplice to that offense.

Unlike most prior statutes, the Model Penal Code contains an explicit provision specifying the mens rea that an accomplice must have with respect to the result of the primary actor's conduct. Section 2.06(4) states:

> When causing a particular result is an element of an offense, an accomplice in the conduct causing such result is an accomplice in the commission of that offense, if he acts with the kind of culpability, if any, with respect to that result that is sufficient for the commission of the crime.

---

[b] The hypothetical is based on People v. Marshall, 362 Mich. 170, 106 N.W.2d 842 (1961), where the court ruled against liability of the secondary party. But see, e.g., Story v. United States, 16 F.2d 342 (D.C.Cir. 1926).

What would the Model Code do in this hypothetical? What issues would the jury have to resolve if *A* were charged with complicity in manslaughter under §§ 2.06 and 210.3? With complicity in negligent homicide under §§ 2.06 and 210.4?

**4. Culpability Required for Circumstances.** In contrast to the explicit treatment of conduct and results, even modern penal codes fail to specify the state of mind required of an accomplice with respect to the attendant *circumstances* of the criminal conduct. There are two obvious possibilities. One is to require that the accomplice know that the circumstance element exists. The alternative is to carry over to the accomplice the level of culpability required of the primary actor by the definition of the offense. The difference between these formulations is posed by the following hypothetical:

> *A* is asked by his friend *B* to assist in the latter's seduction of *C*, a mutual acquaintance. Specifically, *B* wants to borrow *A*'s apartment. *A* agrees, and the seduction is accomplished. To the surprise of both *A* and *B*, *C* turns out to be underage.

Under traditional laws against statutory rape, *B* is strictly liable with respect to the age of his sexual partner. Thus, he may be criminally punished for consensual sexual intercourse with an underage person even if he honestly and reasonably believed *C* to be over the age of consent. The issue here is whether *A* may be held liable on the same basis or whether a special mens-rea requirement of knowledge should be imposed for complicity.

Current law on this question is problematic. Some statutes can be read to say that no special mens rea is required,[c] but most are ambiguous on the point. The absence of any settled common-law understanding is probably due to the infrequency with which the question arises. Obviously, the situation of the accomplice in the hypothetical described above is far less likely to excite prosecutorial interest than is the case of a secondary participant in criminal homicide. Perhaps for that reason, there seems to be no clear rule. If the issue arises, how should it be resolved? Is the discussion of the analogous issue in the law of attempt helpful?

---

# People v. Durham

Supreme Court of California, 1969.
70 Cal.2d 171, 74 Cal.Rptr. 262, 449 P.2d 198.

■ SULLIVAN, JUSTICE. A jury found defendants Gilbert Lee Durham and Edgar Leonard Robinson guilty of murder in the first degree. After a

---

[c] See, e.g., N.Y. Penal Code § 20.00, which reads in its entirety as follows:

> When one person engages in conduct which constitutes an offense, another person is criminally liable for such conduct when, *acting with the mental culpability required for the commission thereof,* he solicits, requests, commands, importunes or intentionally aids such person to engage in such conduct. [Emphasis added.]

penalty trial the same jury fixed the punishment of Durham at life imprisonment and the punishment of Robinson at death, and sentences were rendered accordingly. Durham appeals from the judgment and from the denial of his motion for a new trial. . . .

On October 16, 1966, about 4:00 a.m., Los Angeles Police Officers Treutlein and Du Puis, engaged in routine patrol duties, were driving westward on Pico Boulevard in a marked patrol car. They noticed a beige Thunderbird automobile travelling in the same direction in the lane nearest the curb; it bore Ohio license plates and was occupied by two male Negroes. As the Thunderbird proceeded down the boulevard it swerved slightly to the right at two intersecting streets as if making a right turn into them; on each occasion however it continued westward on Pico. The officers followed the vehicle and at the same time radioed headquarters to ascertain if it had been stolen. Before their radio call was answered, the Thunderbird again made a slight swerving motion to the right at an intersection and the officers decided to stop it and question its occupants. They moved into the curb lane behind the Thunderbird, activated their red light, sounded their horn, and directed their spotlight at the rear window. The vehicle stopped near a streetlight, and the patrol car stopped about six feet behind it.

Defendant Durham, the driver of the Thunderbird, got out and walked back toward the patrol car but his passenger, defendant Robinson, remained seated in the vehicle. The officers, who were in uniform, unsnapped the retaining straps on their holsters and alighted from the patrol car. Officer Treutlein asked Durham for his driver's license and the latter produced what appeared to be a plastic credit card. Officer Du Puis asked Durham the name of his passenger; Durham in reply gave a short name. Office Du Puis then went to the passenger side of the Thunderbird and, using the name which Durham had given him, asked Robinson to come to the rear where Durham and Officer Treutlein were standing.

Robinson complied, and Officer Du Puis asked him to raise his hands so as to check him for weapons. Instead, Robinson sprang to a position between the two vehicles and drew a gun from a concealed holster under his shirt. He pointed the weapon at the two officers and ordered them not to move. Officer Du Puis reached for his own revolver and Robinson fired a shot at him, hitting him in the mouth. As he fell Officer Du Puis, who had apparently succeeded in getting his gun free of the holster, fired at Robinson. At this point, Officer Treutlein, who had also drawn his gun, fired at Robinson and hit him. The latter stumbled backward and fell into the street where he lay face up with his gun still in his hand.

Officer Treutlein then directed his attention to Durham, who was crouched on one knee with his hands half raised and his palms spread at about shoulder level. The officer ordered him not to move. Then, keeping Durham covered with the gun, he stepped to the passenger side of the patrol car and reported the shooting on his radio. At one point during the radio call Durham began to lower his hands and Officer Treutlein again commanded him to keep them raised. Durham obeyed. At this point

Robinson, who was still in the same position, began to raise his gun toward Officer Treutlein; the latter commanded him to drop it. Robinson did not do so, and the officer then fired a shot which struck the pavement close to Robinson's head. Robinson then dropped the gun.

Officer Treutlein ordered both defendants to lie face down on the pavement. Within a few minutes other officers arrived and took them into custody. A search of Durham produced a knife and sheath from his coat pocket.

Eleven days later, on October 27, 1966, Officer Du Puis died as a proximate result of the gunshot wound inflicted upon him.

Evidence of the foregoing facts, the substantiality of which is not here disputed, was admitted at trial. There was also admitted, over the strenuous objection of defendants, a considerable volume of evidence regarding the joint activities of defendants during some three weeks preceding the incident of October 16, 1966. This evidence showed in substance: (i) that on the day of the homicide both defendants were on parole under felony sentences from the state of Ohio; that defendant Robinson was at that time subject to arrest in Ohio for violation of the terms of his parole; and that the presence of defendants in California under the circumstances obtaining involved several violations of the terms of parole relating to each of them; (ii) that on October 5, 1966, eleven days prior to the incident, defendants robbed an A & P store in Toledo, Ohio, of $648; and that in the course of this robbery, Robinson exhibited a pistol similar to that used by him on October 16; (iii) that on October 8, 1966, eight days prior to the incident, defendants robbed the Hinky–Dinky Grocery Store in Omaha, Nebraska, of $2,815; that in the course of this robbery Robinson again exhibited a pistol similar to that used by him on October 16; and that he threatened to shoot a cashier in the store if she did not comply with his demands and Durham told the cashier that he (Robinson) "meant it" ; (iv) that after defendants' departure from the Hinky–Dinky Store the manager ran out to the sidewalk in front of the store after them, and, although he saw neither defendant, he noticed a white car parked in an alley across from the store and heard a loud report which he assumed to be a backfire; that the rear window of a car then driving past the market was shattered by a bullet and an occupant of the car was injured by flying glass; that the bullet was found under the seat of that car, and a cartridge casing was found near the position of the lone car which the manager had noticed in the alley; and that scientific examination and tests had determined that the cartridge casing found in the Omaha alley was ejected from the same gun which Robinson used to kill Officer Du Puis; and (v) that the Thunderbird automobile in which defendants were riding on October 16, 1966, had been stolen from a San Francisco automobile agency on or about October 12, and it bore California license plates at that time . . . .

In the frequently cited case of People v. Villa, 156 Cal.App.2d 128, 318 P.2d 828 (1957), the court set forth the following principles relevant in the case before us:

> To be an abettor the accused must have *instigated or advised the commission of the crime or been present for the purpose of*

*assisting in its commission.* He must share the criminal intent with which the crime was committed.... [W]hile mere presence alone at the scene of the crime is not sufficient to make the accused a participant, and while he is not necessarily guilty if he does not attempt to prevent the crime through fear, such factors may be circumstances that can be considered by the jury with the other evidence in passing on his guilt or innocence. *One may aid or abet in the commission of a crime without having previously entered into a conspiracy to commit it. Moreover, the aider and abettor in a proper case is not only guilty of the particular crime that to his knowledge his confederates are contemplating committing, but he is also liable for the natural and reasonable or probable consequences of any act that he knowingly aided or encouraged. Whether the act committed was the natural and probable consequence of the act encouraged and the extent of defendant's knowledge are questions of fact for the jury.*

In the instant case the prosecution, in support of its sole theory of guilt as to Durham, sought to show that he "instigated or advised the commission of the crime" in that he was a party to a compact of criminal conduct which included within its scope the forcible resistance of arrest *and that he was also* "present for the purposes of assisting in its commission" in that his conduct at the scene of the incident, viewed in its totality, was wholly consistent with such purposes. The jury determined that the evidence produced supported the prosecution theory and accordingly found Durham guilty. The evidence supports the finding....

In view of the evidence in the instant case which we have outlined above the jury could reasonably have found that defendants for some time prior to October 16, 1966, had been engaged in a joint expedition which involved the commission of robberies as they moved westward across the country and which included among its purposes the forcible resistance to arrest; that Durham was fully aware of the fact that Robinson both had exhibited his pistol in the commission of said robberies and had actually fired it at one who had sought to apprehend them in the act of escaping; that at the very time they were stopped by Officers Treutlein and Du Puis, defendants were further engaged in the commission of a crime, namely, the driving of an automobile stolen by them; that Durham knew that Robinson was armed when they emerged from the car; and that in the totality of circumstances Robinson's act was, and was known by Durham to be, a reasonable and probable consequence of the continuing course of action undertaken by the defendants. The finding of such facts would be sufficient to support the finding of Durham's guilt as an aider and abettor under the principles we have above set forth. Since the jury was adequately instructed in the premises, we must conclude that the indicated findings were made—and that the evidence is therefore sufficient to support the verdict as to Durham....

[Judgment affirmed.]

NOTE ON THE RULE OF NATURAL AND PROBABLE
CONSEQUENCES

The rule of natural and probable consequences extends the liability of
an accomplice beyond planned offenses. As traditionally stated, the liability
of an accomplice includes the natural and probable consequences of the
criminal endeavor that the accomplice meant to aid or encourage. This rule
applies chiefly where the principal actor engages in some act of violence not
expressly endorsed by the accomplice. The decisive factor in such cases is
often whether the accomplice knew that the principal was armed.

What is the effect of the rule of natural and probable consequences on
the culpability required for complicity? Under the analysis of *Durham*,
what state of mind must the secondary party have had in order to be held
liable for the conduct of the principal actor? What state of mind would the
primary actor be required to have had? What is the justification for
imposing liability on the secondary participant on the *Durham* basis?

The rule of natural and probable consequences is still good law in
many jurisdictions. It has been abandoned, however, in most states that
have adopted comprehensive revisions of their penal laws. This, at least, is
the implication of those statutes, such as Model Penal Code § 2.06(3)(a),
that expressly require that the accomplice have "the purpose of promoting
or facilitating the commission of the offense" by the principal actor. See,
e.g., Haw.Rev.Stat. § 702–222; Cons.Penn.Stat.Ann. tit. 18, § 306(c); Or.
Rev.Stat. § 161.155. Such provisions presumably preclude liability as an
accomplice where the particular purpose to promote or facilitate the principal's conduct cannot be proved. Note, however, that a few jurisdictions with
recently revised penal codes expressly continue the older rule. Thus, for
example, Kan.Stat.Ann. § 21–3205(2) provides that an accomplice to one
offense "is also liable for any other crime committed in pursuance of the
intended crime if reasonably foreseeable by such person as a probable
consequence of committing or attempting to commit the crime intended."
Cf. Wis.Stat.Ann. § 939.05 (virtually identical). See generally Paul Robinson, Imputed Criminal Liability, 93 Yale L.J. 609, 657–58, 665–68 (1984).

---

SUBSECTION C: GUILT OF THE PRINCIPAL

---

## Regina v. Cogan and Leak

Court of Appeal, 1975.
[1976] Q.B. 217.

■ LAWTON, LORD JUSTICE read the following judgment of the court. The
defendants appeal against their conviction of rape....

The victim of the conduct which the prosecution submitted was rape by both defendants was Leak's wife. . . .

[On July 10, 1974] Leak came home at about 6 p.m. with Cogan. Both had been drinking. Leak told his wife Cogan wanted to have sexual intercourse with her and that he, Leak, was going to see she did. She was frightened of him and what he might do.... He made her go upstairs where he took her clothes off and lowered her on to a bed. Cogan then came into the room. Leak asked him twice whether he wanted sexual intercourse with her. On both occasions he said he did not. Leak then had sexual intercourse with her in the presence of Cogan. When he had finished, Leak again asked Cogan if he wanted sexual intercourse with his wife. This time Cogan said he did. He asked Leak to leave the room but he refused to do so. Cogan then had sexual intercourse with Mrs. Leak. Her husband watched. While all this was going on for most of the time, if not all, Mrs. Leak was sobbing. She did not struggle while Cogan was on top of her but she did try to turn away from him. When he had finished, he left the room. Leak then had intercourse with her again and behaved in a revolting fashion to her. When he had finished he joined Cogan and the pair of them left the house to renew their drinking. Mrs. Leak dressed. She went to a neighbour's house and then to the police. The two defendants were arrested about three-quarters of an hour later. Both defendants made oral and written statements....

Leak's statement amounted to a confession that he had procured Cogan to have sexual intercourse with his wife. He admitted that while Cogan was having sexual intercourse with her she was "sobbing on and off not all the time." There was ample evidence from the terms of his statement that she had not consented to Cogan having intercourse with her. The whole tenor of this statement was that he had procured Cogan to do what he did in order to punish her for past misconduct. He intended that she should be raped and that Cogan's body should provide the physical means to that end.

Cogan, in his written statement, admitted that he had had sexual intercourse with Mrs. Leak at Leak's suggestion and that while he was on top of her she had been upset and had cried. At the trial Cogan gave evidence that he thought Mrs. Leak had consented. The basis for his belief was what he had heard from her husband about her. The drink he had seems to have been a reason, if not the only one, for mistaking her sobs and distress for consent....

[In accord with the law as it then stood, the trial court instructed the jury to find Cogan guilty of rape, notwithstanding that he believed Mrs. Leak had consented, if his belief was unreasonable. The jury returned a verdict of guilty, reporting by special verdict that Cogan believed that she was consenting but that he had no reasonable grounds for his belief. Subsequently, the House of Lords ruled in Regina v. Morgan, [1976] A.C. 182, that even an unreasonable belief that the victim consented precluded conviction for rape. Cogan's conviction was therefore quashed.]

Leak's appeal against conviction was based on the proposition that he could not be found guilty of aiding and abetting Cogan to rape his wife if Cogan was acquitted of that offence as he was deemed in law to have been when his conviction was quashed.... The only case which [Leak's counsel] submitted had a direct bearing upon the problem of Leak's guilt was Walters v. Lunt, [1951] 2 All E.R. 645. In that case the respondents had been charged, under § 33(1) of the Larceny Act 1916, with receiving from a child aged seven years, certain articles knowing them to have been stolen. In 1951, a child under eight years was deemed in law to be incapable of committing a crime: it followed that at the time of receipt by the respondents the articles had not been stolen and that the charge had not been proved. That case is very different from this because here one fact is clear—the wife had been raped. Cogan had had sexual intercourse with her without her consent. The fact that Cogan was innocent of rape because he believed that she was consenting does not affect the position that she was raped.

Her ravishment had come about because Leak had wanted it to happen and had taken action to see that it did by persuading Cogan to use his body as the instrument for the necessary physical act. In the language of the law the act of sexual intercourse without the wife's consent was the actus reus: it had been procured by Leak who had the appropriate mens rea, namely, his intention that Cogan should have sexual intercourse with her without her consent. In our judgment it is irrelevant that the man whom Leak had procured to do the physical act himself did not intend to have sexual intercourse with the wife without her consent....

Appeals against conviction dismissed.

---

## NOTES ON GUILT OF THE PRINCIPAL

**1.  Questions on *Cogan and Leak*.** The *Lunt* case, relied on by Leak's counsel, involved a husband and wife who were charged with receiving a stolen tricycle from their minor child, aged seven. They were held not guilty on the ground that the child was legally incapable of stealing and therefore that the tricycle received by them was not "stolen."

Is the opinion in *Cogan and Leak* correct in distinguishing *Lunt*? If it was clear, as Lord Justice Lawton asserted, that "the wife had been raped," was it not equally clear that the tricycle had been stolen? To put the same question from the other direction, does it make sense to say that Mrs. Leak was not "raped" or the tricycle was not "stolen" because the primary actor lacked the mens rea to be guilty of the crime?

**2.  *Dusenberry v. Commonwealth*: A Contrary View.** That the conclusion reached in *Cogan and Leak* is not everywhere accepted is shown by Dusenbery v. Commonwealth, 220 Va. 770, 263 S.E.2d 392 (1980), where the court unanimously overturned the defendant's conviction for rape on the following facts:

At approximately 10:30 p.m. on September 16, 1978, T_____ M_____ and J_____ G_____, both 16 years of age, parked their car in a secluded area and partially undressed in preparation for sexual intercourse. Defendant, a part-time security guard wearing a uniform, badge, handcuffs, and a holstered pistol, appeared at the window with a flashlight, ordered the couple to get out, and demanded identification. Defendant told them that he would take them to the authorities or report their conduct to their parents unless they finished what they had started and allowed him to watch. The couple entered the back seat of the car, discussed the options, and agreed to attempt to perform the act in defendant's presence. Defendant watched as the couple undressed and the boy assumed the superior position. Complaining that the boy had not penetrated the girl, defendant thrust his head and shoulders through the open window, seized the boy's penis, and forced it "partially in" the girl's vagina.

Defendant contends that the evidence is insufficient to support his conviction under Va. Code § 18.2–61 because "the evidence is clear that [he] did not 'carnally know' the alleged victim" within the meaning of that statute.

In felony cases, principals in the second degree and accessories before the fact are accountable "in all respects as if a principal in the first degree." But, by definition, there can be no accessory without a principal. Although *conviction* of a principal in the first degree is not a condition precedent to conviction of an accessory, "before the accessory to a crime can be convicted as such, it must be shown that the crime has been committed by the principal." Since the evidence fails to show that J_____ G_____ committed rape, defendant cannot be convicted as a principal in the second degree. The question remains whether the evidence is sufficient to prove that defendant committed that crime as a principal in the first degree.

With respect to certain crimes, the law regards a person who acts through an innocent agent as a principal in the first degree. In some jurisdictions, this rule has been applied in rape cases where the accused forced an innocent third party to have carnal knowledge of an unwilling victim. But the "innocent agent" rule cannot be applied here, for it is antithetical to the construction this court has placed upon Virginia's rape statute.

Our prior decisions establish that one element of rape is the penetration of the female sexual organ by the sexual organ of the principal in the first degree. Whether Dusenberry's conduct constituted an offense other than rape is not a question before us on appeal. We hold only that the evidence is insufficient to prove that defendant carnally knew the prosecutrix within the intendment of § 18.2–61 as construed by this court, and the judgment must be reversed. . . .

**3. The Abandonment of Derivative Liability?** Increasingly, *Cogan and Leak* is the prevailing view. As articulated by Professors Smith and Hogan, the modern view holds that the mens rea of the primary actor is irrelevant to the liability of a secondary participant in criminal conduct: "The true principle, it is suggested, is that where the principal has caused an actus reus, the liability of each of the secondary parties should be assessed according to his own mens rea." J. C. Smith & Brian Hogan, Criminal Law 134 (4th ed. 1978). Under this approach, one looks to the primary actor only for the actus reus of the offense. If it exists, a secondary participant may be prosecuted and punished according to his or her own mens rea and without regard to the primary actor's culpability or the lack thereof. Thus, a person may be convicted as a secondary participant where the primary actor has committed no offense. Obviously, this approach rejects the common-law tradition of regarding the liability of secondary parties as derived from the guilt of the primary actor.

**4. *Regina v. Richards* and Degrees of Liability.** A similar problem is posed where a secondary party is charged with a higher degree of criminal liability than the principal. Thus, the question arises whether an accomplice who has the mens rea required for murder may be punished for that crime if the principal actor kills in a sudden heat of passion and is therefore liable only for manslaughter. The traditional answer of English authorities seems to have been "yes." See 1 M. Hale, Pleas of the Crown *438. It should be emphasized, however, that Hale's position on this point does not reflect general abandonment of the traditional common-law conception of derivative liability. Rather, it reflects a special rule based on the characterization of murder and manslaughter as two forms of the more generic offense of criminal homicide and applicable only to the distinction between those two offenses. The reluctance of the common law to extend this principle to other offenses is illustrated by Regina v. Richards, [1974] 1 Q.B. 776.

Mrs. Richards hired Bryant and Squires to beat up her husband. As she later admitted, "I told them I wanted them to beat him up bad enough to put him in the hospital for a month." On the date of the assault, Mrs. Richards gave the agreed signal when her husband left for work. Shortly thereafter, he was attacked in an alley by Bryant and Squires. As it turned out, they inflicted injuries rather less serious than his wife had contemplated, and no hospitalization was required.

The three defendants were charged with violating §§ 18 and 20 of the Offences Against the Person Act, 1961. Both provisions require unlawful wounding. Section 18 further requires a specific intent to do grievous bodily harm and is punished as a felony. Section 20 requires no such intent and is a misdemeanor. At trial, both Bryant and Squires were acquitted of the more serious offense and convicted of the misdemeanor. Mrs. Richards, however, was convicted as a secondary party to the felony offense. She appealed on the ground set forth below:

> Mr. Alpin's submissions [for the accused] are brief. He says that looking at the facts of this case the defendant is in the

position of one who aided and abetted, or counselled and procured, to use the old language, the other two to commit the offence, and that she cannot be guilty of a graver crime than the crime of which the two co-accused were guilty. There was only one offence that was committed by the co-accused, an offence under § 20, and therefore there is no offence under § 18 of the Act of which his client can properly be found guilty on the facts of this case....

That is the short point in the case as we see it. If there is only one offence committed, and that is the offence of unlawful wounding, then the person who has requested that offence to be committed, or advised that that offence be committed, cannot be guilty of a graver offence than that in fact which was committed.

In Complicity, Cause and Blame: A Study in the Interpretation of Doctrine, 73 Cal.L.Rev. 323, 388–89 (1985), Sanford Kadish defends the result in *Richards:*

[T]he decision is supportable, it would seem, on the ground that Mrs. Richards did not *cause* the actions of the men.... She made no misrepresentation to the men she hired. They were not her unwitting instruments, but freely chose to act as they did. Hence their actions, as such, could not be attributed to Mrs. Richards. The innocent-agency doctrine is inapplicable because she did not cause their action.

It is a further question whether Mrs. Richards *should* be liable for assault with intent to do grievous injury, even if I am right that existing doctrine precludes that result. Surely the strongest argument for liability is that the culpability of her hirelings is irrelevant to *her* culpability. But that argument proves too much. If her hirelings committed no assault, but instead went to the police, it is incontrovertible that Mrs. Richards could not be found liable for any assault, let alone an aggravated assault. Yet whether her hirelings chose to do as she bade them or to go to the police is also irrelevant to her culpability. The point would be that however culpable her intentions she could not be blamed for an assault that did not take place. The same retort is applicable on the facts of the case: an actual assault took place (and Mrs. Richards is liable for it) but an aggravated assault did not take place. It did not take place because those committing the assault did not intend to inflict grievous bodily harm. She could properly be held liable for solicitation to commit an aggravated assault, not for aggravated assault.

Is this analysis persuasive? Does it suggest the appropriate way to deal with such situations? Does the answer depend on how the solicitation to commit an aggravated assault is graded?

**5.   The Model Code and Modern Statutes.** Legislation based on the Model Penal Code goes far beyond modifying common-law doctrines governing the relationship between principals and accessories. These newer provisions abandon the common-law categories altogether. In their place, elaborate rules are stated for determining when one person may be held liable for the conduct of another. Section 2.06(1) of the Model Penal Code, for example, begins by providing that: "A person is guilty of an offense if it is committed by his own conduct or by the conduct of another person for which he is legally accountable, or both." Subsection (2) describes three circumstances under which one person is legally accountable for the conduct of another: (i) the innocent agency situation; (ii) cases where the criminal law makes special provision (see, e.g., § 230.1(3)); and (iii) cases where the defendant is an "accomplice." Subsection (3) then defines what it means to be an "accomplice" of another.

The text of the Model Code does not clearly state whether the liability of an accomplice depends upon the guilt of the primary actor. How would *Cogan and Leak*, *Dusenbery*, and *Richards* be decided under its provisions? Is § 5.01(3) relevant?

**6. Study Problems.** A good way to test your understanding of complicity is to consider the following problems.[d] For each situation, assume that *A* initiated the criminal endeavor by suggesting to *B* that they cooperate in the burglary of a store. *B*, who is related to the store owner, fakes acquiescence in order to trap *A*, and the following variations occur.

(i) *A* and *B* go to the store at midnight. *A* helps *B* enter the store and waits outside for *B* to hand out the loot. As B has arranged, the police intervene, and *A* is arrested.

(ii) *A* and *B* go to the store at midnight. *A* brings to the store various implements designed to facilitate surreptitious entry. *A* assists *B* to use these implements to pick the lock of the store's back door. Before either *A* or *B* gain entry to the store, the police intervene, and *A* is arrested.

(iii) Finally, suppose that *B* purports to agree with *A*'s scheme but goes directly to the police without taking any action toward fulfillment of the plan. The police find *A* at home, and *A* is arrested.

What is *A*'s liability in each of these situations at common law? Under the Model Penal Code?

———

## SUBSECTION D: LIMITS OF ACCOMPLICE LIABILITY

———

## Regina v. Tyrrell

Court for Consideration of Crown Cases Reserved, 1893.
[1891–4] All E.R. 1215.

On September 15, 1893, Jane Tyrrell was arraigned before the Central Criminal Court, and pleaded not guilty to an indictment containing counts

———

[d] The fact situation is based on State v. Hayes, 105 Mo. 76, 16 S.W. 514 (1891).

charging (i) that being a girl above the age of 13 years and under the age of 16 years she aided and abetted the commission upon herself of the offence of carnal knowledge, contrary to § 5 of the Criminal Law Amendment Act, 1885;[a] and (ii) that she solicited and incited the commission of such offence upon her. The evidence for the prosecution proved that the defendant, who was under the age of 16, aided and abetted and solicited and incited Thomas Froud to have unlawful carnal connection with her, for which offence the defendant was convicted. . . . [A]t the request of defendant's counsel, the following question was reserved for the opinion of the court: Whether it was an offence for a girl between 13 years and 16 years of age, to aid and abet a male person in the commission of the misdemeanour of having unlawful carnal connection with her, or to solicit and incite a male person to commit that misdemeanour.

LORD COLERIDGE, C. J. I believe that I am expressing the opinion of my learned brothers when I say that this conviction must be quashed. What was intended by the legislature in passing the Act of 1885 was to protect girls against themselves, and it cannot be said that an act which says nothing at all about the girl inciting or anything of that kind, and the whole object of which is to protect women against men, is to be construed so as to render a girl against whom an offence is committed equally liable with the man by whom the offence is committed. In my opinion this conviction cannot be sustained, and must therefore be quashed.

MATHEW, J. I am of the same opinion. I fail to see how this argument on the construction of the statute can be supported. The consequences of upholding this conviction would, as has been pointed out in the course of the argument, be most serious, there being scarcely a section in the act which would not, upon the construction sought to be put upon the act, support a criminal prosecution against a girl. There is no trace anywhere in the act of any intention on the part of the legislature to deal with the woman as a criminal, and I am of the opinion that the act does not create the offence alleged in the indictment. . . .

Conviction quashed.

————

## NOTES ON THE LIMITS OF ACCOMPLICE LIABILITY

**1. Implied Exemption.** What is the precise basis of decision in *Tyrrell*? Is it dispositive that there was no direct evidence of legislative intention to criminalize the girl's conduct? Would you expect to find, in the text or history of a particular criminal offense, explicit legislative attention to the potential scope of accomplice liability? If not, what makes this silence so informative?

[a] The statute in question provided as follows:

[A]ny person who unlawfully and carnally knows, or attempts to have unlawful carnal knowledge of any girl being of or above the age of 13 years, and under the age of 16 years . . . shall be guilty of a misdemeanour. . . .—[Footnote by eds.]

In this connection, note the Model Penal Code effort to generalize on the limits of accomplice liability. Section 2.06(6) provides as follows:

> [U]nless otherwise provided by the Code or by the law defining the offense, a person is not an accomplice in an offense committed by another person if:
>
>    (a) he is a victim of that offense; or
>
>    (b) the offense is so defined that his conduct is inevitably incident to its commission. . . .

What is the rationale for this provision? Why should there be an exception to accomplice liability for the victims of crime? What additional exemption is achieved by the further reference to persons whose conduct is "inevitably incident" to the commission of the offense?

**2.   Withdrawal.** Note also that § 2.06(6) of the Model Penal Code codifies the defense of withdrawal or abandonment as it applies to complicity. Specifically, the provision states that a person is not liable as an accomplice to the offense of another if "he terminates his complicity prior to the commission of the offense and (i) wholly deprives it of effectiveness in the commission of the offense; or (ii) gives timely warning to the law-enforcement authorities or otherwise makes proper effort to prevent commission of the offense." The role of withdrawal or abandonment in the law of complicity is analogous to the similar issue in the law of attempt. The chief differences are, first, that the defense is more widely recognized in the context of complicity, and, second, that most formulations of withdrawal from complicity require that the accomplice make affirmative efforts to give timely warning or otherwise to prevent the commission of the offense.

## SECTION 2:  CONSPIRACY

### INTRODUCTORY NOTES ON THE LAW OF CONSPIRACY

**1.   Background.** The law of conspiracy has several functions. First, conspiracy is an inchoate offense punishing agreement in advance of action. In this respect, conspiracy is like attempt. Additionally, conspiracy usually carries sanctions heavier than, or additional to, those that could be imposed for the same misconduct by an individual acting alone. Thus, conspiracy functions as a ground for aggravation of penalties. Finally, conspiracy is often a way of holding one person liable for the completed conduct of another. In this aspect, conspiracy functions as an alternative to complicity.

Each aspect of the law of conspiracy is dealt with fully in the materials that follow. Also covered are certain subsidiary matters having to do with the scope and duration of a conspiracy and the limitations imposed on prosecution for conspiracy by the definition of certain substantive offenses. Preliminarily, however, three procedural aspects of the law of conspiracy should be noted.

**2. The Co–Conspirator's Exception to the Hearsay Rule.** The hearsay rule is a limitation on the admissibility of evidence. It forbids a witness from testifying to the out-of-court statements of another person (the declarant) where such testimony is offered to prove the truth of those statements. The rationale is that the declarant should be required to take the stand and submit to cross-examination in order to provide a fair opportunity for the veracity of the statement to be tested. Thus, for example, if *A* hears *B* say "I saw *C* rob a bank," the hearsay rule would forbid *A* from repeating *B*'s statement in a robbery prosecution against *C*. The rule would insist that *B* take the stand so that *C*'s attorney would have the opportunity to probe the accuracy of *B*'s observation, memory, and sincerity through cross-examination.

The hearsay rule is riddled with exceptions. One is an admission against interest by a party, as where *A* hears *B* say "I robbed a bank last week" and *A* is called to repeat the statement in the trial of *B*. A closely related, and perhaps derivative, exception is that for the declarations of co-conspirators. Under this rule, a statement against interest by one co-conspirator is admissible against all members of the conspiracy. Thus, if a conspiracy between *B* and *C* is established, *B*'s out-of-court statement that the two of them robbed a bank could be repeated in court by *A* and admitted against both *B* and C.

The administration of the co-conspirator's exception is a matter of some difficulty. The premise for holding the statement of one person admissible against another is the conspiracy between them. It is necessary, therefore, that the existence of the conspiracy be established by some independent evidence before the hearsay becomes admissible against the co-conspirator. Ideally, the independent evidence should be offered before any hearsay is admitted, and many courts attempt to follow this practice. As a practical matter, however, that may be impossible. The problem was aptly described by Justice Jackson in a famous essay on the law of conspiracy in his concurring opinion in Krulewitch v. United States, 336 U.S. 440, 453 (1949):

> When the trial starts, the accused feels the full impact of the conspiracy strategy. Strictly, the prosecution should first establish prima facie the conspiracy and identify the conspirators, after which evidence of acts and declarations of each in the course of its execution are admissible against all. But the order of proof of so sprawling a charge is difficult for a judge to control. As a practical matter, the accused often is confronted with a hodgepodge of acts and statements by others which he may never have authorized or intended or even known about, but which help to persuade the jury of existence of the conspiracy itself. In other words, a conspiracy often is proved by evidence that is admissible only upon assumption that conspiracy existed. The naive assumption that prejudicial effects can be overcome by instructions to the jury, all practicing lawyers know to be unmitigated fiction.

Although many courts have adopted procedures that avoid or mitigate this problem, the situation described by Justice Jackson is difficult to resolve in all cases. For an extended discussion of the operation of the hearsay rule in conspiracy trials, see Paul Marcus, The Prosecution and Defense of Criminal Conspiracy Cases, 5–1 to–72 (1978), and the materials cited therein.

**3. Joint Trial.** Economy may argue for joint trial whenever several defendants are to be prosecuted for crimes arising from the same series of events. In a conspiracy case the necessity of showing that the participants acted in concert creates an especially strong justification for proceeding against all conspirators at once.

From the defendant's point of view, however, joint trial may have disadvantages. The number of peremptory challenges to prospective jurors may have to be divided among the several co-defendants. Moreover, the practical value of an individual's right to counsel may be compromised. The lawyer who wishes to pursue an independent trial strategy may be hindered by the presence in the courtroom of other lawyers pursuing different and perhaps inconsistent lines of defense. Perhaps most important of all is the risk that an arguably innocent defendant who is tried together with patently guilty ones may be prejudiced by the forced association. Again, Justice Jackson made the point in *Krulewitch*:

> A co-defendant in a conspiracy trial occupies an uneasy seat. There generally will be evidence of wrongdoing by somebody. It is difficult for the individual to make his own case stand on its own merits in the minds of jurors who are ready to believe that birds of a feather are flocked together. If he is silent, he is taken to admit it and if, as often happens, co-defendants can be prodded into accusing or contradicting each other, they convict each other.

**4. Venue.** Under both state and federal law, the possible locations for a criminal trial are limited by the requirements of venue. Normally, venue lies where the actus reus of the offense is alleged to have occurred. For conspiracy, however, venue lies not only where the agreement was made but also where any act in furtherance of the agreement was performed. In the words of Justice Jackson:

> [T]he crime is considered so vagrant as to have been committed in any district where any one of the conspirators did any one of the acts, however innocent, intended to accomplish its object. The government may, and often does, compel one to defend at a great distance from any place he ever did any act because some accused confederate did some trivial and by itself innocent act in the chosen district.

**5. Pervasive Issues.** It is important to keep these procedural consequences in mind as you study the materials that follow. They often influence the resolution of substantive questions. Indeed, in some cases, the chief reason that an issue of conspiracy law is raised is that it has a procedural ramification of some practical importance. You should also reflect on the more general questions that pervade these materials—in particular, whether the variety of substantive and procedural issues comprehended by the law of conspiracy can sensibly be addressed through a unitary doctrine and whether any of the several functions of the law of conspiracy justifies the continued existence of this offense.

---

## SUBSECTION A: CONSPIRACY AS AN INCHOATE OFFENSE

---

## People v. Burleson
Appellate Court of Illinois, Fourth District, 1977.
50 Ill.App.3d 629, 8 Ill.Dec. 776, 365 N.E.2d 1162.

■ REARDON, JUSTICE. The defendant, Charles Edward Burleson, was charged in a two-count information filed December 8, 1975, with conspiracy to commit armed robbery and attempt[ed] armed robbery, violations of §§ 8–2(a) and 8–4(a) of the Criminal Code of 1961. The two offenses were alleged to have occurred on September 16, 1975. On April 21, 1976, a third count was added to the information charging the defendant with participating in a second conspiracy to commit armed robbery on September 13, 1975, another violation of § 8–2(a) of the Code.

After being tried before a Logan County jury, the defendant was found guilty on all three counts contained in the information and judgments were entered on the three verdicts. . . . [T]he defendant was sentenced to a one-to five-year sentence for the attempt of September 16, 1975, to run concurrently with a one-to three-year sentence for the conspiracy of September 13, 1975.

The facts pertinent to this appeal are reflected in the trial testimony of defendant's alleged co-conspirator, Bruce Brown. Brown testified that he and the defendant agreed to rob the Middletown State Bank. Pursuant to that agreement, the two "cased" the bank on September 11, 1975. They decided to use two cars in the robbery. One would be left on a rural road near Middletown with a change of clothing for each conspirator. From that location, the two would proceed to the bank wearing nylon stockings and stocking caps over their heads. The defendant agreed to secure a shotgun for use in the robbery and Brown agreed to secure the disguises and a container for the money they expected to remove from the bank. They also decided to commit the crime on Saturday, September 13, 1975.

On September 13, 1975, the conspirators initiated their plan, but decided not to rob the bank on that day because they noticed too many people in town and around the bank. Instead, they made a practice run of their approach to and escape from the bank after agreeing that they would try again on Tuesday, September 16, 1975.

On September 16, 1975, the defendant and Brown again parked their cars along a rural road, changed clothing and drove into the town of

Middletown in a single car with a white suitcase, shotgun and disguises consisting of the nylon stockings and stocking caps. When they arrived in town, they drove to the Middletown State Bank, exited from the car and approached the bank's front door. Brown carried the suitcase and the defendant carried the shotgun. As the duo neared the front door, however, a man bolted the door from the inside. Thereafter, the defendant and Brown scrambled back into the car and returned to their second car which was still parked along the rural road where they had commenced their escapade. Within minutes, Brown was arrested after being chased by the police. The defendant was arrested a few days later.

On appeal, the defendant raises a single issue for our review: whether his conviction for the September 13, 1975, conspiracy to commit armed robbery should be vacated because the alleged conspiracy arose from the same course of conduct that formed the basis for his attempt[ed] armed-robbery conviction.

Section 8–2(a) of the Criminal Code of 1961 provides in pertinent part:

A person commits conspiracy when, with intent that an offense be committed, he *agrees* with another to the commission of that offense. No person may be convicted of conspiracy to commit an offense unless an *act in furtherance* of such agreement is alleged and proved to have been committed by him or by a co-conspirator. (Emphasis added.)[a]

Section 8–4(a) of the code provides:

A person commits an attempt when, with intent to commit a specific offense, he does any act which constitutes a substantial step toward the commission of that offense.[b]

Both of the quoted sections are contained in that part of the code which concerns inchoate or anticipatory offenses. Another of those sections, § 8–5 of the code provides that "[n]o person shall be convicted of both the inchoate and the principal offense."

In Illinois, in order for a defendant to be convicted for the offense of conspiracy, the state must establish three elements beyond a reasonable doubt: (i) that the defendant intended to commit an offense; (ii) that the defendant and another person entered into an agreement to commit the offense; and (iii) that one of the co-conspirators committed an act in furtherance of the agreement. In order for a defendant to be convicted for the offense of attempt, the state must only establish two elements beyond a reasonable doubt: (i) that the defendant intended to commit an offense; and (ii) that the defendant took a "substantial step" toward committing that offense. In comparing these two sections of our criminal code, we note that the conspiracy provision requires a lesser step to fulfill the act requirement, while the attempt provision requires a "substantial step" toward the

---

[a] The maximum term for conspiracy to commit armed robbery was imprisonment for three years.—[Footnote by eds.]

[b] The maximum term for attempt to commit armed robbery was imprisonment for five years.—[Footnote by eds.]

commission of the offense. In each situation, as in situations involving other inchoate offenses, the law makes possible some preventive action by the police and courts before a defendant has come dangerously close to committing the intended crime.

Although § 8–4(a) does not define "substantial step," ... § 5.01(2) of the Model Penal Code contains a list of behavior constituting a "substantial step" which is strongly corroborative of the actor's criminal purpose. Noted on that list is:

> possession ... of materials to be employed in the commission of the crime, at or near the place contemplated for its commission, where such possession ... serves no lawful purpose of the actor under the circumstances.

Here, the defendant and Brown did not enter the bank building on September 16, 1975, although they were in possession of a shotgun, suitcase and disguises which were in place when they approached the bank building. We find these acts sufficient to constitute a "substantial step" toward the commission of an armed robbery in the bank.

In this case, the defendant was also charged with membership in two conspiracies having as their objects the armed robbery of the Middletown State Bank on two separate dates, September 13 and 16, 1975. . . .

Although other courts have [held] that an agreement to violate the same or different statutes on different occasions constitutes a single conspiracy [citing cases], we distinguish those decisions on the ground that the instant defendant entered two separate conspiracies, each of which was composed of the three elements set forth in § 8–2(a) of the Criminal Code of 1961. On September 11, 1975 the defendant and Brown, having the necessary intent, agreed to rob the bank on September 13, 1975. In furtherance of this agreement, they committed the overt acts of "casing" the bank, procuring a weapon and disguises, and going to the bank on September 13, 1975, to commit the crime. This first conspiracy was abandoned when the conspirators observed a large number of persons in and around the bank. Thereafter, the same conspirators, with the necessary intent, agreed to rob the bank on September 16, 1975, after which they committed the overt acts of preserving the disguises, participating in a practice escape from the bank and in approaching the bank on September 16, 1975. The latter act also constituted the "substantial step" necessary to establish the offense of attempt[ed] armed robbery, of which the second conspiracy was a lesser included offense. . . .

We, therefore, hold that a person charged with multiple conspiracies cannot be convicted of more than a single conspiracy if he has with the necessary intent entered into a single agreement to commit a crime even if multiple overt acts are committed in furtherance of that agreement. We further hold, however, that a person charged with multiple conspiracies can be convicted of those multiple conspiracies if, with the necessary intent, he entered into multiple, although partially overlapping agreements to commit crimes so long as overt acts are committed in furtherance of those agreements. It is this latter situation that is presented in the instant case.

As previously noted, § 8–5 of the code prohibits a defendant's conviction for an inchoate offense and the principal offense. Here, however, the defendant has been convicted for two inchoate offenses and not for a principal offense. Recently, our supreme court stated that when more than one offense arises from a single series of closely related acts and when the offenses, by definition, are not lesser included offenses, convictions [for both offenses] may be entered. Lesser included offenses are defined in § 2–9 of the code as an offense which:

> (a) Is established by proof of *the same or less than all of the facts* or a less culpable mental state (or both), than that which is required to establish the commission of the offense charged, or (b) Consists of an attempt to commit the offense charged or an offense included therein. (Emphasis added.)

Here, as already mentioned, the inchoate offenses of attempt and conspiracy require some act for criminal liability to attach to the actor. For an attempt to be committed, "a substantial step" in furtherance of the criminal objective must occur. For a conspiracy to exist, some act amounting to at least a lesser step is required. In the instant case, however, the state has not relied on the same conduct of the defendant to establish the conspiracy to rob the bank on September 13, 1975, and the attempt to rob which was committed on September 16, 1975. We do not view the conspirators' actions in terms of a single course of conduct. Rather, the conspirators' actions originate in separate agreements or impulses to rob the bank on separate dates. With their attempt to rob the bank on September 13, 1975, the conspirator's first agreement to rob the bank came to an end. The attempt of September 16, 1975, was not the result of the original agreement, but of a fresh agreement which was entered into after the attempt of September 13, 1975. Since we have held that the aforementioned offenses arise from separate courses of conduct, we, accordingly, affirm the defendant's convictions for the conspiracy of September 13, 1975, and for the attempted armed robbery of September 16, 1975. In addition, we reverse defendant's conviction for the conspiracy of September 16, 1975, because it is a lesser included offense of attempt. . . .

Affirmed in part. Reversed in part.

---

## NOTES ON CONSPIRACY AS AN INCHOATE OFFENSE

**1. Introduction.** As *Burleson* illustrates, one of the principal functions of the law of conspiracy is to fix criminal liability for anticipatory or inchoate behavior. In this respect, conspiracy supplements attempt. The two offenses are closely parallel. Both confront the same range of problems in assigning criminal liability for uncompleted conduct. The best way to study conspiracy as an inchoate offense is, therefore, to contrast it with the law of attempt. In what ways does conspiracy differ from attempt, and are those differences justified? Does the inchoate offense of conspiracy provide a needed adjunct to the law of attempt, or does it produce unwarranted extensions of penal liability? These and other questions are considered in the following notes.

2.   **The Necessity of Agreement**. The traditional definition of conspiracy is an agreement between two or more persons to do an unlawful act or to do a lawful act by unlawful means. Modern formulations, typified by the Illinois statute quoted in *Burleson*, restrict the offense to agreement to do an act which is itself a crime. The objective need not be achieved for the offense to be made out; the essence of conspiracy is the agreement itself.

At common law, no additional conduct was needed. Many statutes, however, also require that there be an overt act in furtherance of the conspiracy. Under the prevailing view, an act done by any one of the conspirators suffices for all. The significance of the overt-act requirement, however, may well be doubted. Unlike attempt, the law of conspiracy has never elaborated doctrinal tests to determine what kind of act suffices. Instead, the courts have held that virtually any act committed by a conspirator in furtherance of the conspiracy will do. The result is that the independent requirement of an overt act, even where imposed, tends not to be very important. The actus reus of the offense is essentially the act of agreement.

The necessity of proving agreement raises questions both evidentiary and substantive. On the evidentiary side, it is clear that direct proof of criminal agreement is rarely to be had. As is often noted, "[a] conspiracy is seldom born of 'open covenants openly arrived at.'" Usually, the fact of agreement must be inferred from circumstantial evidence. Moreover, as a substantive matter, the agreement need never have been express; a tacit, mutual understanding is enough. The upshot is that conspiracy requires agreement, but the agreement may be highly informal and may be inferred from indirect evidence.

The danger is that a rule of evidence may subsume a rule of law. The unavoidable reliance on circumstantial evidence may lead the trier of fact to find agreement where there was nothing more than concurrent conduct. This issue typically arises as a question of the sufficiency of the evidence, and since that inquiry is inherently fact-specific, generalization is especially difficult. Appellate courts are at pains to require substantial evidence of an actual agreement—"an agreement understood by the defendant, to which the defendant was a party, and to which he meant to be a party." But many defense attorneys nevertheless believe that the necessity of agreement may be lost sight of amidst a welter of evidence that a defendant was somehow involved in criminal activity. For a general discussion of this problem and comments on its practical implications, see Paul Marcus, Conspiracy: The Criminal Agreement in Theory and in Practice, 65 Geo. L.J. 925, 952–57 (1977).

3.   **The Sufficiency of Agreement**. By focusing on agreement, the law of conspiracy allows intervention and punishment at a very early stage

of misconduct. Indeed, one justification for the offense of conspiracy is that it punishes some instances of inchoate misconduct that could not be reached under the law of attempt. The question therefore arises: Is the act of agreeing to commit a crime, standing alone or in connection with an overt act in furtherance of the agreement, a sufficient basis in conduct to support penal liability? Are the underlying concerns of the act requirement adequately protected by this rule?

Perhaps the best defense of agreement as a basis for criminal punishment was offered by the drafters of the Model Penal Code:*

> The act of agreeing with another to commit a crime, like the act of soliciting, is concrete and unambiguous; it does not present the infinite degrees and variations possible in the general category of attempts. The danger that truly equivocal behavior may be misinterpreted as preparation to commit a crime is minimized; purpose must be relatively firm before the commitment involved in agreement is assumed. . . .
>
> In the course of preparation to commit a crime, the act of combining with another is significant both psychologically and practically, the former since it crosses a clear threshold in arousing expectations, the latter since it increases the likelihood that the offense will be committed. Sharing lends fortitude to purpose. The actor knows, moreover, that the future is no longer governed by his will alone; others may complete what he has had a hand in starting, even if he has a change of heart.

ALI, Model Penal Code § 5.03, Comment at 97 (Tent. Draft No. 10, 1960).

This position is criticized in Phillip E. Johnson, The Unnecessary Crime of Conspiracy, 61 Calif.L.Rev. 1137, 1161–64 (1973). In his view, reliance on conspiracy to reach very preliminary conduct made sense when the crime of attempt was limited by strict notions of proximity. According to Johnson, however, the justification for an independent inchoate offense of conspiracy has been substantially vitiated by the modern reformulation of attempt to focus on dangerousness of the actor rather than the proximity of his conduct to the completed offense. Johnson describes the Model Penal Code approach to attempt and examines its relevance to the law of conspiracy as follows:

> Pursued to its logical conclusion, the modern approach [to attempt] would permit the conviction of anyone shown to have had a firm intention to commit a crime, whether or not he had taken any steps towards its commission. The limiting factor, however, is our reluctance to put so much trust in either the omniscience or benevolence of those who administer the law. It is difficult to determine what someone intends to do before he does it, or at least prepares to do it. Even when an individual has plainly said what

_____

* Copyright © 1960 by the American Law Institute. Reprinted with permission.

he intends to do, there remains the question of how serious or definite his intent is. . . .

For this reason the modern codes retain the requirement that a defendant go beyond merely planning or contemplating a crime before he can be convicted of an attempt. He must engage in conduct that is a sufficiently substantial step towards completion of the crime to indicate his firm criminal intent, and to identify him as a dangerous individual who would probably have gone on to complete the crime if his design had not been frustrated. . . .

Under the conspiracy [section] of the Model Penal Code . . . , however, the act of agreement *is* the forbidden conduct whether or not it strongly corroborates the existence of a criminal purpose. In justifying this per se rule, the Model Penal Code commentary relied heavily on the argument . . . that the act of agreeing is so decisive and concrete a step towards the commission of a crime that it ought always to be regarded as a "substantial step." Whether this point is sense or nonsense depends upon how restrictively one defines the term "agreement." Hiring a professional killer to commit murder is an agreement, and surely few would doubt that it is a substantial step toward accomplishing the killing. But the language of the conspiracy [provision] is broad enough to reach conduct far less dangerous or deserving of punishment than letting a contract for murder. As the Model Penal Code commentary concedes, one may be liable for agreeing with another that *he* should commit a particular crime, although this agreement might be insufficient to establish complicity in the completed offense. Furthermore, [the code would not] change the well-established rule that the agreement may be tacit or implied as well as express, and that it may be proved by circumstantial evidence. In short, the term "agreement" may connote anything from firm commitment to engage in criminal activity oneself to reluctant approval of a criminal plot to be carried out entirely by others. To be sure, the Model Penal Code also requires that one enter into the agreement with the purpose of promoting or facilitating the crime, but the existence of that purpose need not be substantiated by any conduct beyond the express or implied agreement and performance in some cases of a single overt act by any party to it. . . .

In summary, insofar as conspiracy adds anything to the attempt provisions of the reform codes under discussion, it adds only overly broad criminal liability. . . . [T]he use of an independent crime of conspiracy to punish inchoate crimes turns out to be unnecessary. . . .

Although Johnson's suggestion is simply to eliminate conspiracy as an inchoate offense, an alternative response to the same concern is to elaborate the conduct required for that offense. A few American jurisdictions have supplemented the requirement of an overt act in conspiracy by analogizing to the law of attempt. In Maine, Ohio, and Washington, conspiracy statutes explicitly require a "substantial step" in furtherance of the conspiracy.[b] Does this make the crime of conspiracy entirely duplicative of attempt?

**4. Bilateral or Unilateral Agreement**. The definition of conspiracy as an agreement between two or more persons has given rise to a requirement of bilateralism. As the court said in Regle v. Maryland, 9 Md.App. 346, 351, 264 A.2d 119, 122 (1970), "it must be shown that at least two persons had a meeting of the minds—a unity of design and purpose—to have an agreement."

The facts of that case highlight the traditional approach. The defendant invited three other persons to participate in an armed robbery. One of them was a police informer, and another an undercover agent, both of whom feigned the intent to go through with the crime. The four men planned the event, obtained a weapon, and drove to the scene of the intended robbery. At that point the undercover officer intervened and arrested the others. Of course, neither the undercover agent nor his informant actually intended to commit the crime. That left only the defendant and the fourth participant, a man named Fields. At his trial for conspiracy to commit armed robbery, the defendant showed that Fields had been insane at the time of the agreement. Therefore, said the court, the defendant could not be guilty of conspiracy:

> By its nature, conspiracy is a joint or group offense requiring a concert of free wills, and the union of the minds of at least two persons is a prerequisite to the commission of the offense. The essence of conspiracy is, therefore, a mental confederation involving at least two persons.... [W]e hold that where only two persons are implicated in a conspiracy, and one is shown to have been insane at the time the agreement was concluded, and hence totally incapable of committing any crime, there is no punishable criminal conspiracy, the requisite joint criminal intent being absent.

Other courts take a different view. The unilateral approach to the agreement of conspiracy was explained in State v. St. Christopher, 305 Minn. 226, 232 N.W.2d 798 (1975), where the facts were as follows:

> On March 16, 1974, defendant (who formerly was named Martin Peter Olson but legally changed his name to Daniel St. Christopher) stated to his cousin, Roger Zobel, that he wanted to kill his mother, Mrs. Marlin Olson, and that he wanted Zobel's help. He would pay him $125,000 over the years, money defendant would get from his father after his mother was dead. Zobel, the key witness against defendant at his trial on the charge of conspir-

[b] Me.Rev.Stat.Ann. § 151(4); Ohio Rev. Code § 2923.01; Rev.Code Wash.Ann. § 9A.28.040. The Maine provision goes on to define "substantial step" in terms strongly reminiscent of the Model Penal Code standard for distinguishing preparation from at- tempt. Under Maine law, there must be "conduct which, under the circumstances in which it occurs, is strongly corroborative of the firmness of the actor's intent to complete commission of the crime."

acy, testified that at no time did he ever intend to participate in the murder but that he discussed the matter with defendant on that and subsequent occasions and acted as if he intended to participate in the plan. On March 18, Zobel contacted the police and told them of defendant's plan and they later told him to continue to cooperate with defendant. The plan, which became definite in some detail as early as March 20, was for Zobel to go to the Olson farmhouse on Saturday, March 23, when defendant's father was at the weekly livestock auction. Since defendant's mother was Zobel's aunt, Zobel could gain entrance readily. The idea was for Zobel to break her neck, hide her body in his automobile trunk, and then attach bricks to it and throw it in a nearby river after dark. Later it developed that defendant's father might not go to the sale on Saturday, so a plan was developed whereby defendant would feign car trouble, call his father for help, then signal Zobel when the father was on his way. Police followed defendant on Saturday when he left his apartment and observed him make a number of telephone calls. In one of these he called his father and told him he was having car trouble and asked him to come and help him pay the bill. In a call to Zobel, which was taped, defendant told Zobel that his father was coming and that Zobel should proceed with the plan. Shortly thereafter, police arrested defendant.

In his prosecution for conspiracy to commit murder, the defendant contended that no conspiracy could be found where the only other party to the scheme had only feigned agreement. The court rejected that claim and construed the Minnesota law to punish one who conspires with another without regard to the other's actual state of mind. In the course of its opinion, the court surveyed the objections to bilateralism:

One criticism by a number of commentators of the [traditional] rule ... is that the courts have reached their conclusion by using as a starting point the definition of conspiracy as an agreement between two or more persons, a definition which was framed in cases not involving the issue.... In other words, the basis for the rule is a strict doctrinal approach toward the conception of conspiracy as an agreement in which two or more parties not only objectively indicate their agreement but actually have a meeting of the minds.

Addressing the rule to be applied as a policy issue, a number of commentators have come to the conclusion that there should be no requirement of a meeting of the minds. Thus, Fridman, Mens Rea in Conspiracy, 19 Mod. L. Rev. 276 (1956), points to cases holding that factual impossibility is no defense to a charge of attempt to commit a crime and argues that, because of close connections between the origins and purposes of the law of conspiracy and of attempt, a similar rule should obtain in conspiracy. Specifically, he argues that "[t]he fact that, unknown to a man who wishes to enter a conspiracy to commit some criminal purpose, the other person has no intention of fulfilling that purpose ought to be irrelevant as long as the first man does intend to fulfill it if he can" because "a man who believes he is conspiring to commit a crime and wishes to conspire to commit a crime has a guilty mind and has done all in his power to plot the commission of an unlawful purpose." ...

[Section 5.03(1) of the Model Penal Code] reads as follows:

A person is guilty of conspiracy with another person or persons to commit a crime if with the purpose of promoting or facilitating its commission he:

(a) agrees with such person or persons that they or one or more of them will engage in conduct which constitutes such crime or an attempt or solicitation to commit such crime; or

(b) agrees to aid such other person or persons in the planning or commission of such crime or of an attempt or solicitation to commit such crime.

In comments explaining this provision, the reporters state as follows:[c]

... The definition of the draft departs from the traditional view of conspiracy as an entirely bilateral or multilateral relationship, the view inherent in the standard formulation cast in terms of "two or more persons" agreeing or combining to commit a crime. Attention is directed instead to each individual's culpability by framing the definition in terms of the conduct which suffices to establish the liability of any given actor, rather than the conduct of a group of which he is charged to be a part—an approach which in this comment we have designated "unilateral."

One consequence of this approach is to make it immaterial to the guilt of a conspirator whose culpability has been established that the person or all of the persons with whom he conspired have not been or cannot be convicted. Present law frequently holds otherwise, reasoning from the definition of conspiracy as an agreement between two or more persons that there must be at least two guilty conspirators or none. The problem arises in a number of contexts....

Where the person with whom the defendant conspired secretly intends not to go through with the plan, ... it is generally held that neither party can be convicted because there was no "agreement" between two persons. Under the

[c] This excerpt is taken from the commentary to the tentative draft version of the conspiracy offense. See A.L.I., Model Penal Code, § 5.03, Comment at 104–05 (Tent. Draft No. 10, 1960).—[Footnote by eds.]

> unilateral approach of the draft, the culpable party's guilt would not be affected by the fact that the other party's agreement was feigned. He has conspired, within the meaning of the definition, in the belief that the other party was with him; apart from the issue of entrapment often presented in such cases, his culpability is not decreased by the other's secret intention. True enough, the project's chances of success have not been increased by the agreement; indeed, its doom may have been sealed by this turn of events. But the major basis of conspiratorial liability—the unequivocal evidence of a firm purpose to commit a crime—remains the same. . . .

In consideration of these arguments, the court pronounced the "scholarly literature persuasive" and affirmed the conviction.

*St. Christopher* states the modern trend. Most recently revised codes follow the Model Code in punishing one who agrees to commit a crime without regard to the actual intention of the supposed collaborator. Yet the unilateral approach is not without its critics. For a sustained and elaborate rebuttal of the Model Code solution, see Paul Marcus, Prosecution and Defense of Criminal Conspiracy Cases, pp. 2–9 to–14 (1978). Marcus argues that in a case such as *St. Christopher*, "[t]he defendant may have wanted to agree, may have intended to agree, and may have even believed he had agreed; but there was no agreement, no true planning by two or more persons, no meeting of the minds between the parties." Moreover, says Marcus, the requirement of bilateralism is not strictly doctrinal. Instead, it reflects the essential rationale for punishing conspiracy in the first place:

> The strongest proponents of conspiracy law argue that the reason the inchoate conspiracy offense is legitimate, and the reason the conspiracy offense can be punished wholly apart from the substantive offense, is that conspirators acting together are dangerous. Group activities, it is said, are more likely to lead to serious anti-social acts than the acts of a single criminal. Reasonable people may disagree on such a rationale, but it is the rationale which has been accepted by the courts and commentators. With the unilateral approach, however, this grave risk will likely be lessened considerably, or actually wholly eliminated. Under such circumstances the rationale for the crime is destroyed, for there is no group danger.

Is this correct? Is the special danger of group criminality the essential rationale for the inchoate offense of conspiracy? Would reliance on this rationale necessarily require bilateral agreement? Or could the unilateral approach be viewed as also consistent with that rationale?

**5. Mens Rea**. Analytically, it seems clear that the mens rea of the inchoate offense of conspiracy should parallel that of attempt. This kinship is suggested by the traditional designation of both conspiracy and attempt as specific-intent offenses. The label connotes some requirement of actual, subjective intention. More elaborate formulations distinguish the intent to agree from the intent to accomplish the objective that makes agreement a crime. One may exist without the other. Assume for example, that $A$ and $B$ agree to remove certain property from the premises of $C$. $A$ has the intent to agree, but if $A$ believes that $C$ has authorized the action, $A$ plainly lacks the intent to commit theft. It is useful to distinguish these two intents chiefly in order to focus on the latter. The intent to agree is implicit in the requirement of agreement and therefore is rarely an issue independent of finding that the agreement exists. There remains the question of the actor's mens rea with respect to the object of the conspiracy. The issue is what state of mind must the actor have with respect to the elements of the underlying substantive crime.

A partial answer is that the actor must have at least the level of culpability required by the underlying crime. The fact that the prosecution is for the inchoate offense of conspiracy is no reason to dilute the mens-rea component of the underlying offense. In the hypothetical noted above, for example, if theft requires an intention permanently to deprive another of his property, conspiracy to commit theft requires the same intention. Similarly, if perjury requires that the actor swear to a statement known to be false, conspiracy to commit perjury also requires awareness of the falsity of the statement agreed to. This much is well settled.

A more difficult issue is whether the inchoate crime of conspiracy imposes mens-rea requirements beyond those of the underlying offense. The question is whether conspiracy requires a higher level of culpability than would be necessary if the object offense were completed. Here the analogy to attempt is exact, and reference should be made to the materials on the mens rea of attempt in Chapter III. The arguments developed there will not be fully rehearsed here, but the following summary may facilitate consideration of the application of those arguments to the inchoate offense of conspiracy.

For conspiracy, as for attempt, it is useful to distinguish among conduct, result, and circumstance elements of the object offense:

(i) **Conduct**. The state of mind required by conspiracy for the conduct elements of the underlying substantive offense is rarely in dispute. An agreement to engage in certain conduct necessarily includes the intention that the conduct be completed. Thus, questions of the actor's mens rea with respect to the conduct elements of the underlying offense are subsumed in the requirement of agreement.

(ii) **Results**. Obviously, it is possible to agree to engage in conduct that would cause a forbidden result without specifically intending that result. Nevertheless, it is well settled that conspiracy requires an actual purpose to cause a proscribed result, even where the underlying substantive offense would allow conviction on proof of lesser culpability. A hypothetical may help frame the issue.

Assume that $A$ and $B$ agree to race their automobiles through an unlighted parking lot even though they are aware of a risk that other people may be present. Assume also that if someone were killed, the driver of the offending vehicle would be guilty of some variety of reckless homicide (probably manslaughter) since his or her conduct, under the circumstances, involved a substantial and unjustifiable risk of death to another. If the scheme were interrupted before any mishap occurred, there could be no prosecution for conspiracy to commit manslaughter. The reason is that *A* and *B* lack the state of mind required by the law of anticipatory offenses for result elements of the substantive crime. An actual purpose to cause that result is required, even where the completed offense would allow conviction for recklessness or negligence.[d]

**(iii) Circumstances.** The only real issue in this area is whether the inchoate offense of conspiracy imposes special mens-rea requirements with respect to the attendant circumstances of an actor's conduct. A hypothetical from the law of theft presents the issue.

Assume that *A* and *B* agree to steal *C*'s watch, which they believe to be worth $100, to support their video-game habit. Suppose the watch is actually worth $2000. Traditionally, the value of the property would be a strict liability component of the completed offense, and *A* and *B* would be guilty of grand larceny rather than petit larceny if they consummated the theft. But what if the scheme is interrupted before the theft occurs, and *A* and *B* are prosecuted for conspiracy to commit grand larceny? If conspiracy is graded at the same level as the object offense, of what grade is their offense, that of petit larceny or that of grand larceny? Is the value of the property still a strict-liability element, or does the law of conspiracy impose a mens-rea requirement where the underlying substantive offense has none?

One answer is suggested by Judge Learned Hand's famous comment in United States v. Crimmins, 123 F.2d 271, 273 (2d Cir. 1941):

> While one may, for instance, be guilty of running past a traffic light of whose existence one is ignorant, one cannot be guilty of conspiring to run past such a light, for one cannot agree to run past a light unless one supposes that there is a light to run past.

The implication is that conspiracy should require awareness of the attendant circumstances of the contemplated conduct, even where the completed offense would require no such awareness. A different answer is derived from the Model Penal Code approach to the mens rea of attempt. Under the approach reflected in § 5.01, circumstance elements require only "the kind of culpability otherwise required for commission of the crime."[e] Which is the better view?

---

[d] Sometimes the conclusion is drawn that there can be no conspiracy to commit an offense of recklessness or negligence. Strictly speaking, this statement may be wrong. In the hypothetical discussed above, there appears to be no reason why *A* and *B* could not be convicted of conspiracy to commit an offense of reckless (or negligent) operation of a motor vehicle. Each has agreed to engage in conduct that would constitute the actus reus of the completed offense, and each has the culpability (recklessness or negligence) required by that offense. The distinctive feature of the hypothetical discussed in text is that it involves a crime requiring recklessness or negligence *with respect to a result* of the contemplated conduct. There can be no crime of conspiracy recklessly or negligently to cause a result.

[e] An arguably special case of the mens rea required for attendant circumstances is presented by the jurisdictional ingredients of

**6.  Impossibility.** The question of impossibility as a defense to the inchoate offense of conspiracy is conceptually analogous to the impossibility issue in the law of attempt. See Chapter III. The law, however, has tended to treat the two crimes differently. Whereas the common law regarded impossibility (at least "legal" impossibility) as a defense to attempt, the authorities generally reject impossibility of any kind as a defense to conspiracy.

The issue arose in United States v. Thomas, 13 U.S.C.M.A. 278, 32 C.M.R. 278 (1962). Thomas and two others went into a bar. One of the three began to dance with a girl, who almost immediately collapsed in his arms. The three companions agreed to take the girl home and on the way took advantage of her unresisting condition to have sexual intercourse. When she did not revive, they became concerned and asked for help. Doctors subsequently agreed that she had died on the dance floor and was therefore not a living person at the time of the events described.

Defendants were convicted of attempted rape and of conspiracy to commit rape. On appeal they claimed that the girl's death prior to sexual intercourse made rape impossible and that "impossibility" should be a defense to both attempt and conspiracy. The majority examined the authorities and concluded, in line with "the advanced and modern position," that impossibility was no defense on these facts. A dissenter, however, after an equally extensive review of the authorities, concluded that the impossibility involved here should be a defense to attempt:

> [T]he barrier to consummation of the crime charged here is not factual but legal. Indeed, accused did everything they set out to do, but they admittedly could not commit the actual crime of rape because their victim was dead and thus outside the protection of the law appertaining to that offense. Because the objective of their loathsome attentions was no longer subject to being raped, it seems to me that there cannot be any liability for an attempt, for ... a legal rather than a factual impediment existed to the offense's consummation.

Interestingly, the same judge concluded that impossibility should not be a defense to conspiracy:

> Despite my position with respect to the charge of attempted rape, I would affirm the conviction of conspiracy to commit rape. Unlike criminal attempts, legal impossibility is not recognized as a defense to the charge of conspiracy. Although both crimes are, in a sense, inchoate offenses, their development has been somewhat different. At common law, conspiracy consisted only of the agree-

federal offenses. In many instances, federal statutes have been construed to require no mens rea with respect to the basis of federal jurisdiction—e.g., the fact that the person assaulted was a federal officer or that the property stolen belonged to the United States. In United States v. Feola, 420 U.S. 671 (1975), the Supreme Court ruled that where a substantive offense requires no mens rea with respect to facts giving rise to federal jurisdiction, conspiracy to commit that offense also requires no mens rea with respect to such facts.

ment to do an unlawful act or a lawful act in an unlawful manner. Although [the relevant statute] requires proof of an overt act in addition to the agreement to commit an offense . . . , we have held that the heart of the crime remains the corrupt meeting of the minds. Here, the accused agreed to have intercourse with an unconscious girl against her will and while she was unable to resist. The averred overt act was also made out. As what these two men thus subjectively agreed to be their objective constitutes in law the offense of rape, and as thereafter one of them performed an overt act, guilt of conspiracy is made out. My objection is simply to the action of my brothers in transferring the subjective approach in conspiracy to the objective questions involved in attempt.

What is the appropriate result on the facts of *Thomas*? Is the impossibility of rape "factual" or "legal," or can you tell? Is an attempt made out on these facts, or should the impossibility (of whatever sort) be a defense? And if impossibility is a defense to the charge of attempt, should it not also apply to conspiracy?

**7. Renunciation and Withdrawal.** The role of conspiracy as an inchoate offense raises the question whether renunciation or abandonment should be a defense. The traditional position is that once agreement (or agreement plus an overt act) is reached, criminal conspiracy is complete, and no subsequent abandonment is a defense. The Model Penal Code, however, has proposed that renunciation be recognized as a defense to conspiracy on similar terms as it is for attempt. Section 5.03(6) of the Model Code provides a defense if "the actor, after conspiring to commit a crime, thwarted the success of the conspiracy, under circumstances manifesting a complete and voluntary renunciation of his criminal purpose."

Renunciation as a claim of defense to liability for conspiracy should be distinguished from the related issue of withdrawal as a means of terminating one's involvement in a conspiracy. Such withdrawal would not exculpate the actor from liability for the conspiracy, but it would limit the actor's liability for substantive offenses committed by co-conspirators after the actor's participation had ceased. Additionally, withdrawal of an individual from an on-going criminal enterprise starts the statute of limitations as against that individual. For a discussion of both withdrawal and true renunciation, see Note, Conspiracy: Statutory Reform Since the Model Penal Code, 75 Colum.L.Rev. 1122 (1975).

---

## NOTE ON CONSPIRACY AND CUMULATIVE PUNISHMENT

In *Burleson* the court noted that Illinois law codified conspiracy as an inchoate offense and provided that "[n]o person shall be convicted of both the inchoate and the principal offense." This rule has long been applied to attempt under the doctrine of merger. The attempt is said to merge into the completed offense, and the actor is therefore protected from punishment for both. At common law merger also applied to conspiracy, but today the majority rule is otherwise. Under federal law and the law of many states, conspiracy is treated as an independent wrong that does not merge into the completed crime that was its object. The result is that a person may be punished both for agreeing to commit a crime and for participation in the crime that was the object of the agreement. In this respect, conspiracy functions as an aggravation of penalties. Cumulative punishment for conspiracy and for its object effectively extends the authorized maxima for substantive crimes whenever they are committed by two or more persons acting in concert.

What is the rationale for this result? The standard explanation, as advanced by the Supreme Court in Callanan v. United States, 364 U.S. 587 (1961), is that the special danger of concerted criminal activity warrants independent punishment. Consider the response of the drafters of the Model Penal Code: "When a conspiracy is declared criminal because its object is a crime, we think it is entirely meaningless to say that the preliminary combination is more dangerous than the forbidden consummation; the measure of its danger is the risk of such a culmination." MPC § 5.03, Comment at 99 (Tent. Draft No. 10, 1960). Is this correct? Is the social danger of conspiracy adequately measured by the gravity of sanctions authorized for the completed offense, or is some aggravation of penalties appropriate?

---

## SUBSECTION B:  THE RELATION OF CONSPIRACY TO COMPLICITY

---

## People v. Lauria

California Court of Appeal, Second District, 1967.
251 Cal.App.2d 471, 59 Cal.Rptr. 628.

■ FLEMING, ASSOCIATE JUSTICE. In an investigation of call-girl activity the police focused their attention on three prostitutes actively plying their trade on call, each of whom was using Lauria's telephone answering service, presumably for business purposes.

On January 8, 1965, Stella Weeks, a policewoman, signed up for telephone service with Lauria's answering service. Mrs. Weeks, in the course of her conversation with Lauria's office manager, hinted broadly that she was a prostitute concerned with the secrecy of her activities and their concealment from the police. She was assured that the operation of the service was discreet and "about as safe as you can get." It was arranged that Mrs. Weeks need not leave her address with the answering service, but could pick up her calls and pay her bills in person.

On February 11, Mrs. Weeks talked to Lauria on the telephone and told him her business was modelling and she had been referred to the answering service by Terry, one of the three prostitutes under investigation. She complained that because of the operation of the service she had lost two valuable customers, referred to as tricks. Lauria defended his service and said that her friends had probably lied to her about having left calls for her. But he did not respond to Mrs. Weeks' hints that she needed customers in order to make money, other than to invite her to his house for a personal visit in order to get better acquainted. In the course of his talk he said "his business was taking messages."

On February 15, Mrs. Weeks talked on the telephone to Lauria's office manager and again complained of two lost calls, which she described as a $50 and a $100 trick. On investigation the office manager could find nothing wrong, but she said she would alert the switchboard operators about slip-ups on calls.

On April 1 Lauria and the three prostitutes were arrested. Lauria complained to the police that this attention was undeserved, stating that Hollywood Call Board had 60 to 70 prostitutes on its board while his own service had only nine or 10, that he kept separate records for known or suspected prostitutes for the convenience of himself and the police. When asked if his records were available to police who might come to the office to investigate call girls, Lauria replied that they were whenever the police had a specific name. However, his service didn't "arbitrarily tell the police about prostitutes on our board. As long as they pay their bills we tolerate them." In a subsequent voluntary appearance before the grand jury Lauria testified he had always cooperated with the police. But he admitted he knew some of his customers were prostitutes, and he knew Terry was a prostitute because he had personally used her services, and he knew she was paying for 500 calls a month.

Lauria and the three prostitutes were indicted for conspiracy to commit prostitution, and nine overt acts were specified. Subsequently the trial court set aside the indictment as having been brought without reasonable or probable cause. The People have appealed, claiming that a sufficient showing of an unlawful agreement to further prostitution was made.

To establish agreement, the People need show no more than a tacit, mutual understanding between conspirators to accomplish an unlawful act. Here the People attempted to establish a conspiracy by showing that Lauria, well aware that his co-defendants were prostitutes who received business calls from customers through his telephone answering service, continued to furnish them with such service. This approach attempts to equate knowledge of another's criminal activity with conspiracy to further such criminal activity, and poses the question of the criminal responsibility of a furnisher of goods or services who knows his product is being used to assist the operation of an illegal business. Under what circumstances does a supplier become part of a conspiracy to further an illegal enterprise by furnishing goods or services which he knows are to be used by the buyer for criminal purposes?

The two leading cases on this point face in opposite directions. In United States v. Falcone, 311 U.S. 205 (1940), the sellers of large quantities of sugar, yeast, and cans were absolved from participation in a moonshining conspiracy among distillers who bought from them, while in Direct Sales Co. v. United States, 319 U.S. 703 (1943), a wholesaler of drugs was convicted of conspiracy to violate the federal narcotic laws by selling drugs in quantity to a co-defendant physician who was supplying them to addicts. The distinction between these two cases appears primarily based on the proposition that distributors of such dangerous products as drugs are required to exercise greater discrimination in the conduct of their business than are distributors of innocuous substances like sugar and yeast.

In the earlier case, *Falcone*, the sellers' knowledge of the illegal use of the goods was insufficient by itself to make the sellers participants in a conspiracy with the distillers who bought from them. Such knowledge fell short of proof of a conspiracy, and evidence on the volume of sales was too vague to support a jury finding that respondents knew of the conspiracy from the size of the sales alone.

In the later case of *Direct Sales*, the conviction of a drug wholesaler for conspiracy to violate federal narcotic laws was affirmed on a showing that it had actively promoted the sale of morphine sulphate in quantity and had sold codefendant physician, who practiced in a small town in South Carolina, more than 300 times his normal requirements of the drug, even though it had been repeatedly warned of the dangers of unrestricted sales of the drug. The court contrasted the restricted goods involved in *Direct Sales* with the articles of free commerce involved in *Falcone*: "All articles of commerce may be put to illegal ends," said the court. "But all do not have inherently the same susceptibility to harmful and illegal use.... This difference is important for two purposes. One is for making certain that the seller knows the buyer's intended illegal use. The other is to show that by the sale he intends to further, promote and cooperate in it. This intent, when given effect by overt act, is the gist of conspiracy. While it is not identical with mere knowledge that another purposes unlawful action, it is not unrelated to such knowledge.... The step from knowledge to intent and agreement may be taken. There is more than suspicion, more than knowledge, acquiescence, carelessness, indifference, lack of concern. There is informed and interested cooperation, stimulation, instigation. And there is also a 'stake in the venture' which, even if it may not be essential, is not irrelevant to the question of conspiracy."

While *Falcone* and *Direct Sales* may not be entirely consistent with each other in their full implications, they do provide us with a framework for the criminal liability of a supplier of lawful goods or services put to unlawful use. Both the element of *knowledge* of the illegal use of the goods or services and the element of *intent* to further that use must be present in order to make the supplier a participant in a criminal conspiracy.

Proof of *knowledge* is ordinarily a question of fact and requires no extended discussion in the present case. The knowledge of the supplier was sufficiently established when Lauria admitted he knew some of his customers were prostitutes and admitted he knew that Terry, an active subscriber of his service, was a prostitute. In the face of these admissions he could scarcely claim to have relied on the normal assumption an operator of a business or service is entitled to make, that his customers are behaving themselves in the eyes of the law. Because Lauria knew in fact that some of his customers were prostitutes, it is a legitimate inference he knew they were subscribing to his answering service for illegal business purposes and were using his service to make assignations for prostitution. On this record we think the prosecution is entitled to claim positive knowledge by Lauria of the use of his service to facilitate the business of prostitution.

The more perplexing issue in the case is the sufficiency of proof of *intent* to further the criminal enterprise. The element of intent may be proved either by direct evidence, or by evidence of circumstances from which an intent to further a criminal enterprise by supplying lawful goods or services may be inferred. Direct evidence of participation, such as advice from the supplier of legal goods or services to the user of those goods or services on their use for illegal purposes ... provides the simplest case. When the intent to further and promote the criminal enterprise comes from the lips of the supplier himself, ambiguities of inference from circumstance need not trouble us. But in cases where direct proof of complicity is lacking, intent to further the conspiracy must be derived from the sale itself and its surrounding circumstances in order to establish the supplier's express or tacit agreement to join the conspiracy.

In the case at bench the prosecution argues that since Lauria knew his customers were using his service for illegal purposes but nevertheless continued to furnish it to them, he must have intended to assist them in carrying out their illegal activities. Thus through a union of knowledge and intent he became a participant in a criminal conspiracy. Essentially, the People argue that knowledge alone of the continuing use of his telephone facilities for criminal purposes provided a sufficient basis from which his intent to participate in those criminal activities could be inferred.

In examining precedents in this field we find that sometimes, but not always, the criminal intent of the supplier may be inferred from his knowledge of the unlawful use made of the product he supplies. Some consideration of characteristic patterns may be helpful.

(i) Intent may be inferred from knowledge, when the purveyor of legal goods for illegal use has acquired a stake in the venture. (United States v. Falcone, 109 F.2d 579, 581 (2d Cir., 1940)). For example, in Regina v. Thomas, 2 All E.R. 181, 342 (1957), a prosecution for living off the earnings of prostitution, the evidence showed that the accused, knowing the woman to be a convicted prostitute, agreed to let her have the use of his room between the hours of 9 p. m. and 2 a. m. for a charge of £3 a night. The Court of Criminal Appeal refused an appeal from the conviction, holding that when the accused rented a room at a grossly inflated rent to a prostitute for the purpose of carrying on her trade, a jury could find he was living on the earnings of prostitution.

In the present case, no proof was offered of inflated charges for the telephone answering services furnished the co-defendants.

(ii) Intent may be inferred from knowledge, when no legitimate use for the goods or services exists. The leading California case is People v. McLaughlin, 111 Cal.App.2d 781, 245 P.2d 1076 (1952), in which the court upheld a conviction of the suppliers of horse-racing information by wire for conspiracy to promote bookmaking, when it had been established that wire-service information had no other use than to supply information needed by bookmakers to conduct illegal gambling operations. . . . In such cases the supplier must necessarily have an intent to further the illegal enterprise since there is no known honest use for his goods.

However, there is nothing in the furnishing of telephone answering service which would necessarily imply assistance in the performance of illegal activities. Nor is any inference to be derived from the use of an answering service by women, either in any particular volume of calls, or outside normal working hours. Night-club entertainers, registered nurses, faith healers, public stenographers, photographic models, and free-lance substitute employees, provide examples of women in legitimate occupations whose employment might cause them to receive a volume of telephone calls at irregular hours.

(iii) Intent may be inferred from knowledge, when the volume of business with the buyer is grossly disproportionate to any legitimate demand, or when sales for illegal use amount to a high proportion of the seller's total business. In such cases an intent to participate in the illegal enterprise may be inferred from the quantity of the business done. For example, in *Direct Sales*, supra, the sale of narcotics to a rural physician in quantities 300 times greater than he would have normal use for provided potent evidence of an intent to further the illegal activity. In the same case the court also found significant the fact that the wholesaler had attracted as customers a disproportionately large group of physicians who had been convicted of violating the Harrison Act. . . .

No evidence of any unusual volume of business with prostitutes was presented by the prosecution against Lauria.

Inflated charges, the sale of goods with no legitimate use, sales in inflated amounts, each may provide a fact of sufficient moment from which the intent of the seller to participate in the criminal enterprise may be inferred. In such instances participation by the supplier of legal goods to the illegal enterprise may be inferred because in one way or another the supplier has acquired a special interest in the operation of the illegal [enterprise]. His intent to participate in the crime of which he has knowledge may be inferred from the existence of his special interest.

Yet there are cases in which it cannot reasonably be said that the supplier has a stake in the venture or has acquired a special interest in the enterprise, but in which he has been held liable as a participant on the basis of knowledge alone. Some suggestion of this appears in *Direct Sales*, supra, where both the knowledge of the illegal use of the drugs and the intent of the supplier to aid that use were inferred. In Regina v. Bainbridge, 3 W.L.R. 656 (C.C.A.1959), a supplier of oxygen-cutting equipment to one known to intend to use it to break into a bank was convicted as an accessory to the crime. In Sykes v. Director of Public Prosecutions, [1962] A.C. 528, one having knowledge of the theft of 100 pistols, four submachine guns, and 1960 rounds of ammunition was convicted of misprision of felony for failure to disclose the theft to the public authorities. It seems apparent from these cases that a supplier who furnishes equipment which he *knows* will be used to commit a serious crime may be deemed from that knowledge alone to have intended to produce the result. Such proof may justify an inference that the furnisher intended to aid the execution of the crime and that he thereby became a participant. For instance, we think the operator of a telephone answering service with positive knowledge that his service was being used to facilitate the extortion of ransom, the distribution of heroin, or the passing of counterfeit money who continued to furnish the service with knowledge of its use, might be chargeable on knowledge alone with participation in a scheme to extort money, to distribute narcotics, or to pass counterfeit money. The same result would follow the seller of gasoline who knew the buyer was using his product to make Molotov cocktails for terroristic use.

Logically, the same reasoning could be extended to crimes of every description. Yet we do not believe an inference of intent drawn from knowledge of criminal use properly applies to the less serious crimes classified as misdemeanors. The duty to take positive action to dissociate oneself from activities helpful to violations of the criminal law is far stronger and more compelling for felonies than it is for misdemeanors or petty offenses. In this respect, as in others, the distinction between felonies and misdemeanors, between more serious and less serious crime, retains continuing vitality. In historically the most serious felony, treason, an individual with knowledge of the treason can be prosecuted for concealing and failing to disclose it. In other felonies, both at common law and under the criminal laws of the United States, an individual knowing of the commission of a felony is criminally liable for concealing it and failing to make it known to proper authority. But this crime, known as misprision of felony, has always been limited to knowledge and concealment of felony and has never extended to misdemeanor. A similar limitation is found in the criminal liability of an accessory [after the fact], which is restricted to aid in the escape of a principal who has committed or been charged with a *felony*. We believe the distinction between the obligations arising from knowledge of a felony and those arising from knowledge of a misdemeanor continues to reflect basic human feelings about the duties owed by individuals to society. Heinous crime must be stamped out, and its suppression is the responsibility of all. Venial crime and crime not evil in itself present less of a danger to society, and perhaps the benefits of their suppression through the modern equivalent of the posse, the hue and cry, the informant, and the citizen's arrest, are outweighed by the disruption to everyday life brought about by amateur law enforcement and private officiousness in relatively inconsequential delicts which do not threaten our basic security. . . .

With respect to misdemeanors, we conclude that positive knowledge of the supplier that his products or services are being used for criminal purposes does not, without more, establish an intent of the supplier to participate in the misdemeanors. With respect to felonies, we do not decide the converse, viz. that in all cases of felony knowledge of criminal use alone may justify an inference of the supplier's intent to participate in the crime. The implications of *Falcone* make the matter uncertain with respect to those felonies which are merely prohibited wrongs. But decision on this point is not compelled, and we leave the matter open.

From this analysis of precedent we deduce the following rule: the intent of a supplier who knows of the criminal use to which his supplies are put to participate in the criminal activity connected with the use of his supplies may be established by (i) direct evidence that he intends to participate, or (ii) through an inference that he intends to participate based on, (a) his special interest in the activity, or (b) the aggravated nature of the crime itself.

When we review Lauria's activities in the light of this analysis, we find no proof that Lauria took any direct action to further, encourage, or direct the call-girl activities of his codefendants and we find an absence of circumstances from which his special interest in their activities could be inferred. Neither excessive charges for standardized services, nor the furnishing of services without a legitimate use, nor an unusual quantity of business with call girls, are present. The offense which he is charged with furthering is a misdemeanor, a category of crime which has never been made a required subject of positive disclosure to public authority. Under these circumstances, although proof of Lauria's knowledge of the criminal activities of his patrons was sufficient to charge him with that fact, there was insufficient evidence that he intended to further their criminal activities, and hence insufficient proof of his participation in a criminal conspiracy with his codefendants to further prostitution. Since the conspiracy centered around the activities of Lauria's telephone answering service, the charges against his codefendants likewise fail for want of proof.

In absolving Lauria of complicity in a criminal conspiracy we do not wish to imply that the public authorities are without remedies to combat modern manifestations of the world's oldest profession. Licensing of telephone answering services under the police power, together with the revocation of licenses for the toleration of prostitution, is a possible civil remedy. The furnishing of telephone answering service in aid of prostitution could be made a crime. Other solutions will doubtless occur to vigilant public authorities if the problem of call-girl activity needs further suppression.

The order is affirmed.

———

## NOTE ON CONSPIRACY AND COMPLICITY

As *Lauria* illustrates, conspiracy often functions as an alternative to complicity. Formally, of course, the doctrines are distinct. Complicity holds one person criminally responsible for the conduct of another. Depending on the jurisdiction, such liability may require aid rendered with intent to promote the criminal venture, or it may rest on knowing assistance of the criminal activity of another. Conspiracy, on the other hand, imposes direct liability for the preliminary step of agreeing with another to commit an offense. A party to such agreement may be held criminally responsible for the object offense even though he or she did not personally complete the actus reus of that crime. In many situations, the two doctrinal categories are functionally interchangeable.

Consider the facts of *Lauria*. Lauria was prosecuted for conspiracy to commit prostitution. Obviously, this charge raises difficult questions about the liability of one who knowingly supplies goods or services to a criminal undertaking. Would these questions have been different if Lauria had been prosecuted for complicity in the acts of prostitution by his customers? Should the determinants of liability turn on which theory is used? In this connection, recall *United States* v. *Peoni* and *Backun* v. *United States*, which are excerpted in the materials on complicity earlier in this chapter. Would these cases have been resolved differently if conspiracy rather than complicity were the offense charged? Should they? What reasons might induce the prosecutor to choose one theory rather than the other?

The fact that conspiracy and complicity overlap has two important implications. First, analysis of the law of conspiracy as an alternative to complicity largely replicates the range of issues dealt with under the doctrine of complicity. An understanding of that subject is, therefore, essential to critical evaluation of this aspect of criminal conspiracy. Second, it is important to remember that conspiracy functions not only as an alternative to prosecution for complicity but also as an inchoate offense and as a basis for aggravation of penalties. There is reason to doubt whether any unified statement of the law of conspiracy can deal coherently with such disparate subjects. The cases and notes that follow illustrate aspects of criminal conspiracy in its role as an alternative to complicity.

----

## Pinkerton v. United States

Supreme Court of the United States, 1946.
328 U.S. 640.

■ MR. JUSTICE DOUGLAS delivered the opinion of the Court.

Walter and Daniel Pinkerton are brothers who live a short distance from each other on Daniel's farm. They were indicted for violations of the Internal Revenue Code. The indictment contained 10 substantive counts and one conspiracy count. The jury found Walter guilty on nine of the substantive counts and on the conspiracy count. It found Daniel guilty on six of the substantive counts and on the conspiracy count. Walter was fined $500 and sentenced generally on the substantive counts to imprisonment for 30 months. On the conspiracy count he was given a two-year sentence to run concurrently with the other sentence. Daniel was fined $1,000 and sentenced generally on the substantive counts to imprisonment for 30 months. On the conspiracy count he was fined $500 and given a two-year sentence to run concurrently with the other sentence. The judgments of conviction were affirmed by the Circuit Court of Appeals. . . .

It is contended that there was insufficient evidence to implicate Daniel in the conspiracy. But we think there was enough evidence for submission of the issue to the jury.

There is, however, no evidence to show that Daniel participated directly in the commission of the substantive offenses on which his conviction has been sustained, although there was evidence to show that these substantive offenses were in fact committed by Walter in furtherance of the unlawful agreement or conspiracy existing between the brothers. The question was submitted to the jury on the theory that each petitioner could be found guilty of the substantive offenses, if it was found at the time those offenses were committed petitioners were parties to an unlawful conspiracy and the substantive offenses charged were in fact committed in furtherance of it.

Daniel relies on United States v. Sall, 116 F.2d 745 (3d Cir. 1940). That case held that participation in the conspiracy was not itself enough to sustain a conviction for the substantive offense even though it was committed in furtherance of the conspiracy. The court held that, in addition to evidence that the offense was in fact committed in furtherance of the conspiracy, evidence of direct participation in the commission of the substantive offense or other evidence from which participation might fairly be inferred was necessary.

We take a different view. We have here a continuous conspiracy. There is here no evidence of the affirmative action on the part of Daniel which is necessary to establish his withdrawal from it. Hyde v. United States, 225 U.S. 347 (1912). As stated in that case,

> [h]aving joined in an unlawful scheme, having constituted agents for its performance, scheme and agency to be continuous until full fruition be secured, until he does some act to disavow or defeat the purpose he is in no situation to claim the delay of the law. As the offense has not been terminated or accomplished he is still offending. And we think, consciously offending, offending as certainly, as we have said, as at the first moment of his confederation, and consciously through every moment of its existence.

And so long as the partnership in crime continues, the partners act for each other in carrying it forward. It is settled that "an overt act of one partner may be the act of all without any new agreement specifically directed to that act." Motive or intent may be proved by the acts or declarations of some of the conspirators in furtherance of the common objective. A scheme to use the mails to defraud, which is joined in by more than one person, is a conspiracy. Yet all members are responsible, though only one did the mailing. The governing principle is the same when the substantive offense is committed by one of the conspirators in furtherance of the unlawful project. The criminal intent to do the act is established by the formation of the conspiracy. Each conspirator instigated the commission of the crime. The unlawful agreement contemplated precisely what was done. It was formed for the purpose. The act done was in execution of the enterprise. The rule which holds responsible one who counsels, procures, or commands another to commit a crime is founded on the same principle. That principle is recognized in the law of conspiracy when the overt act of one partner in crime is attributable to all. An overt act is an essential ingredient of the crime of conspiracy under [18 U.S.C. § 371]. If that can be supplied by the act of one conspirator, we fail to see why the same or other acts in furtherance of the conspiracy are likewise not attributable to the others for the purpose of holding them responsible for the substantive offense.

A different case would arise if the substantive offense committed by one of the conspirators was not in fact done in furtherance of the conspiracy, did not fall within the scope of the unlawful project, or was merely a part of the ramifications of the plan which could not be reasonably foreseen as a necessary or natural consequence of the unlawful agreement. But as we read this record, that is not this case.

Affirmed.

■ MR. JUSTICE JACKSON took no part in the consideration or decision of this case.

■ MR. JUSTICE RUTLEDGE, dissenting in part.

The judgment concerning Daniel Pinkerton should be reversed. In my opinion it is without precedent here and is a dangerous precedent to establish.

Daniel and Walter, who were brothers living near each other, were charged in several counts with substantive offenses, and then a conspiracy count was added naming those offenses as overt acts. The proof showed that Walter alone committed the substantive crimes. There was none to establish that Daniel participated in them, aided and abetted Walter in committing them, or knew that he had done so. Daniel in fact was in the penitentiary, under sentence for other crimes, when some of Walter's crimes were done.

There was evidence, however, to show that over several years Daniel and Walter had confederated to commit similar crimes concerned with unlawful possession, transportation, and dealing in whiskey, in fraud of the federal revenues. On this evidence both were convicted of conspiracy. Walter also was convicted on the substantive counts on the proof of his committing the crimes charged. Then, on that evidence without more than the proof of Daniel's criminal agreement with Walter and the latter's overt acts, which were also the substantive offenses charged, the court told the jury they could find Daniel guilty of those substantive offenses. They did so. . . .

The court's theory seems to be that Daniel and Walter became general partners in crime by virtue of their agreement and because of that agreement without more on his part Daniel became criminally responsible as a principal for everything Walter did thereafter in the nature of a criminal offense of the general sort the agreement contemplated, so long as there was not clear evidence that Daniel had withdrawn from or revoked the agreement. Whether or not his commitment to the penitentiary had that effect, the result is a vicarious criminal responsibility as broad as, or broader than, the vicarious civil liability of a partner for acts done by a co-partner in the course of the firm's business.

Such analogies from private commercial law and the law of torts are dangerous, in my judgment, for transfer to the criminal field. Guilt there with us remains personal, not vicarious, for the more serious offenses. It should be kept so. The effect of Daniel's conviction in this case . . . is either to attribute to him Walter's guilt or to punish him twice for the same offense, namely, agreeing with Walter to engage in crime. Without the agreement Daniel was guilty of no crime on this record. With it and no more, so far as his own conduct is concerned, he was guilty of two. . . .

■ MR. JUSTICE FRANKFURTER . . . agrees in substance with the views expressed in this dissent.

---

## NOTES ON THE *PINKERTON* RULE

**1.  The Scope of Liability for Conspiracy.** *Pinkerton* is the most famous authority for the proposition that a member of a conspiracy is criminally responsible for crimes committed by co-conspirators in furtherance of their agreement. Of course, no such rule is necessary for the particular crime agreed to. The effect of *Pinkerton* is, rather, to extend liability to include additional offenses that may not have been within the actor's contemplation but that were committed by his or her cohorts in the course of the criminal enterprise. The only limit on the scope of the conspirator's liability is that additional offenses must have been reasonably foreseeable consequences of the agreement.

The *Pinkerton* rule is probably the law in a majority of American jurisdictions. Typically, it is enforced without explicit statutory support. Some modern statutes, however, do codify the rule, generally in the provision on complicity rather than in the section on conspiracy. An illustration of this approach comes from the law of Texas. Section 7.02 of the Texas Penal Code is entitled "Criminal Responsibility for the Conduct of Another." Subsection (a) sets forth the general requirements of complicity. Subsection (b) adds the following:

> If, in the attempt to carry out a conspiracy to commit one felony, another felony is committed by one of the conspirators, all conspirators are guilty of the felony actually committed, though having no intent to commit it, if the offense was committed in furtherance of the unlawful purpose and was one that should have been anticipated as a result of the carrying out of the conspiracy.

For other modern provisions to the same general effect, see N.J.Stat.Ann. § 2C:2–5 and Wis.Stat.Ann. § 939.05. The greater number of modern statutes contain no such provision. In some of these jurisdictions, the effect is simply to continue unchanged the decisional authority on the subject. In others, however, the *Pinkerton* rule has been explicitly rejected. See, e.g., Code of Ala., §§ 13A–4–3(f), 13A–2–23; No.Dak.Cent. Code § 12.1–03–01; 17–A Me.Rev.Stat.Ann. § 151.

**2.   Evaluating the *Pinkerton* Rule.** The impact of *Pinkerton* is not easy to assess. In most cases, generally applicable principles of complicity would authorize conviction in any event. There are some cases, however, where *Pinkerton* extends criminal liability, and logically it is on those cases that attention should focus.

Two variables affect the dimensions of the issue. First, the impact of the *Pinkerton* rule depends in large measure on the question, "as compared to what?" If the otherwise applicable principles of complicity limit the liability of an accomplice to crimes which he or she had an actual purpose to aid or encourage, the effect of the *Pinkerton* approach to the scope of liability for conspiracy would be considerable. In such circumstances, *Pinkerton* would effectively dilute the mens-rea requirement from purpose to negligence whenever the primary and secondary actor are bound together by a criminal agreement. But if the scope of an accomplice's liability turned on the natural and probable consequences of the criminal endeavor that he or she meant to aid or encourage (as, for example, in *People* v. *Durham*, supra), the addition of *Pinkerton* would be a matter of little consequence. Thus, the practical impact of embracing the *Pinkerton* approach depends a great deal on the contours of the criminal liability that would otherwise exist.

A second variable concerns the approach taken to determining the size or scope of a single conspiracy. This is a matter considered in more detail in the next subsection, but it is worth noting here that the significance of *Pinkerton* varies with the scope of the activities for which an individual conspirator is held liable. This, in fact, is the principal basis for opposition to *Pinkerton* by the drafters of the Model Penal Code. Consider the following comments made with respect to the tentative draft provision on complicity, MPC § 2.04, Comment at 20–21 (Tent. Draft No. 1, 1953):*

> The most important point at which the draft diverges from the language of the courts is that it does not make "conspiracy," as such, a basis of complicity in substantive offenses committed in furtherance of its aims. It asks, instead, ... more specific questions about the behavior charged to constitute complicity, such as whether the defendant commanded, encouraged, aided or agreed to aid in the commission of the crime.
>
> The reason for this treatment is that there appears to be no other or no better way to confine within reasonable limits the scope of liability to which conspiracy may theoretically give rise. In

* Copyright © 1953 by the American Law Institute. Reprinted with permission.

People v. Luciano, 277 N.Y. 348, 14 N.E.2d 433 (1938), for example, Luciano and others were convicted of 62 counts of compulsory prostitution, each count involving a specific instance of placing a girl in a house of prostitution, receiving money for so doing or receiving money from the earnings of a prostitute, acts proved to have been done pursuant to a combination to control commercialized vice in New York City. The liability was properly imposed with respect to these defendants, who directed and controlled the combination; they commanded, encouraged and aided the commission of numberless specific crimes. But would so extensive a liability be just for each of the prostitutes or runners involved in the plan? They have, of course, committed their own crimes; they may actually have assisted others; but they exerted no substantial influence on the behavior of a hundred other girls or runners, each pursuing his or her own ends within the shelter of the combination. A court would and should hold that they all are parties to a single, large, conspiracy; this is itself, and ought to be, a crime. But it is one crime. Law would lose all sense of just proportion if in virtue of that one crime, each were held accountable for thousands of offenses that he did not influence at all.

**3.** *State v. Stein.* A fascinating application of the *Pinkerton* rule is found in State v. Stein, 70 N.J. 369, 360 A.2d 347 (1976). Defendant Stein was a Trenton attorney with certain unsavory connections. One of them was Pontani, a "professional second-story man" in need of work. Pontani discussed with Stein the possibility of committing a burglary from which they both might benefit. Stein suggested the house of Dr. Arnold Gordon, a dentist who lived in Stein's neighborhood and was known to keep cash at home. At first nothing came of this suggestion, but about a year later two associates of Pontani gained entry to the Gordon home by impersonating policemen. They pulled pistols and demanded money and valuables. While they were tying up Dr. and Mrs. Gordon, a maid called the police. When the police arrived, the two robbers took Mrs. (Edith) Gordon and her 14–year-old daughter (Shelly) as hostages and attempted a getaway. A high-speed chase ensued, and the robbers were captured when their car crashed into a police barrier, seriously wounding two police officers.

As a result of these events, a court sitting without a jury found Stein guilty not only of conspiracy to steal currency from the Gordon home, but also of armed robbery, assaults with an offensive weapon (against Edith and Shelly Gordon), kidnapping, kidnapping while armed, and assaults on a police officer. The intermediate appellate court affirmed the conspiracy and armed robbery convictions but reversed all the rest. The Supreme Court of New Jersey reached a different conclusion:

> The question as to the criminal responsibility of a conspirator for the commission by others of substantive offenses having some causal connection with the conspiracy but not in the contemplation of the conspirator has been a matter of considerable debate and controversy. Here there is no question but that Stein did not

actually contemplate any criminal consequence of his tip to Pontani beyond a burglary and theft of money from the Gordon home....

[T]he generally held rule, exemplified by the leading *Pinkerton* case [is] that so long as a conspiracy is still in existence "an overt act of one partner may be the act of all without any new agreement specifically directed to that act," provided the substantive act could "be reasonably foreseen as a necessary or natural consequence of the unlawful agreement."

We regard the rule as just stated to be sound and viable. We hold it represents the law in this state.

It remains to apply the rule to the instant fact situation. Ordinarily the matter of factual application of the rule would be submitted to the jury under appropriate instructions. Here the matter was for the trial judge in the first instance as fact-finder. The Appellate Division found correct the trial ruling that the armed robbery was within the scope of the conspiracy to steal currency from the Gordon home. We are in agreement. The robbery was a "natural" or "probable" consequence of the conspiracy. But the Appellate Division concluded that the assaults with an offensive weapon on the wife and daughter of Dr. Gordon were "not connected with the robbery as such" but "with the preliminary acts of taking the Gordons as hostages and the eventual kidnappings" and therefore "not fairly . . . part of the conspiratorial agreement." The assault convictions were therefore set aside.

We are not in complete agreement with this last determination. The brandishing of handguns by the robbers when they first encountered Dr. and Mrs. Gordon in the house was clearly a foreseeable event in the course of an unlawful invasion of the house for criminal purposes by armed men. That assault on Mrs. Gordon did not merge with the armed robbery, as the Appellate Division suggested might be the case, since the robbery charged was of Dr. Gordon alone, not the members of his family assaulted. Thus the assault conviction as to Mrs. Gordon should not have been set aside as too remote from the conspiracy.

As to the charge of assault with an offensive weapon on Shelly Gordon (daughter of the Gordons), since the evidence indicates that offense occurred only at the time of the attempted escape from the police, its disposition depends on the determination as to the other associated charges discussed next below.

Liability of the defendant for the kidnapping, kidnapping while armed and assaults on a police officer presents a much closer question. The Appellate Division held that these substantive acts were "offenses committed by the criminals effecting the conspiratorial specific crime after that crime had been committed, as part of a plan to flee when it became evident that they were about to be apprehended'' and that defendant could not be charged therefor. On balance, we are satisfied that this is a correct result, particularly in relation to the kidnapping phases of the episode. This holding will also apply to the reversal by the Appellate Division of the conviction for assault with an offensive weapon on Shelly Gordon. However, we rest our concurrence with the Appellate Division not on the ground that the substantive offenses took place subsequent to the commission of the crime conspired or that the offenses were part of a plan to flee, but rather that it would be unreasonable for a fact-finder to find as a fact beyond a reasonable doubt that they were necessary, natural or probable consequences of the conspiracy, having in mind the unique fact-complex presented.

Is this reasoning persuasive? Does Stein's liability for armed robbery depend on specific awareness by him that guns would be involved, or does it suffice that he agreed generally to some sort of theft? Would it matter if Stein had suggested that the house be burgled when the Gordons were away on vacation, or if he had explicitly directed Pontani not to create risk of bloodshed?

If Stein is responsible for the armed robbery of Dr. Gordon and the assault of his wife, why should he not be held accountable for the other offenses as well? Is the taking of hostages or the assault of police officers really that remote from armed robbery? Would Stein have been liable for malicious wounding or some other aggravated assault offense if the robbers had shot and wounded Dr. Gordon in order to overcome his resistance? Would such an act be a natural and probable consequence of armed robbery? What if the robbers shot and wounded a police officer? Is that any less foreseeable? Can you think of any rationale for distinguishing Stein's liability according to the identity of the victim? If not, how should these issues be addressed? Are you tired of questions? If not, why not?

————

## SUBSECTION C: SCOPE AND DURATION OF CONSPIRACY

————

## Braverman v. United States

Supreme Court of the United States, 1942.
317 U.S. 49.

■ MR. CHIEF JUSTICE STONE delivered the opinion of the Court.

[The question is whether] a conviction upon the several counts of an indictment, each charging conspiracy to violate a different provision of the Internal Revenue laws, where the jury's verdict is supported by evidence of but a single conspiracy, will sustain a sentence of more than two years' imprisonment, the maximum penalty for a single violation of the conspiracy statute[a]. . . .

Petitioners were indicted, with others, on seven counts, each charging a conspiracy to violate a separate and distinct internal revenue law of the United States.[1] On the trial there was evidence from which the jury could have found that, for a considerable period of time, petitioners, with others, collaborated in the illicit manufacture, transportation, and distribution of distilled spirits, involving the violations of statute mentioned in the several counts of the indictment. At the close of the trial, petitioners renewed a motion which they had made at its beginning to require the government to elect one of the seven counts of the indictment upon which to proceed, contending that the proof could not and did not establish more than one agreement. In response the government's attorney took the position that the seven counts of the indictment charged as distinct offenses the several illegal objects of one continuing conspiracy, that if the jury found such a conspiracy it might find the defendants guilty of as many offenses as it had illegal objects, and that for each such offense the two-year statutory penalty could be imposed.

The trial judge submitted the case to the jury on that theory. The jury returned a general verdict finding petitioners "guilty as charged," and the court sentenced each to eight years' imprisonment. On appeal the Court of Appeals for the Sixth Circuit affirmed. . . .

Both courts below recognized that a single agreement to commit an offense does not become several conspiracies because it continues over a period of time and that there may be such a single continuing agreement to commit several offenses. But they thought that, in the latter case, each contemplated offense renders the agreement punishable as a separate conspiracy.

The question whether a single agreement to commit acts in violation of several penal statutes is to be punished as one or several conspiracies is raised on the present record, not by the construction of the indictment, but by the government's concession at the trial and here, reflected in the

---

[a] Section 37 of the Criminal Code, 18 U.S.C. § 88, at this time carried a maximum term of two-years' imprisonment. The general federal conspiracy statute has since been recodified as 18 U.S.C. § 371 and now carries a maximum term of five years in prison.— [Footnote by eds.]

[1] The seven counts respectively charged them with conspiracy, in violation of § 37 of the Criminal Code, unlawfully (i) to carry on the business of wholesale and retail liquor dealers without having the special occupational tax stamps required by statute, 26 U.S.C. § 3253; (ii) to possess distilled spirits, the immediate containers of which did not have stamps affixed denoting the quantity of the distilled spirits which they contained and evidencing payment of all Internal Revenue taxes imposed on such spirits, 26 U.S.C. § 2803; (iii) to transport quantities of distilled spirits, the immediate containers of which did not have affixed the required stamps, 26 U.S.C. § 2803; (iv) to carry on the business of distillers without having given bond as required by law, 26 U.S.C. § 2833; (v) to remove, deposit and conceal distilled spirits in respect whereof a tax is imposed by law, with intent to defraud the United States of such tax, 26 U.S.C. § 3321; (vi) to possess unregistered stills and distilling apparatus, 26 U.S.C. § 2810; and (vii) to make and ferment mash, fit for distillation, on unauthorized premises, 26 U.S.C. § 2834.

charge to the jury, that only a single agreement to commit the offenses alleged was proven. Where each of the counts of an indictment alleges a conspiracy to violate a different penal statute, it may be proper to conclude, in the absence of a bill of exceptions bringing up the evidence, that several conspiracies are charged rather than one, and that the conviction is for each. But it is a different matter to hold, as the court below appears to have done ... that even though a single agreement is entered into, the conspirators are guilty of as many offenses as the agreement has criminal subjects.

The gist of the crime of conspiracy as defined by the statute is the agreement or confederation of the conspirators to commit one or more unlawful acts "where one or more of such parties do any act to effect the object of the conspiracy." The overt act, without proof of which a charge of conspiracy cannot be submitted to the jury, may be that of only a single one of the conspirators and need not be itself a crime. But it is unimportant, for present purposes, whether we regard the overt act as part of the crime which the statute defines and makes punishable or as something apart from it, either an indispensable mode of corroborating the existence of the conspiracy or a device for affording a locus poenitentiae.

For when a single agreement to commit one or more substantive crimes is evidenced by an overt act, as the statute requires, the precise nature and extent of the conspiracy must be determined by reference to the agreement which embraces and defines its objects. Whether the object of a single agreement is to commit one or many crimes, it is in either case that agreement which constitutes the conspiracy which the statute punishes. The one agreement cannot be taken to be several agreements and hence several conspiracies because it envisages the violation of several statutes rather than one....

The single agreement is the prohibited conspiracy, and however diverse its objects it violates but a single statute, § 37 of the Criminal Code. For such a violation, only the single penalty prescribed by the statute can be imposed.

---

## NOTES ON THE SCOPE AND DURATION OF CONSPIRACY

**1. Scope of Conspiracy: The Object Dimension.** The question in *Braverman* is whether an agreement with several criminal objects is one conspiracy or several. When the issue is liability for the inchoate offense of conspiracy—rather than for substantive offenses committed by co-conspirators—the prosecution usually argues for several conspiracies justifying several punishments. The defense, by contrast, tries to lump all the criminal objects into one conspiracy justifying only one punishment. The reaction of the courts is not always consistent.[a]

---

[a] With *Braverman*, compare Lievers v. State, 3 Md.App. 597, 241 A.2d 147 (1968), where the defendant was ringleader of a bad- check operation. Prosecution was based on an effort by Lievers and several cohorts to cash a forged check made out in a fictitious name.

Does *Braverman* set the right standard? In the context of an ongoing criminal enterprise, how realistic is it to inquire into the number of agreements? Such arrangements are not likely to be documented, and indeed may never have been precisely worked out. Given that the agreement may be tacit and that it may evolve from collaborative effort rather than from a particular negotiation, how useful is it to ask whether the objects of the combination were covered by one agreement or several?

Section 5.03 of the Model Penal Code addresses this issue differently:

> If a person conspires to commit a number of crimes, he is guilty of only one conspiracy so long as such multiple crimes are the object of the same agreement or continuous conspiratorial relationship.

Does the concept of "continuous conspiratorial relationship" improve on *Braverman*? Why should conspiracy to commit several crimes be only one conspiracy, while attempt to commit several crimes is several attempts? Is the penalty for agreeing to engage in criminal misconduct unrelated to the number of crimes contemplated?

**2. Scope of Conspiracy: The Party Dimension.** Sometimes the incentives are reversed, and the prosecutor argues for one large conspiracy, while the defense attorney claims that there were several small ones. This is particularly likely to be true when the defendant is charged with various substantive offenses committed by co-conspirators. In that circumstance, the prosecutor wishes to enlarge the conspiracy in order to increase the number of offenses for which each co-conspirator is responsible, and the defense wishes to do exactly the opposite. In other cases, the issue of one or several conspiracies determines the statute of limitations. Under settled doctrine, a member of a single, continuing conspiracy may be prosecuted for that offense, even though prosecution for his or her personal participation in the criminal enterprise would be barred by the statute of limitations. In other cases, the issue of one or several conspiracies determines procedural questions, such as joint trial or the scope of the co-conspirator's exception to the hearsay rule.

Consider a drug ring,[b] consisting of importers who smuggle drugs into the country, distributors who buy from the importers, and one or more groups of dealers who operate in different areas. The importers and the retail dealers may never have direct contact or communication, yet each knows of, and depends on, the existence of the other. Are all these persons involved in one large conspiracy, or is there one conspiracy between the importers and the distributors and another between the distributors and (each group of) dealers? Even at the retail level, the question of scope can be difficult. Is each street-level drug dealer involved in one large conspiracy

---

The Maryland Court of Appeals upheld separate convictions for conspiracy to forge the check, conspiracy to obtain money by false pretenses from the party who cashed the forged check, and conspiracy to use a counterfeit Maryland chauffeur's license in the name of the fictitious payee.

[b] The facts are taken from a famous old case, United States v. Bruno, 105 F.2d 921 (2d Cir. 1939), but there are many examples.

with all other dealers who work for the same boss? Even though they may have no contact or communication with each other? If so, the scope of liability for the substantive offenses committed by co-conspirators may reach very far indeed.

Traditionally, this issue is dealt with by superimposing on the evidence of conspiracy some visualization of its structure. The two most prominent shapes accorded to conspiracies are the chain and the wheel. The chain conspiracy focuses on successive stages of cooperation, as, for example, between *A* and *B*, *B* and *C*, *C* and *D*, and so forth. A person at one end of the chain may be found to have conspired with others with whom that person had no direct dealing. The wheel conspiracy is based on a central figure (the hub) who deals separately with various peripheral figures (the spokes) in a common undertaking. Each of the spokes may be judged a member of the same conspiracy, even though they have no direct relations with one another. Both types are illustrated in the drug hypothetical. The progression from importers to distributors to dealers is a classic chain, while the various street-level dealers who buy from the same source can be seen as separate spokes of a wheel.

The Model Penal Code deals with the scope of conspiracy as follows. Subsection (1) of § 5.03 declares a person guilty of conspiracy with another to commit a crime if, with purpose to promote that crime, he or she "agrees with such other person or persons that they or one or more of them will engage in conduct which constitutes such crime or an attempt or solicitation to commit such crime" or "agrees to aid such other person or persons in the planning or commission of such crime or of an attempt or solicitation to commit such crime." Subsection (2) expands the party dimension of this liability as follows:

> If a person guilty of conspiracy, as defined by Subsection (1) of this Section, knows that a person with whom he conspires to commit a crime has conspired with another person or persons to commit the same crime, he is guilty of conspiring with such other person or persons, whether or not he knows their identity, to commit such crime.

How the drug ring hypothetical be resolved under this standard?

**3. Scope of Conspiracy: Duration.** Another dimension of the scope of a conspiracy is its duration. This may control the statute of limitations, the admissibility of evidence under the co-conspirator's exception to the hearsay rule, and the reach of an individual's liability under *Pinkerton* for the crimes of co-conspirators. The basic propositions in this area are set forth in Model Penal Code § 5.03(7), which essentially codifies prior law. Paragraph (a) states the general rule that conspiracy is a continuing offense; it does not terminate with the agreement but continues until the objective is either accomplished or abandoned. Paragraph (b) imposes a limit on the continuing nature of a conspiracy by creating a presumption of abandonment where no overt act was committed during the applicable period of limitations. Thus, in most cases the defense will simply point to the prosecution's failure to prove an overt act occurring during the relevant time frame as proof that the conspiracy is over. Paragraph (c) deals with the somewhat special case of the individual who claims that an ongoing criminal enterprise is terminated as to that individual by withdrawal from participation. The Code makes such abandonment effective only where it is confirmed by notice to the other participants or by report to the authorities.

Prosecutors have tried to extend the life of a conspiracy by focusing on the subsidiary objective, which surely must be implicit in every criminal agreement, to conceal the activities from the authorities, but the courts have not been sympathetic. See, e.g., Grunewald v. United States, 353 U.S. 391 (1957), and the cases cited therein.

———

## NOTE ON LIMITS ON LIABILITY FOR CONSPIRACY

Recall *Regina v. Tyrrell*, which held that an underage girl who was the victim of statutory rape could not be convicted as an accomplice to that crime. The Model Penal Code generalizes that idea by saying, in § 2.06(6), that a person cannot be an accomplice in the offense of another if "the offense is so defined that his conduct is inevitably incident to its commission." Not surprisingly, liability for conspiracy is limited on the same ground. A good example is Gebardi v. United States, 287 U.S. 112 (1932), which involved prosecution for conspiracy to violate the Mann Act. That statute punished "any person" who knowingly transported in interstate commerce any "any woman or girl for the purpose of prostitution or debauchery. . . ." The defendant was a man, and the person with whom he conspired was the woman to be transported. The Supreme Court disapproved the conviction on the ground that since the Mann Act did not condemn the woman's participation in these interstate transportations, her assent could not form the basis of liability for conspiracy.

Much the same reasoning lies behind the hoary doctrine known as Wharton's rule. Basically, Wharton's rule deals with offenses that are defined to require the participation of more than one person. Classic examples are adultery, incest, bigamy, and duelling. Wharton's rule declares that the agreement between the essential participants to commit such a crime should ordinarily not be prosecuted as conspiracy. As Wharton himself explained, "[w]hen to the idea of an offense plurality of agents is logically necessary, conspiracy, which assumes the voluntary accession of a person to a crime of such a character that it is aggravated by a plurality of agents, cannot be maintained." 2 Francis Wharton, Criminal Law 1862 (12th ed. 1932). The Supreme Court has made clear that this "rule" is actually only a "judicial presumption, to be applied in the absence of legislative intent to the contrary." Iannelli v. United States, 420 U.S. 770, 782 (1975). On that basis, the *Ianelli* Court refused to apply Wharton's rule to a prosecution for conspiracy to violate 18 U.S.C. § 1955, which punished as a federal crime managing or owning an illegal gambling business involving five or more persons. Relying on the history of the statute, the

Court found that the imposition of liability for illegal gambling involving five or more persons was not designed to preclude liability for conspiracy to commit that offense.

## SECTION 3: RICO

## United States v. Turkette

Supreme Court of the United States, 1981.
452 U.S. 576.

■ JUSTICE WHITE delivered the opinion of the Court.

... The question in this case is whether the term "enterprise" as used in [the Racketeer Influenced and Corrupt Organizations Act (RICO)] encompasses both legitimate and illegitimate enterprises or is limited in application to the former. The Court of Appeals ... held that Congress did not intend to include within the definition of "enterprise" those organizations which are exclusively criminal. . . .

I

Count nine of a nine-count indictment charged respondent and 12 others with conspiracy to conduct and participate in the affairs of an enterprise engaged in interstate commerce through a pattern of racketeering activities, in violation of 18 U.S.C. § 1962(d). The indictment described the enterprise as "a group of individuals associated in fact for the purpose of illegally trafficking in narcotics and other dangerous drugs, committing arsons, utilizing the United States mails to defraud insurance companies, bribing and attempting to bribe local police officers, and corruptly influencing and attempting to corruptly influence the outcome of state court proceedings. . . ." The other eight counts of the indictment charged the commission of various substantive criminal acts by those engaged in and associated with the criminal enterprise, including possession with intent to distribute and distribution of controlled substances, and several counts of insurance fraud by arson and other means. The common thread to all counts was respondent's alleged leadership of this criminal organization through which he orchestrated and participated in the commission of the various crimes delineated in the RICO count or charged in the eight preceding counts.

After a six-week jury trial, in which the evidence focused upon both the professional nature of this organization and the execution of a number of distinct criminal acts, respondent was convicted on all nine counts. He was sentenced to a term of 20 years on the substantive counts, as well as a two-year special parole term on the drug count. On the RICO conspiracy count he was sentenced to a 20–year concurrent term and fined $20,000.

On appeal, respondent argued that RICO was intended solely to protect legitimate business enterprises from infiltration by racketeers and that RICO does not make criminal the participation in an association which performs only illegal acts and which has not infiltrated or attempted to infiltrate a legitimate enterprise. The Court of Appeals agreed. We reverse.

## II

... Section 1962(c) makes it unlawful "for any person employed by or associated with any enterprise engaged in, or the activities of which affect, interstate or foreign commerce, to conduct or participate, directly or indirectly, in the conduct of such enterprise's affairs through a pattern of racketeering activity or collection of unlawful debt." The term "enterprise" is defined as including "any individual, partnership, corporation, association, or other legal entity, and any union or group of individuals associated in fact although not a legal entity." § 1961(4). There is no restriction upon the associations embraced by the definition: an enterprise includes any union or group of individuals associated in fact. On its face, the definition appears to include both legitimate and illegitimate enterprises within its scope; it no more excludes criminal enterprises than it does legitimate ones. Had Congress not intended to reach criminal associations, it could easily have narrowed the sweep of the definition by inserting a single word, "legitimate." But it did nothing to indicate that an enterprise consisting of a group of individuals was not covered by RICO if the purpose of the enterprise was exclusively criminal.

The Court of Appeals, however, clearly departed from and limited the statutory language. It gave several reasons for doing so, none of which is adequate. First, it relied in part on the rule of ejusdem generis, an aid to statutory construction problems suggesting that where general words follow a specific enumeration of persons or things, the general words should be limited to persons or things similar to those specifically enumerated. The Court of Appeals ruled that because each of the specific enterprises enumerated in § 1961(4) is a "legitimate" one, the final catchall phrase—"any union or group of individuals associated in fact"—should also be limited to legitimate enterprises. There are at least two flaws in this reasoning. The rule of ejusdem generis is no more than an aid to construction and comes into play only when there is some uncertainty as to the meaning of a particular clause in a statute. Considering the language and structure of § 1961(4), however, we not only perceive no uncertainty in the meaning to be attributed to the phrase, "any union or group of individuals associated in fact" but we are convinced for another reason that ejusdem generis is wholly inapplicable in this context.

Section 1961(4) describes two categories of associations that come within the purview of the "enterprise" definition. The first encompasses organizations such as corporations and partnerships, and other "legal entities." The second covers "any union or group of individuals associated in fact although not a legal entity." The Court of Appeals assumed that the second category was merely a more general description of the first. Having made that assumption, the court concluded that the more generalized description in the second category should be limited by the specific examples enumerated in the first. But that assumption is untenable. Each category describes a separate type of enterprise to be covered by the statute—those that are recognized as legal entities and those that are not. The latter is not a more general description of the former. The second category itself not containing any specific enumeration that is followed by a general description, ejusdem generis has no bearing on the meaning to be attributed to that part of § 1961(4).[4]

A second reason offered by the Court of Appeals in support of its judgment was that giving the definition of "enterprise" its ordinary meaning would create several internal inconsistencies in the act. With respect to § 1962(c), it was said: "If 'a pattern of racketeering' can itself be an 'enterprise' for purposes of § 1962(c), then the two phrases 'employed by or associated with any enterprise' and 'the conduct of such enterprise's affairs through [a pattern of racketeering activity]' add nothing to the meaning of the section. The words of the statute are coherent and logical only if they are read as applying to legitimate enterprises." This conclusion is based on a faulty premise. That a wholly criminal enterprise comes within the ambit of the statute does not mean that a "pattern of racketeering activity" is an "enterprise." In order to secure a conviction under RICO, the government must prove both the existence of an "enterprise" and the connected "pattern of racketeering activity." The enterprise is an entity, for present purposes a group of persons associated together for a common purpose of engaging in a course of conduct. The pattern of racketeering activity is, on the other hand, a series of criminal acts as defined by the statute. The former is proved by evidence of an ongoing organization, formal or informal, and by evidence that the various associates function as a continuing unit. The latter is proved by evidence of the requisite number of acts of racketeering committed by the participants in the enterprise. While the proof used to establish these separate elements may in particular cases coalesce, proof of one does not necessarily establish the other. The "enterprise" is not the "pattern of racketeering activity"; it is an entity separate and apart from the pattern of activity in which it engages. The existence of an enterprise at all times remains a separate element which must be proved by the government.[5]

[4] The Court of Appeals' application of ejusdem generis is further flawed by the assumption that "any individual, partnership, corporation, association or other legal entity" could not act totally beyond the pale of the law. The mere fact that a given enterprise is favored with a legal existence does not prevent that enterprise from proceeding along a wholly illegal course of conduct. Therefore, since legitimacy of purpose is not a universal characteristic of the specifically listed enterprises, it would be improper to engraft this characteristic upon the second category of enterprises.

[5] The government takes the position that proof of a pattern of racketeering activity in

Apart from § 1962(c)'s proscription against participating in an enterprise through a pattern of racketeering activities, RICO also proscribes the investment of income derived from racketeering activity in an enterprise engaged in or which affects interstate commerce as well as the acquisition of an interest in or control of any such enterprise through a pattern of racketeering activity. 18 U.S.C. §§ 1962(a) and (b). The Court of Appeals concluded that these provisions of RICO should be interpreted so as to apply only to legitimate enterprises. If these two sections are so limited, the Court of Appeals held that the proscription in § 1962(c), at issue here, must be similarly limited. Again, we do not accept the premise from which the Court of Appeals derived its conclusion. It is obvious that § 1962(a) and (b) address the infiltration by organized crime of legitimate businesses, but we cannot agree that these sections were not also aimed at preventing racketeers from investing or reinvesting in wholly illegal enterprises and from acquiring through a pattern of racketeering activity wholly illegitimate enterprises such as an illegal gambling business or a loan-sharking operation. There is no inconsistency or anomaly in recognizing that § 1962 applies to both legitimate and illegitimate enterprises. Certainly the language of the statute does not warrant the Court of Appeals' conclusion to the contrary.

Similarly, the Court of Appeals noted that various civil remedies were provided by § 1964, including divestiture, dissolution, reorganization, restrictions on future activities by violators of RICO, and treble damages. These remedies it thought would have utility only with respect to legitimate enterprises. As a general proposition, however, the civil remedies could be useful in eradicating organized crime from the social fabric, whether the enterprise be ostensibly legitimate or admittedly criminal. The aim is to divest the association of the fruits of its ill-gotten gains. Even if one or more of the civil remedies might be inapplicable to a particular illegitimate enterprise, this fact would not serve to limit the enterprise concept. Congress has provided civil remedies for use when the circumstances so warrant. It is untenable to argue that their existence limits the scope of the criminal provisions.

Finally, it is urged that the interpretation of RICO to include both legitimate and illegitimate enterprises will substantially alter the balance between federal and state enforcement of criminal law. This is particularly true, so the argument goes, since included within the definition of racketeering activity are a significant number of acts made criminal under state law. But even assuming that the more inclusive definition of enterprise will have the effect suggested,[9] the language of the statute and its legislative

itself would not be sufficient to establish the existence of an enterprise: "We do not suggest that any two sporadic and isolated offenses by the same actor or actors ipso facto constitute an 'illegitimate' enterprise; rather, the existence of the enterprise as an independent entity must also be shown." But even if that were not the case, the Court of Appeals' position on this point is of little force. Language in a statute is not rendered superfluous merely because in some contexts that language may not be pertinent.

[9] RICO imposes no restrictions upon the criminal justice systems of the states. See 84 Stat. 947 ("Nothing in this title shall super-

history indicate that Congress was well aware that it was entering a new domain of federal involvement through the enactment of this measure. Indeed, the very purpose of the Organized Crime Control Act of 1970 was to enable the federal government to address a large and seemingly neglected problem. The view was that existing law, state and federal, was not adequate to address the problem, which was of national dimensions. That Congress included within the definition of racketeering activities a number of state crimes strongly indicates that RICO criminalized conduct that was also criminal under state law, at least when the requisite elements of a RICO offense are present. As the hearings and legislative debates reveal, Congress was well aware of the fear that RICO would "mov[e] large substantive areas formerly totally within the police power of the state into the federal realm." 116 Cong.Rec. 35217 (1970) (remarks of Rep. Eckhardt). In the face of these objections, Congress nonetheless proceeded to enact the measure, knowing that it would alter somewhat the role of the federal government in the war against organized crime and that the alteration would entail prosecutions involving acts of racketeering that are also crimes under state law. There is no argument that Congress acted beyond its power in so doing. That being the case, the courts are without authority to restrict the application of the statute.

Contrary to the judgment below, neither the language nor structure of RICO limits its application to legitimate "enterprises." Applying it also to criminal organizations does not render any portion of the statute superfluous nor does it create any structural incongruities within the framework of the act. The result is neither absurd nor surprising. On the contrary, insulating the wholly criminal enterprise from prosecution under RICO is the more incongruous position.

Section 904(a) of RICO, 84 Stat. 947, directs that "[t]he provisions of this Title shall be liberally construed to effectuate its remedial purposes." With or without this admonition, we could not agree with the Court of Appeals that illegitimate enterprises should be excluded from coverage. We are also quite sure that nothing in the legislative history of RICO requires a contrary conclusion.

## III

The statement of findings that prefaces the Organized Crime Control Act of 1970 reveals the pervasiveness of the problem that Congress was addressing by this enactment:

> The Congress finds that (1) organized crime in the United
> States is a highly sophisticated, diversified, and widespread activi-
> ty that annually drains billions of dollars from America's economy

---

sede any provision of Federal, State, or other law imposing criminal penalties or affording civil remedies in addition to those provided for in this title"). Thus, under RICO, the states, remain free to exercise their police powers to the fullest constitutional extent in defining and prosecuting crimes within their respective jurisdictions. That some of those crimes may also constitute predicate acts of racketeering under RICO, is no restriction on the separate administration of criminal justice by the states.

by unlawful conduct and the illegal use of force, fraud, and corruption; (2) organized crime derives a major portion of its power through money obtained from such illegal endeavors as syndicated gambling, loan sharking, the theft and fencing of property, the importation and distribution of narcotics and other dangerous drugs, and other forms of social exploitation; (3) this money and power are increasingly used to infiltrate and corrupt legitimate business and labor unions and to subvert and corrupt our democratic processes; (4) organized crime activities in the United States weaken the stability of the nation's economic system, harm innocent investors and competing organizations, interfere with free competition, seriously burden interstate and foreign commerce, threaten the domestic security, and undermine the general welfare of the nation and its citizens; and (5) organized crime continues to grow because of defects in the evidence-gathering process of the law inhibiting the development of the legally admissible evidence necessary to bring criminal and other sanctions or remedies to bear on the unlawful activities of those engaged in organized crime and because the sanctions and remedies available to the government are unnecessarily limited in scope and impact.

84 Stat. 922–23.

In light of the above findings, it was the declared purpose of Congress "to seek the eradication of organized crime in the United States by strengthening the legal tools in the evidence-gathering process, by establishing new penal prohibitions, and by providing enhanced sanctions and new remedies to deal with the unlawful activities of those engaged in organized crime." Id., at 923. The various titles of the act provide the tools through which this goal is to be accomplished. Only three of those titles create substantive offenses, Title VIII, which is directed at illegal gambling operations, Title IX, at issue here, and Title XI, which addresses the importation, distribution, and storage of explosive materials. The other titles provide various procedural and remedial devices to aid in the prosecution and incarceration of persons involved in organized crime.

Considering this statement of the act's broad purposes, the construction of RICO suggested by respondent and the court below is unacceptable. Whole areas of organized criminal activity would be placed beyond the substantive reach of the enactment. For example, associations of persons engaged solely in "loan sharking, the theft and fencing of property, the importation and distribution of narcotics and other dangerous drugs," id., at 922–23, would be immune from prosecution under RICO so long as the association did not deviate from the criminal path. Yet these are among the very crimes that Congress specifically found to be typical of the crimes committed by persons involved in organized crime, and as a major source of revenue and power for such organizations. Along these same lines, Senator McClellan, the principal sponsor of the bill, gave two examples of types of problems RICO was designed to address. Neither is consistent with the view that substantive offenses under RICO would be limited to legitimate enterprises: "Organized criminals, too, have flooded the market with cheap reproductions of hit records and affixed counterfeit popular labels. They are heavily engaged in the illicit prescription drug industry." 116 Cong.Rec. 592 (1970). In view of the purposes and goals of the act, as well as the language of the statute, we are unpersuaded that Congress nevertheless confined the reach of the law to only narrow aspects of organized crime, and, in particular, under RICO, only the infiltration of legitimate business.

This is not to gainsay that the legislative history forcefully supports the view that the major purpose of Title IX is to address the infiltration of legitimate business by organized crime. The point is made time and again during the debates and in the hearings before the House and Senate. But none of these statements requires the negative inference that Title IX did not reach the activities of enterprises organized and existing for criminal purposes.

On the contrary, these statements are in full accord with the proposition that RICO is equally applicable to a criminal enterprise that has no legitimate dimension or has yet to acquire one. Accepting that the primary purpose of RICO is to cope with the infiltration of legitimate businesses, applying the statute in accordance with its terms, so as to reach criminal enterprises, would seek to deal with the problem at its very source. Supporters of the bill recognized that organized crime uses its primary sources of revenue and power—illegal gambling, loan sharking and illicit drug distribution—as a springboard into the sphere of legitimate enterprise. The Senate Report stated:

> What is needed here, the committee believes, are new approaches that will deal not only with individuals, but also with the economic base through which those individuals constitute such a serious threat to the economic well-being of the nation. In short, an attack must be made on *their source of economic power itself*, and the attack must take place on all available fronts.

S.Rep. No. 91–617, p. 79 (1969) (emphasis supplied). Senator Byrd explained in debate on the floor, that "loan sharking paves the way for organized criminals to gain access to and eventually take over the control of thousands of legitimate businesses." 116 Cong.Rec. 606 (1970). Senator Hruska declared that "the combination of criminal and civil penalties in this title offers an extraordinary potential for striking a mortal blow against the property interests of organized crime." Id., at 602. Undoubtedly, the infiltration of legitimate businesses was of great concern, but the means provided to prevent that infiltration plainly included striking at the source of the problem. As Representative Poff, a manager of the bill in the House, stated: "[T]itle IX ... will deal not only with individuals, but also with the economic base through which those individuals constitute such a serious threat to the economic well-being of the nation. In short, an attack must be made on their source of economic power itself...." Id., at 35193.

As a measure to deal with the infiltration of legitimate businesses by organized crime, RICO was both preventive and remedial. Respondent's view would ignore the preventive function of the statute. If Congress had intended the more circumscribed approach espoused by the Court of Appeals, there would have been some positive sign that the law was not to reach organized criminal activities that give rise to the concerns about infiltration. The language of the statute, however—the most reliable evidence of its intent—reveals that Congress opted for a far broader definition of the word "enterprise," and we are unconvinced by anything in the legislative history that this definition should be given less than its full effect.

The judgment of the Court of Appeals is accordingly

Reversed.

■ Justice Stewart agrees with the reasoning and conclusion of the Court of Appeals as to the meaning of the term "enterprise" in this statute. Accordingly, he respectfully dissents.

————

## NOTES ON "ENTERPRISE" AND CONSPIRACY

**1.   The Statute.** The Racketeer Influenced and Corrupt Organizations Act (RICO) was enacted as title IX of the Organized Crime Control Act of 1970. It is codified in 18 U.S.C. §§ 1961–1968. It is an extremely elaborate statute, which reads, in part, as follows:

§ 1961.   Definitions

As used in this chapter—

(1)  "racketeering activity" means

(A) any act or threat involving murder, kidnaping, gambling, arson, robbery, bribery, extortion, dealing in obscene matter, or dealing in narcotic or other dangerous drugs, which is chargeable under State law and punishable by imprisonment for more than one year;

(B) any act which is indictable under any of the following provisions of title 18, United States Code: [Here are cited sections covering, inter alia, bribery, sports bribery, counterfeiting, felonious theft from interstate shipment, embezzlement from pension and welfare funds, extortionate credit transactions, fraud, transmission of gambling information, mail fraud, wire fraud, obscene matter, obstruction of justice, interference with commerce, robbery, extortion, racketeering, interstate transportation of wagering paraphernalia, illegal gambling businesses, laundering of monetary instruments, use of interstate commerce facilities in the commission of murder-for-hire, sexual exploitation of children, interstate transportation of stolen motor vehicles, interstate transportation of stolen property, trafficking in contraband cigarettes, and white slave traffic. Subsection (C) adds certain labor offenses, and subsection (D) adds securities fraud or "the felonious manufacture, importation, receiving, concealment, buying, selling, or otherwise dealing in narcotic or other dangerous drugs, punishable under any law of the United States." Finally, subsection (E) adds certain currency offenses involving the reporting of foreign transactions.]; . . .

(4) "enterprise" includes any individual, partnership, corporation, association, or other legal entity, and any union or group of individuals associated in fact although not a legal entity;

(5) "pattern of racketeering activity" requires at least two acts of racketeering activity, one of which occurred after the effective date of this chapter and the last of which occurred within ten years (excluding any period of imprisonment) after the commission of a prior act of racketeering activity;

(6) "unlawful debt" means a debt

(A) incurred or contracted in gambling activity which was in violation of the law of the United States, a State or political subdivision thereof, or which is unenforceable under State or Federal law in whole or in part as to principal or interest because of the laws relating to usury, and

(B) which was incurred in connection with the business of gambling in violation of the law of the United States, a State or political subdivision thereof, or the business of lending money or a thing of value at a rate usurious under State or Federal law, where the usurious rate is at least twice the enforceable rate; . . . .

## § 1962.   Prohibited activities

(a) It shall be unlawful for any person who has received any income derived, directly or indirectly, from a pattern of racketeering activity or through collection of an unlawful debt in which such person has participated as a principal within the meaning of section 2, title 18, United States Code, to use or invest, directly or indirectly, any part of such income, or the proceeds of such income, in acquisition of any interest in, or the establishment or operation of, any enterprise which is engaged in, or the activities of which affect, interstate or foreign commerce. A purchase of securities on the open market for purposes of investment, and without the intention of controlling or participating in the control of the issuer, or of assisting another to do so, shall not be unlawful under this subsection if the securities of the issuer held by the purchaser, the members of his immediate family, and his or their accomplices in any pattern or racketeering activity or the collection of an unlawful debt after such purchase do not amount in the aggregate to one percent of the outstanding securities of any one class, and do not confer, either in law or in fact, the power to elect one or more directors of the issuer.

(b) It shall be unlawful for any person through a pattern of racketeering activity or through collection of an unlawful debt to acquire or maintain, directly or indirectly, any interest in or control of any enterprise which is engaged in, or the activities of which affect, interstate or foreign commerce.

(c) It shall be unlawful for any person employed by or associated with any enterprise engaged in, or the activities of which affect, interstate or foreign commerce, to conduct or participate, directly or indirectly, in the conduct of such enterprise's affairs through a pattern of racketeering activity or collection of unlawful debt.

(d) It shall be unlawful for any person to conspire to violate any of the provisions of subsection (a), (b), or (c) of this section.

§ 1963.   Criminal penalties

(a) Whoever violates any provision of section 1962 of this chapter shall be fined under this title or imprisoned not more than 20 years (or for life if the violation is based on a racketeering activity for which the maximum penalty includes life imprisonment), or both, and shall forfeit to the United States, irrespective of any provision of State law—

(1) any interest the person has acquired or maintained in violation of section 1962;

(2) any—

(A) interest in;

(B) security of;

(C) claim against; or

(D) property or contractual right of any kind affording a source of influence over;

any enterprise which the person has established, operated, controlled, conducted, or participated in the conduct of, in violation of section 1962; and

(3) any property constituting, or derived from, any proceeds which the person obtained, directly or indirectly, from racketeering activity or unlawful debt collection in violation of section 1962.

The court, in imposing sentence on such person shall order, in addition to any other sentence imposed pursuant to this section, that the person forfeit to the United States all property described in this subsection. In lieu of a fine otherwise authorized by this section, a defendant who derives profits or other proceeds from an offense may be fined not more than twice the gross profits or other proceeds. . . .

§ 1964.   Civil remedies

... (c) Any person injured in his business or property by reason of a violation of section 1962 of this chapter may sue therefor in any appropriate United States district court and shall recover threefold the damages he sustains and the cost of the suit, including a reasonable attorney's fee. . . .

**2.   The RICO "Enterprise."** The place to start in analyzing RICO is with the "enterprise." According to one commentator, RICO was "neatly designed to deal with ... congressional concern with organized criminal infiltration of legitimate business." Gerard E. Lynch, RICO: The Crime of Being a Criminal, Parts I & II, 87 Colum. L. Rev. 661, 681 (1987). On this conception, the purpose of RICO is to protect the public from the tendency of organized crime to take over a legitimate business (the "enterprise") and then operate it by illegal means. Section 1962(c) is designed to punish the completed offense, that is, it punishes running an otherwise lawful business by the methods of organized crime. Sections 1962(a) and 1962(b) are designed to punish inchoate behavior—both deal with methods by which organized crime might acquire the lawful business. Preventing acquisition, the reasoning would go, is one way of preventing operation of the business by illegal means.

*Turkette* departs from this view of the statute. By allowing organized criminal activity to be treated as the "enterprise" under § 1962(c), the focus of RICO is redirected from punishment of the infiltration and operation of legitimate business by organized crime to the punishment of organized crime itself. In effect, *Turkette* allows § 1962(c) to do double duty. Not only does it punish the ultimate harm that Congress had in mind (operation of a lawful business by organized crime) but—like subsections (a) and (b)—it reaches a form of inchoate behavior potentially leading to that harm (in this case, engaging in organized criminal activity in the first place). In order to prevent organized criminals from infiltrating legitimate business, in other words, why not stop organized crime itself?

The *Turkette* approach requires careful definition of the term "enterprise," for it is the existence of the enterprise that distinguishes "ordinary" crime from "organized" crime and triggers the very severe sanctions available under RICO.[a] When does concerted criminal activity become an "enterprise"? Are two persons who carefully plan a series of bank robberies engaged in an ordinary conspiracy (five-year maximum under federal law) or are they conducting the affairs of a RICO "enterprise" through a pattern of racketeering activity (20–year maximum)?

[a] As noted below, the "pattern" of racketeering activity in which the actors must engage can also serve this function.

*Turkette* alluded to this problem, but did not carry the analysis very far. It said:

> [An] enterprise is an entity, for present purposes a group of persons associated together for a common purpose of engaging in a course of conduct. [It] is proved by evidence of an ongoing organization, formal or informal, and by evidence that the various associates function as a continuing unit.... The "enterprise" ... is an entity separate and apart from the pattern of activity in which it engages.

Although the Supreme Court has held there need not be an economic motive,[b] it has not identified the characteristics that make group criminal activity a RICO "enterprise." United States v. Bledsoe, 674 F.2d 647 (8th Cir. 1982), is a well known Circuit Court attempt to do so:

> The primary intent of Congress in enacting 18 U.S.C. § 1962(c) was to prevent organized crime from infiltrating businesses and other legitimate economic entities.... When directed against infiltration of legitimate enterprises, the provisions have a relatively well defined scope of application. Legitimate businesses and other legitimate organizations tend to have a definite structure and clear boundaries which limit the applicability of a criminal statute aimed at the infiltration of criminal elements into these entities. Infiltration of legitimate entities also warrants the act's severe sanctions. The act's drafters perceived a distinct threat to the free market in organized criminal groups gaining control of enterprises operating in that market. These congressmen thought that organized criminal elements exert a monopoly-like power in the legitimate economic sphere. The bill's sponsors also believed that such infiltration was a source of power and protection for organized crime and gave it a permanent base from which it was more likely to perpetrate a continuing pattern of criminal acts.

> But Congress did not draft the statute to apply solely to infiltration of legitimate enterprises. The statute also reaches wholly criminal organizations. However, the act was not intended to reach any criminals who merely associate together and perpetrate two of the specified crimes, rather it was aimed at "organized crime." ... Obviously, no statute could and this statute was not intended to require direct proof that individuals are engaged in something as ill defined as "organized crime." The statute is an attack on organized crime, but it utilizes a per se approach.... Each element of the crime, that is, the predicate acts, the pattern of such acts, and the enterprise requirement, was designed to limit the applicability of the statute and separate individuals engaged in

---

[b] See National Organization for Women, Inc. v. Scheidler, 510 U.S. 249 (1994) (objective of "enterprise" was to close down abortion clinics).

organized crime from ordinary criminals. The enterprise requirement must be interpreted in this light.

[T]he enterprise must be more than an informal group created to perpetrate the acts of racketeering. [It] cannot simply be the undertaking of the acts of racketeering, neither can it be the minimal association which surrounds these acts. Any two criminal acts will necessarily be surrounded by some degree of organization and no two individuals will ever jointly perpetrate a crime without some degree of association apart from the commission of the crime itself. Thus unless the inclusion of the enterprise element requires proof of some structure separate from the racketeering activity and distinct from the organization which is a necessary incident to the racketeering, the act simply punishes the commission of two of the specified crimes within a 10–year period. Congress clearly did not intend such an application of the act.

Although commonality of purpose may be the sine qua non of a criminal enterprise, in many cases this singular test fails to distinguish enterprises from individuals merely associated together for the commission of sporadic crime. Any two wrongdoers who through concerted action commit two or more crimes share a purpose. This suggests that an enterprise must exhibit each of three basic characteristics.

In addition to having a common or shared purpose which animates those associated with it, it is fundamental that the enterprise "function as a continuing unit." In *Turkette*, the Supreme Court stated that an enterprise "is proved by evidence of an *ongoing* organization, formal or informal, and by evidence that the various associates function as a *continuing* unit." (Emphasis added.) This does not mean the scope of the enterprise cannot change as it engages in diverse forms of activity nor does it mean that the participants in the enterprise cannot vary with different individuals managing its affairs at different times and in different places. What is essential, however, is that there is some continuity of both structure and personality. For example, the operatives in a prostitution ring may change through time, but the various roles which the old and new individuals perform remain the same. But if an entirely new set of people begin to operate the ring, it is not the same enterprise as it was before.

Finally, an enterprise must have an "ascertainable structure" distinct from that inherent in the conduct of a pattern of racketeering activity. This distinct structure might be demonstrated by proof that a group engaged in a diverse pattern of crimes or that it has an organizational pattern or system of authority beyond what was necessary to perpetrate the predicate crimes. The command system of a Mafia family is an example of this type of structure as is the hierarchy, planning, and division of profits within a prostitution ring.

Does *Bledsoe* provide a satisfactory basis for distinguishing ordinary crime from "organized" crime? How do the "three basic characteristics" that an "enterprise" must exhibit differentiate a violation of RICO from an ordinary conspiracy? Are they adequate to the task?

**3.   RICO Conspiracy vs. Ordinary Conspiracy: *United States v. Elliott.*** Section 1962(d) complicates the situation by punishing a conspiracy to violate the substantive provisions of RICO. After *Turkette*, one can violate § 1962(c) of RICO by conducting the affairs of an organized crime "enterprise" through criminal behavior that constitutes a "pattern of racketeering activity." Under § 1962(d), one can conspire to violate § 1962(c) by agreeing with others to conduct the affairs of an enterprise in this manner. How does a conspiracy to violate RICO differ from a conspiracy to commit the predicate crimes that constitute the "pattern of racketeering activity"? How does RICO fit with the ordinary law of conspiracy?

These matters were addressed in United States v. Elliott, 571 F.2d 880 (5th Cir. 1978), where the court summarized the facts as follows:

> In this case we deal with the question of whether and, if so, how a free society can protect itself when groups of people, through division of labor, specialization, diversification, complexity of organization, and the accumulation of capital, turn crime into an ongoing business.... Today we review the convictions of six persons accused of conspiring to violate the RICO statute, two of whom were also accused and convicted of substantive RICO violations.... Predictably, the government and the defendants differ as to what this case is about. According to the defendants, what we are dealing with is a leg, a tail, a trunk, an ear—separate entities unaffected by RICO proscriptions. The government, on the other hand, asserts that we have come eyeball to eyeball with a single creature of behemoth proportions, securely within RICO's grasp. After a careful, if laborious study of the facts and the law, we accept, with minor exceptions, the government's view....

> Here, the government proved beyond a reasonable doubt the existence of an enterprise comprised of at least five of the defendants. This enterprise can best be analogized to a large business conglomerate. Metaphorically speaking, J.C. Hawkins was the chairman of the board, functioning as the chief executive officer and overseeing the operations of many separate branches of the corporation. An executive committee in charge of the "Counterfeit Title, Stolen Car, and Amphetamine Sales Department" was comprised of J.C., Delph, and Taylor, who supervised the operations of lower level employees such as Farr, the printer, and Green, Boyd, and Jackson, the car thieves. Another executive committee, comprised of J.C., Recea and Foster, controlled the "Thefts From Interstate Commerce Department", arranging the purchase, concealment, and distribution of such commodities as meat, dairy products, "Career Club" shirts, and heavy construction equip-

ment. An offshoot of this department handled subsidiary activities, such as murder and obstruction of justice, intended to facilitate the smooth operation of its primary activities. Each member of the conglomerate, with the exception of Foster, was responsible for procuring and wholesaling whatever narcotics could be obtained. The thread tying all of these departments, activities, and individuals together was the desire to make money.[c]

In the course of its opinion, the court discussed the differences between a charge of conspiracy under pre-RICO law and under § 1962(d):

All six defendants were convicted under 18 U.S.C. § 1962(d) of having conspired to violate a substantive RICO provision, § 1962(c). In this appeal, [the] defendants . . . argue that while the indictment alleged but one conspiracy, the government's evidence at trial proved the existence of several conspiracies, resulting in a variance which substantially prejudiced their rights and requires reversal. . . . Prior to the enactment of the RICO statute, this argument would have been more persuasive. However, as we explain below, RICO has displaced many of the legal precepts traditionally applied to concerted criminal activity. Its effect in this case is to free the government from the strictures of the multiple conspiracy doctrine and to allow the joint trial of many persons accused of diversified crimes.

[Traditional conspiracy doctrine] applies only insofar as the alleged agreement has "a common end or single unified purpose." Generally, where the government has shown that a number of otherwise diverse activities were performed to achieve a single goal, courts have been willing to find a single conspiracy. This "common objective" test has most often been used to connect the many facets of drug importation and distribution schemes. The rationale falls apart, however, where the remote members of the alleged conspiracy are not truly interdependent or where the various activities sought to be tied together cannot reasonably be said to constitute a unified scheme. . . .

[c] The court affirmed the conviction of five of the six defendants for conspiring to violate RICO. The conspiracy conviction of the sixth defendant—Elliott, whose name adorns the case in the Federal Reporter—was reversed. Elliott was plainly a marginal player. The court was convinced that he " 'associated with the wrong people and was convicted because of guilt by association only.' " Of the other five defendants, J.C. Hawkins and Recea Hawkins (his brother) were convicted both of a substantive RICO count and the count charging conspiracy to violate RICO. Various combinations of the defendants were also convicted of separately stated predicate offenses. Twenty-five overt acts were recited in the conspiracy count, ranging from arson to drug crimes. The "pattern" of racketeering activity alleged in the substantive RICO count (grounded on § 1962(c)) was based on four violations of federal law alleged in separate counts (three involving thefts from interstate shipments and the fourth a counterfeit security), as well as a series of federal drug crimes, an arson in violation of state law, and a murder in violation of state law. J.C. was the ringleader. He was sentenced to 80 years imprisonment. Recea got 50 years. Two other defendants were sentenced to 10 years in prison, and the fifth defendant was sentenced to one year plus five years probation.—[Footnote by eds.]

Applying pre-RICO conspiracy concepts to the facts of this case, we doubt that a single conspiracy could be demonstrated. Foster had no contact with Delph and Taylor during the life of the alleged conspiracy. Delph and Taylor, so far as the evidence revealed, had no contact with Recea Hawkins. The activities allegedly embraced by the illegal agreement in this case are simply too diverse to be tied together on the theory that participation in one activity necessarily implied awareness of others. Even viewing the "common objective" of the conspiracy as the raising of revenue through criminal activity, we could not say, for example, that Foster, when he helped to conceal stolen meat, had to know that J.C. was selling drugs to persons unknown to Foster, or that Delph and Taylor, when they furnished counterfeit titles to a car theft ring, had to know that the man supplying the titles was also stealing goods out of interstate commerce. The enterprise involved in this case probably could not have been successfully prosecuted as a single conspiracy under the general federal conspiracy statute, 18 U.S.C. § 371.

. . . In the context of organized crime, [traditional conspiracy doctrine] inhibited mass prosecutions because a single agreement or "common objective" cannot be inferred from the commission of highly diverse crimes by apparently unrelated individuals. RICO helps to eliminate this problem by creating a substantive offense which ties together these diverse parties and crimes. Thus, the object of a RICO conspiracy is to violate a substantive RICO provision—here, to conduct or participate in the affairs of an enterprise through a pattern of racketeering activity. The gravamen of the conspiracy charge in this case is not that each defendant agreed to commit arson, to steal goods from interstate commerce, to obstruct justice, and to sell narcotics; rather, it is that each agreed to participate, directly and indirectly, in the affairs of the enterprise by committing two or more predicate crimes. Under the statute, it is irrelevant that each defendant participated in the enterprise's affairs through different, even unrelated crimes, so long as we may reasonably infer that each crime was intended to further the enterprise's affairs. To find a single conspiracy, we still must look for agreement on an overall objective. What Congress did was to define that objective through the substantive provisions of the act. . . .

In the instant case, it is clear that "the essential nature of the plan" was to associate for the purpose of making money from repeated criminal activity. Defendant Foster, for example, hired J.C. Hawkins to commit arson, helped him to conceal large quantities of meat and shirts stolen from interstate commerce, and bought a stolen forklift from him. It would be "a perversion of natural thought and of natural language" to deny that these facts give rise to the inference that Foster knew he was directly involved in an enterprise whose purpose was to profit from crime. . . .

Foster also had to know that the enterprise was bigger than his role in it, and that others unknown to him were participating in its affairs. He may have been unaware that others who had agreed to participate in the enterprise's affairs did so by selling drugs and murdering a key witness. That, however, is irrelevant to his own liability, for he is charged with agreeing *to participate* in the enterprise through his own crimes, not with agreeing *to commit* each of the crimes through which the overall affairs of the enterprise were conducted. . . .[31]

We do not lightly dismiss the fact that under this statute four defendants who did not commit murder have been forced to stand trial jointly with, and as confederates of, two others who did. Prejudice inheres in such a trial; great Neptune's ocean could not purge its taint.[33] But the Constitution does not guarantee a trial free from the prejudice that inevitably accompanies any charge of heinous group crime; it demands only that the potential for transference of guilt be minimized to the extent possible under the

---

[31] Although the evidence here supports the inference that each remote member of this enterprise knew he was a part of a much larger criminal venture, we do not wish to imply that each "department" of the enterprise was wholly independent of the others. A close look at the modus operandi of the enterprise reveals a pattern of interdependence which bolsters our conclusion that the functions of each "department" directly contributed to the success of the overall operation. Many of the enterprise's practices were analogous to those common in legitimate businesses:

—*Investment Capital*: Most of the enterprise's activities depended upon the ready availability of investment capital, or "front money", to finance the purchase of stolen goods and narcotics for eventual resale at a profit. In this sense, money brought in from one project could be used to purchase goods in another unrelated project.

—*"Good Will"*: Part of the value of a business is the reputation it has established in the community, its "good will." The enterprise here benefitted from a negative form of "good will." For example, Foster and J.C. exploited their cooperation in the Sparta nursing home arson to gain the confidence of James Gunnells when they needed his help in concealing stolen meat; that earlier endeavor furnished proof that Foster and J.C. could be trusted in criminal pursuits. Similarly, J.C.'s threats of physical harm to many of those involved with the enterprise helped to build a fear in the community which deterred potential witnesses from going to the police. In this way, each successful criminal act and each threat contributed to the success of the enterprise as a whole.

—*Arrangements to Limit Liability*: Like most large business organizations, this enterprise conducted its affairs in a manner calculated to limit its liability for the acts of its agents. J.C. erroneously believed that he could limit each person's liability by keeping him as isolated from the others as possible—in other words, that it would be safer to have the affairs of the enterprise conducted through chains composed of many persons playing limited roles than through a small circle of individuals performing many functions. Where overlap was unavoidable, the enterprise's ongoing operations depended upon each member's confidence that the others would remain silent. When J.C. spoke to Joe Fuchs in January, 1976, for example, he expressed confidence that the government could never make a case against his enterprise. He was certain that James Elliott would not talk because "James is scared." He also assured Fuchs that he, J.C., and Scooter Herring would say nothing: as for Recea, "that's plum out of the question, you can eliminate that." Thus, he concluded, the only other persons who might implicate Fuchs could provide only uncorroborated accounts which would "mean nothing" in court.

[33] Cf. Shakespeare, Macbeth, Act III, Scene I.

circumstances in order "to individualize each defendant in his relation to the mass." Kotteakos v. United States, 328 U.S. 750, 773 (1946). The RICO statute does not offend this principle. Congress, in a proper exercise of its legislative power, has decided that murder, like thefts from interstate commerce and the counterfeiting of securities, qualifies as racketeering activity. This, of course, ups the ante for RICO violators who personally would not contemplate taking a human life. Whether there is a moral imbalance in the equation of thieves and counterfeiters with murderers is a question whose answer lies in the halls of Congress, not in the judicial conscience....

Through RICO, Congress defined a new separate crime to help snare those who make careers of crime. Participation in the affairs of an enterprise through the commission of two or more predicate crimes is now an offense separate and distinct from those predicate crimes. So too is conspiracy to commit this new offense a crime separate and distinct from conspiracy to commit the predicate crimes. The necessity which mothered this statutory invention was caused by the inability of the traditional criminal law to punish and deter organized crime.

**4. Questions and Comments.** Most RICO prosecutions are for violating § 1962(c) under the *Turkette* theory. In this context, RICO has become a significant prosecutorial weapon in the fight against organized crime. What features make it valuable to prosecutors? How is it different from (or better or worse than) charges of pre-RICO crimes and conspiracies?

---

NOTES ON "PATTERN OF RACKETEERING ACTIVITY"

**1. The RICO "Pattern of Racketeering Activity."** Each of the substantive offenses punished by RICO requires that the defendants engage in a "pattern of racketeering activity." Crimes that constitute "racketeering activity" are listed at length in § 1961(1). A "pattern" is defined in § 1961(5) as requiring "at least two acts of racketeering activity."

Further elaboration of this concept is not too important where the "enterprise" being pursued is the organized criminal activity itself. A different situation is presented where a *legitimate* enterprise is the target of the organized criminal activity or the means through which the organized criminal activity is conducted. If it is alleged that a legitimate business has been infiltrated by a pattern of racketeering activity or that the affairs of a legitimate business were conducted by a pattern of racketeering activity, the need to distinguish "ordinary" criminality from "organized" crime once again emerges. Are two acts of mail fraud in conducting an otherwise legitimate "enterprise" a "pattern of racketeering activity"? Three? In this kind of case, the "pattern" of criminality is the only factor separating ordinary criminal sanctions from the elevated sanctions available under RICO. It is therefore necessary, at least in this situation, that "pattern of racketeering activity" be carefully defined.

The primary context in which this issue has arisen is civil litigation under § 1964(c). Mail fraud and wire fraud are potential "racketeering acts" under § 1961(1), and these crimes are so broadly defined that it is often possible to characterize commercial disputes as involving one or both of these offenses. Since treble damages and attorneys fees are available to a civil plaintiff if a violation of RICO can be made out, there is a powerful incentive for private plaintiffs to add a RICO count to what might ordinarily be a typical common law suit for breach of contract. The allegation in such cases is that § 1962(c) has been violated because the "enterprise" (the defendant's otherwise legitimate business entity) has been conducted by a "pattern of racketeering activity" (numerous breaches of contract that amount to mail or wire fraud).

**2. *Sedima, S.P.R.L. v. Imrex Co., Inc.*** The Supreme Court's first attempt to define "pattern of racketeering activity" occurred in a footnote in Sedima, S.P.R.L. v. Imrex Co., Inc., 473 U.S. 479, 497 n.14 (1985). The facts of *Sedima*, fairly typical of such suits, were as follows:

> In 1979, petitioner Sedima, a Belgian corporation, entered into a joint venture with respondent Imrex Co. to provide electronic components to a Belgian firm. The buyer was to order parts through Sedima; Imrex was to obtain the parts in this country and ship them to Europe. The agreement called for Sedima and Imrex to split the net proceeds. Imrex filled roughly $8 million in orders placed with it through Sedima. Sedima became convinced, however, that Imrex was presenting inflated bills, cheating Sedima out of a portion of its proceeds by collecting for nonexistent expenses.

> In 1982, Sedima filed this action.... The complaint set out common-law claims of unjust enrichment, conversion, and breach of contract, fiduciary duty, and a constructive trust. In addition, it asserted RICO claims under § 1964(c) against Imrex and two of its officers. Two counts alleged violations of § 1962(c) based on predicate acts of mail and wire fraud.... Sedima sought treble damages and attorney's fees.

The Court was asked in *Sedima* to adopt several limitations on civil RICO actions that are not material for present purposes.[a] In declining to do so, it held that "Sedima may maintain this action if the defendants conducted the enterprise through a pattern of racketeering activity. The questions whether the defendants committed the requisite predicate acts, and whether the commission of those acts fell into a pattern, are not before us." It did, however, speak in a footnote to what might constitute a pattern:

> As many commentators have pointed out, the definition of a "pattern of racketeering activity" differs from the other provisions

---

[a] Specifically, it was asked to require a special "racketeering injury" as a prerequisite to civil suit under RICO and to hold that a civil RICO claim could not be filed unless there was a prior criminal conviction.

in § 1961 in that it states that a pattern *"requires* at least two acts of racketeering activity," (emphasis added), not that it "means" two such acts. The implication is that while two acts are necessary, they may not be sufficient. Indeed, in common parlance two of anything do not generally form a "pattern." The legislative history supports the view that two isolated acts of racketeering activity do not constitute a pattern. As the Senate Report explained: "The target of [RICO] is thus not sporadic activity. The infiltration of legitimate business normally requires more than one 'racketeering activity' and the threat of continuing activity to be effective. It is this factor of *continuity plus relationship* which combines to produce a pattern." S.Rep. No. 91–617, p. 158 (1969) (emphasis added). Similarly, the sponsor of the Senate bill, after quoting this portion of the Report, pointed out to his colleagues that "[t]he term 'pattern' itself requires the showing of a relationship.... So, therefore, proof of two acts of racketeering activity, without more, does not establish a pattern...." 116 Cong.Rec. 18940 (1970) (statement of Sen. McClellan). See also id., at 35193 (statement of Rep. Poff) (RICO "not aimed at the isolated offender"); House Hearings, at 665. Significantly, in defining "pattern" in a later provision of the same bill, Congress was more enlightening: "[C]riminal conduct forms a pattern if it embraces criminal acts that have the same or similar purposes, results, participants, victims, or methods of commission, or otherwise are interrelated by distinguishing characteristics and are not isolated events." 18 U.S.C. § 3575(e). This language may be useful in interpreting other sections of the act.

**3. *H.J. Inc. v. Northwestern Bell Telephone Company.*** A more elaborate definition of "pattern" was offered in H.J. Inc. v. Northwestern Bell Telephone Company, 492 U.S. 229 (1989). *H.J. Inc.* was also a civil suit. It involved a class action brought by customers of a telephone company who alleged that excessive rates were authorized by the regulatory authorities because they were bribed by officers of the company. The lower courts dismissed the suit because they thought RICO required "multiple illegal schemes" before a "pattern" could be found, whereas what the plaintiffs alleged was a "single fraudulent effort" to obtain higher rates. The Supreme Court reversed. It was unanimous in its conclusion that a series of acts in support of a single scheme or episode could, on appropriate facts, constitute a RICO "pattern."

**(i) Justice Brennan's Opinion.** For the Court, Justice Brennan admitted that "developing a meaningful concept of 'pattern' ... has proved to be no easy task," but made the effort as follows:

We find no support ... for the proposition ... that predicate acts of racketeering may form a pattern only when they are part of separate illegal schemes. Nor can we agree ... that a pattern is established merely by proving two predicate acts ... or ... that the word "pattern" refers only to predicates that are indicative of a perpetrator involved in organized crime or its functional equivalent. In our view, Congress had a more natural and commonsense approach to RICO's pattern element in mind, intending a more stringent requirement than proof simply of two predicates, but also envisioning a concept of sufficient breadth that it might encompass multiple predicates within a single scheme that were related and that amounted to, or threatened the likelihood of, continued criminal activity.

... In normal usage, [a] "pattern" is an "arrangement or order of things or activity," 11 Oxford English Dictionary 357 (2d ed. 1989).... It is not the number of predicates but the relationship that they bear to each other or to some external organizing principle that renders them "ordered" or "arranged." ... It is reasonable to infer ... that Congress intended to take a flexible approach, and envisaged that a pattern might be demonstrated by reference to a range of different ordering principles or relationships between predicates, within the expansive bounds set.... The legislative history ... shows that "[t]he term 'pattern' itself requires the showing of a relationship" between the predicates, 116 Cong. Rec., at 18940 (1970) (Sen. McClellan), and of "the threat of continuing activity," ibid. "It is this factor of *continuity plus relationship* which combines to produce a pattern." Ibid. (emphasis added). RICO's legislative history reveals Congress' intent that to prove a pattern of racketeering activity a plaintiff or prosecutor must show that the racketeering predicates are related, and that they amount to or pose a threat of continued criminal activity.

For analytic purposes these two constituents of RICO's pattern requirement must be stated separately, though in practice their proof will often overlap. The element of relatedness is the easier to define, for we may take guidance from a provision [in another portion of the statute of which RICO formed a part. That section provides:] "[C]riminal conduct forms a pattern if it embraces criminal acts that have the same or similar purposes, results, participants, victims, or methods of commission, or otherwise are interrelated by distinguishing characteristics and are not isolated events." We have no reason to suppose that Congress had in mind for RICO's pattern of racketeering component any more constrained a notion of the relationships between predicates that would suffice.

"Continuity" is both a closed-and open-ended concept, referring either to a closed period of repeated conduct, or to past conduct that by its nature projects into the future with a threat of repetition. It is, in either case, centrally a temporal concept—and particularly so in the RICO context, where what must be continuous, RICO's predicate acts or offenses, and the relationship these predicates must bear one to another, are distinct requirements. A party alleging a RICO violation may demonstrate continuity over a closed period by proving a series of related predicates extending over a substantial period of time. Predicate acts extending over a few weeks or months and threatening no future criminal conduct do not satisfy this requirement: Congress was concerned in RICO with long-term criminal conduct. Often a RICO action will be brought before continuity can be established in this way. In such cases, liability depends on whether the threat of continuity is demonstrated.

Whether the predicates proved establish a threat of continued racketeering activity depends on the specific facts of each case. Without making any claim to cover the field of possibilities—preferring to deal with this issue in the context of concrete factual situations presented for decision—we offer some examples of how this element might be satisfied. A RICO pattern may surely be established if the related predicates themselves involve a distinct threat of long-term racketeering activity, either implicit or explicit. Suppose a hoodlum were to sell "insurance" to a neighborhood's storekeepers to cover them against breakage of their windows, telling his victims he would be reappearing each month to collect the "premium" that would continue their "coverage." Though the number of related predicates involved may be small and they may occur close together in time, the racketeering acts themselves include a specific threat of repetition extending indefinitely into the future, and thus supply the requisite threat of continuity. In other cases, the threat of continuity may be established by showing that the predicate acts or offenses are part of an ongoing entity's regular way of doing business. Thus, the threat of continuity is sufficiently established where the predicates can be attributed to a defendant operating as part of a long-term association that exists for criminal purposes. Such associations include, but extend well beyond, those traditionally grouped under the phrase "organized crime." The continuity requirement is likewise satisfied where it is shown that the predicates are a regular way of conducting defendant's ongoing legitimate business (in the sense that it is not a business that exists for criminal purposes), or of conducting or participating in an ongoing and legitimate RICO "enterprise."

**(ii) Justice Scalia's Opinion.** Justice Scalia, joined by Chief Justice Rehnquist and by Justices O'Connor and Kennedy, wrote separately. His critique was scathing:

Four terms ago, in Sedima, S.P.R.L. v. Imrex Co., 473 U.S. 479, 497 n.14 (1985), we gave lower courts [some] clues concerning the meaning of the enigmatic term "pattern of racketeering activity".... Thus enlightened, the District Courts and Courts of Appeals ... promptly produced the widest and most persistent Circuit split on an issue of federal law in recent memory. Today, four years and countless millions in damages and attorney's fees later (not to mention prison sentences under the criminal provisions of RICO), the Court does little more than repromulgate those hints as to what RICO means, though with the caveat that Congress intended that they be applied using a "flexible approach."

Elevating to the level of statutory text a phrase taken from the legislative history, the Court counsels the lower courts: " 'continuity plus relationship.' " This seems to me about as helpful to the conduct of their affairs as "life is a fountain." Of the two parts of this talismanic phrase, the relatedness requirement is said to be the "easier to define,".... [T]he Court's definition ... has the feel of being solidly rooted in law, since it is a direct quotation of [another statute]. Unfortunately, if normal (and sensible) rules of statutory construction were followed, the existence of [this other statute]—which is the definition contained in another title of the act that was explicitly not rendered applicable to RICO—suggests that whatever "pattern" might mean in RICO, it assuredly does not mean that.... But that does not really matter, since [the Court's language] is utterly uninformative anyway. It hardly closes in on the target to know that "relatedness" refers to acts that are related by "purposes, results, participants, victims, ... methods of commission, or [just in case that is not vague enough] otherwise." Is the fact that the victims of both predicate acts were women enough? Or that both acts had the purpose of enriching the defendant? Or that the different coparticipants of the defendant in both acts were his coemployees? I doubt that the lower courts will find the Court's instructions much more helpful than telling them to look for a "pattern"—which is what the statute already says.

The Court finds "continuity" more difficult to define precisely. "Continuity," it says, "is both a closed-and open-ended concept, referring either to a closed period of repeated conduct, or to past conduct that by its nature projects into the future with a threat of repetition." I have no idea what this concept of a "closed period of repeated conduct" means. Virtually all allegations of racketeering activity, in both civil and criminal suits, will relate to past periods that are "closed" (unless one expects plaintiff or the prosecutor to establish that the defendant not only committed the crimes he did, but is still committing them), and all of them must relate to conduct that is "repeated," because of RICO's multiple-act requirement.... Since the Court has rejected the concept of separate criminal "schemes" or "episodes" as a criterion of "threatening future criminal conduct," I think it must be saying that at least a few months of racketeering activity (and who knows how much more?) is generally for free, as far as RICO is concerned. The "closed period" concept is a sort of safe harbor for racketeering activity that does not last too long, no matter how many different crimes and different schemes are involved, so long as it does not otherwise "establish a threat of continued racketeering activity."

A gang of hoodlums that commits one act of extortion on Monday in New York, a second in Chicago on Tuesday, a third in San Francisco on Wednesday, and so on through an entire week, and then finally and completely disbands, cannot be reached under RICO. I am sure that is not what the statute intends, but I cannot imagine what else the Court's murky discussion can possibly mean.

But Justice Scalia relented a bit:

It is, however, unfair to be so critical of the Court's effort, because I would be unable to provide an interpretation of RICO that gives significantly more guidance concerning its application. It is clear to me ... that the word "pattern" in the phrase "pattern of racketeering activity" was meant to import some requirement beyond the mere existence of multiple predicate acts.... But what that something more is, is beyond me. As I have suggested, it is also beyond the Court.... Today's opinion has added nothing to improve our prior guidance, which has created a kaleidoscope of Circuit positions, except to clarify that RICO may in addition be violated when there is a "threat of continuity." It seems to me this increases rather than removes the vagueness. There is no reason to believe that the Courts of Appeals will be any more unified in the future, than they have in the past, regarding the content of this law.

That situation is bad enough with respect to any statute, but it is intolerable with respect to RICO. For it is not only true, as Justice Marshall commented in *Sedima* that our interpretation of RICO has "quite simply revolutionize[d] private litigation" and "validate[d] the federalization of broad areas of state common law of frauds," so that clarity and predictability in RICO's civil applications are particularly important; but it is also true that RICO, since it has criminal applications as well, must, even in its civil applications, possess the degree of certainty required for criminal laws. No constitutional challenge to this law has been raised in the present case, and so that issue is not before us. That the highest Court in the land has been unable to derive from this statute anything more than today's meager guidance bodes ill for the day when that challenge is presented.

**4. Questions and Comments.** Although most litigation of the "pattern" requirement has arisen in civil suits under RICO, there are occasions when it becomes the crucial determinant of criminal RICO liability. It is possible, for example, for government entities (a governor's or attorney general's office, a mayor's office, a police department) to be the RICO "enterprise" through which corrupt behavior occurs. And although most RICO prosecutions are based on *Turkette*-theory charges of violating § 1962(c), there are scattered prosecutions for criminal activity committed through an otherwise legitimate "enterprise" and for the illegitimate acquisition of legitimate enterprises. In those instances, it is the "pattern of racketeering activity" that determines the applicability of RICO sanctions rather than the sanctions otherwise available for the crimes committed. Has the Court adequately defined "pattern of racketeering activity" in this context? Has it adequately distinguished RICO crime from ordinary crime?

———

# CHAPTER VIII

# HOMICIDE

---

## INTRODUCTORY NOTES ON THE HISTORY OF CRIMINAL HOMICIDE

**1. The Early Law.** From a modern perspective, the most important aspect of early English law was the development of the separate offenses of murder and manslaughter.[a] Prior to 1496, murder was the only homicide offense, and the penalty was death. For those who could come within its terms, however, benefit of clergy was available to avoid the death penalty. By the late 15th century, the categories of offenders who could claim this mitigation had expanded to include virtually all literate persons.

A series of statutes enacted between 1496 and 1547 led to the development of manslaughter as a distinct and lesser homicide offense. The effect of these statutes was to exclude certain of the more serious forms of murder from the benefit of clergy. Those convicted of the excluded offenses became subject to the death penalty, unless they could obtain a royal pardon. As the law matured, the dividing line between murder and manslaughter came to be the concept of "malice prepense" or "malice aforethought." In time, murder came to include all homicides committed with "malice aforethought," and manslaughter all criminal homicides committed without "malice aforethought." As the law evolved, to paraphrase Sir James Fitzjames Stephen, the judges allocated criminal homicides between murder and manslaughter—and gave meaning to the determinative term "malice aforethought"—according to which offenders deserved to be hanged.[b] This initial effort at grading criminal homicide offenses thus used the definition of murder as the device for isolating those homicides for which the death penalty was imposed.[c]

[a] The history of criminal homicide is elaborated in detail in ALI, Model Penal Code and Commentaries, §§ 210.0 to .6, pp. 1–171 (1980). Additional sources are cited in the Model Code commentary. Among the more useful are Royal Comm'n on Capital Punishment, Report, CMND. No. 8932 (1953); 3 Sir James Fitzjames Stephen, A History of the Criminal Law of England 1–107 (1883); Herbert Wechsler and Jerome Michael, A Rationale of the Law of Homicide, 37 Colum.L.Rev. 701, 1261 (1937).

[b] See Royal Comm'n on Capital Punishment, CMND. No. 8932, at 28 (1953). What

Stephen actually said (in 1866), was that "the loose term 'malice' was used, and then when a particular state of mind came to their notice the judges called it 'malice' or not according to their view of the propriety of hanging particular people. That is, in two words, the history of the definition of murder."

[c] The traditional definition of murder, as paraphrased from Coke's rendition in the 17th century, was: "When a man of sound memory and of the age of discretion unlawfully kills any reasonable creature in being and under the King's peace, with malice

**2. The Distinction Between Murder and Manslaughter.** The remaining common-law history of murder and manslaughter principally concerns the content assigned to the two categories as they expanded in scope. Murder came to encompass four different kinds of killings:

(i) those where the actor intended to kill or knew that death would result;

(ii) those where the actor intended to inflict grievous bodily harm or knew that such harm would result;

(iii) those where the actor manifested reckless indifference to death—a state of mind variously described as a "depraved mind," an "abandoned and malignant heart," or "wickedness of disposition, hardness of heart, cruelty, recklessness of consequences, and a mind regardless of social duty";

and (iv) those where the death occurred while the actor was engaged in the commission of a felony.

Malice aforethought became a term of art, if not, as Glanville Williams has said, a term of deception,[d] that encompassed all of these various circumstances and states of mind. The term was thus a token, an arbitrary symbol, used to collect under a single label a wide variety of cases having no more in common than that they were at one time or another deemed appropriate situations for imposition of the death penalty.

Manslaughter was defined as homicide that was committed without malice aforethought. Common-law manslaughter came to include three distinct types of killings:

(i) those where the actor intended to kill but committed the offense in a sudden heat of passion engendered by adequate provocation;

(ii) those where the actor engaged in reckless or negligent behavior that was insufficiently culpable to constitute murder but more culpable than ordinary civil negligence; and

(iii) those where the death occurred while the actor was engaged in the commission of an unlawful act not amounting to a felony.

The term "voluntary manslaughter" was used to refer to the first category. The term "involuntary manslaughter" was used to designate the second and third categories. The distinction between voluntary and involuntary manslaughter had no significance at early common law, although modern statutes frequently use these terms to describe different grading categories.[e]

aforethought, either express or implied by the law, the death taking place within a year and a day." See 3 Coke, Institutes * 47; Royal Comm'n on Capital Punishment, CMND. No. 8932, at 28 (1953).

[d] Glanville Williams, Textbook of Criminal Law 208 (1978).

[e] See, e.g., the Virginia statutes reproduced in Appendix B.

**3.   Modern Developments.** The common-law structure has survived in England, although grading provisions designed to restrict use of the death penalty were adopted in 1957 and the death penalty was abandoned altogether in 1965. In the middle of the last century, England also abolished the felony-murder rule.

In the United States, there have been two broad developments in the law of homicide, each of which has generated a rich and complex jurisprudence. The first development, which began in the 18th century and continues to this day, is the emergence of distinct grades of homicide offenses, each of which carries its own penalty and stigmatic value. As the following materials demonstrate, the common-law structure was enormously influential in the development of modern homicide statutes. That structure remains intact in a few jurisdictions, and, during the codification process, most state legislatures explicitly built upon it. The states continue to treat murder and manslaughter as distinct offense categories, and as they began to subdivide those categories into a number of separate offenses they borrowed heavily from common-law ways of thinking about homicide and fault. Thus, the common law of homicide retains a powerful hold over our legal and popular understandings of which killings are most culpable and why.

For example, despite years of scholarly criticism of the "malice aforethought" construct, many states continue to use the distinct conditions encompassed by the term "malice" as the basis for identifying different degrees of murder. Likewise, many modern statutes rely on the distinction between voluntary and involuntary manslaughter to describe different grading categories.

The second noteworthy development arose from the movement by the United States Supreme Court to constrain the imposition of capital punishment. Commencing in the late 1960's, the Supreme Court entertained a host of procedural and substantive challenges to prevailing capital crime definitions and capital punishment schemes. This litigation produced a series of complicated opinions in which a deeply divided Court struggled to decide when, if ever, imposition of the death penalty was compatible with contemporary constitutional value judgments. Ultimately, the Court upheld the constitutional status of capital punishment in general, but along the way it created a new and complicated body of constitutional death-penalty law. In their turn, the new Supreme Court decisions produced a number of innovations in state capital punishment schemes, which generated new constitutional questions, and so on. Suffice it to say that death-penalty law expanded dramatically in the past several decades, and it now occupies a discrete and unique niche in the criminal homicide landscape.

**4.   Plan of the Chapter.** This Chapter is divided into five sections. Sections 1 and 2 deal with basic divisions between murder and manslaughter in modern law. Section 1 deals with all categories of murder except felony murder, which is postponed because it is advisable to deal with causation first. Section 2 considers manslaughter. Section 3 covers causation, which sets the stage for the treatment of felony murder in Section 4.

Finally, Section 5 considers the capital punishment issue as it applies to murder.

## SECTION 1: MURDER

## State v. Brown

Supreme Court of Tennessee, 1992.
836 S.W.2d 530.

■ MARTHA CRAIG DAUGHTREY, JUDGE. This capital case arose from the death of four-year-old Eddie Eugene Brown and the subsequent conviction of his father for first-degree murder, as well as for child neglect. After careful review, we have reached the conclusion that the evidence introduced at trial is not sufficient to support a conviction for first-degree murder. We therefore hold that the defendant's conviction must be reduced to second-degree murder.

1.  Factual Background

The victim in this case, Eddie Eugene Brown, was born in early February 1982, the son of defendant Mack Edward Brown and his co-defendant, Evajean Bell Brown, who were not living together at the time of Eddie's birth and were later divorced. Evajean was not able to nurse Eddie immediately after his birth because she was hospitalized with hypotoxemia.

According to his pediatrician, this hospitalization and inability to nurse may have contributed to Eddie's being, as the doctor described him, a "failure to thrive baby." When the physician first saw Eddie on March 17, 1982, at a little more than five weeks old, the infant was in good health but smaller than the median for his age. Mack and Evajean were still separated at that time, and relations between them eventually worsened to the point that Evajean asked the pediatrician to change Eddie's name on his records to Justin Michael Brown. Because Eddie had not begun to talk by age two-and-a-half, he was referred to the University of Tennessee Speech and Hearing Clinic. The clinic's report indicates that by age three years and four months, he was not yet toilet-trained and could speak single words, but not whole sentences. Evajean brought Eddie to see his pediatrician on November 5, 1984, because, as the doctor testified, she said he had fallen down fifteen carpeted stairs the night before. Although the physician found no injuries consistent with such a fall, he did note that Eddie's penis was red, swollen, and tender to the touch. His medical records do not give a reason for this condition. Eddie's last visit to his pediatrician's office was on October 16, 1985, with his mother and father, who by that time had reconciled.

According to a Department of Human Services social worker who had investigated the Brown home, Eddie was a hyperactive child with a severe speech problem. She reported that he also had severe emotional and behavioral problems. As an example of his behavior, she reported that during her visit, he ran down the hall directly into a wall....

Mack had been living with his wife and his son for less than a year when Eddie died. The Brown's next-door neighbor testified that, at around 3:40 a.m. on April 10, 1986, she heard yelling and screaming in their apartment. She distinctly heard a man's voice say, "Shut up. Get your ass over here. Sit down. Shut up. I know what I'm doing." She also heard a woman's voice say, "Stop, don't do that. Leave me alone. Stop, don't do that." She testified that the fight went on for 30 minutes and that she heard a sound which she described as a "thump, like something heavy hit the wall." The only other evidence introduced concerning the events of that morning was the tape of Evajean's call for an ambulance. At 8:59 a.m. she telephoned for help for her son, stating that he "fell down some steps and he's not breathing."

The paramedics who answered the call tried to revive Eddie but were unsuccessful. His heartbeat was reestablished at the hospital, but as it turned out, he was already clinically brain-dead. One of the treating nurses later testified that at that point, Eddie was being kept alive only for purposes of potential organ donation.

Various examinations indicated that the child had suffered two, and possibly three, skull fractures. The CT scan revealed a hairline fracture in the front right temporal portion of his skull, as well as a blood clot and swelling in that area of the head. The scan also revealed the possibility of a second fracture in the middle of the frontal bone. Finally, blood coming from Eddie's ear indicated that he had a fracture at the base of his skull which had caused an injury to the middle ear.

The CT scan showed a cerebral edema or swelling of the brain, which was more pronounced on the right side of the brain than the left, and which had shifted the midline of Eddie's brain toward the left. The pathologist who performed the autopsy noted the presence of vomit in Eddie's lungs and explained that swelling in the brain can cause vomiting. He theorized that repeated blows to Eddie's head caused cerebral hemorrhages and swelling. According to the expert, this pressure in the skull resulted in Eddie's aspiration of his own vomit and his ultimate death.

A neurological surgeon testified that Eddie's brain injuries were, at least in part, consistent with contrecoup[1] injuries, which occur when the head is violently shaken back and forth. The surgeon explained that there is a limited amount of fluid between the brain and the skull. That fluid generally serves as a shock absorber, but when the skull and brain are moving at a sufficient velocity and the skull suddenly stops, the fluid is not an adequate buffer between the delicate brain tissue and the hard skull surface. As he described this phenomenon at trial, "when the skull stops the brain slaps up against it," resulting in severe bruising and swelling of the brain.

---

[1] The neurological surgeon testified that "contrecoup" is French for "back and forth."

In addition to his cranial and cerebral injuries, Eddie had several internal injuries. When Eddie's internal organs were removed for donation, the county medical examiner observed hemorrhaging in the duodenum section of his intestine. He testified that such localized hemorrhaging was consistent with a blow by a fist to the upper portion of the abdomen. Additionally, blood was found in the child's stool and urine, and his liver enzymes were elevated. There was testimony to the effect that these conditions may have resulted from cardiac arrest, but that they are also consistent with blows to the abdomen, liver, and kidneys.

Finally, Eddie had bruises of varying ages on his face, scalp, ears, neck, chest, hips, legs, arms, buttocks, and scrotum. He had a large abrasion on his shoulder, scratches on his neck and face, and a round, partially healed wound on his big toe which, according to one of his treating nurses, was consistent with a cigarette burn. He had lacerations on both his ears at the scalp. He had linear bruises consistent with being struck with a straight object. The autopsy revealed an old lesion at the base of his brain which was evidence of a head injury at least two weeks before his death. X-rays revealed a broken arm which had not been treated and which had occurred three to five weeks before his death. The injury to his arm was confirmed by a witness who had noticed his arm hanging limply and then later noticed it in a homemade sling.

The defendant's statement to the police verified the fact that Eddie's broken arm was never properly treated, but Mack Brown also told them that he had tried to help Eddie by making a splint for his arm himself. He explained that he did not take Eddie for medical treatment because he was terrified that no one would believe that he and his wife had not inflicted this injury on the child. He could not explain the old bruises on Eddie's body. He stated that although sometimes they disciplined Eddie by spanking him, they did attempt to discipline him in, as he described it, "alternative ways" such as sending him to his room to let him know that they were upset and wanted him to mind.

Brown's statement indicates that around two or three o'clock on the morning of April 10, 1986, he and his wife both spanked Eddie because Eddie had urinated and defecated on the floor. The defendant admitted to another spanking, after he had sent Eddie to bed, and after he and his wife had a fight over money. As the defendant described it, it was during this spanking that his "mood began to kind of snap and let go." He said that he remembered going to Eddie's bedroom and remembered ordering Evajean out of the room. Although he denied remembering anything other than spanking Eddie's bottom with the open part of his hand, he stated that he was afraid he had beaten Eddie during the time that everything "went blank." The only thing he clearly recalled before that point was Eddie "staring at [him] mean" and saying, "I hate you! I hate you!" He stated that his next memory was of going downstairs and hearing Eddie behind him, falling onto the landing and into the door.

When the police questioned the defendant, his right hand was badly swollen. He explained that several days prior to April 10, he had injured his hand while working on his car and had sought medical treatment at Fort Sanders Hospital. They put a splint on his hand and gave him pain medication. He denied having struck Eddie with his right hand, saying that "it hurts so bad there ain't no way." The hospital's records indicate that on April 3, the defendant's hand was x-rayed and splinted. The records do not indicate that there was any break in the skin on the hand.

With the consent of the defendant, the police searched the apartment and recovered numerous items stained with blood consistent with Eddie's blood type, including an adult pajama top, a brown paper bag from the living room floor, and several towels and wash cloths. Police also found a bandage under the kitchen sink which was stained with blood consistent with Eddie's blood type. The blood on this bandage material was on the outside near the adhesive tape, not on the inner surface, which would have been next to the skin of the person wearing the bandage. The pants the defendant was wearing at the time of his arrest also had blood stains on them that were consistent with Eddie's blood type. A number of other items collected from the apartment tested positive for human blood, but the type of blood could not be determined because there was too little blood or they had been washed. These items included the couch cover, a pillow case and sheets taken from Eddie's bed, paint chips from the wall in Eddie's room, a child's undershirt and socks, and a three-by-five inch section of the living room rug. . . .

2.  Sufficiency of the Evidence

We are asked . . . to decide whether the evidence was sufficient to support the verdict of first-degree murder. The defendant argues principally that premeditation was not shown. . . .

Our consideration of the sufficiency of the evidence is governed by the "well-settled rule that all conflicts in testimony, upon a conviction in the trial court, are resolved in favor of the State, and that upon appeal the State is entitled to the strongest legitimate view of the trial evidence and all reasonable or legitimate inferences which may be drawn therefrom." Nevertheless, the record must demonstrate that the state carried its burden at trial of establishing that the homicide in question was, indeed, first-degree murder. In this case, we conclude, the prosecution failed to discharge its burden. . . .

The statute in effect at the time of the homicide in this case defined first-degree murder as follows:

> Every murder perpetrated by means of poison, lying in wait, or by other kind of willful, deliberate, malicious, and premeditated killing, or committed in the perpetration of, or attempt to perpetrate, any murder in the first degree, arson, rape, robbery, burglary, larceny, kidnaping, aircraft piracy, or the unlawful throwing, placing or discharging of a destructive device or bomb, is murder in the first degree.

Based upon our review of the record, we conclude that the evidence in this case is insufficient to establish deliberation and premeditation. Hence, the defendant's conviction for first-degree murder cannot stand. However, we do find the evidence sufficient to sustain a conviction of second-degree murder.

At common law, there were no degrees of murder, but the tendency to establish a subdivision by statute took root relatively early in the development of American law. The pattern was set by a 1794 Pennsylvania statute that identified the more heinous kinds of murder as murder in the first degree, with all other murders deemed to be murder in the second degree. Some states have subdivided the offense into three or even four degrees of murder, but since the enactment of the first such statute in 1829, Tennessee has maintained the distinction at two. It is one which this Court has found to be "not only founded in mercy and humanity, but ... well fortified by reason."

From the beginning, the statutory definition of first-degree murder required the state to prove that "the killing [was] done willfully, that is, of purpose, with intent that the act by which the life of a party is taken should have that effect; deliberately, that is, with cool purpose; maliciously, that is, with malice aforethought; and with premeditation, that is, a design must be formed to kill, before the act, by which the death is produced, is performed." Because conviction of second-degree murder also requires proof of intent and malice, the two distinctive elements of first-degree murder are deliberation and premeditation.

Even as early as 1872, however, prosecutors and judges had apparently fallen into the error of commingling these two elements by using the terms interchangeably. In Poole v. State, 61 Tenn. 288 (1872), for example, Justice Turney expounded upon the statutory distinction between deliberation and premeditation and the need to maintain them as separate elements of the first-degree murder:

> Proof must be adduced to satisfy the mind that the death of the party slain was the ultimate result which the conquering will, deliberation and premeditation of the party accused sought, making a marked distinction and independence between the terms "deliberation" and "premeditation" and excluding the idea of the substitution of the one for the other, or of the tautology in their use.

Intent to kill had long been the hallmark of common-law murder, and in distinguishing manslaughter from murder on the basis of intent, the courts recognized, in the words of an early Tennessee Supreme Court decision, that the law knows of no specific time within which an intent to kill must be formed so as to make it murder [rather than manslaughter]. If the will accompanies the act, a moment antecedent to the act itself which causes death, it seems to be as completely sufficient to make the offence murder, as if it were a day or any other time. Anderson v. State, 2 Tenn. (2 Overt.) 6, 9 (1804). Of course, the *Anderson* opinion predates the statutory subdivision of murder into first and second degrees. But the temporal concept initially associated in that case with intent, i.e., that no definite period of time is required for the formation of intent, was eventually carried over and applied to the analysis of premeditation. Hence, by the time the opinion in Lewis v. State, 40 Tenn. (3 Head) 127, 147–48, was announced in 1859, the Court had begun the process of commingling the concepts of intent, premeditation, and deliberation, as the following excerpt demonstrates:

> The distinctive characteristic of murder in the first degree, is premeditation. This element is superadded, by the statute, to the common law definition of murder. Premeditation involves a previously formed design, or actual intention to kill. But such design, or intention, may be conceived, and deliberately formed, in an instant. It is not necessary that it should have been conceived, or have pre-existed in the mind, any definite period of time anterior to its execution. It is sufficient that it preceded the assault, however short the interval. The length of time is not of the essence of this constituent of the offense. The purpose to kill is no less premeditated, in the legal sense of the term, if it were deliberately formed but a moment preceding the act by which the death is produced, than if it had been formed an hour before.

It is this language ("premeditation may be formed in an instant") for which *Lewis* is frequently cited. What is often overlooked is the following language, also taken from *Lewis*:

> The mental state of the assailant at the moment, rather than the length of time the act may have been premeditated, is the material point to be considered. The mental process, in the formation of the purpose to kill, may have been instantaneous, and the question of vital importance is—was the mind, at that moment, so far free from the influence of excitement, or passion, as to be capable of reflecting and acting with a sufficient degree of coolness and deliberation of purpose; and was the death of the person assaulted, the object to be accomplished—the end determined upon.

Hence, perhaps the two most oft-repeated propositions with regard to the law of first-degree murder, that the essential ingredient of first-degree murder is premeditation and that premeditation may be formed in an instant, are only partially accurate, because they are rarely quoted in context. In order to establish first-degree murder, the premeditated killing must also have been done deliberately, that is, with coolness and reflection. As noted in Rader v. State, 73 Tenn. 610, 619–20 (1880):

> When the murder is not committed in the perpetration of, or attempt to perpetrate any of the felonies named in the [statute], then, in order to constitute murder in the first degree, it must be perpetrated by poison or lying in wait, or some other kind of willful, deliberate, malicious, and premeditated killing; that is to say, the deliberation and premeditation must be akin to the deliberation and premeditation manifested where the murder is by

poison or lying in wait—the cool purpose must be formed and the deliberate intention conceived in the mind, in the absence of passion, to take the life of the person slain. Murder by poison or lying in wait, are given as instances of this sort of deliberate and premeditated killing, and in such cases no other evidence of the deliberation and premeditation is required; but where the murder is by other means, proof of deliberation and premeditation is required. It is true it has been held several times that the purpose need not be deliberated upon any particular length of time—it is enough if it precede the act, but in all such cases the purpose must be coolly formed, and not in passion, or, if formed in passion, it must be executed after the passion has had time to subside. . . . If the purpose to kill is formed in passion . . ., and executed without time for the passion to cool, it is not murder in the first degree, but murder in the second degree.

The obvious point to be drawn from this discussion is that even if intent (or "purpose to kill") and premeditation ("design") may be formed in an instant, deliberation requires some period of reflection, during which the mind is "free from the influence of excitement, or passion."

Despite admonitions in the opinions of the Tennessee Supreme Court during the nineteenth century and early part of the twentieth century regarding the necessity of maintaining a clear line of demarcation between first-and second-degree murder, that line has been substantially blurred in later cases. The culprit appears to be the shortcutting of analysis, commonly along three or four different tracks.

One of those has been the same error decried by Justice Turney in 1872, i.e., the use of the terms "premeditation" and "deliberation" interchangeably, or sometimes collectively, to refer to the same concept. Thus, in Sikes v. State, 524 S.W.2d 483, 485 (Tenn. 1975), the Court said: "Deliberation and premeditation involve a prior intention or design on the part of the defendant to kill, however short the interval between the plan and its execution." While this statement focuses on premeditation, nowhere in the brief discussion that follows is there any reference to the coolness of purpose or reflection that is required under the older cases to establish deliberation as a separate and distinct element of first-degree murder. . . .

Another weakness in our more recent opinions is the tendency to overemphasize the speed with which premeditation may be formed. The cases convert the proposition that no specific amount of time between the formation of the design to kill and its execution is required to prove first-degree murder, into one that requires virtually no time lapse at all, overlooking the fact that while intent (and perhaps even premeditation) may indeed arise instantaneously, the very nature of deliberation requires time to reflect, a lack of impulse, and, as the older cases had held at least since 1837, a "cool purpose." . . .

One further development in Tennessee law has tended to blur the distinction between the essential elements of first-and second-degree murder, and that is the matter of evidence of "repeated blows" being used as circumstantial evidence of premeditation. Obviously, there may be legitimate first-degree murder cases in which there is no direct evidence of the perpetrator's state of mind. Since that state of mind is crucial to the establishment of the elements of the offense, the cases have long recognized that the necessary elements of first-degree murder may be shown by circumstantial evidence. Relevant circumstances recognized by other courts around the country have included the fact "that a deadly weapon was used upon an unarmed victim; that the homicidal act was part of a conspiracy to kill persons of a particular class; that the killing was particularly cruel; that weapons with which to commit the homicide were procured; that the defendant made declarations of his intent to kill the victim; or that preparations were made before the homicide for concealment of the crime, as by the digging of a grave." This list, although obviously not intended to be exclusive, is notable for the omission of "repeated blows" as circumstantial evidence of premeditation or deliberation.

In Tennessee, the use of repeated blows to establish the premeditation necessary to first-degree murder apparently traces to Bass v. State, 191 Tenn. 259, 231 S.W.2d 707 (1950). There the Court, after noting that "both premeditation and deliberation may be inferred from the circumstances of a homicide," went on to list a series of facts from which the Court concluded that the victim's death constituted first-degree murder. The first (but not the only) such circumstance mentioned was that "the deceased was not only struck and killed by a blow from an iron poker but apparently from the number and nature of his wounds, was beaten to death by a whole series of blows." While the *Bass* court did not interpret the fact of repeated blows to be sufficient, in and of itself, to constitute premeditation and deliberation, subsequent cases have done so. In Houston v. State, 593 S.W.2d 267, 273 (Tenn. 1980), for example, the only circumstance relied upon by the majority to establish premeditation and deliberation was the fact that the victim had sustained "repeated shots or blows."

Logically, of course, the fact that repeated blows (or shots) were inflicted on the victim is not sufficient, by itself, to establish first-degree murder. Repeated blows can be delivered in the heat of passion, with no design or reflection. Only if such blows are inflicted as the result of premeditation and deliberation can they be said to prove first-degree murder....

This discussion leads us inevitably to the conclusion that Mack Brown's conviction for first-degree murder in this case cannot be sustained....

Here, there simply is no evidence in the record that in causing his son's death, Mack Brown acted with the premeditation and deliberation required to establish first-degree murder. There is proof, circumstantial in nature, that the defendant acted maliciously toward the child, in the heat of passion or anger,[2] and without adequate provocation—all of which would

---

[2] "Passion" has been defined as "any of the emotions of the mind [reflecting] anger, rage, sudden resentment, or terror, rendering the mind incapable of cool reflection."

make him guilty of second-degree murder. The only possible legal basis upon which the state might argue that a first-degree conviction can be upheld in this case is the proof in the record that the victim had sustained "repeated blows." It was on this basis, and virtually no other, that we upheld a similar first-degree murder conviction for the death of a victim of prolonged child abuse in State v. LaChance, 524 S.W.2d 933 (Tenn. 1975). In view of our foregoing discussion concerning the shortcomings of such an analysis, we find it necessary to depart from much of the rationale underlying that decision.

In abandoning *LaChance*, we are following the lead of a sister state. In Midgett v. State, 292 Ark. 278, 729 S.W.2d 410 (Ark. 1987), the Arkansas Supreme Court was asked to affirm the first-degree murder conviction of a father who had killed his eight-year-old son by repeated blows of his fist. As was the case here, there was a shocking history of physical abuse to the child, established both by eyewitness testimony and by proof of old bruises and healed fractures.

The Arkansas court faced a precedent much like *LaChance* in Burnett v. State, 287 Ark. 158, 697 S.W.2d 95 (1985). There the court had described the injuries sustained by the child victim and held, without more, that the "required mental state for first-degree murder can be inferred from the evidence of abuse, which is substantial." In confessing error in *Burnett*, the *Midgett* court noted:

> The appellant argues, and we must agree, that in a case of child abuse of long duration the jury could well infer that the perpetrator comes not to expect death of the child from his action, but rather that the child will live so that the abuse may be administered again and again. Had the appellant planned his son's death, he could have accomplished it in a previous beating. . . .

> The evidence in this case supports only the conclusion that the appellant intended not to kill his son but to further abuse him or that his intent, if it was to kill the child, was developed in a drunken, heated, rage while disciplining the child. Neither of those supports a finding of premeditation or deliberation.

The Arkansas court, in strengthening the requirements for proof of premeditation and deliberation in a first-degree murder case involving a victim of child abuse, found it necessary to overrule prior case law to the extent that it was inconsistent with the opinion in *Midgett*. We do the same here. Like the *Midgett* court, we do not condone the homicide in this case, or the sustained abuse of the defenseless victim, Eddie Brown. We simply hold that in order to sustain the defendant's conviction, the proof must conform to the statute. Because the state has failed to establish sufficient evidence of first-degree murder, we reduce the defendant's conviction to second-degree murder and remand the case for resentencing.

———

NOTES ON FIRST–DEGREE MURDER

**1. The "Premeditation and Deliberation" Formula.** As *Brown* explains, Pennsylvania was the first state to recognize degrees of murder. The innovation was made by a Pennsylvania statute adopted in 1794, which created a distinction between "first-degree" and "second-degree" murder. The Pennsylvania statute provided:

> [A]ll murder, which shall be perpetrated by means of poison, or by lying in wait, or by any other kind of wilful, deliberate and premeditated killing, or which shall be committed in the perpetration or attempt to perpetrate any arson, rape, robbery, or burglary, shall be deemed murder in the first degree; and all other kinds of murder shall be deemed murder in the second degree.

The purpose of this legislation was to confine the capital sanction, which remained the mandatory penalty,[a] to first-degree murder. The statute was influential. The majority of American jurisdictions adopted similar provisions early in the 19th century. By 1959, the statutes in 34 jurisdictions were closely derived from the original Pennsylvania formula.

By far the most litigated issue under this statute was the meaning of the phrase "by any other kind of wilful, deliberate and premeditated killing." It clearly referred to an intentional killing, but the question was whether it was meant to include all intentional killings or to be limited to an intent to kill formed in a particular manner.[b]

**(i) The Pennsylvania Construction.** In his article, History of the Pennsylvania Statute Creating Degrees of Murder, 97 U.Pa.L.Rev. 759, 771–73 (1949), Edwin R. Keedy concluded that the Pennsylvania legislature originally intended the words "deliberate" and "premeditated" to be read literally. Nevertheless, the Pennsylvania courts did not construe the language in this manner: "Soon after the statute was enacted the judges began to nullify its requirements by refusing to give effect to the meaning of the words 'deliberate' and 'premeditated,' and by announcing the proposition that killing with an intent to kill constitutes first-degree murder." As early as 1794, the year the degree statute was enacted, a Pennsylvania trial judge adopted this construction. Later pronouncements of the Pennsylvania courts were to the same effect. In Keenan v. Commonwealth, 44 Pa. 55, 56 (1863), the Pennsylvania Supreme Court summarized prior decisions with the comment that "our reported jurisprudence is very uniform in holding that the true criterion of the first degree is the intent to take life."

[a] All states retained the mandatory death penalty for the most serious form of murder until 1838, when Tennessee adopted the first discretionary death penalty statute. Twenty-three American jurisdictions followed suit by the turn of the century, and by 1962 all American jurisdictions had adopted this modification of the common-law system.

[b] Note that the statute begins with the words "all murder," then describes those forms of "murder" that fall into the first-degree category, and concludes by classifying "all other kinds of murder" as of the second degree. The statute thus built upon the common-law definition of murder. Any form of common-law murder not included in the first-degree category fell into the residual second-degree category.

Modern Pennsylvania decisions reaffirmed this interpretation. In Commonwealth v. Carroll, 412 Pa. 525, 526, 194 A.2d 911, 915 (1963), the court said:

> The specific intent to kill which is necessary to constitute ... murder in the first degree may be found from a defendant's words or conduct or from the attendant circumstances together with all reasonable inferences therefrom, and may be inferred from the intentional use of a deadly weapon on a vital part of the body of another human being.... Whether the intention to kill and the killing, that is, the premeditation and the fatal act, were within a brief space of time or a long space of time is immaterial if the killing was in fact intentional, wilful, deliberate and premeditated.

This approach was by no means limited to Pennsylvania. Herbert Wechsler and Jerome Michael, in their classic article, A Rationale of the Law of Homicide I, 37 Colum.L.Rev. 701, 707–09 (1937),[*] summarized the evolution of the American law of murder:

> The most striking phase of the development of the English law was the reduction of "malice aforethought" to a term of art signifying neither "malice" nor "aforethought" in the popular sense. Strikingly analogous in the judicial development of the American law of homicide is the narrow interpretation of "deliberation" and "premeditation" to exclude the two elements which the words normally signify: a determination to kill reached (i) calmly and (ii) some appreciable time prior to the homicide. The elimination of these elements leaves, as Judge Cardozo pointed out, nothing precise as the critical state of mind but intention to kill. Such a result creates particular difficulty in a jurisdiction like New York where "design" to kill is, by statute, the distinguishing feature of second-degree murder.[c] The trial judge must solemnly distinguish in his charge between the two degrees in terms which frequently render them quite indistinguishable, a procedure which obviously confers on the jury a discretion to follow one aspect of the charge or the other, if not a valid excuse for neglecting the charge entirely. The statutory scheme was apparently intended to limit administrative discretion in the selection of capital cases. As so frequently occurs, the discretion which the legislature threw out the door was let in through the window by the courts.[d]

The reference to Judge Cardozo in the preceding excerpt was to a lecture given to the Academy of Medicine in 1928, subsequently published in Law

---

[*] Reprinted with permission of Professor Wechsler and the Columbia Law Review.

[c] The New York statute in effect at this time is reproduced in Appendix B.—[Footnote by eds.]

[d] The early New York cases as well as those of four states that patterned their law on the New York model are analyzed in James K. Knudson, Murder by the Clock, 24 Wash.U.L.Q. 305 (1939). The results confirm the general conclusions advanced by Wechsler and Michael.—[Footnote by eds.]

and Literature 97–101 (1931).* Judge Cardozo said:

> The difficulty arises when we try to discover what is meant by the words deliberate and premeditated. A long series of decisions, beginning many years ago, has given to these words a meaning that differs to some extent from the one revealed upon the surface. To deliberate and premeditate within the meaning of the statute, one does not have to plan the murder days or hours or even minutes in advance, as where one lies in wait for one's enemy or places poison in his food or drink. The law does not say that any particular length of time must intervene between the volition and the act. The human brain, we are reminded, acts at times with extra-ordinary celerity. All that the statute requires is that the act must not be the result of immediate or spontaneous impulse. "If there is hesitation or doubt to be overcome, a choice made as the result of thought, however short the struggle between the intention and the act," there is such deliberation and premeditation as will expose the offender to the punishment of death....

> I think the distinction [between murder in its two degrees] is much too vague to be continued in our law. There can be no intent unless there is a choice, yet by the hypothesis, the choice without more is enough to justify the inference that the intent was deliberate and premeditated. The presence of a sudden impulse is said to mark the dividing line, but how can an impulse be anything but sudden when the time for its formation is measured by the lapse of seconds? Yet the decisions are to the effect that seconds may be enough.... I think the students of the mind should make it clear to the law-makers that the statute is framed along the lines of a defective and unreal psychology. If intent is deliberate and premeditated whenever there is choice, then in truth it is always deliberate and premeditated, since choice is involved in the hypothesis of the intent. What we have is merely a privilege offered to the jury to find the lesser degree, when the suddenness of the intent, the vehemence of the passion, seems to call irresistibly for the exercise of mercy. I have no objection to giving them this dispensing power, but it should be given to them directly and not in a mystifying cloud of words. The present distinction is so obscure that no jury hearing it for the first time can fairly be expected to assimilate and understand it.... Upon the basis of this fine distinction with its obscure and mystifying psychology, scores of men have gone to their death....

    **(ii)** *People v. Anderson.* As *Brown* illustrates, other courts have given the formula a more literal meaning. Consider, for example, People v. Anderson, 70 Cal.2d 15, 73 Cal.Rptr. 550, 447 P.2d 942 (1968). Anderson was convicted of the first-degree murder of a 10–year old girl and sentenced

* From Law and Literature by Benjamin Cardozo, copyright 1931 by Harcourt Brace Jovanovich, Inc.; renewed 1959 by First National Trust Co. Reprinted by permission of the publishers.

to death. He had been living with the girl's mother for about eight months prior to the homicide. On the morning of the murder, the mother went to work, leaving Anderson at home alone with the girl. Anderson had not worked for two days and had been drinking heavily. The girl's nude body was discovered in her bedroom by her brother that evening after the mother returned from work. More than 60 knife wounds, some severe and some superficial, were found on her body, including the partial amputation of her tongue and a post-mortem cut extending from the rectum through the vagina. There was no evidence of sexual molestation prior to the death. Blood was found in every room of the house.

The court held that there was insufficient evidence of premeditation and deliberation and that the killing therefore should be reduced to murder in the second degree. It began by noting that it was "well established that the brutality of a killing cannot in itself support a finding that the killer acted with premeditation and deliberation." The court continued:

> [W]e find no indication that the legislature intended to give the words "deliberate" and "premeditated" other than their ordinary dictionary meanings. Moreover, we have repeatedly pointed out that the legislative classification of murder into two degrees would be meaningless if "deliberation" and "premeditation" were construed as requiring no more reflection than may be involved in the mere formation of a specific intent to kill.

> Thus we have held that in order for a killing with malice aforethought to be first-rather than second-degree murder, " '[t]he intent to kill must be . . . formed upon a *pre-existing* reflection' [and must have] been the subject of actual deliberation or *forethought*." We have therefore [required that the killer act] "as a result of careful thought and weighing of considerations; as a *deliberate* judgment or plan; carried on coolly and steadily, [especially] according to a *preconceived design*."

The court then held that evidence of premeditation and deliberation generally fell into three patterns: evidence of "planning" activity, evidence of "motive," and evidence as to the "manner" of the killing that showed a preconceived design to kill. Most first-degree verdicts that it had sustained, the court said, contained evidence of all three types, though some had consisted of the second in conjunction with one of the other two. But Anderson's case, the court concluded, "lacks evidence of any of the three types." There was no evidence of planning or motive. And "the only inference" which the evidence as to the manner of the killing supports "is that the killing resulted from a 'random,' violent, indiscriminate attack rather than from deliberately placed wounds inflicted according to a preconceived design."[e]

---

[e] Compare Washington v. Bingham, 40 Wash.App. 553, 699 P.2d 262 (1985), where the court said:

[R]eview of [prior Washington] cases reveals that in each one where the evidence has been found sufficient, there has been some evidence beyond time

**2. Questions and Comments on *Brown*.** In *Brown*, the court endeavors to reverse years of judicial erosion of the distinction between killings that merely are intentional, on the one hand, and those that are premeditated and deliberate, on the other. The distinction is of great practical significance: the latter killings are eligible for the most severe punishments known to our law, while the former killings are punished less harshly. The court aims to give each word—"intentional," "premeditated," "deliberate," as well as "maliciously"—a distinct meaning. At one early point in its opinion, the court quotes this effort to define these crucial words:

> [The state must] prove that "the killing [was] done willfully, that is, of purpose, with intent that the act by which the life of a party is taken should have that effect; deliberately, that is, with cool purpose; maliciously, that is with malice aforethought; and with premeditation, that is, a design must be formed to kill, before the act, by which the death is produced, is performed."

Thereafter, the court tries to clarify and illustrate each of these distinctions. Is it successful?

This rhetorical exercise takes on added urgency when one contemplates the need to draft instructions in terms that allow jurors to understand their function and to grasp and apply the crucial terms. Presumably, some version of the preceding language provides the basis for jury instructions in homicide cases in Tennessee. If so, are jurors likely to understand the nuances in meaning that the court has in mind and, most crucially, those that determine the fate of defendants such as Mack Brown? How would one rewrite these instructions to make them more accessible to jurors?

Quite apart from the question of how to define the state of mind signified by "premeditation and deliberation" is the question of how the state proves that a particular killer acted with that state of mind. *Brown* refers to some of the circumstantial evidence that courts have cited as creating an inference of premeditation and deliberation. Such evidence has:

> included the fact "that a deadly weapon was used upon on an unarmed victim; that the homicidal act was part of a conspiracy to kill persons of a particular class; that the killing was particularly cruel; that weapons with which to commit the homicide were procured; that the defendant made declarations of his intent to kill the victim; or that preparations were made before the homicide for concealment of the crime, as by the digging of a grave."

from which a jury could infer the fact of deliberation. This evidence has included, inter alia, motive, acquisition of a weapon, and planning directly related to the killing.

Unless evidence of both time for and fact of deliberation are required, premeditation could be inferred in any case where the means of effecting death requires more than a moment in time. For all practical purposes, it would merge with intent; proof of intent would become proof of premeditation. However, the two elements are separate. Premeditation cannot be inferred from intent.

According to the court, the prosecutors who tried Mack Brown produced none of the evidence on the foregoing list, but relied exclusively on the fact that Brown killed Eddie with "repeated blows." The court then rejects the notion that proof that "repeated blows (or shots) were inflicted on the victim" alone can be sufficient to satisfy the requirements for first-degree murder. If the prosecutors in *Brown* could have predicted that the Tennessee Supreme Court would use this case as the occasion for reinvigorating the distinctions between "intent" and "premeditation-deliberation," is there some other strategy they might have pursued in an effort to prove that Mack Brown did premeditate and deliberate? For example, does further scrutiny of the fact pattern provided by the case yield any of the "circumstantial evidence" of premeditation and deliberation that the court approves? Consider too the various items on that list. Does each of them—alone or in some combination—permit the necessary inference of premeditation and deliberation?

The court reduces Brown's conviction from first-degree murder to second-degree murder. Why is he guilty of second-degree murder? At one point, the court asserts that a conviction for second-degree murder requires proof of "intent and malice." If so and if by "intent" the court means "purpose," does the case contain any evidence that Brown intended to kill Eddie? At the time that Brown was prosecuted, Tennessee authorized second-degree murder liability in some categories of non-intentional homicides, such as those where the actor intended (only) to inflict grievous bodily harm and those that demonstrated extreme indifference to the value of human life. Although it does not say so, the court might have had one or both of those theories in mind when reducing Brown's conviction to second-degree murder.

**3.   Modern Utility of the Formula.** A number of states retain the premeditation-deliberation doctrine to describe the highest category of criminal homicide. Some newer statutes, however, have followed the Model Penal Code in abandoning that formula. In states where the phrase had been interpreted to include every intentional killing, deleting the language in favor of a phrase such as "intent to kill" merely clarifies the inquiry the jury is expected to undertake. In states where the formula had been taken more literally, some legislatures have been convinced that it does not accurately separate the more heinous forms of murder from the less heinous, regardless of whether the most serious class of offenses is punishable by death. They have concluded, in essence, that the formula does not reflect an intelligible policy for the grading of criminal homicides. Long ago, Sir James Fitzjames Stephen made the normative point forcefully:

> As much cruelty, as much indifference to the life of others, a disposition at least as dangerous to society, probably even more dangerous, is shown by sudden as by premeditated murders. The following cases appear to me to set this in a clear light. A man passing along the road, sees a boy sitting on a bridge over a deep river and, out of mere wanton barbarity, pushes him into it and so drowns him. A man makes advances to a girl who repels him. He

deliberately but instantly cuts her throat. A man civilly asked to pay a just debt pretends to get the money, loads a rifle and blows out his creditor's brains. In none of these cases is there premeditation unless the word is used in a sense as unnatural as "afore-thought" in "malice aforethought," but each represents even more diabolical cruelty and ferocity than that which is involved in murders premeditated in the natural sense of the word.

3 A History of the Criminal Law of England 94 (1883).

Quite apart from concerns about capital punishment, does the premeditation-deliberation formula serve a modern function? Should Anderson be included in the highest category of murder? Brown?

Samuel Pillsbury argues that, as a proxy for the worst forms of homicide, the formula is under-and over-inclusive. As he puts it, "[p]remeditation assumes that the worst wrongs involve the most extended, dispassionate consideration of wrongdoing, and while this is often so, it is not always."[f] Pillsbury agrees with Stephen that the spontaneous killer may be as, and sometimes more, culpable than the actor who broods over his crime. He also argues that some premeditated and deliberate killings (say, those committed for profit) are far more culpable than others (say, those committed to relieve the pain of a person who is seriously ill). In other words, "what premeditation misses is the moral importance of the motive for homicide." Hence, Pillsbury proposes that the most serious degree of murder should be defined as a "purposeful" killing that is committed for one of several statutorily specified motives, including "to assert cruel power over another." Would a jury be justified in finding that Mack Brown had killed for that motive?

The Tennessee legislature ultimately came to agree that homicides similar to that perpetrated by Mack Brown should be defined as first-degree murder. Their solution was to add "aggravated child abuse" and "aggravated child neglect" to the list of predicate felonies whose commission qualify offenders for felony-murder liability where the consequence of the abuse or neglect is a death. Is that solution preferable to the more general, open-ended approach endorsed by Pillsbury?

---

# People v. Roe

Court of Appeals of New York, 1989.
74 N.Y.2d 20, 544 N.Y.S.2d 297, 542 N.E.2d 610.

■ HANCOCK, JUDGE. In defendant's appeal from his conviction for depraved indifference murder[1] for the shooting death of a 13–year-old boy, the sole

---

[f] Samuel H. Pillsbury, Judging Evil: Rethinking the Law of Murder and Manslaughter 99 (1998).

[1] Penal Law § 125.25 [provides:]

A person is guilty of murder in the second degree when....

2. Under circumstances evincing a depraved indifference to human life, he

question we address is the legal sufficiency of the evidence. Defendant, a 15½-year-old high school student, deliberately loaded a mix of "live" and "dummy" shells at random into the magazine of a 12–gauge shotgun. He pumped a shell into the firing chamber not knowing whether it was a "dummy" or a "live" round. He raised the gun to his shoulder and pointed it directly at the victim, Darrin Seifert, who was standing approximately 10 feet away. As he did so, he exclaimed "Let's play Polish roulette" and asked "Who is first?" When he pulled the trigger, the gun discharged sending a "live" round into Darrin's chest. Darrin died as a result of the massive injuries.

Defendant was convicted after a bench trial and the Appellate Division unanimously affirmed, holding that the evidence was legally sufficient to establish defendant's guilt.... On our review of the record, we conclude, as did the Appellate Division, that the proof is legally sufficient. Accordingly, there should be an affirmance....

Before analyzing the evidence and its legal sufficiency, a brief examination of the crime of depraved indifference murder and its elements is instructive. Depraved indifference murder, like reckless manslaughter, is a nonintentional homicide. It differs from manslaughter, however, in that it must be shown that the actor's reckless conduct is imminently dangerous and presents a grave risk of death; in manslaughter, the conduct need only present the lesser "substantial risk" of death. See People v. Register, 60 N.Y.2d 270, 276, 469 N.Y.S.2d 599, 457 N.E.2d 704 (1983); see also People v. Gomez, 65 N.Y.2d 9, 11, 489 N.Y.S.2d 156, 478 N.E.2d 759 (1985). Whether the lesser risk sufficient for manslaughter is elevated into the very substantial risk present in murder depends upon the wantonness of defendant's acts—i.e., whether they were committed "[under] circumstances evincing a depraved indifference to human life." This is not a mens rea element which focuses "upon the subjective intent of the defendant, as it is with intentional murder"; rather it involves "an objective assessment of the degree of risk presented by defendant's reckless conduct."

The only culpable mental state required for [depraved indifference] murder ... is recklessness—the same mental state required for [second-degree] manslaughter. In a trial for [depraved indifference] murder, proof of defendant's subjective mental state is, of course, relevant to the element of recklessness, the basic element required for both manslaughter in the second degree and depraved indifference murder. Evidence of the actor's subjective mental state, however, is not pertinent to a determination of the additional element required for depraved indifference murder: whether the objective circumstances bearing on the nature of a defendant's reckless conduct are such that the conduct creates a very substantial risk of death.

Generally, the assessment of the objective circumstances evincing the actor's "depraved indifference to human life"—i.e., those which elevate the risk to the gravity required for a murder conviction—is a qualitative

---

recklessly engages in conduct which creates a grave risk of death to another

person, and thereby causes the death of another person.

judgment to be made by the trier of the facts. If there is evidence which supports the jury's determination, it is this court's obligation to uphold the verdict. Examples of conduct which have been held sufficient to justify a jury's finding of depraved indifference include: driving an automobile on a city sidewalk at excessive speeds and striking a pedestrian without applying the brakes, see *Gomez*;[4] firing several bullets into a house, see People v. Jernatowski, 238 N.Y. 188, 144 N.E. 497 (1924); continually beating an infant over a five-day period, see People v. Poplis, 30 N.Y.2d 85, 330 N.Y.S.2d 365, 281 N.E.2d 167 (1972); and playing "Russian roulette" with one "live" shell in a six-cylinder gun, see Commonwealth v. Malone, 354 Pa. 180, 47 A.2d 445 (1946).

With this background, we turn to the issue before us, now more fully stated: whether, viewing the evidence in the light most favorable to the People, any rational trier of the facts could have concluded that the objective circumstances surrounding defendant's reckless conduct so elevated the gravity of the risk created as to evince the depraved indifference to human life necessary to sustain the murder conviction. A brief summary of the evidence is necessary.

On the afternoon of August 14, 1984, the day of the shooting, defendant was at his home in the Village of Buchanan, Westchester County. There is uncontraverted proof that defendant, who had completed his first year in high school, had an intense interest in and detailed knowledge of weapons, including firearms of various kinds. He was familiar with his father's 12–gauge shotgun and, indeed, had cleaned it approximately 50 times. The cleaning process involved oiling the firing pin and pulling the trigger, using a "dummy" shell to avoid "dry firing" the weapon.[6]

At approximately 3:00 p.m., Darrin and his friend, Dennis Bleakley, also a 13–year-old, stopped by to await the arrival of Darrin's older brother who was expected shortly. Defendant entertained the two boys by showing them his sawed-off shotgun, gravity knife, and Chuka sticks which he kept in a bag under his bed; he demonstrated how he assembled and disassembled the sawed-off shotgun.

Defendant then escorted Darrin and Dennis to his parents' room where he took out his father's 12–gauge shotgun. He asked Darrin to go back to his bedroom to get the five shotgun shells which were on the shelf. Defendant knew that three of these shells were "live" and two were "dummies." He randomly loaded four of the five shells into the magazine and pumped the shotgun, thereby placing one shell in the firing chamber.

---

[4] In attempting to "emphasize the particular escalating depravity facts" in *Gomez*, the dissent overlooks the fact that in *Gomez* we upheld two counts of depraved indifference murder—one for the first victim struck and one for the second. Thus, we obviously did not find it necessary that one person be struck first for the conduct to constitute depraved indifference.

[6] According to defendant, "dry firing" is releasing the firing pin when there is no cartridge in the chamber and nothing for the pin to strike against. To avoid the damage to the pin which "dry firing" can cause, "dummy" cartridges are used.

Because he loaded the magazine without any regard to the order in which the shells were inserted, he did not know if he had chambered a "live" or "dummy" round.

It was at this point, according to Dennis's testimony, that defendant raised the shotgun, pointed it directly at Darrin, and said "Let's play Polish roulette. Who is first?" He pulled the trigger discharging a "live" round which struck the 82–pound Darrin at close range. The shot created a gaping wound in Darrin's upper right chest, destroyed most of his shoulder, produced extensive damage to his lung, and eventually caused his death.

Defendant disputed this version of the incident. He testified that he had one foot on his parents' bed and was resting the butt of the gun on his inner thigh with the barrel pointing up and away from the victim. While he was demonstrating how the gun worked, he claimed, his foot slipped and the shotgun became airborne momentarily. Defendant testified that when he attempted to catch the gun, the butt kicked up under his armpit and he accidentally hit the trigger and discharged the gun.

The evidence of the objective circumstances surrounding defendant's point-blank discharge of the shotgun is, in our view, sufficient to support a finding of the very serious risk of death required for depraved indifference murder. Because the escalating factor—depraved indifference to human life—is based on an objective assessment of the circumstances surrounding the act of shooting and not the mens rea of the actor, the evidence stressed by the dissent concerning defendant's mens rea—his emotional condition in the aftermath of the killing—is beside the point.[7] Also without relevance are the dissent's references to defendant's claimed ignorance concerning the order in which cartridges, once loaded in the magazine, would enter the firing chamber. Such lack of knowledge can make no difference when, as is concededly the case here, the shooter knowingly loaded the mix of "live" and "dummy" cartridges with no regard to the order of their insertion into the magazine.

The comparable case here is not that of a person, uneducated in use of weapons, who, while playing with a gun that he does not know is loaded, accidentally discharges it; rather, the apt analogy is a macabre game of chance where the victim's fate—life or death—may be decreed by the flip of a coin or a roll of a die. It is no different where the odds are even that the shell pumped into the firing chamber of a 12–gauge shotgun is a "live" round, the gun is aimed at the victim standing close by, and the trigger is pulled. See 2 Wayne R. LaFave & Austin W. Scott, Jr., Substantive

---

[7] 2 LaFave & Scott, Substantive Criminal Law § 7.4 (b), at 204–205, cited by the dissent is not to the contrary. Evidence of defendant's conduct and emotional state after the shooting might be relevant to show his subjective awareness of the risk—an element essential to establish the underlying mens rea of recklessness. Here, however, there is no dispute that defendant acted recklessly. The only question is whether the crime conduct creates the very substantial risk of death necessary for depraved indifference. *Gomez* and *Register* make it clear that this element is to be objectively assessed and that defendant's subjective mens rea is not relevant on this point.

Criminal Law § 7.4, at 202 (1986) ("Russian roulette" with one "live" shell in a six-chamber gun is a classic example of depraved indifference murder).

The sheer enormity of the act—putting another's life at such grave peril in this fashion—is not diminished because the sponsor of the game is a youth of 15. As in *Register*, where bullets which might kill or seriously injure someone, or hit no one at all, were fired at random into a crowded bar, the imminent risk of death was present here. That in one case the gamble is that a bullet might not hit anyone and in the other that the gun might not fire is of no moment. In each case, the fact finder could properly conclude that the conduct was so wanton as to amount to depraved indifference to human life.

It is conceivable that another trier of fact hearing this evidence could have been persuaded to arrive at a different verdict. From the dissenter's extensive discussion of the proof and the inferences he would draw therefrom, it is evident that he would have done so. Our proper function on appeal, however, is vastly different from that of the prosecutor in determining which crimes to charge, that of the Judge or jury in hearing the evidence and making factual conclusions, or that of the Appellate Division in reviewing the facts and exercising, where it chooses, its interest of justice jurisdiction. We do not find facts or exercise such discretion. Our sole authority is to review legal questions such as the one considered here: whether the evidence was legally insufficient. As to this question, we have little difficulty in concluding that the unanimous Appellate Division correctly held that the evidence was sufficient to support the verdict....

■ BELLACOSA, JUDGE, dissenting. I vote to reverse this conviction of a 15–year-old person for the highest degree of criminal homicidal responsibility—depraved indifference murder. The evidence adduced, the statutory scheme under which defendant was charged, and the legislative intent behind it do not support the disproportionate level of maximum blameworthiness imposed here. Moreover, this result finalizes the obliteration of the classical demarcation between murder and manslaughter in this State....

From common-law times to modern penal code days, the tragic incident at the heart of this case has qualified as the paradigmatic manslaughter with recklessness as the culpable mental state or mens rea....

One of the three definitions of murder in this State is recklessly engaging in conduct which creates a grave risk of death and causing the death of another under circumstances evincing a depraved indifference to human life. That is the one at issue in this case. Manslaughter, second degree, is defined as recklessly causing the death of another person. This court has held that both of those crimes (the first an "A–I" felony carrying a mandatory sentence of at least 15 years to life, and the lesser being a "C" felony qualifying for 4½ to 15 years) require the same culpable mental state, i.e., acting recklessly when aware of and consciously disregarding a substantial and unjustifiable risk. But that culpable mental state, taken alone, supports and defines only manslaughter unless elevated to murder by reckless conduct, which additionally creates a grave risk under circumstances evincing a depraved indifference to human life. The catapulting ingredients are gravity and depravity. Other synonyms used to try to understand the essence of the escalating difference include malignant, malicious, callous, cruel, wanton, unremorseful, reprehensible and the like. The semantics alone prove that the analysis necessarily includes some subjective, gradational assessment.

While the tangible content of "depraved indifference to human life" is thus elusive, the wantonness of the conduct augmenting the reckless culpable mental state must also manifest a level of callousness and extreme cruelty as to be "equal in blameworthiness to intentional murder." I allude to some of the same case illustrations in this regard as the majority does, except I emphasize the particular escalating depravity facts that the majority avoids: firing a gun three times in a packed barroom, having boasted in advance an intention to kill someone, see People v. Register, 60 N.Y.2d 270, 469 N.Y.S.2d 599, 457 N.E.2d 704 (1983); driving a car at high speed on a crowded urban street and failing to apply the brakes after striking one person, see People v. Gomez, 65 N.Y.2d 9, 489 N.Y.S.2d 156, 478 N.E.2d 759 (1985); continuously beating a young child over a five-day period, see People v. Poplis, 30 N.Y.2d 85, 330 N.Y.S.2d 365, 281 N.E.2d 167 (1972).

The depraved indifference category of murder reflects the Legislature's policy refinement that there is a type of reckless homicide that is so horrendous as to qualify, in a legal fiction way, for blameworthiness in the same degree as the taking of another's life intentionally, purposefully, and knowingly. It is treated equally with the common-law antecedent of pre-meditated murder with malice aforethought. Early cases reveal that the concept of "depraved mind" murder as an escalating factor emerged from this common-law notion and was applied in cases where, despite evidence that a defendant had no desire to kill, the conduct nonetheless demonstrated a substitutive aggravating "malice in the sense of a wicked disposition." Modern statutes have borrowed and recast the concept "of a wicked disposition" to speak in terms of "extreme indifference to the value of human life." The predecessor of New York's present statute used an "act imminently dangerous to others" and was interpreted to apply, consistent with its exceptionability, only in cases where defendant's conduct created a danger to a multitude of persons rather than to just one individual. The language of the statute was expanded in 1967 to apply to persons who engage in "conduct which creates a grave risk of death to another person" and has been construed to apply to an attack directed at a single person.

The latest significant case, involving far more egregious conduct than is present in the instant case and held to constitute depraved indifference murder, evoked a warning, albeit in dissent, of the "evisceration" of the "distinction" between manslaughter and murder, see *Register*, at 284 (Jasen, J., dissenting). In my view, today's application completes the homogenization....

I disagree that defendant's conduct qualifies for this lofty homicidal standard. He acted recklessly, of that there can be no doubt.... But the accusation and the conviction at the highest homicidal level, predicated on callous depravity and complete indifference to human life, are not supportable against this 15–year-old on a sufficiency review and are starkly contradicted by the whole of the evidence adduced.

This "crime is classified as murder and the murder penalty should be imposed 'only when the degree of risk approaches certainty; that is, at the point where reckless homicide becomes knowing homicide.' " Here, defendant's actions cannot be said to have created an almost certain risk of death. The mathematical probabilities, the objective state of mind evidence at and around the critical moment, the ambiguity in the evidence as to the operational order in the firing of the weapon, and all the circumstances surrounding this tragic incident all render the risk uncertain and counter-indicate depravity, callousness, and indifference of the level fictionally equalling premeditated, intentional murder. That central and essential element of the crime charged was not proved beyond a reasonable doubt and that has been for a very long time a classically reviewable issue in this court. . . .

The testimony of the only other eyewitness, Dennis Bleakley, established that defendant was shaken and distraught immediately upon realizing that he had shot their companion. Defendant also immediately ran to his victim and instructed Dennis to call an ambulance; the neighbor testified that when she arrived on the scene, seconds after hearing the shot, defendant was kneeling over his friend's body and crying. Similarly, the police officer who arrived on the scene testified that defendant was extremely distraught and overcome with grief. This is not evidence beyond a reasonable doubt of that hardness of heart or that malignancy of attitude qualifying as "depraved indifference." Frankly, the evidence proves the opposite.

Nor should evidence of the "objective circumstances surrounding the act of the shooting"—the essential elevating element of the crime—be discarded as "beside the point" and artificially cut off as of the moment of the flash of the weapon. This is a substantial and new evidentiary restriction and one that has been rejected by a leading authority. See 2 LaFave & Scott, supra, § 7.4, at 204–05. Indeed, the very section of that text relied upon by the majority is antithetical to the majority's approach and supports the view advanced in this dissent in this regard: "[on] balance, it would seem that, to convict of murder, with its drastic personal consequences, subjective realization should be required," and evidence of a defendant's conduct in stopping and aiding a victim, whom he had struck and fatally injured, was admissible "to 'negative the idea of wickedness of disposition and hardness of heart' required for depraved-heart murder." Under the majority's cramped approach, one must wonder whether res gestae conduct will be foreclosed in a prosecution attempt to prove a real depravity set of circumstances in some other depraved murder case. More to the point here and for the defense side of cases yet to come, the majority appears also to be significantly preventing the evidentiary development of ameliorating or contradicting factors with respect to depravity. Both sides and the truth-seeking process itself lose with this antiseptic evidentiary embargo. . . .

By . . . catapulting the defendant's admittedly reckless criminal act to one "evincing depraved indifference to human life," the court functionally and finally discards and disregards the legislatively drawn distinction between manslaughter and murder. Prosecutors will find the temptation legally and strategically irresistible, and overcharging traditional reckless manslaughter conduct as the more serious murderous conduct will become standard operating procedure in view of the authorized template given for that course of action. Some very disproportionate miscarriages of justice— this case is one of them—will certainly ensue from this prosecutorial leverage in elevating reckless manslaughter to murder. It is difficult to imagine, after this case, any intentional murder situation not being presented to the Grand Jury with a District Attorney's request for a depraved indifference murder count as well. Thus, the exception designed as a special fictional and functional equivalent to intentional murder becomes an automatic alternative and additional top count accusation, carrying significant prejudicial baggage in its terminology alone. That devastating advantage, among others, given to the prosecution provides an unjust double opportunity for a top count murder conviction and an almost certain fallback for conviction on the lesser included crime of manslaughter. . . .

[T]o uphold this defendant's conviction on the uppermost and most heinous level of criminal homicidal responsibility cheapens the gravity with which we treat far more serious murders, e.g., cold-blooded contract killings and the like. In the eyes of the law all the slayers are now made alike, when the perpetrators themselves know and our best instincts and intelligence tell us, too, that they are very different. Justice is disfigured by the punishment of offenders so homogeneously and, yet, so disproportionately.

---

## NOTES ON SECOND–DEGREE MURDER

**1. Common Law Background.** Leaving aside the felony-murder doctrine, which is covered later in this chapter, the common law recognized two kinds of unintentional homicide as murder. The first was based on intent to inflict grievous bodily injury. The second, which effectively subsumes the first, was based on a theory of recklessness or negligence that reached a high degree of callousness or indifference to life.

**(i) _Commonwealth v. Malone._** The second theory is illustrated by the well-known case of Commonwealth v. Malone, 354 Pa. 180, 47 A.2d 445 (1946). Malone, then 17 years old, engaged in a game of Russian Roulette with a 13–year-old friend. He loaded one chamber of a pistol that held five bullets and, with his friend's consent, held the gun to his friend's side and pulled the trigger three times. The gun fired on the third try and Malone's friend died from the wound two days later. Malone was convicted of second-degree murder.

The conviction was affirmed on appeal. The court reasoned that "the 'grand criterion' which 'distinguished murder from other killing' was malice on the part of the killer and this malice was not necessarily 'malevolent to the deceased particularly' but 'any evil design in general; the dictate of a wicked, depraved and malignant heart.' " The court continued:

> When an individual commits an act of gross recklessness for which he must reasonably anticipate that death to another is likely to result, he exhibits that "wickedness of disposition, hardness of heart, cruelty, recklessness of consequences, and a mind regardless of social duty" which proved that there was at that time in him "the state or frame of mind termed malice." This court has declared that if a driver "wantonly, recklessly, and in disregard of consequences" hurls "his car against another, or into a crowd" and death results from that act "he ought . . . to face the same consequences that would be meted out to him if he had accomplished death by wantonly and wickedly firing a gun." . . .
>
> The killing . . . resulted from an act intentionally done . . . , in reckless and wanton disregard of the consequences. . . . The killing was, therefore, murder, for malice in the sense of a wicked disposition is evidenced by the intentional doing of an uncalled-for-act in callous disregard of its likely harmful effects on others. The fact that there was no motive for this homicide does not exculpate the accused. In a trial for murder proof of motive is always relevant but never necessary.

**(ii) Questions and Comments.** As *Malone* reveals, American common law found the existence of malice in unintentional homicides—and distinguished between murder and manslaughter—on the basis of epithetical descriptions of the defendant's behavior. Did Malone have a "wicked, depraved and malignant heart"? Did Roe? How is a jury to be expected to answer such a question?

**2. The Degree of Culpability Sufficient for Murder.** The New York statute at issue in *Roe* is derived from § 210.2(1)(b) of the Model Penal Code, which provides that it is murder if a homicide "is committed recklessly under circumstances manifesting extreme indifference to the value of human life." The Model Penal Code provision, in turn, is derived from the "depraved heart" formulation that constituted malice, and hence justified a murder conviction, at common law. What is the justification for grading this form of murder at the same level as intentional homicide? Are the Model Code and New York formulations an improvement over the questions asked in common law jurisdictions? Are the differences in language between the New York provision and the Model Penal Code significant? Which is better?

Note also that the Model Penal Code, in abandoning the Pennsylvania degree formulation, treats "extreme indifference" homicide in the highest category of murder. Is this justified? The New York grading structure is set forth in Appendix B. Did New York place people like Roe in the right grading category?

In *Roe*, the majority divides the inquiry to be made by factfinders into two parts. First, the jury must determine whether the defendant acted with a mens rea of recklessness. Second, the jury must determine whether the "objective circumstances bearing on the nature of a defendant's reckless conduct are such that the conduct creates a very substantial risk of death." If each of these determinations is made in the affirmative, the jury may convict the defendant of depraved indifference murder. Does the dissenting judge disagree with this statement of doctrine or merely with the sufficiency of the evidence to support the necessary findings?

More generally, precisely what is the element that distinguishes depraved indifference murder from involuntary manslaughter? Does "depraved indifference" refer to a unique mens rea element—to some special kind of recklessness focusing more on the defendant's subjective state of mind? Or does it create an additional objective standard, one that elevates the nature and degree of the risks taken by the actor? How, if at all, will the answer to these questions influence the course of litigation in these cases?

**3.  _Northington v. State._** The revised Alabama statute provides that a person commits murder if:

> Under circumstances manifesting extreme indifference to human life, he recklessly engages in conduct which creates a grave risk of death to a person other than himself, and thereby causes the death of another person.

Northington v. State, 413 So.2d 1169 (Ala.Cr.App.1981), involved a mother convicted of murder for allowing her five-month old daughter to starve to death. The court reversed the conviction because it interpreted the statute to require "universal malice" and no such malice was shown in this case:

> Under whatever name, the doctrine of universal malice, depraved heart murder, or reckless homicide manifesting extreme indifference to human life is intended to embrace those cases where a person has no deliberate intent to kill or injure any _particular_ individual. "The element of 'extreme indifference to human life,' by definition, does not address itself to the life of the victim, but to human life generally." People. By and Through Russel v. District Court, 185 Colo. 78, [83,] 521 P.2d 1254, 1256 (1974)....

The state presented no evidence that the defendant engaged in conduct "under circumstances manifesting extreme indifference to human life" for, while the defendant's conduct did indeed evidence an extreme indifference to the life of her child, there was nothing to show that the conduct displayed an extreme indifference to human life generally. Although the defendant's conduct created a grave risk of death to another and thereby caused the death of that person, the acts of the defendant were aimed at the particular victim and no other. Not only did the defendant's conduct create a grave risk of death to only her daughter and no other, but the defendant's actions (or inactions) were directed specifically against the young infant. This evidence does not support a conviction of murder.... The function of this section is to embrace those homicides caused by such acts as driving an automobile in a grossly wanton manner, shooting a firearm into a crowd or a moving train, and throwing a timber from a roof onto a crowded street.[a]

The court concluded by saying that it was "extremely reluctant to reverse the conviction" because of "the revolting and heartsickening details of this case."[b] "Yet, because our system is one of law and not of men, we have no other choice." Can this be right?

## SECTION 2: MANSLAUGHTER

## Freddo v. State

Supreme Court of Tennessee, 1913.
127 Tenn. 376, 155 S.W. 170.

■ WILLIAMS, J. The plaintiff in error, Raymond Freddo, was indicted . . . for the crime of murder in the first degree . . . and was found by the jury guilty of murder in the second degree; his punishment being fixed at 10 years imprisonment. [It is . . . urged . . . that the facts adduced did not warrant a verdict of guilty of a crime of degree greater than voluntary manslaughter, if guilt of any crime be shown.

[I]n the roundhouse department of the shops of the Nashville & Chattanooga Railway Company from 50 to 60 men were employed, among them being . . . Freddo and the deceased, Higginbotham. Freddo was at the time about 19 years of age; he had been from the age of four years an orphan; he had been reared thereafter in an orphanage, and yet later in the family of a Nashville lady, with result that he had been morally well trained. The proof shows him to have been a quiet, peaceable, high-minded young man of a somewhat retiring disposition. Due, perhaps, to the loss of his mother in his infancy, and to his gratitude to his foster mother, he respected womanhood beyond the average young man, and had a decided antipathy to language of obscene trend or that reflected on womanhood.

Deceased, Higginbotham, was about six years older than Freddo, [was taller than Freddo and outweighed him by about 30 pounds,] and was one of a coterie of the roundhouse employees, . . . given to the use . . . of the expression "son of a bitch"—meant to be taken as an expression of good fellowship or of slight deprecation. Deceased, prior to the date of the difficulty, had applied this epithet to . . . Freddo without meaning offense, but was requested by the latter to discontinue it, as it was not appreciated,

---

[a] The court quoted extensively from State v. Berge, 25 Wash.App. 433, 607 P.2d 1247 (1980), in support of this interpretation of the Alabama statute. *Berge,* in turn, identifies Darry v. People, 10 N.Y. 120 (1854), as the origin of the notion that "depraved mind" murder refers, as the court in *Darry* put it, to "general malice" and not "any affection of the mind having for its object a particular individual."—[Footnote by eds.]

[b] The court's opinion did not elaborate on the facts beyond this cryptic statement.

but resented. It was not discontinued, but repeated, and Freddo so chafed under it that he again warned deceased not to repeat it; and the fact of Freddo's sensitiveness being noted by the mechanic, J.J. Lynch, under whom Freddo served as helper, Lynch sought out deceased in Freddo's behalf and warned him to desist. On Lynch's telling deceased of the offense given to plaintiff in error, and that "he will hurt you some day," deceased replied, "The son of a bitch, he won't do nothing of the kind." [D]eceased is shown to have been habitually foul-mouthed, overbearing, and "nagging and tormenting" in language, and at times in conduct.

On the afternoon of the tragedy, Higginbotham and Freddo were engaged ... in the packing of a locomotive cylinder.... Deceased, so engaged, was in a squatting posture, holding a pinch bar. It appears that some one, thought by deceased to have been Freddo, had spilled oil on deceased's tool box, and as he proceeded with his work the latter, in hearing of the crew, remarked: "Freddo, what in the hell did you want to spill that oil on that box for. If some one spilled oil on your box, you would be raising hell, wouldn't you, you son of a bitch?" Freddo asked Higginbotham if he meant to call the former a son of a bitch, and was replied to in an angry and harsh tone: "Yes, you are a son of a bitch." The plaintiff in error, standing to the left of and about eight feet away from deceased, seeing deceased preparing to rise or rising from his squatting posture, seized a steel bar, one yard long and one inch thick, lying immediately at hand, and advancing struck deceased a blow on the side of his head, above the left ear, and extending slightly to the front and yet more to the rear of the head, but not shown to have been delivered from the rear. Deceased in rising had not gained an erect posture, but is described as stooping at the time the blow was delivered.

Plaintiff in error testified that deceased, in rising, was apparently coming at him; that deceased made a gesture, and had his hand behind him all the time; that he (Freddo) believed that Higginbotham was going to strike; and that he struck because of anger at the epithet and to defend himself, but would not have struck but for deceased's movement. It appears, however, that deceased had not gained a position where he could strike the accused, and it does not appear that he had anything in his hand with which to attack; and the evidence preponderates against the prisoner on the point of deceased's having his hand behind him.

[W]e deem the facts sufficient to show that plaintiff in error killed deceased under the impulse of sudden heat of passion; but, no matter how strong his passionate resentment was, it did not suffice to reduce the grade of the crime from murder to voluntary manslaughter, unless that passion were due to a provocation such as the law deemed reasonable and adequate—that is, a provocation of such a character as would, in the mind of an average reasonable man, stir resentment likely to cause violence, obscuring the reason, and leading to action from passion rather than judgment.

While the testimony indicates that plaintiff in error was peculiarly sensitive in respect of the use by another, as applied to him, of the opprobrious epithet used by deceased, yet we believe the rule to be firmly fixed on authority to the effect that the law proceeds in testing the adequacy of the provocation upon the basis of a mind ordinarily constituted—of the fair average mind and disposition. . . .

The rule in this state is, as it was at common law, that the law regards no mere epithet or language, however violent or offensive, as sufficient provocation for taking life. . . .

It is contended, however, that while the use of such an epithet may not of itself be sufficient cause for provocation, yet that, looked to in connection with the conduct of the deceased at the time of its utterance, in rising from a squatting to a stooping posture, just reached as the blow was delivered, the epithet and the act in combination make a cause of adequate provocation.

The common-law rule appears to be that an assault, too slight in itself to be a sufficient provocation, may become such when accompanied by offensive language. [But the jury was correctly charged on the] proper definitions of and distinctions between murder in the second degree and manslaughter. . . . The stroke having been delivered by plaintiff in error at a moment when deceased may have been found by the jury not to have been in a position to assault him, and since the determination of the fact whether the provocation relied upon in such a case is adequate or reasonable is, under a proper charge, for the jury, we hold that the errors assigned and here treated of are not well taken. . . .

Affirmed.

In view of the very good character of the young plaintiff in error, as disclosed in the record, and of the peculiar motive and the circumstances under which he acted, we feel constrained to and do recommend to the governor of the state that his sentence be commuted to such punishment as the executive may, in the light of this record and opinion, in his discretion think proper. To allow time for such application, execution of sentence is ordered stayed for 10 days from this date.

---

## NOTES ON THE MITIGATION OF MURDER TO MANSLAUGHTER

**1.  The Provocation Formula.** At common law, the distinction between murder and manslaughter originally emerged as a device for isolating a class of offenders who would be subjected to capital punishment. Those convicted of murder received the mandatory death penalty; those convicted of manslaughter received a lesser sentence. It was in this context that the law of provocation developed. When American jurisdictions narrowed the category of murder to which capital punishment applied, the law continued to recognize the distinction between murder and manslaughter as a grading device. The provocation doctrine has proved to be remarkably durable. Today, every state employs some variation of the provocation formula to distinguish between two distinct grades of non-capital criminal homicide.

The origins of the doctrine and its early meaning are summarized in the following excerpt from A.J. Ashworth, The Doctrine of Provocation, 35 Camb.L.J. 292, 293 (1976):*

When in the 17th century the defence of provocation began to assume a recognisable form and function, it took its place within a rigidly structured law of homicide. Killings were presumed to proceed from malice aforethought: if there was no evidence of express malice, then the law would imply malice. Evidence of provocation came to be accepted in rebuttal of this implication of malice, the theory being that such evidence showed that the cause of the killing lay not in some secret hatred or design in the breast of the slayer but rather in provocation given by the deceased which inflamed the slayer's passions. Hale thus "inquired, what is such a provocation, as will take off the presumption of malice in him that kills another," and he discussed the various forms of provocation which the judges had ruled sufficient or insufficient for this purpose. These decisions were conveniently summarised by Lord Holt, C.J., in his judgment in Mawgridge, [1707] Kel. 119, where the categories of provocation are set forth. It was generally agreed that any striking of the accused would be sufficient provocation, and Lord Holt discussed four further types of provocation which had been legally sufficient to rebut the implication of malice: (i) angry words followed by an assault, (ii) the sight of a friend or relative being beaten, (iii) the sight of a citizen being unlawfully deprived of his liberty, and (iv) the sight of a man in adultery with the accused's wife. The categories of provocation insufficient to reduce murder to manslaughter were (i) words alone, (ii) affronting gestures, (iii) trespass to property, (iv) misconduct by a child or servant, and (v) breach of contract.

The rule applied in *Freddo* that "the law regards no mere epithet . . . as sufficient provocation" is thus consistent with early descriptions of provocation. The same rule would be applied with equal rigor in many jurisdictions today. In such jurisdictions, courts refuse to give voluntary manslaughter instructions in cases where the alleged provoking event consisted of "words alone." Similarly, many jurisdictions continue to restrict the events that may constitute sufficient provocation to the categories identified by Ashworth. Where the defendant's evidence of provocation falls outside those categories, the evidence will be excluded. See 1 Paul H. Robinson, Criminal Law Defenses 484–86 (1984).

Beginning in the middle of the 19th century, however, a competing approach to provocation began to develop. For example, Maher v. People, 10 Mich. 212, 220–22 (1862), offered the following description of the provocation doctrine:

* Reprinted by permission of the author and Cambridge University Press.

The principle involved ... would seem to suggest as the true general rule, that reason should, at the time of the act, be disturbed or obscured by passion to an extent which *might render* ordinary men, of fair average disposition, *liable* to act rashly or without due deliberation or reflection, and from passion, rather than judgment....

The judge, it is true, must, to some extent, assume to decide upon the sufficiency of the alleged provocation, when the question arises upon the admission of testimony, and when it is so clear as to admit of no reasonable doubt upon any theory, that the alleged provocation could not have had any tendency to produce such state of mind, in ordinary men, he may properly exclude the evidence; but, if the alleged provocation be such as to admit of any reasonable doubt, whether it might not have had such tendency, it is much safer, ... and more in accordance with principle, to let the evidence go to the jury under the proper instructions. [T]he question of the reasonableness or adequacy of the provocation must depend upon the facts of each particular case.... The law can not with justice assume, by the light of past decisions, to catalogue all the various facts and combinations of facts which shall be held to constitute reasonable or adequate provocation....

By rejecting the notion that the law should identify the precise categories of events that constitute adequate provocation, the *Maher* formulation represents a considerable departure from the traditional view of provocation. *Maher* implies that *any* event—not only those allowed by the traditional doctrine—may be sufficient provocation, as long as the event would inspire a "heat of passion" in the reasonable person. Rather than simply replacing the traditional doctrine with the *Maher* formulation, however, most jurisdictions appear to have merged the two approaches and thereby created a three-stage analysis: (i) the defendant must in fact have acted in a heat of passion based on sudden provocation; (ii) the provoking event must have been "legally adequate," i.e., the courts continue to exclude certain events, such as "mere epithets," from the mitigation even though the event may in fact have provoked "heat of passion" in the defendant; and (iii) the provocation must also have been of a sufficient degree to have excited the passions of a reasonable person. How many of these steps are applied in *Freddo?* Is the *Maher* approach preferable? The pre–19th century rule that ignores the third step?

**2.  Rationale for the Provocation Formula.** These questions can be answered only by thinking about why the rule of provocation developed and, particularly, what (if anything) its modern function should be. It is helpful to subdivide this inquiry into three stages corresponding to the three analytical steps mentioned above.

**(i)  Defendant in Fact Provoked.** Why should it matter that the defendant killed in the "heat of passion" produced by a provoking event? The traditional answer to this question is that a killing which "is the result of temporary excitement" is substantially less blameworthy than a killing which is the result of "wickedness of heart or innate recklessness of disposition." State v. Gounagias, 88 Wash. 304, 311, 153 P. 9, 12 (1915). Glanville Williams offered a utilitarian refinement of this point when he remarked in Provocation and the Reasonable Man, [1954] Crim.L.Rev. 740, 742, that:

> Surely the true view of provocation is that it is a concession to "the frailty of human nature" in those exceptional cases where the legal prohibition fails of effect. It is a compromise, neither conceding the propriety of the act nor exacting the full penalty for it.

Are these explanations satisfactory? Is the person who kills in a "heat of passion" less dangerous than the "cold-blooded" killer? Is "heat of passion" more justified as a mitigation that excludes persons from the death penalty (its original function) than as a mitigation authorizing different terms of imprisonment (its modern function)?

**(ii) Legally Adequate Provocation.** The notion that provocation should be limited to "legally adequate" categories has been rejected by the Model Penal Code and by many American statutes that have followed its lead. The drafters of the Model Code defend this result on the ground that blameworthiness "cannot be resolved successfully by categorization of conduct" and that the correct approach, as *Maher* suggested, is "to abandon preconceived notions of what constitutes adequate provocation and to submit that question to the jury's deliberation." ALI, Model Penal Code and Commentaries, § 210.3, p. 61 (1980). Which formulation is preferable? Does the concept of legally adequate provocation reduce the opportunity for ad hoc determinations by juries and thus contribute to the fairness of the criminal process? Should the requirement be retained for this or any other reason?

**(iii) The Objective Standard.** Why should an objective standard be used to measure the mitigating significance of the provocation to which the defendant reacted? If a reasonable person would have been provoked to the point of losing self-control, is it fair to punish the defendant at all?[a] If the defendant was in fact provoked and acted in the "heat of passion," should not the grade of the offense at least be reduced below that of unprovoked intent-to-kill murders, however confident we are that ordinary people would have remained calm in the face of the provoca-

---

[a] Compare Glanville Williams, Provocation and the Reasonable Man, [1954] Crim. L.Rev. 740, 742:

> Plausible as this formulation may appear, it creates a serious problem. In the law of contract and tort, and elsewhere in the criminal law, the test of the reasonable man indicates an ethical standard; but it seems absurd to say that the reasonable man will commit a felony the possible punishment for which is imprisonment for life. To say that the "ordinary" man will commit this felony is hardly less absurd. The reason why provoked homicide is punished is to deter people from committing the offence; and it is a curious confession of failure on the part of the law to suppose that, notwithstanding the possibility of heavy punishment, an ordinary person will commit it. If the assertion were correct, it would raise serious doubts whether the offense should continue to be punished. [H]ow can it be admitted that the paragon of virtue, the reasonable man, gives way to provocation?

tion? On the other hand, does deterrence theory suggest that provocation should not be recognized as a mitigation, no matter how understandable the accused's passionate reaction? Consider the observations of Jerome Michael and Herbert Wechsler in A Rationale of the Law of Homicide II, 37 Colum.L.Rev. 1261, 1281–82 (1937), in connection with these questions:*

> Provocation may be greater or less, but it cannot be measured by the intensity of the passions aroused in the actor by the provocative circumstances. It must be estimated by the probability that such circumstances would affect most men in like fashion; although the passions stirred up in the actor were violent, the provocation can be said to be great only if the provocative circumstances would have aroused in most men similar desires of comparable intensity. Other things being equal, the greater the provocation, measured in that way, the more ground there is for attributing the intensity of the actor's passions and his lack of self-control on the homicidal occasion to the extraordinary character of the situation in which he was placed rather than to any extraordinary deficiency in his own character. While it is true, it is also beside the point, that most men do not kill on even the gravest provocation; the point is that the more strongly they would be moved to kill by circumstances of the sort which provoked the actor to the homicidal act, and the more difficulty they would experience in resisting the impulse to which he yielded, the less does his succumbing serve to differentiate his character from theirs. But the slighter the provocation, the more basis there is for ascribing the actor's act to an extraordinary susceptibility to intense passion, to an unusual deficiency in those other desires which counteract in most men the desires which impel them to homicidal acts, or to an extraordinary weakness of reason and consequent inability to bring such desires into play. Moreover, since the homicidal act does not always follow closely upon the provocative circumstances and since the passions which they arouse may in the meantime gain or lose in intensity, provocation must be estimated as of the time of the homicidal act and in the light of those additional circumstances which may have intensified or diminished the actor's passions.

Compare the observations in A.J. Ashworth, The Doctrine of Provocation, 35 Camb.L.J. 292, 307–09 (1976):**

> It is contended here that the doctrine of provocation as a qualified defence rests just as much on notions of justification as upon the excusing element of loss of self-control. The term "partial justification" will be used for this, but the term does not necessarily imply a connection with the legal concept of justifiable force (i.e., in self-defence); its closest relationship is with the moral notion that the punishment of wrongdoers is justifiable. This is

---

* Reprinted by permission of Professor Wechsler and Columbia Law Review.

** Reprinted by permission of the author and Cambridge University Press.

not to argue that it is ever morally right to kill a person who does wrong. Rather, the claim implicit in partial justification is that an individual is *to some extent* morally justified in making a punitive return against someone who intentionally causes him serious offence, and that this serves to differentiate someone who is provoked to lose his self-control and kill from the unprovoked killer. Whereas the paradigmatic case of murder might be an attack on an innocent victim, the paradigm of provocation generally involves moral wrongs by both parties. The victim plays an important role in provocation cases, either as instigator of the conflict or by doing something which the accused regards as a wrong against him. Ordinary language reflects this approach, with characteristic phrases such as "he brought it on himself," "she asked for it" and "it served him right." Now the court which tries the accused's case is not standing in judgment upon the victim. But, [contrary to what some judges have said], it does not follow that the court "is not concerned with blame here—the blame attaching to the dead man." The complicity of the victim cannot and should not be ignored, for the blameworthiness of his conduct has a strong bearing on the court's judgment of the seriousness of the provocation and the reasonableness of the accused's failure to control himself. . . .

The objective standard may also be supported by causal reasoning. The offender's responsibility for a provoked killing may be said to be reduced by the fact that the victim's wrongful action was the original cause of the offender's loss of self-control. [T]he objective standard might be defended on the basis that it distinguishes those cases in which the provocation was the substantial cause of the loss of self-control from those in which the provocation was so trivial that the loss of control is attributable rather to an abnormal weakness in the accused's temperament. The defence of provocation implies that the loss of self-control was *caused* by the provocation: if the provocation was objectively slight, this suggests that the substantial cause of the loss of control was not the provocation but rather some weakness (or wickedness) in the accused's character, and the case then becomes one of murder or mental abnormality—not provocation.

When we plead . . . provocation, there is genuine uncertainty or ambiguity as to what we mean—is *he* partly responsible, because he roused a violent impulse or passion in me, so that it wasn't truly or merely me acting "of my own accord" (excuse)? Or is it rather that, he having done me such injury, I was entitled to retaliate (justification)? [W]e have attempted here to defend the law's objective standard on the ground that it respects these elements in the concept of provocation. But, although legal commentators have tended to neglect the element of partial justification, its importance should not be over-emphasized. Standing alone, it would lead the courts to indulge those who take the law into their own hands and deliberately wreak vengeance upon those who insult or wrong them. Without the subjective condition of sudden loss of self-control, as judges have frequently observed, every divorce petitioner who killed the correspondent might be entitled to have his crime reduced from murder to manslaughter. But, [on the other hand], without the objective standard and its flavour of partial justification, everyone who killed another in a fit of temper or rage would be entitled to have his crime reduced to manslaughter upon provocation, irrespective of the seriousness of the provocation and irrespective of whether the substantial cause of his loss of self-control lay in the provocation received or in his own fault or mental abnormality.[b]

**3. Cooling Time.** The traditional provocation doctrine includes a requirement that the killing occur before a sufficient interval has passed "to permit the passions to cool and to allow thought and reflection and reason to reassert itself."[c] Many courts have followed a three-step analysis of the cooling-time question similar to that employed for the main body of the provocation rule: (i) the defendant's passion must not in fact have abated; (ii) the passage of a period of time sufficient for reason to be restored will preclude the defense as a matter of law; and (iii) it is in any event a question for the jury whether a reasonable person would have cooled off in the interval between the provocation and the act of killing.

State v. Gounagias, 88 Wash. 304, 153 P. 9 (1915), is a vivid illustration of the operation of the cooling-time requirement. On the evening of April 19, 1914, the defendant got drunk—so drunk that he fell on the floor almost unconscious. The deceased made many insulting remarks about the defendant and his wife, and then sodomized the defendant while he lay there helpless. The next day, the defendant confronted the deceased about the sodomy; when they parted, the defendant asked the deceased not to tell anyone what had happened. However, the deceased spread the story widely, and numerous acquaintances taunted the defendant about the incident. On April 30, a revolver that the defendant had ordered on April 18 arrived, and he placed it in the mattress of his bed. The continual taunting caused the defendant severe emotional distress and frequent headaches. As a result, he stayed home from work on May 6. That evening, he went to a coffeehouse, where he again was taunted by about 10 of his acquaintances. He became

---

[b] The ethical basis of the provocation mitigation is explored in Joshua Dressler, Rethinking Heat of Passion: A Defense in Search of a Rationale, 73 J.Crim.Law & Criminology 421 (1982). Dressler concludes that the mitigation should be derived from the ethics of excuse, not the ethics of justification. In particular, he argues that the provoked defendant is less blameworthy because his capacity for choice has been limited by the provoking situation. He also argues that under some circumstances—those "which would render the ordinarily reasonable and law-abiding person in the same situation liable to become so emotionally upset that he would be wholly incapable of controlling his conduct"—provocation should be a complete defense. For discussion of the exculpatory effect of situational excuse under present law, see the notes on duress and situational compulsion in Chapter V.—[Footnote by eds.]

[c] State v. Lee, 36 Del. 11, 19, 171 A. 195, 198 (1933). Compare the language of the pre-*Furman* Georgia statute reproduced in Appendix B.

so excited and enraged that, as he sought to testify, "he lost all control of his reason," and resolved to kill the deceased. He went home, picked up his gun and loaded it, went to the house where the deceased lived, entered the house, found the deceased asleep, and, without waking him, emptied the revolver into the deceased's head. He then returned to his house, removed the discharged cartridges, put the gun back in his mattress, and went to bed. He was arrested shortly thereafter.

The trial court excluded evidence of provocation, and the defendant was convicted of murder. On appeal, the Washington Supreme Court affirmed the conviction. The court first reviewed the law on provocation and the cooling-time requirement, and then reasoned:

> The offered evidence makes it clear that the appellant knew and appreciated for days before the killing the full meaning of the words, signs, and vulgar gestures of his [acquaintances] which, as the offer shows, he had encountered from day to day for about three weeks following the original outrage, wherever he went. The final demonstration in the coffeehouse was nothing new. It was exactly what the appellant, from his experience for the prior three weeks, must have anticipated. To say that it alone tended to create the sudden passion and heat of blood essential to mitigation is to ignore the admitted fact that the same thing had created no such condition on its repeated occurrence during the prior three weeks. To say that these repeated demonstrations, coupled with the original outrage, *culminated* in a sudden passion and heat of blood when he encountered the same character of demonstration in the coffeehouse on the night of the killing, is to say that sudden passion and heat of blood in the mitigative sense may be a cumulative result of repeated reminders of a single act of provocation occurring weeks before, and this, whether that provocation be regarded as the original outrage or the spreading of the story among appellant's associates, both of which he knew and fully realized for three weeks before the fatal night. This theory of the cumulative effect of reminders of former wrongs, not of new acts of provocation by the deceased, is contrary to the idea of sudden anger as understood in the doctrine of mitigation. In the nature of the thing *sudden* anger cannot be cumulative. A provocation which does not cause instant resentment, but which is only resented after being thought upon and brooded over, is not a provocation sufficient in law to reduce intentional killing from murder to manslaughter....

The evidence offered had no tendency to prove sudden anger and resentment. On the contrary, it did tend to prove brooding thought, resulting in the design to kill. It was therefore properly excluded.

By contrast, the Supreme Court of California has suggested that the kind of evidence proffered in *Gounagias* may be mitigating, in spite (or, perhaps, because) of the passage of time involved. In People v. Berry, 18

Cal.3d 509, 134 Cal.Rptr. 415, 556 P.2d 777 (1976), the defendant killed his wife, whose name was Rachel, after a 10–day period during which she kept taunting him with the fact that she was sexually attracted to another man. Rachel disclosed that she recently had sexual relations with the other man, claimed she might be pregnant by him, showed the defendant pictures of herself with the other man, and demanded a divorce. On one occasion while the defendant and Rachel were driving, she "demanded immediate sexual intercourse with defendant in the car, which was achieved; however upon reaching their apartment, she again stated that she loved [the other man] and that she would not have intercourse with the defendant in the future." Three days before the killing occurred, the defendant and Rachel engaged in heavy petting at a movie theater. Later, in bed at home, Rachel announced that she had intended to have sex with the defendant, but explained that she had changed her mind because she was saving herself for the other man. The defendant began preparing to leave the apartment, and Rachel started screaming and yelling at him. At this point, the defendant "choked her into unconsciousness," but did not kill her. Rather, he took her to a hospital. A day later, the defendant went to the apartment to talk to Rachel. She was out, and he waited for her there for about 20 hours. When Rachel returned home, she said to the defendant, "I suppose you have come here to kill me." The defendant made an ambivalent response, and Rachel again started screaming. "Defendant grabbed her by the shoulder and tried to stop her screaming. She continued. They struggled and finally defendant strangled her with a telephone cord."

At the defendant's homicide trial, the court refused his request for an instruction on voluntary manslaughter, and the jury convicted him of murder. On appeal, the Supreme Court of California reversed the conviction, agreeing with the defendant's contention "that there is sufficient evidence in the record to show that he committed the homicide while in a state of uncontrollable rage caused by provocation." The court explained:

> [T]here is no specific type of provocation required by [the voluntary manslaughter statute] and ... verbal provocation may be sufficient. [For example, as we held in a prior case,] evidence of admissions of infidelity by the defendant's paramour, taunts directed to him and other conduct, "supports a finding that the defendant killed in wild desperation induced by long continued provocatory conduct." We find this reasoning persuasive in the case now before us. Defendant's testimony chronicles a two-week period of provocatory conduct by his wife Rachel that could arouse a passion of jealousy, pain and sexual rage in an ordinary man of average disposition such as to cause him to act rashly from this passion....
>
> The Attorney General contends that the killing could not have been done in the heat of passion because there was a cooling period, defendant having waited in the apartment for 20 hours. However, the long course of provocatory conduct, which had resulted in intermittent outbreaks of rage under specific provoca-

tion in the past, reached its final culmination in the apartment when Rachel began screaming. Both defendant and [his expert witness] testified that defendant killed in a state of uncontrollable rage, of passion, and there is ample evidence in the record to support the conclusion that this passion was the result of the long course of provocatory conduct by Rachel. . . .

**4.  The Objective Standard.** Both the sufficiency of the provocation and the passage of adequate time to cool down are measured by an objective standard. How "objective" should the inquiry be? To put the question another way, what facts—about the situation leading up to the killing and about the accused—are pertinent to an "objective" inquiry? Especially vexing is the question of whether characteristics personal to the accused should be taken into account. If so, which characteristics? Should the inquiry exclude individual traits that may have made the defendant more or less excitable than the average person? The court in *Maher* reasoned that "the average of men . . . of fair average mind and disposition should be taken as the standard—*unless* . . . the person whose guilt is in question be shown to have some peculiar weakness of mind or infirmity of temper, not arising from wickedness of heart or cruelty of disposition."

At the other extreme is the holding in Bedder v. Director of Public Prosecutions, [1954] 2 All E.R. 801. The defendant was an 18–year-old youth who was sexually impotent and emotionally distressed by his condition. On the night of the offense, he approached a prostitute, who led him to a quiet court off the street. There he attempted in vain to have intercourse with her. She responded by jeering at him and trying to get away. He tried to hold her, and she slapped him in the face and punched him in the stomach. He grabbed her shoulders and pushed her back, whereupon she kicked him in the groin. He then pulled a knife and stabbed her twice. Defendant testified that: "She kicked me in the privates. Whether it was her knee or foot, I do not know. After that I do not know what happened till she fell." She died from the knife wounds, and the defendant was prosecuted for murder. The trial judge instructed on the nature of the objective standard as follows:

> The reasonable person, the ordinary person, is the person you must consider when you are considering the effect which any acts, any conduct, any words, might have to justify the steps which were taken in response thereto, so that an unusually excitable or pugnacious individual, or drunken one or a man who is sexually impotent is not entitled to rely on provocation which would not have led an ordinary person to have acted in the way which was in fact carried out.

Defendant argued on appeal that this instruction was wrong, but his conviction was affirmed. Lord Simonds reasoned in part that:

> It would be plainly illogical not to recognize an unusually excitable or pugnacious temperament in the accused as a matter to be taken into account [as a prior case had established] but yet to recognize for that purpose some unusual physical characteristic, be it impo-

tence or another. Moreover, the proposed distinction appears to me to ignore the fundamental fact that the temper of a man which leads him to react in such and such a way to provocation, is, or may be, itself conditioned by some physical defect. It is too subtle a refinement for my mind or, I think, for that of a jury to grasp that the temper may be ignored but the physical defect taken into account.

Is Lord Simonds correct when he asserts that it is both illogical and too difficult to take account of the accused's physical, but not temperamental, characteristics? Using the facts of *Bedder* as an example, why should the jurors not be instructed to judge the severity of the provocation from the perspective of a sexually impotent man who possesses a reasonable temper?

More recently, in People v. Ogen, 168 Cal.App.3d 611, 215 Cal.Rptr. 16 (1985), the Court of Appeals of California explained why the adequacy of provocation should not be judged by reference to the accused's special sensitivities:

> [T]here are substantial policy reasons to restrict the application of the heat of passion defense to cases where the circumstances are sufficiently provocative to trigger violent reactions in a reasonable person. As members of society, each of us is constantly in contact with family members, friends, acquaintances and strangers under countless circumstances. No social interaction is so placid as to be utterly devoid of interpersonal stress and friction including, we speculate, monastic existence short of becoming a hermit. [The defendant's] suggested rule would limit homicides to manslaughter upon any fancied slight so long as the perpetrator was sufficiently sensitive. Ethnic, racial, or religious slurs, and sexual innuendoes trigger violent reactions and occasionally killings. However, society has a strong interest in deterring violent and homicidal conduct by not allowing individuals to justify their acts by their own standard of conduct. "[Thus], no man of extremely violent passion could so justify or excuse himself if the exciting cause be not adequate, nor could an excessively cowardly man justify himself unless the circumstances were such as to arouse the fears of the ordinarily courageous man."

By contrast, Richard Singer argues that the "solution . . . is to adopt a totally subjective approach" to provocation. Richard Singer, The Resurgence of Mens Rea: I—Provocation, Emotional Disturbance, and the Model Penal Code, 27 B.C. L. Rev. 243, 315 (1986). Since the provocation standard should be defined by reference to the purposes served by criminal punishment, Singer believes that lawmakers must focus on "the question . . . whether a person who has killed in the heat of passion is, for a utilitarian, less deterrable, less dangerous or less in need of rehabilitation than a murderer, or for a retributivist, less morally blameworthy than a murderer and therefore less deserving of the punishment imposed upon a murderer." For Singer, the "singular purpose of the criminal law" is "to measure moral blameworthiness and punish it proportionately." Accordingly, in provocation cases,

> [t]he law should ask only whether (1) the defendant lost control due to some emotional event or series of events; (2) in losing that control, was the defendant as morally blameworthy as a person who deliberately or recklessly kills. In assessing this liability, the jury should consider only the defendant and his emotional characteristics; no suggestions of "reasonable" people or "adequate" provocation should be allowed. This view ... has the virtue of focusing on the critical inquiry: was the defendant blameworthy for having lost his temper, given everything known about the defendant? If so, then his "blameworthy conduct" is in failing to control his temper, *not* in killing once his temper had "replaced his reason."

**5.  Boys' Rules?**[d] Over the past few years, a number of lawyers and commentators have criticized the provocation doctrine on the ground that it incorporates a model of human behavior that may be true of men, but is not true of women. These critics claim that the doctrine was designed and continues to be receptive to the violent rages of the ordinary "man," not those of the ordinary "person." The "sight of adultery" cases are offered to support this claim. The overwhelming majority of defendants in such cases are men who have killed their wives or their wives' lovers. By contrast, when women kill their spouses, they typically do so for reasons other than jealousy over sexual infidelity, but the provocation doctrine does not recognize such reasons as factors that should mitigate their punishment. Thus, for the critics, the assertion that the provocation doctrine is a "concession to the frailty of human nature" is false as a descriptive matter. The doctrine is a concession to the frailty of "male nature," and, as such, it rests not on an "objective" perspective, but on a "male" perspective.

This criticism has been extended by critical race scholars and practitioners, who claim that the provocation formula (like other legal doctrines) endorses the perceptions and experiences of whites, not of blacks or members of other racial minorities. These commentators attack the reasoning employed by the court in *Ogen*, under which "ethnic, racial, or religious slurs" are not "sufficiently provocative to trigger violent reactions in a reasonable person." According to these critics, such reasoning is insensitive to the experiences that tend to provoke rage in minority citizens, including especially the experience of racial discrimination.

These descriptive criticisms have generated different normative criticisms of the provocation doctrine. First, the assertion that the doctrine embodies a male perspective may imply that the doctrine should be abolished altogether. If men, but not women, fly into a homicidal passion when they discover that their spouse has been sexually unfaithful, why should

---

[d] "Most of the time a criminal law that reflects male views and male standards imposes its judgment on men who have injured other men. It is 'boys' rules' applied to a boy's fight." Susan Estrich, Real Rape 60 (1987).

the law recognize such passion as a *mitigating* factor? Why should a man who experiences an overpowering rage in these circumstances not be viewed as more, rather than less, culpable, since a woman would not be similarly provoked? In When "Heterosexual" Men Kill "Homosexual" Men: Reflections on Provocation Law, Sexual Advances, and the "Reasonable Man" Standard, 85 J. Crim. L. & Criminology 726, 735–37, 750–51 (1995),* Joshua Dressler agrees that the provocation defense "is a male-oriented doctrine," but he argues that the law should retain it:

> [A]s long as males are defendants in criminal homicide prosecutions more often than women, men are the primary beneficiaries of *all* criminal law defenses. But having said this, if ever the criminal law follows boys' rules, it does here. Consider, first, that men are far more prone to violence than are women. Both daily experience and crime statistics support this claim. Although the number of women sentenced for violent offenses has risen slightly in recent years, it is still true that "[w]omen rarely kill," and, to the extent that they do, female homicide is so different from male homicide that women and men may be said to live in two different cultures, each with its own "subculture of violence."
>
> What is important here, however, is not simply that the average male is more susceptible to violent loss of self-control than is the average woman. It is also necessary to consider how men and women respond to affronts, i.e., to provocations. Women usually submit stoically to their victimization or deny their status as victims by blaming themselves ("I deserve this treatment"); men are more likely to characterize themselves as victims of injustice, or to think that their self-worth has been attacked, and to act offensively as a result. . . .
>
> The preceding observations might lead to the conclusion that courts should abolish the provocation defense. Arguably, the defense removes an important incentive for persons—primarily men—to learn self-control. And from a feminist perspective, the doctrine specifically "reinforces the conditions in which men are perceived and perceive themselves as natural aggressors, and in particular *women's* natural aggressors." . . .
>
> . . . To the extent that the law can have a salutary effect on human conduct, it is good to tell people, most especially men, that the law does not consider violence an acceptable way to deal with insults, adultery, or violations of any personal interest except, perhaps, bodily integrity. Perhaps the law's message would cause people to learn constructive ways of channeling aggressive feelings.
>
> Deterrence, however, is not the exclusive goal of the criminal law. Another purpose of the law is to differentiate between more and less serious offenses, and "to safeguard offenders against excessive, disproportionate or arbitrary punishment." These goals

* Reprinted by permission of the author
and Northwestern University School of Law.

of the criminal law require consideration of matters of personal culpability.... A system of laws that refuses to recognize any excusing conditions might deter violence and, therefore, might be justifiable in a purely utilitarian system. But excuses, including provocation, are recognized for a non-utilitarian (even counter-utilitarian) reason: they stem from the commitment to afford justice to individual wrongdoers—ensuring that they are not blamed and punished in excess of their personal desert.

Some propose revising the provocation doctrine so that it accords mitigating significance to events that provoke violence in persons who are members of disempowered groups. In Is the Reasonable Man Obsolete? A Critical Perspective on Self–Defense and Provocation, 14 Loyola of L.A.L.Rev. 435 (1981), Delores Donovan and Stephanie Wildman argue that the law of provocation should take account of such factors as race, sex, socio-economic background, traumatic personal experiences, and other factors relevant to the "social reality" of the defendant's behavior. For example, a woman who kills an abusive spouse under circumstances not amounting to self defense should be permitted to offer proof of the abuse in support of a provocation instruction. Donovan and Wildman offer the following jury instruction for cases where provocation is asserted:

> In determining whether the killing was done with malice afore-thought, you must consider whether, in light of all the evidence in the case, the accused was honestly and understandably aroused to the heat of passion. In determining whether [he or she] was understandably aroused to the heat of passion, you must ask yourselves whether [he or she] could have been fairly expected to avoid the act of homicide.

According to Donovan and Wildman, this instruction does not abandon the requirement that an "objective" judgment be made. Rather, the instruction conveys that requirement to the jury in terms that are more likely to produce just results. How does this instruction differ from the "totally subjective approach" proposed by Richard Singer?

**6.  The Relevance of Mistake.** In Criminal Law 578 (1972), Wayne R. LaFave and Austin W. Scott, Jr., assert that:

> It would seem that the provocation is adequate to reduce the homicide to voluntary manslaughter if the killer reasonably believes that the injury to him exists, though actually he has not been injured. In other words, a man's passion directed against another person is reasonable if (i) he reasonably believes that he has been injured by the other, and (ii) a reasonable man who actually has suffered such an injury would be put in a passion directed against the other.

The leading American case for this proposition is State v. Yanz, 74 Conn. 177, 50 A. 37 (1901), where an instruction that "[i]f, in fact, no adultery was going on, and the husband is mistaken as to the fact, though the circumstances were such as to justify a belief ... of adultery, the offense would not be reduced to manslaughter" was held to be reversible error. The court said that:

> The excitement is the effect of a belief, from ocular evidence, of the actual commission of adultery. It is the belief, so reasonably formed, that excites the uncontrollable passion. Such a belief, though a mistaken one, is calculated to induce the same emotions as would be felt were the wrongful act in fact committed.

One judge dissented, reasoning in part that when anger

> is provoked by the wrongful act of the person slain, who thus brings upon himself the fatal blow, given in the first outbreak of rage, caused by himself, the offense is manslaughter; not only because the voluntary act is, in a way, compelled by an ungovernable rage, but also because the victim is the aggressor; and his wrong, although it cannot justify, may modify, the nature of the homicide thus induced. The court therefore correctly told the jury that to make the offense manslaughter, the injury claimed as a provocation must in fact have been done. Our law of homicide recognizes no provocation as legally competent to so modify the cruelty of intentional, unlawful killing as to reduce the offense to manslaughter, except the provocation involved in an actual and adequate injury and insult.

In Provocation and the Reasonable Man, [1954] Crim.L.Rev. 740, 752–53,** Glanville Williams disagrees with LaFave and Scott and with both the majority and the dissent in *Yanz*, at least as to what the law ought to be:

> There seems to be no doubt that a mistaken belief in provocation is equivalent to actual provocation. The mistake is a defence to the same extent as if the facts supposed were true. . . .
>
> It is further submitted that there is no "objective" test in respect of the mistake; in other words, the mistake need not be reasonable. As a general principle in criminal matters, a mistake entitles the accused to be treated on the basis that the facts he supposed existed, whether the mistake was reasonable or not; negligence is not generally a question in issue in criminal law. This is not a denial of the objective test of provocation, for the objective test operates only on the facts as they were believed by the accused to exist. The question asked by the objective test is whether, assuming the facts to be as the accused believed them to be, those facts would come within the legal categories of provocation, or would be provocation for an ordinary man. What the objective test discountenances is unusual deficiency of self-control, not the making of an error of observation or inference in point of fact.
>
> The chief practical importance of this is in connection with drunkenness, for a person under the influence of drink is particularly prone to mistake the intentions of another. (An extraordinary

---

** Reprinted by permission of the author
and Criminal Law Review.

instance is that of Booth the actor—the brother of Lincoln's assassin—who on one occasion when he was playing Macbeth under the influence of liquor, refused to be killed, and chased Macduff murderously all through the stalls.) If the drunkard acts in supposed self-defence, he is entitled (on a charge involving intention or recklessness) to have the facts taken as he supposed them to be, however unreasonable the mistake; and if he acts under supposed provocation, the rule is the same.

How should mistakes be treated in the context of provocation? Should mistakes induced by intoxication be treated differently?

**7. The Relevance of Mental Abnormality.** To what extent is evidence of mental abnormality logically relevant to the criteria governing the reduction of murder to manslaughter? There are two principal contexts in which this question has arisen.

**(i) Provocation.** Is evidence of mental abnormality relevant to the ordinary provocation inquiry? Clearly, such evidence can be probative as to one component of the mitigation—that the defendant in fact acted in the heat of passion generated by the provoking event. For this reason, several courts have admitted such evidence to show that the defendant actually was provoked. But unless the "reasonable person" is to be imbued with the peculiar mental characteristics of the defendant—a step which the courts uniformly have refused to take—the defendant's mental abnormality would not be relevant to whether it was "reasonable" to have been provoked under similar circumstances. Thus, the fact that the standard of adequate provocation requires the application of an objective measure of liability eliminates such evidence from consideration on this branch of the inquiry.

Since evidence of mental abnormality would be relevant on the subjective dimension of the inquiry but not the objective one, should the evidence be admitted or excluded? Could the admission of testimony about the defendant's abnormality mislead and confuse a jury that is told to consider it for one purpose but ignore it for another? Could admission of such evidence push the inquiry too far in a subjective direction? On the other hand, is it fair to foreclose the defendant from a reliable source of evidence on one important aspect of the inquiry?

**(ii) "Imperfect" Justification.** It is a defense to an intentional killing if it can be shown that the defendant believed it a necessary response to unlawful deadly force and that the response was reasonable under the circumstances. Moreover, many courts reduce the offense from murder to manslaughter if only the subjective component of this inquiry is met. The term "imperfect justification" is often used to describe the rule that permits such mitigation.

In jurisdictions that follow this rule, it seems plain that evidence of mental abnormality can be logically relevant to the subjective consideration that will suffice for mitigation of the offense to manslaughter. Such evidence was held admissible in People v. Wells, 33 Cal.2d 330, 202 P.2d 53

(1949), where the defendant was prosecuted under a statute that read: "Every person undergoing a life sentence in a state prison ... who, with malice aforethought, commits an assault upon the person of another ... by any means of force likely to produce great bodily injury, is punishable with death." The defendant sought to introduce evidence that he suffered from a condition that produced an abnormal fear for his own safety causing him to overreact to conduct which he perceived as threatening. He did not claim that he met the objective criterion for exoneration on the ground of self-defense. The court held that "malice aforethought" in the quoted statute had the same meaning as it would in a prosecution for murder, and that because such evidence would be admissible to negate the malice afore-thought required for murder (reducing the offense to manslaughter), it was also logically relevant and admissible to negate an essential element of the offense charged.

Suppose Wells had also claimed self-defense and had sought to show that the objective component of that defense had been satisfied. Would the expert testimony be admissible for that purpose? If not, does this cast doubt on whether it should be admitted in a case where both the complete defense and the mitigation are claimed and the evidence is offered for the sole purpose of establishing the mitigation? Can the jury be expected to keep the two issues separate? Is the provocation situation sufficiently different to suggest that the expert testimony might be excluded entirely in provocation cases but admitted for a limited purpose in a case where the defendant claims both complete and imperfect justification?

---

## NOTES ON "EXTREME EMOTIONAL DISTURBANCE" AS A MITIGATION OF MURDER TO MANSLAUGHTER

**1. The Model Penal Code Formulation.** Section 210.3(b) of the Model Penal Code proposes the following codification of the circumstances that should mitigate murder to manslaughter:

> Criminal homicide constitutes manslaughter when ... a homi-cide which would otherwise be murder is committed under the influence of extreme mental or emotional disturbance for which there is reasonable explanation or excuse. The reasonableness of such explanation or excuse shall be determined from the viewpoint of a person in the actor's situation under the circumstances as he believes them to be.

As the drafters of the Code explain, this provision is designed to modify the common law provocation doctrine. Indeed, their objective in describing the mitigating condition as "extreme mental or emotional disturbance" was to endorse a "substantially enlarged version of the rule of provocation." Thus, the commentary to § 210.3(b) explains:

> ... This formulation effects substantial changes in the tradi-tional notion of provocation. For one thing, the Code does not

require that the actor's emotional distress arise from some injury, affront, or other provocative act perpetrated upon him by the deceased. Under the Code, mitigation may be appropriate where the actor believes that the deceased is responsible for some injustice to another or even where he strikes out in a blinding rage and kills an innocent bystander. In some such cases, the cause and intensity of the actor's emotion may be less indicative of moral depravity than would be a homicidal response to a blow to one's person. By eliminating any reference to provocation in the ordinary sense of improper conduct by the deceased, the Model Code avoids arbitrary exclusion of some circumstances that may justify reducing murder to manslaughter.

Section 210.3 also sweeps away the rigid rules that limited provocation to certain defined circumstances. Instead, it casts the issue in phrases that have no common-law antecedents and hence no accumulated doctrinal content. Where there is evidence of extreme mental or emotional disturbance, it is for the trier of fact to decide, in light of all the circumstances of the case, whether there exists a reasonable explanation or excuse for the actor's mental condition. The issue cannot be resolved successfully by categorization of conduct. It must be confronted directly on the facts of each case. By restating the ultimate inquiry, [the section] avoids the strictures of early precedents and puts the issue in the terms in which it should be considered. This development reflects the trend of many modern decisions to abandon preconceived notions of what constitutes adequate provocation and to submit that question to the jury's deliberation.

Most importantly, the Model Code qualifies the rigorous objectivity with which the common law determined adequacy of provocation. Of course, [the section] does require that the actor's emotional distress be based on "reasonable explanation or excuse." This language preserves the essentially objective character of the inquiry and erects a barrier against debilitating individualization of the legal standard. But the statute further provides that the "reasonableness of such explanation or excuse shall be determined from the viewpoint of a person in the actor's situation under the circumstances as he believes them to be." The last clause clarifies the role of mistake. The trier of fact must evaluate the actor's conduct under the circumstances that the actor believed to exist. Thus, for example, a man who reasonably but mistakenly identifies his wife's rapist and kills the wrong person may be eligible for mitigation if his extreme emotional disturbance were otherwise subject to reasonable explanation or excuse.

The critical element in the Model Code formulation is the clause requiring that reasonableness be assessed "from the viewpoint of a person in the actor's situation." The word "situation" is designedly ambiguous. On the one hand, it is clear that personal handicaps and some external circumstances must be taken into account. Thus, blindness, shock from traumatic injury, and extreme grief are all easily read into the term "situation." This result is sound, for it would be morally obtuse to appraise a crime for mitigation of punishment without reference to these factors. On the other hand, it is equally plain that idiosyncratic moral values are not part of the actor's situation. An assassin who kills a political leader because he believes it is right to do so cannot ask that he be judged by the standard of a reasonable extremist. Any other result would undermine the normative message of the criminal law. In between these two extremes, however, there are matters neither as clearly distinct from individual blameworthiness as blindness or handicap nor as integral a part of moral depravity as a belief in the rightness of killing. Perhaps the classic illustration is the unusual sensitivity to the epithet "bastard" of a person born illegitimate. An exceptionally punctilious sense of personal honor or an abnormally fearful temperament may also serve the differentiate an individual actor from the hypothetical reasonable man, yet none of these factors is wholly irrelevant to the ultimate issue of culpability. The proper role of such factors cannot be resolved satisfactorily by abstract definition of what may constitute adequate provocation.... In the end, the question is whether the actor's loss of self-control can be understood in terms that arouse sympathy in the ordinary citizen. Section 210.3 faces this issue squarely and leaves the ultimate judgment to the ordinary citizen in the function of a juror assigned to resolve the specific case.

The Model Penal Code has led to a reformulation of the law of provocation in at least a dozen states, New York among them. It is clear that it significantly broadens the common-law standard in a number of respects.

Exactly how does it do so? Review the sequence of notes following *Freddo v. State*, supra. How does the Model Code formula differ from common-law provocation on the issues treated in those notes? How would the Model Code be applied to the facts in *Freddo* and the cases discussed in the notes following *Freddo*? Does it do a better job, or is it too permissive and not sufficiently protective of human life? The Oregon statute, reproduced in Appendix B, infra, is worded differently from the Model Code. Is it an improvement?[a]

**2.  *People v. Casassa.*** Victor Casassa was charged with murder in the stabbing death of Victoria Lo Consolo. He waived a jury and was tried by the court. The defense conceded that Casassa had killed Ms. Lo Consolo, but claimed that he had done so "under the influence of extreme mental or emotional disturbance," and that his offense should be mitigated to man- ·

---

[a] The Oregon statute is extensively considered in State v. Ott, 297 Or. 375, 686 P.2d 1001 (1984).

slaughter as provided by § 125.25 (1)(a) of the New York Penal Law, which is identical to the Model Penal Code formulation.[b]

The evidence showed that Casassa and the victim met in August 1976 as a result of their residence in the same apartment complex. Shortly thereafter, he asked her to accompany him to a social function and she agreed. The two apparently dated casually on other occasions until November, 1976 when Ms. Lo Consolo informed him that she was not "falling in love" with him. Devastated by this rejection, Casassa became obsessed with Ms. Lo Consolo. Aware that she was seeing other men, he broke into the apartment below Ms. Lo Consolo's on several occasions to eavesdrop. Thereafter, on one occasion, he broke into her apartment while she was out. He took nothing, but, instead, observed the apartment, disrobed and lay for a time in Miss Lo Consolo's bed. During this break-in, defendant was armed with a knife which, he later told police, he carried "because he knew that he was either going to hurt Victoria or Victoria was going to cause him to commit suicide." Cassasa's final visit to his victim's apartment occurred on February 28, 1977. He brought several bottles of wine and liquor with him to offer as a gift. Upon Ms. Lo Consolo's rejection of this offering, defendant produced a steak knife which he had brought with him, stabbed her several times in the throat, dragged her body to the bathroom and submerged it in a bathtub full of water to "make sure she was dead."

The defense presented only one witness, a psychiatrist, who testified, in essence, that the defendant had become obsessed with Miss Lo Consolo and that the course which their relationship had taken, combined with several personality attributes peculiar to defendant, caused him to be under the influence of extreme emotional disturbance at the time of the killing. In rebuttal, the state's psychiatrist testified that although Casassa was emotionally disturbed, he was not under the influence of "extreme emotional disturbance" within the meaning of § 125.25(1)(a) of the Penal Law because his disturbed state was not the product of external factors but rather was "a stress he created from within himself, dealing mostly with a fantasy, a refusal to accept the reality of the situation."

The trial court in resolving this issue noted that the affirmative defense of extreme emotional disturbance may be based upon a series of events, rather than a single precipitating cause. In order to be entitled to the defense, the court held, a defendant must show that his reaction to such events was reasonable. In determining whether defendant's emotional reaction was reasonable, the court considered the appropriate test to be whether in the totality of the circumstances the finder of fact could understand how a person might have his reason overcome. Concluding that the test was not to be applied solely from the viewpoint of defendant, the court found that defendant's emotional reaction at the time of the commission of the crime was so peculiar to him that it could not be considered reasonable so as to reduce the conviction to manslaughter in the first

[b] The applicable New York statutes are reproduced in Appendix B.

degree. Accordingly, the trial court found defendant guilty of murder in the second degree. The Court of Appeals affirmed:

By suggesting a standard of evaluation which contains both subjective and objective elements, we believe that the drafters of the code adequately achieved their dual goals of broadening the "heat of passion" doctrine to apply to a wider range of circumstances while retaining some element of objectivity in the process. The result of their draftsmanship is a statute which offers the defendant a fair opportunity to seek mitigation without requiring that the trier of fact find mitigation in each case where an emotional disturbance is shown—or as the drafters put it, to offer "room for argument as to the reasonableness of the explanations or excuses offered."

We note also that this interpretation comports with what has long been recognized as the underlying purpose of any mitigation statute. In the words of Mr. Justice Cardozo, referring to an earlier statute: "What we have is merely a privilege offered to the jury to find the lesser degree when the suddenness of the intent, the vehemence of the passion, seems to call irresistibly for the exercise of mercy. I have no objection to giving them this dispensing power, but it should be given to them directly and not in a mystifying cloud of words." Benjamin Cardozo, Law and Literature 100–01.[c] In the end, we believe that what the legislature intended in enacting the statute was to allow the finder of fact the discretionary power to mitigate the penalty when presented with a situation which, under the circumstances, appears to them to have caused an understandable weakness in one of their fellows. Perhaps the chief virtue of the statute is that it allows such discretion without engaging in a detailed explanation of individual circumstances in which the statute would apply, thus avoiding the "mystifying cloud of words" which Mr. Justice Cardozo abhorred.[d]

We conclude that the trial court, in this case, properly applied the statute. The court apparently accepted, as a factual matter, that defendant killed Miss Lo Consolo while under the influence of "extreme emotional disturbance," a threshold question which must be answered in the affirmative before any test of reasonableness is required. The court, however, also recognized that in exercising its function as trier of fact, it must make a further inquiry into the reasonableness of that disturbance. In this regard, the court considered each of the mitigating factors put forward by defendant, including his claimed mental disability, but found that

[c] The passage from which this quotation is taken is reproduced in context in Note 1(i) in the Notes on First–Degree Murder in Section 1 of this Chapter.—[Footnote by eds.]

[d] But see Robert M. Byrn, Homicide Under the Proposed New York Penal Law, 33 Fordham L.Rev. 173, 179 (1964) ("All that has happened is that 'one mystifying cloud of words' has been substituted for another.")—[Footnote by eds.]

the excuse offered by defendant was so peculiar to him that it was unworthy of mitigation. The court obviously made a sincere effort to understand defendant's "situation" and "the circumstances as defendant believed them to be," but concluded that the murder in this case was the result of defendant's malevolence rather than an understandable human response deserving of mercy. We cannot say, as a matter of law, that the court erred in so concluding. Indeed, to do so would subvert the purpose of the statute.

In our opinion, this statute would not require that the jury or the court as trier of fact find mitigation on any particular set of facts, but, rather, allows the finder of fact the opportunity to do so, such opportunity being conditional only upon a finding of extreme emotional disturbance in the first instance. In essence, the statute requires mitigation to be afforded an emotionally disturbed defendant only when the trier of fact, after considering a broad range of mitigating circumstances, believes that such leniency is justified. Since the trier of fact found that defendant failed to establish that he was acting "under the influence of extreme emotional disturbance for which there was a reasonable explanation or excuse," defendant's conviction of murder in the second degree should not be reduced to the crime of manslaughter in the first degree.

Did the Court of Appeals properly apply the Model Penal Code mitigation to Casassa? What if the case had been tried before a jury and the trial judge had refused to give the jury a manslaughter instruction under § 125.25 (1)(a) on the ground that the evidence was legally insufficient to show that there was "a reasonable explanation or excuse" for Casassa's emotional disturbance? How would the Court of Appeals have ruled in that case? What did the drafters of the Model Penal Code intend?

Victoria Nourse has sharply criticized the reforms prompted by the MPC formulation, especially in connection with claims for mitigation such as those presented in *Casassa*. In Passion's Progress: Modern Law Reform and the Provocation Defense, 106 Yale L.J. 1331 (1997), Nourse argues that the reforms "have led us to change our understandings of intimate homicide in ways that we might never have expected." The drafters of the Model Code intended to introduce "modern and enlightened" ways of thinking about the provocation doctrine, but the appellate cases from reform states suggest that the "extreme emotional disturbance" formulation instead has had a pernicious effect. By allowing claims like Casassa's, the formulation "perpetuates ... ideas about men, women, and their relationships that society long ago abandoned." Although the law of domestic relations now acknowledges that women have the right to divorce or separate from their male partners, the reforms of the provocation doctrine have "yielded precisely the opposite result, binding women to the emotional claims of husbands or boyfriends" those women had lawfully and properly rejected. Thus, Nourse wonders whether the Model Code's approach to provocation is an improvement at all. As she puts it, "[i]n this upside-down world of gender relations [promoted by the MPC formulation], it should not be surprising to learn that the common law approach toward the provocation defense, deemed an antique by most legal scholars, provides greater protection for women than do purportedly liberal versions of the defense."

In this connection, note that New York authorizes a maximum prison sentence of 25 years for a person whose offense is mitigated from murder to manslaughter by an "extreme emotional disturbance." The maximum in Oregon is 20 years. By contrast, the maximum in Virginia, which follows the traditional common-law provocation formula, is 10 years. See Appendix B. How is the appropriate choice of formula related to the severity with which the mitigated offense can be punished? Is changing the label from murder to manslaughter under more relaxed standards more tolerable if the offense is still subject to severe punishments approaching those for murder?

**3.  Diminished Responsibility in England.** In the Homicide Act, 1957, 5 & 6 Eliz. 2, c. 11, § 2, England amended the common-law homicide structure as follows:

> Persons suffering from diminished responsibility.
>
> (1) Where a person kills or is a party to the killing of another, he shall not be convicted of murder if he was suffering from such abnormality of mind (whether arising from a condition of arrested or retarded development of mind or any inherent causes or induced by disease or injury) as substantially impaired his mental responsibility for his acts and omissions in doing or being a party to the killing.
>
> (2) On a charge of murder, it shall be for the defence to prove that the person charged is by virtue of this section not liable to be convicted of murder.
>
> (3) A person who but for this section would be liable, whether as principal or as accessory, to be convicted of murder shall be liable instead to be convicted of manslaughter.
>
> (4) The fact that one party to a killing is by virtue of this section not liable to be convicted of murder shall not affect the question whether the killing amounted to murder in the case of any other party to it.

The term "abnormality of mind" has since been defined in Regina v. Byrne, [1960] 2 Q.B. 396, 403, in the following terms:

> "Abnormality of mind," which has to be contrasted with the time-honoured expression in the *M'Naghten* rules, "defect of reason," means a state of mind so different from that of ordinary human beings that the reasonable man would term it abnormal. It appears to us to be wide enough to cover the mind's activities in all its aspects, not only the perception of physical acts and matters and the ability to form a rational judgment whether an act is right or wrong, but also the ability to exercise will-power to control physical acts in accordance with that rational judgment.

The English statute was adopted as part of a package of legislation designed to limit the range of offenses for which the death penalty could be imposed. The death penalty itself was abolished in England in 1965, but the 1957 diminished-responsibility provisions were retained. Note that the effect of the 1957 legislation was to broaden the substantive criteria under which evidence of "abnormality of mind" could be considered as a mitigating factor to reduce murder to manslaughter. Functionally, therefore, it operates much as does the provocation mitigation. Like provocation, it provides the jury with a substantive basis for reducing the grade of the offense, and in so doing broadens the base of evidence that can be introduced for this purpose. Note that it makes evidence of mental abnormality relevant in ways not encompassed by the *M'Naghten* formulation of the insanity defense and also not encompassed by the provocation mitigation. Is this a desirable development?

**4. Diminished Responsibility Under the "Extreme Emotional Disturbance" Formulation.** In what ways does the "extreme emotional disturbance" formulation broaden the base of psychiatric testimony that can be considered for the purpose of reducing an offense from murder to manslaughter? If a defendant is not insane within the applicable definition used by a given jurisdiction for that defense, is it nonetheless desirable that evidence of mental abnormality be considered as a grading factor to distinguish murder from manslaughter? Did the court so use such evidence in *Casassa*? Should it have? Do those states that use the Model Penal Code approach now have a diminished responsibility basis for reducing murder to manslaughter analogous to the English concept discussed above? How is the Model Code formula different from the English concept? Which is the better approach?

**5. Burden of Persuasion.** New York places the burden of persuasion on the defendant to prove "extreme emotional disturbance" by a preponderance of the evidence. As a matter of legislative policy,[e] on whom should the burden be placed on this issue? What factors should be taken into account in resolving this question?

------

# United States v. Robertson

United States Court of Military Appeals, 1993.
37 M.J. 432.

■ Wiss, Judge. After a contested trial, a general court-martial of officer and enlisted members convicted appellant of involuntary manslaughter.... The members sentenced appellant to a bad-conduct discharge, confinement for 1 year, and reduction to the lowest enlisted grade....

------

[e] Constitutional questions posed by placing the burden of persuasion on this issue on the defendant are postponed to Chapter IX. For now it should be assumed, as the United States Supreme Court held in *Patterson v. New York*, that the Constitution permits this issue to be resolved as a matter of legislative policy.

On appeal, the Court of Military Review concluded that "there is insufficient evidence to support a finding of culpable negligence, and thus the manslaughter conviction cannot stand." In the court's view, however, the evidence was both legally and factually sufficient "to support a finding of negligent homicide." Accordingly, the court affirmed only a finding of negligent homicide and, on reassessment of the sentence "on the basis of the errors noted and the entire record," a sentence extending only to reduction to the grade of E–5.

On appellant's petition, this Court agreed to review: "Whether the Army court erred in finding the evidence to be sufficient as a matter of law to support a finding of guilty to negligent homicide...." On further consideration of the decision below, we agree with one prong of appellant's multi-faceted attack within this issue: We hold that the evidence of appellant's negligence—even the simple negligence that is in issue in negligent homicide—is insufficient as a matter of law to support the finding affirmed below.

I

The opinion of the Court of Military Review told the truly sad story of the anorexic/bulimic mission that appellant's son Brad set for himself and the tragic, fatal consequences. Added to this human tragedy for appellant was his own court-martial for alleged negligence in letting his son pursue his suicidal course....

II.A

[Brad lived with his mother after his parents divorced] in 1981, and appellant had not seen his son since then until he visited Brad at his home in Kansas during Christmas of 1987. Their relationship renewed, Brad visited his father in New Jersey during spring break in 1988.

At the time he arrived in New Jersey in early April, Brad was well along on his journey toward self-destruction.... Brad began this pattern of abuse when he discovered during a virus that he had contracted in the fall of 1986 that, if he vomited and did not eat, he would lose weight—a noteworthy discovery to Brad, who had been "quite chunky" at "one point in his life." Before he came into appellant's care in April 1988, Brad already had been hospitalized once for a week in connection with his difficulty in eating and his weight loss, [and he made numerous visits to a medical doctor and a psychiatrist, neither of whom diagnosed anorexia in part because Brad's mother did not tell them about Brad's weight loss and hospitalization.]

[Moreover,] "appellant received essentially no information from Brad's mother at the time of the boy's arrival to alert him to Brad's previous weight loss and erratic eating habits." Appellant's wife testified [that Brad's mother told her only that Brad's stomach was "iffy" because he had a "stomach virus."]

Appellant and his wife noticed, on Brad's arrival, that Brad looked thin. Over the next couple of weeks, Brad seemed mostly to pick at his food rather than to eat much of it. On April 17, Brad complained of dizziness, so appellant took him to the hospital emergency room, where Brad was examined and referred to the pediatric clinic.

On April 20, appellant and Brad saw Dr. (Lieutenant Colonel) Grace Nadhiry at the clinic.... Dr. Nadhiry weighed Brad during her examination, finding that he then weighed 122 pounds; she plotted this weight on a weight chart for boys of Brad's age and found that he was at the 50th percentile. She did notice that his weight on that occasion was less than the 125 pounds that had been recorded as his weight in the emergency room 3 days earlier. When asked, however, whether that weight loss had caused her "any concern," she answered, "Not from the appearance that Brad had. Brad clinically looked perfectly in good health."

Dr. Nadhiry talked to both Brad and appellant about anorexia and the problems associated with it. She talked to Brad in a way intended to elicit his confidence and friendship and asked to have his records from Kansas brought to her. Because the word "psychiatrist really scares most children from Brad's stage and with his type of attitude, which was unfriendly," Dr. Nadhiry "talked to him about a psychologist and counseling." Brad responded that "he didn't need that." ...

Over the next 3 weeks, appellant noticed that Brad still was not eating much, which he believed to be atypical for a 15-year-old. That factor, plus Dr. Nadhiry's advice that she should see him again in 3 to 4 weeks, led appellant to decide that [he should take Brad for a follow-up meeting with Dr. Nadhiry. However, Brad resisted the suggestion; indeed, appellant stated that he thought Brad was going to punch him when he heard about the plan to visit Dr. Nadhiry.]

[A]ppellant decided that physically forcing Brad to return [to the clinic] would be counterproductive.... Brad had told him in conversations about the "stress and turmoil" in the family situation in Kansas, and appellant believed that it was important for Brad to feel comfortable and accepted by appellant. Accordingly, appellant decided on a more "low-keyed" approach of trying to persuade Brad to be more receptive to medical attention (like he had been earlier to eye and dental exams). [Appellant testified that he believed this strategy was working. Brad was scheduled to return to Kansas for a family party, and, about 10 days before his trip, he phoned his mother and asked her to make an appointment with his doctor.]

Throughout the approximately 3 months that Brad spent with appellant and his wife, Brad had followed a pattern of conscious deceit concerning his eating and his weight. For instance, Brad always wore very loose clothes ...; and, since he was almost 15 years old, neither appellant nor his wife ever saw him undressed. Moreover, Brad was an excellent cook, and typically appellant and his wife would arrive home from work about 7:00 p.m. and find that Brad had dinner waiting for them. When they would ask why he was not eating too, he would answer that he had eaten while cooking....

Appellant put Brad on an airplane back to Kansas on July 27, and Brad had an appointment with the doctor the next day. His mother picked him up at the airport, took him home at Brad's insistence even though he looked "[h]ideous," unsuccessfully tried to get him to eat something, and finally let him go to bed. Brad's mother called a doctor that night and was told she could bring him in when the office opened the next morning. She found Brad dead in his bed at 7:00 a.m. The conclusion of the subsequent autopsy was death caused by "cardiac failure due to starvation."

Although a number of witnesses, both expert and lay, testified on both sides on the merits, the only expert witness who addressed actions and reactions of parents of an anorexic or bulimic child was Dr. Neal Satin, a psychiatrist with expertise in eating disorders.... In response to questions asking how parents of anorexic/bulimic children respond and concerning, specifically, appellant's responses [to Brad, Dr. Satin testified:]

> I think that invariably with families, they're no villains, they're only victims. Parents do the best that they can. They often do things that I wouldn't do as an expert, but they try to do what they can to get the individuals either to seek treatment, to eat, to change their behavior, and they are almost invariably unsuccessful.... And so I don't think that in these instances, parents can do anything right or wrong because there isn't a clear answer of what is right or wrong. I think that the best that parents can do is attempt to get the children to accept treatment and to hope that the people that are training are sufficiently competent and have enough expertise in the field that they can raise the likelihood of success a slight higher percentage....

## II.B

[I]n the face of a challenge to the legal sufficiency of the evidence, this Court's charge is to answer "whether, considering the evidence in the light most favorable to the prosecution, a reasonable factfinder could have found all the essential elements beyond a reasonable doubt."

One of the elements of negligent homicide, of course, is simple negligence. See para. 85b(4), Part IV, Manual, supra. Paragraph 85c(2) defines simple negligence for purposes of this crime as follows:

> Simple negligence is the absence of due care, that is, an act or omission of a person who is under a duty to use due care which exhibits a lack of that degree of care of the safety of others which a reasonably careful person would have exercised under the same or similar circumstances.

At the risk of over-simplification, appellant's approach to getting his son the continued medical treatment that appellant ultimately recognized was needed was to persuade his nearly 15–year-old, strong-minded son, who had demonstrated a willingness to physically fight appellant's effort to get him to a doctor. Some parents ... might have pursued more authoritative action, just like some parents are more authoritative than others with their children on virtually all aspects of their upbringing.

[U]rging that negligence cannot be judged by hindsight or by the ultimate result, in essence appellant asks: If the boy's death were unknown (in order to preclude any subconscious impact), does the evidence establish beyond reasonable doubt that his approach was a negligent one? Stated in terms of paragraph 85c(2), did appellant's approach to parenting exhibit a lack of that degree of care for his son which a reasonably prudent parent would have exercised under the same or similar circumstances?

Measured against this standard, we conclude that the evidence is such that a reasonable factfinder could not find beyond a reasonable doubt that appellant's approach to caring for his son was negligent. The uncontroverted evidence demonstrates the following: Appellant had no knowledge of Brad's past medical difficulties relating to eating disorders or weight loss, except for being told Brad had an "iffy" stomach; Brad consciously and creatively concealed both the severity of his weight loss and his non-eating; even when appellant did become aware of these related symptoms, he did not fully appreciate their magnitude because of Brad's determined effort to hide them; and when Brad did exhibit a medical difficulty—dizziness— appellant promptly obtained medical attention for him.

Thereafter, he followed Dr. Nadhiry's advice and closely watched his son, tried to get him to eat, and asked his wife and friends of the family to assist him to persuade his son to eat; when it appeared 3 to 4 weeks later that it was not working, he set out to call Dr. Nadhiry, prompting a physical confrontation with his son who adamantly refused to return to her. Rather than fight his 15–year-old son who was physically and emotionally determined to resist, appellant set out to watch him closely and to persistently try to persuade his son that he needed medical help; indeed, appellant ultimately did exactly that, and his son called his mother to ask her to make an appointment with a doctor back home whom he had seen before.

In light of Dr. Satin's testimony, we are at a loss how reasonable factfinders could find appellant's course of caring for his son to be criminally at odds with what "a reasonably careful" parent would have done under the same or similar circumstances. Absence of negligence does not require that judgment [to be] right, only that it reflect what a reasonably careful person would do. Brad died—and that truly is tragic. But that regrettable result does not necessarily mean that appellant was not reasonably careful. Indeed, Dr. Satin's testimony makes it clear that it does not necessarily mean even that appellant's actions were "wrong."

III

The decision of the United States Army Court of Military Review is reversed. The findings and sentence are set aside. The charge is dismissed.

■ GIERKE, JUDGE, concurring. I agree with the principal opinion. I write separately only to articulate an additional rationale that led me to the conclusion that the evidence in this case is legally insufficient to support appellant's conviction.

Appellant's negligence was based on the allegation that he failed "to provide proper medical and/or psychiatric care" for his son ..., such "failure" being the "proximate cause of" his son's death. The Government's theory was that appellant did not do the "right" thing which, in essence, would have required appellant to physically force his recalcitrant son to go to the hospital at some time prior to his son's death. During her final argument, trial counsel told the members:

> And ask yourselves, if this was your son, if he had gone from healthy to this, 40 pounds less in 3 months, what would you do? Would you let your son say, "I don't want to go to the doctor?" I think what you'd do is tie him up and put him in the car and take him to the hospital and have him admitted. But even if you wouldn't even go that far, you'd go to a doctor. You'd get some care for him.[1]

On appeal, the Government still contends that forced hospitalization would have saved appellant's son's life (or, at least, prolonged it temporarily), and implies that anything short of enlisting the assistance of health-care professionals should be considered negligence under the circumstances.

[T]he question is whether there was any evidence to prove that a reasonable person in appellant's position would have recognized that at some time prior to his son's scheduled appointment, the need for immediate medical intervention made forced hospitalization the only rational option. The evidence is uncontradicted that appellant attempted to persuade his son to seek medical help and was ultimately successful in convincing his son to have his mother schedule an appointment with a doctor in Kansas. More significantly, however, I believe that the evidence fails to establish that a reasonable person in appellant's position would have known, prior to appellant's son's death, that immediate medical intervention was necessary. Accordingly, I concur that the evidence is legally insufficient to support appellant's conviction.

A parent's legal duty to provide medical assistance for his or her children is based upon the "inherent dependency of a child upon his parent to obtain medical aid, i.e., the incapacity of a child to evaluate his condition and summon aid by himself, supports imposition of such a duty upon the

---

[1] As a general rule, it is improper for counsel to identify the "reasonable person" with members of the very jury which is to apply the reasonable person standard. Although there was no objection, trial counsel's suggestion that the members ask themselves what they would do with their own son advocated an incorrect legal standard. Cf. United States v. Shamberger, 1 MJ 377, 379 (CMA 1976) (asking members to place themselves in position of victim's relative invites them to improperly judge issue from a personal rather than objective perspective). Appellant's decision to persuade rather than force his son to receive medical treatment may have been based in part on the unique circumstances facing him as the new guardian of a headstrong teenager whom he previously had not even seen for 7 years.

parent." Commonwealth v. Konz, 498 Pa. 639 (1982). Thus, when a parent knows or should know that his or her child needs immediate medical intervention, failure to act within a reasonable time to seek such aid may be a breach of that duty. Cf. Bergmann v. State, 486 N.E.2d 653 (Ind.App. 4 Dist.1985) (affirming reckless homicide conviction of parents who "treated" 9–month-old daughter who died of bacterial meningitis with prayers and fasting instead of seeking medical care).

On the other hand, consideration must be given to alternative courses of conduct available to a parent. "Parents are vested with a reasonable discretion in regard to when medical attention is needed for their children." It follows then that, absent evidence that a reasonable person would recognize the need for immediate medical intervention, the decision to persuade rather than use force or trickery to get a reluctant adolescent to receive medical care is also within a parent's discretion.

A conviction of negligent homicide requires proof that death resulted from the simple negligence of the accused. Proof of simple negligence requires a showing that the accused failed to use "that degree of care [for] the safety of others which a reasonably careful person would have exercised under the same or similar circumstances." Such a person "is not necessarily a supercautious individual devoid of human frailties." As the late Chief Justice Holmes once noted, a choice "may be mistaken and yet prudent." . . .

Appellant cannot be held criminally responsible for knowledge of medical risks which are neither readily apparent nor known to him. Cf. Fabritz v. Traurig, 583 F.2d 697, 698 (4th Cir.1978) (child-abuse conviction vacated where record lacked evidence indicating that mother had knowledge of fatal nature of 3–year-old daughter's condition when she deferred seeking professional medical care for her). The mere fact that Dr. Nadhiry discussed the "problems" associated with a disease that she did not diagnose appellant's son as having is hardly sufficient evidence to place appellant on notice of the future seriousness of his son's need for medical care.

No evidence established that, at any time during his stay with appellant, appellant's son's illness rendered him helpless and unable to summon aid by himself. Appellant's son suffered from an unusual, long-term psychiatric eating disorder in which receptiveness to treatment was important for its cure. He resisted treatment while continuing to stay active. He attended school and performed routine activities that included mowing a friend's lawn just 2 days before he left appellant.

While likely to become noticeable over a significant period of time, the steady weight loss of appellant's son would be almost imperceptible on a daily basis, especially where the uncontradicted evidence indicates that his son attempted to hide his weight loss and deceive appellant about his eating habits. To say that appellant was negligent for failing to force his son to get medical care sooner than his scheduled appointment based on his son's physical condition at the time of his death begs the question of how much sooner: after his son initially refused to get a follow-up examination?;

after his son lost 20 more pounds?; 30 pounds?; 35½ pounds? The negligence of an individual's conduct (or lack of it) must be determined "in the light of the possibilities apparent to him at the time, and not by looking backward 'with the wisdom born of the event.'" Once appellant was aware his son had an appointment to see a doctor upon his son's return to Kansas, he had no apparent reason to force his son to seek medical treatment in New Jersey ahead of his scheduled appointment.[3] To be sure, there was nothing magic about the fact that his son died of cardiac failure at the weight of 80 pounds. Uncontradicted evidence in the record indicated that, while anorexics may die suddenly after extreme weight loss, they may also live at much lower body weights than Brad's without complication....

■ COX, JUDGE, with whom JUDGE CRAWFORD joins, dissenting. Viewing the evidence in the light most favorable to the prosecution, which is the appropriate mode for reviewing the legal sufficiency of evidence, there can be no serious question that the evidence of appellant's negligence is sufficient to sustain his conviction. The obvious reason for our viewing evidence in the light most favorable to the prosecution is that the defense evidence, for one reason or another, did not sway the factfinder.... The question then is whether the prosecution presented enough evidence such that "any rational trier of fact could have found the essential elements of the crime beyond a reasonable doubt." The logical place to look, therefore, is the prosecution's evidence....

The record does not reveal how much appellant knew, prior to Brad's moving to New Jersey, about his physical and mental condition. [Brad's mother testified that, at the time Brad moved to New Jersey, he weighed between 135 and 140 pounds.] However, there is evidence that appellant was specifically made aware of the general nature of the situation shortly after Brad's arrival. This came about because, on April 17, 1988—2½ to 3½ weeks after his arrival, Brad paid a visit to an emergency room at Fort Dix, due to dizziness and difficulty breathing. By that time, his weight had dropped to 125 pounds.

Three days later, on April 20, he was seen on a follow-up basis by Dr. Grace Nadhiry, a pediatrician at Fort Dix. By this time, Brad's weight had dropped to 122 pounds.... Dr. Nadhiry [testified that she discussed anorexia with Brad and appellant. She made appellant "aware of the problems that could come up," and she asked him to make a follow-up appointment for Brad.]

The April 20 visit with Dr. Nadhiry was Brad's last contact with a doctor until his death—just over 3 months later—when Brad's weight had dropped to about 80 pounds! Despite the multitude of medical, psychological, psychiatric, and social resources available without cost to servicemembers and their dependents by merely picking up a telephone, there is

---

[3] Even the mother of appellant's son admitted that, although she was shocked by her son's condition when she had picked him up at the airport in Kansas and moved up his appointment by several hours, she did not immediately force her son to go to the hospital before taking him to her house because she "didn't honestly believe that he was going to die."

no evidence that appellant ever took any meaningful action during that interval to enlist the assistance of any health care or social professional or agency. Indeed there is no indication that appellant ever so much as notified any person in a position of public trust or authority, or any agency, that he was having a problem with his son! This wholesale failure to seek professional assistance—particularly if normal parental suasion was not working—is the precise theory of negligence upon which appellant was prosecuted and convicted.

Brad flew back to Kansas on July 27, 1988, and was found dead in bed by his mother on the morning of July 28, 1988. An autopsy was conducted July 29, and the pathologist, Dr. (Colonel) Mani Bala, determined the cause of death to be "emaciation and cachexia due to starvation, cardiac failure due to starvation." . . . Dr. Bala described Brad's appearance as

> just like wasted away to the point you can see the bones on the body. It's like—almost like having skin shot on a skeleton. That's what cachexia means, wasted down to the bones. . . . [T]he muscles were all wasted down to the bones. The pictures will tell you all the details,[3] but he was really burned down or cachectic to the point it's almost like a mummy dug out of [the] grave and—

Asked, "If an individual weighed 122 pounds and dropped to 80 within about three and a half months, would that weight loss be noticeable?," Dr. Bala responded, "You bet, absolutely."

Such was the strapping lad appellant feared would "punch . . . [his] running lights out" if appellant sought medical attention. Dr. Bala was confident that, had Brad received medical attention as little as 24 hours before his death, he would have survived.

Dr. Bala's description of Brad's appearance was corroborated by other witnesses. Brad's mother [testified that, when she first saw him at the airport, he was hideous.] "He looked like a walking skeleton." . . . The safety pins he used to hold up his pants caused "sores on his side" that had to be covered by band-aids. . . .

A teacher at Sylvan Learning Center in New Jersey, where Brad received approximately 24 hours of coaching between May and July, 1988, also noted his deterioration. By late July, the teacher described him as being

> very, very thin. I mean his skin was white. You could almost—it's almost like you could see through it. And he had cuts—little cuts down his arm and he was very weak. He had trouble making it through the last hour that I taught with him and he complained that he was perspiring and thirsty.

---

[3] Defense counsel objected to admission of the pictures on the ground that "a couple of the photographs . . . looked like they are straight from Dachau." Indeed, these postmortem photographs, a number of which were received in evidence, are virtually sufficient in and of themselves to overcome a legal sufficiency challenge. They portray a young man who is a virtual skeleton—nothing but skin and bones.

He had to stop the session because "he said he was getting dizzy spells and he was perspiring and he just couldn't concentrate."

Appellant gave the Learning Center director the impression that Brad had recently been released from the hospital and that everything that could be done for Brad was being done. The director "probed a little bit to find out what the illness had been, [but] there was resistance to sharing it with me and so ... [she] respected their privacy." The general supposition at the Center was that Brad had either "AIDS or cancer." ...

[L]ooking only to the prosecution's evidence, I am satisfied it was more than sufficient to sustain the findings of guilty. As I view the prosecution's evidence, the legal adequacy of the evidence of neglect and proximate cause, inter alia, are beyond dispute.

---

## NOTES ON INVOLUNTARY MANSLAUGHTER

**1.   The Degree of Culpability Sufficient for Involuntary Manslaughter**. The common law defined involuntary manslaughter as a killing caused by reckless or negligent conduct that was insufficiently blameworthy to constitute murder but more culpable than ordinary civil negligence. Thus, for purposes of isolating involuntary manslaughter as a distinct degree of homicide, the doctrinal task has been to identify a species of killings that (1) are *less* reckless than those manifesting the "depraved indifference to human life" required for a second-degree murder conviction and (2) are *more* negligent than those required for tort, as opposed to criminal, liability. As the *Roe* case and the note materials on second-degree murder explain, the common law courts tended to fall back on epithets and hyperbole when forced to articulate the difference between depraved-indifference murder and involuntary manslaughter. Thus, according to *Roe*, "[w]hether the lesser risk [of death] sufficient for manslaughter is elevated into the very substantial risk present in murder depends on the wantonness of defendant's acts—i.e., whether they were committed '[under] circumstances evincing a depraved indifference to human life.'"

When it came time to describe the difference between the ordinary negligence sufficient for tort liability and that degree of negligence that will support a conviction for involuntary manslaughter, the common law courts tended to be no more precise. Most agree that it takes "more" negligence than will suffice for an ordinary tort, but there is surprisingly little attention in common-law cases to how that additional ingredient can be formulated in a way that effectively communicates to juries the judgment to be made. Is it likely that a jury would understand the standard the court means to be applying?

**(i)** ***Commonwealth v. Sostilio.*** In Commonwealth v. Sostilio, 325 Mass. 143, 89 N.E.2d 510 (1949), the court said:

The question in this case is whether there is evidence of wanton or reckless conduct on the part of the defendant. Wanton or reckless conduct has been defined as "intentional conduct, by way either of commission or omission where there is a duty to act, which conduct involves a high degree of likelihood that substantial harm will result to another." Wanton or reckless conduct is the legal equivalent of intentional conduct. If by wanton or reckless conduct bodily injury is caused to another, the person guilty of such conduct is guilty of assault and battery. And since manslaughter is simply a battery that causes death, if death results he is guilty of manslaughter.

The court applied this standard to uphold the manslaughter conviction of a driver of midget race-cars who killed another competitor by causing a crash while trying to pass by fitting his four-foot car into a two-foot space.

(ii) *Commonwealth v. Agnew.* Contrast Commonwealth v. Agnew, 263 Pa.Super. 424, 398 A.2d 209 (1979). The defendant was a farmer who was driving his tractor home after disking a field. It was close to midnight and the road, a two-lane highway bounded by guard rails, was unlighted. The road was 33 feet wide from guard rail to guard rail, and the disk the farmer was towing behind his tractor was 17 feet, four inches wide. No lights were placed on the disk. An oncoming car traveling at about 55 miles per hour saw the tractor but not the disk, never slowed down, and hit the disk. The driver and his passenger were killed. The policeman who came to the scene testified that he was unable to see the disk, even with the aid of headlights, until he came to within 30 or 40 feet of the tractor.

The court reversed a conviction of involuntary manslaughter. It reasoned as follows:

The state of mind or mens rea which characterizes involuntary manslaughter is recklessness or gross negligence: a great departure from the standard of ordinary care evidencing a disregard for human life or an indifference to the possible consequences of the actor's conduct. . . .

We feel that the facts in the instant case ... fail to show Agnew's indifference to the possible consequences of his actions. While the evidence shows that Agnew committed two summary offenses under the Motor Vehicle Code[a] which were substantial factors in bringing about the accident, this in itself is not sufficient to sustain a charge of involuntary manslaughter. However, the commonwealth argues that since Agnew drove his tractor at night knowing that the unlighted extremities of the towed disk would encroach upon the oncoming lane, the requisite mens rea was present. However, what must be shown is *disregard* for human life, and an *indifference* to consequences. Here the record shows that Agnew was quite aware of the risk he created and took positive steps to reduce the risk. He placed flashing yellow lights

[a] He violated prohibitions limiting the maximum width of farm equipment on a highway and requiring that one-half of the roadway be yielded to an oncoming vehicle.— [Footnote by eds.]

on the top of the tractor cab, placed warning signs on the tractor disk, and proceeded at a slow rate of speed. Obviously, as the opinion of the lower court concludes, "[t]he precautions were tragically inadequate." Still, the fact that Agnew took these precautions negates the requisite *disregard* of human life. Additionally, when Agnew perceived the oncoming car, he took every possible step to avoid a collision, pulling his tractor over to the right so far as the guard rails would allow . . ., and slowing his tractor down to a stop. This is not indifference to potential consequences, but a conscientious attempt to reduce the risk of an accident. Unhappily, the [driver of the] oncoming car never saw the towed disk in his lane and drove into it at full speed. While a jury could find Agnew guilty of ordinary negligence and impose civil liability on him, we assume, his actions disprove the "disregard of human life and indifference to consequences" mens rea necessary to support the criminal charge of involuntary manslaughter.

**2.  The Degree of Culpability Sufficient for Manslaughter and Negligent Homicide Under the Model Code.** The Model Penal Code divides the former common law offense of involuntary manslaughter into two offenses. Section 210.3 punishes a homicide as manslaughter if "recklessly" committed and § 210.4 punishes a homicide as negligent homicide if "negligently" committed. Many American jurisdictions have followed this approach, both before and after the Model Penal Code was drafted. It is thus not uncommon, as *Robertson* illustrates, for the law of a particular jurisdiction to reflect three grades or levels of criminal homicide based on blameworthy inadvertence: an extreme recklessness that will justify a conviction of some form of murder, a type of recklessness or negligence that will justify a conviction of manslaughter, and a degree of negligence that will warrant a conviction of negligent homicide. What is unique about the Model Penal Code, therefore, is the care with which it attempts to define the concepts of "recklessness" and "negligence" that will suffice.

Is the Model Penal Code approach an improvement over the common law? Are the grading distinctions intelligible? Desirable?

**3.  Questions and Comments on *Robertson*.** Unlike *Roe*, which explores the distinction between depraved-indifference murder and involuntary manslaughter, *Robertson* addresses the distinction between involuntary manslaughter and negligent homicide, and, indeed, the ultimate distinction between criminal liability and (potential) tort liability. Robertson was prosecuted for involuntary manslaughter in connection with Brad's death, which required the government to prove that his behavior "amounted to culpable negligence." The Military Judge's Benchbook offers the following definition of "culpable negligence" to be used when instructing the jury on the elements of involuntary manslaughter:

> Culpable negligence is a degree of carelessness greater than simple negligence. Simple negligence is the absence of due care. The law requires everyone at all times to demonstrate the care for the safety of others that a reasonably careful person would demonstrate under the same or similar circumstances; this is what "due

care" means. Culpable negligence is a negligent act or failure to act accompanied by a gross, reckless, wanton or deliberate disregard for the foreseeable results to others.

Presumably, the judge who presided over Robertson's trial gave a version of this instruction to the members of the court-martial, and they found Robertson guilty. On appeal, the Court of Military Review reduced the conviction from involuntary manslaughter to negligent homicide. In the opinion reproduced above, the Court of Military Appeals reversed again, finding that the evidence was insufficient to support even the finding of "simple negligence" required for conviction of negligent homicide Which body of decisionmakers—the members of the court-martial, the judges on the Court of Military Review, the majority on the Court of Military Appeals—got it right? Was either of the courts of appeal justified in rejecting as insufficient the evidence of Robertson's guilt—either of involuntary manslaughter, as the members of the court-martial found, or of negligent homicide, as the Court of Military Review found? In most jurisdictions, there is a crucial distinction between criminal negligence and tort negligence. The standard that justifies civil recovery of damages is not an adequate basis, the argument would go, for the imposition of a criminal sanction. Did the Court of Military Appeals keep this straight?

In connection with *Robertson*, it is useful to revisit the doctrinal analysis applied in cases where criminal liability is sought to be imposed on the basis of an "omission" rather than an "affirmative act." Presumably, each of the judges on the Court of Military Appeals agreed that Robertson owed a duty of care to Brad, which extended to providing him with medical attention in an emergency. However, it is possible that the judges did not agree on the precise scope of that duty and that this disagreement in part explains their disagreement over the ultimate question of criminal liability. In his concurring opinion, Judge Gierke implies that Robertson had a duty to obtain medical assistance for Brad only when Brad's "illness rendered him helpless and unable to summon aid by himself." Is that a correct statement of the duties that parents owe to their children? To infants? To teenagers? Does the duty of care analysis differ in cases involving failure to assist a person who is suffering from a mental, as opposed to physical, illness or condition?

Might the outcome of the case have been different if Robertson had been Brad's mother rather than his father? If Brad had been a girl instead of a boy? Should these differences matter?

## SECTION 3: CAUSATION

## State v. Pelham

Supreme Court of New Jersey, 2003.
824 A.2d 1082.

■ LaVECCHIA, JUSTICE. This criminal appeal focuses on a disputed jury instruction involving the subject of causation. Defendant was convicted of second-degree death by auto. At trial, the court instructed the jury that a car-accident victim's voluntary removal from a respirator was legally insufficient as an independent intervening cause and thus incapable of breaking the chain of causality between defendant's acts and the victim's death.... The Appellate Division reversed and remanded for a new trial because, in its view, "the charge to the jury on intervening cause deprived defendant of his constitutional right to have the jury in a criminal trial ... decide all elements of the charged offense." We reverse.

It is beyond dispute that individuals have the right to self-determination in respect of medical care generally and, specifically, in respect of rejecting or removing life support devices or techniques. We conclude that the jury may be instructed, as a matter of law, that a victim's determination to be removed from life support is a foreseeable event that does not remove or lessen criminal responsibility for death.

I.

The facts of the horrific car accident in which defendant, Sonney Pelham, was involved are summarized from the trial record. On the evening of December 29, 1995, William Patrick, a sixty-six-year-old lawyer, was driving his Chrysler LeBaron in the right lane of northbound Route 1 in South Brunswick. At approximately 11:42 p.m., a 1993 Toyota Camry driven by defendant struck the LeBaron from behind. The LeBaron sailed over the curb and slid along the guardrail, crashing into a utility pole before it ultimately came to rest 152 feet from the site of impact. The Camry traveled over a curb and came to rest in a grassy area on the side of the highway.

Two nearby police officers heard the collision and rushed to the scene. The officers found Patrick, still wearing his seatbelt, unconscious and slumped forward in the driver's seat. The rear of the LeBaron was crumpled through to the rear tire and the backseat, and the convertible top was crushed. Patrick was making "gurgling" and "wheezing" sounds, and appeared to have difficulty breathing. His passenger, Jocelyn Bobin, was semi-conscious. Emergency crews extricated the two using the "jaws of life" and transported them to [a hospital]. Bobin was treated and later released.

At the accident scene, Officer Heistand smelled an odor of alcohol on defendant's breath, and noted that he was swaying from side to side and front to back. He had no injuries, but was "belligerent." Heistand believed defendant was intoxicated.... Defendant failed [three field sobriety tests. Experts later estimated that his blood alcohol content was] between .19 and .22 at the time of the accident.

Patrick's condition was critical on his arrival at [the hospital]. He had suffered a constellation of injuries, including a spinal column fracture that left him paralyzed from the chest down and a "flailed chest," a condition in which the ribs are broken in multiple places causing uneven chest wall movement during each breath.... The catastrophic injuries Patrick experienced made it virtually impossible for him to breathe on his own.... He was placed on a ventilator. Within five days of the accident, [Patrick's lungs began] to fail. His heart beat was rapid and irregular, and his blood pressure was dropping because of the turmoil within his body. Low blood pressure triggered the start of kidney failure.

Patrick's paralysis rendered him at an increased risk for pulmonary thromboemboli, or blood clots. Accordingly, doctors implanted a vena cava filter through the major vein in the groin area and into the major blood vessel to the heart. The filters were intended to trap clots that form in the lower extremities. A ventilator tube inserted through Patrick's throat was converted to a surgical airway through his neck and into his windpipe. Because Patrick was unable to feed himself, he was fed initially by a tube inserted through his nose to the stomach, and later by a tube directly into the stomach. In addition, because paralysis left him unable to control his bladder or bowels, a Foley catheter was inserted. . . .

On March 13, 1996, Patrick was transferred to [a hospital that] specialized in the care of patients with spinal cord injuries. When he arrived, Patrick was unable to breathe on his own, and was suffering from multi-organ system failure. Medication was required to stabilize his heart rhythm. He was extremely weak, with blood-protein levels that placed him at high risk of death. He was unable to clear secretions in his airways, and thus his oxygen levels would drop requiring medical personnel repeatedly to clear the secretions. Complications from the ventilator caused pneumonia to recur due to his inability to cough or to protect himself from bacteria. Bowel and urinary tract infections continued.

. . . Patrick also was monitored by psychiatric staff. He presented as depressed, confused, uncooperative, and not engaged psychologically. At times he was "hallucinating," even "psychotic." The staff determined that he was "significantly" brain injured. Nonetheless, Patrick was aware of his physical and cognitive disabilities. During lucid moments, he expressed his unhappiness with his situation, and, on occasion, tried to remove his ventilator.

Patrick improved somewhat during the month of April, but then his condition rapidly regressed. By early May, severe infections returned, as well as pneumonia. It was undisputed at trial that Patrick had expressed to his family a preference not to be kept alive on life support. Because of his brain damage, his lack of improvement, and his severe infections Patrick's family decided to act in accordance with his wishes and remove the ventilator. [W]ithin two hours of the ventilator's removal on May 30, 1996, he was pronounced dead. The Deputy Middlesex County Medical Examiner determined that the cause of death was sepsis and bronchopneumonia resulting from multiple injuries from the motor vehicle accident.

Defendant was charged with first-degree aggravated manslaughter. . . .

. . . At trial, [defendant offered no expert testimony] to refute the causal connection between Patrick's death and his accident injuries.

[T]he trial court included in its jury charge on causation an instruction concerning intervening cause and a victim's determination to remove life support. On those points, the trial court instructed the jury as follows:

To establish causation the State must prove two elements beyond a reasonable doubt. First, that but for defendant's conduct William Patrick wouldn't have died. Second, William Patrick's death must have been within the risk of which the defendant was aware. If not it must involve the same kind of injury or harm as the probable result of the defendant's conduct and must also not be too remote, too accidental in its occurrence or too dependant [sic] upon another's volitional act to have a just bearing on the defendant's liability or on the gravity of the offense. In other words, the State must prove beyond a reasonable doubt that William Patrick's death was not so unexpected or unusual that it would be unjust to find the defendant guilty of aggravated manslaughter.

Now, it is alleged that the victim William Patrick died approximately five months after the collision which occurred on December 29, 1995. With regard to the issue of remoteness there is no requirement that the State prove that the victim died immediately or within a certain period of time after the collision. Nevertheless, you may consider the time that elapsed between the collision and Mr. Patrick's death along with all of the other evidence in the case in determining whether the State has proven beyond a reasonable doubt that the defendant caused William Patrick's death as I've defined that term.

The State alleges that William Patrick died as a result of medical complications from the injuries which he sustained in the collision. Subject to the definition of causation which I have already given you the State may satisfy its burden of proving causation by proving beyond a reasonable doubt that William Patrick died from medical complications that resulted from injuries which he sustained in the collision provided that these injuries and medical complications were the precipitating and contributing causes of his death.

With regard to the issue of accident, if you find that Mr. Patrick's death resulted from preexisting medical conditions independent of the injuries and accompanying medical complications which he received as a result of the collision ... then you must find [the defendant] not guilty. If you find that Mr. Patrick died as a result of prior medical conditions being exacerbated or made worse by the collision you are instructed that criminal liability is not lessened because the victim is not in excellent health.

In other words, if you find beyond a reasonable doubt that the defendant's conduct accelerated or worsened any preexisting medical conditions or illness which Mr. Patrick had thereby resulting in his death and meets the other conditions of causation then you should find the defendant caused Mr. Patrick's death.

Let me now instruct you on what an intervening cause is and what it's not. An intervening cause is a cause which breaks the original chain of causation. In that regard you have heard testimony that on May 30, 1996 William Patrick was taken off the ventilator pursuant to his wishes and that he died several hours later. I instruct you that the removal of life supports, in this case a ventilator, is not a sufficient intervening cause to relieve the defendant of criminal liability. In other words, the removal of life supports from Mr. Patrick who is not brain dead was not a sufficient intervening cause to relieve Mr. Pelham from criminal liability.[2]

If you find that the defendant's actions set in motion the victim's need for life support the causal link between the defendant's actions and the victim's death is not broken by the removal or refusal of life support as long as you find that the death was the natural result of the defendant's actions.

The jury acquitted defendant of aggravated manslaughter, but convicted him of the lesser-included offense of second-degree vehicular homicide. He was sentenced to a custodial term of seven years with a mandatory parole ineligibility period of three years. . . .

## II.

New Jersey has been in the forefront of recognizing an individual's right to refuse medical treatment. It is now well settled that competent persons have the right to refuse life-sustaining treatment. Even incompetent persons have the right to refuse life-sustaining treatment through a surrogate decision maker.

The parameters of the right to refuse medical treatment were first addressed in the seminal case In re Quinlan, 70 N.J. 10, 355 A.2d 647, cert. denied sub nom. Garger v. New Jersey, 429 U.S. 922 (1976). We concluded that the right to decide whether to forego life-sustaining treatment was "a valuable incident [to the] right of privacy" afforded by both the New Jersey and United States Constitutions. Any interest the State might have in preservation of life "weakens and the individual's right to privacy grows as the degree of bodily invasion increases and the prognosis dims."

As we explained, because Karen Ann Quinlan's prognosis was "extremely poor," any State-asserted interest in preserving life was out-

---

[2] We do not approve of language in the last two sentences of this paragraph. Nonetheless, reviewing the charge as a whole, we believe that the jury did not misunderstand its obligation to determine the factual question concerning causation in this case, namely, whether Patrick's death resulted from the natural progression of his accident injuries and their complications. To emphasize that the jury must make the causation determination, the court should have added language such as: "Should you make the finding that Mr. Patrick died from medical complications that resulted from injuries he sustained in the collision. . . ." . . .

weighed by her right to self-determination. The "bodily invasion" involved in her care was extensive, including constant nursing care, antibiotics, a catheter, a respirator, and a feeding tube. We held that the only practical way to protect Ms. Quinlan's right to refuse treatment when she was incompetent was to permit her guardian to determine whether Ms. Quinlan would have refused life-sustaining treatment. Cognizant of the liability risk attendant when physicians carry out such wishes, we also made clear that a doctor's termination of treatment, and consequent acceleration of death, is not homicide. Since the 1976 decision in *Quinlan*, numerous other courts, including the United States Supreme Court, have recognized the so-called "right to die." See Cruzan v. Director, Missouri Dept. of Health, 497 U.S. 261 (1990) (recognizing that competent person has Fourteenth Amendment liberty interest in refusing unwanted medical treatment).

[In cases following *Quinlan*, we] observed that the right of self-determination is tempered by the State's countervailing interests, including: (1) preservation of life; (2) prevention of suicide; (3) protection of innocent third parties; and (4) safeguarding the integrity of the medical profession. However, those state interests usually will not preclude a competent person from refusing treatment for himself or herself. As we explained,

> refusing medical intervention merely allows the disease to take its natural course; if death were eventually to occur, it would be the result, primarily, of the underlying disease, and not the result of a self-inflicted injury. . . .

[T]he public policy of this State, as developed by case law and through legislative enactment,[a] clearly recognizes that an individual has the right to refuse devices or techniques for sustaining life, including the withholding of food and the removal of life support. We turn then to examine the effect to be given to a victim's exercise of that right in the context of a homicide trial.

### III.A.

Defendant was charged with aggravated manslaughter, which, according to the New Jersey Code of Criminal Justice (Code), occurs when one "recklessly causes death under circumstances manifesting extreme indifference to human life." The trial court charged the jury on aggravated manslaughter and the lesser-included offense of second-degree vehicular homicide, defined as "criminal homicide . . . caused by driving a vehicle or vessel recklessly." Causation is an essential element of those homicide charges.

The Code defines "causation" as follows:

[a] In 1991, the New Jersey legislature passed a statute that identified procedures for making "living wills," by which people provide "advance directives" concerning their future medical care. The legislative findings included a statement declaring that patients have the right "to accept, to reject, or to choose among alternative courses" of health-care treatment.—[Footnote by eds.]

a.   Conduct is the cause of a result when:

(1) It is an antecedent but for which the result in question would not have occurred; and

(2) The relationship between the conduct and result satisfies any additional causal requirements imposed by the code or by the law defining the offense. . . .

c.   When the offense requires that the defendant recklessly or criminally negligently cause a particular result, the actual result must be within the risk of which the actor is aware or, in the case of criminal negligence, of which he should be aware, or, if not, the actual result must involve the same kind of injury or harm as the probable result and must not be too remote, accidental in its occurrence, or dependent on another's volitional act to have a just bearing on the actor's liability or on the gravity of his offense.

The causation requirement of our Code contains two parts, a "but-for" test under which the defendant's conduct is "deemed a cause of the event if the event would not have occurred without that conduct" and, when applicable, a culpability assessment. Under the culpability assessment, when the actual result is of the same character, but occurred in a different manner from that designed or contemplated [or risked], it is for the jury to determine whether intervening causes or unforeseen conditions lead to the conclusion that it is unjust to find that the defendant's conduct is the cause of the actual result. Although the jury may find that the defendant's conduct was a "but-for" cause of the victim's death . . . it may nevertheless conclude . . . that the death differed in kind from that designed or contemplated [or risked] or that the death was too remote, accidental in its occurrence, or dependent on another's volitional act to justify a murder conviction.

Our Code, like the Model Penal Code (MPC), does not identify what may be an intervening cause. Instead, the Code "deals only with the ultimate criterion by which the significance of such possibilities ought to be judged." Removal of life support, as it relates to causation, should be judged only by the criteria of the Code, assuming that the law recognizes the possibility that removal can be an intervening cause. The dissent . . . suggests that the [Code's] reference to "another's volitional act" supports having the jury determine whether a crime victim's removal from life support constitutes an independent intervening cause. While "another's volitional act" undoubtedly would require a jury to consider whether, for example, a doctor's malpractice in treating a crime victim constituted an intervening cause that had broken the chain of causation after a criminal defendant's act, we do not believe, as the dissent suggests, that the Legislature intended the reference to "another's volitional act" to include a crime victim's decision to be removed from life support.

"Intervening cause" is defined as "an event that comes between the initial event in a sequence and the end result, thereby altering the natural course of events that might have connected a wrongful act to an injury." Generally, to avoid breaking the chain of causation for criminal liability, a variation between the result intended or risked and the actual result of defendant's conduct must not be so out of the ordinary that it is unfair to hold defendant responsible for that result. A defendant may be relieved of criminal liability for a victim's death if an "independent" intervening cause has occurred, meaning "an act of an independent person or entity that destroys the causal connection between the defendant's act and the victim's injury and, thereby becomes the cause of the victim's injury." The question we address, then, is whether the removal of the victim's life support may constitute, as a matter of law, an "independent intervening cause," the significance of which a jury may evaluate as part of a culpability analysis.

B.

The longstanding, clear policy of this State recognizes the constitutional, common-law, and now statutorily based right of an individual to accept, reject, or discontinue medical treatment in the form of life supporting devices or techniques. An ill or injured person has that personal right and is free to exercise it, at his or her discretion, directly or through a family member or guardian acting in accordance with the person's wishes. In other words, a person's choice to have himself or herself removed from life support cannot be viewed as unexpected or extraordinary.

Decisions from other jurisdictions have reasoned similarly and have held that removal of life support is not an independent intervening cause in varied, but related, settings. Courts have confronted whether a victim's removal from life support renders a homicide verdict against the weight of the evidence and have rejected the contention that there was insufficient evidence to support a conviction when the victim expired following his or her removal from life support....

Thus, in People v. Bowles, 461 Mich. 555, 607 N.W.2d 715 (2000), the defendant contended on appeal that the State's evidence on causation was insufficient because "the victim's death was caused by the intervening cause of removal from life support systems that were required to sustain the life of the victim." In its affirmance of the defendant's conviction, the Supreme Court of Michigan observed that "the implementation of a decision to terminate life-support treatment is not the cause of the patient's subsequent death. Instead, the discontinuance of life-support measures merely allows the patient's injury or illness to take its natural and inevitable course." The court concluded that the case involved "no separate intervening cause. Rather, we find in these facts only the unsuccessful efforts of the medical community to overcome the harm inflicted by the defendant, and the acceptance by the victim's family of the reality of the fatal injuries."

Similarly, courts have denied requests by defendants for a jury instruction charging that a victim's removal from life support constitutes an independent intervening cause sufficient to relieve the defendant of criminal liability....

The California Court of Appeals reasoned ... in People v. Funes, 23 Cal. App. 4th 1506, 28 Cal. Rptr. 2d 758 (1994), that the defendant was not entitled to an instruction on intervening causes because "as a matter of law, the decision to withhold antibiotics was not an independent intervening cause. Consequently, the court was not required to instruct on [that] issue." The court noted that a duty exists to instruct on an issue that is supported by the evidence, and conversely, that no such duty arises in respect of an issue unsupported by the evidence. Because an independent intervening cause absolving the defendant from criminal liability must be "unforeseeable" or an "extraordinary and abnormal occurrence," the Court concluded that on the facts of the case before it "the decision to withhold antibiotics was, as a matter of law, not an independent intervening cause. Instead, it was a normal and reasonably foreseeable result of defendant's original [criminal] act." There was no other reasonable inference from the evidence; the removal of life support was determined not to be independent from the defendant's criminal act. . . .

We agree with the widely-recognized principle that removal of life support, as a matter of law, may not constitute an independent intervening cause for purposes of lessening a criminal defendant's liability. Removal of life support in conformity with a victim's expressed wishes is not a legally cognizable cause of death in New Jersey. As aptly put by the District of Columbia Court of Appeals, "the defendant's desire to mitigate his liability may never legally override, in whole, or in part, the decisions of the physicians and the family regarding the treatment of the victim." . . .

Causation is a factual determination for the jury to consider, but the jury may consider only that which the law permits it to consider. The purpose of the charge to the jury is to inform the jury on the law and what the law requires. . . .

Our courts have recognized other circumstances in which a jury is not permitted to consider certain facts. For example, a defendant's criminal liability is not lessened by the existence in the victim of a medical condition that, unbeknownst to the defendant, made the victim particularly vulnerable to attack. The trial court here recognized as much when it correctly instructed the jury to that effect. Similarly, we now hold that a defendant's criminal liability may not be lessened by a victim's subsequent decision to discontinue life support. Therefore, although the trial court must be careful not to suggest that it is directing a verdict on causation, here, the court's instruction viewed in its entirety informed the jury that it could not consider the victim's removal from life support as an intervening cause of his death so long as the death was the natural result of defendant's actions. That is, if defendant's actions set in motion the victim's need for life support, without which death would naturally result, then the causal link is not broken by an unforeseen, extraordinary act when the victim exercises his or her right to be removed from life support and thereupon expires unless there was an intervening volitional act of another, such as gross malpractice by a physician. The trial court's statement was correct as a matter of law and its effect was not the equivalent of directing a verdict when the charge is read as a whole.

. . . In this case, the court did not direct a verdict on causation; rather the jury was instructed on what it could not consider as part of its determination of the causation question. Further, the jury properly was told that it could consider remoteness in respect of the length of time that passed between the date of the accident and the date on which Patrick expired after having been removed from life support (as well as the cause and progression of his medical complications). Thus, the jury could not consider removal as the cause of death when determining causation but it could consider whether the causal link was broken by remoteness in time of death.

IV.

In conclusion, we hold that there was no error in instructing the jury that a victim's decision to invoke his right to terminate life support may not, as a matter of law, be considered an independent intervening cause capable of breaking the chain of causation triggered by defendant's wrongful actions. The judgment of the Appellate Division is reversed and the matter remanded to the trial court for reinstatement of the judgment of conviction.

■ ALBIN, JUSTICE, with whom JUSTICE LONG joins, dissenting. "Hard facts make bad law" is an old saw and an apt description of the resolution of this appeal. In this vehicular homicide case, William Patrick, a sixty-six-year-old lawyer, suffered multiple devastating injuries when his car, which was stopped at a light, was rear-ended by this drunk-driving defendant. The majority opinion describes at length the victim's gruesome injuries, painful hospitalizations, and medical treatment. After the passage of five months during which his condition continued to deteriorate, Patrick, in accordance with his wishes, was taken off a ventilator, and died several hours later. . . .

Proof of causation is an element of every criminal offense and, until today, was no different from other elements that must be submitted to the jury. The New Jersey Code of Criminal Justice (Code) reserves to the jury the ultimate authority to determine whether intervening circumstances break the chain of causation of criminal culpability. In this case, the Code required the jury to determine whether the manner of Patrick's death, which followed from the voluntary removal of life support, was "too remote, accidental in its occurrence, or dependent on another's volitional act to have a just bearing on the actor's liability or on the gravity of his offense." The general and broad language of that provision was intended to apply to the infinite number of variables that arise in the unique circumstances of each new case, including that of this defendant. Causation was a matter that the jury should have been trusted to decide correctly.

Instead, the majority ignores the statutory language that governs this case and imports into the law of causation its own moral and philosophical preferences as it departs from the bedrock principle that a judge cannot direct a verdict against a defendant on an element of an offense, even where evidence of guilt appears overwhelming. The majority has carved from the Code's broad language on causation an inflexible rule that, in all cases, a victim's termination of medical care to support life may never be considered an independent intervening circumstance capable of breaking the chain of causation. The majority has come to that conclusion because it finds that the victim's removal of life-sustaining treatment is always foreseeable.

I object not so much to the wisdom of that new rule of law, as to its failure to find any support in the text of the Code. The Code's drafters left to the jury the commonsense judgment of distinguishing those cases in which intervening circumstances "would have a just bearing on the actor's liability or on the gravity of his offense." Our jurisprudence has traditionally deferred to the jury the delicate and difficult task of deciding the facts on which a defendant's guilt or innocence depends.

The majority's new rule is not only at odds with the Code and the fundamental right of an accused to have the jury decide each element of an offense, but will also have unanticipated consequences as it is reflexively applied to future cases. The jury will no longer be permitted to consider whether the chain of causation is broken in homicide cases where the victim refuses to take antibiotics or other benign medication necessary to sustain life without interfering with the enjoyment of life; where the victim declines a blood transfusion for religious or other reasons; or where the victim decides that he no longer wishes to continue using a medical device, such as a respirator or dialysis machine. The removal of a ventilator or the refusal to take medication or to allow a blood transfusion, all of which may be necessary to sustain life, may or may not, depending on the circumstances, "have a just bearing on the actor's liability or on the gravity of his offense," but the ultimate decision always has been one for the jury.

The application of a general rule, such as the Code's on intervening circumstances, necessarily will lead to varied outcomes, depending on the facts of a particular case. The understanding that two separate juries might decide the same case differently is an acknowledgment of the lack of perfection in our system of justice. That jurors, through their collective experience and humanity, are the conscience of the community is not a weakness, but a strength and the reason why, I suspect, we have not lost faith in the jury as the best means of delivering justice. . . .

[The] patient's right to refuse or terminate life-sustaining medical treatment is . . . not in conflict with a defendant's right to have a jury decide whether he should be held criminally liable for causing the death of a victim who elects to terminate his life. The defendant and prosecutor have no standing to interfere with the patient's decision-making process regarding the course of his medical treatment. It is highly improbable that a crime victim would remain on life support solely for the purpose of assuring that a defendant who victimized him would not be charged with homicide. It is equally improbable that a victim would decline medical intervention for the purpose of assuring a homicide prosecution. . . .

Our causation provision, although not identical to its MPC source, is firmly rooted in MPC § 2.03, and has been construed by this Court accordingly. The premise underlying each code's causation provision is that variations between the actual result of a defendant's conduct and that contemplated, designed, or probable under the circumstances are to be treated as "problems of culpability rather than metaphysical problems of causation." Both codes avoid the vague concept of "proximate cause," and focus on whether a remote result of which a defendant's conduct was a "but-for" cause "bears on the defendant's culpability for the offense."

New Jersey is only one of two states that have adopted MPC § 2.03 and explicitly added the intervening volitional conduct of others as a factor to be considered in determining causation. The inclusion of that factor in cases of human intervention is based on "deeply engrained common sense ideas about causality and responsibility," where the issue "properly turns on the voluntariness of the intervening actor's conduct—to the extent that his intervention is independent and voluntary, the defendant's liability should be diminished." Moreover, only New Jersey has incorporated the term "just" bearing into its causation provision. Despite the American Law Institute's debate on the wisdom of putting "undefined questions of justice to the jury" by including the optional term "just" in its final MPC provision, our Code's drafters, by adopting that term, surely believed its proponents' rationale that its inclusion "had the merit of putting it clearly to the jury that the issue it must decide is whether . . . it would be just to accord" significance to the actual result's remoteness, accidental quality, or dependence on another's volitional act in determining liability.

[The New Jersey causation provisions] "deal explicitly with variations between the actual result and that designed, contemplated or risked." "The actual result is 'to be contrasted with the designed or contemplated []or . . . probable[] result in terms of its specific character and manner of occurrence.'" "Thus, when the actual result occurs in the same manner and is of the same character as the designed or contemplated [or probable] result, the causation requirement is satisfied." On the other hand, if the actual result does not occur in the same manner as the designed, contemplated, or probable result, "'the culpability requirement is not established unless the actual result involved the same kind of injury or harm as that [probable,] designed or contemplated but the precise injury inflicted was different or occurred in a different way.'" Our Code

> makes no attempt to catalogue the possibilities, e.g., to deal with the intervening or concurrent causes, natural or human; unexpected physical conditions; distinctions between the infliction of mortal or non-mortal wounds. It deals only with the ultimate criterion by which the significance of such possibilities ought to be judged, i.e., that the question to be faced is whether the actual result is too accidental in its occurrence or too dependent on another's volitional act to have a just bearing on the actor's liability or on the gravity of his offense.

... In sum, the drafters of our Code clearly contemplated, as previously recognized by this Court, that "when the actual result is of the same character, but occurred in a different manner ..., it is for the jury to determine whether intervening causes or unforeseen conditions lead to the conclusion that it is unjust to find that the defendant's conduct is the cause of the actual result." This is just such a case.

[D]efendant does not dispute that his conduct was a "but-for" cause of the victim's death. Instead, he claims that the State must prove the additional requirement ... that he recklessly caused the actual result, i.e., the victim's death, five months after the accident and two hours after the victim and his family elected to disconnect his ventilator. In order for this defendant to be guilty of vehicular homicide, the State must prove that the specific character and manner of the victim's death was either: (1) within the risk of which defendant was aware; or, (2) if not, then not "too remote, accidental in its occurrence, or dependent on another's volitional act to have a just bearing" on defendant's liability or the gravity of his offense.

The majority holds, in essence, that the risk that a victim will elect to reject or terminate some life-sustaining measure as a result of his injuries is, as a matter of law, within the risk of which defendants are aware. I part with the majority on this point. Whether defendant was aware of the risk was a question for the jury. I do not doubt that under the circumstances of this case, a jury could have found that the manner of Patrick's death was not "too remote, accidental in its occurrence, or dependent on another's volitional act to have a just bearing" on defendant's liability. However, by directing a verdict to the effect that the victim's decision to terminate his life was not a sufficient intervening circumstance to relieve defendant of criminal liability, the trial court deprived defendant of the right to have a jury decide the issue of causation. That ruling directly contravened the Legislature's intent that intervening circumstances be put "squarely to the jury's sense of justice." This Court's affirmance of that ruling eviscerates not only the right to trial by jury, but also the Legislature's intent that our causation provision be "flexible for application to the infinite variety of cases likely to arise."

While asserting the hard-and-fast rule that a victim's decision "to terminate life support, may not, as a matter of law, be considered an independent intervening cause," the majority maintains that a remoteness assessment is viable pursuant to the Code. In approving the trial court's charge, the majority finds that "the jury could not consider removal as the cause of death when determining causation but it could consider whether the causal link was broken by remoteness in time of death." Therefore, the majority must be suggesting that after a period of time, to be fixed by the jury, a victim's decision to terminate life support will not transform an aggravated assault into a homicide. The various factors set forth in the Code that were to have a "just bearing on the actor's liability or on the gravity of his offense" were not meant to be compartmentalized and detached from one another, but considered as a whole in reaching a just verdict. The drafters of the Code expected a jury to consider the interplay between remoteness and the volitional act of another as breaking the chain of causation. In making no allowance for the varied circumstances in which life support may be terminated by a victim, the majority does not permit the jury to consider the level of medical assistance required to sustain life, for example, whether the medical regimen is so burdensome as to deny even a minimal quality of life, or is relatively benign in comparison. The nature and scope of the medical care and the quality of life of the victim are factors that should be considered along with remoteness in determining whether intervening circumstances—including the voluntary termination of life support—should have a just bearing on the outcome of the case. . . .

---

## NOTES ON CAUSATION

**1.   The Relevance of Causation.** Issues of causation arise in the criminal law whenever the definition of the offense specifies a result as an actus reus element. The causation inquiry, as *Pelham* illustrates, concerns a relationship or linkage between the defendant's conduct and the result such that the defendant can properly be punished for the result. Offenses against the person are the predominate context where issues of causation arise, and homicide is the offense where most causation problems are litigated.

Both issues of grading and culpability can turn on causation. This point can be illustrated by assuming on the *Pelham* facts that the court had found that the decision to remove Patrick from life support was an "independent intervening cause" of Patrick's death and that Pelham therefore could not be convicted of homicide in connection with that death. Are there other crimes for which Pelham could be convicted? If so, are the penalties for those other crimes comparable to those imposed for second-degree vehicular homicide? Should they be?

A number of states have adopted reckless-endangering statutes derived from § 211.2 of the Model Penal Code. These offenses require proof that the actor created a grave risk of death, not that he or she caused the risked result. Presumably, Pelham could be prosecuted under such a statute, but the available penalty most likely would be less severe, and most probably far less severe, than that imposed for vehicular homicide. Hence, a significant grading differential turns on the causation inquiry.

The differential is greater still when the defendant is merely negligent. If a death is "caused" by the right quantum of negligence, a conviction of negligent homicide may follow. There may be, in the context of operation of a vehicle, for example, various laws that were broken by a defendant's negligent behavior. But there is no generic "negligent endangering" statute, either in the Model Penal Code or—so far as is known—in any body of American criminal law. So the difference in many cases of negligent behavior "may be between a fairly serious crime and no crime at all."

Causation may have more significance still. Compare the issues explored in Chapter III. To paraphrase a problem presented there, assume an actor who, in the terms of the New Jersey vehicular homicide statute, created a risk that another human being would die by driving a vehicle recklessly. If no death is "caused" by such behavior can there be a conviction for *attempted* vehicular homicide? Are the issues presented by debate of that question similar to those presented by the hypothetical variation of *Pelham* presented above? Why should results matter so much?

Elaborate treatment of these issues can be found in Stephen J. Schulhofer, Harm and Punishment: A Critique of Emphasis on Results of Conduct in the Criminal Law, 122 U. Pa. L. Rev. 1497 (1974). Schulhofer concludes that "many problems associated with mens rea and the law of attempts have never been resolved satisfactorily, due to the absence of acceptable or coherent reasons for attributing significance to the harm caused; the entire field of causation in criminal law is utterly bankrupt for the same reason. Identification of the precise policies served by emphasis on results should provide a basis for more meaningful efforts to tackle these problems." What might these "precise policies" be?

**2.  The Common–Law Approach to Causation.** Most descriptions of the common-law approach to causation divide the problem into two questions. The first is one of factual causation, frequently measured by the so-called "but for" test. This inquiry states a necessary but not sufficient condition of liability, i.e., that the result would not have occurred "but for" the defendant's antecedent conduct. A simple illustration of when this test would not be satisfied would be a case where *A* inflicts a minor flesh wound on *B*, and *C*—acting independently—shoots *B* through the heart and kills *B* instantly. *A*'s conduct in this instance would plainly not be a "but for" cause of *B*'s death, even though *A* may have intended to kill *B*.

It is clear, however, that the law cannot stop by asking the "but for" question. Consider the following case. *D* attempts to kill his wife and fails, and as a result she leaves home, goes to live on a farm with her family, falls off a horse while riding in the woods, lands on a rattlesnake, and dies from the bite of the snake. In this case, *D*'s conduct is related to his wife's death in a "but for" sense; were it not for his attempt to kill her, she would not have left home, would not have been riding in the woods, would not have fallen off her horse, etc. But, although *D* is guilty of attempted murder for his initial conduct, it is clear that he could not be convicted of murder following her death.

The concept used by the common law to describe this conclusion is called "proximate" or "legal" cause. If the defendant's conduct is a "but for" cause of death, the second question that must be asked is whether it was also the "proximate cause" of the death. It is this inquiry that is ordinarily crucial. When deciding whether the actor's conduct was the "sufficiently direct" and, hence, the "proximate" cause of death, courts often ask whether some other cause "intervened" in the chain of events begun by the defendant's conduct such that the defendant should not be held responsible for the ultimate result. The common-law vocabulary for analyzing this question often used the terms "dependent intervening cause" to describe a more immediate causal factor that would not exculpate (e.g., the victim actually died from an infection that resulted from wounds inflicted by the defendant) and "independent intervening cause" to describe a causal factor that would exculpate (e.g., the wife's decision to go horseback riding in the hypothetical used above).

The difficulty with these terms is that they are merely labels that can be attached to conclusions already reached. They do not describe the process or the criteria by which one could reason to those conclusions. They do not explain why a particular actor should be guilty, nor does they establish criteria that can be applied to the next case.

**3. The Model Code Approach.** It is said in H.L.A. Hart and Tony Honoré, Causation in the Law 353 (1959), that "[t]he most lucid, comprehensive, and successful attempt to simplify problems of 'proximate cause' in the criminal law is that contained in the ... Model Penal Code prepared by the American Law Institute." The Model Code made a deliberate attempt "to cut loose from the 'encrusted precedents' of 'proximate cause.'" In doing so, it substituted a new vocabulary and discarded the old common-law terms for reasoning about the proximate-cause question. The New Jersey statute involved in *Pelham* was derived from the Model Code.

The key to the Model Code analysis of causation is recognition that the problem of proximate cause is not a problem of describing physical relationships, but one of assessing their legal significance. Moreover, the criteria against which their significance should be assessed are closely related to the criteria used for measuring responsibility in the criminal law. The question, in other words, is not quantitative, but qualitative; it turns on a judgment of blameworthiness and responsibility and should be thought of in those terms, not in terms of physical causation.

Section 2.03 of the Model Code provides:

(1) Conduct is the cause of a result when:

(a) it is an antecedent but for which the result in question would not have occurred; and

(b) the relationship between the conduct and result satisfies any additional causal requirements imposed by the Code or by the law defining the offense.

(2) When purposely or knowingly causing a particular result is an element of an offense, the element is not established if the actual result is not within the purpose or the contemplation of the actor unless:

(a) the actual result differs from that designed or contemplated, as the case may be, only in the respect that a different person or different property is injured or affected or that the injury or harm designed or contemplated would have been more serious or more extensive than that caused; or

(b) the actual result involves the same kind of injury or harm as that designed or contemplated and is not too remote or accidental in its occurrence to have a [just] bearing on the actor's liability or on the gravity of his offense.

(3) When recklessly or negligently causing a particular result is an element of the offense, the element is not established if the actual result is not within the risk of which the actor is aware or, in the case of negligence, of which he should be aware unless:

> (a) the actual result differs from the probable result only in the respect that a different person or different property is injured or affected or that the probable injury or harm would have been more serious or more extensive than that caused; or

> (b) the actual result involves the same kind of injury or harm as the probable result and is not too remote or accidental in its occurrence to have a [just] bearing on the actor's liability or on the gravity of his offense.

(4) When causing a particular result is a material element of an offense for which absolute liability is imposed by law, the element is not established unless the actual result is a probable consequence of the actor's conduct.

**4.  Problems With the Model Code.** The Model Code provisions on causation have not been received uncritically. Many recently revised codes have not included a comparable provision, at least partly on the ground that the Model Code provision is too complex. There have also been a number of substantive criticisms, among them the following:

**(i) Concurrent Causes.** In 1 Working Papers of the Nat'l Comm'n on Reform of Federal Criminal Laws 144–45 (1970), the Model Code reliance on "but-for" causation in § 2.03(1)(a) is criticized because it "ignores the cases in which ['but-for' causation] is not essential for liability." The example given is a case of concurrent causation:

> Even though all of the senators may have intended to kill Caesar and all of them stabbed him, under the Model Penal Code's formulation none would be criminally liable for his death since (so I shall assume) he would have died even though any one of them had held back his knife. Even a senator who stabbed Caesar through the heart would not be liable, since so Anthony tells us (act 3, scene 2) "sweet Caesar's blood" was streaming from all the wounds.

Is this a likely situation? Is it adequately dealt with by the Model Code?[a] What result under the Model Code if A inflicts a mortal wound on B with

[a] The membership of the American Law Institute debated this issue, "but decided that the language [of the Code] should not be complicated further in an attempt to make more explicit the treatment of extraordinary cases in which persons act concurrently but independently to produce the forbidden consequence." ALI, Model Penal Code and Commentaries, § 2.03, pp. 259–60 (1985). The commentary adds that "[a]ll who have con-

intent to kill, but *C* kills *B* before *A*'s wound can have its natural effect? Should *A* be guilty of murder?

**(ii) Transferred Intent.** Consider the following situation. *A* shoots at *B* with intent to kill. Because it was aimed badly, the shot misses, ricochets off a rock, and kills *C*. The common law would have resolved this case by using the fictional concept of "transferred intent"—by magically "transferring" *A*'s intent from *B* to *C* and holding *A* liable for murder. Under the Model Code, *A* would be liable for murder because *A* acted purposely with respect to the death of another and because the causation requirements of § 2.03(2)(a) would be satisfied; the actual result would have differed from the intended result "only in the respect that a different person . . . is injured."

It is argued in Note, Causation in the Model Penal Code, 78 Colum.L.Rev. 1249, 1267–72 (1978), that the common-law transferred-intent doctrine is a species of strict liability and that the Model Code resolution in effect continues that result and is thus inconsistent with its normal approach to strict liability:

> A difference in victims is not simply a trivial variation in the manner in which harm occurs; the identity of the victim is apt to be of great significance both to the offender and to those affected by the killing. No one would suppose that an offender who fails to kill his intended victim has achieved his basic objective if he inadvertently kills someone else. Admittedly, the harm that ultimately results may be as great as that which would have occurred if the offender had accomplished his precise objective. But if the magnitude of resulting harm were the sole prerequisite for the imposition of liability, there would be no need for any proximity requirement.

The suggested solution is to treat the actor in the transferred-intent situation under the provisions of § 210.2(1)(b) of the Model Code, by adding a presumption of the required recklessness in cases where the death occurs during the attempted murder of another. Is this a better resolution? Does the Model Code embrace a form of strict liability in § 2.03(2)(a)? Is the transferred-intent situation properly treated as a causation problem?

**5. Questions and Comments on *Pelham*.** Some of the most difficult causation problems arise when the defendant sets in motion a series of events that is interrupted by the voluntary action of another person. The Model Code would resolve such a case by asking in § 2.03(3)(b) whether the actual result was "not too remote or accidental in its occurrence to have a

---

sidered the issue agree that each of the assailants should be liable, and it was the intent of the Institute to make them liable." It explains that there is no difficulty when multiple persons act in concert, since each is liable for the acts of the others and in sum "but for" cause is established. "The only difficult case is one that arises most infre-

quently, when the conduct of two actors is completely independent, and each actor's conduct would have been sufficient by itself to produce death. . . ." This situation should perhaps be characterized, the commentary concludes, as " 'death from two mortal blows.' So described, the victim's demise has as but-for causes each assailant's blow."

[just] bearing on the actor's liability or the gravity of his offense." The words "remote or" were added to an earlier draft, partially in response to the criticism of Hart and Honoré that the words "too accidental" put the crucial inquiry in this kind of case "in quite unfamiliar terms." New Jersey responded to this problem by modifying the applicable standard. As *Pelham* explains, New Jersey adopts the basic Model Code structure but modifies § 2.03(3)(b) as follows: "the actual result must involve the same kind of injury or harm as the probable result and must not be too remote, accidental in its occurrence, or dependent on another's volitional act to have a just bearing on the actor's liability or on the gravity of his offense." N.J.Stat.Ann. § 2C:2–3(c). Is the New Jersey statute an improvement on the Model Code? How should liability in this situation be measured?

## SECTION 4: FELONY MURDER

### INTRODUCTORY NOTES ON FELONY MURDER

**1.  The Rule and its Traditional Limitations.** The original statement of the felony-murder rule was that a person who commits any felony and all accomplices in that felony are guilty of murder if a death occurs during the commission or attempted commission of the felony. Liability is strict, in the sense that no inquiry need be made into the felons' culpability as to the death; their culpability for the underlying felony is sufficient. As the Supreme Court of Kansas put the point, "the killer's malignant purpose is established by proof of the collateral felony." State v. Goodseal, 220 Kan. 487, 553 P.2d 279 (1976). Thus, if two persons undertake to commit a robbery, they are both guilty of murder if a victim of the robbery is killed during the commission of the offense, whether or not either robber would have been guilty of murder by the application of the normal mens rea requirements for murder.

The history of felony murder is marked by judicial efforts to limit its scope. The premise of these efforts is that the rule should not be activated by "any" felony, because not all felonies present a likelihood of danger to human life. To pick just a few examples, the list of modern felonies includes offenses related to election returns and voting, securities and insurance violations, conflict of interest, fraud, and a wide variety of other activity in which the prospect of violence or other life-endangering activity is at best remote. Assuming that the rationale for the rule is based on the tendency of certain felonies to threaten life, it follows that some limitation on the kinds of felonies that support application of the felony-murder rule is needed.

The courts have used essentially three devices for limiting the situations to which the rule applies: (i) a requirement that the felony be inherently dangerous, either in general or on the particular facts; (ii) a causation limitation, usually expressed as a requirement that the death be a "natural and probable result" of the felonious conduct; and (iii) a requirement that the felony be "independent" of the homicide, often stated to exclude lesser-included homicide and assault offenses from those felonies to which the rule applies. The first limitation is sometimes expressed as a requirement that the felony must be malum in se rather than malum prohibitum, though this is an obvious overgeneralization since not all malum in se offenses are dangerous to life. The third device is often identified as a "merger" rule; an assault with intent to kill, for example, may be said to "merge" into a resulting homicide and thus not to be an "independent" felony that can result in a felony-murder conviction.

In many states, a form of the first limitation is imposed by statute. For example, murder statutes in those states that have followed the original Pennsylvania degree structure generally include a list of "inherently dangerous" felonies that will support a first-degree murder conviction. Most such statutes define second-degree murder as "all other kinds of murder" recognized by the common law. Thus, in these jurisdictions, second-degree murder includes a residual category of felony-murder based on felonies not found on the first-degree list. Thus the need to address appropriate limitations on the unadorned felony-murder rule exists in states where the highest grade of murder encompasses homicides that occur during the commission of "any" felony,[a] as well as in those states in which a lower grade of murder includes a residual category composed of other homicides that would constitute "murder" at common law.[b]

**2.  Rationale for the Rule.** The felony-murder rule has two principal consequences. First, it criminalizes behavior that absent the rule would not be an independent homicide offense at all. The defendant will be guilty of murder without proof that any traditional culpability standard, independent of that required for the felony that triggered the rule, was satisfied. Thus, an entirely accidental killing—one for which neither an intent to kill nor recklessness or negligence as to the death can be shown—may result in a conviction for murder if it occurs during the commission of a qualifying felony. Second, the felony-murder rule upgrades homicidal behavior that otherwise might be classified as a lesser offense. A negligent killing, for example, might be punished as involuntary manslaughter under normal circumstances, but is upgraded to murder if committed during the course of a qualifying felony. Similarly, provocation that ordinarily might reduce an offense to manslaughter may not have that effect if the charge is felony murder.

Why has the law provided for these results? Given the general reluctance of the common-law system to rely on strict liability, why is strict liability used for one of the most serious criminal offenses? The usual

---

[a] See, e.g., the Kansas statute quoted in State v. Goodseal, 220 Kan. 487, 553 P.2d 279 (1976): "Murder in the first degree is the killing of a human being committed maliciously, willfully, deliberately and with premeditation or committed in the perpetration or attempt to perpetrate any felony."

[b] See, e.g., the original Pennsylvania degree statute quoted in the Notes on First-Degree Murder following *State v. Brown*, above.

answer is the one endorsed by the Supreme Court of Kansas in *Goodseal*: "The only rational function of the felony-murder rule is to furnish an added deterrent to the perpetration of felonies which, by their nature or by the attendant circumstances, create a foreseeable risk of death." A well-known defense, though not necessarily an endorsement, of the rule was offered by Oliver Wendell Holmes in The Common Law 59 (1881):

> [I]f experience shows, or is deemed by the lawmaker to show, that somehow or other deaths which the evidence makes accidental happen disproportionately often in connection with other felonies, or with resistance to officers, or if on any other ground of policy it is deemed desirable to make special efforts for the prevention of such deaths, the lawmaker may consistently treat acts which, under the known circumstances, are felonious, or constitute resistance to officers, as having a sufficiently dangerous tendency to be put under a special ban. The law may, therefore, throw on the actor the peril, not only of the consequences foreseen by him, but also of consequences which, although not predicted by common experience, the legislator apprehends.

It is often noted in response to this contention that there is little empirical evidence that homicides "which the evidence makes accidental happen disproportionately often in connection with other felonies." In ALI, Model Penal Code and Commentaries, § 210.2, p. 38 (1980), statistics are reproduced which show that of 16,273 robberies in New Jersey in 1975, only 66 homicides (or homicides in .41 per cent of the cases) were committed. Similar figures are cited for other felonies and other jurisdictions. Do these statistics show that the felony-murder rule is unnecessary, or that it works? Is Holmes right in considering only those homicides "which the evidence makes accidental?" Are these the only homicides as to which a special rule may be needed?

In an article entitled In Defense of the Felony Murder Doctrine, 8 Harv.J.Law & Pub.Policy 359 (1985), David Crump and Susan Waite Crump offer six rationales for retaining felony murder. First, they argue that the rule "reflects a societal judgment that an intentionally committed robbery that causes ... death ... is qualitatively more serious than an identical robbery that does not." As they remark, the law often classifies offenses on the basis of results. Murder and attempted murder, for example, may be committed with the same mens rea, yet attempted murder is usually graded less severely. The only factor that can account for this grading differential is that the murderer has caused a death. If it is not irrational to grade murder more seriously than attempted murder, they conclude, it is similarly not irrational to classify robbery-that-causes-a-death more seriously than robbery. Second, they argue that the "reinforcement of societal norms" associated with the function of condemnation supports placing the label "murder" on a death that occurs during certain felonies that are by their nature violent. They think this particularly appropriate when, as they argue is the case with felony murder, common social judgment coincides with the classification. Third, they argue that the "felony murder rule is just the sort of simple, commonsense, readily enforceable, and widely known principle that is likely to result in deterrence."

Their remaining arguments list advantages of the rule that cannot stand as independent justifications, but that ought to be considered, in their view, in any rational debate. Their fourth argument is that "the aim of consistent and predictable adjudication" is better served by the felony murder rule than by the convoluted rules that are often used to describe the mens rea of murder. Fifth, the "rule has beneficial allocative consequences because it clearly defines the offense, simplifies the task of judge and jury with respect to questions of law and fact, and thereby promotes efficient administration of justice." Finally, they argue that the rule reduces the incentive to commit perjury by removing defenses that can most readily be proved by the defendant's own testimony.

**3.   Judicial Rejection of the Rule: *People v. Aaron.*** The felony-murder rule was rejected by the Michigan Supreme Court in People v. Aaron, 409 Mich. 672, 299 N.W.2d 304 (1980). The court first addressed the history of the doctrine, noting that "the rule is of questionable origin" and "the reasons for the rule no longer exist, making it an anachronistic remnant, 'a historic survivor for which there is no logical or practical basis for existence in modern law.' " As to its origins, the court referred to scholarship[c] suggesting that the 16th century cases commonly thought to have established the rule were misinterpreted by Lord Coke and some of the other early writers. As to its initial rationale, the court said:

> The failure of the felony-murder rule to consider the defendant's moral culpability is explained by examining the state of the law at the time of the rule's inception. The concept of culpability was not an element of homicide at early common law. The early history of malice aforethought was vague. The concept meant little more than intentional wrongdoing with no other emphasis on intention except to exclude homicides that were committed by misadventure or in some otherwise pardonable manner. Thus, under this early definition of malice aforethought, an intent to commit the felony would itself constitute malice. Furthermore, as all felonies were punished alike, it made little difference whether the felon was hanged for the felony or for the death.

Thus, the felony-murder rule did not broaden the concept of murder at the time of its origin because proof of the intention to commit a felony met the test of culpability based on the vague definition of malice aforethought governing at that time. Today, however, malice is a term of art. It does not include the nebulous definition of intentional wrongdoing. Thus, although the felony-murder rule did not broaden the definition of murder at early

---

[c] E.g., J.M. Kaye, The Early History of Murder and Manslaughter, Part II, 83 Quarterly Rev. 569 (1967); Recent Developments, Felony–Murder Rule—Felon's Responsibility for Death of Accomplice, 65 Colum.L.Rev. 1496 (1965); Note, Felony Murder as a First Degree Offense: An Anachronism Retained, 66 Yale L.J. 427 (1957).

common law, it does so today. We find this enlargement of the scope of murder unacceptable, because it is based on a concept of culpability which is "totally incongruous with the general principles of our jurisprudence" today.

The Michigan statute at issue in *Aaron* was based on the original Pennsylvania degree structure:

> Murder which is perpetrated by means of poison, lying in wait, or other wilful, deliberate, and premeditated killing, or which is committed in the perpetration or attempt to perpetrate [certain listed felonies], is murder in the first degree. . . .

The court held that the purpose of the statute was only "to graduate punishment"; it "only serves to raise an already established *murder* to the first-degree level, not to transform a death, without more, into a murder." Thus, the "use of the term 'murder' in the . . . statute requires that a murder first be established before the statute is applied to elevate the degree."

The question, then, was what constituted a "murder" that could be elevated to "murder in the first degree" when committed in the course of one of the listed felonies. The prosecutor argued that the undefined term "murder" referred to the common law, and that the common law included a felony-murder rule that could trigger the statute. The court recognized the logic of this argument, but held that it was an unsound rule that was "no longer acceptable":

> Accordingly we hold today that malice is the intention to kill, the intention to do great bodily harm, or the wanton and wilful disregard of the likelihood that the natural tendency of the defendant's behavior is to cause death or great bodily harm. We further hold that malice is an essential element of any murder, as that term is judicially defined, whether the murder occurs in the course of a felony or otherwise. The facts and circumstances involved in the perpetration of a felony may evidence an intent to kill, an intent to cause great bodily harm, or a wanton and wilful disregard of the likelihood that the natural tendency of the defendant's behavior is to cause death or great bodily harm; however, the conclusion must be left to the jury to infer from all the evidence.

Finally, the court addressed the practical effect of its abolition of the felony-murder rule. It said:

> From a practical standpoint, the abolition of the category of malice arising from the intent to commit the underlying felony should have little effect on the result of the majority of cases. In many cases where the felony-murder rule has been applied, the use of the doctrine was unnecessary because the other types of malice could have been inferred from the evidence.
>
> Abrogation of this rule does not make irrelevant the fact that a death occurred in the course of a felony. A jury can properly *infer* malice from evidence that a defendant set in motion a force

likely to cause death or great bodily harm. Thus, whenever a killing occurs in the perpetration or attempted perpetration of an inherently dangerous felony, in order to establish malice the jury may consider the "nature of the underlying felony and the circumstances surrounding its commission." If the jury concludes that malice existed, they can find murder and, if they determine that the murder occurred in the perpetration or attempted perpetration of one of the enumerated felonies, by statute the murder would become first-degree murder.

The difference is that the jury may not find malice from the intent to commit the underlying felony alone. The defendant will be permitted to assert any of the applicable defenses relating to mens rea which he would be allowed to assert if charged with premeditated murder. The latter result is reasonable in light of the fact that felony murder is certainly no more heinous than premeditated murder. The prosecution will still be able to prove first-degree murder without proof of premeditation when a homicide is committed with malice, as we have defined it, and the perpetration or attempted perpetration of an enumerated felony is established. Hence, our first-degree statute continues to elevate to first-degree murder a *murder* which is committed in the perpetration or attempted perpetration of one of the enumerated felonies.

Two justices wrote separately to explain the rationale on which they agreed with the result reached by the court's opinion. There were no dissents.

**4.  The Model Penal Code and Modern Statutes.** The Model Penal Code takes the position that the felony-murder rule is indefensible in principle because it bases the most severe sanctions known to the criminal law on strict liability. The Model Code suggests instead that ordinary principles of criminal homicide, causation, and complicity should be used for the prosecution of homicides that occur during the commission of a felony. It does, however, make one concession to the historical momentum of the rule. This is contained in § 210.2(1)(b), which reads as follows:

> [C]riminal homicide constitutes murder when . . . it is committed recklessly under circumstances manifesting extreme indifference to the value of human life. Such recklessness and indifference are presumed if the actor is engaged or is an accomplice in the commission of, or an attempt to commit, or flight after committing or attempting to commit robbery, rape or deviate sexual intercourse by force or threat of force, arson, burglary, kidnapping or felonious escape.

The effect of a presumption under the Model Code is dealt with in § 1.12(5). Is this an effective compromise? Is the point one that should be compromised?

Among the states in which recent penal-code revisions have been undertaken, only Hawaii and Kentucky have abolished the felony-murder rule completely, and only New Hampshire has adopted the Model Penal

Code solution. A couple of states have restricted the rule by engrafting an additional mens rea showing onto the traditional felony-murder elements. For example, Delaware requires that the actor "recklessly cause the death of another person" in order to be guilty of first-degree murder under the felony-murder doctrine, and reduces the offense to second-degree murder if the actor is negligent.

Among the other states, the most important revision is New York's, which is reproduced in Appendix B. The Model Code commentary reports that the New York approach has been copied in at least seven enacted codes. Does the New York approach represent a more principled compromise of the felony-murder debate? What accounts for its greater popularity? What explains the persistence of the felony-murder rule?

––––––

## People v. Hansen

Supreme Court of California, 1994.
9 Cal.4th 300, 36 Cal.Rptr.2d 609, 885 P.2d 1022.

■ GEORGE, JUSTICE. In this case we must determine whether the offense of discharging a firearm at an inhabited dwelling house is a felony "inherently dangerous to human life" for purposes of the second-degree felony-murder doctrine, and, if so, whether that doctrine nonetheless is inapplicable in the present case under the so-called "merger" doctrine applied in People v. Ireland, 70 Cal.2d 522, 75 Cal.Rptr. 188, 450 P.2d 580 (1969), and its progeny. For the reasons explained hereafter, we conclude that this offense, for such purposes, is a felony inherently dangerous to human life and does not "merge" with a resulting homicide so as to preclude application of the felony-murder doctrine. Because the Court of Appeal reached a similar conclusion, we affirm the judgment of that court upholding defendant's conviction of second-degree murder.

I

On September 19, 1991, defendant Michael Hansen, together with Rudolfo Andrade and Alexander Maycott, planned to purchase $40 worth of methamphetamine. With that purpose, defendant, accompanied by his girlfriend Kimberly Geldon and Maycott, drove in defendant's Camaro to an apartment duplex located in the City of San Diego. Upon arriving at the duplex, defendant pounded on the door of the upstairs apartment where Christina Almenar resided with her two children. When he received no response, defendant proceeded to return to his automobile and was approached by Michael Echaves.

Echaves resided in the downstairs apartment with Martha Almenar (Christina's sister) and Martha's two children, Diane Rosalez, 13 years of age, and Louie Miranda, 5 years of age. At the time, Diane and Louie were outside with Echaves helping him with yard work. In response to a question from Echaves, defendant said he was looking for Christina. When Echaves stated he had not seen her, defendant asked whether Echaves would be able to obtain some crystal methamphetamine (speed). After making a telephone call, Echaves informed defendant that he would be able to do so. Defendant said he would attempt to purchase the drug elsewhere but, if unsuccessful, would return.

Defendant and his companions departed but returned approximately 20 minutes later. Defendant, accompanied by Echaves, Maycott, and Geldon, then drove a short distance to another apartment complex. Defendant parked his vehicle, gave Echaves two $20 bills, and told Echaves he would wait while Echaves obtained the methamphetamine. Echaves said he would be back shortly.

When Echaves failed to return, defendant and his companions proceeded to Echaves's apartment. Defendant knocked on the door and the windows. Diane and Louie were inside the apartment alone but did not respond. Their mother, Martha, had left the apartment to meet Echaves, who had telephoned her after eluding defendant. After meeting Echaves at a hardware store, Martha telephoned her children from a public telephone booth. Diane answered and told her mother that the "guys in the Camaro" had returned, pounded on the door, and then had left.

Meanwhile, defendant, Maycott, and Geldon returned to the location where Andrade was waiting for them, acquiring en route a handgun from an acquaintance. The three men then decided to return to Echaves's apartment with the objective either of recovering their money or physically assaulting Echaves. At approximately 7:30 p.m., defendant approached the apartment building in his automobile with the lights turned off, and then from the vehicle fired the handgun repeatedly at the dwelling. At the time, Diane was inside the apartment, in the living room with her brother. The kitchen and living room lights were on. Diane was struck fatally in the head by one of the bullets fired by defendant....

The trial court instructed the jury on several theories of murder, including second-degree felony murder as an unlawful killing that occurs during the commission or attempted commission of a felony inherently dangerous to human life, and further instructed that the felony of shooting at an inhabited dwelling is inherently dangerous to human life. The jury returned a verdict finding defendant guilty of second-degree murder....

On appeal, defendant asserted, among other contentions, that the trial court erred in instructing the jury on second-degree felony-murder based upon the underlying felony of discharging a firearm at an inhabited dwelling, because the latter offense merged with the resulting homicide within the meaning of *People v. Ireland*. [T]he Court of Appeal affirmed the conviction of second-degree murder....

II

Murder is the unlawful killing of a human being, or a fetus, with malice aforethought. (§ 187, subd. (a).) Second degree murder is the unlawful killing of a human being with malice, but without the additional elements (i.e., willfulness, premeditation, and deliberation) that would support a conviction of first degree murder. (§§ 187, subd. (a); 189.)

Malice may be express or implied. (§ 188.) It is express "when there is manifested a deliberate intention unlawfully to take away the life of a fellow creature." (§ 188.) It is implied "when no considerable provocation appears, or when the circumstances attending the killing show an abandoned and malignant heart." (§ 188.) We have held that implied malice has both a physical and a mental component, the physical component being the performance of " 'an act, the natural consequences of which are dangerous to life,' " and the mental component being the requirement that the defendant " 'knows that his conduct endangers the life of another and . . . acts with a conscious disregard for life.' " (People v. Patterson, 49 Cal.3d 615, 626, 262 Cal.Rptr. 195, 778 P.2d 549 (1989); People v. Watson, 30 Cal.3d 290, 300, 179 Cal.Rptr. 43, 637 P.2d 279 (1981).)

The felony-murder rule imputes the requisite malice for a murder conviction to those who commit a homicide during the perpetration of a felony inherently dangerous to human life. "Under well-settled principles of criminal liability a person who kills—whether or not he is engaged in an independent felony at the time—is guilty of murder if he acts with malice aforethought. The felony-murder doctrine, whose ostensible purpose is to deter those engaged in felonies from killing negligently or accidentally, operates to posit the existence of that crucial mental state—and thereby to render irrelevant evidence of actual malice or the lack thereof—when the killer is engaged in a felony whose inherent danger to human life renders logical an imputation of malice on the part of all who commit it." (People v. Satchell, 6 Cal.3d 28, 43, 98 Cal.Rptr. 33, 489 P.2d 1361 (1971).)

The felony-murder rule applies to both first-and second-degree murder. Application of the first-degree felony-murder rule is invoked by the perpetration of one of the felonies enumerated in [the first-degree murder statute]. In People v. Ford, 60 Cal.2d 772, 795, 36 Cal. Rptr. 620, 388 P.2d 892 (1964), the court restricted the felonies that could support a conviction of second-degree murder, based upon a felony-murder theory, to those felonies that are "inherently dangerous to human life." We have explained that the justification for the imputation of implied malice under these circumstances is that, "when society has declared certain inherently dangerous conduct to be felonious, a defendant should not be allowed to excuse himself by saying he was unaware of the danger to life. . . ." (*Patterson,* supra, 49 Cal.3d at 626.) We also have reasoned that, " '[i]f the felony is not inherently dangerous, it is highly improbable that the potential felon will be deterred; he will not anticipate that any injury or death might arise solely from the fact that he will commit the felony.' " (People v. Burroughs, 35 Cal.3d 824, 829, 201 Cal.Rptr. 319, 678 P.2d 894 (1984).) Thus, under the latter circumstances the commission of the felony could not serve logically as the basis for imputation of malice.

In determining whether a felony is inherently dangerous, the court looks to the elements of the felony in the abstract, "not the 'particular' facts of the case," i.e., not to the defendant's specific conduct. (People v. Williams, 63 Cal.2d 452, 47 Cal.Rptr. 7, 406 P.2d 647 (1965).)

Past decisions of this court have explained further the concept of an inherently dangerous felony. In *People v. Burroughs*, supra, we held that an inherently dangerous felony is one which, "by its very nature, . . . cannot be committed without creating a substantial risk that someone will be killed. . . ." And, most recently, in *People v. Patterson*, supra, we specified that, "for purposes of the second degree felony-murder doctrine, an 'inherently dangerous felony' is an offense carrying 'a high probability' that death will result."

Felonies that have been found inherently dangerous to human life, in the abstract—thus supporting application of the second-degree felony-murder rule—include furnishing a poisonous substance (methyl alcohol), reckless or malicious possession of a destructive device, and kidnapping for ransom.

The initial question presented in the case before us is whether the underlying felony involved—willful discharge of a firearm at an inhabited dwelling—is an inherently dangerous felony for purposes of the second-degree felony-murder rule. The offense in question is defined in section 246, which provides in pertinent part:

> Any person who shall maliciously and willfully discharge a firearm at an inhabited dwelling house . . . is guilty of a felony. . . .
> As used in this section, "inhabited" means currently being used for dwelling purposes, whether occupied or not.

As we shall explain, we conclude that this felony, considered in the abstract, involves a high probability that death will result and therefore is an inherently dangerous felony under the governing principles set forth above, for purposes of the second degree felony-murder doctrine.

Although our court has not had occasion previously to render a direct holding on the question whether [this] offense . . . is an inherently dangerous felony for purposes of the second-degree felony-murder doctrine, the reasoning and language of one of our prior decisions provide a rather clear indication of this court's view on this issue. In *People v. Satchell*, the court held the felony of possession of a concealable firearm by a felon, considered in the abstract, was not inherently dangerous to human life and therefore would not support an instruction on second-degree felony-murder. The court concluded that "mere passive possession" of a firearm, even by a felon, could not properly supply the element of malice in a murder prosecution. The court went on to say, however, that if passive possession ripened into a felonious act in which danger to human life was inherent, the purposes of the felony-murder rule would be served by its application, because "it is the deterrence of such acts by felons which the rule is designed to accomplish." The court noted that a "ready example" of such a felony was the act [of] discharging a firearm at an inhabited dwelling.

Although the pertinent language in *Satchell* clearly was dictum, the reasoning underlying this language remains sound. . . . The discharge of a firearm at an inhabited dwelling house ... is a felony whose commission inherently involves a danger to human life. An inhabited dwelling house is one in which persons reside and where occupants "are generally in or *around* the premises." (People v. White, 4 Cal.App.4th 1299, 1303, 6 Cal.Rptr.2d 259 (1992).) In firing a gun at such a structure, there always will exist a significant likelihood that an occupant may be present. Although it is true that a defendant may be guilty of this felony even if, at the time of the shooting, the residents of the inhabited dwelling happen to be absent, the offense nonetheless is one that, viewed in the abstract ..., poses a great risk or "high probability" of death....

Furthermore, application of the second-degree felony-murder rule to a homicide resulting from [such felony] directly would serve the fundamental rationale of the felony-murder rule—the deterrence of negligent or accidental killings in the course of the commission of dangerous felonies. The tragic death of innocent and often random victims, both young and old, as the result of the discharge of firearms, has become an alarmingly common occurrence in our society—a phenomenon of enormous concern to the public. By providing notice to persons inclined to willfully discharge a firearm at an inhabited dwelling—even to those individuals who would do so merely to frighten or intimidate the occupants, or to "leave their calling card"—that such persons will be guilty of murder should their conduct result in the all-too-likely fatal injury of another, the felony-murder rule may serve to deter this type of reprehensible conduct, which has created a climate of fear for significant numbers of Californians even in the privacy of their own homes.

Accordingly, we hold that the offense of discharging a firearm at an inhabited dwelling is an "inherently dangerous felony" for purposes of the second-degree felony-murder rule.

## III

Defendant contends that, even if the ... felony of discharging a firearm is inherently dangerous to human life, the commission of that felony in the present case "merged" with the resulting homicide, within the meaning of *People v. Ireland,* thereby precluding application of the second-degree felony-murder rule.

[D]efendant's contention rests upon an unduly expansive view of the scope of the "merger" doctrine.... Prior to our decision in *Ireland*, the "merger" doctrine had been developed in other jurisdictions as a shorthand explanation for the conclusion that the felony-murder rule should not be applied in circumstances where the only underlying (or "predicate") felony committed by the defendant was assault. The name of the doctrine derived from the characterization of the assault as an offense that "merged" with the resulting homicide. In explaining the basis for the merger doctrine, courts and legal commentators reasoned that, because a homicide generally results from the commission of an assault, every felonious assault ending in death automatically would be elevated to murder in the event a felonious assault could serve as the predicate felony for purposes of the felony-murder doctrine. Consequently, application of the felony-murder rule to felonious assaults would usurp most of the law of homicide, relieve the prosecution in the great majority of homicide cases of the burden of having to prove malice in order to obtain a murder conviction, and thereby frustrate the Legislature's intent to punish certain felonious assaults resulting in death (those committed with malice aforethought, and therefore punishable as murder) more harshly than other felonious assaults that happened to result in death (those committed without malice aforethought, and therefore punishable as manslaughter). [T]he merger rule applied to assaults is supported by the policy of preserving some meaningful domain in which the Legislature's careful gradation of homicide offenses can be implemented.

In *People v. Ireland,* we adopted the merger rule in a case involving the underlying felony of assault with a deadly weapon, where the defendant had shot and killed his wife. The jury was instructed that it could return a second-degree felony-murder verdict based upon the underlying felony of assault with a deadly weapon, and the defendant was convicted of second-degree murder.

On appeal, this court reversed, reasoning that "[t]o allow such use of the felony-murder rule would effectively preclude the jury from considering the issue of malice aforethought in all cases wherein homicide has been committed as a result of a felonious assault—a category which includes the great majority of all homicides. This kind of bootstrapping finds support neither in logic nor in law." The court therefore concluded that the offense of assault with a deadly weapon, which was "an integral part of" and "included in fact" within the homicide, could not support a second-degree felony-murder instruction.

Subsequent decisions have applied the *Ireland* rule to other felonies involving assault . . . , [such as felony child abuse of the assaultive category, burglary with intent to commit the felony of assault with a deadly weapon, and assault with a deadly weapon].

Our court, however, has not extended the *Ireland* doctrine beyond the context of assault, even under circumstances in which the underlying felony plausibly could be characterized as "an integral part of" and "included in fact within" the resulting homicide. The decision in People v. Mattison, 4 Cal.3d 177, 93 Cal.Rptr. 185, 481 P.2d 193 (1971), provides an apt example. In that case, the defendant and the victim both were inmates of a correctional institution. The defendant worked as a technician in the medical laboratory. He previously had offered to sell alcohol to inmates, leading the victim, an alcoholic, to seek alcohol from him. The defendant supplied the victim with methyl alcohol, resulting in the victim's death by methyl alcohol poisoning.

At trial, the court instructed on felony murder based upon the felony of mixing poison with a beverage, an offense proscribed by the then-current version of section 347 ("Every person who wilfully mingles any poison with any food, drink or medicine, with intent that the same shall be taken by any human being to his injury, is guilty of a felony.") The defendant was convicted of second-degree murder. On appeal, contending that the trial court had erred in instructing the jury on felony-murder, the defendant maintained that, on the facts of his case, the underlying felony was "an integral part of" and "included in fact within" the resulting murder, precluding application of the felony-murder rule.

In *Mattison,* [we rejected the defendant's contention because] we found that the predicate felony presented an "entirely different situation from the one that confronted us in *Ireland,*" where the underlying felony was assault with a deadly weapon. We concluded that the merger rule was inapplicable because, in furnishing the methyl alcohol to the victim, the defendant exhibited a collateral and independent felonious design that was separate from the resulting homicide. [W]e held that where the underlying felony is committed with a design collateral to, or independent of, an intent to cause injury that would result in death, "[g]iving a felony-murder instruction in such a situation serves rather than subverts the purpose of the rule."

The Court of Appeal's decision in People v. Taylor, 11 Cal.App.3d 57, 89 Cal.Rptr. 697 (1970), upon which *Mattison* explicitly relied, provides additional guidance.... In *Taylor,* the victim died as a result of an overdose of heroin, which had been furnished to her by the defendant. The defendant was convicted of second degree murder, and the question presented was whether application of the felony-murder rule constituted error under *Ireland.* The Court of Appeal in *Taylor* first acknowledged the confusion that arose from the circumstance that, although *Ireland* involved an assault with a deadly weapon (a felony to which the merger rule traditionally has been applied), the broad language of *Ireland* could be interpreted as extending that rule to all felonies that constitute "an integral part of the homicide," potentially encompassing all felonies closely related to a homicide (and therefore possibly every felony inherently dangerous to human life)....

[In *Taylor,* the court decided] that *Ireland's* "integral part of the homicide" language did not constitute the crucial test [for] merger. [It] held that a felony does not merge with a homicide where the act causing death was committed with a collateral and independent felonious design separate from the intent to inflict the injury that caused death. The court explained its reasoning as follows: when the Legislature has prescribed that an assault resulting in death constitutes second degree murder if the felon acts with malice, it would subvert the legislative intent for a court to apply the felony-murder rule automatically to elevate all felonious assaults resulting in death to second degree murder even where the felon does not act with malice. In other words, if the felony-murder rule were applied to felonious assaults, all such assaults ending in death would constitute murder, effectively eliminating the requirement of malice—a result clearly contrary to legislative intent. The court in *Taylor* further explained, however, that when the underlying or predicate felony is not assault, but rather is a felony such as the furnishing of heroin ..., application of the felony-murder rule would not subvert the legislative intent, because "this is simply not a situation where the Legislature has demanded a showing of actual malice, as distinguished from malice implied in law by way of the felony-murder rule."

We agree ... that *Ireland's* "integral part of the homicide" language [is not the test for] merger. Such a test would be inconsistent with the underlying rule that only felonies "inherently dangerous to human life" are sufficiently indicative of a defendant's culpable mens rea to warrant application of the felony-murder rule. The more dangerous the felony, the more likely it is that a death may result directly from the commission of the felony, but resort to the "integral part of the homicide" language would preclude application of the felony-murder rule for those felonies that are most likely to result in death and that are, consequently, the felonies as to which the felony-murder doctrine is most likely to act as a deterrent (because the perpetrator could foresee the great likelihood that death may result, negligently or accidentally).

[However, we reject *Taylor's* conclusion that merger never applies in cases where the predicate felony was] "committed with a collateral and independent felonious design." Under such a test, a felon who acts with a purpose other than specifically to inflict injury upon someone—for example, with the intent to sell narcotics for financial gain, or to discharge a firearm at a building solely to intimidate the occupants—is subject to greater criminal liability for an act resulting in death than a person who actually intends to injure the person of the victim. Rather than rely upon a somewhat artificial test that may lead to an anomalous result, we focus upon the principles and rationale underlying the foregoing language in *Taylor*, namely, that with respect to certain inherently dangerous felonies, their use as the predicate felony supporting application of the felony-murder rule will not elevate all felonious assaults to murder or otherwise subvert the legislative intent.

In the present case, as in *Mattison* and *Taylor*, application of the second-degree felony-murder rule would not [subvert] legislative intent. Most homicides do not result from [the felony involved here], and thus, unlike the situation in *People v. Ireland,* application of the felony-murder doctrine in the present context will not have the effect of "preclud[ing] the jury from considering the issue of malice aforethought ... [in] the great majority of all homicides." Similarly, application of the felony-murder doctrine in the case before us would not frustrate the Legislature's deliberate calibration of punishment for assaultive conduct resulting in death, based upon the presence or absence of malice aforethought. [Moreover,] application of the felony-murder rule [here] clearly is consistent with the traditionally recognized purpose of the ... doctrine—namely the deterrence of negligent or accidental killings that occur in the course of the commission of dangerous felonies.

The Texas Court of Criminal Appeals recently applied similar reasoning in upholding a murder conviction that occurred after a jury was instructed on felony murder based upon underlying felonious conduct involving the discharge of a firearm into an occupied dwelling. See Aguirre

v. State, 732 S.W.2d 320 (Tex.Crim.App. 1987). The court viewed the defendant's conduct of "attempting to blow open a door with a shotgun" as an offense that did not "merge" with the resulting homicide....

For the foregoing reasons, we conclude that the offense of discharging a firearm at an inhabited dwelling house does not "merge" with a resulting homicide within the meaning of the *Ireland* doctrine, and therefore that this offense will support a conviction of second-degree felony-murder....

■ WERDEGAR, JUSTICE, concurring.... I write separately to express my understanding of the "merger" doctrine, as articulated in People v. Ireland, 70 Cal.2d 522, 75 Cal.Rptr. 188, 450 P.2d 580 (1969), and succeeding decisions, and as applied here.

I join the majority in rejecting the premise [that] *Ireland's* "integral part of the homicide" language is decisive of the merger issue in this case. In my view, however, People v. Mattison, 4 Cal.3d 177, 93 Cal.Rptr. 185, 481 P.2d 193 (1971), adopting the reasoning of the Court of Appeal in People v. Taylor, 11 Cal.App.3d 57, 89 Cal.Rptr. 697 (1970), sets forth the operative test. Those cases require us to determine whether the underlying felony was committed with a "collateral and independent felonious design." Unlike the majority, I see no reason not to follow those decisions. I do not share the majority's concern that application of the *Mattison* and *Taylor* rule leads to the anomalous result of punishing one who does not intend to injure more harshly than one who does. One who commits a felony inherently dangerous to human life with the intent to inflict injury is, in all probability, guilty of second degree murder under the implied malice theory. It follows there likely will be no disparity in the respective criminal liability of the two offenders; thus, the anomaly the majority fears is more apparent than real.

The evidence in this case supports the conclusion defendant entertained a collateral and independent felonious design under *Mattison* and *Taylor*, namely to intimidate Echaves by firing shots into his house. Accordingly, I join in the disposition this court's judgment will effect.

■ MOSK, JUSTICE, dissenting.... I dissent from the judgment to the extent that it affirms the judgment of the Court of Appeal affirming defendant's conviction of murder in the second degree.... This conviction was affected by reversible error when the superior court instructed the jury on second-degree felony-murder based on discharge of a firearm at an inhabited dwelling house.

I

... At issue is the second-degree felony-murder rule. This doctrine arises not from any statute enacted by the Legislature but rather from the common law made by the courts. "[T]he second degree felony-murder rule remains, as it has been since 1872, a judge-made doctrine without any express"—or implied—"basis in the Penal Code...." Contrary to the majority's assertion, the rule does not "impute" the element of malice aforethought. Rather, it omits that element altogether....

The purpose of the ... felony-murder rule is simply "to deter [persons] engaged in felonies from killing negligently or accidentally...." Contrary to the majority's implication at points, the objective is not to deter such persons from committing the underlying felonies themselves.

Pursuant to the so-called "merger" doctrine, the second-degree felony-murder rule is not applicable when, on the evidence adduced at trial, the underlying felony was an "integral part" of, and "included in fact" within, the resulting homicide.

A felony may be so characterized when "there was a single course of conduct with a single purpose," viz., to commit "the very assault which resulted in death...." It has been held that assault is simply a willful act "likely to result in ... physical force" against another.

A felony, however, cannot be so characterized when "there [was] an independent felonious purpose," such as to steal....

At bottom, then, the "merger" doctrine is predicated on, and limited by, the following rationale. When a felony is undertaken with the purpose to engage in an assault, in the sense of a willful act "likely to result in ... physical force" against another, the second-degree felony-murder rule cannot be invoked because its objective—to deter the perpetrator from killing negligently or accidentally—is not likely to be attained. It "can hardly be much of a deterrent to a defendant who has decided" to so act. By contrast, when a felony is undertaken with a different purpose, the rule is allowed to operate because its objective can be reached.

## II

At trial, the superior court instructed the jury on the crime of murder, [including second-degree felony-murder].... After six days of deliberations—almost as much time as was devoted to evidence, arguments, and instructions—the jury returned a verdict finding defendant guilty of murder in the second degree.[4]

## III

... The applicability of the second-degree felony-murder rule, under the governing law, depends on an affirmative answer to this threshold question: is discharge of a firearm at an inhabited dwelling house, considered in the abstract, a felony inherently dangerous to human life? The answer, however, is negative.... Logic dictates that discharge of a firearm

---

[4] It was apparently the second-degree felony-murder rule and not the facts of the case that caused the jury to have trouble reaching its verdict. Ironically, it was also the rule and not the facts that ultimately produced the determination of guilt. One juror subsequently stated: "It makes me sick and ashamed to have been part of a system that would convict someone like [defendant] of murder. Not everyone deserves a second chance but [he] does. The law is what dictated the verdict, not the jury." Another juror added: "If it wasn't for the scenario which said that the murder was a result of an intentional act of shooting into a dwelling which is a felony, then my vote would be for manslaughter. I do think that what [defendant] did was very serious but I would not rank him as a cold blooded killer."

at an inhabited dwelling house cannot carry " 'a high probability' that death will result" when [the statute] expressly does not require the presence of any occupant. Experience provides confirmation: to judge from reported appellate decisions, the prohibited conduct has resulted in death only in rare instances.... Surely, if the dwelling is not occupied at the time of the shooting, the "probability" of death is not "high"—it is zero.

[Thus, the majority errs when it reasons] that "there will always exist a significant likelihood that an occupant may be killed".... At any given time, all occupants may be absent from the dwelling. School, work, shopping, leisure pursuits, and other activities may demand attendance outside, often for the greater part of the day. Even if an occupant is present, he may be in a part of the dwelling away from the shooting. The resident is necessarily smaller than the residence. Usually, thousands of times so. For example, an average adult man may stand in 1 square foot of floor space and take up 6 cubic feet of a room; by contrast, even a modest house may cover as many as 1,500 square feet and, with 8–foot ceilings, fill as much as 12,000 cubic feet. But even if an occupant happens to be near the shooting, the dwelling itself provides significant protection....

Moreover, even if "the offense ... pose[d] a great risk ... of death," it would not matter. The prohibited conduct might be deemed "inherently dangerous to human life" under the former, less demanding definition, which was satisfied by nothing more than a "substantial risk that someone will be killed...." But it would not qualify under the present, more stringent definition, which requires " 'a high probability' that death will result." The implication that a "great risk ... of death" is a " 'high probability' of death" is dead wrong.

The majority then assert: "[A]pplication of the second-degree felony-murder rule to a homicide resulting from [discharging a firearm at a habitation] directly would serve the fundamental rationale of the felony-murder rule—the deterrence of negligent or accidental killings in the course of the commission of dangerous felonies." Are we then to conclude that the rule would lead a person who is minded to discharge a firearm at an inhabited dwelling house—"maliciously and willfully," as [the Penal Code] requires—to blaze away with due caution and circumspection? To ask the question is to provide its answer. As stated above, the rule "can hardly be much of a deterrent to a defendant who has decided" to undertake an assault, in the sense of a willful act "likely to result in ... physical force" against another. That [the felony involved here] does not bear the label of "assault" is not dispositive. It embraces its substance. Because it does, it appears in the Penal Code in the chapter entitled "Assault and Battery."

Next, to the question under the "merger" doctrine, "On the evidence adduced at trial, was defendant's discharge of a firearm at the inhabited dwelling house in question an 'integral part' of, and 'included in fact' within, the resulting homicide?," the majority answer, "No." Again, they are wrong.

In part, the majority would avoid the "merger" doctrine by limiting it to "circumstances where the only underlying ... felony committed by the defendant was assault." Even if this limitation is sound—and apparently it is not—it would not yield the result desired. That is because the only underlying felony committed by defendant here was in fact assault, in the sense of a willful act "likely to result in ... physical force" against another.

Additionally, the majority would avoid the "merger" doctrine by applying it purportedly in accordance with People v. Mattison, 4 Cal.3d 177, 93 Cal.Rptr. 185, 481 P.2d 193 (1971) and People v. Taylor, 11 Cal.App.3d 57, 89 Cal.Rptr. 697 (1970). They recognize that *Mattison* and *Taylor* each held the doctrine unavailable because the evidence adduced at trial therein revealed an "independent felonious purpose." But they seem not to recognize that, as explained, the evidence adduced at trial in this case reveals no such "independent felonious purpose," but only an intent to commit an assault, in the sense indicated above. . . .

Further, the majority attempt to avoid the "merger" doctrine by invoking Aguirre v. State, 732 S.W.2d 320 (Tex.Crim.App. 1987). *Aguirre* is distinguishable. In that case, the felony underlying the resulting homicide was "criminal mischief," a "property offense," which comprised an "attemp[t] to blow open a door with a shotgun;" it was undertaken with the "independent felonious purpose"—in our phrase—to effect an unlawful entrance into a residence. In this case, by contrast, the felony underlying the resulting homicide was discharge of a firearm at an inhabited dwelling house, a crime against the person; it was undertaken simply to effect the ultimately fatal assault, in the sense indicated above.

Unable to avoid the "merger" doctrine, the majority come close to rendering it void. They reason that the doctrine is not available in this case because "[m]ost homicides do not result" from discharge of a firearm at an inhabited dwelling house. It follows that the doctrine would not be available in any case because most homicides do not result from any one felony. Such an outcome is untenable.

■ KENNARD, JUSTICE, concurring and dissenting. . . . The majority concludes, and I agree, that the offense of discharging a firearm at an inhabited dwelling is indeed an inherently dangerous felony for purposes of the second-degree felony-murder rule because it is "an offense carrying 'a high probability' that death will result." This court has never held that for a felony to pose a high probability of death, death must result from the commission of the felony in a majority, or even in a great percentage, of instances. Nor is it necessary in this case to define the outer limits of that term. The drive-by shootings that now plague our cities frequently result in the death of someone inside a residence. Even with no one present in the targeted house, the act of shooting at an inhabited house or apartment creates a substantial or serious risk of death to occupants of neighboring houses or to passersby. . . .

I disagree with the majority, however, when it concludes that the felony of discharging a weapon at an inhabited dwelling is one that does not "merge" with the resulting homicide within the meaning of our decision in

People v. Ireland, 70 Cal.2d 522, 75 Cal.Rptr. 188, 450 P.2d 580 (1969). Under *Ireland*, which has been the law of this state for more than 25 years, a conviction for second degree felony murder cannot rest on a felony assault "that is an integral part of the homicide" and that, based on the prosecution's evidence, is "included in fact" within the resulting homicide. Later decisions have added that a defendant's commission of a felony will support a felony-murder conviction only if the defendant entertained some "independent felonious purpose" beyond mere assault. Here, the prosecution's evidence did not show that defendant had any independent felonious purpose for discharging the firearm at the Echaves residence. That conduct satisfies this court's definition of an assault. As Justice Mosk observes, it was "a willful act 'likely to result in ... physical force' against another." As such, in this case the underlying felony of discharging a firearm at an inhabited dwelling house "merges" with the resulting homicide and cannot support the second-degree murder conviction.

Although from the facts of this case a jury could find that the defendant harbored malice and accordingly could base a second-degree murder conviction on an implied malice theory (rather than a felony-murder theory), I agree with Justice Mosk that defendant's second-degree felony-murder conviction must be reversed because the record does not reveal whether the jury ever made the findings necessary to support a second-degree murder conviction premised on implied malice. I would remand this case to give the prosecution the opportunity to retry the murder charge on a theory of implied malice.

———

## NOTES ON FELONY MURDER

**1. Questions and Comments on *Hansen*.** Each of the traditional limitations on the felony-murder rule summarized in the introductory notes to this section has the effect of modifying the rule by importing some measure of culpability for the offender's conduct in relation to the victim's death—though not that normally associated with murder. The scope of the felony-murder rule in a given jurisdiction thus can be seen as an adjustment of the tension between the deterrent objectives of the rule and limitations based on individual blameworthiness. The arguments made by Judge Mosk in his dissent in *Hansen* are among those frequently offered to illustrate the anomalous results that can arise from such compromises. Do they indicate the fundamental unsoundness of the rule? Or are they inevitable byproducts of the need to draw lines in the implementation of a desirable legislative policy?

Consider also the following aspects of the *Hansen* opinion:

**(i) Determination of Inherent Dangerousness.** In *Hansen*, the court applies one of the traditional, judge-made prerequisites for second-degree felony-murder liability, namely, the requirement that the felony be "inherently dangerous to human life." The court also identifies the methodology to be used in making this essential evaluation: "In determining whether a felony is inherently dangerous, the court looks to the elements of the felony in the abstract." *Hansen* thus demands that felonies be classified according to their general tendencies, not by the facts and circumstances of the particular offense. Other courts have rejected the abstract approach, holding instead that the facts and circumstances surrounding the particular misconduct should be considered in deciding which felonies qualify for operation of the felony-murder rule. Which of these views states the preferable position? Do the purposes of the felony-murder rule suggest an answer?

From another perspective, consider the purposes that are served by the felony-murder rule. Do any of the opinions in *Hansen* clearly articulate a rationale for this strict-liability doctrine? Judge Mosk chides the majority for misstating the objectives of the rule. Does Judge Mosk's opinion offer a convincing explanation for felony murder? An explanation that supports the outcome he prefers?

If the offense is to be classified in the abstract, as *Hansen* concludes, the question to be determined would appear to be one of law for the court. But if the circumstances of the offense are to be considered, should the question be determined by the court or the jury?

**(ii) Merger.** In the *Ireland* case, discussed in *Hansen*, the defendant shot and killed his wife "by firing into her at close range two .38 caliber bullets" from his pistol. The defendant was convicted of second-degree murder based on a jury charge that included instructions authorizing the jury to rely on the felony-murder rule. The theory underlying this instruction was that the defendant had assaulted his wife with a deadly weapon and, in the course of committing that felony, he had caused her death. The court reversed the conviction:

> We have concluded that the utilization of the felony-murder rule in circumstances such as those before us extends the operation of that rule "beyond any rational function that it is designed to serve." To allow such use of the felony-murder rule would effectively preclude the jury from considering the issue of malice aforethought in all cases wherein homicide has been committed as a result of a felonious assault—a category which includes the great majority of all homicides. This kind of bootstrapping finds support neither in logic nor in law.

The court's reasoning in *Ireland* seems irrefutable in one respect: if there were no merger rule of any kind, every person guilty of any felonious grade of homicide would automatically be guilty of felony murder—in effect, for example, one who committed manslaughter would automatically be guilty of murder if the crime of manslaughter could supply the basis for a charge of felony murder. The absence of some merger doctrine thus would erase altogether the distinctions traditionally drawn in grading serious homicides. No court has refused to apply a version of the merger doctrine in this context.

The disputed issue is whether application of the felony-murder rule can be predicated on a felonious assault. In most jurisdictions, intent to injure or recklessness concerning the risk of injury is sufficient to establish the mens rea for some form of felonious assault. What is the proper approach in this situation? Should the felony-murder rule be applied in such a case or should the assault be said to merge with the homicide?

Consider State v. Wanrow, 91 Wash.2d 301, 588 P.2d 1320 (1978), in this connection. The Washington second-degree murder statute covered the killing of a human being, not justifiable or excusable, "committed with a design to effect the death of the person killed or of another, but without premeditation" (subsection (1)) or perpetrated during the commission of "a felony other than those enumerated" on the first-degree list (subsection (2)). The prosecution theory was that the defendant committed a felonious assault when she "wilfully assault[ed]" the victim with a gun, and that this offense established the predicate felony for second-degree felony murder even if she did not intend to kill the victim. The defense argued that this construction of the statute would effectively eliminate the requirement of intent to kill as an element of second-degree murder, and that application of the merger doctrine was necessary to ameliorate the otherwise harsh application of the felony-murder rule.[a] The court rejected these arguments.[b] Was this the proper result?[c]

**2. Distribution of Controlled Substances.** Should the felony-murder rule be applicable to deaths caused by the distribution of controlled substances? At least one state has addressed the question by statute. Section 782.04(1)(a)(3) of the Florida penal code provides that:

> The unlawful killing of a human being ... which resulted from the unlawful distribution of opium or any synthetic or natural salt, compound, derivative, or preparation of opium by a person 18 years of age or older, when such drug is proven to be the proximate cause of the death of the user, is murder in the first degree and constitutes a capital felony....[d]

[a] Ms. Wanrow also attacked the felony-murder rule on constitutional grounds. In rejecting her argument, the court noted that the Supreme Court of the United States had in effect upheld the constitutionality of the rule by its summary order in Thompson v. Washington, 434 U.S. 898 (1977).

[b] The court said that subsection (1) of the statute was not rendered meaningless by its decision "because there are many conceivable circumstances in which an intent to kill is both present and clearly manifested. In these circumstances the state may properly charge under subsection (1). In practice it may be that most second-degree murders are proved through subsection (2), but as long as clear cases of unpremeditated acts with a manifest intent to kill are conceivable, subsection (1) is not meaningless."

[c] The court cited decisions in four other states that had not adopted a merger rule in this context, but added that at least seven states had adopted such a rule.

The merger doctrine is applied in some jurisdictions only where the victim of the assault is also the victim of the homicide. In those jurisdictions, therefore, a felony-murder conviction becomes possible where the defendant assaults one person and accidentally kills another.

[d] The capital punishment aspect of this statute may well be unconstitutional under Enmund v. Florida, 458 U.S. 782 (1982). *Enmund* does not speak, however, to when a non-capital sentence can be imposed for felony murder.

Does this statute establish a wise public policy? What does it mean by "proximate cause"?

In the absence of legislative guidance, this contentious question has been left to the courts, and it has tended to divide them. In *Hansen*, the court cites with approval the decision by the California Court of Appeal in *Taylor*, which held that the "furnishing of heroin" is an appropriate predicate felony for purposes of felony-murder liability. Which of the following cases states the better view?

**(i) *Heacock v. Commonwealth.*** The Virginia statutes contain a traditional category of first-degree felony murder based on the Pennsylvania model, and also provide that the "killing of one accidentally, contrary to the intention of the parties, while in the prosecution of some felonious act other than those specified [in the first-degree statute], is murder of the second degree." In Heacock v. Commonwealth, 228 Va. 397, 323 S.E.2d 90 (1984), the court affirmed the felony-murder conviction of a person who supplied cocaine to the participants at a "drug party." The defendant, with another, "prepared the narcotic mixture in a spoon" prior to a fatal injection and was present at the time of the injection.

The court rejected the "inherently dangerous felony" limitation, concluding that the statute applied to "all felonious acts" except those particularly named in the first-degree statute. The court then said that even if it were prepared to accept that limitation, "which we are not," the evidence was that the defendant "knew, or should have known" that the dosage he helped prepare was inherently dangerous. It based this conclusion on the fact that another person had suffered a violent reaction to the same substance prior to the lethal injection, on medical testimony that "any amount" of cocaine could cause such a reaction in "anyone," and on the fact that the legislature had classified cocaine distribution as a very serious felony (40 years for the first offense; life imprisonment for a second). "Accordingly, we hold as a matter of law, that the unlawful distribution of cocaine is conduct potentially dangerous to human life."

The court then held that any proximate cause limitation that might apply to this class of homicide was satisfied here: "The underlying felony was distribution of cocaine, a drug the defendant should have known was inherently dangerous to human life; [the victim] ingested that drug and, as we have said, it is immaterial who made the injection; [the victim] died of 'acute intravenous cocainism'; thus cause and effect were proximately interrelated." The court concluded:

> [W]e hold that where, as here, death results from ingestion of a controlled substance, classified in law as dangerous to human life, the homicide constitutes murder of the second degree . . . if that substance had been distributed to the decedent in violation of the felony statutes of this commonwealth.

(ii) *Sheriff, Clark County v. Morris.* By contrast, in Sheriff, Clark County v. Morris, 99 Nev. 109, 659 P.2d 852 (1983), the court carefully limited the circumstances that would support conviction of a drug-seller for second-degree felony murder:

> First, it must be established by the evidence that the unauthorized sale and ingestion of [a controlled substance] in the quantities involved are inherently dangerous in the abstract, i.e., without reference to the specific victim. Second, there must be an immediate and causal relationship between the felonious conduct of the defendant and the death of the [victim]. By the term "immediate" we mean without the intervention of some other source or agency. Third, the causal relationship must extend beyond the unlawful sale of the drugs to an involvement by commission or omission in the ingestion of a lethal dosage by the decedent. This element of the rule would be satisfied by the unlawful selling or providing of the drugs and helping the recipient of the drugs to ingest a lethal dose or by unlawfully selling or dispensing the drugs and being present during the consumption of a lethal dose. Thus, absent more, the rule would not apply to a situation involving a sale only or a sale with a nonlethal dosage ingested in the defendant's presence. Although it may be cogently argued that an unlawful sale of drugs is inherently dangerous per se, and therefore an appropriate basis for a charge of murder when death occurs, we leave such a determination to the legislature.

(iii) *State v. Randolph.* In State v. Randolph, 676 S.W.2d 943 (Tenn. 1984), the court declined to embrace a felony-murder theory, but suggested that ordinary principles of culpability could be used in some contexts to convict a drug-seller of second-degree murder or involuntary manslaughter for the death of a drug-purchaser. On the question of causation, the court said "we are of the opinion that the act of the customer in injecting himself is not necessarily so unexpected, unforeseeable or remote as to insulate the seller from criminal responsibility as a matter of law."

3. **Attempted Felony Murder.** In Amlotte v. Florida, 456 So.2d 448 (Fla.1984), the court held that "attempted felony murder is a crime in Florida" and that the "essential elements of the crime are the perpetration or attempt to perpetrate an enumerated felony, together with an intentional overt act, or the aiding and abetting of such an act, which could, but does not, cause the death of another." It added: "Because the attempt occurs during the commission of a felony, the law, as under the felony-murder doctrine, presumes the existence of the specific intent required to prove attempt." The court made these statements in the context of an attempted robbery where two of the felons returned gunfire when a victim of the robbery tried to shoot them. Is this a sound extension of the felony-murder rule?

---

# State v. Sophophone

Supreme Court of Kansas, 2001.
270 Kan. 703, 19 P.3d 70.

■ LARSON, JUDGE. This is Sanexay Sophophone's direct appeal of his felony-murder conviction for the death of his co-felon during flight from an aggravated burglary in which both men participated.

The facts are not in dispute. Sophophone and three other individuals conspired to and broke into a house in Emporia. The resident reported the break-in to the police.

Police officers responded to the call, saw four individuals leaving the back of the house, shined a light on the suspects, identified themselves as police officers, and ordered them to stop. The individuals, one being Sophophone, started to run away. One officer ran down Sophophone, hand-cuffed him, and placed him in a police car.

Other officers arrived to assist in apprehending the other individuals as they were running from the house. An officer chased one of the suspects later identified as Somphone Sysoumphone. Sysoumphone crossed railroad tracks, jumped a fence, and then stopped. The officer approached with his weapon drawn and ordered Sysoumphone to the ground and not to move. Sysoumphone was lying face down but raised up and fired at the officer, who returned fire and killed him. . . .

Sophophone was charged with ... aggravated burglary and felony murder. . . .

Sophophone moved to dismiss the felony-murder charges, contending the complaint was defective because it alleged that he and not the police officer had killed Sysoumphone and further because he was in custody and sitting in the police car when the deceased was killed and therefore not attempting to commit or even fleeing from an inherently dangerous felony. His motion to dismiss was denied by the trial court.

Sophophone was convicted by a jury of all counts. His motion for judgment of acquittal was denied. He was sentenced on all counts. He appeals only his conviction of felony murder. . . .

We consider only the question of law, upon which our review is unlimited, of whether Sophophone can be convicted of felony murder for the killing of a co-felon not caused by his acts but by the lawful acts of a police officer acting in self-defense in the course and scope of his duties in apprehending the co-felon fleeing from an aggravated burglary.

The applicable provisions of K.S.A. 21–3401 read as follows:

> Murder in the first degree is the killing of a human being committed: ...

> (b) in the commission of, attempt to commit, or flight from an inherently dangerous felony as defined in K.S.A. 21–3436. . . . "

Aggravated burglary is one of the inherently dangerous felonies as enumerated by K.S.A. 21–3436(10).

Sophophone does not dispute that aggravated burglary is an inherently dangerous felony which given the right circumstances would support a felony-murder charge. His principal argument centers on his being in custody at the time his co-felon was killed by the lawful act of the officer which he contends was a "break in circumstances" sufficient to insulate him from further criminal responsibility.

This "intervening cause" or "break in circumstances" argument has no merit under the facts of this case. We have held in numerous cases that "time, distance, and the causal relationship between the underlying felony and a killing are factors to be considered in determining whether the killing occurs in the commission of the underlying felony and the defendant is therefore subject to the felony-murder rule." Based on the uncontroverted evidence in this case, the killing took place during flight from the aggravated burglary, and it is only because the act which resulted in the killing was a lawful one by a third party that a question of law exists as to whether Sophophone can be convicted of felony murder. . . .[a]

Our cases are legion in interpreting the felony-murder statute, but we have not previously decided a case where the killing was not by the direct acts of the felon but rather where a co-felon was killed during his flight from the scene of the felony by the lawful acts of a third party (in our case, a law enforcement officer).

A similar scenario took place in State v. Murrell, 224 Kan. 689, 585 P.2d 1017 (1978), where Murrell was charged with felony murder for the death of his co-felon who had been shot by the robbery victim who had returned gunfire from Murrell. However, Murrell was acquitted of felony murder and his appeal involved only issues relating to his other convictions.

Although there were clearly different facts, we held in State v. Hoang, 243 Kan. 40, 755 P.2d 7 (1988), that felony murder may include the accidental death of a co-felon during the commission of arson. The decedents had conspired with Hoang to burn down a building housing a Wichita restaurant/club but died when they were trapped inside the building while starting the fire. Hoang was an active participant in the felony and present at the scene, although he remained outside the building while his three accomplices entered the building with containers of gasoline to start the fire.

We held, in a split decision, that the decedents were killed during the perpetration of a felony inherently dangerous to human life and there was nothing in the statute to exclude the killing of co-felons from its application. It must be pointed out that the facts in *Hoang* involved the wrongful

---

[a] The court identified two purposes of felony murder in omitted portions of its opinion. One was "to deter those engaged in felonies from killing negligently or accidentally." The other was "to relieve the state of the burden of proving premeditation and malice when the victim's death is caused by the killer while he is committing another felony."—[Footnote by eds.]

acts of a co-felon which were directly responsible for the deaths of his co-felons.

The dissent in *Hoang* noted that in previous cases the felony-murder rule had been applied only to the deaths of innocents and not to the deaths of co-felons. The result was deemed by the dissent to be contrary to legislative intent and the strict construction of criminal statutes that is required.

With this brief background of our prior Kansas cases, we look to the prevailing views concerning the applicability of the felony-murder doctrine where the killing has been caused by the acts of a third party. . . . In Joshua Dressler, Understanding Criminal Law (1987), the question is posed of whether the felony-murder rule should apply when the fatal act is performed by a non-felon. Dressler [identifies two approaches]:

. . . The "Agency" Approach

The majority rule is that the felony-murder doctrine does not apply if the person who directly causes the death is a non-felon. . . .

The reasoning of this approach stems from accomplice liability theory. Generally speaking, the acts of the primary party (the person who directly commits the offense) are imputed to an accomplice on the basis of the agency doctrine. It is as if the accomplice says to the primary party: "Your acts are my acts." It follows that [a co-felon] cannot be convicted of the homicides because the primary party was not the person with whom she was an accomplice. It is not possible to impute the acts of the antagonistic party—[the non-felon or] the police officer—to [a co-felon] on the basis of agency.

. . . The "Proximate Causation" Approach

An alternative theory, followed by a few courts . . ., holds that a felon may be held responsible under the felony-murder rule for a killing committed by a non-felon if the felon set in motion the acts which resulted in the victim's death.

Pursuant to this rule, the issue becomes one of proximate causation: if an act by one felon is the proximate cause of the homicidal conduct by [the non-felon] or the police officer, murder liability is permitted.

In 2 Wayne R. LaFave & Austin W. Scott, Jr., Substantive Criminal Law (1986), the author opines: "Although it is now generally accepted that there is no felony-murder liability when one of the felons is shot and killed by the victim, a police officer, or a bystander, it is not easy to explain why this is so."

The author discusses foreseeability, [concludes] that it is not correct to say that a felon is never liable when the death is lawful because it is "justifiable," and goes on to state:

A more plausible explanation, it is submitted, is the feeling that it is not justice (though it may be poetic justice) to hold the felon liable for murder on account of the death, which the felon did not intend, of a co-felon willingly participating in the risky venture. It is true that it is no defense to intentional homicide crimes that the victim voluntarily placed himself in danger of death at the hands of the defendant, or even that he consented to his own death: a mercy killing constitutes murder; and aiding suicide is murder unless special legislation reduces it to manslaughter. But with unintended killings it would seem proper to take the victim's willing participation into account. . . .

As we noted in *Hoang*, it is not very helpful to review case law from other states because of differences in statutory language; however, the high courts which have considered this precise question are divided between the agency approach and the proximate cause approach.

The leading case adopting the agency approach is Commonwealth v. Redline, 391 Pa. 486 (1958), where the underlying principle of the agency theory is described as follows:

> In adjudging a felony-murder, it is to be remembered at all times that the thing which is imputed to a felon for a killing incidental to his felony is malice and not the act of killing. The mere coincidence of homicide and felony is not enough to satisfy the felony-murder doctrine.

The following statement from *Redline* is more persuasive for Sophophone:

> In the present instance, the victim of the homicide was one of the robbers who, while resisting apprehension in his effort to escape, was shot and killed by a policeman in the performance of his duty. Thus, the homicide was justifiable and, obviously, could not be availed of, on any rational legal theory, to support a charge of murder. How can anyone, no matter how much of an outlaw he may be, have a criminal charge lodged against him for the consequences of the lawful conduct of another person? The mere question carries with it its own answer. . . .

The minority of the states whose courts have adopted the proximate cause theory believe their legislatures intended that any person . . . who commits an inherently dangerous felony should be held responsible for any death which is a direct and foreseeable consequence of the actions of those committing the felony. These courts apply the civil law concept of proximate cause to felony-murder situations. . . .

It should be mentioned that some courts have been willing to impose felony-murder liability even where the shooting was by a person other than one of the felons in the so-called "shield" situations where it has been reasoned "that a felon's act of using a victim as a shield in compelling a victim to occupy a place or position of danger constitutes a direct lethal act against the victim."

[We did not] adopt the proximate cause approach . . . in State v. Shaw, 260 Kan. 396, 921 P.2d 779 (1990), where we held that a defendant who bound and gagged an 86–year-old robbery victim with duct tape was liable for the victim's death when he died of a heart attack while so bound and gagged. Although we may speak of causation in such a case, our ruling in *Shaw* is better described [as follows:] "The victim must be taken as the defendant finds him. Death resulting from a heart attack will support a felony-murder conviction if there is a causal connection between the heart attack and the felonious conduct of the defendant." This is not the embracing of a proximate cause approach under the facts we face.

[The State also urges that] in State v. Lamae, 268 Kan. 544, 998 P.2d 106 (2000), we recognized that the killing could be perpetrated ["by the defendant *or another*"]. The case involved the death of a participant in a methamphetamine fire. Our opinion did state: "It is true that there must be a direct causal connection between the commission of the felony and the homicide to invoke the felony-murder rule. However, the general rules of proximate cause used in civil actions do not apply." This language, if taken in isolation, is much more favorable to Sophophone's position. However, we believe that neither this statement nor the "or another" language in *Lamae* should be given undue consideration when we resolve the different question we face here.

There is language in K.S.A. 21–3205(2) that predicates criminal responsibility to an aider or abettor for "any other crime committed in pursuance of the intended crime if reasonably foreseeable by such person as a probable consequence of committing or attempting to commit the crime intended." This wording does not assist us for the killing of the co-felon in our case where it was the lawful act by a law enforcement officer who was in no manner subject to these aider and abettor provisions.

The overriding fact which exists in our case is that neither Sophophone nor any of his accomplices "killed" anyone. The law enforcement officer acted lawfully in committing the act which resulted in the death of the co-felon. This does not fall within the language of K.S.A. 21–3205 since the officer committed no crime.

[To] impute the act of killing to Sophophone when the act was the lawful and courageous one of a law enforcement officer acting in the line of his duties is contrary to the strict construction we are required to give criminal statutes. There is considerable doubt about the meaning of K.S.A. 21–3401(b) as applied to the facts of this case, and we believe that making one criminally responsible for the lawful acts of a law enforcement officer is not the intent of the felony-murder statute as it is currently written. . . .

It does little good to suggest one construction over another would prevent the commission of dangerous felonies or that it would deter those who engage in dangerous felonies from killing purposely, negligently, or accidentally. Actually, innocent parties and victims of crimes appear to be those who are sought to be protected rather than co-felons.

We hold that under the facts of this case where the killing resulted from the lawful acts of a law enforcement officer in attempting to apprehend a co-felon, Sophophone is not criminally responsible for the resulting death of Somphone Sysoumphone, and his felony-murder conviction must be reversed.

This decision is in no manner inconsistent with our rulings in *Hoang* or *Lamae*, which are based on the direct acts of a co-felon and are simply factually different from our case. . . .

Reversed.

■ ABBOT, JUDGE, with whom CHIEF JUDGE McFARLAND and JUDGE DAVIS join, dissenting. The issue facing the court in this case is whether Sophophone may be legally convicted under the felony-murder statute when he did not pull the trigger and where the victim was one of the co-felons. The majority holds that Sophophone cannot be convicted of felony murder. I dissent. . . .

When an issue requires statutory analysis and the statute is unambiguous, we are limited by the wording chosen by the legislature. We are not free to alter the statutory language, regardless of the result. In the present case, the felony-murder statute does not require us to adopt the "agency" theory favored by the majority. Indeed, there is nothing in the statute which establishes an agency approach. The statute does not address the issue at all. The requirements, according to the statute, are: (1) there must be a killing, and (2) the killing must be committed in the commission, attempt to commit, or flight from an inherently dangerous felony. The statute simply does not contain the limitations discussed by the majority. . . .

Moreover, there are sound reasons to adopt the proximate cause approach described in the majority opinion. In State v. Hoang, 243 Kan. 40, 755 P.2d 7 (1988), this court took such an approach, although never referring to it by name. In *Hoang*, Chief Justice McFarland, writing for the court, discussed at length the requirements of the felony-murder rule in Kansas and stated:

> In felony-murder cases, the elements of malice, deliberation, and premeditation which are required for murder in the first degree are deemed to be supplied by felonious conduct alone if a homicide results. To support a conviction for felony murder, all that is required is to prove that a felony was being committed, which felony was inherently dangerous to human life, and that the homicide which followed was a direct result of the commission of that felony. In a felony-murder case, evidence of who the trigger-man is is irrelevant and all participants are principals.

> The purpose of the felony-murder doctrine is to deter all those engaged in felonies from killing negligently or accidentally. . . .

> It is argued in the case before us that felony murder applies only to the deaths of "innocents" rather than co-felons. There is nothing in our statute on which to base such a distinction. . . .

Dung and Thuong, the decedents herein, were human beings who were killed in the perpetration of a felony.... Defendant was an active participant in the felony and present on the scene during all pertinent times. There is nothing in the statute excluding the killing of the co-felons herein from its application. For this court to exclude the co-felons would constitute judicial amendment of a statute on philosophic rather than legal grounds. This would be highly improper. The legislature has defined felony murder. If this definition is to be amended to exclude the killing of co-felons therefrom under circumstances such as are before us, it is up to the legislature to make [the] amendment....

The majority in this case points out that the majority of states have adopted the agency approach when faced with the death of a co-felon. They acknowledge, however, that because statutes vary significantly from state to state, reference to a "majority" rule and a "minority" rule is meaningless. Indeed, an in-depth analysis of the current case law in this area leads me to the following conclusions: (1) While a majority of states would agree with the majority opinion in this case, the margin is slim; (2) many of the states that have adopted the so-called "agency" approach have done so because the statutory language in their state requires them to do so; and (3) several of the states that have adopted the "proximate cause" approach have done so because their statutes are silent on the issue, like Kansas....

In my opinion, our statute is unambiguous and simply does not require the defendant to be the direct cause of the victim's death, nor does it limit application of the felony-murder rule to the death of "innocents."

In People v. Lowery, 178 Ill. 2d 462, 687 N.E.2d 973 (1997), the Illinois Supreme Court discussed the public policy reasons justifying application of a proximate cause approach, stating:

It is equally consistent with reason and sound public policy to hold that when a felon's attempt to commit a forcible felony sets in motion a chain of events which were or should have been within his contemplation when the motion was initiated, he should be held responsible for any death which by direct and almost inevitable sequence results from the initial criminal act. Thus, there is no reason why the principle underlying the doctrine of proximate cause should not apply to criminal cases. Moreover, we believe that the intent behind the felony-murder doctrine would be thwarted if we did not hold felons responsible for the foreseeable consequences of their actions.

In Sheckles v. State, 684 N.E.2d 201 (Ind. Ct. App. 1997), the Indiana Court of Appeals opined:

[A] person who commits or attempts to commit one of the offenses designated in the felony-murder statute is criminally responsible for a homicide which results from the act of one who was not a participant in the original criminal activity. Where the accused reasonably should have ... foreseen that the commission of or attempt to commit the contemplated felony would likely create a situation which would expose another to the danger of death at the hands of a nonparticipant in the felony, and where death in fact occurs as was foreseeable, the creation of such a dangerous situation is a . . . medium in effecting or bringing about the death of the victim.

Likewise, the Supreme Court of New Jersey discussed the historical justification for application of the proximate cause rule in felony-murder cases in State v. Martin, 119 N.J. 2, 573 A.2d 1359 (1990), stating:

> More recently, felony murder has been viewed not as a crime of transferred intent, but as one of absolute or strict liability. Whether the offense is viewed as a crime of transferred intent or as one of absolute liability, the continuing justification for the felony-murder rule is that in some circumstances one who commits a felony should be liable for a resulting, albeit unintended, death. Conversely, other deaths are so remotely related to the underlying felony that the actor should not be held culpable for them. Our task is to ascertain the circumstances in which the Legislature has decided that one who commits a felony should also be culpable for a resulting death.
>
> The historical justification for the rule is that it serves as a general deterrent against the commission of violent crimes. The rationale is that if potential felons realize that they will be culpable as murderers for a death that occurs during the commission of a felony, they will be less likely to commit the felony. From this perspective, the imposition of strict liability without regard to the intent to kill serves to deter the commission of serious crimes.

Here, Sophophone set in motion acts [that] could have very easily resulted in the death of a law enforcement officer, and in my opinion this is exactly the type of case the legislature had in mind when it adopted the felony-murder rule. . . .

---

## FURTHER NOTES ON FELONY MURDER

**1. Homicide Committed by a Non–Participant.** Situations where the homicide is actually committed by the police or a victim have proved particularly troublesome in American litigation over the proper scope of the felony-murder rule. As the opinions in *Sophophone* vividly illustrate, courts have divided sharply over this question, adopting two different approaches to the problem. The first, sometimes called the "proximate-cause" theory, is illustrated by State v. Canola, 135 N.J.Super. 224, 343 A.2d 110 (1975). Four men were engaged in an armed robbery. One of them shot a victim of the offense, who in turn drew a weapon and shot his assailant. Both men died. The defendant was convicted of felony murder for *both* deaths, and his convictions were affirmed. The court said that "[t]he proximate-cause theory simply stated is that when a felon sets in motion a chain of events which were or should have been within his contemplation when the motion was initiated, the felon, and those acting in concert with him, should be held responsible for any death which by direct and almost inevitable consequences results from the initial criminal act.''

Canola's conviction for the murder of his accomplice was reversed by the New Jersey Supreme Court, 73 N.J. 206, 374 A.2d 20 (1977). The court rejected the ''proximate cause'' theory and adopted instead the so-called ''agency theory,'' applied in Commonwealth v. Redline, 391 Pa. 486, 137 A.2d 472 (1958). In *Redline,* the defendant and a co-felon were engaged in the commission of an armed robbery. They engaged in a gun battle with the police, during which the co-felon was killed by police bullets. The Pennsylvania Supreme Court held that ''in order to convict for felony murder, the killing must have been done by the defendant or by an accomplice or confederate or by one acting in furtherance of the felonious undertaking.'' As described in *Canola,* ''the [*Redline*] court held that in order to convict for felony murder the killing must have been done by defendant or someone acting in concert with him in furtherance of the felonious undertaking; that the death must be a consequence of the felony and not merely coincidental; and that a justifiable homicide could not be availed of to support a charge of murder.''

What would be the result on the *Canola* facts under *Sophophone?* Does Kansas squarely endorse the ''agency'' theory of felony murder over the ''proximate cause'' theory? Which theory is to be preferred?

**2.   *People v. Washington.*** In order to answer the last question, one must have in mind the general rationales for felony murder. What justifications for the rule are cited by the majority in *Sophophone?* Which justifications does the dissent endorse? Do the judges explain why those justifications support one approach over the other? Consider as well the arguments of Chief Justice Traynor in People v. Washington, 62 Cal.2d 777, 44 Cal.Rptr. 442, 402 P.2d 130 (1965). The defendant was convicted of felony murder for participating in a robbery in which his accomplice was killed by a victim of the robbery. In reversing the conviction, the court reasoned:

> The purpose of the felony-murder rule is to deter felons from killing negligently or accidentally by holding them strictly responsible for killings they commit. This purpose is not served by punishing them for killings committed by their victims.

> It is contended, however, that another purpose of the felony-murder rule is to prevent the commission of robberies. Neither the common-law rationale of the rule nor the penal code supports this contention. In every robbery there is a possibility that the victim will resist and kill. The robber has little control over such a killing once the robbery is undertaken.... To impose an additional penalty for the killing would discriminate between robbers, not on the basis of any difference in their own conduct, but solely on the basis of the response by others that the robber's conduct happened to induce. An additional penalty for a homicide committed by the

victim would deter robbery haphazardly at best. To "prevent stealing, [the law] would do better to hang one thief in every thousand by lot." Oliver Wendell Holmes, The Common Law 58 (1881)....

A defendant need not do the killing himself, however, to be guilty of murder. He may be vicariously responsible under the rules defining principals and criminal conspiracies. All persons aiding and abetting the commission of a robbery are guilty of first-degree murder when one of them kills while acting in furtherance of the common design. Moreover, when the defendant intends to kill or intentionally commits acts that are likely to kill with a conscious disregard for life, he is guilty of murder even though he uses another person to accomplish his objective.

Defendants who initiate gun battles may also be found guilty of murder if their victims resist and kill. Under such circumstances, "the defendant for a base, anti-social motive and with wanton disregard for human life, does an act that involves a high degree of probability that it will result in death" and it is unnecessary to imply malice by invoking the felony-murder doctrine. To invoke the felony-murder doctrine to imply malice in such a case is unnecessary and overlooks the principles of criminal liability that should govern the responsibility of one person for a killing committed by another.

To invoke the felony-murder doctrine when the killing is not committed by the defendant or by his accomplice could lead to absurd results. Thus, two men rob a grocery store and flee in opposite directions. The owner of the store follows one of the robbers and kills him. Neither robber may have fired a shot. Neither robber may have been armed with a deadly weapon. If the felony-murder doctrine applied, however, the surviving robber could be convicted of first-degree murder, even though he was captured by a policeman and placed under arrest at the time his accomplice was killed.

The felony-murder rule has been criticized on the grounds that in almost all cases in which it is applied it is unnecessary and that it erodes the relation between criminal liability and moral culpability. Although it is the law in this state, it should not be extended beyond any rational function that it is designed to serve. Accordingly, for a defendant to be guilty of murder under the felony-murder rule the act of killing must be committed by the defendant or by his accomplice acting in furtherance of their common design.

Is Chief Justice Traynor's opinion internally consistent? Why is the deterrent purpose of the felony-murder rule accomplished by punishing felons for accidental killings committed by them, but not for intentional or accidental killings committed by their victims? Does the proximate-cause approach extend the rule "beyond any rational function that it is designed to serve"?

**3.   Relation to Principles of Causation.** Causation problems can arise in two distinct ways in connection with felony-murder situations:

**(i)   Application of Felony–Murder Rule.** The first concerns the principles of causation that should control the operation of the felony-murder rule itself. The debate between the "proximate-cause" theory and the "agency" theory for analyzing cases where the homicide is committed by a victim or the police is illustrative. Are those courts which adopt the "agency" theory in effect applying narrower notions of proximate cause to the felony-murder rule than would otherwise be applicable in a prosecution for criminal homicide? If the answer is "yes," then it would seem that a special doctrine of causation is being applied to limit the scope of the felony-murder rule. On the other hand, if the answer is "no," then it would seem that courts adopting the "proximate cause" approach are creating a special doctrine of causation in order to extend the felony-murder rule beyond the limits that ordinary principles of criminal liability would suggest. Which is the more accurate answer to the question? Should special causation principles be applied to limit or to extend the scope of the felony-murder rule?

**(ii)   Independent Prosecution for Murder.** The second way in which causation principles become relevant concerns the possibility of a murder prosecution without resort to the felony-murder rule. Consider the following hypothetical. If *A* initiates a gun battle with intent to kill or in reckless disregard of human life, and if the victim returns fire and accidentally kills a bystander, would normal principles of causation permit *A*'s conviction of murder? Is the action of the victim an "independent intervening cause" of the bystander's death? If the answer to this question is "no," then—as *Washington* indicates—ordinary principles of causation and accessorial liability could handle many cases which have tested the limits of the felony murder rule.

Note also the relationship between these two ways in which causation can be relevant. If an independent prosecution for murder is possible in those cases where the defendant is culpable as to death (albeit not necessarily the one that actually occurred), does this then make the use of narrower causation principles in connection with the operation of the felony-murder rule more justifiable? Should the felony-murder doctrine be discarded entirely in favor of such independent prosecutions for murder? What kinds of murder convictions would be excluded by such an approach? Is the loss significant to the deterrent purposes of the law?

**4.   Relation to Principles of Accessorial Liability.** The felony-murder rule also intersects with problems of accessorial liability. It is again helpful in thinking about this relationship to focus separately on the operation of the felony-murder rule itself and the possibility of an independent prosecution for murder.

**(i) Application of Felony–Murder Rule.** The felony-murder rule operates as an independent basis for accomplice liability. This aspect of the felony-murder rule does not depend on the debate between the "agency" and "proximate cause" theories of felony-murder. Under any formulation of the rule, once its scope is determined all participants in the felony are guilty of murder if any one of them commits an included homicide.

Does this aspect of the felony-murder rule represent an extension of the ordinary principles of accessorial liability that would otherwise determine responsibility for the acts of a confederate? Do the policies underlying the felony-murder rule suggest the need for a separate set of more inclusive principles of accomplice liability? Or is the felony-murder rule on this point simply redundant, i.e., does it lead to the result that ordinary principles of accomplice liability would otherwise accomplish in any event?[a]

**(ii) Independent Prosecution for Murder.** In situations to which the felony-murder rule does not apply, as in *Sophophone*, the way is nonetheless open for the prosecutor to rely on ordinary principles of accomplice liability in an effort to secure a murder conviction. Given the possibility of an ordinary murder prosecution and conviction of accomplices under ordinary principles, is there any need for a special felony-murder rule for accomplices?

5. ***People v. Antick.*** People v. Antick, 15 Cal.3d 79, 123 Cal.Rptr. 475, 539 P.2d 43 (1975), provides a testing situation for application of these principles. Antick was charged, inter alia, with burglary and murder. The burglary was said to have been committed by two people—Antick and Bose. Bose was confronted after the burglary when police spotted him sitting in a stopped car. A person later thought to be Antick was walking away from the car as the police approached. Bose initiated a gun battle, and was killed by a policeman in the exchange of fire. Antick was not apprehended at the scene, but was later identified as the second person involved in the burglary and presumably the person who was walking away from the car when the police approached. The prosecution of Antick for felony murder was based on the theory, as charged in the information, that "during the perpetration of the [September 28] burglary [defendant's] co-partner in the burglary, Donald Joseph Bose, initiated a gun battle which was the direct and unlawful cause of the death of the said Donald Joseph Bose."

Antick was convicted of both burglary and murder, but the murder conviction was set aside on appeal. The court began its discussion as follows:

> [D]efendant's conviction of first-degree murder may have been based upon either of two theories: (i) his participation in the

---

[a] The relationship of the felony-murder rule to principles of accessorial liability is further complicated by the possibility of a conspiracy charge. As developed in the materials on conspiracy in Chapter VII, the liability of a conspirator for crimes committed by other conspirators is frequently measured by the law of conspiracy without reference to the law of accomplice liability. Thus, in felony-murder situations there are three possible bases of accomplice liability: (i) liability under ordinary complicity rules; (ii) liability as a co-conspirator; and (iii) liability under the felony-murder rule.

commission of a burglary which resulted in the death of his accomplice, or (ii) his vicarious liability for the crimes of his accomplice. Defendant contends that on the present record he cannot be convicted of murder under either theory.

Our consideration of defendant's contention requires us at the start to briefly review the basic principles underlying the crime of murder, the felony-murder doctrine and the theory of accomplice liability. A defendant is not guilty of murder unless he is legally chargeable, either by virtue of his own conduct or that of an accomplice, with the two component elements of the crime: its actus reus, a homicide, and its mens rea, malice.[8] "Homicide is the killing of a human being by another human being." Malice is the state of mind of one who has "an intent to kill or an intent with conscious disregard for life to commit acts likely to kill."[9] In addition, "[t]he felony-murder doctrine ascribes malice ... to the felon who kills in the perpetration of an inherently dangerous felony."[10]

The imputation of malice by application of the felony-murder doctrine has been limited by this court to those cases in which the actual killing is committed by the defendant or his accomplice.

> When a killing is not committed by a robber or by his accomplice but by his victim, malice aforethought is not attributable to the robber, for the killing is not committed by him in the perpetration or attempt to perpetrate robbery. It is not enough that the killing was a risk reasonably to be foreseen and that the robbery might therefore be regarded as a proximate cause of the killing. Section 189 requires that the felon or his accomplice commit the killing, for if he does not, the killing is not committed to perpetrate the felony. Indeed, in the present case the killing was committed to thwart a felony. To include such killings within Section 189 would expand the meaning of the words "murder ... which is committed in the perpetration [of] robbery ..." beyond common understanding.

People v. Washington, 62 Cal.2d 777, 781, 44 Cal.Rptr. 442, 445, 402 P.2d 130, 133 (1965).

The court then summarized the applicable principles:

---

[8] Cal.Penal Code § 187 provides in pertinent part: "(a) Murder is the unlawful killing of a human being ... with malice aforethought."

[9] Cal.Penal Code § 188 defines "malice" for purposes of murder: "Such malice may be express or implied. It is express when there is manifested a deliberate intention unlawfully to take away the life of a fellow creature. It is implied, when no considerable provocation appears, or when the circumstances attending the killing show an abandoned and malignant heart."

[10] Under Cal.Penal Code § 189, "[a]ll murder ... which is committed in the perpetration of, or attempt to perpetrate, arson, rape, robbery, burglary, mayhem, or any act punishable under Section 288 [lewd or lascivious acts against children], is murder of the first degree...."

The operation of these principles can best be illustrated by the following example. Three persons agree to commit a robbery, and during its commission *one* of them initiates a gun battle in which the victim or a police officer in reasonable response to such act kills *another* of the robbers. Since the immediate cause of death is the act of the victim or the officer, the felony-murder rule is not applicable to convert the killing into a murder. Nevertheless, the robber initiating the gun battle and the third accomplice are guilty of murder. The former commits a homicide, since his conduct is the proximate cause of the death of another human being; the intervening act of the victim or police officer is not an independent superseding cause, eliminating responsibility for the killing. Furthermore, in initiating the shootout the robber acts with malice, having intentionally and with conscious disregard for life engaged in conduct likely to kill. That this malice is directed at someone other than his crime partner who as a proximate result of the robber's acts is eventually killed "does not prevent the killing from constituting the offense of murder [since] the law transfers the felonious intent from the original object of his attempt to the person killed and the homicide so committed is murder." Since in the posited situation the robber initiating the gun battle is acting in furtherance of the common design of all three participants, the third robber as well may be held vicariously liable for the murder.

The conclusion was:

Applying these principles to the case at bench, we first observe that on the uncontradicted evidence defendant himself did not participate in the immediate events which preceded his accomplice's death. Under the People's version of the facts, which we accept as accurate for purposes of this discussion, Bose initiated a gun battle with the police in order to escape apprehension for a burglary which he and defendant had recently committed. The police officer responded by killing Bose. As the immediate cause of death was the act of the officer, it is clear that the felony-murder rule does not operate to convert the killing into a murder for which defendant may be liable by virtue of his participation in the underlying burglary.[11] *People v. Washington*, supra.

Nor may defendant be held legally accountable for Bose's death based upon his vicarious liability for the crimes of his accomplice. In order to predicate defendant's guilt upon this theory, it is necessary to prove that Bose committed a murder, in other words, that he caused the death of another human being [and] that he acted with malice.

---

[11] The People concede in their brief on appeal that the felony-murder instruction was erroneous and that the only possible legal basis for defendant's murder conviction is his vicarious liability for the consequences of Bose's act in initiating the shootout with the police officers.

It is well settled that Bose's conduct in initiating a shootout with police officers may establish the requisite malice. As we have noted on a number of occasions, a person who initiates a gun battle in the course of committing a felony intentionally and with a conscious disregard for life commits an act that is likely to cause death. However, Bose's malicious conduct did not result in the unlawful killing of *another* human being, but rather in Bose's own death. The only homicide which occurred was the justifiable killing of Bose by the police officer. Defendant's criminal liability certainly cannot be predicated upon the actions of the officer. As Bose could not be found guilty of murder in connection with his own death, it is impossible to base defendant's liability for this offense upon his vicarious responsibility for the crime of his accomplice.

In summary defendant's conviction of the murder of his accomplice Bose cannot be upheld either on the doctrine of felony-murder or on a theory of vicarious liability. We are therefore compelled to conclude that on the instant record defendant as a matter of law cannot be found guilty of murder and that the verdict of the jury to that effect is against the law and the evidence.

**6. Questions and Comments on *Antick*.** Focus on the three-person example given by the *Antick* court. One accomplice (*A1*) is killed by the police after another (*P1*) initiates a gun battle. *P1* is guilty of murder, not because of the felony murder rule but based the application of ordinary actus reus, mens rea, and causation principles. The other accomplice (*A2*) is also guilty of murder, in this case again not because of the felony murder rule but because of the application of ordinary principles of liability as an accessory.

In Antick's case, however, he cannot be convicted of murder under any theory. Felony murder principles do not apply because California adopts the "agency" theory. Accomplice liability principles do not apply either, because Bose did not commit murder. But in terms of personal culpability, personal responsibility, or any other principles relevant to the appropriate imposition of criminal sanctions, how is Antick different from *A2*? Why should he go free of a murder conviction when *A2* is convicted?

Consider the potential application of two Model Penal Code provisions to Antick's situation. Section 2.06(4) provides:

When causing a particular result is an element of an offense, an accomplice in the conduct causing such result is an accomplice in the commission of that offense, if he acts with the kind of culpability, if any, with respect to that result that is sufficient for the commission of the offense.

And § 5.01(3) states:

A person who engages in conduct designed to aid another to commit a crime which would establish his complicity under Section 2.06 if the crime were committed by such other person, is guilty of an attempt to commit the crime, although the crime is not committed or attempted by such other person.

Does this mean that Antick could be convicted of attempted murder under the Model Code? Is this the right outcome?

**7. Duration of the Felony.** Sophophone moved to dismiss the felony-murder charges on the ground that the killing did not occur during the commission or attempted commission of a felony. Indeed, Sophophone argued that the killing did not even take place during a period of flight from the felony because, at the time the officer shot his co-felon, Sophophone "was in custody and sitting in the police car." Since the killing occurred during this "break in the circumstances," he argued, homicide liability could not rest on the felony-murder doctrine.

This argument raises the general problem of determining the operative time span during which the felony-murder rule can be applied—when, in other words, the felony to which the rule attaches begins and when it ends. The normal statement of the rule is that the felony-murder doctrine applies from the time when an attempt to commit the felony has occurred, through its actual commission, and through the period of immediate flight therefrom. One of the ways in which the felony-murder rule can be contracted or expanded is by tinkering with the time during which the felony can be said to be in process. Are there ways in which this issue can be intelligently addressed? Does the purpose of the felony-murder rule suggest how lines of this sort should be drawn? Consider the comments in Herbert Wechsler & Jerome Michael, A Rationale of the Law of Homicide I, 37 Colum.L.Rev. 701, 716–17 (1937):

> The rule has ... been restricted by the contraction of the period during which the felony can be said to be "in the course of" commission. Thus, if a person in flight kills a policeman attempting to interfere with his escape, it is not felony-murder if he was not carrying away spoils. Conceding the ever present legislative necessity for reconciling extremes by drawing arbitrary lines the justice of which must be viewed from afar, the limits of intelligent casuistry have clearly been reached when the question whether judgment of death shall be imposed on a man who went no further than to participate in the planning of a robbery depends upon whether his accomplice shot the victim in his store or on the sidewalk outside.

The court summarily rejected Sophophone's argument as having "no merit under the facts of this case." In the court's view, the "uncontroverted evidence" established that "the killing took place during flight from the aggravated burglary." Is this the right answer?

**8. Modern Statutes.** Most current penal codes do not speak specifically to the situations described in *Antick* and the preceding notes, and the courts are accordingly left to the development of common-law principles to decide such cases. There are, however, exceptions. The criminal code revisions adopted in New York in 1965 were widely copied on the question of felony murder. Section 125.25(3) provided that it would be felony murder when:

> Acting either alone or with one or more other persons, he commits or attempts to commit robbery, burglary, kidnapping, arson, rape in the first degree, sodomy in the first degree, sexual abuse in the first degree, aggravated sexual abuse, escape in the first degree, or escape in the second degree, and, in the course of and in furtherance of such crime or of immediate flight therefrom, he, or another participant, if there be any, causes the death of a person other than one of the participants, except that in any prosecution under this subdivision, in which the defendant was not the only participant in the underlying crime, it is an affirmative defense that the defendant:
>
> > (a) Did not commit the homicidal act or in any way solicit, request, command, importune, cause or aid the commission thereof; and
> >
> > (b) Was not armed with a deadly weapon, or any instrument, article or substance readily capable of causing death or serious physical injury and of a sort not ordinarily carried in public places by law-abiding persons; and
> >
> > (c) Had no reasonable ground to believe that any other participant was armed with such a weapon, instrument, article or substance; and
> >
> > (d) Had no reasonable ground to believe that any other participant intended to engage in conduct likely to result in death or serious physical injury.

Contrast § 782.04(3) of the Florida penal code, which provides:

> When a person is killed in the perpetration of, or in the attempt to perpetrate, any [one of a series of enumerated felonies] by a person other than the person engaged in the perpetration of or attempt to perpetrate such felony, the person perpetrating or attempting to perpetrate such felony is guilty of murder in the second degree, ... punishable by imprisonment for a term of years not exceeding life....

---

### NOTE ON MISDEMEANOR MANSLAUGHTER

Manslaughter was typically defined at common law typically as causing the death of another by an unlawful act or by a lawful act committed in an unlawful manner. The second part of this definition is a reference to liability for recklessness or negligence, which has been dealt with above. The first part is a reference to the so-called misdemeanor-manslaughter rule. This rule provides in effect that when a death occurs during the commission of or attempt to commit a misdemeanor, all participants in the offensive conduct are guilty of manslaughter. As it has been applied in some jurisdictions, the rule encompasses all "unlawful" behavior, i.e., it includes conduct that was not criminal but that only involved the breach of civil standards of liability. In most jurisdictions, however, the rule has been limited to misdemeanors, hence the derivation of the name by which the doctrine is normally called. As in the case of felony-murder, liability is strict as to death in those jurisdictions that follow the rule, and all participants are liable regardless of their culpability as to the death. Analytically, the problems of implementing the misdemeanor-manslaughter rule are directly analogous to problems encountered with felony murder.

The history of the misdemeanor-manslaughter rule also parallels the felony-murder rule. In the main, it consists of a series of judicially derived limitations on its reach. As summarized in Herbert Wechsler and Jerome Michael, A Rationale of the Law of Homicide I, 37 Colum.L.Rev. 701, 722–23 (1937).*

> Homicides resulting from unlawful acts were manslaughter, subject to the single qualification which early appeared, that the unlawful act be malum in se. In the course of time the same impetus was felt as in the case of felony murder, to narrow this category to cases where the unlawful act was dangerous to life. This was accomplished more successfully than in the case of felonies in similar ways, by defining malum in se so as to include misdemeanors dangerous to life or limb and exclude non-dangerous misdemeanors, or by introducing the factor of danger by means of a requirement of proximate causation. But the limitation has resulted in uncertainties similar to those created by efforts to limit the felony-murder rule. Is it sufficient that a misdemeanor involve some kind of behavior which is usually dangerous to life or limb, or must the particular instance of such behavior be dangerous to some serious degree? And if the former, is it also sufficient that the legislature has regarded behavior, such, for example, as driving an automobile at a speed in excess of a statutory limit, as generally dangerous and has therefore forbidden it, or is this legislative judgment open to re-examination by court and jury? And if the latter, is the degree of danger required the same or less than, and the state of mind required the same or different from, what would be required if the behavior were not a misdemeanor? Finally, does the answer to any of these questions vary with the technique employed to limit the rule by a particular court? These are issues which have not received definitive consideration in the cases, and remain for the most part unresolved.

The Model Penal Code does not include a counterpart to the misdemeanor-manslaughter rule. It is reported in ALI, Model Penal Code and Commentaries, § 210.3, p. 77 (1980), that 22 enacted codes and proposals agreed with the Model Code and abolished the rule in its entirety. Eleven

* Reprinted with permission of Professor Wechsler and the Columbia Law Review.

codes and one proposal, on the other hand, retained some form of the rule. There are a number of jurisdictions that have not revised their penal codes in response to the Model Penal Code and that still retain some version of the common-law rule. Should the rule be retained?

## SECTION 5: CAPITAL HOMICIDE

### INTRODUCTORY NOTE ON USE OF THE DEATH PENALTY

Capital punishment was an established feature of American law at the time the Constitution and the Bill of Rights were adopted, as well as when the 14th Amendment was ratified following the Civil War. Although a movement to abolish the death penalty surfaced during the 1830s, only a few states (Michigan in 1847, Rhode Island in 1852, and Wisconsin in 1853) eliminated the capital sanction before the Civil War. Thereafter, occasional surges of abolitionist sentiment led to a gradual reduction of offenses punishable by death.

Abolitionist sentiment emerged on a broad scale after World War II, provoking widespread debate and occasional legislative action. Seven state legislatures eliminated capital punishment between 1957 and 1965, bringing to 10 the number of abolitionist states. Meanwhile, the penalty was carried out with declining frequency: the average annual number of executions gradually dropped from 167 during the 1930s to less than 50 during the late 1950s and early 1960s.

Notwithstanding these trends, public opinion was divided on the issue, and most states defeated abolitionist proposals. In the early 1960s, death penalty opponents began to focus on the courts. Although the constitutionality of capital punishment had traditionally been regarded as settled, there was reason to believe that the Supreme Court would be receptive to the abolitionist cause. The Court had recently shown its willingness—in the school desegregation and reapportionment cases—to use constitutional litigation as a mechanism for changing social and political institutions. Moreover, the claim that the death penalty had been administered in a racially discriminatory fashion[a] implicated one of the central concerns of the Warren Court.

Litigation challenging the constitutionality of capital sentencing proceedings gradually proceeded through the federal courts under the direction of lawyers associated with the NAACP Legal Defense and Educational Fund.[b] In 1968, the Supreme Court invalidated procedures that permitted

---

[a] Of the 3,859 persons executed between 1930 and 1968, 2,066 were black. Of the 455 executed for rape during this period, 405 were black. Of the 2,306 persons executed in the South during these years, 72 percent were black.

[b] An insider's account of the death penalty litigation, culminating in the Supreme

the prosecution to exclude "for cause" any jurors who had "conscientious scruples" against the death penalty. The Court held, in Witherspoon v. Illinois, 391 U.S. 510 (1968), that the exclusion of jurors for cause should be limited to those who were unequivocally opposed to the death penalty in all cases; exclusion of jurors with more ambiguous attitudes, the Court ruled, tended to produce a "hanging jury." The *Witherspoon* decision had the effect of invalidating most death sentences that were pending at the time. A de facto moratorium on executions then took hold as litigants pressed other claims calling into question the constitutionality of the death penalty itself.

Over the next decade, a closely divided Court decided a series of cases that significantly altered the constitutional landscape. Although the Court eventually upheld the constitutionality of capital punishment, it restricted the offenses for which the death penalty may be imposed and restructured the procedures by which capital sentencing must be administered. In response to these decisions, the great majority of states have revised their death penalty statutes.[c] The first execution under this contemporary generation of statutes was carried out in 1977 and, by the end of 2003, more than 850 persons had been executed and about 3600 prisoners were awaiting execution.

It is evident that the death penalty continues to command substantial political support in the United States. For that reason it is likely that there will continue to be executions for the foreseeable future. It is also evident, however, that the debate concerning the merits of capital punishment will continue and that administration of the penalty will be subject to ongoing constitutional scrutiny. Although full coverage of this complex subject is not feasible in these materials, this section is designed, first, to provide an overview of the Supreme Court's decisions and, second, to survey the basic issues that arise under modern capital sentencing statutes.[d]

---

## INTRODUCTORY NOTE ON THE EFFICACY AND MORALITY OF THE DEATH PENALTY

At the outset, it may be useful to review the traditional arguments made for and against the efficacy and morality of the death penalty. The literature on the subject is voluminous,[a] and often polemical. The major

Court's decision in *Furman v. Georgia*, is presented in Michael Meltsner, Cruel and Unusual: The Supreme Court and Capital Punishment (1973).

[c] Thirty-eight states and the federal government had capital sentencing statutes in force on January 1, 2004.

[d] Additional material covering the rulings of the U.S. Supreme Court on the proportionality of capital punishment for partic-

ular offenses and offenders is presented in Section 2 of Chapter 9.

[a] The Model Penal Code Commentaries, quoted below, summarize the literature as of its publication. More recent literature includes Hugo Adam Bedau (ed), Debating the Death Penalty (2004); Franklin E. Zimring, The Contradictions of American Capital Punishment (2003); Roger Hood, The Death Penalty: A World–Wide Perspective (3d ed, 2003);

arguments on both sides of the controversy are summarized in the following excerpt from ALI, Model Penal Code and Commentaries, § 210.6, pp. 111–17 (1980):*

[A] broad societal consensus on the issue of capital punishment seems as elusive as ever. Debate continues, and the literature on the subject grows more and more abundant. Although this commentary makes no attempt to resolve the matter, it may be useful to describe the dimensions of the controversy. Abolitionist sentiment often reflects a profound moral distaste for "official murder." For some, the death penalty is simply an unacceptable contradiction of the intrinsic worth of a human being. As Mr. Justice Brennan made the point, "the calculated killing of a human being by the state involves, by its very nature, a denial of the executed person's humanity." For others, death is a fitting penalty for one who takes another's life and an appropriate expression of societal outrage at such conduct. In any event, judgments of this sort do not readily yield to reasoned support or refutation, at least not in terms within the special competence of lawyers. The debate, therefore, has tended to shift to other grounds.

Chief among them is the efficacy of the death penalty as a deterrent. In a monograph prepared for the [American Law Institute,] Professor Thorsten Sellin collected data on actual imposition of the death penalty and attempted to assess the relationship, if any, between homicide rates and the authorization of death as a possible sanction for murder.[9] Sellin selected clusters of neighboring states with similar social and economic conditions. Within each cluster he compared the experience of abolitionist and retentionist jurisdictions and found no significant or systematic difference between them: "The inevitable conclusion is that executions have no discernible effect on homicide death rates...."

Sellin concluded that a sentence of death is executed in a trivial fraction of the cases in which it might legally be imposed and that there is no quantitative evidence that either its availability or its imposition has noticeable influence upon the frequency of murder. The latter conclusion is not surprising when it is remembered that murders are, upon the whole, either crimes of passion, in which a calculus of consequences has small psychological reality, or crimes of such depravity that the actor reveals himself as

---

Ernst Van den Haag and James Conrad, The Death Penalty: A Debate (1983); Charles Black, Capital Punishment: The Inevitability of Caprice and Mistake (1981); Thorsten Sellin, The Penalty of Death (1980); Walter Berns, For Capital Punishment: Crime and Morality of the Death Penalty (1979); Richard O. Lempert, Desert and Deterrence: An Assessment of The Moral Basis for Capital Punishment, 79 Mich.L.Rev. 1177 (1981).

* Copyright © 1980 by the American Law Institute. Reprinted with permission.

[9] Thorsten Sellin, The Death Penalty (ALI 1959), also printed at MPC § 201.6, p. 221 (Tent.Draft No. 9, 1959). See Thorsten Sellin, Capital Punishment, 25 Fed.Probation, Part 3, at 3 (1961); Thorsten Sellin, Homicides in Retentionist and Abolitionist States, in Capital Punishment (Thorsten Sellin ed. 1967).

doubtfully within the reach of influences that might be especially inhibitory in the case of an ordinary man. These factors, therefore, leave room for substantial doubt that any solid case can be maintained for the death penalty as a deterrent to murder, at least as it is employed in the United States. If this conclusion is correct, it would seem that the social need for grievous condemnation of the act can be met, as it is met in abolition states, without resorting to capital punishment.

Sellin's work proved extremely influential for almost 15 years. It survived without major challenge until Professor Isaac Ehrlich's efforts to test implications of general deterrence theory in the context of capital punishment.[11] Ehrlich looked at the relationship between the homicide rate in the nation as a whole and the "execution risk," that is, the fraction of convicted murderers who are actually put to death. He tried to hold other factors constant by the technique of multiple regression analysis. From experience in the United States from 1933 through 1967 Ehrlich drew the tentative conclusion that execution of an offender tended on the average to deter eight homicides. This finding prompted a storm of controversy that has not yet begun to abate. Sellin's work and Ehrlich's analysis have been attacked and defended on methodological grounds,[13] and each has been tested by replication.[14] These disputes of methodology and statistical technique are largely beyond the competence of those without special training in the field. Further research may clarify the matter, but at present the verdict must be that the existence of a significant deterrent effect from retention of the death penalty has been neither proved nor disproved.[b]

[11] Isaac Ehrlich, The Deterrent Effect of Capital Punishment: A Question of Life or Death, 65 Am.Econ.Rev. 397 (1975); Isaac Ehrlich, The Deterrent Effect of Capital Punishment: A Question of Life or Death (Working Paper No. 18, Center for Economic Analysis of Human Behavior and Social Institutions, 1973).

[13] See, e.g., Hans Zeisel, Deterrent Effect of the Death Penalty: Facts v. Faiths, 1976 Sup.Ct.Rev. 317 (1976); David C. Baldus and James W.L. Cole, A Comparison of the Work of Thorsten Sellin and Isaac Ehrlich on the Deterrent Effect of Capital Punishment, 85 Yale L.J. 170 (1975); William J. Bowers and Glenn L. Pierce, The Illusion of Deterrence in Isaac Ehrlich's Research on Capital Punishment, 85 Yale L.J. 187 (1975); Isaac Ehrlich, Deterrence: Evidence and Inference, 85 Yale L.J. 209 (1975); Jon K. Peck, The Deterrent Effect of Capital Punishment: Ehrlich and his Critics, 85 Yale L.J. 359 (1976); Isaac Ehrlich, Rejoinder, 85 Yale L.J. 368 (1976).

[14] William J. Bowers, Executions in America 137–47 (1974); William C. Bailey, Murder and the Death Penalty, 65 J.Crim.L. & C. 416, 421 (1974); Peter Passel, The Deterrent Effect of the Death Penalty: A Statistical Test, 28 Stan.L.Rev. 61 (1975); Peter Passel and John Taylor, The Deterrent Effect of Capital Punishment: Another View 9–11 (Discussion Paper 74–7509, Columbia Univ. Dept. of Economics, Feb. 1975).

[b] According to the Panel on Research on Deterrent and Incapacitative Effects of the National Academy of Sciences (1978), the Ehrlich study and subsequent re-analysis of the data "provide no useful evidence on the deterrent effect of capital punishment." The panel also noted that it was "skeptical that the death penalty, so long as it is used relatively rarely, can ever be subjected to the kind of statistical analysis that would validly establish the presence or absence of a deterrent effect."—[Footnote by eds.]

Apart from the efficacy of the death penalty as a deterrent, its possible imposition exerts a discernible and baneful effect on the administration of criminal justice. A trial where life is at stake becomes inevitably a morbid and sensational affair, fraught with risk that public sympathy will be aroused for the defendant without reference to guilt or innocence of the crime charged. In the rare cases where a capital sentence is imposed, this unwholesome influence carries through the period preceding execution, reaching a climax when sentence is carried out.

The special sentiment associated with judgment of death is reflected also in the courts, lending added weight to claims of error in the trial and multiplying and protracting the appellate processes, including post-conviction remedies. As astute and realistic an observer as Mr. Justice Jackson observed to the Chief Reporter[c] shortly prior to his death that he opposed capital punishment because of its deleterious effects on the judicial process and stated that he would appear and urge the Institute to favor abolition.

Beyond these considerations, it is obvious that capital punishment is the most difficult of sanctions to administer with even rough equality. A rigid legislative definition of capital murders has proved unworkable in practice, given the infinite variety of homicides and possible mitigating factors. A discretionary system thus becomes inevitable, with equally inevitable differences in judgment depending on the individuals involved and other accidents of time and place.[15] Yet most dramatically when life is at stake, equality is, as it is generally felt to be, a most important element of justice.

Sellin's data showed a total of 3096 civilian executions for murder in the United States during the years 1930–57. This number represents only a small fraction of all murder convictions. The annual number of executions declined noticeably across this time period. The decline resulted in part from a decreasing homicide rate and in part from the removal of mandatory death sentences in a few jurisdictions, but it also reflects a growing reluctance by judges and juries to impose the ultimate sanction. Subsequent experience confirms the point that imposition of the death penalty is an increasingly rare occurrence. The average annual rate of execution dropped from 128 in the 1940's to 72 in the 1950's to 31 in the years 1960–65. These figures give rise to the argument that the death penalty is actually carried out so rarely that its imposition in any particular case must be arbitrary.

---

[c] The reference is to Herbert Wechsler, Chief Reporter for the Model Penal Code.—[Footnote by eds.]

[15] Even when a capital sentence is imposed, the speed as well as the certainty of its execution may depend primarily upon the resignation of the individual or his disposition to pursue appellate and collateral proceedings which may carry on for years. Indeed, as recent experience has shown, even the resignation of the individual to execution will not necessarily bring litigation to an end. See Gilmore v. Utah, 429 U.S. 1012 (1976).

As Mr. Justice Stewart captured the thought in a constitutional context, "death sentences are cruel and unusual in the same way that being struck by lightning is cruel and unusual." Discomfort with the discretionary aspects of the system is aggravated, moreover, by a suspicion that the grounds for differentiating among individuals may include illegitimate factors such as race.[20] Finally, there is the point that erroneous convictions are inevitable and beyond correction in the light of newly discovered evidence when a capital sentence has been carried out.

These, then, are the major arguments against capital punishment for murder. The arguments on the other side may well begin with crediting some deterrent efficacy to the threat of death as punishment, given the weight that such a threat appears to have on introspection. However one evaluates the studies by Sellin and Ehrlich, reported homicide rates per 100,000 of population may be too crude an instrument to reflect all the cases where the threat has been effective; and it may be regarded as sufficient to justify the means that some innocent lives *may* be preserved.

Many would argue, further, that it is appropriate for a society to express its condemnation of murder by associating the offense with the highest sanction that the law can use, however much considerations of humanity should temper the exaction of the penalty when there are extenuations. And some communities may still have cause to fear the greater evil of resort to private violence as reprisal, if the law excludes the possibility that the murderer may lose his life. The problem of equality, to which attention has been drawn, will not appear to all to be dispositive. Arguments based on the discretionary character of the death penalty and the infrequency of its imposition may call for reform and review of the discretionary system rather than abolition of the punishment. And it may be thought enough that the capital penalty is merited in any case in which it actually is imposed. Finally, these arguments may be regarded as outweighing the costs of the penalty to the administration of justice, given the difficulty of measuring the effect of such factors on the deterrence and the condemnation points.

Whatever the merits of the debate, in any event, capital punishment continues to command substantial political support within the American system.[22] It is as clear today as it was when

---

[20] More than half the persons executed in the years 1930–57 were non-white....

[22] As of 1976, 10 states had abolished the death penalty for all crimes: Alaska (1957), Hawaii (1957), Iowa (1965), Maine (1887), Michigan (1847), Minnesota (1911), Oregon (1964), South Dakota (1976), West Virginia (1965), and Wisconsin (1853). Popular support for the death penalty, as indicated by the Gallup polls, declined consistently from 62 percent in 1936 to 42 percent in 1966. After 1966, however, the trend reversed and by 1969 the approval rating had risen to 51 percent. A nationwide Harris survey conducted in 1973 showed that 59 percent of the American people supported the death penalty

the Model Code was drafted that many jurisdictions will continue to authorize the death penalty for at least some offenses for a considerable time to come. Those jurisdictions that elect to retain the penalty must confront the special need to provide a fair and rational system of administration and to meet recently developed constitutional standards. . . .

## SUBSECTION A: THE SUPREME COURT AND CAPITAL PUNISHMENT

### INTRODUCTORY NOTES ON THE SUPREME COURT AND CAPITAL PUNISHMENT

**1. Background.** As opponents of capital punishment prepared to take their challenge to the Supreme Court in the 1960s, 40 states authorized (but did not require) the death penalty for the highest form of murder. Kidnapping was a capital offense in two-thirds of the states, and treason and rape were punishable by death in about half. In trials for capital offenses, juries in most states typically returned a sentence recommendation (often binding) together with the verdict of guilt. No additional criteria or standards were spelled out in the instructions to explain how the jury's discretion should be exercised. Moreover, because the jury decisions on guilt and sentence were made at the same time, no evidence beyond that admissible on the question of guilt was directed specifically to the propriety of a capital sentence. Since evidence concerning the defendant's character, personal background, and prior criminal record is normally inadmissible to determine guilt, the jury was required in many cases to make its sentencing decision without such information.[a]

Constitutional attacks against the death penalty proceeded along two lines. One focused on the capital sanction itself: it was argued that the death penalty contravened "evolving standards of decency in a civilized society" and therefore constituted a cruel and unusual punishment forbidden by the Eighth Amendment.[b] Second, it was argued that even if death is a constitutionally permissible punishment for some offenses, the then-existing capital sentencing procedures were unfair. The following notes summarize the Supreme Court decisions responding to these arguments.

for murder while 31 percent opposed it. The reaction to the *Furman* decision by the national and state legislatures . . . and to the 1976 death-penalty decisions . . . is further evidence of the substantial political support the death penalty commands.

[a] This information could be considered by the judge, however, in states where the jury recommendation was not binding.

[b] The quotation, indicating that the Eighth Amendment has an evolving meaning, is from Chief Justice Warren's plurality opinion in Trop v. Dulles, 356 U.S. 86 (1958) (holding denationalization to be a cruel and unusual punishment).

**2.** *McGautha v. California.* The first major decision focused explicitly on the procedural challenge. In McGautha v. California, 402 U.S. 183 (1971), the Court considered two claims that called into question the constitutionality of every capital sentencing statute then in use. First, the challengers contended that the practice of leaving the sentencing decision to unguided jury discretion was fundamentally unfair because it invited arbitrary and ad-hoc determinations.[c] Second, they argued that the practice of submitting both guilt and punishment to the jury in a single proceeding excluded relevant sentencing information from the jury and thereby deprived the defendant of a fair sentencing hearing.[d] In a six-three decision, the Court held that discretionary jury sentencing, even in a single proceeding, did not violate due process.[e]

**3.** *Furman v. Georgia.* One month after *McGautha* was decided, the Court granted certiorari in four cases to decide whether "the imposition and carrying out of the death penalty [in these cases] constitutes cruel and unusual punishment in violation of the Eighth and 14th Amendments."[f] The cases involved two death sentences for rape and one each for felony murder and murder by a person previously convicted of murder. A year later, a five-four majority set aside the death sentences in all four cases. The result was announced in a short per curiam opinion without supporting explanation. Furman v. Georgia, 408 U.S. 238 (1972). Each member of the Court wrote separately in opinions occupying more than 230 pages in the United States Reports.

The opinions fall into three categories. Justices Brennan and Marshall concluded that the death penalty was unconstitutional no matter what offenses were punished by death and no matter what procedures were used to administer the sanction. Justices Douglas, Stewart, and White concurred on narrower grounds. They seemed to be concerned with the risk that unguided jury discretion would degenerate into unacceptably inconsistent judgments. Chief Justice Burger and Justices Blackmun, Powell, and Rehnquist dissented. The views of each group of Justices are summarized below.

**(i) Brennan and Marshall.** Justice Brennan found the death penalty to be incompatible with evolving conceptions of human dignity for four reasons. First, he argued that the death penalty is so extreme in its severity and so degrading in its character as to be equivalent to the

[c] In McGautha's trial, the jury had been instructed that "the law itself provides no standard for the guidance of the jury in the selection of the penalty, but ... commits the whole matter ... to the judgment, conscience, and absolute discretion of the jury."

[d] Although California was one of the few states with a bifurcated sentencing process, *McGautha* had been consolidated for decision with an Ohio case in which the death penalty had been imposed in a unitary proceeding.

[e] The majority opinion was written by Justice Harlan, who was joined by Chief Justice Burger and Justices Stewart, White, and Blackmun and, in large part, by Justice Black. Justices Douglas, Brennan, and Marshall dissented.

[f] As students of constitutional law will know, the Eighth Amendment in terms applies only to the federal government. The Court had previously held, however, that the cruel-and-unusual-punishment clause of the Eighth Amendment applied to the states through the 14th Amendment.

"barbaric punishments condemned by history," such as the rack, the thumbscrew, and the iron boot. Second, he thought that capital punishment, as administered, was incompatible with the principle that the state "must not arbitrarily inflict a severe punishment." Third, he concluded that the infrequency with which executions actually occurred demonstrated that capital punishment had become morally unacceptable to contemporary society. Finally, Justice Brennan canvassed the various purposes of punishment and concluded that, as administered, the death penalty "serves no penal purpose more effectively than a less severe punishment." With respect to deterrence, he observed that "whatever the speculative validity of the assumption that the threat of death is a superior deterrent, there is no reason to believe that as currently administered, the punishment of death is necessary to deter the commission of capital crimes." As for retribution, he said:

> Obviously concepts of justice change; no immutable moral order requires death for murderers and rapists. The claim that death is a just punishment necessarily refers to the existence of certain public beliefs. The claim must be that for capital crimes death alone comports with society's notion of proper punishment. As administered today, however, the punishment of death cannot be justified as a necessary means of exacting retribution from criminals. When the overwhelming number of criminals who commit capital crimes go to prison, it cannot be concluded that death serves the purpose of retribution more effectively than imprisonment. The asserted public belief that murderers and rapists deserve to die is flatly inconsistent with the execution of a random few. . . .

Justice Marshall reasoned that the average American citizen, if fully informed on the issue, would find the death penalty "shocking to his conscience and sense of justice." He also argued that the death penalty was unconstitutionally excessive because it made no measurable contribution to legitimate legislative objectives. He concluded that "retribution for its own sake is improper" and that the available statistical evidence demonstrated that the death penalty had no significant deterrent effect.

**(ii) Douglas, Stewart, and White.** Justices Douglas, Stewart, and White concluded that the sentencing procedures then in use were constitutionally defective. Justice Douglas noted that discretionary capital sentencing statutes are, in operation, "pregnant with discrimination" against poor, black defendants. Justice Stewart observed that the death penalty is "wantonly and freakishly imposed" and that "death sentences are cruel and unusual in the same way that being struck by lightning is cruel and unusual." Justice White added that "there is no meaningful basis for distinguishing the few cases in which [the death penalty] is imposed from the many cases in which it is not."

**(iii) The Dissenters.** In response to Justices Brennan and Marshall, the dissenters argued that it was institutionally inappropriate for the Supreme Court to foreclose use of the death penalty. They noted that capital punishment was widely used when the Constitution and the Bill of Rights were adopted; that it had been in continuous use since then; and that the declining frequency of imposition indicated that the penalty was being reserved for the most extreme cases, not that it was no longer socially acceptable. As for the argument that the death penalty does not serve valid penological objectives, the dissenters concluded that the Court should defer to rational legislative judgments regarding its retributive and deterrent value. Having concluded that the penalty of death was constitutionally permissible, at least for some offenses, the dissenters also concluded that the procedures by which it was administered did not violate the Eighth Amendment. Chief Justice Burger specifically noted that "all of the arguments and factual contentions accepted [by Justices Douglas, Stewart, and White] were considered and rejected by the Court one year ago" in *McGautha*.

4. **The Aftermath of *Furman*.** Even to the practiced eye, the meaning of *Furman* was obscure. As Chief Justice Burger had observed, the heart of the objection by Justices Douglas, Stewart, and White seemed to be precisely the argument that had failed to command a majority in *McGautha*. It now appeared that the states were not constitutionally permitted to commit the sentencing decision to unguided jury discretion. Since all states followed that procedure, the effect of the decision was to invalidate every death penalty statute then in force.

Thirty-five states responded to *Furman* by reformulating their capital sentencing provisions to restrict sentencing discretion in a way that would meet the objections of at least one of the three Justices whose views had been pivotal in *Furman*.[g] Two approaches seemed plausible, and the states were evenly divided on which would succeed. Eighteen states attempted to eliminate sentencing discretion altogether by making death the mandatory punishment for conviction of a capital crime.[h] The remaining 17 states rejected the mandatory approach but attempted to structure and control the exercise of sentencing discretion. Fifteen adopted statutes, more or less patterned after the Model Penal Code, that provided for bifurcated proceedings and required consideration of specified aggravating and mitigating factors. Two specified aggravating and mitigating factors but did not require bifurcated proceedings.

5. **The 1976 Decisions.** The Court considered a representative group of these statutes in five cases decided in 1976.[i] The Court was again badly divided. Justices Brennan and Marshall adhered to their view that

---

[g] Citations to these provisions can be found in the summary of *Furman* and subsequent decisions contained in ALI, Model Penal Code and Commentaries § 210.6, pp. 153–67 (1980).

[h] Although most of these states restricted the death penalty to a narrowed range of homicides, two (New Mexico and North Carolina) provided that death would be the man-

datory punishment for all cases of first-degree murder as traditionally defined.

[i] Gregg v. Georgia, 428 U.S. 153 (1976); Proffitt v. Florida, 428 U.S. 242 (1976); Jurek v. Texas, 428 U.S. 262 (1976); Woodson v. North Carolina, 428 U.S. 280 (1976); Roberts v. Louisiana, 428 U.S. 325 (1976). The statutes involved in these five decisions are reproduced in Appendix B.

the death penalty was unconstitutional in all cases. The Chief Justice and Justices Blackmun and Rehnquist adhered to their *Furman* dissents. Justice White joined them in voting to sustain all of the statutes, holding that the defect identified in *Furman* could be remedied either by making the death penalty mandatory or by requiring consideration of specified aggravating and mitigating circumstances. Two Justices thus voted to hold all five statutes unconstitutional, and four to sustain them. The three remaining Justices—Stewart, Powell and Stevens (who had succeeded Douglas)—voted to invalidate the mandatory statutes but to uphold the statutes that specified criteria to structure the exercise of discretion. Together, the various opinions in these five cases occupy 210 pages in the United States Reports.

The net result was that a seven-two majority affirmed the constitutionality of three statutes (Georgia, Florida and Texas) that attempted to structure the exercise of discretion. The Court thereby definitively rejected the view that the death penalty was unconstitutional per se, at least as applied to homicide offenses.[j] However, a five-four majority struck down those statutes (North Carolina and Louisiana) that imposed death as a mandatory penalty, even for a narrow class of homicides.[k]

Because the votes of Justices Stewart, Powell and Stevens were determinative of the outcome, their views are generally understood to state the governing constitutional principles. The concluding portion of their joint opinion upholding the Georgia statute explained their rationale:

> The basic concern of *Furman* centered on those defendants who were being condemned to death capriciously and arbitrarily. Under the procedures before the Court in that case, sentencing authorities were not directed to give attention to the nature or circumstances of the crime committed or to the character or record of the defendant. Left unguided, juries imposed the death sentence in a way that could only be called freakish. The new Georgia sentencing procedures, by contrast, focus the jury's attention on the particularized nature of the crime and the particularized characteristics of the individual defendant. While the jury is permitted to consider any aggravating or mitigating circumstances, it must find and identify at least one statutory aggravating factor before it may impose a penalty of death. In this way the jury's discretion is channeled. No longer can a jury wantonly and freakishly impose the death sentence; it is always circumscribed by the legislative guidelines. In addition, the review function of the Su-

---

[j] The Court ruled one year later that the death penalty is an unconstitutionally excessive punishment for the crime of rape. Coker v. Georgia, 433 U.S. 584 (1977). This decision appears as a main case in Chapter IX.

[k] The Court has subsequently made it clear that mandatory death penalty provisions are categorically unconstitutional. In Roberts v. Louisiana, 431 U.S. 633 (1977), it struck down a mandatory death penalty for murder of an on-duty policeman, and in Sumner v. Shuman, 483 U.S. 66 (1987), it invalidated Nevada statute that made a death sentence mandatory for a prison inmate who had been convicted of murder while serving a life sentence without possibility of parole. . . .

preme Court of Georgia affords additional assurance that the concerns that prompted our decision in *Furman* are not present to any significant degree in the Georgia procedure applied here.

In the course of its opinion, the plurality rejected two major arguments against the Georgia system. The first was that the prosecutor in charging and plea bargaining, the jury in convicting the defendant of a non-capital form of criminal homicide, and the governor in exercising his pardoning power can all exercise a kind of unfettered discretion that is inconsistent with the concerns of *Furman*. The plurality responded that:

> Nothing in any of our cases suggests that the decision to afford an individual defendant mercy violates the Constitution. *Furman* held only that, in order to minimize the risk that the death penalty would be imposed on a capriciously selected group of offenders, the decision to impose it had to be guided by standards so that the sentencing authority would focus on the particularized circumstances of the crime and the defendant.

The second argument was that the standards adopted by the Georgia statute were so broad and vague as to provide no meaningful guidance and thus to permit the kind of arbitrary decisions at which *Furman* was aimed. The plurality did not reject this argument out of hand, but held that in context, particularly given the reviewing function exercised by the Georgia Supreme Court, the provisions were not unacceptably vague. In effect, the plurality was unwilling to construe *Furman* as requiring that all possibility of arbitrary action be eliminated. A reasonable effort to guide and control the discretion of the jury was all that could be expected. A more rigid approach would have the effect of outlawing capital punishment altogether. This the plurality was unwilling to do.

By contrast, the plurality held the mandatory North Carolina statute unconstitutional for three reasons. The first was based on history, and the judgment that contemporary values as reflected in a proper interpretation of the cruel-and-unusual-punishment clause were offended by a mandatory death penalty. The second and third arguments are reflected in the following excerpt:

> A separate deficiency of North Carolina's mandatory death-sentence statute is its failure to provide a constitutionally tolerable response to *Furman*'s rejection of unbridled jury discretion in the imposition of capital sentences. Central to the limited holding in *Furman* was the conviction that the vesting of standardless sentencing power in the jury violated the Eighth and 14th Amendments. It is argued that North Carolina has remedied the inadequacies of the death-penalty statutes held unconstitutional in *Furman* by withdrawing all sentencing discretion from juries in capital cases. But when one considers the long and consistent American experience with the death penalty in first-degree murder cases, it becomes evident that mandatory statutes enacted in response to *Furman* have simply papered over the problem of unguided and unchecked jury discretion.

[T]here is general agreement that American juries have persistently refused to convict a significant portion of persons charged with first-degree murder of that offense under mandatory death-penalty statutes. [A]s a matter of historic fact, juries operating under discretionary sentencing statutes have consistently returned death sentences in only a minority of first-degree murder cases. In view of the historic record, it is only reasonable to assume that many juries under mandatory statutes will continue to consider the grave consequences of a conviction in reaching a verdict. North Carolina's mandatory death-penalty statute provides no standards to guide the jury in its inevitable exercise of the power to determine which first-degree murderers shall live and which shall die. And there is no way under the North Carolina law for the judiciary to check arbitrary and capricious exercise of that power through a review of death sentences. Instead of rationalizing the sentencing process, a mandatory scheme may well exacerbate the problem identified in *Furman* by resting the penalty determination on the particular jury's willingness to act lawlessly. While a mandatory death-penalty statute may reasonably be expected to increase the number of persons sentenced to death, it does not fulfill *Furman*'s basic requirement by replacing arbitrary and wanton jury discretion with objective standards to guide, regularize, and make rationally reviewable the process for imposing a sentence of death.

A third constitutional shortcoming of the North Carolina statute is its failure to allow the particularized consideration of relevant aspects of the character and record of each convicted defendant before the imposition upon him of a sentence of death. In *Furman*, members of the Court acknowledged what cannot fairly be denied—that death is a punishment different from all other sanctions in kind rather than degree. A process that accords no significance to relevant facets of the character and record of the individual offender or the circumstances of the particular offense excludes from consideration in fixing the ultimate punishment of death the possibility of compassionate or mitigating factors stemming from the diverse frailties of humankind. It treats all persons convicted of a designated offense not as uniquely individual human beings, but as members of a faceless, undifferentiated mass to be subjected to the blind infliction of the penalty of death.

This Court has previously recognized that "[f]or the determination of sentences, justice generally requires consideration of more than the particular acts by which the crime was committed and that there be taken into account the circumstances of the offense together with the character and propensities of the offender." Consideration of both the offender and the offense in order to arrive at a just and appropriate sentence has been viewed as a progressive and humanizing development. While the prevailing practice of individualizing sentencing determinations generally reflects simply enlightened policy rather than a constitutional imperative, we believe that in capital cases the fundamental respect for humanity underlying the Eighth Amendment requires consideration of the character and record of the individual offender and the circumstances of the particular offense as a constitutionally indispensable part of the process of inflicting the penalty of death.

This conclusion rests squarely on the predicate that the penalty of death is qualitatively different from a sentence of imprisonment, however long. Death, in its finality, differs more from life imprisonment than a 100–year prison term differs from one of only a year or two. Because of that qualitative difference, there is a corresponding difference in the need for reliability in the determination that death is the appropriate punishment in a specific case.

**6.  *Lockett, Eddings,* and *Penry*.** In striking down the mandatory death penalty statutes, Justices Stewart, Powell, and Stevens emphasized that an individualized determination of the death penalty question is "constitutionally indispensable." The Court has elaborated on this theme in subsequent cases.

Sandra Lockett was waiting in a car when an accomplice committed a homicide during the course of a pawn shop robbery.[1] She was convicted of murder under the ordinary rules of complicity. She wanted to argue in mitigation that she was a secondary participant in the offense, that she had not previously committed any major crimes, and that her youth (she was 21) should be taken into account. Under the Ohio statute, the judge was required to impose the death penalty unless the defendant proved one of three mitigating circumstances—that the victim had induced or facilitated the offense, that the defendant was "under duress, coercion or strong provocation," or that the offense was "primarily the product of psychosis or mental deficiency." Because Lockett's mitigating claims did not fall within the factors specified by the statute, the trial judge said he had "no alternative" but to impose a death sentence.

In Lockett v. Ohio, 438 U.S. 586 (1978), the Supreme Court struck down her death sentence by a seven-one vote. (Justice Brennan did not participate.) The plurality opinion by Chief Justice Burger, joined by Justices Stewart, Powell, and Stevens, held that the Ohio statute violated the principle of individualization:

> The Eighth and 14th Amendments require that the sentencer, in all but the rarest kind of capital case, not be precluded from considering, *as a mitigating factor,* any aspect of a defendant's character or record and any of the circumstances of the offense that the defendant proffers as a basis for a sentence less than death.[m]

[1] The person who actually fired the fatal shot pleaded guilty to a non-capital murder charge and was the chief prosecution witness. Lockett twice refused to plead guilty to a reduced charge which would have been punishable by a mandatory life sentence.

[m] Justice Marshall concurred in the result, adhering to his view that the death

Justice Rehnquist's dissent argued that the effect of the plurality decision was to resurrect the discretionary sentencing practices—and the risk of arbitrariness—that *Furman* was designed to eliminate.

In Eddings v. Oklahoma, 455 U.S. 104 (1982), a five-four majority relied on *Lockett* to strike down a death sentence imposed on a 16–year-old defendant for killing a police officer. Although the Court had granted certiorari to consider whether imposition of the death penalty on a minor was forbidden by the Eighth Amendment, it did not reach this question.[n] Instead, it ruled that the sentencing judge had failed to consider evidence of Eddings' "turbulent family history, of beatings by a harsh father and of severe emotional disturbance." Justice Powell explained in the opinion for the Court that "the sentencer [and the appellate court] may determine the weight to be given relevant mitigating evidence. But they may not give it no weight by excluding such evidence from their consideration" as a matter of law. Chief Justice Burger dissented, joined by Justices White, Blackmun and Rehnquist. He questioned the majority's assumption that the mitigating evidence was ignored by the trial judge and concluded that "it is clearly the choice of the Oklahoma courts—a choice not inconsistent with *Lockett* or any other decision of this Court—to accord relatively little weight to Eddings' family background and emotional problems as balanced against the circumstances of his crime and his potential for future dangerousness."

In Penry v. Lynaugh, 492 U.S. 302 (1989), a five-four majority, relying on *Lockett* and *Eddings*, invalidated Texas' jury instructions, as applied to Penry, because they failed to allow the jury "to consider and give effect to mitigating evidence" he had introduced regarding his mental retardation and abused background. The standard Texas instruction directed the jury to impose a death sentence upon affirmative answers to three special issues

penalty is always unconstitutional. Justice Blackmun concurred on the narrow ground that the death penalty could not constitutionally be imposed on a defendant who aided and abetted a murder without considering the degree of the defendant's involvement and the mens rea for the homicide. Justice White also concurred, but would have rested the decision on the principle that the death penalty is unconstitutionally excessive absent a finding that the defendant had a conscious purpose to kill the victim.

*Lockett* is commonly understood to stand for the principle stated by the plurality. However, the Court has subsequently endorsed a version of the principle upon which Justice White relied in his concurring opinion. In Enmund v. Florida, 458 U.S. 782 (1982), as modified by Tison v. Arizona, 481 U.S. 137 (1987), the Court ruled that the Eighth Amendment does not permit imposition of the death penalty on a person who aids and abets a felony in the course of which a murder is committed by others unless the prosecution establishes a constitutionally sufficient level of culpability. Although *Enmund* had implied that the death was impermissible in the absence of intent to kill or of intent for lethal force to be used, *Tison* held that "major participation in the felony committed, combined with reckless indifference to human life" is sufficient to warrant imposition of a death sentence. *Enmund* and *Tison* are discussed below.

[n] The Court subsequently addressed the permissibility of the death penalty for minors in Thompson v. Oklahoma, 487 U.S. 815 (1988), and Stanford v. Kentucky, 492 U.S. 361 (1989). The combined effect of these decisions is to bar the death penalty for defendants who were under 16 at the time of the offense while permitting it for those who were 16 or older. These cases are summarized below.

(whether the killing was deliberate, whether it was unreasonable in response to any provocation, and whether the defendant would constitute a future danger to society). The problem with this instruction, Justice O'Connor observed, was that "if a juror concluded that Penry acted deliberately and was likely to be dangerous in the future, but also concluded that because of his mental retardation he was not sufficiently culpable to deserve the death penalty, that juror would be unable to give effect to that mitigating evidence under the instruction given in this case.... In the absence of instructions informing the jury that it could consider and give effect to the mitigating evidence of Penry's mental retardation and abused background by declining to impose the death penalty, we conclude that the jury was not provided with a vehicle for expressing its 'reasoned moral response' to that evidence in rendering its sentencing decision." Justice Scalia dissented, joined by Chief Justice Rehnquist and Justices White and Kennedy. He argued that the Court's 1976 decisions had "adopted the constitutional rule that the instructions had to render all mitigating circumstances relevant to the jury's verdict, but that the precise *effect* of their consideration could be channeled by law," as Texas had tried to do. "In holding that the jury had to be free to deem Penry's mental retardation and sad childhood relevant for whatever purpose it wished," Justice Scalia concluded, "the Court has come full circle, not only permitting but requiring what *Furman* once condemned." [o]

**7. *Zant v. Stephens.*** As Justice Rehnquist noted in his *Lockett* dissent, there is considerable tension between two themes that underlie the death penalty cases—that capital sentencing decisions must be structured so as to promote consistency and reduce the risk of arbitrariness and that the states may not either eliminate discretion or structure it in such a way as to compromise the defendant's right to an individualized determination of sentence. In Zant v. Stephens, 462 U.S. 862 (1983), the Court addressed this tension. The case involved a Georgia statute that permitted the jury to consider evidence in aggravation beyond the statutory list of aggravating factors and also permitted the jury to exercise unconstrained discretion in determining whether the death penalty should be imposed after a statutory aggravating circumstance was found.

In the course of his opinion for the Court, Justice Stevens summarized the governing constitutional imperatives in the administration of capital sentencing statutes:

[o] Texas retried Penry in 1990. At the sentencing phase, the court instructed the jury to determine Penry's sentence by answering the same three "special issues" that had been put to the jury in *Penry I*. However, in an effort to correct the constitutional defect identified by the Supreme Court in *Penry I*, the jury was also instructed to "give effect and consideration to [mitigating circum-stances] in assessing the defendant's personal culpability at the time you answer the special issues...." The jury returned a death sentence. In Penry v. Johnson (*Penry II*), 532 U.S. 782 (2001), the Supreme Court reversed again, holding that the special issues did not give the jury a vehicle for expressing the view that Penry did not deserve a death sentence based on the mitigating evidence.

The [*Gregg* Court's] approval of Georgia's capital sentencing procedure rested primarily on two features of the scheme: that the jury was required to find at least one valid statutory aggravating circumstance and to identify it in writing, and that the state supreme court reviewed the record of every death penalty proceeding to determine whether the sentence was arbitrary or disproportionate. These elements, the opinion concluded, adequately protected against the wanton and freakish imposition of the death penalty. This conclusion rested ... on the fundamental requirement that ... an aggravating circumstance must genuinely narrow the class of persons eligible for the death penalty and must reasonably justify the imposition of a more severe sentence on the defendant compared to others found guilty of murder....

Our cases indicate, then, that the statutory aggravating circumstances play a constitutionally necessary function at the stage of legislative definition; they circumscribe the class of persons eligible for the death penalty. But the Constitution does not require the jury to ignore other possible aggravating factors in the process of selecting, from among that class, those defendants who will actually be sentenced to death. What is important at the selection stage is an *individualized* determination on the basis of the character of the individual and the circumstances of the crime.

The Georgia scheme provides for categorical narrowing at the definition stage, and for individualized determination and appellate review at the selection stage. We therefore remain convinced, as we were in 1976, that the structure of the statute is constitutional....

Since *Zant v. Stephens* was decided in 1983, six of the nine seats on the Court have changed hands. However, even though the Justices remain closely divided on many issues relating to the administration of the death penalty, a strong majority continues to adhere to the dual principles enunciated in the 1976 decisions and in the cases summarized in the preceding notes, as well as the effort to reconcile them in *Zant v. Stephens*.[P]

---

[P] Justice Scalia has stated that he rejects the "individualization" requirement, see Walton v. Arizona, 497 U.S. 639, 656 (1990) (Scalia, J. concurring), and Justice Thomas has indicated that he accepts only a narrow version of the requirement guaranteeing the right to introduce mitigating evidence, see Graham v. Collins, 506 U.S. 461, 478 (1993) (Thomas, J. concurring).

For general commentary on the Court's effort to develop principles of capital sentencing jurisprudence, see Franklin Zimring, Inheriting The Wind: The Supreme Court and Capital Punishment in the 1990's, 20 Fla.St. U.L.Rev. 7 (1992); Scott Sundby, The Lockett Paradox: Reconciling Guided Discretion and Unguided Mitigation in Capital Sentencing, 38 U.C.L.A. L. Rev. 1147 (1991); Robert Burt, Disorder in the Court: The Death Penalty and The Constitution, 85 Mich.L.Rev. 1741 (1987).

# Godfrey v. Georgia

Supreme Court of the United States, 1980.
446 U.S. 420.

■ MR. JUSTICE STEWART announced the judgment of the Court and delivered an opinion, in which MR. JUSTICE BLACKMUN, MR. JUSTICE POWELL, and MR. JUSTICE STEVENS joined.

Under Georgia law, a person convicted of murder may be sentenced to death if it is found beyond a reasonable doubt that the offense "was outrageously or wantonly vile, horrible or inhuman in that it involved torture, depravity of mind, or an aggravated battery to the victim." In Gregg v. Georgia, 428 U.S. 153 (1976), the Court held that this statutory aggravating circumstance (Subsection (b)(7)) is not unconstitutional on its face.[a] Responding to the argument that the language of the provision is "so broad that capital punishment could be imposed in any murder case," the joint opinion said:

> It is, of course, arguable that any murder involves depravity of mind or an aggravated battery. But this language need not be construed in this way, and there is no reason to assume that the Supreme Court of Georgia will adopt such an open-ended construction. (opinion of Stewart, Powell, and Stevens, JJ.).

Nearly four years have passed since the *Gregg* decision, and during that time many death sentences based in whole or in part on Subsection (b)(7) have been affirmed by the Supreme Court of Georgia. The issue now before us is whether, in affirming the imposition of the sentences of death in the present case, the Georgia Supreme Court has adopted such a broad and vague construction of the Subsection (b)(7) aggravating circumstance as to violate the Eighth and 14th Amendments to the United States Constitution.[2]

## I

On a day in early September in 1977, the petitioner and his wife of 28 years had a heated argument in their home. During the course of this altercation, the petitioner, who had consumed several cans of beer, threatened his wife with a knife and damaged some of her clothing. At this point, the petitioner's wife declared that she was going to leave him, and departed to stay with relatives. That afternoon she went to a justice of the peace and secured a warrant charging the petitioner with aggravated assault. A few days later, while still living away from home, she filed suit for divorce.

[a] The Georgia statute before the Court in *Gregg* and again in *Godfrey* is reprinted in Appendix B.—[Footnote by eds.]

[2] The other statutory aggravating circumstances upon which a death sentence may be based after conviction of murder in Georgia are considerably more specific or objectively measurable than Subsection (b)(7)....

In [a prior decision], the Supreme Court of Georgia held unconstitutional the portion of the first statutory aggravating circumstance encompassing persons who have a "substantial history of serious assaultive criminal convictions" because it did not set "sufficiently 'clear and objective standards.' "

Summons was served on the petitioner, and a court hearing was set on a date some two weeks later. Before the date of the hearing, the petitioner on several occasions asked his wife to return to their home. Each time his efforts were rebuffed. At some point during this period, his wife moved in with her mother. The petitioner believed that his mother-in-law was actively instigating his wife's determination not to consider a possible reconciliation.

In the early evening of September 20, according to the petitioner, his wife telephoned him at home. Once again they argued. She asserted that reconciliation was impossible and allegedly demanded all the proceeds from the planned sale of their house. The conversation was terminated after she said that she would call back later. This she did in an hour or so. The ensuing conversation was, according to the petitioner's account, even more heated than the first. His wife reiterated her stand that reconciliation was out of the question, said that she still wanted all the proceeds from the sale of their house, and mentioned that her mother was supporting her position. Stating that she saw no further use in talking or arguing, she hung up.

At this juncture, the petitioner got out his shotgun and walked with it down the hill from his home to the trailer where his mother-in-law lived. Peering through a window, he observed his wife, his mother-in-law, and his 11–year-old daughter playing a card game. He pointed the shotgun at his wife through the window and pulled the trigger. The charge from the gun struck his wife in the forehead and killed her instantly. He proceeded into the trailer, striking and injuring his fleeing daughter with the barrel of the gun. He then fired the gun at his mother-in-law, striking her in the head and killing her instantly.

The petitioner then called the local sheriff's office, identified himself, said where he was, explained that he had just killed his wife and mother-in-law, and asked that the sheriff come and pick him up. Upon arriving at the trailer, the law-enforcement officers found the petitioner seated on a chair in open view near the driveway. He told one of the officers that "they're dead, I killed them" and directed the officer to the place where he had put the murder weapon. Later the petitioner told a police officer: "I've done a hideous crime, ... but I have been thinking about it for eight years ... I'd do it again."

The petitioner was subsequently indicted on two counts of murder and one of aggravated assault. He pleaded not guilty and relied primarily on a defense of temporary insanity at his trial. The jury returned verdicts of guilty on all three counts.

The sentencing phase of the trial was held before the same jury. No further evidence was tendered, but counsel for each side made arguments to the jury. Three times during the course of his argument, the prosecutor stated that the case involved no allegation of "torture" or of an "aggravated battery." When counsel had completed their arguments, the trial judge instructed the jury orally and in writing on the standards that must guide them in imposing sentence. Both orally and in writing, the judge quoted to the jury the statutory language of the Subsection (b)(7) aggravating circumstance in its entirety.

The jury imposed sentences of death on both of the murder convictions. As to each, the jury specified that the aggravating circumstance they had found beyond a reasonable doubt was "that the offense of murder was outrageously or wantonly vile, horrible and inhuman."

In accord with Georgia law in capital cases, the trial judge prepared a report in the form of answers to a questionnaire for use on appellate review. One question on the form asked whether or not the victim had been "physically harmed or tortured." The trial judge's response was "No, as to both victims, excluding the actual murdering of the two victims."[4]

The Georgia Supreme Court affirmed the judgments of the trial court in all respects. With regard to the imposition of the death sentence for each of the two murder convictions, the court rejected the petitioner's contention that Subsection (b)(7) is unconstitutionally vague. The court noted that Georgia's death-penalty legislation had been upheld in *Gregg* and cited its prior decisions upholding Subsection (b)(7) in the face of similar vagueness challenges. As to the petitioner's argument that the jury's phraseology was, as a matter of law, an inadequate statement of Subsection (b)(7), the court responded by simply observing that the language "was not objectionable." The court found no evidence that the sentence had been "imposed under the influence of passion, prejudice, or any other arbitrary factor," held that the sentence was neither excessive nor disproportionate to the penalty imposed in similar cases, and stated that the evidence supported the jury's finding of the Subsection (b)(7) statutory aggravating circumstance. Two justices dissented.

## II

In Furman v. Georgia, 408 U.S. 238 (1972), the Court held that the penalty of death may not be imposed under sentencing procedures that create a substantial risk that the punishment will be inflicted in an arbitrary and capricious manner. *Gregg* reaffirmed this holding:

> [W]here discretion is afforded a sentencing body on a matter so grave as the determination of whether a human life should be taken or spared, that discretion must be suitably directed and limited so as to minimize the risk of wholly arbitrary and capricious action. (opinion of Stewart, Powell, and Stevens, JJ.).

A capital-sentencing scheme must, in short, provide a "meaningful basis for distinguishing the few cases in which [the penalty] is imposed from the many cases in which it is not."

This means that if a state wishes to authorize capital punishment it has a constitutional responsibility to tailor and apply its law in a manner that avoids the arbitrary and capricious infliction of the death penalty. Part

---

[4] Another question on the form asked the trial judge to list the mitigating circumstances that were in evidence. The judge noted that the petitioner had no significant history of prior criminal activity.

of a state's responsibility in this regard is to define the crimes for which death may be the sentence in a way that obviates "standardless [sentencing] discretion." It must channel the sentencer's discretion by "clear and objective standards" that provide "specific and detailed guidance," and that "make rationally reviewable the process for imposing a sentence of death." As was made clear in *Gregg,* a death-penalty "system could have standards so vague that they would fail adequately to channel the sentencing decision patterns of juries with the result that a pattern of arbitrary and capricious sentencing like that found unconstitutional in *Furman* could occur."

In the case before us, the Georgia Supreme Court has affirmed a sentence of death based upon no more than a finding that the offense was "outrageously or wantonly vile, horrible and inhuman." There is nothing in these few words, standing alone, that implies any inherent restraint on the arbitrary and capricious infliction of the death sentence. A person of ordinary sensibility could fairly characterize almost every murder as "outrageously or wantonly vile, horrible and inhuman." Such a view may, in fact, have been one to which the members of the jury in this case subscribed. If so, their preconceptions were not dispelled by the trial judge's sentencing instructions. These gave the jury no guidance concerning the meaning of any of Subsection (b)(7)'s terms. In fact, the jury's interpretation of Subsection (b)(7) can only be the subject of sheer speculation.

The standardless and unchanneled imposition of death sentences in the uncontrolled discretion of a basically uninstructed jury in this case was in no way cured by the affirmance of those sentences by the Georgia Supreme Court. Under state law that court may not affirm a judgment of death until it has independently assessed the evidence of record and determined that such evidence supports the trial judge's or jury's finding of an aggravating circumstance.

In past cases the state supreme court has apparently understood this obligation as carrying with it the responsibility to keep Subsection (b)(7) within constitutional bounds. Recognizing that "there is a possibility of abuse of [the Subsection (b)(7)] statutory aggravating circumstance," the court has emphasized that it will not permit the language of that subsection simply to become a "catchall" for cases which do not fit within any other statutory aggravating circumstance. Thus, in exercising its function of death-sentence review, the court has said that it will restrict its "approval of the death penalty under this statutory aggravating circumstance to those cases that lie at the core."

When *Gregg* was decided by this Court in 1976, the Georgia Supreme Court had affirmed two death sentences based wholly on Subsection (b)(7). The homicide in [the first case] was "a horrifying torture-murder." There, the victim had been beaten, burned, raped, and otherwise severely abused before her death by strangulation. The homicide in [the second case] was of a similar ilk. In that case, the convicted murderer had choked two seven-year-old boys to death after having forced each of them to submit to anal sodomy.

[Subsequent decisions] suggest that the Georgia Supreme Court had by 1977 reached three separate but consistent conclusions respecting the Subsection (b)(7) aggravating circumstance. The first was that the evidence that the offense was "outrageously or wantonly vile, horrible or inhuman" had to demonstrate "torture, depravity of mind, or an aggravated battery to the victim." The second was that the phrase, "depravity of mind," comprehended only the kind of mental state that led the murderer to torture or to commit an aggravated battery before killing his victim. The third ... was that the word, "torture," must be construed in pari materia with "aggravated battery" so as to require evidence of serious physical abuse of the victim before death. Indeed, the circumstances proved in a number of the Subsection (b)(7) death-sentence cases affirmed by the Georgia Supreme Court have met all three of these criteria.

The Georgia courts did not, however, so limit Subsection (b)(7) in the present case. No claim was made, and nothing in the record before us suggests, that the petitioner committed an aggravated battery upon his wife or mother-in-law or, in fact, caused either of them to suffer any physical injury preceding their deaths. Moreover, in the trial court, the prosecutor repeatedly told the jury—and the trial judge wrote in his sentencing report—that the murders did not involve "torture." Nothing said on appeal by the Georgia Supreme Court indicates that it took a different view of the evidence. The circumstances of this case, therefore, do not satisfy the criteria laid out by the Georgia Supreme Court itself in [the prior] cases. In holding that the evidence supported the jury's Subsection (b)(7) finding, the state Supreme Court simply asserted that the verdict was "factually substantiated."

Thus, the validity of the petitioner's death sentences turns on whether, in light of the facts and circumstances of the murders that Godfrey was convicted of committing, the Georgia Supreme Court can be said to have applied a constitutional construction of the phrase "outrageously or wantonly vile, horrible or inhuman in that [they] involved ... depravity of mind...."[15] We conclude that the answer must be no. The petitioner's crimes cannot be said to have reflected a consciousness materially more "depraved" than that of any person guilty of murder. His victims were killed instantaneously.[16] They were members of his family who were causing him extreme emotional trauma. Shortly after the killings, he acknowledged his responsibility and the heinous nature of his crimes. These factors certainly did not remove the criminality from the petitioner's acts. But ... it "is of vital importance to the defendant and to the

---

[15] The sentence of death in this case rested exclusively on Subsection (b)(7). Accordingly, we intimate no view as to whether or not the petitioner might constitutionally have received the same sentences on some other basis. Georgia does not, as do some states, make multiple murders an aggravating circumstance, as such.

[16] In light of this fact, it is constitutionally irrelevant that the petitioner used a shotgun instead of a rifle as the murder weapon, resulting in a gruesome spectacle in his mother-in-law's trailer. An interpretation of Subsection (b)(7) so as to include all murders resulting in gruesome scenes would be totally irrational.

community that any decision to impose the death sentence be, and appear to be, based on reason rather than caprice or emotion.''

That cannot be said here. There is no principled way to distinguish this case, in which the death penalty was imposed, from the many cases in which it was not. Accordingly, the judgment of the Georgia Supreme Court insofar as it leaves standing the petitioner's death sentences is reversed, and the case is remanded to that court for further proceedings.

It is so ordered.

■ MR. JUSTICE MARSHALL, with whom MR. JUSTICE BRENNAN joins, concurring in the judgment.

I continue to believe that the death penalty is in all circumstances cruel and unusual punishment forbidden by the Eighth and 14th Amendments. In addition, I agree with the plurality that the Georgia Supreme Court's construction of the provision at issue in this case is unconstitutionally vague under Gregg v. Georgia, 428 U.S. 153 (1976). I write separately, first, to examine the Georgia Supreme Court's application of this provision, and second, to suggest why the enterprise on which the Court embarked in *Gregg* increasingly appears to be doomed to failure.

I

... The Court's conclusion in *Gregg* was ... expressly based on the assumption that the Georgia Supreme Court would adopt a narrowing construction that would give some discernible content to Subsection (b)(7). In the present case, no such narrowing construction was read to the jury or applied by the Georgia Supreme Court on appeal. As it has so many times in the past, that court upheld the jury's finding with a simple notation that it was supported by the evidence. The premise on which *Gregg* relied has thus proved demonstrably false. . . .

In addition I think it necessary to emphasize that even under the prevailing view that the death penalty may, in some circumstances, constitutionally be imposed, it is not enough for a reviewing court to apply a narrowing construction to otherwise ambiguous statutory language. The jury must be instructed on the proper, narrow construction of the statute. The Court's cases make clear that it is the *sentencer's* discretion that must be channeled and guided by clear, objective, and specific standards. To give the jury an instruction in the form of the bare words of the statute—words that are hopelessly ambiguous and could be understood to apply to any murder—would effectively grant it unbridled discretion to impose the death penalty. Such a defect could not be cured by the post hoc narrowing construction of an appellate court. The reviewing court can determine only whether a rational jury might have imposed the death penalty if it had been properly instructed; it is impossible for it to say whether a particular jury would have so exercised its discretion if it had known the law. . . .

II

The preceding discussion leads me to what I regard as a more fundamental defect in the Court's approach to death-penalty cases. In *Gregg*, the

Court rejected the position, expressed by my Brother Brennan and myself, that the death penalty is in all circumstances cruel and unusual punishment forbidden by the Eighth and 14th Amendments. Instead it was concluded that in "a matter so grave as the determination of whether a human life should be taken or spared," it would be both necessary and sufficient to insist on sentencing procedures that would minimize or eliminate the "risk that [the death penalty] would be inflicted in an arbitrary and capricious manner." (opinion of Stewart, Powell, and Stevens, JJ.). Contrary to the statutes at issue in *Furman,* under which the death penalty was "infrequently imposed" upon "a capriciously selected random handful," (Stewart, J., concurring), and "the threat of execution [was] too attenuated to be of substantial service to criminal justice," (White, J., concurring), it was anticipated that the Georgia scheme would produce an evenhanded, objective procedure rationally " 'distinguishing the few cases in which [the death penalty] is imposed from the many cases in which it is not.' " (White, J., concurring).

For reasons I expressed in *Furman* and *Gregg,* I believe that the death penalty may not constitutionally be imposed even if it were possible to do so in an evenhanded manner. But events since *Gregg* make that possibility seem increasingly remote. Nearly every week of every year, this Court is presented with at least one petition for certiorari raising troubling issues of non-compliance with the strictures of *Gregg* and its progeny. On numerous occasions since *Gregg,* the Court has reversed decisions of state supreme courts upholding the imposition of capital punishment, [citing 14 cases over a three-year period], frequently on the ground that the sentencing proceeding allowed undue discretion, causing dangers of arbitrariness in violation of *Gregg* and its companion cases. These developments, coupled with other pervasive evidence,[6] strongly suggest that appellate courts are incapable of guaranteeing the kind of objectivity and evenhandedness that the Court contemplated and hoped for in *Gregg.* The disgraceful distorting effects of racial discrimination and poverty continue to be painfully visible in the imposition of death sentences.[7] And while hundreds have been placed on death row in the years since *Gregg,*[8] only three persons have been executed.[9] Two of them made no effort to challenge their sentence and were thus

[6] See generally George Dix, Appellate Review of the Decision To Impose Death, 68 Geo.L.J. 97 (1979). Dix's meticulous study of the process of appellate review in Georgia, Florida, and Texas since 1976 demonstrates that "objective standards" for the imposition of the death penalty have not been achieved and probably are impossible to achieve, and concludes that *Gregg* and its companion cases "mandate pursuit of an impossible goal."

[7] On April 20, 1980, for example, over 40 percent of the persons on death row were Negroes.

[8] See NAACP Legal Defense and Educational Fund, Death Row, U.S.A. (April 20, 1980) (642 people on death row); U.S. Department of Justice, Capital Punishment 1978, p. 1 (1979) (445 people on death row as of December 31, 1978).

[9] In *Furman,* my Brothers Stewart and White concurred in the judgment largely on the ground that the death penalty had been so infrequently imposed that it made no contribution to the goals of punishment. Mr. Justice Stewart stated that "the petitioners are among a capriciously selected random handful upon whom the sentence of death has in fact been imposed." Mr. Justice White relied on his conclusion that "the penalty is so infrequently imposed that the threat of

permitted to commit what I have elsewhere described as "state-administered suicide." The task of eliminating arbitrariness in the infliction of capital punishment is proving to be one which our criminal justice system—and perhaps any criminal justice system—is unable to perform. In short, it is now apparent that the defects that led my Brothers Douglas, Stewart, and White to concur in the judgment in *Furman* are present as well in the statutory schemes under which defendants are currently sentenced to death.

The issue presented in this case usefully illustrates the point. The Georgia Supreme Court has given no real content to Subsection (b)(7) in by far the majority of the cases in which it has had an opportunity to do so. In the four years since *Gregg*, the Georgia court has *never* reversed a jury's finding of a Subsection (b)(7) aggravating circumstance. With considerable frequency the Georgia court has, as here, upheld the imposition of the death penalty on the basis of a simple conclusory statement that the evidence supported the jury's finding under Subsection (b)(7). Instances of a narrowing construction are difficult to find, and those narrowing constructions that can be found have not been adhered to with any regularity. In no case has the Georgia court required a narrowing construction to be given to the jury—an indispensable method for avoiding the "standardless and unchanneled imposition of death sentences." Genuinely independent review has been exceedingly rare. . . .

The Georgia court's inability to administer its capital-punishment statute in an evenhanded fashion is not necessarily attributable to any bad faith on its part; it is, I believe, symptomatic of a deeper problem that is proving to be genuinely intractable. Just five years before *Gregg*, Mr. Justice Harlan stated for the Court that the tasks of identifying "before the fact those characteristics of criminal homicides and their perpetrators which call for the death penalty, and [of] express[ing] these characteristics in language which can be fairly understood and applied by the sentencing authority, appear to be ... beyond present human ability." McGautha v. California, 402 U.S. 183, 204 (1971). From this premise, the Court in *McGautha* drew the conclusion that the effort to eliminate arbitrariness in the imposition of the death penalty need not be attempted at all. In *Furman*, the Court concluded that the arbitrary infliction of the death penalty was constitutionally intolerable. And in *Gregg*, the Court rejected the premise of *McGautha* and approved a statutory scheme under which, as the Court then perceived it, the death penalty would be imposed in an evenhanded manner.

There can be no doubt that the conclusion drawn in *McGautha* was properly repudiated in *Furman*, where the Court made clear that the arbitrary imposition of the death penalty is forbidden by the Eighth and 14th Amendments. But I believe that the Court in *McGautha* was substantially correct in concluding that the task of selecting in some objective way those persons who should be condemned to die is one that remains beyond

execution is too attenuated to be of substantial service to criminal justice." These conclusions have proved to be equally valid under the sentencing schemes upheld in *Gregg*.

the capacities of the criminal justice system. For this reason, I remain hopeful that even if the Court is unwilling to accept the view that the death penalty is so barbaric that it is in all circumstances cruel and unusual punishment forbidden by the Eighth and 14th Amendments, it may eventually conclude that the effort to eliminate arbitrariness in the infliction of that ultimate sanction is so plainly doomed to failure that it—and the death penalty—must be abandoned altogether.

■ Mr. Chief Justice Burger, dissenting.

After murdering his wife and mother-in-law, petitioner informed the police that he had committed a "hideous" crime. The dictionary defines hideous as "morally offensive," "shocking," or "horrible." Thus, the very curious feature of this case is that petitioner himself characterized his crime in terms equivalent to those employed in the Georgia statute. For my part, I prefer petitioner's characterization of his conduct to the plurality's effort to excuse and rationalize that conduct as just another killing. The jurors in this case, who heard all relevant mitigating evidence obviously shared that preference; they concluded that this "hideous" crime was "outrageously or wantonly vile, horrible and inhuman" within the meaning of Subsection (b)(7).

More troubling than the plurality's characterization of petitioner's crime is the new responsibility that it assumes with today's decision—the task of determining on a case-by-case basis whether a defendant's conduct is egregious enough to warrant a death sentence. . . . I am convinced that the course the plurality embarks on today is sadly mistaken. . . .

■ Mr. Justice White, with whom Mr. Justice Rehnquist joins, dissenting. . . .

The question [is] whether the facts of this case bear sufficient relation to Subsection (b)(7) to conclude that the Georgia Supreme Court responsibly and constitutionally discharged its review function. I believe that they do.

[P]etitioner, in a cold blooded executioner's style, murdered his wife and his mother-in-law and, in passing, struck his young daughter on the head with the barrel of his gun. The weapon, a shotgun, is hardly known for the surgical precision with which it perforates its target. The murder scene, in consequence, can only be described in the most unpleasant terms. Petitioner's wife lay prone on the floor. Mrs. Godfrey's head had a hole described as "[a]pproximately the size of a silver dollar" on the side where the shot entered, and much less decipherable and more extensive damage on the side where the shot exited. Pellets that had passed through Mrs. Godfrey's head were found embedded in the kitchen cabinet.

It will be remembered that after petitioner inflicted this much damage, he took out time not only to strike his daughter on the head, but also to reload his single-shot shotgun and to enter the house. Only then did he get around to shooting his mother-in-law, Mrs. Wilkerson, whose last several moments as a sentient being must have been as terrifying as the human mind can imagine. The police eventually found her face down on the floor with a substantial portion of her head missing and her brain, no longer cabined by her skull, protruding for some distance onto the floor. Blood not only covered the floor and table, but dripped from the ceiling as well.

The Georgia Supreme Court held that these facts supported the jury's finding of the existence of statutory aggravating circumstance Subsection (b)(7). A majority of this Court disagrees. But this disagreement, founded as it is on the notion that the lower court's construction of the provision was overly broad, in fact reveals a conception of this Court's role in backstopping the Georgia Supreme Court that is itself overly broad. Our role is to correct genuine errors of constitutional significance resulting from the application of Georgia's capital sentencing procedures; our role is not to peer majestically over the lower court's shoulder so that we might second-guess its interpretation of facts that quite reasonably—perhaps even quite plainly—fit within the statutory language.[2]

Who is to say that the murders of Mrs. Godfrey and Mrs. Wilkerson were not "vile," or "inhuman," or "horrible"? In performing his murderous chore, petitioner employed a weapon known for its disfiguring effects on targets, human or other, and he succeeded in creating a scene so macabre and revolting that, if anything, "vile," "horrible," and "inhuman" are descriptively inadequate.

And who among us can honestly say that Mrs. Wilkerson did not feel "torture" in her last sentient moments. Her daughter, an instant ago a living being sitting across the table from Mrs. Wilkerson, lay prone on the floor, a bloodied and mutilated corpse. The seconds ticked by; enough time for her son-in-law to reload his gun, to enter the home, and to take a gratuitous swipe at his daughter. What terror must have run through her veins as she first witnessed her daughter's hideous demise and then came to terms with the imminence of her own. Was this not torture? And if this was not torture, can it honestly be said that petitioner did not exhibit a "depravity of mind" in carrying out this cruel drama to its mischievous and murderous conclusion? I should have thought, moreover, that the Georgia court could reasonably have deemed the scene awaiting the investigating policemen as involving "an aggravated battery to the victim[s]."

---

[2] The plurality opinion states that "[A]n interpretation of Subsection (b)(7) so as to include all murders resulting in gruesome scenes would be totally irrational" and that the fact that both "victims were killed instantaneously" makes the gruesomeness of the scene irrelevant. This view ignores the indisputable truth that Mrs. Wilkerson did not die "instantaneously"; she had many moments to contemplate her impending death, assuming that the stark terror she must have felt permitted any contemplation. More importantly, it also ignores the obvious correlation between gruesomeness and "depravity of mind," between gruesomeness and "aggravated battery," between gruesomeness and "horrible," between gruesomeness and "vile," and between gruesomeness and "inhuman." Mere gruesomeness, to be sure, would not itself serve to establish the existence of Subsection (b)(7). But it certainly fares sufficiently well as an indicator of this particular aggravating circumstance to signal to a reviewing court the distinct possibility that the terms of the provision, upon further investigation, might well be met in the circumstances of the case.

The point is not that, in my view, petitioner's crimes were definitively vile, horrible, or inhuman, or that, as I assay the evidence, they beyond *any* doubt involved torture, depravity of mind, or an aggravated battery to the victims. Rather, the lesson is a much more elementary one, an instruction that, I should have thought, this Court would have taken to heart long ago. Our mandate does not extend to interfering with factfinders in state criminal proceedings or with state courts that are responsibly and consistently interpreting state law, unless that interference is predicated on a violation of the Constitution. No convincing showing of such a violation is made here, for, as Mr. Justice Stewart has written in another place, the issue here is not what *our* verdict would have been, but whether "any rational factfinder" could have found the existence of aggravating circumstance Subsection (b)(7). Faithful adherence to this standard of review compels our affirmance of the judgment below. . . .

Under the present statutory regime, adopted in response to *Furman,* the Georgia Supreme Court has responsibly and consistently performed its review function pursuant to the Georgia capital-sentencing procedures. The state reports, that at the time its brief was written, the Georgia Supreme Court had reviewed some 99 cases in which the death penalty has been imposed. Of these, 66 had been affirmed, five had been reversed for errors in the guilt phase; and 22 had been reversed for errors in the sentencing phase. This reversal rate of over 27 percent is not substantially lower than the historic reversal rate of state supreme courts. See Courting Reversal: The Supervisory Role of State Supreme Courts, 87 Yale L.J. 1191, 1198, 1209 (1978), where it is indicated that 16 state supreme courts over a 100–year period, in deciding 5,133 cases, had a reversal rate of 38.5 percent; for criminal cases, the reversal rate was 35.6 percent. To the extent that the reversal rate is lower than the historic level, it doubtless can be attributed to the great and admirable extent to which discretion and uncertainty have been removed from Georgia's capital-sentencing procedures since our decision in *Furman* and to the fact that review is mandatory.

The Georgia Supreme Court has vacated a death sentence where it believed that the statutory sentencing procedures, as passed by the legislature, were defective; it has held that jurors must be instructed that they can impose a life sentence even though they find the existence of a statutory aggravating circumstance; it has reversed the imposition of the death penalty where the prosecutor made an improper comment during his argument to the jury in the sentencing phase; it has reversed a trial court's decision limiting the type of mitigating evidence that could be presented; it has set aside a death sentence when jurors failed to specify which aggravating circumstances they found to exist; it has reversed a death sentence imposed on a partial finding of an aggravating circumstance; it has disapproved a death penalty because of errors in admitting evidence; it has reversed a capital sentence where a co-defendant received only a life sentence; and it has held a statutory aggravating circumstance to be unconstitutional.

The Georgia Supreme Court has also been responsible and consistent in its construction of Subsection (b)(7). The provision has been the exclusive or nonexclusive basis for imposition of the death penalty in over 30 cases. In one excursus on the provision's language, the court in effect held that the section is to be read as a whole, construing "depravity of mind," "torture," and "aggravated battery" to flesh out the meaning of "vile," "horrible," and "inhuman." I see no constitutional error resulting from this understanding of the provision.... And the court has noted that it would apply the provision only in "core" cases and would not permit Subsection (b)(7) to become a "catchall."

Nor do the facts of this case stand out as an aberration. A jury found Subsection (b)(7) satisfied, for example, when a child was senselessly and ruthlessly executed by a murderer who, like petitioner, accomplished this end with a shotgun. The Georgia Supreme Court affirmed. The court has also affirmed a jury's finding of Subsection (b)(7) where, as here, there was substantial disfigurement of the victim, and where, as arguably with Mrs. Wilkerson, there was torture of the victim.

The majority's attempt to drive a wedge between this case and others in which Subsection (b)(7) has been applied is thus unconvincing, as is any suggestion that the Georgia Supreme Court has somehow failed overall in performance of its review function.

In the circumstances of this case, the majority today endorses the argument that I thought we had rejected in *Gregg:* namely, "that no matter how effective the death penalty may be as a punishment, government, created and run as it must be by humans, is inevitably incompetent to administer it." The Georgia Supreme Court, faced with a seemingly endless train of macabre scenes, has endeavored in a responsible, rational, and consistent fashion to effectuate its statutory mandate as illuminated by our judgment in *Gregg.* Today, a majority of this Court, its arguments shredded by its own illogic, informs the Georgia Supreme Court that, to some extent, its efforts have been outside the Constitution. I reject this as an unwarranted invasion into the realm of state law, for, as in *Gregg,* "I decline to interfere with the manner in which Georgia has chosen to enforce [its] laws" until a genuine error of constitutional magnitude surfaces.

I would affirm the judgment of the Supreme Court of Georgia.

———

## NOTES ON *GODFREY*

**1. The Constitutional Defect in Godfrey's Death Sentence.** Although the Supreme Court held that Godfrey's death sentence was unconstitutional, the rationale for the decision is elusive. Did the Court hold that subsection (b)(7) is void for vagueness? If not, what is the holding of the case?

The plurality and dissenting opinions appear to view the outcome in *Godfrey* through different lenses. Justice White asserts that the case does not "stand out as an aberration" when compared with other cases in which death sentences had been imposed under subsection (b)(7). In contrast, Justice Stewart observes that "there is no meaningful way to distinguish [Godfrey's] case in which the death penalty was imposed from the many cases in which it was not." Which is the right question to ask? How did Justice Stewart know about the cases in which the death penalty had not been imposed?

**2. The Proper Role of the Supreme Court.** The *Godfrey* opinions reflect continuing disagreement about the proper role of the Supreme Court. The plurality appears willing to pursue a relatively aggressive role in supervising state administration of capital sentencing. This approach is flanked on one side by the more passive position of Justices White, Rehnquist, and Burger, who object, in White's words, to the plurality's effort to "backstop" the Georgia Supreme Court and to the Court's "unwarranted invasion into the realm of state law." The plurality is flanked on the other side by Justices Marshall and Brennan, who assert that "the effort to eliminate arbitrariness" in the administration of the death penalty is "so plainly doomed to failure" that capital punishment should be declared unconstitutional. What position should the Court take?[a]

**3. Subsequent History.** After Godfrey's case was remanded to the Georgia courts, the prosecution again sought the death penalty. This time another statutory circumstance was advanced to establish the predicate for a death sentence—that the murder "was committed while the offender was engaged in the commission of another capital felony." The jury found that this circumstance had been proved and recommended death sentences for each murder. On appeal, the Georgia Supreme Court affirmed. Godfrey v. State, 248 Ga. 616, 284 S.E.2d 422 (1981). The court held that Godfrey's retrial and the reimposition of the death sentences did not violate the double jeopardy provisions of the state or federal Constitutions. The court also rejected Godfrey's contention that the particular aggravating circumstance had been improperly applied:

> [Godfrey] argues that since both murders were separate in time, although only moments apart, and each was instantaneous, one could not have occurred while in the commission of another. However, this argument has been raised before and decided in a manner contrary to Godfrey's position [citing a 1981 case]. Furthermore, under the plain meaning of the statute, multiple murders are included as "another capital felony."

Was Godfrey's second death sentence constitutional?

---

[a] The positions reflected in Justice Stewart's plurality opinion and in Justice White's dissenting opinion in *Godfrey* continue to represent the main division on the Court. Although the abolitionist position is no longer held by any of the active Justices, Justice Blackmun endorsed this view, for reasons similar to those expressed by Justice Marshall in his *Godfrey* concurrence, just before he resigned from the Court. See Callins v. Collins, 510 U.S. 1141 (1994) (Blackmun, J., dissenting from denial of certiorari).

**4. The Structure of Modern Capital Sentencing Statutes: An Overview.** The Supreme Court has established certain conditions that must be met by capital sentencing procedures. Within these boundaries the legislatures have considerable flexibility. Thus, while the Supreme Court's death penalty decisions provide an essential foundation for further study, a complete understanding of the place of the death penalty in the modern law of homicide requires attention to the formulation and administration of contemporary capital sentencing statutes. The next section considers these questions in some detail. The following overview illustrates the questions raised.

**(i) Criteria of Inclusion.** Although the Supreme Court's decisions have not yet marked a clear line regarding the level of culpability that is constitutionally required to support a death sentence, it appears that intent to kill (or to use lethal force) or extreme indifference to the value of human life must be shown.[b] In addition, the line of decisions culminating in *Zant v. Stephens* stands for the proposition that the state is required to establish additional substantive criteria so as to "genuinely narrow the class of persons eligible for the death penalty." The state may provide such criteria in the definition of the elements of capital homicide, as has been done in Texas and Virginia, or in the definition of aggravating circumstances that must be proved at the sentencing stage, as has been done in Georgia and Florida. It may be useful at this point to review § 210.6 of the Model Penal Code and the capital sentencing statutes of Alabama, Florida, Georgia, New York, North Carolina, Texas, and Virginia reprinted in Appendix B. These statutes reflect varying judgments concerning appropriate criteria of inclusion. Have they specified substantive predicates for imposition of the death penalty in a way that "genuinely narrows the class" of intentional homicides to those for which the ultimate sanction is reasonably justified?

**(ii) Criteria of Exclusion.** The Supreme Court has held that the Eighth Amendment precludes execution of defendants who are mentally retarded,[c] and is considering whether the constitution bans the death penalty for a person who was under 18 years of age at the time of the homicide, as provided by the laws of at least 16 states.[d] What is the basis of these judgments? Are there other factors that should preclude imposition of the death penalty for a homicide otherwise properly punishable as a capital offense?

---

[b] See Enmund v. Florida, 458 U.S. 782 (1982), and Tison v. Arizona, 481 U.S. 137 (1987), discussed below.

[c] See Atkins v. Virginia, 536 U.S. 304 (2002), discussed below and in Chapter 9.

[d] The Supreme Court has agreed to review the Missouri Supreme Court's decision in Simmons v. Roper, 112 S.W.3d 397 (Mo. 2003). See Roper v. Simmons, ___ U.S. ___, 124 S.Ct. 1171 (2004). Previously, in a series of five-four decisions, the Supreme Court held that the death penalty is constitutionally precluded for persons who were under 16 years of age at the time of the offense but is not categorically precluded for older adolescents or for mentally retarded defendants. The cases are summarized below.

**(iii) Criteria of Mitigation and Selection.** Once the legislature has defined the class of intentional homicides for which the death penalty is permissible, what additional criteria should be considered? The Supreme Court has made it clear that the death sentence cannot be mandatory and that the sentencer is constitutionally required to "consider" any evidence proffered by the defendant in mitigation. Within this framework, should the sentencer's discretion be subject to normative constraint or guidance? In this connection, compare the Model Penal Code and the Georgia and Florida statutes reproduced in Appendix B. Under the Georgia statute, the sentencer's discretion "to recommend" a death sentence for a death-eligible offender is unconstrained by normative criteria. In contrast, the Model Penal Code provides that the sentencing court is permitted to consider a death sentence only if it (or the jury) finds that "there are no mitigating circumstances sufficiently substantial to call for leniency." Even in the absence of such a finding, moreover, it appears that the court has residual discretion to impose a life sentence. The Florida statute appears to tip the scale in the other direction, requiring a death sentence to be imposed if "there are insufficient mitigating circumstances to outweigh the aggravating circumstances." Are these variations significant? Which is preferable?

**(iv) Comparative Review.** Appellate review serves the same functions in capital cases as in any other case—assuring, for example, that the trial court has properly interpreted and applied the governing law and that the evidence is legally sufficient to establish the necessary substantive predicates for the disposition of the case below. In addition to the standard functions, however, appellate courts in most states also have a unique responsibility in capital cases—conducting "comparative review" of each death sentence to determine whether the imposition of the capital sanction is consistent with the sentences imposed in similar cases. Although the Supreme Court has held that comparative review is not constitutionally required, Pulley v. Harris, 465 U.S. 37 (1984), most state statutes include provisions, modeled on the Georgia statute, which direct the appellate court to determine "whether the sentence of death is excessive or disproportionate to the penalty imposed in similar cases, considering both the crime and the defendant." Comparative review is designed to promote consistency in the administration of the death penalty in each state and thereby to respond to the concerns underlying the Supreme Court's decision in *Furman*. Can work for this purpose? On what data should the comparisons be based? Are any two offenses likely to be identical in *all* relevant respects? What kinds of variations are tolerable?

In a general sense, these questions go to the heart of the constitutional issue raised by *Furman*. The Supreme Court has apparently determined that the *Furman* defect is adequately remedied, from a constitutional standpoint, if the state statute "genuinely narrows the class" of death-eligible offenders. The risk of arbitrary selection within the class is apparently tolerable as a constitutional matter. Is the Court right? Even if the risk is not of constitutional magnitude, what should state appellate courts do to reduce it?

———

## SUBSECTION B: ADMINISTRATION OF MODERN CAPITAL SENTENCING STATUTES

———

## State v. Moose

Supreme Court of North Carolina, 1984.
310 N.C. 482, 313 S.E.2d 507.

■ MEYER, JUSTICE. [The defendant was convicted of first-degree murder for killing Ransom Connelly and was sentenced to death.]

. . . Phillip Kincaid, a surviving eye-witness to the murder, testified that he and Ransom Connelly were driving down Zion Road at about 10:30 p.m. on the night of 26 March 1982. As they crossed the intersection of Zion Road and Settlemyer Road, they noticed a pickup truck. The truck followed them for a distance of 1.3 miles to the intersection of Zion Road and Highway 64–70. The truck followed Connelly's Pontiac Bonneville very closely, repeatedly honking its horn, and bumping the back of the car as it came to a stop at the 64–70 intersection. Although there was no traffic and the pickup truck had numerous opportunities to pass, it did not. The pickup truck continued to follow Connelly's car as it turned left on 64–70, at which point Connelly and Kincaid became alarmed and decided to pull off the road into the parking lot of the Drexel Discount Drug Store. Kincaid watched as the pickup truck drove up along the driver's side of the car, and the barrel of a shotgun emerged from the window on the passenger side of the truck. Kincaid testified that the shotgun remained pointed at them for approximately five seconds before the blast which shattered the driver's window of the Pontiac and killed Ransom Connelly.

The defendant testified on his own behalf to the effect that he and two women, Lynn Whisnant and Carolyn Bradshaw Chapman, left the American Legion Hut on Settlemyer Road in defendant's pickup truck. He and Whisnant were living together at the home of Whisnant's father in Morganton. Defendant had been drinking beer and liquor all day. He pulled up behind a vehicle on Zion Road and attempted to pass it twice. He blew his horn when he reached the stop sign at the 64–70 intersection. He followed the car as it turned left on 64–70 because he was going to visit a friend in Valdese. He attempted to pass the car again, but it veered to the middle of the road. He was carrying two shotguns in the cab of his truck. He asked Whisnant to pass him one of the guns because "Well, we were sitting there at the stop sign and there were several cars coming by, and he was taking longer than he should to be turning, and stuff, and I, you know, got a little irritated sitting there behind him, and after we turned, you know, the idea struck me to fire over him and scare him."

The defendant placed the shotgun "across the upper part of the door frame, where the window rolls down, inside there. It was laid across that and my leg, with my hand on it." Defendant testified that he remembered being off the road and "the doorpost of the truck being approximately even with the front window of the car." He then testified, "I thought somebody hollered at me, but anyway, I had the impression that I was about to hit something and I swerved to the left, as instinct, to get the truck turned as fast as I could, and as I started to turn, I brought my right hand up to grab for the wheel and the shotgun went off." He maintained that he did not bring the truck to a complete stop, did not aim the shotgun at anyone, and did not know that he had shot anyone until after he was arrested. Nevertheless, immediately after the blast, defendant fled the scene, colliding with another automobile as he entered highway 64–70. He drove his truck into the M & C Auto Parts Store lot, located a short distance down the road, and began to repair a broken fuel line "busted during the impact." Shortly afterwards the defendant and Whisnant were apprehended. Carolyn Bradshaw disappeared before the police arrived. She would not testify at trial.

Lynn Whisnant testified that as they drove down Zion Road defendant did follow a car which she knew to be occupied by two black men. Although she and the defendant had decided to go to Morganton after leaving the American Legion Hut, when they reached the intersection of 64–70, rather than turning right to Morganton as she had asked him to do, the defendant turned left. He continued to follow the Pontiac until it pulled into the Drexel Discount Drug parking lot. The truck pulled up nearly parallel to the car. She remembered the blast of the shotgun and hearing glass shatter.

Ronnie Glenn Bowen testified for the state. Bowen occupied the same jail cell with the defendant in the Burke County jail and the two discussed the murder of Ransom Connelly. Moose described to Bowen the events leading up to the murder, repeatedly referred to the victim as an "old man" or a "nigger," expressed no regret for his actions, and said he wished that he had shot one of the arresting officers.

[The jury found Moose guilty of a "willful, deliberate and premeditated killing." A separate verdict was returned on sentence. Under North Carolina's capital sentencing statute, the jury is instructed that it may recommend the death penalty if it finds that one or more statutory aggravating circumstances exist, that the aggravating circumstances are sufficiently substantial to call for the death penalty, and that the aggravating circumstances outweigh the mitigating circumstances. The jury found two aggravating circumstances: that "the murder was especially heinous, atrocious or cruel" and that "the defendant knowingly created a great risk of death to more than one person by means of a weapon or device which would normally be hazardous to the lives of more than one person." The jury also found, as mitigating factors, that the defendant had "exhibited good behavior" while in jail and that he had a "history of alcohol abuse."[a] Based on its judgment that the aggravating circumstances outweighed the mitigating circumstances, the jury recommended a death sentence. Moose sought to set aside his death sentence on a variety of grounds.]

Defendant first contends that the evidence . . . was insufficient to support a finding . . . that the murder was especially heinous, atrocious, or cruel.

[T]he state argued that because the victim was "stalked" for a period of time prior to the murder, he suffered psychological torture in excess of that normally present in a first-degree murder case. We agree . . . that where the facts . . . support a finding that a victim is stalked and during the stalking the victim is aware of it and in fear that death is likely to result, the issue of whether the murder is especially heinous, atrocious, or cruel may be properly submitted for jury consideration.

Thus the issue before us is whether, as a matter of law, there is sufficient evidence to submit the issue to the jury. . . .

[T]he state was permitted to present the testimony of Phillip Kincaid for the purpose of [proving] that through a continuing and escalating course of events culminating in the murder, the victim became increasingly fearful for his life, and thereby underwent psychological torture. Kincaid testified that shortly after the defendant appeared behind them, he discovered that he and Mr. Connelly were not being pursued by a police car and informed Connelly of the fact. They "were asking each other, wondering who was that behind us." The vehicle behind them continued to bump them and at the intersection they thought the truck was going to pull around them. Connelly then said, "Well, maybe we can make it on to Fender's." They continued to wonder "who was that behind us blowing the horn." As they turned into the Drexel Discount Drug Connelly said, "I'll just pull off here, maybe whoever it is will go on by." Kincaid's testimony concluded with:

> Q. Was there anything stated about the ability to make it to Fender's?
>
> A. Well, we thought we would have been safe if we got to Fender's.
>
> Q. Was there anything said by Ransom Connelly when the shotgun came out the window and during the time that it was pointed at him and you?
>
> A. He said "Oh God, what are they going to do?"

---

[a] The trial judge had submitted a list of other factors in mitigation which the jury apparently rejected. These included two statutory factors (that "the defendant has no significant history of prior criminal activity" and that his "capacity to appreciate the criminality of his conduct or to conform his conduct to the requirements of the law was impaired.") and several other factors proposed by the defense concerning the defendant's relationship with his mother and children.—[Footnote by eds.]

> Q. What conversation during the entire time, beginning from Zion Road and coming on down No. 64–70 what, if anything, did Ransom Connelly say about wanting the vehicle behind to go on and pass to leave you alone?
>
> A. Yeah, he said I wish they'd go ahead and pass and leave us alone.

Kincaid's testimony before the jury essentially paralleled that given during the voir dire hearing. He did state before the jury, however, that they "drove up the road frightened" and that he [Kincaid] "was beginning to get more frightened after [the defendant] wouldn't pass" and "after we pulled off the road, and after the shotgun came out of the window I just froze."

It seems then that although there was a considerable amount of "wondering" about the intentions of their pursuer, and some very legitimate concern and apprehension engendered by defendant's inexplicable behavior, there is no evidence that either Kincaid or Connelly believed that the ultimate result of the pursuit would be death—at least not until the shotgun appeared. In fact, Connelly's final utterance, "Oh God, what are they going to do?" suggests that even then, the controlling factor was as much incredulity as it was fear.

We do not consider this evidence sufficient to support the state's theory that Ransom Connelly suffered excessive psychological torture as he was being "stalked for the kill." . . .

Defendant [also] contends that the evidence was insufficient to support the aggravating circumstance that "[t]he defendant knowingly created a great risk of death to more than one person by means of a weapon or device which would normally be hazardous to the lives of more than one person." This court has not previously spoken to this particular aggravating circumstance. . . .

The aggravating factor requires a showing that defendant (i) knowingly created a great risk of death to more than one person, (ii) by means of a weapon or device which would normally be hazardous to the lives of more than one person. This factor thus addresses essentially two considerations: a great risk of death knowingly created and the weapon by which it is created. We therefore address ourselves to both the risk and the weapon.

With regard to the risk element, the evidence is certainly sufficient to support a jury finding that the defendant knew there were two people in the front seat of Connelly's car. While much of the evidence is conflicting, it is clear that defendant's passenger, Mrs. Whisnant, testified that she knew there were two men in the victim's car and that they were black, and said in a statement given three days after the incident that the driver was wearing a hat and the passenger was not. The defendant . . . drove right on the bumper of the victim's car for . . . 1.3 miles and . . . bumped it at least twice. The defendant stopped his car in the parking lot within several feet of the victim's car and . . . fired the shotgun into the occupied vehicle within two or three feet of the victim and his passenger.... It cannot be said that the defendant did not knowingly create the risk.

When a shotgun is fired at close range into the passenger compartment of an automobile, the risk created is not simply a risk of injury but a risk of death. The risk of death to Connelly and Kincaid was ''great'' and not merely negligible. The risk did not exist as to only one of the occupants but to both. The fact that only one of the occupants was killed does not refute the fact that both were placed at risk of death.

As to the weapon, the crucial consideration ... is its potential to kill more than one person ... The focus must be upon the destructive capabilities of the weapon or device. Whether used for sporting purposes against game birds, water fowl and animals, or as a weapon against man, the shotgun is selected for the very reason that it is capable of firing more than one, and in fact, many projectiles in a pattern over a wide impact area rather than a specifically aimed single projectile such as from a rifle or pistol. It is used by law enforcement officers and the military alike for its widespread destructive power in close places or at close range. It is axiomatic that a shotgun is a weapon which would normally be hazardous to more than one person if it is fired into a group of two or more persons in close proximity to one another.

... We note [that the shell used] would have contained ... approximately 253 pellets.... We further note that only approximately 40 pellets were recovered from the victim's body.

We hold that a shotgun falls within the category of weapon envisioned in [the statute] and that there was sufficient evidence from which the jury could conclude that the defendant knowingly created a great risk of death to Ransom Connelly and Phillip Kincaid by means of a weapon or device which would normally be hazardous to the lives of more than one person. The jury's finding of this factor is supported by the evidence....

Defendant additionally asserts that the state impermissibly appealed to racial fears and biases when [the prosecution] argued that the murder was racially motivated. We held in [upholding the conviction] that arguments relating to the racially motivated character of this murder were supported by the evidence and relevant to refute defendant's contention that he did not intend to harm Mr. Connelly. Likewise, this evidence and the argument based thereon was relevant at sentencing to illustrate the depravity of defendant's character....

In the guilt phase we find no error. The case is remanded to the Superior Court, Burke County, for resentencing.

■ MARTIN, JUSTICE, dissenting in part. [I] respectfully dissent from the remanding of the case for a new sentencing hearing. The majority finds the evidence insufficient to submit the issue to the jury of whether the capital crime was especially heinous, atrocious, or cruel. In this finding I cannot concur. I do concur in that portion of the majority opinion concerning whether the shotgun in this case was a weapon within the meaning of [the statute].

This blatant murder in cold blood of a black man by this white defendant was racially motivated. A racially motivated murder evidences abnormal brutality and depravity not found in other murders. It is especially heinous, atrocious, or cruel.

The majority concedes that for the purpose of evaluating the prosecution's jury argument, the evidence supports a finding that the murder was racially motivated. The deceased, Ransom Connelly, was a 62–year-old black man driving his car through a white community in the night-time. He was accompanied by another black man, the witness Phillip Kincaid. When defendant and his women friends, Lynn Whisnant and Carolyn Bradshaw, left the American Legion hut, they intended to go to Morganton. However, after following Connelly and Kincaid on Zion Hill Road for 1.3 miles, defendant changed his mind. Even though Lynn asked him to turn right on highway 64–70 toward Morganton, defendant turned left and continued to follow his intended victims. All during this travel, defendant had repeatedly honked the car horn, followed Connelly's Pontiac car very closely, and bumped the rear of the car at least twice.

The testimony of Ronnie Bowen supports a finding that defendant murdered Connelly for racial reasons. Bowen was in jail with defendant for about two months after the murder and before the trial. He testified that he talked with defendant several times about defendant's case and:

Q. State whether or not you told him what you were charged with and if he told you about things he was charged with.

A. Yes sir, I told him I was charged with forgery and he was in there for shooting a nigger, is what he told me ... He told me that he had followed a dude, that he followed a nigger into, down the road into a parking lot drug store and pulled up beside of him, that he shot the man with a shotgun out of the window, was rolled down on the truck.... Yes sir, he said something about it wasn't on his conscience and that he had killed the nigger, but since he was in jail he regretted it, but that it didn't bother him, though....

Q. By what names did he refer to the person that he told you that he had shot; what did he call that person?

A. Old man. Nigger; most of all nigger....

Q. And did you tell me in that statement the names, or three different names that he referred to the dead man by? What he called the dead man.

A. Nigger. Old man and damn nigger. [H]e told me that he did kill the damn nigger....

Q. Has he ever said that he was sorry that he shot the man?

A. Naw, he ain't never said that. He was sorry. He said that he wished it hadn't happened, but he never said that he was sorry.

This testimony as to what the defendant said evidences on his part a hatred for black people, a feeling of his superiority to them, and a cruel indifference to their fate. He was not sorry that he murdered the black man, it was not on his conscience. He only regretted being in jail. There is no other cause for this murder except defendant's racist attitude toward black people in general and toward Ransom Connelly in particular. Such evidence indicates abnormal brutality and depravity in the commission of the capital crime and is sufficient to submit the issue of especially heinous, atrocious, or cruel to the jury.

In analyzing this assignment of error, the majority only discusses the evidence that defendant stalked the deceased prior to the killing, thereby causing psychological torture to him. Contrary to the majority, I also find the evidence sufficient on this theory to submit the issue to the jury. Although the surviving witness failed to testify that Ransom Connelly was in panic because of the conduct of defendant in following Connelly's car, the evidence is sufficient to support a finding by the jury that Connelly suffered psychological torture during this period of time. When defendant failed to turn right on U.S. 64 toward Morganton as he had planned to do, it demonstrated an intent on his part to further inflict psychological torture on Connelly. The most potent evidence supporting this theory is that of the defendant ordering one of the women to hand him the shotgun, directing that the window be rolled down on the passenger side of his pickup truck, and coolly pointing the shotgun at Ransom Connelly's head for a period of five seconds before blowing him away. Five seconds is a short time in most circumstances, but when looking into the muzzle of a shotgun, it can be as an eternity. Ransom Connelly's remarks during the drive and as he faced the shotgun manifest the mental torture he was suffering. He said he wished they would go ahead and pass and leave us alone; maybe we could make it on to Fender's store; we will be safe if we can get to Fender's; I'll just pull in here (at the Drexel Discount Drugstore) and maybe whoever it is will go on by. Finally, as the gun was leveled at his head, Connelly said, "Oh God, what are they going to do?" The majority characterizes the last statement as being one of incredulity. I find it to be a despairing prayer. Just as the hunter stalks his frightened and cornered prey, defendant stalked Connelly for the kill.

Further, the conduct of defendant after the murder, which I will not repeat, also supports a finding of depravity on the part of defendant within the holding of State v. Oliver, 309 N.C. 326, 307 S.E.2d 304 (1983).[b]

[b] In *Oliver*, two defendants were sentenced to death in connection with two murders committed in the course of an armed robbery of a convenience store. The Court upheld the "heinous, atrocious or cruel" finding against one of defendants on the following basis:

[T]he evidence justifies a conclusion that the murder [of the store attendant], committed in total disregard for the val-

ue of human life, was a senseless murder, executed in cold blood as the victim pleaded "please don't shoot me"; and that the defendant showed no remorse. In fact, [the defendant] later laughingly boasted to his fellow inmates that he pointed the gun at [the victim] who begged not to be shot and offered the defendant more money, and that the de-

The majority correctly states the rule to be applied in determining the sufficiency of the evidence to submit an aggravating circumstance to the jury. Upon applying the rule to the evidence in this case, I find it sufficient to support the issue on the theories that (i) defendant stalked his victim, causing him to suffer psychological torture; (ii) the conduct of defendant was abnormally depraved under *Oliver*; and (iii) the capital crime was a racially motivated murder. The evidence was sufficient to submit the aggravating circumstance of especially heinous, atrocious, or cruel to the jury for its determination.

I am authorized to state that JUSTICES COPELAND and MITCHELL join in this dissenting opinion.

———

## NOTES ON SUBSTANTIVE PREDICATES FOR IMPOSITION OF THE DEATH PENALTY

**1.   Statutory Criteria of Inclusion.** What criteria should be used to define the class of homicides punishable by death? The statutes now in force reveal a number of common legislative judgments about the characteristics of the offense or of the defendant that are regarded as sufficient to support a death sentence. They are summarized below.

**(i) Identity of the Victim.** Under most modern statutes, an intentional killing is punishable by death if the victim falls within certain specified categories. A basis for the death penalty is established in most states[a] if the victim is a law enforcement officer or a correctional officer. In addition, many states make a killing punishable by death if the victim is a fireman, a judge, a prosecutor, a witness, or an elected official, or, in a smaller number of states, a kidnap victim, a hostage, or a shield.

**(ii) Accompanying Criminal Offenses.** In most states, an intentional killing is punishable by death if it occurred while the defendant was committing, attempting to commit, or fleeing after committing, a variety of specified felonies—usually rape, robbery, burglary, arson and kidnapping. About a third of the states make multiple murders punishable by death, and a few make a killing capital if the defendant committed other crimes of violence against persons other than the murder victim at the same time or in the same course of conduct.

**(iii) Hazardous Conduct.** As *Moose* illustrates, many state statutes make intentional homicide punishable by death if the defendant "knowingly created a great risk of death to many persons" or if the defendant "knowingly created a great risk of death to more than one person in a public place by means of a weapon or device which would normally be hazardous to the lives of more than one person." In other states, a killing is capital if it is committed by use of explosives.

fendant "kind of liked the idea of it."— [Footnote by eds.]

a The reference here, and below, is limited to those states that retain capital punishment.

**(iv) Pecuniary Motive.** About half the states make murder punishable by death if the defendant was hired to commit it or hired someone else to do so; in a few other states, only the hired killer is punishable by death. Under a related provision in several states, a killing is death-eligible if the defendant caused or directed another to commit it or committed it as the agent or employee of another. In a number of additional states, the standard is more broadly defined: a killing is punishable by death if "it was committed . . . for the purpose of receiving anything of monetary value" or "for pecuniary gain."

**(v) Hindrance of Law Enforcement.** A large number of statutes make a killing capital if it was committed to avoid or prevent arrest or to effect escape, and a few others make a killing punishable by death if it was committed for the purpose of disrupting or hindering law enforcement or governmental functions.

**(vi) Unusual Cruelty or Depravity.** In about three-quarters of the states a killing is capital if it is "especially heinous, atrocious or cruel" or "unwantonly vile, horrible or inhuman in that it involved torture, depravity of mind or aggravated battery to the victim" or especially cruel by some similar epithetical description. These criteria have a catch-all quality, requiring interpretation and application in a manner that provides some objective basis for distinguishing between killings that are punishable by death and those that are not.

**(vii) In Custody.** In most states, an intentional killing is punishable by death if the actor is confined in a correctional institution or otherwise "in custody" at the time of the offense.

**(viii) Prior Criminal Conduct.** In most states, an intentional killing is punishable by death if the offender has previously been convicted of murder. In about half of the states, the predicate for a death sentence is established if the defendant has previously been convicted of any felony involving the use or threat of violence. In a few additional states, it is sufficient if the defendant has a "substantial history of serious assaultive convictions" or a significant history of "criminal activity."

**(ix) Prediction of Future Criminal Conduct.** The "prior criminal record" provisions discussed above should be contrasted with the unusual provisions found in Oklahoma and Idaho, which make an intentional killing punishable by death if the sentencer finds that there is a "probability that the defendant would commit criminal acts of violence that would constitute a continuing threat to society."[b] These provisions rest explicitly on an incapacitative rationale.

**2. Questions and Comments on *Moose*.** As has been noted, creating a risk of death to more than one person is a common predicate for a death sentence in modern capital sentencing statutes. According to the court's interpretation, the circumstance is established whenever the intend-

---

[b] In two other states, Virginia and Texas, such a finding constitutes an aggravating circumstance but is not sufficient, in itself, to establish the substantive predicate for a death sentence for an intentional killing.

ed victim is in the company of one other person and the offender uses a shotgun. Thus, the offense would not have been punishable by death if Ransom Connelly had been driving alone or if Moose had used a rifle and endangered only one person. Should the death penalty hinge on such considerations? Does the Court's interpretation "reasonably justify" the imposition of a death sentence? Does it establish a "meaningful difference" between those homicides that are punishable by death and those that are not?

Assume that the North Carolina statute had not included the aggravating factor discussed above. In that event, Moose's offense would be punishable by death only if the offense had been properly found to be "heinous, atrocious or cruel." Although a majority of the court ruled that the evidence was not legally sufficient to establish this circumstance, Justice Martin argued in dissent that three dimensions of the case were sufficient to establish that the offense was "heinous, atrocious or cruel": (i) that Moose caused his victim "psychological torture" by "stalking" him; (ii) that the killing was "racially motivated"; and (iii) that Moose's conduct after the murder (his failure to express remorse) demonstrated "abnormal depravity." Is any of these three factors, standing alone, a proper predicate for a death sentence? Would it matter if the legislature had specified intentionally placing the victim in mortal fear, racial antipathy, or failure to express remorse as aggravating factors? If none of these factors is independently sufficient, should all these together be sufficient to support a finding that Moose's offense was "heinous, atrocious or cruel"? Would such a determination survive constitutional scrutiny under *Godfrey v. Georgia*?[c]

**3.   Relevance of the Premeditation–Deliberation Formula.** Under the contemporary generation of capital sentencing statutes, the premeditation-deliberation formula no longer provides a sufficient basis for imposing a death sentence; other factors relating to the offender and the offense, reviewed in the preceding notes, are now required. However, even though the formula no longer establishes a legally sufficient predicate for a capital sentence, the statutes of at least 20 states, including North Carolina, still retain it in the definition of capital homicide. In these states, the formula remains a necessary predicate for imposition of the death penalty in cases not involving torture, lying in wait, or felony murder.

Abandonment of the original mandatory approach to the capital punishment of premeditated killings indicates that lawmakers concluded long ago that the formula does not isolate a class of homicide offenders all of whom should be executed. The question remains, however, whether the formula is nonetheless useful as a screening device. Does it accurately sort intentional homicides into a class for which the death penalty should be foreclosed and a class for which the death penalty should be considered if other criteria are met? Reconsider the discussion of the meaning of the

---

[c] For a subsequent North Carolina case holding the evidence insufficient to support the "heinous, atrocious or cruel" circumstance, see State v. Lloyd, 552 S.E.2d 596 (N.C. 2001) (defendant shot his former girlfriend four times at close range and then left as dying woman was found by her son and five-year old grandson).

formula summarized in the Introductory Notes to this Chapter. Does its utility depend on what it means? Should Anderson (also discussed in those notes) be excluded from the death penalty because there was no evidence that he "deliberated" and "premeditated" before he killed a 13–year-old girl by inflicting some 60 knife wounds? Did Moose "premeditate and deliberate" before shooting his victim? Should it matter?

---

## State of Alabama v. Judith Ann Neelley

Circuit Court of DeKalb County, Alabama, April 18, 1983.
Sentencing Order

■ DONALD L. COLE, CIRCUIT JUDGE. The defendant was charged by indictment with the murder of Lisa Ann Millican during a kidnapping in the first degree, a capital offense. A jury returned a verdict on March 22, 1983, finding the defendant guilty of the capital offense, whereupon the court adjudged the defendant guilty in accordance with the jury's verdict.

Following the adjudication of guilt, a separate sentence hearing was conducted before the same jury, and the jury returned a recommendation that the defendant be sentenced to life without parole.[a]

The court has ordered and received a written pre-sentence investigation report and has conducted an additional sentence hearing pursuant to Ala.Code § 13A–5–47. At the sentence hearing, the state, through its district attorney, urged that the court fix the defendant's punishment at death. The defendant, through her counsel, argued that the court should fix her punishment, in accordance with the jury's recommendation, at life in prison without parole.

### FINDING OF FACTS SUMMARIZING THE CRIME
### AND THE DEFENDANT'S PARTICIPATION IN IT

The body of Lisa Ann Millican, age 13, was found in a gorge known as Little River Canyon near Fort Payne on September 29, 1982. Lisa was a resident of the Ethel Harpst Home, a Methodist home for neglected children located in Cedartown, Georgia.

Lisa and five other girls from the home were taken by a house parent on an outing to Riverbend Mall in Rome, Georgia on September 25, 1982. While at the mall, Lisa became separated from the others. During this separation, she was abducted by the defendant, who asked Lisa to go "riding around." Lisa hesitated at first, but then agreed. The events which followed the abduction led to the death of Lisa when the defendant shot her in the back on September 28, 1982, and threw her body into the canyon.

The abduction of Lisa Ann Millican was part of a bizarre scheme whereby the defendant attempted to lure girls and young women into the car with her for the ultimate purpose of making them available to her

[a] The vote was ten jurors for life without parole and two for death.—[Footnote by eds.]

husband, Alvin Neelley, for sex with him. For several days immediately prior to Lisa's abduction, the defendant and Alvin drove up and down Rome streets in separate automobiles looking for girls who would be suitable. When Alvin would see one who appealed to him, he would communicate with the defendant by C–B radio, and the defendant would invite the girl to go riding around with her. Numerous girls refused the defendant's invitation; her first successful pick-up was Lisa Ann Millican.

The defendant took Lisa to a motel in Franklin, Georgia, where she tried to persuade Lisa to submit to sex with Alvin, but Lisa resisted. Finally, Alvin told Lisa that if she did not submit to sex, the defendant would kill her. Following this threat, Alvin engaged in sex with Lisa, and later that night, Lisa was handcuffed to the bed to prevent her escape.

The next day, the defendant and Alvin, traveling in two cars, took Lisa with them to Cleveland, Tennessee, where they picked up their two-year-old twins who were being cared for by Alvin's mother. Later that day, they traveled to Scottsboro, Alabama where they rented a motel room. Shortly after their arrival at the motel, the defendant hit Lisa in the head several times with a slapjack in an attempt to render her unconscious, but she was unsuccessful in achieving that result. Alvin then had sex with Lisa, and afterward Lisa slept overnight on the floor, unclothed, and handcuffed to the bed.

The following day, Alvin had sex with Lisa twice more despite her cries and pleas that he stop. The defendant was present during these sexual encounters and at one point during the day, she handcuffed Lisa to the plumbing in the bathroom and interrogated her about a man she had appeared to know at a dairy bar near the motel.

The next morning, Lisa was taken to Little River Canyon by the defendant where the defendant instructed Lisa to lie face down and place her hands around a tree. The defendant then handcuffed Lisa's hands. She explained to Lisa that she was going to give her a shot that would make her fall asleep and that when she waked up, Lisa would be free to go. Using a needle and syringe, the defendant injected Lisa in the neck with liquid drain cleaner. When Lisa did not die in five minutes, the defendant injected her again in the neck. She injected Lisa four additional times, twice in the arms and twice in the buttocks, waiting about five minutes after each injection for Lisa to die. Twice during the infliction of these injections, Lisa requested to get up and "use the bathroom" in the woods. She was allowed to do so, and each time she returned and resumed her position on the ground with her hands around the tree.

Following the last injection, the defendant instructed Lisa to walk around for awhile to hasten the work of the poison in her body. When it finally appeared that Lisa was not going to die from the drain cleaner, the defendant marched Lisa to the rim of the canyon to shoot her in the back in a manner that would cause her body to fall into the canyon. Lisa begged to go back to the Harpst Home and promised not to tell what had happened. The defendant told Lisa to be quiet and then shot her in the back. Lisa fell backward toward the defendant instead of falling into the canyon. The defendant picked up the body and, using her knee, propelled it into the canyon.

During the defendant's trial testimony, she testified that Alvin was present at the canyon directing her every action. However, in an out-of-court statement made shortly after her arrest, the defendant stated that Alvin was not present at the canyon.

Five days after the death of Lisa Ann Millican, the defendant picked up a young woman named Janice Chapman and her common-law husband, John Hancock, from a street in Rome. Later that night, the defendant shot John Hancock in the back and left him for dead. He survived, however, and was present at the trial to testify to the incident.

The defendant and Alvin took Janice Chapman to a motel in Rome where Alvin engaged in sex with Janice. The next day, the defendant killed Janice Chapman, shooting her once in the back and twice in the chest. During the defendant's trial testimony, she testified that Alvin was present during the shooting of John Hancock and Janice Chapman and that he directed her to shoot them; however, in her out-of-court statement given shortly after her arrest, she stated that Alvin was present when she shot John Hancock but that he was not present when she killed Janice Chapman.

On October 9, 1982, the day before the defendant's arrest, she picked up another young woman in Nashville, Tennessee, who was present with the defendant and Alvin in a motel room in Murfreesboro, Tennessee, on October 10, 1982, when the defendant was arrested on a bad check charge. Later, this woman was released by Alvin unharmed.

Alvin was arrested in Murfreesboro on October 13, 1982, also on a bad check charge. While the defendant and Alvin were in custody on the bad check charges, additional charges were placed against them arising from the murders of Lisa Ann Millican and Janice Chapman, and the shooting of John Hancock.

## FINDINGS CONCERNING THE EXISTENCE OR NON–EXISTENCE OF AGGRAVATING CIRCUMSTANCES

In compliance with the requirements of the law that the trial court shall enter specific findings concerning the existence or non-existence of each aggravating circumstance enumerated by statute, the court finds that none of the aggravating circumstances enumerated by statute [was] proved beyond a reasonable doubt in the proceedings before this court except the following, which the court finds were proved beyond a reasonable doubt:

1. The capital offense was committed while the defendant was engaged in kidnapping. The jury's verdict establishes the existence of this aggravating circumstance, and the verdict is supported by the evidence.

2. The capital offense was especially heinous, atrocious and cruel compared to other capital offenses. The court reaches the conclusion that this aggravating circumstance exists based upon uncontroverted evidence of the following:

a. The victim of the crime was a child, age 13.

b. Repeatedly, the child was abused and violated sexually causing her enormous fright and pain. While the evidence is insufficient to establish that the defendant participated in sex acts upon the child, she was an accomplice to the sexual abuse perpetrated upon the child by Alvin Neelley.

c. The defendant inflicted pain and suffering upon the child by hitting her on the head with a slapjack in an attempt to knock her unconscious.

d. The defendant physically restrained the child much of the time following her abduction by the use of handcuffs.

e. The defendant made the child lie on the ground with her hands handcuffed around a tree while the defendant injected her six times with liquid drain cleaner.

f. The defendant marched the child to the rim of the deep canyon, with the child begging to be released, where the defendant shot her in the back.

By any standard acceptable to civilized society, this crime was extremely wicked and shockingly evil. It was perpetrated with a design to inflict a high degree of pain with utter indifference to the suffering of the victim. The court recognizes that all capital offenses are heinous, atrocious and cruel to some extent, but the degree of heinousness, atrociousness and cruelty which characterizes this offense exceeds that which is common to all capital offenses.

## FINDINGS CONCERNING THE EXISTENCE OR NON–EXISTENCE OF MITIGATING CIRCUMSTANCES

I.

In compliance with the statutory requirement that the trial court enter specific findings concerning the existence or non-existence of each mitigating circumstance enumerated by statute, the court finds that none of the following mitigating circumstances [existed] in this case:

1. That the defendant has no significant history of prior criminal activity. The defendant testified to a significant history of criminal conduct. When she was 16 years of age, she robbed a woman of her purse at gunpoint. As a result of this offense, she was committed to the Georgia Youth Development Center, and her husband, Alvin, who was an accomplice to the robbery, was sentenced to a term in the Georgia State Penitentiary.

The defendant was released from the Georgia Youth Development Center in December, 1981, and Alvin was released from the penitentiary several months later. The defendant testified that upon Alvin's release, he was obsessed with the notion that she had been sexually abused by employees at the Youth Development Centers in Rome and Macon. To avenge the alleged wrong, Alvin and the defendant set out to kill or terrorize employees of the YDC. Pursuant to this objective, they shot into the house of one employee and attempted to firebomb the automobile of another in Rome. In Macon, the defendant attempted to lure YDC employees to a motel room where Alvin was prepared to kill them. The defendant was unsuccessful in luring any employees to the motel, and none [was] harmed.

Additional criminal activity by the defendant, according to her own testimony, includes writing bad checks, raising the amounts on money orders, stealing checks from post office boxes and cashing them with false identification, and stealing from convenience stores where Alvin was employed.

2. That the capital offense was committed while the defendant was under the influence of extreme mental or emotional disturbance. When the defendant was arraigned on December 17, 1982, her counsel requested that the defendant be committed to Bryce Hospital for psychiatric examination and evaluation. The court granted the request, and the defendant thereafter underwent psychiatric examination and evaluation at Bryce Hospital. Dr. Alexander Salillas, a staff psychiatrist at Taylor Hardin Secure Medical Facility and a consultant at Bryce, testified that as a result of his examination of the defendant, he found no mental disease or defect and that, in his opinion, she knew right from wrong at the time of the offense and that she acted with deliberation and premeditation.

While the court recognizes that this mitigating circumstance contemplates a disturbance of the mind which might exist separate and apart from a mental disease or defect, and that the testimony of the psychiatrist is, by no means, conclusive, the court finds from a consideration of all the evidence that the defendant was not under the influence of extreme mental or emotional disturbance.

3. That the victim was a participant in the defendant's conduct or consented to it. There is no support for this mitigating circumstance. Although Lisa Ann Millican initially agreed to go with the defendant when the defendant picked her up at the mall in Rome, the fact that Lisa was less than 16 years old and that the Harpst Home, which had legal custody of her, had not acquiesced to her being taken by the defendant, makes any consent given by Lisa legally ineffectual. Any consent given by the child to the acts of violence and abuse committed upon her was the result of threats or false promises and provides no support for this mitigating circumstance.

4. That the defendant was an accomplice in the capital offense committed by another person and her participation was relatively minor. The evidence is uncontroverted that the defendant abducted Lisa Ann Millican, that the defendant injected her six times with liquid drain cleaners, and that the defendant shot her in the back and threw her body into the canyon. Although there is evidence that the defendant's husband, Alvin, was also involved in this criminal conduct, there is no support for a finding that the defendant's participation was relatively minor.

5. That the defendant acted under extreme duress or under the substantial [domination] of another person. The defendant's primary con-

tention throughout the trial and the sentence hearings was that she had become completely submissive to the will of her husband, Alvin, and that he exercised total control over her. Perhaps the strongest support for this contention is found in the following:

a. testimony by Alvin's former wife that Alvin dominated their relationship and imposed his will upon her;

b. evidence, including pictures of the defendant's bruised body, that Alvin beat the defendant frequently;

c. letters written by Alvin while he was incarcerated in the penitentiary which portray him as a vile and dominant husband; and

d. the fact that the defendant had no record of criminal activity prior to her association with Alvin Neelley.

The evidence cited above, together with the defendant's testimony, convinces the court that the defendant was substantially influenced by her husband, but the court concludes that the husband's influence did not constitute extreme duress or substantial domination.

The defendant is an intelligent person capable of making independent choices. The evidence is substantial that she made a willing choice to follow her husband's influence rather than to depart from it. There were numerous opportunities for the defendant to break with her husband and seek help had she felt the need or been so inclined. These opportunities were enhanced by the fact that the defendant was armed and traveling in a separate vehicle during most of their exploits. Ultimately, the defendant chose, rather than to make the break or turn on her husband, to brutally murder Lisa Ann Millican.

The court finds that the defendant was not brainwashed and that she retained her will and her capacity to make independent choices.

6. That the capacity of the defendant to appreciate the criminality of her conduct or to conform her conduct to the requirements of law was substantially impaired. The defendant entered a plea of not guilty by reason of mental disease or defect. With regard to this defense, the court instructed the jury that a person is not responsible for criminal conduct if at the time of such conduct, as a result of mental disease or defect, such person lacks substantial capacity to appreciate the criminality of his conduct or to conform his conduct to the requirements of law. By its verdict of guilt, the jury found the evidence insufficient to support the plea of insanity, and the jury's finding is supported by the evidence. While the court recognizes that this mitigating circumstance contemplates impaired capacity which might exist separate and apart from a mental disease or defect, the court finds from a consideration of Dr. Salillas' testimony and the evidence as a whole that this mitigating circumstance does not exist.

II.

The court finds that the following mitigating circumstance enumerated by statute does exist in this case:

1.   The age of the defendant at the time of the crime. The defendant was 18 years of age at the time she committed the capital offense of which she is convicted. While the court finds the defendant's age to be a mitigating circumstance, the court considers the weight to be given this circumstance lessened by the fact that the defendant, since a much earlier age, had adopted the lifestyle of an adult. She commenced a marital relationship with Alvin Neelley when she was age 15, and gave birth to twins when she was age 16. The criminal activity in which the defendant engaged was less akin to the behavior of a teenager and more akin to the conduct of a seasoned criminal.

### III.

The court finds two additional mitigating circumstances not enumerated by the statute:

1.   The defendant was substantially influenced by her husband. Although the court has heretofore found that the husband's influence did not constitute extreme duress or substantial domination, it seems appropriate that such influence should be given weight as a mitigating circumstance.

2.   The defendant voluntarily and intentionally set in motion the events which led to her arrest and the arrest of her husband, thus ending the reign of terror which they had perpetrated throughout three states. The defendant did this while at her mother's house in Murfreesboro by instructing her mother to notify the police that she was in the area and could be arrested on bad check charges pending against her. In the defendant's testimony, she could not explain what prompted her to give her mother these instructions, but it is fair to infer that conscience had a hand in it.

### CONCLUSION

The court has carefully weighed the aggravating and mitigating circumstances which it finds to exist in this case, and has given consideration to the recommendation of the jury contained in its advisory verdict. While the mitigating circumstances and the jury's recommendation of life without parole have weighed heavily in the court's consideration, it is the judgment of this court that they are outweighed by the aggravating circumstances of this horrible crime. Accordingly, it is ordered, adjudged, and decreed that the defendant shall be punished by death.

A formal sentencing entry shall be made by separate order.

––––––

## Neelley v. State

Court of Criminal Appeals of Alabama, 1985.
494 So.2d 669.

■ BOWEN, PRESIDING JUDGE. . . . In reviewing any case in which the death penalty has been imposed, this Court must follow the guidelines set out in § 13A–5–53.[a]

In accordance with § 13A–5–53(a), we have reviewed the entire record ... for any error adversely affecting the rights of the defendant and have found no error.

The trial court properly found the existence of two aggravating circumstances: "The capital offense was committed while the defendant was engaged ... in ... kidnapping" and that it was "especially heinous, atrocious and cruel compared to other capital offenses." Even a cursory reading of the record and the trial judge's reasons for finding these two aggravating circumstances reveals that his findings are supported by the evidence.

The trial judge stated his reasons for finding the nonexistence of statutory mitigating circumstances identified in § 13A–5–51(1) through (6). The only statutory mitigating circumstance found to exist was the age of the defendant at the time of the crime (§ 13A–5–51(7)).

The trial judge did find the existence of two nonstatutory mitigating circumstances. Although he found that the offense was not committed while the defendant was under the influence of extreme mental or emotional disturbance, he did find, as a nonstatutory mitigating circumstance, that the "defendant was substantially influenced by her husband." As a second nonstatutory mitigating circumstance, the trial judge considered the fact that Mrs. Neelley "voluntarily and intentionally set in motion the events which led to her arrest and the arrest of her husband." The judge's findings concerning the statutory and nonstatutory mitigating circumstances are supported by the evidence.

The following findings are in compliance with § 13A–5–53(b). First, despite the shocking nature of the criminal acts involved, the record reveals

---

[a] Section 13A–5–53 provides in relevant part:

(a) In any case in which the death penalty is imposed, in addition to reviewing the case for any error involving the conviction, the Alabama Court of Criminal Appeals, subject to review by the Alabama Supreme Court, shall also review the propriety of the death sentence. This review shall include the determination of whether any error adversely affecting the rights of the defendant was made in the sentence proceedings, whether the trial court's findings concerning the aggravating and mitigating circumstances were supported by the evidence, and whether death was the proper sentence in the case....

(b) In determining whether death was the proper sentence in the case the Alabama Court of Criminal Appeals, subject to review by the Alabama Supreme Court, shall determine:

(1) Whether the sentence of death was imposed under the influence of passion, prejudice, or any other arbitrary factor;

(2) Whether an independent weighing of the aggravating and mitigating circumstances at the appellate level indicates that death was the proper sentence; and

(3) Whether the sentence of death is excessive or disproportionate to the penalty imposed in similar cases, considering both the crime and the defendant.

(c) The Court of Criminal Appeals shall explicitly address each of the three questions specified in subsection (b) of this section in every case it reviews in which a sentence of death has been imposed....—[Footnote by eds.]

no evidence that the sentence of death was imposed under the influence of passion, prejudice, or any other arbitrary factor. In this dramatic trial, there is no evidence of prejudicial sensationalism. . . .

Second, our independent weighing of the aggravating and mitigating circumstances indicates that death was the proper sentence. This Court has read and reread the testimony of clinical psychologist Margaret Nichols. At the hearing on the motion for new trial, she testified that Mrs. Neelley "probably fits the battered women's syndrome to the most severe extent that [she had] seen." She stated that Alvin's mental state was substituted for hers so that Mrs. Neelley "had no intents of her own." This Court is not insensitive to Mrs. Neelley's defense.[b] However, the Court is also aware of the trial testimony of psychiatrist Alexander Salillas that Mrs. Neelley's actions were not those "of a crazy person, but a demented person," and that, if Mrs. Neelley had been beaten and abused to the extent she testified, she would "probably be dead by now and so disfigured and mentally impaired as to be unable to do anything else at this point in time. . . . She would probably have every bone broken in her body."

There are four conceivable legal issues upon which evidence of the abuse suffered by Mrs. Neelley might have been relevant, namely: (i) duress, (ii) insanity, (iii) diminished capacity, and (iv) mitigation of punishment.[c]

The first, duress, is unavailable as a defense to Mrs. Neelley. Alabama Code § 13A–3–30 provides that duress is no defense "in a prosecution for murder or any killing of another under aggravated circumstances."

While the second, insanity, has been used as a defense in other cases dealing with battered women . . . there was absolutely no evidence—expert or lay—presented by the defense that Mrs. Neelley was legally insane. . . . The following observation by the court in McKinnon v. State, 405 So.2d 78 (Ala.Crim.App.1981), applies with equal force here:

> Insanity which will excuse a crime, even under the new criminal code test, must be the result of a "mental disease or defect." Emotional insanity or temporary mania, not associated with a disease of the mind, does not constitute insanity. . . .

The third legal theory, diminished capacity, is not recognized as a defense in Alabama. Some commentators have suggested an additional

[b] In an omitted portion of Judge Bowen's opinion, Mrs. Neelley's defense was described as a "combination of duress and coercive persuasion":

The defense was that Alvin had subjected Mrs. Neelley to such violent and gross mental, emotional, physical, and sexual abuse that she would have done anything, and did do everything he asked. A picture was painted, in the terminology used at trial, of Alvin as "Frankenstein" and Mrs. Neelley as "the Bride of Frankenstein." The jury was exposed to accounts of "putrid, pornographic, degrading, disgusting sex" as Mrs. Neelley testified how she had been dominated, manipulated, and trained like an animal. She described herself as feeling like a "piece of meat" and it was argued that she had been reduced to a nonhuman.—[Footnote by eds.]

[c] The relevance of the "battered wife syndrome" to claims of self-defense is considered in Chapter 5.—[Footnote by eds.]

defense for crimes committed by those who suffer from the kind of abuse alleged by Mrs. Neelley. "One researcher suggests that the psychological effects of the battered spouse syndrome can be compared to classic brainwashing," see Suzanne K. Steinmetz, Wife Beating: A Critique and Reformulation of Existing Theory, 6 Amer. Acad. of Psych. & Law Bull. 322, 327 (1978) (quoted in Comment, The Battered Spouse Syndrome as a Defense to a Homicide, 26 Vill.L.Rev. 105, 111 (1980)). See also Richard Delgado, Ascription of Criminal States of Mind: Toward A Defense Theory For The Coercively Persuaded ("Brainwashed") Defendant, 63 Minn.L.Rev. 1 (1978). The "brainwashing" defense has not achieved acceptance in any jurisdiction, see Joshua Dressler, Professor Delgado's "Brainwashing" Defense: Courting A Determinist Legal System, 63 Minn.L.Rev. 335 (1979).

Finally, the only legal theory upon which Mrs. Neelley's alleged treatment by her husband was relevant was the one the jury properly considered—mitigation of sentence. While the factfinders determined Mrs. Neelley guilty of the crime charged, they apparently considered the evidence of her abuse as indicative of one or more of the following mitigating circumstances outlined in Ala.Code § 13A–5–51:

> (2) The capital offense was committed while the defendant was under the influence of extreme mental or emotional disturbance; . . .

> (5) The defendant acted under extreme duress or under the substantial domination of another person;

> (6) The capacity of the defendant to appreciate the criminality of his conduct or to conform his conduct to the requirements of law was substantially impaired.

The brutal reality of the cruel abuse and calculated murder of 13–year old Lisa Ann Millican stands in stark contrast to Mrs. Neelley's allegations of her own abuse and mental condition. This Court agrees with the trial court that "[w]hile the mitigating circumstances and the jury's recommendation of life without parole have weighed heavy in the court's consideration, . . . they are outweighed by the aggravating circumstances of this horrible crime."

Finally, the sentence of death in this case is neither excessive nor disproportionate to the penalty imposed in similar cases, considering both the crime and the defendant. The death sentence for a murder/kidnapping was imposed in [two other cases]. Although a factor to consider, the fact that Alvin Neelley has not been prosecuted for his involvement in Miss Millican's murder does not render Mrs. Neelley's death sentence disproportionate.

Mrs. Neelley's own defense counsel described her as the "Bride of Frankenstein." Her actions were overwhelmingly demonic and savagely inhuman, generating fear, horror, and shock.

After careful review and consideration, this court concludes that Judith Ann Neelley received a fair trial and that the sentence of death is proper under the laws of Alabama and of the United States. The judgment of the circuit court is affirmed.

Affirmed.

All judges concur.[d]

———

## NOTES ON CRITERIA OF MITIGATION AND SELECTION IN CAPITAL CASES

**1.   Questions on *Neelley*.** There can be little doubt about the adequacy of the substantive predicate for Mrs. Neelley's death sentence.[a] Her case calls attention, instead, to the procedures and criteria for deciding which offenders within the death-eligible class should be sentenced to death. Was the trial judge correct that aside from Mrs. Neelley's youthfulness, none of the statutory criteria in mitigation had been demonstrated? Would it have mattered if the jury had made a specific finding that she had acted under the "substantial domination" of her husband? Should any of Mrs. Neelley's claims in mitigation, if believed, have precluded imposition of the death penalty?

Under Alabama law, the ultimate sentencing determination turned on a "weighing" of the aggravating and mitigating circumstances. Ten of the 12 jurors apparently concluded that the mitigating evidence was compelling enough to outweigh the aggravating circumstances. Should the judge have had the authority to override the jury's decision?[b] What is the proper role of the appellate court in such a case?

**2.   Statutory Mitigating Circumstances.** Of the 38 states with capital punishment statutes in force on January 1, 1996, 30 specify a list of mitigating circumstances. Typically, they are based on § 210.6 of the Model Penal Code. In most instances, these criteria of mitigation reflect judgments about reduced culpability and proportionate punishment that parallel the defenses considered in earlier chapters of this book.

It is important to remember that the statutory lists of mitigating factors are not exclusive. The Supreme Court held, in *Lockett v. Ohio*,

---

[d] The decision of the Court of Criminal Appeals was affirmed by the Supreme Court of Alabama in Ex Parte Neelley, 494 So. 2d 697 (1986) certiorari. denied 480 U.S. 926 (1987).

[a] Indeed, a review of current statutes indicates that the evidence would have established a proper statutory predicate in most death penalty states.

[b] In most death penalty states, a jury's rejection of a death sentence is final. In only three states (Alabama, Florida, and Indiana) is a judge authorized to override a jury's recommendation of a life sentence. In four other states, the sentencing process is conducted solely by the judge, with no jury participation. In Spaziano v. Florida, 468 U.S. 447 (1984), the Supreme Court held that jury sentencing in capital cases is not constitutionally required and also upheld Florida's jury-override procedure. Although the holding in *Spaziano* remains authoritative, the Supreme Court may be inclined to reconsider it in light of its decision in Ring v. Arizona, 536 U.S. 584 (2002) (holding that aggravating circumstances establishing statutory predicates for a death sentence must be proved to a jury beyond a reasonable doubt).

summarized in the Introductory Notes to subsection A of this section, that a capital defendant is entitled to offer any evidence concerning character, record, or the circumstances of the offense as a basis for mitigation. Moreover, in several states the trial judge is required to include in the jury instructions any mitigating claims raised by the evidence, whether or not they are included in the statutory list. In short, evidence that does not satisfy the criteria of mitigation specified in the statutes is nonetheless considered in sentencing.

Note that § 210.6 of the Model Code does not give determinative significance to the statutory mitigating criteria. Instead it is left to the judge or jury to determine whether any of the mitigating factors is "sufficiently substantial to call for leniency." Should the death penalty be precluded, as a matter of law, if one of these statutory mitigating criteria exists?[c] Suppose that Judge Cole had found one of the circumstances in the Alabama statute (other than the defendant's youthfulness) to have been proved in *Neelley*. In that event, what would be the moral justification for imposing the death penalty in her case? Or should such a finding have required the imposition of a life sentence?

The following notes address mitigating criteria commonly specified in capital sentencing statutes. In light of the fact that these criteria are neither preclusive nor exclusive, should they play a significant role in the administration of the death penalty? In what way?

**3.   Youth.** Many states follow the lead of the Model Penal Code and preclude execution of a defendant who was younger than 18 at the time of the offense. In the remaining states, youthfulness does not foreclose imposition of a death sentence on any offender who is properly within the jurisdiction of the criminal courts.[d] In 1989, the Supreme Court held that death sentences for 16 or 17–year old adolescents are not constitutionally forbidden, although a majority of the Court would probably not uphold a death sentence for a minor who was under 16 at the time of the offense.[e]

In the absence of a categorical exclusion, the significance of the defendant's youthfulness is considered on a case-by-case basis. All except two of the states with statutory lists of mitigating circumstances include the "age" or "youth" of the defendant. But why should youthfulness matter? Should Mrs. Neelley's age (18) be regarded as a mitigating factor? Is youthfulness significant because the offender does not bear the full measure of responsibility for criminal conduct? Because younger defendants have better prospects for rehabilitation? Compare the following two cases to *Neelley* in this respect.

---

[c] Recall that Alabama, like many states, directs the decision-maker to determine whether the mitigating factors outweigh the aggravating factors, or vice-versa.

[d] The doctrines governing the respective jurisdictions of the juvenile justice and criminal justice systems are discussed in Chapter VI.

[e] The Court's decisions in Thompson v. Oklahoma, 487 U.S. 815 (1988), and Stanford v. Kentucky, 492 U.S. 361 (1989), summarized in Chapter IX, Section 2, are under reconsideration in Roper v. Simmons, ___ U.S. ___, 124 S.Ct. 1171 (2004).

**(i) *State v. Valencia.*** Frank Valencia, age 16, was convicted of first-degree murder for ambushing and shooting a woman in a parking garage in the course of a robbery attempt. He was also convicted for kidnapping, robbing, and raping another victim at gunpoint. He was sentenced to death. Death sentences imposed by the trial judge (juries are not involved in capital sentencing in Arizona) were twice set aside by the Arizona Supreme Court, and the case was remanded for resentencing. A third death sentence was imposed by another judge. Finally, on the third appeal, the Arizona Supreme Court reversed the death sentence, holding that the defendant's age was a mitigating factor "sufficiently substantial" to call for leniency. State v. Valencia, 132 Ariz. 248, 645 P.2d 239 (1982). The Court explained that "while we do not hold that age alone will always [preclude a death sentence] in every case of first-degree murder, it is a substantial and relevant factor which must be given great weight." The Court did not elaborate.

**(ii) *Trimble v. State.*** A different result was reached in Trimble v. State, 300 Md. 387, 478 A.2d 1143 (1984). Trimble was convicted of raping the victim, assaulting her with a baseball bat, and then killing her by slitting her throat. He was 17 at the time. Prosecution and defense experts agreed that he met the criteria for antisocial personality disorder, had a history of substance abuse, and was mildly mentally retarded (64 IQ).[f] The defense expert testified that it was possible that Trimble had experienced temporary organic psychosis as a result of his drug use. The trial judge sentenced him to death. The Court of Appeals affirmed the sentence, making the following observations concerning the significance of Trimble's youthfulness:

> Even though society's interest in retribution is focused mainly on the crime, not the defendant, we do not believe that consideration of the defendant's age is irrelevant. Society's "moral outrage" may be tempered somewhat by the youthful age of the perpetrator; hence the alternate "response" of treatment in the juvenile system. Nevertheless, society's interest in retribution is by no means inapplicable in juvenile cases. In extreme cases, the benign goals of the juvenile system are subordinated to the more broad-based and immediate interest in retribution. In short, a particularly heinous act can take the juvenile outside of the protective umbrella of the juvenile system.

> We believe that such a crime was committed here. Trimble's crime was not a youthful prank; it was a cold, brutal act of repeated and sadistic violence. The trial judge was presented with psychiatric testimony indicating that Trimble's prospects of rehabilitation were bleak. Thus, the one factor that could temper society's justifiable moral outrage was noticeably absent. In these circumstances, the death penalty is not an unjustified response

---

[f] Several states preclude a death sentence in cases in which the defendant is found to be mentally retarded. See, e.g. O.C.G.A. § 17–7–131. The constitutional significance of mental retardation in capital sentencing is considered below.

solely because the perpetrator of these acts was four months shy of his 18th birthday. . . .

[W]hile the youthful age of the offender is a relevant mitigating factor, it alone does not end the weighing process. Here, the sentencing authority had before it a wealth of information about Trimble's character. Trimble was expelled from school while in the 10th grade after several suspensions. At the time of the offense, he had been steadily employed at an airport for seven months. He maintained a steady relationship with a girlfriend. In addition to his low intelligence, he was diagnosed as having antisocial personality, possible temporary organic psychosis, and possible schizophrenia but nevertheless criminally responsible. These characteristics were exacerbated by his drug and alcohol abuse.

According to the psychiatric testimony, his criminal behavior was part of his lifestyle (he regarded Charles Manson as a role model) and a matter of choice. Trimble freely admitted his involvement in 10 breaking and entering crimes, a handgun violation, an assault, and several drug arrests. He further admitted a pattern of sadistic behavior toward his girlfriend and animals. The psychiatrists determined his prospects for rehabilitation to be bleak because he had no respect for the rights of others. In our view, the trial judge who sentenced him to death could reasonably conclude that Trimble was an adult beyond repair rather than a juvenile in need of treatment.

**4.   Degree of Participation.** Under the law of complicity, more than one person may be liable for a single murder. Although the capital sentencing statutes of a number of states permit a death sentence only for the person who actually caused the victim's death, most states permit a death sentence to be imposed on accomplices. Moreover, because of the combined operation of the law of complicity and the felony murder rule, an accomplice to a felony may be convicted of a capital homicide in many of these states without any specific finding of culpable participation in the homicide itself. Once convicted, however, such a defendant is typically permitted to establish, in mitigation, that his participation was "relatively minor."

These statutory provisions do not tell the whole story, however, because the Supreme Court has held that some level of culpability with regard to the homicide must be shown for the accomplice. Although the Court has not yet specified the requisite finding, it is most likely to come to rest on the proposition that a death sentence is constitutionally impermissible unless the defendant's participation was substantial enough to manifest extreme indifference to the value of human life. See Tison v. Arizona, 481 U.S. 137 (1987).

**5.   Duress or Domination By Another.** Mrs. Neelley claimed that her will was subordinated to that of her husband. Alabama's statute, like those of most other states, recognizes the mitigating significance of a claim that the defendant acted under duress or under the "substantial influence" or "domination" of another person. As the Alabama Supreme Court notes, this factor takes into account actual coercive threats which do not provide a defense in homicide cases. In People v. Gleckler, 82 Ill.2d 145, 411 N.E.2d 849 (1980), for example, the Illinois Supreme Court determined that a death sentence was excessive for a defendant "with no criminal history, the personality of a doormat, and a problem with alcohol" who succumbed to an accomplice's threats when he fatally shot two robbery victims who had already been wounded by the accomplice.

The mitigating significance of this factor explicitly extends beyond coercive threats in a substantial number of states. In State v. McIlvoy, 629 S.W.2d 333 (Mo.1982), a closely divided (four-three) court set aside a death sentence imposed on a defendant who had been recruited by one Nicki Williams to kill her husband. The Court explained that McIlvoy "appears to be a person with only minimal juvenile criminal record, limited education (ninth grade) and limited intelligence (81 IQ), substantial alcohol problems, and appears to [have been] a weakling and follower in executing the murder scheme perpetrated by Nicki Williams."

*Gleckler* and *McIlvoy* both reflect the moral judgment that the death penalty is not appropriate for psychologically weak and vulnerable offenders who are used as instruments for achieving the criminal ambitions of others. In this sense, the factor represents a version of diminished responsibility.

**6.   Mental Retardation and Low Intelligence.** As indicated in the previous note, low intelligence is often raised as a mitigating factor in cases involving offenders who were pressured or manipulated by others. In addition, very low intelligence has traditionally been regarded as a basis for diminished responsibility because it can be associated with impulsiveness and impaired appreciation of the consequences or significance of one's actions, as discussed in the next note. Beginning in the 1980's, however, a consensus emerged in favor of banning the death penalty altogether in cases involving offenders whose intelligence and adaptive functioning was so deficient as to meet the clinical definition of mental retardation. Eventually the Supreme Court concluded that this consensus had become so clear that it anchored a constitutional ban against executing persons with mental retardation.[g] As a result, proof of mental retardation in capital proceedings now precludes a death sentence. However, even when a diagnosis of mental retardation has not been proved, a defendant's low intelligence still serves as a mitigating factor on its own or as a manifestation of diminished responsibility.

**7.   Diminished Responsibility.** Evidence of mental abnormality plays a somewhat complicated role in the administration of the death penalty and, more generally, in the law of homicide. Recall the two meanings of "diminished responsibility" or "diminished capacity" explored in the notes on this subject in Chapter 6. One refers to a rule of evidence allowing testimony concerning mental abnormality whenever it is logically relevant to the existence of a mental state determinative of the fact or

---

[g] See Atkins v. Virginia, 536 U.S. 304 (2002), discussed in Chapter 9, Section 2.

grade of criminal liability. The other refers to a substantive concept denoting an "intermediate" degree of cognitive or volitional impairment falling short of insanity but entitling the defendant to reduction of the grade of the offense or mitigation of the punishment.

Historically, evidence of mental abnormality was pressed upon the courts with greatest frequency in homicide cases. A review of the extensive literature on the question between 1880 and 1950 demonstrates that proponents of broader rules of admissibility were aiming primarily at capital prosecutions. It was the image of the executioner that drove the engines of reform. However, the courts were slow to accept such evidence for any purpose beyond the insanity defense. In 1925, Sheldon Glueck summarized the law regarding what he called "partial responsibility":

> Does mental disease, though not of sufficient degree to excuse entirely from criminal responsibility, ever operate to *reduce the degree* of the criminal offense? For example, a person is charged with murder: Is it possible that, though he can not be acquitted entirely, yet, by reason of his mental abnormality he cannot be said to have had the "malice aforethought" or deliberation or premeditation, or any other condition of mind which must be proved . . .? Can evidence of some degree of mental unsoundness reduce to murder in the second degree or manslaughter a crime which, had the defendant been perfectly sound mentally, would have been first-degree murder? Is there room in the law for the "semi-responsible" in this sense of the term? As a general rule, no.[h]

Today, in a majority of jurisdictions the answer is "yes," at least when the evidence is offered on a charge of first-degree murder. The logical relevance of mental abnormality to such a charge is readily apparent. It can, for example, negate an intent to kill, which is prerequisite to the first-degree offense in most states. In those states that also require actual reflection and deliberation, expert testimony can shed light on whether the defendant consciously thought about the homicide before it occurred and whether the required reflection took place. Most states today give evidence of mental abnormality its full logical import when relevant to the issues involved in a first-degree murder prosecution.

More importantly for present purposes, evidence of mental abnormality is virtually unrestricted in capital sentencing proceedings. The statutes of most states include provisions, based on the Model Penal Code, which accord mitigating significance to claims of diminished or partial responsibility. The two pertinent provisions of § 210.6(4) of the Model Code are:

> (b) the murder was committed while the defendant was under the influence of extreme mental or emotional disturbance . . . .; and

> (g) at the time of the murder, the capacity of the defendant to appreciate the criminality [wrongfulness] of his conduct or to

[h] Sheldon Glueck, Mental Disorder and the Criminal Law 199–200 (1925).

conform his conduct to the requirements of law was impaired as a result of mental disease or defect or intoxication.

Most capital sentencing statutes include formulations based on subsections (4)(b) and (4)(g). These provisions reflect a virtually unanimous legislative judgment that the presence of mens rea for capital homicide and a determination that the defendant is legally sane, however these concepts are defined, do not exhaust the significance of mental abnormality in determining the moral propriety of the death penalty. Unhinged from the technical concepts of malice, premeditation, deliberation, and insanity, the evidence of mental abnormality is measured explicitly by criteria of diminished responsibility.

(i) **Extreme Mental or Emotional Disturbance.** The concept of provocation, recognized in § 210.3(1)(b) of the Model Code, is dealt with in the next section of these materials. For present purposes, it is sufficient to note that the presence of provocation permits mitigation of murder to manslaughter, and that its scope is restricted by an objective inquiry into whether the defendant's homicidal reaction was a "reasonable" (or at least understandable) response to the provoking event. The language of § 210.6(4)(b) resembles the language of § 210.3(b), but with an important difference. Section 210.6(4)(b) does not include the limitation "for which there is a reasonable explanation or excuse." Does this mean that virtually any psychiatric evidence of "extreme mental or emotional disturbance" can establish this basis for mitigation? Was this circumstance proved in *Godfrey?* Did Judge Cole correctly rule that it had not been proved in *Neelley?* Would it be appropriate for a court to instruct a jury that a claimed mental disturbance does not have mitigating significance under this standard if it is attributable to voluntary intoxication? A few states have omitted the word "extreme" from their formulations of this criterion. Is this a significant omission?

(ii) **Impaired Capacity for Appreciation or Control.** Section 210.6(4)(g) is derived from the Model Code insanity defense, provided in § 4.01(1). Note two key differences. First, subsection (4)(g) encompasses impairments attributable to intoxication as well as mental disease. Impairment due to voluntary intoxication, no matter how extreme, is without significance under the insanity test unless it is related to an independent mental disease. Under subsection (4)(g), however, any impairment affecting behavioral controls could have mitigating significance. Second, the Model Code insanity test focuses on whether defendants lack "substantial" capacity to appreciate the criminality of their conduct or conform their behavior to the requirements of law. The question asked in a capital-sentencing proceeding is whether the offender's cognitive or volitional capacity was sufficiently impaired by mental disease or intoxication to warrant some penalty other than death even though it was not so substantially impaired as to require exculpation.

What is the purpose of the "mental disease or defect" requirement in subsection (4)(g)? Is it undermined by the provisions of subsection (4)(b)? Of the states that include a criterion of impaired capacity, about half omit the threshold condition of "mental disease or defect or intoxication." However, many of these states require instead that the defendant's capacity be "substantially" or "significantly" impaired. It has been observed that deletion of the "mental disease" threshold is not a "minor editorial omission" since "the concept of mitigating mental abnormality has been detached from the medical model [opening the door] to the full spectrum of explanations that may be offered."[i] Does this modification make sense? Alabama is one of the states which has deleted the mental disease requirement. Did Judge Cole properly interpret the provision when he determined that Mrs. Neeley had not established the mitigating circumstance?

**8.  The Double–Edged Sword.** The tension between subjective criteria of blameworthiness and the incapacitative functions of the penal law has been highlighted frequently in these materials. The problem is raised most vividly in the administration of capital punishment. Often the most compelling claims of diminished responsibility arise in cases presenting the most demonstrable need for incapacitation. Consider, in this connection, Miller v. State, 373 So.2d 882 (Fla.1979).

After being released one morning from jail, where he had been incarcerated for possession of a concealed weapon (a fishing knife), Miller wandered around Ft. Myers and bought a fishing knife similar to the one which had been taken from him by the police. An employee in the store where the weapon was purchased stated that Miller was "wild looking" and was mumbling angrily to himself. This employee called the police and followed Miller to two nearby bars. Eventually, when he saw Miller leaving in a taxicab with a woman driver, he contacted the taxi company to inform them of the apparent danger. The woman taxi driver was found murdered soon thereafter. She had been stabbed nine times and raped. When Miller was arrested at the bus station that evening, his pants were still covered with blood. Blood-soaked money, some of which had been taken from the taxi driver, was found in his pockets.

Soon after his arrest, Miller was found incompetent to stand trial and was committed to a state mental hospital. Two-and-a-half years later, when his mental illness was found to be sufficiently controlled by medication to render him competent to stand trial, he was convicted of first-degree murder. The jury recommended a death sentence, which the judge imposed. The Florida Supreme Court affirmed the conviction but reversed the sentence on the ground that the trial judge should have granted a continuance to permit the defendant to present psychiatric testimony at the sentencing hearing. On remand, a new jury again recommended death, and the trial judge followed the jury's recommendation.

Undisputed psychiatric testimony presented at the sentencing hearing showed that Miller was suffering from paranoid schizophrenia, had been committed to mental hospitals on several previous occasions, and had a

---

[i] Richard J. Bonnie, Psychiatry and the Death Penalty: Emerging Problems in Virginia, 66 Va.L.Rev. 167, 184 (1980).

long history of drug abuse. The evidence showed that Miller had been raised primarily by his mother, who had been married four times. For many years prior to this crime, Miller's mother had refused any contact with him. On several previous occasions, Miller had experienced hallucinations in which he saw his mother in the faces of other persons. He had once assaulted a woman while experiencing such an hallucination. Miller testified that he hated his mother and had planned to kill her after his release from jail on the day of the murder. He also testified that at the time of the murder, he saw his mother's face on this 56-year-old woman taxi driver, in a "yellow haze," and proceeded to stab her to death.

The trial court found that three statutory aggravating circumstances had been proved: (i) the defendant had previously been convicted of a felony involving the threat of violence to another person; (ii) the murder was committed while the defendant was engaged in the commission of or attempt to commit robbery, and was thus committed for pecuniary gain; and (iii) the murder was especially heinous, atrocious, and cruel.

The trial court also found, as mitigating circumstances, that (i) the murder was committed while the defendant was under the influence of extreme mental disturbance; (ii) the defendant acted under mental duress; (iii) due to mental sickness, the defendant's capacity and ability to conform his conduct to the requirements of law were substantially impaired. However, the trial court concluded that the defendant could and did appreciate the criminality of his conduct.

Having made these findings, the trial judge explained:

[In] weighing the aggravating and mitigating factors, I [take into account] the reality of Florida law [that] life imprisonment ... doesn't mean life imprisonment and there is a substantial chance he could be released into society. And the testimony overwhelmingly establishes that the mental sickness or illness that he suffers from is such that he will never recover [and that] it will only be repressed by the use of drugs. . . .

If the law in Florida were such that life imprisonment meant the ability to live in a prison environment for the entire remainder of one's life, I would [reach] the conclusion that there would be sufficient mitigating factors to offset the aggravating factors, and allow him to live in prison. But since this is not the case, the reality is that life imprisonment does not mean that, I conclude in this case that the aggravating factors heavily outweigh the mitigating factors. . . .

The Florida Supreme Court unanimously reversed:

It is clear [that the trial judge] considered as an aggravating factor the defendant's alleged incurable and dangerous mental illness. The use of this nonstatutory aggravating factor as a controlling circumstance tipping the balance in favor of the death penalty was improper. The aggravating circumstances specified in the statute are exclusive, and no others may be used for that purpose. This court [has] stated: "We must guard against any unauthorized aggravating factor going into the equation which might tip the scales of the weighing process in favor of death."

Strict application of the sentencing statute is necessary because the sentencing authority's discretion must be "guided and channeled" by requiring an examination of specific factors that argue in favor of or against imposition of the death penalty, thus eliminating total arbitrariness and capriciousness in its imposition. The trial judge's use of the defendant's mental illness, and his resulting propensity to commit violent acts, as an aggravating factor favoring the imposition of the death penalty appears contrary to the legislative intent set forth in the statute. The legislature has not authorized consideration of the probability of recurring violent acts by the defendant if he is released on parole in the distant future. To the contrary, a large number of the statutory mitigating factors reflect a legislative determination to mitigate the death penalty in favor of a life sentence for those persons whose responsibility for their violent actions has been substantially diminished as a result of a mental illness, uncontrolled emotional state of mind, or drug abuse.

It appears likely that at least one of the aggravating circumstances proven at the sentencing hearing, the heinous nature of the offense, resulted from the defendant's mental illness. . . .

In light of the trial court's findings that the defendant was suffering from mental illness at the time he committed this crime, the motivating role the defendant's mental illness played in this crime, and the apparent causal relationship between the aggravating circumstances and his mental illness, it was reversible error for the trial court to consider as an additional aggravating circumstance, not enumerated by the statute, the possibility that Miller might commit similar acts of violence if he were ever to be released on parole. Whether a defendant who is convicted of a capital crime and receives a life sentence should be allowed a chance of parole after 25 years is a policy determination for the legislature or the parole authorities rather than for the courts. Therefore, the sentence of death is vacated and the cause remanded to the trial court for resentencing in a manner not inconsistent with this opinion.

Suppose the defendant's propensity for violence had been specified as an aggravating circumstance, as it is in a few states. Or suppose that consideration of non-statutory aggravating factors is permissible, as it is in many states, so long as a statutory predicate for a death sentence has been properly established. Would Miller's death sentence then have been proper?[j]

---

[j] Compare State v. Gretzler, 135 Ariz. 42, 659 P.2d 1 (1983). The trial judge had found that Gretzler's "capacity to appreciate the wrongfulness of his conduct or to conform his conduct to the requirements of the law was significantly impaired." Gretzler argued that

**9. Limits on Mitigating Evidence.** As previously noted, the Supreme Court held in *Lockett v. Ohio* that a capital defendant is entitled to put before the sentencer "any aspect of [his or her] character or record, and any circumstances of the offense that [he or she] proffers as a basis for a sentence less than death." A statute restricting mitigating claims is unconstitutional, Chief Justice Burger said, because it "creates the risk that the death penalty will be imposed in spite of factors which may call for a less severe penalty." However, in a footnote, the Chief Justice cautioned that "nothing in this opinion limits the traditional authority of a court to exclude, as irrelevant, evidence not bearing on the defendant's character, prior record, or the circumstances of [his or her] offense."

Is it true that evidence not bearing on the defendant's character, prior record, or the circumstances of the offense is "irrelevant" to the propriety of a death sentence in a particular case? Some have argued that the defendant should be permitted to offer any evidence that might persuade the jury to preclude a death sentence, including evidence calling into question the morality or efficacy of the death penalty or describing the process of execution.[k] Although no court has permitted defendants to introduce evidence on these questions, some courts have admitted evidence calculated to arouse the jury's sympathy and compassion. For example, the Georgia Supreme Court has permitted the defense to elicit testimony from the defendant's grandfather that he did not want his grandson executed for killing his parents. Romine v. State, 251 Ga. 208, 305 S.E.2d 93 (1983).

What are the arguments favoring and opposing admissibility of evidence designed to dampen the jurors' retributive instincts or arouse their compassion, but which has no bearing on the defendant's blameworthiness or potential for rehabilitation? Should the defense be permitted to present testimony by members of the defendant's family regarding the impact on them of the defendant's execution?[l] Recall the *Godfrey* case. Should Godfrey have been permitted to introduce evidence showing that he continued to provide financial support for his children after killing their mother and grandmother? Should he have been permitted to introduce statistical evi-

---

this finding should have precluded the imposition of the death penalty for kidnapping, robbing, and murdering a young couple. (This crime was only part of a spree of 17 aggravated murders committed by Gretzler and an accomplice.) The court rejected the claim:

> Incarceration is intended to serve the goal of isolation of dangerous individuals, but the prison system is a human enterprise, and thus it cannot serve this goal perfectly no matter how diligent the effort. This state has learned through sad experience that even after incarceration a violent person may become a menace to

other prisoners or may escape and become a menace to the public at large. At some point a violent individual has caused so much harm and destruction of human life that society is entitled to foreclose the possibility of further deprivation.

[k] See, e.g., Bruce Ledewitz, The Requirement of Death: Mandatory Language in the Pennsylvania Death Penalty Statute, 21 Duq. L.Rev. 103 (1982).

[l] Compare Houston v. State, 593 S.W.2d 267 (Tenn.1980) (no), with Cofield v. State, 247 Ga. 98, 274 S.E.2d 530 (1981) (yes).

dence on the frequency with which death sentences have been imposed for domestic homicides?[m]

**10.   Limits on Discretion to be Lenient.** Proper resolution of these evidentiary questions may depend on underlying substantive judgments about proper grounds for leniency. Specifically, should the sentencer's discretion to be lenient be unconstrained, or should leniency be permitted only for prescribed reasons? In Gregg v. Georgia, 428 U.S. 153 (1976), Justices Stewart, Powell and Stevens interpreted *Furman* to stand for the proposition that "where discretion is afforded a sentencing body on a matter so grave as the determination of whether a human life should be taken or spared, that discretion must be suitably directed and limited so as to minimize the risk of wholly arbitrary and capricious action." It has become clear, however, that discretion to *take* life and discretion to *spare* life are not constitutionally equivalent.[n]

Under Georgia's capital sentencing statute, the jury's discretion to be lenient is essentially unconstrained. The constitutionality of this feature of the Georgia statute was explicitly upheld by a majority of the Supreme Court in Zant v. Stephens, 462 U.S. 862 (1983). The Court held that the "mandate of *Furman* is [not] violated by a scheme that permits the jury to exercise unbridled discretion in determining whether the death penalty should be imposed after it has found that the defendant is a member of the class made eligible for the penalty by statute."

Statutes of about half of the death penalty states give the sentencer unfettered discretion to be lenient.[o] In the other states, however, the statutes seek to constrain the sentencer's discretion. Most of these states use a balancing formula which directs the sentencer to impose a death sentence if it finds that the aggravating circumstances outweigh the mitigating circumstances (or that the mitigating circumstances do not outweigh the aggravating circumstances). Some statutes, such as Pennsylvania's, explicitly require the jury to impose a death sentence if it finds at least one aggravating circumstance and no mitigating circumstances.

In a series of three cases decided in 1990, a narrowly divided Supreme Court upheld a variety of sentencing formulas designed to constrain discretion to be lenient. (Justices Brennan, Marshall, Blackmun and Stevens dissented in all three cases.) In Boyde v. California, 494 U.S. 370 (1990), the Court upheld California's "balancing" instruction which directed the

---

[m] The Georgia Supreme Court held that the evidence had been properly excluded. Godfrey v. Francis, 251 Ga. 652, 308 S.E.2d 806 (1983).

[n] The plurality opinion in *Gregg* had also stated that "[n]othing in any of the cases suggests that the decision to afford an individual defendant mercy violates the Constitution." 428 U.S. at 199.

[o] The statutes differ, however, on the conditions which must be satisfied before a death sentence may be imposed. In Georgia, one statutory aggravating circumstance is enough. In Mississippi, by comparison, a death sentence is permitted only if the jury finds that "sufficient aggravating factors exist," *and* that mitigating circumstances are insufficient to outweigh the aggravating circumstances. Even if these conditions are satisfied, however, the sentencer still has absolute discretion not to impose a death sentence.

jury to impose a death sentence if it concluded "that the aggravating circumstances outweigh the mitigating circumstances." Chief Justice Rehnquist explained that "there is no ... constitutional requirement of unfettered sentencing discretion in the jury, and the states are free to structure and shape consideration of mitigating evidence 'in an effort to achieve a more rational and equitable administration of the death penalty.' "

The Court also upheld Pennsylvania's "quasi-mandatory" formula (requiring the jury to impose a death sentence if it finds one aggravating circumstance and no mitigating circumstance) in a case involving a murder in the course of armed robbery. Blystone v. Pennsylvania, 494 U.S. 299 (1990). In response to the argument that Pennsylvania's instruction was incompatible with the principle of individualized sentencing, Chief Justice Rehnquist observed that "th[is] requirement ... is satisfied by allowing the jury to consider all relevant mitigating evidence." In dissent, Justice Brennan observed that the opportunity to have the jury consider mitigating evidence does not "satisfy the constitutional demand for an individualized sentencing hearing" and insisted that the Court had ignored the "mandatory" feature of the Pennsylvania statute:

> *Woodson* and its progeny are distinguishable from this case because the Pennsylvania statute allows the jury to consider mitigating circumstances. But once a Pennsylvania jury finds that no mitigating circumstances are proved by a preponderance of the evidence, it is required to impose the death penalty. The mandatory provision of the Pennsylvania statute may be effective in a smaller set of cases than the North Carolina statute at issue in *Woodson*. Nevertheless the effect of the mandatory provision in both statutes is the same; it substitutes a legislative judgment about the severity of the crime for a jury's determination that the death penalty is appropriate for the individual.

In the third in this series of cases, Walton v. Arizona, 497 U.S. 639 (1990), the Court upheld Arizona's formula which imposes on the defendant the burden of proving mitigating circumstances by a preponderance of the evidence and which directs the sentencing judge to impose a death sentence upon finding one or more aggravating circumstances and no mitigating circumstances "sufficiently substantial to call for leniency." *Walton* is less noteworthy for its result than for what it revealed about the Court's continuing inability to muster a common understanding of the principles emerging from the 1976 decisions.

Justice White announced the judgment of the Court. His opinion upholding the Arizona sentencing formula was joined by Chief Justice Rehnquist and Justices O'Connor and Kennedy.[p] Justice Blackmun, joined

---

[p] In upholding the feature of Arizona's statute placing the burden of proving mitigating circumstances on the defendant, the Court relied on a series of cases, considered in Chapter IX, which elaborate on the due process principle that the defendant's guilt must be proven beyond a reasonable doubt. The dissenters insisted that the dispositive constitutional principle was found in *Lockett* because the effect of the Arizona scheme was

by Justices Brennan, Marshall and Stevens, concluded that the Arizona statute was incompatible with *Lockett* because it directs the sentencing judge to ignore evidence offered in support of each mitigating claim unless it crosses the threshold of substantiality, and thereby "impermissibly limits the sentencer's consideration of relevant mitigating evidence."

The Court was thus divided four-four on whether the Arizona sentencing formula violated the principles emerging from *Woodson* and *Lockett*. In an extraordinary opinion, Justice Scalia joined in the result while refusing to resolve the substantive issue. Instead, he announced that he would no longer adhere to *Woodson* and *Lockett* at all:

> Despite the fact that I think *Woodson* and *Lockett* find no proper basis in the Constitution, they have some claim to my adherence because of the doctrine of *stare decisis*. I do not reject that claim lightly, but I must reject it here. My initial and my fundamental problem ... is not that *Woodson* and *Lockett* are wrong, but that [they] are rationally irreconcilable with *Furman*.... I would not know how to apply them—or, more precisely, how to apply both of them and *Furman*—if I wanted to. I cannot continue to say, in case after case, what degree of "narrowing" is sufficient to achieve the constitutional objective enunciated in *Furman* when I know that that objective is in any case impossible of achievement because of *Woodson-Lockett*. And I cannot continue to say, in case after case, what sort of restraints upon sentencer discretion are unconstitutional under *Woodson-Lockett* when I know that the Constitution positively *favors* constraints under *Furman*. *Stare decisis* cannot command the impossible. Since I cannot possibly be guided by what seem to me incompatible principles, I must reject the one that is plainly in error.

> The objectives of the doctrine of *stare decisis* are not furthered by adhering to *Woodson-Lockett* in any event. The doctrine exists for the purpose of introducing certainty and stability into the law and protecting the expectations of individuals and institutions that have acted in reliance on existing rules. As I have described, the *Woodson-Lockett* principle has frustrated this very purpose from the outset—contradicting the basic thrust of much of our death penalty jurisprudence, laying traps for unwary States, and generating a fundamental uncertainty in the law that shows no signs of ending or even diminishing.

> I cannot adhere to a principle so lacking in support in constitutional text and so plainly unworthy of respect under *stare decisis*. Accordingly, I will not, in this case or in the future, vote to uphold an Eighth Amendment claim that the sentencer's discretion has been unlawfully restricted.

Is there merit to Scalia's assessment of the "*Woodson-Lockett* principle"?[q] If so, is it too late to change course?

---

to limit the sentencer's consideration of relevant mitigating evidence.

[q] Justice Thomas has also indicated that he disagrees with the Court's decision in

**11. Intracase Disparity as a Basis for Leniency.** Consider the problem presented in Biondi v. State, 699 P.2d 1062 (Nev.1985). The facts were summarized in the court's opinion as follows:

> Timothy Smith, a parole officer, was stabbed in the parking lot of a Las Vegas bar in the early morning hours of February 4, 1981. Smith, who was off duty, arrived at the bar around 12:45 a.m. with a friend, Carl Blair. Appellant Biondi and his friends, including Michael Phillips, Ron and Becky Lacey, and Steve Izzi, were in the bar. They were drinking, and they were intoxicated. When in the bar Timothy Smith and Ron Lacey began an argument. They left the bar and went outside to "settle" the dispute. A fight ensued between Timothy Smith and Blair and Ron Lacey. Lacey cut the two men with a knife. After this fight had ended, four of those present saw Timothy Smith struggling with Biondi and Phillips between two parked cars. One of the witnesses, Becky Lacey, testified that Biondi and Phillips each stabbed Smith. Blair testified that only Biondi stabbed Smith. Izzy testified that Biondi held Smith while Phillips stabbed him. Biondi and Phillips fled the scene. Biondi discarded the knife he was carrying. The knife was not recovered. Smith had been stabbed in the chest. He suffered brain death from loss of blood. He was pronounced dead two days later.

Biondi and Phillips were both charged with first-degree murder. Phillips pleaded guilty and was sentenced to life in prison without parole. At Biondi's trial, the prosecution argued that Biondi was guilty of first-degree murder on either of two theories—that both Biondi and Phillips had stabbed Smith or that Biondi had aided and abetted Phillips by holding Smith while Phillips stabbed him. The jury found Biondi guilty of first-degree murder. At the penalty hearing, the jury returned a special verdict finding that Biondi had stabbed Smith, and found, as an aggravating circumstance, that Biondi had previously been convicted of a felony (armed robbery) involving the use of violence. The jury sentenced Biondi to death.

The Nevada Supreme Court affirmed the conviction but set aside the sentence. The court found the disparity between the sentences for Phillips and Biondi "strikingly significant":

> Biondi and Phillips each had one prior felony conviction for a violent crime; Biondi pleaded guilty to armed robbery in 1976; Phillips was convicted in 1977 or 1978 for assault with a deadly weapon. Biondi's participation in the murder was no more significant than Phillips'. In fact, one eyewitness testified that Biondi had held Smith while Phillips stabbed him. The state has provided no explanation for its decision to allow Phillips to plead guilty and be sentenced to life with the possibility of parole but to seek the

---

*Woodson* striking down mandatory statutes and with the prevailing reading of the *Lockett-Eddings* line of cases under which sen-tencing discretion may not be curtailed. Graham v. Collins, 506 U.S. 461, 478 (1993) (Thomas, J., concurring).

death penalty for Biondi. Nor does any justification for this disparity appear in the record. This is a case where similar defendants
were sentenced differently for the identical crime. For this reason,
and for [other] reasons discussed above, we hold the death penalty
imposed on Biondi is disproportionate.

Compare Miller v. State, 415 So.2d 1262 (Fla.1982). Ernest Miller and
his step-brother William Jent were charged with first degree murder for
the death of a young woman known only as "Tammy," and were tried
before separate juries. Three eyewitnesses testified that during the course
of a swimming party, at which the participants had been using drugs and
drinking heavily, Jent and Miller had beaten Tammy and transported her
in the trunk of a car to Miller's home where four men raped her while their
female companions watched. She was placed back in the trunk and taken to
a game preserve where Jent and Miller poured gasoline on her and set her
on fire. The medical examiner testified that she had been alive when
ignited and that the burns caused her death.

The respective juries convicted Miller and Jent of first-degree murder,
but Miller's jury recommended life imprisonment while Jent's recommended a death sentence. In a combined sentencing order, the trial judge
imposed the death penalty on both defendants, based on his conclusion that
the mitigating evidence offered in Miller's behalf did not outweigh the
aggravating evidence and that following the recommendation of Miller's
jury would result in an unwarranted disparity in sentences. The Florida
Supreme Court affirmed, holding that the judge had properly overridden
the jury's recommendation under the applicable standard (that "on the
totality of the circumstances, no reasonable person would differ on the
appropriateness of the death penalty"). Two Justices dissented. They found
the different sentences to be justifiable in light of psychological testimony
that Miller was a "follower" with a "weak ego" who tended to "go along
with the group."

Recall that Judith Neelley's counsel had brought to the appellate
court's attention the fact that Alvin Neelley had not been prosecuted for
Lisa Ann Millican's death. Was this fact pertinent? Would it have mattered
if Alvin Neelley had been prosecuted, convicted of murder, and sentenced to
life imprisonment?

---

## INTRODUCTORY NOTES ON COMPARATIVE REVIEW OF DEATH SENTENCES

**1. Introduction.** The Supreme Court's death penalty decisions have
indicated that "meaningful appellate review" of death sentences by a court
with statewide jurisdiction is an indispensable feature of a constitutional
capital sentencing scheme. Many of the functions performed by appellate
courts in capital cases merely extend to the sentencing phase the same
form of review exercised with respect to adjudication of guilt. This includes
review of trial court decisions concerning the admissibility of evidence in

aggravation or mitigation, and the sufficiency of the evidence to prove aggravating circumstances. In addition, however, most appellate courts have a further responsibility of reviewing the correctness of the sentencer's decision to impose a death sentence in each case. That is, even if a legally adequate predicate for a death sentence was established, and even if the sentencing process was untainted by error, the appellate court has an independent obligation to review the correctness of the sentence. Capital sentence review takes two basic forms:

**2.   Case-by-Case Proportionality Review.** The appellate courts of most death penalty states have authority to set aside a death sentence adjudged to be excessive in the particular case. Proportionality review[a] in this sense refers to a qualitative judgment concerning the suitability of the punishment for a given offense or offender. A court might determine, for example, that the offense was not sufficiently aggravated to warrant the death penalty even though an adequate statutory predicate for the sentence was established. Or a court might set aside a sentence in light of factors relating to the reduced responsibility, character, or background of the offender.

**3.   Comparative Review.** In a large number of states, appellate courts—normally because mandated to do so by statute, but in a few states in the absence of statutory directive—undertake an additional responsibility: to determine whether a defendant's death sentence is excessive in comparison with the penalty imposed in "similar" cases. The justifying premise for comparative review is that even if a death sentence does not strike the judicial mind as disproportionate when the case is viewed on its own terms, such a sentence is nonetheless objectionable if death sentences have not ordinarily been imposed in "similar" cases. Unlike case-by-case proportionality review, which is entirely qualitative in nature, judgments about "comparative excessiveness" have a quantitative dimension; the courts require a systematic method of compiling information regarding the characteristics and outcomes of a pool of "similar" cases.[b] Issues relating to the exercise of comparative review are explored in the following materials.

———

## State v. Yates

Supreme Court of South Carolina, 1982.
280 S.C. 29, 310 S.E.2d 805.

■ PER CURIAM:

Appellant, Dale Robert Yates, was indicted and convicted of murder, armed robbery, assault and battery with intent to kill, and conspiracy.

---

[a] The Supreme Court has determined that a death sentence is constitutionally excessive for the crime of rape or for an accomplice to homicide if the defendant did not manifest reckless indifference to human life. It has also determined that some non-death sentences can be constitutionally disproportionate. These cases are considered together in Chapter IX. As used here, the term "pro-portionality review" refers to case-by-case assessments by the state courts of the propriety of a death sentence.

[b] See generally, David Baldus, Charles Pulaski, George Woodworth and Frederick Kyle, Identifying Comparatively Excessive Sentences of Death: A Quantitative Approach, 33 Stan.L.Rev. 1 (1980).

After being found guilty of murder, the jury recommended at the second phase of the bifurcated trial, that he should die by electrocution. From these convictions and sentence, he appeals. The basic issue involved in the appeal is whether the death sentence should be carried out.

On February 12, 1981, David Loftis (not on trial), Henry Davis (killed in the robbery), and appellant Yates talked about various places to rob and rode around in the car of Davis looking for a store which could be easily robbed. As a part of the plan, they borrowed a gun from the appellant's brother. On the following day, February 13, they continued to ride around, casing places to rob. The appellant and Davis left Loftis (who turned state's evidence) at a shopping mall and drove away with the pistol under the passenger's side of the front seat. The appellant and Davis subsequently entered Wood's rural store, by the appellant's own testimony, for the purpose of committing armed robbery. Appellant was armed with the pistol and Davis with a knife. They demanded and received approximately $3,000 from Willie Wood, who was alone and in charge of the store operation. When Willie Wood failed to cooperate to the satisfaction of the robbers, the appellant shot him, but not fatally. About that time, the mother of Willie Wood, who was the postmistress in the adjoining building, came upon the scene. The appellant ran out of the store, taking the money and the gun. Davis remained in the store, and stabbed Mrs. Wood to death with his knife. Willie Wood succeeded in obtaining a gun and killed Davis. After appellant waited in Davis' car and concluded that Davis had been caught, he drove off, hid the money and pistol in a wooded area, and was later apprehended.

The appellant testified in his own behalf. His testimony was not inconsistent with the facts recited above. It was his contention that he did not kill Mrs. Wood and that it was his intent all along to abandon the robbery without hurting anybody if the victims refused to cooperate.

[The prosecution's theory of liability was that "Yates and Davis were present aiding and abetting each other in the commission of a planned armed robbery and that the hand of one was the hand of all." The court concluded that Yates "is equally responsible for the stabbing death of Mrs. Wood, even though he did not actually cast the fatal blows. [Yates] and Henry Davis entered the store armed and did commit a robbery. As a direct result of their joint actions in committing the armed robbery, Mrs. Wood was killed." The court upheld Yates' conviction for murder and the jury's finding of the aggravating circumstance that the "murder was committed while in the commission of . . . robbery while armed with a deadly weapon."]

Appellant challenges the trial court's refusal to enjoin the solicitor from seeking the death penalty in his case. Appellant based this challenge on the prosecutor's record of handling previous death penalty cases involving triggermen and nontriggermen. . . . Appellant argues that the solicitor normally sought the death penalty only against the triggerman.

It would be error for the trial judge to tell a solicitor how to determine whether the death penalty should be sought. This is the prerogative of the solicitor....

The appellant requested the trial judge to charge the jury as a mitigating circumstance: "That Dale Robert Yates did not kill the victim Helen Wood." ... The judge very properly told counsel, in lieu of granting the request, "you may argue it [to the jury] all you wish to." Presumably, counsel did exactly that. The fact that Yates did not do the stabbing personally was one of the facts upon which counsel relied in hopes of obtaining a life sentence. Instead of charging the jury in the language suggested by counsel, the judge [charged]:

> [T]he defendant asks you to consider that [he] was an accomplice to the murder, committed by another person, and his participation was relatively minor. In other words, that embraces the theory that the defendant did not, himself, personally strike the fatal blow.

The charge, first orally and then in writing, to the jury, let it know that it should give consideration to the fact that Yates did not personally stab Mrs. Wood. The thought counsel wished the judge to convey was actually given to the jury, although not in the exact verbiage requested....

The last questions raised ... call upon this Court to perform the duty imposed upon it by § 16–3–25(C) of our Code[:]

> (C) With regard to the sentence, the court shall determine:

> (1) Whether the sentence of death was imposed under the influence of passion, prejudice, or any other arbitrary factor, and

> (2) Whether the evidence supports the jury's or judge's finding of a statutory aggravating circumstance as enumerated in § 16–3–20, and

> (3) Whether the sentence of death is excessive or disproportionate to the penalty imposed in similar cases, considering both the crime and the defendant.

... We discussed the duty of the Court under the statutory requirements in the recent case of State v. Copeland, 278 S.C. 572, 300 S.E.2d 63 (1982)....[a] While the duty imposed is a difficult one because no two

[a] In *Copeland*, after reviewing the United States Supreme Court's capital sentencing decisions, the court stated:

> [These decisions] encourage, while not mandating, an appellate review which accords priority to the particular and distinctive features of each defendant as well as the specific circumstances of the crime for which the death sentence has been imposed. The ultimate outcome, it is suggested by these decisions, should be the infliction of capital punishment upon only those individuals who have been culled from all other defendants by a process which highlights the unique attributes of their personalities and their crimes.

> From a logical standpoint, of course, that which is unique is also incommensurable. Herein lies the conflict between particularized sentencing (and review) and the notion of comparing "similar cases." Clearly, a comparative review

defendants and no two crimes are exactly alike, it is not an unsurmountable chore. Prior to imposition of sentence, the trial judge ... made this finding:

> Mr. Yates, as the trial judge in the case just concluded in which you are indicted for the crime of murder, prior to imposing the death sentence upon you, I find as an affirmative fact beyond any reasonable doubt that the evidence warrants the imposition of the death penalty and that its imposition is not a result of prejudice, passion, or any other arbitrary factor.

The ... record ... supports the trial judge's finding. We agree that the evidence warrants the death penalty and our independent finding and conclusion is that the penalty was not the result of prejudice, passion or any other arbitrary factor.

The appellant [argues] that the sentence is disproportionate to penalties imposed in similar cases. He argues that he personally did not stab and cause the death of Mrs. Wood. He testified during the trial that at the time of her death he was not in the store but had departed to the getaway car.

[The Court first ruled that the death penalty was not unconstitutionally excessive under Enmund v. Florida, 458 U.S. 782 (1982), because Yates intended for life to be taken: "[H]e failed to kill Willie Wood merely because his aim was less than perfect. It is of little significance that the life he intended to take and attempted to take was that of Willie Wood instead of his mother, who was actually stabbed."]

In determining whether ... the sentence ... is excessive or disproportionate in light of the crime and the defendant, this Court has reviewed the entire record. We have also considered the circumstances of State v. Gilbert, 277 S.C. 53, 283 S.E.2d 179 (1981) the only prior holding of this court suitable for comparison. In that case, the two defendants, Gilbert and Gleaton, spent a morning cruising in search of a target to rob.... In the instant case, appellant with Davis and Loftis apparently contemplated robbery for over a day, making a diligent search of Greenville County for just the right setting. Indeed, Loftis, one of the accomplices, withdrew from the enterprise before the actual robbery and testified to this lengthy prologue.

As in *Gilbert,* appellant and his cohort, Davis, found a solitary, apparently unarmed victim in Mr. Willie Wood. In almost every respect, the robbery unfolded as in the case of Gilbert and Gleaton with one assailant wielding a knife and the other a pistol. Mr. Wood was directed to lean over

---

cannot be permitted to diminish the particularized quality of sentencing, since the latter is now an absolute command of the U.S. Constitution. By the same token, the final resolution of a given appeal, if sentence is to be affirmed, should rest upon the unique correctness of the result in the given instance rather than its coarse resemblance to other cases....

In our view, the search for "similar cases" can only begin with an actual conviction and sentence of death rendered by a trier of fact.... We consider such findings by the trial court to be a threshold requirement for comparative study and indeed the only foundation of "similarity" consonant with our role as an appellate court.—[Footnote by eds.]

the store counter by Davis who appeared ready to stab him with the knife. At this point, however, the victim refused to obey. At Davis' command, the appellant fired two bullets at Wood from close range and fled. From this a jury could conclude beyond a reasonable doubt that appellant fully intended Wood's death, either by Davis' hand or his own, in the course of this armed robbery.

Hereafter the facts diverge from [*Gilbert*]. Mr. Wood did not die from his wound but instead seized his own gun and fought off Davis. Willie Wood's sixty-eight year-old mother then came upon the scene and was stabbed to death by Davis, who in turn was shot and killed by Wood. Although this outcome sets the instant case apart from previous capital sentences we have affirmed, it is sufficient for our purposes that the appellant displayed the same intent and followed the same pattern of preparation as Gilbert [and] Gleaton . . . before him.

In mitigation, appellant offered his own testimony and that of his mother. The jury learned that appellant had been a poor student in school, achieving basically a ninth grade education. In appellant's own words, he was more interested in "getting out and having fun, shooting pool." If given a life sentence, however, he intended to write a book, study, and improve the prison system. Appellant frankly conceded that he had not managed to do these things during ten previous periods of incarceration. Both appellant and his mother testified generally that he had some history of drug abuse and that, most importantly, he allowed himself to be influenced by Davis, the deceased accomplice. Appellant did not contend, however, that he was actually inebriated at the time of the robbery nor that Henry Davis forced him to participate.

The trial judge meticulously instructed the jury on the available mitigating circumstances under [the statute]. In addition, the trial court orally and in writing directed the jury to consider any other mitigating circumstances presented by the defendant.

In our view, the appellant had the benefit of every reasonable explanation for his acts. We are satisfied that the jury properly found the aggravating circumstance of robbery while armed with a deadly weapon and did so without any influence of passion, prejudice or other arbitrary factor. The testimony in mitigation is comparable to that in *Gilbert,* if not somewhat less impressive, given the claim of Gilbert and Gleaton that they had partaken of drugs and were acting solely on impulse. We are satisfied that the penalty here imposed is neither excessive nor disproportionate in light of this crime and this defendant. Given that we have upheld a comparable sentence in the comparable case of *State v. Gilbert*, we are confident that the finding of this jury represents consistent application of the ultimate sanction in this category of capital crime.

... The convictions and sentence of the appellant, Dale Robert Yates, are, accordingly,

Affirmed.[b]

## State v. Young

Supreme Court of North Carolina, 1985.
312 N.C. 669, 325 S.E.2d 181.

After finishing a bottle of vodka in [a] parking lot, defendant, Presnell, and Jackson began to talk about how they might obtain more liquor.... Since the men had no money, defendant suggested that the three men go to [J.O.] Cooke's house, rob and kill him, and take money. Presnell and Jackson testified that they thought defendant was joking.... The three men left the ... parking lot and began walking to Cooke's house. On the way defendant suggested that Jackson hold Cooke, defendant stab him, and Presnell "finish" him. When the men arrived at Cooke's house, Jackson knocked on the door and told Cooke that they wanted to buy liquor. Cooke let the men inside and went into the kitchen to get the liquor. When he returned with the vodka, defendant suddenly reached into his pants, pulled out a knife and stabbed Cooke twice in the chest. Cooke said "What are you doing?" and fell to the floor. Cooke was able to take the knife from his own chest, at which point defendant told Presnell to "finish him." Presnell stabbed the victim five or six times in the back.

Defendant searched through Cooke's pockets and wallet and divided the money he found among the three men. The men then searched the house for other valuables and found a coin collection which they divided. They left the house, and Jackson placed the knife in a nearby snowbank.

[D]efendant was charged with first-degree murder, first-degree burglary, and robbery with a dangerous weapon. At trial defendant offered no evidence. The jury found defendant guilty of first-degree murder, first-degree burglary, and robbery with a dangerous weapon.

In the sentencing phase of the trial, ... the trial court submitted three aggravating circumstances: (i) whether the murder was committed while defendant was engaged in a commission of robbery with a dangerous weapon or first-degree burglary; (ii) whether the murder was committed for pecuniary gain; and (iii) whether the murder was especially heinous, atrocious, or cruel. The trial court submitted two mitigating circumstances for consideration by the jury: (i) the age (19) of defendant; and (ii) any other circumstance deemed to have mitigating value. The jury found ... that the murder was committed while in the commission of a robbery or burglary and that it was committed for pecuniary gain. The jury found evidence of one or more mitigating circumstances, but found them insufficient to outweigh the aggravating circumstances. The jury recommended

[b] Yates' death sentence was subsequently set aside by the Supreme Court due to an improper burden-shifting instruction on the issue of malice. Yates v. Aiken, 484 U.S. 211 (1988).—[Footnote by eds.]

that defendant be sentenced to death and the trial court entered judgment accordingly. . . .

■ BRANCH, CHIEF JUSTICE. [The Court affirmed Young's conviction and held that the sentencing proceedings had been conducted in conformity with state and federal law.]

As a final matter in every capital case, we are directed by [statute] to review the record and determine (i) whether the record supports the jury's findings of any aggravating . . . circumstances upon which the sentencing court based its sentence of death; (ii) whether the sentence was imposed under the influence of passion, prejudice or any other arbitrary factor; and (iii) whether the sentence of death is excessive or disproportionate to the penalty imposed in similar cases, considering both the crime and the defendant.

[W]e find that the evidence supports the two aggravating factors found by the jury . . . We also conclude that there is nothing in the record which suggests that the sentence of death was influenced by passion, prejudice or any other arbitrary factor. We thus turn to our final statutory duty of proportionality review.

In determining whether the death sentence in this case is disproportionate to the penalty imposed in similar cases, we first refer to the now familiar "pool" of cases established [by a prior case]:

In comparing "similar cases" for purposes of proportionality review, we use as a pool for comparison purposes *all cases* arising since the effective date of our capital punishment statute, 1 June 1977, which have been tried as capital cases and reviewed on direct appeal by this court and in which the jury recommended death or life imprisonment or in which the trial court imposed life imprisonment after the jury's failure to agree upon a sentencing recommendation within a reasonable period of time.

. . . The pool "includes only those cases which have been affirmed by this court."

We have held that our task on proportionality review is to compare the case "with other cases in the pool which are roughly similar with regard to the crime and the defendant. . . ."

In conducting our proportionality review in this case, we have reviewed the approximately 28 robbery murder cases in the "pool." We note that in 23 of these cases, juries imposed sentences of life imprisonment rather than death. The death penalty was imposed in five cases. While we wish to make it *abundantly clear* that we do not consider this numerical disparity dispositive . . . , our careful examination of these cases has led us to the conclusion that although the crime here committed was a tragic killing, "it does not rise to the level of those murders in which we have approved the death sentence upon proportionality review." The facts presented by this appeal more closely resemble those cases in which the jury recommended life imprisonment than those in which the defendant was sentenced to death.

In this case, the evidence essentially reveals that defendant, a young man 19 years of age, and two companions went to the victim's home.... They gained entry to Cooke's dwelling by trick. Defendant stabbed Cooke twice in the chest and his companion Presnell "finished him" by stabbing him several more times. Young and his two friends then stole the victim's money and some valuable coins and fled the scene. The pathologist testified that the victim died shortly after he was stabbed.

Although we have not in the past, and will not in the future "necessarily feel bound during [our] proportionality review to give a citation to every case in the pool of 'similar cases' used for comparison," we find it instructive to discuss several cases which impelled our conclusion that the death penalty is disproportionate in this case.

A case with facts similar to the murder here under review is State v. Whisenant, 308 N.C. 791, 303 S.E.2d 784 (1983). In *Whisenant,* the defendant, a 43–year-old male, discussed with several witnesses his intention to rob the Leonhardt home in Morganton, North Carolina. [He] went to the Leonhardt residence and shot and killed the owner, a 79–year-old male, and the housekeeper, a 66–year-old female. The jury found as aggravating circumstances that defendant had previously been convicted of a felony involving the use of violence against another person; the murder was committed while defendant was engaged in the commission of armed robbery; the murder was perpetrated for pecuniary gain; and the murder was committed while defendant was engaged in a course of conduct which included the commission of another crime of violence against another person. No mitigating circumstances were found. Despite the presence of four aggravating circumstances and the failure of the jury to find a single circumstance in mitigation of defendant's punishment, defendant was sentenced to consecutive life sentences after the jury was unable to agree upon the recommendation of punishment.

State v. Hunt, 305 N.C. 238, 287 S.E.2d 818 (1982) is another capital case in which the crime committed by the defendant was much worse than that committed by Phillip Young....

In *Hunt,* the deceased, Walter Ray, lived alone in a trailer in Henderson, North Carolina. Ray operated an illegal bar in his residence. As Ray was closing the bar one night, defendant put on gloves, walked up behind the victim, grabbed him and put a knife against his throat. Defendant then forced Ray back to the bedroom where defendant searched a closet and removed approximately $400.00 and a pistol from it. As defendant prepared to shoot Ray with the pistol, Ray begged him not to kill him that way. Defendant agreed to employ another method.

After forcing Ray to drink beer and a pint of liquor, defendant slashed one of Ray's forearms near the wrist with a knife. He slashed him again and waited while the victim slowly bled to death. Defendant then left the trailer carrying the pistol and the money with him.

The jury found six aggravating circumstances, but specified no mitigating circumstances since they found that the aggravating circumstances were insufficient to support the death penalty.

Finally,[3] we agree with defendant's contention that this case is very similar to State v. Jackson, 309 N.C. 26, 305 S.E.2d 703 (1983) in which this Court overturned a death sentence as disproportionate to the penalty imposed in similar cases.

In *Jackson,* three men conspired to ambush and rob a 71–year-old ailing man. The trio faked car trouble and the elderly victim, George McAulay, stopped to offer aid. One of the three men told McAulay that they needed jumper cables. McAulay replied that he did not have any with him, but would give one of the men a ride to town. Defendant got into the car with him. When the victim refused to give Jackson money, Jackson murdered McAulay by shooting him twice in the head. Jackson took the money, met his companions and reported to them that he had killed McAulay because he had refused to relinquish the money.

The jury found as an aggravating circumstance that the crime was committed for pecuniary gain. They found as the sole mitigating circumstance that defendant had no significant history of prior criminal activity. In the instant case, the jury found the two aggravating circumstances earlier mentioned, that is, that the murder was committed while defendant was engaged in the commission of armed robbery and that it was committed for pecuniary gain. The jury did not specify the mitigating circumstances they found.

In contrast to *Whisenant, Hunt, Jackson* and other cases [where the death penalty was either not imposed or set aside on appeal] are those armed robbery cases in which this Court affirmed the jury's recommendation of the death penalty.... We do not deem it necessary to discuss each of these cases; suffice it to say that we have carefully reviewed each of them and are convinced that defendant Young did not commit a crime as egregious as those committed by the defendants in [those cases]. In nearly all those cases, the jury found as an aggravating circumstance that the defendants were engaged in a course of conduct which included the commission of another crime of violence against another person. Furthermore, in [two of them], the jury found that the murder was especially atrocious, heinous or cruel.... In this case, however, the jury specifically found that this aggravating circumstance did *not* exist.

In conclusion, we hold as a matter of law that the death sentence imposed in this case is disproportionate. ... We are therefore required by the statute to sentence defendant to life imprisonment in lieu of the death sentence....

Guilt–Innocence Phase: No Error;

---

[3] By singling out these few cases for discussion, we do not mean to imply that these were the only cases reviewed by this court in conducting our proportionality review. We considered carefully each of the cases in the "pool"....

Sentencing Phase: Death Sentence Vacated, Sentence of Life Imprisonment Imposed.

■ VAUGHN, J., did not participate in the consideration or decision of this case.

————

## NOTES ON COMPARATIVE REVIEW OF DEATH SENTENCES

**1.  Questions on *Yates* and *Young*.** *Yates* and *Young* take very different approaches to comparative review. The South Carolina Supreme Court's earlier decision in *Gilbert* demonstrates that Yates' death sentence is not unprecedented, but does it show that such a sentence is "consistently" imposed in similar cases? By contrast, the North Carolina Supreme Court examines a broader base of cases and concludes that *Young* "more closely resembles" cases in which death sentences were not imposed. In light of the highly individualized nature of the sentencing inquiry, is it possible for the court to know which cases *Young* "more closely resembles?" Won't it always be possible to find cases "worse" than the one being considered in which the death sentence was not imposed? One could interpret *Young* to indicate that a death sentence for robbery-murder is likely to be found comparatively excessive unless more than one person was killed[a] or the offense was found to be "heinous, atrocious or cruel."[b] If this is what *Young* means, has the court rewritten the statute?

[a] See State v. Benson, 323 N.C. 318, 372 S.E.2d 517 (1988) in which the court invalidated another death sentence imposed in an armed robbery-murder case. The court explained:

> Approximately 51 robbery-murder cases are in the pool. Of these, life sentences have been imposed in 44 cases and death sentences in seven. In five of these robbery-murder cases, the only aggravating circumstance was pecuniary gain. Life sentences were imposed in four of the five. The fifth case [was *State v. Jackson*]. On appeal that death sentence was found to be disproportionate. Here, the mitigating circumstances are stronger than in *Jackson* . . . .

> In the robbery-murder cases where the death sentence has been upheld, all but two involved multiple killings. Of those two, one involved the shooting of a second victim and one involved the kidnapping of the female victim. The case at issue cannot be equated with the robbery-murder convictions where the death sentence was upheld. . . .

The North Carolina Supreme Court has not set aside a death sentence based on proportionality review since *Benson*.

[b] See State v. Fletcher, 354 N.C. 455, 555 S.E.2d 534 (2001) in which the court explained why the defendant's death sentence for robbery murder was not disproportionate:

> In four of the seven cases in which this Court has concluded that the death penalty was disproportionate, the especially heinous, atrocious, or cruel aggravating circumstance was not submitted to the jury (*Benson, Rogers, Hill,* and *Jackson*) whereas in a fifth the circumstance was submitted to but not found by the jury (*Young*). As the jury in the present case found this aggravating circumstance existed, this case is clearly distinguishable from those five cases. The evidence in this case showed that defendant beat and stabbed the victim repeatedly while taking her from room to room, forcing her to identify the location of her valuables. The victim tried to fend off defendant's attack to no avail. After attacking the victim with two different weapons, defendant left the victim conscious and dying. The victim managed to

**2. Methodology of Comparative Review: Defining the Universe of Relevant Cases.** The first question that must be resolved by appellate courts conducting comparative review is how to define the universe of relevant cases. Courts in more than half the death penalty states limit their review to appealed cases, although most of these courts follow the approach taken by the North Carolina Supreme Court in *Young* (including appealed life sentences) rather than that taken by the South Carolina Supreme Court in *Yates* (including only appealed death sentences). The remaining states broaden the universe to include some portion of unappealed cases. The information in these states is typically provided by reports which must be filed by the trial court. Some of these states define the universe to include all cases in which a capital sentencing proceeding was held, thus excluding all those in which the death penalty was not sought by the prosecution; others include all convictions for capital crimes, thus including some cases in which the prosecution did not seek the death penalty; and one state, Louisiana, includes all cases initiated by indictments for capital crimes, encompassing cases in which the defendant was convicted of a non-capital murder and thereby reaching all exercises of prosecutorial discretion.[c]

These approaches reflect different responses to two basic questions. First, should comparative review be limited to cases in which death sentences have been imposed? Second, even if the pool is broadened to include life sentences, should it be limited to cases in which the prosecution sought the death sentence, i.e., to cases in which capital sentencing proceedings were held? These issues are addressed in turn below.

**(i) Should Comparison be Limited to Cases in Which Death Sentences Were Imposed?** The argument against a pool limited to

move to a chair in a bedroom before succumbing to her wounds. Furthermore, defendant was convicted in part under a theory of premeditation and deliberation. In the other two cases in which we have concluded that the death penalty was disproportionate, the jury did find that the murders were especially heinous, atrocious, or cruel (*Stokes* and *Bondurant*). However, both cases are distinguishable from the case at hand on other grounds.

In *Stokes* the Court emphasized that the defendant was found guilty of first-degree murder based only upon the felony murder rule; that there was little, if any, evidence of premeditation and deliberation; and that the defendant acted in concert with a considerably older co-felon. To the contrary, in the present case there was no proper evidence that defendant acted in concert with someone else; and the trial jury found defendant guilty of first-degree murder on the basis of

premeditation and deliberation as well as under the felony murder rule. In *Bondurant* the defendant shot the victim but then immediately directed the driver of the car in which they had been riding to proceed to an emergency room. In concluding that the death penalty was disproportionate, the Court focused on the defendant's immediate attempt to obtain medical assistance for the victim and the lack of any apparent motive for the killing. In contrast, defendant in this case left the house while the victim lay conscious and dying. Furthermore, the trial jury found that defendant committed the murder in the course of a burglary, thus establishing his motivation for this senseless killing.

[c] Another unique feature of the Louisiana scheme is that the statute directs the court to compare only those cases arising in the same parish. In every other state, the review is statewide, and some courts occasionally consult cases arising in other states.

appealed death sentences was stated by Justice Exum of the North Carolina Supreme Court:[d]

> The basic purpose of [comparative] review is to make sure that the death sentence in the case before us is not "excessive" to sentences "imposed in similar cases." If we look for comparison only to cases in which the death penalty has been imposed, the sentence in the case under review could never be excessive because one death sentence never "exceeds" another. It is only by comparing the case being reviewed in which a death sentence was imposed with other similar cases in which life was imposed that we can determine whether the death penalty in the case being reviewed is really excessive to the penalty being imposed in similar cases. For, to reiterate what the Supreme Court said in *Gregg v. Georgia,* if there are certain kinds of murder cases in which our juries are generally not recommending death, then an occasional death sentence imposed in those kinds of cases ought to be set aside by this court.
>
> We ought not limit ourselves only to cases where the death sentence was imposed and affirmed. To do so means that we only ask whether the case under review is as bad as the other death cases. The legislature intended us not only to make that determination but also to determine whether the case under review is more deserving of the death penalty than similar cases in which life sentences have been imposed. The statute's plain language requires that we make both kinds of comparisons. Of the two, the latter is the more meaningful and is probably constitutionally required.

The Supreme Court of South Carolina disagreed:[e]

> We recognize that [some feel] that the reviewing court should compare a given death sentence with a "universe" of cases which includes sentences of life imprisonment, acquittals, reversals and even mere indictments and arrests. Under such a regime, the review court could only determine the size of its sample or "universe" by some arbitrary device. Fact findings of the trial court [supporting a sentence of death], by contrast, provide a fundamental line of demarcation well recognized in and even exalted by our legal tradition....
>
> To expand the notion of a "universe" would also entail intolerable speculation by this court. Under the South Carolina statute, a jury is not required to state its reasons for failing to recommend a sentence of death. In a given case, the alleged

---

[d] State v. Pinch, 306 N.C. 1, 292 S.E.2d 203, 242–43 (1982) (Exum, J., dissenting). The North Carolina Supreme Court adopted Justice Exum's view in State v. Williams, 308 N.C. 47, 301 S.E.2d 335 (1983).

[e] State v. Copeland, 278 S.C. 572, 300 S.E.2d 63 (1982).

aggravating circumstance may not have been proven to the satisfaction of the jury, while in another "similar case" (expansively defined) the statutory mitigating circumstances or some mitigating factor "otherwise authorized or allowed by law" may have deterred imposition of the death sentence.

This Court would enter a realm of pure conjecture if it attempted to compare and contrast such verdicts with an actual sentence of death. They represent acts of mercy which have not yet been held to offend the United States Constitution. Moreover, they reflect the emphasis upon individualized sentencing mandated by the United States Supreme Court. We will not subject these verdicts to scrutiny in pursuit of phantom "similar cases," when a meaningful sample lies ready at hand in those cases where the jury has spoken unequivocally.

**(ii) Should Comparison be Limited to Cases in Which the Prosecution Sought a Death Sentence?** In Tichnell v. State, 297 Md. 432, 468 A.2d 1 (1983), the Maryland Court of Appeals concluded "that the legislatively intended inventory of cases from which 'similar cases' are to be culled encompasses only those first-degree murder cases in which the state sought the death penalty . . . whether it was imposed or not."[f]

Three members of the court objected:

"[D]eath eligible murder cases in which the prosecutor could have, but did not seek the death penalty" must be included in the inventory of relevant cases in order to achieve the goal of proportionality review—the consistent and fair application of the death penalty. . . .

[T]his Court has before it data concerning the exercise of prosecutorial discretion in death penalty cases. This data dramatically demonstrates that the inventory of relevant cases for proportionality review must include all death-eligible murder cases—not only those in which the prosecutor sought the death penalty, but also those in which he did not.

This data reveals that in Maryland prosecutors seek the death penalty in only 7.8 percent of the death-eligible cases, whereas in 92.2 percent of the death-eligible cases the death penalty is not sought. Consequently, this data establishes that Maryland prosecutors rarely seek the death penalty, a fact that is relevant, in and of itself, in determining whether the death penalty is disproportionate. . . .

In addition, the data [show] that in cases in which the death penalty has been sought juries in Garrett County have imposed the death penalty in 50 percent of the cases, whereas juries in Balti-

---

[f] The court noted, however, that "we do not preclude any defendant whose death sentence is under appellate review from presenting argument, with relevant facts, that designated non-capital murder cases are similar to the case then under scrutiny and should be taken into account in the exercise of our proportionality review function."

more City have imposed the death penalty in 33 percent. This data suggests that in these two jurisdictions the death penalty has been imposed in a somewhat consistent manner. The data further reveals [that] there is a substantial variation in the exercise of prosecutorial discretion. In Garrett County prosecutors seek the death penalty in 100 percent of the death-eligible cases, whereas in Baltimore City, they seek that penalty in only 1.8 percent. [J]uries in Garrett County have imposed the death penalty in 50 percent of all the death-eligible cases, whereas juries in Baltimore City have imposed the death penalty in only .6 percent. [I]n these two jurisdictions the death penalty has been imposed in an inconsistent manner. If death-eligible cases in which the death penalty has not been sought are excluded from the inventory, a person who has committed a crime in Garrett County is deprived of a realistic comparison of the treatment accorded to other persons of similar background who committed a similar crime under similar circumstances in Baltimore City and, indeed, throughout the state. . . .

It is . . . apparent that the existence of such data raises the question whether the relevant inventory of cases must include those in which the death penalty was not sought in order for proportionality review to be constitutional. . . .

Is it feasible for courts to broaden in this manner the universe of cases to be considered? Prosecutors are not required to articulate reasons for their decisions to negotiate plea arrangements, to reduce charges, or not to seek the death penalty. If the courts were to include such cases within the universe of comparative review, how would they determine whether the evidence in the case would have been legally sufficient to support a death sentence? How would the court obtain other information relevant to the prosecutor's decision and, ultimately, to its own comparison?

Recall that Yates sought to "enjoin" the prosecution from seeking the death penalty because the prosecutor's normal policy was to seek the capital sanction only against the "triggerman." If this were the normal policy, would it demonstrate that the decision to seek the death penalty against Yates was arbitrary or unjustified? Does it matter that the "triggerman" was dead? Would it matter if Yates had more previous convictions for violent felonies than most of the other accomplices against whom the prosecutor decided not to seek a death sentence? Or that Yates' claims in mitigation were weaker? In the absence of adjudication of these issues, how could the court evaluate them?

**3. Methodology of Comparative Review: Selecting and Comparing "Similar" Cases.** Within the universe of cases available for comparative review, the court must develop a methodology for deciding which features make cases similar or dissimilar to one another and for determining whether the death sentence being reviewed is "comparatively excessive." Baldus and his colleagues have recommended that courts develop quantitative approaches using statistical techniques for classifying cases and developing measures of comparative excessiveness. See David Baldus,

Charles Pulaski, George Woodworth, and Frederick Kyle, Comparative Review of Death Sentences: An Empirical Study of the Georgia Experience, 74 J.Crim.L. and Criminology 661 (1983). Is this feasible or desirable? The Supreme Court of North Carolina has expressly refused to adopt a highly quantitative methodology for conducting comparative review, explaining why in State v. Williams, 308 N.C. 47, 301 S.E.2d 335 (1983):

> We do not propose to attempt to employ mathematical or statistical models involving multiple regression analysis or other scientific techniques, currently in vogue among social scientists, which have been described as having "the seductive appeal of science and mathematics." The factors to be considered and their relevancy during [comparative] review in a given capital case are not readily subject to complete enumeration and definition. Those factors will be as numerous and as varied as the cases coming before us on appeal. This truth is readily revealed by a comparison of the opinions of the Justices of the Supreme Court of the United States concerning the relevancy of certain factors as revealed in *Godfrey v. Georgia*. Even those with extensive training in data collection and statistical evaluation and analysis are unable to agree concerning the type of statistical methodology which should be employed if statistical or mathematical models are adopted for purposes of proportionality review. E.g., David Baldus, Charles Pulaski, George Woodworth, and Frederick Kyle, Identifying Comparatively Excessive Sentences of Death: A Quantitative Approach, 33 Stan. L.Rev. 1 (1980); George Dix, Appellate Review of the Decision to Impose Death, 68 Geo.L.J. 97 (1979). Additionally, the categories of factors which would be used in setting up any statistical model for quantitative analysis, no matter how numerous those factors, would have a natural tendency to become the last word on the subject of proportionality rather than serving as an initial point of inquiry. After making numerical determinations concerning the number of similar and dissimilar characteristics in the case before it and in other cases in which the death sentence was or was not imposed, a reviewing court might well tend to disregard the experienced judgments of its own members in favor of the "scientific" evidence resulting from quantitative analysis. To the extent that a reviewing court allowed itself to be so swayed, it would tend to deny the defendant before it the constitutional right to "individualized consideration" as that concept was expounded in *Lockett v. Ohio*. This is so because, a "close reading of the actual records of cases identified as 'similar' by a quantitative measure may reveal factual distinctions which make them legally dissimilar." David Baldus, Charles Pulaski, George Woodworth, and Frederick Kyle, Identifying Comparatively Excessive Sentences of Death: A Quantitative Approach, 33 Stan.L.Rev. 1, 68 (1980). Further, the reviewing court would still be required to rely upon a "best estimate" of the factors that actually influenced the sentencing juries. Id. at 24–25. Therefore, this court will not attempt to engage in

the systematic and scientific collection of statistical data or its evaluation and analysis through the theory of probability, multiple regression analysis, graphs or the other tools of statistical analysis which are of value to scientists engaged in the physical sciences and dealing with matters other than [comparative] review in capital cases.

Although the North Carolina Supreme Court rejected sophisticated statistical methodologies, it does appear to employ one of the quantitative techniques (the "salient factors method") described by Baldus and his colleagues: in *Young,* it selected cases involving the same statutory aggravating circumstance (murder in the course of armed robbery) as the pool for comparison; within that group, it identified those features of the cases which appear to explain the variation in outcome between the five death sentences and the 23 life sentences; it then concluded that in the absence of these distinguishing characteristics, the death sentence in *Young* was comparatively excessive. Does this approach give undue emphasis to the characteristics of the offense? Is it possible that Young's case was dissimilar to the life-sentence cases in other respects, such as the absence of any compelling claim in mitigation? Is comparative review of individualized death sentences a self-contradiction?

**4. The New Jersey Experience.** The New Jersey Supreme Court is the only state court that has adopted a statistical approach to comparative review. In 1988, the court commissioned a comprehensive study of different approaches and appointed Professor David Baldus to develop a system using statistical methodologies of the kind that he had described in his writings. In 1992, the court adopted his principal recommendations, which combined various types of "frequency analysis" with a traditional "precedent-seeking" analysis comparing the case under review with prior cases. Initially, the "frequency" analysis consisted of three different methods of characterizing the "culpability level" of the cases: the "salient factor" approach (categorizing cases into 55 factually comparable groups organized around statutory aggravating factors in a hierarchy of "culpability);" a "numerical preponderance" approach counting and weighting the aggravating and mitigating factors; and an "index of outcomes" approach using multiple regression analyses to rank the overall "culpability" level of each case. After a few years, however, the court appointed a special master— Judge David Baime, from the intermediate appellate court—to review the system. In 1999, based on Judge Baime's recommendations, the court substantially modified the system to reduce its complexity. Specifically, the court abandoned the numerical preponderance and index of outcomes approaches, and significantly modified the salient factors approach by reducing the number of categories and removing subjective judgments from the task of ranking them. The court's current approach to comparative review is described by Judge Baime as follows:

> The salient factor table in force today consists of the statutory aggravating factors ranked in descending order of aggravation determined by the historical frequency of death outcomes. Only

three of the statutory aggravating factors contain subcategories: sexual assaults, robberies and multiple victim cases. Sexual assaults are divided into "aggravated" and "non-aggravated" categories, the former comprised of cases characterized by extreme violence. Robberies are divided into three groups in descending order of aggravation depending upon whether the crime is committed in a residence, a business establishment or other place. Multiple victim cases are divided into "aggravated" and "non-aggravated" subcategories, the former comprised of multiple killings which occur in the commission of some other crime.

Deathworthiness is measured by calculating three ratios, representing significant decision making points in the criminal justice system: (i) the ratio of death sentences to capital penalty trails; (ii) the ratio of death sentences to the total number of "death-eligible" cases in the salient factor category or subgrouping; and (iii) the ratio of capital penalty trials to the total number of "death-eligible" cases in the salient factor category or subgroup. The higher the ratios for a category or subgroup, the more deathworthy the crimes in that category or subgroup, and correspondingly, the more likely the death sentence in a case assigned to that category or subgroup will be considered proportionate. Although the New Jersey Supreme Court has declined to adopt any numerical threshold of disproportionality on the grounds that individualized sentencing and jury mercy militate against reliance on a purely quantitative analysis, the salient factor tests benefits from its "transparency." Deathworthiness of a category of crimes can be easily determined by lawypersons. . . .

[P]recedent-seeking review is the more traditional, less quantitative comparison of factually similar cases. As a general rule, the comparison cases are drawn from the category or subcategory into which the case under review is assigned for the purpose of the salient factors test. While the reliability of the salient factors test is undoubtedly enhanced by the increase in the number of comparable cases in each category, the corresponding growth in the number of cases to be examined, at a certain point, tends to render precedent-seeking review unwieldy. To avoid this problem, [the "master" appointed by the Supreme Court to assist the comparative review process] recommends comparison cases after hearing arguments from the parties. A bench memorandum is prepared for the Supreme Court, setting forth summaries of the parties' arguments, the [master's] recommendations, and an appendix containing descriptions of the cases upon which the parties agree and descriptions of the cases upon which the parties disagree. Generally, the court utilizes approximately twenty comparison cases in rendering its decision.

The court examines the case under review with the comparison cases, applying three factors: (i) the degree of moral blameworthiness in terms of motive, premeditation, justification or excuse, evidence of mental defect or disturbance, knowledge of helplessness of the victim, the defendant's age or maturity level, and the defendant's involvement in planning the murder; (ii) the degree of victimization, including the violence or brutality of the murder, and the injury to non-decedent victims; and (iii) the character of the defendant in terms of his prior record, involvement in crimes of violence, degree of cooperation, remorse and capacity for rehabilitation. The court makes detailed findings respecting those elements in its opinions.

David Baime, Comparative Proportionality Review in New Jersey, 39 Crim. L. Bull. 227 (2003).[g] For a recent example of comparative review in New Jersey, in which a death sentence was affirmed over two dissents, see New Jersey v. Harris, 757 A.2d 221 (N.J.2000).

**5.** *Godfrey* **Reconsidered.** As previously noted, Godfrey was resentenced to death after the United States Supreme Court remanded the case to the Georgia courts. This time, the sentence rested on the jury's finding that the murder "was committed while the offender was engaged in the commission of another capital felony." On appeal, Godfrey argued that the sentence should have been set aside because death sentences for domestic murders are comparatively rare. In Godfrey v. State, 248 Ga. 616, 284 S.E.2d 422 (1981), the Georgia Supreme Court rejected his contention:

> Appellant [argues] that the death penalty in domestic cases is such a rarity that, considering the mitigation, i.e., lack of prior criminal record and psychiatric history, the death penalty as applied to appellant is disproportionate and is also "unusual" and therefore violates the Eighth and 14th Amendments of the United States Constitution. In reviewing the death penalties in this case, we have considered the cases appealed to this court since January 1, 1970, in which a death or life sentence was imposed. Cases selected for comparison included those involving a death sentence or those involving a life sentence for domestic homicides, that is where the victim was a girlfriend, spouse, or ex-spouse of the perpetrator, or a relative of the girlfriend, spouse, or ex-spouse. As we [have previously noted,] "although lesser sentences than death are frequently imposed in domestic murder cases, it does not follow that the death penalty would not be authorized for the murder of one spouse by another under any circumstances. Some of the more vile, horrible or inhuman homicides have been perpetrated by family members against one another." Since January 1, 1970, juries throughout the state have given the death penalty in seven domestic murder cases.... Therefore, domestic murders are

[g] For a more detailed account of the New Jersey experience, see In the Matter of the Proportionality Review Project, 585 A.2d 358 (N.J. 1990); In re Proportionality Review Project, 735 A.2d 528 (N.J. 1999); Barry Lat-zer, The Failure of Comparative Proportionality Review of Capital Cases (With Lessons from New Jersey), 64 Albany L. Rev. 1161 (2001).

not a "capriciously selected group of offenders." In addition, multiple murder cases were selected for comparison.... In three of the seven cases in which the death penalty was returned, not only did defendant have no prior record, but also there was a history of prior psychiatric disorder, as in the instant case. Therefore, we find the appellant's sentence to death for murder is not excessive or disproportionate to the penalty imposed in similar cases considering both the crime and the defendant....

Was this a satisfactory response to Godfrey's argument? The court concludes that Godfrey's death sentence was not "capricious" because seven other domestic killers had received death sentences since 1970. Is the court's conclusion supported by the data upon which it relies?

6. *Pulley v. Harris.* Appellate courts in some states have no statutory obligation to conduct comparative review.[h] In Pulley v. Harris, 465 U.S. 37 (1984), the Supreme Court held that comparative review was not constitutionally required so long as the state's statutory scheme otherwise provides adequate safeguards against arbitrary application of the death penalty. The Court concluded that by limiting the death sentence to a "small sub-class of capital-eligible cases," and by specifying a statutory list of "relevant factors" to be considered by the jury at the penalty phase, California had adopted a facially constitutional statute notwithstanding the absence of a requirement for comparative review. Justice White concluded the Court's opinion with the following observations:

> Any capital sentencing scheme may occasionally produce aberrational outcomes. Such inconsistencies are a far cry from the major systemic defects identified in *Furman*. As we have acknowledged in the past, "there can be 'no perfect procedure for deciding in which cases governmental authority should be used to impose death.'" As we are presently informed, we cannot say that the California procedures provided Harris inadequate protection against the evil identified in *Furman*.

Justice Stevens wrote a separate concurring opinion, agreeing with the Court's conclusion that comparative review is not constitutionally required but emphasizing that "some form of meaningful appellate review is an essential safeguard against the arbitrary and capricious imposition of death sentences by individual juries and judges." Justices Brennan and Marshall dissented. They argued that comparative review should be constitutionally required because it "serves to eliminate some, if only a small part, of the irrationality that infects the current imposition of death sentences in the United States," and that judicial experience demonstrates "that such review can be administered without much difficulty...."

7. **Efficacy of Comparative Review.** Although the courts of most states exercise comparative review, they have set aside very few death sentences on the basis of comparative excessiveness. How should this experience be interpreted? Does it show that comparative review cannot

---

[h] The courts in some of these states do conduct a case-by-case proportionality review.

work? Does it show that comparative review is exercised deficiently by most courts? Or does it show that comparative review is superfluous in light of other safeguards against arbitrary sentences?

---

## SUBSECTION C: RACE AND THE DEATH PENALTY

---

## McCleskey v. Kemp
Supreme Court of the United States, 1987.
481 U.S. 279.

■ JUSTICE POWELL delivered the opinion of the Court.

This case presents the question whether a complex statistical study that indicates a risk that racial considerations enter into capital sentencing determinations proves that petitioner McCleskey's capital sentence is unconstitutional under the Eighth or 14th Amendment.

### I

McCleskey, a black man, was convicted of two counts of armed robbery and one count of murder in the Superior Court of Fulton County, Georgia, on October 12, 1978. McCleskey's convictions arose out of the robbery of a furniture store and the killing of a white police officer during the course of the robbery. The evidence at trial indicated that McCleskey and three accomplices planned and carried out the robbery. All four were armed. McCleskey entered the front of the store while the other three entered the rear. McCleskey secured the front of the store by rounding up the customers and forcing them to lie face down on the floor. The other three rounded up the employees in the rear and tied them up with tape. The manager was forced at gunpoint to turn over the store receipts, his watch, and six dollars. During the course of the robbery, a police officer, answering a silent alarm, entered the store through the front door. As he was walking down the center aisle of the store, two shots were fired. Both struck the officer. One hit him in the face and killed him.

Several weeks later, McCleskey was arrested in connection with an unrelated offense. He confessed that he had participated in the furniture store robbery, but denied that he had shot the police officer. At trial, the state introduced evidence that at least one of the bullets that struck the officer was fired from a .38 caliber Rossi revolver. This description matched the description of the gun that McCleskey had carried during the robbery. The state also introduced the testimony of two witnesses who had heard McCleskey admit to the shooting.

The jury convicted McCleskey of murder.[1] At the penalty hearing,[2] the jury heard arguments as to the appropriate sentence. Under Georgia law,

---

[1] The Georgia Code contains only one degree of murder. A person commits murder "when he unlawfully and with malice aforethought, either express or implied, causes the

the jury could not consider imposing the death penalty unless it found beyond a reasonable doubt that the murder was accompanied by one of the statutory aggravating circumstances. The jury in this case found two aggravating circumstances to exist beyond a reasonable doubt: the murder was committed during the course of an armed robbery; and the murder was committed upon a peace officer engaged in the performance of his duties. In making its decision whether to impose the death sentence, the jury considered the mitigating and aggravating circumstances of McCleskey's conduct. McCleskey offered no mitigating evidence. The jury recommended that he be sentenced to death on the murder charge and to consecutive life sentences on the armed robbery charges. The court followed the jury's recommendation and sentenced McCleskey to death.

[McCleskey's death sentence was affirmed on direct appeal and in state habeas corpus proceedings, and he next filed a habeas corpus petition in the federal district court.] His petition raised 18 claims, one of which was that the Georgia capital sentencing process is administered in a racially discriminatory manner in violation of the Eighth and 14th Amendments to the United States constitution. In support of his claim, McCleskey proffered a statistical study performed by Professors David C. Baldus, Charles Pulaski, and George Woodworth (the Baldus study) that purports to show a disparity in the imposition of the death sentence in Georgia based on the race of the murder victim and, to a lesser extent, the race of the defendant. The Baldus study is actually two sophisticated statistical studies that examine over 2,000 murder cases that occurred in Georgia during the 1970s. The raw numbers collected by Professor Baldus indicate that defendants charged with killing white persons received the death penalty in 11 percent of the cases, but defendants charged with killing blacks received the death penalty in only one percent of the cases. The raw numbers also indicate a reverse racial disparity according to the race of the defendant: four percent of the black defendants received the death penalty, as opposed to seven percent of the white defendants.

Baldus also divided the cases according to the combination of the race of the defendant and the race of the victim. He found that the death penalty was assessed in 22 percent of the cases involving black defendants and white victims; eight percent of the cases involving white defendants and white victims; one percent of the cases involving black defendants and

---

death of another human being." Ga. Code Ann. § 16–5–1(a) (1984). A person convicted of murder "shall be punished by death or by imprisonment for life." § 16–5–1(d).

2 Georgia Code Ann. § 17–10–2(c) (1982) provides that when a jury convicts a defendant of murder, "the court shall resume the trial and conduct a presentence hearing before the jury." This subsection suggests that a defendant convicted of murder always is subjected to a penalty hearing at which the jury considers imposing a death sentence. But as a matter of practice, penalty hearings seem to be held only if the prosecutor affirmatively seeks the death penalty. If he does not, the defendant receives a sentence of life imprisonment. See David C. Baldus, Charles R. Pulaski, Jr., and George Woodworth, Comparative Review of Death Sentences: An Empirical Study of the Georgia Experience, 74 J. Crim. L. & C. 661, 674, n. 56 (1983).

black victims; and three percent of the cases involving white defendants and black victims. Similarly, Baldus found that prosecutors sought the death penalty in 70 percent of the cases involving black defendants and white victims; 32 percent of the cases involving white defendants and white victims; 15 percent of the cases involving black defendants and black victims; and 19 percent of the cases involving white defendants and black victims.

Baldus subjected his data to an extensive analysis, taking account of 230 variables that could have explained the disparities on nonracial grounds. One of his models concludes that, even after taking account of 39 nonracial variables, defendants charged with killing white victims were 4.3 times as likely to receive a death sentence as defendants charged with killing blacks. According to this model, black defendants were 1.1 times as likely to receive a death sentence as other defendants. Thus, the Baldus study indicates that black defendants, such as McCleskey, who kill white victims have the greatest likelihood of receiving the death penalty.[5]

The district court held an extensive evidentiary hearing on McCleskey's petition.... It concluded that McCleskey's "statistics do not demonstrate a prima facie case in support of the contention that the death penalty was imposed upon him because of his race, because of the race of the victim, or because of any Eighth Amendment concern." As to McCleskey's 14th Amendment claim, the court found that the methodology of the Baldus study was flawed in several respects. Because of these defects, the court held that the Baldus study "fail[ed] to contribute anything of value" to McCleskey's claim. Accordingly, the court denied the petition insofar as it was based upon the Baldus study.

The Court of Appeals for the Eleventh Circuit, sitting en banc, carefully reviewed the district court's decision on McCleskey's claim. It assumed the validity of the study itself and addressed the merits of McCleskey's Eighth and 14th Amendment claims. That is, the court assumed that the study "showed that systematic and substantial disparities existed in the penalties imposed upon homicide defendants in Georgia based on race of the homicide victim, that the disparities existed at a less substantial rate in death sentencing based on race of defendants, and that the factors of race of the victim and defendant were at work in Fulton County." Even assuming the study's validity, the court of appeals found the statistics "insufficient to demonstrate discriminatory intent or unconstitutional dis-

---

[5] Baldus' 230–variable model divided cases into eight different ranges, according to the estimated aggravation level of the offense. Baldus argued in his testimony to the district court that the effects of racial bias were most striking in the midrange cases. "When the cases become tremendously aggravated so that everybody would agree that if we're going to have a death sentence, these are the cases that should get it, the race effects go away. It's only in the mid-range of cases where the decision-makers have a real choice as to what to do. If there's room for the exercise of discretion, then the [racial] factors begin to play a role." Under this model, Baldus found that 14.4 percent of the black-victim midrange cases received the death penalty, and 34.4 percent of the white-victim cases received the death penalty. According to Baldus, the facts of McCleskey's case placed it within the midrange.

crimination in the 14th Amendment context, [and] insufficient to show irrationality, arbitrariness and capriciousness under any kind of Eighth Amendment analysis." . . .

The Court of Appeals affirmed the denial by the district court of McCleskey's petition for a writ of habeas corpus insofar as the petition was based upon the Baldus study, with three judges dissenting as to McCleskey's claims based on the Baldus study. We granted certiorari and now affirm.

[The Court rejected McClesky's equal protection challenge to Georgia's capital sentencing statute on the ground that the evidence failed to show either that any of the decision-makers in his case acted with a discriminatory purpose or that the Georgia Legislature had enacted or perpetuated its capital sentencing statute to further a racially discriminatory purpose. The court then turned to his Eighth Amendment claim.]

In light of our precedents under the Eighth Amendment, McCleskey cannot argue successfully that his sentence is "disproportionate to the crime in the traditional sense." See Pulley v. Harris, 465 U.S. 37, 43 (1984). He does not deny that he committed a murder in the course of a planned robbery, a crime for which this Court has determined that the death penalty constitutionally may be imposed. Gregg v. Georgia, 428 U.S. 153, 187 (1976). His disproportionality claim "is of a different sort." *Pulley v. Harris*, supra. McCleskey argues that the sentence in his case is disproportionate to the sentences in other murder cases.

On the one hand, he cannot base a constitutional claim on an argument that his case differs from other cases in which defendants did receive the death penalty. On automatic appeal, the Georgia Supreme Court found that McCleskey's death sentence was not disproportionate to other death sentences imposed in the state. The court supported this conclusion with an appendix containing citations to 13 cases involving generally similar murders. See Ga. Code Ann. § 17–10–35(e) (1982). Moreover, where the statutory procedures adequately channel the sentencer's discretion, such proportionality review is not constitutionally required. *Pulley v. Harris*, supra.

On the other hand, absent a showing that the Georgia capital punishment system operates in an arbitrary and capricious manner, McCleskey cannot prove a constitutional violation by demonstrating that other defendants who may be similarly situated did not receive the death penalty. In *Gregg*, the Court confronted the argument that "the opportunities for discretionary action that are inherent in the processing of any murder case under Georgia law," specifically the opportunities for discretionary leniency, rendered the capital sentences imposed arbitrary and capricious. We rejected this contention:

> The existence of these discretionary stages is not determinative of the issues before us. At each of these stages an actor in the criminal justice system makes a decision which may remove a defendant from consideration as a candidate for the death penalty.

*Furman*, in contrast, dealt with the decision to impose the death sentence on a specific individual who had been convicted of a capital offense. Nothing in any of our cases suggests that the decision to afford an individual defendant mercy violates the constitution. *Furman* held only that, in order to minimize the risk that the death penalty would be imposed on a capriciously selected group of offenders, the decision to impose it had to be guided by standards so that the sentencing authority would focus on the particularized circumstances of the crime and the defendant.[28]

Because McCleskey's sentence was imposed under Georgia sentencing procedures that focus discretion "on the particularized nature of the crime and the particularized characteristics of the individual defendant," we lawfully may presume that McCleskey's death sentence was not "wantonly and freakishly" imposed, and thus that the sentence is not disproportionate within any recognized meaning under the Eighth Amendment.

Although our decision in *Gregg* as to the facial validity of the Georgia capital punishment statute appears to foreclose McCleskey's disproportionality argument, he further contends that the Georgia capital punishment system is arbitrary and capricious in application, and therefore his sentence is excessive, because racial considerations may influence capital sentencing decisions in Georgia. We now address this claim.

To evaluate McCleskey's challenge, we must examine exactly what the Baldus study may show. Even Professor Baldus does not contend that his statistics *prove* that race enters into any capital sentencing decisions or that race was a factor in McCleskey's particular case. Statistics at most may show only a likelihood that a particular factor entered into some decisions. There is, of course, some risk of racial prejudice influencing a jury's decision in a criminal case. There are similar risks that other kinds of prejudice will influence other criminal trials. The question "is at what point that risk becomes constitutionally unacceptable." McCleskey asks us to accept the likelihood allegedly shown by the Baldus study as the constitutional measure of an unacceptable risk of racial prejudice influencing capital sentencing decisions. This we decline to do.

Because of the risk that the factor of race may enter the criminal justice process, we have engaged in "unceasing efforts" to eradicate racial prejudice from our criminal justice system. Batson v. Kentucky, 476 U.S.

---

[28] The constitution is not offended by inconsistency in results based on the objective circumstances of the crime. Numerous legitimate factors may influence the outcome of a trial and a defendant's ultimate sentence, even though they may be irrelevant to his actual guilt. If sufficient evidence to link a suspect to a crime cannot be found, he will not be charged. The capability of the responsible law enforcement agency can vary widely. Also, the strength of the available evidence remains a variable throughout the criminal justice process and may influence a prosecutor's decision to offer a plea bargain or to go to trial. Witness availability, credibility, and memory also influence the results of prosecutions. Finally, sentencing in state courts is generally discretionary, so a defendant's ultimate sentence necessarily will vary according to the judgment of the sentencing authority. The foregoing factors necessarily exist in varying degrees throughout our criminal justice system.

79, 85 (1986).[30] Our efforts have been guided by our recognition that "the inestimable privilege of trial by jury . . . is a vital principle, underlying the whole administration of criminal justice." Thus, it is the jury that is a criminal defendant's fundamental "protection of life and liberty against race or color prejudice." Strauder v. West Virginia, 100 U.S. 303, 309 (1880). Specifically, a capital sentencing jury representative of a criminal defendant's community assures a " 'diffused impartiality,' " in the jury's task of "express[ing] the conscience of the community on the ultimate question of life or death," Witherspoon v. Illinois, 391 U.S. 510, 519 (1968).

Individual jurors bring to their deliberations "qualities of human nature and varieties of human experience, the range of which is unknown and perhaps unknowable." Peters v. Kiff, 407 U.S. 493, 503 (1972) (opinion of Marshall, J.). The capital sentencing decision requires the individual jurors to focus their collective judgment on the unique characteristics of a particular criminal defendant. It is not surprising that such collective judgments often are difficult to explain. But the inherent lack of predictability of jury decisions does not justify their condemnation. On the contrary, it is the jury's function to make the difficult and uniquely human judgments that defy codification and that "buil[d] discretion, equity, and flexibility into a legal system." Harry Kalven and Hans Zeisel, The American Jury 498 (1966).

McCleskey's argument that the constitution condemns the discretion allowed decisionmakers in the Georgia capital sentencing system is antithetical to the fundamental role of discretion in our criminal justice system. Discretion in the criminal justice system offers substantial benefits to the criminal defendant. Not only can a jury decline to impose the death sentence, it can decline to convict, or choose to convict of a lesser offense. Whereas decisions against a defendant's interest may be reversed by the trial judge or on appeal, these discretionary exercises of leniency are final and unreviewable. Similarly, the capacity of prosecutorial discretion to provide individualized justice is "firmly entrenched in American law." As we have noted, a prosecutor can decline to charge, offer a plea bargain, or decline to seek a death sentence in any particular case. Of course, "the power to be lenient [also] is the power to discriminate," but a capital-punishment system that did not allow for discretionary acts of leniency

---

[30] This Court has repeatedly stated that prosecutorial discretion cannot be exercised on the basis of race. Nor can a prosecutor exercise peremptory challenges on the basis of race. Batson v. Kentucky, 476 U.S. 79 (1986). More generally, this Court has condemned state efforts to exclude blacks from grand and petit juries. Vasquez v. Hillery, 474 U.S. 254 (1986). . . .

Other protections apply to the trial and jury deliberation process. Widespread bias in the community can make a change of venue constitutionally required. The constitution prohibits racially biased prosecutorial arguments. If the circumstances of a particular case indicate a significant likelihood that racial bias may influence a jury, the constitution requires questioning as to such bias. Finally, in a capital sentencing hearing, a defendant convicted of an interracial murder is entitled to such questioning without regard to the circumstances of the particular case. Turner v. Murray, 476 U.S. 28 (1986).

"would be totally alien to our notions of criminal justice." *Gregg v. Georgia*.

At most, the Baldus study indicates a discrepancy that appears to correlate with race. Apparent disparities in sentencing are an inevitable part of our criminal justice system.[35] The discrepancy indicated by the Baldus study is "a far cry from the major systemic defects identified in *Furman*," *Pulley v. Harris*, supra.[36] As this Court has recognized, any mode for determining guilt or punishment "has its weaknesses and the potential for misuse." Specifically, "there can be 'no perfect procedure for deciding in which cases governmental authority should be used to impose death.' " Despite these imperfections, our consistent rule has been that constitutional guarantees are met when "the mode [for determining guilt or punishment] itself has been surrounded with safeguards to make it as fair as possible." Where the discretion that is fundamental to our criminal process is involved, we decline to assume that what is unexplained is invidious. In light of the safeguards designed to minimize racial bias in the process, the fundamental value of jury trial in our criminal justice system, and the benefits that discretion provides to criminal defendants, we hold that the Baldus study does not demonstrate a constitutionally significant risk of racial bias affecting the Georgia capital-sentencing process.

Two additional concerns inform our decision in this case. First, McCleskey's claim, taken to its logical conclusion, throws into serious question the principles that underlie our entire criminal justice system. The Eighth Amendment is not limited in application to capital punishment, but applies to all penalties. Solem v. Helm, 463 U.S. 277 (1983). Thus, if we accepted McCleskey's claim that racial bias has impermissibly tainted the capital sentencing decision, we could soon be faced with similar claims as to other types of penalty.[38] Moreover, the claim that his sentence rests on the irrelevant factor of race easily could be extended to apply to claims based

[35] Congress has acknowledged that existence of such discrepancies in criminal sentences, and in 1984 created the United States Sentencing Commission to develop sentencing guidelines. The objective of the guidelines "is to avoid *unwarranted* sentencing disparities among defendants with similar records who have been found guilty of similar criminal conduct, while maintaining sufficient flexibility to permit individualized sentencing when warranted by mitigating or aggravating factors not taken into account in the guidelines." 52 Fed. Reg. 3920 (1987) (emphasis added). No one contends that all sentencing disparities can be eliminated. The guidelines, like the safeguards in the *Gregg*-type statute, further an essential need of the Anglo–American criminal justice system—to balance the desirability of a high degree of uniformity against the necessity for the exercise of discretion.

[36] The Baldus study in fact confirms that the Georgia system results in a reasonable level of proportionality among the class of murderers eligible for the death penalty. As Professor Baldus confirmed, the system sorts out cases where the sentence of death is highly likely and highly unlikely, leaving a mid-range of cases where the imposition of the death penalty in any particular case is less predictable.

[38] Studies already exist that allegedly demonstrate a racial disparity in the length of prison sentences. See, e.g., Cassia Spohn, John Gruhl, and Susan Welch, The Effect of Race on Sentencing: A Reexamination of an Unsettled Question, 16 Law & Soc. Rev. 71 (1981–1982); James D. Unnever, Charles E. Frazier, and John C. Henretta, Race Differences in Criminal Sentencing, 21 Sociological Q. 197 (1980).

on unexplained discrepancies that correlate to membership in other minority groups, and even to gender. Similarly, since McCleskey's claim relates to the race of his victim, other claims could apply with equally logical force to statistical disparities that correlate with the race or sex of other actors in the criminal justice system, such as defense attorneys, or judges. Also, there is no logical reason that such a claim need be limited to racial or sexual bias. If arbitrary and capricious punishment is the touchstone under the Eighth Amendment, such a claim could at least in theory be based upon any arbitrary variable, such as the defendant's facial characteristics, or the physical attractiveness of the defendant or the victim, that some statistical study indicates may be influential in jury decisionmaking. As these examples illustrate, there is no limiting principle to the type of challenge brought by McCleskey. The constitution does not require that a state eliminate any demonstrable disparity that correlates with a potentially irrelevant factor in order to operate a criminal justice system that includes capital punishment. As we have stated specifically in the context of capital punishment, the Constitution does not "plac[e] totally unrealistic conditions on its use." *Gregg v. Georgia.*

Second, McCleskey's arguments are best presented to the legislative bodies. It is not the responsibility—or indeed even the right—of this Court to determine the appropriate punishment for particular crimes. It is the legislatures, the elected representatives of the people, that are "constituted to respond to the will and consequently the moral values of the people." Legislatures also are better qualified to weigh and "evaluate the results of statistical studies in terms of their own local conditions and with a flexibility of approach that is not available to the courts." Capital punishment is now the law in more than two thirds of our states. It is the ultimate duty of courts to determine on a case-by-case basis whether these laws are applied consistently with the constitution. Despite McCleskey's wide ranging arguments that basically challenge the validity of capital punishment in our multi-racial society, the only question before us is whether in his case, the law of Georgia was properly applied. We agree with the district court and the Court of Appeals for the Eleventh Circuit that this was carefully and correctly done in this case. . . .

■ JUSTICE BRENNAN, with whom JUSTICE MARSHALL joins, and with whom JUSTICE BLACKMUN and JUSTICE STEVENS join in all but Part I, dissenting.

I

Adhering to my view that the death penalty is in all circumstances cruel and unusual punishment forbidden by the Eighth and 14th Amendments, I would vacate the decision below insofar as it left undisturbed the death sentence imposed in this case. Gregg v. Georgia, 428 U.S. 153, 227 (1976) (Brennan, J., dissenting). The Court observes that "the *Gregg*-type statute imposes unprecedented safeguards in the special context of capital punishment," which "ensure a degree of care in the imposition of the death penalty that can be described only as unique." Notwithstanding these efforts, murder defendants in Georgia with white victims are more than four times as likely to receive the death sentence as are defendants with black victims. Nothing could convey more powerfully the intractable reality of the death penalty: "that the effort to eliminate arbitrariness in the infliction of that ultimate sanction is so plainly doomed to failure that it—and the death penalty—must be abandoned altogether." Godfrey v. Georgia, 446 U.S. 420, 442 (1980) (Marshall, J., concurring in judgment).

Even if I did not hold this position, however, I would reverse the Court of Appeals, for petitioner McCleskey has clearly demonstrated that his death sentence was imposed in violation of the Eighth and 14th Amendments. . . .

## II

At some point in this case, Warren McCleskey doubtless asked his lawyer whether a jury was likely to sentence him to die. A candid reply to this question would have been disturbing. First, counsel would have to tell McCleskey that few of the details of the crime or of McCleskey's past criminal conduct were more important than the fact that his victim was white. Furthermore, counsel would feel bound to tell McCleskey that defendants charged with killing white victims in Georgia are 4.3 times as likely to be sentenced to death as defendants charged with killing blacks. In addition, frankness would compel the disclosure that it was more likely than not that the race of McCleskey's victim would determine whether he received a death sentence: six of every 11 defendants convicted of killing a white person would not have received the death penalty if their victims had been black, while, among defendants with aggravating and mitigating factors comparable to McCleskey's, 20 of every 34 would not have been sentenced to die if their victims had been black. Finally, the assessment would not be complete without the information that cases involving black defendants and white victims are more likely to result in a death sentence than cases featuring any other racial combination of defendant and victim. The story could be told in a variety of ways, but McCleskey could not fail to grasp its essential narrative line: there was a significant chance that race would play a prominent role in determining if he lived or died.

The Court today holds that Warren McCleskey's sentence was constitutionally imposed. It finds no fault in a system in which lawyers must tell their clients that race casts a large shadow on the capital sentencing process. The Court arrives at this conclusion by stating that the Baldus study cannot "prove that race enters into any capital sentencing decisions or that race was a factor in McCleskey's particular case." Since, according to Professor Baldus, we cannot say "to a moral certainty" that race influenced a decision, we can identify only "a likelihood that a particular factor entered into some decisions," and "a discrepancy that appears to correlate with race." This "likelihood" and "discrepancy," holds the Court, is insufficient to establish a constitutional violation. The Court reaches this conclusion by placing four factors on the scales opposite McCleskey's evidence: the desire to encourage sentencing discretion, the existence of "statutory safeguards" in the Georgia scheme, the fear of encouraging widespread challenges to other sentencing decisions, and the limits of the judicial role. The Court's evaluation of the significance of petitioner's evidence is fundamentally at odds with our consistent concern for rationality in capital sentencing, and the considerations that the majority invokes to discount that evidence cannot justify ignoring its force.

### III.A.

... The Court assumes the statistical validity of the Baldus study, and acknowledges that McCleskey has demonstrated a risk that racial prejudice plays a role in capital sentencing in Georgia. Nonetheless, it finds the probability of prejudice insufficient to create constitutional concern. Close analysis of the Baldus study, however, in light of both statistical principles and human experience, reveals that the risk that race influenced McCleskey's sentence is intolerable by any imaginable standard.

### B.

The Baldus study indicates that, after taking into account some 230 nonracial factors that might legitimately influence a sentencer, the jury more likely than not would have spared McCleskey's life had his victim been black. The study distinguishes between those cases in which (1) the jury exercises virtually no discretion because the strength or weakness of aggravating factors usually suggests that only one outcome is appropriate;[2] and (2) cases reflecting an "intermediate" level of aggravation, in which the jury has considerable discretion in choosing a sentence.[3] McCleskey's case falls into the intermediate range. In such cases, death is imposed in 34 percent of white-victim crimes and 14 percent of black-victim crimes, a difference of 139 percent in the rate of imposition of the death penalty. In other words, just under 59 percent—almost six in 10—defendants comparable to McCleskey would not have received the death penalty if their victims had been black.[4]

---

[2] The first two and the last of the study's eight case categories represent those cases in which the jury typically sees little leeway in deciding on a sentence. Cases in the first two categories are those that feature aggravating factors so minimal that juries imposed no death sentences in the 88 cases with these factors during the period of the study. Cases in the Eighth category feature aggravating factors so extreme that the jury imposed the death penalty in 88 percent of the 58 cases with these factors in the same period. Ibid.

[3] In the five categories characterized as intermediate, the rate at which the death penalty was imposed ranged from eight percent to 41 percent. The overall rate for the 326 cases in these categories was 20 percent.

[4] The considerable racial disparity in sentencing rates among these cases is consistent with the "liberation hypothesis" of H. Kalven and H. Zeisel in their landmark work, The American Jury (1966). These authors found that, in close cases in which jurors were most often in disagreement, "the closeness of the evidence makes it possible for the jury to respond to sentiment by liberating it from the discipline of the evidence." While "the jury does not often consciously and explicitly yield to sentiment in the teeth of the law ... it yields to sentiment in the apparent process of resolving doubts as to evidence. The jury, therefore, is able to conduct its revolt from the law within the etiquette of resolving issues of fact." Thus, it is those cases in which sentencing evidence seems to dictate neither

Furthermore, even examination of the sentencing system as a whole, factoring in those cases in which the jury exercises little discretion, indicates the influence of race on capital sentencing. For the Georgia system as a whole, race accounts for a six percentage point difference in the rate at which capital punishment is imposed. Since death is imposed in 11 percent of all white-victim cases, the rate in comparably aggravated black-victim cases is five percent. The rate of capital sentencing in a white-victim case is thus 120 percent greater than the rate in a black-victim case. Put another way, over half—55 percent—of defendants in white-victim crimes in Georgia would not have been sentenced to die if their victims had been black. Of the more than 200 variables potentially relevant to a sentencing decision, race of the victim is a powerful explanation for variation in death sentence rates—as powerful as nonracial aggravating factors such as a prior murder conviction or acting as the principal planner of the homicide.[5]

These adjusted figures are only the most conservative indication of the risk that race will influence the death sentences of defendants in Georgia. Data unadjusted for the mitigating or aggravating effect of other factors show an even more pronounced disparity by race. The capital sentencing rate for all white-victim cases was almost 11 times greater than the rate for black-victim cases. Furthermore, blacks who kill whites are sentenced to death at nearly 22 times the rate of blacks who kill blacks, and more than seven times the rate of whites who kill blacks. In addition, prosecutors seek the death penalty for 70 percent of black defendants with white victims, but for only 15 percent of black defendants with black victims, and only 19 percent of white defendants with black victims. Since our decision upholding the Georgia capital sentencing system in *Gregg*, the state has executed seven persons. All of the seven were convicted of killing whites, and six of the seven executed were black.[6] Such execution figures are especially striking in light of the fact that, during the period encompassed by the Baldus study, only 9.2 percent of Georgia homicides involved black defendants and white victims, while 60.7 percent involved black victims....

The statistical evidence in this case thus relentlessly documents the risk that McCleskey's sentence was influenced by racial considerations. This evidence shows that there is a better than even chance in Georgia that race will influence the decision to impose the death penalty: a majority of defendants in white-victim crimes would not have been sentenced to die if their victims had been black. In determining whether this risk is acceptable, our judgment must be shaped by the awareness that "the risk of racial prejudice infecting a capital sentencing proceeding is especially serious in light of the complete finality of the death sentence," Turner v. Murray, 476 U.S. 28, 35 (1986), and that "it is of vital importance to the

life imprisonment nor the death penalty that impermissible factors such as race play the most prominent role.

[5] The fact that a victim was white accounts for a nine percentage point difference in the rate at which the death penalty is imposed, which is the same difference attrib-

utable to a prior murder conviction or the fact that the defendant was the "prime mover" in planning a murder.

[6] NAACP Legal Defense and Educational Fund, Death Row, U. S. A. 4 (Aug. 1, 1986).

defendant and to the community that any decision to impose the death sentence be, and appear to be, based on reason rather than caprice or emotion." Gardner v. Florida, 430 U.S. 349, 358 (1977). In determining the guilt of a defendant, a state must prove its case beyond a reasonable doubt. That is, we refuse to convict if the chance of error is simply less likely than not. Surely, we should not be willing to take a person's life if the chance that his death sentence was irrationally imposed is more likely than not. In light of the gravity of the interest at stake, petitioner's statistics on their face are a powerful demonstration of the type of risk that our Eighth Amendment jurisprudence has consistently condemned.

C.

Evaluation of McCleskey's evidence cannot rest solely on the numbers themselves. We must also ask whether the conclusion suggested by those numbers is consonant with our understanding of history and human experience. Georgia's legacy of a race-conscious criminal justice system, as well as this Court's own recognition of the persistent danger that racial attitudes may affect criminal proceedings, indicates that McCleskey's claim is not a fanciful product of mere statistical artifice.

For many years, Georgia operated openly and formally precisely the type of dual system the evidence shows is still effectively in place. The criminal law expressly differentiated between crimes committed by and against blacks and whites, distinctions whose lineage traced back to the time of slavery. During the colonial period, black slaves who killed whites in Georgia, regardless of whether in self-defense or in defense of another, were automatically executed. A. Leon Higginbotham, Jr., In the Matter of Color: Race in the American Legal Process 256 (1978).

By the time of the Civil War, a dual system of crime and punishment was well established in Georgia. See Ga. Penal Code (1861). The state criminal code contained separate sections for "Slaves and Free Persons of Color," and for all other persons. The code provided, for instance, for an automatic death sentence for murder committed by blacks, but declared that anyone else convicted of murder might receive life imprisonment if the conviction were founded solely on circumstantial testimony or simply if the jury so recommended. The code established that the rape of a free white female by a black "shall be" punishable by death. However, rape by anyone else of a free white female was punishable by a prison term not less than two nor more than 20 years. The rape of blacks was punishable "by fine and imprisonment, at the discretion of the court." A black convicted of assaulting a free white person with intent to murder could be put to death at the discretion of the court, but the same offense committed against a black, slave or free, was classified as a "minor" offense whose punishment lay in the discretion of the court, as long as such punishment did not "extend to life, limb, or health." Assault with intent to murder by a white person was punishable by a prison term of from two to 10 years. While sufficient provocation could reduce a charge of murder to manslaughter, the code provided that "obedience and submission being the duty of a slave, much greater provocation is necessary to reduce a homicide of a white person by him to voluntary manslaughter, than is prescribed for white persons."

In more recent times, some 40 years ago, Gunnar Myrdal's epochal study of American race relations produced findings mirroring McCleskey's evidence:

> As long as only Negroes are concerned and no whites are disturbed, great leniency will be shown in most cases.... The sentences for even major crimes are ordinarily reduced when the victim is another Negro....

> For offenses which involve any actual or potential danger to whites, however, Negroes are punished more severely than whites....

> On the other hand, it is quite common for a white criminal to be set free if his crime was against a Negro. Gunnar Myrdal, An American Dilemma 551–553 (1944).

This Court has invalidated portions of the Georgia capital sentencing system three times over the past 15 years. The specter of race discrimination was acknowledged by the Court in striking down the Georgia death penalty statute in *Furman*....

Five years later, the Court struck down the imposition of the death penalty in Georgia for the crime of rape. Coker v. Georgia, 433 U.S. 584 (1977). Although the Court did not explicitly mention race, the decision had to have been informed by the specific observations on rape by both the Chief Justice and Justice Powell in *Furman*. Furthermore, evidence submitted to the Court indicated that black men who committed rape, particularly of white women, were considerably more likely to be sentenced to death than white rapists. For instance, by 1977 Georgia had executed 62 men for rape since the federal government began compiling statistics in 1930. Of these men, 58 were black and 4 were white....

[This] historical review of Georgia criminal law is not intended as a bill of indictment calling the state to account for past transgressions. Citation of past practices does not justify the automatic condemnation of current ones. But it would be unrealistic to ignore the influence of history in assessing the plausible implications of McCleskey's evidence....

The ongoing influence of history is acknowledged, as the majority observes, by our " 'unceasing efforts' to eradicate racial prejudice from our criminal justice system." These efforts, however, signify not the elimination of the problem but its persistence. Our cases reflect a realization of the myriad of opportunities for racial considerations to influence criminal proceedings: in the exercise of peremptory challenges, Batson v. Kentucky, 476 U.S. 79 (1986); in the selection of the grand jury, Vasquez v. Hillery, 474 U.S. 254 (1986); in the selection of the petit jury, Whitus v. Georgia, 385 U.S. 545 (1967); in the exercise of prosecutorial discretion, Wayte v. United States, 470 U.S. 598 (1985); in the conduct of argument, Donnelly v. DeChristoforo, 416 U.S. 637 (1974); and in the conscious or unconscious bias of jurors, Turner v. Murray, 476 U.S. 28 (1986); Ristaino v. Ross, 424 U.S. 589 (1976).

The discretion afforded prosecutors and jurors in the Georgia capital sentencing system creates such opportunities. No guidelines govern prose-cutorial decisions to seek the death penalty, and Georgia provides juries with no list of aggravating and mitigating factors, nor any standard for balancing them against one another. Once a jury identifies one aggravating factor, it has complete discretion in choosing life or death, and need not articulate its basis for selecting life imprisonment. The Georgia sentencing system therefore provides considerable opportunity for racial consider-ations, however subtle and unconscious, to influence charging and sentenc-ing decisions.

History and its continuing legacy thus buttress the probative force of McCleskey's statistics. Formal dual criminal laws may no longer be in effect, and intentional discrimination may no longer be prominent. None-theless, as we acknowledged in *Turner*, "subtle, less consciously held racial attitudes" continue to be of concern and the Georgia system gives such attitudes considerable room to operate. The conclusions drawn from McCleskey's statistical evidence are therefore consistent with the lessons of social experience.

The majority thus misreads our Eighth Amendment jurisprudence in concluding that McCleskey has not demonstrated a degree of risk sufficient to raise constitutional concern. The determination of the significance of his evidence is at its core an exercise in human moral judgment, not a mechanical statistical analysis.... It is true that every nuance of decision cannot be statistically captured, nor can any individual judgment be plumbed with absolute certainty. Yet the fact that we must always act without the illumination of complete knowledge cannot induce paralysis when we confront what is literally an issue of life and death. Sentencing data, history, and experience all counsel that Georgia has provided insuffi-cient assurance of the heightened rationality we have required in order to take a human life.

## IV

The Court cites four reasons for shrinking from the implications of McCleskey's evidence: the desirability of discretion for actors in the crimi-nal justice system, the existence of statutory safeguards against abuse of that discretion, the potential consequences for broader challenges to crimi-nal sentencing, and an understanding of the contours of the judicial role. While these concerns underscore the need for sober deliberation, they do not justify rejecting evidence as convincing as McCleskey has presented....

Our desire for individualized moral judgments may lead us to accept some inconsistencies in sentencing outcomes. Since such decisions are not reducible to mathematical formulae, we are willing to assume that a certain degree of variation reflects the fact that no two defendants are completely alike. There is thus a presumption that actors in the criminal justice system exercise their discretion in responsible fashion, and we do not automatically infer that sentencing patterns that do not comport with ideal rationality are suspect.

As we made clear in Batson v. Kentucky, 476 U.S. 79 (1986), however, that presumption is rebuttable. *Batson* dealt with another arena in which considerable discretion traditionally has been afforded, the exercise of peremptory challenges. Those challenges are normally exercised without any indication whatsoever of the grounds for doing so. The rationale for this deference has been a belief that the unique characteristics of particular prospective jurors may raise concern on the part of the prosecution or defense, despite the fact that counsel may not be able to articulate that concern in a manner sufficient to support exclusion for cause. As with sentencing, therefore, peremptory challenges are justified as an occasion for particularized determinations related to specific individuals, and, as with sentencing, we presume that such challenges normally are not made on the basis of a factor such as race. As we said in *Batson*, however, such features do not justify imposing a "crippling burden of proof," in order to rebut that presumption. The Court in this case apparently seeks to do just that. On the basis of the need for individualized decisions, it rejects evidence, drawn from the most sophisticated capital sentencing analysis ever performed, that reveals that race more likely than not infects capital sentencing decisions. The Court's position converts a rebuttable presumption into a virtually conclusive one. . . .

It has now been over 13 years since Georgia adopted the provisions upheld in *Gregg*. Professor Baldus and his colleagues have compiled data on almost 2,500 homicides committed during the period 1973–79. They have taken into account the influence of 230 nonracial variables, using a multitude of data from the state itself, and have produced striking evidence that the odds of being sentenced to death are significantly greater than average if a defendant is black or his or her victim is white. The challenge to the Georgia system is not speculative or theoretical; it is empirical. As a result, the Court cannot rely on the statutory safeguards in discounting McCleskey's evidence, for it is the very effectiveness of those safeguards that such evidence calls into question. . . .

The Court next states that its unwillingness to regard petitioner's evidence as sufficient is based in part on the fear that recognition of McCleskey's claim would open the door to widespread challenges to all aspects of criminal sentencing. Taken on its face, such a statement seems to suggest a fear of too much justice. Yet surely the majority would acknowledge that if striking evidence indicated that other minority groups, or women, or even persons with blond hair, were disproportionately sentenced to death, such a state of affairs would be repugnant to deeply rooted conceptions of fairness. The prospect that there may be more widespread abuse than McCleskey documents may be dismaying, but it does not justify complete abdication of our judicial role. . . .

In fairness, the Court's fear that McCleskey's claim is an invitation to descend a slippery slope also rests on the realization that any humanly imposed system of penalties will exhibit some imperfection. Yet to reject

McCleskey's powerful evidence on this basis is to ignore both the qualitatively different character of the death penalty and the particular repugnance of racial discrimination, considerations which may properly be taken into account in determining whether various punishments are "cruel and unusual." Furthermore, it fails to take account of the unprecedented refinement and strength of the Baldus study. . . .

Finally, the Court justifies its rejection of McCleskey's claim by cautioning against usurpation of the legislatures' role in devising and monitoring criminal punishment. The Court is, of course, correct to emphasize the gravity of constitutional intervention and the importance that it be sparingly employed. The fact that "capital punishment is now the law in more than two thirds of our states," however, does not diminish the fact that capital punishment is the most awesome act that a state can perform. The judiciary's role in this society counts for little if the use of governmental power to extinguish life does not elicit close scrutiny. . . .

Those whom we would banish from society or from the human community itself often speak in too faint a voice to be heard above society's demand for punishment. It is the particular role of courts to hear these voices, for the constitution declares that the majoritarian chorus may not alone dictate the conditions of social life. The Court thus fulfills, rather than disrupts, the scheme of separation of powers by closely scrutinizing the imposition of the death penalty, for no decision of a society is more deserving of "sober second thought." Harlan F. Stone, The Common Law in the United States, 50 Harv. L. Rev. 4, 25 (1936).

V

At the time our Constitution was framed 200 years ago this year, blacks "had for more than a century before been regarded as beings of an inferior order, and altogether unfit to associate with the white race, either in social or political relations; and so far inferior, that they had no rights which the white man was bound to respect." Dred Scott v. Sandford, 60 U.S. (19 How.) 393, 407 (1857). Only 130 years ago, this Court relied on these observations to deny American citizenship to blacks. A mere three generations ago, this Court sanctioned racial segregation, stating that "if one race be inferior to the other socially, the Constitution of the United States cannot put them upon the same plane." Plessy v. Ferguson, 163 U.S. 537, 552 (1896).

In more recent times, we have sought to free ourselves from the burden of this history. Yet it has been scarcely a generation since this Court's first decision striking down racial segregation, and barely two decades since the legislative prohibition of racial discrimination in major domains of national life. These have been honorable steps, but we cannot pretend that in three decades we have completely escaped the grip of a historical legacy spanning centuries. Warren McCleskey's evidence confronts us with the subtle and persistent influence of the past. His message is a disturbing one to a society that has formally repudiated racism, and a frustrating one to a Nation accustomed to regarding its destiny as the product of its own will. Nonetheless, we ignore him at our peril, for we remain imprisoned by the past as long as we deny its influence in the present.

It is tempting to pretend that minorities on death row share a fate in no way connected to our own, that our treatment of them sounds no echoes beyond the chambers in which they die. Such an illusion is ultimately corrosive, for the reverberations of injustice are not so easily confined. "The destinies of the two races in this country are indissolubly linked together," id., at 560 (Harlan, J., dissenting), and the way in which we choose those who will die reveals the depth of moral commitment among the living.

The Court's decision today will not change what attorneys in Georgia tell other Warren McCleskeys about their chances of execution. Nothing will soften the harsh message they must convey, nor alter the prospect that race undoubtedly will continue to be a topic of discussion. McCleskey's evidence will not have obtained judicial acceptance, but that will not affect what is said on death row. However many criticisms of today's decision may be rendered, these painful conversations will serve as the most eloquent dissents of all.

■ [Justice Blackmun's dissenting opinion has been omitted.]

■ JUSTICE STEVENS, with whom JUSTICE BLACKMUN joins, dissenting. . . .

In this case it is claimed—and the claim is supported by elaborate studies which the Court properly assumes to be valid—that the jury's sentencing process was likely distorted by racial prejudice. The studies demonstrate a strong probability that McCleskey's sentencing jury, which expressed "the community's outrage—its sense that an individual has lost his moral entitlement to live," Spaziano v. Florida, 468 U.S. 447, 469 (1984) (Stevens, J., dissenting)—was influenced by the fact that McCleskey is black and his victim was white, and that this same outrage would not have been generated if he had killed a member of his own race. This sort of disparity is constitutionally intolerable. It flagrantly violates the Court's prior "insistence that capital punishment be imposed fairly, and with reasonable consistency, or not at all." Eddings v. Oklahoma, 455 U.S. 104, 112 (1982).

The Court's decision appears to be based on a fear that the acceptance of McCleskey's claim would sound the death knell for capital punishment in Georgia. If society were indeed forced to choose between a racially discriminatory death penalty (one that provides heightened protection against murder "for whites only") and no death penalty at all, the choice mandated by the constitution would be plain. But the Court's fear is unfounded. One of the lessons of the Baldus study is that there exist certain categories of extremely serious crimes for which prosecutors consistently seek, and juries consistently impose, the death penalty without regard to the race of the victim or the race of the offender. If Georgia were to narrow the class of death-eligible defendants to those categories, the danger of arbitrary and discriminatory imposition of the death penalty would be significantly decreased, if not eradicated. As Justice Brennan has demonstrated in his dissenting opinion, such a restructuring of the sentencing scheme is surely not too high a price to pay.

Like Justice Brennan, I would therefore reverse the judgment of the Court of Appeals. I believe, however, that further proceedings are necessary in order to determine whether McCleskey's death sentence should be set aside. First, the Court of Appeals must decide whether the Baldus study is valid. I am persuaded that it is, but orderly procedure requires that the Court of Appeals address this issue before we actually decide the question. Second, it is necessary for the District Court to determine whether the particular facts of McCleskey's crime and his background place this case within the range of cases that present an unacceptable risk that race played a decisive role in McCleskey's sentencing.

Accordingly, I respectfully dissent.

———

## NOTES ON RACE AND THE DEATH PENALTY

**1. Introduction.** The risk of arbitrariness in capital sentencing condemned in *Furman* has two dimensions: (i) random or capricious decisions that are not grounded in any discernible normative criteria that could justify differential outcomes; and (ii) "discriminatory" decisions that are based on impermissible factors. The preceding materials have focused mainly on the first dimension of *Furman*. *McCleskey* addresses the second.

Empirical studies conducted before *Furman* suggested two respects in which the death penalty may have been discriminatory: first, black defendants were more likely to receive the death penalty than white defendants in the South, although this finding was not consistently demonstrated elsewhere; and second, the death penalty was less likely to be imposed for homicides with black victims than for those with white victims.[a] In 1976, a majority of the Supreme Court expressed confidence that the contemporary generation of capital sentencing statutes had substantially reduced the risk of discrimination in the administration of the death penalty. During the following decade, social scientists sought to test the Court's supposition in studies of sentencing patterns under the post-*Furman* statutes. Although the Baldus study is generally acknowledged to be the most sophisticated of these investigations, other rigorous studies were conducted during the 1970s in Florida,[b]

[a] These studies are summarized in Gary Kleck, Racial Discrimination in Criminal Sentencing: A Critical Evaluation of the Evidence with Additional Evidence on the Death Penalty, 46 Am.Soc.Rev. 783 (1981).

[b] William Bowers and Glenn Pierce, Arbitrariness and Discrimination Under Post–Furman Capital Statutes, 26 Crime and Del-

inq 563 (1980); Michael Radalet, Racial Characteristics and the Imposition of the Death Penalty, 46 Amer. Sociolog. Rev. 918 (1981); Hans Zeisel, Race Bias in the Administration of the Death Penalty: The Florida Experience, 95 Harv. L. Rev. 456 (1981); Linda Foley and Richard Powell, The Discretion of Prosecutors, Judges and Juries in Capital

South Carolina,[c] and North Carolina.[d] This body of research yields a surprisingly consistent pattern: although most investigators found no systematic evidence of discrimination based on race of the defendant, almost all of the studies found a pronounced race-of-victim effect similar to the one found by Baldus and his colleagues.

**2.   The Gross and Mauro Study.** The pervasiveness of the race-of-victim effect is evident in a multi-state study conducted by Samuel Gross and Robert Mauro. They examined death sentencing patterns from 1976 through 1980 in eight states, using data obtained primarily from reports on homicide cases filed by local police agencies with the FBI. The FBI reports included data on: (i) the sex, age, and race of the victim(s); (ii) the sex, age, and race of the suspect(s); (iii) the date and place of the homicide; (iv) the weapon used; (v) the commission of any accompanying felony; and (vi) the relationship between the victim(s) and the suspected killer(s). The findings from this study are described and discussed in Samuel Gross and Robert Mauro, Patterns of Death: An Analysis of Racial Disparities in Capital Sentencing and Homicide Victimization, 37 Stan.L.Rev. 27 (1984). The portions of this article summarized below pertain to the three states (Georgia, Florida, and Illinois) that had the highest number of death sentences.

Gross and Mauro presented their aggregate findings as follows:*

In each state a large proportion of homicide victims in this period were black: a majority in Georgia and Illinois (63.5 percent and 58.6 percent, respectively) and nearly half in Florida (43.3 percent). This is consistent with the national pattern of homicides; blacks and other racial minorities are far more likely than whites to be the victims of homicides.... At the same time, the risk of a death sentence was far lower for those suspects charged with killing black people in Georgia, Florida, and Illinois than for those charged with killing whites. In Georgia, those who killed whites were almost ten times as likely to be sentenced to death as those who killed blacks; in Florida the ratio was about eight to one, and in Illinois about six to one.

In Georgia and Florida, white homicide suspects were, on the whole, about twice as likely to get death sentences as black homicide suspects: 5.5 percent versus 2.9 percent in Georgia, 5.2 percent versus 2.4 percent in Florida. In Illinois, there was a similar but smaller difference.... In each state, however, the relationship between the suspect's race and the likelihood of a

Cases, 7 Crim. Just. Rev. 16 (1982); Steven Arkin, Discrimination and Arbitrariness in Capital Punishment: An Analysis of Post–Furman Murder Cases in Dade County, Florida, 1973–1976, 33 Stan. L. Rev. 75 (1980); William Bowers, The Pervasiveness of Arbitrariness and Discrimination Under Post–Furman Capital Statutes, 74 J. Crim. L. and Criminol. 1067 (1983).

[c] Raymond Paternoster, Prosecutorial Discretion in Requesting the Death Penalty: A Case of Victim–Based Racial Discrimination, 18 L. & Soc'y Rev. 437 (1984).

[d] Barry Nakell and Kenneth Hardy, The Arbitrariness of the Death Penalty (1987).

* The excerpts below are reproduced with permission of the authors and the Stanford Law Review.

death sentence appears to be due entirely to the fact that black suspects were more likely to kill black victims and white suspects were more likely to kill white victims. Indeed, when we control for the race of the victim, blacks who killed whites were several times more likely to be sentenced to death than whites who killed whites in each state.

Next, Gross and Mauro turned to the relation between outcome and the nonracial variables included in the FBI data. They found that three of these factors had a strong aggregate effect on the likelihood of death sentences in each state: the commission of a homicide in the course of another felony, the killing of a stranger, and the killing of multiple victims.[e] They then sought to determine whether the race-of-victim disparities could be explained by any of these nonracial effects:

> (i) Felony circumstances. Although only a minority of all reported homicides in each state involved other felonies—17.5 percent in Georgia, 18.1 percent in Florida, and 27.1 percent in Illinois—the great majority of death sentences fell in this category—over 80 percent in Georgia and Florida, and about 75 percent in Illinois. Among homicides with suspects over fourteen years old, the commission of a separate felony increased the likelihood of a death sentence by a factor of about twelve in Illinois, twenty-six in Georgia, and nearly twenty-four in Florida. . . . Nevertheless, the disparities in capital sentencing by race of victim persist when we control for the felony circumstance of the homicide. For both felony and nonfelony homicides, white-victim cases were far more likely to result in death sentences in each state[:]

TABLE 4

Percentage of Death Sentences by Felony Circumstance and Race of Victim

|  | Georgia | | Florida | | Illinois | |
|---|---|---|---|---|---|---|
|  | Felony | Non-Felony | Felony | Non-Felony | Felony | Non-Felony |
| White Victim | 35.0% (57/163) | 1.9% (10/520) | 27.5% (95/346) | 1.5% (19/1272) | 9.4% (24/256) | 1.2% (11/890) |
| Black Victim | 6.6% (7/106) | 0.4% (5/1165) | 7.0% (9/128) | 0.3% (5/1468) | 3.0% (10/330) | 0% (0/1475) |

> Controlling for both the race of the suspect and felony circumstance does not dilute the capital sentencing disparities by race of victim, but it does change the race of suspect pattern seen in [the aggregated data]. When we consider felony and nonfelony homi-

---

[e] Two other factors (killing a female and using a gun) had less pronounced and less consistent aggregate effects on outcome. In addition, rural homicides were somewhat more likely than urban homicides to result in death sentences in Georgia and Florida, but not in Illinois.

cides separately, there are no substantial differences in capital sentencing rates between blacks who kill whites and whites who kill whites in Florida; in Illinois there is a sizable difference between these two racial groups of suspects among nonfelony homicides, and essentially none among felony homicides; and in Georgia there are disparities between whites who kill whites and blacks who kill whites in both felony and nonfelony homicides . . . . [:]

## TABLE 5

Percentage of Death Sentences by Race of Suspect and Victim and Felony Circumstance

|  | Georgia | | Florida | | Illinois | |
|---|---|---|---|---|---|---|
|  | Felony | Non-Felony | Felony | Non-Felony | Felony | Non-Felony |
| Black Kills White | 38.5% (30/78) | 4.2% (2/48) | 28.8% (32/111) | 2.5% (2/79) | 8.8% (10/114) | 7.2% (6/83) |
| White Kills White | 31.8% (27/85) | 1.7% (8/472) | 26.9% (63/234) | 1.4% (17/1187) | 10.2% (14/137) | 0.6% (5/791) |
| Black Kills Black | 6.3 (6/96) | 0.4% (5/1146) | 6.0% (7/116) | 0.3% (4/1414) | 3.1% (10/321) | 0% (0/1429) |
| White Kills Black | 11.1% (1/9) | 0% (0/19) | 18.2% (2/11) | 1.9% (1/53) | 0% (0/9) | 0% (0/45) |

(ii) Relationship of victim to suspect. Relatively few homicide victims in these three states were killed by strangers—17 percent in Georgia, 17 percent in Florida, and 22 percent in Illinois—but the majority of death sentences in each state were pronounced in those cases: over half in Florida, nearly two-thirds in Georgia, and about 70 percent in Illinois. Those who killed strangers were far more likely to be sentenced to death than those who killed family members, friends, or acquaintances: ten times as likely in Georgia, four times as likely in Florida, and over six times as likely in Illinois.

Controlling for the relationship of the suspect to the victim, however, does little to change the pattern of disparities in capital sentencing by the race of the victim. Those who killed whites were much more likely to be sentenced to death, in each state, regardless of their relationship to the victim[:]

TABLE 7

Percentage of Death Sentences by Race of Victim and Relationship of Victim to Suspect

| | Georgia | | Florida | | Illinois | |
|---|---|---|---|---|---|---|
| | Strangers | Non-Strangers | Strangers | Non-Strangers | Strangers | Non-Strangers |
| White Victim | 26.6% (47/177) | 3.4% (20/591) | 14.5% (68/469) | 3.7% (46/1227) | 5.8% (26/448) | 1.2% (9/745) |
| Black Victim | 3.1% (4/130) | 0.7% (8/1207) | 1.2% (3/257) | 0.8% (11/1337) | 1.5% (6/389) | 0.3% (4/1450) |

Controlling further for the race of the suspect does not alter this pattern. In addition, among both stranger and nonstranger homicides, blacks who killed whites were more likely to be sentenced to death in each state than whites who killed whites[:]

TABLE 8

Percentage of Death Sentences by Race of Victim and Suspect and Their Relationship

| | Georgia | | Florida | | Illinois | |
|---|---|---|---|---|---|---|
| | Strangers | Non-Strangers | Strangers | Non-Strangers | Strangers | Non-Strangers |
| Black Kills White | 28.6% (28/98) | 6.6% (4/61) | 19.3% (29/150) | 6.5% (5/77) | 8.4% (13/155) | 5.6% (3/54) |
| White Kills White | 24.1% (19/79) | 3.0% (16/530) | 12.3% (39/318) | 3.6% (41/1146) | 4.6% (13/285) | 0.9% (6/678) |
| Black Kills Black | 2.6% (3/115) | 0.7% (8/1189) | 1.3% (3/227) | 0.6% (8/1302) | 1.7% (6/360) | 0.3% (4/1425) |
| White Kills Black | 6.7% (1/15) | 0% (0/18) | 0% (0/29) | 8.8% (3/34) | 0% (0/29) | 0% (0/24) |

(iii) Number of victims. Multiple homicides are quite rare; they accounted for only about two percent of all homicides reported to the FBI from Georgia and Florida, and about four percent from Illinois. Killing more than one victim increased the probability of a death sentence greatly in Georgia and Florida—by a factor of about six—and even more dramatically in Illinois—by a factor of more than eighteen. Despite the small proportion of multiple homicides in Illinois, 44 percent of those sentenced to death in Illinois from 1976 through 1980 killed more than one victim. But the higher death sentencing rate for multiple homicides does not explain the racial disparities that we have observed. Disparities by race of victim persist in each state after we control for the number of victims; [and] among homicides with white victims, [black] suspects were more likely to be sentenced to death than white suspects[:]

TABLE 10

Percentages of Death Sentences by Race of Victim and Number of Victims

|  | Georgia | | Florida | | Illinois | |
|---|---|---|---|---|---|---|
|  | Multiple | Single | Multiple | Single | Multiple | Single |
| White Victim | 27.6% (8/29) | 7.9% (59/744) | 20.4% (20/98) | 5.5% (94/1705) | 22.5% (16/71) | 1.7% (19/1143) |
| Black Victim | 6.3% (1/16) | 0.8% (11/1329) | 11.1% (3/27) | 0.7% (11/1656) | 6.8% (4/59) | 0.3% (6/1807) |

TABLE 11

Percentage of Death Sentences by Race of Victim and Defendant and Number of Victims

|  | Georgia | | Florida | | Illinois | |
|---|---|---|---|---|---|---|
|  | Multiple | Single | Multiple | Single | Multiple | Single |
| Black Kills White | 42.9% (3/7) | 19.1% (29/152) | 26.7% (4/15) | 12.8% (30/234) | 41.2% (7/17) | 4.6% (9/196) |
| White Kills White | 22.7% (5/22) | 5.1% (30/592) | 19.3% (16/83) | 4.4% (64/1464) | 16.7% (9/54) | 1.1% (10/926) |
| Black Kills Black | 6.3% (1/16) | 0.8% (10/1294) | 12% (3/25) | 0.5% (8/1587) | 6.8% (4/59) | 0.3% (6/1750) |
| White Kills Black | — | 2.9% (1/34) | 0% (0/2) | 4.5% (3/67) | — | 0% (0/56) |

Having determined that none of the nonracial variables, standing alone, could account for the observed racial disparities, Gross and Mauro turned to the possibility that the racial patterns are a byproduct of the *combined* effects of the other variables. They used two techniques to control simultaneously for the effects of nonracial variables. First, they constructed a scale of aggravation by scoring each homicide on a scale of zero to three, according to the number of major aggravating factors (felony circumstance, stranger victim, and multiple victims) present in the case. As their Table 21 shows, this score was a good predictor of the probability of a death sentence:

TABLE 21

Percentage of Death Sentences by Level of Aggravation
Number of Major Aggravating Circumstances

|  | 0 | 1 | 2 | 3 |
|---|---|---|---|---|
| Georgia | 0.4% (6/1635) | 7.7% (26/339) | 31.6% (43/136) | 57.1% (4/7) |
| Florida | 0.6% (14/2295) | 4.7% (41/874) | 21.9% (62/283) | 44.0% (11/25) |
| Illinois | 0.1% (2/1924) | 1.0% (7/711) | 7.4% (29/392) | 22.6% (7/31) |

However, as their Table 23 shows, this aggregate measure of aggravation did not account for the race-of-victim effect in any state: at each level of aggravation, killers of white victims were substantially more likely to receive death sentences than killers of black victims:[f]

## TABLE 23

### Percentage of Death Sentences by Level of Aggravation and Race of Victim

Number of Major Aggravating Circumstances

|  | 0 | 1 | 2–3 |
|---|---|---|---|
| **Georgia** | | | |
| White Victim | 0.8% ($^{4}/_{499}$) | 10.1% ($^{18}/_{179}$) | 47.4% ($^{45}/_{95}$) |
| Black Victim | 0.2% ($^{2}/_{1136}$) | 5.0% ($^{8}/_{160}$) | 4.2% ($^{2}/_{48}$) |
| **Florida** | | | |
| White Victim | 1.0% ($^{10}/_{1044}$) | 7.0% ($^{36}/_{511}$) | 28.2% ($^{68}/_{241}$) |
| Black Victim | 0.3% ($^{4}/_{1251}$) | 1.4% ($^{5}/_{363}$) | 7.5% ($^{5}/_{67}$) |
| **Illinois** | | | |
| White Victim | 0.3% ($^{2}/_{646}$) | 1.8% ($^{6}/_{329}$) | 12.4% ($^{27}/_{218}$) |
| Black Victim | 0% ($^{0}/_{1278}$) | 0.3% ($^{1}/_{382}$) | 4.4% ($^{9}/_{205}$) |

The second technique used to control simultaneously for all nonracial variables was "multiple regression analysis." This technique produces a mathematical model of the data that estimates the effect of each independent variable on the dependent variable (the outcome). Gross and Mauro summarized their findings as follows:

> In each state, the race of the victim had a sizable and statistically significant effect on the odds of a defendant receiving a death sentence. In Florida the overall odds of an offender receiving the death penalty for killing a white victim were 4.8 times greater than for killing a black victim. In Illinois the overall

[f] Controlling for the level of aggravation did eliminate any independent race-of-suspect effect.

odds of an offender receiving the death penalty for killing a white were 4.0 times greater than for killing a black. In Georgia ... the odds of receiving the death penalty for killing a white are approximately 7.2 times greater than the odds of receiving the death penalty for killing a black....

The magnitude of the racial effects ... can also be described by comparing the predicted probabilities of receiving the death penalty generated by these models for hypothetical homicide cases that differ only in the race of the victim. In Table 25 these predicted probabilities are compared for hypothetical "high aggravation" and "low aggravation" homicides[:]

### TABLE 25

Best Logistic Regression Models: Predicted Probability of a Death Sentence in Hypothetical High and Low Aggravation Cases, by Race of Victim

|                         | Georgia | Florida | Illinois |
|-------------------------|---------|---------|----------|
| High-Aggravation Case[a] |         |         |          |
| White Victim            | .653    | .362    | .352     |
| Black Victim            | .025    | .107    | .120     |
|                         |         |         |          |
| Low-Aggravation Case[b]  |         |         |          |
| White Victim            | .0048   | .010    | .0020    |
| Black Victim            | .0006   | .002    | .0006    |

[a] Multiple homicide of at least one female during the course of a felony in which a gun was used; all victims were strangers to the offender.

[b] Single victim homicide of a male relative, friend, or acquaintance not committed with a gun; no other felonies involved.

... As Table 25 demonstrates, these regression analyses indicate substantial racial disparities in each of these three states at both ends of the continuum of aggravation....

Multiple logistic regression analysis reveals large and statistically significant race-of-victim effects on capital sentencing in Georgia, Florida, and Illinois. After controlling for the effects of all of the other variables in our data set, the killing of a white victim increased the odds of a death sentence by an estimated factor of four in Illinois, about five in Florida, and about seven in Georgia. This method of analysis reveals some evidence that the race of the suspect had an independent effect on capital sentencing in Illinois, but no evidence of independent race-of-suspect effects in Georgia or Florida.[g]

[g] Gross and Mauro also found that these racial patterns persisted when the analysis was restricted to affirmed death sentences in Georgia and Florida, thereby taking into account the effect of appellate review. They also found similar racial effects in the other five

Gross and Mauro also tried to anticipate the methodological objections that could be raised to their analysis. In particular, they focus on the possibility that information not included in the FBI files (concerning the strength of evidence or the suspects' prior record, for example) could account for the observed racial disparities. Although they concede that the inclusion of information on other variables would probably affect the magnitude of the effects yielded by the regression analysis, they insist that there is little likelihood that the omitted variables would substantially explain the racial disparities. "In sum," they conclude, "we are aware of no plausible alternative hypothesis that might explain the observed racial patterns in capital sentencing in legitimate, nondiscriminatory terms."[h]

**3.   Comments and Questions on *McCleskey*.** Justice Powell concluded that the Baldus study failed to demonstrate "a constitutionally significant risk of racial bias" in the administration of Georgia's dealth penalty. Why not? Would the result have been different if the Baldus study had revealed an equally pronounced race-of-defendant effect? Would it have mattered if the race-of-victim effect had been larger or more pervasive (e.g. if it had appeared in the most aggravated cases as well as in the mid-range cases)? In their comments on the *McCleskey* decision, Baldus and his colleagues suggest that the Court's refusal "to accept statistical proof of discrimination to support an Eighth Amendment claim" reflects "an unwillingness to destabilize the capital sentencing process."[i] Assume that McCleskey had prevailed. What would have been the impact of such a ruling on other death sentences in Georgia? On death sentences in other states?

**4.   Post-*McCleskey* Research.** In the wake of *McCleskey*, Congress asked the Government Accounting Office (GAO) to determine the extent to

states that they studied although some of the findings were not statistically significant due to the low numbers of death sentences in those states.

[h] The analysis leading to this conclusion is illustrated by their assessment of the possible significance of the suspect's prior record:

[T]he criminal record of the suspect undoubtedly has an effect on the chances of a death sentence. Moreover, we know that black defendants in general are more likely to have serious criminal records than white defendants, and we can safely assume that this general relationship applies to the homicide suspects in our study. This association, however, explains very little. After controlling for level of aggravation, the race of the suspect is not a significant predictive variable, and the principal racial pattern that we did find—discrimination by race of victim—persisted when we controlled for the race of the suspect. Indeed, we were careful to make sure that the effect of the race of the victim could be determined separately from any possible race-of-suspect effect. To assert that the criminal records of the *suspects* might account for discrimination by the race of the *victim* one would have to suppose that, controlling for the nature of the homicide and for their relationship to the victims, the killers of whites, regardless of their own race, were more likely to have serious criminal records than the killers of blacks. We know of no empirical or logical basis for such a supposition, and it seems unlikely that any unforeseen effect of this type could be large enough and consistent enough to have the power to explain the racial patterns that we have reported.

[i] David C. Baldus, George Woodworth and Charles R. Pulaski, Jr., Equal Justice and the Death Penalty and A Legal and Empirical Analysis 380 (1990).

which race was a factor in the administration of the death penalty. The GAO's 1990 report summarized post-*Furman* research regarding race-of-victim discrimination as follows:

> In 82% of the studies, race-of-victim was found to influence the likelihood of being charged with capital murder or receiving a death sentence.... This finding was remarkably consistent across data sets, states, data collection methods, and analytic techniques.

With regard to race-of-defendant discrimination, the GAO concluded that the evidence was more equivocal. Although more than half of the studies found that race-of-defendant influenced the likelihood of being charged with a capital crime or receiving the death penalty, the nature of the relationship varied across studies.

Since the GOA report was prepared, 18 additional studies have been published. David Baldus and George Woodworth, Race Discrimination in the Administration of the Death Penalty: An Overview of the Empirical Evidence with Special Emphasis on the Post–1990 Research, 39 Crim. L Bull. 194 (2003), summarized the findings of these studies as follows:

> Overall, their results indicate that the patterns documented in the GAO study persist. Specifically, on the issue of race-of-victim discrimination, there is a consistent pattern of white-victim disparities across the systems for which we have data. However, they are not apparent in all jurisdictions [or] at all states of the charging and sentencing processes in which they do occur. On the issue of race-of-defendant discrimination in the system, with few exceptions the pre–1990 pattern of minimal minority-defendant disparities persists, although in some states, black defendants in white victim cases are at higher risk of being charged capitally and sentenced to death than are all other cases with different defendant/victim racial combinations.

---

# CHAPTER IX

# PROOF AND PROPORTIONALITY

---

## SECTION 1: PROOF BEYOND A REASONABLE DOUBT

### INTRODUCTORY NOTE ON *IN RE WINSHIP*

Proof beyond a reasonable doubt has long been thought fundamental to the American system of criminal justice. Only in 1970, however, did the Supreme Court make this standard a constitutional requirement. The issue arose under a New York statute that permitted adjudication of juvenile delinquency on a preponderance of the evidence. The Court declared that scheme unconstitutional in In re Winship, 397 U.S. 358 (1970). The Court held that criminal conviction had to be based on proof beyond a reasonable doubt and that the same standard applied to delinquency proceedings. The Court's conclusion was made unmistakably plain: "Lest there remain any doubt about the constitutional stature of the reasonable-doubt standard, we explicitly hold that the due-process clause protects the accused against conviction except upon proof beyond a reasonable doubt of every fact necessary to constitute the crime with which he is charged."

This requirement seemed unremarkable. By the time of *Winship,* every American jurisdiction required that conviction of an adult be based on proof beyond a reasonable doubt. Aside from extending that standard to delinquency proceedings, *Winship* seemed to have little impact.

The issue lurking in *Winship,* however, was the scope of the reasonable-doubt requirement. What, exactly, would be included by the phrase "every fact necessary to constitute the crime ... charged?" Should it cover only those facts formally made elements of the crime by the definition of the offense? Or should it also include matters technically extrinsic to the definition of the offense, such as a fact relevant only to a defense? Or should the constitutional requirement of proof beyond a reasonable doubt perhaps be limited to those facts constitutionally necessary to constitute the crime charged? If so, what facts are constitutionally necessary?

These and other possible interpretations surfaced in the years following *Winship.* By the end of the decade, a constitutional pronouncement that originally had seemed largely symbolic had become the subject of intense debate. The essential problem is how to mesh a judicial requirement of proof beyond a reasonable doubt with legislative control over the substance of the penal law. The Supreme Court's efforts to resolve this issue are revealed in the cases that follow.

---

## SUBSECTION A: MITIGATIONS AND DEFENSES

---

## Mullaney v. Wilbur

Supreme Court of the United States, 1975.
421 U.S. 684.

■ MR. JUSTICE POWELL delivered the opinion of the Court.

The State of Maine requires a defendant charged with murder to prove that he acted "in the heat of passion on sudden provocation" in order to reduce the homicide to manslaughter. We must decide whether this rule comports with the due-process requirement, as defined in In re Winship, 397 U.S. 358 (1970), that the prosecution prove beyond a reasonable doubt every fact necessary to constitute the crime charged.

I

In June 1966 a jury found respondent Stillman E. Wilbur, Jr., guilty of murder. The case against him rested on his own pretrial statement and on circumstantial evidence showing that he fatally assaulted Claude Hebert in the latter's hotel room. Respondent's statement, introduced by the prosecution, claimed that he had attacked Hebert in a frenzy provoked by Hebert's homosexual advance. The defense offered no evidence, but argued that the homicide was not unlawful since respondent lacked criminal intent. Alternatively, Wilbur's counsel asserted that at most the homicide was manslaughter rather than murder, since it occurred in the heat of passion provoked by the homosexual assault.

The trial court instructed the jury that Maine law recognizes two kinds of homicide, murder and manslaughter, and that these offenses are not subdivided into different degrees. The common elements of both are that the homicide be unlawful—i.e., neither justifiable nor excusable—and that it be intentional.[2] The prosecution is required to prove these elements by proof beyond a reasonable doubt, and only if they are so proved is the jury to consider the distinction between murder and manslaughter.

In view of the evidence the trial court drew particular attention to the difference between murder and manslaughter. After reading the statutory definitions of both offenses,[3] the court charged that "malice aforethought is

---

[2] The court elaborated that an intentional homicide required the jury to find "either that the defendant intended death, or that he intended an act which was calculated and should have been understood by [a] person of reason to be one likely to do great bodily harm and that death resulted."

[3] The Maine murder statute, 17 Me.Rev. Stat.Ann. § 2651, provides:

Whoever unlawfully kills a human being with malice aforethought, either express or implied, is guilty of murder and shall be punished by imprisonment for life.

The manslaughter statute, 17 Me.Rev. Stat.Ann. § 2551, in relevant part provides:

Whoever unlawfully kills a human being in the heat of passion, on sudden provocation, without express or implied

an essential and indispensable element of the crime of murder," without which the homicide would be manslaughter. The jury was further instructed, however, that if the prosecution established that the homicide was both intentional and unlawful, malice aforethought was to be conclusively implied unless the defendant proved by a fair preponderance of the evidence that he acted in the heat of passion on sudden provocation. The court emphasized that "malice aforethought and heat of passion on sudden provocation are two inconsistent things"; thus, by proving the latter the defendant would negate the former and reduce the homicide from murder to manslaughter. The court then concluded its charge with elaborate definitions of "heat of passion" and "sudden provocation."

After retiring to consider its verdict, the jury twice returned to request further instruction. It first sought reinstruction on the doctrine of implied malice aforethought, and later on the definition of "heat of passion." Shortly after the second reinstruction, the jury found respondent guilty of murder.

Respondent appealed to the Maine Supreme Judicial Court, arguing that he had been denied due process because he was required to negate the element of malice aforethought by proving that he had acted in the heat of passion on sudden provocation. . . .

[The state court affirmed the conviction. There ensued a rather complicated series of proceedings resulting in a decision by the United States Court of Appeals for the First Circuit upholding Wilbur's constitutional contention. The First Circuit ordered that he be either released or retried. The state authorities then sought certiorari to review that judgment, and the Supreme Court granted that petition. After describing these proceedings, the Court resolved in part II of its opinion a dispute about Maine law. It then undertook in part III of its opinion to analyze Wilbur's federal constitutional claim.]

### III

The Maine law of homicide, as it bears on this case, can be stated succinctly: Absent justification or excuse, all intentional or criminally reckless killings are felonious homicides. Felonious homicide is punished as murder—i.e., by life imprisonment—unless the defendant proves by a fair preponderance of the evidence that it was committed in the heat of passion on sudden provocation, in which case it is punished as manslaughter. . . . The issue is whether the Maine rule requiring the defendant to prove that he acted in the heat of passion on sudden provocation accords with due process.

### A

Our analysis may be illuminated if this issue is placed in historical context. At early common law only those homicides committed in the

malice aforethought . . . shall be punished by a fine of not more than $1,000 or by imprisonment for not more than 20 years. . . .

enforcement of justice were considered justifiable; all others were deemed unlawful and were punished by death. Gradually, however, the severity of the common-law punishment for homicide abated. Between the 13th and 16th centuries the class of justifiable homicides expanded to include, for example, accidental homicides and those committed in self-defense. Concurrently, the widespread use of capital punishment was ameliorated further by extension of the ecclesiastic jurisdiction. Almost any person able to read was eligible for "benefit of clergy," a procedural device that effected a transfer from the secular to the ecclesiastic jurisdiction. And under ecclesiastic law a person who committed an unlawful homicide was not executed; instead he received a one-year sentence, had his thumb branded and was required to forfeit his goods. At the turn of the 16th century, English rulers, concerned with the accretion of ecclesiastic jurisdiction at the expense of the secular, enacted a series of statutes eliminating the benefit of clergy in all cases of "murder of malice prepensed." Unlawful homicides that were committed without such malice were designated "manslaughter," and their perpetrators remained eligible for the benefit of clergy.

Even after ecclesiastic jurisdiction was eliminated for all secular offenses the distinction between murder and manslaughter persisted. It was said that "manslaughter, when voluntary, arises from the sudden heat of the passions, murder, from the wickedness of the heart." 4 W. Blackstone, Commentaries *190. Malice aforethought was designated as the element that distinguished the two crimes, but it was recognized that such malice could be implied by law as well as proved by evidence. Absent proof that an unlawful homicide resulted from "sudden and sufficiently violent provocation," the homicide was "presumed to be malicious." In view of this presumption, the early English authorities held that once the prosecution proved that the accused had committed the homicide, it was "incumbent upon the prisoner to make out, to the satisfaction of the court and jury all . . . circumstances of justification, excuse, or alleviation." Thus, at common law the burden of proving heat of passion on sudden provocation appears to have rested on the defendant.

In this country the concept of malice aforethought took on two distinct meanings: In some jurisdictions it came to signify a substantive element of intent, requiring the prosecution to prove that the defendant intended to kill or to inflict great bodily harm; in other jurisdictions it remained a policy presumption, indicating only that absent proof to the contrary a homicide was presumed not to have occurred in the heat of passion. In a landmark case, Commonwealth v. York, 50 Mass. (9 Met.) 93 (1845), Chief Justice Shaw of the Massachusetts Supreme Judicial Court held that the defendant was required to negate malice aforethought by proving by a preponderance of the evidence that he acted in the heat of passion. Initially, *York* was adopted in Maine as well as several other jurisdictions. In 1895, however, in the context of deciding a question of federal criminal procedure, this Court explicitly considered and unanimously rejected the general approach articulated in *York*. Davis v. United States, 160 U.S. 469 (1895). And, in the past half century, the large majority of states have abandoned *York* and now require the prosecution to prove the absence of the heat of passion on sudden provocation beyond a reasonable doubt.

This historical review establishes two important points. First, the fact at issue here—the presence or absence of the heat of passion on sudden provocation—has been, almost from the inception of the common law of homicide, the single most important factor in determining the degree of culpability attaching to an unlawful homicide. And, second, the clear trend has been toward requiring the prosecution to bear the ultimate burden of proving this fact.

B

Petitioners, the warden of the Maine Prison and the state of Maine, argue that despite these considerations *Winship* should not be extended to the present case. They note that as a formal matter the absence of the heat of passion on sudden provocation is not a "fact necessary to constitute the *crime*" of felonious homicide in Maine. This distinction is relevant, according to petitioners, because in *Winship* the facts at issue were essential to establish criminality in the first instance, whereas the fact in question here does not come into play until the jury already has determined that the defendant is guilty and may be punished at least for manslaughter. In this situation, petitioners maintain, the defendant's critical interests in liberty and reputation are no longer of paramount concern since, irrespective of the presence or absence of the heat of passion on sudden provocation, he is likely to lose his liberty and certain to be stigmatized. In short, petitioners would limit *Winship* to those facts which, if not proved, would wholly exonerate the defendant.

This analysis fails to recognize that the criminal law of Maine, like that of other jurisdictions, is concerned not only with guilt or innocence in the abstract but also with the degree of criminal culpability. Maine has chosen to distinguish those who kill in the heat of passion from those who kill in the absence of this factor. Because the former are less "blameworth[y]," they are subject to substantially less severe penalties. By drawing this distinction, while refusing to require the prosecution to establish beyond a reasonable doubt the fact upon which it turns, Maine denigrates the interests found critical in *Winship*.

The safeguards of due process are not rendered unavailing simply because a determination may already have been reached that would stigmatize the defendant and that might lead to a significant impairment of personal liberty. The fact remains that the consequences resulting from a verdict of murder, as compared with a verdict of manslaughter, differ significantly. Indeed, when viewed in terms of the potential difference in restrictions of personal liberty attendant to each conviction, the distinction established by Maine between murder and manslaughter may be of greater importance than the difference between guilt or innocence for many lesser crimes.

Moreover, if *Winship* were limited to those facts that constitute a crime as defined by state law, a state could undermine many of the interests that decision sought to protect without effecting any substantive change in its law. It would only be necessary to redefine the elements that constitute different crimes, characterizing them as factors that bear solely on the extent of punishment. An extreme example of this approach can be fashioned from the law challenged in this case. Maine divides the single generic offenses of felonious homicide into three distinct punishment categories—murder, voluntary manslaughter, and involuntary manslaughter. Only the first two of these categories require that the homicidal act either be intentional or the result of criminally reckless conduct. But under Maine law these facts of intent are not general elements of the crime of felonious homicide. Instead, they bear only on the appropriate punishment category. Thus, if petitioners' argument were accepted, Maine could impose a life sentence for any felonious homicide—even those that traditionally might be considered involuntary manslaughter—unless the *defendant* was able to prove that his act was neither intentional nor criminally reckless.[24]

*Winship* is concerned with substance rather than this kind of formalism. The rationale of that case requires an analysis that looks to the "operation and effect of the law as applied and enforced by the state," and to the interests of both the state and the defendant as affected by the allocation of the burden of proof.

In *Winship* the Court emphasized the societal interests in the reliability of jury verdicts:

> The requirement of proof beyond a reasonable doubt has [a] vital role in our criminal procedure for cogent reasons. The accused during a criminal prosecution has at stake interests of immense importance, both because of the possibility that he may lose his liberty upon conviction and because of the certainty that he would be stigmatized by the conviction....

> Moreover, use of the reasonable-doubt standard is indispensable to command the respect and confidence of the community in applications of the criminal law. It is critical that the moral force of the criminal law not be diluted by a standard of proof that leaves people in doubt whether innocent men are being condemned.

The interests are implicated to a greater degree in this case than they were in *Winship* itself. Petitioner there faced an 18–month sentence, with a maximum possible extension of an additional four and one-half years, whereas respondent here faces a differential in sentencing ranging from a nominal fine to a mandatory life sentence. Both the stigma to the defendant and the community's confidence in the administration of the criminal law are also of greater consequence in this case, since the adjudication of

---

[24] Many states impose different statutory sentences on different degrees of assault. If *Winship* were limited to a state's definition of the elements of a crime, these states could define all assaults as a single offense and then require the defendant to disprove the elements of aggravation—e.g., intent to kill or intent to rob....

delinquency involved in *Winship* was "benevolent" in intention, seeking to provide "a generously conceived program of compassionate treatment."

Not only are the interests underlying *Winship* implicated to a greater degree in this case, but in one respect the protection afforded those interests is less here. In *Winship* the ultimate burden of persuasion remained with the prosecution, although the standard had been reduced to proof by a fair preponderance of the evidence. In this case, by contrast, the state has affirmatively shifted the burden of proof to the defendant. The result, in a case such as this one where the defendant is required to prove the critical fact in dispute, is to increase further the likelihood of an erroneous murder conviction....

### C

It has been suggested that because of the difficulties in negating an argument that the homicide was committed in the heat of passion the burden of proving this fact should rest on the defendant. No doubt this is often a heavy burden for the prosecution to satisfy. The same may be said of the requirement of proof beyond a reasonable doubt of many controverted facts in a criminal trial. But this is the traditional burden which our system of criminal justice deems essential.

Indeed, the Maine Supreme Judicial Court itself acknowledged that most states require the prosecution to prove the absence of passion beyond a reasonable doubt.[28] Moreover, the difficulty of meeting such an exacting burden is mitigated in Maine where the fact at issue is largely an "objective, rather than a subjective, behavioral criterion." In this respect, proving that the defendant did not act in the heat of passion on sudden provocation is similar to proving any other element of intent; it may be established by adducing evidence of the factual circumstances surrounding the commission of the homicide. And although intent is typically considered a fact peculiarly within the knowledge of the defendant, this does not, as this Court has long recognized, justify shifting the burden to him.

Nor is the requirement of proving a negative unique in our system of criminal jurisprudence. Maine itself requires the prosecution to prove the absence of self-defense beyond a reasonable doubt. Satisfying this burden imposes an obligation that, in all practical effect, is identical to the burden involved in negating the heat of passion on sudden provocation. Thus, we discern no unique hardship on the prosecution that would justify requiring the defendant to carry the burden of proving a fact so critical to criminal culpability.

### IV

Maine law requires a defendant to establish by a preponderance of the evidence that he acted in the heat of passion on sudden provocation in

---

[28] Many states do require the defendant to show that there is "some evidence" indicating that he acted in the heat of passion before requiring the prosecution to negate this element by proving the absence of passion beyond a reasonable doubt. Nothing in this opinion is intended to affect that requirement.

order to reduce murder to manslaughter. Under this burden of proof a defendant can be given a life sentence when the evidence indicates that it is *as likely as not* that he deserves a significantly lesser sentence. This is an intolerable result in a society where, to paraphrase Mr. Justice Harlan, it is far worse to sentence one guilty only of manslaughter as a murderer than to sentence a murderer for the lesser crime of manslaughter. In re Winship, 397 U.S. at 372 (concurring opinion). We therefore hold that the due-process clause requires the prosecution to prove beyond a reasonable doubt the absence of the heat of passion on sudden provocation when the issue is properly presented in a homicide case. Accordingly, the judgment below is

Affirmed.

■ [The concurring opinion of Justice Rehnquist, with whom Chief Justice Burger joined, has been omitted.]

---

## Patterson v. New York

Supreme Court of the United States, 1977.
432 U.S. 197.

■ MR. JUSTICE WHITE delivered the opinion of the Court.

The question here is the constitutionality under the 14th Amendment's due-process clause of burdening the defendant in a New York state murder trial with proving the affirmative defense[a] of extreme emotional disturbance as defined by New York law.

### I

After a brief and unstable marriage, the appellant, Gordon Patterson, Jr., became estranged from his wife, Roberta. Roberta resumed an association with John Northrup, a neighbor to whom she had been engaged prior to her marriage to appellant. On December 27, 1970, Patterson borrowed a rifle from an acquaintance and went to the residence of his father-in-law. There, he observed his wife through a window in a state of semi-undress in the presence of John Northrup. He entered the house and killed Northrup by shooting him twice in the head.

Patterson was charged with second-degree murder. In New York there are two elements of the crime: (i) "intent to cause the death of another person"; and (ii) "caus[ing] the death of such person or of a third person."

---

[a] "Affirmative defense" is used here to indicate a defense that shifts to the defendant both the burden of production (which means that the issue will be resolved against him if it is not raised by the evidence) and the burden of persuasion (which means that the issue will be resolved against him if, after considering the evidence, the trier of fact remains uncertain whether the required standard of proof has been met). An "affirmative defense" is thus distinguished from an ordinary "defense," which shifts to the defendant only the burden of production. This usage is increasingly widespread, but not uniform. See, e.g., MPC § 1.12, which uses the term "affirmative defense" even where there is no shift in the burden of persuasion.—[Footnote by eds.]

N.Y. Penal Law § 125.25. Malice aforethought is not an element of the crime. In addition, the state permits a person accused of murder to raise an affirmative defense that he "acted under the influence of extreme emotional disturbance for which there was a reasonable explanation or excuse."[b]

New York also recognizes the crime of manslaughter. A person is guilty of manslaughter if he intentionally kills another person "under circumstances which do not constitute murder because he acts under the influence of extreme emotional disturbance." Appellant confessed before trial to killing Northrup, but at trial he raised the defense of extreme emotional disturbance.

The jury was instructed as to the elements of the crime of murder. Focusing on the element of intent, the trial court charged:

> Before you, considering all of the evidence, can convict this defendant or anyone of murder, you must believe and decide that the People have established beyond a reasonable doubt that he intended, in firing the gun, to kill either the victim himself or some other human being. . . .

> Always remember that you must not expect or require the defendant to prove to your satisfaction that his acts were done without the intent to kill. Whatever proof he may have attempted, however far he may have gone in an effort to convince you of his innocence or guiltlessness, he is not obliged, he is not obligated to prove anything. It is always the People's burden to prove his guilt, and to prove that he intended to kill in this instance beyond a reasonable doubt.

The jury was further instructed, consistently with New York law, that the defendant had the burden of proving his affirmative defense by a preponderance of the evidence. The jury was told that if it found beyond a reasonable doubt that appellant had intentionally killed Northrup but that appellant had demonstrated by a preponderance of the evidence that he had acted under the influence of extreme emotional disturbance, it had to find appellant guilty of manslaughter instead of murder.

The jury found appellant guilty of murder. Judgment was entered on the verdict, and the appellate division affirmed. While appeal to the New York Court of Appeals was pending, this Court decided Mullaney v. Wilbur, 421 U.S. 684 (1975). . . . In the court of appeals appellant urged that New York's murder statute is functionally equivalent to the one struck down in *Mullaney* and that therefore his conviction should be reversed.

The Court of Appeals rejected appellant's argument, holding that the New York murder statute is consistent with due process. The court distinguished *Mullaney* on the ground that the New York statute involved no shifting of the burden to the defendant to disprove any fact essential to the offense charged since the New York affirmative defense of extreme

---

[b] The New York homicide provisions are reprinted in Appendix B.—[Footnote by eds.]

emotional disturbance bears no direct relationship to any element of murder. This appeal ensued.... We affirm.

## II

It goes without saying that preventing and dealing with crime is much more the business of the states than it is of the federal government, and that we should not lightly construe the Constitution so as to intrude upon the administration of justice by the individual states. Among other things, it is normally "within the power of the state to regulate procedures under which its laws are carried out, including the burden of producing evidence and the burden of persuasion," and its decision in this regard is not subject to proscription under the due process clause unless "it offends some principle of justice so rooted in the traditions and conscience of our people as to be ranked as fundamental." Speiser v. Randall, 357 U.S. 513 (1958).

In determining whether New York's allocation to the defendant of proving the mitigating circumstances of severe emotional disturbance is consistent with due process, it is therefore relevant to note that this defense is a considerably expanded version of the common-law defense of heat of passion on sudden provocation and that at common law the burden of proving the latter, as well as other affirmative defenses—indeed, "all ... circumstances of justification, excuse or alleviation"—rested on the defendant. This was the rule when the Fifth Amendment was adopted, and it was the American rule when the 14th Amendment was ratified....

## III

We cannot conclude that Patterson's conviction under the New York law deprived him of due process of law. The crime of murder is defined by the statute, which represents a recent revision of the state criminal code, as causing the death of another person with intent to do so. The death, the intent to kill, and causation are the facts that the state is required to prove beyond a reasonable doubt if a person is to be convicted of murder. No further facts are either presumed or inferred in order to constitute the crime. The statute does provide an affirmative defense—that the defendant acted under the influence of extreme emotional disturbance for which there was a reasonable explanation—which, if proved by a preponderance of the evidence, would reduce the crime to manslaughter, an offense defined in a separate section of the statute. It is plain enough that if the intentional killing is shown, the state intends to deal with the defendant as a murderer unless he demonstrates the mitigating circumstances.

Here, the jury was instructed in accordance with the statute, and the guilty verdict confirms that the state successfully carried its burden of proving the facts of the crime beyond a reasonable doubt. Nothing in the evidence, including any evidence that might have been offered with respect to Patterson's mental state at the time of the crime, raised a reasonable doubt about his guilt as a murderer; and clearly the evidence failed to convince the jury that Patterson's affirmative defense had been made out. It seems to us that the state satisfied the mandate of *Winship* that it prove beyond a reasonable doubt "every fact necessary to constitute the crime with which [Patterson was] charged." . . .

Here, in revising its criminal code, New York provided the affirmative defense of extreme emotional disturbance, a substantially expanded version of the older heat-of-passion concept; but it was willing to do so only if the facts making out the defense were established by the defendant with sufficient certainty. The state was itself unwilling to undertake to establish the absence of those facts beyond a reasonable doubt, perhaps fearing that proof would be too difficult and that too many persons deserving treatment as murderers would escape that punishment if the evidence need merely raise a reasonable doubt about the defendant's emotional state. It has been said that the new criminal code of New York contains some 25 affirmative defenses which exculpate or mitigate but which must be established by the defendant to be operative.[10] The due-process clause, as we see it, does not put New York to the choice of abandoning those defenses or undertaking to disprove their existence in order to convict of a crime which otherwise is within its constitutional powers to sanction by substantial punishment.

The requirement of proof beyond a reasonable doubt in a criminal case is "bottomed on a fundamental value determination of our society that it is far worse to convict an innocent man than to let a guilty man go free." The social cost of placing the burden on the prosecution to prove guilt beyond a reasonable doubt is thus an increased risk that the guilty will go free. While it is clear that our society has willingly chosen to bear a substantial burden in order to protect the innocent, it is equally clear that the risk it must bear is not without limits; and Mr. Justice Harlan's aphorism provides little guidance for determining what those limits are. Due process does not require that every conceivable step be taken, at whatever cost, to eliminate the possibility of convicting an innocent person. Punishment of those found guilty by a jury, for example, is not forbidden merely because there is a remote possibility in some instances that an innocent person might go to jail.

It is said that the common-law rule [requiring the accused to prove heat of passion based on sudden provocation] permits a state to punish one as a murderer when it is as likely as not that he acted in the heat of passion or under severe emotional distress and when, if he did, he is guilty only of manslaughter. But this has always been the case in those jurisdic-

---

[10] The State of New York is not alone in this result:

> Since the Model Penal Code was completed in 1962, some 22 states have codified and reformed their criminal laws. At least 12 of these jurisdictions have used the concept of an "affirmative defense" and have defined that phrase to require that the defendant prove the existence of an "affirmative defense" by a preponderance of the evidence. Additionally, at least six proposed state codes and each of the four successive versions of a revised federal code use the same procedural device. Finally, many jurisdictions that do not generally employ this concept of "affirmative defense" nevertheless shift the burden of proof to the defendant on particular issues.

Peter W. Low & John C. Jeffries, DICTA: Constitutionalizing the Criminal Law?, 29 Va. Law Weekly, No. 18, p. 1 (1977) (footnotes omitted). . . .

tions adhering to the traditional rule. It is also very likely true that fewer convictions of murder would occur if New York were required to negative the affirmative defense at issue here. But in each instance of a murder conviction under the present law, New York will have proved beyond a reasonable doubt that the defendant has intentionally killed another person, an act which it is not disputed the state may constitutionally criminalize and punish. If the state nevertheless chooses to recognize a factor that mitigates the degree of criminality or punishment, we think the state may assure itself that the fact has been established with reasonable certainty. To recognize at all a mitigating circumstance does not require the state to prove its non-existence in each case in which the fact is put in issue, if in its judgment this would be too cumbersome, too expensive, and too inaccurate.

We thus decline to adopt as a constitutional imperative, operative countrywide, that a state must disprove beyond a reasonable doubt every fact constituting any and all affirmative defenses related to the culpability of the accused. Traditionally, due process has required that only the most basic procedural safeguards be observed; more subtle balancing of society's interests against those of the accused have been left to the legislative branch. We therefore will not disturb the balance struck in previous cases holding that the due-process clause requires the prosecution to prove beyond a reasonable doubt all of the elements included in the definition of the offense of which the defendant is charged. Proof of the non-existence of all affirmative defenses has never been constitutionally required; and we perceive no reason to fashion such a rule in this case and apply it to the statutory defense at issue here.

This view may seem to permit state legislatures to reallocate burdens of proof by labeling as affirmative defenses at least some elements of the crime, now defined in their statutes. But there are obviously constitutional limits beyond which the states may not go in this regard. "[I]t is not within the province of a legislature to declare an individual guilty or presumptively guilty of a crime." McFarland v. American Sugar Rfg. Co., 241 U.S. 79, 86 (1916). The legislature cannot "validly command that the finding of an indictment, or mere proof of the identity of the accused, should create a presumption of the existence of all the facts essential to guilt." Tot v. United States, 319 U.S. 463, 469 (1943).

Long before *Winship*, the universal rule in this country was that the prosecution must prove guilt beyond a reasonable doubt. At the same time, the long-accepted rule was that it was constitutionally permissible to provide that various affirmative defenses were to be proved by the defendant. This did not lead to such abuses or to such widespread redefinition of crime and reduction of the prosecutor's burden that a new constitutional rule was required. This was not the problem to which *Winship* was addressed. Nor does the fact that a majority of the states have now assumed the burden of disproving affirmative defenses—for whatever reasons—mean that those states that strike a different balance are in violation of the Constitution.

## IV

It is urged that *Mullaney* necessarily invalidates Patterson's conviction....

*Mullaney*'s holding, it is argued, is that the state may not permit the blameworthiness of an act or the severity of punishment authorized for its commission to depend on the presence or absence of an identified fact without assuming the burden of proving the presence or absence of that fact, as the case may be, beyond a reasonable doubt. In our view, the *Mullaney* holding should not be so broadly read....

*Mullaney* surely held that a state must prove every ingredient of an offense beyond a reasonable doubt, and that it may not shift the burden of proof to the defendant by presuming that ingredient upon proof of the other elements of the offense. This is true even though the state's practice, as in Maine, had been traditionally to the contrary. Such shifting of the burden of persuasion with respect to a fact which the state deems so important that it must be either proved or presumed is impermissible under the due process clause.

It was unnecessary to go further in *Mullaney*. The Maine Supreme Judicial Court made it clear that ... a killing became murder in Maine when it resulted from a deliberate, cruel act committed by one person against another, "suddenly without any, or without a considerable provocation." ... [M]alice, in the sense of the absence of provocation, was part of the definition of that crime. Yet malice, i.e., lack of provocation, was presumed and could be rebutted by the defendant only by proving by a preponderance of the evidence that he acted with heat of passion upon sudden provocation. In *Mullaney* we held that however traditional this mode of proceeding might have been, it is contrary to the due process clause as construed in *Winship*.

As we have explained, nothing was presumed or implied against Patterson; and his conviction is not invalid under any of our prior cases. The judgment of the New York Court of Appeals is affirmed.

■ MR. JUSTICE REHNQUIST took no part in the consideration or decision of this case.

■ MR. JUSTICE POWELL, with whom MR. JUSTICE BRENNAN and MR. JUSTICE MARSHALL join, dissenting.

In the name of preserving legislative flexibility, the Court today drains *In re Winship* of much of its vitality. Legislatures do require broad discretion in the drafting of criminal laws, but the Court surrenders to the legislative branch a significant part of its responsibility to protect the presumption of innocence.

## I

An understanding of the import of today's decision requires a comparison of the statutes at issue here with the statutes and practices of Maine struck down by a unanimous Court just two years ago in Mullaney v. Wilbur, 421 U.S. 684 (1975).

### A

Maine's homicide laws embodied the common-law distinctions along with the colorful common-law language. Murder was defined as the unlawful killing of a human being "with malice aforethought, either express or implied." Manslaughter was a killing "in the heat of passion, on sudden provocation, without express or implied malice aforethought." . . .

New York's present homicide laws had their genesis in lingering dissatisfaction with certain aspects of the common-law framework that this Court confronted in *Mullaney*. Critics charged that the archaic language tended to obscure the factors of real importance in the jury's decision. Also, only a limited range of aggravations would lead to mitigation under the common-law formula, usually only those resulting from direct provocation by the victim himself. It was thought that actors whose emotions were stirred by other forms of outrageous conduct, even conduct by someone other than the ultimate victim, also should be punished as manslaughterers rather than murderers. Moreover, the common-law formula was generally applied with strict objectivity. Only provocations that might cause the hypothetical reasonable man to lose control could be considered. And even provocations of that sort were inadequate to reduce the crime to manslaughter if enough time had passed for the reasonable man's passions to cool, regardless of whether the actor's own thermometer had registered any decline.

The American Law Institute took the lead in moving to remedy these difficulties. As part of its commendable undertaking to prepare a Model Penal Code, it endeavored to bring modern insights to bear on the law of homicide. The result was a proposal to replace "heat of passion" with the moderately broader concept of "extreme mental or emotional disturbance." . . .

At about this time the New York legislature undertook the preparation of a new criminal code, and the Revised Penal Law of 1967 was the ultimate result. The new code adopted virtually word for word the ALI formula for distinguishing murder from manslaughter. Under current New York law . . . the last traces of confusing archaic language have been removed. There is no mention of malice aforethought, no attempt to give a name to the state of mind that exists when extreme emotional disturbance is not present. . . .

### B

*Mullaney* held invalid Maine's requirement that the defendant prove heat of passion. The Court today, without disavowing the unanimous holding of *Mullaney*, approves New York's requirement that the defendant prove extreme emotional disturbance. The Court manages to run a constitutional boundary line through the barely visible space that separates

Maine's law from New York's. It does so on the basis of distinctions in language that are formalistic rather than substantive.

This result is achieved by a narrowly literal parsing of the holding in *Winship*: "[T]he due-process clause protects the accused against conviction except upon proof beyond a reasonable doubt of every fact necessary to constitute the crime with which he is charged." The only "facts" necessary to constitute a crime are said to be those that appear on the face of the statute as a part of the definition of the crime. Maine's statute was invalid, the Court reasons, because it "defined [murder] as the unlawful killing of a human being 'with malice aforethought, either express or implied.'" "[M]alice," the Court reiterates, "in the sense of the absence of provocation, was part of the definition of that crime." *Winship* was violated only because this "fact"—malice—was "presumed" unless the defendant persuaded the jury otherwise by showing that he acted in the heat of passion. New York, in form presuming no affirmative "fact" against Patterson, and blessed with a statute drafted in the leaner language of the 20th century, escapes constitutional scrutiny unscathed even though the effect on the defendant of New York's placement of the burden of persuasion is exactly the same as Maine's.

This explanation of the *Mullaney* holding bears little resemblance to the basic rationale of that decision. But this is not the cause of greatest concern. The test the Court today establishes allows a legislature to shift, virtually at will, the burden of persuasion with respect to any factor in a criminal case, so long as it is careful not to mention the non-existence of that factor in the statutory language that defines the crime. The sole requirement is that any references to the factor be confined to those sections that provide for an affirmative defense.

Perhaps the Court's interpretation of *Winship* is consistent with the letter of the holding in that case. But little of the spirit survives. Indeed, the Court scarcely could distinguish this case from *Mullaney* without closing its eyes to the constitutional values for which *Winship* stands. As Mr. Justice Harlan observed in *Winship*, "a standard of proof represents an attempt to instruct the factfinder concerning the degree of confidence our society thinks he should have in the correctness of actual conclusions for a particular type of adjudication." Explaining *Mullaney*, the Court says today, in effect, that society demands full confidence before a Maine factfinder determines that heat of passion is missing—a demand so insistent that this Court invoked the Constitution to enforce it over the contrary decision by the state. But we are told that society is willing to tolerate far less confidence in New York's factual determination of precisely the same functional issue. One must ask what possibly could explain this difference in societal demands. According to the Court, it is because Maine happened to attach a name—"malice aforethought"—to the absence of heat of passion, whereas New York refrained from giving a name to the absence of extreme emotional disturbance.

With all respect, this type of constitutional adjudication is indefensibly formalistic. A limited but significant check on possible abuses in the criminal law now becomes an exercise in arid formalities. What *Winship* and *Mullaney* had sought to teach about the limits a free society places on its procedures to safeguard the liberty of its citizens becomes a rather simplistic lesson in statutory draftsmanship. Nothing in the Court's opinion prevents a legislature from applying this new learning to many of the classical elements of the crimes it punishes.[8] It would be preferable, if the Court has found reason to reject the rationale of *Winship* and *Mullaney*, simply and straightforwardly to overrule those precedents.

The Court understandably manifests some uneasiness that its formalistic approach will give legislatures too much latitude in shifting the burden of persuasion. And so it issues a warning that "there are obviously constitutional limits beyond which the states may not go in this regard." The Court thereby concedes that legislative abuses may occur and that they must be curbed by the judicial branch. But if the state is careful to conform to the drafting formulas articulated today, the constitutional limits are anything but "obvious." This decision simply leaves us without a conceptual framework for distinguishing abuses from legitimate legislative adjustments of the burden of persuasion in criminal cases.

## II

It is unnecessary for the Court to retreat to a formalistic test for applying *Winship*. Careful attention to the *Mullaney* decision reveals the principles that should control in this and like cases. *Winship* held that the prosecution must bear the burden of proving beyond a reasonable doubt " 'the existence of every fact necessary to constitute the crime charged.' " In *Mullaney* we concluded that heat of passion was one of the "facts" described in *Winship*—that is, a factor as to which the prosecution must bear the burden of persuasion beyond a reasonable doubt. We reached that result only after making two careful inquiries. First, we noted that the presence or absence of heat of passion made a substantial difference in punishment of the offender and in the stigma associated with the conviction. Second, we reviewed the history, in England and this country, of the factor at issue. Central to the holding in *Mullaney* was our conclusion that heat of passion "has been, almost from the inception of the common law of homicide, the single most important factor in determining the degree of culpability attaching to an unlawful homicide."

Implicit in these two inquiries are the principles that should govern this case. The due-process clause requires that the prosecutor bear the burden of persuasion beyond a reasonable doubt only if the factor at issue makes a substantial difference in punishment and stigma. The requirement of course applies a fortiori if the factor makes the difference between guilt

---

[8] For example, a state statute could pass muster under the only solid standard that appears in the Court's opinion if it defined murder as mere physical contact between the defendant and the victim leading to the victim's death, but then set up an affirmative defense leaving it to the defendant to prove that he acted without culpable mens rea. The state, in other words, could be relieved altogether of responsibility for proving *anything* regarding the defendant's state of mind, provided only that the face of the statute meets the Court's drafting formulas....

and innocence. But a substantial difference in punishment alone is not enough. It also must be shown that in the Anglo–American legal tradition the factor in question historically has held that level of importance. If either branch of the test is not met, then the legislature retains its traditional authority over matters of proof. But to permit a shift in the burden of persuasion when both branches of this test are satisfied would invite the undermining of the presumption of innocence, "that bedrock 'axiomatic and elementary' principle whose 'enforcement lies at the foundation of the administration of our criminal law.' "

I hardly need add that New York's provisions allocating the burden of persuasion as to "extreme emotional disturbance" are unconstitutional when judged by these standards. "[E]xtreme emotional disturbance" is . . . the direct descendant of the "heat of passion" factor considered at length in *Mullaney*. I recognize, of course, that the differences between Maine and New York law are not unimportant to the defendant; there is a somewhat broader opportunity for mitigation. But none of those distinctions is relevant here. The presence or absence of extreme emotional disturbance makes a critical difference in punishment and stigma, and throughout our history the resolution of this issue of fact, although expressed in somewhat different terms, has distinguished manslaughter from murder.

### III

The Court beats its retreat from *Winship* apparently because of a concern that otherwise the federal judiciary will intrude too far into the substantive choices concerning the content of a state's criminal law. The concern is legitimate, but misplaced. *Winship* and *Mullaney* are no more than what they purport to be: decisions addressing the procedural requirements that states must meet to comply with due process. They are not outposts for policing the substantive boundaries of the criminal law.

The *Winship/Mullaney* test identifies those factors of such importance, historically, in determining punishment and stigma that the Constitution forbids shifting to the defendant the burden of persuasion when such a factor is at issue. *Winship* and *Mullaney* specify only the procedure that is required when a state elects to use such a factor as part of its substantive criminal law. They do not say that the state must elect to use it. For example, where a state has chosen to retain the traditional distinction between murder and manslaughter, as have New York and Maine, the burden of persuasion must remain on the prosecution with respect to the distinguishing factor, in view of its decisive historical importance. But nothing in *Mullaney* or *Winship* precludes a state from abolishing the distinction between murder and manslaughter and treating all unjustifiable homicide as murder.[13] In this significant respect, neither *Winship* nor

[13] Perhaps under other principles of due-process jurisprudence, certain factors are so fundamental that a state could not, as a substantive matter, refrain from recognizing them so long as it chooses to punish given conduct as a crime. . . . But substantive limits were not at issue in *Winship* or *Mullaney*, and they are not at issue here. . . .

*Mullaney* eliminates the substantive flexibility that should remain in legislative hands.

Moreover, it is unlikely that more than a few factors—although important ones—for which a shift in the burden of persuasion seriously would be considered will come within the *Mullaney* holding. With some exceptions, then, the state has the authority "to recognize a factor that mitigates the degree of criminality or punishment" without having "to prove its non-existence in each case in which the fact is put in issue." New ameliorative affirmative defenses, about which the Court expresses concern, generally remain undisturbed by the holdings in *Winship* and *Mullaney*—and need not be disturbed by a sound holding reversing Patterson's conviction.

Furthermore, as we indicated in *Mullaney*, even as to those factors upon which the prosecution must bear the burden of persuasion, the state retains an important procedural device to avoid jury confusion and prevent the prosecution from being unduly hampered. The state normally may shift to the defendant the burden of production, that is, the burden of going forward with sufficient evidence "to justify [a reasonable] doubt upon the issue." If the defendant's evidence does not cross this threshold, the issue—be it malice, extreme emotional disturbance, self-defense, or whatever—will not be submitted to the jury. . . .

To be sure, there will be many instances when the *Winship/Mullaney* test as I perceive it will be more difficult to apply than the Court's formula. Where I see the need for a careful and discriminating review of history, the Court finds a brightline standard that can be applied with a quick glance at the face of the statute. But this facile test invites tinkering with the procedural safeguards of the presumption of innocence, an invitation to disregard the principles of *Winship* that I would not extend.

———

## NOTES ON BURDEN OF PROOF FOR MITIGATIONS AND DEFENSES

**1. The Distinction Between *Mullaney* and *Patterson*.** Note that the *Patterson* majority purported to distinguish rather than to overrule *Mullaney*. Presumably, that means that *Mullaney* is still good law for certain situations. What are those situations? What is the dividing line between the continuing authority of *Mullaney* and the superseding rule of *Patterson*? Is the effort to distinguish them, as Justice Powell charged, "indefensibly formalistic?" Is there any rationale for *Mullaney* that does not apply with equal force to *Patterson*?

**2. The Procedural Interpretation of *Winship*.** If *Mullaney* and *Patterson* are inconsistent, it follows that one of them is wrong. For a time, at least, the prevailing reaction was that *Mullaney* was right and *Patterson* wrong. This position is founded on what may be called the procedural interpretation of *Winship*. Under this view, the constitutional commitment to proof beyond a reasonable doubt should extend to every fact determinative of criminal liability. The prosecution would be required to prove beyond a reasonable doubt not only every element of the offense charged but also the absence of justification, excuse, or other grounds of defense or mitigation. This is termed the procedural interpretation of *Winship* because it treats the reasonable-doubt standard as a procedural requirement to be enforced without regard to legislative control over the substance of the penal law. In other words, the value of requiring proof beyond a reasonable doubt is thought to be entirely independent of the substantive issue of what must be proved.

An articulate exponent of this view is Barbara Underwood. In her article, The Thumb on the Scales of Justice: Burdens of Persuasion in Criminal Cases, 86 Yale L.J. 1299 (1977), she postulates two distinct purposes for requiring proof beyond a reasonable doubt: "First, the rule is meant to affect the outcome of individual cases, reducing the likelihood of an erroneous conviction. Second, the rule is meant to symbolize for society the great significance of a criminal conviction."

In Underwood's view, these considerations support an insistence on proof beyond a reasonable doubt even in the face of undoubted legislative authority over what must be proved. She denies that legislative power to eliminate altogether a ground of defense or mitigation should entail the lesser power to shift to the defendant the burden of establishing its existence. In her view, the fact that a defense is gratuitous—i.e., may be granted or withheld at the legislature's option—provides no basis for treating it as an exception to the reasonable-doubt requirement.

The result of this approach would be to force legislatures to extreme choices. Thus, under the procedural interpretation of *Winship*, a legislature could choose to require that the prosecution disprove a defense beyond a reasonable doubt, *or* it could choose to eliminate the defense entirely. But it could not adopt the compromise solution of recognizing the defense and requiring the defendant to establish its existence. In the following passage, Underwood confronts these implications of her argument and explains why she regards the compromise solution as constitutionally inappropriate:*

> Broad application of the requirement of proof beyond a reasonable doubt operates to foreclose certain kinds of compromise in the formulation of criminal law policy. In general, compromise is a desirable and indeed essential part of the lawmaking process. If this reading of the constitutional requirement [i.e., the procedural interpretation of *Winship*] seemed to foreclose sensible legislative options for no good reason, that would count heavily for a different and more felicitous reading. But the kind of compromise prohibited by the reasonable-doubt rule is less satisfactory than other forms of compromise that remain available, and therefore its loss is no ground for concern. . . .
>
> A substantive disagreement about whether to recognize a defense amounts to a disagreement about whether the person with

---

* Reprinted by permission of the author, The Yale Law Journal Company, and Fred B. Rothman & Company from The Yale Law Journal, vol. 86, pp. 1320–22.

the proposed defense is less suitable than other offenders for specified criminal sanctions. By shifting the burden of persuasion to the defendant, a legislature limits the defense to those for whom the evidence is most abundant. That group, however, is not necessarily the least culpable, least harmful, or least deterrable. For there is no reason to think that the continuum of culpability, harm, or deterrability bears any relationship to the continuum of available evidence. The person for whom the evidence is strongest may not be the person whose claim, if believed, has the strongest relationship to the policies behind the defense. A disagreement about the proper scope of the substantive criminal law can be compromised by an intermediate definition of the facts that constitute crimes and defenses. Tinkering with the reasonable-doubt rule, which determines when to believe a defendant's version of the facts, requires an explanation in terms of the purposes of that rule. But those purposes are no less relevant to factfinding when a controversial gratuitous defense is at issue than they are to the determination of any other fact in a criminal case. Indeed, any controversy over the defense may enhance the threat to the values the reasonable-doubt rule was designed to protect.

. . . A legislature uncertain about the merits of a proposed defense might reasonably wish to change its assessment of the relative costs of errors. But a constitutional valuation of the relative costs of errors cannot be avoided by legislative fiat. So long as the factual determination has the function and consequences that characterize other issues in a criminal case, such as enhanced stigma and an increased period of potential incarceration, the reasons for the constitutional rule remain. The costs of erroneous convictions and erroneous acquittals are not different by virtue of the gratuitous character of the defense. . . .

**3. Criticisms of the Procedural Approach.** The procedural interpretation of *Winship* has been attacked on a number of grounds. Representative criticisms are made by John C. Jeffries, Jr. and Paul B. Stephan III in Defenses, Presumptions, and Burden of Proof in the Criminal Law, 88 Yale L.J. 1325 (1979).[a] In their opinion, the rationales for the reasonable-doubt requirement demand that *something* be proved beyond a reasonable doubt, but "do not establish that *every* fact relevant to the imposition or grade of penal liability be subject to that standard." They focus squarely on the gratuitous defense. In their view, the constitutional insistence on proof beyond a reasonable doubt "no longer makes sense" when applied to a gratuitous defense. "Such a rule would purport to preserve individual liberty and the societal sense of commitment to it by forcing the govern-

[a] See also Ronald J. Allen, The Restoration of *In re Winship*: A Comment on Burdens of Persuasion in Criminal Cases After *Patterson* v. *New York*, 76 Mich.L.Rev. 30 (1977), and Ronald J. Allen, *Mullaney* v. *Wilbur*, The Supreme Court and the Substantive Criminal Law—An Examination of the Limits of Legitimate Intervention, 55 Tex.L.Rev. 269 (1977).

ment *either* to disprove the defense beyond a reasonable doubt *or* to eliminate the defense altogether." The government could cure the purported unconstitutionality *either* by proving more *or* by proving less, as it saw fit. "The latter solution results in an extension of penal liability despite the presence of mitigating or exculpatory facts. It is difficult to see this result as constitutionally compelled and harder still to believe that it flows from a general policy, whether actual or symbolic, in favor of individual liberty."

In addition to the theoretical criticism stated above, Jeffries and Stephan also make a practical evaluation of the procedural interpretation of *Winship*:*

> The procedural interpretation of *Winship* would not only be illogical in concept; it would also be potentially pernicious in effect. It is at least plausible, indeed we think it likely, that a rule barring reallocation of the burden of proof would thwart legislative reform of the penal law and stifle efforts to undo injustice in the traditional law of crimes. Even if one were to believe that rigid insistence on proof beyond a reasonable doubt might in some purely symbolic sense reaffirm the "presumption of innocence," it would do so at the risk of a harsh and regressive expansion in the definition of guilt.

> This is a point of some importance, for, quite surprisingly, proponents of a procedural interpretation of *Winship* have made exactly the contrary argument. They assume that forcing legislatures to choose between proving more and proving less would produce good choices. In other words, they argue that a legislature required to abandon an affirmative defense would be likely to force the prosecution to disprove the existence of a ground of exculpation beyond a reasonable doubt rather than to eliminate it altogether. Popular pressure, it is asserted, would act as a check against untoward expansion of criminal liability. The net effect, therefore, of disallowing the intermediate solution of an affirmative defense would be a benign and progressive influence on the substance of the penal law.

> Aside from failing to demonstrate whether this supposition, even if true, would be sufficient basis for constitutional adjudication, advocates of the procedural approach fail to produce evidence to support the supposition. The best evidence of what legislatures would do if they were forced to abandon the affirmative defense is the catalogue of uses to which that device is currently put. If it were used to disguise harsh innovations in the law of crimes, one might reasonably infer that elimination of the procedural device would have an ameliorative effect on substance. In point of fact, however, the burden-shifting defense quite generally is employed to moderate traditional rigors in the law of crimes. There is,

* Reprinted by permission of the authors, The Yale Law Journal Company, and Fred B.    Rothman & Company from The Yale Law Journal, vol. 88, pp. 1353–56.

therefore, reason to believe that rejection of this device would result in abandonment of the underlying substantive innovations and reversion to older and harsher rules of penal liability.

In order to test this proposition, we surveyed the practices of the 33 American states that have recently enacted comprehensive revisions of their penal laws. These are the jurisdictions that in modern times have had an occasion to confront the issues here under discussion. Eight of these states provide no statutory guidance on this point, and six more expressly require that the prosecution bear the burden of proof beyond a reasonable doubt for every fact needed to obtain conviction. However, 19 states have enacted revised codes that include burden-shifting defenses. Virtually all of these uses of the burden-shifting defense mark instances of benevolent innovation in the penal law. Thirteen states recognize an affirmative defense of renunciation for the crime of attempt. Nine permit reasonable mistake as to age as an affirmative defense to statutory rape. Eight create an affirmative defense to liability for felony murder, and six exonerate the accused if he can show reasonable reliance on an official misstatement of law. In each of these cases, the affirmative defense is used to introduce a new ground of exculpation, often in circumstances where an obligation to disprove its existence beyond a reasonable doubt would be especially onerous. None of the named defenses existed at common law, and none is a traditional feature of American statutes. A plausible conclusion is that shifting the burden of proof is often politically necessary to secure legislative reform. It seems quite possible, therefore, that disallowance of this procedural device would work to inhibit reform and induce retrogression in the penal law.

**4.  An Alternative Reformulation of *Mullaney*: The *Patterson* Dissent.** While the *Patterson* majority reinterpreted *Mullaney* in order to avoid it, the *Patterson* dissent reinterpreted *Mullaney* in order to save it. Interestingly, even Justice Powell's *Patterson* dissent does not take *Mullaney* at face value, but instead finds implicit in that decision two limiting criteria. First, "[t]he due-process clause requires that the prosecution bear the burden of persuasion beyond a reasonable doubt only if the factor at issue makes a substantial difference in punishment and stigma." Second, "[i]t must also be shown that in the Anglo–American legal tradition the factor in question historically has held that level of importance." Only where both conditions are met would burden-shifting be disallowed. But, as Justice Powell was at pains to point out, these criteria would not limit legislative authority over substance. Even where both criteria were met (and burden-shifting consequently forbidden), the legislature would remain free to eliminate altogether the mitigating or exculpatory effect of the fact in issue.

This approach has the advantage of reducing the risk of thwarting legislative reform, as few of the "benevolent innovations" described above would be barred by Powell's revised formulation. Yet he plainly would disallow the law in *Patterson*, which not only shifted to defendants the burden of persuasion but also broadened significantly the substantive criteria of mitigation. Should that be cause for concern?

One might also ask why the "Anglo–American legal tradition" should play so decisive a role in constitutional adjudication. Is there necessarily virtue in antiquity? Should the constitutionality of modern legislation depend on its consistency with the common law? And if history is to be decisive in limiting shifts in the burden of persuasion, why should it not also be decisive in limiting legislative power over the substance of the law? If the historic importance of provocation in the law of homicide precludes the legislature from shifting the burden of persuasion, why does it not also prevent the legislature from taking the much greater step of eliminating provocation altogether?

**5. Burden of Proof and Substantive Justice.** It seems clear that the underlying concern in much of the debate over burden of proof is not procedural regularity but substantive justice. This concern surfaces in the "horror stories" used to describe what a legislature might do if burden-shifting were allowed. Recall, for example, the *Patterson* footnote where Justice Powell speculates that a state might define murder "as mere physical contact between the defendant and the victim leading to the victim's death, but then set up an affirmative defense leaving it to the defendant to prove that he acted without culpable mens rea." By this device, says Justice Powell, the prosecution "could be relieved altogether of responsibility for proving *anything* regarding the defendant's state of mind...." Barbara Underwood advances a similar concern. What if, she asks, the legislature were to replace the entire range of homicide and assault offenses with the single crime of "personal attack?" Unless burden-shifting were disallowed, she continues, the legislature could authorize major penalties "on proof of a trivial assault, with the burden on the defendant to establish the mitigating defenses of the victim's survival, his freedom from injury, or the defendant's lack of intent to harm or injure."

These hypotheticals have much in common. Both envision serious punishment on proof beyond a reasonable doubt of no more than trivial wrongdoing. The result would be the use of burden-shifting defenses to impose criminal penalties far out of proportion to any proven misconduct by the accused.

Does the danger posed by these hypotheticals has any necessary connection with shifting the burden of proof? Consider the response of Jeffries and Stephan:

> The trouble [with this argument] lies in the unspoken assumption that excessive punishment is somehow a product of shifting the burden of proof. In fact, use of a burden-shifting defense ... does not necessarily result in excessive punishment, nor does excessive punishment necessarily involve reallocation of the burden of proof. Thus, to forbid burden-shifting devices *in order to* reduce disparity between proven fault and authorized

penalties is a non sequitur. In point of fact, a constitutional stricture against shifting the burden of proof would not prevent the injustice of unwarranted or disproportionate criminal punishment.... The hypothetical legislature that would assign the fact of the victim's survival to an affirmative defense to a "personal attack" charge just as easily could eliminate the victim's death as a grading factor for assaultive behavior. The state could simply authorize serious sanctions for any physical assault, whether fatal or trivial, and leave distinctions among cases to the sentencing stage. This scheme involves no reallocation of the burden of proof, but it is just as objectionable as Underwood's original hypothetical. Both schemes would authorize major felony sanctions on proof of nothing more than a trivial assault; both involve the infliction of punishment grossly disproportionate to any proven blameworthiness of the defendant.

The excerpt from Jeffries and Stephan also suggests their alternative construction of *In re Winship*. In their view, the constitutional insistence on proof beyond a reasonable doubt should extend only to facts constitutionally required to be proved. "In other words, *Winship* should be read to assert a constitutional requirement of proof beyond a reasonable doubt of a constitutionally adequate basis for imposing the punishment authorized." The state could shift to the defendant the burden of persuasion for any additional or gratuitous factor which it chose to take into account. The focus would be not on what the government invited the defendant to prove by way of mitigation or excuse, but rather on what the prosecution had to prove beyond a reasonable doubt in order to establish liability in the first instance. For Jeffries and Stephan, therefore, the question in both *Mullaney* and *Patterson* would be whether the facts required to be proved beyond a reasonable doubt established a constitutionally adequate basis for imposing the authorized maximum of life imprisonment. If so, "nothing would bar the state from going beyond the constitutional minimum to allow mitigation when the defendant can prove his claim to it." If not, the state would be required to establish a constitutionally adequate basis for life imprisonment by disproving heat of passion or extreme emotional disturbance beyond a reasonable doubt.

The Supreme Court's response to an argument of this sort is revealed in the following case.

————

## Martin v. Ohio

Supreme Court of the United States, 1987.
480 U.S. 228.

■ JUSTICE WHITE delivered the opinion of the Court.

The Ohio Code provides that "[e]very person accused of an offense is presumed innocent until proved guilty beyond a reasonable doubt, and the burden of proof for all elements of the offense is upon the prosecution. The burden of going forward with the evidence of an affirmative defense, and the burden of proof by a preponderance of the evidence, for an affirmative defense is upon the accused." Ohio Rev. Code Ann. § 2901.05(A) (1982).... The Ohio courts have "long determined that self-defense is an affirmative defense," 21 Ohio St. 3d 91, 93 (1986), and that the defendant has the burden of proving it as required by § 2901.05(A).

... The question before us is whether the due process clause of the 14th Amendment forbids placing the burden of proving self-defense on the defendant when she is charged by the state of Ohio with committing the crime of aggravated murder, which, as relevant tot his case, is defined by the Revised Code of Ohio as "purposely, and with prior calculation and design, caus[ing] the death of another." Ohio Rev. Code Ann. § 2903.1 (1982).

... On July 21, 1983, petitioner Earline Martin and her husband, Walter Martin, argued over grocery money. Petitioner claimed that her husband struck her in the head during the argument. Petitioner's version of what then transpired was that she went upstairs, put on a robe, and later came back down with her husband's gun which she intended to dispose of. Her husband saw something in her hand and questioned her about it. He came at her, she lost her head and fired the gun at him. Five or six shots were fired, three of them striking and killing Mr. Martin. She was charged with and tried for aggravated murder. She pleaded self-defense and testified in her own defense. The judge charged the jury with respect to the elements of the crime and of self-defense and rejected petitioner's due process clause challenge to the charge placing on her the burden of proving self-defense. The jury found her guilty....

In re Winship, 397 U.S. 358, 364 (1970), declared that the due process clause "protects the accused against conviction except upon proof beyond a reasonable doubt of every fact necessary to constitute the crime with which he is charged." A few years later, we held that *Winship*'s mandate was fully satisfied where the state of New York had proved beyond reasonable doubt each of the elements of murder, but placed on the defendant the burden of proving the affirmative defense of extreme emotional disturbance, which, if proved, would have reduced the crime from murder to manslaughter. Patterson v. New York, 432 U.S. 197 (1977)....

As in *Patterson*, the jury was here instructed that to convict it must find, in light of all the evidence, that each of the elements of the crime of aggravated murder has been proved by the state beyond reasonable doubt and that the burden of proof with respect to these elements did not shift. To find guilt, the jury had to be convinced that none of the evidence, whether offered by the state or by Martin in connection with her plea of self-defense, raised a reasonable doubt that Martin had killed her husband, that she had the specific purpose and intent to cause his death, or that she had done so with prior calculation and design. It was also told, however, that it could acquit if it found by a preponderance of the evidence that Martin had not precipitated the confrontation, that she had an honest belief that she was in imminent danger of death or great bodily harm, and that she had satisfied any duty to retreat or avoid danger. The jury convicted Martin.

We agree with the state ... that this conviction did not violate the due process clause. The state did not exceed its authority in defining the crime of murder as purposely causing the death of another with prior calculation or design. It did not seek to shift to Martin the burden of proving any of those elements, and the jury's verdict reflects that none of her self-defense evidence raised a reasonable doubt about the state's proof that she purposefully killed with prior calculation and design. She nevertheless had the opportunity under state law and the instructions given to justify the killing and show herself to be blameless by proving that she acted in self-defense. The jury thought she had failed to do so, and Ohio is as entitled to punish Martin as one guilty of murder as New York was to punish Patterson.

It would be quite different if the jury had been instructed that self-defense evidence could not be considered in determining whether there was a reasonable doubt about the state's case, i.e., that self-defense evidence must be put aside for all purposes unless it satisfied the preponderance standard. Such instruction would relieve the state of its burden and plainly run afoul of *Winship*'s mandate. The instructions in this case could be clearer in this respect, but when read as a whole, we think they are adequate to convey to the jury that all of the evidence, including the evidence going to self-defense, must be considered in deciding whether there was a reasonable doubt about the sufficiency of the state's proof of the elements of the crime. ...

As we noted in *Patterson*, the common-law rule was that affirmative defenses, including self-defense, were matters for the defendant to prove. ... We are aware that all but two of the states, Ohio and South Carolina, have abandoned the common-law rule and require the prosecution to prove the absence of self-defense when it is properly raised by the defendant. But the question remains whether those states are in violation of the Constitution; and, as we observed in *Patterson*, that question is not answered by cataloging the practices of other states. We are no more convinced that the Ohio practice of requiring self-defense to be proved by the defendant is unconstitutional than we are that the Constitution requires the prosecution to prove the sanity of a defendant who pleads not guilty by reason of insanity[, a proposition rejected in Leland v. Oregon, 343 U.S. 790 (1952), and again in Rivera v. Delaware, 429 U.S. 877 (1976).] The judgment of the Ohio Supreme Court is accordingly affirmed.

■ JUSTICE POWELL, with whom JUSTICE BRENNAN and JUSTICE MARSHALL join, and with whom JUSTICE BLACKMUN joins with respect to parts I and III, dissenting.

Today the Court holds that a defendant can be convicted of aggravated murder even though the jury may have a reasonable doubt whether the accused acted in self-defense, and thus, whether he is guilty of a crime. Because I think this decision is inconsistent with both precedent and fundamental fairness, I dissent.

I

Petitioner Earline Martin was tried in state court for the aggravated murder of her husband. Under Ohio law, the elements of the crime are that the defendant has purposely killed another with "prior calculation and design." Ohio Rev. Code Ann. § 2903.1 (1982). Martin admitted that she shot her husband, but claimed that she acted in self-defense. Because self-defense is classified as an "affirmative" defense in Ohio, the jury was instructed that Martin had the burden of proving her claim by a preponderance of the evidence. Martin apparently failed to carry this burden, and the jury found her guilty....

In Patterson v. New York, 432 U.S. 197 (1977), the Court upheld a state statute that shifted the burden of proof for an affirmative defense to the accused. New York law required the prosecutor to prove all of the statutorily defined elements of murder beyond a reasonable doubt, but permitted a defendant to reduce the charge to manslaughter by showing that he acted while suffering an "extreme emotional disturbance." The Court found that this burden-shifting did not violate due process because the affirmative defense did "not serve to negative any facts of the crime which the state is to prove in order to convict of murder." Id., at 207. The clear implication of this ruling is that when an affirmative defense *does* negate an element of the crime, the state may not shift the burden....

The reason for treating a defense that negates an element of the crime differently from other affirmative defenses is plain. If the jury is told that the prosecution has the burden of proving all the elements of a crime, but then also is instructed that the defendant has the burden of *dis*proving one of those same elements, there is a danger that the jurors will resolve the inconsistency in a way that lessens the presumption of innocence. For example, the jury might reasonable believe that by raising the defense, the accused has assumed the ultimate burden of proving that particular element. Or, it might reconcile the instructions simply by balancing the prosecutor's case against the evidence supporting the affirmative defense, and conclude that the state has satisfied its burden if the prosecution's version is more persuasive. In either case, the jury is given the unmistakable but erroneous impression that the defendant shares the risk of nonpersuasion as to a fact necessary for conviction.

Given these principles, the Court's reliance on *Patterson* is puzzling. Under Ohio law, the element of "prior calculation and design" is satisfied only when the accused has engaged in a "definite process of reasoning *in advance* of the killing," i.e., when he has given the plan at least some "studied consideration," [citing jury instructions, emphasis added]. In contrast, when a defendant such as Martin raises a claim of self-defense, the jury also is instructed that the accused must prove that she "had an honest belief that she was in *imminent* danger of death of great bodily harm." Id. (emphasis added). In many cases, a defendant who finds himself in immediate danger and reacts with deadly force will not have formed a prior intent to kill.... Under *Patterson*, this conclusion should suggest that Ohio is precluded from shifting the burden as to self-defense....

## II

Although I believe that this case is wrongly decided even under the principles set forth in *Patterson*, my differences with the Court's approach are more fundamental. I continue to believe that the better method for deciding when a state may shift the burden of proof is outlined in the Court's opinion in Mullaney v. Wilbur, 421 U.S. 684 (1975), and in my dissenting opinion in *Patterson*. In *Mullaney*, we emphasized that the state's obligation to prove certain facts beyond a reasonable doubt was not necessarily restricted to legislative distinctions between offenses and affirmative defenses. The boundaries of the state's authority in this respect were elaborated in the *Patterson* dissent, where I proposed a two-part inquiry:

> The due process clause requires that the prosecutor bear the burden of persuasion beyond a reasonable doubt only if the factor at issue makes a substantial difference in punishment and stigma. The requirement of course applies a fortiori if the factor makes the difference between guilt and innocence.... It also must be shown that in the Anglo–American legal tradition the factor in question historically has held that level of importance. If either branch of the test is not met, then the legislature retains its traditional authority over matters of proof. 432 U.S., at 226–27 (footnotes omitted)....

There are at least two benefits to this approach. First, it ensures that the critical facts necessary to sustain a conviction will be proved by the state. Because the Court would be willing to look beyond the text of a state statute, legislatures would have no incentive to redefine essential elements of an offense to make them part of an affirmative defense, thereby shifting the burden of proof in a manner inconsistent with *Winship* and *Mullaney*. Second, it would leave the states free in all other respects to recognize new factors that may mitigate the degree of criminality or punishment, without requiring that they also bear the burden of disproving these defenses.

Under this analysis, it plainly is impermissible to require the accused to prove self-defense. If petitioner could have carried her burden, the result would have been decisively different as to both guilt and punishment. There also is no dispute that self-defense historically is one of the primary justifications for otherwise unlawful conduct. Thus, while I acknowledge that the two-part test may be difficult to apply at times, it is hard to imagine a more clear-cut application than the one presented here.

## III

In its willingness to defer to the state's legislative definitions of crimes and defenses, the Court apparently has failed to recognize the practical effect of its decision. Martin alleged that she was innocent because she acted in self-defense, a complete justification under Ohio law. Because she had the burden of proof on this issue, the jury could have believed that it was just as likely as not that Martin's conduct was justified, and yet still have voted to convict. In other words, even though the jury may have had a substantial doubt whether Martin committed a crime, she was found guilty under Ohio law. I do not agree that the Court's authority to review state legislative choices is so limited that is justifies increasing the risk of convicting a person who may not be blameworthy. See *Patterson v. New York*, supra, at 201–02 (state definition of criminal law must yield when it " 'offends some principle of justice so rooted in the traditions and conscience of our people as to be ranked as fundamental' " (quoting Speiser v. Randall, 357 U.S. 513, 123 (1958)). The complexity of the inquiry as to when a state may shift the burden of proof should not lead the Court to fashion simple rules of deference that could lead to such unjust results.

_____

### NOTE ON *MARTIN v. OHIO*

*Martin* is complicated by the fact that the offense of aggravated murder, requiring "prior calculation and design," and the defense of self-defense seem to overlap. This overlap allows the majority to say that *Patterson* was observed, because "prior calculation and design" had to be proved beyond a reasonable doubt. The overlap also allows the dissent to argue that *Patterson* was violated, because the jury might not have required proof beyond a reasonable doubt, given the burden-shifting instructions on self defense.

What would have happened had there been no overlap between offense and defense? What if Ohio law had defined murder simply as "intentional homicide" and required the accused to prove self-defense? *Patterson* would be satisfied, because the burden of proof is not shifted with respect to any element of the crime charged. Would the dissent have found that scheme acceptable?

A similar question could be posed to the dissent. Suppose that Ohio, fearing frequent abuse, eliminated self-defense as a defense to liability and relegated it to the discretion of the trial judge in imposing sentence. There would be no violation of *Patterson* or *Mullaney* because there would be no burden-shifting. Would that scheme be acceptable under either of the views expressed in *Martin*?

_____

## SUBSECTION B: PRESUMPTIONS

_____

## Sandstrom v. Montana

Supreme Court of the United States, 1979.
442 U.S. 510.

■ MR. JUSTICE BRENNAN delivered the opinion of the Court.

The question presented is whether, in a case in which intent is an element of the crime charged, the jury instruction "the law presumes that a person intends the ordinary consequences of his voluntary acts," violates the 14th Amendment's requirement that the state prove every element of a criminal offense beyond a reasonable doubt.

## I

On November 22, 1976, 18–year-old David Sandstrom confessed to the slaying of Annie Jessen. Based upon the confession and corroborating evidence, petitioner was charged on December 2 with "deliberate homicide," Rev. Code Mont. § 45–5–102, in that he "purposely or knowingly caused the death of Annie Jessen."[1] At trial, Sandstrom's attorney informed the jury that, although his client admitted killing Jessen, he did not do so "purposely or knowingly," and was therefore not guilty of "deliberate homicide" but of a lesser crime. The basic support for this contention was the testimony of two court-appointed mental health experts, each of whom described for the jury petitioner's mental state at the time of the incident. Sandstrom's attorney argued that this testimony demonstrated that petitioner, due to a personality disorder aggravated by alcohol consumption, did not kill Annie Jessen "purposely or knowingly."

The prosecution requested the trial judge to instruct the jury that "[t]he law presumes that a person intends the ordinary consequences of his voluntary acts." Petitioner's counsel objected, arguing that "the instruction has the effect of shifting the burden of proof on the issue of" purpose or knowledge to the defense, and that "that is impermissible under the federal Constitution, due process of law." He offered to provide a number of federal decisions in support of the objection, including this Court's holding in Mullaney v. Wilbur, 421 U.S. 684 (1975), but was told by the judge: "You can give those to the Supreme Court. The objection is overruled." The instruction was delivered, the jury found petitioner guilty of deliberate homicide, and petitioner was sentenced to 100 years in prison.

Sandstrom appealed to the Supreme Court of Montana, again contending that the instruction shifted to the defendant the burden of disproving an element of the crime charged, in violation of *Mullaney* v. *Wilbur*, supra, In re Winship, 397 U.S. 358 (1970), and Patterson v. New York, 432 U.S. 197 (1977). The Montana court conceded that these cases did prohibit shifting the burden of proof to the defendant by means of a presumption, but held that these cases "do not prohibit allocation of *some* burden of

---

[1] The statute provides:

§ 45–5–101. Criminal homicide.

(1) A person commits the offense of criminal homicide if he purposely, knowingly, or negligently causes the death of another human being.

(2) Criminal homicide is deliberate homicide, mitigated deliberate homicide, or negligent homicide.

§ 45–5–102. Deliberate homicide.

(1) Except as provided in 45–5–103(1), criminal homicide constitutes deliberate homicide if:

(a) it is committed purposely or knowingly. . . .

proof to a defendant under certain circumstances." Since in the court's view "[d]efendant's sole burden ... was to produce *some* evidence that he did not intend the ordinary consequences of his voluntary acts, not to disprove that he acted 'purposely' or 'knowingly,' ... the instruction does not violate due process standards as defined by the United States or Montana Constitution...." [Emphasis added].

Both federal and state courts have held, under a variety of rationales, that the giving of an instruction similar to that challenged here is fatal to the validity of a criminal conviction. We granted certiorari to decide the important question of the instruction's constitutionality. We reverse.

## II

The threshold inquiry in ascertaining the constitutional analysis applicable to this kind of jury instruction is to determine the nature of the presumption it describes. That determination requires careful attention to the words actually spoken to the jury, for whether a defendant has been accorded his constitutional rights depends upon the way in which a reasonable juror could have interpreted the instruction.

Respondent argues, first, that the instruction merely described a permissive inference—that is, it allowed but did not require the jury to draw conclusions about defendant's intent from his actions—and that such inferences are constitutional. These arguments need not detain us long, for even respondent admits that "it's possible" that the jury believed they were required to apply the presumption. Sandstrom's jurors were told that "[t]he law presumes that a person intends the ordinary consequences of his voluntary acts." They were not told that they had a choice, or that they might infer that conclusion; they were told only that the law presumed it. It is clear that a reasonable juror could easily have viewed such an instruction as mandatory.

In the alternative, respondent urges that, even if viewed as a mandatory presumption rather than as a permissive inference, the presumption did not conclusively establish intent but rather could be rebutted. On this view, the instruction required the jury, if satisfied as to the facts which trigger the presumption, to find intent *unless* the defendant offered evidence to the contrary. Moreover, according to the state, all the defendant had to do to rebut the presumption was produce "some" contrary evidence; he did not have to "prove" that he lacked the required mental state. Thus, "[a]t most, it placed a *burden of production* on the petitioner," but "did not shift to petitioner the *burden of persuasion* with respect to any element of the offense...." [Emphasis added.] Again, respondent contends that presumptions with this limited effect pass constitutional muster.

We need not review respondent's constitutional argument on this point either, however, for we reject this characterization of the presumption as well. Respondent concedes there is a "risk" that the jury, once having found petitioner's act voluntary, would interpret the instruction as automatically directing a finding of intent. Moreover, the state also concedes that numerous courts "have differed as to the effect of the presumption when given as a jury instruction without further explanation as to its use by the jury," and that some have found it to shift more than the burden of production, and even to have conclusive effect. Nonetheless, the state contends that the only authoritative reading of the effect of the presumption resides in the Supreme Court of Montana. And the state argues that by holding that "[d]efendant's sole burden ... was to produce *some* evidence that he did not intend the ordinary consequences of his voluntary acts, not to disprove that he acted 'purposely' or 'knowingly,' " (emphasis added), the Montana Supreme Court decisively established that the presumption at most affected only the burden of going forward with evidence of intent—that is, the burden of production.

The Supreme Court of Montana is, of course, the final authority on the legal weight to be given a presumption under Montana law, but it is not the final authority on the interpretation which a jury could have given the instruction. If Montana intended its presumption to have only the effect described by its Supreme Court, then we are convinced that a reasonable juror could well have been misled by the instruction given, and could have believed that the presumption was not limited to requiring the defendant to satisfy only a burden of production. Petitioner's jury was told that "the law *presumes* that a person intends the ordinary consequences of his voluntary acts." They were not told that the presumption could be rebutted, as the Montana Supreme Court held, by the defendant's simple presentation of "some" evidence; nor even that it could be rebutted at all. Given the common definition of "presume" as "to suppose to be true without proof," and given the lack of qualifying instructions as to the legal effect of the presumption, we cannot discount the possibility that the jury may have interpreted the instruction in either of two more stringent ways.

First, a reasonable jury could well have interpreted the presumption as "conclusive," that is, not technically as a presumption at all, but rather as an irrebuttable direction by the court to find intent once convinced of the facts triggering the presumption. Alternatively, the jury may have interpreted the instruction as a direction to find intent upon proof of the defendant's voluntary actions (and their "ordinary" consequences), unless *the defendant* proved the contrary by some quantum of proof which may well have been considerably greater than "some" evidence—thus effectively shifting the burden of persuasion on the element of intent. Numerous federal and state courts have warned that instructions of the type given here can be interpreted in just these ways. And although the Montana Supreme Court held to the contrary in this case, Montana's own Rules of Evidence expressly state that the presumption at issue here may be overcome only "by a preponderance of evidence contrary to the presumption." Montana Rule of Evidence 301(b)(2). Such a requirement shifts not only the burden of production, but also the ultimate burden of persuasion on the issue of intent.[7]

---

[7] The potential for these interpretations of the presumption was not removed by the other instructions given at the trial. It is true that the jury was instructed generally that the accused was presumed innocent until proved guilty, and that the state had the

We do not reject the possibility that some jurors may have interpreted the challenged instruction as permissive, or, if mandatory, as requiring only that the defendant come forward with "some" evidence in rebuttal. However, the fact that a reasonable juror could have given the presumption conclusive or persuasion-shifting effect means that we cannot discount the possibility that Sandstrom's jurors actually did proceed upon one or the other of these latter interpretations. And that means that unless these kinds of presumptions are constitutional, the instruction cannot be adjudged valid. It is the line of cases urged by the petitioner, and exemplified by In re Winship, 397 U.S. 358 (1970), that provides the appropriate mode of constitutional analysis for these kinds of presumptions.

### III

In *Winship*, the Court stated:

> Lest there remain any doubt about the constitutional stature of the reasonable-doubt standard, we explicitly hold that the due process clause protects the accused against conviction except upon proof beyond a reasonable doubt of every *fact* necessary to constitute the crime with which he is charged. [Emphasis added.]

Accord, *Patterson* v. *New York*, supra. The petitioner here was charged with and convicted of deliberate homicide, committed purposely or knowingly.... It is clear that under Montana law, whether the crime was committed purposely or knowingly is a fact necessary to constitute the crime of deliberate homicide. Indeed, it was the lone element of the offense at issue in Sandstrom's trial, as he confessed to causing the death of the victim, told the jury that knowledge and purpose were the only questions he was controverting, and introduced evidence solely on those points. Moreover, it is conceded that proof of defendant's "intent" would be sufficient to establish this element. Thus, the question before this Court is whether the challenged jury instruction had the effect of relieving the state of the burden of proof enunciated in *Winship* on the critical question of petitioner's state of mind. We conclude that under either of the two possible interpretations of the instruction set out above, precisely that effect would result, and that the instruction therefore represents constitutional error.

We consider first the validity of a conclusive presumption. This Court has [previously] considered such a presumption.... In Morissette v. United States, 342 U.S. 246 (1952), the defendant was charged with willful and knowing theft of government property. Although his attorney argued that

burden of proving beyond a reasonable doubt that the defendant caused the death of the deceased purposely or knowingly. But this is not rhetorically inconsistent with a conclusive or burden-shifting presumption. The jury could have interpreted the two sets of instructions as indicating that the presumption was a means by which proof beyond a reason-able doubt as to intent could be satisfied. For example, if the presumption were viewed as conclusive, the jury could have believed that although intent must be proved beyond a reasonable doubt, proof of the voluntary slaying and its ordinary consequences constituted proof of intent beyond a reasonable doubt....

for his client to be found guilty, "the taking must have been with felonious intent," the trial judge ruled that "[t]hat is presumed by his own act." After first concluding that intent was in fact an element of the crime charged, and after declaring that "[w]here intent of the accused is an ingredient of the crime charged, its existence is . . . a jury issue," *Morissette* held:

> *It follows that the trial court may not withdraw or prejudge the issue by instruction that the law raises a presumption of intent from an act.* It often is tempting to cast in terms of a "presumption" a conclusion which a court thinks probable from given facts. . . . [But we] think presumptive intent has no place in this case. *A conclusive presumption which testimony could not overthrow would effectively eliminate intent as an ingredient of the offense.* A presumption which would permit but not require the jury to assume intent from an isolated fact would prejudge a conclusion which the jury should reach of its own volition. A presumption which would permit the jury to make an assumption which all the evidence considered together does not logically establish would give to a proven fact an artificial and fictional effect. In either case, *this presumption would conflict with the overriding presumption of innocence with which the law endows the accused and which extends to every element of the crime.* [Emphasis added.]
>
> . . .

As in *Morissette* . . ., a conclusive presumption in this case would "conflict with the overriding presumption of innocence with which the law endows the accused and which extends to every element of the crime," and would "invade [the] factfinding function" which in a criminal case the law assigns solely to the jury. The instruction announced to David Sandstrom's jury may well have had exactly these consequences. Upon finding proof of one element of the crime (causing death), and of facts insufficient to establish the second (the voluntariness and "ordinary consequences" of defendant's action), Sandstrom's jurors could reasonably have concluded that they were directed to find against defendant on the element of intent. The state was thus not forced to prove "beyond a reasonable doubt . . . every fact necessary to constitute the crime . . . charged," and defendant was deprived of his constitutional rights as explicated in *Winship.*

A presumption which, although not conclusive, had the effect of shifting the burden of persuasion to the defendant, would have suffered from similar infirmities. If Sandstrom's jury interpreted the presumption in that manner, it could have concluded that upon proof by the state of the slaying, and of additional facts not themselves establishing the element of intent, the burden was shifted to the defendant to prove that he lacked the requisite mental state. Such a presumption was found constitutionally deficient in Mullaney v. Wilbur, 421 U.S. 684 (1975). In *Mullaney* the charge was murder, which under Maine law required proof not only of intent but of malice. The trial court charged the jury that " 'malice aforethought is an essential and indispensable element of the crime of murder.' " However, it also instructed that if the prosecution established that the homicide was both intentional and unlawful, malice aforethought was to be implied unless the defendant proved by a fair preponderance of the evidence that he acted in the heat of passion on sudden provocation. As we recounted just two terms ago in *Patterson* v. *New York*, supra, "[t]his Court ... unanimously agreed with the Court of Appeals that Wilbur's due process rights had been invaded by the presumption casting upon him the burden of proving by a preponderance of the evidence that he had acted in the heat of passion upon sudden provocation." And *Patterson* reaffirmed that "a state must prove every ingredient of an offense beyond a reasonable doubt, and ... may not shift the burden of proof to the defendant" by means of such a presumption.

Because David Sandstrom's jury may have interpreted the judge's instruction as constituting either a burden-shifting presumption like that in *Mullaney*, or a conclusive presumption like that in *Morissette* ..., and because either interpretation would have deprived defendant of his right to the due process of law, we hold the instruction given in this case unconstitutional....

[The concurring opinion of Mr. Justice Rehnquist, with whom the Chief Justice joined, is omitted.]

--------

### NOTES ON PRESUMPTIONS AND THE BURDEN OF PROOF

**1. Introduction.** A presumption arises when the existence of one fact is "presumed" from proof of another. Unfortunately, this description covers a variety of evidentiary relationships. The *Sandstrom* Court's classification of conclusive presumptions, rebuttable presumptions, and permissive inferences is helpful, but this usage is not uniformly followed. Moreover, as the facts of *Sandstrom* illustrate, courts often identify "presumptions" without further specifying their procedural consequences. For these reasons it is important that any use of the label "presumption" be approached with caution and that care be taken to determine precisely what the term is used to designate. For an excellent survey, see Graham Lilly, An Introduction to the Law of Evidence 55–80 (2d ed. 1987).

**2. Conclusive Presumptions.** The *Sandstrom* Court was concerned that the jury might have construed the instruction on intending the ordinary consequences of one's voluntary acts as creating a conclusive or mandatory presumption. Perhaps it might have been so understood, but in fact the true conclusive presumption is extremely rare in the criminal law. The effect of this device is, of course, simply to redefine the substantive law. If fact *A* is *conclusively* presumed from fact *B*, proof of *B* becomes sufficient, and *A* is rendered unnecessary and irrelevant. Thus, on the facts of *Sandstrom*, a conclusive presumption would have redefined the crime of murder to require not a subjective intent to kill, but an objective determination that death of another was an "ordinary consequence" of the fendant's voluntary acts. Cf. *Director of Public Prosecutions v. Smith*, Chapter II, supra.

The *Sandstrom* Court declared that this construction would be unconstitutional. Why? Would a conclusive presumption of intent from proof of the ordinary consequences of one's voluntary acts "conflict with the overriding presumption of innocence"? Would it "invade [the] factfinding function" of the jury? Perhaps the answer to these questions depends on whether Montana would have constitutional authority to base liability for the crime of "deliberate homicide" on proof of negligence. Does *Sandstrom* stand for the proposition that it would be unconstitutional to impose sanctions typically associated with murder on proof of merely negligent homicide? If not, what exactly is the discussion of conclusive presumptions designed to forbid?

**3. Rebuttable Presumptions.** A second possibility considered in *Sandstrom* is that the jury might have construed the instruction as creating a rebuttable or burden-shifting presumption. Under this interpretation, proof that death of another was an "ordinary consequence" of the defendant's voluntary acts would shift to him the obligation to disprove that he killed purposely or knowingly. The *Sandstrom* Court concluded that this kind of presumption would be constitutionally invalid under *Mullaney*. Is that conclusion sound? Does it depend on whether the state could constitutionally have imprisoned the defendant for 100 years merely on proof that he killed by voluntary acts the ordinary consequence of which was death of another?

A different way to approach this issue is to ask whether the following hypothetical statute would be unconstitutional under the authority of *Sandstrom*:

Section 101. Criminal homicide.

(1) A person commits the offense of criminal homicide if he causes the death of another human being by voluntary acts the ordinary consequence of which is death of another.

(2) Criminal homicide is aggravated criminal homicide [carrying a maximum term of life imprisonment] or simple criminal homicide [carrying a maximum term of imprisonment for five years].

(3) It is an affirmative defense to aggravated criminal homicide, but not to simple criminal homicide, that the actor did not kill purposely or knowingly.

Does *Sandstrom* stand for the invalidity of such a statute? If not, can the state of Montana achieve substantively the same result deemed unconstitutional by the Supreme Court simply by rephrasing its law to avoid use of the language of presumption? Is the message of *Sandstrom* merely to avoid a confusing vocabulary, or are there substantive concerns at stake?

**4. Shift in the Burden of Production.** Another possibility raised by the state's argument in *Sandstrom* is that a presumption might be construed to shift to the defendant only the burden of production. So construed, the presumption would not affect the prosecution's obligation to persuade the trier of fact beyond a reasonable doubt, but would place on the defendant the obligation to see that a particular issue is raised by the evidence. This is the functional description of a defense, and most devices that shift to the defendant only the burden of production are called defenses. On such an issue, if the burden of production is not met, the issue is simply not raised, and the jury is given no instruction on the subject. Whether many such devices would be labeled presumptions seems doubtful, but in any event, *Mullaney* and *Patterson* make clear that a device that shifts to the defendant only the burden of production is constitutionally permissible.

**5.   Permissive Inferences.** The final possibility considered by the *Sandstrom* Court is that the trial judge's instruction only stated a permissive inference. Under this view, the jury would have been allowed, but not required, to consider the ordinary consequences of the defendant's voluntary acts in determining whether he killed purposely or knowingly, but would have been instructed to make the ultimate finding of purpose or knowledge beyond a reasonable doubt. Apparently, this sort of evidentiary device is constitutional, and presumably, there would have been no defect in the *Sandstrom* conviction if the trial court had explicitly couched the instruction in these terms. Is the basis for this conclusion clear? Why does the Supreme Court attach so much importance to the explicit differentiation of presumptions and permissive inferences? Could juries be expected to make the distinction with equal care?

Ronald Allen has argued that presumptions (of whatever sort) and permissive inferences are not so clearly different and that in fact both have a lot in common with other devices such as defenses, affirmative defenses, and comments on the evidence. Allen's conclusion is that all these devices should be constitutionally permissible so long as they are not used to undermine the state's obligation to prove beyond a reasonable doubt a constitutionally sufficient basis to support the punishment authorized. See Ronald J. Allen, Structuring Jury Decisionmaking in Criminal Cases: A Unified Constitutional Approach to Evidentiary Devices, 94 Harv.L.Rev. 321 (1980). Charles Nesson, on the other hand, shares Allen's view that these various evidentiary devices are not readily distinguishable, but believes that they should generally be condemned as unconstitutional. See Charles R. Nesson, Reasonable Doubt and Permissive Inferences: The Value of Complexity, 92 Harv.L.Rev. 1187 (1979). Both Allen and Nesson have written in rebuttal of the other's view. See Charles R. Nesson, Rationality, Presumptions, and Judicial Comment: A Response to Professor Allen, 94 Harv.L.Rev. 1574 (1981), and Ronald J. Allen, More on Constitutional Process-of-Proof Problems in Criminal Cases, 94 Harv.L.Rev. 1795 (1981).

**6.   Defenses, Presumptions, and Legislative Candor.** An argument occasionally advanced in the context of affirmative defenses, and more forcefully pressed in the context of presumptions, is that such devices should be declared unconstitutional in order to induce legislative candor. The contention is that legislatures use presumptions to disadvantage defendants in ways that the people would find unacceptable if they understood the legislative action. If presumptions are outlawed, the argument continues, the legislative intention will be forced out in the open and thus made amenable to popular control through the political process.

This argument was first developed in Harold A. Ashford and D. Michael Risinger, Presumptions, Assumptions, and Due Process in Criminal Cases: A Theoretical Overview, 79 Yale L.J. 165, 177–78 (1969). Their discussion was based on a hypothetical suggesting the following three statutes:

> (i) It shall be a crime for an individual to be present in a house where he knows narcotics are illegally kept.

> (ii) It shall be a crime for an individual to be present in a house where narcotics are illegally kept, whether or not he knows that the narcotics are so kept.

> (iii) It shall be a crime for an individual to be present in a house where he knows narcotics are illegally kept, but such knowledge may be presumed from the fact that the defendant was present in a house where narcotics were so kept.

In the first hypothetical statute, the legislature has made liability turn on three factors: presence of the individual, presence of narcotics in the house, and the defendant's knowledge. In the second statute, only two factors are made relevant to liability: presence of the individual and presence of narcotics in the house. In the view of Ashford and Risinger, the third statute is designed to look like the first but work like the second. The risk, therefore, is that the legislature might use a presumption to undermine the political process:

> If the legislature nominally recognizes knowledge as germane (as it did in the first statute) and further, as the type of germane issue to be proved by the state, and then arranges its processes so that most of those who lack knowledge are still sent to jail (as though the second statute had been passed), then those individuals are punished for a crime which has never undergone the political checks guaranteed by representative government. This, we believe, is a violation of due process.

Is this persuasive? Certainly, the use of presumptions may render penal statutes obscure and inaccessible. But does that make them unconstitutional? If so, should criminal statutes be declared unconstitutional whenever they use (or rely on the courts to use) obscure language? Arguably, this proposition might require that the entire mens-rea structure of the common law be declared unconstitutional. Would the political electorate would understand the meaning of "malice aforethought" or the difference between "specific" and "general" intent? Should the legislature be prohibited from using such formulations on the ground that the general public might not understand them? If not, what is the basis for invalidating presumptions that have the same effect?

————

## SUBSECTION C: SENTENCING

————

### INTRODUCTORY NOTE ON *WINSHIP* AND SENTENCING

Up to this point, the materials have addressed applications of *Winship* to facts bearing on whether the defendant should be convicted of an offense and, if so, the grade of that offense. When these facts are contested, they are adjudicated at trial where a defendant charged with felonies or serious misdemeanors is entitled by the Sixth Amendment to have the jury decide the facts. The following case and its accompanying notes address whether, and under what circumstances, the due process clause requires the factual predicates for decisions regarding the severity of *sentences* to be proved beyond a reasonable doubt.

Before studying these materials, it is important to recognize that the sentencing hearing has traditionally been much less formal than the trial, and that sentencing decisions in non-capital cases are made by judges rather than juries in most states and in the federal courts. In making sentencing decisions, judges almost always make factual determinations about the offender's background, character and record, and often take evidence relating to circumstances of the offense beyond the facts that are embedded in the conviction. It should come as no surprise, then, that defense attorneys have argued that at least some of the factual predicates for sentencing judgments should be subject to a heightened standard of proof, especially if they make the defendant eligible for greater punishment than the offense for which he was convicted (and are functionally equivalent to increasing the grade of the offense). Similar arguments have been raised about factual findings that make the defendant eligible for a minimum sentence, thereby curtailing the discretion of the sentencing judge.

These questions implicate fundamental questions about the sentencing process and go well beyond the coverage of an introductory course in criminal law. It should come as no surprise, for example, that arguments for applying *Winship* to factual predicates of enhanced sentences and minimum sentences are often accompanied by arguments that these findings should be made by juries, rather than judges. All of these issues cannot be covered here, but the next main case, *Apprendi v. New Jersey*, provides a digestible introduction to due process in sentencing.

————

# Apprendi v. New Jersey

Supreme Court of the United States, 2000.
530 U.S. 466.

■ JUSTICE STEVENS delivered the opinion of the Court.

A New Jersey statute classifies the possession of a firearm for an unlawful purpose as a "second-degree" offense. Such an offense is punishable by imprisonment for "between five years and 10 years." A separate statute, described by that State's Supreme Court as a "hate crime" law, provides for an "extended term" of imprisonment if the trial judge finds, by a preponderance of the evidence, that "the defendant in committing the crime acted with a purpose to intimidate an individual or group of individuals because of race, color, gender, handicap, religion, sexual orientation or ethnicity." The extended term authorized by the hate crime law for second-degree offenses is imprisonment for "between 10 and 20 years."

The question presented is whether the due process clause of the 14th Amendment requires that a factual determination authorizing an increase in the maximum prison sentence for an offense from 10 to 20 years be made by a jury on the basis of proof beyond a reasonable doubt.

I

At 2:04 a.m. on December 22, 1994, petitioner Charles C. Apprendi, Jr., fired several .22–caliber bullets into the home of an African–American family that had recently moved into a previously all-white neighborhood in Vineland, New Jersey. Apprendi was promptly arrested and, at 3:05 a.m., admitted that he was the shooter. After further questioning, at 6:04 a.m., he made a statement—which he later retracted—that even though he did not know the occupants of the house personally, "because they are black in color he does not want them in the neighborhood."

A New Jersey grand jury returned a 23–count indictment charging Apprendi with four first-degree, eight second-degree, six third-degree, and five fourth-degree offenses. The charges alleged shootings on four different dates, as well as the unlawful possession of various weapons. None of the counts referred to the hate crime statute, and none alleged that Apprendi acted with a racially biased purpose.

The parties entered into a plea agreement, pursuant to which Apprendi pleaded guilty to two counts (3 and 18) of second-degree possession of a firearm for an unlawful purpose, and one count (22) of the third-degree offense of unlawful possession of an antipersonnel bomb; the prosecutor dismissed the other 20 counts. Under state law, a second-degree offense carries a penalty range of 5 to 10 years; a third-degree offense carries a penalty range of between 3 and 5 years. As part of the plea agreement, however, the State reserved the right to request the court to impose a higher "enhanced" sentence on count 18 (which was based on the December 22 shooting) on the ground that that offense was committed with a biased purpose. Apprendi, correspondingly, reserved the right to challenge the hate crime sentence enhancement on the ground that it violates the United States constitution.

At the plea hearing, the trial judge heard sufficient evidence to establish Apprendi's guilt on counts 3, 18, and 22; the judge then confirmed that Apprendi understood the maximum sentences that could be imposed on those counts. Because the plea agreement provided that the sentence on the sole third-degree offense (count 22) would run concurrently with the other sentences, the potential sentences on the two second-degree counts were critical. If the judge found no basis for the biased purpose enhancement, the maximum consecutive sentences on those counts would amount to 20 years in aggregate; if, however, the judge enhanced the sentence on count 18, the maximum on that count alone would be 20 years and the maximum for the two counts in aggregate would be 30 years, with a 15–year period of parole ineligibility.

After the trial judge accepted the three guilty pleas, the prosecutor filed a formal motion for an extended term. The trial judge thereafter held an evidentiary hearing on the issue of Apprendi's "purpose" for the shooting on December 22. Apprendi adduced evidence from a psychologist and from seven character witnesses who testified that he did not have a reputation for racial bias. He also took the stand himself, explaining that the incident was an unintended consequence of overindulgence in alcohol, denying that he was in any way biased against African–Americans, and denying that his statement to the police had been accurately described. The judge, however, found the police officer's testimony credible, and concluded that the evidence supported a finding "that the crime was motivated by racial bias." Having found "by a preponderance of the evidence" that Apprendi's actions were taken "with a purpose to intimidate" as provided by the statute, the trial judge held that the hate crime enhancement applied. Rejecting Apprendi's constitutional challenge to the statute, the judge sentenced him to a 12–year term of imprisonment on count 18, and to shorter concurrent sentences on the other two counts.

Apprendi appealed, arguing, inter alia, that the due process clause of the United States Constitution requires that the finding of bias upon which his hate crime sentence was based must be proved to a jury beyond a reasonable doubt. Over dissent, the Appellate Division of the Superior Court of New Jersey upheld the enhanced sentence. Relying on our decision in McMillan v. Pennsylvania, 477 U.S. 79 (1986), the appeals court found that the state legislature decided to make the hate crime enhancement a "sentencing factor," rather than an element of an underlying offense—and that decision was within the state's established power to define the elements of its crimes. The hate crime statute did not create a presumption of guilt, the court determined, and did not appear "tailored to permit the . . . finding to be a tail which wags the dog of the substantive offense" (quoting McMillan). Characterizing the required finding as one of "motive," the court described it as a traditional "sentencing factor," one not considered an "essential element" of any crime unless the legislature so provides. While recognizing that the hate crime law did expose defendants to "greater and additional punishment," (quoting *McMillan*), the court held that that "one factor standing alone" was not sufficient to render the statute unconstitutional.

A divided New Jersey Supreme Court affirmed. ...We granted certiorari and now reverse....

### III

In his 1881 lecture on the criminal law, Oliver Wendell Holmes, Jr., observed: "The law threatens certain pains if you do certain things, intending thereby to give you a new motive for not doing them. If you persist in doing them, it has to inflict the pains in order that its threats may continue to be believed." New Jersey threatened Apprendi with certain pains if he unlawfully possessed a weapon and with additional pains if he selected his victims with a purpose to intimidate them because of their race. As a matter of simple justice, it seems obvious that the procedural safeguards designed to protect Apprendi from unwarranted pains should apply equally to the two acts that New Jersey has singled out for punishment. Merely using the label "sentence enhancement" to describe the latter surely does not provide a principled basis for treating them differently.

At stake in this case are constitutional protections of surpassing importance: the proscription of any deprivation of liberty without "due process of law," and the guarantee that "in all criminal prosecutions, the accused shall enjoy the right to a speedy and public trial, by an impartial jury." Taken together, these rights indisputably entitle a criminal defendant to "a jury determination that [he] is guilty of every element of the crime with which he is charged, beyond a reasonable doubt." ...

Since *Winship*, we have made clear beyond peradventure that *Winship*'s due process and associated jury protections extend, to some degree, "to determinations that [go] not to a defendant's guilt or innocence, but simply to the length of his sentence." This was a primary lesson of *Mullaney v. Wilbur,* in which we invalidated a Maine statute that presumed that a defendant who acted with an intent to kill possessed the "malice aforethought" necessary to constitute the State's murder offense (and therefore, was subject to that crime's associated punishment of life imprisonment). The statute placed the burden on the defendant of proving, in rebutting the statutory presumption, that he acted with a lesser degree of culpability, such as in the heat of passion, to win a reduction in the offense from murder to manslaughter (and thus a reduction of the maximum punishment of 20 years).

The state had posited in *Mullaney* that requiring a defendant to prove heat-of-passion intent to overcome a presumption of murderous intent did not implicate *Winship* protections because, upon conviction of either offense, the defendant would lose his liberty and face societal stigma just the same. Rejecting this argument, we acknowledged that criminal law "is concerned not only with guilt or innocence in the abstract, but also with the degree of criminal culpability" assessed. Because the "*consequences*" of a guilty verdict for murder and for manslaughter differed substantially, we dismissed the possibility that a State could circumvent the protections of *Winship* merely by "redefining the elements that constitute different crimes, characterizing them as factors that bear solely on the extent of punishment."[12]

## IV

It was in *McMillan v. Pennsylvania* that this Court, for the first time, coined the term "sentencing factor" to refer to a fact that was not found by a jury but that could affect the sentence imposed by the judge. That case involved a challenge to the State's Mandatory Minimum Sentencing Act. According to its provisions, anyone convicted of certain felonies would be subject to a mandatory minimum penalty of five years imprisonment if the judge found, by a preponderance of the evidence, that the person "visibly possessed a firearm" in the course of committing one of the specified felonies. Articulating for the first time, and then applying, a multifactor set of criteria for determining whether the *Winship* protections applied to bar such a system, we concluded that the Pennsylvania statute did not run afoul of our previous admonitions against relieving the state of its burden of proving guilt, or tailoring the mere form of a criminal statute solely to avoid *Winship*'s strictures.

We did not, however, there budge from the position that (1) constitutional limits exist to states' authority to define away facts necessary to constitute a criminal offense, and (2) that a state scheme that keeps from the jury facts that "expose [defendants] to greater or additional punishment," may raise serious constitutional concern. As we explained:

> [The Pennsylvania statute] neither alters the maximum penalty for the crime committed nor creates a separate offense calling for a separate penalty; it operates solely to limit the sentencing court's discretion in selecting a penalty within the range already available to it without the special finding of visible possession of a firearm.... The statute gives no impression of having been tailored to permit the visible possession finding to be a tail which wags the dog of the substantive offense. Petitioners' claim that visible possession under the Pennsylvania statute is "really" an element of the offenses for which they are being punished—that Pennsylvania has in effect defined a new set of upgraded felonies—

---

[12] Contrary to the principal dissent's suggestion, *Patterson v. New York* posed no direct challenge to this aspect of *Mullaney*. In upholding a New York law allowing defendants to raise and prove extreme emotional distress as an affirmative defense to murder, *Patterson* made clear that the state law still required the State to prove every element of that State's offense of murder and its accompanying punishment. "No further facts are either presumed or inferred in order to constitute the crime." New York, unlike Maine, had not made malice aforethought, or any described *mens rea*, part of its statutory definition of second-degree murder; one could tell from the face of the statute that if one intended to cause the death of another person and did cause that death, one could be subject to sentence for a second-degree offense. Responding to the argument that our view could be seen "to permit state legislatures to reallocate burdens of proof by labeling as affirmative defenses at least some elements of the crimes now defined in their statutes," the Court made clear in the very next breath that there were "obviously constitutional limits beyond which the States may not go in this regard."

would have at least more superficial appeal if a finding of visible possession exposed them to greater or additional punishment, cf. *18 U.S.C. § 2113*(d) (providing separate and greater punishment for bank robberies accomplished through "use of a dangerous weapon or device"), but it does not.[13]

[Justice Stevens then reviewed recent cases involving federal prosecutions holding that *Winship* did not apply to sentence enhancements based on prior convictions and summarizes the principle emerging from these cases:] Other than the fact of a prior conviction, any fact that increases the penalty for a crime beyond the prescribed statutory maximum must be submitted to a jury, and proved beyond a reasonable doubt.... [16]

## V

The New Jersey statutory scheme that Apprendi asks us to invalidate allows a jury to convict a defendant of a second-degree offense based on its

[13] The principal dissent accuses us of today "overruling *McMillan*." We do not overrule *McMillan*. We limit its holding to cases that do not involve the imposition of a sentence more severe than the statutory maximum for the offense established by the jury's verdict—a limitation identified in the *McMillan* opinion itself. Conscious of the likelihood that legislative decisions may have been made in reliance on *McMillan*, we reserve for another day the question whether *stare decisis* considerations preclude reconsideration of its narrower holding.

[16] The principal dissent would reject the Court's rule as a "meaningless formalism," because it can conceive of hypothetical statutes that would comply with the rule and achieve the same result as the New Jersey statute. While a state could, hypothetically, undertake to revise its entire criminal code in the manner the dissent suggests—extending all statutory maximum sentences to, for example, 50 years and giving judges guided discretion as to a few specially selected factors within that range—this possibility seems remote. Among other reasons, structural democratic constraints exist to discourage legislatures from enacting penal statutes that expose *every* defendant convicted of, for example, weapons possession, to a maximum sentence exceeding that which is, in the legislature's judgment, generally proportional to the crime. This is as it should be. Our rule ensures that a state is obliged "to make its choices concerning the substantive content of its criminal laws with full awareness of the consequence, unable to mask substantive policy choices" of exposing all who are convicted to the maximum sentence it provides. *Patterson v. New York* (Powell, J., dissenting). So exposed, "the political check on potentially harsh legislative action is then more likely to operate."

In all events, if such an extensive revision of the state's entire criminal code were enacted for the purpose the dissent suggests, or if New Jersey simply reversed the burden of the hate crime finding (effectively assuming a crime was performed with a purpose to intimidate and then requiring a defendant to prove that it was not), we would be required to question whether the revision was constitutional under this Court's prior decisions.

Finally, the principal dissent ignores the distinction the Court has often recognized, see, *e.g.*, *Martin v. Ohio*, between facts in aggravation of punishment and facts in mitigation. If facts found by a jury support a guilty verdict of murder, the judge is authorized by that jury verdict to sentence the defendant to the maximum sentence provided by the murder statute. If the defendant can escape the statutory maximum by showing, for example, that he is a war veteran, then a judge that finds the fact of veteran status is neither exposing the defendant to a deprivation of liberty greater than that authorized by the verdict according to statute, nor is the Judge imposing upon the defendant a greater stigma than that accompanying the jury verdict alone. Core concerns animating the jury and burden-of-proof requirements are thus absent from such a scheme.

finding beyond a reasonable doubt that he unlawfully possessed a prohibited weapon; after a subsequent and separate proceeding, it then allows a judge to impose punishment identical to that New Jersey provides for crimes of the first degree, based upon the judge's finding, by a preponderance of the evidence, that the defendant's "purpose" for unlawfully possessing the weapon was "to intimidate" his victim on the basis of a particular characteristic the victim possessed. In light of the constitutional rule explained above, and all of the cases supporting it, this practice cannot stand.

[New Jersey's argument that] the required finding of biased purpose is not an "element" of a distinct hate crime offense, but rather the traditional "sentencing factor" of motive ... is nothing more than a disagreement with the rule we apply today. Beyond this, we do not see how the argument can succeed on its own terms.... The text of the statute requires the factfinder to determine whether the defendant possessed, at the time he committed the subject act, a "purpose to intimidate" on account of, inter alia, race. By its very terms, this statute mandates an examination of the defendant's state of mind—a concept known well to the criminal law as the defendant's mens rea. It makes no difference in identifying the nature of this finding that Apprendi was also required, in order to receive the sentence he did for weapons possession, to have possessed the weapon with a "purpose to use [the weapon] unlawfully against the person or property of another." A second mens rea requirement hardly defeats the reality that the enhancement statute imposes of its own force an intent requirement necessary for the imposition of sentence. On the contrary, the fact that the language and structure of the "purpose to use" criminal offense is identical in relevant respects to the language and structure of the "purpose to intimidate" provision demonstrates to us that it is precisely a particular criminal mens rea that the hate crime enhancement statute seeks to target. The defendant's intent in committing a crime is perhaps as close as one might hope to come to a core criminal offense "element."

The foregoing notwithstanding, however, the New Jersey Supreme Court correctly recognized that it does not matter whether the required finding is characterized as one of intent or of motive, because "labels do not afford an acceptable answer." That point applies as well to the constitutionally novel and elusive distinction between "elements" and "sentencing factors." *McMillan* (noting that the sentencing factor—visible possession of a firearm—"might well have been included as an element of the enumerated offenses"). Despite what appears to us the clear "elemental" nature of the factor here, the relevant inquiry is one not of form, but of effect—does the required finding expose the defendant to a greater punishment than that authorized by the jury's guilty verdict?[19] ...

---

[19] This is not to suggest that the term "sentencing factor" is devoid of meaning. The term appropriately describes a circumstance, which may be either aggravating or mitigating in character, that supports a specific sentence *within the range* authorized by the jury's finding that the defendant is guilty of a particular offense. On the other hand, when the term "sentence enhancement" is used to describe an increase beyond the maxi-

The preceding discussion should make clear why the state's reliance on *McMillan* is likewise misplaced. The differential in sentence between what Apprendi would have received without the finding of biased purpose and what he could receive with it is not, it is true, as extreme as the difference between a small fine and mandatory life imprisonment. *Mullaney*. But it can hardly be said that the potential doubling of one's sentence—from 10 years to 20—has no more than a nominal effect. Both in terms of absolute years behind bars, and because of the more severe stigma attached, the differential here is unquestionably of constitutional significance. When a judge's finding based on a mere preponderance of the evidence authorizes an increase in the maximum punishment, it is appropriately characterized as "a tail which wags the dog of the substantive offense." *McMillan*.

New Jersey would also point to the fact that the state did not, in placing the required biased purpose finding in a sentencing enhancement provision, create a "separate offense calling for a separate penalty." As for this, we agree wholeheartedly with the New Jersey Supreme Court that merely because the state legislature placed its hate crime sentence "enhancer" "within the sentencing provisions" of the criminal code "does not mean that the finding of a biased purpose to intimidate is not an essential element of the offense." Indeed, the fact that New Jersey, along with numerous other states, has also made precisely the same conduct the subject of an independent substantive offense makes it clear that the mere presence of this "enhancement" in a sentencing statute does not define its character.[20] . . .

[T]he judgment of the Supreme Court of New Jersey is reversed, and the case is remanded for further proceedings not inconsistent with this opinion.

It is so ordered.

■ [JUSTICE SCALIA's concurring opinion is omitted.]

■ JUSTICE THOMAS, with whom JUSTICE SCALIA joins as to Parts I and II, concurring.

I join the opinion of the Court in full. I write separately to explain my view that the Constitution requires a broader rule than the Court adopts.

## I

[A long line of] authority establishes that a "crime" includes every fact that is by law a basis for imposing or increasing punishment (in contrast

---

mum authorized statutory sentence, it is the functional equivalent of an element of a greater offense than the one covered by the jury's guilty verdict. Indeed, it fits squarely within the usual definition of an "element" of the offense.

[20] Including New Jersey, N. J. Stat. Ann. § 2C:33–4 (West Supp. 2000) ("A person commits a crime of the fourth degree if in committing an offense [of harassment] under

this section, he acted with a purpose to intimidate an individual or group of individuals because of race, color, religion, gender, handicap, sexual orientation or ethnicity"), 26 States currently have laws making certain acts of racial or other bias freestanding violations of the criminal law, see generally F. Lawrence, Punishing Hate: Bias Crimes Under American Law 178–189 (1999) (listing current state hate crime laws).

with a fact that mitigates punishment). Thus, if the legislature defines some core crime and then provides for increasing the punishment of that crime upon a finding of some aggravating fact—of whatever sort, including the fact of a prior conviction—the core crime and the aggravating fact together constitute an aggravated crime, just as much as grand larceny is an aggravated form of petit larceny. The aggravating fact is an element of the aggravated crime. Similarly, if the legislature, rather than creating grades of crimes, has provided for setting the punishment of a crime based on some fact—such as a fine that is proportional to the value of stolen goods—that fact is also an element. No multi-factor parsing of statutes, of the sort that we have attempted since *McMillan*, is necessary. One need only look to the kind, degree, or range of punishment to which the prosecution is by law entitled for a given set of facts. Each fact necessary for that entitlement is an element.

[Justice Thomas then reviewed case law and commentary from the Founding through the 19th century and concluded:]

[The] traditional understanding—that a "crime" includes every fact that is by law a basis for imposing or increasing punishment—continued well into the 20th century, at least until the middle of the century. In fact, it is fair to say that *McMillan* began a revolution in the law regarding the definition of "crime." Today's decision, far from being a sharp break with the past, marks nothing more than a return to the status quo ante—the status quo that reflected the original meaning of the Fifth and Sixth Amendments.

### III

. . . [O]ne of the chief errors of [the Court's earlier cases]—an error to which I succumbed—was to attempt to discern whether a particular fact is traditionally (or typically) a basis for a sentencing court to increase an offender's sentence. For the reasons I have given, it should be clear that this approach just defines away the real issue. What matters is the way by which a fact enters into the sentence. If a fact is by law the basis for imposing or increasing punishment—for establishing or increasing the prosecution's entitlement—it is an element. (To put the point differently, I am aware of no historical basis for treating as a non-element a fact that by law sets or increases punishment.) When one considers the question from this perspective, it is evident why the fact of a prior conviction is an element under a recidivism statute. . . .

. . . I think it clear that the [traditional understanding] would cover the *McMillan* situation of a mandatory minimum sentence (in that case, for visible possession of a firearm during the commission of certain crimes). No doubt a defendant could, under such a scheme, find himself sentenced to the same term to which he could have been sentenced absent the mandatory minimum. The range for his underlying crime could be 0 to 10 years, with the mandatory minimum of 5 years, and he could be sentenced to 7. (Of course, a similar scenario is possible with an increased maximum.) But it is equally true that his expected punishment has increased as a result of the narrowed range and that the prosecution is empowered, by invoking the mandatory minimum, to require the judge to impose a higher punishment than he might wish. The mandatory minimum "entitles the government" to more than it would otherwise be entitled (5 to 10 years, rather than 0 to 10 and the risk of a sentence below 5). . . .

For the foregoing reasons, as well as those given in the Court's opinion, I agree that the New Jersey procedure at issue is unconstitutional.

■ JUSTICE O'CONNOR, with whom THE CHIEF JUSTICE, JUSTICE KENNEDY, and JUSTICE BREYER join, dissenting. . . .

## I

Our Court has long recognized that not every fact that bears on a defendant's punishment need be charged in an indictment, submitted to a jury, and proved by the government beyond a reasonable doubt. Rather, we have held that the "legislature's definition of the elements of the offense is usually dispositive." Although we have recognized that "there are obviously constitutional limits beyond which the States may not go in this regard," and that "in certain limited circumstances *Winship*'s reasonable-doubt requirement applies to facts not formally identified as elements of the offense charged," we have proceeded with caution before deciding that a certain fact must be treated as an offense element despite the legislature's choice not to characterize it as such. We have therefore declined to establish any bright-line rule for making such judgments and have instead approached each case individually, sifting through the considerations most relevant to determining whether the legislature has acted properly within its broad power to define crimes and their punishments or instead has sought to evade the constitutional requirements associated with the characterization of a fact as an offense element.

In one bold stroke the Court today casts aside our traditional cautious approach and instead embraces a universal and seemingly bright-line rule limiting the power of Congress and state legislatures to define criminal offenses and the sentences that follow from convictions thereunder. The Court states: "Other than the fact of a prior conviction, any fact that increases the penalty for a crime beyond the prescribed statutory maximum must be submitted to a jury, and proved beyond a reasonable doubt." In its opinion, the Court marshals virtually no authority to support its extraordinary rule. Indeed, it is remarkable that the Court cannot identify a *single instance*, in the over 200 years since the ratification of the Bill of Rights, that our Court has applied, as a constitutional requirement, the rule it announces today. . . .

[The Court] cites our decision in *Mullaney v. Wilbur* to demonstrate the "lesson" that due process and jury protections extend beyond those factual determinations that affect a defendant's guilt or innocence. The Court explains *Mullaney* as having held that the due process proof-beyond-a-reasonable-doubt requirement applies to those factual determinations that, under a State's criminal law, make a difference in the degree of punishment the defendant receives. The Court chooses to ignore, however, the decision we issued two years later, *Patterson v. New York,* which clearly rejected the Court's broad reading of *Mullaney.* . . .

*Patterson* is important because it plainly refutes the Court's expansive reading of *Mullaney.* Indeed, the defendant in *Patterson* characterized *Mullaney* exactly as the Court has today and we *rejected* that interpretation:

> *Mullaney*'s holding, it is argued, is that the State may not permit the blameworthiness of an act *or the severity of punishment authorized for its commission* to depend on the presence or absence of an identified fact without assuming the burden of proving the presence or absence of that fact, as the case may be, beyond a reasonable doubt. In our view, the *Mullaney* holding should not be so broadly read.

We explained *Mullaney* instead as holding only "that a state must prove every ingredient of an offense beyond a reasonable doubt, and that it may not shift the burden of proof to the defendant by presuming that ingredient upon proof of the other elements of the offense." Because nothing had been presumed against Patterson under New York law, we found no due process violation. Ever since our decision in *Patterson,* we have consistently explained the holding in *Mullaney* in these limited terms and have rejected the broad interpretation the Court gives *Mullaney* today. . . .

[T]he Court appears to hold that any fact that increases or alters *the range* of penalties to which a defendant is exposed—which, by definition, must include increases or alterations to either the minimum or maximum penalties—must be proved to a jury beyond a reasonable doubt. In *McMillan,* however, we rejected such a rule to the extent it concerned those facts that increase or alter the minimum penalty to which a defendant is exposed. Accordingly, it is incumbent on the Court not only to admit that it is overruling *McMillan,* but also to explain why such a course of action is appropriate under normal principles of *stare decisis.* . . .

## II

. . . [T]here appear to be several plausible interpretations of the constitutional principle on which the Court's decision rests.

For example, under one reading, the Court appears to hold that the constitution requires that a fact be submitted to a jury and proved beyond a reasonable doubt only if that fact, as a formal matter, extends the range of punishment *beyond the prescribed statutory maximum.* A state could, however, remove from the jury (and subject to a standard of proof below "beyond a reasonable doubt") the assessment of those facts that define narrower ranges of punishment, *within the overall statutory range,* to which the defendant may be sentenced. Thus, apparently New Jersey could cure its sentencing scheme, and achieve virtually the same results, by drafting its weapons possession statute in the following manner: First, New Jersey could prescribe, in the weapons possession statute itself, a range of 5 to 20 years' imprisonment for one who commits that criminal offense. Second, New Jersey could provide that only those defendants convicted under the statute who are found by a judge, by a preponderance of the evidence, to have acted with a purpose to intimidate an individual on the basis of race may receive a sentence greater than 10 years' imprisonment....

Under another reading of the Court's decision, it may mean only that the Constitution requires that a fact be submitted to a jury and proved beyond a reasonable doubt if it, as a formal matter, *increases* the range of punishment *beyond that which could legally be imposed absent that fact*. A state could, however, remove from the jury (and subject to a standard of proof below "beyond a reasonable doubt") the assessment of those facts that, as a formal matter, *decrease* the range of punishment *below that which could legally be imposed absent that fact*. Thus, consistent with our decision in *Patterson*, New Jersey could cure its sentencing scheme, and achieve virtually the same results, by drafting its weapons possession statute in the following manner: First, New Jersey could prescribe, in the weapons possession statute itself, a range of 5 to 20 years' imprisonment for one who commits that criminal offense. Second, New Jersey could provide that a defendant convicted under the statute whom a judge finds, by a preponderance of the evidence, *not* to have acted with a purpose to intimidate an individual on the basis of race may receive a sentence no greater than 10 years' imprisonment.

The rule that Justice Thomas advocates in his concurring opinion embraces this precise distinction between a fact that increases punishment and a fact that decreases punishment.... [W]hether a fact is responsible for an increase or a decrease in punishment rests in the eye of the beholder. Again, it is difficult to understand, and neither the Court nor Justice Thomas explains, why the constitution would require a state legislature to follow such a meaningless and formalistic difference in drafting its criminal statutes.

If either of the above readings is all that the Court's decision means, "the Court's principle amounts to nothing more than chastising [the New Jersey legislature] for failing to use the approved phrasing in expressing its intent as to how [unlawful weapons possession] should be punished." If New Jersey can, consistent with the constitution, make precisely the same differences in punishment turn on precisely the same facts, and can remove the assessment of those facts from the jury and subject them to a standard of proof below "beyond a reasonable doubt," it is impossible to say that the Fifth, Sixth, and 14th Amendments require the Court's rule. For the same reason, the "structural democratic constraints" that might discourage a legislature from enacting either of the above hypothetical statutes would be no more significant than those that would discourage the enactment of New Jersey's present sentence-enhancement statute. In all three cases, the legislature is able to calibrate punishment perfectly, and subject to a maximum penalty only those defendants whose cases satisfy the sentence-enhancement criterion....

Given the pure formalism of the above readings of the Court's opinion, one suspects that the constitutional principle underlying its decision is more far reaching. The actual principle underlying the Court's decision may be that any fact (other than prior conviction) that has the effect, *in real terms*, of increasing the maximum punishment beyond an otherwise applicable range must be submitted to a jury and proved beyond a reasonable doubt. ("The relevant inquiry is one not of form, but of effect—does the required finding expose the defendant to a greater punishment than that authorized by the jury's guilty verdict?"). The principle thus would apply not only to schemes like New Jersey's, under which a factual determination exposes a defendant to a sentence beyond the prescribed statutory maximum, but also to all determinate-sentencing schemes in which the length of a defendant's sentence within the statutory range turns on specific factual determinations (*e.g.*, the federal sentencing guidelines). . . .

I would reject any such principle. . . .

As the Court acknowledges, we have never doubted that the constitution permits Congress and the state legislatures to define criminal offenses, to prescribe broad ranges of punishment for those offenses, and to give judges discretion to decide where within those ranges a particular defendant's punishment should be set. That view accords with historical practice under the Constitution. "From the beginning of the Republic, federal judges were entrusted with wide sentencing discretion. The great majority of federal criminal statutes have stated only a maximum term of years and a maximum monetary fine, permitting the sentencing judge to impose any term of imprisonment and any fine up to the statutory maximum." Kate Stith & Jose Cabranes, Fear of Judging: Sentencing Guidelines in the Federal Courts 9 (1998) (footnote omitted). Under discretionary-sentencing schemes, a judge bases the defendant's sentence on any number of facts neither presented at trial nor found by a jury beyond a reasonable doubt. . . .

Under our precedent, then, a state may leave the determination of a defendant's sentence to a judge's discretionary decision within a prescribed range of penalties. When a judge, pursuant to that sentencing scheme, decides to increase a defendant's sentence on the basis of certain contested facts, those facts need not be proved to a jury beyond a reasonable doubt. The judge's findings, whether by proof beyond a reasonable doubt or less, suffice for purposes of the constitution. Under the Court's decision today, however, it appears that once a legislature constrains judges' sentencing discretion by prescribing certain sentences that may only be imposed (or must be imposed) in connection with the same determinations of the same contested facts, the constitution requires that the facts instead be proved to a jury beyond a reasonable doubt. I see no reason to treat the two schemes differently. See, *e.g.*, *McMillan* ("We have some difficulty fathoming why the due process calculus would change simply because the legislature has seen fit to provide sentencing courts with additional guidance"). In this respect, I agree with the Solicitor General that "[a] sentence that is constitutionally permissible when selected by a court on the basis of whatever factors it deems appropriate does not become impermissible simply because the court is permitted to select that sentence only after making a finding prescribed by the legislature." Although the Court acknowledges the legitimacy of discretionary sentencing by judges, it never provides a sound reason for treating judicial factfinding under determinate-sentencing schemes differently under the constitution. . . .

Prior to the most recent wave of sentencing reform, the federal government and the states employed indeterminate-sentencing schemes in which judges and executive branch officials (e.g., parole board officials) had substantial discretion to determine the actual length of a defendant's sentence. Studies of indeterminate-sentencing schemes found that similarly situated defendants often received widely disparate sentences. Although indeterminate sentencing was intended to soften the harsh and uniform sentences formerly imposed under mandatory-sentencing systems, some studies revealed that indeterminate sentencing actually had the opposite effect.

In response, Congress and the state legislatures shifted to determinate-sentencing schemes that aimed to limit judges' sentencing discretion and, thereby, afford similarly situated offenders equivalent treatment. The most well known of these reforms was the federal Sentencing Reform Act of 1984, 18 U.S.C. § 3551 et seq. In the Act, Congress created the United States Sentencing Commission, which in turn promulgated the Sentencing Guidelines that now govern sentencing by federal judges. [T]he apparent effect of the Court's opinion today is to halt the current debate on sentencing reform in its tracks and to invalidate with the stroke of a pen three decades' worth of nationwide reform, all in the name of a principle with a questionable constitutional pedigree. Indeed, it is ironic that the Court, in the name of constitutional rights meant to protect criminal defendants from the potentially arbitrary exercise of power by prosecutors and judges, appears to rest its decision on a principle that would render unconstitutional efforts by Congress and the state legislatures to place constraints on that very power in the sentencing context.

Finally, perhaps the most significant impact of the Court's decision will be a practical one—its unsettling effect on sentencing conducted under current federal and state determinate-sentencing schemes. As I have explained, the Court does not say whether these schemes are constitutional, but its reasoning strongly suggests that they are not. Thus, with respect to past sentences handed down by judges under determinate-sentencing schemes, the Court's decision threatens to unleash a flood of petitions by convicted defendants seeking to invalidate their sentences in whole or in part on the authority of the Court's decision today. Statistics compiled by the United States Sentencing Commission reveal that almost a half-million cases have been sentenced under the Sentencing Guidelines since 1989. Federal cases constitute only the tip of the iceberg. In 1998, for example, federal criminal prosecutions represented only about 0.4% of the total number of criminal prosecutions in federal and state courts. ([In] 1998,

57,691 criminal cases were filed in federal court compared to 14,623,330 in state courts). Because many states, like New Jersey, have determinate-sentencing schemes, the number of individual sentences drawn into question by the Court's decision could be colossal.

The decision will likely have an even more damaging effect on sentencing conducted in the immediate future under current determinate-sentencing schemes. Because the Court fails to clarify the precise contours of the constitutional principle underlying its decision, federal and state judges are left in a state of limbo. Should they continue to assume the constitutionality of the determinate-sentencing schemes under which they have operated for so long, and proceed to sentence convicted defendants in accord with those governing statutes and guidelines? The Court provides no answer, yet its reasoning suggests that each new sentence will rest on shaky ground. The most unfortunate aspect of today's decision is that our precedents did not foreordain this disruption in the world of sentencing. Rather, our cases traditionally took a cautious approach to questions like the one presented in this case. The Court throws that caution to the wind and, in the process, threatens to cast sentencing in the United States into what will likely prove to be a lengthy period of considerable confusion.

### III

Because I do not believe that the Court's "increase in the maximum penalty" rule is required by the constitution, I would evaluate New Jersey's sentence-enhancement statute by analyzing the factors we have examined in past cases. First, the New Jersey statute does not shift the burden of proof on an essential ingredient of the offense by presuming that ingredient upon proof of other elements of the offense. Second, the magnitude of the New Jersey sentence enhancement, as applied in petitioner's case, is constitutionally permissible. Under New Jersey law, the weapons possession offense to which petitioner pleaded guilty carries a sentence range of 5 to 10 years' imprisonment. The fact that petitioner, in committing that offense, acted with a purpose to intimidate because of race exposed him to a higher sentence range of 10 to 20 years' imprisonment. The 10–year increase in the maximum penalty to which petitioner was exposed falls well within the range we have found permissible. Third, the New Jersey statute gives no impression of having been enacted to evade the constitutional requirements that attach when a State makes a fact an element of the charged offense. For example, New Jersey did not take what had previously been an element of the weapons possession offense and transform it into a sentencing factor.

In sum, New Jersey "simply took one factor that has always been considered by sentencing courts to bear on punishment"—a defendant's motive for committing the criminal offense—"and dictated the precise weight to be given that factor" when the motive is to intimidate a person because of race. . . .

The New Jersey statute resembles the Pennsylvania statute we upheld in *McMillan* in every respect but one. That difference—that the New

Jersey statute increases the maximum punishment to which petitioner was exposed—does not persuade me that New Jersey "sought to evade the constitutional requirements associated with the characterization of a fact as an offense element." There is no question that New Jersey could prescribe a range of 5 to 20 years' imprisonment as punishment for its weapons possession offense. Thus, as explained above, the specific means by which the State chooses to control judges' discretion within that permissible range is of no moment. Cf. *Patterson* ("The due process clause, as we see it, does not put New York to the choice of abandoning [the affirmative defense] or undertaking to disprove [its] existence in order to convict of a crime which otherwise is within its constitutional powers to sanction by substantial punishment"). . . .

■ JUSTICE BREYER, with whom CHIEF JUSTICE REHNQUIST joins, dissenting.

The majority holds that the constitution contains the following requirement: "any fact [other than recidivism] that increases the penalty for a crime beyond the prescribed statutory maximum must be submitted to a jury, and proved beyond a reasonable doubt." This rule would seem to promote a procedural ideal—that of juries, not judges, determining the existence of those facts upon which increased punishment turns. But the real world of criminal justice cannot hope to meet any such ideal. It can function only with the help of procedural compromises, particularly in respect to sentencing. And those compromises, which are themselves necessary for the fair functioning of the criminal justice system, preclude implementation of the procedural model that today's decision reflects. At the very least, the impractical nature of the requirement that the majority now recognizes supports the proposition that the constitution was not intended to embody it.

I

In modern times the law has left it to the sentencing judge to find those facts which (within broad sentencing limits set by the legislature) determine the sentence of a convicted offender. The judge's factfinding role is not inevitable. One could imagine, for example, a pure "charge offense" sentencing system in which the degree of punishment depended only upon the crime charged (e.g., eight mandatory years for robbery, six for arson, three for assault). But such a system would ignore many harms and risks of harm that the offender caused or created, and it would ignore many relevant offender characteristics. See United States Sentencing Commission, Sentencing Guidelines and Policy Statements, Part A, at 1.5 (1987) (hereinafter Sentencing Guidelines or Guidelines) (pointing out that a "charge offense" system by definition would ignore any fact "that did not constitute [a] statutory element of the offense of which the defendant was convicted"). Hence, that imaginary "charge offense" system would not be a fair system, for it would lack proportionality, i.e., it would treat different offenders similarly despite major differences in the manner in which each committed the same crime.

There are many such manner-related differences in respect to criminal behavior. Empirical data collected by the Sentencing Commission makes clear that, before the Guidelines, judges who exercised discretion within broad legislatively determined sentencing limits (say, a range of 0 to 20 years) would impose very different sentences upon offenders engaged in the same basic criminal conduct, depending, for example, upon the amount of drugs distributed (in respect to drug crimes), the amount of money taken (in respect to robbery, theft, or fraud), the presence or use of a weapon, injury to a victim, the vulnerability of a victim, the offender's role in the offense, recidivism, and many other offense-related or offender-related factors. The majority does not deny that judges have exercised, and, constitutionally speaking, *may* exercise sentencing discretion in this way.

Nonetheless, it is important for present purposes to understand why *judges*, rather than *juries*, traditionally have determined the presence or absence of such sentence-affecting facts in any given case. And it is important to realize that the reason is not a theoretical one, but a practical one. It does not reflect an ideal of procedural "fairness," but rather an administrative need for procedural *compromise*. There are, to put it simply, far too many potentially relevant sentencing factors to permit submission of all (or even many) of them to a jury. As the Sentencing Guidelines state the matter,

> [a] bank robber with (or without) a gun, which the robber kept hidden (or brandished), might have frightened (or merely warned), injured seriously (or less seriously), tied up (or simply pushed) a guard, a teller or a customer, at night (or at noon), for a bad (or arguably less bad) motive, in an effort to obtain money for other crimes (or for other purposes), in the company of a few (or many) other robbers, for the first (or fourth) time that day, while sober (or under the influence of drugs or alcohol), and so forth.

The Guidelines note that "a sentencing system tailored to fit every conceivable wrinkle of each case can become unworkable and seriously compromise the certainty of punishment and its deterrent effect." To ask a jury to consider all, or many, such matters would do the same.

At the same time, to require jury consideration of all such factors—say, during trial where the issue is guilt or innocence—could easily place the defendant in the awkward (and conceivably unfair) position of having to deny he committed the crime yet offer proof about how he committed it, e.g., "I did not sell drugs, but I sold no more than 500 grams." And while special postverdict sentencing juries could cure this problem, they have seemed (but for capital cases) not worth their administrative costs. Hence, before the Guidelines, federal sentencing judges typically would obtain relevant factual sentencing information from probation officers' presentence reports, while permitting a convicted offender to challenge the information's accuracy at a hearing before the judge without benefit of trial-type evidentiary rules. See Williams v. New York, 337 U.S. 241, 249–251 (1949) (describing the modern "practice of individualizing punishments" under which judges often consider otherwise inadmissible information gleaned from probation reports); see also Sanford Kadish, Legal Norm And Discretion In The Police And Sentencing Processes, 75 Harv. L. Rev. 904, 915–917 (1962).

It is also important to understand how a judge traditionally determined which factors should be taken into account for sentencing purposes. In principle, the number of potentially relevant behavioral characteristics is endless. A judge might ask, for example, whether an unlawfully possessed knife was "a switchblade, drawn or concealed, opened or closed, large or small, used in connection with a car theft (where victim confrontation is rare), a burglary (where confrontation is unintended) or a robbery (where confrontation is intentional)." Again, the method reflects practical, rather than theoretical, considerations. Prior to the Sentencing Guidelines, federal law left the individual sentencing judge free to determine which factors were relevant. That freedom meant that each judge, in an effort to tailor punishment to the individual offense and offender, was guided primarily by experience, relevance, and a sense of proportional fairness.

Finally, it is important to understand how a legislature decides which factual circumstances among all those potentially related to generally harmful behavior it should transform into elements of a statutorily defined crime (where they would become relevant to the guilt or innocence of an accused), and which factual circumstances it should leave to the sentencing process (where, as sentencing factors, they would help to determine the sentence imposed upon one who has been found guilty). Again, theory does not provide an answer. Legislatures, in defining crimes in terms of elements, have looked for guidance to common-law tradition, to history, and to current social need. And, traditionally, the Court has left legislatures considerable freedom to make the element determination.

... A sentencing system in which judges have discretion to find sentencing-related factors is a workable system and one that has long been thought consistent with the Constitution; why, then, would the Constitution treat sentencing *statutes* any differently?

## II

As Justice Thomas suggests, until fairly recent times many legislatures rarely focused upon sentencing factors. Rather, it appears they simply identified typical forms of antisocial conduct, defined basic "crimes," and attached a broad sentencing range to each definition—leaving judges free to decide how to sentence within those ranges in light of such factors as they found relevant. But the Constitution does not freeze 19th-century sentencing practices into permanent law. And dissatisfaction with the traditional sentencing system (reflecting its tendency to treat similar cases differently) has led modern legislatures to write new laws that refer specifically to sentencing factors.

Legislatures have tended to address the problem of too much judicial sentencing discretion in two ways. First, legislatures sometimes have created sentencing commissions armed with delegated authority to make more uniform judicial exercise of that discretion. Congress, for example, has created a federal Sentencing Commission, giving it the power to create guidelines that (within the sentencing range set by individual statutes) reflect the host of factors that might be used to determine the actual sentence imposed for each individual crime. Federal judges must apply those guidelines in typical cases (those that lie in the "heartland" of the crime as the statute defines it) while retaining freedom to depart in atypical cases.

Second, legislatures sometimes have directly limited the use (by judges or by a commission) of particular factors in sentencing, either by specifying statutorily how a particular factor will affect the sentence imposed or by specifying how a commission should use a particular factor when writing a guideline. Such a statute might state explicitly, for example, that a particular factor, say, use of a weapon, recidivism, injury to a victim, or bad motive, "shall" increase, or "may" increase, a particular sentence in a particular way. See, e.g., *McMillan* (Pennsylvania statute expressly treated "visible possession of a firearm" as a sentencing consideration that subjected a defendant to a mandatory 5–year term of imprisonment).

The issue the Court decides today involves this second kind of legislation. The Court holds that a legislature cannot enact such legislation (where an increase in the maximum is involved) unless the factor at issue has been charged, tried to a jury, and found to exist beyond a reasonable doubt. My question in respect to this holding is, simply, "*why* would the constitution contain such a requirement"?

### III

... [T]he majority raises no objection to traditional pre-Guidelines sentencing procedures under which judges, not juries, made the factual findings that would lead to an increase in an individual offender's sentence. How does a legislative determination differ in any significant way? For example, if a judge may on his or her own decide that victim injury or bad motive should increase a bank robber's sentence from 5 years to 10, why does it matter that a legislature instead enacts a statute that increases a bank robber's sentence from 5 years to 10 based on this same judicial finding?

... [T]he majority also makes no constitutional objection to a legislative delegation to a commission of the authority to create guidelines that determine how a judge is to exercise sentencing discretion. But if the constitution permits guidelines, why does it not permit Congress similarly to guide the exercise of a judge's sentencing discretion? That is, if the constitution permits a delegatee (the commission) to exercise sentencing-related rulemaking power, how can it deny the delegator (the legislature) what is, in effect, the same rulemaking power?

The majority appears to offer two responses. First, it argues for a limiting principle that would prevent a legislature with broad authority from transforming (jury-determined) facts that constitute elements of a crime into (judge-determined) sentencing factors, thereby removing procedural protections that the constitution would otherwise require ("constitutional limits" prevent states from "defining away facts necessary to constitute a criminal offense"). The majority's cure, however, is not aimed at the disease.

The same "transformational" problem exists under traditional sentencing law, where legislation, silent as to sentencing factors, grants the judge virtually unchecked discretion to sentence within a broad range. Under such a system, judges or prosecutors can similarly "transform" crimes, punishing an offender convicted of one crime as if he had committed another. A prosecutor, for example, might charge an offender with five counts of embezzlement (each subject to a 10–year maximum penalty), while asking the judge to impose maximum and consecutive sentences because the embezzler murdered his employer. And, as part of the traditional sentencing discretion that the majority concedes judges retain, the judge, not a jury, would determine the last-mentioned relevant fact, i.e., that the murder actually occurred.

This egregious example shows the problem's complexity. The source of the problem lies not in a legislature's power to enact sentencing factors, but in the traditional legislative power to select elements defining a crime, the traditional legislative power to set broad sentencing ranges, and the traditional judicial power to choose a sentence within that range on the basis of relevant offender conduct. Conversely, the solution to the problem lies, not in prohibiting legislatures from enacting sentencing factors, but in sentencing rules that determine punishments on the basis of properly defined relevant conduct, with sensitivity to the need for procedural protections where sentencing factors are determined by a judge (for example, use of a "reasonable doubt" standard), and invocation of the Due Process Clause where the history of the crime at issue, together with the nature of the facts to be proved, reveals unusual and serious procedural unfairness. Cf. *McMillan* (upholding statute in part because it "gives no impression of having been tailored to permit the [sentencing factor] to be a tail which wags the dog of the substantive offense").

Second, the majority, in support of its constitutional rule, emphasizes the concept of a statutory "maximum." The Court points out that a sentencing judge (or a commission) traditionally has determined, and now still determines, sentences *within* a legislated range capped by a maximum (a range that the legislature itself sets). I concede the truth of the majority's statement, but I do not understand its relevance.

From a defendant's perspective, the legislature's decision to cap the possible range of punishment at a statutorily prescribed "maximum" would affect the actual sentence imposed no differently than a sentencing commission's (or a sentencing judge's) similar determination. Indeed, as a practical matter, a legislated mandatory "minimum" is far more important to an actual defendant. A judge and a commission, after all, are legally free to select any sentence below a statute's maximum, but they are not free to subvert a statutory minimum. And, as Justice Thomas indicates, all the considerations of fairness that might support submission to a jury of a factual matter that increases a statutory maximum, apply a fortiori to any matter that would increase a statutory minimum. To repeat, I do not understand why, when a legislature *authorizes* a judge to impose a higher penalty for bank robbery (based, say, on the court's finding that a victim was injured or the defendant's motive was bad), a new crime is born; but where a legislature *requires* a judge to impose a higher penalty than he otherwise would (within a pre-existing statutory range) based on similar criteria, it is not.

IV

... [I] am willing, consequently, to assume that the majority's rule would provide a degree of increased procedural protection in respect to those particular sentencing factors currently embodied in statutes. I nonetheless believe that any such increased protection provides little practical help and comes at too high a price. For one thing, by leaving mandatory minimum sentences untouched, the majority's rule simply encourages any legislature interested in asserting control over the sentencing process to do so by creating those minimums. That result would mean significantly less procedural fairness, not more.

For another thing, this Court's case law led legislatures to believe that they were permitted to increase a statutory maximum sentence on the basis of a sentencing factor [and] legislatures may well have relied upon that belief. See, e.g., 21 U.S.C. § 841(b) (1994 ed. and Supp. III) (providing penalties for, among other things, possessing a "controlled substance" with intent to distribute it, which sentences vary dramatically depending upon the amount of the drug possessed, without requiring jury determination of the amount); N. J. Stat. Ann. §§ 2C:43–6, 2C:43–7, 2C:44–1a-f, 2C:44–3 (West 1995 and Supp. 1999–2000) (setting sentencing ranges for crimes, while providing for lesser or greater punishments depending upon judicial findings regarding certain "aggravating" or "mitigating" factors); Cal. Penal Code Ann. § 1170 (West Supp. 2000) (similar); see also Cal. Court Rule 420(b) (1996) (providing that "circumstances in aggravation and mitigation" are to be established by the sentencing judge based on "the case record, the probation officer's report, [and] other reports and statements properly received").

As Justice O'Connor points out, the majority's rule creates serious uncertainty about the constitutionality of such statutes and about the constitutionality of the confinement of those punished under them. ...

Finally, the Court's new rule will likely impede legislative attempts to provide authoritative guidance as to how courts should respond to the presence of traditional sentencing factors. The factor at issue here—motive—is such a factor. Whether a robber takes money to finance other crimes or to feed a starving family can matter, and long has mattered, when the length of a sentence is at issue. The state of New Jersey has determined that one motive—racial hatred—is particularly bad and ought to make a difference in respect to punishment for a crime. That determination is reasonable. The procedures mandated are consistent with traditional sentencing practice. Though additional procedural protections might well be desirable, for the reasons Justice O'Connor discusses and those I have discussed, I do not believe the Constitution requires them where ordinary sentencing factors are at issue. Consequently, in my view, New Jersey's statute is constitutional.

I respectfully dissent.

———

## NOTES ON *APPRENDI* AND ITS IMPLICATIONS

**1.   The Reach of *Apprendi*.** New Jersey treated the factual finding relating to Apprendi's motive as a feature of the sentencing process rather than an "element of the offense," and therefore argued that this fact was properly determined by the judge based on a preponderance standard, rather than by the a jury based on proof beyond a reasonable doubt. The Supreme Court disagreed, and ruled instead that the fact at issue in *Apprendi* is the functional equivalent of an element of the crime. To some extent, *Apprendi* redrew the line between trial and sentencing, applying not only the *Winship* requirement but also the Sixth Amendment jury trial right to facts that are typically adjudicated at sentencing under contemporary determinate sentencing statutes.

In a lengthy historical analysis, Justice Thomas sought to show that *Apprendi* simply applied a well-rooted principle to contemporary statutory innovations, and did not mark a significant break with the traditional understanding of the line between crime-definition and sentencing. In her dissenting opinion, however, Justice O'Connor characterized the decision as a "watershed change in constitutional law" and expressed concern that it would unsettle the law of criminal sentencing and cast doubt on the validity of numerous sentences imposed under pre-*Apprendi* statutes. Justice Breyer forecast the unraveling of the federal sentencing guidelines and other contemporary forms of determinate sentencing.

Not surprisingly, *Apprendi* evoked extensive commentary and litigation.[a] What are its limits? Is every factual determination at sentencing that bears on sentence severity subject to *Winship* (and the right to a jury)? Does it apply to findings regarding aggravating or mitigating factors that allow or require a judge to increase or reduce a presumptive sentence prescribed by sentencing guidelines? Or is the holding limited to findings that increase the possible sentence beyond the statutory maximum prescribed for the convicted offense? If it is so limited, is it simply an empty formalism, as Justice O'Connor suggested?

[a] See, e.g., Symposium [*Apprendi v. New Jersey*]. 38 Am. Crim. L. Rev. 241 (2001); Stephanos Bibas, How *Apprendi* Affects Institutional Allocations of Power, 87 Iowa L. Rev. 465 (2002); Douglas Berman (ed), *Apprendi*'s Progeny, 15 Federal Sentencing Reporter 75–118 (2002); Nancy J. King and Susan R. Klein, *Apprendi* and Plea Bargaining, 54 Stan. L Rev. 295 (2001); Jacqueline Ross, Unanticipated Consequences of Turning Sentencing Factors into Offense Elements: The *Apprendi* Debate, 12 Federal Sentencing Reporter 197 (2000).

One of the puzzles about *Apprendi* is why none of the Justices separated the *Winship* requirement from the right to a jury trial. Consider, for example, the possibility of requiring factual predicates for significant enhancements of allowable punishment to be proved beyond a reasonable doubt, but without requiring that they be decided by a jury. Would that be a better approach?

In the immediate aftermath of *Apprendi*, lower courts grappled with its implications for proving the factual predicates for minimum punishments and for death sentences. Both of these issues were soon resolved by the Supreme Court.

**2.   Mandatory Minimum Sentences.** The first question to be answered was whether *McMillan* (holding that the factual predicates for mandatory minimum sentences did not have to be proved beyond a reasonable doubt) survived *Apprendi*. Although Justices Thomas and O'Connor both speculated that it would not, Justice Stevens' majority opinion reserved the issue "for another day." That day came two years later in Harris v. United States, 536 U.S. 545 (2002).

Harris sold marijuana to an undercover agent on two occasions. Both times he was carrying a handgun in an unconcealed holster. He pled guilty to drug distribution, and after a bench trial, he was also convicted of carrying a firearm "during and in relation to any crime of violence or drug trafficking." At sentencing, however, applying a preponderance standard, the district court found that Harris had "brandished" his handgun during one of the drug sales. That finding triggered a seven-year mandatory minimum sentence (as compared with the five-year mandatory minimum otherwise applicable).[b] The Fourth Circuit affirmed.

The Supreme Court also affirmed. Justice Kennedy's opinion for the Court, joined by Justices Rehnquist, O'Connor and Scalia in relevant part, took note of tension between *Apprendi*'s requirement that factual predicates for maximum sentences be proved beyond a reasonable doubt to a jury and *McMillan*'s holding allowing factual predicates for mandatory minimum sentences to be proved to sentencing judges under a preponderance standard:

> Petitioner argues that the concerns underlying *Apprendi* apply with equal or more force to facts increasing the defendant's minimum sentence. Those factual findings, he contends, often have a greater impact on the defendant than the findings at issue in *Apprendi*. This is so because when a fact increasing the statuto-

---

[b] 18 U.S.C. § 924 (c)(1)(A) provides as follows:

[A]ny person who, during and in relation to any crime of violence or drug trafficking crime . . . uses or carries a firearm, or who, in furtherance of any such crime, possesses a firearm, shall, in addition to the punishment provided for such crime of violence or drug trafficking crime—

(i) be sentenced to a term of imprisonment of not less than 5 years;

(ii) if the firearm is brandished, be sentenced to a term of imprisonment of not less than 7 years; and

(iii) if the firearm is discharged, be sentenced to a term of imprisonment of not less than 10 years.

ry maximum is found, the judge may still impose a sentence far below that maximum; but when a fact increasing the minimum is found, the judge has no choice but to impose that minimum, even if he or she otherwise would have chosen a lower sentence. Why, petitioner asks, would fairness not also require the latter sort of fact to be alleged in the indictment and found by the jury under a reasonable-doubt standard? The answer is that because it is beyond dispute that the judge's choice of sentences within the authorized range may be influenced by facts not considered by the jury, a factual finding's practical effect cannot by itself control the constitutional analysis. The Fifth and Sixth Amendments ensure that the defendant "will never get *more* punishment than he bargained for when he did the crime," but they do not promise that he will receive "anything less" than that. If the grand jury has alleged, and the trial jury has found, all the facts necessary to impose the maximum, the barriers between government and defendant fall. The judge may select any sentence within the range, based on facts not alleged in the indictment or proved to the jury— even if those facts are specified by the legislature, and even if they persuade the judge to choose a much higher sentence than he or she otherwise would have imposed. That a fact affects the defendant's sentence, even dramatically so, does not by itself make it an element. . . .

Read together, *McMillan* and *Apprendi* mean that those facts setting the outer limits of a sentence, and of the judicial power to impose it, are the elements of the crime for the purposes of the constitutional analysis. Within the range authorized by the jury's verdict, however, the political system may channel judicial discretion—and rely upon judicial expertise—by requiring defendants to serve minimum terms after judges make certain factual findings. It is critical not to abandon that understanding at this late date. Legislatures and their constituents have relied upon *McMillan* to exercise control over sentencing through dozens of statutes like the one the Court approved in that case. Congress and the States have conditioned mandatory minimum sentences upon judicial findings that, as here, a firearm was possessed, brandished, or discharged; or among other examples, that the victim was over 60 years of age, that the defendant possessed a certain quantity of drugs, that the victim was related to the defendant, and that the defendant was a repeat offender. We see no reason to overturn those statutes or cast uncertainty upon the sentences imposed under them.

Reaffirming *McMillan* and employing the approach outlined in that case, we conclude that the federal provision at issue is constitutional. Basing a 2–year increase in the defendant's minimum sentence on a judicial finding of brandishing does not evade the requirements of the Fifth and Sixth Amendments. Congress "simply took one factor that has always been considered by sentencing courts to bear on punishment ... and dictated the precise weight to be given that factor." That factor need not be alleged in the indictment, submitted to the jury, or proved beyond a reasonable doubt.

The Court is well aware that many question the wisdom of mandatory minimum sentencing. Mandatory minimums, it is often said, fail to account for the unique circumstances of offenders who warrant a lesser penalty. These criticisms may be sound, but they would persist whether the judge or the jury found the facts giving rise to the minimum. We hold only that the Constitution permits the judge to do so, and we leave the other questions to Congress, the States, and the democratic processes.

Justice Thomas's dissenting opinion, joined by Justices Stevens, Souter and Ginsburg, expressed the view that *McMillan* was inconsistent with *Apprendi* and should be overruled.

Justice Breyer concurred separately. While conceding that Harris's case could not easily be distinguished from *Apprendi* "in terms of logic," and expressing serious reservations about the wisdom of mandatory minimum sentences, he explained that he was joining the Court's judgment because extending *Apprendi* to mandatory minimums would have adverse practical as well as legal consequences:

> Mandatory minimum statutes are fundamentally inconsistent with Congress' simultaneous effort to create a fair, honest, and rational sentencing system through the use of Sentencing Guidelines. Unlike Guideline sentences, statutory mandatory minimums generally deny the judge the legal power to depart downward, no matter how unusual the special circumstances that call for leniency. They rarely reflect an effort to achieve sentencing proportionality—a key element of sentencing fairness that demands that the law punish a drug "kingpin" and a "mule" differently. They transfer sentencing power to prosecutors, who can determine sentences through the charges they decide to bring, and who thereby have reintroduced much of the sentencing disparity that Congress created Guidelines to eliminate. They rarely are based upon empirical study. And there is evidence that they encourage subterfuge, leading to more frequent downward departures (on a random basis), thereby making them a comparatively ineffective means of guaranteeing tough sentences.

> Applying *Apprendi* in this case would not, however, lead Congress to abolish, or to modify, mandatory minimum sentencing statutes. Rather, it would simply require the prosecutor to charge, and the jury to find beyond a reasonable doubt, the existence of the "factor," say, the amount of unlawful drugs, that triggers the mandatory minimum. In many cases, a defendant, claiming innocence and arguing, say, mistaken identity, will find it impossible simultaneously to argue to the jury that the prosecutor has overstated the drug amount. How, the jury might ask, could this

"innocent" defendant know anything about that matter? The upshot is that in many such cases defendant and prosecutor will enter into a stipulation before trial as to drug amounts to be used at sentencing (if the jury finds the defendant guilty). To that extent, application of *Apprendi* would take from the judge the power to make a factual determination, while giving that power not to juries, but to prosecutors. And such consequences, when viewed through the prism of an open, fair sentencing system, are seriously adverse.

The legal consequences of extending *Apprendi* to the mandatory minimum sentencing context are also seriously adverse. Doing so would diminish further Congress' otherwise broad constitutional authority to define crimes through the specification of elements, to shape criminal sentences through the specification of sentencing factors, and to limit judicial discretion in applying those factors in particular cases. I have discussed these matters fully in my *Apprendi* dissent. For the reasons set forth there, I would not apply *Apprendi* in this case.

**3.  Capital Sentencing**. Under all contemporary capital sentencing statutes, a defendant convicted of a capital offense cannot be sentenced to death unless the prosecution proves one or more "aggravating circumstances" at the sentencing phase of the case. Most capital sentencing statutes require the substantive factual predicates for a death sentence to be proved to a jury beyond a reasonable doubt. However, some states repose sentencing authority in judges and do not explicitly require the requisite findings to be made beyond a reasonable doubt. When the issue first came before the Supreme Court in Walton v. Arizona, 497 U.S. 639 (1990), the Court that specific findings required for imposition of a death sentence are not constitutionally equivalent to elements of the offense, and that the Constitution did not require jury determinations. *Walton* also implied that the findings need not be made beyond a reasonable doubt. Although the issue was sidestepped in *Apprendi*, the Court overruled *Walton* in Ring v. Arizona, 536 U.S. 584 (2002), holding that these findings must be made by a jury and, although the Court had no reason to say so explicitly in *Ring*, the implication is inescapable that they must be proved beyond a reasonable doubt.[c]

---

[c] Capital sentencing is more fully covered in Chapter 8.

## SECTION 2: PROPORTIONALITY
## SUBSECTION A: PROPORTIONALITY AND CAPITAL PUNISHMENT

---

### Coker v. Georgia
Supreme Court of the United States, 1977.
433 U.S. 584.

■ MR. JUSTICE WHITE announced the judgment of the Court and filed an opinion in which MR. JUSTICE STEWART, MR. JUSTICE BLACKMUN, and MR. JUSTICE STEVENS, joined.

. . . Petitioner Coker was convicted of rape and sentenced to death. Both the conviction and the sentence were affirmed by the Georgia Supreme Court. Coker was granted a writ of certiorari limited to the single claim, rejected by the Georgia court, that the punishment of death for rape violates the Eighth Amendment, which proscribes "cruel and unusual punishments" and which must be observed by the states as well as the federal government. Robinson v. California, 370 U.S. 660 (1962).

### I

While serving various sentences for murder, rape, kidnapping, and aggravated assault, petitioner escaped from the Ware Correctional Institution near Waycross, Ga., on September 2, 1974. At approximately 11 o'clock that night, petitioner entered the house of Allen and Elnita Carver through an unlocked kitchen door. Threatening the couple with a "board," he tied up Mr. Carver in the bathroom, obtained a knife from the kitchen, and took Mr. Carver's money and the keys to the family car. Brandishing the knife and saying "you know what's going to happen to you if you try anything, don't you," Coker then raped Mrs. Carver. Soon thereafter, petitioner drove away in the Carver car, taking Mrs. Carver with him. Mr. Carver, freeing himself, notified the police; and not long thereafter petitioner was apprehended. Mrs. Carver was unharmed.

Petitioner was [tried on charges of] escape, armed robbery, motor vehicle theft, kidnapping, and rape. . . . The jury returned a verdict of guilty, rejecting his general plea of insanity. A sentencing hearing was then conducted in accordance with the procedures dealt with at length in Gregg v. Georgia, 428 U.S. 153 (1976). . . . The jury's verdict on the rape count was death by electrocution. . . .

### II

[The Court's prior capital punishment decisions] make unnecessary the recanvassing of certain critical aspects of the controversy about the constitutionality of capital punishment. It is now settled that the death penalty is not invariably cruel and unusual punishment within the meaning of the Eighth Amendment; it is not inherently barbaric or an unacceptable mode of punishment for crime; neither is it always disproportionate to the crime for which it is imposed. . . .

In sustaining the imposition of the death penalty, however, the Court [has] firmly embraced the holdings and dicta from prior cases, to the effect that the Eighth Amendment bars not only those punishments that are "barbaric" but also those that are "excessive" in relation to the crime committed. Under *Gregg v. Georgia,* supra, a punishment is "excessive" and unconstitutional if it (i) makes no measurable contribution to acceptable goals of punishment and hence is nothing more than the purposeless and needless imposition of pain and suffering; or (ii) is grossly out of proportion to the severity of the crime. A punishment might fail the test on either ground. Furthermore, these Eighth Amendment judgments should not be, or appear to be, merely the subjective views of individual Justices; judgment should be informed by objective factors to the maximum possible extent. To this end, attention must be given to the public attitudes concerning a particular sentence—history and precedent, legislative attitudes, and the response of juries reflected in their sentencing decisions are to be consulted. In *Gregg,* after giving due regard to such sources, the Court's judgment was that the death penalty for deliberate murder was neither the purposeless imposition of severe punishment nor a punishment grossly disproportionate to the crime. But the Court reserved the question of the constitutionality of the death penalty when imposed for other crimes.

### III

That question, with respect to rape of an adult woman, is now before us. We have concluded that a sentence of death is grossly disproportionate and excessive punishment for the crime of rape and is therefore forbidden by the Eighth Amendment as cruel and unusual punishment.[4]

### A

As advised by recent cases, we seek guidance in history and from the objective evidence of the country's present judgment concerning the acceptability of death as a penalty for rape of an adult woman. At no time in the last 50 years have a majority of the states authorized death as a punishment for rape. In 1925, 18 states, the District of Columbia, and the federal government authorized capital punishment for the rape of an adult female. By 1971 just prior to the decision in Furman v. Georgia, 408 U.S. 238 (1972), that number had declined, but not substantially, to 16 states plus the federal government. *Furman* then invalidated most of the capital-punishment statutes in this country, including the rape statutes, because, among other reasons, of the manner in which the death penalty was imposed and utilized under those laws.

With their death-penalty statutes for the most part invalidated, the states were faced with the choice of enacting modified capital-punishment laws in an attempt to satisfy the requirements of *Furman* or of being satisfied with life imprisonment as the ultimate punishment for *any* offense. Thirty-five states immediately reinstituted the death penalty for at

---

[4] Because the death sentence is a disproportionate punishment for rape, it is cruel and unusual punishment within the meaning of the Eighth Amendment even though it may measurably serve the legitimate ends of punishment and therefore is not invalid for its failure to do so. We observe that in the light of the legislative decisions in almost all of the states and in most of the countries around the world, it would be difficult to support a claim that the death penalty for rape is an indispensable part of the states' criminal justice system.

least limited kinds of crime. This public judgment as to the acceptability of capital punishment, evidenced by the immediate, post-*Furman* legislative reaction in a large majority of the states, heavily influenced the Court to sustain the death penalty for murder in *Gregg v. Georgia,* supra.

But if the "most marked indication of society's endorsement of the death penalty for murder is the legislative response to *Furman,*" it should also be telling datum that the public judgment with respect to rape, as reflected in the statutes providing the punishment for that crime, has been dramatically different. In reviving death-penalty laws to satisfy *Furman's* mandate, none of the states that had not previously authorized death for rape chose to include rape among capital felonies. Of the 16 states in which rape had been a capital offense, only three provided the death penalty for rape of an adult woman in their revised statutes—Georgia, North Carolina, and Louisiana. In the latter two states, the death penalty was mandatory for those found guilty, and those laws were invalidated by Woodson v. North Carolina, 428 U.S. 280 (1976), and Roberts v. Louisiana, 428 U.S. 325 (1976). When Louisiana and North Carolina, responding to those decisions, again revised their capital punishment laws, they re-enacted the death penalty for murder but not for rape; none of the seven other legislatures that to our knowledge have amended or replaced their death penalty statutes since July 2, 1976, . . . included rape among the crimes for which death was an authorized punishment.

Georgia argues that 11 of the 16 states that authorized death for rape in 1972 attempted to comply with *Furman* by enacting arguably mandatory death-penalty legislation and that it is very likely that, aside from Louisiana and North Carolina, these states simply chose to eliminate rape as a capital offense rather than to *require* death for *each* and *every* instance of rape. The argument is not without force; but four of the 16 states did not take the mandatory course and also did *not* continue rape of an adult woman as a capital offense. Further, as we have indicated, the legislatures of six of the 11 arguably mandatory states have revised their death-penalty laws since *Woodson* and *Roberts* without enacting a new death penalty for rape. And this is to say nothing of 19 other states that enacted nonmandatory, post-*Furman* statutes and chose not to sentence rapists to death.

It should be noted that Florida, Mississippi, and Tennessee also authorized the death penalty in some rape cases, but only where the victim was a child and the rapist an adult. The Tennessee statute has since been invalidated because the death sentence was mandatory. The upshot is that Georgia is the sole jurisdiction in the United States at the present time that authorizes a sentence of death when the rape victim is an adult woman and only two other jurisdictions provide capital punishment when the victim is a child.

The current judgment with respect to the death penalty for rape is not wholly unanimous among state legislatures, but it obviously weighs very heavily on the side of rejecting capital punishment as a suitable penalty for raping an adult woman.[10]

## B

It was also observed in *Gregg* that "[t]he jury ... is a significant and reliable objective index of contemporary values because it is so directly involved," and that it is thus important to look to the sentencing decisions that juries have made in the course of assessing whether capital punishment is an appropriate penalty for the crime being tried. Of course, the jury's judgment is meaningful only where the jury has an appropriate measure of choice as to whether the death penalty is to be imposed. As far as execution for rape is concerned, this is now true only in Georgia and in Florida; and in the latter state, capital punishment is authorized only for the rape of children.

According to the factual submissions in this Court, out of all rape convictions in Georgia since 1973—and that total number has not been tendered—63 cases had been reviewed by the Georgia Supreme Court as of the time of oral argument; and of these, six involved a death sentence, one of which was set aside, leaving five convicted rapists now under sentence of death in the state of Georgia. Georgia juries have thus sentenced rapists to death six times since 1973. This obviously is not a negligible number; and the state argues that as a practical matter juries simply reserve the extreme sanction for extreme cases of rape and that recent experience surely does not prove that jurors consider the death penalty to be a disproportionate punishment for every conceivable instance of rape, no matter how aggravated. Nevertheless, it is true that in the vast majority of cases, at least nine out of 10, juries have not imposed the death sentence.

## IV

These recent events evidencing the attitude of state legislatures and sentencing juries do not wholly determine this controversy, for the Constitution contemplates that in the end our own judgment will be brought to bear on the question of the acceptability of the death penalty under the Eighth Amendment. Nevertheless, the legislative rejection of capital punishment for rape strongly confirms our own judgment, which is that death is indeed a disproportionate penalty for the crime of raping an adult woman.

We do not discount the seriousness of rape as a crime. It is highly reprehensible, both in a moral sense and in its almost total contempt for the personal integrity and autonomy of the female victim and for the latter's privilege of choosing those with whom intimate relationships are to be established. Short of homicide, it is the "ultimate violation of self." It is also a violent crime because it normally involves force, or the threat of

---

[10] In Trop v. Dulles, 356 U.S. 86, 102 (1958), the plurality took pains to note the climate of international opinion concerning the acceptability of a particular punishment. It is thus not irrelevant here that out of 60 major nations in the world surveyed in 1965, only three retained the death penalty for rape where death did not ensue. United Nations, Department of Economic and Social Affairs, Capital Punishment 40, 86 (1968).

force or intimidation, to overcome the will and the capacity of the victim to resist. Rape is very often accompanied by physical injury to the female and can also inflict mental and psychological damage. Because it undermines the community's sense of security, there is public injury as well.

Rape is without doubt deserving of serious punishment; but in terms of moral depravity and of the injury to the person and to the public, it does not compare with murder, which does involve the unjustified taking of human life. Although it may be accompanied by another crime, rape by definition does not include the death of or even the serious injury to another person. The murderer kills; the rapist, if no more than that, does not. Life is over for the victim of the murderer; for the rape victim, life may not be nearly so happy as it was, but it is not over and normally is not beyond repair. We have the abiding conviction that the death penalty, which "is unique in its severity and irrevocability," is an excessive penalty for the rapist who, as such, does not take human life.

This does not end the matter; for under Georgia law, death may not be imposed for any capital offense, including rape, unless the jury or judge finds one of the statutory aggravating circumstances and then elects to impose that sentence. For the rapist to be executed in Georgia, it must therefore be found not only that he committed rape but also that one or more of the following aggravating circumstances were present: (i) that the rape was committed by a person with a prior record of conviction for a capital felony; (ii) that the rape was committed while the offender was engaged in the commission of another capital felony, or aggravated battery; or (iii) the rape "was outrageously or wantonly vile, horrible or inhuman in that it involved torture, depravity of mind, or aggravated battery to the victim."[a] Here, the first two of these aggravating circumstances were alleged and found by the jury.

Neither of these circumstances, nor both of them together, change our conclusion that the death sentence imposed on Coker is a disproportionate punishment for rape. Coker had prior convictions for capital felonies—rape, murder, and kidnapping—but these prior convictions do not change the fact that the instant crime being punished is a rape not involving the taking of life.

It is also true that the present rape occurred while Coker was committing armed robbery, a felony for which the Georgia statutes authorize the death penalty. But Coker was tried for the robbery offense as well as for rape and received a separate life sentence for this crime; the jury did not deem the robbery itself deserving of the death penalty, even though accompanied by the aggravating circumstance, which was stipulated, that Coker had been convicted of a prior capital crime.[16]

---

[a] The applicable Georgia statutes are reprinted in Appendix B.—[Footnote by eds.]

[16] Where the accompanying capital crime is murder, it is most likely that the defendant would be tried for murder, rather than rape; and it is perhaps academic to deal with the death sentence for rape in such a circumstance. It is likewise unnecessary to consider the rape-felony murder—a rape accompanied by the death of the victim which was unlaw-

We note finally that in Georgia a person commits murder when he unlawfully and with malice aforethought, either express or implied, causes the death of another human being. He also commits that crime when in the commission of a felony he causes the death of another human being, irrespective of malice. But even where the killing is deliberate, it is not punishable by death absent proof of aggravating circumstances. It is difficult to accept the notion, and we do not, that the rapist, with or without aggravating circumstances, should be punished more heavily than the deliberate killer as long as the rapist does not himself take the life of his victim. The judgment of the Georgia Supreme Court upholding the death sentence is reversed, and the case is remanded to that court for further proceedings not inconsistent with this opinion.

So ordered.

■ Mr. Justice Brennan, concurring in the judgment.

Adhering to my view that the death penalty is in all circumstances cruel and unusual punishment prohibited by the eighth and 14th Amendments, I concur in the judgment of the Court setting aside the death sentence imposed under the Georgia rape statute.

■ Mr. Justice Marshall, concurring in the judgment.

... I continue to adhere to [my previously expressed view that the death penalty is a cruel and unusual punishment prohibited by the eighth and 14th Amendments] in concurring in the judgment of the Court in this case.

■ Mr. Justice Powell, concurring in the judgment in part and dissenting in part.

I concur in the judgment of the Court on the facts of this case, and also in the plurality's reasoning supporting the view that ordinarily death is disproportionate punishment for the crime of raping an adult woman. Although rape invariably is a reprehensible crime, there is no indication that petitioner's offense was committed with excessive brutality or that the victim sustained serious or lasting injury. The plurality, however, does not limit its holding to the case before us or to similar cases. Rather, in an opinion that ranges well beyond what is necessary, it holds that capital punishment *always*—regardless of the circumstances—is a disproportionate penalty for the crime of rape.

The Georgia statute specifies [three] aggravating circumstances [for the crime of rape]: (i) the offense was committed by a person with a prior record of conviction for a capital felony; (ii) the offense was committed while the offender was engaged in another capital felony or in aggravated battery; and (iii) the offense was "outrageously or wantonly vile, horrible or

---

fully but nonmaliciously caused by the defendant.

Where the third aggravating circumstance mentioned in the text is present—that the rape is particularly vile or involves tor-

ture or aggravated battery—it would seem that the defendant could very likely be convicted, tried, and appropriately punished for this additional conduct.

inhuman in that it involved torture, depravity of mind, or an aggravated battery to the victim." Only the third circumstance describes in general the offense of aggravated rape, often identified as a separate and more heinous offense than rape. See, e.g., ALI, Model Penal Code § 213.1. That third circumstance was not submitted to the jury in this case, as the evidence would not have supported such a finding. It is therefore quite unnecessary for the plurality to write in terms so sweeping as to foreclose each of the 50 state legislatures from creating a narrowly defined substantive crime of aggravated rape punishable by death.[1] ...

Today, in a case that does not require such an expansive pronouncement, the plurality draws a bright line between murder and all rapes—regardless of the degree of brutality of the rape or the effect upon the victim. I dissent because I am not persuaded that such a bright line is appropriate. "[There] is extreme variation in the degree of culpability of rapists." The deliberate viciousness of the rapist may be greater than that of the murderer. Rape is never an act committed accidentally. Rarely can it be said to be unpremeditated. There also is wide variation in the effect on the victim. The plurality opinion says that "[l]ife is over for the victim of the murderer; for the rape victim, life may not be nearly so happy as it was, but it is not over and normally is not beyond repair." But there is indeed "extreme variation" in the crime of rape. Some victims are so grievously injured physically or psychologically that life *is* beyond repair.

Thus, it may be that the death penalty is not disproportionate punishment for the crime of aggravated rape. Final resolution of the question must await careful inquiry into objective indicators of society's "evolving standards of decency," particularly legislative enactments and the responses of juries in capital cases.[2] The plurality properly examines these indicia, which do support the conclusion that society finds the death penalty unacceptable for the crime of rape in the absence of excessive brutality or severe injury. But it has not been shown that society finds the penalty disproportionate for all rapes. In a proper case a more discriminating inquiry than the plurality undertakes well might discover that both juries and legislatures have reserved the ultimate penalty for the case of an outrageous rape resulting in serious, lasting harm to the victim. I would not prejudge the issue. To this extent, I respectfully dissent.

---

[1] It is not this Court's function to formulate the relevant criteria that might distinguish aggravated rape from the more usual case, but perhaps a workable test would embrace the factors identified by Georgia: the cruelty or viciousness of the offender, the circumstances and manner in which the offense was committed, and the consequences suffered by the victim. The legislative task of defining, with appropriate specificity, the elements of the offense of aggravated rape would not be easy, but certainly this Court should not assume that the task is impossible. ...

[2] These objective indicators are highly relevant, but the ultimate decision as to the appropriateness of the death penalty under the Eighth Amendment ... must be decided on the basis of our own judgment in light of the precedents of this Court.

■ Mr. Chief Justice Burger, with whom Mr. Justice Rehnquist joins, dissenting.

In a case such as this, confusion often arises as to the Court's proper role in reaching a decision. Our task is not to give effect to our individual views on capital punishment; rather, we must determine what the Constitution permits a state to do under its reserved powers. In striking down the death penalty imposed upon the petitioner in this case, the Court has overstepped the bounds of proper constitutional adjudication by substituting its policy judgment for that of the state legislature. I accept that the Eighth Amendment's concept of disproportionality bars the death penalty for minor crimes. But rapeslls is not a minor crime. . . .

(1)

On December 5, 1971, the petitioner, Ehrlich Anthony Coker, raped and then stabbed to death a young woman. Less than eight months later Coker kidnapped and raped a second young woman. After twice raping this 16–year-old victim, he stripped her, severely beat her with a club, and dragged her into a wooded area where he left her for dead. He was apprehended and pleaded guilty to offenses stemming from these incidents. He was sentenced by three separate courts to three life terms, two 20–year terms, and one eight-year term of imprisonment. Each judgment specified that the sentences it imposed were to run consecutively rather than concurrently. Approximately one and one-half years later, on September 2, 1974, petitioner escaped from the state prison where he was serving these sentences. He promptly raped another 16–year-old woman in the presence of her husband, abducted her from her home, and threatened her with death and serious bodily harm. It is this crime for which the sentence now under review was imposed.

The Court today holds that the state of Georgia may not impose the death penalty on Coker. In so doing, it prevents the state from imposing any effective punishment upon Coker for his latest rape. The Court's holding, moreover, bars Georgia from guaranteeing its citizens that they will suffer no further attacks by this habitual rapist. In fact, given the lengthy sentences Coker must serve for the crimes he has already committed, the Court's holding assures that petitioner—as well as others in his position—will henceforth feel no compunction whatsoever about committing further rapes as frequently as he may be able to escape from confinement and indeed even within the walls of the prison itself. To what extent we have left states "elbow-room" to protect innocent persons from depraved human beings like Coker remains in doubt.

(2)

My first disagreement with the Court's holding is its unnecessary breadth. The narrow issue here presented is whether the state of Georgia may constitutionally execute this petitioner for the particular rape which he has committed, in light of all the facts and circumstances shown by this record. The plurality opinion goes to great lengths to consider societal mores and attitudes toward the generic crime of rape and the punishment for it; however, the opinion gives little attention to the special circumstances which bear directly on whether imposition of the death penalty is an appropriate societal response to Coker's criminal acts: (i) On account of his prior offenses, Coker is already serving such lengthy prison sentences that imposition of additional periods of imprisonment would have no incremental punitive effect; (ii) by his life pattern Coker has shown that he presents a particular danger to the safety, welfare, and chastity of women, and on his record the likelihood is therefore great that he will repeat his crime at the first opportunity; (iii) petitioner escaped from prison, only a year and a half after he commenced serving his latest sentences; he has nothing to lose by further escape attempts; and (iv) should he again succeed in escaping from prison, it is reasonably predictable that he will repeat his pattern of attacks on women—and with impunity since the threat of added prison sentences will be no deterrent.

Unlike the plurality, I would narrow the inquiry in this case to the question actually presented: Does the Eighth Amendment's ban against cruel and unusual punishment prohibit the state of Georgia from executing a person who has, within the space of three years, raped three separate women, killing one and attempting to kill another, who is serving prison terms exceeding his probable lifetime and who has not hesitated to escape confinement at the first available opportunity? Whatever one's view may be as to the state's constitutional power to impose the death penalty upon a rapist who stands before a court convicted for the first time, this case reveals a chronic rapist whose continuing danger to the community is abundantly clear.

Mr. Justice Powell would hold the death sentence inappropriate in *this* case because "there is no indication that petitioner's offense was committed with excessive brutality or that the victim sustained serious or lasting injury." Apart from the reality that rape is inherently one of the most egregiously brutal acts one human being can inflict upon another, there is nothing in the Eighth Amendment that so narrowly limits the factors which may be considered by a state legislature in determining whether a particular punishment is grossly excessive. Surely recidivism, especially the repeated commission of heinous crimes, is a factor which may properly be weighed as an aggravating circumstance, permitting the imposition of a punishment more severe than for one isolated offense.... As a factual matter, the plurality opinion is correct in stating that Coker's "prior convictions do not change the fact that the instant crime being punished is a rape not involving the taking of life"; however, it cannot be disputed that the existence of these prior convictions makes Coker a substantially more serious menace to society than a first-time offender:[4]

---

[4] This special danger is demonstrated by the very record in this case. After tying and gagging the victim's husband, and raping the victim, petitioner sought to make his getaway in their automobile. Leaving the victim's husband tied and gagged in his bathroom, Coker took the victim with him. As he started to leave, he brandished the kitchen knife he was carrying and warned the husband that "if he would get pulled over or the police was following him in any way that he would kill—he would kill my wife. *He said he didn't have nothing to lose—that he was in prison for the rest of his life, anyway....*" Testimony of the victim's husband, App. 121 (emphasis added).

There is a widely held view that those who present the strongest case for severe measures of incapacitation are not murderers as a group (their offenses often are situational) *but rather those who have repeatedly engaged in violent, combative behavior.* A well-demonstrated propensity for life-endangering behavior is thought to provide a more solid basis for infliction of the most severe measures of incapacitation than does the fortuity of a single homicidal incident. Packer, Making the Punishment Fit the Crime, 77 Harv.L.Rev. 1071, 1080 (1964). (Emphasis added.)

In my view, the Eighth Amendment does not prevent the state from taking an individual's "well-demonstrated propensity for life-endangering behavior" into account in devising punitive measures which will prevent inflicting further harm upon innocent victims. Only one year ago Mr. Justice White succinctly noted: "[D]eath finally forecloses the possibility that a prisoner will commit further crimes, whereas life imprisonment does not."

In sum, once the Court has held that "the punishment of death does not invariably violate the Constitution," it seriously impinges upon the state's legislative judgment to hold that it may not impose such sentence upon an individual who has shown total and repeated disregard for the welfare, safety, personal integrity, and human worth of others, and who seemingly cannot be deterred from continuing such conduct.[5] I therefore would hold that the death sentence here imposed is within the power reserved to the state and leave for another day the question of whether such sanction would be proper under other circumstances. The dangers which inhere whenever the Court casts its constitutional decisions in terms sweeping beyond the facts of the case presented, are magnified in the context of the Eighth Amendment. In *Furman v. Georgia,* Mr. Justice Powell, in dissent, stated:

[W]here, as here, the language of the applicable [constitutional] provision provides great leeway and where the underlying social policies are felt to be of vital importance, the temptation to read personal preference into the Constitution is understandably great. *It is too easy to propound our subjective standards of wise policy under the rubric of more or less universally held standards of decency.* (Emphasis added.)

---

[5] Professor Packer addressed this:

What are we to do with those whom we cannot reform, and, in particular, those who by our failure are thought to remain menaces to life? Current penal theories admit, indeed insist upon, the need for permanent incapacitation in such cases. Once this need is recognized, the death penalty as a means of incapacitation for the violent psychopath can hardly be objected to on grounds that will survive rational scrutiny, *if the use of the death penalty in any situation is to be permitted.* And its use in rape cases as a class, while inept, is no more so than its use for any other specific offense involving danger to life and limb. Making the Punishment Fit the Crime, 77 Harv. L.Rev. 1071, 1081 (1964). (Emphasis added.)

Since the Court now invalidates the death penalty as a sanction for all rapes of adults at all times under all circumstances, I reluctantly turn to what I see as the broader issues raised by this holding.

(3)

The plurality acknowledges the gross nature of the crime of rape. A rapist not only violates a victim's privacy and personal integrity, but inevitably causes serious psychological as well as physical harm in the process. The long-range effect upon the victim's life and health is likely to be irreparable; it is impossible to measure the harm which results. Volumes have been written by victims, physicians, and psychiatric specialists on the lasting injury suffered by rape victims. Rape is not a mere physical attack—it is destructive of the human personality. The remainder of the victim's life may be gravely affected, and this in turn may have a serious detrimental effect upon her husband and any children she may have. I therefore wholly agree with Mr. Justice White's conclusion as far as it goes—that "[s]hort of homicide, [rape] is the 'ultimate violation of self.'" Victims may recover from the physical damage of knife or bullet wounds, or a beating with fists or a club, but recovery from such a gross assault on the human personality is not healed by medicine or surgery. To speak blandly, as the plurality does, of rape victims who are "unharmed," or to classify the human outrage of rape, as does Mr. Justice Powell, in terms of "excessively brutal," versus "moderately brutal," takes too little account of the profound suffering the crime imposes upon the victims and their loved ones.

Despite its strong condemnation of rape, the Court reaches the inexplicable conclusion that "the death penalty ... is an excessive penalty" for the perpetrator of this heinous offense. This, the Court holds, is true even though in Georgia the death penalty may be imposed only where the rape is coupled with one or more aggravating circumstances. The process by which this conclusion is reached is as startling as it is disquieting. It represents a clear departure from precedent by making this Court "under the aegis of the cruel and unusual punishments clause, the ultimate arbiter of the standards of criminal responsibility in diverse areas of the criminal law, throughout the country." This seriously strains and distorts our federal system, removing much of the flexibility from which it has drawn strength for two centuries.

The analysis of the plurality opinion is divided into two parts: (i) an "objective" determination that most American jurisdictions do not presently make rape a capital offense, and (ii) a subjective judgment that death is an excessive punishment for rape because the crime does not, in and of itself, cause the death of the victim. I take issue with each of these points.

(a)

The plurality opinion bases its analysis, in part, on the fact that "Georgia is the sole jurisdiction in the United States at the present time that authorizes a sentence of death when the rape victim is an adult woman." Surely, however, this statistic cannot be deemed determinative, or even particularly relevant. As the opinion concedes, two other states— Louisiana and North Carolina—have enacted death penalty statutes for adult rape since this Court's 1972 decision in *Furman v. Georgia.* If the Court is to rely on some "public opinion" process, does this not suggest the beginning of a "trend"?

More to the point, however, it is myopic to base sweeping constitutional principles upon the narrow experience of the past five years. Considerable uncertainty was introduced into this area of the law by this Court's *Furman* decision. A large number of states found their death-penalty statutes invalidated; legislatures were left in serious doubt by the expressions vacillating between discretionary and mandatory death penalties, as to whether this Court would sustain *any* statute imposing death as a criminal sanction. Failure of more states to enact statutes imposing death for rape of an adult woman may thus reflect hasty legislative compromise occasioned by time pressures following *Furman,* a desire to wait on the experience of those states which did enact such statutes, or simply an accurate forecast of today's holding.

In any case, when considered in light of the experience since the turn of this century, where more than one-third of American jurisdictions have consistently provided the death penalty for rape, the plurality's focus on the experience of the immediate past must be viewed as truly disingenuous. Having in mind the swift changes in positions of some members of this Court in the short span of five years, can it rationally be considered a relevant indicator of what our society deems "cruel and unusual" to look solely to what legislatures have *refrained* from doing under conditions of great uncertainty arising from our less than lucid holdings on the Eighth Amendment? Far more representative of societal mores of the 20th century is the accepted practice in a substantial number of jurisdictions preceding the *Furman* decision. "[The] problem ... is the suddenness of the Court's perception of progress in the human attitude since decisions of only a short while ago."

However, even were one to give the most charitable acceptance to the plurality's statistical analysis, it still does not, to my mind, support its conclusion. The most that can be claimed is that for the past year Georgia has been the only state whose adult rape death penalty statute has not otherwise been invalidated; two other state legislatures had enacted rape death penalty statutes in the last five years, but these were invalidated for reasons unrelated to rape under the Court's decisions. ...Even if these figures could be read as indicating that no other states view the death penalty as an appropriate punishment for the rape of an adult woman, it would not necessarily follow that Georgia's imposition of such sanction violates the Eighth Amendment.

The Court has repeatedly pointed to the reserve strength of our federal system which allows state legislatures, within broad limits, to experiment with laws, both criminal and civil, in the effort to achieve socially desirable results. Various provisions of the Constitution, including the Eighth Amendment and the due process clause, of course place substantive limitations on the type of experimentation a state may undertake. However, as the plurality admits, the crime of rape is second perhaps only to murder in its gravity. It follows then that Georgia did not approach such substantive constraints by enacting the statute here in question.

Statutory provisions in criminal justice applied in one part of the country can be carefully watched by other state legislatures, so that the experience of one state becomes available to all. Although human lives are in the balance, it must be remembered that failure to allow flexibility may also jeopardize human lives—those of the victims of undeterred criminal conduct. Our concern for the accused ought not foreclose legislative judgments showing a modicum of consideration for the potential victims.

Three state legislatures have, in the past five years, determined that the taking of human life and the devastating consequences of rape will be minimized if rapists may, in a limited class of cases, be executed for their offenses. That these states are presently a minority does not, in my view, make their judgment less worthy of deference. Our concern for human life must not be confined to the guilty; a state legislature is not to be thought insensitive to human values because it acts firmly to protect the lives and related values of the innocent. In this area, the choices for legislatures are at best painful and difficult and deserve a high degree of deference. Only last Term Mr. Justice White observed:

> It will not do to denigrate these legislative judgments as some form of vestigial savagery or as purely retributive in motivation; for they are solemn judgments, reasonably based, that imposition of the death penalty will save the lives of innocent persons. This concern for life and human values and the sincere efforts of the states to pursue them are matters of the greatest moment *with which the judiciary should be most reluctant to interfere.* Roberts v. Louisiana, 428 U.S., at 355 (dissenting opinion). (Emphasis added.)

The question of whether the death penalty is an appropriate punishment for rape is surely an open one. It is arguable that many prospective rapists would be deterred by the possibility that they could suffer death for their offense; it is also arguable that the death penalty would have only minimal deterrent effect. It may well be that rape victims would become more willing to report the crime and aid in the apprehension of the criminals if they knew that community disapproval of rapists was sufficiently strong to inflict the extreme penalty; or perhaps they would be reluctant to cooperate in the prosecution of rapists if they knew that a conviction might result in the imposition of the death penalty. Quite possibly, the occasional, well-publicized execution of egregious rapists may cause citizens to feel greater security in their daily lives; or, on the contrary, it may be that members of a civilized community will suffer the pangs of a heavy conscience because such punishment will be perceived as excessive.[13] We cannot know which among this range of possibilities is

[13] Obviously I have no special competence to make these judgments, but by the same token no other member of the Court is competent to make a contrary judgment. This

correct, but today's holding forecloses the very exploration we have said federalism was intended to foster. It is difficult to believe that Georgia would long remain alone in punishing rape by death if the next decade demonstrated a drastic reduction in its incidence of rape, an increased cooperation by rape victims in the apprehension and prosecution of rapists, and a greater confidence in the rule of law on the part of the populace.

In order for Georgia's legislative program to develop it must be given time to take effect so that data may be evaluated for comparison with the experience of states which have not enacted death penalty statutes. Today, the Court repudiates the state's solemn judgment on how best to deal with the crime of rape before anyone can know whether the death penalty is an effective deterrent for one of the most horrible of all crimes.... To deprive states of this authority as the Court does, on the basis that "[t]he current judgment with respect to the death penalty for rape ... weighs very heavily on the side of rejecting capital punishment as a suitable penalty for raping an adult woman" is impermissibly rash.... Social change on great issues generally reveals itself in small increments, and the "current judgment" of many states could well be altered on the basis of Georgia's experience, were we to allow its statute to stand.

(b)

The subjective judgment that the death penalty is simply disproportionate to the crime of rape is even more disturbing than the "objective" analysis discussed supra. The plurality's conclusion on this point is based upon the bare fact that murder necessarily results in the physical death of the victim, while rape does not. However, no member of the Court explains why this distinction has relevance, much less constitutional significance. It is, after all, not irrational—nor constitutionally impermissible—for a legislature to make the penalty more severe than the criminal act it punishes in the hope it would deter wrongdoing....

It begs the question to state, as does the plurality opinion: "Life is over for the victim of the murderer; for the rape victim, life may not be nearly so happy as it was, but it is not over and normally is not beyond repair." Until now, the issue under the Eighth Amendment has not been the state of any particular victim after the crime, but rather whether the punishment imposed is grossly disproportionate to the evil committed by the perpetrator. As a matter of constitutional principle, that test cannot have the primitive simplicity of "life for life, eye for eye, tooth for tooth." Rather states must be permitted to engage in a more sophisticated weighing of values in dealing with criminal activity which consistently poses serious danger of death or grave bodily harm. If innocent life and limb are to be preserved I see no constitutional barrier in punishing by death all who engage in such activity, regardless of whether the risk comes to fruition in any particular instance.

is why our system has, until now, left these difficult policy choices to the state legislatures, which may be no wiser, but surely are more attuned to the mores of their communities, than are we.

... The clear implication of today's holding appears to be that the death penalty may be properly imposed only as to crimes resulting in death of the victim. This casts serious doubt upon the constitutional validity of statutes imposing the death penalty for a variety of conduct which, though dangerous, may not necessarily result in any immediate death, e.g., treason, airplane hijacking, and kidnapping. In that respect, today's holding does even more harm than is initially apparent. We cannot avoid taking judicial notice that crimes such as airplane hijacking, kidnapping, and mass terrorist activity constitute a serious and increasing danger to the safety of the public. It would be unfortunate indeed if the effect of today's holding were to inhibit states and the federal government from experimenting with various remedies—including possibly imposition of the penalty of death—to prevent and deter such crimes.

Some sound observations, made only a few years ago, deserve repetition:

> Our task here, as must so frequently be emphasized and re-emphasized, is to pass upon the constitutionality of legislation that has been enacted and that is challenged. This is the sole task for judges. We should not allow our personal preferences as to the wisdom of legislative and congressional action, or our distaste for such action, to guide our judicial decision in cases such as these. The temptations to cross that policy line are very great. In fact, as today's decision reveals, they are almost irresistible. Furman v. Georgia, 408 U.S., at 411 (Blackmun, J., dissenting).

Whatever our individual views as to the wisdom of capital punishment, I cannot agree that it is constitutionally impermissible for a state legislature to make the "solemn judgment" to impose such penalty for the crime of rape. Accordingly, I would leave to the states the task of legislating in this area of the law.

―――――

## NOTES ON PROPORTIONALITY AND CAPITAL OFFENSES

**1. Questions and Comments on *Coker*.** *Coker* should be approached on the Court's assumption that capital punishment is *sometimes* permissible for *some* offenses. Obviously, one could take the view—as Justices Brennan and Marshall do—that capital punishment is always unconstitutional. From this perspective, *Coker* is an easy case. It is a hard case, and worth talking about as a problem independent of the legitimacy of capital punishment in general, only if one is prepared to assume that the capital sanction is sometimes constitutional.

On this assumption, the case may be evaluated from at least two perspectives. The first concerns the Court's methodology. Justice White argues that the judgment involved "should not be, or appear to be, merely the subjective views of individual Justices; judgment should be informed by objective factors to the maximum possible extent." To what "objective factors'' does he look? Does the Chief Justice disagree about what factors are relevant, or only about their application to the case at hand? Are the factors to which either opinion looks really "objective," or does the case in the end turn on "merely the subjective views of the individual Justices?"

Secondly, there is the question on the merits: whether rapists in general, or Coker in particular, can appropriately be distinguished from those murderers constitutionally punishable by death. Do you agree with Justice White's treatment of this issue? With the Chief Justice's? Or should Justice Powell's view—that some rapists may be executed but not Coker—prevail?[a]

At least one state supreme court has interpreted *Coker* to apply only to rape of an adult woman. In State v. Wilson, 685 So.2d 1063 (La. 1996), the Louisiana Supreme Court held that a death sentence is constitutionally permissible for rape of a minor, and allowed a capital charge to proceed against an HIV-positive defendant accused of raping three girls, ages five, seven and nine, one of whom was his daughter. Is this a correct reading of *Coker*?

**2.  *Enmund v. Florida.*** The Court addressed the use of capital punishment for an accomplice to murder in Enmund v. Florida, 458 U.S. 782 (1982). Enmund planned the robbery of an elderly couple, Thomas and Eunice Kersey, who were known to keep large sums of cash in their home. He waited in a car some distance from the victims' house while two accomplices, Sampson and Jeanette Armstrong, approached the house on the pretense of asking for water for an overheated radiator. After Thomas Kersey retrieved a water jug, Sampson Armstrong held a gun to him while Jeanette tried to get his wallet. Hearing her husband's cry for help, Eunice Kersey came around the side of the house with a gun and shot Jeanette Armstrong. Sampson, and perhaps Jeanette, returned Eunice's fire, killing both her and her husband. They then dragged the bodies into the kitchen, took what money they could find, and fled in the waiting car. Sampson Armstrong and Enmund were tried together, and both were sentenced to death. Jeanette Armstrong was tried separately. She was convicted of two counts of second-degree murder and one of robbery, and given three consecutive life sentences.

Under Florida law, the "felony-murder rule and the law of principals combine to make a felon generally responsible for the lethal acts of his co-felon." No findings were required as to whether Enmund planned the killings or actually anticipated that lethal force might be used. The imposition of capital punishment for felony murder was limited, however, by the requirement that the defendant be classified in common-law terms as a principal in the second degree rather than an accessory before the fact—that is, that he be actually or constructively present at the scene of the crime. The Florida courts held that Enmund satisfied this condition.

[a] The constitutional and jurisprudential aspects of the issue presented in *Coker* are extensively examined in Margaret Radin, The Jurisprudence of Death: Evolving Standards for the Cruel and Unusual Punishments Clause, 126 U.Pa.L.Rev. 989 (1978).

The Supreme Court set aside Enmund's death sentence, holding that the Eighth Amendment does not permit "imposition of the death penalty on one such as Enmund who aids and abets a felony in the course of which a murder is committed by others but who does not himself kill, attempt to kill or intend that a killing take place or that lethal force will be employed." Justice White wrote for the majority, which included Justices Brennan, Marshall, Blackmun, and Stevens. Justice O'Connor wrote a dissent on behalf of herself, Chief Justice Burger, and Justices Powell and Rehnquist.

(i) **The Indicators of Societal Judgment.** Justice White began his majority opinion by referring to the methodology of *Coker:*

> [I]t was stressed that our judgment "should be informed by objective factors to the maximum possible extent." Accordingly, the Court looked to the historical development of the punishment at issue, legislative judgments, international opinion, and the sentencing decisions juries have made before bringing its own judgment to bear on the matter. We proceed to analyze the punishment at issue in this case in a similar manner.

He began by undertaking a complex analysis of the felony-murder provisions of the 36 American jurisdictions that authorize the death penalty. Essentially, he divided the states into three categories: (i) nine states in which the death penalty is authorized "solely for participation in a robbery in which another robber takes life"; (ii) nine states in which conviction of a capital offense for unadorned felony murder is permissible, but in which various combinations of aggravating and mitigating circumstances must be satisfied before a capital sentence can be imposed; and (iii) the remainder of the states, in three of which felony murder is not a capital offense, in four of which Enmund could not have been convicted of a capital offense because of various limitations in the statutes, and in the remaining 11 of which some culpability as to the death must be proved in order to justify conviction of a capital crime. Justice White concluded:

> Thus only a small minority of jurisdictions—nine—allow the death penalty to be imposed solely because the defendant somehow participated in a robbery in the course of which a murder was committed. Even if the nine states are included where such a defendant could be executed for an unintended felony murder if sufficient aggravating circumstances are present to outweigh mitigating circumstances—which often include the defendant's minimal participation in the murder—only about a third of American jurisdictions would ever permit a defendant who somehow participated in a robbery where a murder occurred to be sentenced to die. Moreover, of the eight states which have enacted new death-penalty statutes since 1978, only one authorizes capital punishment in such circumstances. While the current legislative judgment with respect to imposition of the death penalty where a defendant did not take life, attempt to take it, or intend to take life is neither "wholly unanimous among state legislatures," nor as

compelling as the legislative judgments considered in *Coker,* it nevertheless weighs on the side of rejecting capital punishment for the crime at issue.

Justice White then turned to the second "objective" factor relied upon in *Coker*. He asserted that "[s]ociety's rejection of the death penalty for accomplice liability in felony murders is also indicated by the sentencing decisions that juries have made. ...The evidence is overwhelming that American juries have repudiated imposition of the death penalty for crimes such as petitioner's." Justice White cited in support of this conclusion a search by Enmund's lawyer of all reported appellate court decisions since 1954 involving defendants who were executed for homicide. The study showed that of 362 executions, the defendant personally committed the homicide in 339. In two cases, the defendant hired the killer, and in 16 others it could not be determined from the reported facts who committed the homicide:

> The survey revealed only six cases out of 362 where a nontrigger-man felony murderer was executed. All six executions took place in 1955. By contrast, there were 72 executions for rape in this country between 1955 and this Court's decision in *Coker v. Georgia* in 1977.

Justice White also cited a study by counsel of the nation's death row population as of October 1, 1981. There were 796 inmates under a capital sentence for homicide. Of the 739 for whom the data were sufficient, only 41 did not actually participate in the fatal assault. Of these 41, only 16 were not actually present at the homicide, and 13 of these 16 either hired or solicited someone else to commit the offense or participated in a scheme designed to kill the victim. Thus only three offenders, including Enmund, did not take life themselves, attempt to take life, or intend to take life. Of the 45 felony murderers on Florida's death row, moreover, Enmund was the only one in this category.[b]

"[W]e are not aware," Justice White concluded, "of a single person convicted of felony murder over the past quarter century who did not kill or attempt to kill, and did not intend the death of the victim, who has been executed." And "only three persons in that category are presently sentenced to die."

Justice O'Connor's dissent accepted the premise that the factors to be examined were those identified by the *Coker* plurality. She concluded, however, that "the available data do not show that society has rejected conclusively the death penalty for felony murderers."

---

[b] Justice White added a footnote to this part of his discussion:

"The climate of international opinion concerning the acceptability of a particular punishment" is an additional consideration which is "not irrelevant." It is thus worth noting that the doctrine of felony murder has been abolished in England and India, severely restricted in Canada and a number of other Commonwealth countries, and is unknown in continental Europe....

She first noted that historically—beginning with the English law from which the American tradition is derived—the death penalty was an accepted sanction for felony murder. She then examined Enmund's evidence as to contemporary attitudes: the study of reported appellate opinions since 1954, the examination of the prisoners currently on death row, and the conclusions drawn from current death penalty legislation. As to the first two points, she argued:

> Impressive as these statistics are at first glance, they cannot be accepted uncritically. So stated, the data do not reveal the number or fraction of homicides that were charged as felony murders, or the number or fraction of cases in which the state sought the death penalty for an accomplice guilty of felony murder. Consequently, we cannot know the fraction of cases in which juries rejected the death penalty for accomplice felony murder.[c] Moreover, ... much of these data classify defendants by whether they "personally committed homicidal assault," and do not show the fraction of capital defendants who were shown to have an intent to kill. While the petitioner relies on the fact that he did not pull the trigger, his principal argument is, and must be, that death is an unconstitutional penalty absent an intent to kill, for otherwise, defendants who hire others to kill would escape the death penalty. Thus, the data he presents are not entirely relevant. Even accepting the petitioner's facts as meaningful, they may only reflect that sentencers are especially cautious in imposing the death penalty, and reserve that punishment for those defendants who are sufficiently involved in the homicide, whether or not there was specific intent to kill.

With respect to the third point—the current status of state legislation authorizing the death penalty for felony murder—Justice O'Connor disagreed strongly with Justice White's characterization of the statutes. She divided the states into a different three categories: (i) 21 states that "permit imposition of the death penalty for felony murder even though the defendant did not commit the homicidal act, and even though he had no actual intent to kill"; she added three additional states to this category that do not require a purpose to take life, but do require some form of recklessness or negligence; (ii) seven states that "authorize the death penalty only if the defendant had the specific intent (or some rough equivalent) to kill the victim"; and (iii) three states that "restrict the application of the death penalty to those felony murderers who actually

---

[c] Justice White responded as follows:

The dissent criticizes these statistics on the ground that they do not reveal the percentage of homicides that were charged as felony murders or the percentage of cases where the state sought the death penalty for an accomplice guilty of felony murder. We doubt whether it is possible to gather such information, and at any rate, it would be relevant if prosecutors rarely sought the death penalty for accomplice felony murder, for it would tend to indicate that prosecutors, who represent society's interest in punishing crime, consider the death penalty excessive for accomplice felony murder.—[Footnote by eds.]

commit the homicide." Thus, she regarded the laws of 24 states as permitting an execution that would violate the principle underlying the majority opinion, whereas Justice White considered that only nine—or at most 18—would permit such an execution. Justice O'Connor concluded as follows:

> Thus, in nearly half the states, and in two-thirds of the states that permit the death penalty for murder, a defendant who neither killed the victim nor specifically intended that the victim die may be sentenced to death for his participation in the robbery-murder. Far from "[w]eighing very heavily on the side of rejecting capital punishment as a suitable penalty for" felony murder, these legislative judgments indicate that our "evolving standards of decency" still embrace capital punishment for this crime. For this reason, I conclude that the petitioner has failed to meet the standards in *Coker* . . . that the "two crucial indicators of evolving standards of decency . . . —jury determinations and legislative enactments—*both point conclusively* to the repudiation" of capital punishment for felony murder. In short, the death penalty for felony murder does not fall short of our "national standards of decency".

**(ii) The "Ultimate" Judgment.** After his review of the "objective" indicators of society's judgment on the death penalty for persons in Enmund's situation, Justice White concluded his opinion for the Court as follows:

> Although the judgments of legislatures, juries and prosecutors [who may have contributed to the low death-row population of people in Enmund's situation by not seeking the death penalty] weigh heavily in the balance, it is for us ultimately to judge whether the Eighth Amendment permits imposition of the death penalty on one such as Enmund who aids and abets a felony in the course of which a murder is committed by others but who does not himself kill, attempt to kill, or intend that a killing take place or that lethal force will be employed. We have concluded, along with most legislatures and juries, that it does not.

> We have no doubt that robbery is a serious crime deserving serious punishment. It is not, however, a crime "so grievous an affront to humanity that the only adequate response may be the penalty of death." "[I]t does not compare with murder, which does involve the unjustified taking of human life. Although it may be accompanied by another crime, [robbery] by definition does not include the death of or even the serious injury to another person. The murderer kills; the [robber], if no more than that, does not. Life is over for the victim of the murderer; for the [robbery] victim, life . . . is not over and normally is not beyond repair." Coker v. Georgia, 433 U.S. 584, 598 (1977). As was said of the crime of rape in *Coker,* we have the abiding conviction that the death penalty, which is "unique in its severity and irrevocability,"

is an excessive penalty for the robber who, as such, does not take human life.

Here the robbers did commit murder; but they were subjected to the death penalty only because they killed as well as robbed. The question before us is not the disproportionality of death as a penalty for murder, but is rather the validity of capital punishment for Enmund's own conduct. The focus must be on *his* culpability, not on that of those who committed the robbery and shot the victims, for we insist on "individualized consideration as a constitutional requirement in imposing the death sentence," which means that we must focus on "relevant facets of the character and record of the individual offender."[d] Enmund himself did not kill or attempt to kill; and as construed by the Florida Supreme Court, the record before us does not warrant a finding that Enmund had any intention of participating in or facilitating a murder....

In Gregg v. Georgia, 428 U.S. 153, 183 (1976), the prevailing opinion observed that "[t]he death penalty is said to serve two principal social purposes: retribution and deterrence of capital crimes by prospective offenders." Unless the death penalty when applied to those in Enmund's position measurably contributes to one or both of these goals, it "is nothing more than the purposeless and needless imposition of pain and suffering," and hence an unconstitutional punishment. We are quite unconvinced, however, that the threat that the death penalty will be imposed for murder will measurably deter one who does not kill and has no intention or purpose that life will be taken. Instead, it seems likely that "capital punishment can serve as a deterrent only when murder is the result of premeditation and deliberation," for if a person does not intend that life be taken or contemplate that lethal force will be employed by others, the possibility that the death penalty will be imposed for vicarious felony murder will not "enter into the cold calculus that precedes the decision to act."

It would be very different if the likelihood of a killing in the course of a robbery were so substantial that one should share the blame for the killing if he somehow participated in the felony. But competent observers have concluded that there is no basis in experience for the notion that death so frequently occurs in the course of a felony for which killing is not an essential ingredient that the death penalty should be considered as a justifiable deterrent to the felony itself. ALI, Model Penal Code § 210.2, Comment at 38 & n. 96 (Official Draft and Revised Comments, 1980). This conclusion was based on three comparisons of robbery statistics, each of which showed that only about one-half of one per cent of robberies resulted in homicide.[e] The most recent national crime

---

[d] The reference is to the individualization requirements of *Lockett* and *Eddings,* which are discussed in Chapter VIII.—[Footnote by eds.]

[e] The cited discussion in the Model Penal Code Commentaries occurs in the context of whether there should be a felony-murder rule

statistics strongly support this conclusion. In addition to the evidence that killings only rarely occur during robberies is the fact, already noted, that however often death occurs in the course of a felony such as robbery, the death penalty is rarely imposed on one only vicariously guilty of the murder, a fact which further attenuates its possible utility as an effective deterrent.

As for retribution as a justification for executing Enmund, we think this very much depends on the degree of Enmund's culpability—what Enmund's intentions, expectations, and actions were. American criminal law has long considered a defendant's intention—and therefore his moral guilt—to be critical to "the degree of [his] criminal culpability" and the Court has found criminal penalties to be unconstitutionally excessive in the absence of intentional wrongdoing. [Citing Robinson v. California, 370 U.S. 660 (1962), which held a statute unconstitutional under the Eighth Amendment because it punished an "illness which may be contracted innocently or involuntarily" and Godfrey v. Georgia, 446 U.S. 420 (1980), which held a death sentence in violation of the Eighth Amendment because "the defendant's crime did not reflect" a consciousness materially more "depraved" than that of any person guilty of murder.]

For purposes of imposing the death penalty, Enmund's criminal culpability must be limited to his participation in the robbery, and his punishment must be tailored to his personal responsibility and moral guilt. Putting Enmund to death to avenge two killings that he did not commit and had no intention of committing or causing does not measurably contribute to the retributive end of ensuring that the criminal gets his just deserts. This is the judgment of most of the legislatures that have recently addressed the matter, and we have no reason to disagree with that judgment for purposes of construing and applying the Eighth Amendment.

Justice O'Connor's dissent also addressed the requirement of *Coker* that "the penalty imposed in a capital case be proportional to the harm caused and the defendant's blameworthiness." On this point, she concluded:

Although the Court disingenuously seeks to characterize Enmund as only a "robber," it cannot be disputed that he is responsible, along with Sampson and Jeanette Armstrong, for the murders of the Kerseys. There is no dispute that their lives were unjustifiably taken, and that the petitioner, as one who aided and abetted the armed robbery, is legally liable for their deaths. Quite unlike the defendant in *Coker,* the petitioner cannot claim that the

in the first place, not whether the death penalty should be authorized if there is to be such a rule. The Model Penal Code rejects the traditional formulation of the felony-murder rule, as discussed in Chapter VIII.— [Footnote by eds.]

penalty imposed is "grossly out of proportion" to the harm for which he admittedly is at least partly responsible.

The Court's holding today is especially disturbing because it makes intent a matter of federal constitutional law, requiring this Court both to review highly subjective definitional problems customarily left to state criminal law and to develop an Eighth Amendment meaning of intent.... Although the Court's opinion suggests that intent can be ascertained as if it were some historical fact, in fact it is a legal concept, not easily defined. Thus, while proportionality requires a nexus between the punishment imposed and the defendant's blameworthiness, the Court fails to explain why the Eighth Amendment concept of proportionality requires rejection of standards of blameworthiness based on other levels of intent, such as, for example, the intent to commit an armed robbery coupled with knowledge that armed robberies involve substantial risk of death or serious injury to other persons. Moreover, the intent-to-kill requirement is crudely crafted; it fails to take into account the complex picture of the defendant's knowledge of his accomplice's intent and whether he was armed, the defendant's contribution to the planning and success of the crime, and the defendant's actual participation during the commission of the crime. Under the circumstances, the determination of the degree of blameworthiness is best left to the sentencer, who can sift through the facts unique to each case. Consequently, while the type of mens rea of the defendant must be considered carefully in assessing the proper penalty, it is not so critical a factor in determining blameworthiness as to require a finding of intent to kill in order to impose the death penalty for felony murder.

In sum, the petitioner and the Court have failed to show that contemporary standards, as reflected in both jury determinations and legislative enactments, preclude imposition of the death penalty for accomplice felony murder. Moreover, examination of the qualitative factors underlying the concept of proportionality do not show that the death penalty is disproportionate as applied to Earl Enmund. In contrast to the crime in *Coker,* the petitioner's crime involves the very type of harm that this Court has held justifies the death penalty. Finally, because of the unique and complex mixture of facts involving a defendant's actions, knowledge, motives, and participation during the commission of a felony murder, I believe that the factfinder is best able to assess the defendant's blameworthiness. Accordingly, I conclude that the death penalty is not disproportionate to the crime of felony murder even though the defendant did not actually kill or intend to kill his victims.[f]

At this point, Justice O'Connor appended a footnote:

[f] Justice O'Connor went on to argue on other grounds, however, that the case should have been remanded for a new sentencing hearing.—[Footnote by eds.]

The petitioner and the Court also contend that capital punishment for felony murder violates the Eighth Amendment because it "makes no measurable contribution to acceptable goals of punishment." In brief, the petitioner and the Court reason that since he did not specifically intend to kill the Kerseys, since the probability of death during an armed robbery is so low, and since the death penalty is so rarely imposed on nontriggermen, capital punishment could not have deterred him or anyone else from participating in the armed robbery. The petitioner and the Court also reject the notion that the goal of retribution might be served because his "moral guilt" is too insignificant.

At their core, these considerations are legislative judgment decisions regarding the efficacy of capital punishment as a tool in achieving retributive justice and deterring violent crime. Surely, neither the petitioner nor the Court has shown that capital punishment is ineffective as a deterrent for his crime; the most the Court can do is speculate as to its effect on other felony murderers and rely on "competent observers" rather than legislative judgments. Moreover, the decision of whether or not a particular punishment serves the admittedly legitimate goal of retribution seems uniquely suited to legislative resolution. Because an armed robber takes a serious risk that someone will die during the course of his crime, and because of the obviousness of that risk, we cannot conclude that the death penalty "makes no measurable contribution to acceptable goals of punishment."

**3.  *Tison v. Arizona.*** The principle announced by the majority in *Enmund* was modified in Tison v. Arizona, 481 U.S. 137 (1987), another 5–4 decision,[g] in which the Court affirmed death sentences imposed on two brothers, Raymond and Ricky Tison. The facts were summarized in Justice O'Connor's majority opinion:

> Gary Tison was sentenced to life imprisonment as the result of a prison escape during the course of which he had killed a guard. After he had been in prison a number of years, Gary Tison's wife, their three sons Donald, Ricky, and Raymond, Gary's brother Joseph, and other relatives made plans to help Gary Tison escape again. The Tison family assembled a large arsenal of weapons for this purpose. Plans for escape were discussed with Gary Tison, who insisted that his cellmate, Randy Greenawalt, also a convicted murderer, be included in the prison break. The following facts are largely evidenced by [Raymond and Ricky Tison's] detailed confessions given as part of a plea bargain according to the terms of which the State agreed not to seek the death sentence. The Arizona courts interpreted the plea agreement to require that petitioners testify to the planning stages of the

---

[g] The *Tison* majority comprised Justices O'Connor and Powell and Chief Justice Rehnquist (all of whom dissented in *En-* *mund*), Justice White (who wrote the majority opinion in *Enmund*), and Justice Scalia (who had succeeded Chief Justice Burger).

breakout. When they refused to do so, the bargain was rescinded and they were tried, convicted, and sentenced to death.

On July 30, 1978, the three Tison brothers entered the Arizona State Prison at Florence carrying a large ice chest filled with guns. The Tisons armed Greenawalt and their father, and the group, brandishing their weapons, locked the prison guards and visitors present in a storage closet. The five men fled the prison grounds in the Tisons' Ford Galaxy automobile. No shots were fired at the prison.

After leaving the prison, the men abandoned the Ford automobile and proceeded on to an isolated house in a white Lincoln automobile that the brothers had parked at a hospital near the prison. At the house, the Lincoln automobile had a flat tire; the only spare tire was pressed into service. After two nights at the house, the group drove towards Flagstaff. As the group traveled on back roads and secondary highways through the desert, another tire blew out. The group decided to flag down a passing motorist and steal a car. Raymond stood out in front of the Lincoln; the other four armed themselves and laid in wait by the side of the road. One car passed by without stopping, but a second car, a Mazda occupied by John Lyons, his wife Donelda, his two-year-old son Christopher and his 15–year-old niece, Theresa Tyson, pulled over to render aid.

As Raymond showed John Lyons the flat tire on the Lincoln, the other Tisons and Greenawalt emerged. The Lyons family was forced into the back seat of the Lincoln. Raymond and Donald drove the Lincoln down a dirt road off the highway and then down a gas line service road farther into the desert; Gary Tison, Ricky Tison and Randy Greenawalt followed in the Lyons' Mazda. The two cars were parked trunk to trunk and the Lyons family was ordered to stand in front of the Lincoln's headlights. The Tisons transferred their belongings from the Lincoln into the Mazda. They discovered guns and money in the Mazda which they kept and they put the rest of the Lyons' possessions in the Lincoln.

Gary Tison then told Raymond to drive the Lincoln still farther into the desert. Raymond did so, and, while the others guarded the Lyons and Theresa Tyson, Gary fired his shotgun into the radiator, presumably to completely disable the vehicle. The Lyons and Theresa Tyson were then escorted to the Lincoln and again ordered to stand in its headlights. Ricky Tison reported that John Lyons begged, in comments "more or less directed at everybody," "Jesus, don't kill me." Gary Tison said he was "thinking about it." John Lyons asked the Tisons and Greenawalt to "[g]ive us some water ... just leave us out here, and you all go home." Gary Tison then told his sons to go back to the Mazda and get some water. Raymond later explained that his father "was like in conflict with himself . . . [w]hat it was, I think it was the baby being there and all this, and he wasn't sure about what to do."

The petitioners' statements diverge to some extent, but it appears that both of them went back towards the Mazda, along with Donald, while Randy Greenawalt and Gary Tison stayed at the Lincoln guarding the victims. Raymond recalled being at the Mazda filling the water jug "hen we started hearing the shots." Ricky said that the brothers gave the water jug to Gary Tison who then, with Randy Greenawalt went behind the Lincoln where they spoke briefly, then raised the shotguns and started firing. In any event, petitioners agree they saw Greenawalt and their father brutally murder their four captives with repeated blasts from their shotguns. Neither made an effort to help the victims, though both later stated they were surprised by the shooting. The Tisons got into the Mazda and drove away, continuing their flight. Physical evidence suggested that Theresa Tyson managed to crawl away from the bloodbath, severely injured. She died in the desert after the Tisons left.

Several days later the Tisons and Greenawalt were apprehended after a shootout at a police roadblock. Donald Tison was killed. Gary Tison escaped into the desert where he subsequently died of exposure. . . .

[Raymond and Ricky Tison were tried] for capital murder of the four victims as well as for the associated crimes of armed robbery, kidnaping, and car theft. The capital murder charges were based on Arizona felony-murder law providing that a killing occurring during the perpetration of robbery or kidnaping is capital murder, and that each participant in the kidnaping or robbery is legally responsible for the acts of his accomplices. Each [was] convicted of the four murders under these accomplice liability and felony-murder statutes.

The trial judge sentenced each of the Tison brothers to death based on findings of three aggravating factors which he found to outweigh the mitigating factors, including the brothers' youth and the absence of any prior felony record. He also specifically found that their "participation . . . in the crimes giving rise to the application of the felony murder rule" had been "very substantial," and that each of them "could reasonably have foreseen that his conduct . . . would cause or create a grave risk of . . . death." On direct appeal, the Arizona Supreme Court affirmed the death sentences, noting that:

The record establishes that both Ricky and Raymond Tison were present when the homicides took place and that they occurred as part of and in the course of the escape and continuous attempt to prevent recapture. The deaths would not have occurred but for their assistance. That they did not specifically intend that the Lyonses and Theresa Tyson die, that they did not plot in advance that these homicides would take place, or that they did not actually pull the triggers on the guns which inflicted the fatal wounds is of little significance.

In habeas proceedings brought after the Supreme Court's decision in *Enmund*, the Tisons sought to set aside the death sentences on the ground that *Enmund* required a finding of intent to kill. Finding that the Tisons "could anticipate the use of lethal force" and "played an active part in the events that led to the murders," the Arizona Supreme Court held that this amounted to "intent to kill" within the meaning of *Enmund*, because "intent to kill includes the situation in which the defendant intended, contemplated, or anticipated that lethal force would or might be used or that life would or might be taken in accomplishing the underlying felony."

Justice O'Connor acknowledged that the Arizona Supreme Court's definition of intent "is broader than that described by the *Enmund* Court" and that the Tisons "do not fall within the 'intent to kill' category of felony murderers for which *Enmund* explicitly finds the death penalty permissible...." On the other hand, she observed, "it is equally clear" that they "fall outside the category of felony murderers for whom *Enmund* explicitly held the death penalty disproportional"—cases involving "the minor actor in an armed robbery, not on the scene, who neither intended to kill nor was found to have had any culpable mental state." She continued:

> [The] facts not only indicate that the Tison brothers' participation in the crime was anything but minor, they also would clearly support a finding that they both subjectively appreciated that their acts were likely to result in the taking of innocent life. The issue raised by this case is whether the Eighth Amendment prohibits the death penalty in the intermediate case of the defendant whose participation is major and whose mental state is one of reckless indifference to the value of human life. *Enmund* does not specifically address this point. We now take up the task of determining whether the Eighth Amendment proportionality requirement bars the death penalty under these circumstances.

> Like the *Enmund* Court, we find the state legislatures' judgment as to proportionality in these circumstances relevant to this constitutional inquiry. The largest number of States still fall into the two intermediate categories discussed in *Enmund*. Four States authorize the death penalty in felony-murder cases upon a showing of culpable mental state such as recklessness or extreme indifference to human life. Two jurisdictions require that the defendant's participation be substantial and the statutes of at least six more, including Arizona, take minor participation in the felony expressly into account in mitigation of the murder. These requirements significantly overlap both in this case and in general, for the greater the defendant's participation in the felony murder, the more likely that he acted with reckless indifference to human life. At a minimum, however, it can be said that all these jurisdictions, as well as six States which *Enmund* classified along with Florida as permitting capital punishment for felony-murder *simpliciter*,

and the three States which simply require some additional aggravation before imposing the death penalty upon a felony murderer, specifically authorize the death penalty in a felony-murder case where, though the defendant's mental state fell short of intent to kill, the defendant was a major actor in a felony in which he knew death was highly likely to occur. On the other hand, even after *Enmund*, only 11 States authorizing capital punishment forbid imposition of the death penalty even though the defendant's participation in the felony murder is major and the likelihood of killing is so substantial as to raise an inference of extreme recklessness. This substantial and recent legislative authorization of the death penalty for the crime of felony murder regardless of the absence of a finding of an intent to kill powerfully suggests that our society does *not* reject the death penalty as grossly excessive under these circumstances.

Moreover, a number of state courts have interpreted *Enmund* to permit the imposition of the death penalty in such aggravated felony murders. . . .

Against this backdrop, we now consider the proportionality of the death penalty in these mid range felony-murder cases for which the majority of American jurisdictions clearly authorize capital punishment and for which American courts have not been nearly so reluctant to impose death as they are in the case of felony-murder *simpliciter*.

A critical facet of the individualized determination of culpability required in capital cases is the mental state with which the defendant commits the crime. Deeply ingrained in our legal tradition is the idea that the more purposeful is the criminal conduct, the more serious is the offense, and, therefore, the more severely it ought to be punished. . . .

A narrow focus on the question of whether or not a given defendant "intended to kill," however, is a highly unsatisfactory means of definitively distinguishing the most culpable and dangerous of murderers. . . . [S]ome nonintentional murderers may be among the most dangerous and inhumane of all—the person who tortures another not caring whether the victim lives or dies, or the robber who shoots someone in the course of the robbery, utterly indifferent to the fact that the desire to rob may have the unintended consequence of killing the victim as well as taking the victim's property. This reckless indifference to the value of human life may be every bit as shocking to the moral sense as an "intent to kill." Indeed it is for this very reason that the common law and modern criminal codes alike have classified behavior such as occurred in this case along with intentional murders. *Enmund* held that when "intent to kill" results in its logical though not inevitable consequence—the taking of human life—the Eighth Amendment permits the State to exact the death penalty after a careful weighing of the aggravating and mitigating circumstances. Similarly, we hold that the reckless disregard for human life implicit in knowingly engaging in criminal activities known to carry a grave risk of death represents a highly culpable mental state, a mental state that may be taken into account in making a capital sentencing judgment when that conduct causes its natural, though also not inevitable, lethal result.

Only a small minority of those jurisdictions imposing capital punishment for felony murder have rejected the possibility of a capital sentence absent an intent to kill and we do not find this minority position constitutionally required. We will not attempt to precisely delineate the particular types of conduct and states of mind warranting imposition of the death penalty here. Rather, we simply hold that major participation in the felony committed, combined with reckless indifference to human life, is sufficient to satisfy the *Enmund* culpability requirement....

Justice Brennan dissented, in an opinion joined by Justices Marshall, Blackmun and Stevens:

... Creation of a new category of culpability is not enough to distinguish this case from *Enmund*. The Court must also establish that death is a proportionate punishment for individuals in this category. In other words, the Court must demonstrate that major participation in a felony with a state of mind of reckless indifference to human life deserves the same punishment as intending to commit a murder or actually committing a murder. The Court does not attempt to conduct a proportionality review of the kind performed in past cases raising a proportionality question.

One reason the Court offers for its conclusion that death is proportionate punishment for persons falling within its new category is that limiting the death penalty to those who intend to kill "is a highly unsatisfactory means of definitively distinguishing the most culpable and dangerous of murderers." To illustrate that intention cannot be dispositive, the Court offers as examples "the person *who tortures* another not caring whether the victim lives or dies, or the robber *who shoots* someone in the course of the robbery, utterly indifferent to the fact that the desire to rob may have the unintended consequence of killing the victim as well as taking the victim's property." (Emphasis added.) Influential commentators and some States have approved the use of the death penalty for persons, like those given in the Court's examples, *who kill* others in circumstances manifesting an extreme indifference to the value of human life. Thus an exception to the requirement that only intentional murders be punished with death might be made for persons who actually commit an act of homicide; *Enmund*, by distinguishing from the accomplice case "those who kill," clearly reserved that question. But the constitutionality of the death penalty for those individuals is no more relevant to this case than it was to *Enmund*, because this case, like *Enmund*, involves accomplices *who did not kill*. Thus, although some of the "most culpable and dangerous of murderers" may be those who killed without specifically intending to kill, it is considerably more difficult to apply that rubric convincingly to those who not only did not intend to kill, but who also have not killed.

It is precisely in this context—where the defendant has not killed—that a finding that he or she nevertheless intended to kill seems indispensable to establishing capital culpability. It is important first to note that such a defendant has not committed an *act* for which he or she could be sentenced to death. The applicability of the death penalty therefore turns entirely on the defendant's mental state with regard to an act committed by another. Factors such as the defendant's major participation in the events surrounding the killing or the defendant's presence at the scene are relevant insofar as they illuminate the defendant's mental state with regard to the killings. They cannot serve, however, as independent grounds for imposing the death penalty.

Second, when evaluating such a defendant's mental state, a determination that the defendant acted with intent is qualitatively different from a determination that the defendant acted with reckless indifference to human life. The difference lies in the nature of the choice each has made. The reckless actor has not *chosen* to bring about the killing in the way the intentional actor has. The person who chooses to act recklessly and is indifferent to the possibility of fatal consequences often deserves serious punishment. But because that person has not chosen to kill, his or her moral and criminal culpability is of a different degree than that of one who killed or intended to kill.... The Court's decision today to approve the death penalty for accomplices who lack this mental state is inconsistent with *Enmund* and with the only justifications this Court has put forth for imposing the death penalty in any case.

In *Enmund*, the Court explained at length the reasons a finding of intent is a necessary prerequisite to the imposition of the death penalty. In any given case, the Court said, the death penalty must "measurably contribut[e]" to one or both of the two "social purposes"—deterrence and retribution—which this Court has accepted as justifications for the death penalty.... The Court's second reason for abandoning the intent requirement is based on its survey of state statutes authorizing the death penalty for felony murder, and on a handful of state cases. On this basis, the Court concludes that "[o]nly a small minority *of those jurisdictions imposing capital punishment for felony murder have* rejected the possibility of a capital sentence absent an intent to kill and we do not find this minority position constitutionally required." (Emphasis added.) The Court would thus have us believe that "the majority of American jurisdictions clearly authorize capital punishment" in cases such as this. This is not the case. First, the Court excludes from its survey those jurisdictions that have abolished the death penalty and those that have authorized it only in circumstances different from those presented here. When these jurisdictions are included, and are considered with those jurisdictions that require a finding of intent to kill in order to impose the death sentence for felony murder, one discovers that approximately three-fifths of American jurisdictions do not authorize the death penalty for a non-triggerman absent a finding that he intended to kill. Thus, contrary to the Court's implication that its view is consonant with that of "the majority of American jurisdictions," the Court's view is itself distinctly the minority position.

Second, it is critical examine not simply those jurisdictions that authorize the death penalty in a given circumstance, but those that actually *impose* it. Evidence that a penalty is imposed only infrequently suggests not only that jurisdictions are reluctant to apply it but also that, when it is applied, its imposition is arbitrary and therefore unconstitutional. Thus, the Court in *Enmund* examined the relevant statistics on the imposition of the death penalty for accomplices in a felony murder. . . .

The Court today neither reviews nor updates this evidence. Had it done so, it would have discovered that, even including the 65 executions since *Enmund*, "[t]he fact remains that we are not aware of a single person convicted of felony murder over the past quarter century who did not kill or attempt to kill, and did not intend the death of the victim, who has been executed. . . ." Of the 64 persons on death row in Arizona, all of those who have raised and lost an *Enmund* challenge in the Arizona Supreme Court have been found either to have killed or to have specifically intended to kill. Thus, like Enmund, the Tisons' sentence appears to be an aberration within Arizona itself as well as nationally and internationally. The Court's objective evidence that the statutes of roughly 20 States appear to authorize the death penalty for defendants in the Court's new category is therefore an inadequate substitute for a proper proportionality analysis, and is not persuasive evidence that the punishment that was unconstitutional for Enmund is constitutional for the Tisons.

**4. Questions on *Enmund* and *Tison*.** Can *Tison* be reconciled with *Enmund*? If you were sitting on a state supreme court, what culpability finding would you regard as constitutionally prerequisite to the imposition of a death sentence on an accomplice to a felony-murder? What culpability finding is constitutionally required for a person who kills? Justice Brennan argues that reckless indifference to human life should not be constitutionally sufficient for an accomplice even though it might be sufficient for the killer. Is this a defensible position?

It is also helpful to think about *Enmund* and *Tison* from the standpoint of constitutional interpretation. Consider the methodology employed in the various opinions. Do the Justices disagree about what "objective" factors are relevant or only about their application to the cases at hand? And on the merits of the "ultimate" issue, did the Court reach the right results in these two cases?[h]

———

### NOTES ON DIMINISHED RESPONSIBILITY, PROPORTIONALITY, AND THE DEATH PENALTY

**1. Introduction.** *Coker* and the preceding notes address the constitutionally necessary *offense* elements (conduct and mens rea) required for capital punishment. Another line of cases has addressed the capacities of *offenders*—specifically the levels of maturity and intellectual capacity—that are constitutionally necessary predicates for execution. In both contexts, it has been argued that death is a grossly disproportionate punishment even though the offender's youthfulness or intellectual deficiency does not bar criminal conviction and punishment. These claims of diminished responsibility echo the concepts explored in Chapter VI.

**2. Mental Retardation.** In Penry v. Lynaugh, 492 U.S. 302 (1989), a five-four majority of the Supreme Court held that the death penalty is not categorically precluded for mentally retarded defendants. At the time *Penry* was decided, only one state (Georgia) and the federal government explicitly barred execution of a retarded person who had been convicted of a capital crime, and no data were available on sentencing practices. Thus, neither of the "objective indicators" utilized in previous cases demonstrated an evolving societal consensus against execution of the mentally retarded. Justice Scalia, joined by Chief Justice Rehnquist and Justices White and Kennedy, thought that the Court's inquiry was at an end. The plurality refused to undertake any "subjective" analysis of proportionality, which "has no place in our eighth-amendment jurisprudence." If "an objective examination of laws and jury determinations fails to demonstrate society's disapproval of it, the punishment is not unconstitutional even if out of accord with the theories of penology favored by the Justices of the Court."

The five remaining Justices endorsed the legitimacy of the proportionality inquiry, and all except Justice O'Connor were prepared to bar execution of mentally retarded defendants. The basis for this conclusion was most fully developed by Justice Brennan, in an opinion joined by Justice Marshall:

> The impairment of a mentally retarded offender's reasoning abilities, control over impulsive behavior and moral development in my view limits his culpability so that, whatever other punish-

---

[h] For a thorough discussion of *Enmund* and *Tison*, see David McCord, State Death Sentencing for Felony Murder Accomplices under the *Enmund* and *Tison* Standards, 32 Ariz. St. L. J. 843 (2000).

ment might be appropriate, the ultimate penalty of death is always and necessarily disproportionate to his blameworthiness and hence is unconstitutional.

Even if mental retardation alone were not invariably associated with a lack of the degree of culpability upon which death as a proportionate punishment is predicated, I would still hold the execution of the mentally retarded to be unconstitutional. If there are among the mentally retarded exceptional individuals as responsible for their actions as persons who suffer no such disability, the individualized consideration afforded at sentencing fails to ensure that they are the only mentally retarded offenders who will be picked out to receive a death sentence. The consideration of mental retardation as a mitigating factor is inadequate to guarantee, as the Constitution requires, that an individual who is not fully blameworthy for her crime because of a mental disability does not receive the death penalty.

That "sentencers can consider and give effect to mitigating evidence of mental retardation in imposing sentence" provides no assurance that an adequate individualized determination of whether the death penalty is a proportionate punishment will be made at the conclusion of each capital trial. At sentencing, the judge or jury considers an offender's level of blameworthiness only along with a host of other factors that the sentencer may decide outweigh any want of responsibility. The sentencer is free to weigh a mentally retarded offender's relative lack of culpability against the heinousness of the crime and other aggravating factors and to decide that even the most retarded and irresponsible of offenders should die.... Lack of culpability as a result of mental retardation is simply not isolated at the sentencing stage as a factor that determinatively bars a death sentence; for individualized consideration at sentencing is not designed to ensure that mentally retarded offenders are not sentenced to death if they are not culpable to the degree necessary to render execution a proportionate response to their crimes....

There is a second ground upon which I would conclude that the execution of mentally retarded offenders violates the Eighth Amendment: killing mentally retarded offenders does not measurably further the penal goals of either retribution or deterrence....

Justice O'Connor's vote was determinative. Although recognizing that mental retardation might diminish culpability, she was unwilling to accept the view that the Eighth Amendment "precludes the execution of any mentally retarded person of Penry's ability convicted of a capital offense simply by virtue of their mental retardation alone." She explained:

It is clear that mental retardation has long been regarded as a factor that may diminish an individual's culpability for a criminal act. In its most severe forms, mental retardation may result in complete exculpation from criminal responsibility. Moreover, virtually all of the States with death penalty statutes that list statutory mitigating factors include as a mitigating circumstance evidence that "[t]he capacity of the defendant to appreciate the criminality of his conduct or to conform his conduct to the requirements of law was substantially impaired." A number of States explicitly mention "mental defect" in connection with such mitigating circumstance.

On the record before the Court today, however, I cannot conclude that all mentally retarded people of Penry's ability—by virtue of their mental retardation alone, and apart from any individualized consideration of their personal responsibility—inevitably lack the cognitive, volitional, and moral capacity to act with the degree of culpability associated with the death penalty. Mentally retarded persons are individuals whose abilities and experiences can vary greatly.... In addition to the varying degrees of mental retardation, the consequences of a retarded person's mental impairment, including the deficits in their adaptive behavior, "may be ameliorated through education and habilitation." Although retarded persons generally have difficulty learning from experience, some are fully "capable of learning, working, and living in their communities." In light of the diverse capacities and life experiences of mentally retarded persons, it cannot be said on the record before us today that all mentally retarded people, by definition, can never act with the level of culpability associated with the death penalty.

Thirteen years after *Penry*, the Court revisited the issue in Atkins v. Virginia, 536 U.S. 304 (2002). By this time, 17 states had joined Georgia in enacting statutes prohibiting the execution of mentally retarded offenders. The Court's opinion, written by Justice Stevens and joined by Justices O'Connor, Kennedy, Souter, Ginsburg and Breyer, concluded a societal consensus had formed against the use of the death penalty for mentally retarded defendants:

Much has changed since [*Penry*]. Responding to the national attention received by [a juvenile] execution and our decision in *Penry*, state legislatures across the country began to address the issue....

It is not so much the number of these states that is significant, but the consistency of the direction of change. Given the well-known fact that anticrime legislature is far more popular than legislation providing protections for persons guilty of violent crime, the large number of states prohibiting the execution of mentally retarded persons (and the complete absence of states passing legislation reinstating the power to conduct such executions) provides powerful evidence that today our society views mentally retarded offenders as categorically less culpable than the average criminal. The evidence carries even greater force when it is noted that the legislatures that have addressed the issue have voted overwhelmingly in favor of the prohibition. Moreover, in those states that allow the execution of mentally retarded offenders, the practice is uncommon. Some states, for example New Hampshire and New Jersey, continue to authorize executions, but none have been carried out in decades. Thus there is little need to pursue legislation barring the execution of the mentally retarded in those States. And it appears that even among those states that regularly execute offenders and that have no prohibition with regard to the mentally retarded, only five have executed offenders possessing a known IQ less than 70 since we decided *Penry*. The practice, therefore, has become truly unusual, and it is fair to say that a national consensus has developed against it. . . .

This consensus unquestionably reflects widespread judgment about the relative culpability of mentally retarded offenders, and the relationship between mental retardation and the penological purposes served by the death penalty. Additionally, it suggests that some characteristics of mental retardation undermine the strength of the procedural protections that our capital jurisprudence steadfastly guards.

[C]linical definitions of mental retardation require not only subaverage intellectual functioning, but also significant limitations in adaptive skills such as communications, self-care, and self-direction that became manifest before age 18. Mentally retarded persons frequently know the difference between right and wrong and are competent to stand trial. Because of their impairments, however, by definition they have diminished capacities to understand and process information, to communicate, to abstract from mistakes and learn from experience, to engage in logical reasoning, to control impulses, and to understand the reactions of others. There is no evidence that they are more likely to engage in criminal conduct than others, but there is abundant evidence that they often act on impulse rather than pursuant to a premeditated plan, and that in group settings they are followers rather than leaders. Their deficiencies do not warrant an exemption from criminal sanctions, but they do diminish their personal culpability.

In light of these deficiencies, our death penalty jurisprudence provides two reasons consistent with the legislative consensus that the mentally retarded should be categorically excluded from execution. First, there is a serious question as to whether either justification that we have recognized as a basis for the death penalty applies to mentally retarded offenders. *Gregg v. Georgia* identified "retribution and deterrence of capital crimes by prospective offenders" as the social purposes served by the death penalty. Unless the imposition of the death penalty on a mentally retarded person "measurably contributes" to one or both of these goals, it "is nothing more than the purposeless and needless imposition of pain and suffering," and hence an unconstitutional punishment. *Enmund....*

Our independent evaluation of the issue reveals no reason to disagree with the judgments of "the legislatures that have recently addressed the matter" and concluded that death is not a suitable punishment for a mentally retarded criminal. We are not persuaded that the execution of mentally retarded criminals will measurably advance the deterrent or the retributive purpose of the death penalty. Construing and applying the Eighth Amendment in the light of our "evolving standards of decency," we therefore conclude that such punishment is excessive and that the constitution "places a substantive restriction on the state's power to take the life" of a mentally retarded offender.

Chief Justice Rehnquist and Justices Scalia and Thomas dissented. In his dissenting opinion, Justice Scalia objected to the Court's methodology as well as its application to the issue of mental retardation:

Today's decision is the pinnacle of our Eighth Amendment death-is-different jurisprudence. Not only does it, like all of that jurisprudence, find no support in the text or history of the Eighth Amendment; it does not even have support in current social attitudes regarding the conditions that render an otherwise just death penalty inappropriate. Seldom has an opinion of this Court rested so obviously upon nothing but the personal views of its members....

[Atkins'] mental retardation was a *central issue* at sentencing. The jury concluded, however, that his alleged retardation was not a compelling reason to exempt him from the death penalty in light of the brutality of his crime and his long demonstrated propensity for violence. In upsetting this particularized judgment on the basis of a constitutional absolute, the Court concludes that no one who is even slightly mentally retarded can have sufficient moral responsibility to be subjected to capital punishment for any crime. As a sociological and moral conclusion that is implausible; and it is doubly implausible as an interpretation of the United States constitution.

The Court makes no pretense that execution of the mildly mentally retarded would have been considered "cruel and unusual" in 1791. Only the *severely* or *profoundly* mentally retarded, commonly known as "idiots," enjoyed any special status under the law at that time.... Mentally retarded offenders with less severe impairments–those who were not "idiots"—suffered criminal prosecution and punishment, including capital punishment....

The Court is left to argue, therefore, that execution of the mildly retarded is inconsistent with the "evolving standards of decency that mark the progress of a maturing society." ... [It] miraculously extracts a "national consensus" forbidding execution of the mentally retarded ... from the fact that 18 states-less than *half* (47%) of the 38 States that permit capital punishment (for whom the issue exists)-have very recently enacted legislation barring execution of the mentally retarded. Even that 47% figure is a distorted one. If one is to say, as the Court does today, that *all* executions of the mentally retarded are so morally repugnant as to violate our national "standards of decency," surely the "consensus" it points to must be one that has set its righteous face against *all* such executions. Not 18 States, but only seven–18% of death penalty jurisdictions-have legislation of that scope. Eleven of those that the Court counts enacted statutes prohibiting execution of mentally retarded defendants *convicted after, or convicted of crimes committed after, the effective date* of the legislation; those already on death row, or consigned there before the statute's effective date, or even (in those State using the date of the crime as the criterion of retroactivity) tried in the future for murders committed many years ago, could be put to death. That is not a statement of absolute moral repugnance, but one of current preference between two tolerable approaches. Two of these States permit execution of the mentally retarded in other situations as well: Kansas apparently permits execution of all except the *severely* mentally retarded; New York permits execution of the mentally retarded who commit murder in a correctional facility....

Moreover, a major fact that the Court entirely disregards is that the legislation of all 18 states it relies on is still in its infancy. The oldest of the statutes is only 14 years old; five were enacted last year; over half were enacted within the past eight years. Few, if any, of the States have had sufficient experience with these laws to know whether they are sensible in the long term. It is "myopic to base sweeping constitutional principles upon the narrow experience of [a few] years." ...

The genuinely operative portion of the opinion, then, is the Court's statement of the reasons why it agrees with the contrived consensus it has found, that the "diminished capacities" of the mentally retarded render the death penalty excessive. The Court's analysis rests on two fundamental assumptions: that the Eighth Amendment prohibits excessive punishments, and that sentencing juries or judges are unable to account properly for the "diminished capacities" of the retarded. The first assumption is wrong, as I explained at length in Harmelin v. Michigan, 501 U.S. 957, 966–990 (1991).[a] The Eighth Amendment is addressed to always-and-everywhere "cruel" punishments, such as the rack and the thumbscrew. But where the punishment is in itself permissible, "[t]he Eighth Amendment is not a ratchet, whereby a temporary consensus on leniency for a particular crime fixes a permanent constitutional maximum, disabling the States from giving effect to altered

---

[a] *Harmelin* appears as a main case in the next subsection.—[Footnote by eds.]

beliefs and responding to changed social conditions." The second assumption–inability of judges or juries to take proper account of mental retardation–is not only unsubstantiated, but contradicts the immemorial belief, here and in England, that they play an *indispensable* role in such matters. . . .

[W]hat scientific analysis can possibly show that a mildly retarded individual who commits an exquisite torture-killing is "no more culpable" than the "average" murderer in a holdup-gone-wrong or a domestic dispute? Or a moderately retarded individual who commits a series of 20 exquisite torture-killings? Surely culpability, and deservedness of the most severe retribution, depends not merely (if at all) upon the mental capacity of the criminal (above the level where he is able to distinguish right from wrong) but also upon the depravity of the crime—which is precisely why this sort of question has traditionally been thought answerable not by a categorical rule of the sort the Court today imposes upon all trials, but rather by the sentencer's weighing of the circumstances (both degree of retardation and depravity of crime) in the particular case. The fact that juries continue to sentence mentally retarded offenders to death for extreme crimes shows that society's moral outrage sometimes demands execution of retarded offenders. By what principle of law, science, or logic can the Court pronounce that this is wrong? There is none. Once the Court admits (as it does) that mental retardation does not render the offender morally *blameless*, there is no basis for saying that the death penalty is *never* appropriate retribution, no matter *how* heinous the crime. As long as a mentally retarded offender knows "the difference between right and wrong," only the sentencer can assess whether his retardation reduces his culpability enough to exempt him from the death penalty for the particular murder in question. . . .

[S]urely the deterrent effect of a penalty is adequately vindicated if it successfully deters many, but not all, of the target class. Virginia's death penalty, for example, does not fail of its deterrent effect simply because *some* criminals are unaware that Virginia *has* the death penalty. In other words, the supposed fact that *some* retarded criminals cannot fully appreciate the death penalty has nothing to do with the deterrence rationale, but is simply an echo of the arguments denying a retribution rationale, discussed and rejected above. . . .

Today's opinion adds one more to the long list of substantive and procedural requirements impeding imposition of the death penalty imposed under this Court's assumed power to invent a death-is-different jurisprudence. . . .

This newest invention promises to be more effective than any of the others in turning the process of capital trial into a game. One need only read the definitions of mental retardation adopted by the American Association on Mental Retardation and the American Psychiatric Association to realize that the symptoms of this condition can readily be feigned....

Perhaps these practical difficulties will not be experienced by the minority of capital-punishment States that have very recently changed mental retardation from a mitigating factor (to be accepted or rejected by the sentencer) to an absolute immunity. Time will tell—and the brief time those States have had the new disposition in place (an average of 6.8 years) is surely not enough. But if the practical difficulties do not appear, and if the other states share the Court's perceived moral consensus that *all* mental retardation renders the death penalty inappropriate for *all* crimes, then that majority will presumably follow suit. But there is no justification for this Court's pushing them into the experiment—and turning the experiment into a permanent practice—on constitutional pretext. Nothing has changed the accuracy of Matthew Hale's endorsement of the common law's traditional method for taking account of guilt-reducing factors, written over three centuries ago:

> [Determination of a person's incapacity] is a matter of great difficulty, partly from the easiness of counterfeiting this disability ... and partly from the variety of the degrees of this infirmity, whereof some are sufficient, and some are insufficient to excuse persons in capital offenses....

> Yet the law of England hath afforded the best method of trial, that is possible, of this and all other matters of fact, namely, by a jury of twelve men all concurring in the same judgment, by the testimony of witnesses ..., and by the inspection and direction of the judge. 1 Pleas of the Crown, at 32–33.

*Atkins* raises many interesting questions of both theory and implementation. On the methodology of proportionality analysis, who has the better of the argument, Justice Stevens or Justice Scalia? What should be the relative weight between the "objective indicators" of societal consensus and the Court's "subjective" judgment about the suitability of the death penalty in relation to the culpability of the offender? How significant was the legislative activity between 1989 and 2002? In omitted portions of the opinions, the Justices disagreed about the relevance of evidence of international law and practice and public opinion polls. Do you think that international human rights norms should have any bearing on the interpretation of the Eighth Amendment?

One of the intriguing aspects of *Atkins* is that the Court declined to define mental retardation, leaving it to the states to do so. Most states have adopted a clinical definition drawn from the diagnostic criteria in the American Psychiatric Association's diagnostic manual (DSM–IV) or the manual of the American Association on Mental Retardation. However, as Justice Scalia points out, one state (Kansas) exempts offenders with mental retardation only if they are found to meet the Model Penal Code criteria for the insanity defense (lack of substantial capacity to appreciate the wrongfulness of the conduct or conform conduct to the requirements of law). Is this constitutional? Whatever the definition, *Atkins* has invited the proverbial "battle of the experts" on the diagnosis of mental retardation. Contrary to Justice Scalia's assertion, fabrication does not seem to be a significant problem in the diagnosis of mental retardation. This is not to say, however, that there will be no "practical difficulties" in administering *Atkins*. Under the prevailing definition, mental retardation is characterized by significant deficits in both intellectual and adaptive functioning. Typically the diagnosis must be based on the defendant's performance on standardized measures of intelligence and "adaptive behavior" that is two standard deviations from the mean. But a score on any psychological test is subject to measurement error, so a score of, say 70 doesn't "mean" 70–it means a prediction that, for example, the person would score between 66 and 74 on this test 66% of the time. Should the constitutional permissibility of the death penalty turn on whether a judge or jury "finds" that the defendant "is mentally retarded"?

**3. Immaturity.** In 1989, the same year that *Penry v. Lynaugh* was decided, the Supreme Court also addressed the constitutionality of death sentences for adolescents. In Stanford v. Kentucky, 492 U.S. 361 (1989), a five-four majority of the Court held that the Eighth Amendment does not forbid execution of offenders who committed capital offenses while they were 16 or 17.[b] Of the 38 death penalty statutes in force in 1989, 18 expressly established a minimum age for acts that can be punished by death—12 set the age at 18, three at 17 and three at 16. In the remaining states, a death sentence was permitted for any person within the criminal court's jurisdiction, and in most states this could include older adolescents over whom the juvenile court has waived jurisdiction. As for actual practice, death sentences have rarely been imposed on youthful offenders, especially in recent years.

Writing for a plurality of the Court, including Chief Justice Rehnquist and Justices White and Kennedy, Justice Scalia (the same plurality that prevailed in *Penry*) reviewed the objective evidence regarding legislative action and sentencing practice. The evidence showed, he concluded, that a majority of states permitting capital punishment authorized it for crimes committed at age 16 or above, and that the only consensus that could be inferred from actual practice is that prosecutors and juries believe the

[b] In Thompson v. Oklahoma, 487 U.S. 815 (1988), a five-three majority (Justice Kennedy not participating) set aside the death sentence of a defendant who was 15 at the time of the offense. Although Justice O'Connor joined Justices Brennan, Marshall, Stevens and Blackmun in this case, she did not endorse their view that the Eighth Amendment barred a death sentence in such a case, concluding that definitive resolution of this question was unnecessary. Instead, she rested her decision on the narrower ground that offenders younger than 16 "may not be executed under the authority of a capital punishment statute that fails to specify a minimum age at which the commission of a capital crime can lead to the offender's execution." None of the 18 states with statutes specifying a minimum age authorizes a capital sentence for offenders younger than 16.

death sentence is rarely appropriate for youthful offenders, not that it is categorically unacceptable. Having discerned "neither a historical nor a modern societal consensus forbidding imposition of capital punishment on any person who murders at 16 or 17 years of age," Justice Scalia concluded that the constitutional inquiry was at an end. "To say ... that 'it is for *us* ultimately to judge whether the Eighth Amendment permits imposition of the death penalty' ... and to mean ... that it is for *us* to judge, not on the basis of what we perceive the society through its democratic processes now overwhelmingly disapproved, but on the basis of what we think 'proportionate' and 'measurably contributory to acceptable goals of punishment'—to say and mean that, is to replace judges of the law with a committee of philosopher kings." Although conceding that the Court had engaged in "so-called 'proportionality' analysis" in earlier cases, he noted that "we have never invalidated a punishment on this basis alone." Citing *Enmund* and *Coker*, Justice Scalia observed that "[a]ll of our cases condemning a punishment under this mode of analysis also found that the objective indicators of state laws or jury determinations evidenced a societal consensus against the penalty."

The dissenting Justices in *Penry* also dissented in *Stanford*. Writing for himself and Justices Marshall, Stevens and Blackmun, Justice Brennan first reviewed the objective indicators of contemporary standards. He concluded that "the rejection of the death penalty for juveniles by a majority of the states, the rarity of the sentence for juveniles, both as an absolute and a comparative matter, the decisions of respected organizations in relevant fields that this punishment is unacceptable, and its rejection generally throughout the world, provide ... a strong grounding for the view that it is not constitutionally tolerable that certain states persist in authorizing the execution of adolescent offenders." Justice Brennan then turned to what he characterized as "two well-established and independent Eighth Amendment requirements—that a punishment not be disproportionate and that it make a contribution to acceptable goals of punishment." He continued:

> There may be exceptional individuals who mature more quickly than their peers, and who might be considered fully responsible for their actions prior to the age of 18, despite their lack of experience upon which judgment depends. In my view, however, it is not sufficient to accommodate the facts about juveniles that an individual youth's culpability may be taken into account in the decision to transfer him or her from the juvenile to adult court systems for trial, or that a capital sentencing jury is instructed to consider youth and other mitigating factors. I believe that the Eighth Amendment requires that a person who lacks the full degree of responsibility for his or her actions associated with adulthood not be sentenced to death. Hence it is constitutionally inadequate that a juvenile offender's level of responsibility be taken into account only along with a host of other factors that the court or jury may decide outweigh that want of responsibility.

Immaturity that constitutionally should operate as a bar to a disproportionate death sentence does *not* guarantee that a minor will not be transferred for trial to the adult court system. Rather, the most important considerations in the decision to transfer a juvenile offender are the seriousness of the offense, the extent of prior delinquency, and the response to prior treatment within the juvenile justice system. Psychological, intellectual and other personal characteristics of juvenile offenders receive little attention at the transfer stage, and cannot account for differences between those transferred and those who remain in the juvenile court system. Nor is an adolescent's lack of full culpability isolated at the sentencing stage as a factor that determinatively bars a death sentence. A jury is free to weigh a juvenile offender's youth and lack of full responsibility against the heinousness of the crime and other aggravating factors—and, finding the aggravating factors weightier, to sentence even the most immature of 16–or 17–year olds to be killed. By no stretch of the imagination, then, are the transfer and sentencing decisions designed to isolate those juvenile offenders who are exceptionally mature and responsible, and who thus stand out from their peers as a class.

It is thus unsurprising that individualized consideration at transfer and sentencing has not in fact ensured that juvenile offenders lacking an adult's culpability are not sentenced to die. Quite the contrary. Adolescents on death row appear typically to have a battery of psychological, emotional, and other problems going to their likely capacity for judgment and level of blameworthiness. . . .

Juveniles very generally lack that degree of blameworthiness that is, in my view, a constitutional prerequisite for the imposition of capital punishment under our precedents concerning the Eighth Amendment proportionality principle. The individualized consideration of an offender's youth and culpability at the transfer stage and at sentencing has not operated to ensure that the only offenders under 18 singled out for the ultimate penalty are exceptional individuals whose level of responsibility is more developed than that of their peers. In that circumstance, I believe that the same categorical assumption that juveniles as a class are insufficiently mature to be regarded as fully responsible that we make in so many other areas is appropriately made in determining whether minors may be subjected to the death penalty. . . .

Under a second strand of Eighth Amendment inquiry into whether a particular sentence is excessive and hence unconstitutional we ask whether the sentence makes a measurable contribution to acceptable goals of punishment. . . .A punishment that fails the Eighth Amendment test of proportionality because disproportionate to the offender's blameworthiness by definition is not justly deserved.

Nor does the execution of juvenile offenders measurably contribute to the goal of deterrence. Excluding juveniles from the class of persons eligible to receive the death penalty will have little effect on any deterrent value capital punishment may have for potential offenders who are over 18: these adult offenders may of course remain eligible for a death sentence. The potential deterrent effect of juvenile executions on adolescent offenders is also insignificant. "The likelihood that the teenage offender has made the kind of cost-benefit analysis that attaches any weight to the possibility of execution is so remote as to be virtually nonexistent." First, juveniles "have less capacity ... to think in long-range terms than adults," and their careful weighing of a distant, uncertain, and indeed highly unlikely consequence prior to action is most improbable. In addition, juveniles have little fear of death, because they have "a profound conviction of their own omnipotence and immortality." Because imposition of the death penalty on persons for offenses committed under the age of 18 makes no measurable contribution to the goals of either retribution or deterrence, it is "nothing more than the purposeless and needless imposition of pain and suffering." and is thus excessive and unconstitutional.

In her decisive opinion, Justice O'Connor agreed with the plurality's judgment "that no national consensus forbids the imposition of capital punishment on 16 or 17–year old capital murderers," although she rejected the plurality's view that this conclusion ended the constitutional inquiry. "In my view, this Court does have a constitutional obligation to conduct proportionality analysis." Nonetheless, in applying proportionality analysis, she concluded that the special characteristics of juveniles that underlie differential legal treatment vary widely among individuals of the same age and "I would not substitute our inevitably subjective judgment about the best age at which to draw a line in the capital punishment context for the judgments of the nation's legislatures."[c]

In the wake of *Atkins v. Virginia*, holding that a societal consensus has emerged since 1989 against executing people with mental retardation, a closely divided Missouri Supreme Court ruled in Simmons v. Roper, 112 S.W.3d 397 (Mo. 2003), that execution of 16 and 17 year-old offenders now violates "evolving standards of decency in a civilized society." Specifically, the Missouri Supreme Court observed that 5 additional states had banned execution of juveniles since 1989, bringing the total to 16; that no state has lowered the minimum age since then; and that only 6 states have actually executed a juvenile since 1989. A body of scientific literature on adolescent development bearing on the diminished culpability of juveniles has also emerged. See Elizabeth Scott and Laurence Steinberg, Less Guilty by Reason of Adolescence: Developmental Immaturity, Diminished Responsibility and the Juvenile Death Penalty, 58 American Psychologist 1009

---

[c] The quoted statement actually appears in Justice O'Connor's opinion in Thompson v. Oklahoma, 487 U.S. 815 (1988), to which she referred in her *Stanford* opinion.

(2003). The Supreme Court granted certiorari in *Roper v. Simmons*, and a ruling is expected in 2005. How should the Court rule?

———

## SUBSECTION B: PROPORTIONALITY AND IMPRISONMENT

———

## Harmelin v. Michigan

Supreme Court of the United States, 1991.
501 U.S. 957.

■ JUSTICE SCALIA announced the judgment of the Court and delivered the opinion of the Court with respect to Part IV, and an opinion with respect to Parts I, II, and III, in which CHIEF JUSTICE REHNQUIST joins.

Petitioner was convicted of possessing 672 grams of cocaine and sentenced to a mandatory term of life in prison without possibility of parole.[1] [He] claims that his sentence is unconstitutionally "cruel and unusual" for two reasons: first, because it is "significantly disproportionate" to the crime he committed; second, because the sentencing judge was statutorily required to impose it, without taking into account the particularized circumstances of the crime and of the criminal.

I

A

The Eighth Amendment, which applies against the states by virtue of the 14th Amendment, provides: "Excessive bail shall not be required, nor excessive fines imposed, nor cruel and unusual punishments inflicted." In Rummel v. Estelle, 445 U.S. 263 (1980), we held that it did not constitute "cruel and unusual punishment" to impose a life sentence, under a recidivist statute, upon a defendant who had been convicted, successively, of fraudulent use of a credit card to obtain $80 worth of goods or services, passing a forged check in the amount of $28.36, and obtaining $120.75 by false pretenses. We said that "one could argue without fear of contradiction by any decision of this Court that for crimes concededly classified and classifiable as felonies, that is, as punishable by significant terms of imprisonment in a state penitentiary, the length of the sentence actually imposed is purely a matter of legislative prerogative." We specifically rejected the proposition asserted by the dissent, (opinion of Powell, J.), that

---

[1] Mich. Comp. Laws Ann. § 333.7403(2)(a)(i) (West Supp. 1990–1991) provides a mandatory sentence of life in prison for possession of 650 grams or more of "any mixture containing [a schedule 2] controlled substance"; § 333.7214(a)(iv) defines cocaine as a schedule 2 controlled substance. Section 791.234(4) provides eligibility for parole after 10 years in prison, except for those convicted of either first-degree murder or "a major controlled substance offense"; § 791.233b[1](b) defines "major controlled substance offense" as, inter alia, a violation of § 333.7403.

unconstitutional disproportionality could be established by weighing three factors: (1) gravity of the offense compared to severity of the penalty, (2) penalties imposed within the same jurisdiction for similar crimes, and (3) penalties imposed in other jurisdictions for the same offense. A footnote in the opinion, however, said: "This is not to say that a proportionality principle would not come into play in the extreme example mentioned by the dissent ... if a legislature made overtime parking a felony punishable by life imprisonment."

Two years later, in Hutto v. Davis, 454 U.S. 370 (1982), we similarly rejected an Eighth Amendment challenge to a prison term of 40 years and fine of $20,000 for possession and distribution of approximately nine ounces of marijuana....

A year and a half after *Davis* we uttered what has been our last word on this subject to date. Solem v. Helm, 463 U.S. 277 (1983), set aside under the Eighth Amendment, because it was disproportionate, a sentence of life imprisonment without possibility of parole, imposed under a South Dakota recividist statute for successive offenses that included three convictions of third-degree burglary, one of obtaining money by false pretenses, one of grand larceny, one of third-offense driving while intoxicated, and one of writing a "no account" check with intent to defraud.... Having decreed that a general principle of disproportionality exists, the Court used as the criterion for its application the three-factor test that had been explicitly rejected in both *Rummel* and *Davis*....

It should be apparent from the above discussion that our five-to-four decision eight years ago in *Solem* was scarcely the expression of clear and well accepted constitutional law. We have long recognized, of course, that the doctrine of *stare decisis* is less rigid in its application to constitutional precedents, and we think that to be especially true of a constitutional precedent that is both recent and in apparent tension with other decisions. Accordingly, we have addressed anew, and in greater detail, the question whether the Eighth Amendment contains a proportionality guarantee—with particular attention to the background of the Eighth Amendment and to the understanding of the Eighth Amendment before the end of the 19th century. We conclude from this examination that *Solem* was simply wrong; the Eighth Amendment contains no proportionality guarantee....

[Justice Scalia presented an extensive analysis of the "cruell and unusuall punishments" provision of the English Declaration of Rights of 1689, the antecedent of the analogous clause of the Eighth Amendment. He concluded that it is "most unlikely" that the English clause was intended to forbid disproportionate punishments. He then analyzed the language of the Eighth Amendment and the history of its adoption and concluded that the clause was meant to outlaw only certain barbaric *modes* of punishment and was not intended to incorporate a requirement of proportionality.]

## II

We think it enough that those who framed and approved the federal constitution chose, for whatever reason, not to include within it the guarantee against disproportionate sentences that some state constitutions contained. It is worth noting, however, that there was good reason for that choice—a reason that reinforces the necessity of overruling *Solem*. While there are relatively clear historical guidelines and accepted practices that enable judges to determine which modes of punishment are "cruel and unusual," proportionality does not lend itself to such analysis. [O]ne can imagine extreme examples that no rational person, in no time or place, could accept. But for the same reason these examples are easy to decide, they are certain never to occur. The real function of a constitutional proportionality principle, if it exists, is to enable judges to evaluate a penalty that some assemblage of men and women has considered proportionate—and to say that it is not. For that real-world enterprise, the standards seem so inadequate that the proportionality principle becomes an invitation to imposition of subjective values.

This becomes clear, we think, from a consideration of the three factors that *Solem* found relevant to the proportionality determination: (i) the inherent gravity of the offense, (ii) the sentences imposed for similarly grave offenses in the same jurisdiction, and (iii) sentences imposed for the same crime in other jurisdictions. As to the first factor: Of course some offenses, involving violent harm to human beings, will always and every-where be regarded as serious, but that is only half the equation. The issue is what else should be regarded to be as serious as these offenses, or even to be more serious than some of them. On that point, judging by the statutes that Americans have enacted, there is enormous variation—even within a given age, not to mention across the many generations ruled by the Bill of Rights. The State of Massachusetts punishes sodomy more severely than assault and battery, compare Mass. Gen. Laws § 272:34 (1988) ("not more than twenty years" in prison for sodomy) with § 265:13A ("not more than two and one half years" in prison for assault and battery); whereas in several states, sodomy is not unlawful at all. In Louisiana, one who assaults another with a dangerous weapon faces the same maximum prison term as one who removes a shopping basket "from the parking area or grounds of any store ... without authorization." La. Rev. Stat. Ann. §§ 14:37, 14:68.1 (West 1986). A battery that results in "protracted and obvious disfigure-ment" merits imprisonment "for not more than five years," § 14:34.1, one half the maximum penalty for theft of livestock or an oilfield seismograph, §§ 14:67.1, 14:67.8. We may think that the First Congress punished with clear disproportionality when it provided up to seven years in prison and up to $1,000 in fine for "cutting off the ear or ears, ... cutting out or disabling the tongue, ... putting out an eye, ... cutting off ... any limb or member of any person with intention ... to maim or disfigure," but provided the death penalty for "running away with [a] ship or vessel, or any goods or merchandise to the value of fifty dollars." Act of Apr. 30, 1790, ch. 9, §§ 8, 13, 1 Stat. 113–15. But then perhaps the citizens of 1791 would think that today's Congress punishes with clear disproportionality when it sanctions "assault by ... wounding" with up to six months in prison, 18 U.S.C. § 113(d), unauthorized reproduction of the "Smokey Bear" character or name with the same penalty, 18 U.S.C. § 711, offering to barter a migratory bird with up to two years in prison, 16 U.S.C. § 707(b), and purloining a "key suited to any lock adopted by the Post Office Department" with a prison term of up to 10 years, 18 U.S.C. § 1704. Perhaps both we and they would be right, but the point is that there are no textual or historical standards for saying so.

The difficulty of assessing gravity is demonstrated in the very context of the present case: Petitioner acknowledges that a mandatory life sentence might not be "grossly excessive" for possession of cocaine with intent to distribute, see *Hutto v. Davis*. But surely whether it is a "grave" offense merely to possess a significant quantity of drugs—thereby facilitating distribution, subjecting the holder to the temptation of distribution, and raising the possibility of theft by others who might distribute—depends entirely upon how odious and socially threatening one believes drug use to be. Would it be "grossly excessive" to provide life imprisonment for "mere possession" of a certain quantity of heavy weaponry? If not, then the only issue is whether the possible dissemination of drugs can be as "grave" as the possible dissemination of heavy weapons. Who are we to say no? The members of the Michigan legislature, and not we, know the situation on the streets of Detroit.

The second factor suggested in *Solem* fails for the same reason. One cannot compare the sentences imposed by the jurisdiction for "similarly grave" offenses if there is no objective standard of gravity. Judges will be comparing what they consider comparable. Or, to put the same point differently: When it happens that two offenses judicially determined to be "similarly grave" receive significantly dissimilar penalties, what follows is not that the harsher penalty is unconstitutional, but merely that the legislature does not share the judges' view that the offenses are similarly grave. Moreover, even if "similarly grave" crimes could be identified, the penalties for them would not necessarily be comparable, since there are many other justifications for a difference. For example, since deterrent effect depends not only upon the amount of the penalty but upon its certainty, crimes that are less grave but significantly more difficult to detect may warrant substantially higher penalties. Grave crimes of the sort that will not be deterred by penalty may warrant substantially lower penalties, as may grave crimes of the sort that are normally committed once in a lifetime by otherwise law-abiding citizens who will not profit from rehabilitation. Whether these differences will occur, and to what extent, depends, of course, upon the weight the society accords to deterrence and rehabilitation, rather than retribution, as the objective of criminal punishment (which is an eminently legislative judgment). In fact, it becomes difficult even to speak intelligently of "proportionality," once deterrence and rehabilitation are given significant weight. Proportionality is inherently a retributive concept, and perfect proportionality is the talionic law. Cf. Bill For Proportioning Punishments, 1 Writings of Thomas Jefferson, at 218, 228–29 ("Whoever ... shall maim another, or shall disfigure him ... shall be maimed or disfigured in like sort").

As for the third factor mentioned by *Solem*—the character of the sentences imposed by other states for the same crime—it must be acknowledged that that can be applied with clarity and ease. The only difficulty is that it has no conceivable relevance to the Eighth Amendment. That a state is entitled to treat with stern disapproval an act that other states punish with the mildest of sanctions follows a *fortiori* from the undoubted fact that a state may criminalize an act that other states do not criminalize at all. Indeed, a State may criminalize an act that other states choose to reward— punishing, for example, the killing of endangered wild animals for which other states are offering a bounty. What greater disproportion could there be than that? "Absent a constitutionally imposed uniformity inimical to traditional notions of federalism, some state will always bear the distinction of treating particular offenders more severely than any other state." *Rummel*, supra, 445 U.S. at 282. Diversity not only in policy, but in the means of implementing policy, is the very raison d'etre of our federal system. Though the different needs and concerns of other states may induce them to treat simple possession of 672 grams of cocaine as a relatively minor offense, see Wyo. Stat. § 35–7–1031(c) (1988) (6 months); W. Va. Code § 60A–4–401(c) (1989) (6 months), nothing in the constitution requires Michigan to follow suit. The Eighth Amendment is not a ratchet, whereby a temporary consensus on leniency for a particular crime fixes a permanent constitutional maximum, disabling the states from giving effect to altered beliefs and responding to changed social conditions.

### III

Our 20th-century jurisprudence has not remained entirely in accord with the proposition that there is no proportionality requirement in the Eighth Amendment, but neither has it departed to the extent that *Solem* suggests. In Weems v. United States, 217 U.S. 349 (1910), a government disbursing officer convicted of making false entries of small sums in his account book was sentenced by Philippine courts to 15 years of cadena temporal. That punishment, based upon the Spanish Penal Code, called for incarceration at " 'hard and painful labor' " with chains fastened to the wrists and ankles at all times. Several "accessories" were superadded, including permanent disqualification from holding any position of public trust, subjection to "[government] surveillance" for life, and "civil interdiction," which consisted of deprivation of "the rights of parental authority, guardianship of person or property, participation in the family council [, etc.]' "

Justice McKenna, writing for himself and three others, held that the imposition of cadena temporal was "cruel and unusual punishment." (Justice White, joined by Justice Holmes, dissented.) That holding, and some of the reasoning upon which it was based, was not at all out of accord with the traditional understanding of the provision we have described above. The punishment was both (i) severe and (ii) unknown to Anglo–American tradition. As to the former, Justice McKenna wrote:

No circumstance of degradation is omitted. It may be that even the cruelty of pain is not omitted. He must bear a chain night and day. He is condemned to painful as well as hard labor. What painful labor may mean we have no exact measure. It must be something more than hard labor. It may be hard labor pressed to the point of pain. 217 U.S. at 366–67.

As to the latter:

It has no fellow in American legislation. Let us remember that it has come to us from a government of a different form and genius from ours. It is cruel in its excess of imprisonment and that which accompanies and follows imprisonment. It is unusual in its character.

Other portions of the opinion, however, suggest that mere disproportionality, by itself, might make a punishment cruel and unusual:

Such penalties for such offenses amaze those who . . . believe that it is a precept of justice that punishment for crime should be graduated and proportioned to offense.

The inhibition [of the cruel and unusual punishments clause] was directed, not only against punishments which inflict torture, "but against all punishments which by their excessive length or severity are greatly disproportioned to the offenses charged." Id., at 371, quoting O'Neil v. Vermont, 144 U.S. 323, 339–40, (1892) (Field, J., dissenting).

Since it contains language that will support either theory, our later opinions have used *Weems*, as the occasion required, to represent either the principle that "the Eighth Amendment bars not only those punishments that are 'barbaric' but also those that are 'excessive' in relation to the crime committed," Coker v. Georgia, 433 U.S. 584, 592 (1977), or the principle that only a "unique . . . punishment," a form of imprisonment different from the "more traditional forms . . . imposed under the Anglo–Saxon system," can violate the Eighth Amendment, Rummel, 445 U.S. at 274. . . .

The first holding of this Court unqualifiedly applying a requirement of proportionality to criminal penalties was issued 185 years after the Eighth Amendment was adopted. In Coker v. Georgia, 433 U.S. 584 (1977), the Court held that, because of the disproportionality, it was a violation of the cruel and unusual punishments clause to impose capital punishment for rape of an adult woman. Five years later, in Enmund v. Florida, 458 U.S. 782 (1982), we held that it violates the Eighth Amendment, because of disproportionality, to impose the death penalty upon a participant in a felony that results in murder, without any inquiry into the participant's intent to kill. *Rummel* treated this line of authority as an aspect of our death penalty jurisprudence, rather than a generalizable aspect of Eighth Amendment law. We think that is an accurate explanation, and we reassert it. Proportionality review is one of several respects in which we have held that "death is different," and have imposed protections that the Constitution nowhere else provides. We would leave it there, but will not extend it further.

## IV

Petitioner claims that his sentence violates the Eighth Amendment for a reason in addition to its alleged disproportionality. He argues that it is "cruel and unusual" to impose a mandatory sentence of such severity, without any consideration of so-called mitigating factors such as, in his case, the fact that he had no prior felony convictions. He apparently contends that the Eighth Amendment requires Michigan to create a sentencing scheme whereby life in prison without possibility of parole is simply the most severe of a range of available penalties that the sentencer may impose after hearing evidence in mitigation and aggravation.

As our earlier discussion should make clear, this claim has no support in the text and history of the Eighth Amendment. Severe, mandatory penalties may be cruel, but they are not unusual in the constitutional sense, having been employed in various forms throughout our nation's history. As noted earlier, mandatory death sentences abounded in our first penal code. They were also common in the several states—both at the time of the founding and throughout the 19th century. See Woodson v. North Carolina, 428 U.S. 280 (1976). There can be no serious contention, then, that a sentence which is not otherwise cruel and unusual becomes so simply because it is "mandatory."

Petitioner's "required mitigation" claim, like his proportionality claim, does find support in our death penalty jurisprudence. We have held that a capital sentence is cruel and unusual under the Eighth Amendment if it is imposed without an individualized determination that that punishment is "appropriate"—whether or not the sentence is "grossly disproportionate." Petitioner asks us to extend this so-called "individualized capital-sentencing doctrine," to an "individualized mandatory life in prison without parole sentencing doctrine." We refuse to do so.

Our cases creating and clarifying the "individualized capital sentencing doctrine" have repeatedly suggested that there is no comparable requirement outside the capital context, because of the qualitative difference between death and all other penalties. . . .

It is true that petitioner's sentence is unique in that it is the second most severe known to the law; but life imprisonment with possibility of parole is also unique in that it is the third most severe. And if petitioner's sentence forecloses some "flexible techniques" for later reducing his sentence, it does not foreclose all of them, since there remain the possibilities of retroactive legislative reduction and executive clemency. In some cases, moreover, there will be negligible difference between life without parole and other sentences of imprisonment—for example, a life sentence with eligibility for parole after 20 years, or even a lengthy term sentence without eligibility for parole, given to a 65–year-old man. But even where the difference is the greatest, it cannot be compared with death. We have drawn the line of required individualized sentencing at capital cases, and see no basis for extending it further.

The judgment of the Michigan Court of Appeals is

Affirmed.

■ JUSTICE KENNEDY, with whom JUSTICE O'CONNOR and JUSTICE SOUTER join, concurring in part and concurring in the judgment.

I concur in Part IV of the Court's opinion and in the judgment. I write this separate opinion because my approach to the Eighth Amendment proportionality analysis differs from Justice Scalia's. Regardless of whether Justice Scalia or the dissent has the best of the historical argument, *stare decisis* counsels our adherence to the narrow proportionality principle that has existed in our Eighth Amendment jurisprudence for 80 years. Although our proportionality decisions have not been clear or consistent in all respects, they can be reconciled, and they require us to uphold petitioner's sentence.

## I

### A

Our decisions recognize that the cruel and unusual punishments clause encompasses a narrow proportionality principle. We first interpreted the Eighth Amendment to prohibit " 'greatly disproportioned' " sentences in Weems v. United States, 217 U.S. 349, 371. Since *Weems*, we have applied the principle in different Eighth Amendment contexts. Its most extensive application has been in death penalty cases. . . .

### B

Though our decisions recognize a proportionality principle, its precise contours are unclear. This is so in part because we have applied the rule in few cases and even then to sentences of different types. Our most recent pronouncement on the subject in Solem v. Helm, 463 U.S. 277 (1983), furthermore, appeared to apply a different analysis than in Rummel v. Estelle, 445 U.S. 263 (1980), and Hutto v. Davis, 454 U.S. 370 (1982). *Solem* twice stated, however, that its decision was consistent with *Rummel* and thus did not overrule it. Despite these tensions, close analysis of our decisions yields some common principles that give content to the uses and limits of proportionality review.

The first of these principles is that the fixing of prison terms for specific crimes involves a substantive penological judgment that, as a general matter, is "properly within the province of legislatures, not courts." Determinations about the nature and purposes of punishment for criminal acts implicate difficult and enduring questions respecting the sanctity of the individual, the nature of law, and the relation between law and the social order. "As a moral or political issue [the punishment of offenders] provokes intemperate emotions, deeply conflicting interests, and intractable disagreements." D. Garland, Punishment and Modern Society 1 (1990). The efficacy of any sentencing system cannot be assessed absent agreement on the purposes and objectives of the penal system. And the responsibility for making these fundamental choices and implementing them lies with the legislature.... Thus, "reviewing courts ... should grant substantial deference to the broad authority that legislatures necessarily possess in determining the types and limits of punishments for crimes." *Solem*, supra, 463 U.S. at 290.

The second principle is that the Eighth Amendment does not mandate adoption of any one penological theory. ...The federal and state criminal systems have accorded different weights at different times to the penological goals of retribution, deterrence, incapacitation, and rehabilitation. And competing theories of mandatory and discretionary sentencing have been in varying degrees of ascendancy or decline since the beginning of the republic.

Third, marked divergences both in underlying theories of sentencing and in the length of prescribed prison terms are the inevitable, often beneficial, result of the federal structure.... state sentencing schemes may embody different penological assumptions, making interstate comparison of sentences a difficult and imperfect enterprise.... And even assuming identical philosophies, differing attitudes and perceptions of local conditions may yield different, yet rational, conclusions regarding the appropriate length of prison terms for particular crimes. Thus, the circumstance that a state has the most severe punishment for a particular crime does not by itself render the punishment grossly disproportionate....

The fourth principle at work in our cases is that proportionality review by federal courts should be informed by " 'objective factors to the maximum possible extent.' " The most prominent objective factor is the type of punishment imposed. In *Weems*, "the Court could differentiate in an objective fashion between the highly unusual cadena temporal and more traditional forms of imprisonment imposed under the Anglo–Saxon system." In a similar fashion, because " 'the penalty of death differs from all other forms of criminal punishment,' " the objective line between capital punishment and imprisonment for a term of years finds frequent mention in our Eighth Amendment jurisprudence. By contrast, our decisions recognize that we lack clear objective standards to distinguish between sentences for different terms of years. *Solem*, 463 U.S. at 294 ("It is clear that a 25–year sentence generally is more severe than a 15–year sentence, but in most cases it would be difficult to decide that the former violates the Eighth Amendment while the latter does not"). Although "no penalty is *per se* constitutional," the relative lack of objective standards concerning terms of imprisonment has meant that " 'outside the context of capital punishment, successful challenges to the proportionality of particular sentences [are] exceedingly rare.' " Id. at 289.

All of these principles—the primacy of the legislature, the variety of legitimate penological schemes, the nature of our federal system, and the requirement that proportionality review be guided by objective factors—inform the final one: the Eighth Amendment does not require strict proportionality between crime and sentence. Rather, it forbids only extreme sentences that are "grossly disproportionate" to the crime....

## II

With these considerations stated, it is necessary to examine the challenged aspects of petitioner's sentence: its severe length and its mandatory operation.

## A

Petitioner's life sentence without parole is the second most severe penalty permitted by law. It is the same sentence received by the petitioner in *Solem*. Petitioner's crime, however, was far more grave than the crime at issue in *Solem*.

The crime of uttering a no account check at issue in *Solem* was " 'one of the most passive felonies a person could commit.' " It "involved neither violence nor threat of violence to any person," and was "viewed by society as among the less serious offenses." The felonies underlying the defendant's recidivism conviction, moreover, were "all relatively minor." The *Solem* court contrasted these "minor" offenses with "very serious offenses" such as "a third offense of heroin dealing," and stated that "no one suggests that [a statute providing for life imprisonment without parole] may not be applied constitutionally to fourth-time heroin dealers or other violent criminals."

Petitioner was convicted of possession of more than 650 grams (over 1.5 pounds) of cocaine. This amount of pure cocaine has a potential yield of between 32,500 and 65,000 doses. From any standpoint, this crime falls in a different category from the relatively minor, nonviolent crime at issue in *Solem*. Possession, use, and distribution of illegal drugs represents "one of the greatest problems affecting the health and welfare of our population." Petitioner's suggestion that his crime was nonviolent and victimless, echoed by the dissent, is false to the point of absurdity. To the contrary, petitioner's crime threatened to cause grave harm to society.

Quite apart from the pernicious effects on the individual who consumes illegal drugs, such drugs relate to crime in at least three ways: (1) A drug user may commit crime because of drug-induced changes in physiological functions, cognitive ability, and mood; (2) A drug user may commit crime in order to obtain money to buy drugs; and (3) A violent crime may occur as part of the drug business or culture. See Paul J. Goldstein, Drugs and Violent Crime, in Pathways to Criminal Violence 16, 24–36 (Neil Alan Weiner, Marvin Wolfgang eds. 1989). Studies bear out these possibilities, and demonstrate a direct nexus between illegal drugs and crimes of violence. To mention but a few examples, 57 percent of a national sample of males arrested in 1989 for homicide tested positive for illegal drugs. National Institute of Justice, 1989 Drug Use Forecasting Annual Report 9 (June 1990). The comparable statistics for assault, robbery, and weapons arrests were 55, 73 and 63 percent, respectively. In Detroit, Michigan in 1988, 68 percent of a sample of male arrestees and 81 percent of a sample of female arrestees tested positive for illegal drugs. National Institute of Justice, 1988 Drug Use Forecasting Annual Report 4 (Mar. 1990). Fifty-one percent of males and 71 percent of females tested positive for cocaine. And last year an estimated 60 percent of the homicides in Detroit were drug-related, primarily cocaine-related. U.S. Department of Health and Human Services, Epidemiologic Trends in Drug Abuse 107 (Dec. 1990).

These and other facts and reports detailing the pernicious effects of the drug epidemic in this country do not establish that Michigan's penalty scheme is correct or the most just in any abstract sense. But they do demonstrate that the Michigan legislature could with reason conclude that the threat posed to the individual and society by possession of this large an amount of cocaine—in terms of violence, crime, and social displacement—is momentous enough to warrant the deterrence and retribution of a life sentence without parole. . . .

Petitioner and amici contend that our proportionality decisions require a comparative analysis between petitioner's sentence and sentences imposed for other crimes in Michigan and sentences imposed for the same crime in other jurisdictions. Given the serious nature of petitioner's crime, no such comparative analysis is necessary. Although *Solem* considered these comparative factors after analyzing "the gravity of the offense and the harshness of the penalty," it did not announce a rigid three-part test. In fact, *Solem* stated that in determining unconstitutional disproportionality, "no one factor will be dispositive in a given case." ("No single criterion can identify when a sentence is so grossly disproportionate that it violates the Eighth Amendment").

On the other hand, one factor may be sufficient to determine the constitutionality of a particular sentence. Consistent with its admonition that "a reviewing court rarely will be required to engage in extended analysis to determine that a sentence is not constitutionally disproportionate," *Solem* is best understood as holding that comparative analysis within and between jurisdictions is not always relevant to proportionality review. The Court stated that "it may be helpful to compare sentences imposed on other criminals in the same jurisdiction," and that "courts may find it useful to compare the sentences imposed for commission of the same crime in other jurisdictions." It did not mandate such inquiries.

A better reading of our cases leads to the conclusion that intra-and inter-jurisdictional analyses are appropriate only in the rare case in which a threshold comparison of the crime committed and the sentence imposed leads to an inference of gross disproportionality. . . .

The proper role for comparative analysis of sentences, then, is to validate an initial judgment that a sentence is grossly disproportionate to a crime. This conclusion neither "eviscerates" *Solem*, nor "abandons" its second and third factors, as the dissent charges, and it takes full account of *Rummel* and *Davis*, cases ignored by the dissent. In light of the gravity of petitioner's offense, a comparison of his crime with his sentence does not give rise to an inference of gross disproportionality, and comparative analysis of his sentence with others in Michigan and across the nation need not be performed.

B

Petitioner also attacks his sentence because of its mandatory nature. Petitioner would have us hold that any severe penalty scheme requires individualized sentencing so that a judicial official may consider mitigating circumstances. Our precedents do not support this proposition, and petitioner presents no convincing reason to fashion an exception or adopt a new rule in the case before us. The Court demonstrates that our Eighth Amendment capital decisions reject any requirement of individualized sentencing in noncapital cases.

The mandatory nature of this sentence comports with our noncapital proportionality decisions as well. The statute at issue in *Solem* made the offender liable to a maximum, not a mandatory, sentence of life imprisonment without parole. Because a "lesser sentence ... could have been entirely consistent with both the statute and the Eighth Amendment," the Court's decision "did not question the legislature's judgment," but rather challenged the sentencing court's selection of a penalty at the top of the authorized sentencing range. Here, by contrast, the Michigan legislature has mandated the penalty and has given the state judge no discretion in implementing it. It is beyond question that the legislature "has the power to define criminal punishments without giving the courts any sentencing discretion." Since the beginning of the republic, Congress and the states have enacted mandatory sentencing schemes. To set aside petitioner's mandatory sentence would require rejection not of the judgment of a single jurist, as in *Solem*, but rather the collective wisdom of the Michigan legislature and, as a consequence, the Michigan citizenry. We have never invalidated a penalty mandated by a legislature based only on the length of sentence, and, especially with a crime as severe as this one, we should do so only in the most extreme circumstance.

In asserting the constitutionality of this mandatory sentence, I offer no judgment on its wisdom. Mandatory sentencing schemes can be criticized for depriving judges of the power to exercise individual discretion when remorse and acknowledgment of guilt, or other extenuating facts, present what might seem a compelling case for departure from the maximum. On the other hand, broad and unreviewed discretion exercised by sentencing judges leads to the perception that no clear standards are being applied, and that the rule of law is imperiled by sentences imposed for no discernible reason other than the subjective reactions of the sentencing judge. The debate illustrates that, as noted at the outset, arguments for and against particular sentencing schemes are for legislatures to resolve.

Michigan's sentencing scheme establishes graduated punishment for offenses involving varying amounts of mixtures containing controlled substances. Possession of controlled substances in schedule 1 or 2 in an amount less than 50 grams results in a sentence of up to 20 years imprisonment; possession of more than 50 but less than 225 grams results in a mandatory minimum prison sentence of 10 years with a maximum sentence of 20 years; possession of more than 225 but less than 650 grams results in a mandatory minimum prison sentence of 20 years with a maximum sentence of 30 years; and possession of 650 grams or more results in a mandatory life sentence. Sentencing courts may depart from the minimum terms specified for all amounts, except those exceeding 650 grams, "if the court finds on the record that there are substantial and compelling reasons to do so." This system is not an ancient one revived in a sudden or surprising way; it is, rather, a recent enactment calibrated with care, clarity, and much deliberation to address a most serious contemporary social problem. The scheme provides clear notice of the severe consequences that attach to possession of drugs in wholesale amounts, thereby giving force to one of the first purposes of criminal law—deterrence. In this sense, the Michigan scheme may be as fair, if not more so, than other sentencing systems in which the sentencer's discretion or the complexity of the scheme obscures the possible sanction for a crime, resulting in a shock to the offender who learns the severity of his sentence only after he commits the crime.

The Michigan scheme does possess mechanisms for consideration of individual circumstances. Prosecutorial discretion before sentence and executive or legislative clemency afterwards provide means for the State to avert or correct unjust sentences. Here the prosecutor may have chosen to seek the maximum penalty because petitioner possessed 672.5 grams of undiluted cocaine and several other trappings of a drug trafficker, including marijuana cigarettes, four brass cocaine straws, a cocaine spoon, 12 percodan tablets, 25 tablets of phendimetrazine tartrate, a Motorola beeper, plastic bags containing cocaine, a coded address book, and $3500 in cash.

\* \* \*

A penalty as severe and unforgiving as the one imposed here would make this a most difficult and troubling case for any judicial officer. Reasonable minds may differ about the efficacy of Michigan's sentencing scheme, and it is far from certain that Michigan's bold experiment will succeed. The accounts of pickpockets at Tyburn hangings are a reminder of the limits of the law's deterrent force, but we cannot say the law before us has no chance of success and is on that account so disproportionate as to be cruel and unusual punishment. The dangers flowing from drug offenses and the circumstances of the crime committed here demonstrate that the Michigan penalty scheme does not surpass constitutional bounds. Michigan may use its criminal law to address the issue of drug possession in wholesale amounts in the manner that it has in this sentencing scheme. For the foregoing reasons, I conclude that petitioner's sentence of life imprisonment without parole for his crime of possession of more than 650 grams of cocaine does not violate the Eighth Amendment.

■ JUSTICE WHITE, with whom JUSTICE BLACKMUN and JUSTICE STEVENS join, dissenting.

[Justice White briefly surveyed the historical record and concluded that construing the cruel and unusual punishments clause to include a ban on disproportionate punishment is not precluded by either the text or the original understanding and that, in any event, "there can be no doubt" that the Court's prior decisions have construed the language to include a proportionality principle.]

. . . The Court's capital punishment cases requiring proportionality reject Justice Scalia's notion that the amendment bars only cruel and unusual modes or methods of punishment. Under that view, capital punishment—a mode of punishment—would either be completely barred or left to the discretion of the legislature. Yet neither is true. The death penalty is appropriate in some cases and not in others. The same should be true of punishment by imprisonment.

What is more, the Court's prohibition against cruel and unusual punishments has long understood the limitations of a purely historical analysis. Trop v. Dulles, 356 U.S. 86 (1958). . . . Thus, "this Court has 'not confined the prohibition embodied in the Eighth Amendment to 'barbarous' methods that were generally outlawed in the 18th century,' but instead has interpreted the amendment 'in a flexible and dynamic manner.' " Stanford v. Kentucky, 492 U.S. 361, 369 (1989). . . .

The Court therefore has recognized that a punishment may violate the Eighth Amendment if it is contrary to the "evolving standards of decency that mark the progress of a maturing society." *Trop*, supra at 101. In evaluating a punishment under this test, "we have looked not to our own conceptions of decency, but to those of modern American society as a whole" in determining what standards have "evolved," and thus have focused not on "the subjective views of individual Justices," but on "objective factors to the maximum possible extent." Coker v. Georgia, 433 U.S. 584, 592 (1977). It is this type of objective factor which forms the basis for the tripartite proportionality analysis set forth in *Solem*.

Contrary to Justice Scalia's suggestion, the *Solem* analysis has worked well in practice. Courts appear to have had little difficulty applying the analysis to a given sentence, and application of the test by numerous state and federal appellate courts has resulted in a mere handful of sentences being declared unconstitutional.[2] Thus, it is clear that reviewing courts have not baldly substituted their own subjective moral values for those of the legislature. Instead, courts have demonstrated that they are "capable of

[2] Indeed, the parties have cited only four cases decided in the years since *Solem* in which sentences have been reversed on the basis of a proportionality analysis. See Clowers v. State, 522 So. 2d 762 (Miss. 1988) (holding that trial court had discretion to reduce a mandatory sentence of fifteen years without parole under a recidivist statute for a defendant who uttered a forged check); Ashley v. State, 538 So. 2d 1181 (Miss. 1989) (reaching a similar result for a defendant who burgled a home to get $4.00 to pay a grocer for food eaten in the store); State v. Gilham, 48 Ohio App. 3d 293, 549 N.E.2d 555 (1988). In addition, in Naovarath v. State, 105 Nev. 525, 779 P.2d 944 (1989), the court relied on both state and federal constitutions to strike a sentence of life without parole imposed on an adolescent who killed and then robbed an individual who had repeatedly molested him.

applying the Eighth Amendment to disproportionate noncapital sentences with a high degree of sensitivity to principles of federalism and state autonomy." *Solem* is wholly consistent with this approach, and when properly applied, its analysis affords "substantial deference to the broad authority that legislatures necessarily possess in determining the types and limits of punishments for crimes, as well as to the discretion that trial courts possess in sentencing convicted criminals," and will only rarely result in a sentence failing constitutional muster. The fact that this is one of those rare instances is no reason to abandon the analysis. . . .

Two dangers lurk in Justice Scalia's analysis. First, he provides no mechanism for addressing a situation such as that proposed in *Rummel*, in which a legislature makes overtime parking a felony punishable by life imprisonment. He concedes that "one can imagine extreme examples"— perhaps such as the one described in *Rummel*—"that no rational person, in no time or place, could accept," but attempts to offer reassurance by claiming that "for the same reason these examples are easy to decide, they are certain never to occur." This is cold comfort indeed, for absent a proportionality guarantee, there would be no basis for deciding such cases should they arise.

Second, as I have indicated, Justice Scalia's position that the Eighth Amendment addresses only modes or methods of punishment is quite inconsistent with our capital punishment cases, which do not outlaw death as a mode or method of punishment, but instead put limits on its application. If the concept of proportionality is downgraded in the Eighth Amendment calculus, much of this Court's capital penalty jurisprudence will rest on quicksand.

While Justice Scalia seeks to deliver a swift death sentence to *Solem*, Justice Kennedy prefers to eviscerate it, leaving only an empty shell. The analysis Justice Kennedy proffers is contradicted by the language of *Solem* itself and by our other cases interpreting the Eighth Amendment. . . .

Justice Kennedy's abandonment of the second and third factors set forth in *Solem* makes any attempt at an objective proportionality analysis futile. The first prong of *Solem* requires a court to consider two discrete factors—the gravity of the offense and the severity of the punishment. A court is not expected to consider the interaction of these two elements and determine whether "the sentence imposed was grossly excessive punishment for the crime committed." Were a court to attempt such an assessment, it would have no basis for its determination that a sentence was—or was not—disproportionate, other than the "subjective views of individual [judges]," which is the very sort of analysis our Eighth Amendment jurisprudence has shunned. Justice Kennedy asserts that "our decisions recognize that we lack clear objective standards to distinguish between sentences for different terms of years," citing *Rummel* and *Solem* as support. But *Solem* recognized that

> [f]or sentences of imprisonment, the problem is not so much one of ordering, but one of line-drawing. It is clear that a 25–year sentence generally is more severe than a 15–year sentence, but in

most cases it would be difficult to decide that the former violates the Eighth Amendment while the latter does not. Decisions of this kind, although troubling, are not unique to this area. The courts are constantly called upon to draw similar lines in a variety of contexts. 463 U.S. at 294.

The Court compared line-drawing in the Eighth Amendment context to that regarding the sixth amendment right to a speedy trial and right to a jury before concluding that "courts properly may look to the practices in other jurisdictions in deciding where lines between sentences should be drawn." Indeed, only when a comparison is made with penalties for other crimes and in other jurisdictions can a court begin to make an objective assessment about a given sentence's constitutional proportionality, giving due deference to "public attitudes concerning a particular sentence."

Because there is no justification for overruling or limiting *Solem*, it remains to apply that case's proportionality analysis to the sentence imposed on petitioner. Application of the *Solem* factors to the statutorily mandated punishment at issue here reveals that the punishment fails muster under *Solem* and, consequently, under the Eighth Amendment to the Constitution.

Petitioner, a first-time offender, was convicted of possession of 672 grams of cocaine. The statute under which he was convicted, provides that a person who knowingly or intentionally possesses any of various narcotics, including cocaine, "which is in an amount of 650 grams or more of any mixture containing that substance is guilty of a felony and shall be imprisoned for life." No particular degree of drug purity is required for a conviction. Other statutes make clear that an individual convicted of possessing this quantity of drugs is not eligible for parole. A related statute, which was enacted at the same time as the statute under which petitioner was convicted, mandates the same penalty of life imprisonment without possibility of parole for someone who "manufactures, delivers, or possesses with intent to manufacture or deliver," 650 grams or more of a narcotic mixture.[3] There is no room for judicial discretion in the imposition of the life sentence upon conviction. . . .

The first *Solem* factor requires a reviewing court to assess the gravity of the offense and the harshness of the penalty. The mandatory sentence of life imprisonment without possibility of parole "is the most severe punishment that the state could have imposed on any criminal for any crime," for Michigan has no death penalty.

Although these factors are "by no means exhaustive," in evaluating the gravity of the offense, it is appropriate to consider "the harm caused or threatened to the victim or society," based on such things as the degree of violence involved in the crime and "the absolute magnitude of the crime,"

---

[3] The two statutes also set forth penalties for those convicted based on lesser quantities of drugs. They provide for parallel penalties for all amounts greater than 50 grams, but below that point the penalties under the two statutes diverge.

and "the culpability of the offender," including the degree of requisite intent and the offender's motive in committing the crime.

Drugs are without doubt a serious societal problem. To justify such a harsh mandatory penalty as that imposed here, however, the offense should be one which will always warrant that punishment. Mere possession of drugs—even in such a large quantity—is not so serious an offense that it will always warrant, much less mandate, life imprisonment without possibility of parole. Unlike crimes directed against the persons and property of others, possession of drugs affects the criminal who uses the drugs most directly. The ripple effect on society caused by possession of drugs, through related crimes, lost productivity, health problems, and the like, is often not the direct consequence of possession, but of the resulting addiction. . . .

To be constitutionally proportionate, punishment must be tailored to a defendant's personal responsibility and moral guilt. See *Enmund v. Florida*, 458 U.S. at 801. Justice Kennedy attempts to justify the harsh mandatory sentence imposed on petitioner by focusing on the subsidiary effects of drug use, and thereby ignores this aspect of our Eighth Amendment jurisprudence. While the collateral consequences of drugs such as cocaine are indisputably severe, they are not unlike those which flow from the misuse of other, legal, substances. . . . It is one thing to uphold a checkpoint designed to detect drivers then under the influence of a drug that creates a present risk that they will harm others. It is quite something else to uphold petitioner's sentence because of the collateral consequences which might issue, however indirectly, from the drugs he possessed. Indeed, it is inconceivable that a state could rationally choose to penalize one who possesses large quantities of alcohol in a manner similar to that in which Michigan has chosen to punish petitioner for cocaine possession, because of the tangential effects which might ultimately be traced to the alcohol at issue. . . .

The "absolute magnitude" of petitioner's crime is not exceptionally serious. Because possession is necessarily a lesser included offense of possession with intent to distribute, it is odd to punish the former as severely as the latter. Nor is the requisite intent for the crime sufficient to render it particularly grave. To convict someone under the possession statute, it is only necessary to prove that the defendant knowingly possessed a mixture containing narcotics which weighs at least 650 grams. There is no mens rea requirement of intent to distribute the drugs, as there is in the parallel statute. Indeed, the presence of a separate statute which reaches manufacture, delivery, or possession with intent to do either, undermines the state's position that the purpose of the possession statute was to reach drug dealers. Although "intent to deliver can be inferred from the amount of a controlled substance possessed by the accused," the inference is one to be drawn by the jury. In addition, while there is usually a pecuniary motive when someone possesses a drug with intent to deliver it, such a motive need not exist in the case of mere possession. Finally, this statute applies equally to first-time offenders, such as petitioner, and recidivists. Consequently, the particular concerns reflected in recidivist statutes such as those in *Rummel* and *Solem* are not at issue here.

There is an additional concern present here. The state has conceded that it chose not to prosecute Harmelin under the statute prohibiting possession with intent to deliver, because it was "not necessary and not prudent to make it more difficult for us to win a prosecution." The state thus aimed to avoid having to establish Harmelin's intent to distribute by prosecuting him instead under the possession statute.[4] Because the statutory punishment for the two crimes is the same, the state succeeded in punishing Harmelin as if he had been convicted of the more serious crime without being put to the test of proving his guilt on those charges.

The second prong of the *Solem* analysis is an examination of "the sentences imposed on other criminals in the same jurisdiction." As noted above, there is no death penalty in Michigan; consequently, life without parole, the punishment mandated here, is the harshest penalty available. It is reserved for three crimes: first-degree murder, manufacture, distribution, or possession with intent to manufacture or distribute 650 grams or more of narcotics; and possession of 650 grams or more of narcotics. Crimes directed against the persons and property of others—such as second-degree murder, rape, and armed robbery,—do not carry such a harsh mandatory sentence, although they do provide for the possibility of a life sentence in the exercise of judicial discretion. It is clear that petitioner "has been treated in the same manner as, or more severely than, criminals who have committed far more serious crimes."

The third factor set forth in *Solem* examines "the sentences imposed for commission of the same crime in other jurisdictions." No other jurisdiction imposes a punishment nearly as severe as Michigan's for possession of the amount of drugs at issue here. Of the remaining 49 states, only Alabama provides for a mandatory sentence of life imprisonment without possibility of parole for a first-time drug offender, and then only when a defendant possesses ten kilograms or more of cocaine. Possession of the amount of cocaine at issue here would subject an Alabama defendant to a mandatory minimum sentence of only five years in prison. Even under the Federal Sentencing Guidelines, with all relevant enhancements, petitioner's sentence would barely exceed ten years. Thus, "it appears that [petitioner] was treated more severely than he would have been in any other state." Indeed, the fact that no other jurisdiction provides such a severe, mandatory penalty for possession of this quantity of drugs is enough to establish "the degree of national consensus this Court has previously thought sufficient to label a particular punishment cruel and unusual."

---

[4] Both the state and Justice Kennedy, point to the fact that the amount and purity of the drugs, and Harmelin's possession of a beeper, coded phone book, and gun all were noted in the presentence report and provided circumstantial evidence of an intent to distribute. None of this information, however, was relevant to a prosecution under the possession statute. Indeed, because the sentence is statutorily mandated for mere possession, there was no reason for defense counsel to challenge the presence of this information in the presentence report. It would likewise be inappropriate to consider petitioner's characteristics in assessing the constitutionality of the penalty.

Application of *Solem's* proportionality analysis leaves no doubt that the Michigan statute at issue fails constitutional muster.[5] The statutorily mandated penalty of life without possibility of parole for possession of narcotics is unconstitutionally disproportionate in that it violates the Eighth Amendment's prohibition against cruel and unusual punishment. Consequently, I would reverse the decision of the Michigan Court of Appeals.

■ [JUSTICE MARSHALL's dissenting opinion has been omitted.]

■ JUSTICE STEVENS, with whom JUSTICE BLACKMUN joins, dissenting.

While I agree wholeheartedly with Justice White's dissenting opinion, I believe an additional comment is appropriate.

The severity of the sentence that Michigan has mandated for the crime of possession of more than 650 grams of cocaine, whether diluted or undiluted, does not place the sentence in the same category as capital punishment. I remain convinced that Justice Stewart correctly characterized the penalty of death as "unique" because of "its absolute renunciation of all that is embodied in our concept of humanity." Furman v. Georgia, 408 U.S. 238, 306 (1972). Nevertheless, a mandatory sentence of life imprisonment without the possibility of parole does share one important characteristic of a death sentence: The offender will never regain his freedom. Because such a sentence does not even purport to serve a rehabilitative function, the sentence must rest on a rational determination that the punished "criminal conduct is so atrocious that society's interest in deterrence and retribution wholly outweighs any considerations of reform or rehabilitation of the perpetrator." Id. at 307. Serious as this defendant's crime was, I believe it is irrational to conclude that every similar offender is wholly incorrigible.

The death sentences that were at issue and invalidated in *Furman* were "cruel and unusual in the same way that being struck by lightning is cruel and unusual." Id. at 309. In my opinion the imposition of a life sentence without possibility of parole on this petitioner is equally capricious. As Justice White has pointed out, under the Federal Sentencing Guidelines, with all relevant enhancements, petitioner's sentence would barely exceed 10 years. In most states, the period of incarceration for a first offender like petitioner would be substantially shorter. No jurisdiction except Michigan has concluded that the offense belongs in a category where reform and rehabilitation are considered totally unattainable. Accordingly, the notion that this sentence satisfies any meaningful requirement of proportionality is itself both cruel and unusual.

I respectfully dissent.

---

[5] Because the statute under which petitioner was convinced is unconstitutional under *Solem*, there is no need to reach his remaining argument that imposition of a life sentence without the possibility of parole necessitates the sort of individualized sentencing determination heretofore reserved for defendants subject to the death penalty.

NOTES ON PROPORTIONALITY AND IMPRISONMENT

**1. Questions and Comments on *Harmelin v. Michigan*.** One year after *Harmelin* was decided, the Michigan Supreme Court ruled that the statute violated the Michigan constitution's ban on "cruel and unusual punishment." People v. Bullock, 440 Mich. 15, 485 N.W.2d 866 (1992). A four-three majority of the Michigan Supreme Court relied on *Solem's* three-factor analysis and embraced Justice White's reasoning in *Harmelin*. One of the dissenting justices concluded that the Michigan constitution did not include a proportionality requirement at all, relying upon arguments analogous to those stated by Justice Scalia in *Harmelin*. A second dissenting justice opined that the Michigan constitution's proportionality requirement is coextensive with the Eighth Amendment prohibition and therefore concluded that the Michigan cocaine penalty is not unconstitutionally disproportionate for the reasons stated by Justice Kennedy in *Harmelin*.[a] To what extent are the concerns about proportionality review raised by Justices Scalia and Kennedy in *Harmelin* ameliorated when this function is carried out by state supreme courts under state constitutions rather than by the federal courts under the federal constitution?

**2. *State v. Bartlett* and Statutory Rape.** Although the *Harmelin* Court rebuffed the proportionality challenge to the Michigan cocaine statute, it left the door just barely ajar for challenges to other penalties. The Arizona Supreme Court entertained such a challenge in State v. Bartlett, 171 Ariz. 302, 830 P.2d 823 (1992). Joseph Bartlett, Jr. was convicted in 1987 of two counts of sexual conduct with a minor under A.R.S. § 13–1405, a class 2 felony.[b] The circumstances of the offense, as summarized by the court, were as follows:

> In September 1986, defendant, age 23, was introduced to Mary, age 14½. A few months later, Mary introduced defendant to her friend Susan, of approximately the same age. Mary had voluntary sexual intercourse with defendant in December 1986, when she was 14 years and ten months of age. Susan also had voluntary sexual intercourse with defendant in December 1986, when she was 14 years and six months of age.

> In January 1987, Susan's mother filed a complaint with the police, alleging that defendant had forcibly sexually assaulted Susan. When defendant learned from neighbors that the police were inquiring about him, he voluntarily went to the police station. Defendant admitted to the police that he had had consensual

---

[a] A third justice dissented on the ground that the constitutional flaw of the Michigan statute is not its no-parole feature but rather its "mandatory, uniform and blanket application to all defendants." In light of this conclusion, he would have remanded the case for determination whether a non-parolable life sentence is unconstitutionally disproportionate as applied to particular defendants.

[b] At the time of Bartlett's offense, sexual conduct with a minor was a class 2 felony if the minor was under 15 and a class 6 felony if the minor was over 15 (and under 18). In 1990, the Arizona legislature amended the statute to draw the line between the two offenses at age 14.

sexual intercourse with both Susan and Mary knowing that they were under 15 years old at the time. Both girls testified at trial that the intercourse with defendant had been voluntary....

Under the applicable sentencing provisions, Bartlett's convictions for two class 2 felonies triggered the application of the "dangerous crimes against children act." Under this sentencing scheme, the mandatory minimum sentence for a first offense is 15 years, with a presumptive term of 20 years and a maximum term of 25 years. Because Bartlett's first offense was a predicate felony for enhancement purposes, the minimum term for his second offense was 25 years, with a presumptive term of 30 years and a maximum of 35 years. In addition, the statute required the sentences for the two offenses to be served consecutively as "hard time" with no possibility of early release or parole. The trial judge imposed the mandatory minimum terms of 15 and 25 years for the two offenses, amounting to a 40–year sentence.[c]

In 1990, the Supreme Court of Arizona held that Bartlett's sentence was unconstitutionally disproportionate under the Eighth Amendment as interpreted in *Solem v. Helm*. State v. Bartlett, 164 Ariz. 229, 792 P.2d 692 (1990).[d] Arizona petitioned the United States Supreme Court for a writ of certiorari and the Court remanded the case to the Arizona Supreme Court for reconsideration in light of the Court's recent decision in *Harmelin*. On remand, a 3–2 majority of the Arizona court reaffirmed its previous ruling, holding that *Solem* survives *Harmelin* and that nothing in *Harmelin* altered its earlier analysis of the three *Solem* factors.

With respect to the gravity of Bartlett's offenses, the court noted:

> Although the minor's consent will not decriminalize the sexual conduct, that consent is relevant to our inquiry into the gravity of the offense. In this case, both minors were close to the maturity line that the legislature has drawn for less serious offenses. According to their testimonies, both were willing participants in defendant's conduct. Defendant used no violent force or threats against them. Neither girl was physically injured or testified to any emotional trauma. Under these circumstances, we must certainly consider these offenses less grave than the others punishable under the same statutory scheme: second degree murder, sexual assault, taking a child for the purposes of prostitution, child prostitution, involving a minor in drug offenses, aggravated assault, molestation of a child, sexual exploitation of a minor, child abuse, or kidnapping.

[c] Apparently the prosecution offered a stipulated, five-year sentence (on reduced charges) in return for a guilty plea. However, against counsel's advice, Bartlett rejected the state's offer and refused to plead guilty.

[d] The Court remanded the case for re-sentencing, directing the trial court to sentence Bartlett for the two class 2 felonies but without applying the stringent provisions of the dangerous crimes against the children act. The trial judge imposed the minimum available terms for a class 2 felony, sentencing Bartlett to 5¼ years on one count and seven years on the other, with the sentences to run concurrently.

Additionally, we must consider the minors' proximities to their 15th birthdays. Although the legislature may be forced to draw a "bright line" at a particular age (in this case, at the age of 15) in distinguishing between class 6 and class 2 sexual conduct felonies, a reviewing court can look at a more graduated line, depending on the nature of the individual offense, in deciding the proportionality of the punishment to the crime. Thus, although the fact that both consenting girls were close to their 15th birthdays cannot be used to reduce the crimes from class 2 felonies to class 6 felonies, the punishment imposed for those harsher class 2 felonies must be proportionate to these individual offenses. And although the legislature has determined that a minor's "consent" to sexual conduct does not excuse its commission, certainly the punishment for consensual sexual conduct with a minor over 14½ years old should be closer to the punishment for sexual conduct with a 15–year-old than to punishment for sexual conduct with a two-year-old. We thus examine what punishment defendant would have received if the minors were 15.

If Mary and Susan had been two months and six months older, respectively, defendant would have faced sentencing for two counts of a class 6 felony for sexual conduct with a minor 15 years of age. The range of sentencing for the *first* offense would have been a minimum term of nine months, a presumptive term of 1.5 years, and a maximum term of 1.875 years. The trial court would have had discretion to place defendant on probation and to designate the offense as a class 1 misdemeanor upon successful completion of that probation. If imprisoned, defendant would have been eligible for early release after one-half the sentence had been served. The range of sentencing for the *second* offense, as a repetitive felony, would have been a minimum term of 1.5 years, a presumptive term of 2.25 years, and a maximum term of three years. Defendant would not have been eligible for probation for the second offense, but would have been eligible for early release after one-half the sentence had been served. Defendant's terms could have been imposed either consecutively or concurrently, within the trial court's discretion. The sentences defendant actually received were significantly more harsh.

As to defendant's personal culpability, the record indicates that he was an "immature" young man who associated with a younger peer group because of his emotional insecurities, which included a pending divorce after marriage at a young age. He had no prior felony record and no history of assaulting young children. No evidence was presented that he intended to harm these girls, either physically or emotionally.

With regard to sentences prescribed by Arizona law for other crimes, the court observed:

[A] comparison of the other crimes punishable under the same mandatory sentencing provisions is helpful in this case to show that more serious offenses do not receive any greater punishment. For example, second degree murder, forcible sexual assault, taking a child for the purposes of prostitution, or involving a child in a drug offense are all considered first degree crimes against children, subject to the same mandatory minimum sentences of 15 and 25 years that defendant received. More potentially serious crimes than those committed here, such as aggravated assault, child molestation, child abuse, or kidnapping, are subject to a lesser minimum sentence of 12 years for the first offense and 23 years for the second offense.

Other more serious crimes that do not involve children similarly receive lesser penalties than those mandated in this case. . . .

Finally, the Court examined the punishments imposed by other jurisdictions for comparable crimes—"consensual, nonincestuous, heterosexual intercourse with a 14–year old" by a person without any prior felony convictions—for first and second offenses:

In 10 jurisdictions, defendant's offenses would either not be a crime or would be punishable only as a misdemeanor with a sentence of less than one year and/or a fine. For a *first* felony offense in the remaining jurisdictions, defendant would have faced a minimum penalty of one, two or three years, with probation often available. Thus, our statute is unique among all jurisdictions in that it imposes a minimum mandatory term of 15 years, which is 5 times higher than the imposed in any other jurisdiction. In all jurisdictions but Arizona, the sentencing judge has a wide range of discretion in imposing a sentence at the bottom of the statutory range that fits the individual circumstances of the crime. Although the *maximum* allowable sentence in some jurisdictions would have fallen within the range of sentencing provided for a first offender under [Arizona law], in no jurisdiction would the sentencing judge be *required* to impose a sentence of more than 3 years for the identical offense. . . . Additionally, defendant's appellate counsel has avowed to the court that he "has diligently searched two centuries of case law of each of our 50 sister states. This required the review of just over 2,600 cases. Not one case was found where a similarly situated defendant received an aggravated sentence remotely comparable to that imposed as a mandatory minimum upon Mr. Bartlett." . . .

A comparison of the 25–year mandatory minimum sentence defendant received for the *second* offense with those imposed in other jurisdictions is complicated by the enhancement of defendant's second sentence because the first count was treated as a prior predicate felony. . . .

Also complicating our analysis is the mandatory consecutive nature of the two sentences, along with the absence of the availability of parole....

Despite these difficulties, a comparison of what penalties defendant would face for a second offense in other jurisdictions, although not as clear as the comparison for a first offense, compels the conclusion that defendant would be subject to a much lighter minimum mandatory sentence for his second offense in all but one state.

In Nebraska, defendant would be subject to a statutory range of 25 to 50 years for a second conviction of sexual assault involving a consenting child less than 16 years old, and would not be eligible for parole.... [W]e have not been advised by the state of any defendant charged in Nebraska with offenses similar to Bartlett's actually receiving such a harsh sentence. Rather, the published cases that we have found challenging the mandatory Nebraska sentence for a second offense have involved more heinous offenses, including forcible rape with serious physical injuries to the victim....

Except for Nebraska, no other jurisdiction imposes a mandatory minimum sentence of more than 10 years for a second offense similar to defendant's. In no jurisdiction did we find the particularly harsh combination of provisions present here, including both mandatory consecutive sentencing and nonavailability of parole. We must conclude, therefore, that the 25–year mandatory minimum imposed for defendant's second offense is also disproportionate to the sentences imposed on similarly situated defendants in other jurisdictions.

Did the Arizona Supreme Court properly interpret *Harmelin*?[e]

**3. Mandatory Life Sentences for Juveniles.** Does the Eighth Amendment permit a mandatory life sentence with a minimum term of 30 years for a defendant convicted of first-degree murder who was 15 at the time of the offense? Recall that the U.S. Supreme Court has barred death sentences for juveniles who were younger than 15 at the time of the offense. (See the preceding subsection of this chapter.) The Supreme Court of Minnesota rejected constitutional challenges to such a sentence in State v. Mitchell, 577 N.W.2d 481 (Minn. 1998), a case involving a 15–year-old first offender with a history of serious physical and emotional abuse and multiple suicide attempts who shot a convenience store clerk during a robbery that was planned by three older teenagers. See also Harris v. Wright, 93 F.3d 581 (9th Cir. 1996)(holding that no societal consensus

---

[e] Four years after *Bartlett*, a new majority of the Arizona Supreme Court disavowed the *Bartlett* majority's interpretation of Justice Kennedy's pivotal opinion in *Harmelin*. Arizona v. DePiano, 187 Ariz. 27, 926 P.2d 494 (1996). Although *Bartlett* was not overruled, the *DePiano* majority opined that "the initial threshold disproportionality analysis is to be measured by the nature of the offense generally and not specifically."

exists against lengthy mandatory sentences for juveniles convicted of murder). How would you frame and analyze the issues in such a case?

**4. Three Strikes Laws: *Ewing v. California*.** Between 1993 and 2002, more than half of the states enacted so-called "three strikes" laws designed to incapacitate violent recidivist offenders. Under the California version of the three-strikes law, enacted in response to strong public pressure in 1994, a defendant convicted of a felony is subject to the law if he has previously been convicted of one or more prior felonies defined as "serious" or "violent." If he has one prior qualifying conviction, he must be sentenced to "twice the term otherwise provided as punishment for the current felony conviction." If he has two or more prior "serious" or "violent" felony convictions, he must receive "an indeterminate term of life imprisonment." Defendants sentenced to life under the three strikes law become eligible for parole on a date calculated by reference to a "minimum term," which is the greater of (i) three times the term otherwise provided for the current conviction, (ii) 25 years, or (iii) the term determined by the court for the underlying conviction, including any enhancements.

On parole from a 9–year prison term, petitioner Gary Ewing walked into the pro shop of the El Segundo Golf Course in Los Angeles County in March, 2000. He walked out with three golf clubs, priced at $399 apiece, concealed in his pants leg. A shop employee, whose suspicions were aroused when he observed Ewing limp out of the pro shop, telephoned the police. The police apprehended Ewing in the parking lot. Ewing was charged with and ultimately convicted of felony grand theft of personal property valued at more than $400. As required by the three strikes law, the prosecutor formally alleged, and the trial court later found, that Ewing had been convicted previously of four serious or violent felonies for three burglaries and a robbery in Committed over a five-week period in October and November 1993.[f] He was sentenced to nine years and eight months in prison for these offenses and was paroled in 1999.

At the sentencing hearing for the golf club theft, Ewing asked the court to reduce the conviction for grand theft, a "wobbler" under California law,[g] to a misdemeanor so as to avoid a three strikes sentence. Ewing

---

[f] Ewing awakened one of his victims, asleep on her living room sofa, as he tried to disconnect her video cassette recorder from the television in that room. When she screamed, Ewing ran out the front door. On another occasion, Ewing accosted a victim in the mailroom of the apartment complex. Ewing claimed to have a gun and ordered the victim to hand over his wallet. When the victim resisted, Ewing produced a knife and forced the victim back to the apartment itself. While Ewing rifled through the bedroom, the victim fled the apartment screaming for help. Ewing absconded with the victim's money and credit cards.

[g] Under California law, certain offenses may be classified as either felonies or misdemeanors. These crimes are known as "wobblers." Some crimes that would otherwise be misdemeanors become "wobblers" because of the defendant's prior record. For example, petty theft, a misdemeanor, becomes a "wobbler" when the defendant has previously served a prison term for committing specified theft-related crimes. Other crimes, such as grand theft, are "wobblers" regardless of the defendant's prior record. Both types of "wobblers" are triggering offenses under the three strikes law only when they are treated as felonies. California, prosecutors may exercise their discretion to charge a "wobbler" as

also asked the trial court to exercise its discretion to dismiss the allegations of some or all of his prior serious or violent felony convictions, again for purposes of avoiding a three strikes sentence. Before sentencing Ewing, the trial court took note of his entire criminal history, including the fact that he was on parole when he committed his latest offense. In the end, the trial judge determined that the grand theft should remain a felony. The court also ruled that the four prior strikes for the three burglaries and the robbery should stand. As a newly convicted felon with two or more "serious" or "violent" felony convictions in his past, Ewing was sentenced under the three strikes law to 25 years to life.

The California Court of Appeal rejected Ewing's claim that his sentence was grossly disproportionate under the Eighth Amendment. Enhanced sentences under recidivist statutes like strikes law, the court reasoned, serve the "legitimate goal" of deterring and incapacitating repeat offenders. After the California Supreme Court denied Ewing's petition for review, U.S. Supreme Court granted certiorari and affirmed in *Ewing v. California*, 538 U.S. 11 (2003). As in *Rummel*, *Solem* and *Harmelin*, the Supreme Court was divided five-to-four.

Justice O'Connor announced the judgment of the Court in an opinion joined only by Chief Justice Rehnquist and Justice Kennedy. Using the principles "distilled" by Justice Kennedy in his *Harmelin* opinion, Justice O'Connor concluded that Ewing's sentence was not a "grossly disproportionate" punishment fore his offense taking into account his "long criminal history" and the incapacitative aims of the "three-strikes" laws:

> When the California Legislature enacted the three strikes law, it made a judgment that protecting the public safety requires incapacitating criminals who have already been convicted of at least one serious or violent crime. Nothing in the Eighth Amendment prohibits California from making that choice. To the contrary, our cases establish that "states have a valid interest in deterring and segregating habitual criminals." Recidivism has long been recognized as a legitimate basis for increased punishment. California's justification is no pretext. Recidivism is a serious public safety concern in California and throughout the Nation. According to a recent report, approximately 67 percent of former inmates released from state prisons were charged with at least one "serious" new crime within three years of their release. See U.S. Dept. of Justice, Bureau of Justice Statistics, Special Report: Recidivism of Prisoners Released in 1994, p. 1 (June 2002). In particular, released property offenders like Ewing had higher recidivism rates than those released after committing violent,

either a felony or a misdemeanor. Likewise, California trial courts have discretion to reduce a "wobbler" charged as a felony to a misdemeanor either before preliminary examination or at sentencing to avoid imposing a three strikes sentence. In exercising this discretion, the court may consider "those factors that direct similar sentencing decisions," such as "the nature and circumstances of the offense, the defendant's appreciation of and attitude toward the offense, ... [and] the general objectives of sentencing."

drug, or public-order offenses. Approximately 73 percent of the property offenders released in 1994 were arrested again within three years, compared to approximately 61 percent of the violent offenders, 62 percent of the public-order offenders, and 66 percent of the drug offenders.

In 1996, when the Sacramento Bee studied 233 three strikes offenders in California, it found that they had an aggregate of 1,165 prior felony convictions, an average of 5 apiece. See Furillo, Three Strikes—The Verdict: Most Offenders Have Long Criminal Histories, Sacramento Bee, Mar. 31, 1996, p. A1. The prior convictions included 322 robberies and 262 burglaries. About 84 percent of the 233 three strikes offenders had been convicted of at least one violent crime. In all, they were responsible for 17 homicides, 7 attempted slayings, and 91 sexual assaults and child molestations. The Sacramento Bee concluded, based on its investigation, that "[i]n the vast majority of the cases, regardless of the third strike, the [three strikes] law is snaring [the] long-term habitual offenders with multiple felony convictions. . . ."

The state's interest in deterring crime also lends some support to the three strikes law. We have long viewed both incapacitation and deterrence as rationales for recidivism statutes: "[A] recidivist statute['s] . . . primary goals are to deter repeat offenders and, at some point in the life of one who repeatedly commits criminal offenses serious enough to be punished as felonies, to segregate that person from the rest of society for an extended period of time." *Rummel*, at 284. Four years after the passage of California's three strikes law, the recidivism rate of parolees returned to prison for the commission of a new crime dropped by nearly 25 percent. California Dept. of Justice, Office of the Attorney General, Three Strikes and You're Out—Its Impact on the California Criminal Justice System After Four Years, p. 10 (1998). Even more dramatically:

> An unintended but positive consequence of "Three Strikes" has been the impact on parolees leaving the state. More California parolees are now leaving the state than parolees from other jurisdictions entering California. This striking turnaround started in 1994. It was the first time more parolees left the state than entered since 1976. This trend has continued and in 1997 more than 1,000 net parolees left California. *Id.*

To be sure, California's three strikes law has sparked controversy. Critics have doubted the law's wisdom, cost-efficiency, and effectiveness in reaching its goals. See, e.g., Franklin Zimring, Gordon Hawkins, & Sam Kamin, Punishment and Democracy: Three Strikes and You're Out in California (2001); Michael Vitiello, Three Strikes: Can We Return to Rationality?, 87 J. Crim. L. & C. 395, 423 (1997). This criticism is appropriately directed at the legislature, which has primary responsibility for making the difficult policy choices that underlie any criminal sentencing scheme. We do not sit as a "superlegislature" to second-guess these policy choices. It is enough that the State of California has a reasonable basis for believing that dramatically enhanced sentences for habitual felons "advance[s] the goals of [its] criminal justice system in any substantial way." See *Solem*, 463 U.S., at 297, n. 22.

Justice O'Connor then applied the Eighth Amendment to Ewing's sentence and concluded that it did not cross the "threshold" under Justice Kennedy's formulation:

> In weighing the gravity of Ewing's offense, we must place on the scales not only his current felony, but also his long history of felony recidivism. Any other approach would fail to accord proper deference to the policy judgments that find expression in the legislature's choice of sanctions. In imposing a three strikes sentence, the State's interest is not merely punishing the offense of conviction, or the "triggering" offense: "[I]t is in addition the interest ... in dealing in a harsher manner with those who by repeated criminal acts have shown that they are simply incapable of conforming to the norms of society as established by its criminal law." *Rummel*, 445 U.S., at 276. To give full effect to the state's choice of this legitimate penological goal, our proportionality review of Ewing's sentence must take that goal into account.

> Ewing's sentence is justified by the State's public-safety interest in incapacitating and deterring recidivist felons, and amply supported by his own long, serious criminal record. Ewing has been convicted of numerous misdemeanor and felony offenses, served nine separate terms of incarceration, and committed most of his crimes while on probation or parole. His prior "strikes" were serious felonies including robbery and three residential burglaries. To be sure, Ewing's sentence is a long one. But it reflects a rational legislative judgment, entitled to deference, that offenders who have committed serious or violent felonies and who continue to commit felonies must be incapacitated. The State of California "was entitled to place upon [Ewing] the onus of one who is simply unable to bring his conduct within the social norms prescribed by the criminal law of the state." *Rummel, supra*, at 284. Ewing's is not "the rare case in which a threshold comparison of the crime committed and the sentence imposed leads to an inference of gross disproportionality." *Harmelin*, 501 U.S., at 1005 (Kennedy, J., concurring in part and concurring in judgment).

Justices Scalia and Thomas concurred in the judgment, adhering to their view, expressed in *Harmelin*, that the Eighth Amendment does not include a ban against disproportionate sentences. Justice Scalia also pointed out that, even if it did, such a principle "could not be intelligently applied" to sentences for recidivists based on incapacitation—sentences that reflect a policy judgment that deterrence and incapacitation trump proportionality concerns:

> ... Perhaps the plurality should revise its terminology, so that what it reads into the Eighth Amendment is not the unstated proposition that all punishment should be reasonably proportionate to the gravity of the offense, but rather the unstated proposition that all punishment should reasonably pursue the multiple purposes of the criminal law. That formulation would make it clearer than ever, of course, that the plurality is not applying law but evaluating policy.

Justices Stevens, Souter, Ginsburg and Breyer dissented. The main dissent, written by Justice Breyer, applied Justice Kennedy's *Harmelin* framework, and concluded that Ewing's case was one of the "rare" cases in which the punishment imposed was "grossly disproportionate" to the crime. Justice Breyer first reasoned that Ewing's claim passed the "threshold" because "one of most severe sentences available" (in between the sentences in *Solem* and *Rummel*) had been imposed "upon a recidivist who subsequently engaged in one of the less serious forms of criminal conduct," and because such a sentence would be considered "disproportionately harsh" by "many experienced judges." He pointed out for example that the federal sentencing guidelines, based on actual sentencing patterns, do not include shoplifting among the crimes that trigger lengthy recidivist sentences. Turning to the comparative analysis (unaddressed in Justice O'Connor's opinion), Justice Breyer concluded that, before 1994, Ewing could not have served more than 10 years for grand theft, even as a recidivist. As for other jurisdictions, data regarding actual time served are sparse, but a review of the law shows that "Ewing's sentence is, at a minimum, two to three times the length of sentences that other jurisdictions would impose in similar circumstances." Justice Breyer appended to his opinion a state-by-state legal analysis showing that 33 jurisdictions, as well as the federal courts, preclude a sentence longer than 10 years in prison for a similarly situated offender, four additional states preclude a sentence of more than 15 years, and four additional states preclude a sentence of more than 20 years. Although the remaining nine states might permit sentences in excess of 25 years, the offender would be parole-eligible before 25 years in five of these states. Finally, Justice Breyer could find no "special criminal justice concerns that might justify this sentence," especially in light the many "anomalies" created by classifying a "wobbler" theft offense as a trigger for a 25-to-life sentence under a statute designed to incapacitate offenders who have committed "serious" and "violent" offenses.

The sequence of 5–4 rulings in *Solem*, *Rummel* and *Ewing* does not mark a straight path, to say the least. What role should the Supreme Court play in reviewing the proportionality of incapacitative sentences for recidivists? None, as Justices Scalia and Thomas contend? Or the more aggressive role envisioned by Justice Breyer? Is there an alternative?

# APPENDIX A

# THE MODEL PENAL CODE

## INTRODUCTORY NOTE ON THE MODEL PENAL CODE

The American Law Institute was founded in 1923. It is a private organization of lawyers, judges, and law teachers. Together with the American Bar Association, the Institute sponsors an extensive program of continuing legal education. It has published Restatements of American law in several areas, including property, torts, and contracts; has prepared model statutes on subjects as diverse as federal income taxation, federal securities, criminal procedure, federal jurisdiction, and land development; and was a major contributor to the drafting of the Uniform Commercial Code. Of more relevance to students of the criminal law, the Institute published the Model Penal Code in 1962.

Examination of the substantive criminal law in the United States was on the Institute's initial agenda in 1923. An early proposal to restate the law was rejected, however, largely on the ground that a more prescriptive document, looking toward major reform, should be attempted. The first proposal for a "model code" of criminal law was considered in 1931. For various reasons, the project was sidetracked until 1950, when an Advisory Committee was established to take another look at the problem. By 1952, funds had been secured from the Rockefeller Foundation, and the drafting of a model penal code began in earnest.

Herbert Wechsler of the Columbia University Law School was appointed the Chief Reporter for the project. Louis B. Schwartz of the University of Pennsylvania Law School became the Reporter for Part II of the Code, dealing with substantive crimes. The elaborate process of producing the Model Code extended over a period of 10 years. Drafts were reviewed by a specially appointed Advisory Committee, by the Council of the Institute, and by the entire Institute membership at annual meetings. During the period from 1953 to 1962, Tentative Drafts of the Model Code, numbered one through 13, were published and reviewed at the annual meetings. A Proposed Final Draft was reviewed by the membership in 1961, and the text of the Proposed Official Draft was approved in 1962.

Extensive explanatory commentary was included in the various Tentative Drafts. This commentary provides a rich source of research and reflection on the content of the criminal law. Shortly after the completion of the text of the Model Code in 1962, an effort was undertaken to prepare a final commentary on each provision. Although that project was also delayed for various reasons, three volumes, consisting of commentary on Part II (specific crimes), were published in the fall of 1980. Three additional volumes on Part I (the general provisions) were published in 1985, together with a fourth volume containing the final text of the Code. This commentary explains the rationale underlying each section of the Model Code and examines the extent to which the Code provisions have been influential in recent reform efforts.

It is impossible to estimate the number of people who have had a hand in the Model Penal Code since the inception of the project in 1950. What can be said, however, is that the list of those who participated at one time or another is a virtual Who's Who of practitioners, judges, and academics interested in the subject of criminal law both in the United States and abroad.   Additionally, the Tentative Drafts of the Code sparked a considerable body of commentary from academics, judges, and practitioners, all of which was taken into account as the drafting process progressed.   Suffice it to say that the Model Penal Code is the product of an impressive intellectual effort.   Moreover, it has been, as Kadish put it, "stunningly successful in accomplishing the comprehensive rethinking of the criminal law that Wechsler and his colleagues sought."[a]

Wechsler stated the objective of the Institute in promulgating a Model Penal Code in his article, Codification of Criminal Law in the United States: The Model Penal Code, 68 Colum. L. Rev. 1425, 1427 (1968), as follows:

> "It should be noted, however, that it was not the purpose of the Institute to achieve uniformity in penal law throughout the nation, since it was deemed inevitable that substantial differences of social situation or of point of view among the states should be reflected in substantial variation in their penal laws.   The hope was rather that the model would stimulate and facilitate the systematic re-examination of the subject needed to assure that the prevailing law does truly represent the mature sentiment of our respective jurisdictions, sentiment formed after a fresh appraisal of the problems and their possible solutions.   Of course, the Institute was not without ambition that in such an enterprise the model might seem worthy of adoption or, at least, of adaptation."[b]

One need only examine the volume of criminal code reform that has occurred in this country since the Model Code project was undertaken in order to appreciate the extent to which this ambition has been achieved.   Prior to 1952, the date the drafting of the Model Code was begun, only one state, Louisiana in 1942, had significantly revised its criminal code in the 20th century.   As a result, criminal codes in the United States were a clumsy collection of common-law principles and ad hoc modifications.   Dramatic inconsistencies, particularly in penalty structure but also in the definition of offenses, could easily be found in virtually any penal code. Legislatures responded piecemeal to particular problems as they arose, and little effort was devoted to examining the criminal code as a whole or to integrating newly adopted provisions into an overall scheme or plan.

Although four states prepared new codes while the Model Code itself was being drafted, the first new enactment that was animated entirely by the spirit of the Model Code was adopted in New York in 1965 and became effective in 1967.   The New York code itself became a kind of model.   Subsequent enactments were influenced substantially both by the fact that criminal code reform had been successful in New York and by the particular adaptations of the Model Code enacted in that state.

Code revision proceeded at a moderate pace over the next several years. During the decade of the 1970's, however, substantial reform was achieved in a majority of American jurisdictions.   By May of 1982, new legislation in 37 American jurisdictions had been substantially influenced by the Model Penal Code.   In at least 11 jurisdictions, new criminal codes had been completed as of 1982, but had failed of enactment.   The remaining states were at one stage or another in study of

---

[a] Sanford Kadish, Codifiers of the Criminal Law: Wechsler's Predecessors, 78 Colum. L. Rev. 1098, 1140 (1978).

[b] See also Herbert Wechsler, The Challenge of a Model Penal Code, 65 Harv.L. Rev. 1097 (1952), which was prepared at the outset of the Model Code project.

the question.[c]  A few of the states in which new legislation has been enacted have adopted only minor revisions, essentially retaining the common-law orientation of their previous codes.  But in many of the 37 jurisdictions listed above, a thorough re-examination of fundamental issues was conducted by a locally-appointed drafting body and the codes were substantially revised along lines suggested by the Model Penal Code.

The extent to which the judiciary has been influenced by the Model Code should also be taken into account.  Many of the cases reproduced in this book illustrate that influence.  More subtly, many of the analytical techniques of the Model Code have become an integral part of judicial reasoning about the criminal law.  The vocabulary of the Model Code, particularly in its culpability structure, has also been influential in this manner.  The Model Code is thus to a considerable degree working its way into the common law of the country even in jurisdictions that have not explicitly adopted its provisions by legislation.

To a large extent, the Model Penal Code actually illustrates existing law in most American jurisdictions.  More importantly, the provisions of the Model Code define the terms of the debate on virtually every issue of penal law of general significance.  Thus, it is now clear after more than three decades of effort that the development of the criminal law in the United States will be dominated by the Model Penal Code for many years to come.

––––––––

[c] This information was extracted from the Annual Report of the American Law Institute, May 1982.

# AMERICAN LAW INSTITUTE
## MODEL PENAL CODE[a]
### (OFFICIAL DRAFT, 1962)

———

[Copyright © 1962 by the American Law Institute.
Reprinted with permission of the American Law Institute.]

———

## Table of Contents

### PART I.  GENERAL PROVISIONS

#### ARTICLE 1.  PRELIMINARY

#### ARTICLE 2.  GENERAL PRINCIPLES OF LIABILITY

[a] The Model Penal Code consists of four parts.  Parts I and II are reproduced in full on the following pages.  Part III (dealing with treatment and correction) and Part IV (dealing with organization of correctional facilities) have been omitted.

## ARTICLE 3.  GENERAL PRINCIPLES OF JUSTIFICATION

## ARTICLE 4.  RESPONSIBILITY

## ARTICLE 5.  INCHOATE CRIMES

### ARTICLE 6.  AUTHORIZED DISPOSITION OF OFFENDERS

### ARTICLE 7.  AUTHORITY OF COURT IN SENTENCING

**A-9**

---

## PART I.   GENERAL PROVISIONS

---

### ARTICLE 1.   PRELIMINARY

#### Section 1.01.   Title and Effective Date

(1) This Act is called the Penal and Correctional Code and may be cited as P.C.C.  It shall become effective on....

(2) Except as provided in Subsections (3) and (4) of this Section, the Code does not apply to offenses committed prior to its effective date and prosecutions for such offenses shall be governed by the prior law, which is continued in effect for that purpose, as if this Code were not in force.  For the purposes of this Section, an offense was committed prior to the effective date of the Code if any of the elements of the offense occurred prior thereto.

(3) In any case pending on or after the effective date of the Code, involving an offense committed prior to such date:

(a) procedural provisions of the Code shall govern, insofar as they are justly applicable and their application does not introduce confusion or delay;

(b) provisions of the Code according a defense or mitigation shall apply, with the consent of the defendant;

(c) the Court, with the consent of the defendant, may impose sentence under the provisions of the Code applicable to the offense and the offender.

(4) Provisions of the Code governing the treatment and the release or discharge of prisoners, probationers and parolees shall apply to persons under sentence for offenses committed prior to the effective date of the Code, except that the minimum or maximum period of their detention or supervision shall in no case be increased.

#### Section 1.02.   Purposes; Principles of Construction

(1) The general purposes of the provisions governing the definition of offenses are:

(a) to forbid and prevent conduct that unjustifiably and inexcusably inflicts or threatens substantial harm to individual or public interests;

(b) to subject to public control persons whose conduct indicates that they are disposed to commit crimes;

(c) to safeguard conduct that is without fault from condemnation as criminal;

(d) to give fair warning of the nature of the conduct declared to constitute an offense;

(e) to differentiate on reasonable grounds between serious and minor offenses.

(2) The general purposes of the provisions governing the sentencing and treatment of offenders are:

(a) to prevent the commission of offenses;

(b) to promote the correction and rehabilitation of offenders;

(c) to safeguard offenders against excessive, disproportionate or arbitrary punishment;

(d) to give fair warning of the nature of the sentences that may be imposed on conviction of an offense;

(e) to differentiate among offenders with a view to a just individualization in their treatment;

(f) to define, coordinate and harmonize the powers, duties and functions of the courts and of administrative officers and agencies responsible for dealing with offenders;

(g) to advance the use of generally accepted scientific methods and knowledge in the sentencing and treatment of offenders;

(h) to integrate responsibility for the administration of the correctional system in a State Department of Correction [or other single department or agency].

(3) The provisions of the Code shall be construed according to the fair import of their terms but when the language is susceptible of differing constructions it shall be interpreted to further the general purposes stated in this Section and the special purposes of the particular provision involved.  The discretionary powers conferred by the Code shall be exercised in accordance with the criteria stated in the Code and, insofar as such criteria are not decisive, to further the general purposes stated in this Section.

### Section 1.03.  Territorial Applicability

(1) Except as otherwise provided in this Section, a person may be convicted under the law of this State of an offense committed by his own conduct or the conduct of another for which he is legally accountable if:

(a) either the conduct which is an element of the offense or the result which is such an element occurs within this State;  or

(b) conduct occurring outside the State is sufficient under the law of this State to constitute an attempt to commit an offense within the State;  or

(c) conduct occurring outside the State is sufficient under the law of this State to constitute a conspiracy to commit an offense within the State and an overt act in furtherance of such conspiracy occurs within the State;  or

**A-11**

(d) conduct occurring within the State establishes complicity in the commission of, or an attempt, solicitation or conspiracy to commit, an offense in another jurisdiction which also is an offense under the law of this State; or

(e) the offense consists of the omission to perform a legal duty imposed by the law of this State with respect to domicile, residence or a relationship to a person, thing or transaction in the State; or

(f) the offense is based on a statute of this State which expressly prohibits conduct outside the State, when the conduct bears a reasonable relation to a legitimate interest of this State and the actor knows or should know that his conduct is likely to affect that interest.

(2) Subsection (1)(a) does not apply when either causing a specified result or a purpose to cause or danger of causing such a result is an element of an offense and the result occurs or is designed or likely to occur only in another jurisdiction where the conduct charged would not constitute an offense, unless a legislative purpose plainly appears to declare the conduct criminal regardless of the place of the result.

(3) Subsection (1)(a) does not apply when causing a particular result is an element of an offense and the result is caused by conduct occurring outside the State which would not constitute an offense if the result had occurred there, unless the actor purposely or knowingly caused the result within the State.

(4) When the offense is homicide, either the death of the victim or the bodily impact causing death constitutes a "result," within the meaning of Subsection (1)(a) and if the body of a homicide victim is found within the State, it is presumed that such result occurred within the State.

(5) This State includes the land and water and the air space above such land and water with respect to which the State has legislative jurisdiction.

### Section 1.04. Classes of Crimes; Violations

(1) An offense defined by this Code or by any other statute of this State, for which a sentence of [death or of] imprisonment is authorized, constitutes a crime. Crimes are classified as felonies, misdemeanors or petty misdemeanors.

(2) A crime is a felony if it is so designated in this Code or if persons convicted thereof may be sentenced [to death or] to imprisonment for a term which, apart from an extended term, is in excess of one year.

(3) A crime is a misdemeanor if it is so designated in this Code or in a statute other than this Code enacted subsequent thereto.

(4) A crime is a petty misdemeanor if it is so designated in this Code or in a statute other than this Code enacted subsequent thereto or if it is defined by a statute other than this Code which now provides that persons convicted thereof may be sentenced to imprisonment for a term of which the maximum is less than one year.

(5) An offense defined by this Code or by any other statute of this State constitutes a violation if it is so designated in this Code or in the law defining the offense or if no other sentence than a fine, or fine and forfeiture or other civil penalty is authorized upon conviction or if it is defined by a statute other than this Code which now provides that the offense shall not constitute a crime. A violation does not constitute a crime and conviction of a violation shall not give rise to any disability or legal disadvantage based on conviction of a criminal offense.

(6) Any offense declared by law to constitute a crime, without specification of the grade thereof or of the sentence authorized upon conviction, is a misdemeanor.

(7) An offense defined by any statute of this State other than this Code shall be classified as provided in this Section and the sentence that may be imposed upon conviction thereof shall hereafter be governed by this Code.

### Section 1.05. All Offenses Defined by Statute; Application of General Provisions of the Code

(1) No conduct constitutes an offense unless it is a crime or violation under this Code or another statute of this State.

(2) The provisions of Part I of the Code are applicable to offenses defined by other statutes, unless the Code otherwise provides.

(3) This Section does not affect the power of a court to punish for contempt or to employ any sanction authorized by law for the enforcement of an order or a civil judgment or decree.

### Section 1.06. Time Limitations

(1) A prosecution for murder may be commenced at any time.

(2) Except as otherwise provided in this Section, prosecutions for other offenses are subject to the following periods of limitation:

(a) a prosecution for a felony of the first degree must be commenced within six years after it is committed;

(b) a prosecution for any other felony must be commenced within three years after it is committed;

(c) a prosecution for a misdemeanor must be commenced within two years after it is committed;

(d) a prosecution for a petty misdemeanor or a violation must be commenced within six months after it is committed.

(3) If the period prescribed in Subsection (2) has expired, a prosecution may nevertheless be commenced for:

(a) any offense a material element of which is either fraud or a breach of fiduciary obligation within one year after discovery of the offense by an aggrieved party or by a person who has legal duty to represent an aggrieved party and who is himself not a party to the offense, but in no case shall this provision extend the period of limitation otherwise applicable by more than three years; and

(b) any offense based upon misconduct in office by a public officer or employee at any time when the defendant is in public office or employment or within two years thereafter, but in no case shall this provision extend the period of limitation otherwise applicable by more than three years.

(4) An offense is committed either when every element occurs, or, if a legislative purpose to prohibit a continuing course of conduct plainly appears, at the time when the course of conduct or the defendant's complicity therein is terminated. Time starts to run on the day after the offense is committed.

**A-13**

(5) A prosecution is commenced either when an indictment is found [or an information filed] or when a warrant or other process is issued, provided that such warrant or process is executed without unreasonable delay.

(6) The period of limitation does not run:

(a) during any time when the accused is continuously absent from the State or has no reasonably ascertainable place of abode or work within the State, but in no case shall this provision extend the period of limitation otherwise applicable by more than three years; or

(b) during any time when a prosecution against the accused for the same conduct is pending in this State.

### Section 1.07.　Method of Prosecution When Conduct Constitutes More Than One Offense

(1) Prosecution for Multiple Offenses; Limitation on Convictions. When the same conduct of a defendant may establish the commission of more than one offense, the defendant may be prosecuted for each such offense. He may not, however, be convicted of more than one offense if:

(a) one offense is included in the other, as defined in Subsection (4) of this Section; or

(b) one offense consists only of a conspiracy or other form of preparation to commit the other; or

(c) inconsistent findings of fact are required to establish the commission of the offenses; or

(d) the offenses differ only in that one is defined to prohibit a designated kind of conduct generally and the other to prohibit a specific instance of such conduct; or

(e) the offense is defined as a continuing course of conduct and the defendant's course of conduct was uninterrupted, unless the law provides that specific periods of such conduct constitute separate offenses.

(2) Limitation on Separate Trials for Multiple Offenses. Except as provided in Subsection (3) of this Section, a defendant shall not be subject to separate trials for multiple offenses based on the same conduct or arising from the same criminal episode, if such offenses are known to the appropriate prosecuting officer at the time of the commencement of the first trial and are within the jurisdiction of a single court.

(3) Authority of Court to Order Separate Trials. When a defendant is charged with two or more offenses based on the same conduct or arising from the same criminal episode, the Court, on application of the prosecuting attorney or of the defendant, may order any such charge to be tried separately, if it is satisfied that justice so requires.

(4) Conviction of Included Offense Permitted. A defendant may be convicted of an offense included in an offense charged in the indictment [or the information]. An offense is so included when:

(a) it is established by proof of the same or less than all the facts required to establish the commission of the offense charged; or

(b) it consists of an attempt or solicitation to commit the offense charged or to commit an offense otherwise included therein; or

(c) it differs from the offense charged only in the respect that a less serious injury or risk of injury to the same person, property or public interest or a lesser kind of culpability suffices to establish its commission.

(5) <u>Submission of Included Offense to Jury.</u>  The Court shall not be obligated to charge the jury with respect to an included offense unless there is a rational basis for a verdict acquitting the defendant of the offense charged and convicting him of the included offense.

### Section 1.08.  When Prosecution Barred by Former Prosecution for the Same Offense

When a prosecution is for a violation of the same provision of the statutes and is based upon the same facts as a former prosecution, it is barred by such former prosecution under the following circumstances:

(1) The former prosecution resulted in an acquittal.  There is an acquittal if the prosecution resulted in a finding of not guilty by the trier of fact or in a determination that there was insufficient evidence to warrant a conviction.  A finding of guilty of a lesser included offense is an acquittal of the greater inclusive offense, although the conviction is subsequently set aside.

(2) The former prosecution was terminated, after the information had been filed or the indictment found, by a final order or judgment for the defendant, which has not been set aside, reversed, or vacated and which necessarily required a determination inconsistent with a fact or a legal proposition that must be established for conviction of the offense.

(3) The former prosecution resulted in a conviction.  There is a conviction if the prosecution resulted in a judgment of conviction which has not been reversed or vacated, a verdict of guilty which has not been set aside and which is capable of supporting a judgment, or a plea of guilty accepted by the Court.  In the latter two cases failure to enter judgment must be for a reason other than a motion of the defendant.

(4) The former prosecution was improperly terminated.  Except as provided in this Subsection, there is an improper termination of a prosecution if the termination is for reasons not amounting to an acquittal, and it takes place after the first witness is sworn but before verdict.  Termination under any of the following circumstances is not improper:

(a) The defendant consents to the termination or waives, by motion to dismiss or otherwise, his right to object to the termination.

(b) The trial court finds that the termination is necessary because:

(1) it is physically impossible to proceed with the trial in conformity with law; or

(2) there is a legal defect in the proceedings which would make any judgment entered upon a verdict reversible as a matter of law; or

(3) prejudicial conduct, in or outside the courtroom, makes it impossible to proceed with the trial without injustice to either the defendant or the State; or

(4) the jury is unable to agree upon a verdict; or

(5) false statements of a juror on voir dire prevent a fair trial.

**A-15**

### Section 1.09.   When Prosecution Barred by Former Prosecution for Different Offense

Although a prosecution is for a violation of a different provision of the statutes than a former prosecution or is based on different facts, it is barred by such former prosecution under the following circumstances:

(1) The former prosecution resulted in an acquittal or in a conviction as defined in Section 1.08 and the subsequent prosecution is for:

(a) any offense of which the defendant could have been convicted on the first prosecution; or

(b) any offense for which the defendant should have been tried on the first prosecution under Section 1.07, unless the Court ordered a separate trial of the charge of such offense; or

(c) the same conduct, unless (i) the offense of which the defendant was formerly convicted or acquitted and the offense for which he is subsequently prosecuted each requires proof of a fact not required by the other and the law defining each of such offenses is intended to prevent a substantially different harm or evil, or (ii) the second offense was not consummated when the former trial began.

(2) The former prosecution was terminated, after the information was filed or the indictment found, by an acquittal or by a final order or judgment for the defendant which has not been set aside, reversed or vacated and which acquittal, final order or judgment necessarily required a determination inconsistent with a fact which must be established for conviction of the second offense.

(3) The former prosecution was improperly terminated, as improper termination is defined in Section 1.08, and the subsequent prosecution is for an offense of which the defendant could have been convicted had the former prosecution not been improperly terminated.

### Section 1.10.   Former Prosecution in Another Jurisdiction: When a Bar

When conduct constitutes an offense within the concurrent jurisdiction of this State and of the United States or another State, a prosecution in any such other jurisdiction is a bar to a subsequent prosecution in this State under the following circumstances:

(1) The first prosecution resulted in an acquittal or in a conviction as defined in Section 1.08 and the subsequent prosecution is based on the same conduct, unless (a) the offense of which the defendant was formerly convicted or acquitted and the offense for which he is subsequently prosecuted each requires proof of a fact not required by the other and the law defining each of such offenses is intended to prevent a substantially different harm or evil or (b) the second offense was not consummated when the former trial began; or

(2) The former prosecution was terminated, after the information was filed or the indictment found, by an acquittal or by a final order or judgment for the defendant which has not been set aside, reversed or vacated and which acquittal, final order or judgment necessarily required a determination inconsistent with a fact which must be established for conviction of the offense of which the defendant is subsequently prosecuted.

**Section 1.11.   Former Prosecution Before Court Lacking Jurisdiction or When Fraudulently Procured by the Defendant**

A prosecution is not a bar within the meaning of Sections 1.08, 1.09 and 1.10 under any of the following circumstances:

(1) The former prosecution was before a court which lacked jurisdiction over the defendant or the offense; or

(2) The former prosecution was procured by the defendant without the knowledge of the appropriate prosecuting officer and with the purpose of avoiding the sentence which might otherwise be imposed; or

(3) The former prosecution resulted in a judgment of conviction which was held invalid in a subsequent proceeding on a writ of habeas corpus, coram nobis or similar process.

**Section 1.12.   Proof Beyond a Reasonable Doubt; Affirmative Defenses; Burden of Proving Fact When Not an Element of an Offense; Presumptions**

(1) No person may be convicted of an offense unless each element of such offense is proved beyond a reasonable doubt. In the absence of such proof, the innocence of the defendant is assumed.

(2) Subsection (1) of this Section does not:

(a) require the disproof of an affirmative defense unless and until there is evidence supporting such defense; or

(b) apply to any defense which the Code or another statute plainly requires the defendant to prove by a preponderance of evidence.

(3) A ground of defense is affirmative, within the meaning of Subsection (2)(a) of this Section, when:

(a) it arises under a section of the Code which so provides; or

(b) it relates to an offense defined by a statute other than the Code and such statute so provides; or

(c) it involves a matter of excuse or justification peculiarly within the knowledge of the defendant on which he can fairly be required to adduce supporting evidence.

(4) When the application of the Code depends upon the finding of a fact which is not an element of an offense, unless the Code otherwise provides:

(a) the burden of proving the fact is on the prosecution or defendant, depending on whose interest or contention will be furthered if the finding should be made; and

(b) the fact must be proved to the satisfaction of the Court or jury, as the case may be.

(5) When the Code establishes a presumption with respect to any fact which is an element of an offense, it has the following consequences:

(a) when there is evidence of the facts which give rise to the presumption, the issue of the existence of the presumed fact must be submitted to the jury, unless the Court is satisfied that the evidence as a whole clearly negatives the presumed fact; and

**A-17**

(b) when the issue of the existence of the presumed fact is submitted to the jury, the Court shall charge that while the presumed fact must, on all the evidence, be proved beyond a reasonable doubt, the law declares that the jury may regard the facts giving rise to the presumption as sufficient evidence of the presumed fact.

(6) A presumption not established by the Code or inconsistent with it has the consequences otherwise accorded it by law.

### Section 1.13.  General Definitions

In this Code, unless a different meaning plainly is required:

(1) "statute" includes the Constitution and a local law or ordinance of a political subdivision of the State;

(2) "act" or "action" means a bodily movement whether voluntary or involuntary;

(3) "voluntary" has the meaning specified in Section 2.01;

(4) "omission" means a failure to act;

(5) "conduct" means an action or omission and its accompanying state of mind, or, where relevant, a series of acts and omissions;

(6) "actor" includes, where relevant, a person guilty of an omission;

(7) "acted" includes, where relevant, "omitted to act" ;

(8) "person," "he" and "actor" include any natural person and, where relevant, a corporation or an unincorporated association;

(9) "element of an offense" means (i) such conduct or (ii) such attendant circumstances or (iii) such a result of conduct as

(a) is included in the description of the forbidden conduct in the definition of the offense; or

(b) establishes the required kind of culpability; or

(c) negatives an excuse or justification for such conduct; or

(d) negatives a defense under the statute of limitations; or

(e) establishes jurisdiction or venue;

(10) "material element of an offense" means an element that does not relate exclusively to the statute of limitations, jurisdiction, venue or to any other matter similarly unconnected with (i) the harm or evil, incident to conduct, sought to be prevented by the law defining the offense, or (ii) the existence of a justification or excuse for such conduct;

(11) "purposely" has the meaning specified in Section 2.02 and equivalent terms such as "with purpose," "designed" or "with design" have the same meaning;

(12) "intentionally" or "with intent" means purposely;

(13) "knowingly" has the meaning specified in Section 2.02 and equivalent terms such as "knowing" or "with knowledge" have the same meaning;

(14) "recklessly" has the meaning specified in Section 2.02 and equivalent terms such as "recklessness" or "with recklessness" have the same meaning;

(15) "negligently" has the meaning specified in Section 2.02 and equivalent terms such as "negligence" or "with negligence" have the same meaning;

(16) "reasonably believes" or "reasonable belief" designates a belief which the actor is not reckless or negligent in holding.

## ARTICLE 2.  GENERAL PRINCIPLES OF LIABILITY

### Section 2.01.  Requirement of Voluntary Act; Omission as Basis of Liability; Possession as an Act

(1) A person is not guilty of an offense unless his liability is based on conduct which includes a voluntary act or the omission to perform an act of which he is physically capable.

(2) The following are not voluntary acts within the meaning of this Section:

(a) a reflex or convulsion;

(b) a bodily movement during unconsciousness or sleep;

(c) conduct during hypnosis or resulting from hypnotic suggestion;

(d) a bodily movement that otherwise is not a product of the effort or determination of the actor, either conscious or habitual.

(3) Liability for the commission of an offense may not be based on an omission unaccompanied by action unless:

(a) the omission is expressly made sufficient by the law defining the offense;  or

(b) a duty to perform the omitted act is otherwise imposed by law.

(4) Possession is an act, within the meaning of this Section, if the possessor knowingly procured or received the thing possessed or was aware of his control thereof for a sufficient period to have been able to terminate his possession.

### Section 2.02.  General Requirements of Culpability

(1) Minimum Requirements of Culpability.  Except as provided in Section 2.05, a person is not guilty of an offense unless he acted purposely, knowingly, recklessly or negligently, as the law may require, with respect to each material element of the offense.

(2) Kinds of Culpability Defined.

(a) Purposely.

A person acts purposely with respect to a material element of an offense when:

(i) if the element involves the nature of his conduct or a result thereof, it is his conscious object to engage in conduct of that nature or to cause such a result; and

(ii) if the element involves the attendant circumstances, he is aware of the existence of such circumstances or he believes or hopes that they exist.

(b) Knowingly.

A person acts knowingly with respect to a material element of an offense when:

(i) if the element involves the nature of his conduct or the attendant circumstances, he is aware that his conduct is of that nature or that such circumstances exist; and

**A-19**

(ii) if the element involves a result of his conduct, he is aware that it is practically certain that his conduct will cause such a result.

(c) _Recklessly._

A person acts recklessly with respect to a material element of an offense when he consciously disregards a substantial and unjustifiable risk that the material element exists or will result from his conduct. The risk must be of such a nature and degree that, considering the nature and purpose of the actor's conduct and the circumstances known to him, its disregard involves a gross deviation from the standard of conduct that a law-abiding person would observe in the actor's situation.

(d) _Negligently._

A person acts negligently with respect to a material element of an offense when he should be aware of a substantial and unjustifiable risk that the material element exists or will result from his conduct. The risk must be of such a nature and degree that the actor's failure to perceive it, considering the nature and purpose of his conduct and the circumstances known to him, involves a gross deviation from the standard of care that a reasonable person would observe in the actor's situation.

(3) _Culpability Required Unless Otherwise Provided._ When the culpability sufficient to establish a material element of an offense is not prescribed by law, such element is established if a person acts purposely, knowingly or recklessly with respect thereto.

(4) _Prescribed Culpability Requirement Applies to All Material Elements._ When the law defining an offense prescribes the kind of culpability that is sufficient for the commission of an offense, without distinguishing among the material elements thereof, such provision shall apply to all the material elements of the offense, unless a contrary purpose plainly appears.

(5) _Substitutes for Negligence, Recklessness and Knowledge._ When the law provides that negligence suffices to establish an element of an offense, such element also is established if a person acts purposely, knowingly or recklessly. When recklessness suffices to establish an element, such element also is established if a person acts purposely or knowingly. When acting knowingly suffices to establish an element, such element also is established if a person acts purposely.

(6) _Requirement of Purpose Satisfied if Purpose Is Conditional._ When a particular purpose is an element of an offense, the element is established although such purpose is conditional, unless the condition negatives the harm or evil sought to be prevented by the law defining the offense.

(7) _Requirement of Knowledge Satisfied by Knowledge of High Probability._ When knowledge of the existence of a particular fact is an element of an offense, such knowledge is established if a person is aware of a high probability of its existence, unless he actually believes that it does not exist.

(8) _Requirement of Wilfulness Satisfied by Acting Knowingly._ A requirement that an offense be committed wilfully is satisfied if a person acts knowingly with respect to the material elements of the offense, unless a purpose to impose further requirements appears.

(9) _Culpability as to Illegality of Conduct._ Neither knowledge nor recklessness or negligence as to whether conduct constitutes an offense or as to the existence, meaning or application of the law determining the elements of an offense is an element of such offense, unless the definition of the offense or the Code so provides.

(10) Culpability as Determinant of Grade of Offense. When the grade or degree of an offense depends on whether the offense is committed purposely, knowingly, recklessly or negligently, its grade or degree shall be the lowest for which the determinative kind of culpability is established with respect to any material element of the offense.

**Section 2.03.  Causal Relationship Between Conduct and Result;  Divergence Between Result Designed or Contemplated and Actual Result or Between Probable and Actual Result**

(1) Conduct is the cause of a result when:

(a) it is an antecedent but for which the result in question would not have occurred; and

(b) the relationship between the conduct and result satisfies any additional causal requirements imposed by the Code or by the law defining the offense.

(2) When purposely or knowingly causing a particular result is an element of an offense, the element is not established if the actual result is not within the purpose or the contemplation of the actor unless:

(a) the actual result differs from that designed or contemplated, as the case may be, only in the respect that a different person or different property is injured or affected or that the injury or harm designed or contemplated would have been more serious or more extensive than that caused; or

(b) the actual result involves the same kind of injury or harm as that designed or contemplated and is not too remote or accidental in its occurrence to have a [just] bearing on the actor's liability or on the gravity of his offense.

(3) When recklessly or negligently causing a particular result is an element of an offense, the element is not established if the actual result is not within the risk of which the actor is aware or, in the case of negligence, of which he should be aware unless:

(a) the actual result differs from the probable result only in the respect that a different person or different property is injured or affected or that the probable injury or harm would have been more serious or more extensive than that caused; or

(b) the actual result involves the same kind of injury or harm as the probable result and is not too remote or accidental in its occurrence to have a [just] bearing on the actor's liability or on the gravity of his offense.

(4) When causing a particular result is a material element of an offense for which absolute liability is imposed by law, the element is not established unless the actual result is a probable consequence of the actor's conduct.

**Section 2.04.  Ignorance or Mistake**

(1) Ignorance or mistake as to a matter of fact or law is a defense if:

(a) the ignorance or mistake negatives the purpose, knowledge, belief, recklessness or negligence required to establish a material element of the offense; or

(b) the law provides that the state of mind established by such ignorance or mistake constitutes a defense.

**A-21**

(2) Although ignorance or mistake would otherwise afford a defense to the offense charged, the defense is not available if the defendant would be guilty of another offense had the situation been as he supposed. In such case, however, the ignorance or mistake of the defendant shall reduce the grade and degree of the offense of which he may be convicted to those of the offense of which he would be guilty had the situation been as he supposed.

(3) A belief that conduct does not legally constitute an offense is a defense to a prosecution for that offense based upon such conduct when:

(a) the statute or other enactment defining the offense is not known to the actor and has not been published or otherwise reasonably made available prior to the conduct alleged; or

(b) he acts in reasonable reliance upon an official statement of the law, afterward determined to be invalid or erroneous, contained in (i) a statute or other enactment; (ii) a judicial decision, opinion or judgment; (iii) an administrative order or grant of permission; or (iv) an official interpretation of the public officer or body charged by law with responsibility for the interpretation, administration or enforcement of the law defining the offense.

(4) The defendant must prove a defense arising under Subsection (3) of this Section by a preponderance of evidence.

### Section 2.05.  When Culpability Requirements Are Inapplicable to Violations and to Offenses Defined by Other Statutes; Effect of Absolute Liability in Reducing Grade of Offense to Violation

(1) The requirements of culpability prescribed by Sections 2.01 and 2.02 do not apply to:

(a) offenses which constitute violations, unless the requirement involved is included in the definition of the offense or the Court determines that its application is consistent with effective enforcement of the law defining the offense; or

(b) offenses defined by statutes other than the Code, insofar as a legislative purpose to impose absolute liability for such offenses or with respect to any material element thereof plainly appears.

(2) Notwithstanding any other provision of existing law and unless a subsequent statute otherwise provides:

(a) when absolute liability is imposed with respect to any material element of an offense defined by a statute other than the Code and a conviction is based upon such liability, the offense constitutes a violation; and

(b) although absolute liability is imposed by law with respect to one or more of the material elements of an offense defined by a statute other than the Code, the culpable commission of the offense may be charged and proved, in which event negligence with respect to such elements constitutes sufficient culpability and the classification of the offense and the sentence that may be imposed therefor upon conviction are determined by Section 1.04 and Article 6 of the Code.

## Section 2.06.  Liability for Conduct of Another;  Complicity

(1) A person is guilty of an offense if it is committed by his own conduct or by the conduct of another person for which he is legally accountable, or both.

(2) A person is legally accountable for the conduct of another person when:

(a) acting with the kind of culpability that is sufficient for the commission of the offense, he causes an innocent or irresponsible person to engage in such conduct; or

(b) he is made accountable for the conduct of such other person by the Code or by the law defining the offense; or

(c) he is an accomplice of such other person in the commission of the offense.

(3) A person is an accomplice of another person in the commission of an offense if:

(a) with the purpose of promoting or facilitating the commission of the offense, he

(i) solicits such other person to commit it;  or

(ii) aids or agrees or attempts to aid such other person in planning or committing it;  or

(iii) having a legal duty to prevent the commission of the offense, fails to make proper effort so to do;  or

(b) his conduct is expressly declared by law to establish his complicity.

(4) When causing a particular result is an element of an offense, an accomplice in the conduct causing such result is an accomplice in the commission of that offense, if he acts with the kind of culpability, if any, with respect to that result that is sufficient for the commission of the offense.

(5) A person who is legally incapable of committing a particular offense himself may be guilty thereof if it is committed by the conduct of another person for which he is legally accountable, unless such liability is inconsistent with the purpose of the provision establishing his incapacity.

(6) Unless otherwise provided by the Code or by the law defining the offense, a person is not an accomplice in an offense committed by another person if:

(a) he is a victim of that offense;  or

(b) the offense is so defined that his conduct is inevitably incident to its commission;  or

(c) he terminates his complicity prior to the commission of the offense and

(i) wholly deprives it of effectiveness in the commission of the offense;  or

(ii) gives timely warning to the law enforcement authorities or otherwise makes proper effort to prevent the commission of the offense.

(7) An accomplice may be convicted on proof of the commission of the offense and of his complicity therein, though the person claimed to have committed the offense has not been prosecuted or convicted or has been convicted of a different offense or degree of offense or has an immunity to prosecution or conviction or has been acquitted.

**Section 2.07.   Liability of Corporations, Unincorporated Associations and Persons Acting, or Under a Duty to Act, in Their Behalf**

(1) A corporation may be convicted of the commission of an offense if:

(a) the offense is a violation or the offense is defined by a statute other than the Code in which a legislative purpose to impose liability on corporations plainly appears and the conduct is performed by an agent of the corporation acting in behalf of the corporation within the scope of his office or employment, except that if the law defining the offense designates the agents for whose conduct the corporation is accountable or the circumstances under which it is accountable, such provisions shall apply;  or

(b) the offense consists of an omission to discharge a specific duty of affirmative performance imposed on corporations by law;  or

(c) the commission of the offense was authorized, requested, commanded, performed or recklessly tolerated by the board of directors or by a high managerial agent acting in behalf of the corporation within the scope of his office or employment.

(2) When absolute liability is imposed for the commission of an offense, a legislative purpose to impose liability on a corporation shall be assumed, unless the contrary plainly appears.

(3) An unincorporated association may be convicted of the commission of an offense if:

(a) the offense is defined by a statute other than the Code which expressly provides for the liability of such an association and the conduct is performed by an agent of the association acting in behalf of the association within the scope of his office or employment, except that if the law defining the offense designates the agents for whose conduct the association is accountable or the circumstances under which it is accountable, such provisions shall apply;  or

(b) the offense consists of an omission to discharge a specific duty of affirmative performance imposed on associations by law.

(4) As used in this Section:

(a) "corporation" does not include an entity organized as or by a governmental agency for the execution of a governmental program;

(b) "agent" means any director, officer, servant, employee or other person authorized to act in behalf of the corporation or association and, in the case of an unincorporated association, a member of such association;

(c) "high managerial agent" means an officer of a corporation or an unincorporated association, or, in the case of a partnership, a partner, or any other agent of a corporation or association having duties of such responsibility that his conduct may fairly be assumed to represent the policy of the corporation or association.

(5) In any prosecution of a corporation or an unincorporated association for the commission of an offense included within the terms of Subsection (1)(a) or Subsection (3)(a) of this Section, other than an offense for which absolute liability has been imposed, it shall be a defense if the defendant proves by a preponderance of evidence that the high managerial agent having supervisory responsibility over the subject matter of the offense employed due diligence to prevent its commission.

This paragraph shall not apply if it is plainly inconsistent with the legislative purpose in defining the particular offense.

(6)(a) A person is legally accountable for any conduct he performs or causes to be performed in the name of the corporation or an unincorporated association or in its behalf to the same extent as if it were performed in his own name or behalf.

(b) Whenever a duty to act is imposed by law upon a corporation or an unincorporated association, any agent of the corporation or association having primary responsibility for the discharge of the duty is legally accountable for a reckless omission to perform the required act to the same extent as if the duty were imposed by law directly upon himself.

(c) When a person is convicted of an offense by reason of his legal accountability for the conduct of a corporation or an unincorporated association, he is subject to the sentence authorized by law when a natural person is convicted of an offense of the grade and the degree involved.

### Section 2.08.   Intoxication

(1) Except as provided in Subsection (4) of this Section, intoxication of the actor is not a defense unless it negatives an element of the offense.

(2) When recklessness establishes an element of the offense, if the actor, due to self-induced intoxication, is unaware of a risk of which he would have been aware had he been sober, such unawareness is immaterial.

(3) Intoxication does not, in itself, constitute mental disease within the meaning of Section 4.01.

(4) Intoxication which (a) is not self-induced or (b) is pathological is an affirmative defense if by reason of such intoxication the actor at the time of his conduct lacks substantial capacity either to appreciate its criminality [wrongfulness] or to conform his conduct to the requirements of law.

(5) Definitions.   In this Section unless a different meaning plainly is required:

(a) "intoxication" means a disturbance of mental or physical capacities resulting from the introduction of substances into the body;

(b) "self-induced intoxication" means intoxication caused by substances which the actor knowingly introduces into his body, the tendency of which to cause intoxication he knows or ought to know, unless he introduces them pursuant to medical advice or under such circumstances as would afford a defense to a charge of crime;

(c) "pathological intoxication" means intoxication grossly excessive in degree, given the amount of the intoxicant, to which the actor does not know he is susceptible.

### Section 2.09.   Duress

(1) It is an affirmative defense that the actor engaged in the conduct charged to constitute an offense because he was coerced to do so by the use of, or a threat to use, unlawful force against his person or the person of another, which a person of reasonable firmness in his situation would have been unable to resist.

(2) The defense provided by this Section is unavailable if the actor recklessly placed himself in a situation in which it was probable that he would be subjected to duress.   The defense is also unavailable if he was negligent in placing himself in

such a situation, whenever negligence suffices to establish culpability for the offense charged.

(3) It is not a defense that a woman acted on the command of her husband, unless she acted under such coercion as would establish a defense under this Section. [The presumption that a woman, acting in the presence of her husband, is coerced is abolished.]

(4) When the conduct of the actor would otherwise be justifiable under Section 3.02, this Section does not preclude such defense.

### Section 2.10.  Military Orders

It is an affirmative defense that the actor, in engaging in the conduct charged to constitute an offense, does no more than execute an order of his superior in the armed services which he does not know to be unlawful.

### Section 2.11.  Consent

(1) In General.  The consent of the victim to conduct charged to constitute an offense or to the result thereof is a defense if such consent negatives an element of the offense or precludes the infliction of the harm or evil sought to be prevented by the law defining the offense.

(2) Consent to Bodily Harm.  When conduct is charged to constitute an offense because it causes or threatens bodily harm, consent to such conduct or to the infliction of such harm is a defense if:

(a) the bodily harm consented to or threatened by the conduct consented to is not serious; or

(b) the conduct and the harm are reasonably foreseeable hazards of joint participation in a lawful athletic contest or competitive sport; or

(c) the consent establishes a justification for the conduct under Article 3 of the Code.

(3) Ineffective Consent.  Unless otherwise provided by the Code or by the law defining the offense, assent does not constitute consent if:

(a) it is given by a person who is legally incompetent to authorize the conduct charged to constitute the offense; or

(b) it is given by a person who by reason of youth, mental disease or defect or intoxication is manifestly unable or known by the actor to be unable to make a reasonable judgment as to the nature or harmfulness of the conduct charged to constitute the offense; or

(c) it is given by a person whose improvident consent is sought to be prevented by the law defining the offense; or

(d) it is induced by force, duress or deception of a kind sought to be prevented by the law defining the offense.

### Section 2.12.  De Minimis Infractions

The Court shall dismiss a prosecution if, having regard to the nature of the conduct charged to constitute an offense and the nature of the attendant circumstances, it finds that the defendant's conduct:

(1) was within a customary license or tolerance, neither expressly negatived by the person whose interest was infringed nor inconsistent with the purpose of the law defining the offense; or

(2) did not actually cause or threaten the harm or evil sought to be prevented by the law defining the offense or did so only to an extent too trivial to warrant the condemnation of conviction; or

(3) presents such other extenuations that it cannot reasonably be regarded as envisaged by the legislature in forbidding the offense.

The Court shall not dismiss a prosecution under Subsection (3) of this Section without filing a written statement of its reasons.

## Section 2.13.  Entrapment

(1) A public law enforcement official or a person acting in cooperation with such an official perpetrates an entrapment if for the purpose of obtaining evidence of the commission of an offense, he induces or encourages another person to engage in conduct constituting such offense by either:

(a) making knowingly false representations designed to induce the belief that such conduct is not prohibited; or

(b) employing methods of persuasion or inducement which create a substantial risk that such an offense will be committed by persons other than those who are ready to commit it.

(2) Except as provided in Subsection (3) of this Section, a person prosecuted for an offense shall be acquitted if he proves by a preponderance of evidence that his conduct occurred in response to an entrapment.  The issue of entrapment shall be tried by the Court in the absence of the jury.

(3) The defense afforded by this Section is unavailable when causing or threatening bodily injury is an element of the offense charged and the prosecution is based on conduct causing or threatening such injury to a person other than the person perpetrating the entrapment.

## ARTICLE 3.   GENERAL PRINCIPLES OF JUSTIFICATION

## Section 3.01.   Justification an Affirmative Defense;  Civil Remedies Unaffected

(1) In any prosecution based on conduct which is justifiable under this Article, justification is an affirmative defense.

(2) The fact that conduct is justifiable under this Article does not abolish or impair any remedy for such conduct which is available in any civil action.

## Section 3.02.  Justification Generally:  Choice of Evils

(1) Conduct which the actor believes to be necessary to avoid a harm or evil to himself or to another is justifiable, provided that:

(a) the harm or evil sought to be avoided by such conduct is greater than that sought to be prevented by the law defining the offense charged;  and

(b) neither the Code nor other law defining the offense provides exceptions or defenses dealing with the specific situation involved;  and

**A-27**

(c) a legislative purpose to exclude the justification claimed does not otherwise plainly appear.

(2) When the actor was reckless or negligent in bringing about the situation requiring a choice of harms or evils or in appraising the necessity for his conduct, the justification afforded by this Section is unavailable in a prosecution for any offense for which recklessness or negligence, as the case may be, suffices to establish culpability.

### Section 3.03.  Execution of Public Duty

(1) Except as provided in Subsection (2) of this Section, conduct is justifiable when it is required or authorized by:

(a) the law defining the duties or functions of a public officer or the assistance to be rendered to such officer in the performance of his duties;  or

(b) the law governing the execution of legal process;  or

(c) the judgment or order of a competent court or tribunal;  or

(d) the law governing the armed services or the lawful conduct of war;  or

(e) any other provision of law imposing a public duty.

(2) The other sections of this Article apply to:

(a) the use of force upon or toward the person of another for any of the purposes dealt with in such sections;  and

(b) the use of deadly force for any purpose, unless the use of such force is otherwise expressly authorized by law or occurs in the lawful conduct of war.

(3) The justification afforded by Subsection (1) of this Section applies:

(a) when the actor believes his conduct to be required or authorized by the judgment or direction of a competent court or tribunal or in the lawful execution of legal process, notwithstanding lack of jurisdiction of the court or defect in the legal process;  and

(b) when the actor believes his conduct to be required or authorized to assist a public officer in the performance of his duties, notwithstanding that the officer exceeded his legal authority.

### Section 3.04.  Use of Force in Self–Protection

(1) Use of Force Justifiable for Protection of the Person.  Subject to the provisions of this Section and of Section 3.09, the use of force upon or toward another person is justifiable when the actor believes that such force is immediately necessary for the purpose of protecting himself against the use of unlawful force by such other person on the present occasion.

(2) Limitations on Justifying Necessity for Use of Force.

(a) The use of force is not justifiable under this Section:

(i) to resist an arrest which the actor knows is being made by a peace officer, although the arrest is unlawful;  or

(ii) to resist force used by the occupier or possessor of property or by another person on his behalf, where the actor knows that the person using the force is doing so under a claim of right to protect the property, except that this limitation shall not apply if:

(1) the actor is a public officer acting in the performance of his duties or a person lawfully assisting him therein or a person making or assisting in a lawful arrest; or

(2) the actor has been unlawfully dispossessed of the property and is making a re-entry or recaption justified by Section 3.06; or

(3) the actor believes that such force is necessary to protect himself against death or serious bodily harm.

(b) The use of deadly force is not justifiable under this Section unless the actor believes that such force is necessary to protect himself against death, serious bodily harm, kidnapping or sexual intercourse compelled by force or threat; nor is it justifiable if:

(i) the actor, with the purpose of causing death or serious bodily harm, provoked the use of force against himself in the same encounter; or

(ii) the actor knows that he can avoid the necessity of using such force with complete safety by retreating or by surrendering possession of a thing to a person asserting a claim of right thereto or by complying with a demand that he abstain from any action which he has no duty to take, except that:

(1) the actor is not obliged to retreat from his dwelling or place of work, unless he was the initial aggressor or is assailed in his place of work by another person whose place of work the actor knows it to be; and

(2) a public officer justified in using force in the performance of his duties or a person justified in using force in his assistance or a person justified in using force in making an arrest or preventing an escape is not obliged to desist from efforts to perform such duty, effect such arrest or prevent such escape because of resistance or threatened resistance by or on behalf of the person against whom such action is directed.

(c) Except as required by paragraphs (a) and (b) of this Subsection, a person employing protective force may estimate the necessity thereof under the circumstances as he believes them to be when the force is used, without retreating, surrendering possession, doing any other act which he has no legal duty to do or abstaining from any lawful action.

(3) Use of Confinement as Protective Force. The justification afforded by this Section extends to the use of confinement as protective force only if the actor takes all reasonable measures to terminate the confinement as soon as he knows that he safely can, unless the person confined has been arrested on a charge of crime.

## Section 3.05.  Use of Force for the Protection of Other Persons

(1) Subject to the provisions of this Section and of Section 3.09, the use of force upon or toward the person of another is justifiable to protect a third person when:

(a) the actor would be justified under Section 3.04 in using such force to protect himself against the injury he believes to be threatened to the person whom he seeks to protect; and

(b) under the circumstances as the actor believes them to be, the person whom he seeks to protect would be justified in using such protective force; and

(c) the actor believes that his intervention is necessary for the protection of such other person.

(2) Notwithstanding Subsection (1) of this Section:

(a) when the actor would be obliged under Section 3.04 to retreat, to surrender the possession of a thing or to comply with a demand before using force in self-protection, he is not obliged to do so before using force for the protection of another person, unless he knows that he can thereby secure the complete safety of such other person; and

(b) when the person whom the actor seeks to protect would be obliged under Section 3.04 to retreat, to surrender the possession of a thing or to comply with a demand if he knew that he could obtain complete safety by so doing, the actor is obliged to try to cause him to do so before using force in his protection if the actor knows that he can obtain complete safety in that way; and

(c) neither the actor nor the person whom he seeks to protect is obliged to retreat when in the other's dwelling or place of work to any greater extent than in his own.

### Section 3.06. Use of Force for the Protection of Property

(1) Use of Force Justifiable for Protection of Property. Subject to the provisions of this Section and of Section 3.09, the use of force upon or toward the person of another is justifiable when the actor believes that such force is immediately necessary:

(a) to prevent or terminate an unlawful entry or other trespass upon land or a trespass against or the unlawful carrying away of tangible, movable property, provided that such land or movable property is, or is believed by the actor to be, in his possession or in the possession of another person for whose protection he acts; or

(b) to effect an entry or re-entry upon land or to retake tangible movable property, provided that the actor believes that he or the person by whose authority he acts or a person from whom he or such other person derives title was unlawfully dispossessed of such land or movable property and is entitled to possession, and provided, further, that:

(i) the force is used immediately or on fresh pursuit after such dispossession; or

(ii) the actor believes that the person against whom he uses force has no claim of right to the possession of the property and, in the case of land, the circumstances, as the actor believes them to be, are of such urgency that it would be an exceptional hardship to postpone the entry or re-entry until a court order is obtained.

(2) Meaning of Possession. For the purposes of Subsection (1) of this Section:

(a) a person who has parted with the custody of property to another who refuses to restore it to him is no longer in possession, unless the property is movable and was and still is located on land in his possession;

(b) a person who has been dispossessed of land does not regain possession thereof merely by setting foot thereon;

(c) a person who has a license to use or occupy real property is deemed to be in possession thereof except against the licensor acting under claim of right.

(3) Limitations on Justifiable Use of Force.

(a) Request to Desist.   The use of force is justifiable under this Section only if the actor first requests the person against whom such force is used to desist from his interference with the property, unless the actor believes that:

(i) such request would be useless; or

(ii) it would be dangerous to himself or another person to make the request; or

(iii) substantial harm will be done to the physical condition of the property which is sought to be protected before the request can effectively be made.

(b) Exclusion of Trespasser.   The use of force to prevent or terminate a trespass is not justifiable under this Section if the actor knows that the exclusion of the trespasser will expose him to substantial danger or serious bodily harm.

(c) Resistance of Lawful Re-entry or Recaption.   The use of force to prevent an entry or re-entry upon land or the recaption of movable property is not justifiable under this Section, although the actor believes that such re-entry or recaption is unlawful, if:

(i) the re-entry or recaption is made by or on behalf of a person who was actually dispossessed of the property; and

(ii) it is otherwise justifiable under paragraph (1)(b) of this Section.

(d) Use of Deadly Force.   The use of deadly force is not justifiable under this Section unless the actor believes that:

(i) the person against whom the force is used is attempting to dispossess him of his dwelling otherwise than under a claim of right to its possession; or

(ii) the person against whom the force is used is attempting to commit or consummate arson, burglary, robbery or other felonious theft or property destruction and either:

(1) has employed or threatened deadly force against or in the presence of the actor; or

(2) the use of force other than deadly force to prevent the commission or the consummation of the crime would expose the actor or another in his presence to substantial danger of serious bodily harm.

(4) Use of Confinement as Protective Force.   The justification afforded by this Section extends to the use of confinement as protective force only if the actor takes all reasonable measures to terminate the confinement as soon as he knows that he can do so with safety to the property, unless the person confined has been arrested on a charge of crime.

(5) Use of Device to Protect Property.   The justification afforded by this Section extends to the use of a device for the purpose of protecting property only if:

(a) the device is not designed to cause or known to create a substantial risk of causing death or serious bodily harm; and

**A-31**

(b) the use of the particular device to protect the property from entry or trespass is reasonable under the circumstances, as the actor believes them to be; and

(c) the device is one customarily used for such a purpose or reasonable care is taken to make known to probable intruders the fact that it is used.

(6) Use of Force to Pass Wrongful Obstructor. The use of force to pass a person whom the actor believes to be purposely or knowingly and unjustifiably obstructing the actor from going to a place to which he may lawfully go is justifiable, provided that:

(a) the actor believes that the person against whom he uses force has no claim of right to obstruct the actor; and

(b) the actor is not being obstructed from entry or movement on land which he knows to be in the possession or custody of the person obstructing him, or in the possession or custody of another person by whose authority the obstructor acts, unless the circumstances, as the actor believes them to be, are of such urgency that it would not be reasonable to postpone the entry or movement on such land until a court order is obtained; and

(c) the force used is not greater than would be justifiable if the person obstructing the actor were using force against him to prevent his passage.

**Section 3.07.  Use of Force in Law Enforcement**

(1) Use of Force Justifiable to Effect an Arrest. Subject to the provisions of this Section and of Section 3.09, the use of force upon or toward the person of another is justifiable when the actor is making or assisting in making an arrest and the actor believes that such force is immediately necessary to effect a lawful arrest.

(2) Limitations on the Use of Force.

(a) The use of force is not justifiable under this Section unless:

(i) the actor makes known the purpose of the arrest or believes that it is otherwise known by or cannot reasonably be made known to the person to be arrested; and

(ii) when the arrest is made under a warrant, the warrant is valid or believed by the actor to be valid.

(b) The use of deadly force is not justifiable under this Section unless:

(i) the arrest is for a felony; and

(ii) the person effecting the arrest is authorized to act as a peace officer or is assisting a person whom he believes to be authorized to act as a peace officer; and

(iii) the actor believes that the force employed creates no substantial risk of injury to innocent persons; and

(iv) the actor believes that:

(1) the crime for which the arrest is made involved conduct including the use or threatened use of deadly force; or

(2) there is a substantial risk that the person to be arrested will cause death or serious bodily harm if his apprehension is delayed.

(3) Use of Force to Prevent Escape From Custody. The use of force to prevent the escape of an arrested person from custody is justifiable when the force could justifiably have been employed to effect the arrest under which the person is in custody, except that a guard or other person authorized to act as a peace officer is justified in using any force, including deadly force, which he believes to be immediately necessary to prevent the escape of a person from a jail, prison, or other institution for the detention of persons charged with or convicted of a crime.

(4) Use of Force by Private Person Assisting an Unlawful Arrest.

(a) A private person who is summoned by a peace officer to assist in effecting an unlawful arrest, is justified in using any force which he would be justified in using if the arrest were lawful, provided that he does not believe the arrest is unlawful.

(b) A private person who assists another private person in effecting an unlawful arrest, or who, not being summoned, assists a peace officer in effecting an unlawful arrest, is justified in using any force which he would be justified in using if the arrest were lawful, provided that (i) he believes the arrest is lawful, and (ii) the arrest would be lawful if the facts were as he believes them to be.

(5) Use of Force to Prevent Suicide or the Commission of a Crime.

(a) The use of force upon or toward the person of another is justifiable when the actor believes that such force is immediately necessary to prevent such other person from committing suicide, inflicting serious bodily harm upon himself, committing or consummating the commission of a crime involving or threatening bodily harm, damage to or loss of property or a breach of the peace, except that:

(i) any limitations imposed by the other provisions of this Article on the justifiable use of force in self-protection, for the protection of others, the protection of property, the effectuation of an arrest or the prevention of an escape from custody shall apply notwithstanding the criminality of the conduct against which such force is used; and

(ii) the use of deadly force is not in any event justifiable under this Subsection unless:

(1) the actor believes that there is a substantial risk that the person whom he seeks to prevent from committing a crime will cause death or serious bodily harm to another unless the commission or the consummation of the crime is prevented and that the use of such force presents no substantial risk of injury to innocent persons; or

(2) the actor believes that the use of such force is necessary to suppress a riot or mutiny after the rioters or mutineers have been ordered to disperse and warned, in any particular manner that the law may require, that such force will be used if they do not obey.

(b) The justification afforded by this Subsection extends to the use of confinement as preventive force only if the actor takes all reasonable measures to terminate the confinement as soon as he knows that he safely can, unless the person confined has been arrested on a charge of crime.

**A-33**

### Section 3.08.   Use of Force by Persons With Special Responsibility for Care, Discipline or Safety of Others

The use of force upon or toward the person of another is justifiable if:

(1) the actor is the parent or guardian or other person similarly responsible for the general care and supervision of a minor or a person acting at the request of such parent, guardian or other responsible person and:

(a) the force is used for the purpose of safeguarding or promoting the welfare of the minor, including the prevention or punishment of his misconduct; and

(b) the force used is not designed to cause or known to create a substantial risk of causing death, serious bodily harm, disfigurement, extreme pain or mental distress or gross degradation; or

(2) the actor is a teacher or a person otherwise entrusted with the care or supervision for a special purpose of a minor and:

(a) the actor believes that the force used is necessary to further such special purpose, including the maintenance of reasonable discipline in a school, class or other group, and that the use of such force is consistent with the welfare of the minor; and

(b) the degree of force, if it had been used by the parent or guardian of the minor, would not be unjustifiable under Subsection (1)(b) of this Section; or

(3) the actor is the guardian or other person similarly responsible for the general care and supervision of an incompetent person; and:

(a) the force is used for the purpose of safeguarding or promoting the welfare of the incompetent person, including the prevention of his misconduct, or, when such incompetent person is in a hospital or other institution for his care and custody, for the maintenance of reasonable discipline in such institution; and

(b) the force used is not designed to cause or known to create a substantial risk of causing death, serious bodily harm, disfigurement, extreme or unnecessary pain, mental distress, or humiliation; or

(4) the actor is a doctor or other therapist or a person assisting him at his direction, and:

(a) the force is used for the purpose of administering a recognized form of treatment which the actor believes to be adapted to promoting the physical or mental health of the patient; and

(b) the treatment is administered with the consent of the patient or, if the patient is a minor or an incompetent person, with the consent of his parent or guardian or other person legally competent to consent in his behalf, or the treatment is administered in an emergency when the actor believes that no one competent to consent can be consulted and that a reasonable person, wishing to safeguard the welfare of the patient, would consent; or

(5) the actor is a warden or other authorized official of a correctional institution, and:

(a) he believes that the force used is necessary for the purpose of enforcing the lawful rules or procedures of the institution, unless his belief in the lawfulness of the rule or procedure sought to be enforced is erroneous and his error is due to ignorance or mistake as to the provisions of the Code, any other provision of the criminal law or the law governing the administration of the institution; and

(b) the nature or degree of force used is not forbidden by Article 303 or 304 of the Code; and

(c) if deadly force is used, its use is otherwise justifiable under this Article; or

(6) the actor is a person responsible for the safety of a vessel or an aircraft or a person acting at his direction, and:

(a) he believes that the force used is necessary to prevent interference with the operation of the vessel or aircraft or obstruction of the execution of a lawful order, unless his belief in the lawfulness of the order is erroneous and his error is due to ignorance or mistake as to the law defining his authority; and

(b) if deadly force is used, its use is otherwise justifiable under this Article; or

(7) the actor is a person who is authorized or required by law to maintain order or decorum in a vehicle, train or other carrier or in a place where others are assembled, and:

(a) he believes that the force used is necessary for such purpose; and

(b) the force used is not designed to cause or known to create a substantial risk of causing death, bodily harm, or extreme mental distress.

### Section 3.09.  Mistake of Law as to Unlawfulness of Force or Legality of Arrest; Reckless or Negligent Use of Otherwise Justifiable Force; Reckless or Negligent Injury or Risk of Injury to Innocent Persons

(1) The justification afforded by Sections 3.04 to 3.07, inclusive, is unavailable when:

(a) the actor's belief in the unlawfulness of the force or conduct against which he employs protective force or his belief in the lawfulness of an arrest which he endeavors to effect by force is erroneous; and

(b) his error is due to ignorance or mistake as to the provisions of the Code, any other provision of the criminal law or the law governing the legality of an arrest or search.

(2) When the actor believes that the use of force upon or toward the person of another is necessary for any of the purposes for which such belief would establish a justification under Sections 3.03 to 3.08 but the actor is reckless or negligent in having such belief or in acquiring or failing to acquire any knowledge or belief which is material to the justifiability of his use of force, the justification afforded by those Sections is unavailable in a prosecution for an offense for which recklessness or negligence, as the case may be, suffices to establish culpability.

(3) When the actor is justified under Sections 3.03 to 3.08 in using force upon or toward the person of another but he recklessly or negligently injures or creates a risk of injury to innocent persons, the justification afforded by those Sections is unavailable in a prosecution for such recklessness or negligence towards innocent persons.

### Section 3.10.  Justification in Property Crimes

Conduct involving the appropriation, seizure or destruction of, damage to, intrusion on or interference with property is justifiable under circumstances which would establish a defense of privilege in a civil action based thereon, unless:

(1) the Code or the law defining the offense deals with the specific situation involved;  or

(2) a legislative purpose to exclude the justification claimed otherwise plainly appears.

### Section 3.11.  Definitions

In this Article, unless a different meaning plainly is required:

(1) "unlawful force" means force, including confinement, which is employed without the consent of the person against whom it is directed and the employment of which constitutes an offense or actionable tort or would constitute such offense or tort except for a defense (such as the absence of intent, negligence, or mental capacity;  duress;  youth;  or diplomatic status) not amounting to a privilege to use the force.  Assent constitutes consent, within the meaning of this Section, whether or not it otherwise is legally effective, except assent to the infliction of death or serious bodily harm.

(2) "deadly force" means force which the actor uses with the purpose of causing or which he knows to create a substantial risk of causing death or serious bodily harm.  Purposely firing a firearm in the direction of another person or at a vehicle in which another person is believed to be constitutes deadly force.  A threat to cause death or serious bodily harm, by the production of a weapon or otherwise, so long as the actor's purpose is limited to creating an apprehension that he will use deadly force if necessary, does not constitute deadly force;

(3) "dwelling" means any building or structure, though movable or temporary, or a portion thereof, which is for the time being the actor's home or place of lodging.

### ARTICLE 4.   RESPONSIBILITY

### Section 4.01.  Mental Disease or Defect Excluding Responsibility

(1) A person is not responsible for criminal conduct if at the time of such conduct as a result of mental disease or defect he lacks substantial capacity either to appreciate the criminality [wrongfulness] of his conduct or to conform his conduct to the requirements of law.

(2) As used in this Article, the terms "mental disease or defect" do not include an abnormality manifested only by repeated criminal or otherwise anti-social conduct.

### Section 4.02.   Evidence of Mental Disease or Defect Admissible When Relevant to Element of the Offense; [Mental Disease or Defect Impairing Capacity as Ground for Mitigation of Punishment in Capital Cases]

(1) Evidence that the defendant suffered from a mental disease or defect is admissible whenever it is relevant to prove that the defendant did or did not have a state of mind which is an element of the offense.

[(2) Whenever the jury or the Court is authorized to determine or to recommend whether or not the defendant shall be sentenced to death or imprisonment upon conviction, evidence that the capacity of the defendant to appreciate the criminality [wrongfulness] of his conduct or to conform his conduct to the requirements of law was impaired as a result of mental disease or defect is admissible in favor of sentence of imprisonment.]

## Section 4.03.  Mental Disease or Defect Excluding Responsibility Is Affirmative Defense; Requirement of Notice; Form of Verdict and Judgment When Finding of Irresponsibility Is Made

(1) Mental disease or defect excluding responsibility is an affirmative defense.

(2) Evidence of mental disease or defect excluding responsibility is not admissible unless the defendant, at the time of entering his plea of not guilty or within ten days thereafter or at such later time as the Court may for good cause permit, files a written notice of his purpose to rely on such defense.

(3) When the defendant is acquitted on the ground of mental disease or defect excluding responsibility, the verdict and the judgment shall so state.

## Section 4.04.  Mental Disease or Defect Excluding Fitness to Proceed

No person who as a result of mental disease or defect lacks capacity to understand the proceedings against him or to assist in his own defense shall be tried, convicted or sentenced for the commission of an offense so long as such incapacity endures.

## Section 4.05.  Psychiatric Examination of Defendant With Respect to Mental Disease or Defect

(1) Whenever the defendant has filed a notice of intention to rely on the defense of mental disease or defect excluding responsibility, or there is reason to doubt his fitness to proceed, or reason to believe that mental disease or defect of the defendant will otherwise become an issue in the cause, the Court shall appoint at least one qualified psychiatrist or shall request the Superintendent of the _____ Hospital to designate at least one qualified psychiatrist, which designation may be or include himself, to examine and report upon the mental condition of the defendant.  The Court may order the defendant to be committed to a hospital or other suitable facility for the purpose of the examination for a period of not exceeding sixty days or such longer period as the Court determines to be necessary for the purpose and may direct that a qualified psychiatrist retained by the defendant be permitted to witness and participate in the examination.

(2) In such examination any method may be employed which is accepted by the medical profession for the examination of those alleged to be suffering from mental disease or defect.

(3) The report of the examination shall include the following: (a) a description of the nature of the examination; (b) a diagnosis of the mental condition of the defendant; (c) if the defendant suffers from a mental disease or defect, an opinion as to his capacity to understand the proceedings against him and to assist in his own defense; (d) when a notice of intention to rely on the defense of irresponsibility has been filed, an opinion as to the extent, if any, to which the capacity of the defendant to appreciate the criminality [wrongfulness] of his conduct or to conform

his conduct to the requirements of law was impaired at the time of the criminal conduct charged; and (e) when directed by the Court, an opinion as to the capacity of the defendant to have a particular state of mind which is an element of the offense charged.

If the examination can not be conducted by reason of the unwillingness of the defendant to participate therein, the report shall so state and shall include, if possible, an opinion as to whether such unwillingness of the defendant was the result of mental disease or defect.

The report of the examination shall be filed [in triplicate] with the clerk of the Court, who shall cause copies to be delivered to the district attorney and to counsel for the defendant.

### Section 4.06.   Determination of Fitness to Proceed;  Effect of Finding of Unfitness;  Proceedings if Fitness Is Regained [;  Post–Commitment Hearing]

(1) When the defendant's fitness to proceed is drawn in question, the issue shall be determined by the Court.  If neither the prosecuting attorney nor counsel for the defendant contests the finding of the report filed pursuant to Section 4.05, the Court may make the determination on the basis of such report.  If the finding is contested, the Court shall hold a hearing on the issue.  If the report is received in evidence upon such hearing, the party who contests the finding thereof shall have the right to summon and to cross-examine the psychiatrists who joined in the report and to offer evidence upon the issue.

(2) If the Court determines that the defendant lacks fitness to proceed, the proceeding against him shall be suspended, except as provided in Subsection (3) [Subsections (3) and (4)] of this Section, and the Court shall commit him to the custody of the Commissioner of Mental Hygiene [Public Health or Correction] to be placed in an appropriate institution of the Department of Mental Hygiene [Public Health or Correction] for so long as such unfitness shall endure.  When the Court, on its own motion or upon the application of the Commissioner of Mental Hygiene [Public Health or Correction] or the prosecuting attorney, determines, after a hearing if a hearing is requested, that the defendant has regained fitness to proceed, the proceeding shall be resumed.  If, however, the Court is of the view that so much time has elapsed since the commitment of the defendant that it would be unjust to resume the criminal proceeding, the Court may dismiss the charge and may order the defendant to be discharged or, subject to the law governing the civil commitment of persons suffering from mental disease or defect, order the defendant to be committed to an appropriate institution of the Department of Mental Hygiene [Public Health].

(3) The fact that the defendant is unfit to proceed does not preclude any legal objection to the prosecution which is susceptible of fair determination prior to trial and without the personal participation of the defendant.

[Alternative: (3) At any time within ninety days after commitment as provided in Subsection (2) of this Section, or at any later time with permission of the Court granted for good cause, the defendant or his counsel or the Commissioner of Mental Hygiene [Public Health or Correction] may apply for a special post-commitment hearing.  If the application is made by or on behalf of a defendant not represented by counsel, he shall be afforded a reasonable opportunity to obtain counsel, and if he lacks funds to do so, counsel shall be assigned by the Court.  The application shall be granted only if the counsel for the defendant satisfies the Court by affidavit or otherwise that as an attorney he has reasonable grounds for a good faith belief that his client has, on the facts and the law, a defense to the charge other than mental disease or defect excluding responsibility.

[(4) If the motion for a special post-commitment hearing is granted, the hearing shall be by the Court without a jury. No evidence shall be offered at the hearing by either party on the issue of mental disease or defect as a defense to, or in mitigation of, the crime charged. After hearing, the Court may in an appropriate case quash the indictment or other charge, or find it to be defective or insufficient, or determine that it is not proved beyond a reasonable doubt by the evidence, or otherwise terminate the proceedings on the evidence or the law. In any such case, unless all defects in the proceedings are promptly cured, the Court shall terminate the commitment ordered under Subsection (2) of this Section and order the defendant to be discharged or, subject to the law governing the civil commitment of persons suffering from mental disease or defect, order the defendant to be committed to an appropriate institution of the Department of Mental Hygiene [Public Health].]

### Section 4.07. Determination of Irresponsibility on Basis of Report; Access to Defendant by Psychiatrist of His Own Choice; Form of Expert Testimony When Issue of Responsibility Is Tried

(1) If the report filed pursuant to Section 4.05 finds that the defendant at the time of the criminal conduct charged suffered from a mental disease or defect which substantially impaired his capacity to appreciate the criminality [wrongfulness] of his conduct or to conform his conduct to the requirements of law, and the Court, after a hearing if a hearing is requested by the prosecuting attorney or the defendant, is satisfied that such impairment was sufficient to exclude responsibility, the Court on motion of the defendant shall enter judgment of acquittal on the ground of mental disease or defect excluding responsibility.

(2) When, notwithstanding the report filed pursuant to Section 4.05, the defendant wishes to be examined by a qualified psychiatrist or other expert of his own choice, such examiner shall be permitted to have reasonable access to the defendant for the purposes of such examination.

(3) Upon the trial, the psychiatrists who reported pursuant to Section 4.05 may be called as witnesses by the prosecution, the defendant or the Court. If the issue is being tried before a jury, the jury may be informed that the psychiatrists were designated by the Court or by the Superintendent of the _____ Hospital at the request of the Court, as the case may be. If called by the Court, the witness shall be subject to cross-examination by the prosecution and by the defendant. Both the prosecution and the defendant may summon any other qualified psychiatrist or other expert to testify, but no one who has not examined the defendant shall be competent to testify to an expert opinion with respect to the mental condition or responsibility of the defendant, as distinguished from the validity of the procedure followed by, or the general scientific propositions stated by, another witness.

(4) When a psychiatrist or other expert who has examined the defendant testifies concerning his mental condition, he shall be permitted to make a statement as to the nature of his examination, his diagnosis of the mental condition of the defendant at the time of the commission of the offense charged and his opinion as to the extent, if any, to which the capacity of the defendant to appreciate the

**A-39**

criminality [wrongfulness] of his conduct or to conform his conduct to the requirements of law or to have a particular state of mind which is an element of the offense charged was impaired as a result of mental disease or defect at that time. He shall be permitted to make any explanation reasonably serving to clarify his diagnosis and opinion and may be cross-examined as to any matter bearing on his competency or credibility or the validity of his diagnosis or opinion.

### Section 4.08.  Legal Effect of Acquittal on the Ground of Mental Disease or Defect Excluding Responsibility; Commitment; Release or Discharge

(1) When a defendant is acquitted on the ground of mental disease or defect excluding responsibility, the Court shall order him to be committed to the custody of the Commissioner of Mental Hygiene [Public Health] to be placed in an appropriate institution for custody, care and treatment.

(2) If the Commissioner of Mental Hygiene [Public Health] is of the view that a person committed to his custody, pursuant to paragraph (1) of this Section, may be discharged or released on condition without danger to himself or to others, he shall make application for the discharge or release of such person in a report to the Court by which such person was committed and shall transmit a copy of such application and report to the prosecuting attorney of the county [parish] from which the defendant was committed. The Court shall thereupon appoint at least two qualified psychiatrists to examine such person and to report within sixty days, or such longer period as the Court determines to be necessary for the purpose, their opinion as to his mental condition. To facilitate such examination and the proceedings thereon, the Court may cause such person to be confined in any institution located near the place where the Court sits, which may hereafter be designated by the Commissioner of Mental Hygiene [Public Health] as suitable for the temporary detention of irresponsible persons.

(3) If the Court is satisfied by the report filed pursuant to paragraph (2) of this Section and such testimony of the reporting psychiatrists as the Court deems necessary that the committed person may be discharged or released on condition without danger to himself or others, the Court shall order his discharge or his release on such conditions as the Court determines to be necessary. If the Court is not so satisfied, it shall promptly order a hearing to determine whether such person may safely be discharged or released. Any such hearing shall be deemed a civil proceeding and the burden shall be upon the committed person to prove that he may safely be discharged or released. According to the determination of the Court upon the hearing, the committed person shall thereupon be discharged or released on such conditions as the Court determines to be necessary, or shall be recommitted to the custody of the Commissioner of Mental Hygiene [Public Health], subject to discharge or release only in accordance with the procedure prescribed above for a first hearing.

(4) If, within [five] years after the conditional release of a committed person, the court shall determine, after hearing evidence, that the conditions of release have not been fulfilled and that for the safety of such person or for the safety of others his conditional release should be revoked, the Court shall forthwith order him to be recommitted to the Commissioner of Mental Hygiene [Public Health], subject to discharge or release only in accordance with the procedure prescribed above for a first hearing.

(5) A committed person may make application for his discharge or release to the Court by which he was committed, and the procedure to be followed upon such application shall be the same as that prescribed above in the case of an application by the Commissioner of Mental Hygiene [Public Health]. However, no such application by a committed person need be considered until he has been confined for a period of not less than [six months] from the date of the order of commitment, and if the determination of the Court be adverse to the application, such person shall not be permitted to file a further application until [one year] has elapsed from the date of any preceding hearing on an application for his release or discharge.

### Section 4.09.   Statements for Purposes of Examination or Treatment Inadmissible Except on Issue of Mental Condition

A statement made by a person subjected to psychiatric examination or treatment pursuant to Sections 4.05, 4.06 or 4.08 for the purposes of such examination or treatment shall not be admissible in evidence against him in any criminal proceeding on any issue other than that of his mental condition but it shall be admissible upon that issue, whether or not it would otherwise be deemed a privileged communication [, unless such statement constitutes an admission of guilt of the crime charged].

### Section 4.10.   Immaturity Excluding Criminal Conviction;   Transfer of Proceedings to Juvenile Court

(1) A person shall not be tried for or convicted of an offense if:

(a) at the time of the conduct charged to constitute the offense he was less than sixteen years of age [, in which case the Juvenile Court shall have exclusive jurisdiction];  or

(b) at the time of the conduct charged to constitute the offense he was sixteen or seventeen years of age, unless:

(i) the Juvenile Court has no jurisdiction over him, or,

(ii) the Juvenile Court has entered an order waiving jurisdiction and consenting to the institution of criminal proceedings against him.

(2) No court shall have jurisdiction to try or convict a person of an offense if criminal proceedings against him are barred by Subsection (1) of this Section. When it appears that a person charged with the commission of an offense may be of such an age that criminal proceedings may be barred under Subsection (1) of this Section, the Court shall hold a hearing thereon, and the burden shall be on the prosecution to establish to the satisfaction of the Court that the criminal proceeding is not barred upon such grounds. If the Court determines that the proceeding is barred, custody of the person charged shall be surrendered to the Juvenile Court, and the case, including all papers and processes relating thereto, shall be transferred.

### ARTICLE 5.   INCHOATE CRIMES

### Section 5.01.   Criminal Attempt

(1) Definition of Attempt.  A person is guilty of an attempt to commit a crime if, acting with the kind of culpability otherwise required for commission of the crime, he:

**A-41**

(a) purposely engages in conduct which would constitute the crime if the attendant circumstances were as he believes them to be; or

(b) when causing a particular result is an element of the crime, does or omits to do anything with the purpose of causing or with the belief that it will cause such result without further conduct on his part; or

(c) purposely does or omits to do anything which, under the circumstances as he believes them to be, is an act or omission constituting a substantial step in a course of conduct planned to culminate in his commission of the crime.

(2) Conduct Which May Be Held Substantial Step Under Subsection (1)(c). Conduct shall not be held to constitute a substantial step under Subsection (1)(c) of this Section unless it is strongly corroborative of the actor's criminal purpose. Without negativing the sufficiency of other conduct, the following, if strongly corroborative of the actor's criminal purpose, shall not be held insufficient as a matter of law:

(a) lying in wait, searching for or following the contemplated victim of the crime;

(b) enticing or seeking to entice the contemplated victim of the crime to go to the place contemplated for its commission;

(c) reconnoitering the place contemplated for the commission of the crime;

(d) unlawful entry of a structure, vehicle or enclosure in which it is contemplated that the crime will be committed;

(e) possession of materials to be employed in the commission of the crime, which are specially designed for such unlawful use or which can serve no lawful purpose of the actor under the circumstances;

(f) possession, collection or fabrication of materials to be employed in the commission of the crime, at or near the place contemplated for its commission, where such possession, collection or fabrication serves no lawful purpose of the actor under the circumstances;

(g) soliciting an innocent agent to engage in conduct constituting an element of the crime.

(3) Conduct Designed to Aid Another in Commission of a Crime. A person who engages in conduct designed to aid another to commit a crime which would establish his complicity under Section 2.06 if the crime were committed by such other person, is guilty of an attempt to commit the crime, although the crime is not committed or attempted by such other person.

(4) Renunciation of Criminal Purpose. When the actor's conduct would otherwise constitute an attempt under Subsection (1)(b) or (1)(c) of this Section, it is an affirmative defense that he abandoned his effort to commit the crime or otherwise prevented its commission, under circumstances manifesting a complete and voluntary renunciation of his criminal purpose. The establishment of such defense does not, however, affect the liability of an accomplice who did not join in such abandonment or prevention.

Within the meaning of this Article, renunciation of criminal purpose is not voluntary if it is motivated, in whole or in part, by circumstances, not present or apparent at the inception of the actor's course of conduct, which increase the probability of detection or apprehension or which make more difficult the accomplishment of the criminal purpose. Renunciation is not complete if it is motivated by a decision to postpone the criminal conduct until a more advantageous time or to transfer the criminal effort to another but similar objective or victim.

### Section 5.02.  Criminal Solicitation

(1) Definition of Solicitation.  A person is guilty of solicitation to commit a crime if with the purpose of promoting or facilitating its commission he commands, encourages or requests another person to engage in specific conduct which would constitute such crime or an attempt to commit such crime or which would establish his complicity in its commission or attempted commission.

(2) Uncommunicated Solicitation.  It is immaterial under Subsection (1) of this Section that the actor fails to communicate with the person he solicits to commit a crime if his conduct was designed to effect such communication.

(3) Renunciation of Criminal Purpose.  It is an affirmative defense that the actor, after soliciting another person to commit a crime, persuaded him not to do so or otherwise prevented the commission of the crime, under circumstances manifesting a complete and voluntary renunciation of his criminal purpose.

### Section 5.03.  Criminal Conspiracy

(1) Definition of Conspiracy.  A person is guilty of conspiracy with another person or persons to commit a crime if with the purpose of promoting or facilitating its commission he:

(a) agrees with such other person or persons that they or one or more of them will engage in conduct which constitutes such crime or an attempt or solicitation to commit such crime; or

(b) agrees to aid such other person or persons in the planning or commission of such crime or of an attempt or solicitation to commit such crime.

(2) Scope of Conspiratorial Relationship.  If a person guilty of conspiracy, as defined by Subsection (1) of this Section, knows that a person with whom he conspires to commit a crime has conspired with another person or persons to commit the same crime, he is guilty of conspiring with such other person or persons, whether or not he knows their identity, to commit such crime.

(3) Conspiracy With Multiple Criminal Objectives.  If a person conspires to commit a number of crimes, he is guilty of only one conspiracy so long as such multiple crimes are the object of the same agreement or continuous conspiratorial relationship.

(4) Joinder and Venue in Conspiracy Prosecutions.

(a) Subject to the provisions of paragraph (b) of this Subsection, two or more persons charged with criminal conspiracy may be prosecuted jointly if:

(i) they are charged with conspiring with one another; or

(ii) the conspiracies alleged, whether they have the same or different parties, are so related that they constitute different aspects of a scheme of organized criminal conduct.

(b) In any joint prosecution under paragraph (a) of this Subsection:

(i) no defendant shall be charged with a conspiracy in any county [parish or district] other than one in which he entered into such conspiracy or in which an overt act pursuant to such conspiracy was done by him or by a person with whom he conspired; and

**A-43**

(ii) neither the liability of any defendant nor the admissibility against him of evidence of acts or declarations of another shall be enlarged by such joinder; and

(iii) the Court shall order a severance or take a special verdict as to any defendant who so requests, if it deems it necessary or appropriate to promote the fair determination of his guilt or innocence, and shall take any other proper measures to protect the fairness of the trial.

(5) Overt Act. No person may be convicted of conspiracy to commit a crime, other than a felony of the first or second degree, unless an overt act in pursuance of such conspiracy is alleged and proved to have been done by him or by a person with whom he conspired.

(6) Renunciation of Criminal Purpose. It is an affirmative defense that the actor, after conspiring to commit a crime, thwarted the success of the conspiracy, under circumstances manifesting a complete and voluntary renunciation of his criminal purpose.

(7) Duration of Conspiracy. For purposes of Section 1.06(4):

(a) conspiracy is a continuing course of conduct which terminates when the crime or crimes which are its object are committed or the agreement that they be committed is abandoned by the defendant and by those with whom he conspired; and

(b) such abandonment is presumed if neither the defendant nor anyone with whom he conspired does any overt act in pursuance of the conspiracy during the applicable period of limitation; and

(c) if an individual abandons the agreement, the conspiracy is terminated as to him only if and when he advises those with whom he conspired of his abandonment or he informs the law enforcement authorities of the existence of the conspiracy and of his participation therein.

### Section 5.04. Incapacity, Irresponsibility or Immunity of Party to Solicitation or Conspiracy

(1) Except as provided in Subsection (2) of this Section, it is immaterial to the liability of a person who solicits or conspires with another to commit a crime that:

(a) he or the person whom he solicits or with whom he conspires does not occupy a particular position or have a particular characteristic which is an element of such crime, if he believes that one of them does; or

(b) the person whom he solicits or with whom he conspires is irresponsible or has an immunity to prosecution or conviction for the commission of the crime.

(2) It is a defense to a charge of solicitation or conspiracy to commit a crime that if the criminal object were achieved, the actor would not be guilty of a crime under the law defining the offense or as an accomplice under Section 2.06(5) or 2.06(6)(a) or (b).

### Section 5.05. Grading of Criminal Attempt, Solicitation and Conspiracy; Mitigation in Cases of Lesser Danger; Multiple Convictions Barred

(1) Grading. Except as otherwise provided in this Section, attempt, solicitation and conspiracy are crimes of the same grade and degree as the most serious offense

which is attempted or solicited or is an object of the conspiracy.  An attempt, solicitation or conspiracy to commit a [capital crime or a] felony of the first degree is a felony of the second degree.

(2) Mitigation.  If the particular conduct charged to constitute a criminal attempt, solicitation or conspiracy is so inherently unlikely to result or culminate in the commission of a crime that neither such conduct nor the actor presents a public danger warranting the grading of such offense under this Section, the Court shall exercise its power under Section 6.12 to enter judgment and impose sentence for a crime of lower grade or degree or, in extreme cases, may dismiss the prosecution.

(3) Multiple Convictions.  A person may not be convicted of more than one offense defined by this Article for conduct designed to commit or to culminate in the commission of the same crime.

## Section 5.06.  Possessing Instruments of Crime;  Weapons

(1) Criminal Instruments Generally.  A person commits a misdemeanor if he possesses any instrument of crime with purpose to employ it criminally.  "Instrument of crime" means:

(a) anything specially made or specially adapted for criminal use;  or

(b) anything commonly used for criminal purposes and possessed by the actor under circumstances which do not negative unlawful purpose.

(2) Presumption of Criminal Purpose from Possession of Weapon.  If a person possesses a firearm or other weapon on or about his person, in a vehicle occupied by him, or otherwise readily available for use, it is presumed that he had the purpose to employ it criminally, unless:

(a) the weapon is possessed in the actor's home or place of business;

(b) the actor is licensed or otherwise authorized by law to possess such weapon;  or

(c) the weapon is of a type commonly used in lawful sport.

"Weapon" means anything readily capable of lethal use and possessed under circumstances not manifestly appropriate for lawful uses which it may have; the term includes a firearm which is not loaded or lacks a clip or other component to render it immediately operable, and components which can readily be assembled into a weapon.

(3) Presumptions as to Possession of Criminal Instruments in Automobiles. Where a weapon or other instrument of crime is found in an automobile, it shall be presumed to be in the possession of the occupant if there is but one.  If there is more than one occupant, it shall be presumed to be in the possession of all, except under the following circumstances:

(a) where it is found upon the person of one of the occupants;

(b) where the automobile is not a stolen one and the weapon or instrument is found out of view in a glove compartment, car trunk, or other enclosed customary depository, in which case it shall be presumed to be in the possession of the occupant or occupants who own or have authority to operate the automobile;

(c) in the case of a taxicab, a weapon or instrument found in the passengers' portion of the vehicle shall be presumed to be in the possession of all the passengers, if there are any, and, if not, in the possession of the driver.

**A-45**

### Section 5.07. Prohibited Offensive Weapons

A person commits a misdemeanor if, except as authorized by law, he makes, repairs, sells, or otherwise deals in, uses, or possesses any offensive weapon. "Offensive weapon" means any bomb, machine gun, sawed-off shotgun, firearm specially made or specially adapted for concealment or silent discharge, any blackjack, sandbag, metal knuckles, dagger, or other implement for the infliction of serious bodily injury which serves no common lawful purpose. It is a defense under this Section for the defendant to prove by a preponderance of evidence that he possessed or dealt with the weapon solely as a curio or in a dramatic performance, or that he possessed it briefly in consequence of having found it or taken it from an aggressor, or under circumstances similarly negativing any purpose or likelihood that the weapon would be used unlawfully. The presumptions provided in Section 5.06(3) are applicable to prosecutions under this Section.

## ARTICLE 6.  AUTHORIZED DISPOSITION OF OFFENDERS

### Section 6.01. Degrees of Felonies

(1) Felonies defined by this Code are classified, for the purpose of sentence, into three degrees, as follows:

(a) felonies of the first degree;

(b) felonies of the second degree;

(c) felonies of the third degree.

A felony is of the first or second degree when it is so designated by the Code. A crime declared to be a felony, without specification of degree, is of the third degree.

(2) Notwithstanding any other provision of law, a felony defined by any statute of this State other than this Code shall constitute for the purpose of sentence a felony of the third degree.

### Section 6.02. Sentence in Accordance With Code; Authorized Dispositions

(1) No person convicted of an offense shall be sentenced otherwise than in accordance with this Article.

[(2) The Court shall sentence a person who has been convicted of murder to death or imprisonment, in accordance with Section 210.6.]

(3) Except as provided in Subsection (2) of this Section and subject to the applicable provisions of the Code, the Court may suspend the imposition of sentence on a person who has been convicted of a crime, may order him to be committed in lieu of sentence, in accordance with Section 6.13, or may sentence him as follows:

(a) to pay a fine authorized by Section 6.03; or

(b) to be placed on probation [, and, in the case of a person convicted of a felony or misdemeanor to imprisonment for a term fixed by the Court not exceeding thirty days to be served as a condition of probation]; or

(c) to imprisonment for a term authorized by Sections 6.05, 6.06, 6.07, 6.08, 6.09, or 7.06; or

(d) to fine and probation or fine and imprisonment, but not to probation and imprisonment [, except as authorized in paragraph (b) of this Subsection].

(4) The Court may suspend the imposition of sentence on a person who has been convicted of a violation or may sentence him to pay a fine authorized by Section 6.03.

(5) This Article does not deprive the Court of any authority conferred by law to decree a forfeiture of property, suspend or cancel a license, remove a person from office, or impose any other civil penalty. Such a judgment or order may be included in the sentence.

### Section 6.03.  Fines

A person who has been convicted of an offense may be sentenced to pay a fine not exceeding:

(1) $10,000, when the conviction is of a felony of the first or second degree;

(2) $5,000, when the conviction is of a felony of the third degree;

(3) $1,000, when the conviction is of a misdemeanor;

(4) $500, when the conviction is of a petty misdemeanor or a violation;

(5) any higher amount equal to double the pecuniary gain derived from the offense by the offender;

(6) any higher amount specifically authorized by statute.

### Section 6.04.  Penalties Against Corporations and Unincorporated Associations; Forfeiture of Corporate Charter or Revocation of Certificate Authorizing Foreign Corporation to Do Business in the State

(1) The Court may suspend the sentence of a corporation or an unincorporated association which has been convicted of an offense or may sentence it to pay a fine authorized by Section 6.03.

(2) (a) The [prosecuting attorney] is authorized to institute civil proceedings in the appropriate court of general jurisdiction to forfeit the charter of a corporation organized under the laws of this State or to revoke the certificate authorizing a foreign corporation to conduct business in this State. The Court may order the charter forfeited or the certificate revoked upon finding (i) that the board of directors or a high managerial agent acting in behalf of the corporation has, in conducting the corporation's affairs, purposely engaged in a persistent course of criminal conduct and (ii) that for the prevention of future criminal conduct of the same character, the public interest requires the charter of the corporation to be forfeited and the corporation to be dissolved or the certificate to be revoked.

(b) When a corporation is convicted of a crime or a high managerial agent of a corporation, as defined in Section 2.07, is convicted of a crime committed in the conduct of the affairs of the corporation, the Court, in sentencing the corporation or the agent, may direct the [prosecuting attorney] to institute proceedings authorized by paragraph (a) of this Subsection.

(c) The proceedings authorized by paragraph (a) of this Subsection shall be conducted in accordance with the procedures authorized by law for the involuntary dissolution of a corporation or the revocation of the certificate authorizing a foreign corporation to conduct business in this State. Such proceedings shall be deemed additional to any other proceedings authorized by law for the purpose of forfeiting the charter of a corporation or revoking the certificate of a foreign corporation.

**A-47**

### Section 6.05.  Young Adult Offenders

(1) <u>Specialized Correctional Treatment.</u>  A young adult offender is a person convicted of a crime who, at the time of sentencing, is sixteen but less than twenty-two years of age.  A young adult offender who is sentenced to a term of imprisonment which may exceed thirty days [alternatives: (1) ninety days; (2) one year] shall be committed to the custody of the Division of Young Adult Correction of the Department of Correction, and shall receive, as far as practicable, such special and individualized correctional and rehabilitative treatment as may be appropriate to his needs.

(2) <u>Special Term.</u>  A young adult offender convicted of a felony may, in lieu of any other sentence of imprisonment authorized by this Article, be sentenced to a special term of imprisonment without a minimum and with a maximum of four years, regardless of the degree of the felony involved, if the Court is of the opinion that such special term is adequate for his correction and rehabilitation and will not jeopardize the protection of the public.

[(3) <u>Removal of Disabilities; Vacation of Conviction.</u>

(a) In sentencing a young adult offender to the special term provided by this Section or to any sentence other than one of imprisonment, the Court may order that so long as he is not convicted of another felony, the judgment shall not constitute a conviction for the purposes of any disqualification or disability imposed by law upon conviction of a crime.

(b) When any young adult offender is unconditionally discharged from probation or parole before the expiration of the maximum term thereof, the Court may enter an order vacating the judgment of conviction.]

[(4) <u>Commitment for Observation.</u>  If, after pre-sentence investigation, the Court desires additional information concerning a young adult offender before imposing sentence, it may order that he be committed, for a period not exceeding ninety days, to the custody of the Division of Young Adult Correction of the Department of Correction for observation and study at an appropriate reception or classification center.  Such Division of the Department of Correction and the [Young Adult Division of the] Board of Parole shall advise the Court of their findings and recommendations on or before the expiration of such ninety-day period.]

### Section 6.06.  Sentence of Imprisonment for Felony;  Ordinary Terms

A person who has been convicted of a felony may be sentenced to imprisonment, as follows:

(1) in the case of a felony of the first degree, for a term the minimum of which shall be fixed by the Court at not less than one year nor more than ten years, and the maximum of which shall be life imprisonment;

(2) in the case of a felony of the second degree, for a term the minimum of which shall be fixed by the Court at not less than one year nor more than three years, and the maximum of which shall be ten years;

(3) in the case of a felony of the third degree, for a term the minimum of which shall be fixed by the Court at not less than one year nor more than two years, and the maximum of which shall be five years.

**Alternate Section 6.06.  Sentence of Imprisonment for Felony;  Ordinary Terms**

A person who has been convicted of a felony may be sentenced to imprisonment, as follows:

(1) in the case of a felony of the first degree, for a term the minimum of which shall be fixed by the Court at not less than one year nor more than ten years, and the maximum at not more than twenty years or at life imprisonment;

(2) in the case of a felony of the second degree, for a term the minimum of which shall be fixed by the Court at not less than one year nor more than three years, and the maximum at not more than ten years;

(3) in the case of a felony of the third degree, for a term the minimum of which shall be fixed by the Court at not less than one year nor more than two years, and the maximum at not more than five years.

No sentence shall be imposed under this Section of which the minimum is longer than one-half the maximum, or, when the maximum is life imprisonment, longer than ten years.

**Section 6.07.  Sentence of Imprisonment for Felony;  Extended Terms**

In the cases designated in Section 7.03, a person who has been convicted of a felony may be sentenced to an extended term of imprisonment, as follows:

(1) in the case of a felony of the first degree, for a term the minimum of which shall be fixed by the Court at not less than five years nor more than ten years, and the maximum of which shall be life imprisonment;

(2) in the case of a felony of the second degree, for a term the minimum of which shall be fixed by the Court at not less than one year nor more than five years, and the maximum of which shall be fixed by the Court at not less than ten nor more than twenty years;

(3) in the case of a felony of the third degree, for a term the minimum of which shall be fixed by the Court at not less than one year nor more than three years, and the maximum of which shall be fixed by the Court at not less than five nor more than ten years.

**Section 6.08.  Sentence of Imprisonment for Misdemeanors and Petty Misdemeanors;  Ordinary Terms**

A person who has been convicted of a misdemeanor or a petty misdemeanor may be sentenced to imprisonment for a definite term which shall be fixed by the Court and shall not exceed one year in the case of a misdemeanor or thirty days in the case of a petty misdemeanor.

**Section 6.09.  Sentence of Imprisonment for Misdemeanors and Petty Misdemeanors;  Extended Terms**

(1) In the cases designated in Section 7.04, a person who has been convicted of a misdemeanor or a petty misdemeanor may be sentenced to an extended term of imprisonment, as follows:

(a) in the case of a misdemeanor, for a term the minimum of which shall be fixed by the Court at not more than one year and the maximum of which shall be three years;

**A-49**

(b) in the case of a petty misdemeanor, for a term the minimum of which shall be fixed by the Court at not more than six months and the maximum of which shall be two years.

(2) No such sentence for an extended term shall be imposed unless:

(a) the Director of Correction has certified that there is an institution in the Department of Correction, or in a county, city [or other appropriate political subdivision of the State] which is appropriate for the detention and correctional treatment of such misdemeanants or petty misdemeanants, and that such institution is available to receive such commitments; and

(b) the [Board of Parole] [Parole Administrator] has certified that the Board of Parole is able to visit such institution and to assume responsibility for the release of such prisoners on parole and for their parole supervision.

### Section 6.10.   First Release of All Offenders on Parole;  Sentence of Imprisonment Includes Separate Parole Term;  Length of Parole Term;  Length of Recommitment and Reparole After Revocation of Parole;  Final Unconditional Release

(1) First Release of All Offenders on Parole.   An offender sentenced to an indefinite term of imprisonment in excess of one year under Section 6.05, 6.06, 6.07, 6.09 or 7.06 shall be released conditionally on parole at or before the expiration of the maximum of such term, in accordance with Article 305.

(2) Sentence of Imprisonment Includes Separate Parole Term;  Length of Parole Term.   A sentence to an indefinite term of imprisonment in excess of one year under Section 6.05, 6.06, 6.07, 6.09 or 7.06 includes as a separate portion of the sentence a term of parole or of recommitment for violation of the conditions of parole which governs the duration of parole or recommitment after the offender's first conditional release on parole.   The minimum of such term is one year and the maximum is five years, unless the sentence was imposed under Section 6.05(2) or Section 6.09, in which case the maximum is two years.

(3) Length of Recommitment and Reparole After Revocation of Parole.   If an offender is recommitted upon revocation of his parole, the term of further imprisonment upon such recommitment and of any subsequent reparole or recommitment under the same sentence shall be fixed by the Board of Parole but shall not exceed in aggregate length the unserved balance of the maximum parole term provided by Subsection (2) of this Section.

(4) Final Unconditional Release.   When the maximum of his parole term has expired or he has been sooner discharged from parole under Section 305.12, an offender shall be deemed to have served his sentence and shall be released unconditionally.

### Section 6.11.  Place of Imprisonment

(1) When a person is sentenced to imprisonment for an indefinite term with a maximum in excess of one year, the Court shall commit him to the custody of the Department of Correction [or other single department or agency] for the term of his sentence and until released in accordance with law.

(2) When a person is sentenced to imprisonment for a definite term, the Court shall designate the institution or agency to which he is committed for the term of his sentence and until released in accordance with law.

### Section 6.12.   Reduction of Conviction by Court to Lesser Degree of Felony or to Misdemeanor

If, when a person has been convicted of a felony, the Court, having regard to the nature and circumstances of the crime and to the history and character of the defendant, is of the view that it would be unduly harsh to sentence the offender in accordance with the Code, the Court may enter judgment of conviction for a lesser degree of felony or for a misdemeanor and impose sentence accordingly.

### Section 6.13.   Civil Commitment in Lieu of Prosecution or of Sentence

(1) When a person prosecuted for a [felony of the third degree,] misdemeanor or petty misdemeanor is a chronic alcoholic, narcotic addict [or prostitute] or person suffering from mental abnormality and the Court is authorized by law to order the civil commitment of such person to a hospital or other institution for medical, psychiatric or other rehabilitative treatment, the Court may order such commitment and dismiss the prosecution. The order of commitment may be made after conviction, in which event the Court may set aside the verdict or judgment of conviction and dismiss the prosecution.

(2) The Court shall not make an order under Subsection (1) of this Section unless it is of the view that it will substantially further the rehabilitation of the defendant and will not jeopardize the protection of the public.

## ARTICLE 7.   AUTHORITY OF COURT IN SENTENCING

### Section 7.01.   Criteria for Withholding Sentence of Imprisonment and for Placing Defendant on Probation

(1) The Court shall deal with a person who has been convicted of a crime without imposing sentence of imprisonment unless, having regard to the nature and circumstances of the crime and the history, character and condition of the defendant, it is of the opinion that his imprisonment is necessary for protection of the public because:

(a) there is undue risk that during the period of a suspended sentence or probation the defendant will commit another crime; or

(b) the defendant is in need of correctional treatment that can be provided most effectively by his commitment to an institution; or

(c) a lesser sentence will depreciate the seriousness of the defendant's crime.

(2) The following grounds, while not controlling the discretion of the Court, shall be accorded weight in favor of withholding sentence of imprisonment:

(a) the defendant's criminal conduct neither caused nor threatened serious harm;

(b) the defendant did not contemplate that his criminal conduct would cause or threaten serious harm;

(c) the defendant acted under a strong provocation;

**A-51**

(d) there were substantial grounds tending to excuse or justify the defendant's criminal conduct, though failing to establish a defense;

(e) the victim of the defendant's criminal conduct induced or facilitated its commission;

(f) the defendant has compensated or will compensate the victim of his criminal conduct for the damage or injury that he sustained;

(g) the defendant has no history of prior delinquency or criminal activity or has led a law-abiding life for a substantial period of time before the commission of the present crime;

(h) the defendant's criminal conduct was the result of circumstances unlikely to recur;

(i) the character and attitudes of the defendant indicate that he is unlikely to commit another crime;

(j) the defendant is particularly likely to respond affirmatively to probationary treatment;

(k) the imprisonment of the defendant would entail excessive hardship to himself or his dependents.

(3) When a person who has been convicted of a crime is not sentenced to imprisonment, the Court shall place him on probation if he is in need of the supervision, guidance, assistance or direction that the probation service can provide.

### Section 7.02.  Criteria for Imposing Fines

(1) The Court shall not sentence a defendant only to pay a fine, when any other disposition is authorized by law, unless having regard to the nature and circumstances of the crime and to the history and character of the defendant, it is of the opinion that the fine alone suffices for protection of the public.

(2) The Court shall not sentence a defendant to pay a fine in addition to a sentence of imprisonment or probation unless:

(a) the defendant has derived a pecuniary gain from the crime;  or

(b) the Court is of opinion that a fine is specially adapted to deterrence of the crime involved or to the correction of the offender.

(3) The Court shall not sentence a defendant to pay a fine unless:

(a) the defendant is or will be able to pay the fine;  and

(b) the fine will not prevent the defendant from making restitution or reparation to the victim of the crime.

(4) In determining the amount and method of payment of a fine, the Court shall take into account the financial resources of the defendant and the nature of the burden that its payment will impose.

### Section 7.03.  Criteria for Sentence of Extended Term of Imprisonment; Felonies

The Court may sentence a person who has been convicted of a felony to an extended term of imprisonment if it finds one or more of the grounds specified in this Section.  The finding of the Court shall be incorporated in the record.

(1) The defendant is a persistent offender whose commitment for an extended term is necessary for protection of the public.

The Court shall not make such a finding unless the defendant is over twenty-one years of age and has previously been convicted of two felonies or of one felony and two misdemeanors, committed at different times when he was over [insert Juvenile Court age] years of age.

(2) The defendant is a professional criminal whose commitment for an extended term is necessary for protection of the public.

The Court shall not make such a finding unless the defendant is over twenty-one years of age and:

(a) the circumstances of the crime show that the defendant has knowingly devoted himself to criminal activity as a major source of livelihood;  or

(b) the defendant has substantial income or resources not explained to be derived from a source other than criminal activity.

(3) The defendant is a dangerous, mentally abnormal person whose commitment for an extended term is necessary for protection of the public.

The Court shall not make such a finding unless the defendant has been subjected to a psychiatric examination resulting in the conclusions that his mental condition is gravely abnormal; that his criminal conduct has been characterized by a pattern of repetitive or compulsive behavior or by persistent aggressive behavior with heedless indifference to consequences;  and that such condition makes him a serious danger to others.

(4) The defendant is a multiple offender whose criminality was so extensive that a sentence of imprisonment for an extended term is warranted.

The Court shall not make such a finding unless:

(a) the defendant is being sentenced for two or more felonies, or is already under sentence of imprisonment for felony, and the sentences of imprisonment involved will run concurrently under Section 7.06;  or

(b) the defendant admits in open court the commission of one or more other felonies and asks that they be taken into account when he is sentenced;  and

(c) the longest sentences of imprisonment authorized for each of the defendant's crimes, including admitted crimes taken into account, if made to run consecutively would exceed in length the minimum and maximum of the extended term imposed.

### Section 7.04.  Criteria for Sentence of Extended Term of Imprisonment; Misdemeanors and Petty Misdemeanors

The Court may sentence a person who has been convicted of a misdemeanor or petty misdemeanor to an extended term of imprisonment if it finds one or more of the grounds specified in this Section.  The finding of the Court shall be incorporated in the record.

(1) The defendant is a persistent offender whose commitment for an extended term is necessary for protection of the public.

**A-53**

The Court shall not make such a finding unless the defendant has previously been convicted of two crimes, committed at different times when he was over [insert Juvenile Court age] years of age.

(2) The defendant is a professional criminal whose commitment for an extended term is necessary for protection of the public.

The Court shall not make such a finding unless:

(a) the circumstances of the crime show that the defendant has knowingly devoted himself to criminal activity as a major source of livelihood;  or

(b) the defendant has substantial income or resources not explained to be derived from a source other than criminal activity.

(3) The defendant is a chronic alcoholic, narcotic addict, prostitute or person of abnormal mental condition who requires rehabilitative treatment for a substantial period of time.

The Court shall not make such a finding unless, with respect to the particular category to which the defendant belongs, the Director of Correction has certified that there is a specialized institution or facility which is satisfactory for the rehabilitative treatment of such persons and which otherwise meets the requirements of Section 6.09, Subsection (2).

(4) The defendant is a multiple offender whose criminality was so extensive that a sentence of imprisonment for an extended term is warranted.

The Court shall not make such a finding unless:

(a) the defendant is being sentenced for a number of misdemeanors or petty misdemeanors or is already under sentence of imprisonment for crime of such grades, or admits in open court the commission of one or more such crimes and asks that they be taken into account when he is sentenced;  and

(b) maximum fixed sentences of imprisonment for each of the defendant's crimes, including admitted crimes taken into account, if made to run consecutively, would exceed in length the maximum period of the extended term imposed.

### Section 7.05.  Former Conviction in Another Jurisdiction;  Definition and Proof of Conviction;  Sentence Taking into Account Admitted Crimes Bars Subsequent Conviction for Such Crimes

(1) For purposes of paragraph (1) of Section 7.03 or 7.04, a conviction of the commission of a crime in another jurisdiction shall constitute a previous conviction. Such conviction shall be deemed to have been of a felony if sentence of death or of imprisonment in excess of one year was authorized under the law of such other jurisdiction, of a misdemeanor if sentence of imprisonment in excess of thirty days but not in excess of a year was authorized and of a petty misdemeanor if sentence of imprisonment for not more than thirty days was authorized.

(2) An adjudication by a court of competent jurisdiction that the defendant committed a crime constitutes a conviction for purposes of Sections 7.03 to 7.05 inclusive, although sentence or the execution thereof was suspended, provided that the time to appeal has expired and that the defendant was not pardoned on the ground of innocence.

(3) Prior conviction may be proved by any evidence, including fingerprint records made in connection with arrest, conviction or imprisonment, that reasonably satisfies the Court that the defendant was convicted.

(4) When the defendant has asked that other crimes admitted in open court be taken into account when he is sentenced and the Court has not rejected such request, the sentence shall bar the prosecution or conviction of the defendant in this State for any such admitted crime.

### Section 7.06.  Multiple Sentences; Concurrent and Consecutive Terms

(1) Sentences of Imprisonment for More Than One Crime.  When multiple sentences of imprisonment are imposed on a defendant for more than one crime, including a crime for which a previous suspended sentence or sentence of probation has been revoked, such multiple sentences shall run concurrently or consecutively as the Court determines at the time of sentence, except that:

(a) a definite and an indefinite term shall run concurrently and both sentences shall be satisfied by service of the indefinite term; and

(b) the aggregate of consecutive definite terms shall not exceed one year; and

(c) the aggregate of consecutive indefinite terms shall not exceed in minimum or maximum length the longest extended term authorized for the highest grade and degree of crime for which any of the sentences was imposed; and

(d) not more than one sentence for an extended term shall be imposed.

(2) Sentences of Imprisonment Imposed at Different Times.  When a defendant who has previously been sentenced to imprisonment is subsequently sentenced to another term for a crime committed prior to the former sentence, other than a crime committed while in custody:

(a) the multiple sentences imposed shall so far as possible conform to Subsection (1) of this Section; and

(b) whether the Court determines that the terms shall run concurrently or consecutively, the defendant shall be credited with time served in imprisonment on the prior sentence in determining the permissible aggregate length of the term or terms remaining to be served; and

(c) when a new sentence is imposed on a prisoner who is on parole, the balance of the parole term on the former sentence shall be deemed to run during the period of the new imprisonment.

(3) Sentence of Imprisonment for Crime Committed While on Parole.  When a defendant is sentenced to imprisonment for a crime committed while on parole in this State, such term of imprisonment and any period of reimprisonment that the Board of Parole may require the defendant to serve upon the revocation of his parole shall run concurrently, unless the Court orders them to run consecutively.

(4) Multiple Sentences of Imprisonment in Other Cases.  Except as otherwise provided in this Section, multiple terms of imprisonment shall run concurrently or consecutively as the Court determines when the second or subsequent sentence is imposed.

(5) Calculation of Concurrent and Consecutive Terms of Imprisonment.

(a) When indefinite terms run concurrently, the shorter minimum terms merge in and are satisfied by serving the longest minimum term and the

**A-55**

shorter maximum terms merge in and are satisfied by discharge of the longest maximum term.

(b) When indefinite terms run consecutively, the minimum terms are added to arrive at an aggregate minimum to be served equal to the sum of all minimum terms and the maximum terms are added to arrive at an aggregate maximum equal to the sum of all maximum terms.

(c) When a definite and an indefinite term run consecutively, the period of the definite term is added to both the minimum and maximum of the indefinite term and both sentences are satisfied by serving the indefinite term.

(6) Suspension of Sentence or Probation and Imprisonment; Multiple Terms of Suspension and Probation.  When a defendant is sentenced for more than one offense or a defendant already under sentence is sentenced for another offense committed prior to the former sentence:

(a) the Court shall not sentence to probation a defendant who is under sentence of imprisonment [with more than thirty days to run] or impose a sentence of probation and a sentence of imprisonment [, except as authorized by Section 6.02(3)(b)];  and

(b) multiple periods of suspension or probation shall run concurrently from the date of the first such disposition;  and

(c) when a sentence of imprisonment is imposed for an indefinite term, the service of such sentence shall satisfy a suspended sentence on another count or a prior suspended sentence or sentence to probation;  and

(d) when a sentence of imprisonment is imposed for a definite term, the period of a suspended sentence on another count or a prior suspended sentence or sentence to probation shall run during the period of such imprisonment.

(7) Offense Committed While Under Suspension of Sentence or Probation. When a defendant is convicted of an offense committed while under suspension of sentence or on probation and such suspension or probation is not revoked:

(a) if the defendant is sentenced to imprisonment for an indefinite term, the service of such sentence shall satisfy the prior suspended sentence or sentence to probation;  and

(b) if the defendant is sentenced to imprisonment for a definite term, the period of the suspension or probation shall not run during the period of such imprisonment;  and

(c) if sentence is suspended or the defendant is sentenced to probation, the period of such suspension or probation shall run concurrently with or consecutively to the remainder of the prior periods, as the Court determines at the time of sentence.

### Section 7.07.  Procedure on Sentence; Pre-sentence Investigation and Report; Remand for Psychiatric Examination; Transmission of Records to Department of Correction

(1) The Court shall not impose sentence without first ordering a pre-sentence investigation of the defendant and according due consideration to a written report of such investigation where:

(a) the defendant has been convicted of a felony;  or

(b) the defendant is less than twenty-two years of age and has been convicted of a crime; or

(c) the defendant will be [placed on probation or] sentenced to imprisonment for an extended term.

(2) The Court may order a pre-sentence investigation in any other case.

(3) The pre-sentence investigation shall include an analysis of the circumstances attending the commission of the crime, the defendant's history of delinquency or criminality, physical and mental condition, family situation and background, economic status, education, occupation and personal habits and any other matters that the probation officer deems relevant or the Court directs to be included.

(4) Before imposing sentence, the Court may order the defendant to submit to psychiatric observation and examination for a period of not exceeding sixty days or such longer period as the Court determines to be necessary for the purpose. The defendant may be remanded for this purpose to any available clinic or mental hospital or the Court may appoint a qualified psychiatrist to make the examination. The report of the examination shall be submitted to the Court.

(5) Before imposing sentence, the Court shall advise the defendant or his counsel of the factual contents and the conclusions of any pre-sentence investigation or psychiatric examination and afford fair opportunity, if the defendant so requests, to controvert them. The sources of confidential information need not, however, be disclosed.

(6) The Court shall not impose a sentence of imprisonment for an extended term unless the ground therefor has been established at a hearing after the conviction of the defendant and on written notice to him of the ground proposed. Subject to the limitation of Subsection (5) of this Section, the defendant shall have the right to hear and controvert the evidence against him and to offer evidence upon the issue.

(7) If the defendant is sentenced to imprisonment, a copy of the report of any pre-sentence investigation or psychiatric examination shall be transmitted forthwith to the Department of Correction [or other state department or agency] or, when the defendant is committed to the custody of a specific institution, to such institution.

### Section 7.08.   Commitment for Observation;   Sentence of Imprisonment for Felony Deemed Tentative for Period of One Year; Re-sentence on Petition of Commissioner of Correction

(1) If, after pre-sentence investigation, the Court desires additional information concerning an offender convicted of a felony or misdemeanor before imposing sentence, it may order that he be committed, for a period not exceeding ninety days, to the custody of the Department of Correction, or, in the case of a young adult offender, to the custody of the Division of Young Adult Correction, for observation and study at an appropriate reception or classification center. The Department and the Board of Parole, or the Young Adult Divisions thereof, shall advise the Court of their findings and recommendations on or before the expiration of such ninety-day period. If the offender is thereafter sentenced to imprisonment, the period of such commitment for observation shall be deducted from the maximum term and from the minimum, if any, of such sentence.

(2) When a person has been sentenced to imprisonment upon conviction of a felony, whether for an ordinary or extended term, the sentence shall be deemed tentative, to the extent provided in this Section, for the period of one year following the date when the offender is received in custody by the Department of Correction [or other state department or agency].

(3) If, as a result of the examination and classification by the Department of Correction [or other state department or agency] of a person under sentence of imprisonment upon conviction of a felony, the Commissioner of Correction [or other department head] is satisfied that the sentence of the Court may have been based upon a misapprehension as to the history, character or physical or mental condition of the offender, the Commissioner, during the period when the offender's sentence is deemed tentative under Subsection (2) of this Section shall file in the sentencing Court a petition to re-sentence the offender. The petition shall set forth the information as to the offender that is deemed to warrant his re-sentence and may include a recommendation as to the sentence to be imposed.

(4) The Court may dismiss a petition filed under Subsection (3) of this Section without a hearing if it deems the information set forth insufficient to warrant reconsideration of the sentence. If the Court is of the view that the petition warrants such reconsideration, a copy of the petition shall be served on the offender, who shall have the right to be heard on the issue and to be represented by counsel.

(5) When the Court grants a petition filed under Subsection (3) of this Section, it shall re-sentence the offender and may impose any sentence that might have been imposed originally for the felony of which the defendant was convicted. The period of his imprisonment prior to re-sentence and any reduction for good behavior to which he is entitled shall be applied in satisfaction of the final sentence.

(6) For all purposes other than this Section, a sentence of imprisonment has the same finality when it is imposed that it would have if this Section were not in force.

(7) Nothing in this Section shall alter the remedies provided by law for vacating or correcting an illegal sentence.

### Section 7.09.   Credit for Time of Detention Prior to Sentence; Credit for Imprisonment Under Earlier Sentence for the Same Crime

(1) When a defendant who is sentenced to imprisonment has previously been detained in any state or local correctional or other institution following his [conviction of] [arrest for] the crime for which such sentence is imposed, such period of detention following his [conviction] [arrest] shall be deducted from the maximum term, and from the minimum, if any, of such sentence. The officer having custody of the defendant shall furnish a certificate to the Court at the time of sentence, showing the length of such detention of the defendant prior to sentence in any state or local correctional or other institution, and the certificate shall be annexed to the official records of the defendant's commitment.

(2) When a judgment of conviction is vacated and a new sentence is thereafter imposed upon the defendant for the same crime, the period of detention and imprisonment theretofore served shall be deducted from the maximum term, and from the minimum, if any, of the new sentence. The officer having custody of the defendant shall furnish a certificate to the Court at the time of sentence, showing

the period of imprisonment served under the original sentence, and the certificate shall be annexed to the official records of the defendant's new commitment.

---

## PART II.  DEFINITION OF SPECIFIC CRIMES

---

### OFFENSES AGAINST EXISTENCE OR STABILITY OF THE STATE

[Reporter's note: This category of offenses, including treason, sedition, espionage and like crimes, was excluded from the scope of the Model Penal Code.  These offenses are peculiarly the concern of the federal government.  The Constitution itself defines treason: "Treason against the United States shall consist only in levying War against them, or in adhering to their Enemies, giving them Aid and Comfort...."  Article III, Section 3; cf. Pennsylvania v. Nelson, 350 U.S. 497 (1956)(supersession of state sedition legislation by federal law).  Also, the definition of offenses against the stability of the state is inevitably affected by special political considerations.  These factors militated against the use of the Institute's limited resources to attempt to draft "model" provisions in this area.  However we provide at this point in the Plan of the Model Penal Code for an Article 200, where definitions of offenses against the existence or stability of the state may be incorporated.]

---

### OFFENSES INVOLVING DANGER TO THE PERSON

---

### ARTICLE 210.  CRIMINAL HOMICIDE

#### Section 210.0.  Definitions

In Articles 210–213, unless a different meaning plainly is required:

(1) "human being" means a person who has been born and is alive;

(2) "bodily injury" means physical pain, illness or any impairment of physical condition;

(3) "serious bodily injury" means bodily injury which creates a substantial risk of death or which causes serious, permanent disfigurement, or protracted loss or impairment of the function of any bodily member or organ;

(4) "deadly weapon" means any firearm, or other weapon, device, instrument, material or substance, whether animate or inanimate, which in the manner it is used or is intended to be used is known to be capable of producing death or serious bodily injury.

**A-59**

### Section 210.1.  Criminal Homicide

(1) A person is guilty of criminal homicide if he purposely, knowingly, recklessly or negligently causes the death of another human being.

(2) Criminal homicide is murder, manslaughter or negligent homicide.

### Section 210.2.  Murder

(1) Except as provided in Section 210.3(1)(b), criminal homicide constitutes murder when:

(a) it is committed purposely or knowingly;  or

(b) it is committed recklessly under circumstances manifesting extreme indifference to the value of human life.  Such recklessness and indifference are presumed if the actor is engaged or is an accomplice in the commission of, or an attempt to commit, or flight after committing or attempting to commit robbery, rape or deviate sexual intercourse by force or threat of force, arson, burglary, kidnapping or felonious escape.

(2) Murder is a felony of the first degree [but a person convicted of murder may be sentenced to death, as provided in Section 210.6].[b]

### Section 210.3.  Manslaughter

(1) Criminal homicide constitutes manslaughter when:

(a) it is committed recklessly;  or

(b) a homicide which would otherwise be murder is committed under the influence of extreme mental or emotional disturbance for which there is reasonable explanation or excuse.  The reasonableness of such explanation or excuse shall be determined from the viewpoint of a person in the actor's situation under the circumstances as he believes them to be.

(2) Manslaughter is a felony of the second degree.

### Section 210.4.  Negligent Homicide

(1) Criminal homicide constitutes negligent homicide when it is committed negligently.

(2) Negligent homicide is a felony of the third degree.

### Section 210.5.  Causing or Aiding Suicide

(1) Causing Suicide as Criminal Homicide.  A person may be convicted of criminal homicide for causing another to commit suicide only if he purposely causes such suicide by force, duress or deception.

(2) Aiding or Soliciting Suicide as an Independent Offense.  A person who purposely aids or solicits another to commit suicide is guilty of a felony of the second degree if his conduct causes such suicide or an attempted suicide, and otherwise of a misdemeanor.

---

[b] The American Law Institute took no position on whether the capital sanction should be provided.  The bracketed portion of this provision, as well as Section 210.6, was included to address the procedures for imposition of the death penalty for jurisdictions that wished to retain it.—[Footnote by eds.]

**[Section 210.6.   Sentence of Death for Murder;   Further Proceedings to Determine Sentence**

(1) <u>Death Sentence Excluded.</u>   When a defendant is found guilty of murder, the Court shall impose sentence for a felony of the first degree if it is satisfied that:

(a) none of the aggravating circumstances enumerated in Subsection (3) of this Section was established by the evidence at the trial or will be established if further proceedings are initiated under Subsection (2) of this Section;   or

(b) substantial mitigating circumstances, established by the evidence at the trial, call for leniency;   or

(c) the defendant, with the consent of the prosecuting attorney and the approval of the Court, pleaded guilty to murder as a felony of the first degree; or

(d) the defendant was under 18 years of age at the time of the commission of the crime;   or

(e) the defendant's physical or mental condition calls for leniency;   or

(f) although the evidence suffices to sustain the verdict, it does not foreclose all doubt respecting the defendant's guilt.

(2) <u>Determination by Court or by Court and Jury.</u>   Unless the Court imposes sentence under Subsection (1) of this Section, it shall conduct a separate proceeding to determine whether the defendant should be sentenced for a felony of the first degree or sentenced to death.   The proceeding shall be conducted before the Court alone if the defendant was convicted by a Court sitting without a jury or upon his plea of guilty or if the prosecuting attorney and the defendant waive a jury with respect to sentence.   In other cases it shall be conducted before the Court sitting with the jury which determined the defendant's guilt or, if the Court for good cause shown discharges that jury, with a new jury empaneled for the purpose.

In the proceeding, evidence may be presented as to any matter that the Court deems relevant to sentence, including but not limited to the nature and circumstances of the crime, the defendant's character, background, history, mental and physical condition and any of the aggravating or mitigating circumstances enumerated in Subsections (3) and (4) of this Section.   Any such evidence, not legally privileged, which the Court deems to have probative force, may be received, regardless of its admissibility under the exclusionary rules of evidence, provided that the defendant's counsel is accorded a fair opportunity to rebut such evidence. The prosecuting attorney and the defendant or his counsel shall be permitted to present argument for or against sentence of death.

The determination whether sentence of death shall be imposed shall be in the discretion of the Court, except that when the proceeding is conducted before the Court sitting with a jury, the Court shall not impose sentence of death unless it submits to the jury the issue whether the defendant should be sentenced to death or to imprisonment and the jury returns a verdict that the sentence should be death. If the jury is unable to reach a unanimous verdict, the Court shall dismiss the jury and impose sentence for a felony of the first degree.

The Court, in exercising its discretion as to sentence, and the jury, in determining upon its verdict, shall take into account the aggravating and mitigating circumstances enumerated in Subsections (3) and (4) and any other facts that it deems relevant, but it shall not impose or recommend sentence of death unless it finds one of the aggravating circumstances enumerated in Subsection (3) and

**A-61**

further finds that there are no mitigating circumstances sufficiently substantial to call for leniency. When the issue is submitted to the jury, the Court shall so instruct and also shall inform the jury of the nature of the sentence of imprisonment that may be imposed, including its implication with respect to possible release upon parole, if the jury verdict is against sentence of death.

Alternative formulation of Subsection (2):

(2) Determination by Court. Unless the Court imposes sentence under Subsection (1) of this Section, it shall conduct a separate proceeding to determine whether the defendant should be sentenced for a felony of the first degree or sentenced to death. In the proceeding, the Court, in accordance with Section 7.07, shall consider the report of the pre-sentence investigation and, if a psychiatric examination has been ordered, the report of such examination. In addition, evidence may be presented as to any matter that the Court deems relevant to sentence, including but not limited to the nature and circumstances of the crime, the defendant's character, background, history, mental and physical condition and any of the aggravating or mitigating circumstances enumerated in Subsections (3) and (4) of this Section. Any such evidence, not legally privileged, which the Court deems to have probative force, may be received, regardless of its admissibility under the exclusionary rules of evidence, provided that the defendant's counsel is accorded a fair opportunity to rebut such evidence. The prosecuting attorney and the defendant or his counsel shall be permitted to present argument for or against sentence of death.

The determination whether sentence of death shall be imposed shall be in the discretion of the Court. In exercising such discretion, the Court shall take into account the aggravating and mitigating circumstances enumerated in Subsections (3) and (4) and any other facts that it deems relevant but shall not impose sentence of death unless it finds one of the aggravating circumstances enumerated in Subsection (3) and further finds that there are no mitigating circumstances sufficiently substantial to call for leniency.

(3) Aggravating Circumstances.

(a) The murder was committed by a convict under sentence of imprisonment.

(b) The defendant was previously convicted of another murder or of a felony involving the use or threat of violence to the person.

(c) At the time the murder was committed the defendant also committed another murder.

(d) The defendant knowingly created a great risk of death to many persons.

(e) The murder was committed while the defendant was engaged or was an accomplice in the commission of, or an attempt to commit, or flight after committing or attempting to commit robbery, rape or deviate sexual intercourse by force or threat of force, arson, burglary or kidnapping.

(f) The murder was committed for the purpose of avoiding or preventing a lawful arrest or effecting an escape from lawful custody.

(g) The murder was committed for pecuniary gain.

(h) The murder was especially heinous, atrocious or cruel, manifesting exceptional depravity.

(4) <u>Mitigating Circumstances.</u>

(a) The defendant has no significant history of prior criminal activity.

(b) The murder was committed while the defendant was under the influence of extreme mental or emotional disturbance.

(c) The victim was a participant in the defendant's homicidal conduct or consented to the homicidal act.

(d) The murder was committed under circumstances which the defendant believed to provide a moral justification or extenuation for his conduct.

(e) The defendant was an accomplice in a murder committed by another person and his participation in the homicidal act was relatively minor.

(f) The defendant acted under duress or under the domination of another person.

(g) At the time of the murder, the capacity of the defendant to appreciate the criminality [wrongfulness] of his conduct or to conform his conduct to the requirements of law was impaired as a result of mental disease or defect or intoxication.

(h) The youth of the defendant at the time of the crime.]

## ARTICLE 211.  ASSAULT; RECKLESS ENDANGERING; THREATS

### Section 211.0.  Definitions

In this Article, the definitions given in Section 210.0 apply unless a different meaning plainly is required.

### Section 211.1.  Assault

(1) <u>Simple Assault.</u>  A person is guilty of assault if he:

(a) attempts to cause or purposely, knowingly or recklessly causes bodily injury to another; or

(b) negligently causes bodily injury to another with a deadly weapon; or

(c) attempts by physical menace to put another in fear of imminent serious bodily injury.

Simple assault is a misdemeanor unless committed in a fight or scuffle entered into by mutual consent, in which case it is a petty misdemeanor.

(2) <u>Aggravated Assault.</u>  A person is guilty of aggravated assault if he:

(a) attempts to cause serious bodily injury to another, or causes such injury purposely, knowingly or recklessly under circumstances manifesting extreme indifference to the value of human life; or

(b) attempts to cause or purposely or knowingly causes bodily injury to another with a deadly weapon.

Aggravated assault under paragraph (a) is a felony of the second degree; aggravated assault under paragraph (b) is a felony of the third degree.

### Section 211.2.  Recklessly Endangering Another Person

A person commits a misdemeanor if he recklessly engages in conduct which places or may place another person in danger of death or serious bodily injury.

Recklessness and danger shall be presumed where a person knowingly points a firearm at or in the direction of another, whether or not the actor believed the firearm to be loaded.

### Section 211.3.  Terroristic Threats

A person is guilty of a felony of the third degree if he threatens to commit any crime of violence with purpose to terrorize another or to cause evacuation of a building, place of assembly, or facility of public transportation, or otherwise to cause serious public inconvenience, or in reckless disregard of the risk of causing such terror or inconvenience.

### ARTICLE 212.  KIDNAPPING AND RELATED OFFENSES;  COERCION

### Section 212.0.  Definitions

In this Article, the definitions given in Section 210.0 apply unless a different meaning plainly is required.

### Section 212.1.  Kidnapping

A person is guilty of kidnapping if he unlawfully removes another from his place of residence or business, or a substantial distance from the vicinity where he is found, or if he unlawfully confines another for a substantial period in a place of isolation, with any of the following purposes:

(a)  to hold for ransom or reward, or as a shield or hostage;  or

(b)  to facilitate commission of any felony or flight thereafter;  or

(c)  to inflict bodily injury on or to terrorize the victim or another;  or

(d)  to interfere with the performance of any governmental or political function.

Kidnapping is a felony of the first degree unless the actor voluntarily releases the victim alive and in a safe place prior to trial, in which case it is a felony of the second degree.  A removal or confinement is unlawful within the meaning of this Section if it is accomplished by force, threat or deception, or, in the case of a person who is under the age of 14 or incompetent, if it is accomplished without the consent of a parent, guardian or other person responsible for general supervision of his welfare.

### Section 212.2.  Felonious Restraint

A person commits a felony of the third degree if he knowingly:

(a)  restrains another unlawfully in circumstances exposing him to risk of serious bodily injury;  or

(b)  holds another in a condition of involuntary servitude.

### Section 212.3.  False Imprisonment

A person commits a misdemeanor if he knowingly restrains another unlawfully so as to interfere substantially with his liberty.

## Section 212.4. Interference With Custody

(1) Custody of Children. A person commits an offense if he knowingly or recklessly takes or entices any child under the age of 18 from the custody of its parent, guardian or other lawful custodian, when he has no privilege to do so. It is an affirmative defense that:

(a) the actor believed that his action was necessary to preserve the child from danger to its welfare; or

(b) the child, being at the time not less than 14 years old, was taken away at its own instigation without enticement and without purpose to commit a criminal offense with or against the child.

Proof that the child was below the critical age gives rise to a presumption that the actor knew the child's age or acted in reckless disregard thereof. The offense is a misdemeanor unless the actor, not being a parent or person in equivalent relation to the child, acted with knowledge that his conduct would cause serious alarm for the child's safety, or in reckless disregard of a likelihood of causing such alarm, in which case the offense is a felony of the third degree.

(2) Custody of Committed Persons. A person is guilty of a misdemeanor if he knowingly or recklessly takes or entices any committed person away from lawful custody when he is not privileged to do so. "Committed person" means, in addition to anyone committed under judicial warrant, any orphan, neglected or delinquent child, mentally defective or insane person, or other dependent or incompetent person entrusted to another's custody by or through a recognized social agency or otherwise by authority of law.

## Section 212.5. Criminal Coercion

(1) Offense Defined. A person is guilty of criminal coercion if, with purpose unlawfully to restrict another's freedom of action to his detriment, he threatens to:

(a) commit any criminal offense; or

(b) accuse anyone of a criminal offense; or

(c) expose any secret tending to subject any person to hatred, contempt or ridicule, or to impair his credit or business repute; or

(d) take or withhold action as an official, or cause an official to take or withhold action.

It is an affirmative defense to prosecution based on paragraphs (b), (c) or (d) that the actor believed the accusation or secret to be true or the proposed official action justified and that his purpose was limited to compelling the other to behave in a way reasonably related to the circumstances which were the subject of the accusation, exposure or proposed official action, as by desisting from further misbehavior, making good a wrong done, refraining from taking any action or responsibility for which the actor believes the other disqualified.

(2) Grading. Criminal coercion is a misdemeanor unless the threat is to commit a felony or the actor's purpose is felonious, in which cases the offense is a felony of the third degree.

### ARTICLE 213. SEXUAL OFFENSES

## Section 213.0. Definitions

In this Article, unless a different meaning plainly is required:

**A-65**

(1) the definitions given in Section 210.0 apply;

(2) "Sexual intercourse" includes intercourse per os or per anum, with some penetration however slight; emission is not required;

(3) "Deviate sexual intercourse" means sexual intercourse per os or per anum between human beings who are not husband and wife, and any form of sexual intercourse with an animal.

### Section 213.1.   Rape and Related Offenses

(1) Rape.  A male who has sexual intercourse with a female not his wife is guilty of rape if:

(a) he compels her to submit by force or by threat of imminent death, serious bodily injury, extreme pain or kidnapping, to be inflicted on anyone; or

(b) he has substantially impaired her power to appraise or control her conduct by administering or employing without her knowledge drugs, intoxicants or other means for the purpose of preventing resistance; or

(c) the female is unconscious; or

(d) the female is less than 10 years old.

Rape is a felony of the second degree unless (i) in the course thereof the actor inflicts serious bodily injury upon anyone, or (ii) the victim was not a voluntary social companion of the actor upon the occasion of the crime and had not previously permitted him sexual liberties, in which cases the offense is a felony of the first degree.

(2) Gross Sexual Imposition.  A male who has sexual intercourse with a female not his wife commits a felony of the third degree if:

(a) he compels her to submit by any threat that would prevent resistance by a woman of ordinary resolution; or

(b) he knows that she suffers from a mental disease or defect which renders her incapable of appraising the nature of her conduct; or

(c) he knows that she is unaware that a sexual act is being committed upon her or that she submits because she mistakenly supposes that he is her husband.

### Section 213.2.   Deviate Sexual Intercourse by Force or Imposition

(1) By Force or Its Equivalent.  A person who engages in deviate sexual intercourse with another person, or who causes another to engage in deviate sexual intercourse, commits a felony of the second degree if:

(a) he compels the other person to participate by force or by threat of imminent death, serious bodily injury, extreme pain or kidnapping, to be inflicted on anyone; or

(b) he has substantially impaired the other person's power to appraise or control his conduct, by administering or employing without the knowledge of the other person drugs, intoxicants or other means for the purpose of preventing resistance; or

(c) the other person is unconscious; or

(d) the other person is less than 10 years old.

(2) <u>By Other Imposition.</u>  A person who engages in deviate sexual intercourse with another person, or who causes another to engage in deviate sexual intercourse, commits a felony of the third degree if:

(a) he compels the other person to participate by any threat that would prevent resistance by a person of ordinary resolution;  or

(b) he knows that the other person suffers from a mental disease or defect which renders him incapable of appraising the nature of his conduct;  or

(c) he knows that the other person submits because he is unaware that a sexual act is being committed upon him.

### Section 213.3.  Corruption of Minors and Seduction

(1) <u>Offense Defined.</u>  A male who has sexual intercourse with a female not his wife, or any person who engages in deviate sexual intercourse or causes another to engage in deviate sexual intercourse, is guilty of an offense if:

(a) the other person is less than [16] years old and the actor is at least [four] years older than the other person;  or

(b) the other person is less than 21 years old and the actor is his guardian or otherwise responsible for general supervision of his welfare;  or

(c) the other person is in custody of law or detained in a hospital or other institution and the actor has supervisory or disciplinary authority over him;  or

(d) the other person is a female who is induced to participate by a promise of marriage which the actor does not mean to perform.

(2) <u>Grading.</u>  An offense under paragraph (a) of Subsection (1) is a felony of the third degree.  Otherwise an offense under this section is a misdemeanor.

### Section 213.4.  Sexual Assault

A person who has sexual contact with another not his spouse, or causes such other to have sexual contact with him, is guilty of sexual assault, a misdemeanor, if:

(1) he knows that the contact is offensive to the other person;  or

(2) he knows that the other person suffers from a mental disease or defect which renders him or her incapable of appraising the nature of his or her conduct;  or

(3) he knows that the other person is unaware that a sexual act is being committed;  or

(4) the other person is less than 10 years old;  or

(5) he has substantially impaired the other person's power to appraise or control his or her conduct, by administering or employing without the other's knowledge drugs, intoxicants or other means for the purpose of preventing resistance;  or

(6) the other person is less than [16] years old and the actor is at least [four] years older than the other person;  or

(7) the other person is less than 21 years old and the actor is his guardian or otherwise responsible for general supervision of his welfare;  or

(8) the other person is in custody of law or detained in a hospital or other institution and the actor has supervisory or disciplinary authority over him.

**A-67**

Sexual contact is any touching of the sexual or other intimate parts of the person for the purpose of arousing or gratifying sexual desire.

### Section 213.5.  Indecent Exposure

A person commits a misdemeanor if, for the purpose of arousing or gratifying sexual desire of himself or of any person other than his spouse, he exposes his genitals under circumstances in which he knows his conduct is likely to cause affront or alarm.

### Section 213.6.  Provisions Generally Applicable to Article 213

(1) Mistake as to Age.  Whenever in this Article the criminality of conduct depends on a child's being below the age of 10, it is no defense that the actor did not know the child's age, or reasonably believed the child to be older than 10.  When criminality depends on the child's being below a critical age other than 10, it is a defense for the actor to prove by a preponderance of the evidence that he reasonably believed the child to be above the critical age.

(2) Spouse Relationships.  Whenever in this Article the definition of an offense excludes conduct with a spouse, the exclusion shall be deemed to extend to persons living as man and wife, regardless of the legal status of their relationship.  The exclusion shall be inoperative as respects spouses living apart under a decree of judicial separation.  Where the definition of an offense excludes conduct with a spouse or conduct by a woman, this shall not preclude conviction of a spouse or woman as accomplice in a sexual act which he or she causes another person, not within the exclusion, to perform.

(3) Sexually Promiscuous Complainants.  It is a defense to prosecution under Section 213.3 and paragraphs (6), (7) and (8) of Section 213.4 for the actor to prove by a preponderance of the evidence that the alleged victim had, prior to the time of the offense charged, engaged promiscuously in sexual relations with others.

(4) Prompt Complaint.  No prosecution may be instituted or maintained under this Article unless the alleged offense was brought to the notice of public authority within [3] months of its occurrence or, where the alleged victim was less than [16] years old or otherwise incompetent to make complaint, within [3] months after a parent, guardian or other competent person specially interested in the victim learns of the offense.

(5) Testimony of Complainants.  No person shall be convicted of any felony under this Article upon the uncorroborated testimony of the alleged victim.  Corroboration may be circumstantial.  In any prosecution before a jury for an offense under this Article, the jury shall be instructed to evaluate the testimony of a victim or complaining witness with special care in view of the emotional involvement of the witness and the difficulty of determining the truth with respect to alleged sexual activities carried out in private.

## OFFENSES AGAINST PROPERTY

---

### ARTICLE 220.   ARSON, CRIMINAL MISCHIEF, AND OTHER PROPERTY DESTRUCTION

#### Section 220.1.   Arson and Related Offenses

(1) Arson.  A person is guilty of arson, a felony of the second degree, if he starts a fire or causes an explosion with the purpose of:

(a) destroying a building or occupied structure of another; or

(b) destroying or damaging any property, whether his own or another's, to collect insurance for such loss.  It shall be an affirmative defense to prosecution under this paragraph that the actor's conduct did not recklessly endanger any building or occupied structure of another or place any other person in danger of death or bodily injury.

(2) Reckless Burning or Exploding.  A person commits a felony of the third degree if he purposely starts a fire or causes an explosion, whether on his own property or another's, and thereby recklessly:

(a) places another person in danger of death or bodily injury; or

(b) places a building or occupied structure of another in danger of damage or destruction.

(3) Failure to Control or Report Dangerous Fire.  A person who knows that a fire is endangering life or a substantial amount of property of another and fails to take reasonable measures to put out or control the fire, when he can do so without substantial risk to himself, or to give a prompt fire alarm, commits a misdemeanor if:

(a) he knows that he is under an official, contractual, or other legal duty to prevent or combat the fire;  or

(b) the fire was started, albeit lawfully, by him or with his assent, or on property in his custody or control.

(4) Definitions.  "Occupied structure" means any structure, vehicle or place adapted for overnight accommodation of persons, or for carrying on business therein, whether or not a person is actually present.  Property is that of another, for the purposes of this section, if anyone other than the actor has a possessory or proprietary interest therein.  If a building or structure is divided into separately occupied units, any unit not occupied by the actor is an occupied structure of another.

#### Section 220.2.   Causing or Risking Catastrophe

(1) Causing Catastrophe.  A person who causes a catastrophe by explosion, fire, flood, avalanche, collapse of building, release of poison gas, radioactive material or other harmful or destructive force or substance, or by any other means of causing potentially widespread injury or damage, commits a felony of the second degree if he does so purposely or knowingly, or a felony of the third degree if he does so recklessly.

(2) Risking Catastrophe.  A person is guilty of a misdemeanor if he recklessly creates a risk of catastrophe in the employment of fire, explosives or other dangerous means listed in Subsection (1).

**A-69**

(3) <u>Failure to Prevent Catastrophe.</u>  A person who knowingly or recklessly fails to take reasonable measures to prevent or mitigate a catastrophe commits a misdemeanor if:

(a) he knows that he is under an official, contractual or other legal duty to take such measures; or

(b) he did or assented to the act causing or threatening the catastrophe.

## Section 220.3.  Criminal Mischief

(1) <u>Offense Defined.</u>  A person is guilty of criminal mischief if he:

(a) damages tangible property of another purposely, recklessly, or by negligence in the employment of fire, explosives, or other dangerous means listed in Section 220.2(1); or

(b) purposely or recklessly tampers with tangible property of another so as to endanger person or property; or

(c) purposely or recklessly causes another to suffer pecuniary loss by deception or threat.

(2) <u>Grading.</u>  Criminal mischief is a felony of the third degree if the actor purposely causes pecuniary loss in excess of $5,000, or a substantial interruption or impairment of public communication, transportation, supply of water, gas or power, or other public service.  It is a misdemeanor if the actor purposely causes pecuniary loss in excess of $100, or a petty misdemeanor if he purposely or recklessly causes pecuniary loss in excess of $25.  Otherwise criminal mischief is a violation.

## ARTICLE 221.  BURGLARY AND OTHER CRIMINAL INTRUSION

## Section 221.0.  Definitions

In this Article, unless a different meaning plainly is required:

(1) "occupied structure" means any structure, vehicle or place adapted for overnight accommodation of persons, or for carrying on business therein, whether or not a person is actually present.

(2) "night" means the period between thirty minutes past sunset and thirty minutes before sunrise.

## Section 221.1.  Burglary

(1) <u>Burglary Defined.</u>  A person is guilty of burglary if he enters a building or occupied structure, or separately secured or occupied portion thereof, with purpose to commit a crime therein, unless the premises are at the time open to the public or the actor is licensed or privileged to enter.  It is an affirmative defense to prosecution for burglary that the building or structure was abandoned.

(2) <u>Grading.</u>  Burglary is a felony of the second degree if it is perpetrated in the dwelling of another at night, or if, in the course of committing the offense, the actor:

(a) purposely, knowingly or recklessly inflicts or attempts to inflict bodily injury on anyone; or

(b) is armed with explosives or a deadly weapon.

Otherwise, burglary is a felony of the third degree.  An act shall be deemed "in the course of committing" an offense if it occurs in an attempt to commit the offense or in flight after the attempt or commission.

(3) Multiple Convictions.  A person may not be convicted both for burglary and for the offense which it was his purpose to commit after the burglarious entry or for an attempt to commit that offense, unless the additional offense constitutes a felony of the first or second degree.

### Section 221.2.  Criminal Trespass

(1) Buildings and Occupied Structures.  A person commits an offense if, knowing that he is not licensed or privileged to do so, he enters or surreptitiously remains in any building or occupied structure, or separately secured or occupied portion thereof.  An offense under this Subsection is a misdemeanor if it is committed in a dwelling at night.  Otherwise it is a petty misdemeanor.

(2) Defiant Trespasser.  A person commits an offense if, knowing that he is not licensed or privileged to do so, he enters or remains in any place as to which notice against trespass is given by:

(a) actual communication to the actor;  or

(b) posting in a manner prescribed by law or reasonably likely to come to the attention of intruders;  or

(c) fencing or other enclosure manifestly designed to exclude intruders.

An offense under this Subsection constitutes a petty misdemeanor if the offender defies an order to leave personally communicated to him by the owner of the premises or other authorized person.  Otherwise it is a violation.

(3) Defenses.  It is an affirmative defense to prosecution under this Section that:

(a) a building or occupied structure involved in an offense under Subsection (1) was abandoned;  or

(b) the premises were at the time open to members of the public and the actor complied with all lawful conditions imposed on access to or remaining in the premises;  or

(c) the actor reasonably believed that the owner of the premises, or other person empowered to license access thereto, would have licensed him to enter or remain.

## ARTICLE 222.  ROBBERY

### Section 222.1.  Robbery

(1) Robbery Defined.  A person is guilty of robbery if, in the course of committing a theft, he:

(a) inflicts serious bodily injury upon another;  or

(b) threatens another with or purposely puts him in fear of immediate serious bodily injury;  or

(c) commits or threatens immediately to commit any felony of the first or second degree.

**A-71**

An act shall be deemed "in the course of committing a theft" if it occurs in an attempt to commit theft or in flight after the attempt or commission.

(2) Grading.  Robbery is a felony of the second degree, except that it is a felony of the first degree if in the course of committing the theft the actor attempts to kill anyone, or purposely inflicts or attempts to inflict serious bodily injury.

## ARTICLE 223.   THEFT AND RELATED OFFENSES

### Section 223.0.  Definitions

In this Article, unless a different meaning plainly is required:

(1) "deprive" means:  (a) to withhold property of another permanently or for so extended a period as to appropriate a major portion of its economic value, or with intent to restore only upon payment of reward or other compensation;  or (b) to dispose of the property so as to make it unlikely that the owner will recover it.

(2) "financial institution" means a bank, insurance company, credit union, building and loan association, investment trust or other organization held out to the public as a place of deposit of funds or medium of savings or collective investment.

(3) "government" means the United States, any State, county, municipality, or other political unit, or any department, agency or subdivision of any of the foregoing, or any corporation or other association carrying out the functions of government.

(4) "movable property" means property the location of which can be changed, including things growing on, affixed to, or found in land, and documents although the rights represented thereby have no physical location.  "Immovable property" is all other property.

(5) "obtain" means:  (a) in relation to property, to bring about a transfer or purported transfer of a legal interest in the property, whether to the obtainer or another;  or (b) in relation to labor or service, to secure performance thereof.

(6) "property" means anything of value, including real estate, tangible and intangible personal property, contract rights, choses-in-action and other interests in or claims to wealth, admission or transportation tickets, captured or domestic animals, food and drink, electric or other power.

(7) "property of another" includes property in which any person other than the actor has an interest which the actor is not privileged to infringe, regardless of the fact that the actor also has an interest in the property and regardless of the fact that the other person might be precluded from civil recovery because the property was used in an unlawful transaction or was subject to forfeiture as contraband. Property in possession of the actor shall not be deemed property of another who has only a security interest therein, even if legal title is in the creditor pursuant to a conditional sales contract or other security agreement.

### Section 223.1.  Consolidation of Theft Offenses;  Grading;  Provisions Applicable to Theft Generally

(1) Consolidation of Theft Offenses.  Conduct denominated theft in this Article constitutes a single offense.  An accusation of theft may be supported by evidence that it was committed in any manner that would be theft under this Article, notwithstanding the specification of a different manner in the indictment or information, subject only to the power of the Court to ensure fair trial by granting a

continuance or other appropriate relief where the conduct of the defense would be prejudiced by lack of fair notice or by surprise.

(2) Grading of Theft Offenses.

(a) Theft constitutes a felony of the third degree if the amount involved exceeds $500, or if the property stolen is a firearm, automobile, airplane, motorcycle, motorboat, or other motor-propelled vehicle, or in the case of theft by receiving stolen property, if the receiver is in the business of buying or selling stolen property.

(b) Theft not within the preceding paragraph constitutes a misdemeanor, except that if the property was not taken from the person or by threat, or in breach of a fiduciary obligation, and the actor proves by a preponderance of the evidence that the amount involved was less than $50, the offense constitutes a petty misdemeanor.

(c) The amount involved in a theft shall be deemed to be the highest value, by any reasonable standard, of the property or services which the actor stole or attempted to steal.   Amounts involved in thefts committed pursuant to one scheme or course of conduct, whether from the same person or several persons, may be aggregated in determining the grade of the offense.

(3) Claim of Right.  It is an affirmative defense to prosecution for theft that the actor:

(a) was unaware that the property or service was that of another;  or

(b) acted under an honest claim of right to the property or service involved or that he had a right to acquire or dispose of it as he did;  or

(c) took property exposed for sale, intending to purchase and pay for it promptly, or reasonably believing that the owner, if present, would have consented.

(4) Theft From Spouse.  It is no defense that theft was from the actor's spouse, except that misappropriation of household and personal effects, or other property normally accessible to both spouses, is theft only if it occurs after the parties have ceased living together.

## Section 223.2.  Theft by Unlawful Taking or Disposition

(1) Movable Property.  A person is guilty of theft if he unlawfully takes, or exercises unlawful control over, movable property of another with purpose to deprive him thereof.

(2) Immovable Property.  A person is guilty of theft if he unlawfully transfers immovable property of another or any interest therein with purpose to benefit himself or another not entitled thereto.

## Section 223.3.  Theft by Deception

A person is guilty of theft if he purposely obtains property of another by deception.  A person deceives if he purposely:

(1) creates or reinforces a false impression, including false impressions as to law, value, intention or other state of mind;  but deception as to a person's intention to perform a promise shall not be inferred from the fact alone that he did not subsequently perform the promise;  or

(2) prevents another from acquiring information which would affect his judgment of a transaction; or

(3) fails to correct a false impression which the deceiver previously created or reinforced, or which the deceiver knows to be influencing another to whom he stands in a fiduciary or confidential relationship; or

(4) fails to disclose a known lien, adverse claim or other legal impediment to the enjoyment of property which he transfers or encumbers in consideration for the property obtained, whether such impediment is or is not valid, or is or is not a matter of official record.

The term "deceive" does not, however, include falsity as to matters having no pecuniary significance, or puffing by statements unlikely to deceive ordinary persons in the group addressed.

### Section 223.4.   Theft by Extortion

A person is guilty of theft if he purposely obtains property of another by threatening to:

(1) inflict bodily injury on anyone or commit any other criminal offense; or

(2) accuse anyone of a criminal offense; or

(3) expose any secret tending to subject any person to hatred, contempt or ridicule, or to impair his credit or business repute; or

(4) take or withhold action as an official, or cause an official to take or withhold action; or

(5) bring about or continue a strike, boycott or other collective unofficial action, if the property is not demanded or received for the benefit of the group in whose interest the actor purports to act; or

(6) testify or provide information or withhold testimony or information with respect to another's legal claim or defense; or

(7) inflict any other harm which would not benefit the actor.

It is an affirmative defense to prosecution based on paragraphs (2), (3) or (4) that the property obtained by threat of accusation, exposure, lawsuit or other invocation of official action was honestly claimed as restitution or indemnification for harm done in the circumstances to which such accusation, exposure, lawsuit or other official action relates, or as compensation for property or lawful services.

### Section 223.5.   Theft of Property Lost, Mislaid, or Delivered by Mistake

A person who comes into control of property of another that he knows to have been lost, mislaid, or delivered under a mistake as to the nature or amount of the property or the identity of the recipient is guilty of theft if, with purpose to deprive the owner thereof, he fails to take reasonable measures to restore the property to a person entitled to have it.

### Section 223.6.   Receiving Stolen Property

(1) Receiving.  A person is guilty of theft if he purposely receives, retains, or disposes of movable property of another knowing that it has been stolen, or believing that it has probably been stolen, unless the property is received, retained, or disposed with purpose to restore it to the owner.  "Receiving" means acquiring possession, control or title, or lending on the security of the property.

(2) Presumption of Knowledge.  The requisite knowledge or belief is presumed in the case of a dealer who:

(a) is found in possession or control of property stolen from two or more persons on separate occasions; or

(b) has received stolen property in another transaction within the year preceding the transaction charged;  or

(c) being a dealer in property of the sort received, acquires it for a consideration which he knows is far below its reasonable value.

"Dealer" means a person in the business of buying or selling goods including a pawnbroker.

### Section 223.7.  Theft of Services

(1) A person is guilty of theft if he purposely obtains services which he knows are available only for compensation, by deception or threat, or by false token or other means to avoid payment for the service.  "Services" includes labor, professional service, transportation, telephone or other public service, accommodation in hotels, restaurants or elsewhere, admission to exhibitions, use of vehicles or other movable property.  Where compensation for service is ordinarily paid immediately upon the rendering of such service, as in the case of hotels and restaurants, refusal to pay or absconding without payment or offer to pay gives rise to a presumption that the service was obtained by deception as to intention to pay.

(2) A person commits theft if, having control over the disposition of services of others, to which he is not entitled, he knowingly diverts such services to his own benefit or to the benefit of another not entitled thereto.

### Section 223.8.  Theft by Failure to Make Required Disposition of Funds Received

A person who purposely obtains property upon agreement, or subject to a known legal obligation, to make specified payment or other disposition, whether from such property or its proceeds or from his own property to be reserved in equivalent amount, is guilty of theft if he deals with the property obtained as his own and fails to make the required payment or disposition.  The foregoing applies notwithstanding that it may be impossible to identify particular property as belonging to the victim at the time of the actor's failure to make the required payment or disposition.  An officer or employee of the government or of a financial institution is presumed: (i) to know any legal obligation relevant to his criminal liability under this Section, and (ii) to have dealt with the property as his own if he fails to pay or account upon lawful demand, or if an audit reveals a shortage or falsification of accounts.

### Section 223.9.  Unauthorized Use of Automobiles and Other Vehicles

A person commits a misdemeanor if he operates another's automobile, airplane, motorcycle, motorboat, or other motor-propelled vehicle without consent of the owner.  It is an affirmative defense to prosecution under this Section that the actor reasonably believed that the owner would have consented to the operation had he known of it.

## ARTICLE 224.  FORGERY AND FRAUDULENT PRACTICES

### Section 224.0.  Definitions

In this Article, the definitions given in Section 223.0 apply unless a different meaning plainly is required.

### Section 224.1.  Forgery

(1) Definition.  A person is guilty of forgery if, with purpose to defraud or injure anyone, or with knowledge that he is facilitating a fraud or injury to be perpetrated by anyone, the actor:

  (a) alters any writing of another without his authority;  or

  (b) makes, completes, executes, authenticates, issues or transfers any writing so that it purports to be the act of another who did not authorize that act, or to have been executed at a time or place or in a numbered sequence other than was in fact the case, or to be a copy of an original when no such original existed;  or

  (c) utters any writing which he knows to be forged in a manner specified in paragraphs (a) or (b).

"Writing" includes printing or any other method of recording information, money, coins, tokens, stamps, seals, credit cards, badges, trade-marks, and other symbols of value, right, privilege, or identification.

(2) Grading.  Forgery is a felony of the second degree if the writing is or purports to be part of an issue of money, securities, postage or revenue stamps, or other instruments issued by the government, or part of an issue of stock, bonds or other instruments representing interests in or claims against any property or enterprise.  Forgery is a felony of the third degree if the writing is or purports to be a will, deed, contract, release, commercial instrument, or other document evidencing, creating, transferring, altering, terminating, or otherwise affecting legal relations.  Otherwise forgery is a misdemeanor.

### Section 224.2.  Simulating Objects of Antiquity, Rarity, Etc.

A person commits a misdemeanor if, with purpose to defraud anyone or with knowledge that he is facilitating a fraud to be perpetrated by anyone, he makes, alters or utters any object so that it appears to have value because of antiquity, rarity, source, or authorship which it does not possess.

### Section 224.3.  Fraudulent Destruction, Removal or Concealment of Recordable Instruments

A person commits a felony of the third degree if, with purpose to deceive or injure anyone, he destroys, removes or conceals any will, deed, mortgage, security instrument or other writing for which the law provides public recording.

### Section 224.4.  Tampering With Records

A person commits a misdemeanor if, knowing that he has no privilege to do so, he falsifies, destroys, removes or conceals any writing or record, with purpose to deceive or injure anyone or to conceal any wrongdoing.

## Section 224.5.  Bad Checks

A person who issues or passes a check or similar sight order for the payment of money, knowing that it will not be honored by the drawee, commits a misdemeanor. For the purposes of this Section as well as in any prosecution for theft committed by means of a bad check, an issuer is presumed to know that the check or order (other than a post-dated check or order) would not be paid, if:

(1) the issuer had no account with the drawee at the time the check or order was issued; or

(2) payment was refused by the drawee for lack of funds, upon presentation within 30 days after issue, and the issuer failed to make good within 10 days after receiving notice of that refusal.

## Section 224.6.  Credit Cards

A person commits an offense if he uses a credit card for the purpose of obtaining property or services with knowledge that:

(1) the card is stolen or forged; or

(2) the card has been revoked or canceled; or

(3) for any other reason his use of the card is unauthorized by the issuer.

It is an affirmative defense to prosecution under paragraph (c) if the actor proves by a preponderance of the evidence that he had the purpose and ability to meet all obligations to the issuer arising out of his use of the card. "Credit card" means a writing or other evidence of an undertaking to pay for property or services delivered or rendered to or upon the order of a designated person or bearer. An offense under this Section is a felony of the third degree if the value of the property or services secured or sought to be secured by means of the credit card exceeds $500; otherwise it is a misdemeanor.

## Section 224.7.  Deceptive Business Practices

A person commits a misdemeanor if in the course of business he:

(1) uses or possesses for use a false weight or measure, or any other device for falsely determining or recording any quality or quantity; or

(2) sells, offers or exposes for sale, or delivers less than the represented quantity of any commodity or service; or

(3) takes or attempts to take more than the represented quantity of any commodity or service when as buyer he furnishes the weight or measure; or

(4) sells, offers or exposes for sale adulterated or mislabeled commodities. "Adulterated" means varying from the standard of composition or quality prescribed by or pursuant to any statute providing criminal penalties for such variance, or set by established commercial usage. "Mislabeled" means varying from the standard of truth or disclosure in labeling prescribed by or pursuant to any statute providing criminal penalties for such variance, or set by established commercial usage; or

(5) makes a false or misleading statement in any advertisement addressed to the public or to a substantial segment thereof for the purpose of promoting the purchase or sale of property or services; or

**A-77**

(6) makes a false or misleading written statement for the purpose of obtaining property or credit; or

(7) makes a false or misleading written statement for the purpose of promoting the sale of securities, or omits information required by law to be disclosed in written documents relating to securities.

It is an affirmative defense to prosecution under this Section if the defendant proves by a preponderance of the evidence that his conduct was not knowingly or recklessly deceptive.

### Section 224.8.  Commercial Bribery and Breach of Duty to Act Disinterestedly

(1) A person commits a misdemeanor if he solicits, accepts or agrees to accept any benefit as consideration for knowingly violating or agreeing to violate a duty of fidelity to which he is subject as:

(a) partner, agent, or employee of another;

(b) trustee, guardian, or other fiduciary;

(c) lawyer, physician, accountant, appraiser, or other professional adviser or informant;

(d) officer, director, manager or other participant in the direction of the affairs of an incorporated or unincorporated association;  or

(e) arbitrator or other purportedly disinterested adjudicator or referee.

(2) A person who holds himself out to the public as being engaged in the business of making disinterested selection, appraisal, or criticism of commodities or services commits a misdemeanor if he solicits, accepts or agrees to accept any benefit to influence his selection, appraisal or criticism.

(3) A person commits a misdemeanor if he confers, or offers or agrees to confer, any benefit the acceptance of which would be criminal under this Section.

### Section 224.9.  Rigging Publicly Exhibited Contest

(1) A person commits a misdemeanor if, with purpose to prevent a publicly exhibited contest from being conducted in accordance with the rules and usages purporting to govern it, he:

(a) confers or offers or agrees to confer any benefit upon, or threatens any injury to a participant, official or other person associated with the contest or exhibition; or

(b) tampers with any person, animal or thing.

(2) Soliciting or Accepting Benefit for Rigging.  A person commits a misdemeanor if he knowingly solicits, accepts or agrees to accept any benefit the giving of which would be criminal under Subsection (1).

(3) Participation in Rigged Contest.  A person commits a misdemeanor if he knowingly engages in, sponsors, produces, judges, or otherwise participates in a publicly exhibited contest knowing that the contest is not being conducted in compliance with the rules and usages purporting to govern it, by reason of conduct which would be criminal under this Section.

## Section 224.10.  Defrauding Secured Creditors

A person commits a misdemeanor if he destroys, removes, conceals, encumbers, transfers or otherwise deals with property subject to a security interest with purpose to hinder enforcement of that interest.

## Section 224.11.  Fraud in Insolvency

A person commits a misdemeanor if, knowing that proceedings have been or are about to be instituted for the appointment of a receiver or other person entitled to administer property for the benefit of creditors, or that any other composition or liquidation for the benefit of creditors has been or is about to be made, he:

(1) destroys, removes, conceals, encumbers, transfers, or otherwise deals with any property with purpose to defeat or obstruct the claim of any creditor, or otherwise to obstruct the operation of any law relating to administration of property for the benefit of creditors;  or

(2) knowingly falsifies any writing or record relating to the property;  or

(3) knowingly misrepresents or refuses to disclose to a receiver or other person entitled to administer property for the benefit of creditors, the existence, amount or location of the property, or any other information which the actor could be legally required to furnish in relation to such administration.

## Section 224.12.  Receiving Deposits in a Failing Financial Institution

An officer, manager or other person directing or participating in the direction of a financial institution commits a misdemeanor if he receives or permits the receipt of a deposit, premium payment or other investment in the institution knowing that:

(1) due to financial difficulties the institution is about to suspend operations or go into receivership or reorganization;  and

(2) the person making the deposit or other payment is unaware of the precarious situation of the institution.

## Section 224.13.  Misapplication of Entrusted Property and Property of Government or Financial Institution

A person commits an offense if he applies or disposes of property that has been entrusted to him as a fiduciary, or property of the government or of a financial institution, in a manner which he knows is unlawful and involves substantial risk of loss or detriment to the owner of the property or to a person for whose benefit the property was entrusted.  The offense is a misdemeanor if the amount involved exceeds $50;  otherwise it is a petty misdemeanor.  "Fiduciary" includes trustee, guardian, executor, administrator, receiver and any person carrying on fiduciary functions on behalf of a corporation or other organization which is a fiduciary.

## Section 224.14.  Securing Execution of Documents by Deception

A person commits a misdemeanor if by deception he causes another to execute any instrument affecting, purporting to affect, or likely to affect the pecuniary interest of any person.

---

## OFFENSES AGAINST THE FAMILY

---

### ARTICLE 230.   OFFENSES AGAINST THE FAMILY

#### Section 230.1.   Bigamy and Polygamy

(1) Bigamy. A married person is guilty of bigamy, a misdemeanor, if he contracts or purports to contract another marriage, unless at the time of the subsequent marriage:

(a) the actor believes that the prior spouse is dead; or

(b) the actor and the prior spouse have been living apart for five consecutive years throughout which the prior spouse was not known by the actor to be alive; or

(c) a Court has entered a judgment purporting to terminate or annul any prior disqualifying marriage, and the actor does not know that judgment to be invalid; or

(d) the actor reasonably believes that he is legally eligible to remarry.

(2) Polygamy. A person is guilty of polygamy, a felony of the third degree, if he marries or cohabits with more than one spouse at a time in purported exercise of the right of plural marriage. The offense is a continuing one until all cohabitation and claim of marriage with more than one spouse terminates. This section does not apply to parties to a polygamous marriage, lawful in the country of which they are residents or nationals, while they are in transit through or temporarily visiting this State.

(3) Other Party to Bigamous or Polygamous Marriage. A person is guilty of bigamy or polygamy, as the case may be, if he contracts or purports to contract marriage with another knowing that the other is thereby committing bigamy or polygamy.

#### Section 230.2.   Incest

A person is guilty of incest, a felony of the third degree, if he knowingly marries or cohabits or has sexual intercourse with an ancestor or descendant, a brother or sister of the whole or half blood [or an uncle, aunt, nephew or niece of the whole blood]. "Cohabit" means to live together under the representation or appearance of being married. The relationships referred to herein include blood relationships without regard to legitimacy, and relationship of parent and child by adoption.

#### Section 230.3.   Abortion

(1) Unjustified Abortion. A person who purposely and unjustifiably terminates the pregnancy of another otherwise than by a live birth commits a felony of the third degree or, where the pregnancy has continued beyond the twenty-sixth week, a felony of the second degree.

(2) Justifiable Abortion. A licensed physician is justified in terminating a pregnancy if he believes there is substantial risk that continuance of the pregnancy would gravely impair the physical or mental health of the mother or that the child would be born with grave physical or mental defect, or that the pregnancy resulted from rape, incest, or other felonious intercourse. All illicit intercourse with a girl

below the age of 16 shall be deemed felonious for purposes of this Subsection. Justifiable abortions shall be performed only in a licensed hospital except in case of emergency when hospital facilities are unavailable. [Additional exceptions from the requirement of hospitalization may be incorporated here to take account of situations in sparsely settled areas where hospitals are not generally accessible.]

(3) Physicians' Certificates; Presumption From Non–Compliance. No abortion shall be performed unless two physicians, one of whom may be the person performing the abortion, shall have certified in writing the circumstances which they believe to justify the abortion. Such certificate shall be submitted before the abortion to the hospital where it is to be performed and, in the case of abortion following felonious intercourse, to the prosecuting attorney or the police. Failure to comply with any of the requirements of this Subsection gives rise to a presumption that the abortion was unjustified.

(4) Self–Abortion. A woman whose pregnancy has continued beyond the twenty-sixth week commits a felony of the third degree if she purposely terminates her own pregnancy otherwise than by a live birth, or if she uses instruments, drugs or violence upon herself for that purpose. Except as justified under Subsection (2), a person who induces or knowingly aids a woman to use instruments, drugs or violence upon herself for the purpose of terminating her pregnancy otherwise than by a live birth commits a felony of the third degree whether or not the pregnancy has continued beyond the twenty-sixth week.

(5) Pretended Abortion. A person commits a felony of the third degree if, representing that it is his purpose to perform an abortion, he does an act adapted to cause abortion in a pregnant woman although the woman is in fact not pregnant, or the actor does not believe she is. A person charged with unjustified abortion under Subsection (1) or an attempt to commit that offense may be convicted thereof upon proof of conduct prohibited by this Subsection.

(6) Distribution of Abortifacients. A person who sells, offers to sell, possesses with intent to sell, advertises, or displays for sale anything specially designed to terminate a pregnancy, or held out by the actor as useful for that purpose, commits a misdemeanor, unless:

(a) the sale, offer or display is to a physician or druggist or to an intermediary in a chain of distribution to physicians or druggists; or

(b) the sale is made upon prescription or order of a physician; or

(c) the possession is with intent to sell as authorized in paragraphs (a) and (b); or

(d) the advertising is addressed to persons named in paragraph (a) and confined to trade or professional channels not likely to reach the general public.

(7) Section Inapplicable to Prevention of Pregnancy. Nothing in this Section shall be deemed applicable to the prescription, administration or distribution of drugs or other substances for avoiding pregnancy, whether by preventing implantation of a fertilized ovum or by any other method that operates before, at or immediately after fertilization.

### Section 230.4. Endangering Welfare of Children

A parent, guardian, or other person supervising the welfare of a child under 18 commits a misdemeanor if he knowingly endangers the child's welfare by violating a duty of care, protection or support.

### Section 230.5.  Persistent Non–Support

A person commits a misdemeanor if he persistently fails to provide support which he can provide and which he knows he is legally obliged to provide to a spouse, child or other dependent.

––––––

## OFFENSES AGAINST PUBLIC ADMINISTRATION

––––––

## ARTICLE 240.  BRIBERY AND CORRUPT INFLUENCE

### Section 240.0.  Definitions

In Articles 240–243, unless a different meaning plainly is required:

(1) "benefit" means gain or advantage, or anything regarded by the beneficiary as gain or advantage, including benefit to any other person or entity in whose welfare he is interested, but not an advantage promised generally to a group or class of voters as a consequence of public measures which a candidate engages to support or oppose;

(2) "government" includes any branch, subdivision or agency of the government of the State or any locality within it;

(3) "harm" means loss, disadvantage or injury, or anything so regarded by the person affected, including loss, disadvantage or injury to any other person or entity in whose welfare he is interested;

(4) "official proceeding" means a proceeding heard or which may be heard before any legislative, judicial, administrative or other governmental agency or official authorized to take evidence under oath, including any referee, hearing examiner, commissioner, notary or other person taking testimony or deposition in connection with any such proceeding;

(5) "party official" means a person who holds an elective or appointive post in a political party in the United States by virtue of which he directs or conducts, or participates in directing or conducting party affairs at any level of responsibility;

(6) "pecuniary benefit" is benefit in the form of money, property, commercial interests or anything else the primary significance of which is economic gain;

(7) "public servant" means any officer or employee of government, including legislators and judges, and any person participating as juror, advisor, consultant or otherwise, in performing a governmental function;  but the term does not include witnesses;

(8) "administrative proceeding" means any proceeding, other than a judicial proceeding, the outcome of which is required to be based on a record or documentation prescribed by law, or in which law or regulation is particularized in application to individuals.

### Section 240.1.  Bribery in Official and Political Matters

A person is guilty of bribery, a felony of the third degree, if he offers, confers or agrees to confer upon another, or solicits, accepts or agrees to accept from another:

(1) any pecuniary benefit as consideration for the recipient's decision, opinion, recommendation, vote or other exercise of discretion as a public servant, party official or voter; or

(2) any benefit as consideration for the recipient's decision, vote, recommendation or other exercise of official discretion in a judicial or administrative proceeding; or

(3) any benefit as consideration for a violation of a known legal duty as public servant or party official.

It is no defense to prosecution under this section that a person whom the actor sought to influence was not qualified to act in the desired way whether because he had not yet assumed office, or lacked jurisdiction, or for any other reason.

## Section 240.2.   Threats and Other Improper Influence in Official and Political Matters

(1) <u>Offenses Defined.</u>   A person commits an offense if he:

(a) threatens unlawful harm to any person with purpose to influence his decision, opinion, recommendation, vote or other exercise of discretion as a public servant, party official or voter; or

(b) threatens harm to any public servant with purpose to influence his decision, opinion, recommendation, vote or other exercise of discretion in a judicial or administrative proceeding; or

(c) threatens harm to any public servant or party official with purpose to influence him to violate his known legal duty; or

(d) privately addresses to any public servant who has or will have an official discretion in a judicial or administrative proceeding any representation, entreaty, argument or other communication with purpose to influence the outcome on the basis of considerations other than those authorized by law.

It is no defense to prosecution under this Section that a person whom the actor sought to influence was not qualified to act in the desired way, whether because he had not yet assumed office, or lacked jurisdiction, or for any other reason.

(2) <u>Grading.</u>   An offense under this Section is a misdemeanor unless the actor threatened to commit a crime or made a threat with purpose to influence a judicial or administrative proceeding, in which cases the offense is a felony of the third degree.

## Section 240.3.   Compensation for Past Official Behavior

A person commits a misdemeanor if he solicits, accepts or agrees to accept any pecuniary benefit as compensation for having, as public servant, given a decision, opinion, recommendation or vote favorable to another, or for having otherwise exercised a discretion in his favor, or for having violated his duty.   A person commits a misdemeanor if he offers, confers or agrees to confer compensation acceptance of which is prohibited by this Section.

## Section 240.4.   Retaliation for Past Official Action

A person commits a misdemeanor if he harms another by any unlawful act in retaliation for anything lawfully done by the latter in the capacity of public servant.

### Section 240.5. Gifts to Public Servants by Persons Subject to Their Jurisdiction

(1) Regulatory and Law Enforcement Officials. No public servant in any department or agency exercising regulatory functions, or conducting inspections or investigations, or carrying on civil or criminal litigation on behalf of the government, or having custody of prisoners, shall solicit, accept or agree to accept any pecuniary benefit from a person known to be subject to such regulation, inspection, investigation or custody, or against whom such litigation is known to be pending or contemplated.

(2) Officials Concerned with Government Contracts and Pecuniary Transactions. No public servant having any discretionary function to perform in connection with contracts, purchases, payments, claims or other pecuniary transactions of the government shall solicit, accept or agree to accept any pecuniary benefit from any person known to be interested in or likely to become interested in any such contract, purchase, payment, claim or transaction.

(3) Judicial and Administrative Officials. No public servant having judicial or administrative authority and no public servant employed by or in a court or other tribunal having such authority, or participating in the enforcement of its decisions, shall solicit, accept or agree to accept any pecuniary benefit from a person known to be interested in or likely to become interested in any matter before such public servant or a tribunal with which he is associated.

(4) Legislative Officials. No legislator or public servant employed by the legislature or by any committee or agency thereof shall solicit, accept or agree to accept any pecuniary benefit from any person known to be interested in a bill, transaction or proceeding, pending or contemplated, before the legislature or any committee or agency thereof.

(5) Exceptions. This Section shall not apply to:

(a) fees prescribed by law to be received by a public servant, or any other benefit for which the recipient gives legitimate consideration or to which he is otherwise legally entitled; or

(b) gifts or other benefits conferred on account of kinship or other personal, professional or business relationship independent of the official status of the receiver; or

(c) trivial benefits incidental to personal, professional or business contacts and involving no substantial risk of undermining official impartiality.

(6) Offering Benefits Prohibited. No person shall knowingly confer, or offer or agree to confer, any benefit prohibited by the foregoing Subsections.

(7) Grade of Offense. An offense under this Section is a misdemeanor.

### Section 240.6. Compensating Public Servant for Assisting Private Interests in Relation to Matters Before Him

(1) Receiving Compensation. A public servant commits a misdemeanor if he solicits, accepts or agrees to accept compensation for advice or other assistance in preparing or promoting a bill, contract, claim, or other transaction or proposal as to which he knows that he has or is likely to have an official discretion to exercise.

(2) Paying Compensation.  A person commits a misdemeanor if he pays or offers or agrees to pay compensation to a public servant with knowledge that acceptance by the public servant is unlawful.

### Section 240.7.  Selling Political Endorsement;  Special Influence

(1) Selling Political Endorsement.  A person commits a misdemeanor if he solicits, receives, agrees to receive, or agrees that any political party or other person shall receive, any pecuniary benefit as consideration for approval or disapproval of an appointment or advancement in public service, or for approval or disapproval of any person or transaction for any benefit conferred by an official or agency of government.  "Approval" includes recommendation, failure to disapprove, or any other manifestation of favor or acquiescence.  "Disapproval" includes failure to approve, or any other manifestation of disfavor or nonacquiescence.

(2) Other Trading in Special Influence.  A person commits a misdemeanor if he solicits, receives or agrees to receive any pecuniary benefit as consideration for exerting special influence upon a public servant or procuring another to do so.  "Special influence" means power to influence through kinship, friendship or other relationship, apart from the merits of the transaction.

(3) Paying for Endorsement or Special Influence.  A person commits a misdemeanor if he offers, confers or agrees to confer any pecuniary benefit receipt of which is prohibited by this Section.

### ARTICLE 241.  PERJURY AND OTHER FALSIFICATION IN OFFICIAL MATTERS

### Section 241.0.  Definitions

In this Article, unless a different meaning plainly is required:

(1) the definitions given in Section 240.0 apply;  and

(2) "statement" means any representation, but includes a representation of opinion, belief or other state of mind only if the representation clearly relates to state of mind apart from or in addition to any facts which are the subject of the representation.

### Section 241.1.  Perjury

(1) Offense Defined.  A person is guilty of perjury, a felony of the third degree, if in any official proceeding he makes a false statement under oath or equivalent affirmation, or swears or affirms the truth of a statement previously made, when the statement is material and he does not believe it to be true.

(2) Materiality.  Falsification is material, regardless of the admissibility of the statement under rules of evidence, if it could have affected the course or outcome of the proceeding.  It is no defense that the declarant mistakenly believed the falsification to be immaterial.  Whether a falsification is material in a given factual situation is a question of law.

(3) Irregularities No Defense.  It is not a defense to prosecution under this Section that the oath or affirmation was administered or taken in an irregular manner or that the declarant was not competent to make the statement.  A document purporting to be made upon oath or affirmation at any time when the actor presents it as being so verified shall be deemed to have been duly sworn or affirmed.

(4) Retraction. No person shall be guilty of an offense under this Section if he retracted the falsification in the course of the proceeding in which it was made before it became manifest that the falsification was or would be exposed and before the falsification substantially affected the proceeding.

(5) Inconsistent Statements. Where the defendant made inconsistent statements under oath or equivalent affirmation, both having been made within the period of the statute of limitations, the prosecution may proceed by setting forth the inconsistent statements in a single count alleging in the alternative that one or the other was false and not believed by the defendant. In such case it shall not be necessary for the prosecution to prove which statement was false but only that one or the other was false and not believed by the defendant to be true.

(6) Corroboration. No person shall be convicted of an offense under this Section where proof of falsity rests solely upon contradiction by testimony of a single person other than the defendant.

### Section 241.2.  False Swearing

(1) False Swearing in Official Matters. A person who makes a false statement under oath or equivalent affirmation, or swears or affirms the truth of such a statement previously made, when he does not believe the statement to be true, is guilty of a misdemeanor if:

(a) the falsification occurs in an official proceeding; or

(b) the falsification is intended to mislead a public servant in performing his official function.

(2) Other False Swearing. A person who makes a false statement under oath or equivalent affirmation, or swears or affirms the truth of such a statement previously made, when he does not believe the statement to be true, is guilty of a petty misdemeanor, if the statement is one which is required by law to be sworn or affirmed before a notary or other person authorized to administer oaths.

(3) Perjury Provisions Applicable. Subsections (3) to (6) of Section 241.1 apply to the present Section.

### Section 241.3.  Unsworn Falsification to Authorities

(1) In General. A person commits a misdemeanor if, with purpose to mislead a public servant in performing his official function, he:

(a) makes any written false statement which he does not believe to be true; or

(b) purposely creates a false impression in a written application for any pecuniary or other benefit, by omitting information necessary to prevent statements therein from being misleading; or

(c) submits or invites reliance on any writing which he knows to be forged, altered or otherwise lacking in authenticity; or

(d) submits or invites reliance on any sample, specimen, map, boundary-mark, or other object which he knows to be false.

(2) Statements "Under Penalty." A person commits a petty misdemeanor if he makes a written false statement which he does not believe to be true, on or pursuant to a form bearing notice, authorized by law, to the effect that false statements made therein are punishable.

(3) Perjury Provisions Applicable.  Subsections (3) to (6) of Section 241.1 apply to the present section.

### Section 241.4.  False Alarms to Agencies of Public Safety

A person who knowingly causes a false alarm of fire or other emergency to be transmitted to or within any organization, official or volunteer, for dealing with emergencies involving danger to life or property commits a misdemeanor.

### Section 241.5.  False Reports to Law Enforcement Authorities

(1) Falsely Incriminating Another.  A person who knowingly gives false information to any law enforcement officer with purpose to implicate another commits a misdemeanor.

(2) Fictitious Reports.  A person commits a petty misdemeanor if he:

(a) reports to law enforcement authorities an offense or other incident within their concern knowing that it did not occur; or

(b) pretends to furnish such authorities with information relating to an offense or incident when he knows he has no information relating to such offense or incident.

### Section 241.6.  Tampering With Witnesses and Informants;  Retaliation Against Them

(1) Tampering.  A person commits an offense if, believing that an official proceeding or investigation is pending or about to be instituted, he attempts to induce or otherwise cause a witness or informant to:

(a) testify or inform falsely;  or

(b) withhold any testimony, information, document or thing;  or

(c) elude legal process summoning him to testify or supply evidence;  or

(d) absent himself from any proceeding or investigation to which he has been legally summoned.

The offense is a felony of the third degree if the actor employs force, deception, threat or offer of pecuniary benefit.  Otherwise it is a misdemeanor.

(2) Retaliation Against Witness or Informant.  A person commits a misdemeanor if he harms another by any unlawful act in retaliation for anything lawfully done in the capacity of witness or informant.

(3) Witness or Informant Taking Bribe.  A person commits a felony of the third degree if he solicits, accepts or agrees to accept any benefit in consideration of his doing any of the things specified in clauses (a) to (d) of Subsection (1).

### Section 241.7.  Tampering With or Fabricating Physical Evidence

A person commits a misdemeanor if, believing that an official proceeding or investigation is pending or about to be instituted, he:

(1) alters, destroys, conceals or removes any record, document or thing with purpose to impair its verity or availability in such proceeding or investigation; or

(2) makes, presents or uses any record, document or thing knowing it to be false and with purpose to mislead a public servant who is or may be engaged in such proceeding or investigation.

**A-87**

### Section 241.8.  Tampering With Public Records or Information

(1) <u>Offense Defined.</u>  A person commits an offense if he:

(a) knowingly makes a false entry in, or false alteration of, any record, document or thing belonging to, or received or kept by, the government for information or record, or required by law to be kept by others for information of the government; or

(b) makes, presents or uses any record, document or thing knowing it to be false, and with purpose that it be taken as a genuine part of information or records referred to in paragraph (a); or

(c) purposely and unlawfully destroys, conceals, removes or otherwise impairs the verity or availability of any such record, document or thing.

(2) <u>Grading.</u>  An offense under this Section is a misdemeanor unless the actor's purpose is to defraud or injure anyone, in which case the offense is a felony of the third degree.

### Section 241.9.  Impersonating a Public Servant

A person commits a misdemeanor if he falsely pretends to hold a position in the public service with purpose to induce another to submit to such pretended official authority or otherwise to act in reliance upon that pretense to his prejudice.

### ARTICLE 242.  OBSTRUCTING GOVERNMENTAL OPERATIONS; ESCAPES

### Section 242.0.  Definitions

In this Article, unless another meaning plainly is required, the definitions given in Section 240.0 apply.

### Section 242.1.  Obstructing Administration of Law or Other Governmental Function

A person commits a misdemeanor if he purposely obstructs, impairs or perverts the administration of law or other governmental function by force, violence, physical interference or obstacle, breach of official duty, or any other unlawful act, except that this Section does not apply to flight by a person charged with crime, refusal to submit to arrest, failure to perform a legal duty other than an official duty, or any other means of avoiding compliance with law without affirmative interference with governmental functions.

### Section 242.2.  Resisting Arrest or Other Law Enforcement

A person commits a misdemeanor if, for the purpose of preventing a public servant from effecting a lawful arrest or discharging any other duty, the person creates a substantial risk of bodily injury to the public servant or anyone else, or employs means justifying or requiring substantial force to overcome the resistance.

### Section 242.3.  Hindering Apprehension or Prosecution

A person commits an offense if, with purpose to hinder the apprehension, prosecution, conviction or punishment of another for crime, he:

(1) harbors or conceals the other; or

(2) provides or aids in providing a weapon, transportation, disguise or other means of avoiding apprehension or effecting escape; or

(3) conceals or destroys evidence of the crime, or tampers with a witness, informant, document or other source of information, regardless of its admissibility in evidence; or

(4) warns the other of impending discovery or apprehension, except that this paragraph does not apply to a warning given in connection with an effort to bring another into compliance with law; or

(5) volunteers false information to a law enforcement officer.

The offense is a felony of the third degree if the conduct which the actor knows has been charged or is liable to be charged against the person aided would constitute a felony of the first or second degree. Otherwise it is a misdemeanor.

### Section 242.4.  Aiding Consummation of Crime

A person commits an offense if he purposely aids another to accomplish an unlawful object of a crime, as by safeguarding the proceeds thereof or converting the proceeds into negotiable funds. The offense is a felony of the third degree if the principal offense was a felony of the first or second degree. Otherwise it is a misdemeanor.

### Section 242.5.  Compounding

A person commits a misdemeanor if he accepts or agrees to accept any pecuniary benefit in consideration of refraining from reporting to law enforcement authorities the commission or suspected commission of any offense or information relating to an offense. It is an affirmative defense to prosecution under this Section that the pecuniary benefit did not exceed an amount which the actor believed to be due as restitution or indemnification for harm caused by the offense.

### Section 242.6.  Escape

(1) Escape.  A person commits an offense if he unlawfully removes himself from official detention or fails to return to official detention following temporary leave granted for a specific purpose or limited period. "Official detention" means arrest, detention in any facility for custody of persons under charge or conviction of crime or alleged or found to be delinquent, detention for extradition or deportation, or any other detention for law enforcement purposes; but "official detention" does not include supervision of probation or parole, or constraint incidental to release on bail.

(2) Permitting or Facilitating Escape.  A public servant concerned in detention commits an offense if he knowingly or recklessly permits an escape. Any person who knowingly causes or facilitates an escape commits an offense.

(3) Effect of Legal Irregularity in Detention.  Irregularity in bringing about or maintaining detention, or lack of jurisdiction of the committing or detaining authority, shall not be a defense to prosecution under this Section if the escape is from a prison or other custodial facility or from detention pursuant to commitment by official proceedings. In the case of other detentions, irregularity or lack of jurisdiction shall be a defense only if:

(a) the escape involved no substantial risk of harm to the person or property of anyone other than the detainee; or

(b) the detaining authority did not act in good faith under color of law.

(4) Grading of Offenses.  An offense under this Section is a felony of the third degree where:

(a) the actor was under arrest for or detained on a charge of felony or following conviction of crime; or

(b) the actor employs force, threat, deadly weapon or other dangerous instrumentality to effect the escape; or

(c) a public servant concerned in detention of persons convicted of crime purposely facilitates or permits an escape from a detention facility.

Otherwise an offense under this section is a misdemeanor.

### Section 242.7.  Implements for Escape;  Other Contraband

(1) Escape Implements.  A person commits a misdemeanor if he unlawfully introduces within a detention facility, or unlawfully provides an inmate with, any weapon, tool or other thing which may be useful for escape.  An inmate commits a misdemeanor if he unlawfully procures, makes, or otherwise provides himself with, or has in his possession, any such implement of escape.  "Unlawfully" means surreptitiously or contrary to law, regulation or order of the detaining authority.

(2) Other Contraband.  A person commits a petty misdemeanor if he provides an inmate with anything which the actor knows it is unlawful for the inmate to possess.

### Section 242.8.  Bail Jumping;  Default in Required Appearance

A person set at liberty by court order, with or without bail, upon condition that he will subsequently appear at a specified time and place, commits a misdemeanor if, without lawful excuse, he fails to appear at that time and place.  The offense constitutes a felony of the third degree where the required appearance was to answer to a charge of felony, or for disposition of any such charge, and the actor took flight or went into hiding to avoid apprehension, trial or punishment.  This Section does not apply to obligations to appear incident to release under suspended sentence or on probation or parole.

## ARTICLE 243.  ABUSE OF OFFICE

### Section 243.0.  Definitions

In this Article, unless a different meaning plainly is required, the definitions given in Section 240.0 apply.

### Section 243.1.  Official Oppression

A person acting or purporting to act in an official capacity or taking advantage of such actual or purported capacity commits a misdemeanor if, knowing that his conduct is illegal, he:

(1) subjects another to arrest, detention, search, seizure, mistreatment, dispossession, assessment, lien or other infringement of personal or property rights; or

(2) denies or impedes another in the exercise or enjoyment of any right, privilege, power or immunity.

### Section 243.2.  Speculating or Wagering on Official Action or Information

A public servant commits a misdemeanor if, in contemplation of official action by himself or by a governmental unit with which he is associated, or in reliance on information to which he has access in his official capacity and which has not been made public, he:

(1) acquires a pecuniary interest in any property, transaction or enterprise which may be affected by such information or official action;  or

(2) speculates or wagers on the basis of such information or official action;  or

(3) aids another to do any of the foregoing.

---

## OFFENSES AGAINST PUBLIC ORDER AND DECENCY

---

## ARTICLE 250.  RIOT, DISORDERLY CONDUCT, AND RELATED OFFENSES

### Section 250.1.  Riot;  Failure to Disperse

(1) Riot.  A person is guilty of riot, a felony of the third degree, if he participates with [two] or more others in a course of disorderly conduct:

(a) with purpose to commit or facilitate the commission of a felony or misdemeanor;

(b) with purpose to prevent or coerce official action;  or

(c) when the actor or any other participant to the knowledge of the actor uses or plans to use a firearm or other deadly weapon.

(2) Failure of Disorderly Persons to Disperse Upon Official Order.  Where [three] or more persons are participating in a course of disorderly conduct likely to cause substantial harm or serious inconvenience, annoyance or alarm, a peace officer or other public servant engaged in executing or enforcing the law may order the participants and others in the immediate vicinity to disperse.  A person who refuses or knowingly fails to obey such an order commits a misdemeanor.

### Section 250.2.  Disorderly Conduct

(1) Offense Defined.  A person is guilty of disorderly conduct if, with purpose to cause public inconvenience, annoyance or alarm, or recklessly creating a risk thereof, he:

(a) engages in fighting or threatening, or in violent or tumultuous behavior;  or

(b) makes unreasonable noise or offensively coarse utterance, gesture or display, or addresses abusive language to any person present;  or

(c) creates a hazardous or physically offensive condition by any act which serves no legitimate purpose of the actor.

"Public" means affecting or likely to affect persons in a place to which the public or a substantial group has access;  among the places included are highways, transport

**A-91**

facilities, schools, prisons, apartment houses, places of business or amusement, or any neighborhood.

(2) Grading. An offense under this Section is a petty misdemeanor if the actor's purpose is to cause substantial harm or serious inconvenience, or if he persists in disorderly conduct after reasonable warning or request to desist. Otherwise disorderly conduct is a violation.

### Section 250.3.  False Public Alarms

A person is guilty of a misdemeanor if he initiates or circulates a report or warning of an impending bombing or other crime or catastrophe, knowing that the report or warning is false or baseless and that it is likely to cause evacuation of a building, place of assembly, or facility of public transport, or to cause public inconvenience or alarm.

### Section 250.4.  Harassment

A person commits a petty misdemeanor if, with purpose to harass another, he:

(1) makes a telephone call without purpose of legitimate communication; or

(2) insults, taunts or challenges another in a manner likely to provoke violent or disorderly response; or

(3) makes repeated communications anonymously or at extremely inconvenient hours, or in offensively coarse language; or

(4) subjects another to an offensive touching; or

(5) engages in any other course of alarming conduct serving no legitimate purpose of the actor.

### Section 250.5.  Public Drunkenness;  Drug Incapacitation

A person is guilty of an offense if he appears in any public place manifestly under the influence of alcohol, narcotics or other drug, not therapeutically administered, to the degree that he may endanger himself or other persons or property, or annoy persons in his vicinity. An offense under this Section constitutes a petty misdemeanor if the actor has been convicted hereunder twice before within a period of one year. Otherwise the offense constitutes a violation.

### Section 250.6.  Loitering or Prowling

A person commits a violation if he loiters or prowls in a place, at a time, or in a manner not usual for law-abiding individuals under circumstances that warrant alarm for the safety of persons or property in the vicinity. Among the circumstances which may be considered in determining whether such alarm is warranted is the fact that the actor takes flight upon appearance of a peace officer, refuses to identify himself, or manifestly endeavors to conceal himself or any object. Unless flight by the actor or other circumstance makes it impracticable, a peace officer shall prior to any arrest for an offense under this section afford the actor an opportunity to dispel any alarm which would otherwise be warranted, by requesting him to identify himself and explain his presence and conduct. No person shall be convicted of an offense under this Section if the peace officer did not comply with the preceding sentence, or if it appears at trial that the explanation given by the actor was true and, if believed by the peace officer at the time, would have dispelled the alarm.

## Section 250.7.  Obstructing Highways and Other Public Passages

(1) A person, who, having no legal privilege to do so, purposely or recklessly obstructs any highway or other public passage, whether alone or with others, commits a violation, or, in case he persists after warning by a law officer, a petty misdemeanor. "Obstructs" means renders impassable without unreasonable inconvenience or hazard. No person shall be deemed guilty of recklessly obstructing in violation of this Subsection solely because of a gathering of persons to hear him speak or otherwise communicate, or solely because of being a member of such a gathering.

(2) A person in a gathering commits a violation if he refuses to obey a reasonable official request or order to move:

(a) to prevent obstruction of a highway or other public passage; or

(b) to maintain public safety by dispersing those gathered in dangerous proximity to a fire or other hazard.

An order to move, addressed to a person whose speech or other lawful behavior attracts an obstructing audience, shall not be deemed reasonable if the obstruction can be readily remedied by police control of the size or location of the gathering.

## Section 250.8.  Disrupting Meetings and Processions

A person commits a misdemeanor if, with purpose to prevent or disrupt a lawful meeting, procession or gathering, he does any act tending to obstruct or interfere with it physically, or makes any utterance, gesture or display designed to outrage the sensibilities of the group.

## Section 250.9.  Desecration of Venerated Objects

A person commits a misdemeanor if he purposely desecrates any public monument or structure, or place of worship or burial, or if he purposely desecrates the national flag or any other object of veneration by the public or a substantial segment thereof in any public place. "Desecrate" means defacing, damaging, polluting or otherwise physically mistreating in a way that the actor knows will outrage the sensibilities of persons likely to observe or discover his action.

## Section 250.10.  Abuse of Corpse

Except as authorized by law, a person who treats a corpse in a way that he knows would outrage ordinary family sensibilities commits a misdemeanor.

## Section 250.11.  Cruelty to Animals

A person commits a misdemeanor if he purposely or recklessly:

(1) subjects any animal to cruel mistreatment; or

(2) subjects any animal in his custody to cruel neglect; or

(3) kills or injures any animal belonging to another without legal privilege or consent of the owner.

Subsections (1) and (2) shall not be deemed applicable to accepted veterinary practices and activities carried on for scientific research.

**Section 250.12. Violation of Privacy**

(1) <u>Unlawful Eavesdropping or Surveillance.</u> A person commits a misdemeanor if, except as authorized by law, he:

(a) trespasses on property with purpose to subject anyone to eavesdropping or other surveillance in a private place; or

(b) installs in any private place, without the consent of the person or persons entitled to privacy there, any device for observing, photographing, recording, amplifying or broadcasting sounds or events in such place, or uses any such unauthorized installation; or

(c) installs or uses outside a private place any device for hearing, recording, amplifying or broadcasting sounds originating in such place which would not ordinarily be audible or comprehensible outside, without the consent of the person or persons entitled to privacy there.

"Private place" means a place where one may reasonably expect to be safe from casual or hostile intrusion or surveillance, but does not include a place to which the public or a substantial group thereof has access.

(2) <u>Other Breach of Privacy of Messages.</u> A person commits a misdemeanor if, except as authorized by law, he:

(a) intercepts without the consent of the sender or receiver a message by telephone, telegraph, letter or other means of communicating privately; but this paragraph does not extend to (i) overhearing of messages through a regularly installed instrument on a telephone party line or on an extension, or (ii) interception by the telephone company or subscriber incident to enforcement of regulations limiting use of the facilities or incident to other normal operation and use; or

(b) divulges without the consent of the sender or receiver the existence or contents of any such message if the actor knows that the message was illegally intercepted, or if he learned of the message in the course of employment with an agency engaged in transmitting it.

### ARTICLE 251.  PUBLIC INDECENCY

**Section 251.1. Open Lewdness**

A person commits a petty misdemeanor if he does any lewd act which he knows is likely to be observed by others who would be affronted or alarmed.

**Section 251.2. Prostitution and Related Offenses**

(1) <u>Prostitution.</u> A person is guilty of prostitution, a petty misdemeanor, if he or she:

(a) is an inmate of a house of prostitution or otherwise engages in sexual activity as a business; or

(b) loiters in or within view of any public place for the purpose of being hired to engage in sexual activity.

"Sexual activity" includes homosexual and other deviate sexual relations. A "house of prostitution" is any place where prostitution or promotion of prostitution is regularly carried on by one person under the control, management or supervision of another. An "inmate" is a person who engages in prostitution in or through the agency of a house of prostitution. "Public place" means any place to which the public or any substantial group thereof has access.

(2) <u>Promoting Prostitution.</u> A person who knowingly promotes prostitution of another commits a misdemeanor or felony as provided in Subsection (3). The following acts shall, without limitation of the foregoing, constitute promoting prostitution:

(a) owning, controlling, managing, supervising or otherwise keeping, alone or in association with others, a house of prostitution or a prostitution business; or

(b) procuring an inmate for a house of prostitution or a place in a house of prostitution for one who would be an inmate; or

(c) encouraging, inducing, or otherwise purposely causing another to become or remain a prostitute; or

(d) soliciting a person to patronize a prostitute; or

(e) procuring a prostitute for a patron; or

(f) transporting a person into or within this state with purpose to promote that person's engaging in prostitution, or procuring or paying for transportation with that purpose; or

(g) leasing or otherwise permitting a place controlled by the actor, alone or in association with others, to be regularly used for prostitution or the promotion of prostitution, or failure to make reasonable effort to abate such use by ejecting the tenant, notifying law enforcement authorities, or other legally available means; or

(h) soliciting, receiving, or agreeing to receive any benefit for doing or agreeing to do anything forbidden by this Subsection.

(3) <u>Grading of Offenses Under Subsection (2).</u> An offense under Subsection (2) constitutes a felony of the third degree if:

(a) the offense falls within paragraph (a), (b) or (c) of Subsection (2); or

(b) the actor compels another to engage in or promote prostitution; or

(c) the actor promotes prostitution of a child under 16, whether or not he is aware of the child's age; or

(d) the actor promotes prostitution of his wife, child, ward or any person for whose care, protection or support he is responsible.

Otherwise the offense is a misdemeanor.

(4) <u>Presumption from Living off Prostitutes.</u> A person, other than the prostitute or the prostitute's minor child or other legal dependent incapable of self-support, who is supported in whole or substantial part by the proceeds of prostitution is presumed to be knowingly promoting prostitution in violation of Subsection (2).

(5) <u>Patronizing Prostitutes.</u> A person commits a violation if he hires a prostitute to engage in sexual activity with him, or if he enters or remains in a house of prostitution for the purpose of engaging in sexual activity.

(6) <u>Evidence.</u> On the issue whether a place is a house of prostitution the following shall be admissible evidence: its general repute; the repute of the persons who reside in or frequent the place; the frequency, timing and duration of visits by

non-residents. Testimony of a person against his spouse shall be admissible to prove offenses under this Section.

### Section 251.3.  Loitering to Solicit Deviate Sexual Relations

A person is guilty of a petty misdemeanor if he loiters in or near any public place for the purpose of soliciting or being solicited to engage in deviate sexual relations.

### Section 251.4.  Obscenity

(1) Obscene Defined.  Material is obscene if, considered as a whole, its predominant appeal is to prurient interest, that is, a shameful or morbid interest, in nudity, sex or excretion, and if in addition it goes substantially beyond customary limits of candor in describing or representing such matters.  Predominant appeal shall be judged with reference to ordinary adults unless it appears from the character of the material or the circumstances of its dissemination to be designed for children or other specially susceptible audience.  Undeveloped photographs, molds, printing plates, and the like, shall be deemed obscene notwithstanding that processing or other acts may be required to make the obscenity patent or to disseminate it.

(2) Offenses.  Subject to the affirmative defense provided in Subsection (3), a person commits a misdemeanor if he knowingly or recklessly:

(a) sells, delivers or provides, or offers or agrees to sell, deliver or provide, any obscene writing, picture, record or other representation or embodiment of the obscene; or

(b) presents or directs an obscene play, dance or performance, or participates in that portion thereof which makes it obscene; or

(c) publishes, exhibits or otherwise makes available any obscene material; or

(d) possesses any obscene material for purposes of sale or other commercial dissemination; or

(e) sells, advertises or otherwise commercially disseminates material, whether or not obscene, by representing or suggesting that it is obscene.

A person who disseminates or possesses obscene material in the course of his business is presumed to do so knowingly or recklessly.

(3) Justifiable and Non–Commercial Private Dissemination.  It is an affirmative defense to prosecution under this Section that dissemination was restricted to:

(a) institutions or persons having scientific, educational, governmental or other similar justification for possessing obscene material; or

(b) non-commercial dissemination to personal associates of the actor.

(4) Evidence; Adjudication of Obscenity.  In any prosecution under this Section evidence shall be admissible to show:

(a) the character of the audience for which the material was designed or to which it was directed;

(b) what the predominant appeal of the material would be for ordinary adults or any special audience to which it was directed, and what effect, if any, it would probably have on conduct of such people;

(c) artistic, literary, scientific, educational or other merits of the material;

(d) the degree of public acceptance of the material in the United States;

(e) appeal to prurient interest, or absence thereof, in advertising or other promotion of the material; and

(f) the good repute of the author, creator, publisher or other person from whom the material originated.

Expert testimony and testimony of the author, creator, publisher or other person from whom the material originated, relating to factors entering into the determination of the issue of obscenity, shall be admissible. The Court shall dismiss a prosecution for obscenity if it is satisfied that the material is not obscene.

---

## ADDITIONAL ARTICLES

[Reporter's note: At this point, a State enacting a new Penal Code may insert additional Articles dealing with special topics such as narcotics, alcoholic beverages, gambling and offenses against tax and trade laws. The Model Penal Code project did not extend to these, partly because a higher priority on limited time and resources was accorded to branches of the penal law which have not received close legislative scrutiny. Also, in legislation dealing with narcotics, liquor, tax evasion, and the like, penal provisions have been so intermingled with regulatory and procedural provisions that the task of segregating one group from the other presents special difficulty for model legislation.]

---

\*

# TABLE OF MODEL PENAL CODE REFERENCES

*

APPENDIX B

# Selected Penal Statutes

---

TABLE OF CONTENTS

---

### (A) CONTEMPORARY RAPE STATUTES

### 1. New Jersey Statutes Annotated:

§ 2C:14–2.  Sexual assault

a. An actor is guilty of aggravated sexual assault if he commits an act of sexual penetration with another person under any one of the following circumstances:

(1) The victim is less than 13 years old;

(2) The victim is at least 13 but less than 16 years old; and

(a) The actor is related to the victim by blood or affinity to the third degree, or

(b) The actor has supervisory or disciplinary power over the victim by virtue of the actor's legal, professional, or occupational status, or

(c) The actor is a foster parent, a guardian, or stands in loco parentis within the household;

(3) The act is committed during the commission, or attempted commission, whether alone or with one or more other persons, of robbery, kidnapping, homicide, aggravated assault on another, burglary, arson or criminal escape;

(4) The actor is armed with a weapon or any object fashioned in such a manner as to lead the victim to reasonably believe it to be a weapon and threatens by word or gesture to use the weapon or object;

(5) The actor is aided or abetted by one or more other persons and the actor uses physical force or coercion;

(6) The actor uses physical force or coercion and severe personal injury is sustained by the victim;

(7) The victim is one whom the actor knew or should have known was physically helpless, mentally defective or mentally incapacitated.

Aggravated sexual assault is a crime of the first degree [20–year maximum].

b.  An actor is guilty of sexual assault if he commits an act of sexual contact with a victim who is less than 13 years old and the actor is at least four years older than the victim.

c.  An actor is guilty of sexual assault if he commits an act of sexual penetration with another person under any one of the following circumstances:

(1) The actor uses physical force or coercion, but the victim does not sustain severe personal injury;

(2) The victim is on probation or parole, or is detained in a hospital, prison or other institution and the actor has supervisory or disciplinary power over the victim by virtue of the actor's legal, professional or occupational status;

(3) The victim is at least 16 but less than 18 years old and:

(a) The actor is related to the victim by blood or affinity to the third degree; or

(b) The actor has supervisory or disciplinary power of any nature or in any capacity over the victim; or

(c) The actor is a foster parent, a guardian, or stands in loco parentis within the household;

(4) The victim is at least 13 but less than 16 years old and the actor is at least four years older than the victim.

Sexual assault is a crime of the second degree [10–year maximum].

§ 2C:14–2.1.  Right of victim to consult with prosecuting authority

Whenever there is a prosecution for a violation of N.J.S.A.2C: 14–2, the victim of the sexual assault shall be provided an opportunity to consult with the prosecuting authority prior to the conclusion of any plea negotiations.

Nothing contained herein shall be construed to alter or limit the authority or discretion of the prosecutor to enter into any plea agreement which the prosecutor deems appropriate.

§ 2C:14–3.  Criminal sexual contact

a.   An actor is guilty of aggravated criminal sexual contact if he commits an act of sexual contact with the victim under any of the circumstances set forth in 2C:14–2a. (2) through (7).

Aggravated criminal sexual contact is a crime of the third degree.

b.   An actor is guilty of criminal sexual contact if he commits an act of sexual contact with the victim under any of the circumstances set forth in section 2C:14–2c. (1) through (4).

Criminal sexual contact is a crime of the fourth degree [18–month maximum].

**2.  Code of Virginia:**

§ 18.2–61   Rape.

A.   If any person has sexual intercourse with a complaining witness who is not his or her spouse or causes a complaining witness, whether or not his or her spouse, to engage in sexual intercourse with any other person and such act is accomplished

(i) against the complaining witness's will, by force, threat or intimidation of or against the complaining witness or another person, or

(ii) through the use of the complaining witness's mental incapacity or physical helplessness, or

(iii) with a child under age thirteen as the victim,

he or she shall be guilty of rape.

B.   If any person has sexual intercourse with his or her spouse and such act is accomplished against the spouse's will by force, threat or intimidation of or against the spouse or another, he or she shall be guilty of rape.[a]

C.   A violation of this section shall be punishable, in the discretion of the court or jury, by confinement in a state correctional facility for life or for any term not less than five years. There shall be a rebuttable presumption that a juvenile over the age of 10 but less than 12,[b] does not possess the physical capacity to commit a violation of this section. In any case deemed appropriate by the court, all or part of

---

[a] Prior to 1999, this provision contained the following limitation:

However, no person shall be found guilty under this subsection unless, at the time of the alleged offense,

(i) the spouses were living separate and apart, or

(ii) the defendant caused serious physical injury to the spouse by the use of force or violence.

The phrase "serious physical injury" was changed to "bodily injury" in 1999, and the entire limitation was deleted in 2002.—[Footnote by eds.]

[b] The age used to be 14.—[Footnote by eds.]

any sentence imposed for a violation of subsection B may be suspended upon the defendant's completion of counseling or therapy, if not already provided, in the manner prescribed under § 19.2–218.1 if, after consideration of the views of the complaining witness and such other evidence as may be relevant, the court finds such action will promote maintenance of the family unit and will be in the best interest of the complaining witness.

D.  Upon a finding of guilt under subsection B in any case tried by the court without a jury, the court, without entering a judgment of guilt, upon motion of the defendant and with the consent of the complaining witness and the attorney for the Commonwealth, may defer further proceedings and place the defendant on probation pending completion of counseling or therapy, if not already provided, in the manner prescribed under § 19.2–218.1. If the defendant fails to so complete such counseling or therapy, the court may make final disposition of the case and proceed as otherwise provided. If such counseling is completed as prescribed under § 19.2–218.1, the court may discharge the defendant and dismiss the proceedings against him if, after consideration of the views of the complaining witness and such other evidence as may be relevant, the court finds such action will promote maintenance of the family unit and be in the best interest of the complaining witness.

§ 18.2–63  Carnal knowledge of child between thirteen and fifteen years of age.

If any person carnally knows, without the use of force, a child thirteen years of age or older but under fifteen years of age, such person shall be guilty of a Class 4 felony [10–year maximum].

However, if such child is thirteen years of age or older but under fifteen years of age and consents to sexual intercourse and the accused is a minor and such consenting child is three years or more the accused's junior, the accused shall be guilty of a Class 6 felony [five-year maximum]. If such consenting child is less than three years the accused's junior, the accused shall be guilty of a Class 4 misdemeanor [maximum: fine not exceeding $250].

In calculating whether such child is three years or more a junior of the accused minor, the actual dates of birth of the child and the accused, respectively, shall be used.

For the purposes of this section,

(i) a child under the age of thirteen years shall not be considered a consenting child and

(ii) "carnal knowledge" includes the acts of sexual intercourse, cunnilingus, fellatio, anallingus, anal intercourse, and animate and inanimate object sexual penetration.

§ 18.2–63.1  Death of victim.

When the death of the victim occurs in connection with an offense under this article, it shall be immaterial in the prosecution thereof whether the alleged offense occurred before or after the death of the victim.

§ 18.2–64.1  Carnal knowledge of certain minors.

If any person providing services, paid or unpaid, to juveniles under the purview of the Juvenile and Domestic Relations District Court Law, or to juveniles who have been committed to the custody of the State Department of Juvenile Justice, carnally knows, without the use of force, any minor fifteen years of age or older, when such minor is confined or detained in jail, is detained in any facility mentioned in § 16.1–249, or has been committed to the custody of the Department of Juvenile Justice pursuant to § 16.1–278.8, knowing or having good reason to believe that

(i)  such minor is in such confinement or detention status,

(ii)  such minor is a ward of the Department of Juvenile Justice, or

(iii)  such minor is on probation, furlough, or leave from or has escaped or absconded from such confinement, detention, or custody, he shall be guilty of a Class 6 felony [five-year maximum].

For the purposes of this section, "carnal knowledge" includes the acts of sexual intercourse, cunnilingus, fellatio, anallingus, anal intercourse, and animate and inanimate object sexual penetration.

§ 18.2–66   Effect of subsequent marriage to child over fourteen years of age.

If the carnal knowledge is with the consent of the child and such child is fourteen years of age or older, the subsequent marriage of the parties may be pleaded to any indictment found against the accused. The court, upon proof of such marriage, and that the parties are living together as husband and wife, and that the accused has properly provided for, supported, and maintained and is at the time properly providing, supporting and maintaining the spouse and the issue of such marriage, if any, shall continue the case from time to time and from term to term, until the spouse reaches the age of sixteen years. Thereupon the court shall dismiss the indictment already found against the accused for the aforesaid offense. However, if the accused deserts such spouse before the spouse reaches the age of sixteen without just cause, any indictment found against the accused for such offense shall be tried without regard to the number of times the case has been continued, and whether such continuance is entered upon the order book.

§ 18.2–67.1   Forcible sodomy.

A.   An accused shall be guilty of forcible sodomy if he or she engages in cunnilingus, fellatio, anallingus, or anal intercourse with a complaining witness who is not his or her spouse, or causes a complaining witness, whether or not his or her spouse, to engage in such acts with any other person, and

1.   The complaining witness is less than thirteen years of age, or

2.   The act is accomplished against the will of the complaining witness, by force, threat or intimidation of or against the complaining witness or another person, or through the use of the complaining witness's mental incapacity or physical helplessness.

B.   An accused shall be guilty of forcible sodomy if

(i)  he or she engages in cunnilingus, fellatio, anallingus, or anal intercourse with his or her spouse, and

(ii)  such act is accomplished against the will of the spouse, by force, threat or intimidation of or against the spouse or another person.

However, no person shall be found guilty under this subsection unless, at the time of the alleged offense,

(i)  the spouses were living separate and apart, or

(ii) the defendant caused bodily injury[c] to the spouse by the use of force or violence.

C.   Forcible sodomy is a felony punishable by confinement in a state correctional facility for life or for any term not less than five years. In any case deemed appropriate by the court, all or part of any sentence imposed for a violation of subsection B may be suspended upon the defendant's completion of counseling or therapy, if not already provided, in the manner prescribed under § 19.2–218.1 if, after consideration of the views of the complaining witness and such other evidence as may be relevant, the court finds such action will promote maintenance of the family unit and will be in the best interest of the complaining witness.

D.   Upon a finding of guilt under subsection B in any case tried by the court without a jury, the court, without entering a judgment of guilt, upon motion of the defendant and with the consent of the complaining witness and the attorney for the Commonwealth, may defer further proceedings and place the defendant on probation pending completion of counseling or therapy, if not already provided, in the manner prescribed under § 19.2–218.1. If the defendant fails to so complete such counseling or therapy, the court may make final disposition of the case and proceed as otherwise provided. If such counseling is completed as prescribed under § 19.2–218.1, the court may discharge the defendant and dismiss the proceedings against him if, after consideration of the views of the complaining witness and such other evidence as may be relevant, the court finds such action will promote maintenance of the family unit and be in the best interest of the complaining witness.

§ 18.2–67.2   Object sexual penetration; penalty.

A.   An accused shall be guilty of inanimate or animate object sexual penetration if he or she penetrates the labia majora or anus of a complaining witness who is not his or her spouse with any object, other than for a bona fide medical purpose, or causes such complaining witness to so penetrate his or her own body with an object or causes a complaining witness, whether or not his or her spouse, to engage in such acts with any other person or to penetrate, or to be penetrated by, an animal, and

1.   The complaining witness is less than thirteen years of age, or

2.   The act is accomplished against the will of the complaining witness, by force, threat or intimidation of or against the complaining witness or another person, or through the use of the complaining witness's mental incapacity or physical helplessness.

B.   An accused shall be guilty of inanimate or animate object sexual penetration if

(i) he or she penetrates the labia majora or anus of his or her spouse with any object other than for a bona fide medical purpose, or causes such spouse to so penetrate his or her own body with an object and

(ii) such act is accomplished against the spouse's will by force, threat or intimidation of or against the spouse or another person.

[c] This used to read "serious physical injury." The change was made in 1999. Compare footnote a, above.—[Footnote by eds.]

However, no person shall be found guilty under this subsection unless, at the time of the alleged offense,

(i) the spouses were living separate and apart or

(ii) the defendant caused serious physical injury to the spouse by the use of force or violence.

C.   Inanimate or animate object sexual penetration is a felony punishable by confinement in the state correctional facility for life or for any term not less than five years. In any case deemed appropriate by the court, all or part of any sentence imposed for a violation of subsection B may be suspended upon the defendant's completion of counseling or therapy, if not already provided, in the manner prescribed under § 19.2–218.1 if, after consideration of the views of the complaining witness and such other evidence as may be relevant, the court finds such action will promote maintenance of the family unit and will be in the best interest of the complaining witness.

D.   Upon a finding of guilt under subsection B in any case tried by the court without a jury, the court, without entering a judgment of guilt, upon motion of the defendant and with the consent of the complaining witness and the attorney for the Commonwealth, may defer further proceedings and place the defendant on probation pending completion of counseling or therapy, if not already provided, in the manner prescribed under § 19.2–218.1. If the defendant fails to so complete such counseling or therapy, the court may make final disposition of the case and proceed as otherwise provided. If such counseling is completed as prescribed under § 19.2–218.1, the court may discharge the defendant and dismiss the proceedings against him if, after consideration of the views of the complaining witness and such other evidence as may be relevant, the court finds such action will promote maintenance of the family unit and be in the best interest of the complaining witness.

§ 18.2–67.2:1   Marital sexual assault.

A.   An accused shall be guilty of marital sexual assault if

(i) he or she engages in sexual intercourse, cunnilingus, fellatio, anallingus or anal intercourse with his or her spouse, or penetrates the labia majora or anus of his or her spouse with any object other than for a bona fide medical purpose, or causes such spouse to so penetrate his or her own body with an object, and

(ii) such act is accomplished against the spouse's will by force or a present threat of force or intimidation of or against the spouse or another person.

B.   A violation of this section shall be punishable by confinement in a state correctional facility for a term of not less than one year nor more than twenty years or, in the discretion of the court or jury, by confinement in jail for not more than twelve months and a fine of not more than $1,000, either or both. In any case deemed appropriate by the court, all or part of any sentence may be suspended upon the defendant's completion of counseling or therapy if not already provided, in the manner prescribed under § 19.2–218.1 if, after consideration of the views of the complaining witness and such other evidence as may be relevant, the court finds such action will promote maintenance of the family unit and will be in the best interest of the complaining witness.

C.   Upon a finding of guilt under this section in any case tried by the court without a jury, the court, without entering a judgment of guilt, upon motion of the defendant and with the consent of the complaining witness and the attorney for the Commonwealth, may defer further proceedings and place the defendant on probation pending completion of counseling or therapy, if not already provided, in the manner prescribed under § 19.2–218.1. If the defendant fails to so complete such counseling or therapy, the court may enter an adjudication of guilt and proceed as otherwise provided. If such counseling is completed as prescribed under § 19.2–218.1, the court may discharge the defendant and dismiss the proceedings against him if, after consideration of the views of the complaining witness and such other evidence as may be relevant, the court finds such action will promote maintenance of the family unit and be in the best interest of the complaining witness.

D.  A violation of this section shall constitute a lesser, included offense of the respective violation set forth in §§ 18.2–61 B, 18.2–67.1 B or § 18.2–67.2 B.

§ 18.2–67.3  Aggravated sexual battery.

A.  An accused shall be guilty of aggravated sexual battery if he or she sexually abuses the complaining witness, and

    1.  The complaining witness is less than thirteen years of age, or

    2.  The act is accomplished against the will of the complaining witness, by force, threat or intimidation, or through the use of the complaining witness's mental incapacity or physical helplessness, and

        a.  The complaining witness is at least thirteen but less than fifteen years of age, or

        b.  The accused causes serious bodily or mental injury to the complaining witness, or

        c.  The accused uses or threatens to use a dangerous weapon.

B.  Aggravated sexual battery is a felony punishable by confinement in a state correctional facility for a term of not less than one nor more than twenty years and by a fine of not more than $100,000.

§ 18.2–67.4  Sexual battery.

A.  An accused shall be guilty of sexual battery if he or she sexually abuses, as defined in § 18.2–67.10,

    (i) the complaining witness against the will of the complaining witness, by force, threat, intimidation or ruse, or through the use of the complaining witness's mental incapacity or physical helplessness, or

    (ii) an inmate who has been committed to jail or convicted and sentenced to confinement in a state or local correctional facility or regional jail, and the accused is an employee or contractual employee of, or a volunteer with, the state or local correctional facility or regional jail; is in a position of authority over the inmate; and knows that the inmate is under the jurisdiction of the state or local correctional facility or regional jail, or

    (iii) a probationer, parolee, or a pretrial or posttrial offender under the jurisdiction of the Department of Corrections, a local community-based probation program, a pretrial services program, a local or regional jail for the purposes of imprisonment, a work program or any other parole/probationary or pretrial services program and the accused is an employee or contractual employee of, or a volunteer with, the Department of Corrections, a local community-based probation program, a pretrial services program or a local or regional jail; is in a position of authority over an offender; and knows that the offender is under the jurisdiction of the Department of Corrections, a local community-based probation program, a pretrial services program or a local or regional jail.

B.    Sexual battery is a Class 1 misdemeanor [12–month maximum].

§ 18.2–67.4:1    Infected sexual battery; penalty.

Any person who, knowing he is infected with HIV, syphilis, or hepatitis B, has sexual intercourse, cunnilingus, fellatio, anallingus or anal intercourse with the intent to transmit the infection to another person shall be guilty of a Class 6 felony [five-year maximum].

"HIV" means the human immunodeficiency virus or any other related virus that causes acquired immunodeficiency syndrome (AIDS).

Nothing in this section shall prevent the prosecution of any other crime against persons under Chapter 4 (§ 18.2–30 et seq.) of this title. Any person charged with a violation of this section alleging he is infected with HIV shall be subject to the testing provisions of § 18.2–62.

§ 18.2–67.5    Attempted rape, forcible sodomy, object sexual penetration, aggravated sexual battery, and sexual battery.

A.    An attempt to commit rape, forcible sodomy, or inanimate or animate object sexual penetration shall be punishable as a Class 4 felony [10–year maximum].

B.    An attempt to commit aggravated sexual battery shall be a felony punishable as a Class 6 felony [five-year maximum].

C.    An attempt to commit sexual battery is a Class 1 misdemeanor [12–month maximum].

### 3.  Michigan Compiled Laws Annotated:

§ 750.520a.    Definitions

As used in this chapter:

(a) "Actor" means a person accused of criminal sexual conduct.

(b) "Developmental disability" means an impairment of general intellectual functioning or adaptive behavior which meets the following criteria:

(*i*) It originated before the person became 18 years of age.

(*ii*) It has continued since its origination or can be expected to continue indefinitely.

(*iii*) It constitutes a substantial burden to the impaired person's ability to perform in society.

(*iv*) It is attributable to 1 or more of the following:

(A) Mental retardation, cerebral palsy, epilepsy, or autism.

(B) Any other condition of a person found to be closely related to mental retardation because it produces a similar impairment or requires treatment and services similar to those required for a person who is mentally retarded.

**B-9**

(c) "Intimate parts" includes the primary genital area, groin, inner thigh, buttock, or breast of a human being.

(d) "Mental health professional" means that term as defined in section 100b of the mental health code, 1974 PA 258, MCL 330.1100b.

(e) "Mental illness" means a substantial disorder of thought or mood which significantly impairs judgment, behavior, capacity to recognize reality, or ability to cope with the ordinary demands of life.

(f) "Mentally disabled" means that a person has a mental illness, is mentally retarded, or has a developmental disability.

(g) "Mentally incapable" means that a person suffers from a mental disease or defect which renders that person temporarily or permanently incapable of appraising the nature of his or her conduct.

(h) "Mentally incapacitated" means that a person is rendered temporarily incapable of appraising or controlling his or her conduct due to the influence of a narcotic, anesthetic, or other substance administered to that person without his or her consent, or due to any other act committed upon that person without his or her consent.

(i) "Mentally retarded" means significantly subaverage general intellectual functioning which originates during the developmental period and is associated with impairment in adaptive behavior.

(j) "Nonpublic school" means that term as defined in section 5 of the revised school code, 1976 PA 451, MCL 380.5.

(k) "Physically helpless" means that a person is unconscious, asleep, or for any other reason is physically unable to communicate unwillingness to an act.

(*l*) "Personal injury" means bodily injury, disfigurement, mental anguish, chronic pain, pregnancy, disease, or loss or impairment of a sexual or reproductive organ.

(m) "Public school" means that term as defined in section 5 of the revised school code, 1976 PA 451, MCL 380.5.

(n) "Sexual contact" includes the intentional touching of the victim's or actor's intimate parts or the intentional touching of the clothing covering the immediate area of the victim's or actor's intimate parts, if that intentional touching can reasonably be construed as being for the purpose of sexual arousal or gratification, done for a sexual purpose, or in a sexual manner for:

(*i*) Revenge.

(*ii*) To inflict humiliation.

(*iii*) Out of anger.

(*o*) "Sexual penetration" means sexual intercourse, cunnilingus, fellatio, anal intercourse, or any other intrusion, however slight, of any part of a person's body or of any object into the genital or anal openings of another person's body, but emission of semen is not required.

(p) "Victim" means the person alleging to have been subjected to criminal sexual conduct.

§ 750.520b. First degree criminal sexual conduct

(1) A person is guilty of criminal sexual conduct in the first degree if he or she engages in sexual penetration with another person and if any of the following circumstances exists:

(a) That other person is under 13 years of age.

(b) That other person is at least 13 but less than 16 years of age and any of the following:

(*i*) The actor is a member of the same household as the victim.

(*ii*) The actor is related to the victim by blood or affinity to the fourth degree.

(*iii*) The actor is in a position of authority over the victim and used this authority to coerce the victim to submit.

(*iv*) The actor is a teacher, substitute teacher, or administrator of the public or nonpublic school in which that other person is enrolled.

(c) Sexual penetration occurs under circumstances involving the commission of any other felony.

(d) The actor is aided or abetted by 1 or more other persons and either of the following circumstances exists:

(*i*) The actor knows or has reason to know that the victim is mentally incapable, mentally incapacitated, or physically helpless.

(*ii*) The actor uses force or coercion to accomplish the sexual penetration. Force or coercion includes but is not limited to any of the circumstances listed in subdivision (f)(*i*) to (*v*).

(e) The actor is armed with a weapon or any article used or fashioned in a manner to lead the victim to reasonably believe it to be a weapon.

(f) The actor causes personal injury to the victim and force or coercion is used to accomplish sexual penetration. Force or coercion includes but is not limited to any of the following circumstances:

(*i*) When the actor overcomes the victim through the actual application of physical force or physical violence.

(*ii*) When the actor coerces the victim to submit by threatening to use force or violence on the victim, and the victim believes that the actor has the present ability to execute these threats.

(*iii*) When the actor coerces the victim to submit by threatening to retaliate in the future against the victim, or any other person, and the victim believes that the actor has the ability to execute this threat. As used in this subdivision, "to retaliate" includes threats of physical punishment, kidnapping, or extortion.

(*iv*) When the actor engages in the medical treatment or examination of the victim in a manner or for purposes which are medically recognized as unethical or unacceptable.

(*v*) When the actor, through concealment or by the element of surprise, is able to overcome the victim.

(g) The actor causes personal injury to the victim, and the actor knows or has reason to know that the victim is mentally incapable, mentally incapacitated, or physically helpless.

(h) That other person is mentally incapable, mentally disabled, mentally incapacitated, or physically helpless, and any of the following:

(*i*) The actor is related to the victim by blood or affinity to the fourth degree.

(*ii*) The actor is in a position of authority over the victim and used this authority to coerce the victim to submit.

(2) Criminal sexual conduct in the first degree is a felony punishable by imprisonment in the state prison for life or for any term of years.

§ 750.520c.  Second degree criminal sexual conduct

(1) A person is guilty of criminal sexual conduct in the second degree if the person engages in sexual contact with another person and if any of the following circumstances exists:

(a) That other person is under 13 years of age.

(b) That other person is at least 13 but less than 16 years of age and any of the following:

(*i*) The actor is a member of the same household as the victim.

(*ii*) The actor is related by blood or affinity to the fourth degree to the victim.

(*iii*) The actor is in a position of authority over the victim and the actor used this authority to coerce the victim to submit.

(*iv*) The actor is a teacher, substitute teacher, or administrator of the public or nonpublic school in which that other person is enrolled.

(c) Sexual contact occurs under circumstances involving the commission of any other felony.

(d) The actor is aided or abetted by 1 or more other persons and either of the following circumstances exists:

(*i*) The actor knows or has reason to know that the victim is mentally incapable, mentally incapacitated, or physically helpless.

(*ii*) The actor uses force or coercion to accomplish the sexual contact. Force or coercion includes but is not limited to any of the circumstances listed in sections 520b(1)(f)(*i*) to (*v*).

(e) The actor is armed with a weapon, or any article used or fashioned in a manner to lead a person to reasonably believe it to be a weapon.

(f) The actor causes personal injury to the victim and force or coercion is used to accomplish the sexual contact. Force or coercion includes but is not limited to any of the circumstances listed in section 520b(1)(f)(*i*) to (*v*).

(g) The actor causes personal injury to the victim and the actor knows or has reason to know that the victim is mentally incapable, mentally incapacitated, or physically helpless.

(h) That other person is mentally incapable, mentally disabled, mentally incapacitated, or physically helpless, and any of the following:

(*i*) The actor is related to the victim by blood or affinity to the fourth degree.

(*ii*) The actor is in a position of authority over the victim and used this authority to coerce the victim to submit.

(i) That other person is under the jurisdiction of the department of corrections and the actor is an employee or a contractual employee of, or a volunteer with, the department of corrections who knows that the other person is under the jurisdiction of the department of corrections.

(j) That other person is under the jurisdiction of the department of corrections and the actor is an employee or a contractual employee of, or a volunteer with, a private vendor that operates a youth correctional facility under section 20g of 1953 PA 232, MCL 791.220g, who knows that the other person is under the jurisdiction of the department of corrections.

(k) That other person is a prisoner or probationer under the jurisdiction of a county for purposes of imprisonment or a work program or other probationary program and the actor is an employee or a contractual employee of or a volunteer with the county or the department of corrections who knows that the other person is under the county's jurisdiction.

(*l*) The actor knows or has reason to know that a court has detained the victim in a facility while the victim is awaiting a trial or hearing, or committed the victim to a facility as a result of the victim having been found responsible for committing an act that would be a crime if committed by an adult, and the actor is an employee or contractual employee of, or a volunteer with, the facility in which the victim is detained or to which the victim was committed.

(2) Criminal sexual conduct in the second degree is a felony punishable by imprisonment for not more than 15 years.

§ 750.520d.   Third degree criminal sexual conduct

(1) A person is guilty of criminal sexual conduct in the third degree if the person engages in sexual penetration with another person and if any of the following circumstances exist:

(a) That other person is at least 13 years of age and under 16 years of age.

(b) Force or coercion is used to accomplish the sexual penetration. Force or coercion includes but is not limited to any of the circumstances listed in section 520b(1)(f)(*i*) to (*v*).

(c) The actor knows or has reason to know that the victim is mentally incapable, mentally incapacitated, or physically helpless.

(d) That other person is related to the actor by blood or affinity to the third degree and the sexual penetration occurs under circumstances not otherwise prohibited by this chapter. It is an affirmative defense to a prosecution under this subdivision that the other person was in a position of authority over the defendant and used this authority to coerce the defendant to violate this subdivision. The defendant has the burden of proving this defense by a preponderance of the evidence. This subdivision does not apply if both persons are lawfully married to each other at the time of the alleged violation.

(e) That other person is at least 16 years of age but less than 18 years of age and a student at a public or nonpublic school, and the actor is a teacher, substitute teacher, or administrator of that public or nonpublic school. This subdivision does not apply if the other person is emancipated or if both persons are lawfully married to each other at the time of the alleged violation.

(2) Criminal sexual conduct in the third degree is a felony punishable by imprisonment for not more than 15 years.

§ 750.520e.   Fourth degree criminal sexual conduct

(1) A person is guilty of criminal sexual conduct in the fourth degree if he or she engages in sexual contact with another person and if any of the following circumstances exist:

(a) That other person is at least 13 years of age but less than 16 years of age, and the actor is 5 or more years older than that other person.

(b) Force or coercion is used to accomplish the sexual contact. Force or coercion includes, but is not limited to, any of the following circumstances:

(*i*) When the actor overcomes the victim through the actual application of physical force or physical violence.

(*ii*) When the actor coerces the victim to submit by threatening to use force or violence on the victim, and the victim believes that the actor has the present ability to execute that threat.

(*iii*) When the actor coerces the victim to submit by threatening to retaliate in the future against the victim, or any other person, and the victim believes that the actor has the ability to execute that threat. As used in this subparagraph, "to retaliate" includes threats of physical punishment, kidnapping, or extortion.

(*iv*) When the actor engages in the medical treatment or examination of the victim in a manner or for purposes which are medically recognized as unethical or unacceptable.

(*v*) When the actor achieves the sexual contact through concealment or by the element of surprise.

(c) The actor knows or has reason to know that the victim is mentally incapable, mentally incapacitated, or physically helpless.

(d) That other person is related to the actor by blood or affinity to the third degree and the sexual contact occurs under circumstances not otherwise prohibited by this chapter. It is an affirmative defense to a prosecution under this subdivision that the other person was in a position of authority over the defendant and used this authority to coerce the defendant to violate this subdivision. The defendant has the burden of proving this defense by a preponderance of the evidence. This subdivision does not apply if both persons are lawfully married to each other at the time of the alleged violation.

(e) The actor is a mental health professional and the sexual contact occurs during or within 2 years after the period in which the victim is his or her client or patient and not his or her spouse. The consent of the victim is not a defense to a prosecution under this subdivision. A prosecution under this subsection shall not be used as evidence that the victim is mentally incompetent.

(f) That other person is at least 16 years of age but less than 18 years of age and a student at a public or nonpublic school, and the actor is a teacher, substitute teacher, or administrator of that public or nonpublic school. This subdivision does not apply if the other person is emancipated or if both persons are lawfully married to each other at the time of the alleged violation.

(2) Criminal sexual conduct in the fourth degree is a misdemeanor punishable by imprisonment for not more than 2 years or a fine of not more than $500.00, or both.

§ 750.520f.  Second or subsequent offenses

(1) If a person is convicted of a second or subsequent offense under section 520b, 520c, or 520d, the sentence imposed under those sections for the second or subsequent offense shall provide for a mandatory minimum sentence of at least 5 years.

(2) For purposes of this section, an offense is considered a second or subsequent offense if, prior to conviction of the second or subsequent offense, the actor has at any time been convicted under section 520b, 520c, or 520d or under any similar statute of the United States or any state for a criminal sexual offense including rape, carnal knowledge, indecent liberties, gross indecency, or an attempt to commit such an offense.

§ 750.520g.  Assault with intent to commit criminal sexual conduct

(1) Assault with intent to commit criminal sexual conduct involving sexual penetration shall be a felony punishable by imprisonment for not more than 10 years.

(2) Assault with intent to commit criminal sexual conduct in the second degree is a felony punishable by imprisonment for not more than 5 years.

---

## (B) VIRGINIA HOMICIDE STATUTES

### 1.  2 Va. Stat. §§ 2, 4, 14 (Shepherd 1796):

II.  And whereas, The several offenses which are included under the general denomination of murder, differ so greatly from each other in the degree of their atrociousness, that it is unjust to involve them in the same punishment; Be it ... enacted, That all murder which shall be perpetrated by means of poison, or by lying in wait, or by any other kind of wilful, deliberate, and premeditated killing, or which shall be committed in the perpetration or attempt to perpetrate any arson, rape, robbery or burglary, shall be deemed murder of the first degree; and all other kinds of murder shall be deemed murder of the second degree....

IV.  ... Every person duly convicted of the crime of murder in the second degree, shall be sentenced to ... confinement for a period not less than five years, nor more than 18 years....

XIV.  Every person convicted of murder of the first degree ... shall suffer death by hanging by the neck.

### 2.  Va. Code, tit. 52 (1887):

§ 3662.  **Murder, first and second degree, defined.**—Murder by poison, lying in wait, imprisonment, starving, or any wilful, deliberate, and premeditated killing, or in the commission of, or attempt to commit arson, rape, robbery, or burglary, is murder of the first degree. All other murder is murder of the second degree.

§ 3663.   **First degree, how punished**.—Murder of the first degree shall be punished with death.

§ 3664.   **Second degree, how punished**.—Murder of the second degree shall be punished by confinement in the penitentiary not less than five nor more than 18 years.

§ 3665.   **Voluntary manslaughter, how punished**.—Voluntary manslaughter, shall be punished by confinement in the penitentiary not less than one nor more than five years.

§ 3666.   **Involuntary manslaughter, a misdemeanor**.—Involuntary manslaughter, shall be a misdemeanor.

**3.   Va. Acts, ch. 240, § 1 (1914):**

1.   Be it enacted by the General Assembly of Virginia, That section 3663, be amended and reenacted so as to read as follows:

Sec. 3663. Murder of the first degree shall be punished with death, or in the discretion of the jury by confinement in the penitentiary for life.

**4.   Va. Code Ann. (Michie 1996 & Supp 2003):**

§ 18.2–10. **Punishment for conviction of felony**.—The authorized punishments for conviction of a felony are:

(a) For Class 1 felonies, death, if the person so convicted was 16 years of age or older at the time of the offense and is not determined to be mentally retarded pursuant to § 19.2–264.3:1.1, or imprisonment for life and, subject to subdivision (g), a fine of not more than $100,000. If the person was under 16 years of age at the time of the offense or is determined to be mentally retarded pursuant to § 19.2–264.3:1.1, the punishment shall be imprisonment for life and, subject to subdivision (g), a fine of not more than $100,000.

(b) For Class 2 felonies, imprisonment for life or for any term not less than 20 years and, subject to subdivision (g), a fine of not more than $100,000.

(c) For Class 3 felonies, a term of imprisonment of not less than five years nor more than 20 years and, subject to subdivision (g), a fine of not more than $100,000.

(d) For Class 4 felonies, a term of imprisonment of not less than two years nor more than 10 years and, subject to subdivision (g), a fine of not more than $100,000.

(e) For Class 5 felonies, a term of imprisonment of not less than one year nor more than 10 years, or in the discretion of the jury or the court trying the case without a jury, confinement in jail for not more than 12 months and a fine of not more than $2,500, either or both.

(f) For Class 6 felonies, a term of imprisonment of not less than one year nor more than five years, or in the discretion of the jury or the court trying the case without a jury, confinement in jail for not more than 12 months and a fine of not more than $2,500, either or both.

(g) Except as specifically authorized in subdivision (e) or (f), or in Class 1 felonies for which a sentence of death is imposed, the court shall impose either a sentence of imprisonment together with a fine, or imprisonment only. However, if the defendant is not a natural person, the court shall impose only a fine.

For any felony offense committed (i) on or after January 1, 1995, the court may, and (ii) on or after July 1, 2000, shall, except in cases in which the court orders a suspended term of confinement of at least six months, impose an additional term of not less than six months nor more than three years, which shall be suspended conditioned upon successful completion of a period of post-release supervision pursuant to § 19.2–295.2 and compliance with such other terms as the sentencing court may require. However, such additional term may only be imposed when the sentence includes an active term of incarceration in a correctional facility.

For a felony offense prohibiting proximity to children as described in subsection A of § 18.2–370.2, the sentencing court is authorized to impose the punishment set forth in subsection B of that section in addition to any other penalty provided by law.

**§ 18.2–30. Murder and manslaughter declared felonies.**—Any person who commits capital murder, murder of the first degree, murder of the second degree, voluntary manslaughter, or involuntary manslaughter, shall be guilty of a felony.

**§ 18.2–31. Capital murder defined; punishment.**—The following offenses shall constitute capital murder, punishable as a Class 1 felony:

1.   The willful, deliberate and premeditated killing of any person in the commission of abduction, as defined in § 18.2–48, when such abduction was committed with the intent to extort money, or a pecuniary benefit or with the intent to defile the victim of such abduction;

2.   The willful, deliberate, and premeditated killing of any person by another for hire;

3.   The willful, deliberate, and premeditated killing of any person by a prisoner confined in a state or local correctional facility as defined in § 53.1–1, or while in the custody of an employee thereof;

4.   The willful, deliberate, and premeditated killing of any person in the commission of robbery or attempted robbery;

5.   The willful, deliberate, and premeditated killing of any person in the commission of, or subsequent to, rape or attempted rape, forcible sodomy or attempted forcible sodomy or object sexual penetration;

6.   The willful, deliberate, and premeditated killing of a law-enforcement officer as defined in § 9.1–101 or any law-enforcement officer of another state or the United States having the power to arrest for a felony under the laws of such state or the United States, when such killing is for the purpose of interfering with the performance of his official duties;

7.   The willful, deliberate, and premeditated killing of more than one person as a part of the same act or transaction;

8.   The willful, deliberate, and premeditated killing of more than one person within a three-year period;

9.   The willful, deliberate, and premeditated killing of any person in the commission of or attempted commission of a violation of § 18.2–248, involving a Schedule I or II controlled substance, when such killing is for the purpose of furthering the commission or attempted commission of such violation.

10.   The willful, deliberate, and premeditated killing of any person by another pursuant to the direction or order of one who is engaged in a continuing criminal enterprise as defined in subsection I of § 18.2–248;

**B-17**

11.   The willful, deliberate and premeditated killing of a pregnant woman by one who knows that the woman is pregnant and has the intent to cause the involuntary termination of the woman's pregnancy without a live birth;

12.   The willful, deliberate and premeditated killing of a person under the age of fourteen by a person age twenty-one or older; and

13.   The willful, deliberate and premeditated killing of any person by another in the commission of or attempted commission of an act of terrorism as defined in § 18.2–46.4.

If any one or more subsections, sentences, or parts of this section shall be judged unconstitutional or invalid, such adjudication shall not affect, impair, or invalidate the remaining provisions thereof but shall be confined in its operation to the specific provisions so held unconstitutional or invalid.

**§ 18.2–32. First-and second-degree murder defined; punishment**.—Murder, other than capital murder, by poison, lying in wait, imprisonment, starving, or by any willful, deliberate, and premeditated killing, or in the commission of, or attempt to commit, arson, rape, forcible sodomy, inanimate or animate object sexual penetration, robbery, burglary or abduction, except as provided in § 18.2–31, is murder of the first degree, punishable as a Class 2 felony.

All murder other than capital murder and murder in the first degree is murder of the second degree and is punishable by confinement in a state correctional facility for not less than five nor more than forty years.

**§ 18.2–32.1. Murder of a pregnant woman; penalty**

The willful and deliberate killing of a pregnant woman without premeditation by one who knows that the woman is pregnant and has the intent to cause the involuntary termination of the woman's pregnancy without a live birth shall be punished by a term of imprisonment of not less than ten years nor more than forty years.

**§ 18.2–33. Felony homicide defined; punishment**.—The killing of one accidentally, contrary to the intention of the parties, while in the prosecution of some felonious act other than those specified in §§ 18.2–31 and 18.2–32, is murder of the second degree and is punishable by confinement in a state correctional facility for not less than five years nor more than forty years.

**§ 18.2–35. How voluntary manslaughter punished**.—Voluntary manslaughter is punishable as a Class 5 felony.

**§ 18.2–36. How involuntary manslaughter punished**.—Involuntary manslaughter is punishable as a Class 5 felony.

**§ 19.2–264.2. Conditions for imposition of death sentence**.—In assessing the penalty of any person convicted of an offense for which the death penalty may be imposed, a sentence of death shall not be imposed unless the court or jury shall (1) after consideration of the past criminal record of convictions of the defendant, find that there is a probability that the defendant would commit criminal acts of violence that would constitute a continuing serious threat to society or that his conduct in committing the offense for which he stands charged was outrageously or wantonly vile, horrible or inhuman in that it involved torture, depravity of mind or an aggravated battery to the victim; and (2) recommend that the penalty of death be imposed.

**§ 19.2–264.3. Procedure for trial by jury.—**

A.   In any case in which the offense may be punishable by death which is tried before a jury the court shall first submit to the jury the issue of guilt or innocence of the defendant of the offense charged in the indictment, or any other offense supported by the evidence for which a lesser punishment is provided by law and the penalties therefor.

B. If the jury finds the defendant guilty of an offense for which the death penalty may not be imposed, it shall fix the punishment for such offense as provided in § 19.2–295.1.

C. If the jury finds the defendant guilty of an offense which may be punishable by death, then a separate proceeding before the same jury shall be held as soon as is practicable on the issue of the penalty, which shall be fixed as is provided in § 19.2–264.4.

If the sentence of death is subsequently set aside or found invalid, and the defendant or the Commonwealth requests a jury for purposes of resentencing, the court shall impanel a different jury on the issue of penalty.

### § 19.2–264.4. Sentence proceeding.—

A. Upon a finding that the defendant is guilty of an offense which may be punishable by death, a proceeding shall be held which shall be limited to a determination as to whether the defendant shall be sentenced to death or life imprisonment. Upon request of the defendant, a jury shall be instructed that for all Class 1 felony offenses committed after January 1, 1995, a defendant shall not be eligible for parole if sentenced to imprisonment for life. In case of trial by jury, where a sentence of death is not recommended, the defendant shall be sentenced to imprisonment for life.

A1. In any proceeding conducted pursuant to this section, the court shall permit the victim, as defined in § 19.2–11.01, upon the motion of the attorney for the Commonwealth, and with the consent of the victim, to testify in the presence of the accused regarding the impact of the offense upon the victim. The court shall limit the victim's testimony to the factors set forth in clauses (i) through (vi) of subsection A of § 19.2–299.1.

B. In cases of trial by jury, evidence may be presented as to any matter which the court deems relevant to sentence, except that reports under the provisions of § 19.2–299, or under any Rule of Court, shall not be admitted into evidence.

Evidence which may be admissible, subject to the rules of evidence governing admissibility, may include the circumstances surrounding the offense, the history and background of the defendant, and any other facts in mitigation of the offense. Facts in mitigation may include, but shall not be limited to, the following:

(i) The defendant has no significant history of prior criminal activity,

(ii) the capital felony was committed while the defendant was under the influence of extreme mental or emotional disturbance,

(iii) the victim was a participant in the defendant's conduct or consented to the act,

(iv) at the time of the commission of the capital felony, the capacity of the defendant to appreciate the criminality of his conduct or to conform his conduct to the requirements of law was significantly impaired,

(v) the age of the defendant at the time of the commission of the capital offense or

(vi) even if § 19.2–264.3:1.1 is inapplicable as a bar to the death penalty, the subaverage intellectual functioning of the defendant.

C.   The penalty of death shall not be imposed unless the Commonwealth shall prove beyond a reasonable doubt that there is a probability based upon evidence of the prior history of the defendant or of the circumstances surrounding the commission of the offense of which he is accused that he would commit criminal acts of violence that would constitute a continuing serious threat to society, or that his conduct in committing the offense was outrageously or wantonly vile, horrible or inhuman, in that it involved torture, depravity of mind or aggravated battery to the victim.

D.   The verdict of the jury shall be in writing, and in one of the following forms:

(1) "We, the jury, on the issue joined, having found the defendant guilty of (here set out statutory language of the offense charged) and that (after consideration of his prior history that there is a probability that he would commit criminal acts of violence that would constitute a continuing serious threat to society) or his conduct in committing the offense is outrageously or wantonly vile, horrible or inhuman in that it involved (torture) (depravity of mind) (aggravated battery to the victim), and having considered the evidence in mitigation of the offense, unanimously fix his punishment at death.

Signed _____ foreman"

or

(2) "We, the jury, on the issue joined, having found the defendant guilty of (here set out statutory language of the offense charged) and having considered all of the evidence in aggravation and mitigation of such offense, fix his punishment at (i) imprisonment for life; or (ii) imprisonment for life and a fine of $ . . . . . . . . . .

Signed _____ foreman"

E.   In the event the jury cannot agree as to the penalty, the court shall dismiss the jury, and impose a sentence of imprisonment for life.

**§ 19.2–264.5. Post sentence reports**.—When the punishment of any person has been fixed at death, the court shall, before imposing sentence, direct a probation officer of the court to thoroughly investigate the history of the defendant and any and all other relevant facts, to the end that the court may be fully advised as to whether the sentence of death is appropriate and just. Reports shall be made, presented and filed as provided in § 19.2–299 except that, notwithstanding any other provision of law, such reports shall in all cases contain a Victim Impact Statement. Such statement shall contain the same information and be prepared in the same manner as Victim Impact Statements prepared pursuant to § 19.2–299.1. After consideration of the report, and upon good cause shown, the court may set aside the sentence of death and impose a sentence of imprisonment for life.

**§ 17.1–313. Review of death sentence**.—

A.   A sentence of death, upon the judgment thereon becoming final in the circuit court, shall be reviewed on the record by the Supreme Court.

B.   The proceeding in the circuit court shall be transcribed as expeditiously as practicable, and the transcript filed forthwith upon transcription with the clerk of the circuit court, who shall, within ten days after receipt of the transcript, compile the record as provided in Rule 5:14 and transmit it to the Supreme Court.

C.  In addition to consideration of any errors in the trial enumerated by appeal, the court shall consider and determine:

1.  Whether the sentence of death was imposed under the influence of passion, prejudice or any other arbitrary factor; and

2.  Whether the sentence of death is excessive or disproportionate to the penalty imposed in similar cases, considering both the crime and the defendant.

D.  In addition to the review and correction of errors in the trial of the case, with respect to review of the sentence of death, the court may:

1.  Affirm the sentence of death;

2.  Commute the sentence of death to imprisonment for life; or

3.  Remand to the trial court for a new sentence proceeding.

E.  The Supreme Court may accumulate the records of all capital felony cases tried within such period of time as the court may determine. The court shall consider such records as are available as a guide in determining whether the sentence imposed in the case under review is excessive. Such records as are accumulated shall be made available to the circuit courts.

F.  Sentence review shall be in addition to appeals, if taken, and review and appeal may be consolidated. The defendant and the Commonwealth shall have the right to submit briefs within time limits imposed by the court, either by rule or order, and to present oral argument.

G.  The Supreme Court shall, in setting its docket, give priority to the review of cases in which the sentence of death has been imposed over other cases pending in the Court. In setting its docket, the Court shall also give priority to the consideration and disposition of petitions for writs of habeas corpus filed by prisoners held under sentence of death.

––––––––

### (C) PRE-*FURMAN* GEORGIA HOMICIDE STATUTES

**1.  Ga. Laws, 1968 Sess., pp. 1276–77, 1335, before the Supreme Court in Furman v. Georgia, 408 U.S. 238 (1972):**

§ **26–1101. Murder.**—(a) A person commits murder when he unlawfully and with malice aforethought, either express or implied, causes the death of another human being. Express malice is that deliberate intention unlawfully to take away the life of a fellow creature, which is manifested by external circumstances capable of proof. Malice shall be implied where no considerable provocation appears, and where all the circumstances of the killing show an abandoned and malignant heart.

(b) A person also commits the crime of murder when in the commission of a felony he causes the death of another human being, irrespective of malice.

(c) A person convicted of murder shall be punished by death or by imprisonment for life.

§ **26–1102. Voluntary Manslaughter**. A person commits voluntary manslaughter when he causes the death of another human being, under circumstances which would otherwise be murder, if he acts solely as the result of a sudden, violent, and irresistible passion resulting from serious provocation sufficient to excite such passion in a reasonable person; however, if there should have been an interval between the provocation and the killing sufficient for the voice of reason and humanity to be heard, of which the jury in all cases shall be the judge, the killing shall be attributed to deliberate revenge and be punished as murder. A person convicted of voluntary manslaughter shall be punished by imprisonment for not less than one nor more than 20 years.

**§ 26–1103. Involuntary Manslaughter**. (a) A person commits involuntary manslaughter in the commission of an unlawful act when he causes the death of another human being without any intention to do so, by the commission of an unlawful act other than a felony. A person convicted under this subsection shall be punished by imprisonment for not less than one year nor more than five years.

(b) A person commits involuntary manslaughter in the commission of a lawful act in an unlawful manner when he causes the death of another human being, without any intention to do so, by the commission of a lawful act in an unlawful manner likely to cause death or great bodily harm. A person convicted under this subsection shall be punished as for a misdemeanor.

**§ 26–3102. Capital Offenses**.—Jury Verdict and Sentence. Where, upon a trial by jury, a person is convicted of an offense which may be punishable by death, a sentence of death shall not be imposed unless the jury verdict includes a recommendation that such sentence be imposed. Where a recommendation of death is made, the court shall sentence the defendant to death. Where a sentence of death is not recommended by the jury, the court shall sentence the defendant to imprisonment as provided by law. Unless the jury trying the case recommends the death sentence in its verdict, the court shall not sentence the defendant to death.

---

### (D) NEW YORK HOMICIDE STATUTES

**1.  Bender's N.Y. Penal Law (1942):**

**§ 1044.  Murder in first degree defined**.

The killing of a human being, unless it is excusable or justifiable, is murder in the first degree, when committed:

1.  From a deliberate and premeditated design to effect the death of the person killed, or of another; or,

2.  By an act imminently dangerous to others, and evincing a depraved mind, regardless of human life, although without a premeditated design to effect the death of any individual; or without a design to effect death, by a person engaged in the commission of, or in an attempt to commit a felony, either upon or affecting the person killed or otherwise; or

3.  When perpetrated in committing the crime of arson in the first degree. . . .

**§ 1045.  Punishment for murder in first degree**.

Murder in the first degree is punishable by death, unless the jury recommends life imprisonment as provided by section 1045–a.

**§ 1045–a.  Life imprisonment for felony murder; jury may recommend**.

A jury finding a person guilty of murder in the first degree, as defined by Section 1044(2), may, as a part of its verdict, recommend that the defendant be imprisoned for the term of his natural life. Upon such recommendation, the court may sentence the defendant to imprisonment for the term of his natural life.

**§ 1046.  Murder in second degree defined**.

Such killing of a human being is murder in the second degree, when committed with a design to effect the death of the person killed, or of another, but without deliberation and premeditation.

**§ 1048.  Punishment for murder in the second degree**.

Murder in the second degree is punishable by imprisonment under an indeterminate sentence, the minimum of which shall be not less than 20 years and the maximum of which shall be for the offender's natural life. . . .

**§ 1049.  Manslaughter defined**.

In a case other than one of those specified in Sections 1044 [and] 1046 . . ., homicide, not being justifiable or excusable, is manslaughter.

**§ 1050.  Manslaughter in first degree**.

Such homicide is manslaughter in the first degree, when committed without a design to effect death:

1.  By a person engaged in committing, or attempting to commit a misdemeanor, affecting the person or property, either of the person killed, or of another; or,

2.  In the heat of passion, but in a cruel and unusual manner, or by means of a dangerous weapon. . . .

**§ 1051.  Punishment for manslaughter in first degree**.

Manslaughter in the first degree is punishable by imprisonment for a term not exceeding 20 years.

**§ 1052.  Manslaughter in second degree defined**.

Such homicide is manslaughter in the second degree, when committed without a design to effect death:

1.  By a person committing or attempting to commit a trespass, or other invasion of a private right, either of the person killed, or of another, not amounting to a crime; or,

2.  In the heat of passion, but not by a dangerous weapon or by the use of means of either cruel or unusual; or,

3.  By any act, procurement or culpable negligence of any person, which, according to the provisions of this article, does not constitute the crime of murder in the first or second degree, nor manslaughter in the first degree. . . .

**§ 1053.  Punishment for manslaughter in second degree**.

Manslaughter in the second degree is punishable by imprisonment for a term not exceeding 15 years, or by a fine of not more than $1,000, or by both.

**§ 1053–a.  Criminal negligence in operation of a vehicle resulting in death**.

A person who operates or drives any vehicle of any kind in a reckless or culpably negligent manner, whereby a human being is killed, is guilty of criminal negligence in the operation of a vehicle resulting in death.

**B-23**

### § 1053–b.  Punishment for criminal negligence in operation of vehicle resulting in death.

A person convicted of the crime defined by section 1053–a is punishable by imprisonment for a term of not exceeding five years or by a fine of not more than $1000, or by both.

### 2.  N.Y. Penal Law (McKinney 1998 & Supp. 2004):

### § 125.10.  Criminally negligent homicide.

A person is guilty of criminally negligent homicide when, with criminal negligence, he causes the death of another person.

Criminally negligent homicide is a class E felony [four-year maximum].

### § 125.15.  Manslaughter in the second degree.

A person is guilty of manslaughter in the second degree when:

1.  He recklessly causes the death of another person. . . .

Manslaughter in the second degree is a class C felony [15–year maximum].

### § 125.20.  Manslaughter in the first degree.

A person is guilty of manslaughter in the first degree when:

1.  With intent to cause serious physical injury to another person, he causes the death of such person or of a third person; or

2.  With intent to cause the death of another person, he causes the death of such person or of a third person under circumstances which do not constitute murder because he acts under the influence of extreme emotional disturbance, as defined in paragraph (a) of subdivision one of section 125.25. The fact that homicide was committed under the influence of extreme emotional disturbance constitutes a mitigating circumstance reducing murder to manslaughter in the first degree and need not be proved in any prosecution initiated under this subdivision. . . .

Manslaughter in the first degree is a class B felony [25–year maximum].

### § 125.25.  Murder in the second degree.

A person is guilty of murder in the second degree [punishable by a 20–year minimum and maximum of life imprisonment] when:

1.  With intent to cause the death of another person, he causes the death of such person or of a third person; except that in any prosecution under this subdivision, it is an affirmative defense that:

   (a) The defendant acted under the influence of extreme emotional disturbance for which there was a reasonable explanation or excuse, the reasonableness of which is to be determined from the viewpoint of a person in the defendant's situation under the circumstances as the defendant believed them to be. Nothing contained in this paragraph shall constitute a defense to a prosecution for, or preclude a conviction of, manslaughter in the first degree or any other crime; or

   (b) The defendant's conduct consisted of causing or aiding, without the use of duress or deception, another person to commit suicide. Nothing contained in this paragraph shall constitute a defense to a prosecution for, or preclude a conviction of, manslaughter in the second degree or any other crime; or

2. Under circumstances evincing a depraved indifference to human life, he recklessly engages in conduct which creates a grave risk of death to another person, and thereby causes the death of another person; or

3. Acting either alone or with one or more other persons, he commits or attempts to commit robbery, burglary, kidnapping, arson, rape in the first degree, criminal sexual act in the first degree, sexual abuse in the first degree, aggravated sexual abuse, escape in the first degree, or escape in the second degree, and, in the course of and in furtherance of such crime or of immediate flight therefrom, he, or another participant, if there be any, causes the death of a person other than one of the participants; except that in any prosecution under this subdivision, in which the defendant was not the only participant in the underlying crime, it is an affirmative defense that the defendant:

(a) Did not commit the homicidal act or in any way solicit, request, command, importune, cause or aid the commission thereof; and

(b) Was not armed with a deadly weapon, or any instrument, article or substance readily capable of causing death or serious physical injury and of a sort not ordinarily carried in public places by law-abiding persons; and

(c) Had no reasonable ground to believe that any other participant was armed with such a weapon, instrument, article or substance; and

(d) Had no reasonable ground to believe that any other participant intended to engage in conduct likely to result in death or serious physical injury; or

4. Under circumstances evincing a depraved indifference to human life, and being eighteen years old or more the defendant recklessly engages in conduct which creates a grave risk of serious physical injury or death to another person less than eleven years old and thereby causes the death of such person.

Murder in the second degree is a class A–I felony.

### § 125.27.  Murder in the first degree.[d]

A person is guilty of murder in the first degree when:

1. With intent to cause the death of another person, he causes the death of such person or of a third person; and

(a) Either:

(i) the intended victim was a police officer . . . who was at the time of the killing engaged in the course of performing his official duties, and the defendant knew or reasonably should have known that the intended victim was a police officer; or

(ii) the intended victim was a peace officer . . . who was at the time of the killing engaged in the course of performing his official duties, and the defendant knew or reasonably should have known that the intended victim was such a uniformed court officer, parole officer, probation officer, or employee of the division for youth; or

(iii) the intended victim was an employee of a state correctional institution or was an employee of a local correctional facility . . ., who was at the time of the killing engaged in the course of performing his official duties, and the defendant knew or reasonably should have known that the

[d] This section was substantially revised in 1995 when New York revived the death penalty for first-degree murder.—[Footnote by eds.]

intended victim was an employee of a state correctional institution or a local correctional facility; or

(iv) at the time of the commission of the killing, the defendant was confined in a state correctional institution or was otherwise in custody upon a sentence for the term of his natural life, or upon a sentence commuted to one of natural life, or upon a sentence for an indeterminate term the minimum of which was at least fifteen years and the maximum of which was natural life, or at the time of the commission of the killing, the defendant had escaped from such confinement or custody while serving such a sentence and had not yet been returned to such confinement or custody; or

(v) the intended victim was a witness to a crime committed on a prior occasion and the death was caused for the purpose of preventing the intended victim's testimony in any criminal action or proceeding whether or not such action or proceeding had been commenced, or the intended victim had previously testified in a criminal action or proceeding and the killing was committed for the purpose of exacting retribution for such prior testimony, or the intended victim was an immediate family member of a witness to a crime committed on a prior occasion and the killing was committed for the purpose of preventing or influencing the testimony of such witness, or the intended victim was an immediate family member of a witness who had previously testified in a criminal action or proceeding and the killing was committed for the purpose of exacting retribution upon such witness for such prior testimony. As used in this subparagraph "immediate family member" means a husband, wife, father, mother, daughter, son, brother, sister, stepparent, grandparent, stepchild or grandchild; or

(vi) the defendant committed the killing or procured commission of the killing pursuant to an agreement with a person other than the intended victim to commit the same for the receipt, or in expectation of the receipt, of anything of pecuniary value from a party to the agreement or from a person other than the intended victim acting at the direction of a party to such agreement; or

(vii) the victim was killed while the defendant was in the course of committing or attempting to commit and in furtherance of robbery, burglary in the first degree or second degree, kidnapping in the first degree, arson in the first degree or second degree, rape in the first degree, criminal sexual act in the first degree, sexual abuse in the first degree, aggravated sexual abuse in the first degree or escape in the first degree, or in the course of and furtherance of immediate flight after committing or attempting to commit any such crime or in the course of and furtherance of immediate flight after attempting to commit the crime of murder in the second degree; provided however, the victim is not a participant in one of the aforementioned crimes and, provided further that, unless the defendant's criminal liability under this subparagraph is based upon the defendant having commanded another person to cause the death of the victim or intended victim ..., this subparagraph shall not apply where the defendant's criminal liability is based upon the conduct of another ...; or

(viii) as part of the same criminal transaction, the defendant, with intent to cause serious physical injury to or the death of an additional person or persons, causes the death of an additional person or persons; provided, however, the victim is not a participant in the criminal transaction; or

(ix) prior to committing the killing, the defendant had been convicted of murder as defined in this section or section 125.25 of this article, or had been convicted in another jurisdiction of an offense which, if committed in this state, would constitute a violation of either of such sections; or

(x) the defendant acted in an especially cruel and wanton manner pursuant to a course of conduct intended to inflict and inflicting torture upon the victim prior to the victim's death. As used in this subparagraph, "torture" means the intentional and depraved infliction of extreme physical pain; "depraved" means the defendant relished the infliction of extreme physical pain upon the victim evidencing debasement or perversion or that the defendant evidenced a sense of pleasure in the infliction of extreme physical pain; or

(xi) the defendant intentionally caused the death of two or more additional persons within the state in separate criminal transactions within a period of twenty-four months when committed in a similar fashion or pursuant to a common scheme or plan; or

(xii) the intended victim was a judge ... and the defendant killed such victim because such victim was, at the time of the killing, a judge; or

(xiii) the victim was killed in furtherance of an act of terrorism, as defined in paragraph (b) of subdivision one of section 490.05 of this chapter; and

(b) The defendant was more than eighteen years old at the time of the commission of the crime.

2. In any prosecution under subdivision one, it is an affirmative defense that:

(a) The defendant acted under the influence of extreme emotional disturbance for which there was a reasonable explanation or excuse, the reasonableness of which is to be determined from the viewpoint of a person in the defendant's situation under the circumstances as the defendant believed them to be. Nothing contained in this paragraph shall constitute a defense to a prosecution for, or preclude a conviction of, manslaughter in the first degree or any other crime except murder in the second degree; or

(b) The defendant's conduct consisted of causing or aiding, without the use of duress or deception, another person to commit suicide. Nothing contained in this paragraph shall constitute a defense to a prosecution for, or preclude a conviction of, manslaughter in the second degree or any other crime except murder in the second degree.

Murder in the first degree is a class A–I felony.

**3.   N.Y. Crim. Proc. Law (McKinney Supp. 2004)**

**§ 400.27.   Procedure for determining sentence upon conviction for the offense of murder in the first degree.**

1. Upon the conviction of a defendant for the offense of murder in the first degree as defined by section 125.27 of the penal law, the court shall promptly conduct a separate sentencing proceeding to determine whether the defendant shall be sentenced to death or to life imprisonment without parole.... Nothing in this

section shall be deemed to preclude the people at any time from determining that the death penalty shall not be sought in a particular case, in which case the separate sentencing proceeding shall not be conducted and the court may sentence such defendant to life imprisonment without parole or to a sentence of imprisonment [not less than 20 years] other than a sentence of life imprisonment without parole.

2. The separate sentencing proceeding provided for by this section shall be conducted before the court sitting with the jury that found the defendant guilty. The court may discharge the jury and impanel another jury only in extraordinary circumstances and upon a showing of good cause, which may include, but is not limited to, a finding of prejudice to either party.... Before proceeding with the jury that found the defendant guilty, the court shall determine whether any juror has a state of mind that is likely to preclude the juror from rendering an impartial decision based upon the evidence adduced during the proceeding. In making such determination the court shall personally examine each juror individually outside the presence of the other jurors. The scope of the examination shall be within the discretion of the court and may include questions supplied by the parties as the court deems proper. The proceedings provided for in this subdivision shall be conducted on the record; provided, however, that upon motion of either party, and for good cause shown, the court may direct that all or a portion of the record of such proceedings be sealed. In the event the court determines that a juror has such a state of mind, the court shall discharge the juror and replace the juror with the alternate juror whose name was first drawn and called. If no alternate juror is available, the court must discharge the jury and impanel another jury....

3. For the purposes of a proceeding under this section each subparagraph of paragraph (a) of subdivision one of section 125.27 of the penal law shall be deemed to define an aggravating factor. Except as provided in subdivision seven of this section, at a sentencing proceeding pursuant to this section the only aggravating factors that the jury may consider are those proven beyond a reasonable doubt at trial, and no other aggravating factors may be considered. Whether a sentencing proceeding is conducted before the jury that found the defendant guilty or before another jury, the aggravating factor or factors proved at trial shall be deemed established beyond a reasonable doubt at the separate sentencing proceeding and shall not be relitigated. Where the jury is to determine sentences for concurrent counts of murder in the first degree, the aggravating factor included in each count shall be deemed to be an aggravating factor for the purpose of the jury's consideration in determining the sentence to be imposed on each such count....

6. At the sentencing proceeding the people shall not relitigate the existence of aggravating factors proved at the trial or otherwise present evidence, except, subject to the rules governing admission of evidence in the trial of a criminal action, in rebuttal of the defendant's evidence. However, when the sentencing proceeding is conducted before a newly impaneled jury, the people may present evidence to the extent reasonably necessary to inform the jury of the nature and circumstances of the count or counts of murder in the first degree for which the defendant was convicted in sufficient detail to permit the jury to determine the weight to be accorded the aggravating factor or factors established at trial. Whenever the people present such evidence, the court must instruct the jury in its charge that any facts elicited by the people that are not essential to the verdict of guilty on such count or counts shall not be deemed established beyond a reasonable doubt. Subject to the rules governing the admission of evidence in the trial of a criminal action, the

defendant may present any evidence relevant to any mitigating factor set forth in subdivision nine of this section; provided, however, the defendant shall not be precluded from the admission of reliable hearsay evidence. The burden of establishing any of the mitigating factors set forth in subdivision nine of this section shall be on the defendant, and must be proven by a preponderance of the evidence. The people shall not offer evidence or argument relating to any mitigating factor except in rebuttal of evidence offered by the defendant.

7.   (a) The people may present evidence at the sentencing proceeding to prove that in the ten-year period prior to the commission of the crime of murder in the first degree for which the defendant was convicted, the defendant has previously been convicted of two or more offenses committed on different occasions; provided, that each such offense shall be either (i) [specified violent felonies or attempted violent felonies] or a felony offense under the penal law a necessary element of which involves either the use or attempted use or threatened use of a deadly weapon or the intentional infliction of or the attempted intentional infliction of serious physical injury or death, or (ii) an offense under the laws of another state or of the United States punishable by a term of imprisonment of more than one year a necessary element of which involves either the use or attempted use or threatened use of a deadly weapon or the intentional infliction of or the attempted intentional infliction of serious physical injury or death.... In calculating the ten-year period under this paragraph, any period of time during which the defendant was incarcerated for any reason between the time of commission of any of the prior felony offenses and the time of commission of the crime of murder in the first degree shall be excluded and such ten year period shall be extended by a period or periods equal to the time served under such incarceration. The defendant's conviction of two or more such offenses shall, if proven at the sentencing proceeding, constitute an aggravating factor.

(b) In order to be deemed established, an aggravating factor set forth in this subdivision must be proven by the people beyond a reasonable doubt and the jury must unanimously find such factor to have been so proven....

8.   Consistent with the provisions of this section, the people and the defendant shall be given fair opportunity to rebut any evidence received at the separate sentencing proceeding.

9.   Mitigating factors shall include the following:

(a) The defendant has no significant history of prior criminal convictions involving the use of violence against another person;

(b) The defendant was mentally retarded at the time of the crime, or the defendant's mental capacity was impaired or his ability to conform his conduct to the requirements of law was impaired but not so impaired in either case as to constitute a defense to prosecution;

(c) The defendant was under duress or under the domination of another person, although not such duress or domination as to constitute a defense to prosecution;

(d) The defendant was criminally liable for the present offense of murder committed by another, but his participation in the offense was relatively minor although not so minor as to constitute a defense to prosecution;

**B-29**

(e) The murder was committed while the defendant was mentally or emotionally disturbed or under the influence of alcohol or any drug, although not to such an extent as to constitute a defense to prosecution; or

(f) Any other circumstance concerning the crime, the defendant's state of mind or condition at the time of the crime, or the defendant's character, background or record that would be relevant to mitigation or punishment for the crime.

10. At the conclusion of all the evidence, the people and the defendant may present argument in summation for or against the sentence sought by the people. The people may deliver the first summation and the defendant may then deliver the last summation. Thereafter, the court shall deliver a charge to the jury on any matters appropriate in the circumstances. In its charge, the court must instruct the jury that with respect to each count of murder in the first degree the jury should consider whether or not a sentence of death should be imposed and whether or not a sentence of life imprisonment without parole should be imposed, and that the jury must be unanimous with respect to either sentence. The court must also instruct the jury that in the event the jury fails to reach unanimous agreement with respect to the sentence, the court will sentence the defendant to a term of imprisonment with a minimum term of between twenty and twenty-five years and a maximum term of life. . . .

11. (a) The jury may not direct imposition of a sentence of death unless it unanimously finds beyond a reasonable doubt that the aggravating factor or factors substantially outweigh the mitigating factor or factors established, if any, and unanimously determines that the penalty of death should be imposed. Any member or members of the jury who find a mitigating factor to have been proven by the defendant by a preponderance of the evidence may consider such factor established regardless of the number of jurors who concur that the factor has been established.

(b) If the jury directs imposition of either a sentence of death or life imprisonment without parole, it shall specify on the record those mitigating and aggravating factors considered and those mitigating factors established by the defendant, if any. . . .

12. (a) Upon the conviction of a defendant for the offense of murder in the first degree as defined in section 125.27 of the penal law, the court shall, upon oral or written motion of the defendant based upon a showing that there is reasonable cause to believe that the defendant is mentally retarded, promptly conduct a hearing without a jury to determine whether the defendant is mentally retarded. Upon the consent of both parties, such a hearing, or a portion thereof, may be conducted by the court contemporaneously with the separate sentencing proceeding in the presence of the sentencing jury, which in no event shall be the trier of fact with respect to the hearing. At such hearing the defendant has the burden of proof by a preponderance of the evidence that he or she is mentally retarded. The court shall defer rendering any finding pursuant to this subdivision as to whether the defendant is mentally retarded until a sentence is imposed pursuant to this section.

(b) In the event the defendant is sentenced pursuant to this section to life imprisonment without parole or to a term of imprisonment for the class A–I felony of murder in the first degree other than a sentence of life imprisonment without parole, the court shall not render a finding with respect to whether the defendant is mentally retarded.

(c) In the event the defendant is sentenced pursuant to this section to death, the court shall thereupon render a finding with respect to whether the defendant is mentally retarded. If the court finds the defendant is mentally retarded, the court shall set aside the sentence of death and sentence the defendant either to life imprisonment without parole or to a term of imprisonment for the class A–I felony of murder in the first degree other than a sentence of life imprisonment without parole. If the court finds the defendant is not mentally retarded, then such sentence of death shall not be set aside pursuant to this subdivision.

(d) In the event that a defendant is convicted of murder in the first degree pursuant to subparagraph (iii) of paragraph (a) of subdivision one of section 125.27 of the penal law, and the killing occurred while the defendant was confined or under custody in a state correctional facility or local correctional institution, and a sentence of death is imposed, such sentence may not be set aside pursuant to this subdivision upon the ground that the defendant is mentally retarded. Nothing in this paragraph or paragraph (a) of this subdivision shall preclude a defendant from presenting mitigating evidence of mental retardation at the separate sentencing proceeding.

(e) The foregoing provisions of this subdivision notwithstanding, at a reasonable time prior to the commencement of trial the defendant may, upon a written motion alleging reasonable cause to believe the defendant is mentally retarded, apply for an order directing that a mental retardation hearing be conducted prior to trial. If, upon review of the defendant's motion and any response thereto, the court finds reasonable cause to believe the defendant is mentally retarded, it shall promptly conduct a hearing without a jury to determine whether the defendant is mentally retarded. In the event the court finds after the hearing that the defendant is not mentally retarded, the court must, prior to commencement of trial, enter an order so stating, but nothing in this paragraph shall preclude a defendant from presenting mitigating evidence of mental retardation at a separate sentencing proceeding. In the event the court finds after the hearing that the defendant, based upon a preponderance of the evidence, is mentally retarded, the court must, prior to commencement of trial, enter an order so stating. Unless the order is reversed on an appeal by the people or unless the provisions of paragraph (d) of this subdivision apply, a separate sentencing proceeding under this section shall not be conducted if the defendant is thereafter convicted of murder in the first degree. In the event a separate sentencing proceeding is not conducted, the court, upon conviction of a defendant for the crime of murder in the first degree, shall sentence the defendant to life imprisonment without parole or to a sentence of imprisonment for the class A–I felony of murder in the first degree other than a sentence of life imprisonment without parole. Whenever a mental retardation hearing is held and a finding is rendered pursuant to this paragraph, the court may not conduct a hearing pursuant to paragraph (a) of this subdivision. For purposes of this subdivision and paragraph (b) of subdivision nine of this section, "mental retardation" mens significantly subaverage general intellectual functioning existing concurrently with deficits in adaptive behavior which were manifested before the age of eighteen. . . .

### § 470.30.  Determination by court of appeals of appeals. . . .

2.  Whenever a sentence of death is imposed, the judgment and sentence shall be reviewed on the record by the court of appeals. Review by the court of appeals . . . may not be waived.

3.  With regard to the sentence, the court shall, in addition to exercising the powers and scope of review [otherwise granted], determine:

(a) whether the sentence of death was imposed under the influence of passion, prejudice, or any other arbitrary or legally impermissible factor including whether the imposition of the verdict or sentence was based upon the race of the defendant or a victim of the crime for which the defendant was convicted;

(b) whether the sentence of death is excessive or disproportionate to the penalty imposed in similar cases considering both the crime and the defendant. In conducting such review the court, upon request of the defendant, in addition to any other determination, shall review whether the sentence of death is excessive or disproportionate to the penalty imposed in similar cases by virtue of the race of the defendant or a victim of the crime for which the defendant was convicted; and

(c) whether the decision to impose the sentence of death was against the weight of the evidence.

4. The court shall include in its decision: (a) the aggravating and mitigating factors established in the record on appeal; and (b) those similar cases it took into consideration. . . .

---

### (E) OREGON HOMICIDE AND ASSAULT OFFENSES AND PROVISIONS ON ATTEMPT

#### 1.  Ore. Rev. Stat. Ann. (West 2003):

HOMICIDE

#### § 163.005.  Criminal homicide

(1) A person commits criminal homicide if, without justification or excuse, the person intentionally, knowingly, recklessly or with criminal negligence causes the death of another human being.

(2) "Criminal homicide" is murder, manslaughter or criminally negligent homicide.

(3) "Human being" means a person who has been born and was alive at the time of the criminal act.

#### § 163.115.  Murder; affirmative defenses; felony murder; sentence

(1) Except as provided in ORS 163.118 and 163.125, criminal homicide constitutes murder:

(a) When it is committed intentionally, except that it is an affirmative defense that, at the time of the homicide, the defendant was under the influence of an extreme emotional disturbance;

(b) When it is committed by a person, acting either alone or with one or more persons, who commits or attempts to commit any of the following crimes and in the course of and in furtherance of the crime the person is committing or attempting to commit, or during the immediate flight therefrom, the person, or another participant if there be any, causes the death of a person other than one of the participants:

(A) Arson in the first degree as defined in ORS 164.325;

(B) Criminal mischief in the first degree by means of an explosive as defined in ORS 164.365;

(C) Burglary in the first degree as defined in ORS 164.225;

(D) Escape in the first degree as defined in ORS 162.165;

(E) Kidnapping in the second degree as defined in ORS 163.225;

(F) Kidnapping in the first degree as defined in ORS 163.235;

(G) Robbery in the first degree as defined in ORS 164.415;

(H) Any felony sexual offense in the first degree defined in this chapter; or

(I) Compelling prostitution as defined in ORS 167.017; or

(J) Assault in the first degree, as defined in ORS 163.185, and the victim is under 14 years of age, or assault in the second degree, as defined in ORS 163.175 (1)(a) or (b), and the victim is under 14 years of age; or

(c) By abuse when a person, recklessly under circumstances manifesting extreme indifference to the value of human life, causes the death of a child under 14 years of age or a dependent person . . ., and:

(A) The person has previously engaged in a pattern or practice of assault or torture of the victim or another child under 14 years of age or a dependent person; or

(B) The person causes the death by neglect or maltreatment. . . .

(3) It is an affirmative defense to a charge of violating subsection (1)(b) of subsection (1) of this section that the defendant:

(a) Was not the only participant in the underlying crime;

(b) Did not commit the homicidal act or in any way solicit, request, command, importune, cause or aid in the commission thereof;

(c) Was not armed with a dangerous or deadly weapon;

(d) Had no reasonable ground to believe that any other participant was armed with a dangerous or deadly weapon; and

(e) Had no reasonable ground to believe that any other participant intended to engage in conduct likely to result in death.

(4) It is an affirmative defense to a charge of violating subsection (1)(c)(B) of this section that the child or dependent person was under care or treatment solely by spiritual means pursuant to the religious beliefs or practices of the child or person or the parent or guardian of the child or person.

(5)(a) A person convicted of murder, who was at least 15 years of age at the time of committing the murder, shall be punished by imprisonment for life [with a minimum non-parolable term of 25 years]. . . .

### § 163.118.  First degree manslaughter

(1) Criminal homicide constitutes manslaughter in the first degree when:

(a) It is committed recklessly under circumstances manifesting extreme indifference to the value of human life;

(b) It is committed intentionally by a defendant under the influence of extreme emotional disturbance as provided in ORS 163.135, which constitutes a mitigating circumstance reducing the homicide that would otherwise be murder to manslaughter in the first degree and need not be proved in any prosecution; or

(c) A person recklessly causes the death of a child under 14 years of age or a dependent person, as defined in ORS 163.205, and:

(A) The person has previously engaged in a pattern or practice of assault or torture of the victim or another child under 14 years of age or a dependent person; or

(B) The person causes the death by neglect or maltreatment, as defined in ORS 163.115.

(2) Manslaughter in the first degree is a Class A felony.

(3) It is an affirmative defense to a charge of violating subsection (1)(c)(B) of this section that the child or dependent person was under care or treatment solely by spiritual means pursuant to the religious beliefs or practices of the child or person or the parent or guardian of the child or person.

### § 163.125.  Second Degree Manslaughter

(1) Criminal homicide constitutes manslaughter in the second degree when:

(a) It is committed recklessly;

(b) A person intentionally causes or aids another person to commit suicide; or

(c) A person, with criminal negligence, causes the death of a child under 14 years of age or a dependent person, as defined in ORS 163.205, and:

(A) The person has previously engaged in a pattern or practice of assault or torture of the victim or another child under 14 years of age or a dependent person; or

(B) The person causes the death by neglect or maltreatment, as defined in ORS 163.115.

(2) Manslaughter in the second degree is a Class B felony.

### § 163.135.  Extreme emotional disturbance....

(1) It is an affirmative defense to murder for purposes of ORS 163.115 (1)(a) that the homicide was committed under the influence of extreme emotional disturbance if the disturbance is not the result of the person's own intentional, knowing, reckless or criminally negligent act and if there is a reasonable explanation for the disturbance. The reasonableness of the explanation for the disturbance must be determined from the standpoint of an ordinary person in the actor's situation under the circumstances that the actor reasonably believed them to be. Extreme emotional disturbance does not constitute a defense to a prosecution for, or preclude a conviction of, manslaughter in the first degree or any other crime....

### § 163.145.

[This section punishes criminally negligent homicide as a Class B felony.]

### ASSAULT AND RELATED OFFENSES

### § 163.160.  Assault in the fourth degree.

(1) A person commits the crime of assault in the fourth degree if the person:

(a) Intentionally, knowingly or recklessly causes physical injury to another; or

(b) With criminal negligence causes physical injury to another by means of a deadly weapon.

(2) Assault in the fourth degree is a Class A misdemeanor.

(3) Notwithstanding subsection (2) of this section, assault in the fourth degree is a Class C felony if the person commits the crime of assault in the fourth degree and:

(a) The person has previously been convicted of assaulting the same victim;

(b) The person has previously been convicted at least three times under this section or under equivalent laws of another jurisdiction and all of the assaults involved domestic violence, as defined in ORS 135.230; or

(c) The assault is committed in the immediate presence of, or is witnessed by, the person's or the victim's minor child or stepchild or a minor child residing within the household of the person or victim.

(4) For the purposes of subsection (3) of this section, an assault is witnessed if the assault is seen or directly perceived in any other manner by the child.

### § 163.165.  Assault in the third degree.

(1) A person commits the crime of assault in the third degree if the person:

(a) Recklessly causes serious physical injury to another by means of a deadly or dangerous weapon;

(b) Recklessly causes serious physical injury to another under circumstances manifesting extreme indifference to the value of human life;

(c) Recklessly causes physical injury to another by means of a deadly or dangerous weapon under circumstances manifesting extreme indifference to the value of human life;

(d) Intentionally, knowingly or recklessly causes, by means other than a motor vehicle, physical injury to the operator of a public transit vehicle while the operator is in control of or operating the vehicle....

(e) While being aided by another person actually present, intentionally or knowingly causes physical injury to another;

(f) While committed to a youth correction facility, intentionally or knowingly causes physical injury to another knowing the other person is a staff member of a youth correction facility while the other person is acting in the course of official duty;

(g) Intentionally, knowingly or recklessly causes physical injury to an emergency medical technician or paramedic, ... while the technician or paramedic is performing official duties; or

(h) Being at least 18 years of age, intentionally or knowingly causes physical injury to a child 10 years of age or younger.

(i) Knowing the other person is a staff member [of defined correctional facilities], intentionally or knowingly propels any dangerous substance at the staff member while the staff member is acting in the course of official duty or as a result of the staff member's official duties; or

**B-35**

(j) Intentionally, knowingly or recklessly causes, by means other than a motor vehicle, physical injury to the operator of a taxi while the operator is in control of the taxi.

(2) Assault in the third degree is a Class C felony. . . .

### § 163.175.   Assault in the second degree.

(1) A person commits the crime of assault in the second degree if the person:

(a) Intentionally or knowingly causes serious physical injury to another; or

(b) Intentionally or knowingly causes physical injury to another by means of a deadly or dangerous weapon; or

(c) Recklessly causes serious physical injury to another by means of a deadly or dangerous weapon under circumstances manifesting extreme indifference to the value of human life.

(2) Assault in the second degree is a Class B felony.

### § 163.185.   Assault in the first degree.

(1) A person commits the crime of assault in the first degree if the person intentionally causes serious physical injury to another by means of a deadly or dangerous weapon.

(2) Assault in the first degree is a Class A felony.

### § 163.190.   Menacing.

(1) A person commits the crime of menacing if by word or conduct the person intentionally attempts to place another person in fear of imminent serious physical injury.

(2) Menacing is a Class A misdemeanor.

### § 163.195.   Recklessly endangering another person.

(1) A person commits the crime of recklessly endangering another person if the person recklessly engages in conduct which creates a substantial risk of serious physical injury to another person.

(2) Recklessly endangering another person is a Class A misdemeanor.

## INCHOATE CRIMES

### § 161.405.   Attempt

(1) A person is guilty of an attempt to commit a crime when the person intentionally engages in conduct which constitutes a substantial step toward commission of the crime.

(2) An attempt is a:

(a) Class A felony if the offense attempted is murder or treason.

(b) Class B felony if the offense attempted is a Class A felony.

(c) Class C felony if the offense attempted is a Class B felony.

(d) Class A misdemeanor if the offense attempted is a Class C felony or an unclassified felony.

(e) Class B misdemeanor if the offense attempted is a Class A misdemeanor.

(f) Class C misdemeanor if the offense attempted is a Class B misdemeanor.

(g) Violation if the offense attempted is a Class C misdemeanor or an unclassified misdemeanor.

### § 161.425.  Impossibility as defense.

In a prosecution for an attempt, it is no defense that it was impossible to commit the crime which was the object of the attempt where the conduct engaged in by the actor would be a crime if the circumstances were as the actor believed them to be.

### § 161.430.  Renunciation; defense to attempt

(1) A person is not liable under ORS 161.405 if, under circumstances manifesting a voluntary and complete renunciation of the criminal intent of the person, the person avoids the commission of the crime attempted by abandoning the criminal effort and, if mere abandonment is insufficient to accomplish this avoidance, doing everything necessary to prevent the commission of the attempted crime.

(2) The defense of renunciation is an affirmative defense.

## DISPOSITION OF OFFENDERS

### § 161.605.  Maximum terms of imprisonment; felonies.

The maximum term of an indeterminate sentence of imprisonment for a felony is as follows:

(1) For a Class A felony, 20 years.

(2) For a Class B felony, 10 years.

(3) For a Class C felony, 5 years.

(4) For an unclassified felony as provided in the statute defining the crime.

### § 161.615.  Sentences for misdemeanors.

Sentences for misdemeanors shall be for a definite term. The court shall fix the term of imprisonment within the following maximum limitations:

(1) For a Class A misdemeanor, 1 year.

(2) For a Class B misdemeanor, 6 months.

(3) For a Class C misdemeanor, 30 days.

(4) For an unclassified misdemeanor, as provided in the statute defining the crime.

----

### (F) SELECTED COLORADO STATUTES

### 1.  Colo. Rev. Stat. (2003):

## PRINCIPLES OF CRIMINAL CULPABILITY

### § 18–1–501.  Definitions

The following definitions are applicable to the determination of culpability requirements for offenses defined in this code:

**B-37**

(1) "Act" means a bodily movement, and includes words and possession of property.

(2) "Conduct" means an act or omission and its accompanying state of mind or, where relevant, a series of acts or omissions.

(3) "Criminal negligence". A person acts with criminal negligence when, through a gross deviation from the standard of care that a reasonable person would exercise, he fails to perceive a substantial and unjustifiable risk that a result will occur or that a circumstance exists.

(4) "Culpable mental state" means intentionally, or with intent, or knowingly, or willfully, or recklessly, or with criminal negligence, as these terms are defined in this section.

(5) "Intentionally" or "with intent". All offenses defined in this code in which the mental culpability requirement is expressed as "intentionally" or "with intent" are declared to be specific intent offenses. A person acts "intentionally" or "with intent" when his conscious objective is to cause the specific result proscribed by the statute defining the offense. It is immaterial to the issue of specific intent whether or not the result actually occurred.

(6) "Knowingly" or "willfully". All offenses defined in this code in which the mental culpability requirement is expressed as "knowingly" or "willfully" are declared to be general intent crimes. A person acts "knowingly" or "willfully" with respect to conduct or to a circumstance described by a statute defining an offense when he is aware that his conduct is of such nature or that such circumstance exists. A person acts "knowingly" or "willfully", with respect to a result of his conduct, when he is aware that his conduct is practically certain to cause the result.

(7) "Omission" means a failure to perform an act as to which a duty of performance is imposed by law.

(8) "Recklessly". A person acts recklessly when he consciously disregards a substantial and unjustifiable risk that a result will occur or that a circumstance exists.

(9) "Voluntary act" means an act performed consciously as a result of effort or determination, and includes the possession of property if the actor was aware of his physical possession or control thereof for a sufficient period to have been able to terminate it.

## ATTEMPTS

### § 18–2–101.   Criminal attempt

(1) A person commits criminal attempt if, acting with the kind of culpability otherwise required for commission of an offense, he engages in conduct constituting a substantial step toward the commission of the offense. A substantial step is any conduct, whether act, omission, or possession, which is strongly corroborative of the firmness of the actor's purpose to complete the commission of the offense. Factual or legal impossibility of committing the offense is not a defense if the offense could have been committed had the attendant circumstances been as the actor believed them to be, nor is it a defense that the crime attempted was actually perpetrated by the accused.

(2) A person who engages in conduct intending to aid another to commit an offense commits criminal attempt if the conduct would establish his complicity

under section 18–1–603 were the offense committed by the other person, even if the other is not guilty of committing or attempting the offense.

(3) It is an affirmative defense to a charge under this section that the defendant abandoned his effort to commit the crime or otherwise prevented its commission, under circumstances manifesting the complete and voluntary renunciation of his criminal intent. . . .

(4) Criminal attempt to commit a class 1 felony is a class 2 felony; criminal attempt to commit a class 2 felony is a class 3 felony; criminal attempt to commit a class 3 felony is a class 4 felony; criminal attempt to commit a class 4 felony is a class 5 felony; criminal attempt to commit a class 5 or 6 felony is a class 6 felony. . . .

## HOMICIDE

### § 18–3–101.  Homicide—Definition of terms.

As used in this part 1, unless the context otherwise requires:

(1) "Homicide" means the killing of a person by another.

(2) "Person", when referring to the victim of a homicide, means a human being who had been born and was alive at the time of the homicidal act.

(2.5) One in a "position of trust" includes, but is not limited to, any person who is a parent or acting in the place of a parent and charged with any of a parent's rights, duties, or responsibilities concerning a child, including a guardian or someone otherwise responsible for the general supervision of a child's welfare, or a person who is charged with any duty or responsibility for the health, education, welfare, or supervision of a child, including foster care, child care, family care, or institutional care, either independently or through another, no matter how brief, at the time of an unlawful act.

(3) The term "after deliberation" means not only intentionally but also that the decision to commit the act has been made after the exercise of reflection and judgment concerning the act. An act committed after deliberation is never one which has been committed in a hasty or impulsive manner.

### § 18–3–102. Murder in the first degree.

(1) A person commits the crime of murder in the first degree if:

(a) After deliberation and with the intent to cause the death of a person other than himself, he causes the death of that person or of another person; or

(b) Acting either alone or with one or more persons, he or she commits or attempts to commit arson, robbery, burglary, kidnapping, sexual assault . . ., or a class 3 felony for sexual assault on a child . . ., or the crime of escape . . ., and, in the course of or in furtherance of the crime that he or she is committing or attempting to commit, or of immediate flight therefrom, the death of a person, other than one of the participants, is caused by anyone; or

(c) By perjury or subornation of perjury he procures the conviction and execution of any innocent person; or

(d) Under circumstances evidencing an attitude of universal malice manifesting extreme indifference to the value of human life generally, he knowingly engages in conduct which creates a grave risk of death to a person, or persons, other than himself, and thereby causes the death of another; or

**B-39**

(e) He or she commits unlawful distribution, dispensation, or sale of a controlled substance to a person under the age of eighteen years on school grounds ..., and the death of such person is caused by the use of such controlled substance; or

(f) The person knowingly causes the death of a child who has not yet attained twelve years of age and the person committing the offense is one in a position of trust with respect to the victim.

(2) It is an affirmative defense to a charge of violating subsection (1)(b) of this section that the defendant:

(a) Was not the only participant in the underlying crime; and

(b) Did not commit the homicidal act or in any way solicit, request, command, importune, cause, or aid the commission thereof; and

(c) Was not armed with a deadly weapon; and

(d) Had no reasonable ground to believe that any other participant was armed with such a weapon, instrument, article, or substance; and

(e) Did not engage himself in or intend to engage in and had no reasonable ground to believe that any other participant intended to engage in conduct likely to result in death or serious bodily injury; and

(f) Endeavored to disengage himself from the commission of the underlying crime or flight therefrom immediately upon having reasonable grounds to believe that another participant is armed with a deadly weapon, instrument, article, or substance, or intended to engage in conduct likely to result in death or serious bodily injury.

(3) Murder in the first degree is a class 1 felony....

### § 18–3–103. Murder in the second degree

(1) A person commits the crime of murder in the second degree if the person knowingly causes the death of a person.

(2) Diminished responsibility due to self-induced intoxication is not a defense to murder in the second degree.

(3)(a) Except as otherwise provided in paragraph (b) of this subsection (3), murder in the second degree is a class 2 felony.

(b) Notwithstanding the provisions of paragraph (a) of this subsection (3), murder in the second degree is a class 3 felony where the act causing the death was performed upon a sudden heat of passion, caused by a serious and highly provoking act of the intended victim, affecting the defendant sufficiently to excite an irresistible passion in a reasonable person; but, if between the provocation and the killing there is an interval sufficient for the voice of reason and humanity to be heard, the killing is a class 2 felony....

### § 18–3–104. Manslaughter.

(1) A person commits the crime of manslaughter if:

(a) Such person recklessly causes the death of another person[e] ....

---

[e] Prior to 1996, this section contained a paragraph (c) that read:

Such person knowingly causes the death of another person under circumstances where the act causing the death

(2) Manslaughter is a class 4 felony.

### § 18–3–105. Criminally negligent homicide.

Any person who causes the death of another person by conduct amounting to criminal negligence commits criminally negligent homicide which is a class 5 felony.

### ASSAULTS

### § 18–3–202. Assault in the first degree.

(1) A person commits the crime of assault in the first degree if:

(a) With intent to cause serious bodily injury to another person, he causes serious bodily injury to any person by means of a deadly weapon; or

(b) With intent to disfigure another person seriously and permanently, or to destroy, amputate, or disable permanently a member or organ of his body, he causes such an injury to any person; or

(c) Under circumstances manifesting extreme indifference to the value of human life, he knowingly engages in conduct which creates a grave risk of death to another person, and thereby causes serious bodily injury to any person; or. . . .

(2)(a) If assault in the first degree is committed under circumstances where the act causing the injury is performed upon a sudden heat of passion, caused by a serious and highly provoking act of the intended victim, affecting the person causing the injury sufficiently to excite an irresistible passion in a reasonable person, and without an interval between the provocation and the injury sufficient for the voice of reason and humanity to be heard, it is a class 5 felony.

(b) If assault in the first degree is committed without the circumstances provided in paragraph (a) of this subsection (2), it is a class 3 felony. . . .

### § 18–3–203. Assault in the second degree.

(1) A person commits the crime of assault in the second degree if: . . .

(b) With intent to cause bodily injury to another person, he or she causes such injury to any person by means of a deadly weapon; or . . .

(d) He recklessly causes serious bodily injury to another person by means of a deadly weapon; or . . .

(g) With intent to cause bodily injury to another person, he causes serious bodily injury to that person or another.

(2)(a) If assault in the second degree is committed under circumstances where the act causing the injury is performed upon a sudden heat of passion, caused by a serious and highly provoking act of the intended victim, affecting the person causing the injury sufficiently to excite an irresistible passion in a reasonable person, and without an interval between the provocation and the injury sufficient for the voice of reason and humanity to be heard, it is a class 6 felony.

was performed upon a sudden heat of passion, caused by a serious and highly provoking act of the intended victim, affecting the person who performs the killing sufficiently to excite an irresistible passion in a reasonable person; but, if between the provocation and the killing there is an interval sufficient for the voice of reason and humanity to be heard, the killing is murder.

The penalty was that of a Class 3 felony. Subsection (b) deals with assisted suicide.— [Footnote by eds.]

**B-41**

(b) If assault in the second degree is committed without the circumstances provided in paragraph (a) of this subsection (2), it is a class 4 felony....

### § 18–3–204. Assault in the third degree.

A person commits the crime of assault in the third degree if he knowingly or recklessly causes bodily injury to another person or with criminal negligence he causes bodily injury to another person by means of a deadly weapon. Assault in the third degree is a class 1 misdemeanor.

### § 18–3–206. Menacing.

A person commits the crime of menacing if, by any threat or physical action, he or she knowingly places or attempts to place another person in fear of imminent serious bodily injury. Menacing is a class 3 misdemeanor, but, it is a class 5 felony if committed:

(a) By the use of a deadly weapon or any article used or fashioned in a manner to cause a person to reasonably believe that the article is a deadly weapon; or

(b) By the person representing verbally or otherwise that he or she is armed with a deadly weapon.

### § 18–3–208. Reckless endangerment.

A person who recklessly engages in conduct which creates a substantial risk of serious bodily injury to another person commits reckless endangerment, which is a class 3 misdemeanor.

————

### (G) CAPITAL PUNISHMENT STATUTES BEFORE THE SUPREME COURT IN 1976 DECISIONS

**1. Ga. Laws, 1973 Sess., pp. 164–67, 170, before the Supreme Court in Gregg v. Georgia, 428 U.S. 153 (1976):**

**§ 26–3102. Capital offenses; jury verdict and sentence**. Where, upon a trial by jury, a person is convicted of an offense which may be punishable by death, a sentence of death shall not be imposed unless the jury verdict includes a finding of at least one statutory aggravating circumstance and a recommendation that such sentence be imposed. Where a statutory aggravating circumstance is found and a recommendation of death is made, the court shall sentence the defendant to death. Where a sentence of death is not recommended by the jury, the court shall sentence the defendant to imprisonment as provided by law. Unless the jury trying the case makes a finding of at least one statutory aggravating circumstance and recommends the death sentence in its verdict, the court shall not sentence the defendant to death, provided that no such finding of statutory aggravating circumstance shall be necessary in offenses of treason or aircraft hijacking. The provisions of this section shall not affect a sentence when the case is tried without a jury or when the judge accepts a plea of guilty.

**§ 27–2534.1. Mitigating and aggravating circumstances; death penalty**.—(a) The death penalty may be imposed for the offenses of aircraft hijacking or treason, in any case.

(b) In all cases of other offenses for which the death penalty may be authorized, the judge shall consider, or he shall include in his instructions to the jury for it to consider, any mitigating circumstances or aggravating circumstances otherwise authorized by law and any of the following statutory aggravating circumstances which may be supported by the evidence:

(1) The offense of murder, rape, armed robbery, or kidnapping was committed by a person with a prior record of conviction for a capital felony, or the offense of murder was committed by a person who has a substantial history of serious assaultive criminal convictions.

(2) The offense of murder, rape, armed robbery, or kidnapping was committed while the offender was engaged in the commission of another capital felony, or aggravated battery, or the offense of murder was committed while the offender was engaged in the commission of burglary or arson in the first degree.

(3) The offender by his act of murder, armed robbery, or kidnapping knowingly created a great risk of death to more than one person in a public place by means of a weapon or device which would normally be hazardous to the lives of more than one person.

(4) The offender committed the offense of murder for himself or another, for the purpose of receiving money or any other thing of monetary value.

(5) The murder of a judicial officer, former judicial officer, district attorney or solicitor or former district attorney or solicitor during or because of the exercise of his official duty.

(6) The offender caused or directed another to commit murder or committed murder as an agent or employee of another person.

(7) The offense of murder, rape, armed robbery, or kidnapping was outrageously or wantonly vile, horrible or inhuman in that it involved torture, depravity of mind, or an aggravated battery to the victim.

(8) The offense of murder was committed against any peace officer, corrections employee or fireman while engaged in the performance of his official duties.

(9) The offense of murder was committed by a person in, or who has escaped from, the lawful custody of a peace officer or place of lawful confinement.

(10) The murder was committed for the purpose of avoiding, interfering with, or preventing a lawful arrest or custody in a place of lawful confinement, of himself or another.

(c) The statutory instructions as determined by the trial judge to be warranted by the evidence shall be given in charge and in writing to the jury for its deliberation. The jury, if its verdict be a recommendation of death, shall designate in writing, signed by the foreman of the jury, the aggravating circumstance or circumstances which it found beyond a reasonable doubt. In non-jury cases the judge shall make such designation. Except in cases of treason or aircraft hijacking, unless at least one of the statutory aggravating circumstances enumerated in Code Section 27–2534.1(b) is so found, the death penalty shall not be imposed.

§ 27–2537. **Review of death sentences.**—(a) Whenever the death penalty is imposed, and upon the judgment becoming final in the trial court, the sentence shall be reviewed on the record by the Supreme Court of Georgia. The clerk of the trial court, within ten days after receiving the transcript, shall transmit the entire record and transcript to the Supreme Court of Georgia together with a notice prepared by the clerk and a report prepared by the trial judge. The notice shall set forth the title and docket number of the case, the name of the defendant and the name and address of his attorney, a narrative statement of the judgment, the offense, and the punishment prescribed. The report shall be in the form of a standard questionnaire prepared and supplied by the Supreme Court of Georgia.

(b) The Supreme Court of Georgia shall consider the punishment as well as any errors enumerated by way of appeal.

(c) With regard to the sentence, the court shall determine:

(1) Whether the sentence of death was imposed under the influence of passion, prejudice, or any other arbitrary factor, and

(2) Whether, in cases other than treason or aircraft hijacking, the evidence supports the jury's or judge's finding of a statutory aggravating circumstance as enumerated in Code Section 27–2534.1(b), and

(3) Whether the sentence of death is excessive or disproportionate to the penalty imposed in similar cases, considering both the crime and the defendant.

(d) Both the defendant and the State shall have the right to submit briefs within the time provided by the court, and to present oral argument to the court.

(e) The court shall include in its decision a reference to those similar cases which it took into consideration. In addition to its authority regarding correction of errors, the court, with regard to review of death sentences, shall be authorized to:

(1) Affirm the sentence of death; or

(2) Set the sentence aside and remand the case for resentencing by the trial judge based on the record and argument of counsel. The records of those similar cases referred to by the Supreme Court of Georgia in its decision, and the extracts prepared as hereinafter provided for, shall be provided to the resentencing judge for his consideration.

(f) There shall be an Assistant to the Supreme Court, who shall be an attorney appointed by the Chief Justice of Georgia and who shall serve at the pleasure of the court. The court shall accumulate the records of all capital felony cases in which sentence was imposed after January 1, 1970, or such earlier date as the court may deem appropriate. The Assistant shall provide the court with whatever extracted information it desires with respect thereto, including but not limited to a synopsis or brief of the facts in the record concerning the crime and the defendant.

(g) The court shall be authorized to employ an appropriate staff and such methods to compile such data as are deemed by the Chief Justice to be appropriate and relevant to the statutory questions concerning the validity of the sentence.

(h) The office of the Assistant shall be attached to the office of the Clerk of the Supreme Court of Georgia for administrative purposes.

(i) The sentence review shall be in addition to direct appeal, if taken, and the review and appeal shall be consolidated for consideration. The court shall render its decision on legal errors enumerated, the factual substantiation of the verdict, and the validity of the sentence.

**2. Fla. Laws, 1975, ch. 75–298, § 6; Fla. Laws, 1972, ch. 72–724, §§ 2, 9, before the Supreme Court in Proffitt v. Florida, 428 U.S. 242 (1976):**

**§ 782.04. Murder—**

(1)(a) The unlawful killing of a human being, when perpetrated from a premeditated design to effect the death of the person killed or any human being, or when committed by a person engaged in the perpetration of, or in the attempt to perpetrate, any arson, involuntary sexual battery, robbery, burglary, kidnapping, aircraft piracy, or unlawful throwing, placing, or discharging of a destructive device or bomb, or which resulted from the unlawful distribution of heroin by a person 18 years of age or older when such drug is proven to be the proximate cause of the death of the user, shall be murder in the first degree and shall constitute a capital felony, punishable as provided in § 775.082.

(b) In all cases under this section, the procedure set forth in § 921.141 shall be followed in order to determine sentence of death or life imprisonment.

### § 775.082.  Penalties for felonies and misdemeanors.—

(1) A person who has been convicted of a capital felony shall be punished by life imprisonment and shall be required to serve no less than 25 calendar years before becoming eligible for parole unless the proceeding held to determine sentence according to the procedure set forth in § 921.141 results in findings by the court that such person shall be punished by death, and in the latter event such person shall be punished by death.

### § 921.141.  Sentence of death or life imprisonment for capital felonies; further proceedings to determine sentence.—

(1) Upon conviction or adjudication of guilt of a defendant of a capital felony the court shall conduct a separate sentencing proceeding to determine whether the defendant should be sentenced to death or life imprisonment as authorized by Section 775.082. The proceeding shall be conducted by the trial judge before the trial jury as soon as practicable. If the trial jury has been waived or if the defendant pleaded guilty, the sentencing proceeding shall be conducted before a jury empaneled for that purpose unless waived by the defendant. In the proceeding, evidence may be presented as to any matter that the court deems relevant to sentence, and shall include matters relating to any of the aggravating or mitigating circumstances enumerated in Subsections (6) and (7) of this section. Any such evidence which the court deems to have probative value may be received, regardless of its admissibility under the exclusionary rules of evidence, provided that the defendant is accorded a fair opportunity to rebut any hearsay statements; and further provided that this subsection shall not be construed to authorize the introduction of any evidence secured in violation of the Constitution of the United States or of the State of Florida. The state and the defendant or his counsel shall be permitted to present argument for or against sentence of death.

(2) After hearing all the evidence, the jury shall deliberate and render an advisory sentence to the court based upon the following matters:

(a) Whether sufficient aggravating circumstances exist as enumerated in Subsection (6), and

(b) Whether sufficient mitigating circumstances exist as enumerated in Subsection (7), which outweigh aggravating circumstances found to exist, and

(c) Based on these considerations whether the defendant should be sentenced to life or death.

(3) Notwithstanding the recommendation of a majority of the jury, the court after weighing the aggravating and mitigating circumstances shall enter a sentence of life imprisonment or death, but if the court imposes a sentence of death, it shall

set forth in writing its findings upon which the sentence of death is based as to the facts:

(a) That sufficient aggravating circumstances exist as enumerated in Subsection (6), and

(b) That there are insufficient mitigating circumstances, as enumerated in Subsection (7), to outweigh the aggravating circumstances.

In each case in which the court imposes the death sentence, the determination of the court shall be supported by specific written findings of fact based upon the circumstances in Subsections (6) and (7) and based upon the records of the trial and the sentencing proceedings.

(4) If the court does not make the findings requiring the death sentence, the court shall impose sentence of life imprisonment in accordance with Section 775.082.

(5) The judgment of conviction and sentence of death shall be subject to automatic review by the Supreme Court of Florida within 60 days after certification by the sentencing court of the entire record unless time is extended an additional period not to exceed 30 days by the Supreme Court for good cause shown. Such review by the Supreme Court shall have priority over all other cases, and shall be heard in accordance with rules promulgated by the Supreme Court.

(6) Aggravating circumstances.—Aggravating circumstances shall be limited to the following:

(a) The capital felony was committed by a person under sentence of imprisonment;

(b) The defendant was previously convicted of another capital felony or of a felony involving the use or threat of violence to the person;

(c) The defendant knowingly created a great risk of death to many persons;

(d) The capital felony was committed while the defendant was engaged or was an accomplice in the commission of, or an attempt to commit, or flight after committing or attempting to commit any robbery, rape, arson, burglary, kidnaping, aircraft piracy, or the unlawful throwing, placing or discharging of a destructive device or bomb;

(e) The capital felony was committed for the purpose of avoiding or preventing a lawful arrest or effecting an escape from custody;

(f) The capital felony was committed for pecuniary gain;

(g) The capital felony was committed to disrupt or hinder the lawful exercise of any governmental function or the enforcement of laws;

(h) The capital felony was especially heinous, atrocious or cruel.

(7) Mitigating circumstances.—Mitigating circumstances shall be the following:

(a) The defendant has no significant history of prior criminal activity;

(b) The capital felony was committed while the defendant was under the influence of extreme mental or emotional disturbance;

(c) The victim was a participant in the defendant's conduct or consented to the act;

(d) The defendant was an accomplice in the capital felony committed by another person and his participation was relatively minor;

(e) The defendant acted under extreme duress or under the substantial domination of another person;

(f) The capacity of the defendant to appreciate the criminality of his conduct or to conform his conduct to the requirements of law was substantially impaired;

(g) The age of the defendant at the time of the crime.

**3.   Tex. Gen. Laws, 63rd Leg., ch. 426, art. 1, § 1, p. 1122, art. 3, § 1, pp. 1125–26, before the Supreme Court in Jurek v. Texas, 428 U.S. 262 (1976):**

### Art. 1257. Punishment for murder.

(a) Except as provided in Subsection (b) of this Article, the punishment for murder shall be confinement in the penitentiary for life or for any term of years not less than two.

(b) The punishment for murder with malice aforethought shall be death or imprisonment for life if:

(1) the person murdered a peace officer or fireman who was acting in the lawful discharge of an official duty and who the defendant knew was a peace officer or fireman;

(2) the person intentionally committed the murder in the course of committing or attempting to commit kidnapping, burglary, robbery, forcible rape, or arson;

(3) the person committed the murder for remuneration or the promise of remuneration or employed another to commit the murder for remuneration or the promise of remuneration;

(4) the person committed the murder while escaping or attempting to escape from a penal institution;

(5) the person, while incarcerated in a penal institution, murdered another who was employed in the operation of the penal institution.

(c) If the jury does not find beyond a reasonable doubt that the murder was committed under one of the circumstances or conditions enumerated in Subsection (b) of this Article, the defendant may be convicted of murder, with or without malice, under Subsection (a) of this Article or of any other lesser included offense. . . .

### Art. 37.071. Procedure in capital case.

(a) Upon a finding that the defendant is guilty of a capital offense, the court shall conduct a separate sentencing proceeding to determine whether the defendant shall be sentenced to death or life imprisonment. The proceeding shall be conducted in the trial court before the trial jury as soon as practicable. In the proceeding, evidence may be presented as to any matter that the court deems relevant to sentence. This subsection shall not be construed to authorize the introduction of any evidence secured in violation of the Constitution of the United States or of the State of Texas. The state and the defendant or his counsel shall be permitted to present argument for or against sentence of death.

(b) On conclusion of the presentation of the evidence, the court shall submit the following issues to the jury:

(1) whether the conduct of the defendant that caused the death of the deceased was committed deliberately and with the reasonable expectation that the death of the deceased or another would result;

(2) whether there is a probability that the defendant would commit criminal acts of violence that would constitute a continuing threat to society; and

(3) if raised by the evidence, whether the conduct of the defendant in killing the deceased was unreasonable in response to the provocation, if any, by the deceased.

(c) The state must prove each issue submitted beyond a reasonable doubt, and the jury shall return a special verdict of "yes" or "no" on each issue submitted.

(d) The court shall charge the jury that:

(1) it may not answer any issue "yes" unless it agrees unanimously; and

(2) it may not answer any issue "no" unless 10 or more jurors agree.

(e) If the jury returns an affirmative finding on each issue submitted under this article, the court shall sentence the defendant to death. If the jury returns a negative finding on any issue submitted under this article, the court shall sentence the defendant to confinement in the Texas Department of Corrections for life.

(f) The judgment of conviction and sentence of death shall be subject to automatic review by the Court of Criminal Appeals within 60 days after certification by the sentencing court of the entire record unless time is extended an additional period not to exceed 30 days by the Court of Criminal Appeals for good cause shown. Such review by the Court of Criminal Appeals shall have priority over all other cases, and shall be heard in accordance with rules promulgated by the Court of Criminal Appeals.

**4. N.C. Sess. Laws, 1973, ch. 1201, § 1, p. 323, before the Supreme Court in Woodson v. North Carolina, 428 U.S. 280 (1976):**

**§ 14–17. Murder in the first and second degree defined; punishment.—** A murder which shall be perpetrated by means of poison, lying in wait, imprisonment, starving, torture, or by any other kind of willful, deliberate and premeditated killing, or which shall be committed in the perpetration or attempt to perpetrate any arson, rape, robbery, kidnapping, burglary or other felony, shall be deemed to be murder in the first degree and shall be punished with death. All other kinds of murder shall be deemed murder in the second degree, and shall be punished by imprisonment for a term of not less than two years nor more than life imprisonment in the State's prison.

**5. La. Acts, 1973, No. 109, § 1, p. 218, before the Supreme Court in Roberts v. Louisiana, 428 U.S. 325 (1976):**

**§ 30.  First-degree murder.**

First-degree murder is the killing of a human being:

(1) When the offender has a specific intent to kill or to inflict great bodily harm and is engaged in the perpetration or attempted perpetration of aggravated kidnapping, aggravated rape or armed robbery; or

(2) When the offender has a specific intent to kill, or to inflict great bodily harm upon, a fireman or a peace officer who was engaged in the performance of his lawful duties; or

(3) Where the offender has a specific intent to kill or to inflict great bodily harm and has previously been convicted of an unrelated murder or is serving a life sentence; or

(4) When the offender has a specific intent to kill or to inflict great bodily harm upon more than one person.

(5) When the offender has specific intent to commit murder and has been offered or has received anything of value for committing the murder.

For the purposes of Paragraph (2) herein, the term peace officer shall be defined and include any constable, sheriff, deputy sheriff, local or state policeman, game warden, federal law enforcement officer, jail or prison guard, parole officer, probation officer, judge, district attorney, assistant district attorney or district attorneys' investigator.

Whoever commits the crime of first-degree murder shall be punished by death.

————

## (H) ADDITIONAL CONTEMPORARY CAPITAL SENTENCING STATUTES

### 1.  Alabama Code (1994 & Supp. 2003):

### § 13A–6–1. Definitions.

The following terms shall have the meanings ascribed to them by this section:

(1) _Homicide._ A person commits criminal homicide if he intentionally, knowingly, recklessly or with criminal negligence causes the death of another person.

(2) _Person._ Such term, when referring to the victim of a criminal homicide, means a human being who had been born and was alive at the time of the homicidal act.

(3) _Criminal Homicide._ Murder, manslaughter, or criminally negligent homicide.

### § 13A–6–2. Murder.

(a) A person commits the crime of murder if:

(1) With intent to cause the death of another person, he causes the death of that person or of another person; or

(2) Under circumstances manifesting extreme indifference to human life, he recklessly engages in conduct which creates a grave risk of death to a person other than himself, and thereby causes the death of another person; or

(3) He commits or attempts to commit arson in the first degree, burglary in the first or second degree, escape in the first degree, kidnapping in the first degree, rape in the first degree, robbery in any degree, sodomy in the first degree or any other felony clearly dangerous to human life and, in the course of and in furtherance of the crime that he is committing or attempting to commit, or in immediate flight therefrom, he, or another participant if there be any, causes the death of any person.

(b) A person does not commit murder under subdivisions (a)(1) or (a)(2) of this section if he was moved to act by a sudden heat of passion caused by provocation recognized by law, and before there had been a reasonable time for the passion to

**B-49**

cool and for reason to reassert itself. The burden of injecting the issue of killing under legal provocation is on the defendant, but this does not shift the burden of proof. This subsection does not apply to a prosecution for, or preclude a conviction of, manslaughter or other crime.

(c) Murder is a Class A felony; provided, that the punishment for murder or any offense committed under aggravated circumstances, as provided by Article 2 of Chapter 5 of this title, is death or life imprisonment without parole, which punishment shall be determined and fixed as provided by Article 2 of Chapter 5 of this title or any amendments thereto.

### § 13A–5–40. Capital offenses.

(a) The following are capital offenses:

(1) Murder by the defendant during a kidnapping in the first degree or an attempt thereof committed by the defendant;

(2) Murder by the defendant during a robbery in the first degree or an attempt thereof committed by the defendant;

(3) Murder by the defendant during a rape in the first or second degree or an attempt thereof committed by the defendant; or murder by the defendant during sodomy in the first or second degree or an attempt thereof committed by the defendant;

(4) Murder by the defendant during a burglary in the first or second degree or an attempt thereof committed by the defendant;

(5) Murder of any police officer, sheriff, deputy, state trooper, federal law enforcement officer, or any other state or federal peace officer of any kind, or prison or jail guard, while such officer or guard is on duty, regardless of whether the defendant knew or should have known the victim was an officer or guard on duty, or because of some official or job-related act or performance of such officer or guard;

(6) Murder committed while the defendant is under sentence of life imprisonment;

(7) Murder done for a pecuniary or other valuable consideration or pursuant to a contract or for hire;

(8) Murder by the defendant during sexual abuse in the first or second degree or an attempt thereof committed by the defendant;

(9) Murder by the defendant during arson in the first or second degree committed by the defendant; or murder by the defendant by means of explosives or explosion;

(10) Murder wherein two or more persons are murdered by the defendant by one act or pursuant to one scheme or course of conduct;

(11) Murder by the defendant when the victim is a state or federal public official or former public official and the murder stems from or is caused by or is related to his official position, act, or capacity;

(12) Murder by the defendant during the act of unlawfully assuming control of any aircraft by use of threats or force with intent to obtain any valuable consideration for the release of said aircraft or any passenger or crewmen thereon or to direct the route or movement of said aircraft, or otherwise exert control over said aircraft;

(13) Murder by a defendant who has been convicted of any other murder in the 20 years preceding the crime; provided that the murder which constitutes the capital crime shall be murder as defined in subsection (b) of this section; and provided further that the prior murder conviction referred to shall include murder in any degree as defined at the time and place of the prior conviction;

(14) Murder when the victim is subpoenaed, or has been subpoenaed, to testify, or the victim had testified, in any preliminary hearing, grand jury proceeding, criminal trial or criminal proceeding of whatever nature, or civil trial or civil proceeding of whatever nature, in any municipal, state, or federal court, when the murder stems from, is caused by, or is related to the capacity or role of the victim as a witness.

(15) Murder when the victim is less than fourteen years of age.

(16) Murder committed by or through the use of a deadly weapon fired or otherwise used from outside a dwelling while the victim is in a dwelling.

(17) Murder committed by or through the use of a deadly weapon while the victim is in a vehicle.

(18) Murder committed by or through the use of a deadly weapon fired or otherwise used within or from a vehicle.

(b) Except as specifically provided to the contrary in the last part of subdivision (a)(13) of this section, the terms "murder" and "murder by the defendant" as used in this section to define capital offenses mean murder as defined in Section 13A–6–2(a)(1), but not as defined in Section 13A–6–2(a)(2) and (3). Subject to the provisions of Section 13A–5–41, murder as defined in Section 13A–6–2(a)(2) and (3), as well as murder as defined in Section 13A–6–2(a)(1), may be a lesser included offense of the capital offenses defined in subsection (a) of this section.

(c) A defendant who does not personally commit the act of killing which constitutes the murder is not guilty of a capital offense defined in subsection (a) of this section unless that defendant is legally accountable for the murder because of complicity in the murder itself under the provisions of Section 13A–2–23, in addition to being guilty of the other elements of the capital offense as defined in subsection (a) of this section.

(d) To the extent that a crime other than murder is an element of a capital offense defined in subsection (a) of this section, a defendant's guilt of that other crime may also be established under Section 13A–2–23. When the defendant's guilt of that other crime is established under Section 13A–2–23, that crime shall be deemed to have been "committed by the defendant" within the meaning of that phrase as it is used in subsection (a) of this section.

§ 13A–5–47. Determination of sentence by court; pre-sentence investigation report; presentation of arguments on aggravating and mitigating circumstances; court to enter written findings; court not bound by sentence recommended by jury.

(a) After the sentence hearing has been conducted, and after the jury has returned an advisory verdict, or after such a verdict has been waived as provided in Section 13A–5–46(a) or Section 13A–5–46(g), the trial court shall proceed to determine the sentence.

(b) Before making the sentence determination, the trial court shall order and receive a written pre-sentence investigation report. The report shall contain the information prescribed by law or court rule for felony cases generally and any additional information specified by the trial court. No part of the report shall be kept confidential, and the parties shall have the right to respond to it and to present evidence to the court about any part of the report which is the subject of factual dispute. The report and any evidence submitted in connection with it shall be made part of the record in the case.

(c) Before imposing sentence the trial court shall permit the parties to present arguments concerning the existence of aggravating and mitigating circumstances and the proper sentence to be imposed in the case. The order of the arguments shall be the same as at the trial of a case.

(d) Based upon the evidence presented at trial, the evidence presented during the sentence hearing, and the pre-sentence investigation report and any evidence submitted in connection with it, the trial court shall enter specific written findings concerning the existence or nonexistence of each aggravating circumstance enumerated in Section 13A–5–49, each mitigating circumstance enumerated in Section 13A–5–51, and any additional mitigating circumstances offered pursuant to Section 13A–5–52. The trial court shall also enter written findings of facts summarizing the crime and the defendant's participation in it.

(e) In deciding upon the sentence, the trial court shall determine whether the aggravating circumstances it finds to exist outweigh the mitigating circumstances it finds to exist, and in doing so the trial court shall consider the recommendation of the jury contained in its advisory verdict, unless such a verdict has been waived pursuant to Section 13A–5–46(a) or 13A–5–46(g). While the jury's recommendation concerning sentence shall be given consideration, it is not binding upon the court.

### § 13A–5–48. Process of weighing aggravating and mitigating circumstances defined.

The process described in Sections 13A–5–46(e)(2), 13A–5–46(e)(3) and Section 13A–5–47(e) of weighing the aggravating and mitigating circumstances to determine the sentence shall not be defined to mean a mere tallying of aggravating and mitigating circumstances for the purpose of numerical comparison. Instead, it shall be defined to mean a process by which circumstances relevant to sentence are marshalled and considered in an organized fashion for the purpose of determining whether the proper sentence in view of all the relevant circumstances in an individual case is life imprisonment without parole or death.

### § 13A–5–49. Aggravating circumstances.

Aggravating circumstances shall be the following:

(1) The capital offense was committed by a person under sentence of imprisonment;

(2) The defendant was previously convicted of another capital offense or a felony involving the use or threat of violence to the person;

(3) The defendant knowingly created a great risk of death to many persons;

(4) The capital offense was committed while the defendant was engaged or was an accomplice in the commission of, or an attempt to commit, or flight after committing, or attempting to commit, rape, robbery, burglary or kidnapping;

(5) The capital offense was committed for the purpose of avoiding or preventing a lawful arrest or effecting an escape from custody;

(6) The capital offense was committed for pecuniary gain;

(7) The capital offense was committed to disrupt or hinder the lawful exercise of any governmental function or the enforcement of laws;

(8) The capital offense was especially heinous, atrocious or cruel compared to other capital offenses.

(9) The defendant intentionally caused the death of two or more persons by one act or pursuant to one scheme or course of conduct; or

(10) The capital offense was one of a series of intentional killings committed by the defendant.

## § 13A–5–50. Consideration of aggravating circumstances in sentence determination.

The fact that a particular capital offense as defined in Section 13A–5–40(a) necessarily includes one or more aggravating circumstances as specified in Section 13A–5–49 shall not be construed to preclude the finding and consideration of that relevant circumstance or circumstances in determining sentence. By way of illustration and not limitation, the aggravating circumstance specified in Section 13A–5–49(4) shall be found and considered in determining sentence in every case in which a defendant is convicted of the capital offenses defined in subdivisions (1) through (4) of subsection (a) of Section 13A–5–40.

## § 13A–5–51. Mitigating circumstances—Generally.

Mitigating circumstances shall include, but not be limited to, the following:

(1) The defendant has no significant history of prior criminal activity;

(2) The capital offense was committed while the defendant was under the influence of extreme mental or emotional disturbance;

(3) The victim was a participant in the defendant's conduct or consented to it;

(4) The defendant was an accomplice in the capital offense committed by another person and his participation was relatively minor;

(5) The defendant acted under extreme duress or under the substantial domination of another person;

(6) The capacity of the defendant to appreciate the criminality of his conduct or to conform his conduct to the requirements of law was substantially impaired; and

(7) The age of the defendant at the time of the crime.

## § 13A–5–52. Mitigating Circumstances—Inclusion of defendant's character, record, etc.

In addition to the mitigating circumstances specified in Section 13A–5–51, mitigating circumstances shall include any aspect of a defendant's character or record and any of the circumstances of the offense that the defendant offers as a basis for a sentence of life imprisonment without parole instead of death, and any other relevant mitigating circumstance which the defendant offers as a basis for a sentence of life imprisonment without parole instead of death.

## § 13A–5–53. Appellate review of death sentence; scope; remand; specific determinations to be made by court; authority of court following review.

(a) In any case in which the death penalty is imposed, in addition to reviewing the case for any error involving the conviction, the Alabama Court of Criminal Appeals, subject to review by the Alabama Supreme Court, shall also review the propriety of the death sentence. This review shall include the determination of whether any error adversely affecting the rights of the defendant was made in the sentence proceedings, whether the trial court's findings concerning the aggravating and mitigating circumstances were supported by the evidence, and whether death was the proper sentence in the case. If the court determines that an error adversely affecting the rights of the defendant was made in the sentence proceedings or that one or more of the trial court's findings concerning aggravating and mitigating circumstances were not supported by the evidence, it shall remand the case for new proceedings to the extent necessary to correct the error or errors. If the appellate court finds that no error adversely affecting the rights of the defendant was made in the sentence proceedings and that the trial court's findings concerning aggravating and mitigating circumstances were supported by the evidence, it shall proceed to review the propriety of the decision that death was the proper sentence.

(b) In determining whether death was the proper sentence in the case the Alabama Court of Criminal Appeals, subject to review by the Alabama Supreme Court, shall determine:

(1) Whether the sentence of death was imposed under the influence of passion, prejudice, or any other arbitrary factor;

(2) Whether an independent weighing of the aggravating and mitigating circumstances at the appellate level indicates that death was the proper sentence; and

(3) Whether the sentence of death is excessive or disproportionate to the penalty imposed in similar cases, considering both the crime and the defendant.

(c) The Court of Criminal Appeals shall explicitly address each of the three questions specified in subsection (b) of this section in every case it reviews in which a sentence of death has been imposed.

(d) After performing the review specified in this section, the Alabama Court of Criminal Appeals, subject to review by the Alabama Supreme Court, shall be authorized to:

(1) Affirm the sentence of death;

(2) Set the sentence of death aside and remand to the trial court for correction of any errors occurring during the sentence proceedings and for imposition of the appropriate penalty after any new sentence proceedings that are necessary, provided that such errors shall not affect the determination of guilt and shall not preclude the imposition of a sentence of death where it is determined to be proper after any new sentence proceedings that are deemed necessary; or

(3) In cases in which the death penalty is deemed inappropriate under subdivision (b)(2) or (b)(3) of this section, set the sentence of death aside and remand to the trial court with directions that the defendant be sentenced to life imprisonment without parole.

## § 13A–5–55. Conviction and sentence of death subject to automatic review.

In all cases in which a defendant is sentenced to death, the judgment of conviction shall be subject to automatic review. The sentence of death shall be subject to review as provided in Section 13A–5–53.

### 2.   Gen. Stat. North Carolina (West 2000 & Supp. 2003):

### ARTICLE 6.   HOMICIDE

### § 14–17.   Murder in the first and second degree defined; punishment.

A murder which shall be perpetrated by means of nuclear, biological, or chemical weapon of mass destruction as defined in G.S. 14–288.21, poison, lying in wait, imprisonment, starving, torture, or by any other kind of willful, deliberate, and premeditated killing, or which shall be committed in the perpetration or attempted perpetration of any arson, rape or a sex offense, robbery, kidnapping, burglary, or other felony committed or attempted with the use of a deadly weapon shall be deemed to be murder in the first degree, a Class A felony, and any person who commits such murder shall be punished with death or imprisonment in the State's prison for life without parole as the court shall determine pursuant to G.S. 15A–2000, except that any such person who was under 17 years of age at the time of the murder shall be punished with imprisonment in the State's prison for life without parole. Provided, however, any person under the age of 17 who commits murder in the first degree while serving a prison sentence imposed for a prior murder or while on escape from a prison sentence imposed for a prior murder shall be punished with death or imprisonment in the State's prison for life without parole as the court shall determine pursuant to G.S. 15A–2000. All other kinds of murder, including that which shall be proximately caused by the unlawful distribution of opium or any synthetic or natural salt, compound, derivative, or preparation of opium, or cocaine or other [controlled substance] when the ingestion of such substance causes the death of the user, shall be deemed murder in the second degree, and any person who commits such murder shall be punished as a Class B2 felon.

### ARTICLE 100.   CAPITAL PUNISHMENT

### § 15A–2000. Sentence of death or life imprisonment for capital felonies; further proceedings to determine sentence.

(a) Separate Proceedings on Issue of Penalty.—

(1) [U]pon conviction or adjudication of guilt of a defendant of a capital felony in which the State has given notice of its intent to seek the death penalty, the court shall conduct a separate sentencing proceeding to determine whether the defendant should be sentenced to death or life imprisonment. A capital felony is one which may be punishable by death.

(2) The proceeding shall be conducted by the trial judge before the trial jury as soon as practicable after the guilty verdict is returned. If prior to the time that the trial jury begins its deliberations on the issue of penalty, any juror dies, becomes incapacitated or disqualified, or is discharged for any reason, an alternate juror shall become a part of the jury and serve in all respects as those selected on the regular trial panel. An alternate juror shall become a part of the jury in the order in which he was selected. If the trial jury is unable to reconvene for a hearing on the issue of penalty after having

determined the guilt of the accused, the trial judge shall impanel a new jury to determine the issue of the punishment. If the defendant pleads guilty, the sentencing proceeding shall be conducted before a jury impaneled for that purpose. A jury selected for the purpose of determining punishment in a capital case shall be selected in the same manner as juries are selected for the trial of capital cases.

(3) In the proceeding there shall not be any requirement to resubmit evidence presented during the guilt determination phase of the case, unless a new jury is impaneled, but all such evidence is competent for the jury's consideration in passing on punishment. Evidence may be presented as to any matter that the court deems relevant to sentence, and may include matters relating to any of the aggravating or mitigating circumstances enumerated in subsections (e) and (f). Any evidence which the court deems to have probative value may be received.

(4) The State and the defendant or his counsel shall be permitted to present argument for or against sentence of death. The defendant or defendant's counsel shall have the right to the last argument.

(b) Sentence Recommendation by the Jury.—Instructions determined by the trial judge to be warranted by the evidence shall be given by the court in its charge to the jury prior to its deliberation in determining sentence. The court shall give appropriate instructions in those cases in which evidence of the defendant's mental retardation requires the consideration by the jury of the provisions of G.S. 15A–2005. In all cases in which the death penalty may be authorized, the judge shall include in his instructions to the jury that it must consider any aggravating circumstance or circumstances or mitigating circumstance or circumstances from the lists provided in subsections (e) and (f) which may be supported by the evidence, and shall furnish to the jury a written list of issues relating to such aggravating or mitigating circumstance or circumstances.

After hearing the evidence, argument of counsel, and instructions of the court, the jury shall deliberate and render a sentence recommendation to the court, based upon the following matters:

(1) Whether any sufficient aggravating circumstance or circumstances as enumerated in subsection (e) exist;

(2) Whether any sufficient mitigating circumstance or circumstances as enumerated in subsection (f), which outweigh the aggravating circumstance or circumstances found, exist; and

(3) Based on these considerations, whether the defendant should be sentenced to death or to imprisonment in the State's prison for life.

The sentence recommendation must be agreed upon by a unanimous vote of the 12 jurors. Upon delivery of the sentence recommendation by the foreman of the jury, the jury shall be individually polled to establish whether each juror concurs and agrees to the sentence recommendation returned.

If the jury cannot, within a reasonable time, unanimously agree to its sentence recommendation, the judge shall impose a sentence of life imprisonment; provided, however, that the judge shall in no instance impose the death penalty when the jury cannot agree unanimously to its sentence recommendation.

(c) Findings in Support of Sentence of Death.—When the jury recommends a sentence of death, the foreman of the jury shall sign a writing on behalf of the jury which writing shall show:

(1) The statutory aggravating circumstance or circumstances which the jury finds beyond a reasonable doubt; and

(2) That the statutory aggravating circumstance or circumstances found by the jury are sufficiently substantial to call for the imposition of the death penalty; and

(3) That the mitigating circumstance or circumstances are insufficient to outweigh the aggravating circumstance or circumstances found.

(d)  Review of Judgment and Sentence.—

(1) The judgment of conviction and sentence of death shall be subject to automatic review by the Supreme Court of North Carolina pursuant to procedures established by the Rules of Appellate Procedure. In its review, the Supreme Court shall consider the punishment imposed as well as any errors assigned on appeal.

(2) The sentence of death shall be overturned and a sentence of life imprisonment imposed in lieu thereof by the Supreme Court upon a finding that the record does not support the jury's findings of any aggravating circumstance or circumstances upon which the sentencing court based its sentence of death, or upon a finding that the sentence of death was imposed under the influence of passion, prejudice, or any other arbitrary factor, or upon a finding that the sentence of death is excessive or disproportionate to the penalty imposed in similar cases, considering both the crime and the defendant. The Supreme Court may suspend consideration of death penalty cases until such time as the court determines it is prepared to make the comparisons required under the provisions of this section.

(3) If the sentence of death and the judgment of the trial court are reversed on appeal for error in the post-verdict sentencing proceeding, the Supreme Court shall order that a new sentencing hearing be conducted in conformity with the procedures of this Article.

(e) Aggravating Circumstances.—Aggravating circumstances which may be considered shall be limited to the following:

(1) The capital felony was committed by a person lawfully incarcerated.

(2) The defendant had been previously convicted of another capital felony or had been previously adjudicated delinquent in a juvenile proceeding for committing an offense that would be a capital felony if committed by an adult.

(3) The defendant had been previously convicted of a felony involving the use or threat of violence to the person or had been previously adjudicated delinquent in a juvenile proceeding for committing an offense that would be a Class A, B1, B2, C, D, or E felony involving the use or threat of violence to the person if the offense had been committed by an adult.

(4) The capital felony was committed for the purpose of avoiding or preventing a lawful arrest or effecting an escape from custody.

(5) The capital felony was committed while the defendant was engaged, or was an aider or abettor, in the commission of, or an attempt to commit, or flight after committing or attempting to commit, any homicide, robbery, rape or

a sex offense, arson, burglary, kidnapping, or aircraft piracy or the unlawful throwing, placing, or discharging of a destructive device or bomb.

(6) The capital felony was committed for pecuniary gain.

(7) The capital felony was committed to disrupt or hinder the lawful exercise of any governmental function or the enforcement of laws.

(8) The capital felony was committed against a law-enforcement officer, employee of the Department of Correction, jailer, fireman, judge or justice, former judge or justice, prosecutor or former prosecutor, juror or former juror, or witness or former witness against the defendant, while engaged in the performance of his official duties or because of the exercise of his official duty.

(9) The capital felony was especially heinous, atrocious, or cruel.

(10) The defendant knowingly created a great risk of death to more than one person by means of a weapon or device which would normally be hazardous to the lives of more than one person.

(11) The murder for which the defendant stands convicted was part of a course of conduct in which the defendant engaged and which included the commission by the defendant of other crimes of violence against another person or persons.

(f) Mitigating Circumstances.—Mitigating circumstances which may be considered shall include, but not be limited to, the following:

(1) The defendant has no significant history of prior criminal activity.

(2) The capital felony was committed while the defendant was under the influence of mental or emotional disturbance.

(3) The victim was a voluntary participant in the defendant's homicidal conduct or consented to the homicidal act.

(4) The defendant was an accomplice in or accessory to the capital felony committed by another person and his participation was relatively minor.

(5) The defendant acted under duress or under the domination of another person.

(6) The capacity of the defendant to appreciate the criminality of his conduct or to conform his conduct to the requirements of law was impaired.

(7) The age of the defendant at the time of the crime.

(8) The defendant aided in the apprehension of another capital felon or testified truthfully on behalf of the prosecution in another prosecution of a felony.

(9) Any other circumstance arising from the evidence which the jury deems to have mitigating value.

---

†

1-58778-720-2